ARCHB

G000253119

2009

THIRD SUPPLEMENT TO THE 2009 EDITION

EDITOR

P. J. RICHARDSON, LL.M. (Lond.), Dip.Crim. (CANTAB.)
of Gray's Inn and the Inner Temple, Barrister

SUPPLEMENT EDITORS

WILLIAM CARTER, B.A. (OXON.)
of Gray's Inn, Barrister

STEPHEN SHAY, B.A. (OXON.)
of the Middle Temple, Barrister

SWEET & MAXWELL   THOMSON REUTERS

Published and typeset in 2009 by Thomson Reuters (Legal)
Limited (Registered in England & Wales, Company No
1679046. Registered Office and address for service:
100 Avenue Rd, London, NW3 3PF)
trading as Sweet & Maxwell
Printed in the UK by CPI William Clowes Beccles NR34 7TL
For further information on our products and services, visit:
http://www.sweetandmaxwell.co.uk

No natural forests were destroyed to make this product;
only farmed timber was used and replanted.

**A CIP catalogue record for this book is available from
the British Library**

ISBN MAIN WORK 978-1-84703-583-7
ISBN THIRD SUPPLEMENT
978-1-84703-587-5

All rights reserved. Crown Copyright Legislation is
reproduced under the terms of Crown Copyright Policy
Guidance issued by HMSO.No part of this publication may
be reproduced or transmitted, in any form or by any
means, or stored in any retrieval system of any nature
without prior written permission, except for permitted fair
dealing under the Copyright, Designs and Patents Act
1988, or in accordance with the terms of a licence issued
by the Copyright Licensing Agency in respect of
photocopying and/or reprographic reproduction.
Application for permission for other use of copyright
material including permission to reproduce extracts in
other published works shall be made to the publishers.
Full acknowledgement of author, publisher and source
must be given. Application for permission for other use of
copyright material controlled by the publisher shall be
made to the publishers. Material is contained in this
publication for which publishing permission has been
sought, and for which copyright is acknowledged.
Permission to reproduce such material cannot be granted
by the publishers and application must be made to the
copyright holder.
Thomson Reuters and the Thomson Reuters Logo are
trademarks of Thomson Reuters. Sweet & Maxwell® is a
registered trademark of Thomson Reuters (Legal) Limited.

©
Thomson Reuters (Legal) Limited
2009

SERVICE INFORMATION

The Archbold service

Archbold: Criminal Pleading, Evidence and Practice consists of one main text volume (including the tables and index). This volume is re-issued annually, and is updated by cumulative supplements and *Archbold News*.

The supplement

Three cumulative supplements, containing updating material for the main volume, are published in each year as part of the service.

This is the third supplement of 2009.

New material is incorporated into this supplement using the same paragraph numbers as appear in the main work. All material new to this supplement is marked in the text by a **bold** star in the margin.

After consulting the main work on any given subject, reference should always be made to the same paragraph number in the current supplement to check that there have been no new developments since the main text volume was published. The supplement will also track material which has been removed or relocated as part of the re-issue process.

The back cover contains a list of all important developments included in this supplement for the first time and where they can be found.

All references in the text to cases, statutes and statutory instruments are contained in the tables printed at the beginning of this supplement.

Please email *smg.archbold@thomson.com* with comments/suggestions for any of the Archbold services, particularly any notes on the index to the mainwork.

TABLE OF CONTENTS

vi

TABLE OF STATUTES

References in bold indicate where legislation is reproduced in full

Northern Ireland

TABLE OF STATUTORY INSTRUMENTS

Northern Ireland

TABLE OF CASES

ABBREVIATIONS OF LEGISLATION

The following abbreviations have been adopted throughout.

AFA	Armed Forces Act
CAA	Criminal Appeal Act
CDA	Crime and Disorder Act
CDDA	Company Directors Disqualification Act
CEMA	Customs and Excise Management Act
CJA	Criminal Justice Act
CJCSA	Criminal Justice and Court Services Act
CJIA	Criminal Justice and Immigration Act
CJPA	Criminal Justice and Police Act
CJPOA	Criminal Justice and Public Order Act
CLA	Criminal Law Act
CPIA	Criminal Procedure and Investigations Act
C(S)A	Crime (Sentences) Act
CYPA	Children and Young Persons Act
DTA	Drug Trafficking Act
DTOA	Drug Trafficking Offences Act
ECHR	European Convention on Human Rights
FSMA	Financial Services and Markets Act
MCA	Magistrates' Courts Act
MHA	Mental Health Act
PACE	Police and Criminal Evidence
PCA	Proceeds of Crime Act
PCCA	Powers of Criminal Courts Act
PCC(S)A	Powers of Criminal Courts (Sentencing) Act
PJA	Police and Justice Act
RIPA	Regulation of Investigatory Powers Act
RSA	Road Safety Act
RSC	Rules of the Supreme Court (Revision)
RTA	Road Traffic Act
RTOA	Road Traffic Offenders Act
SCA	Serious Crime Act
SOA	Sexual Offences Act
SOCPA	Serious Organised Crime and Police Act
VCRA	Violent Crime Reduction Act
YJCEA	Youth Justice and Criminal Evidence Act

CHAPTER 1

THE INDICTMENT

III. SENDINGS, TRANSFERS AND COMMITTALS FOR TRIAL OF INDICTABLE OFFENCES

B. SENDINGS FOR TRIAL

(5) Procedure

Crime and Disorder Act 1998, Sched. 3

Procedure where no indictable-only offence remains

The replacement of paragraph 9(5)(b) of Schedule 3 to the 1998 Act with a   ★**1–33**
new paragraph 9(5)(b) by the *AFA* 2006 (see § 1–35 in the main work) comes
into force on October 31, 2009: *Armed Forces Act 2006 (Commencement No. 5)
Order* 2009 (S.I. 2009 No. 1167). In connection with that commencement, see
the transitional provision in the *Armed Forces Act 2006 (Transitional Provisions
etc.) Order* 2009 (S.I. 2009 No. 1059), Sched. 1, para. 43 (interpretation of
references to "service offence" and "previous conviction").

D. COMMITTALS FOR TRIAL

(2) Determination of mode of trial

(a) *Statutory provisions*

Magistrates' Courts Act 1980, s.19

Decision as to allocation

The amendment of the replacement section 19 of the 1980 Act effected by   ★**1–74**
the *AFA* 2006 comes into force on October 31, 2009: *Armed Forces Act 2006
(Commencement No. 5) Order* 2009 (S.I. 2009 No. 1167). In connection with
that commencement, see the transitional provision in the *Armed Forces Act
2006 (Transitional Provisions etc.) Order* 2009 (S.I. 2009 No. 1059), Sched. 1,
para. 18(1) (interpretation of references to "service offence" and "previous
conviction").

IV. AGAINST WHOM AN INDICTMENT LIES

B. EXEMPTIONS

(6) Children between 10 and 14

The decision of the Court of Appeal in *R. v. T.* has been upheld by the   ★**1–91**
House of Lords: see *R. v. J.T.B.* [2009] 2 W.L.R. 1088.

1

C. Indicting Extradited Persons

Extradition Act 2003, ss.146–151

Dealing with person for other offences

★**1–97**   It was held in *R. v. Seddon*, unreported, March 10, 2009, CA ([2009] EWCA Crim. 483), that section 146(3)(b) of the 2003 Act does not enable the court to deal with the offender for an offence which is wholly extraneous and additional to the offence in respect of which the person has been surrendered, and to which there is the merest passing reference in the arrest warrant. The court said that where a prosecutor wishes to prosecute a fugitive for a bail offence, the preferred route should be to include in the warrant a specific reference to that offence as one of the extradition offences for which surrender is sought. The court also noted that section 146(3)(b) allowed the fugitive to be dealt with for a lesser included offence such as manslaughter on a murder charge, but left open the question whether he could be proceeded against for an "ancillary offence", *e.g.* where the warrant seeks surrender for an offence of robbery and where the facts of the robbery disclosed in the warrant reveal that the robber was armed.

V. THE FORM OF AN INDICTMENT

E. Duplicity

(3) Application of the general rule

★**1–137**   In *R. v. K. (Robert)* [2009] 1 Cr.App.R. 24, CA, during the trial of the appellant for an offence of rape of a child under 13 (*SOA* 2003, s.5 (§ 20–49 in the main work)), it became unclear whether, in respect of a single incident, the complainant was alleging that she had been penetrated vaginally or anally. Therefore, the indictment, which had originally charged one count of vaginal rape, was amended so that it alleged instead rape by penetration either vaginally or anally. The Court of Appeal held that the indictment was not bad for duplicity. It was not charging two offences, since under the 2003 Act there is only one offence of rape either by penetration of the vagina, anus or mouth. The court said that the rules in relation to duplicity are intended to ensure fairness to a defendant so that he may know and understand what the case against him is and to enable a jury's verdict to be clear and understandable for the purposes of sentence. Here, there was no prejudice to the defendant, since the only doubt was whether the penetration was vaginal or anal, and there was no materiality in whether it was one or the other, given that the defendant denied that the act had taken place at all. As to the direction to the jury, see *post*, § 4–391.

G. Joinder

(1) Joinder of counts in one indictment

"founded on the same facts"

1–157   (4) *R. v. Roberts* [2009] 1 Cr.App.R. 20, CA (counts of possessing a controlled drug with intent to supply and of possessing a firearm when

prohibited were properly joined in the same indictment where
drugs and firearms were found at the appellant's home during a
search; the factual connection was sufficiently established by the coincidence of time and place; and the fact that the appellant's
explanations were different was nothing to the point; the propriety
of an indictment must be judged at the time it is drawn; it is not
for the prosecution to second-guess the defence).

XI. POWERS AND DUTIES OF PARTICULAR PROSECUTION AGENCIES

A. CROWN PROSECUTION SERVICE

(5) Private prosecutions

R. (Dacre and Associated Newspapers) v. City of Westminster Magistrates' Court   **1–259**
is now reported at [2009] 1 Cr.App.R. 6, *sub nom. R. (Dacre) v. Westminster
Magistrates' Court.*

(8) Guidelines for Crown Prosecutors

For a further example of a successful application for judicial review of a de-   **1–263**
cision to discontinue a prosecution, see *R. (F.B.) v. DPP* [2009] 1 Cr.App.R.
38, DC, where the decision was held to involve a misapplication of the Code
for Crown Prosecutors (see *post*, § E–12e) and a violation of the claimant's
right under Article 3 of the ECHR (§ 16–39 in the main work) not to be
subjected to inhuman or degrading treatment (see *post*, § 16–40a).

In *Guest v. DPP* [2009] 4 *Archbold News* 2, DC, a decision to impose a   ★
conditional caution under the *CJA* 2003 was quashed. The court rejected an
argument that quashing the caution would serve no purpose as it was not
inevitable that any subsequent proceedings instituted by the CPS would be
stayed as an abuse of process (referring to *Jones v. Whalley* (§ 4–59 in the
main work)).

A challenge to the *vires* of the prosecutor should be made by way of an ap-   ★
plication for judicial review of the decision to prosecute: *R. (Securiplan) v. Security Industry Authority* [2009] 2 All E.R. 211, DC (see also *post*, § 7–12).

CHAPTER 2

THE CRIMINAL JURISDICTION OF THE CROWN COURT

I. THE CROWN COURT

C. CONSTITUTION

(1) Judges of the Crown Court

Supreme Court [Senior Courts] Act 1981, s.8

The Crown Court
Where a restraint order had been made under section 41 of the *PCA* 2002   ★**2–3**

(§ 5–602 in the main work) freezing the assets of a father, and where the mother made an application in the High Court under Schedule 1 to the *Children Act* 1989 for maintenance in the form of periodical payments in respect of their daughter, a judge of the High Court hearing that application was entitled, pursuant to section 8(1) of the 1981 Act (see the main work), to sit simultaneously both as a Family Division judge and as a judge of the Crown Court, and to exercise the powers of the Crown Court if he thought it appropriate and had all the relevant material before him (including by way of making an order under section 42 of the 2002 Act discharging or varying the restraint order): *T. v. B. and Revenue and Customs Prosecutions Office* [2009] 1 F.L.R. 1231, Fam D (Sir Mark Potter P.) (observing that such a course was not to be encouraged, the proper place for consideration of restraint orders being in the Crown Court).

III. JURISDICTION IN RESPECT OF ACTS PERFORMED ABROAD AND IN RESPECT OF FOREIGN NATIONALS

D. PARTICULAR OFFENCES

(1) Sexual offences

(b) *Sexual Offences Act 2003*

Sexual Offences Act 2003, s.72

Offences outside United Kingdom

2–36f   The amendments to section 72 of the 2003 Act effected by the *Sexual Offences (Northern Ireland Consequential Amendments) Order* 2008 (S.I. 2008 No. 1779) came into force on February 2, 2009: see article 2(3) of that order and the *Sexual Offences (Northern Ireland) Order 2008 (Commencement) Order* 2008 (S.R.N.I. 2008 No. 510).

Sexual Offences Act 2003, Sched. 2

Sexual offences to which section 72 applies

2–36g   The amendments to Schedule 2 to the 2003 Act effected by S.I. 2008 No. 1779 came into force on February 2, 2009: see article 2(3) of that order and the *Sexual Offences (Northern Ireland) Order 2008 (Commencement) Order* 2008 (S.R.N.I. 2008 No. 510).

(12) Offshore activities

Petroleum Act 1987

2–81   As from April 6, 2009 (*Energy Act 2008 (Commencement No. 1 and Savings) Order* 2009 (S.I. 2009 No. 45)), sections 21, 23 and 24 of the *Petroleum Act* 1987 (provision for safety zones around offshore installations) apply to carbon storage installations: *Energy Act* 2008, ss.30(1) and 32.

V. JURISDICTION TO OBTAIN EVIDENCE FOR USE OVERSEAS

Crime (International Co-operation) Act 2003

★2–154   *R. (Hafner) v. Westminster Magistrates' Court* is now reported at [2009] 1 W.L.R. 1005.

VI. *APPELLATE JURISDICTION OF CROWN COURT IN CRIMINAL CASES*

A. Concurrent Jurisdiction of High Court

(2) Practice

R. (White) v. Crown Court at Blackfriars is now reported at [2008] 2   **2–160**
Cr.App.R.(S.) 97, *sub nom. R. (White) v. Blackfriars Crown Court.*

D. Cessation and Abandonment of Right to Appeal

(1) Cessation of right of appeal

Magistrates' Courts Act 1980, s.111

Statement of case by magistrates' court
A new subsection has been inserted in section 111 of the 1980 Act by the   **★2–174**
Access to Justice Act 1999 (Destination of Appeals) (Family Proceedings) Order
2009 (S.I. 2009 No. 871). This provides that section 111 has no application to
family proceedings within the meaning of section 111A (inserted by the same
order).

F. Procedure

(9) Change of plea – equivocal plea

(a) *Plea of guilty recorded and magistrates pass sentence*

Procedure

As from April 6, 2009, the procedure to be followed where a defendant   **2–199a**
seeks to vacate a plea of guilty entered in summary proceedings is prescribed
by rule 37.9 of the *Criminal Procedure Rules* 2005: *Criminal Procedure (Amendment No. 2) Rules* 2008 (S.I. 2008 No. 3269). The new Part 37 (trial and
sentence in a magistrates' court) is designed to consolidate, revise and simplify
the rules about procedure at trial in magistrates' courts. The procedure
remains effectively unchanged.

VII. *CRIMINAL PROCEDURE RULES*

Criminal Procedure Rules 2005 (S.I. 2005 No. 384), Pt 2

As from April 6, 2009, the *Criminal Procedure (Amendment No. 2) Rules* 2008   **2–206**
(S.I. 2008 No. 3269) amend rule 2.1 of the 2005 rules by the addition of new
paragraphs (13) to (15), as follows—

"(13) The rules in Part 21 apply unless the court otherwise directs under rule
21.1(2). If it does so, the rules replaced by those rules apply.
(14) The rules in Part 37 apply in cases in which on or after 6th April 2009—
(a) the court tries a case; or
(b) the defendant pleads guilty.

In other cases, the rules in Parts 37 and 38 apply as if the *Criminal Procedure (Amendment No. 2) Rules* 2008 had not been made.

(15) The rules in Part 44 apply in cases in which an application to which that Part applies is made on or after 6th April 2009. In other cases, the rules in Parts 38 and 44 apply as if the *Criminal Procedure (Amendment No. 2) Rules* 2008 had not been made.".

As from April 6, 2009, the *Criminal Procedure (Amendment No. 2) Rules* 2008 (S.I. 2008 No. 3269) amend rule 2.2 of the 2005 rules by the insertion of the following definition after the definition of "court officer"—

"'justices' legal adviser' means a justices' clerk or an assistant to a justices' clerk;".

Criminal Procedure Rules 2005 (S.I. 2005 No. 384), Pt 5

Forms

2–219   The *Consolidated Criminal Practice Direction (Amendment No. 21) (Criminal Proceedings: Witness Anonymity Orders; Forms)* is now reported at [2009] 1 Cr.App.R. 5.

★   As from May 14, 2009, new forms are prescribed for use in connection with the 2005 rules, Parts 19 (bail), 37 (trial and sentence in a magistrates' court), 68 (appeal to the Court of Appeal against conviction or sentence) and 74 (application for leave to appeal to the House of Lords): *Practice Direction (Criminal proceedings: victim personal statements; pleas of guilty in the Crown Court; forms)*, *The Times*, May 19, 2009, Supreme Court.

CHAPTER 3

BAIL, APPEARANCE OF ACCUSED FOR TRIAL, PRESENCE DURING TRIAL

I. BAIL

A. GENERAL

(2) The Bail Act 1976

(c) *Text of the Act*

Bail Act 1976, ss.1, 2

Other definitions

★**3–7**   The amendment to section 2 of the 1976 Act effected by the *AFA* 2006 comes into force on October 31, 2009: *Armed Forces Act 2006 (Commencement No. 5) Order* 2009 (S.I. 2009 No. 1167).

Bail Act 1976, s.3

General provisions

3–11   Section 51 of, and Schedule 11 to, the *CJIA* 2008 came into force on November 3, 2008: *Criminal Justice and Immigration Act 2008 (Commencement No. 3 and Transitional Provisions) Order* 2008 (S.I. 2008 No. 2712).

Bail Act 1976, s.3AA

*Conditions for the imposition of electronic monitoring requirements: children and
    young persons*
    Section 51 of, and Schedule 11 to, the *CJIA* 2008 came into force on   **3-12**
November 3, 2008: *Criminal Justice and Immigration Act 2008 (Commencement
No. 3 and Transitional Provisions) Order* 2008 (S.I. 2008 No. 2712).

Bail Act 1976, ss.3AB, 3AC

Conditions for the imposition of electronic monitoring requirements: other persons
    Section 51 of, and Schedule 11 to, the *CJIA* 2008 came into force on   **3-12a**
November 3, 2008: *Criminal Justice and Immigration Act 2008 (Commencement
No. 3 and Transitional Provisions) Order* 2008 (S.I. 2008 No. 2712).

Electronic monitoring: general provisions
    Section 51 of, and Schedule 11 to, the *CJIA* 2008 came into force on   **3-12b**
November 3, 2008: *Criminal Justice and Immigration Act 2008 (Commencement
No. 3 and Transitional Provisions) Order* 2008 (S.I. 2008 No. 2712).

Bail Act 1976, s.4

Withdrawal of bail

    It is not reasonable for a court to withdraw bail unless it is necessary to do   **3-19a**
so, especially as any decision to withdraw bail engages Article 5 of the ECHR
(right to liberty and security (§ 16–43 in the main work)); any decision to
withdraw bail must explain why bail should be withdrawn, and the reasons
must relate to the particular facts: *R. (Fergus) v. Crown Court at Southampton*,
unreported, December 4, 2008, QBD (Silber J.) ([2008] EWHC 3273
(Admin.)).

Bail Act 1976, s.5

Supplementary provisions about decisions on bail
    The amendment to section 5(10) of the 1976 Act effected by the *AFA* 2006   **★3-24**
comes into force on October 31, 2009: *Armed Forces Act 2006 (Commencement
No. 5) Order* 2009 (S.I. 2009 No. 1167).

Bail Act 1976, ss.5B, 6

Offence of absconding by person released on bail
    The amendment to section 6(9) of the 1976 Act effected by the *AFA* 2006   **★3-29**
comes into force on October 31, 2009: *Armed Forces Act 2006 (Commencement
No. 5) Order* 2009 (S.I. 2009 No. 1167).

Bail Act 1976, s.7

Liability to arrest for absconding or breaking conditions of bail
    It was held in *R. (Thomas) v. Greenwich Magistrates' Court*, unreported, May   **★3-39**
11, 2009, QBD (Hickinbottom J.), that when considering whether a person
"has broken or is likely to break any condition of bail" (s.7(5)(b) (§ 3–38 in the

main work)) a justice is entitled to rely on written hearsay, so long as it is properly evaluated. His Lordship stated that the decision in *R. (DPP v. Havering Magistrates' Court*; *R. (McKeown) v. Wirral Borough Magistrates' Court* (see the main work), had not been overtaken by (i) the changes to the hearsay rules in the *CJA* 2003 because (a) the Act did not impose stricter hearsay rules than had previously applied to bail proceedings, (b) it did not bring bail proceedings within the ambit of criminal proceedings for the purposes of Article 6(3) of the ECHR (§ 16–57 in the main work), and (c) it could not have changed the well-established law as to the type of evidence upon which a decision can be made, nor the approach to be taken to such evidence, (ii) the decision of the European Court of Human Rights in *Al-Khawaja v. U.K.*; *Tahery v. U.K.* (*post*, § 16–91), because the comments made in that case were clearly and expressly in the context of criminal proceedings within the meaning of Article 6(3), or (iii) *R. (Cleary) v. Highbury Corner Magistrates' Court (Practice Note)* [2007] 1 W.L.R. 1272, DC (*Civil Evidence Act* 1995 applies to closure proceedings), because the 1995 Act pre-dated *Havering Magistrates' Court* and, in any event, that case made it clear that there should be no technical evidential rules in relation to evidence adduced at a bail hearing.

Bail Act 1976, s.8

Bail with sureties

★3–42   The amendments to section 8 of the 1976 Act effected by the *AFA* 2006 come into force on October 31, 2009: *Armed Forces Act 2006 (Commencement No. 5) Order* 2009 (S.I. 2009 No. 1167).

Bail Act 1976, Sched. 1

Exceptions to right to bail

★3–48   As to the commencement of the amendment to paragraph 4 of Part I of Schedule 1 to the 1976 Act effected by the *AFA* 2006, see *post*, § 3–52.

Exceptions to right to bail

★3–51   As to the commencement of the amendment to paragraph 4 of Part II of Schedule 1 to the 1976 Act effected by the *AFA* 2006, see *post*, § 3–52.

Interpretation

★3–52   The amendments to Schedule 1 to the 1976 Act effected by the *AFA* 2006 come into force on October 31, 2009: *Armed Forces Act 2006 (Commencement No. 5) Order* 2009 (S.I. 2009 No. 1167). In connection with that commencement, see the transitional provision in the *Armed Forces Act 2006 (Transitional Provisions etc.) Order* 2009 (S.I. 2009 No. 1059), Sched. 1, para. 15 (interpretation of references to "a sentence imposed by an officer").

(3) Limitation on right to bail

Criminal Justice and Public Order Act 1994, s.25

No bail for defendants charged with or convicted of homicide or rape after previous conviction of such offences

3–55   The amendments to section 25 of the 1994 Act effected by the *Sexual Of-*

fences (Northern Ireland Consequential Amendments) Order 2008 (S.I. 2008 No.
1779) came into force on February 2, 2009: see article 2(3) of that order and
the *Sexual Offences (Northern Ireland) Order 2008 (Commencement) Order* 2008
(S.R.N.I. 2008 No. 510).

(6) Place of remand

Children and Young Persons Act 1969, s.23AA

Electronic monitoring of conditions of remand
  The amendments effected by the *CJIA* 2008 to section 23AA of the 1969   **3–76a**
Act came into force on November 3, 2008: *Criminal Justice and Immigration
Act 2008 (Commencement No. 3 and Transitional Provisions) Order* 2008 (S.I.
2008 No. 2712). Note, however, that the reference to Schedule 29 to the 2008
Act in the main work should be a reference to Schedule 28.

(7) Transfer to hospital of persons in custody otherwise than under sentence

Mental Health Act 1983, s.51

Further provisions as to detained persons
  Section 51(3) of the 1983 Act has been amended by the *Transfer of Tribunal*   **3–83**
Functions Order 2008 (S.I. 2008 No. 2833), art. 9(1), and Sched. 3, para. 43.

B. Specific Provisions

(1) The police

(a) *The Police and Criminal Evidence Act 1984*

Police and Criminal Evidence Act 1984, s.34

Limitations on police detention
  The *PJA* 2006, s.46, came into force on November 14, 2008 *(Police and*   **3–93**
Justice Act 2006 (Commencement No. 10) Order 2008 (S.I. 2008 No. 2785)) in
the following further local justice areas: in London, Barking and Dagenham,
Barnet, Bexley, Brent, Bromley, Camden and Islington, City of London, City
of Westminster, Croydon, Ealing, Enfield, Greenwich and Lewisham, Hackney
and Tower Hamlets, Hammersmith and Fulham and Kensington and Chelsea,
Haringey, Harrow Gore, Havering, Hillingdon, Hounslow, Kingston-upon-
Thames, Merton, Newham, Redbridge, Richmond-upon-Thames, Sutton,
Waltham Forest, and Wandsworth, and in Kent, Central Kent, East Kent and
North Kent.

Police and Criminal Evidence Act 1984, s.46ZA

Persons granted live link bail
  As to the further commencement of the *PJA* 2006, s.46, see *ante*, § 3–93.   **3–128a**

Police and Criminal Evidence Act 1984, s.46A

Power of arrest for failure to answer police bail
  As to the further commencement of the *PJA* 2006, s.46, see *ante*, § 3–93.   **3–129**

Police and Criminal Evidence Act 1984, s.47

Bail after arrest

3–131   As to the further commencement of the *PJA* 2006, s.46, see *ante*, § 3–93.

Savings

★3–131a   The repeal of section 51(c) of the 1984 Act comes into force on October 31, 2009: *Armed Forces Act 2006 (Commencement No. 5) Order* 2009 (S.I. 2009 No. 1167).

(2) Magistrates' courts

(b) *Criminal Procedure Rules 2005 (S.I. 2005 No. 384)*

Criminal Procedure Rules 2005 (S.I. 2005 No. 384), rr.19.1-19.8

Application to a magistrates' court to vary conditions of police bail

3–159   With effect from April 6, 2009, the *Criminal Procedure (Amendment No. 2) Rules* 2008 (S.I. 2008 No. 3269), r.7(b), revokes the word "police" in the heading to rule 19.1 of the 2005 rules.

With effect from April 6, 2009, the *Criminal Procedure (Amendment No. 2) Rules* 2008 (S.I. 2008 No. 3269), r.7(c)(i) to (iii), amend rule 19.1(1) of the 2005 rules, so as (i) to insert the words ", to vary conditions of police bail," after "1984", (ii) to revoke the word "and" at the end of paragraph (d); and (iii) to insert at the end, "; and (f) specify the address at which the applicant would reside, if the court imposed a condition of residence".

With effect from April 6, 2009, the *Criminal Procedure (Amendment No. 2) Rules* 2008 (S.I. 2008 No. 3269), r.7(c)(iv), amends rule 19.1(3) of the 2005 rules, so as to insert the words "not less than 24 hours" after the words "shall serve".

With effect from April 6, 2009, the *Criminal Procedure (Amendment No. 2) Rules* 2008 (S.I. 2008 No. 3269), r.7(c)(v), amends rule 19.1 of the 2005 rules, so as to insert a new paragraph (5), as follows—

> "(5) A party who wants a magistrates' court to vary or to impose conditions of bail under section 3(8) of the *Bail Act* 1976, must—
>> (a) serve notice, not less than 24 hours before the hearing at which that party intends to apply, on—
>>> (i) the court officer, and
>>> (ii) the other party; and
>> (b) in that notice—
>>> (i) specify the variation or conditions proposed, and
>>> (ii) explain the reasons.".

With effect from April 6, 2009, the *Criminal Procedure (Amendment No. 2) Rules* 2008 (S.I. 2008 No. 3269), r.7(c)(vi), amends rule 19.1 of the 2005 rules, so as to substitute a new paragraph (7), as follows—

> "(7) The court may—
>> (a) vary or waive a time limit under paragraph (3) or (5) of this rule; and
>> (b) allow a notice to be—
>>> (i) in a different form to one set out in the Practice Direction, or
>>> (ii) given orally.".

(3) The Crown Court

(e) *Criminal Procedure Rules 2005 (S.I. 2005 No. 384)*

With effect from April 6, 2009, the *Criminal Procedure (Amendment No. 2)*   **3–185**
Rules 2008 (S.I. 2008 No. 3269), r.7(e), inserts a new rule 19.25.

Criminal Procedure Rules 2005 (S.I. 2005 No. 384), r.19.25

Grant of bail subject to a condition of residence

19.25—(1) The defendant must notify the prosecutor of the address at which
the defendant would reside if released on bail with a condition of residence—

    (a) as soon as practicable after the institution of proceedings, unless already
done; and

    (b) as soon as practicable after any change of that address.

(2) The prosecutor must help the court to assess the suitability of an address
proposed as a condition of residence.

III. PRESENCE OF THE ACCUSED IN COURT DURING HEARING

B. LIMITATIONS

(1) Preliminary and sentencing hearings

Crime and Disorder Act 1998, ss.57A–57E

Use of live link in sentencing hearings

    It should be noted that the insertion of section 57C of the 1998 Act took ef-   **3–204**
fect on April 1, 2007, only in the local justice areas of Lambeth and Southwark.
On November 14, 2008 (*Police and Justice Act 2006 (Commencement No. 10)*
Order 2008 (S.I. 2008 No. 2785)), it took effect in the following further local
justice areas: in London, Barking and Dagenham, Barnet, Bexley, Brent,
Bromley, Camden and Islington, City of London, City of Westminster, Croy-
don, Ealing, Enfield, Greenwich and Lewisham, Hackney and Tower Hamlets,
Hammersmith and Fulham and Kensington and Chelsea, Haringey, Harrow
Gore, Havering, Hillingdon, Hounslow, Kingston-upon-Thames, Merton, Ne-
wham, Redbridge, Richmond-upon-Thames, Sutton, Waltham Forest, and
Wandsworth, and in Kent, Central Kent, East Kent and North Kent.

(2) Defendant unruly, obstructive, etc.

    It was held in *R. v. Horden* [2009] 3 *Archbold News* 3, CA, that the fact that   ★**3–205**
it is wise for a prison to warn prison escort and dock security contractors that
there might be some risk of escape does not automatically mean that such a
risk is strong enough to justify the handcuffing of a defendant in court.
Furthermore, whereas applications for the handcuffing of a defendant at a
jury trial by contractors are made routinely and often with minimal supporting facts, contractors must exercise a degree of judgment before making such
an application and it is essential that they take steps to ensure that there is a
proper basis for it. An application must also be properly scrutinised by the
judge. The test to be applied is as stated in *R. v. Vratsides* and *R. v. Mullen* (as

to which, see the main work), and alternative methods of guarding against the risk of violence or escape (such as having police officers strategically positioned in or outside the courtroom) must have been investigated.

CHAPTER 4

TRIAL

I. PRELIMINARIES

C. PUBLICITY

(2) Restrictions

(b) *Child or young person as victim, witness or defendant*

Youth Justice and Criminal Evidence Act 1999, ss.44, 45

Restrictions on reporting alleged offences involving persons under 18

★4–29a   As to the commencement of the amendment to section 44(13) of the 1999 Act effected by the *AFA* 2006, see *post*, § 3–29b.

Power to restrict reporting of criminal proceedings involving persons under 18

★4–29b   The amendments to section 44(13) of the 1999 Act effected by the *AFA* 2006 come into force on October 31, 2009: *Armed Forces Act 2006 (Commencement No. 5) Order* 2009 (S.I. 2009 No. 1167). In connection with that commencement, see the transitional provision in the *Armed Forces Act 2006 (Transitional Provisions etc.) Order* 2009 (S.I. 2009 No. 1059), Sched. 1, para. 44(1) (interpretation of references to "a person subject to service law").

(c) *Certain adult witnesses and victims*

Youth Justice and Criminal Evidence Act 1999, s.46

4–29c   *R. v. Davis* is now reported at [2008] 1 A.C. 1128.

Youth Justice and Criminal Evidence Act 1999, Sched. 7, para. 6

Transitional

★4–29i   The amendment of paragraph 6(6) of Schedule 7 to the 1999 Act comes into force on October 31, 2009: *Armed Forces Act 2006 (Commencement No. 5) Order* 2009 (S.I. 2009 No. 1167).

D. IDENTITY AND IMPARTIALITY OF JUDGE

Impartiality

★4–32   *R. v. Khyam, Amin, Akbar, Garcia and Mahmood* is now reported at [2009] 1 Cr.App.R.(S.) 77, *sub nom. R. v. Khyam.*

It being of importance that a judge who has presided over a trial, especially one lasting several weeks, should be the judge who passes sentence, a judge had been entitled to refuse to recuse herself where it had become known after the trial that two of the defendants had been arrested on suspicion of jury tampering and of uttering a threat to kill the judge; whilst the judge had been in a difficult position, she would have been able to put on one side for sentencing purposes the allegations made against the defendants, especially where she had no means of knowing whether they could be substantiated: *R. v. Mehta, Sharman, Reardon and Ratcliff, The Times*, October 3, 2008, CA.

It was held by the House of Lords in *Helow v. Secretary of State for the Home Department* [2008] 1 W.L.R. 2416, that absent anything to indicate that a judge by word or deed associated himself with the views of an association of which he was a member, membership of an association generally connotes no such approval or endorsement of that which is said or done by the association's representatives or officers, or of its communications or the material it publishes, as could lead a fair-minded and informed observer (who is neither unduly sensitive nor suspicious (*Johnson v. Johnson* (2000) 201 C.L.R. 488, High Court of Australia)) to conclude that there existed a real possibility that the judge was biased by reason of such membership (*Porter v. Magill*; *Weeks v. Magill* [2002] 2 A.C. 357, HL). Their Lordships said that although it is possible to conceive of circumstances involving words or conduct so extreme that an association member might be expected to become aware of them and disassociate himself by resignation if he did not approve or wish to be thought to approve of them, this was not the case where the aims of the association to which a judge had expressly subscribed were entirely unobjectionable and where the extreme material complained of was an incomplete and one-sided selection of the association's output. Nor, they said, could mere membership give rise in the eyes of a fair-minded observer to a real possibility that a judge would be unconsciously influenced, through some form of osmosis, by the content and general attitude of the extreme material. A judge could be assumed, by virtue of the office for which he had been selected, to be intelligent and well able to form his own views about anything that he read, and to be capable of detaching his own mind from things with which he did not agree.

K. Limited Discretionary Power to Prevent Prosecution Proceeding

(2) Abuse of process

(d) *Application of the principles*

Misuse, manipulation, etc. of process of court

Decisions as to the institution/continuation of prosecutions

    R. v. Arnold is now reported at [2008] 2 Cr.App.R. 37. **4–58**

    R. (Dacre and Associated Newspapers) v. City of Westminster Magistrates' Court **4–59** is now reported at [2009] 1 Cr.App.R. 6, *sub nom. R. (Dacre) v. Westminster Magistrates' Court.*

    R. v. Asfaw (United Nations High Commr for Refugees intervening) is now reported at [2008] 1 A.C. 1061.

    Jones v. Whalley (see the main work) was considered in *Guest v. DPP* (*ante*, § 1–263).

Evidential matters and the impossibility of a fair trial

★**4–65**   In *R. v. Redmond* [2009] 1 Cr.App.R. 25, the Court of Appeal made an *obiter* observation that where the prosecution seek to rely on evidence obtained abroad and in breach of the local rules relating to the obtaining of evidence, and where British investigators were party to the obtaining of that evidence, on an application for a stay of the proceedings, it will be open to the judge, in the exercise of his discretion, to permit the prosecution to proceed save where the British investigators had knowingly ridden roughshod over the local rules. The crucial issue is whether the authorities have knowingly abused their powers.

Delay and the right to trial "within a reasonable time"

Impact of Article 6 of the European Convention on Human Rights

4–67   *Spiers (Procurator Fiscal) v. Ruddy* is now reported at [2008] 1 A.C. 873.

Directing the jury

4–71a   As to directing the jury as to possible explanations for a delayed complaint in a case of rape, see *R. v. Doody, post,* § 20–27a.

L. Access to Judge

(2) Pleas and sentence

★**4–78**   Paragraph IV.45 of the consolidated criminal practice direction has been reissued with effect from May 14, 2009: *Practice Direction (Criminal proceedings: victim personal statements; pleas of guilty in the Crown Court; forms), The Times,* May 19, 2009, Supreme Court. Paragraphs IV.45.1 to IV.45.3 are set out below. As to paragraph IV.45 of the practice direction, see also *post,* §§ 4–108, 5–73 and 5–79b and Appendix A–281 *et seq.*

Practice Direction (Criminal Proceedings: Consolidation), paras IV.45.1–IV.45.3 (as substituted by Practice Direction (Criminal proceedings: victim personal statements; pleas of guilty in the Crown Court; forms), The Times, May 19, 2009)

Pleas of guilty in the Crown Court

    IV.45.1   Advocates must be free to perform their duty namely to give the accused the best advice possible and, if need be, in strong terms. It will often include advice that, in accordance with the relevant authorities and sentencing guidelines, a court will normally reduce a sentence as a result of a guilty plea and that the level of reduction will reflect the stage in the proceedings at which willingness to admit guilt was indicated. The advocate will, of course, emphasise that the defendant must not plead guilty unless he or she is guilty of the offence(s) charged.

    IV.45.2   The defendant, having considered the advocate's advice, must have complete freedom of choice whether to plead guilty or not guilty.

    IV.45.3   There must be freedom of access between advocate and judge. Any discussion must, however, be between the judge and the advocates on both sides. If an advocate is instructed by a solicitor who is in court, he or she, too, should be allowed to attend the discussion. This freedom of access is important because there may be matters calling for communication or discussion of such a nature that the advocate cannot, in the client's interest, mention them in open court, *e.g.* the advocate, by way of mitigation, may wish to tell the judge that reliable medical evidence shows that the defendant is suffering from a terminal illness and may not have long to live. It is imperative that, so far as possible, justice must be administered in open court. Advocates should, therefore, only ask to see the judge when it is felt to be really necessary. The judge must be careful only to treat such communications as private where, in the interests of justice, this is necessary. Where any such discussion takes place it should be recorded either by a tape recorder or shorthand writer.

II. ARRAIGNMENT AND PLEA

B. PLEA

(4) Plea of guilty

(b) *To lesser offence*

As to the respective roles of prosecution and judge in relation to the acceptance of a plea to a lesser offence, see also paragraphs IV.45.5 to IV.45.8 of the consolidated criminal practice direction, as substituted by *Practice Direction (Criminal proceedings: victim personal statements; pleas of guilty in the Crown Court; forms), The Times*, May 19, 2009, Supreme Court. Effective from May 14, 2009, this says nothing new (see the Attorney-General's guidelines as to the acceptance of pleas, para. A.4 (*post*, Appendix A–259) and paragraph 7 of the Farquharson Guidelines on the Role and Responsibilities of the Prosecution Advocate (*post*, Appendix E–42 *et seq.*)), but reiterates, in particular, that if the prosecution seek the approval of the judge for their proposed course of action, they are bound by the judge's view and that, if they do not seek such approval, the judge may nevertheless express his disapproval, and that, if of the view that the course proposed may lead to serious injustice, the judge may adjourn the proceedings so that consideration may be given to the matter by the local chief crown prosecutor in the first instance, the Director of Public Prosecutions if that does not resolve the matter, and ultimately, and in extreme circumstances, by the Attorney-General.   **★4–108**

(9) Autrefois acquit and autrefois convict

(b) *A man may not be tried for a crime in respect of which he has previously been acquitted or convicted*

Army Act 1955, s.133(1)

The repeals of the *Army Act* 1955, the *Air Force Act* 1955 and the *Naval Discipline Act* 1957 come into force on October 31, 2009: *Armed Forces Act 2006 (Commencement No. 5) Order* 2009 (S.I. 2009 No. 1167).   **★4–125**

Armed Forces Act 2006, s.64

Section 64 of the 2006 Act comes into force on October 31, 2009: *Armed Forces Act 2006 (Commencement No. 5) Order* 2009 (S.I. 2009 No. 1167).   **★4–125a**

Sections 65 and 127 of the 2006 Act come into force on October 31, 2009: *Armed Forces Act 2006 (Commencement No. 5) Order* 2009 (S.I. 2009 No. 1167).   **★4–125b**

(13) Defendant unfit to plead or take his trial

(a) *Procedure, evidence and burden of proof*

Criminal Procedure (Insanity) Act 1964, ss.4, 4A

Finding that the accused did the act or made the omission charged against him

4–168   Where one of two or more defendants is found unfit to plead and proceedings are to take place under section 4A of the 1964 Act (see the main work) for the determination of the question whether he did the act or made the omission charged against him, the wording of subsection (5) and of section 11(4) of the *Juries Act* 1974 ("(4) Subject to subsection (5) … , the jury selected by any one ballot shall try only one issue … ." (§ 4–233 in the main work)), when read together, do not preclude a jury from hearing both those proceedings and the trial of the fit defendants simultaneously; the "one issue" for the purposes of section 11(4) refers to an empanelled jury deciding whether allegations contained in an indictment are proved by the evidence presented to them, and that includes deciding whether the unfit defendant did the act or made the omission charged against him; if during the course of a trial of co-defendants one becomes unfit, the proceedings simply continue with the jury then deciding the more limited issue of whether or not that defendant committed the *actus reus* of the offence; and the same principle applies where one of the defendants has been found to be unfit before a jury are empanelled: *R. v. B., W., S., H. and W.* [2009] 1 Cr.App.R. 19, CA.

C. CHANGE OF PLEA

Application to change a plea of guilty

4–187a   With effect from April 6, 2009, Part 37 of the *Criminal Procedure Rules* 2005 (S.I. 2005 No. 384) is substituted by a new Part 37. Rule 37.9 corresponds in substance to the original rule 37.6.

VI. THE JURY

B. QUALIFICATION

Juries Act 1974, Sched. 1

Persons disqualified

★4–202   The amendments to Part 2 of Schedule 1 to the 1974 Act effected by the *AFA* 2006 come into force on October 31, 2009: *Armed Forces Act 2006 (Commencement No. 5) Order* 2009 (S.I. 2009 No. 1167). In connection with that commencement, see the transitional provision in the *Armed Forces Act 2006 (Transitional Provisions etc.) Order* 2009 (S.I. 2009 No. 1059), Sched. 1, para. 15 (interpretation of reference to "a service offence").

C. SUMMONING AND PANELS

Juries Act 1974, s.18

Effect of non-compliance on verdict

★4–222   See *R. v. Jalil, post,* § 4–233.

E. The Ballot and Swearing of Jurors

Juries Act 1974, s.11

In connection with subsection (4), see *R. v. B.*, *ante*, § 4–168.   **4–233**

Whereas it was held in *R. v. Mulkerrings and Sansom* (see the main work)   ★
that a jury ballot required more than 12 entrants, a ballot had taken place
where, of the 14 jurors put forward for the ballot, the prosecution had — at
the suggestion of the judge following unsuccessful defence attempts to have
them excluded by reason of their connection to the armed forces and/or the
police — stood two of them by when their names were called; standing by
only put the potential juror to the back of the line and if there had been a
successful challenge to one of the other twelve, or if for any reason one of
them could not sit, one of those two potential jurors would have served; the
question which arose in relation to the two jurors was not a question of qualification to sit but was one of possible challenge for cause and the time for
making such a challenge was after the ballot (*Juries Act* 1974, s.12(3) (§ 4–234
in the main work)); however, that did not mean that the oft-followed and convenient procedure of inviting the judge, where all parties agree, to rule in
anticipation upon a possible challenge for cause was wrong, or ought not to
be followed; and, in any event, no objection to the procedure having been
taken at the time, section 18(1)(a) and (2) of the 1974 Act (§ 4–222 in the main
work) effectively precluded it being raised as a ground of appeal: *R. v. Jalil*
[2009] Crim.L.R. 443, CA.

F. The Judge's Discretion to Stand Jurors Down

It was held in *R. v. G.C.* [2008] Crim.L.R. 984, CA, that a jury's verdict was   **4–233a**
safe where a serving police officer who worked on a unit undertaking
investigations into allegations of child abuse was a juror in a case where the
appellant was charged with a number of offences of sexual abuse against his
daughter, where the appellant was also a police officer and where the defence
case involved criticism of the conduct of the interviews of the complainant by
the police. The court said that whilst the fact that a police officer is a juror
does not of itself give rise to an appearance of bias (see *R. v. Abdroikov*; *R. v.
Green*; *R. v. Williamson* and *R. v. Khan* in the main work), there may be an appearance of bias in a number of situations including where a police officer
shares some connection, *e.g.* by place of service, with a police officer whose evidence in the case is going to be in dispute. However, here it was said that the
evidence of the police officer was not in dispute and the criticism of the way
she conducted the interview with the complainant was on an issue of comparatively narrow significance. Furthermore, it was taking the application of the
question whether there was a real danger or a real risk of bias a step too far to
suggest that the juror might as a result of her time working on investigations
of this kind have taken the view that complainants are generally truthful; this
was an assumption that could not be made.

J. Discharge of Juror or Jury

(4) Misconduct or bias

For a case, the facts of which illustrate the desirability of a special warning   **★4–256**
to a juror who is stood down at the outset because of his knowledge of the de-

fendant as to the imperative need not to discuss any aspect of the case with the remaining jurors, see *R. v. Hambleton* [2009] 2 *Archbold News* 2, CA.

L. Miscellaneous

(2) Direction to jury as to how to approach their role

★**4–264b**   It was held in *R. v. Thakrar* [2009] Crim.L.R. 357, CA, that the presumption that jurors follow the directions they receive (*Montgomery v. H.M. Advocate*; *Coulter v. H.M. Advocate* [2003] 1 A.C. 641, PC) had been rebutted in respect of a judge's summing up in which he told the jury to ignore as irrelevant the defendant's previous convictions that had come to their attention when they should not have done, where (a) one member of the jury had already failed to comply with at least the spirit of the judge's direction at the beginning of the trial (*viz.* to seek nobody else's opinion about the case) by researching the internet to see what he could find out about the defendant, (b) all members of the jury had already failed to comply with at least the spirit of that direction by receiving and not disclosing to the judge the information that that juror had found and, even more seriously, keeping quiet about it until the defendant had given evidence-in-chief, and (c) the defendant having given evidence without disclosing his previous convictions, there was a real risk that the jurors had formed an adverse view of him and his evidence at that time of which they would later be unable to divest themselves. The court found that there was a real possibility that a member or members of the jury had not followed the direction in the summing-up such that the conviction was unsafe.

XII. SUBMISSION OF NO CASE TO ANSWER

A. Practice

4–292   *R. v. N. Ltd* is now reported at [2009] 1 Cr.App.R. 3.

XIII. THE DEFENCE CASE

B. Warning as to Giving of Evidence by Defendant

Criminal Justice and Public Order Act 1994, s.35

Effect of accused's silence at trial

★**4–305**   The amendment of section 35 of the 1994 Act effected by the *AFA* 2006 comes into force on October 31, 2009: *Armed Forces Act 2006 (Commencement No. 5) Order* 2009 (S.I. 2009 No. 1167).

★**4–305a**   *R. (DPP) v. Kavanagh* (see the main work) was applied in *R. v. Tabbakh*, 173 J.P. 201, CA, where it was held that whilst the terms of section 35(1)(b) of the 1994 Act make it clear that the test it poses is required to be answered according to the physical or mental condition of the accused, it does not follow that all the circumstances of the case (including the potential importance of the defendant's evidence) do not fall to be taken into account in deciding whether it is undesirable for the accused to give evidence; and it is plainly not sufficient that the defendant suffers from some physical or mental condition that may cause him some difficulty in giving evidence; it must be a condition which is such as to make it undesirable for him to give evidence; many, if not most, difficulties that a defendant or any other witness may have in giving evidence are things that have to be assessed by the tribunal of fact.

XVII. SUMMING UP

C. Miscellaneous

(6) Scope of judge's task

As to directions in law needing do no more than guide the jury as to the essential factual dispute and the conclusions to be drawn from the different findings open to them on the evidence, see *R. v. Harvey* [2009] 4 *Archbold News* 2, CA.   ★4–376

F. What Degree of Unanimity is Required of a Jury?

R. v. Brown (K.) (see the main work), was distinguished in *R. v. K. (Robert)* [2009] 1 Cr.App.R. 24, CA. During the trial of the appellant for an offence of rape of a child under 13 (*SOA* 2003, s.5 (§ 20–49 in the main work)), it became unclear whether, in respect of a single incident, the complainant was alleging that she had been penetrated vaginally or anally. The Court of Appeal held that the judge had been entitled to direct the jury that it mattered not "for example that six of you are sure that it was the anus and the other six are sure it was within the labia". As to the form of the indictment, see *ante*, § 1–137.   ★4–391

G. Comment

(1) On the merits

As to commenting on how to approach a delay in making a complaint of rape, see *R. v. Doody, post*, § 20–27a.   4–394

XVIII. RETIREMENT OF JURY UNTIL VERDICT

D. Majority Verdicts

**Practice Direction (Criminal Proceedings: Consolidation), para. IV.46.2–46.8
[2002] 1 W.L.R. 2870**

It was said in *R. v. Stringfellow, The Times*, November 14, 2008, CA, that where there was a failure to follow the procedure for taking a verdict, as prescribed by paragraph IV.46 of the consolidated criminal practice direction, it was desirable that counsel should interrupt the procedure in order that it might be started again, rather than make an unnecessary excursion to the Court of Appeal.   4–435

XIX. VERDICT

A. GENERAL

4–443   It was held in *R. v. McEvilly* [2008] Crim.L.R. 968, CA, that where an indictment contains alternative charges of differing seriousness, the judge should not take a verdict on the less serious count until finality has been reached on the more serious charge. Such finality may take the form of a not guilty verdict, or a decision to discharge the jury because there is no realistic prospect of agreement. If a verdict is prematurely returned on an alternative count, the judge should decline to accept it. However, the court said that if the judge does accept it, it is liable to be quashed on appeal where the jury subsequently return a verdict of guilty on the more serious count (*R. v. Fernandez* (see § 21–288 in the main work)).

CHAPTER 5

SENTENCES AND ORDERS ON CONVICTION

I. GENERAL INTERPRETATION

(2) Legislation

Powers of Criminal Courts (Sentencing) Act 2000, ss.161, 163, 164

General definitions

★**5–3**   The amendment of section 163 of the 2000 Act effected by the *AFA* 2006 comes into force on October 31, 2009: *Armed Forces Act 2006 (Commencement No. 5) Order* 2009 (S.I. 2009 No. 1167).

★   The commencement of the *CJA* 2003 amendments due to take effect on April 4, 2009 has been postponed to April 4, 2010 (*Criminal Justice Act 2003 (Commencement No. 8 and Transitional and Saving Provisions) (Amendment) Order* 2009 (S.I. 2009 No. 616)), but it is expected that they will in due course (anticipated to be November 30, 2009) be overtaken by the commencement of the repeals effected by the *CJIA* 2008, the net effect being that they never come into force.

Criminal Justice Act 2003, ss.176, 305

Interpretation of Part 12

★**5–7**   The amendments of section 305 of the 2003 Act effected by the *AFA* 2006 come into force on October 31, 2009: *Armed Forces Act 2006 (Commencement No. 5) Order* 2009 (S.I. 2009 No. 1167).

III. GENERAL PRINCIPLES

B. Determining the Seriousness of an Offence

(1) Statute

Criminal Justice Act 2003, s.143

The amendment of section 143 of the 2003 Act effected by the *AFA* 2006   ★**5-54**
comes into force on October 31, 2009: *Armed Forces Act 2006 (Commencement
No. 5) Order* 2009 (S.I. 2009 No. 1167). In connection with that commencement, see the transitional provision in the *Armed Forces Act 2006 (Transitional
Provisions etc.) Order* 2009 (S.I. 2009 No. 1059), Sched. 1, para. 53(5) (interpretation of references to "previous conviction").

As to whether it is legitimate in assessing the seriousness of an offence to
take account of the impact of the offence on persons other than the immediate victim, see *R. v. Darwin (Anne) and Darwin (John)*, *post* § 5–77a.

Offences with a terrorist connection

See section 30 of the *Counter-Terrorism Act* 2008, *post*, § 25–142q.   **5-63a**

(2) Factual basis of sentence

(b) *Following plea of guilty*

The defence case

The correct reference for *R. v. Underwood* is [2005] 1 Cr.App.R. 13.   ★**5-73**

In connection with *R. v. Underwood*, reference should also be made to   ★
paragraphs IV.45.10 to IV.45.14 of the consolidated criminal practice direction as inserted by *Practice Direction (Criminal proceedings: victim personal statements; pleas of guilty in the Crown Court; forms)*, *The Times*, May 19, 2009,
Supreme Court, with effect from May 14, 2009.

Practice Direction (Criminal Proceedings: Consolidation), paras IV.45.10–IV.45.14 (as inserted by Practice Direction (Criminal proceedings: victim personal statements; pleas of guilty in the Crown Court; forms), The Times, May 19, 2009)

IV.45.10   The prosecution may reach an agreement with the defendant as to the
factual basis on which the defendant will plead guilty, often known as an "agreed
basis of plea". It is always subject to the approval of the court, which will consider
whether it is fair and in the interests of justice.

IV.45.11   *R. v. Underwood* ... outlines the principles to be applied where the defendant admits that he or she is guilty, but disputes the basis of offending alleged by
the prosecution:

    (a) the prosecution may accept and agree the defendant's account of the
        disputed facts or reject it in its entirety; if the prosecution accepts the
        defendant's basis of plea, it must ensure that the basis of plea is factually ac-
        curate and enables the sentencing judge to impose a sentence appropriate to
        reflect the justice of the case;

    (b) in resolving any disputed factual matters, the prosecution must consider its primary duty to the court and must not agree with or acquiesce in an agreement which contains material factual disputes;

    (c) if the prosecution does accept the defendant's basis of plea, it must be reduced to writing, be signed by advocates for both sides, and made available to the judge prior to the prosecution's opening;

    (d) an agreed basis of plea that has been reached between the parties must not contain any matters which are in dispute;

    (e) on occasion the prosecution may lack the evidence positively to dispute the defendant's account, for example, where the defendant asserts a matter outside the knowledge of the prosecution; simply because the prosecution does not have evidence to contradict the defendant's assertions does not mean those assertions should be agreed; in such a case, the prosecution should test the defendant's evidence and submissions by requesting a *Newton* hearing [see § 5–74 in the main work], following the procedure set out in paragraph IV.45.13, below;

    (f) if it is not possible for the parties to resolve a factual dispute when attempting to reach a plea agreement under this part, it is the responsibility of the prosecution to consider whether the matter should proceed to trial, or to invite the court to hold a *Newton* hearing as necessary;

    (g) subject to paragraph IV.45.12, where the prosecution has not invited the court to hold a *Newton* hearing, and where the factual dispute between the prosecution and the defence is likely to have a material impact on the sentence, if the defence does not invite the court to hold a *Newton* hearing the court is entitled to reach its own conclusion of the facts on the evidence before it.

    IV.45.12   *R. v. Underwood* emphasises that whether or not pleas have been "agreed" the judge is not bound by any such agreement and is entitled of his or her own motion to insist that any evidence relevant to the facts in dispute (or upon which the judge requires further evidence for whatever reason) should be called. Any view formed by the prosecution on a proposed basis of plea is deemed to be conditional on the judge's acceptance of the basis of plea.

    IV.45.13   Where the defendant pleads guilty, but disputes the basis of offending alleged by the prosecution, the following procedure should be followed:

    (a) the defendant's basis of plea must be set out in writing, identifying what is in dispute;

    (b) the court may invite the parties to make representations about whether the dispute is material to sentence; and

    (c) if the court decides that it is a material dispute, the court will invite such further representations or evidence as it may require and decide the dispute in accordance with the principles set out in *R. v. Newton*.

    IV.45.14   Where the disputed issue arises from facts which are within the exclusive knowledge of the defendant and the defendant is willing to give evidence in support of his case, the defence advocate should be prepared to call the defendant. If the defendant is not willing to testify, and subject to any explanation which may be given, the judge may draw such inferences as appear appropriate. Paragraphs 6 to 10 of *Underwood* provide additional guidance regarding the Newton hearing procedure.

★   Paragraphs IV.45.18 to IV.45.28 of the consolidated criminal practice direction, also as inserted by *Practice Direction (Criminal proceedings: victim personal statements; pleas of guilty in the Crown Court; forms)*, *ante*, make provision as to the practice to be followed in cases of serious fraud where a plea agreement has been reached pursuant to the Attorney-General's guidelines on plea discussions in such cases and where a joint sentencing submission is to be placed before the court. For convenience, these paragraphs of the practice direction are set out in Appendix A, together with the guidelines: see A–281 *et seq*.

Resolution of disputed issues

A judge is entitled to refuse to give any credit for a plea of guilty where   ★**5–74**
there is an overwhelming case, and where thereafter there has been a *Newton*
hearing (see the main work) during which the defendant has clearly lied as to
his involvement in the offence (see para. 4.3(iv) of the Sentencing Guideline
Council's revised guideline on guilty pleas (*post*, Appendix K–6)): *R. v. Elicin
and Moore* [2009] 1 Cr.App.R.(S.) 98, CA.

(3) Information about the effect of the offence on the victim

Paragraphs III.28.1 and III.28.2 of the consolidated criminal practice   ★**5–77a**
direction have been reissued with effect from May 14, 2009: *Practice Direction
(Criminal proceedings: victim personal statements; pleas of guilty in the Crown
Court; forms)*, *The Times*, May 19, 2009, Supreme Court. The changes are
limited to pointing out that the family of a victim may make a victim personal
statement in certain circumstances (as where the victim has died as a result of
relevant criminal conduct) and that it will not normally be appropriate for a
victim personal statement to be made or updated following the disposal of a
case, but that this may be necessary on certain rare occasions (as between
sentence and appeal where a final prognosis was not available at the time of
the first instance hearing).

It was held in *R. v. Darwin (Anne) and Darwin (John)*, *The Times*, April 1,   ★
2009, CA, that, when considering the seriousness of an offence of fraud, pursuant to section 143 of the *CJA* 2003 (see § 5–54 in the main work), the
protection of the law could not be confined to those who had lost financially.
Human beings on whom the crime has had a devastating impact are
legitimately and properly to be considered. See also *post*, § 21–368.

C. Reduction in Sentence for Guilty Plea

Advance indication of sentence

Paragraphs IV.45.29 to IV.45.33 of the consolidated criminal practice   ★**5–79b**
direction, as inserted by *Practice Direction (Criminal proceedings: victim personal
statements; pleas of guilty in the Crown Court; forms)*, *The Times*, May 19, 2009,
Supreme Court, effective from May 14, 2009, summarise the effect of *R. v.
Goodyear* (see the main work). Apart from the points dealt with in the main
work, they emphasise that an indication should not be given if there is a
dispute as to the basis of plea unless the judge concludes that he can properly
deal with the case without the need for a *Newton* hearing (as to which, see
§ 5–74 in the main work) and that the embargo on the prosecution saying
anything to indicate their approval or support for any indication given applies
in all circumstances, including where joint sentencing submissions have been
made pursuant to the Attorney-General's guidelines on plea discussions in
cases of serious fraud (as to which, see post, Appendix A–274 *et seq.*). Where a
dispute arises, the procedure set out in paragraphs IV.45.11 to IV.45.13
(*ante*, § 5–73) should be followed prior to further consideration being given to
an indication.

It was held in *R. v. Patel* [2009] 3 *Archbold News* 4, CA, that, when indicat-   ★
ing sentence pursuant to *R. v. Goodyear*, a judge is only entitled to commit
himself to the maximum sentence that he would impose if the defendant were
then and there to plead guilty. Even where the judge expresses his indication

by reference to a notional post-trial sentence, this cannot bind him or any other judge when sentencing after a trial. Furthermore, it was reiterated that if a defendant decides not to accept an indication, it lapses and is thereafter irrelevant. At the end of the trial, a judge's assessment of the seriousness of the offence may be significantly different, whether because the evidence against the defendant has worsened or simply because the judge has a fuller picture of the criminality involved.

Withholding the discount

5–82   It should be noted in relation to *Att.-Gen.'s References (Nos 117 and 118 of 2006) (R. v. Jesus and De Oliviera)* (cited in the main work) that whilst the Court of Appeal rejected a suggestion that the judge in that case should not have allowed the full discount for the pleas of guilty, its approach was that it was "very much a matter for the judge" whether to allow a full discount where a *Newton* hearing has been prepared for, but has not been required.

D. Increase in Sentences for Racial or Religious Aggravation or Aggravation Related to Disability or Sexual Orientation

Meaning of "racially or religiously aggravated"

5–88   Where the appellant, a British National Party member, had stuck a series of posters in a high street bearing the slogan "Illegal Immigrant Murder Scum", photographs of three black men who had been convicted of the manslaughter of a woman holding a baby at a christening, and contact details for the British National Party and where it would not have necessarily been apparent to passers-by that the men depicted in the photographs were the convicted killers, it was held in *Kendall v. South East Magistrates' Court*, 72 J.C.L. 484, DC ([2008] EWHC 1848 (Admin.)), that, on the facts, it was reasonably open to the magistrates: (i) to conclude that the posters were conveying the message that black people were scum because they were the sort of people who came to the country illegally and who either did commit, or were capable of committing, crimes like murder, and that the posters were therefore threatening and abusive, contrary to section 5(1) of the *Public Order Act* 1986, (ii) to conclude that the appellant was aware that the posters were conveying that message and they may therefore have been found by others to be threatening, abusive or insulting (thereby satisfying the *mens rea* requirement for the s.5 offence set out in s.6(4) of the 1986 Act (§ 29–35 in the main work)), and (iii) (despite the fact that the appellant's primary motivation may have been simply to recruit new members by highlighting issues relating to immigration) to treat as significant the fact that the appellant chose to illustrate the prevalence of crimes committed by illegal immigrants with black men, which, together with the use of the highly derogatory word "scum" and the notion that the immigrant community should be judged by the action of these particular illegal immigrants, justified the conclusion that his conduct amounted (in addition to his primary motivation) to a manifestation of his hostility to immigrants, within section 28(1)(b) of the *CDA* 1998 (§ 5–84 in the main work), and contrary to section 31 of the 1998 *Act* (§ 29–38a in the main work)), in that their non-Britishness was perceived by him to derive from their race or colour (*cf. Att.-Gen.'s Reference (No. 4 of 2004)* (cited in the main work)). Furthermore, the court rejected the argument that the posters amounted to no more than might appear in a tabloid newspaper and that "scum" was also a word often used by such publications.

F. Sentencing Guidelines

Criminal Justice Act 2003, s.172

Duty of court to have regard to sentencing guidelines

The Sentencing Guidelines Council has issued two further definitive   **5–100**
guidelines relating to breach of an anti-social behaviour order (*post*, Appendix
K–196 *et seq.*) and theft and burglary other than in a dwelling (*post*, Appendix
K–209 *et seq.*).

Even a definitive sentencing guideline is not to be used or approached as if
each offence can be put into fixed and inflexible compartments; assessing the
seriousness of an offence involves a broad judgment of overall criminality: *R.
v. Herbert* [2009] 2 Cr.App.R.(S.) 9, CA. In that case, the trial judge's decision
to place a case at the top of the most serious category of case under the
Sentencing Guidelines Council's definitive guideline for offences contrary to
the *Offences against the Person Act* 1861, s.18 (§ 19–199 in the main work) was
upheld, on the basis that the judge had rated it the worst case he had
encountered in 30 years at the bar and on the bench, notwithstanding that
it did not fall within the council's description of cases falling into that category by reason of it not involving a weapon, nor being premeditated.

For a further example of the Court of Appeal taking a robust approach to
an attempt by counsel to rely on a draft guideline, see *R. v. Abbas* [2009]
R.T.R. 3, CA, where the court stated that the Sentencing Guidelines Council's
draft guideline on causing death by driving was not a guideline "to which it is
appropriate for this court to have any reference at all".

H. Taking Offences Into Consideration

Significance

It was held in *R. v. Lavery*, 172 J.P. 561, CA, that there was no reason in   **5–109a**
principle why an offence to be taken into consideration, which was of a more
serious nature than the index offence or offences, should not result in a
higher sentence than would otherwise have been the case, as the sentence
would then reflect the defendant's overall criminality (considering *R. v. Miles*
(see the main work)). The court added, however, that inappropriate non-
charging and under-charging were inimical to the administration of justice.

V. COMMUNITY SENTENCES

A. Introduction

Criminal Justice Act 2003

As to the continued application of the former statutory provisions to of-   **5–121e**
fences committed by persons aged 16 or 17 beyond April 4, 2009, see *ante*,
§ 5–3.

Criminal Justice and Immigration Act 2008

As at June, 2009, it was anticipated that the provisions of the 2008 Act re-   **5–122**
lating to youth rehabilitation orders would be commenced on November 30,

2009, and accordingly those provisions will be included in the 2010 edition (to be published on November 19, 2009). The commencement of the provisions due to come into force on April 4, 2009, has been delayed: see *ante*, § 5–3.

AA. COMMUNITY REHABILITATION, COMMUNITY PUNISHMENT, DRUG TREATMENT AND TESTING, AND DRUG ABSTINENCE ORDERS

(1) General provisions

Powers of Criminal Courts (Sentencing) Act 2000, ss.33–36

Meaning of "community order" and "community sentence"

5–122a   **33.**—(1) In this Act, "community order" means any of the following orders—
(a) a curfew order;
(aa) an exclusion order;
(b) a community rehabilitation order;
(c) a community punishment order;
(d) a community punishment and rehabilitation order;
(e) a drug treatment and testing order;
(ee) a drug abstinence order;
(f) an attendance centre order;
(g) a supervision order;
(h) an action plan order.

(2) In this Act, "community sentence" means a sentence which consists of or includes one or more community orders.

[This section is printed as amended by the *CJCSA* 2000, s.74, and Sched. 7, paras 1 to 3 and 161.]

Community orders not available where sentence fixed by law etc.

5–122b   **34.** None of the powers to make community orders which are conferred by this Part is exercisable in respect of an offence for which the sentence—
(a) is fixed by law; or
(b) falls to be imposed under section 109(2), 110(2) or 111(2) below (requirement to impose custodial sentences for certain repeated offences committed by offenders aged 18 or over).

[This section was repealed as from April 4, 2005 (*Criminal Justice Act 2003 (Commencement No. 8 and Transitional and Saving Provisions) Order* 2005 (S.I. 2005 No. 950)): *CJA* 2003, s.332, and Sched. 7, Pt 7. For the relevant saving provisions, see *ante*, § 5–1a.]

As to (b), see section 164(3), § 5–5 in the main work.

Restrictions on imposing community sentences

5–122c   **35.**—(1) A court shall not pass a community sentence on an offender unless it is of the opinion that the offence, or the combination of the offence and one or more offences associated with it, was serious enough to warrant such a sentence.

(2) In consequence of the provision made by section 51 below with respect to community punishment and rehabilitation orders, a community sentence shall not

consist of or include both a community rehabilitation order and a community punishment order.

(3) Subject to subsection (2) above and to section 69(5) below (which limits the community orders that may be combined with an action plan order), where a court passes a community sentence—

(a) the particular order or orders comprising or forming part of the sentence shall be such as in the opinion of the court is, or taken together are, the most suitable for the offender; and

(b) the restrictions on liberty imposed by the order or orders shall be such as in the opinion of the court are commensurate with the seriousness of the offence, or the combination of the offence and one or more offences associated with it.

(4) Subsections (1) and (3)(b) above have effect subject to section 59 below (curfew orders and community punishment orders for persistent petty offenders).

[This section is printed as amended by the *CJCSA* 2000, s.74 and Sched. 7, paras 1 to 3. It is repealed as from April 4, 2005 (*Criminal Justice Act 2003 (Commencement No. 8 and Transitional and Saving Provisions) Order* 2005 (S.I. 2005 No. 950)): *CJA* 2003, s.332, and Sched. 7, Pt 7. For the relevant saving provisions, see § 5–1a in the main work.]

Procedural requirements for community sentences: pre-sentence reports etc.

36.—(1) In forming any such opinion as is mentioned in subsection (1) or (3)(b)   **5–122d**
of section 35 above, a court shall take into account all such information as is available to it about the circumstances of the offence or (as the case may be) of the offence and the offence or offences associated with it, including any aggravating or mitigating factors.

(2) In forming any such opinion as is mentioned in subsection (3)(a) of that section, a court may take into account any information about the offender which is before it.

(3) The following provisions of this section apply in relation to—

(a) a community rehabilitation order which includes additional requirements authorised by Schedule 2 to this Act;

(b) a community punishment order;

(c) a community punishment and rehabilitation order;

(d) a drug treatment and testing order;

(e) a supervision order which includes requirements authorised by Schedule 6 to this Act.

(4) Subject to subsection (5) below, a court shall obtain and consider a pre-sentence report before forming an opinion as to the suitability for the offender of one or more of the orders mentioned in subsection (3) above.

(5) Subsection (4) above does not apply if, in the circumstances of the case, the court is of the opinion that it is unnecessary to obtain a pre-sentence report.

(6) In a case where the offender is aged under 18 and the offence is not triable only on indictment and there is no other offence associated with it that is triable only on indictment, the court shall not form such an opinion as is mentioned in subsection (5) above unless—

(a) there exists a previous pre-sentence report obtained in respect of the offender; and

(b) the court has had regard to the information contained in that report, or, if there is more than one such report, the most recent report.

(7) No community sentence which consists of or includes such an order as is mentioned in subsection (3) above shall be invalidated by the failure of a court to obtain and consider a pre-sentence report before forming an opinion as to the suitability of the order for the offender, but any court on an appeal against such a sentence—

(a) shall, subject to subsection (8) below, obtain a pre-sentence report if none was obtained by the court below; and

(b) shall consider any such report obtained by it or by that court.

(8) Subsection (7)(a) above does not apply if the court is of the opinion—

(a) that the court below was justified in forming an opinion that it was unnecessary to obtain a pre-sentence report; or

(b) that, although the court below was not justified in forming that opinion, in the circumstances of the case at the time it is before the court, it is unnecessary to obtain a pre-sentence report.

(9) In a case where the offender is aged under 18 and the offence is not triable only on indictment and there is no other offence associated with it that is triable only on indictment, the court shall not form such an opinion as is mentioned in subsection (8) above unless—

(a) there exists a previous pre-sentence report obtained in respect of the offender; and

(b) the court has had regard to the information contained in that report, or, if there is more than one such report, the most recent report.

(10) Section 156 below (disclosure of pre-sentence report to offender etc.) applies to any pre-sentence report obtained in pursuance of this section.

[This section is printed as amended by the *CJCSA* 2000, s.74, and Sched. 7, paras 1 to 3. It is repealed as from April 4, 2005 (*Criminal Justice Act 2003 (Commencement No. 8 and Transitional and Saving Provisions) Order* 2005 (S.I. 2005 No. 950)): *CJA* 2003, s.332, and Sched. 7, Pt 7. For the relevant saving provisions, see § 5–1a in the main work.]

5–122e   Apart from the matters specifically referred to in section 36, a court, in forming an opinion as to the suitability of a community order, should have regard, in particular to sections 151 (effect of previous convictions and offending while on bail) (now section 143 of the *CJA* 2003 (§ 5–54 in the main work)) and 158 (savings for mitigation and mentally disordered offenders) of the *PCC(S)A* 2000 (now section 166 of the *CJA* 2003 (§ 5–90 in the main work)).

Powers of Criminal Courts (Sentencing) Act 2000, s.36A

Pre-sentence drug testing

5–122f   **36A.**—(1) Where a person aged 18 or over is convicted of an offence and the court is considering passing a community sentence, it may make an order under subsection (2) below for the purpose of ascertaining whether the offender has any specified Class A drug in his body.

(2) The order shall require the offender to provide, in accordance with the order, samples of any description specified in the order.

(3) If it is proved to the satisfaction of the court that the offender has, without reasonable excuse, failed to comply with the order it may impose on him a fine of an amount not exceeding level 4.

In this subsection, "level 4" means the amount which, in relation to a fine for a summary offence, is level 4 on the standard scale.

(4) The court shall not make an order under subsection (2) above unless it has been notified by the Secretary of State that the power to make such orders is exercisable by the court and the notice has not been withdrawn.

[This section was inserted by the *CJCSA* 2000, s.48. It is repealed as from April 4, 2005 (*Criminal Justice Act 2003 (Commencement No. 8 and Transitional and Saving Provisions) Order* 2005 (S.I. 2005 No. 950)): *CJA* 2003, s.332, and Sched. 7, Pt 7. For the relevant saving provisions, see § 5–1a in the main work.]

The court may make a similar order under section 52(4) (*post*, § 5–123d), if it is contemplating a drug treatment and testing order. Failure to express willingness to comply with an order under section 52(4) may empower the court to pass a custodial sentence: see the *PCC(S)A* 2000, s.79(3) (*post*, § 5–275a).

(2) Particular orders

(a) *Community rehabilitation orders*

Powers of Criminal Courts (Sentencing) Act 2000, ss.41–44

Community rehabilitation orders

41.—(1) Where a person aged 16 or over is convicted of an offence and the court by or before which he is convicted is of the opinion that his supervision is desirable in the interests of— **5–122g**

(a) securing his rehabilitation, or

(b) protecting the public from harm from him or preventing the commission by him of further offences,

the court may (subject to sections 34 to 36 above) make an order requiring him to be under supervision for a period specified in the order of not less than six months nor more than three years.

(2) An order under subsection (1) above is in this Act referred to as a "community rehabilitation order".

(3) A community rehabilitation order shall specify the petty sessions area in which the offender resides or will reside.

(4) If the offender is aged 18 or over at the time when the community rehabilitation order is made, he shall, subject to paragraph 18 of Schedule 3 to this Act (offender's change of area), be required to be under the supervision of an officer of a local probation board appointed for or assigned to the petty sessions area specified in the order, or (as the case may be) an officer of a provider of probation services acting in the local justice area specified in the order.

(5) If the offender is aged under 18 at that time, he shall, subject to paragraph 18 of Schedule 3, be required to be under the supervision of—

(a) an officer of a local probation board appointed for or assigned to the petty sessions area specified in the order, or (as the case may be) an officer of a provider of probation services acting in the local justice area specified in the order; or

(b) a member of a youth offending team established by a local authority specified in the order;

and if an order specifies a local authority for the purposes of paragraph (b) above, the authority specified must be the local authority within whose area it appears to the court that the offender resides or will reside.

(6) In this Act, "responsible officer", in relation to an offender who is subject to a community rehabilitation order, means the officer of a local probation board, officer of a provider of probation services or member of a youth offending team responsible for his supervision.

(7) Before making a community rehabilitation order, the court shall explain to the offender in ordinary language—

(a) the effect of the order (including any additional requirements proposed to be included in the order in accordance with section 42 below);

(b) the consequences which may follow (under Part II of Schedule 3 to this Act) if he fails to comply with any of the requirements of the order; and

(c) that the court has power (under Parts III and IV of that Schedule) to

29

review the order on the application *either* of the offender *or of the responsible officer* [, of the responsible officer or any affected person].

(8) On making a community rehabilitation order, the court may, if it thinks it expedient for the purpose of the offender's reformation, allow any person who consents to do so to give security for the good behaviour of the offender.

(9) The court by which a community rehabilitation order is made shall forthwith give copies of the order to—

(a) if the offender is aged 18 or over, an officer of a local probation board assigned to the court or an officer of a provider of probation services acting at the court (as the case may be), or

(b) if the offender is aged under 18—

(i) an officer of a local probation board assigned to the court or an officer of a provider of probation services acting at the court (as the case may be); or

(ii) a member of a youth offending team assigned to the court,

and he shall give a copy to the offender, to the responsible officer and to the person in charge of any institution in which the offender is required by the order to reside.

[(9A) The court by which such an order is made shall give to any affected person any information relating to the order which the court considers it appropriate for him to have.]

(10) The court by which such an order is made shall also, except where it itself acts for the petty sessions area specified in the order, send to the clerk to the justices for that area—

(a) a copy of the order; and

(b) such documents and information relating to the case as it considers likely to be of assistance to a court acting for that area in the exercise of its functions in relation to the order.

(11) An offender in respect of whom a community rehabilitation order is made shall keep in touch with the responsible officer in accordance with such instructions as he may from time to time be given by that officer, and shall notify him of any change of address.

[(12) For the purposes of this Act, a person is an affected person in relation to a community rehabilitation order if—

(a) a requirement under section 36B(1) above is included in the order by virtue of his consent; or

(b) a requirement is included in the order under paragraph 8(1) of Schedule 2 to this Act for the purpose (or partly for the purpose) of protecting him from being approached by the offender.]

[This section is printed as amended by the *CJCSA* 2000, ss.43 and 74, and Sched. 7, para. 1; and the *Offender Management Act 2007 (Consequential Amendments) Order* 2008 (S.I. 2008 No. 912), art. 3, and Sched. 1, para. 14(1) and (4); and, as from a day to be appointed, para. 165 (omission of italicised words, insertion of words in square brackets). It is repealed as from April 4, 2005 (*Criminal Justice Act 2003 (Commencement No. 8 and Transitional and Saving Provisions) Order* 2005 (S.I. 2005 No. 950)): *CJA* 2003, s.332, and Sched. 7, Pt 7. For the relevant saving provisions, see § 5–1a in the main work; and *post*, §§ 5–130 *et seq.*]

A community rehabilitation order is a "community order" (s.33(1)), and thus a court must not make such an order without complying with sections 35 and 36 (*ante*, §§ 5–122c, 5–122d).

Additional requirements which may be included in community rehabilitation orders

5-122h   42.—(1) Subject to subsection (3) below, a community rehabilitation order may in addition require the offender to comply during the whole or any part of the community rehabilitation period with such requirements as the court, having regard to the circumstances of the case, considers desirable in the interests of—

    (a) securing the rehabilitation of the offender; or

    (b) protecting the public from harm from him or preventing the commission by him of further offences.

(2) Without prejudice to the generality of subsection (1) above,

    (a) the additional requirements which may be included in a community rehabilitation order shall include the requirements which are authorised by Schedule 2 to this Act.

    (b) subject to subsections (2D) and (2F) below, the order shall, if the first set of conditions is satisfied, include a drug abstinence requirement and may include such a requirement if the second set of conditions is satisfied.

(2A) For the purposes of this Part of this Act, a drug abstinence requirement is a requirement for the offender—

    (a) to abstain from misusing specified Class A drugs; and

    (b) to provide, when instructed to do so by the responsible officer, any sample mentioned in the instruction for the purpose of ascertaining whether he has any specified Class A drug in his body.

(2B) The first set of conditions is—

    (a) that the offender was aged 18 or over on the date of his conviction for the offence;

    (b) that, in the opinion of the court, the offender is dependent on or has a propensity to misuse specified Class A drugs; and

    (c) that the offence is a trigger offence.

(2C) The second set of conditions is—

    (a) that the offender was aged 18 or over on the date of his conviction for the offence; and

    (b) that, in the opinion of the court—

        (i) the offender is dependent on or has a propensity to misuse specified Class A drugs; and

        (ii) the misuse by the offender of any specified Class A drug caused or contributed to the offence.

(2D) The order may not include a drug abstinence requirement if—

    (a) the community rehabilitation order includes any requirement in respect of drugs under paragraph 6 of Schedule 2 to this Act; or

    (b) the community sentence includes a drug treatment and testing order or a drug abstinence order.

(2E) The function of giving instructions for the purposes of subsection (2A)(b) above shall be exercised in accordance with guidance given from time to time by the Secretary of State; and the Secretary of State may make rules for regulating the provision of samples in pursuance of such instructions.

(2F) The court shall not include a drug abstinence requirement in the order unless the court has been notified by the Secretary of State that arrangements for implementing such requirements are available in the area proposed to be specified under section 41(3) above and the notice has not been withdrawn.

(3) Without prejudice to the power of the court under section 130 below to make a compensation order, the payment of sums by way of damages for injury or compensation for loss shall not be included among the additional requirements of a community rehabilitation order.

[This section is printed as amended by the *CJCSA* 2000, ss.49 and 74, and Sched. 7, paras 1 and 166. It is repealed as from April 4, 2005 (*Criminal Justice Act 2003 (Commencement No. 8 and Transitional and Saving Provisions) Order* 2005 (S.I. 2005 No. 950)): *CJA* 2003, s.332, and Sched. 7, Pt 7. For the relevant saving provisions, see § 5–1a in the main work; and *post*, §§ 5–131a *et seq.*]

As to what is a "trigger offence", see the *CJCSA* 2000, Sched. 6 (§ 15–246b in the main work).

As to "specified Class A drugs", see § 15–245c in the main work.

Breach, revocation and amendment of community rehabilitation order

5–122i　　　**43.** [*Gives effect to Sched. 3, post, §§ 5–123p et seq.*]

Offenders residing in Scotland or Northern Ireland

5–122j　　　**44.** [*Gives effect to Sched. 4.*]

Powers of Criminal Courts (Sentencing) Act 2000, Sched. 2

SCHEDULE 2

ADDITIONAL REQUIREMENTS WHICH MAY BE INCLUDED IN COMMUNITY
REHABILITATION ORDERS

Requirements as to residence

5–122k　　　1.—(1) Subject to sub-paragraphs (2) and (3) below, a community rehabilitation order may include requirements as to the residence of the offender.

(2) Before making a community rehabilitation order containing any such requirement, the court shall consider the home surroundings of the offender.

(3) Where a community rehabilitation order requires the offender to reside in an approved hostel or any other institution, the period for which he is required to reside there shall be specified in the order.

Requirements as to activities etc.

5–122l　　　2.—(1) Subject to the provisions of this paragraph, a community rehabilitation order may require the offender—

(a) to present himself to a person or persons specified in the order at a place or places so specified;

(b) to participate or refrain from participating in activities specified in the order—

(i) on a day or days so specified; or

(ii) during the community rehabilitation period or such portion of it as may be so specified.

(2) A court shall not include in a community rehabilitation order a requirement such as is mentioned in sub-paragraph (1) above unless—

(a) it has consulted—

(i) in the case of an offender aged 18 or over, an officer of a local probation board; or

(ii) in the case of an offender aged under 18, either an officer of a local probation board or a member of a youth offending team; and

(b) it is satisfied that it is feasible to secure compliance with the requirement.

(3) A court shall not include a requirement such as is mentioned in sub-paragraph (1)(a) above or a requirement to participate in activities if it would involve the co-operation of a person other than the offender and the offender's responsible officer, unless that other person consents to its inclusion.

(4) A requirement such as is mentioned in sub-paragraph (1)(a) above shall operate to require the offender—

(a) in accordance with instructions given by his responsible officer, to present himself at a place or places for not more than 60 days in the aggregate; and

(b) while at any place, to comply with instructions given by, or under the
authority of, the person in charge of that place.

(5) A place specified in an order shall have been approved by the local probation
board for the area in which the premises are situated as providing facilities suitable
for persons subject to community rehabilitation orders.

(6) A requirement to participate in activities shall operate to require the offender—

(a) in accordance with instructions given by his responsible officer, to participate in activities for not more than 60 days in the aggregate; and

(b) while participating, to comply with instructions given by, or under the
authority of, the person in charge of the activities.

(7) Instructions given by the offender's responsible officer under sub-paragraph
(4) or (6) above shall, as far as practicable, be such as to avoid—

(a) any conflict with the offender's religious beliefs or with the requirements
of any other community order to which he may be subject; and

(b) any interference with the times, if any, at which he normally works or attends school or any other educational establishment.

Requirements as to attendance at community rehabilitation centre

3.—(1) Subject to the provisions of this paragraph, a community rehabilitation or-   **5–122m**
der may require the offender during the community rehabilitation period to attend
at a community rehabilitation centre specified in the order.

(2) A court shall not include in a community rehabilitation order such a requirement as is mentioned in sub-paragraph (1) above unless it has consulted—

(a) in the case of an offender aged 18 or over, an officer of a local probation
board; or

(b) in the case of an offender aged under 18, either an officer of a local probation board or a member of a youth offending team.

(3) A court shall not include such a requirement in a community rehabilitation order unless it is satisfied—

(a) that arrangements can be made for the offender's attendance at a centre;
and

(b) that the person in charge of the centre consents to the inclusion of the
requirement.

(4) A requirement under sub-paragraph (1) above shall operate to require the offender—

(a) in accordance with instructions given by his responsible officer, to attend
on not more than 60 days at the centre specified in the order; and

(b) while attending there to comply with instructions given by, or under the
authority of, the person in charge of the centre.

(5) Instructions given by the offender's responsible officer under sub-paragraph
(4) above shall, as far as practicable, be such as to avoid—

(a) any conflict with the offender's religious beliefs or with the requirements
of any other community order to which he may be subject; and

(b) any interference with the times, if any, at which he normally works or attends school or any other educational establishment.

(6) References in this paragraph to attendance at a community rehabilitation centre include references to attendance elsewhere than at the centre for the purpose of
participating in activities in accordance with instructions given by, or under the
authority of, the person in charge of the centre.

(7) The Secretary of State may make rules for regulating the provision and carrying on of community rehabilitation centres and the attendance at such centres of
persons subject to community rehabilitation orders; and such rules may in particular
include provision with respect to hours of attendance, the reckoning of days of attendance and the keeping of attendance records.

(8) In this paragraph "community rehabilitation centre" means premises—

    (a) at which non-residential facilities are provided for use in connection with the rehabilitation of offenders; and

    (b) which are for the time being approved by the Secretary of State as providing facilities suitable for persons subject to probation orders.

Extension of requirements for sexual offenders

5–122n   4. If the court so directs in the case of an offender who has been convicted of a sexual offence—

    (a) sub-paragraphs (4) and (6) of paragraph 2 above, and

    (b) sub-paragraph (4) of paragraph 3 above,

shall each have effect as if for the reference to 60 days there were substituted a reference to such greater number of days as may be specified in the direction.

Requirements as to treatment for mental condition etc.

5–122o   5.—(1) This paragraph applies where a court proposing to make a community rehabilitation order is satisfied, on the evidence of a registered medical practitioner approved for the purposes of section 12 of the *Mental Health Act* 1983, that the mental condition of the offender—

    (a) is such as requires and may be susceptible to treatment; but

    (b) is not such as to warrant the making of a hospital order or guardianship order within the meaning of that Act.

(2) Subject to sub-paragraph (4) below, the community rehabilitation order may include a requirement that the offender shall submit, during the whole of the community rehabilitation period or during such part or parts of that period as may be specified in the order, to treatment by or under the direction of a registered medical practitioner or a chartered psychologist (or both, for different parts) with a view to the improvement of the offender's mental condition.

(3) The treatment required by any such order shall be such one of the following kinds of treatment as may be specified in the order, that is to say—

    (a) treatment as a resident patient in an independent hospital or care home within the meaning of the *Care Standards Act* 2000 or a hospital within the meaning of the *Mental Health Act* 1983, but not hospital premises at which high security psychiatric services within the meaning of that Act are provided;

    (b) treatment as a non-resident patient at such institution or place as may be specified in the order;

    (c) treatment by or under the direction of such registered medical practitioner or chartered psychologist (or both) as may be so specified;

but the nature of the treatment shall not be specified in the order except as mentioned in paragraph (a), (b) or (c) above.

(4) A court shall not by virtue of this paragraph include in a community rehabilitation order a requirement that the offender shall submit to treatment for his mental condition unless—

    (a) it is satisfied that arrangements have been or can be made for the treatment intended to be specified in the order (including arrangements for the reception of the offender where he is to be required to submit to treatment as a resident patient); and

    (b) the offender has expressed his willingness to comply with such a requirement.

(5) While the offender is under treatment as a resident patient in pursuance of a requirement of the community rehabilitation order, his responsible officer shall carry out the supervision of the offender to such extent only as may be necessary for the purpose of the revocation or amendment of the order.

(6) Where the medical practitioner or chartered psychologist by whom or under whose direction an offender is being treated for his mental condition in pursuance of a community rehabilitation order is of the opinion that part of the treatment can be better or more conveniently given in or at an institution or place which—

(a) is not specified in the order, and

(b) is one in or at which the treatment of the offender will be given by or under the direction of a registered medical practitioner or chartered psychologist,

he may, with the consent of the offender, make arrangements for him to be treated accordingly.

(7) Such arrangements as are mentioned in sub-paragraph (6) above may provide for the offender to receive part of his treatment as a resident patient in an institution or place notwithstanding that the institution or place is not one which could have been specified for that purpose in the community rehabilitation order.

(8) Where any such arrangements as are mentioned in sub-paragraph (6) above are made for the treatment of an offender—

(a) the medical practitioner or chartered psychologist by whom the arrangements are made shall give notice in writing to the offender's responsible officer, specifying the institution or place in or at which the treatment is to be carried out; and

(b) the treatment provided for by the arrangements shall be deemed to be treatment to which he is required to submit in pursuance of the community rehabilitation order.

(9) Subsections (2) and (3) of section 54 of the *Mental Health Act* 1983 shall have effect with respect to proof for the purposes of sub-paragraph (1) above of an offender's mental condition as they have effect with respect to proof of an offender's mental condition for the purposes of section 37(2)(a) of that Act.

(10) In this paragraph, "chartered psychologist" means a person for the time being listed in the British Psychological Society's Register of Chartered Psychologists.

Requirements as to treatment for drug or alcohol dependency

6.—(1) Subject to sub-paragraph (2) below, this paragraph applies where a court **5–122p** proposing to make a community rehabilitation order is satisfied—

(a) that the offender is dependent on drugs or alcohol;

(b) that his dependency caused or contributed to the offence in respect of which the order is proposed to be made; and

(c) that his dependency is such as requires and may be susceptible to treatment.

(2) If the court has been notified by the Secretary of State that arrangements for implementing drug treatment and testing orders are available in the area proposed to be specified in the probation order, and the notice has not been withdrawn, this paragraph shall have effect as if the words "drugs or", in each place where they occur, were omitted.

(3) Subject to sub-paragraph (5) below, the community rehabilitation order may include a requirement that the offender shall submit, during the whole of the community rehabilitation period or during such part of that period as may be specified in the order, to treatment by or under the direction of a person having the necessary qualifications or experience with a view to the reduction or elimination of the offender's dependency on drugs or alcohol.

(4) The treatment required by any such order shall be such one of the following kinds of treatment as may be specified in the order, that is to say—

(a) treatment as a resident in such institution or place as may be specified in the order;

(b) treatment as a non-resident in or at such institution or place as may be so specified;

(c) treatment by or under the direction of such person having the necessary qualifications or experience as may be so specified;

but the nature of the treatment shall not be specified in the order except as mentioned in paragraph (a), (b) or (c) above.

(5) A court shall not by virtue of this paragraph include in a community rehabilitation order a requirement that the offender shall submit to treatment for his dependency on drugs or alcohol unless—

35

(a) it is satisfied that arrangements have been or can be made for the treatment intended to be specified in the order (including arrangements for the reception of the offender where he is to be required to submit to treatment as a resident); and

(b) the offender has expressed his willingness to comply with such a requirement.

(6) While the offender is under treatment as a resident in pursuance of a requirement of the community rehabilitation order, his responsible officer shall carry out the offender's supervision to such extent only as may be necessary for the purpose of the revocation or amendment of the order.

(7) Where the person by whom or under whose direction an offender is being treated for dependency on drugs or alcohol in pursuance of a community rehabilitation order is of the opinion that part of the treatment can be better or more conveniently given in or at an institution or place which—

(a) is not specified in the order, and

(b) is one in or at which the treatment of the offender will be given by or under the direction of a person having the necessary qualifications or experience,

he may, with the consent of the offender, make arrangements for him to be treated accordingly.

(8) Where any such arrangements as are mentioned in sub-paragraph (7) above are made for the treatment of an offender—

(a) the person by whom the arrangements are made shall give notice in writing to the offender's responsible officer, specifying the institution or place in or at which the treatment is to be carried out; and

(b) the treatment provided for by the arrangements shall be deemed to be treatment to which he is required to submit in pursuance of the community rehabilitation order.

(9) In this paragraph, the reference to the offender being dependent on drugs or alcohol includes a reference to his having a propensity towards the misuse of drugs or alcohol; and references to his dependency on drugs or alcohol shall be construed accordingly.

Curfew requirements

5–122q   7.—(1) Subject to the provisions of this paragraph, a community rehabilitation order may include a requirement that the offender remain, for periods specified in the requirement, at a place so specified.

(2) A requirement under sub-paragraph (1) above may specify different places or different periods for different days, but shall not specify—

(a) periods which fall outside the period of six months beginning with the day on which the order is made; or

(b) periods which amount to less than two hours or more than twelve hours in any one day.

(3) A requirement under sub-paragraph (1) above shall, as far as practicable, be such as to avoid—

(a) any conflict with the offender's religious beliefs or with the requirements of any other community order to which he may be subject; and

(b) any interference with the times, if any, at which he normally works or attends school or any other educational establishment.

(4) An order which includes a requirement under sub-paragraph (1) above shall include provision for making a person responsible for monitoring the offender's whereabouts during the curfew periods specified in the requirement; and a person who is made so responsible shall be of a description specified in an order made by the Secretary of State.

(5) A court shall not include in a community rehabilitation order such a requirement as is mentioned in sub-paragraph (1) above unless the court has been notified by the Secretary of State that arrangements for monitoring the offender's where-

abouts are available in the area in which the place proposed to be specified in the requirement is situated and the notice has not been withdrawn.

(6) A court shall not include in a community rehabilitation order such a requirement as is mentioned in sub-paragraph (1) above if the community sentence includes a curfew order.

(7) Before including in a community rehabilitation order such a requirement as is mentioned in sub-paragraph (1) above, the court shall obtain and consider information about the place proposed to be specified in the requirement (including information as to the attitude of persons likely to be affected by the enforced presence there of the offender).

(8) The Secretary of State may make rules for regulating—

    (a) the monitoring of the whereabouts of an offender who is subject to a requirement under sub-paragraph (1) above; and

    (b) without prejudice to the generality of paragraph (a) above, the functions of any person responsible for monitoring the offender's whereabouts during the curfew periods specified in the requirement.

(9) The Secretary of State may by order direct that sub-paragraph (3) above shall have effect with such additional restrictions as may be specified in the order.

[Exclusion requirements

8.—(1) Subject to the provisions of this paragraph, a community rehabilitation order may include a requirement prohibiting the offender from entering a place specified in the requirement for a period so specified of not more than two years.   **5–122r**

(2) A requirement under sub-paragraph (1) above—

    (a) may provide for the prohibition to operate only during the periods specified in the order;

    (b) may specify different places for different periods or days.

(3) *[Identical to para. 7(3), ante.]*

(4) An order which includes a requirement under sub-paragraph (1) above shall include provision for making a person responsible for monitoring the offender's whereabouts during the periods when the prohibition operates; and a person who is made so responsible shall be of a description specified in an order made by the Secretary of State.

(5) A court shall not include in a community rehabilitation order such a requirement as is mentioned in sub-paragraph (1) above unless the court has been notified by the Secretary of State that arrangements for monitoring the offender's whereabouts are available in the area in which the place proposed to be specified in the order is situated and the notice has not been withdrawn.

(6) A court shall not include in a community rehabilitation order such a requirement as is mentioned in sub-paragraph (1) above if the community sentence includes an exclusion order.

(7) The Secretary of State may make rules for regulating—

    (a) the monitoring of the whereabouts of an offender who is subject to a requirement under sub-paragraph (1) above; and

    (b) without prejudice to the generality of paragraph (a) above, the functions of any person responsible for monitoring the offender's whereabouts during the periods when the prohibition operates.

(8) *[Identical to para. 7(8), ante.]*

(9) In this paragraph, "place" includes an area.]

[This Schedule is printed as amended by the *CJCSA* 2000, s.49, 50 and 74, and Sched. 7, paras 1, 4 and 198; and the *Care Standards Act* 2000, s.116 and Sched. 4, para. 28(2); and as amended, as from a day to be appointed, by the *CJCSA* 2000, s.51 (insertion of para. 8). It is repealed as from April 4, 2005 (*Criminal Justice Act 2003 (Commencement No. 8 and Transitional and Saving Provisions) Order* 2005 (S.I. 2005 No. 950)): *CJA* 2003, s.332, and Sched. 7, Pt 7. For the relevant saving provisions, see § 5–1a in the main work; and *post*, §§ 5–131a *et seq.*]

Willingness to comply with requirements of order

5–122s   The general requirement that an offender should express his willingness to comply with the requirements of a probation order was abolished by the *C(S)A* 1997, s.38(2), with reference to probation orders made for offences committed on or after October 1, 1997 (*Crime (Sentences) Act 1997 (Commencement No. 2 and Transitional Provisions) Order* 1997 (S.I. 1997 No. 2200)). Where a court proposes to make a community rehabilitation order for an offence committed before that date, the requirement remains: see Sched. 11, para. 4(1)(b) to the 2000 Act. An offender must still express his willingness to comply with requirements relating to psychiatric treatment, or treatment for drug or alcohol dependency (Sched. 2, paras 5(4) and 6(5)).

For cases on the meaning of "willingness", see *R. v. Marquis*, 59 Cr.App.R. 228, CA, and *R. v. Barnett*, 8 Cr.App.R.(S.) 200, CA.

Combined with custodial sentence

5–122t   A community sentence may not be imposed on the same occasion as an offender is made the subject of a suspended sentence: s.118(6) of the 2000 Act. There is no such express bar on a community sentence being imposed at the same time as an immediate custodial sentence, but the spirit of section 118(6) would seem to apply *a fortiori*.

Where, however, the offender is already serving a custodial sentence, it has been held that there is no objection to the imposition of a community sentence provided that the sentence could have practical effect, as where the custodial sentence had only a short time to run: see *Fontenau v. DPP* [2001] 1 Cr.App.R.(S.) 15, DC. This is contrary to the approach of the Court of Appeal in *R. v. Carr Thompson* [2000] 2 Cr.App.R.(S.) 335, where a probation order which had been made on the same occasion as the Crown Court dismissed an appeal against a custodial sentence was quashed. The court relied on *R. v. Evans*, 43 Cr.App.R. 66, CCA. *Evans* was, however, decided at a time when the legislation expressly declared that probation was instead of punishment. The rationale of the decision, *viz.* that it was fundamentally inconsistent to impose an avowedly punitive sentence at the same time as making a probation order, disappeared with the legislative changes made by the *CJA* 1991. Probation then became a form of punishment, and the rationale underlying *Evans* disappeared. It is submitted that the more flexible approach in *Fontenau* is to be preferred to that in *Carr Thompson*.

Contempt of court

5–122u   A community rehabilitation order may not be made against a person adjudged guilty of contempt of court: *R. v. Palmer*, 95 Cr.App.R. 170, CA.

Electronic monitoring

5–122v   As to the electronic monitoring of a curfew requirement under paragraph 7, see section 36B (§ 5–179 in the main work). Rule 48.1 of the *Criminal Procedure Rules* 2005 (S.I. 2005 No. 384) makes provision as to the service of notice of the order on the defendant, on the person responsible for electronically monitoring compliance, and on the local probation board or youth offending team.

Enforcement

5–122w   See Schedule 3 to the 2000 Act, see *post*, §§ 5–123p *et seq.*

(b) *Community punishment orders*

Powers of Criminal Courts (Sentencing) Act 2000, ss.46–49

Community punishment orders

46.—(1) Where a person aged 16 or over is convicted of an offence punishable **5–122x** with imprisonment, the court by or before which he is convicted may (subject to sections 34 to 36 above) make an order requiring him to perform unpaid work in accordance with section 47 below.

(2) An order under subsection (1) above is in this Act referred to as a "community punishment order".

(3) The number of hours which a person may be required to work under a community punishment order shall be specified in the order and shall be in the aggregate—

(a) not less than 40; and

(b) not more than 240.

(3A) Subject to subsection (3B) below, the community punishment order shall, if the set of conditions in section 42(2B) above is satisfied, include a drug abstinence requirement and may include such a requirement if the set of conditions in section 42(2C) above is satisfied.

(3B) The order may not include a drug abstinence requirement if the community sentence includes a drug treatment and testing order or a drug abstinence order.

(3C) Subsections (2E) and (2F) of section 42 above apply for the purposes of this section as they apply for the purposes of that.

(4) A court shall not make a community punishment order in respect of an offender unless, after hearing (if the court thinks it necessary) an appropriate officer, the court is satisfied that the offender is a suitable person to perform work under such an order.

(5) In subsection (4) above "an appropriate officer" means—

(a) in the case of an offender aged 18 or over, an officer of a local probation board, an officer of a provider of probation services or social worker of a local authority social services department; and

(b) in the case of an offender aged under 18, an officer of a local probation board, an officer of a provider of probation services, a social worker of a local authority social services department or a member of a youth offending team.

(6) A court shall not make a community punishment order in respect of an offender unless it is satisfied that provision for him to perform work under such an order can be made under the arrangements for persons to perform work under such orders which exist in the petty sessions area in which he resides or will reside.

(7) Subsection (6) above has effect subject to paragraphs 3 and 4 of Schedule 4 to this Act (transfer of order to Scotland or Northern Ireland).

(8) Where a court makes community punishment orders in respect of two or more offences of which the offender has been convicted by or before the court, the court may direct that the hours of work specified in any of those orders shall be concurrent with or additional to those specified in any other of those orders, but so that the total number of hours which are not concurrent shall not exceed the maximum specified in subsection (3)(b) above.

(9) A community punishment order—

(a) shall specify the petty sessions area in which the offender resides or will reside; and

(b) where the offender is aged under 18 at the time the order is made, may also specify a local authority for the purposes of section 47(5)(b) below (cases where functions are to be discharged by member of a youth offending team);

and if the order specifies a local authority for those purposes; the authority specified must be the local authority within whose area it appears to the court that the offender resides or will reside.

(10) Before making a community punishment order, the court shall explain to the offender in ordinary language—

    (a) the purpose and effect of the order (and in particular the requirements of the order as specified in section 47(1) to (3) below);

    (b) the consequences which may follow (under Part II of Schedule 3 to this Act) if he fails to comply with any of those requirements; and

    (c) that the court has power (under Parts III and IV of that Schedule) to review the order on the application either of the offender or of the responsible officer.

(11) The court by which a community punishment order is made shall forthwith give copies of the order to—

    (a) if the offender is aged 18 or over, an officer of a local probation board assigned to the court or an officer of a provider of probation services acting at the court (as the case may be), or

    (b) if the offender is under 18—

        (i) an officer of a local probation board assigned to the court or an officer of a provider of probation services acting at the court; or

        (ii) a member of a youth offending team assigned to the court,

    and he shall give a copy to the offender and to the responsible officer.

(12) The court by which such an order is made shall also, except where it itself acts for the petty sessions area specified in the order, send to the clerk to the justices for that area—

    (a) a copy of the order; and

    (b) such documents and information relating to the case as it considers likely to be of assistance to a court acting for that area in the exercise of its functions in relation to the order.

(13) In this section and Schedule 3 to this Act "responsible officer", in relation to an offender subject to a community punishment order, means the person mentioned in subsection (4)(a) or (b) or (5)(b) of section 47 below who, as respects the order, is responsible for discharging the functions conferred by that section.

[This section is printed as amended by the *CJCSA* 2000, ss.45, 49(2) and 74, and Sched. 7, paras 2, 4 and 168; and the *Offender Management Act 2007 (Consequential Amendments) Order* 2008 (S.I. 2008 No. 912), art. 3, and Sched. 1, para. 14(1) and (5). It is repealed as from April 4, 2005 (*Criminal Justice Act 2003 (Commencement No. 8 and Transitional and Saving Provisions) Order* 2005 (S.I. 2005 No. 950)): *CJA* 2003, s.332, and Sched. 7, Pt 7. For the relevant saving provisions, see § 5–1a in the main work; and *post*, §§ 5–131a *et seq.*]

A community punishment order is a "community order" within Part IV of the Act (s.33(1), *ante*, § 5–122a), and thus a court must not make such an order without complying with sections 35 and 36 (*ante*, §§ 5–122c, 5–122d), unless the case falls within section 59 (*post*, § 5–123o).

Obligations of person subject to community punishment order

5–122y   47.—(1) An offender in respect of whom a community punishment order is in force shall—

    (a) keep in touch with the responsible officer in accordance with such instructions as he may from time to time be given by that officer and notify him of any change of address; and

    (b) perform for the number of hours specified in the order such work at such times as he may be instructed by the responsible officer.

(2) The instructions given by the responsible officer under this section shall, as far as practicable, be such as to avoid—

    (a) any conflict with the offender's religious beliefs or with the requirements of any other community order to which he may be subject; and

(b) any interference with the times, if any, at which he normally works or attends school or any other educational establishment.

(3) Subject to paragraph 22 of Schedule 3 to this Act (power to extend order), the work required to be performed under a community punishment order shall be performed during the period of twelve months beginning with the date of the order; but, unless revoked, the order shall remain in force until the offender has worked under it for the number of hours specified in it.

(4) If the offender is aged 18 or over at the time when the order is made, the functions conferred by this section on "the responsible officer" shall be discharged by an officer of a local probation board or (as the case may be) an officer of a provider of probation services acting in the local justice area specified in the order.

(5) If the offender is aged under 18 at that time, those functions shall be discharged by—

(a) a person mentioned in subsection (4) above; or

(b) a member of a youth offending team established by a local authority specified in the order.

(6) The reference in subsection (4) above to the petty sessions area specified in the order and the reference in subsection (5) above to a local authority so specified are references to the area or an authority for the time being so specified, whether under section 46(9) above or by virtue of Part IV of Schedule 3 to this Act (power to amend orders).

[This section is printed as amended by the *CJCSA* 2000, s.74 and Sched. 7, paras 2, 5 and 169; and the *Offender Management Act 2007 (Consequential Amendments) Order* 2008 (S.I. 2008 No. 912), art. 3, and Sched. 1, para. 14(1) and (6). It is repealed as from April 4, 2005 (*Criminal Justice Act 2003 (Commencement No. 8 and Transitional and Saving Provisions) Order* 2005 (S.I. 2005 No. 950)): *CJA* 2003, s.332, and Sched. 7, Pt 7. For the relevant saving provisions, see § 5–1a in the main work; and *post*, §§ 5–130 *et seq.*]

Breach, revocation and amendment of community punishment orders
48. [*Gives effect to Sched. 3*, post, §§ 5–123p *et seq.*]

Offenders residing in Scotland or Northern Ireland
49. [*Gives effect to Sched. 4.*]

Combined with other forms of sentence

Section 118(6) of the *PCC(S)A* 2000 provides that a court which imposes a suspended sentence may not make any form of community order on the same occasion. A magistrates' court should not make a community punishment order in respect of an offence committed while the offender is subject to a suspended sentence imposed by the Crown Court: the offender should be committed to the Crown Court for both matters to be dealt with together (see *R. v. Stewart*, 6 Cr.App.R.(S.) 166, CA). Where a community punishment order is made by one court for one offence, the making of the order does not prevent another court, dealing with the offender for offences committed before the order was made, from imposing a custodial sentence (see *R. v. Bennett*, 2 Cr.App.R.(S.) 96, CA).   **5–122z**

Consecutive orders

See section 46(2), *ante*.   **5–123a**

When a community punishment order is made against an offender who is subject to an existing community punishment order which has been partly performed, the total number of hours outstanding should not generally exceed 240 (see *R. v. Siha*, 13 Cr.App.R.(S.) 588, CA). The Court of Appeal held in *R. v. Meredith*, 15 Cr.App.R.(S.) 528, that where an offender was ordered to perform a number of hours of community service by a magistrates' court and then ordered to perform a further number of hours by the Crown Court in the form of a consecutive community service order, both orders became for all practical purposes one order and a breach of one became a breach of both. It is submitted that this case is wrongly decided, at least where one order is made by a magistrates' court and the other by the Crown Court, as an order made by a magistrates' court can be revoked (following a failure to comply with the order) only by a magistrates' court, and an order made by the Crown Court can be revoked only by the Crown Court: see Sched. 3, paras 4 and 5 (*post*, §§ 5–123t, 5–123v).

Enforcement

5–123b   The enforcement of community punishment orders is governed by the provisions of Schedule 3 (*post*, §§ 5–123p *et seq.*).

(c) *Community punishment and rehabilitation orders*

Powers of Criminal Courts (Sentencing) Act 2000, s.51

Community punishment and rehabilitation orders

5–123c   **51.**—(1) Where a person aged 16 or over is convicted of an offence punishable with imprisonment and the court by or before which he is convicted is of the opinion mentioned in subsection (3) below, the court may (subject to sections 34 to 36 above) make an order requiring him both—

(a) to be under supervision for a period specified in the order, being not less than twelve months nor more than three years; and

(b) to perform unpaid work for a number of hours so specified, being in the aggregate not less than 40 nor more than 100.

(2) An order under subsection (1) above is in this Act referred to as a "community punishment and rehabilitation order".

(3) The opinion referred to in subsection (1) above is that the making of a community punishment and rehabilitation order is desirable in the interests of—

(a) securing the rehabilitation of the offender; or

(b) protecting the public from harm from him or preventing the commission by him of further offences.

(4) Subject to subsection (1) above, sections 41, 42, 46 and 47 above and Schedule 2 to this Act shall apply in relation to community punishment and rehabilitation orders—

(a) in so far as those orders impose such a requirement as is mentioned in paragraph (a) of subsection (1) above, as if they were community rehabilitation orders; and

(b) in so far as they impose such a requirement as is mentioned in paragraph (b) of that subsection, as if they were community punishment orders.

(5) [*Gives effect to Sched. 3 (enforcement), post, §§ 5–123p et seq.*]

(6) [*Gives effect to Sched. 4 (offenders residing in Scotland or Northern Ireland).*]

[This section is printed as amended by the *CJCSA* 2000, ss.45 and 75, and Sched. 7, para. 3. It is repealed as from April 4, 2005 (*Criminal Justice Act 2003 (Commencement No. 8 and Transitional and Saving Provisions) Order* 2005 (S.I. 2005 No. 950)): *CJA* 2003, s.332, and Sched. 7, Pt 7. For the relevant saving provisions, see § 5–1a in the main work; and *post*, §§ 5–131a *et seq.*]

A community punishment and rehabilitation order is a "community order" (s.33(1), *ante*, § 5–122a) and thus a court must not make such an order without complying with sections 35 and 36 (*ante*, §§ 5–122c, 5–122d).

As to the enforcement of community punishment and rehabilitation orders, see Schedule 3, *post*, §§ 5–123p *et seq.*

(d) *Drug treatment and testing orders*

Powers of Criminal Courts (Sentencing) Act 2000, ss.52–57

Drug treatment and testing orders

52.—(1) Where a person aged 16 or over is convicted of an offence, the court   **5–123d** by or before which he is convicted may (subject to sections 34 to 36 above) make an order which—

    (a) has effect for a period specified in the order of not less than six months nor more than three years ("the treatment and testing period"); and

    (b) includes the requirements and provisions mentioned in sections 53 and 54 below;

but this section does not apply in relation to an offence committed before 30th September 1998.

(2) An order under subsection (1) above is in this Act referred to as a "drug treatment and testing order".

(3) A court shall not make a drug treatment and testing order in respect of an offender unless it is satisfied—

    (a) that he is dependent on or has a propensity to misuse drugs; and

    (b) that his dependency or propensity is such as requires and may be susceptible to treatment.

(4) For the purpose of ascertaining for the purposes of subsection (3) above whether the offender has any drug in his body [(in a case where, at the time of conviction, he was aged under 18)], the court may by order require him to provide samples of such description as it may specify; but the court shall not make such an order unless the offender expresses his willingness to comply with its requirements.

(5) A court shall not make a drug treatment and testing order unless it has been notified by the Secretary of State that arrangements for implementing such orders are available in the area proposed to be specified in the order under section 54(1) below and the notice has not been withdrawn.

(6) Before making a drug treatment and testing order, the court shall explain to the offender in ordinary language—

    (a) the effect of the order and of the requirements proposed to be included in it;

    (b) the consequences which may follow (under Part II of Schedule 3 to this Act) if he fails to comply with any of those requirements;

    (c) that the order will be periodically reviewed at intervals as provided for in the order (by virtue of section 54(6) below); and

    (d) that the order may be reviewed (under Parts III and IV of Schedule 3) on the application either of the offender or of the responsible officer;

and "responsible officer" here has the meaning given by section 54(3) below.

(7) A court shall not make a drug treatment and testing order unless the offender expresses his willingness to comply with its requirements.

[This section is printed as amended, as from a day to be appointed, by the *CJCSA* 2000, s.74, and Sched. 7, para. 170 (insertion of words in square brackets). It is repealed as from April 4, 2005 (*Criminal Justice Act 2003 (Commencement No. 8 and Transitional and Saving Provisions) Order* 2005 (S.I. 2005 No. 950)): *CJA* 2003, s.332, and Sched. 7, Pt 7. For the relevant saving provisions, see § 5–1a in the main work; and *post*, §§ 5–131a *et seq.*]

A drug treatment and testing order is a "community order" (s.33(1), *ante*) and thus a court must not make such an order without complying with sections 35 and 36 (*ante*, §§ 5–122c, 5–122d).

The treatment and testing requirements

5–123e   **53.**—(1) A drug treatment and testing order shall include a requirement ("the treatment requirement") that the offender shall submit, during the whole of the treatment and testing period, to treatment by or under the direction of a specified person having the necessary qualifications or experience ("the treatment provider") with a view to the reduction or elimination of the offender's dependency on or propensity to misuse drugs.

(2) The required treatment for any particular period shall be—

(a) treatment as a resident in such institution or place as may be specified in the order; or

(b) treatment as a non-resident in or at such institution or place, and at such intervals, as may be so specified;

but the nature of the treatment shall not be specified in the order except as mentioned in paragraph (a) or (b) above.

(3) A court shall not make a drug treatment and testing order unless it is satisfied that arrangements have been or can be made for the treatment intended to be specified in the order (including arrangements for the reception of the offender where he is to be required to submit to treatment as a resident).

(4) A drug treatment and testing order shall include a requirement ("the testing requirement") that, for the purpose of ascertaining whether he has any drug in his body during the treatment and testing period, the offender shall during that period, at such times or in such circumstances as may (subject to the provisions of the order) be determined by the treatment provider, provide samples of such description as may be so determined.

(5) The testing requirement shall specify for each month the minimum number of occasions on which samples are to be provided.

[This section was repealed as from April 4, 2005 (*Criminal Justice Act 2003 (Commencement No. 8 and Transitional and Saving Provisions) Order* 2005 (S.I. 2005 No. 950)): *CJA* 2003, s.332, and Sched. 7, Pt 7. For the relevant saving provisions, see § 5–1a in the main work; and *post*, §§ 5–131a *et seq.*]

Provisions of order as to supervision and periodic review

5–123f   **54.**—(1) A drug treatment and testing order shall include a provision specifying the petty sessions area in which it appears to the court making the order that the offender resides or will reside.

(2) A drug treatment and testing order shall provide that, for the treatment and testing period, the offender shall be under the supervision of an officer of a local probation board appointed for or assigned to the petty sessions area specified in the order or (as the case may be) an officer of a provider of probation services acting in the local justice area specified in the order.

(3) In this Act "responsible officer", in relation to an offender who is subject to a drug treatment and testing order, means the officer of a local probation board or officer of a provider of probation services responsible for his supervision.

(4) A drug treatment and testing order shall—

(a) require the offender to keep in touch with the responsible officer in accordance with such instructions as he may from time to time be given by that officer, and to notify him of any change of address; and

(b) provide that the results of the tests carried out on the samples provided by the offender in pursuance of the testing requirement shall be communicated to the responsible officer.

(5) Supervision by the responsible officer shall be carried out to such extent only as may be necessary for the purpose of enabling him—

(a) to report on the offender's progress to the court responsible for the order;

(b) to report to that court any failure by the offender to comply with the requirements of the order; and

(c) to determine whether the circumstances are such that he should apply to that court for the revocation or amendment of the order.

(6) A drug treatment and testing order shall—

(a) provide for the order to be reviewed periodically at intervals of not less than one month;

(b) provide for each review of the order to be made, subject to section 55(6) below, at a hearing held for the purpose by the court responsible for the order (a "review hearing");

(c) require the offender to attend each review hearing;

(d) provide for the responsible officer to make to the court responsible for the order, before each review, a report in writing on the offender's progress under the order; and

(e) provide for each such report to include the test results communicated to the responsible officer under subsection (4)(b) above and the views of the treatment provider as to the treatment and testing of the offender.

(7) In this section references to the court responsible for a drug treatment and testing order are references to—

(a) where a court is specified in the order in accordance with subsection (8) below, that court;

(b) in any other case, the court by which the order is made.

(8) Where the area specified in a drug treatment and testing order made by a magistrates' court is not the area for which the court acts, the court may, if it thinks fit, include in the order provision specifying for the purposes of subsection (7) above a magistrates' court which acts for the area specified in the order.

(9) Where a drug treatment and testing order has been made on an appeal brought from the Crown Court or from the criminal division of the Court of Appeal, for the purposes of subsection (7)(b) above it shall be deemed to have been made by the Crown Court.

[This section is printed as amended by the *CJCSA* 2000, s.74, and Sched. 7, para. 4; and the *Offender Management Act 2007 (Consequential Amendments) Order* 2008 (S.I. 2008 No. 912), art. 3, and Sched. 1, para. 14(1) and (7). It is repealed as from April 4, 2005 (*Criminal Justice Act 2003 (Commencement No. 8 and Transitional and Saving Provisions) Order* 2005 (S.I. 2005 No. 950)): *CJA* 2003, s.332, and Sched. 7, Pt 7. For the relevant saving provisions, see § 5–1a in the main work; and *post*, §§ 5–131a *et seq.*]

Periodic reviews

55.—(1) At a review hearing (within the meaning given by subsection (6) of section 54 above) the court may, after considering the responsible officer's report referred to in that subsection, amend any requirement or provision of the drug treatment and testing order.   **5–123g**

(2) The court—

(a) shall not amend the treatment or testing requirement unless the offender expresses his willingness to comply with the requirement as amended;

(b) shall not amend any provision of the order so as to reduce the treatment and testing period below the minimum specified in section 52(1) above, or to increase it above the maximum so specified; and

(c) except with the consent of the offender, shall not amend any requirement or provision of the order while an appeal against the order is pending.

(3) If the offender fails to express his willingness to comply with the treatment or testing requirement as proposed to be amended by the court, the court may—

    (a) revoke the order; and

    (b) deal with him, for the offence in respect of which the order was made, in any way in which it could deal with him if he had just been convicted by the court of the offence.

(4) In dealing with the offender under subsection (3)(b) above, the court—

    (a) shall take into account the extent to which the offender has complied with the requirements of the order; and

    (b) may impose a custodial sentence (where the order was made in respect of an offence punishable with such a sentence) notwithstanding anything in section 79(2) below.

(5) Where the order was made by a magistrates' court in the case of an offender under 18 years of age in respect of an offence triable only on indictment in the case of an adult, any powers exercisable under subsection (3)(b) above in respect of the offender after he attains the age of 18 shall be powers to do either or both of the following—

    (a) to impose a fine not exceeding £5,000 for the offence in respect of which the order was made;

    (b) to deal with the offender for that offence in any way in which the court could deal with him if it had just convicted him of an offence punishable with imprisonment for a term not exceeding six months.

(6) If at a review hearing the court, after considering the responsible officer's report, is of the opinion that the offender's progress under the order is satisfactory, the court may so amend the order as to provide for each subsequent review to be made by the court without a hearing.

(7) If at a review without a hearing the court, after considering the responsible officer's report, is of the opinion that the offender's progress under the order is no longer satisfactory, the court may require the offender to attend a hearing of the court at a specified time and place.

(8) At that hearing the court, after considering that report, may—

    (a) exercise the powers conferred by this section as if the hearing were a review hearing; and

    (b) so amend the order as to provide for each subsequent review to be made at a review hearing.

(9) In this section any reference to the court, in relation to a review without a hearing, shall be construed—

    (a) in the case of the Crown Court, as a reference to a judge of the court;

    (b) in the case of magistrates' court, as a reference to a justice of the peace acting for the commission area for which the court acts.

[This section was repealed as from April 4, 2005 (*Criminal Justice Act 2003 (Commencement No. 8 and Transitional and Saving Provisions) Order* 2005 (S.I. 2005 No. 950)): *CJA* 2003, s.332, and Sched. 7, Pt 7. For the relevant saving provisions, see § 5–1a in the main work; and *post*, §§ 5–131a *et seq.*]

Breach, revocation and amendment of drug treatment and testing orders

56. [*Gives effect to Sched. 3, post, §§ 5–123p et seq.*]

Copies of orders

57.—(1) Where a drug treatment and testing order is made, the court making the order shall (subject to subsection (3) below) forthwith give copies of the order to an officer of a local probation board assigned to the court, or (as the case may be) an officer of a provider of probation services acting at the court.

(2) Where such an order is amended under section 55(1) above, the court amending the order shall (subject to subsection (3A) below) forthwith give copies of the or-

der as amended to an officer of a local probation board assigned to the court, or (as the case may be) an officer of a provider of probation services operating at the court.

(3) Where a drug treatment and testing order is made by a magistrates' court and another magistrates' court is responsible for the order (within the meaning given by section 54(7) above) by virtue of being specified in the order in accordance with section 54(8)—

- (a) the court making the order shall not give copies of it as mentioned in subsection (1) above but shall forthwith send copies of it to the court responsible for the order; and
- (b) the court shall, as soon as reasonably practicable after the order is made, give copies of it to a probation officer assigned to that court, or (as the case may be) an officer of a provider of probation services acting at that court.

(3A) Where—

- (a) a magistrates' court amends a drug treatment and testing order under section 55(1) above; and
- (b) the order as amended provides for a magistrates' court other than that mentioned in paragraph (a) above to be responsible for the order;

the court amending the order shall not give copies of the order as amended as mentioned in subsection (2) above but shall forthwith send copies of it to the court responsible for the order and that court shall, as soon as reasonably practicable after the order is amended, give copies to an officer of a local probation board assigned to that court, or (as the case may be) an officer of a provider of probation services acting at that court.

(4) An officer of a local probation board or officer of a provider of probation services to whom copies of an order are given under this section shall give a copy to—

- (a) the offender;
- (b) the treatment provider; and
- (c) the responsible officer.

[This section is printed as amended by the *CJCSA* 2000, s.74, and Sched. 7, paras 4 and 71; and the *Offender Management Act 2007 (Consequential Amendments) Order* 2008 (S.I. 2008 No. 912), art. 3, and Sched. 1, para. 14(1) and (8). It is repealed as from April 4, 2005 (*Criminal Justice Act 2003 (Commencement No. 8 and Transitional and Saving Provisions) Order* 2005 (S.I. 2005 No. 950)): *CJA* 2003, s.332, and Sched. 7, Pt 7. For the relevant saving provisions, see § 5–1a in the main work; and *post*, §§ 5–131a *et seq.*]

A drug treatment and testing order may be made only by a court which has **5–123j** been notified that arrangements for implementing the order have been made in the relevant area, and if the general requirements of sections 35 and 36 (*ante*, §§ 5–122c, 5–122d), relating to community orders are satisfied.

In order to ascertain whether an offender has drugs in his body, the court may order him to provide samples of such description as may be specified (s.52(4)), provided that the offender expresses his willingness to comply with the requirements of the order. A similar order may be made in respect of an offender over 18 by virtue of section 36A (*ante*, § 5–122f).

The order must be for a period of between six months and three years, and must contain the requirements specified in section 53. An order may not be made unless the offender expresses his willingness to comply with the requirements of the order (s.52(7)). An offender who fails to express his willingness to comply with a requirement proposed to be included in such an order may be sentenced to a custodial sentence for the offence (s.79(3), § 5–263 in the main work). There is no power to include requirements in a drug treatment and testing order other than those specified in section 53, but there appears to be no restriction on making such an order in conjunction with any other form of sentence, including a community punishment order or community rehabilita-

47

tion order. For an analysis of the statutory requirements which must be satisfied before a drug treatment and testing order may be made, see *R. (Inner London Probation Service) v. Tower Bridge Magistrates' Court* [2002] 1 Cr.App.R.(S.) 43, DC.

Regular reviews of drug treatment and testing orders will be carried out by the court which made the order. An order made by the Court of Appeal, on appeal from the Crown Court, or by the House of Lords on an appeal from the Court of Appeal, is treated as if it had been made by the Crown Court (s.54(9)). The frequency of review hearings must be specified in the order (intervals of not less than one month), and the offender must attend unless the court subsequently releases him from the obligation to do so. At a review hearing, the court may amend the requirements of the order, but may not reduce the period of the order to less than the minimum or extend it beyond the maximum permissible period.

Where a defendant is to be sentenced shortly after being made the subject of a drug treatment and testing order by another court, and whether in respect of an offence committed before or after the order was imposed, the normal course to adopt where the court wishes the drug treatment and testing order to continue in effect, would be to make a further such order in identical terms (assuming the statutory criteria are met); if the court felt that further requirements were necessary, a community rehabilitation order would be an appropriate alternative; if, however, a custodial sentence is to be imposed, three options are open to the Crown Court in relation to the drug treatment and testing order; the first, and normal, option would be to revoke it and pass a custodial sentence for the original offence (*PCC(S)A* 2000, Sched. 3, para. 11 (*post*, § 5–123z)); the second possibility would be to leave the order in force, but, whilst there is no statutory bar to such course, it is unlikely ever to be appropriate and feasible; thirdly, it would be possible to revoke the order and to impose a drug abstinence order under section 58A of the 2000 Act (provided the statutory criteria were met); but, as with the second option, this is unlikely ever to be practical: *R. v. Robinson* [2002] 2 Cr.App.R.(S.) 95, CA.

In *R. v. Woods and Collins* [2006] 1 Cr.App.R.(S.) 83, CA, the authorities in relation to drug treatment and testing orders were reviewed. It was said: (i) that these orders were designed for, amongst others, repeat offenders whose offending is driven by drug dependence; such offenders will often be those who would otherwise have to be sent to prison, and, it may well be, not for a short period; that the defendant was a prolific offender did not necessarily militate against an order, but there would be cases in which the nature of the offence or the scale of the offending was such that only a custodial sentence was justified; such orders are expensive and it is in the interests neither of the public nor the offender for one to be made where there are no reasonable prospects of it succeeding; that said, 100 per cent success rate should not be expected (some lapse often being a feature of an order which turns out to be substantially successful); (ii) as to the decisions to be made by a sentencer, these are (a) whether the case warrants adjournment for a report on the availability of such an order and (b) where such a report has been obtained and is favourable, whether such an order is appropriate; (iii) as to whether to adjourn for a report, there is no obligation to do so in every case in which it is represented to the sentencer that the cause of the offending was drug dependence and that the offender would welcome an order (where there is no prospect of such an order being made, obtaining a report would be wasteful and would unjustifiably raise false expectations); experienced sentencers know to look, *inter alia*, for signs that such an order might be effective; generally they will have the assistance of the standard pre-sentence report and they will look

for indications that the defendant is likely to engage with the order, and that
he has sufficient stability in his home life for there to be a reasonable prospect
of its succeeding; it is also right at this stage to consider the nature of the offending, since the gravity of the offences or the personal characteristics of the
defendant (*e.g.* repeated breaches of community orders) might demonstrate
that such an order would plainly be inappropriate; but the possibility of such
an order should not be rejected simply on the ground that the defendant is a
repeat offender for whom otherwise a custodial sentence would be inevitable
(such an offender being precisely the person for whom an order may be suitable), (iv) as to whether to make an order following a favourable report, this is
for the court and not the probation officer; the public interest as well as the
interests of the defendant are to be weighed in the balance, together with the
criminality of the defendant and the desirability and prospects of rehabilitation; (v) as to appeals, if at either stage, the sentencer has properly addressed
the issue before him and exercised his judgment, the cases in which it would
be right for the Court of Appeal to say that he erred in principle would be
comparatively rare.

In *Att.-Gen.'s Reference (No. 82 of 2005) (R. v. Toulson)* [2006] 1
Cr.App.R.(S.) 118, CA, it was said that whilst the general principle in *Att.-
Gen.'s Reference (No. 28 of 2001) (R. v. McCollins)* [2002] 1 Cr.App.R.(S.) 59,
CA, and *Att.-Gen.'s Reference (No. 64 of 2003)* [2004] 2 Cr.App.R.(S.) 22, CA,
was that a drug treatment and testing order would be inappropriate in cases
of serious offending (particularly where significant violence or threats were
involved), no straitjacket had been imposed on sentencers in cases where they
considered that in the public interest some course other than a deterrent
sentence should at least be tried.

Pre-sentence drug testing

The *PCC(S)A* 2000, s.36A (*ante*, § 5–122f) empowers a court which is deal-   **5–123k**
ing with an offender over the age of 18 and considering whether to pass any
community sentence, to make an order requiring the offender to provide
samples of any description specified in the order for the purpose of ascertaining whether the offender has any specified Class A drugs (heroin or cocaine)
in his body. Such an order may be made only if the court has been notified
that the power is available. The power is limited to testing for heroin and
cocaine, and not any other kind of drug. The power contained in section
52(4), *ante*, allows a court which is considering a drug treatment and testing
order in respect of an offender over 16 to order a defendant to provide
samples to ascertain whether he has any drug in his body. As the consequence
of failing to comply with an order to provide a specimen differ according to
the power which is exercised, it is important for the court to specify whether
the order is made under section 36A or section 52(4). When (and if) the
amendment to section 52(4) effected by the *CJCSA* 2000 takes effect, there
will be no overlap in the powers as section 52(4) will be restricted to offenders aged under 18 at the time of conviction.

(e) *Drug abstinence orders*

Powers of Criminal Courts (Sentencing) Act 2000, ss.58A, 58B

Drug abstinence orders
58A.—(1) Where a person aged 18 or over is convicted of an offence, the court   **5–123l**

by or before which he is convicted may (subject to sections 34 to 36 above) make an order which requires the offender—

(a) to abstain from misusing specified Class A drugs; and

(b) to provide, when instructed to do so by the responsible officer, any sample mentioned in the instruction for the purpose of ascertaining whether he has any specified Class A drug in his body.

(2) An order under subsection (1) above is in this Act referred to as a "drug abstinence order".

(3) The court shall not make a drug abstinence order in respect of an offender unless—

(a) in the opinion of the court, the offender is dependent on, or has a propensity to misuse, specified Class A drugs; and

(b) the offence in question is a trigger offence or, in the opinion of the court, the misuse by the offender of any specified Class A drug caused or contributed to the offence in question.

(4) A drug abstinence order shall provide that, for the period for which the order has effect, the offender shall be under the supervision of a person, being a person of a description specified in an order made by the Secretary of State.

(5) In this Act, "responsible officer", in relation to an offender who is subject to a drug abstinence order, means the person who is responsible for his supervision.

(6) The function of giving instructions for the purposes of subsection (1)(b) above shall be exercised in accordance with guidance given from time to time by the Secretary of State.

(7) A drug abstinence order shall have effect for a period specified in the order of not less than six months nor more than three years.

(8) The Secretary of State may make rules for regulating the provision of samples in pursuance of such instructions.

(9) A court shall not make a drug abstinence order unless the court has been notified by the Secretary of State that arrangements for implementing such orders are available in the area proposed to be specified in the order under section 54(1) above (as applied by section 58B(2) below) and the notice has not been withdrawn.

[See the note to s.58B, *post.*]

Drug abstinence orders: supplementary

5-123m   **58B.**—(1) Before making a drug abstinence order, the court shall explain to the offender in ordinary language—

(a) the effect of the order and of the requirements proposed to be included in it;

(b) the consequences which may follow (under Part II of Schedule 3 to this Act) if he fails to comply with any of those requirements; and

(c) that the order may be reviewed (under Parts III and IV of that Schedule) on the application either of the offender or of the responsible officer.

(2) Section 54 above (except subsections (2), (3) and (6)) and section 57 above (except subsections (2), (3A) and (4)(b)) shall apply for the purposes of section 58A above and this section as if references to drug treatment and testing orders were references to drug abstinence orders.]

(3) [*Gives effect to Sched. 3 (enforcement), post, §§ 5–123p et seq.*]

[Sections 58A and 58B were inserted as from July 2, 2001, by the *CJCSA* 2000, s.47. They were repealed as from April 4, 2005 (*Criminal Justice Act 2003 (Commencement No. 8 and Transitional and Saving Provisions) Order* 2005 (S.I. 2005 No. 950)): *CJA* 2003, s.332, and Sched. 7, Pt 7. For the relevant saving provisions, see § 5–1a in the main work; and *post*, §§ 5–131a *et seq.*]

(3) Persistent petty offenders

If the conditions specified in section 59 are satisfied, the court may make a   **5–123n**
community punishment order or curfew order even though the offences
concerned are not serious enough to warrant a community order, as would
otherwise be required by section 35.

Powers of Criminal Courts (Sentencing) Act 2000, s.59

Curfew orders and community punishment orders for persistent petty offenders
59.—(1) This section applies where—   **5–123o**
    (a) a person aged 16 or over is convicted of an offence;
    (b) the court by or before which he is convicted is satisfied that each of the
        conditions mentioned in subsection (2) below is fulfilled; and
    (c) if it were not so satisfied, the court would be minded to impose a fine in re-
        spect of the offence.
  (2) The conditions are that—
    (a) one or more fines imposed on the offender in respect of one or more previ-
        ous offences have not been paid; and
    (b) if a fine were imposed in an amount which was commensurate with the
        seriousness of the offence, the offender would not have sufficient means to
        pay it.
  (3) The court may—
    (a) subject to subsections (5) and (7) below, make a curfew order under section
        37(1) above, or
    (b) subject to subsections (6) and (7) below, make a community punishment or-
        der under section 46(1) above,
in respect of the offender instead of imposing a fine.
  (4) Subsection (3) above applies notwithstanding anything in subsections (1) and
(3)(b) of section 35 above (restrictions on imposing community sentences).
  (5) Section 37(1) above (curfew orders) shall apply for the purposes of subsection
(3)(a) above as if for the words from the beginning to "make" there were substituted
"Where section 59 below applies, the court may make in respect of the offender";
and—
    (a) section 37(3), (5) to (8) and (10) to (12), and
    (b) so far as applicable, the other provisions of this Part relating to curfew
        orders,
have effect in relation to a curfew order made by virtue of this section as they
have effect in relation to any other curfew order.
  (6) Section 46(1) above (community punishment orders) shall apply for the
purposes of subsection (3)(b) above as if for the words from the beginning to "make"
there were substituted "Where section 59 below applies, the court may make in respect of the offender"; and—
    (a) section 46(3) and (4), and
    (b) so far as applicable, the following provisions of section 46 and the other
        provisions of this Part relating to community punishment orders,
have effect in relation to a community punishment order made by virtue of this
section as they have effect in relation to any other community punishment order.
  (7) A court shall not make an order by virtue of subsection (3)(a) or (b) above unless the court has been notified by the Secretary of State that arrangements for
implementing orders so made are available in the relevant area and the notice has
not been withdrawn.
  (8) In subsection (7) above "the relevant area" means—
    (a) in relation to a curfew order, the area in which the place proposed to be
        specified in the order is situated;
    (b) in relation to a community punishment order, the area proposed to be

specified in the order.

[This section is printed as amended by the *CJCSA* 2000, s.74, Sched. 7, para. 2. It is repealed as from April 4, 2005 (*Criminal Justice Act 2003 (Commencement No. 8 and Transitional and Saving Provisions) Order* 2005 (S.I. 2005 No. 950)): *CJA* 2003, s.332, and Sched. 7, Pt 7. For the relevant saving provisions, see § 5–1a in the main work; and *post*, §§ 5–131a *et seq.*]

For section 37 of the Act, see § 5–157 in the main work.

(4) Enforcement, etc.

Powers of Criminal Courts (Sentencing) Act 2000, Sched. 3, Pts I–III

SCHEDULE 3

BREACH, REVOCATION AND AMENDMENT OF CERTAIN COMMUNITY ORDERS

PART I

PRELIMINARY

Definitions

5–123p   1.—(1) In this Schedule "relevant order" means any of the following orders—

   (a) a curfew order;

  (aa) an exclusion order;

   (b) a community rehabilitation order;

   (c) a community punishment order;

   (d) a community punishment and rehabilitation order;

   (e) a drug treatment and testing order;

   (f) a drug abstinence order.

[(1A) The orders mentioned in paragraphs (a) to (d) and (f) of sub-paragraph (1) above and, if an order made by the Secretary of State so provides, any other order mentioned in that sub-paragraph are referred to in this Schedule as orders to which the warning provisions apply.]

(2) In this Schedule "the petty sessions area concerned" means—

   (a) in relation to a curfew order, the petty sessions area in which the place for the time being specified in the order is situated; and

   (b) in relation to an exclusion, community rehabilitation, community punishment, community punishment and rehabilitation, drug treatment and testing or drug abstinence order, the petty sessions area for the time being specified in the order.

(3) In this Schedule, references to the court responsible for a drug treatment and testing order or drug abstinence order shall be construed in accordance with section 54(7) of this Act (or that subsection as applied by section 58B(2) of this Act).

(4) In this Schedule—

   (a) references to the community rehabilitation element of a community punishment and rehabilitation order are references to the order in so far as it imposes such a requirement as is mentioned in section 51(1)(a) of this Act (and in so far as it imposes any additional requirements included in the order by virtue of section 42); and

   (b) references to the community punishment element of such an order are references to the order in so far as it imposes such a requirement as is mentioned in section 51(1)(b).

Orders made on appeal

5–123q   2.—(1) Where a curfew, exclusion, community rehabilitation, community punishment, community punishment and rehabilitation or drug abstinence order has been made on appeal, for the purposes of this Schedule it shall be deemed—

(a) if it was made on an appeal brought from a magistrates' court, to have been made by a magistrates' court;

(b) if it was made on an appeal brought from the Crown Court or from the criminal division of the Court of Appeal, to have been made by the Crown Court.

(2) Where a drug treatment and testing order has been made on an appeal brought from the Crown Court or from the criminal division of the Court of Appeal, for the purposes of this Schedule it shall be deemed to have been made by the Crown Court.

PART II

BREACH OF REQUIREMENT OF ORDER

[Functions of responsible officer

2A.—(1) Sub-paragraphs (2) and (3) below apply if the responsible officer is of the   **5–123r**
opinion that a person aged 18 or over ("the offender") has failed without reasonable excuse to comply with any of the requirements of an order to which the warning provisions apply other than a requirement to abstain from misusing specified Class A drugs.

(2) The officer shall give him a warning under this paragraph if—

(a) the offender has not within the specified period been given a warning under this paragraph in respect of a failure to comply with any of the requirements of the order; and

(b) the officer does not cause an information to be laid before a justice of the peace in respect of the failure in question.

(3) If the offender has within the specified period been given such a warning, the officer shall cause an information to be laid before a justice of the peace in respect of the failure in question.

(4) In sub-paragraphs (2) and (3) above, "specified period" means—

(a) in the case of a curfew order, the period of six months;

(b) in any other case, the period of twelve months;

ending with the failure in question.

(5) A warning under this paragraph must—

(a) describe the circumstances of the failure;

(b) state that the failure is unacceptable;

(c) inform the offender that if within the next six or (as the case may be) twelve months he again fails to comply with any requirement of the order, he will be liable to be brought before a court;

and the officer shall, as soon as is practicable after the warning has been given, record that fact.

(6) If a community sentence consists of or includes two or more orders to which the warning provisions apply, being orders in respect of the same offence—

(a) the preceding provisions of this paragraph shall have effect as if those orders were a single order to which the warning provisions apply; and

(b) where one of those orders is a curfew order that fact shall be disregarded for the purposes of sub-paragraph (4) above.]

Issue of summons or warrant

3.—(1) If at any time while a relevant order is in force in respect of an offender it appears on information to a justice of the peace that the offender has failed to comply with any of the requirements of the order, the justice may—

(a) issue a summons requiring the offender to appear at the place and time specified in it; or

(b) if the information is in writing and on oath, issue a warrant for his arrest.

(2) Any summons or warrant issued under this paragraph shall direct the offender to appear or be brought—

53

(a) in the case of a drug treatment and testing order or a drug abstinence order, before the court responsible for the order;

(b) in the case of any other relevant order which was made by the Crown Court and included a direction that any failure to comply with any of the requirements of the order be dealt with by the Crown Court, before the Crown Court; and

(c) in the case of a relevant order which is not an order to which paragraph (a) or (b) applies, before a magistrates' court acting for the petty sessions area in which the offender resides or, if it is not known where he resides, before a magistrates' court acting for the petty sessions area concerned.

(3) Where a summons issued under sub-paragraph (1)(a) above requires an offender to appear before the Crown Court and the offender does not appear in answer to the summons, the Crown Court may issue a further summons requiring the offender to appear at the place and time specified in it.

(4) Where a summons issued under sub-paragraph (1)(a) above or a further summons issued under sub-paragraph (3) above requires an offender to appear before the Crown Court and the offender does not appear in answer to the summons, the Crown Court may issue a warrant for the arrest of the offender.

Powers of magistrates' court

5–123s   4.—(1) *If it is proved to the satisfaction of a magistrates' court before which an offender appears or is brought under paragraph 3 above that he has failed without reasonable excuse to comply with any of the requirements of the relevant order, the court may deal with him in respect of the failure in any one of the following ways—*

(a) *it may impose on him a fine not exceeding £1,000;*

(b) *where the offender is aged 16 or over it may, subject to paragraph 7 below, make a community service order in respect of him;*

(c) *where—*

     (i) *the relevant order is a curfew order and the offender is aged under 16, or*

     (ii) *the relevant order is a probation order or combination order and the offender is aged under 21,*

it may, subject to paragraph 8 below, make an attendance centre order in respect of him; or

(d) *where the relevant order was made by a magistrates' court, it may deal with him, for the offence in respect of which the order was made, in any way in which it could deal with him if he had just been convicted by the court of the offence.*

[(1) This paragraph applies if it is proved to the satisfaction of a magistrates' court before which an offender appears or is brought under paragraph 3 above that he has failed without reasonable excuse to comply with any of the requirements of the relevant order.

(1A) In a case where the offender is aged 18 or over and the order is one to which the warning provisions apply, the magistrates' court shall impose a sentence of imprisonment for the offence in respect of which the order was made unless it is of the opinion—

(a) that the offender is likely to comply with the requirements of the order during the period for which it remains in force; or

(b) that the exceptional circumstances of the case justify not imposing a sentence of imprisonment.

(1B) The sentence of imprisonment—

(a) where the offence was an offence punishable by imprisonment, shall be for the term which, if—

     (i) he had just been convicted of the offence by the court, and

     (ii) section 79(2) of this Act did not apply,

the court would impose on him for that offence; and

(b) in any other case, shall be for a term not exceeding three months;

taking account of the extent to which he has complied with the requirements of the order.

(1C) If in a case within sub-paragraph (1A) above the court does not impose a sentence of imprisonment or if the case is not within that sub-paragraph, the magistrates' court may deal with him in respect of the failure in one of the following ways (and must deal with him in one of those ways if the relevant order is in force)—

(a) by making a curfew order in respect of him (subject to paragraph 6A below);

(b) where the offender is aged 16 or over, by making a community punishment order in respect of him (subject to paragraph 7 below);

(c) where the offender is aged under 21, by making an attendance centre order in respect of him (subject to paragraph 8 below); or

(d) where the relevant order was made by a magistrates' court, by dealing with him, for the offence in respect of which the order was made, in any way in which the court could deal with him if he had just been convicted by it of the offence.]

(2) In dealing with an offender under sub-paragraph *(1)(d)* [(1C)(d)] above, a magistrates' court—

(a) shall take into account the extent to which the offender has complied with the requirements of the relevant order; and

(b) in the case of an offender who has wilfully and persistently failed to comply with those requirements, may impose a custodial sentence (where the relevant order was made in respect of an offence punishable with such a sentence) notwithstanding anything in section 79(2) of this Act.

(3) Where a magistrates' court deals with an offender under sub-paragraph *(1)(d)* [(1A) or (1C)(d)] above, it shall revoke the relevant order if it is still in force.

(3A) Where a magistrates' court dealing with an offender under sub-paragraph (1)(a), (b) or (c) above would not otherwise have the power to amend the relevant order under paragraph 18 below (amendment by reason of change of residence), that paragraph has effect as if the reference to a magistrates' court acting for the petty sessions area concerned were a reference to the court dealing with the offender.

(4) Where a relevant order was made by the Crown Court and a magistrates' court has power to deal with the offender under sub-paragraph *(1)(a)* [(1C)(a)], (b) or (c) above, it may instead commit him to custody or release him on bail until he can be brought or appear before the Crown Court.

(5) A magistrates' court which deals with an offender's case under sub-paragraph (4) above shall send to the Crown Court—

(a) a certificate signed by a justice of the peace certifying that the offender has failed to comply with the requirements of the relevant order in the respect specified in the certificate; and

(b) such other particulars of the case as may be desirable;

and a certificate purporting to be so signed shall be admissible as evidence of the failure before the Crown Court.

(6) A person sentenced under sub-paragraph *(1)(d)* [(1A) or (1C)(d)] above for an offence may appeal to the Crown Court against the sentence.

Powers of Crown Court

5.—(1) *Where under paragraph 3 or by virtue of paragraph 4(4) above an offender is brought or appears before the Crown Court and it is proved to the satisfaction of that court that he has failed without reasonable excuse to comply with any of the requirements of the relevant order, the Crown Court may deal with him in respect of the failure in any one of the following ways—*   **5–123t**

(a)–(c) *[identical to para. 4(1)(a)–(c), ante];*

(d) *it may deal with him, for the offence in respect of which the order was made, in any way in which it could deal with him if he had just been convicted before the Crown Court of the offence.*

[(1) This paragraph applies where under paragraph 3 or by virtue of paragraph 4(4) above an offender is brought or appears before the Crown Court and it is proved to the satisfaction of that court that he has failed without reasonable excuse to comply with any of the requirements of the relevant order.

(1A) In a case where the offender is aged 18 or over and the order is one to which the warning provisions apply, the Crown Court shall impose a sentence of imprisonment for the offence in respect of which the order was made unless it is of the opinion—

    (a) that the offender is likely to comply with the requirements of the order during the period for which it remains in force; or

    (b) that the exceptional circumstances of the case justify not imposing a sentence of imprisonment.

(1B) The sentence of imprisonment—

    (a) where the offence was an offence punishable by imprisonment, shall be for the term which, if—

        (i) he had just been convicted of the offence by the court, and

        (ii) section 79(2) of this Act did not apply,

    the court would impose on him for that offence; and

    (b) in any other case, shall be for a term not exceeding three months;

taking account of the extent to which he has complied with the requirements of the order.

(1C) If in a case within sub-paragraph (1A) above the court does not impose a sentence of imprisonment or if the case is not within that sub-paragraph, the Crown Court may deal with him in respect of the failure in one of the following ways (and must deal with him in one of those ways if the relevant order is in force)—

    (a) by making a curfew order in respect of him (subject to paragraph 6A below);

    (b) where the offender is aged 16 or over, by making a community punishment order in respect of him (subject to paragraph 7 below);

    (c) where the offender is aged under 21, by making an attendance centre order in respect of him (subject to paragraph 8 below); or

    (d) by dealing with him, for the offence in respect of which the order was made, in any way in which the Crown Court could deal with him if he had just been convicted before it of the offence.]

(2) In dealing with an offender under sub-paragraph (1)(d) above, the Crown Court—

    (a), (b) [*identical to para. 4(2)(a), (b),* ante, *save that for the reference to* "section 79(2) of this Act" *there is substituted a reference to* "section 152(3) of the *Criminal Justice Act* 2003"];

(3) Where the Crown Court deals with an offender under sub-paragraph *(1)(d)* [(1A) or (1C)(d)] above, it shall revoke the relevant order if it is still in force.

(4) In proceedings before the Crown Court under this paragraph any question whether the offender has failed to comply with the requirements of the relevant order shall be determined by the court and not by the verdict of a jury.

Exclusions from paragraphs 4 and 5

6.—(1) Without prejudice to paragraphs 10 and 11 below, an offender who is convicted of a further offence while a relevant order is in force in respect of him shall not on that account be liable to be dealt with under paragraph 4 or 5 above in respect of a failure to comply with any requirement of the order.

(2) An offender who—

    (a) is required by a probation order or combination order to submit to treatment for his mental condition, or his dependency on or propensity to misuse drugs or alcohol, or

    (b) is required by a drug treatment and testing order to submit to treatment for his dependency on or propensity to misuse drugs,

shall not be treated for the purposes of paragraph 4 or 5 above as having failed to comply with that requirement on the ground only that he has refused to undergo any surgical, electrical or other treatment if, in the opinion of the court, his refusal was reasonable having regard to all the circumstances.

[(3) Paragraphs 4(1A) and 5(1A) above do not apply in respect of a failure to comply with a requirement to abstain from misusing specified Class A drugs.]

[Curfew orders imposed for breach of relevant order

6A.—(1) Section 37(1) of this Act (curfew orders) shall apply for the purposes of paragraphs 4(1C)(a) and 5(1C)(a) above as if for the words from the beginning to "make" there were substituted "Where a court has power to deal with an offender under Part II of Schedule 3 to this Act for failure to comply with any of the requirements of a relevant order, the court may make in respect of the offender".

(2) In this paragraph—

"secondary order" means a curfew order made by virtue of paragraph 4(1C)(a) or 5(1C)(a) above;

"original order" means the relevant order the failure to comply with which led to the making of the secondary order.

(3) A secondary order—

(a) shall specify a period of not less than 14 nor more than 28 days for which the order is to be in force; and

(b) may specify different places, or different periods (within the period for which the order is in force), for different days, but shall not specify periods which amount to less than two hours or more than twelve hours in any one day.

(4) Part IV of this Act, except sections 35, 36, 37(3) and (4), 39 and 40(2)(a), has effect in relation to a secondary order as it has effect in relation to any other curfew order, but subject to the further modifications made below.

(5) Section 37(9) applies as if the reference to an offender who on conviction is under 16 were a reference to a person who on the date when his failure to comply with the original order is proved to the court is under 16.

(6) Paragraphs 2A, 4(1A) to (2) and 5(1A) to (2) above and 10 and 11 below apply as if, in respect of the period for which the secondary order is in force, the requirements of that order were requirements of the original order.

But in paragraphs 4 and 5 above, sub-paragraph (1C)(c) applies as if references to the relevant order were to the original order or the secondary order.

(7) In paragraphs 4 and 5 above, sub-paragraph (3) applies as if references to the relevant order were to the original order and the secondary order

(8) Paragraph 19(3) below applies as if the reference to six months from the date of the original order were a reference to 28 days from the date of the secondary order.]

Community punishment orders imposed for breach of relevant order

7.—(1) Section 46(1) of this Act (community service orders) shall apply for the   **5–123v**
purposes of paragraphs *4(1)(b) and 5(1)(b)* [4(1C) and 5(1C)(b)] above as if for the words from the beginning to "make" there were substituted "Where a court has power to deal with an offender aged 16 or over under Part II of Schedule 3 to this Act for failure to comply with any of the requirements of a relevant order, the court may make in respect of the offender".

(2) In this paragraph a "secondary order" means a community service order made by virtue of paragraph *4(1)(b) or 5(1)(b) above* [4(1C)(b) or 5(1C)(b) and "original order" means the relevant order the failure to comply with which led to the making of the secondary order].

(3) The number of hours which an offender may be required to work under a secondary order shall be specified in the order and shall not exceed 60 in the aggregate; and—

(a) where the relevant order is a community service order, the number of hours which the offender may be required to work under the secondary order shall not be such that the total number of hours under both orders exceeds the maximum specified in section 46(3) of this Act; and

(b) where the relevant order is a combination order, the number of hours which the offender may be required to work under the secondary order shall not be such that the total number of hours under—

(i) the secondary order, and

(ii) the community punishment element of the combination order,

exceeds the maximum specified in section 51(1)(b) of this Act.

(4) *Section 46(4) of this Act and, so far as applicable—*

(a) *section 46(5) to (7) and (9) to (13), and*

(b) *section 47 and the provisions of this Schedule so far as relating to community service orders,*

have effect in relation to a secondary order as they have effect in relation to any other community service order, subject to sub-paragraph (6) below.

(5) *Sections 148 and 156 of the* Criminal Justice Act *2003 (restrictions and procedural requirements for community sentences) do not apply in relation to a secondary order.*

(6) *Where the provisions of this Schedule have effect as mentioned in sub-paragraph (4) above in relation to a secondary order—*

(a) *the power conferred on the court by each of paragraphs 4(1)(d) and 5(1)(d) above and paragraph 10(3)(b) below to deal with the offender for the offence in respect of which the order was made shall be construed as a power to deal with the offender, for his failure to comply with the original order, in any way in which the court could deal with him if that failure had just been proved to the satisfaction of the court;*

(b) *the references in paragraphs 10(1)(b) and 11(1)(a) below to the offence in respect of which the order was made shall be construed as references to the failure to comply in respect of which the order was made; and*

(c) *the power conferred on the Crown Court by paragraph 11(2)(b) below to deal with the offender for the offence in respect of which the order was made shall be construed as a power to deal with the offender, for his failure to comply with the original order, in any way in which a magistrates' court (if the original order was made by a magistrates' court) or the Crown Court (if the original order was made by the Crown Court) could deal with him if that failure had just been proved to its satisfaction;*

and in this sub-paragraph "the original order" means the relevant order the failure to comply with which led to the making of the secondary order.

[(4) Part IV of this Act, except sections 35, 36, 46(3) and (8) and 48 to 50, has effect in relation to a secondary order as it has effect in relation to any other community punishment order, but subject to the further modifications made below.

(5) Paragraphs 2A, 4(1A) to (3) and 5(1A) to (3) above and 10 and 11 below apply as if, in respect of the period for which the secondary order is in force, the requirements of that order were requirements of the original order.

But in paragraphs 4 and 5 above, sub-paragraph (1C)(c) applies as if references to the relevant order were to the original order or the secondary order.

(6) In paragraphs 4 and 5 above, sub-paragraph (3) applies as if references to the relevant order were to the original order and the secondary order.

(7) Paragraph 19(3) below applies as if the reference to six months from the date of the original order were a reference to 28 days from the date of the secondary order.]

Attendance centre orders imposed for breach of relevant order

5-123w   8.—(1) Section 60(1) of this Act (attendance centre orders) shall apply for the purposes of paragraphs *4(1)(c) and 5(1)(c)* [4(1C)(c) and 5(1C)(c)] above as if for the words from the beginning to "the court may," there were substituted

"Where a court—

(a) *has power to deal with an offender aged under 16 under Part II of Schedule 3 to this Act for failure to comply with any of the requirements of a curfew order, or*

(b) *has power to deal with an offender aged under 21 under that Part of that Schedule for failure to comply with any of the requirements of a probation or combination order,*

the court may, [has power to deal with an offender under Part II of Schedule 3 to this Act for failure to comply with any of the requirements of a relevant order, the court may,]".

(2) The following provisions of this Act, namely—

(a) subsections (3) to (11) of section 60, and

(b) so far as applicable, section 36B and Schedule 5,

have effect in relation to an attendance centre order made by virtue of paragraph *4(1)(c) or 5(1)(c)* [4(1C)(c) or 5(1C)(c)] above as they have effect in relation to any other attendance centre order, but as if there were omitted from each of paragraphs 2(1)(b), 3(1) and 4(3) of Schedule 5 the words ", for the offence in respect of which the order was made," and "for that offence".

(3) Sections 148 and 156 of the *Criminal Justice Act* 2003 (restrictions and procedural requirements for community sentences) do not apply in relation to an attendance centre order made by virtue of paragraph *4(1)(c) or 5(1)(c)* [4(1C)(c) or 5(1C)(c)] above.

Supplementary

9.—(1) Any exercise by a court of its powers under paragraph *4(1)(a), (b) or (c) or* **5–123x** *5(1)(a), (b) or (c)* [4(1C)(a), (b) or (c) or 5(1C)(a), (b) or (c)] above shall be without prejudice to the continuance of the relevant order.

(2) *A fine imposed under paragraph 4(1)(a) or 5(1)(a) above shall be deemed, for the purposes of any enactment, to be a sum adjudged to be paid by a conviction.*

(3) Where a relevant order was made by a magistrates' court in the case of an offender under 18 years of age in respect of an offence triable only on indictment in the case of an adult, any powers exercisable under paragraph *4(1)(d)* [4(1C)(d)] above in respect of the offender after he attains the age of 18 shall be powers to do either or both of the following—

(a) to impose a fine not exceeding £5,000 for the offence in respect of which the order was made;

(b) to deal with the offender for that offence in any way in which a magistrates' court could deal with him if it had just convicted him of an offence punishable with imprisonment for a term not exceeding six months.

PART III

REVOCATION OF ORDER

Revocation of order with or without re-sentencing: powers of magistrates' court

10.—(1) This paragraph applies where a relevant order made by a magistrates' **5–123y** court is in force in respect of any offender and on the application of the offender or the responsible officer it appears to the appropriate magistrates' court that, having regard to circumstances which have arisen since the order was made, it would be in the interests of justice—

(a) for the order to be revoked; or

(b) for the offender to be dealt with in some other way for the offence in respect of which the order was made.

(2) In this paragraph "the appropriate magistrates court" means—

(a) in the case of a drug treatment and testing order or a drug abstinence order, the magistrates' court responsible for the order;

(b) in the case of any other relevant order, a magistrates' court acting for the petty sessions area concerned.

(3) The appropriate magistrates' court may—

(a) revoke the order; or

(b) both—

(i) revoke the order; and

(ii) deal with the offender, for the offence in respect of which the order was made, in any way in which it could deal with him if he had just been convicted by the court of the offence.

(4) The circumstances in which a community rehabilitation, community punishment and rehabilitation or drug treatment and testing order may be revoked under

sub-paragraph (3)(a) above shall include the offender's making good progress or his responding satisfactorily to supervision or, as the case may be, treatment.

(5) In dealing with an offender under sub-paragraph (3)(b) above, a magistrates' court shall take into account the extent to which the offender has complied with the requirements of the relevant order.

(6) A person sentenced under sub-paragraph (3)(b) above for an offence may appeal to the Crown Court against the sentence.

(7) Where a magistrates' court proposes to exercise its powers under this paragraph otherwise than on the application of the offender, it shall summon him to appear before the court and, if he does not appear in answer to the summons, may issue a warrant for his arrest.

(8) No application may be made by the offender under sub-paragraph (1) above while an appeal against the relevant order is pending.

Revocation of order with or without re-sentencing: powers of
Crown Court on conviction etc.

5–123z   11.—(1) This paragraph applies where—

    (a) a relevant order made by the Crown Court is in force in respect of an offender and the offender or the responsible officer applies to the Crown Court for the order to be revoked or for the offender to be dealt with in some other way for the offence in respect of which the order was made; or

    (b) an offender in respect of whom a relevant order is in force is convicted of an offence before the Crown Court or, having been committed by a magistrates' court to the Crown Court for sentence, is brought or appears before the Crown Court.

(2) If it appears to the Crown Court to be in the interests of justice to do so, having regard to circumstances which have arisen since the order was made, the Crown Court may—

    (a) revoke the order; or

    (b) both—

      (i) revoke the order; and

      (ii) deal with the offender, for the offence in respect of which the order was made, in any way in which the court which made the order could deal with him if he had just been convicted of that offence by or before the court which made the order.

(3) The circumstances in which a community rehabilitation, community punishment and rehabilitation or drug treatment and testing order may be revoked under sub-paragraph (2)(a) above shall include the offender's making good progress or his responding satisfactorily to supervision or, as the case may be, treatment.

(4) In dealing with an offender under sub-paragraph (2)(b) above, the Crown Court shall take into account the extent to which the offender has complied with the requirements of the relevant order.

Substitution of conditional discharge for community rehabilitation
or community punishment and rehabilitation order

5–124a   12.—(1) This paragraph applies where a community rehabilitation order or community punishment and rehabilitation order is in force in respect of any offender and on the application of the offender or the responsible officer to the appropriate court it appears to the court that, having regard to circumstances which have arisen since the order was made, it would be in the interests of justice—

    (a) for the order to be revoked; and

    (b) for an order to be made under section 12(1)(b) of this Act discharging the offender conditionally for the offence for which the community rehabilitation or community punishment and rehabilitation order was made.

(2) In this paragraph "the appropriate court" means—

    (a) where the community rehabilitation or community punishment and rehabilitation order was made by a magistrates' court, a magistrates' court acting for the petty sessions area concerned;

(b) where the community rehabilitation or community punishment and rehabilitation order was made by the Crown Court, the Crown Court.

(3) No application may be made under paragraph 10 or 11 above for a probation order or combination order to be revoked and replaced with an order for conditional discharge under section 12(1)(b); but otherwise nothing in this paragraph shall affect the operation of paragraphs 10 and 11 above.

(4) Where this paragraph applies—

(a) the appropriate court may revoke the community rehabilitation or community punishment and rehabilitation order and make an order under section 12(1)(b) of this Act discharging the offender in respect of the offence for which the community rehabilitation or community punishment and rehabilitation order was made, subject to the condition that he commits no offence during the period specified in the order under section 12(1)(b); and

(b) the period specified in the order under section 12(1)(b) shall be the period beginning with the making of that order and ending with the date when the community rehabilitation period specified in the community rehabilitation or community punishment and rehabilitation order would have ended.

(5) For the purposes of sub-paragraph (4) above, subsection (1) of section 12 of this Act shall apply as if—

(a) for the words from the beginning to "may make an order either" there were substituted the words "Where paragraph 12 of Schedule 3 to this Act applies, the appropriate court may (subject to the provisions of sub-paragraph (4) of that paragraph) make an order in respect of the offender"; and

(b) paragraph (a) of that subsection were omitted.

(6) An application under this paragraph may be heard in the offender's absence if—

(a) the application is made by the responsible officer; and

(b) that officer produces to the court a statement by the offender that he understands the effect of an order for conditional discharge and consents to the making of the application;

and where the application is so heard section 12(4) of this Act shall not apply.

(7) No application may be made under this paragraph while an appeal against the community rehabilitation or community punishment and rehabilitation order is pending.

(8) Without prejudice to paragraph 15 below, on the making of an order under section 12(1)(b) of this Act by virtue of this paragraph the court shall forthwith give copies of the order to the responsible officer, and the responsible officer shall give a copy to the offender.

(9) Each of sections 1(11), 2(9) and 66(4) of the *Crime and Disorder Act* 1998 (which prevent a court from making an order for conditional discharge in certain cases) shall have effect as if the reference to the court by or before which a person is convicted of an offence there mentioned included a reference to a court dealing with an application under this paragraph in respect of the offence.

Revocation following custodial sentence by magistrates' court unconnected with order

13.—(1) This paragraph applies where— **5–124b**

(a) an offender in respect of whom a relevant order is in force is convicted of an offence by a magistrates' court unconnected with the order;

(b) the court imposes a custodial sentence on the offender; and

(c) it appears to the court, on the application of the offender or the responsible officer, that it would be in the interests of justice to exercise its powers under this paragraph, having regard to circumstances which have arisen since the order was made.

(2) In sub-paragraph (1) above "a magistrates' court unconnected with the order" means—

    (a) in the case of a drug treatment and testing order or a drug abstinence order, a magistrates' court which is not responsible for the order;

    (b) in the case of any other relevant order, a magistrates' court not acting for the petty sessions area concerned.

(3) The court may—

    (a) if the order was made by a magistrates' court, revoke it;

    (b) if the order was made by the Crown Court, commit the offender in custody or release him on bail until he can be brought or appear before the Crown Court.

(4) Where the court deals with an offender's case under sub-paragraph (3)(b) above, it shall send to the Crown Court such particulars of the case as may be desirable.

14. Where by virtue of paragraph 13(3)(b) above an offender is brought or appears before the Crown Court and it appears to the Crown Court to be in the interests of justice to do so, having regard to circumstances which have arisen since the relevant order was made, the Crown Court may revoke the order.

Supplementary

15.—(1) On the making under this Part of this Schedule of an order revoking a relevant order, the proper officer of the court shall forthwith give copies of the revoking order to the responsible officer.

(2) In sub-paragraph (1) above "proper officer" means—

    (a) in relation to a magistrates' court, the justices' chief executive for the court; and

    (b) in relation to the Crown Court, the appropriate officer.

(3) A responsible officer to whom in accordance with sub-paragraph (1) above copies of a revoking order are given shall give a copy to the offender and to the person in charge of any institution in which the offender was required by the order to reside.

16. Paragraph 9(3) above shall apply for the purposes of paragraphs 10 and 11 above as it applies for the purposes of paragraph 4 above, but as if for the words "paragraph *4(1)(d)* [4(1C)(d)] above" there were substituted "paragraph 10(3)(b)(ii) or 11(2)(b)(ii) below".

17. Where under this Part of this Schedule a relevant order is revoked and replaced by an order for conditional discharge under section 12(1)(b) of this Act and—

    (a) the order for conditional discharge is not made in the circumstances mentioned in section 13(9) of this Act (order made by magistrates' court in the case of an offender under 18 in respect of offence triable only on indictment in the case of an adult), but

    (b) the relevant order was made in those circumstances,

section 13(9) shall have effect as if the order for conditional discharge had been made in those circumstances.

[Paras 1 to 17 are printed as amended, and as amended as from a day to be appointed, by the *CJCSA* 2000, ss.53, 54 and 74, and Sched. 7, paras 1 to 3, and 199(1) to (19) (italicised words are omitted and words in square brackets are inserted as from a day to be appointed). The amendments effected by s.53 of the 2000 Act (insertion of paras 1(1A), 2A and 6(3), and substitution of new paras 4(1) to (1C) for 4(1), and new paras 5(1) to (1C) for 5(1)) have no application in relation to any community order made before the commencement date of that section: *CJCSA* 2000, s.70(5). Paragraphs 3 and 4 are printed as further amended by the *Domestic Violence, Crime and Victims Act* 2004, s.29, and Sched. 5, para. 4. It should be further noted in relation to this schedule: (i) its substitution by a new Schedule 3 (set out in the main work, §§ 5–201 *et seq.*), by virtue of the *CJA* 2003, s.304, and Sched. 32, para. 125, is to take effect on April 4, 2009 (but as to the likely postponement of this date, see *post*, § 5–210): *Criminal Justice Act 2003 (Commencement No. 8 and Transitional and Saving Provisions) Order* 2005 (S.I. 2005 No. 950), as amended by the *Criminal Justice Act 2003 (Commencement No. 8 and Transitional Provisions) (Amendment) Order* 2007 (S.I. 2007 No. 391); (ii) until that substitution takes effect, the schedule "shall continue to have effect (subject to any necessary modifications) as if" the reference in paragraphs 5(2) and 21(6)(b) to "section 79(2) of this Act" were to "section 152(3)" of the 2003 Act, and as if the reference in paragraphs 7(5) and 8(3) to "sections 35 and 36 of this Act" were to "sections 148 and 156" of the 2003 Act: S.I. 2005 No. 950, art. 4(1), and Sched. 2, para. 11; (iii) the modifications referred to in (ii) have been incorporated into the text of the schedule (*ante*), but the first of these modifications raises the issue whether paragraph 4(2) should be read as being similarly so modified; (iv) all the amending provisions of the *CJCSA* 2000 (*ante*) which had not been brought into force as at April 4, 2005, were repealed on that day by a combination of the *CJA* 2003, Sched. 37, Pt 7, and S.I. 2005 No. 950; but (v) even though repealed without ever being brought into force, their repeal is of no effect in relation to offences committed before that date: S.I. 2005 No. 950, art. 2(1), and Sched. 2, para. 5.]

Orders made prior to the commencement of the CJCSA 2000, s.53

The criminal standard of proof applies where an information is laid alleging a failure to comply with a community rehabilitation order; upon proof of a breach, the defendant was at risk of being sentenced to imprisonment (a sharp potential increase in penalty), and that should not occur unless the factual basis of the breach had been proved beyond reasonable doubt: *West Yorkshire Probation Board v. Boulter* [2006] 1 W.L.R. 232, DC. **5–124d**

Where a court re-sentences under paragraph 4(1)(d), 5(1)(d), 10(3)(b) or 11(2)(b) it must observe the provisions of sections 79 and 80 of the *PCC(S)A* 2000 (*post*, §§ 5–275a, 5–275b) before imposing a custodial sentence; but paragraphs 4(2)(b) and 5(2)(b) permit a custodial sentence notwithstanding anything in section 79(2). The fact that the offence was originally dealt with by a community sentence does not exclude the possibility of a custodial sentence under section 79(2) ("so serious that only such a sentence can be justified"): see *R. v. Webster*, 12 Cr.App.R.(S.) 760, CA; *R. v. Oliver and Little*, 96 Cr.App.R. 426, CA.

Where an offender has spent time in custody on remand before being sentenced to a community rehabilitation or community punishment order, and is later sentenced to a custodial sentence for the offence for which the community order was made, time spent in custody on remand will not count as part of that sentence for the purposes of the *CJA* 1967, s.67 (*rep.*). The Court of Appeal has held that the custodial sentence imposed in such circumstances should be reduced by an appropriate amount to compensate the offender for this time. (For cases dealing with probation orders, see *R. v. McDonald*, 10 Cr.App.R.(S.) 458, CA; *R. v. Gyorgy*, 11 Cr.App.R.(S.) 1, CA; *R. v. Needham, ibid.* at 506, CA; for cases dealing with community service orders, see *R. v. McIntyre*, 7 Cr.App.R.(S.) 196, CA; *R. v. MacKenzie*, 10 Cr.App.R.(S.) 299, CA.) In normal circumstances, it will be appropriate to reduce the intended sentence by a period equivalent to twice the time spent in custody on remand in connection with the original proceedings.

In *R. v. Henderson* [1997] 2 Cr.App.R.(S.) 266, CA, it was held that the amount of time to be allowed is a matter for the sentencer's discretion. If a court takes into account time spent in custody before the making of a community order, it should state that fact when passing sentence, and indicate the extent to which the matter has been taken into account. See also *R. v. Armstrong* [2002] 2 Cr.App.R.(S.) 87, CA (court not bound to reduce sentence by fixed amount).

The requirement that a court which re-sentences for an offence for which a community order was originally imposed should have regard to the extent to which the offender has complied with the requirements of the order (see paras 4(2)(a), 5(2)(a), 10(5) and 11(4)) was considered in *R. v. Neville*, 14 Cr.App.R.(S.) 768, CA.

Where a court makes a community order in a case where there is power to disqualify the offender from driving, and that power is exercised at the time the community order is made, there is no power to impose a further period of disqualification if the offender is later sentenced for a breach of the order: see *R. v. Coy*, 13 Cr.App.R.(S.) 619, CA, decided on the *PCCA* 1973, s.16 (*rep.*).

Where an offender commits an offence during the period of a community order, but is not convicted of that offence until after the community order has expired, there is no power to revoke the community order and pass a further sentence for the original offence: see *R. v. Bennett*, 15 Cr.App.R.(S.) 213; and *R. v. Cousin*, *ibid.* at 516, CA.

Where an offender is subject to a "relevant order" (see Sched. 3, para. 1) at the time of conviction by, or of being brought or appearing before, the Crown Court, that court has power to revoke the community order or to revoke and re-sentence for the original offence even though the community order had not been made at the time of the commission of the new offence (para. 11); what order should be made in any given case should be decided according to the demands of justice and not according to any prescriptive principle: *R. v. Newton* [1999] 2 Cr.App.R.(S.) 172, CA.

Where an offender applies for a community order to be revoked on the ground that he is unable to perform the order because of injury or ill health, the court should not, on revoking the order, impose a custodial sentence for the original offence, or a suspended sentence: *R. v. Fielding*, 14 Cr.App.R.(S.) 494, CA; *R. v. Jackson* [2000] 1 Cr.App.R.(S.) 405, CA.

Where an offender consents to a community service order, knowing that he is subject to a medical condition which will make performance of the order impossible, or will limit the type of work which he can perform, and the offence would justify a custodial sentence, the court may, on application to vary the order, revoke the order and substitute a custodial sentence: see *R. v. Hammon* [1998] 2 Cr.App.R.(S.) 202, CA.

Orders made after the commencement of the CJCSA 2000, s.53

5-124e   The *CJCSA* 2000, s.53 (repealed without ever being brought into force with effect from April 4, 2005, but subject to a saving provision declaring the repeal to be of no effect in relation to offences committed before that date), makes major amendments to the treatment of offenders who fail to comply with the requirements of community orders. These amendments apply only to orders made after the commencement of section 53: *CJCSA* 2000, s.70(5). The amendments are effected by a series of amendments to Schedule 3 to the *PCC(S)A* 2000, which will continue to exist in two versions until the last of the pre-commencement orders has been served.

Under the new scheme, an offender over the age of 18 who fails for a second time to comply with a requirement of a community order, other than a drug treatment and testing order or a requirement not to misuse specified class A drugs, must be brought before the appropriate court; if the court finds that the failure is proved, the court must impose a sentence of imprisonment unless either the court is of the opinion that the offender is likely to comply with the order during the remaining period of the order, or that there are "exceptional circumstances". In imposing a sentence of imprisonment, the court is not bound by the *PCC(S)A* 2000, s.79 (custody threshold) but it is bound by section 80 (term of sentence to be commensurate with offence). If a court imposes a mandatory sentence of imprisonment under paragraph 4(1A) or 5(1A), it must revoke the community order.

If the court finds that there are grounds for not imposing the mandatory sentence of imprisonment, or the obligation to impose imprisonment does not apply, the court may deal with the case in one of the alternative ways set out in paragraphs 4(1C) or 5(1C). The power to deal with a breach of a requirement by a fine is abolished.

(5) Amendment

Part IV (paras 18– 25) of Schedule 3 to the *PCC(S)A* 2000 provides for the   **5–124f**
amendment of community orders. Paragraph 18 relates to amendment on the ground of the offender's change of residence, but does not apply to a drug treatment and testing order. Paragraphs 19 and 20 make provision for the amendment of the requirements of a community rehabilitation order or curfew order, and amendment of particular requirements of a community rehabilitation order or community punishment and rehabilitation order. Paragraph 22 provides for the extension of a community punishment or community punishment and rehabilitation order. Orders under paragraphs 18 to 20 and 22 are to be made by the magistrates' court acting for the petty sessions area concerned. The amendment of drug treatment and testing orders is regulated by paragraph 21 (*post*). Paragraphs 23 to 25 contain supplemental provisions.

**Powers of Criminal Courts (Sentencing) Act 2000, Sched. 3, Pt IV,
paras 21, 23–25**

Amendment of drug treatment and testing order

21.—(1) Without prejudice to the provisions of section 55(1), (6) and (8) of this   **5–124g**
Act, the court responsible for a drug treatment and testing order may by order—

    (a) vary or cancel any of the requirements or provisions of the order on an application by the responsible officer under sub-paragraph (2) or (3)(a) or (b) below; or

    (b) amend the order on an application by that officer under sub-paragraph (3)(c) below.

(2) Where the treatment provider is of the opinion that the treatment or testing requirement of the order should be varied or cancelled—

    (a) he shall make a report in writing to that effect to the responsible officer; and

    (b) that officer shall apply to the court for the variation or cancellation of the requirement.

(3) Where the responsible officer is of the opinion—

    (a) that the treatment or testing requirement of the order should be so varied as to specify a different treatment provider,

(b) that any other requirement of the order, or a provision of the order, should be varied or cancelled, or

(c) that the order should be so amended as to provide for each subsequent periodic review (required by section 54(6)(a) of this Act) to be made without a hearing instead of at a review hearing, or vice versa,

he shall apply to the court for the variation or cancellation of the requirement or provision or the amendment of the order.

(4) The court—

(a) shall not amend the treatment or testing requirement unless the offender expresses his willingness to comply with the requirement as amended; and

(b) shall not amend any provision of the order so as to reduce the treatment and testing period below the minimum specified in section 52(1) of this Act, or to increase it above the maximum so specified.

(5) If the offender fails to express his willingness to comply with the treatment or testing requirement as proposed to be amended by the court, the court may—

(a) revoke the order; and

(b) deal with him, for the offence in respect of which the order was made, in any way in which it could deal with him if he had just been convicted by or before the court of the offence.

(6) In dealing with the offender under sub-paragraph (5)(b) above, the court—

(a) shall take into account the extent to which the offender has complied with the requirements of the order; and

(b) may impose a custodial sentence (where the order was made in respect of an offence punishable with such a sentence) notwithstanding anything in section 152(3) of the *Criminal Justice Act* 2003.

(7) Paragraph 9(3) above shall apply for the purposes of this paragraph as it applies for the purposes of paragraph 4 above, but as if for the words "paragraph *4(1)(d)* [4(1C)(d)] above" there were substituted "paragraph 21(5)(b) below".

Supplementary

5–124h   23. No order may be made under paragraph 18 above, and no application may be made under paragraph 19 or 22 above or, except with the consent of the offender, under paragraph 21 above, while an appeal against the relevant order is pending.

24.—(1) Subject to sub-paragraph (2) below, where a court proposes to exercise its powers under this Part of this Schedule, otherwise than on the application of the offender, the court—

(a) shall summon him to appear before the court; and

(b) if he does not appear in answer to the summons, may issue a warrant for his arrest.

(2) This paragraph shall not apply to an order cancelling a requirement of a relevant order or reducing the period of any requirement, or [to an order under paragraph 18 above] substituting a new petty sessions area or a new place for the one specified in a relevant order.

25. [*Copies of amending orders.*]

26. [*Copies of orders amending drug treatment and testing orders.*]

[Paras 21 and 24 are printed as amended, as from a day to be appointed, by the *CJCSA* 2000, s.74 and Sched. 7, para. 199(19) and (24) (omission of italicised words, insertion of words in square brackets). As to this schedule, see the annotations to paras 1 to 17, *ante*, § 5–124c.]

B. GENERAL RESTRICTIONS

Criminal Justice Act 2003, ss.147–151

[Community order [[or youth rehabilitation order]] for persistent offender previously fined

★5–129   The amendments of section 151 of the 2003 Act effected by the *AFA* 2006

come into force on October 31, 2009: *Armed Forces Act 2006 (Commencement
No. 5) Order* 2009 (S.I. 2009 No. 1167). In connection with that commencement, see the transitional provision in the *Armed Forces Act 2006 (Transitional
Provisions etc.) Order* 2009 (S.I. 2009 No. 1059), Sched. 1, para. 53(6) (interpretation of references to "conviction in service disciplinary proceedings"
and "service offence").

C. COMMUNITY ORDERS

(1) General

Criminal Justice Act 2003, s.177

Community orders

    Sections 178 and 182 of the *AFA* 2006 come into force on October 31,   ★**5–130**
2009: *Armed Forces Act 2006 (Commencement No. 5) Order* 2009 (S.I. 2009 No.
1167).

    The commencement of sections 177, 179 and 180 of the 2003 Act, in rela-   ★**5–131**
tion to a person aged 16 or 17 convicted of an offence, has been postponed to
April 4, 2010 (*Criminal Justice Act 2003 (Commencement No. 8 and Transitional
and Saving Provisions) (Amendment) Order* 2009 (S.I. 2009 No. 616)), but it is
expected that this will be overtaken by the commencement (anticipated in
June, 2009, to be on November 30, 2009) of Part 1 of the *CJIA* 2008, which
will render the commencement redundant in any event.

**Criminal Justice Act 2003 (Commencement No. 8 and Transitional and
Saving Provisions) Order 2005 (S.I. 2005 No. 950), Sched. 2, paras 7–13**

Transitional provisions

    7. Until the coming into force of sections 177 and 179 to 180 (community orders)   **5–131a**
of the 2003 Act in accordance with article 2(2) of this Order, the transitional provisions in paragraphs 8 to 10 shall have effect.

    8. Sections 41 to 58 of and Schedules 2 and 4 to the *Sentencing Act* shall continue   **5–131b**
to have effect (subject to any necessary modifications) where a person aged 16 or 17
is convicted of an offence as if—

    (a) for "sections 34 to 36 above" in sections 41(1), 46(1), 51(1) and 52(1) there
         were substituted "sections 148, 150 and 156 of the *Criminal Justice Act*
         2003";

    (b) sections 41(4), (7) and (9)(a); 42(2)(b) to (3); 46(5)(a), (10), 11(a); 47(3A) to
         (4); and 52(6) were omitted;

    (c) paragraphs 2(2)(a)(i) and 3(2)(a) of Schedule 2 were omitted; and

    (d) paragraphs 1(3)(a) and 2(3)(a) of Schedule 4, in so far as they relate to
         paragraph 2(2)(a)(i) of Schedule 2 to the *Sentencing Act*, were omitted.

    9. Notwithstanding the substitution of section 33 (community orders) and the   **5–131c**
amendment to section 165 (interpretation) of the *Sentencing Act* by Schedule 32 to
the 2003 Act, orders made under sections 41 to 58 of the *Sentencing Act* (community
rehabilitation orders, community punishment orders, community punishment and
rehabilitation orders and drug treating and testing orders) shall continue to be
regarded as community orders and community sentences for the purposes of the
Sentencing Act.

    10. Notwithstanding sections 147 (meaning of community sentence), 177 (com-   **5–131d**
munity orders) and 305 (interpretation) of the 2003 Act, orders made under sections
41 to 58 of the *Sentencing Act* shall also be regarded as community orders and community sentences for the purposes of the provisions specified in paragraphs (a) and
(b)—

(a) sections 148 to 150, 152, 156, 166 and 174 of the 2003 Act; and

(b) the amendments made by paragraphs 8, 12(4) and 5, 13(2) and (3), 18(3), 21(3), 31, 38, 73, 89, 123(4), 131, 132 and 134(a) of Schedule 32 to the 2003 Act.

5–131e   11. Until the coming into force of paragraph 125 (substitution of Schedule 3 to the *Sentencing Act*) of Schedule 32 to the 2003 Act in accordance with article 4 of this Order, Schedule 3 to the *Sentencing Act* shall continue to have effect (subject to any necessary modifications) as if—

(a) the reference in paragraphs 5(2) and 21(6)(b) to "section 79(2) of this Act" were to "section 152(3) of the *Criminal Justice Act* 2003"; and

(b) the reference in paragraphs 7(5) and 8(3) to "sections 35 and 36 of this Act" were to "sections 148 and 156 of the *Criminal Justice Act* 2003".

Savings

5–131f   12. Until the coming into force of sections 177 and 179 to 180 of the 2003 Act in accordance with article 2(2) of this Order, the provisions of the 2003 Act specified in paragraph 13 shall have no effect where a person aged 16 or 17 is convicted of an offence or in relation to orders made under sections 41 to 58 of the *Sentencing Act* by virtue of paragraph 8.

5–131g   13. The provisions referred to paragraph 12 are—

(a) section 303(d)(i) (repeal of Chapter 3 of Part 4 of the *Sentencing Act*);

(b) in Schedule 32, the amendments made by paragraphs 5, 14, 32, 36, 64, 69 to 72, 78(3), 96, 97(2)(a) and (3), 98, 100(2)(a) in so far as it substitutes "16" for "21", (2)(c) and (3), 101, 102(2)(a) and (4), 104(3) and 106(2);

(c) in Schedule 37, the entries relating to—

(i) section 94(1) of the *Social Work (Scotland) Act* 1968;

(ii) sections 35(2), 36B, 37(9) and 41 to 58 of and Schedules 2 and 4 to the *Sentencing Act*.

(2) Definitions

Criminal Justice Act 2003, s.196

Meaning of "relevant order"

★**5–132**   Sections 178 and 182 of the *AFA* 2006 come into force on October 31, 2009: *Armed Forces Act 2006 (Commencement No. 5) Order* 2009 (S.I. 2009 No. 1167).

(3) Requirements in case of all offenders

Criminal Justice Act 2003, ss.199–213

Prohibited activity requirement

5–139   The primary purpose of a prohibited activity requirement under section 203 of the 2003 Act or of an exclusion requirement under section 205 (§ 5–141 in the main work) being not to punish the offender but to prevent, or at least reduce, the risk of further offending, any such requirement must be proportionate to the risk of further offending: *R. v. J.*, 172 J.P. 513, CA.

Exclusion requirement

5–141   See *R. v. J., ante*, § 5–139.

Mental health treatment requirement

★**5–143**   As from July 1, 2009 (*Health Care and Associated Professions (Miscellaneous*

Amendments and Practitioner Psychologists) Order 2009 (Commencement No. 1 and Transitional Provisions) Order of Council 2009 (S.I. 2009 No. 1357)), the *Health Care and Associated Professions (Miscellaneous Amendments and Practitioner Psychologists) Order* 2009 (S.I. 2009 No. 1182), Sched. 5, para. 7(a)(i) and (b), amends section 207 of the 2003 Act by (i) substituting the word "registered" for the word "chartered" in subsections (1) and (2)(c), and (ii) substituting a new subsection (6), as follows—

"(6) In this section and section 208, 'registered psychologist' means a person registered in the part of the register maintained under the *Health Professions Order* 2001 (S.I. 2002 No. 254) which relates to practitioner psychologists.".

Mental health treatment at place other than that specified in order
As from July 1, 2009 (S.I. 2009 No. 1357 (*ante*, § 5–143)), the *Health Care and Associated Professions (Miscellaneous Amendments and Practitioner Psychologists) Order* 2009 (S.I. 2009 No. 1182), Sched. 5, para. 7(a)(ii), amends section 208 of the 2003 Act by substituting the word "registered" for the word "chartered" wherever it occurs in subsections (1) and (3)(a).   ★5–144

Drug rehabilitation requirement: provision for review by court
Sections 179 and 203 of the *AFA* 2006 come into force on October 31, 2009: *Armed Forces Act 2006 (Commencement No. 5) Order* 2009 (S.I. 2009 No. 1167).   ★5–146

Periodic review of drug rehabilitation requirement
Sections 179 and 203 of the *AFA* 2006 come into force on October 31, 2009: *Armed Forces Act 2006 (Commencement No. 5) Order* 2009 (S.I. 2009 No. 1167). In connection with the commencement of those sections, see the transitory provisions in the *Armed Forces Act 2006 (Transitional Provisions etc.) Order* 2009 (S.I. 2009 No. 1059), Sched. 2, para. 3 (references to "12 months" to have effect as references to "6 months" pending commencement of repeal of *CJCSA* 2000, s.78).   ★5–147

D. Youth Community Orders

(1) Curfew orders

Powers of Criminal Courts (Sentencing) Act 2000, s.37

Curfew orders
As to the substitution of the date of April 4, 2009 (see the main work) by a later date, see *ante*, §§ 5–3, 5–121e, 5–122, 5–131.   ★5–157

(2) Exclusion orders

Powers of Criminal Courts (Sentencing) Act 2000, s.40A

Exclusion orders
As to the substitution of the date of April 4, 2009 (see the main work) by a later date, see *ante*, §§ 5–3, 5–121e, 5–122, 5–131.   ★5–160

(3) Attendance centre orders

Powers of Criminal Courts (Sentencing) Act 2000, s.60

Attendance centre orders

★**5–162** As to the substitution of the date of April 4, 2009 (see the main work) by a later date, see *ante*, §§ 5–3, 5–121e, 5–122, 5–131.

(4) Supervision orders

Requirement to live for specified period with local authority foster parent

5–171a As from a day to be appointed "22C" is substituted for "23(2)(a)" in paragraph 5A(3) of Schedule 6 to the *PCC(S)A* 2000 by the *CYPA* 2008, s.8(2), and Sched. 1, para. 10.

Requirements as to treatment for mental condition

★**5–172** As from July 1, 2009 (S.I. 2009 No. 1357 (*ante*, § 5–143)), the *Health Care and Associated Professions (Miscellaneous Amendments and Practitioner Psychologists) Order* 2009 (S.I. 2009 No. 1182), Sched. 5, para. 5, amends paragraph 6 of Schedule 6 to the *PCC(S)A* 2000 by (i) substituting the word "registered" for the word "chartered" in sub-paragraph (2)(d) and (ii) by inserting a new sub-paragraph (5), as follows—

> "(5) In sub-paragraph (2), 'registered psychologist' means a person registered in the part of the register maintained under the *Health Professions Order* 2001 (S.I. 2002 No. 254) which relates to practitioner psychologists.".

(5) Action plan orders

Powers of Criminal Courts (Sentencing) Act 2000, ss.69-72

Action plan orders

★**5–175** As to the substitution of the date of April 4, 2009 (see the main work) by a later date, see *ante*, §§ 5–3, 5–121e, 5–122, 5–131.

(6) Electronic monitoring

Powers of Criminal Courts (Sentencing) Act 2000, s.36B

Electronic monitoring of requirements in [youth] community orders

★**5–178a** As to the substitution of the date of April 4, 2009 (see the main work) by a later date, see *ante*, §§ 5–3, 5–121e, 5–122, 5–131.

F. ENFORCEMENT

(1) Of community orders

(b) *Amendment, revocation and re-sentencing*

Criminal Justice Act 2003, Sched. 8

Supplementary

★**5–200** Section 181 of, and Schedule 5 to, the *AFA* 2006 come into force on

October 31, 2009: *Armed Forces Act 2006 (Commencement No. 5) Order* 2009
(S.I. 2009 No. 1167).

(2) Of youth community orders

(a) *Curfew and exclusion orders*

Powers of Criminal Courts (Sentencing) Act 2000, Sched. 3

Supplementary
    The substitution of Schedule 3 has been postponed to April 4, 2010 (*Crimi-*   **★5–210**
nal Justice Act 2003 (Commencement No. 8 and Transitional and Saving Provi-
sions) (Amendment) Order 2009 (S.I. 2009 No. 616)), but it is anticipated that
this will be overtaken by the commencement (probably on November 30,
2009) of Part 1 of the *CJIA* 2008, which will render the substitution
redundant in any event (see the main work).

VI. *CUSTODIAL SENTENCES*

A. MANDATORY LIFE SENTENCE

(2) Legislation

Criminal Justice Act 2003, ss.269, 270, 276, 277

Determination of minimum term in relation to mandatory life sentence
    Section 22 of the *CJIA* 2008 came into force on November 3, 2008: *Crimi-*   **5–239**
nal Justice and Immigration Act 2008 (Commencement No. 3 and Transitional Pro-
visions) Order 2008 (S.I. 2008 No. 2712).
    The amendment of section 269 of the 2003 Act effected by the *AFA* 2006   **★**
comes into force on October 31, 2009: *Armed Forces Act 2006 (Commencement*
No. 5) Order 2009 (S.I. 2009 No. 1167).

Fixing the minimum term

Lack of intent to kill/ plea of guilty
    Suggestions that there had been provocative conduct and a lack of intent to   **5–239g**
kill and of premeditation carried little weight where a significant degree of
force had been required to inflict the fatal wound (considering *R. v. Peters*; *R.*
v. Palmer; *R. v. Campbell* (see the main work)) and where there was evidence
that the appellant had taken the murder weapon (a knife) with a view to using it in a punitive rather than merely defensive fashion: *R. v. Blue* [2009] 1
Cr.App.R.(S.) 2, CA.

Starting points generally
    R. v. Bonellie, Hughes and Miller is now reported at [2009] 1 Cr.App.R.(S.)   **5–239j**
55, *sub nom. R. v. Bonellie*.
    It was held in *R. v. Height and Anderson* [2009] 1 Cr.App.R.(S.) 117, CA,
that whereas paragraph 4(1) of Schedule 21 to the *CJA* 2003 (see § 5–246 in
the main work) provides for a whole life starting point where the seriousness of the offence is "exceptionally high", whereas paragraph 5(1) provides

for a 30-year starting point in cases of "particularly high" seriousness, whereas paragraphs 4(2) and 5(2) list cases that would "normally" fall within paragraph 4(1) or 5(1) respectively, and whereas paragraph 6, read literally and in isolation from the remaining paragraphs, may suggest that any case which falls outside the cases listed in paragraphs 4(2) and 5(2) should have a 15-year starting point, such an inflexible approach would be inconsistent with the terms of the statutory framework and is problematic. The court said that the use of the word "normally" means that the listings are not exhaustive, from which it follows that in some cases, probably rare, the seriousness may be such as to justify the "exceptionally high" or "particularly high" starting point, although they do not fall within paragraph 4(2) or 5(2). Where, therefore, D1 wished to have his wife murdered "simply to get rid of her", where he had arranged and agreed to pay D2 to carry out the murder and where he had eventually carried out the killing himself in D2's presence, it was held that there was something wrong with the conclusion that the starting point for D1's sentence should differ from D2's simply because D2's case fell squarely within paragraph 5(2)(c) ("a murder done for gain") and D1's did not. It was difficult to conceive of many cases in which one defendant, acting for gain, should be subject to a different starting point to the individual who paid or agreed to pay him, at any rate where the money asked for was willingly paid. Accordingly, it was said that the judge should have applied the same (30-year) starting point to both defendants.

As to it making little difference to the seriousness of an offence whether the killing was committed in the course of attempting to obtain money from the victim or after such an attempt had failed, see *Att.-Gen.'s Reference (No. 12 of 2008) (R. v. Cole)* [2009] 1 Cr.App.R.(S.) 18, CA.

A judge was entitled to find that a murder was "done for gain" (within Sched. 21, para. 5(2)(c)), notwithstanding the absence of a separate count (and conviction) for robbery; robbery is but one example of murder for gain; and some forms of gain would not be capable of being pleaded as a separate count; furthermore, a number of the factors set out in paragraph 5(2) as matters which would normally cause a case to fall within the higher starting point are factors which would not involve guilt of a discrete criminal offence: *R. v. Healy* [2009] 2 Cr.App.R.(S.) 3, CA.

★ Where one offender had raped the victim and the other had attempted to do so before they killed her, that the case fell within paragraph 5(2)(e) of Schedule 21 to the *CJA* 2003 as being a murder involving "sexual conduct" was beyond argument; sexual conduct was the common thread from start to finish; the violence that led to the victim's death and the sexual conduct were inextricably interwoven: *Att.-Gen.'s References (Nos 25 and 26 of 2008) (R. v. McCarry George and Waters)* [2009] 1 Cr.App.R.(S.) 116, CA.

When sentencing a person for two or more murders committed when he was under 18, the judge should decide on the appropriate minimum term for each offence separately in accordance with the principles set out in Schedule 21 to the 2003 Act, then aggregate the two terms and discount the aggregated figure to allow for the totality principle; and the resulting figure should then be fixed as the minimum term for each offence: *R. v. Malasi* [2009] 1 Cr.App.R.(S.) 51, CA. Where, therefore, the appropriate minimum terms for two murders were 24 years and 12 years, the judge had been correct to discount the total of 36 years to 30 years.

Aggravating factors

5–239k *R. v. Davies* is now reported at [2009] 1 Cr.App.R.(S.) 15.

A judge was entitled to find a racial element to an offence despite having
indicated that he would not be relying on racial aggravation so as to justify a
30-year starting point under paragraph 5(2)(g) of Schedule 21 to the *CJA*
2003 (§ 5–246 in the main work): *R. v. Blue* [2009] 1 Cr.App.R.(S.) 6(2), CA.

Secondary parties

Sentencing of a person convicted of murder as a secondary party is   ★5–239o
governed by section 269 of, and Schedule 21 to, the CJA 2003 as much is the
sentencing of a person convicted as a principal: *Att.-Gen.'s Reference (No. 24 of
2008) (R. v. Sanchez)*, unreported, December 5, 2008, CA ([2008] EWCA
Crim. 2936).

Interpretation of Chapter 7

The amendment of section 277 of the 2003 Act effected by the *AFA* 2006   ★5–242
comes into force on October 31, 2009: *Armed Forces Act 2006 (Commencement
No. 5) Order* 2009 (S.I. 2009 No. 1167).

Crime (Sentences) Act 1997, s.34

The amendments of section 34 of the 1997 Act effected by the *AFA* 2006   ★5–244
come into force on October 31, 2009: *Armed Forces Act 2006 (Commencement
No. 5) Order* 2009 (S.I. 2009 No. 1167). In connection with that commencement, see the transitional provisions in the *Armed Forces Act 2006 (Transitional
Provisions etc.) Order* 2009 (S.I. 2009 No. 1059), Sched. 1, para. 40 (interpretation of references to sections 90, 91, 93 and 94 of the *PCC(S)A* 2000).

Criminal Justice Act 2003, Sched. 21

Determination of minimum terms in relation to mandatory life sentence

As from February 16, 2009 (*Counter-Terrorism Act 2008 (Commencement No.   **5–246**
2) Order* 2009 (S.I. 2009 No. 58)), ", racial" is inserted after "religious" in
paragraph 4(2)(c) of Schedule 21 to the 2003 Act: *Counter-Terrorism Act 2008*,
s.75(1) and (2)(c).

Aggravating and mitigating factors

The amendment of Schedule 21 to the 2003 Act effected by the *AFA* 2006   ★5–247
comes into force on October 31, 2009: *Armed Forces Act 2006 (Commencement
No. 5) Order* 2009 (S.I. 2009 No. 1167).

Criminal Justice Act 2003, Sched. 22, paras 1, 2, 9 and 10

Section 276   SCHEDULE 22

MANDATORY LIFE SENTENCES: TRANSITIONAL CASES

Interpretation

1. In this Schedule—   **5–248**
    "the commencement date" means the day on which section 269 comes into force;
    "the early release provisions" means the provisions of section 28(5) to (8) of the
        Crime (Sentences) Act 1997;
    "existing prisoner" means a person serving one or more mandatory life sentences
        passed before the commencement date (whether or not he is also serving any
        other sentence);

"life sentence" means a sentence of imprisonment for life or custody for life passed in England and Wales or by a court-martial outside England and Wales;

"mandatory life sentence" means a life sentence passed in circumstances where the sentence was fixed by law.

Existing prisoners notified by Secretary of State

5-249   2. Paragraph 3 applies in relation to any existing prisoner who, in respect of any mandatory life sentence, has before the commencement date been notified in writing by the Secretary of State (otherwise than in a notice that is expressed to be provisional) either—

(a) of a minimum period which in the view of the Secretary of State should be served before the prisoner's release on licence, or

(b) that the Secretary of State does not intend that the prisoner should ever be released on licence.

Sentences passed on or after commencement date in respect of offences committed before that date

5-250   9. Paragraph 10 applies where—

(a) on or after the commencement date a court passes a life sentence in circumstances where the sentence is fixed by law, and

(b) the offence to which the sentence relates was committed before the commencement date.

10. The court—

(a) may not make an order under subsection (2) of section 269 specifying a part of the sentence which in the opinion of the court is greater than that which, under the practice followed by the Secretary of State before December 2002, the Secretary of State would have been likely to notify as mentioned in paragraph 2(a), and

(b) may not make an order under subsection (4) of section 269 unless the court is of the opinion that, under the practice followed by the Secretary of State before December 2002, the Secretary of State would have been likely to give the prisoner a notification falling within paragraph 2(b).

(3) Practice

Practice Direction (Criminal Proceedings: Consolidation), para. IV.49.14–IV.49.37 (as substituted by Practice Direction (Crime: Mandatory Life Sentences) (No. 2) [2004] 1 W.L.R. 2551

Transitional arrangements for new sentences where the offence was committed before 18 December 2003

5-251a   IV.49.14   Where the court is passing a sentence of mandatory life imprisonment for an offence committed before 18 December 2003, the court should take a fourth step in determining the minimum term in accordance with section 276 and Schedule 22 ... .

IV.49.15   The purpose of those provisions is to ensure that the sentence does not breach the principle of non-retroactivity by ensuring that a lower minimum term would not have been imposed for the offence when it was committed. Before setting the minimum term the court must check whether the proposed term is greater than that which the term [*sic*] the Secretary of State would probably have notified under the practice followed by the Secretary of State before December 2002.

IV.49.16   The decision in *Sullivan* ... gives detailed guidance as to the correct approach to this practice and judges passing mandatory life sentences where the murder was committed prior to 18 December 2003 are well advised to read that judgment before proceeding.

IV.49.17 The practical result of that judgment is that in sentences where the murder was committed before 31 May 2002, the best guide to what would have been the practice of the Secretary of State is the letter sent to judges by Lord Bingham C.J. on 10th February 1997, the relevant parts of which are set out at paras IV.49.18 to IV.49.21 below.

IV.49.18 The practice of Lord Bingham, as set out in his letter ... was to take 14 years as the period actually to be served for the "average", "normal" or "unexceptional" murder. Examples of factors he outlined as capable, in appropriate cases, of mitigating the normal penalty were:

> Youth.
>
> Age (where relevant to physical capacity on release or the likelihood of the defendant dying in prison).
>
> Subnormality or mental abnormality.
>
> Provocation (in a non-technical sense), or an excessive response to a personal threat.
>
> The absence of an intention to kill.
>
> Spontaneity and lack of premeditation (beyond that necessary to constitute the offence: *e.g.* a sudden response to family pressure or to prolonged and eventually unsupportable stress).
>
> Mercy killing.
>
> A plea of guilty, or hard evidence of remorse or contrition.

IV.49.19 Lord Bingham then listed the following factors as likely to call for a sentence more severe than the norm:

> Evidence of a planned, professional, revenge or contract killing.
>
> The killing of a child or a very old or otherwise vulnerable victim.
>
> Evidence of sadism, gratuitous violence, or sexual maltreatment, humiliation or degradation before the killing.
>
> Killing for gain (in the course of burglary, robbery, blackmail, insurance fraud, etc.).
>
> Multiple killings.
>
> The killing of a witness or potential witness to defeat the ends of justice.
>
> The killing of those doing their public duty (policemen, prison officers, postmasters, firemen, judges, etc).
>
> Terrorist or politically motivated killings.
>
> The use of firearms or other dangerous weapons, whether carried for defensive or offensive reasons.
>
> A substantial record of serious violence.
>
> Macabre attempts to dismember or conceal the body.

IV.49.20 Lord Bingham further stated that the fact that a defendant was under the influence of drink or drugs at the time of the killing is so common he would be inclined to treat it as neutral. But in the not unfamiliar case in which a married couple, or two derelicts, or two homosexuals, inflamed by drink, indulge in a violent quarrel in which one dies, often against a background of long-standing drunken violence, then he would tend to recommend a term somewhat below the norm.

IV.49.21 Lord Bingham went on to say that given the intent necessary for proof of murder, the consequences of taking life and the understandable reaction of relatives of the deceased, a substantial term will almost always be called for, save perhaps in a truly venial case of mercy killing. While a recommendation of a punitive term longer than, say, 30 years will be very rare indeed, there should not be any upper limit. Some crimes will certainly call for terms very well in excess of the norm.

IV.49.22 For the purposes of sentences where the murder was committed after 31 May 2002 and before 18 December 2003, the judge should apply the practice statement handed down on 31 May 2002 reproduced at paras 49.23 to 49.33 below. **5–251b**

IV.49.23 This statement replaces the previous single normal tariff of 14 years by substituting: a higher and a normal starting point of respectively 16 (comparable to 32 years) and 12 years (comparable to 24 years). These starting points have then to be increased or reduced because of aggravating or mitigating factors such as those referred to below. It is emphasised that they are no more than starting points.

The normal starting point of 12 years

5–251c   IV.49.24 Cases falling within this starting point will normally involve the killing of an adult victim, arising from a quarrel or loss of temper between two people known to each other. It will not have the characteristics referred to in paragraph 49.26. Exceptionally, the starting point may be reduced because of the sort of circumstances described in the next paragraph.

IV.49.25 The normal starting point can be reduced because the murder is one where the offender's culpability is significantly reduced, for example, because: the case came close to the borderline between murder and manslaughter; or the offender suffered from mental disorder, or from a mental disability which lowered the degree of his criminal responsibility for the killing, although not affording a defence of diminished responsibility; or the offender was provoked (in a non-technical sense) such as by prolonged and eventually unsupportable stress; or the case involved an over reaction in self-defence; or the offence was a mercy killing. These factors could justify a reduction to 8/9 years (equivalent to 16/18 years).

The higher starting point of 15/16 years

5–251d   IV.49.26 The higher starting point will apply to cases where the offender's culpability was exceptionally high or the victim was in a particularly vulnerable position. Such cases will be characterised by a feature which makes the crime especially serious, such as: the killing was "professional" or a contract killing; the killing was politically motivated; the killing was done for gain (in the course of a burglary, robbery etc.); the killing was intended to defeat the ends of justice (as in the killing of a witness or potential witness); the victim was providing a public service; the victim was a child or was otherwise vulnerable; the killing was racially aggravated; the victim was deliberately targeted because of his or her sexual orientation; there was evidence of sadism, gratuitous violence or sexual maltreatment, humiliation or degradation of the victim before the killing; extensive and/or multiple injuries were inflicted on the victim before death; the offender committed multiple murders.

Variation of the starting point

5–251e   IV.49.27 Whichever starting point is selected in a particular case, it may be appropriate for the trial judge to vary the starting point upwards or downwards, to take account of aggravating or mitigating factors, which relate to either the offence or the offender, in the particular case.

IV.49.28 Aggravating factors relating to the offence can include: the fact that the killing was planned; the use of a firearm; arming with a weapon in advance; concealment of the body, destruction of the crime scene and/or dismemberment of the body; particularly in domestic violence cases, the fact that the murder was the culmination of cruel and violent behaviour by the offender over a period of time.

IV.49.29 Aggravating factors relating to the offender will include the offender's previous record and failures to respond to previous sentences, to the extent that this is relevant to culpability rather than to risk.

IV.49.30 Mitigating factors relating to the offence will include: an intention to cause grievous bodily harm, rather than to kill; spontaneity and lack of premeditation.

IV.49.31 Mitigating factors relating to the offender may include: the offender's age; clear evidence of remorse or contrition; a timely plea of guilt.

Very serious cases

5–251f   IV.49.32 A substantial upward adjustment may be appropriate in the most serious cases, for example, those involving a substantial number of murders, or if there are several factors identified as attracting the higher starting point present. In suitable cases, the result might even be a minimum term of 30 years (equivalent to 60 years) which would offer little or no hope of the offender's eventual release. In cases of exceptional gravity, the judge, rather than setting a whole life minimum term, can state that there is no minimum period which could properly be set in that particular case.

IV.49.33 Among the categories of case referred to in paragraph IV.49.26 some offences may be especially grave. These include cases where the victim was performing his duties as a prison officer at the time of the crime or the offence was a terrorist or sexual or sadistic murder or involved a young child. In such a case, a term of 20 years and upwards could be appropriate.

IV.49.34 In following this guidance, judges should bear in mind the conclusion of the court in *Sullivan* that the general effect of both these statements is the same. While Lord Bingham does not identify as many starting points, it is open to the judge to come to exactly the same decision irrespective of which was followed. Both pieces of guidance give the judge a considerable degree of discretion.

Procedure for announcing the minimum term in open court

IV.49.35 Having gone through the three or four steps outlined above, the court   **5–251g**
is then under a duty under section 270 of the Act, to state in open court, in ordinary language, its reasons for deciding on the minimum term or for passing a whole life order.

IV.49.36 In order to comply with this duty the court should state clearly the minimum term it has determined. In doing so, it should state which of the starting points it has chosen and its reasons for doing so. Where the court has departed from that starting point due to mitigating or aggravating features it must state the reasons for that departure and any aggravating or mitigating features which have led to that departure. At that point the court should also declare how much, if any, time is being deducted for time spent in custody. The court must then explain that the minimum term is the minimum amount of time the prisoner will spend in prison, from the date of sentence, before the Parole Board can order early release. If it remains necessary for the protection of the public, the prisoner will continue to be detained after that date. The court should also state that where the prisoner has served the minimum term and the Parole Board has decided to direct release the prisoner will remain on licence for the rest of his life and may be recalled to prison at any time.

IV.49.37 Where the offender was 21 or over when he committed the offence and the court considers that the seriousness of the offence is so exceptionally high that a "whole life order" is appropriate, the court should state clearly its reasons for reaching this conclusion. It should also explain that the early release provisions will not apply.

As to the authority referred to in IV.49.16, see *R. v. Sullivan*; *R. v. Gibbs*; *R. v. Elener (Barry) and Elener (Derek)* [2005] 1 Cr.App.R. 3, CA.

B. Automatic Life Sentences

Powers of Criminal Courts (Sentencing) Act 2000, s.109

Life sentence for second serious offence
109.—(1) *This section applies where—*   **5–251j**

    (a) *a person is convicted of a serious offence committed after 30th September 1997; and*

    (b) *at the time when that offence was committed, he was 18 or over and had been convicted in any part of the United Kingdom of another serious offence.*

  (2) *The court shall impose a life sentence, that is to say—*

    (a) *where the offender is 21 or over when convicted of the offence mentioned in subsection (1)(a) above, a sentence of imprisonment for life,*

    (b) *where he is under 21 at that time, a sentence of custody for life under section 94 above,*

[a sentence of imprisonment for life] unless the court is of the opinion that there are exceptional circumstances relating to either of the offences or to the offender which justify its not doing so.

  (3) *Where the court does not impose a life sentence, it shall state in open court that it is of that opinion and what the exceptional circumstances are.*

(4) *An offence the sentence for which is imposed under subsection (2) above shall not be regarded as an offence the sentence for which is fixed by law.*

(5) *An offence committed in England and Wales is a serious offence for the purposes of this section if it is any of the following, namely—*

    (a) *an attempt to commit murder, a conspiracy to commit murder or an incitement to murder;*

    (b) *an offence under section 4 of the* Offences Against the Person Act *1861 (soliciting murder);*

    (c) *manslaughter;*

    (d) *an offence under section 18 of the* Offences Against the Person Act *1861 (wounding, or causing grievous bodily harm, with intent);*

    (e) *rape or an attempt to commit rape;*

    (f) *an offence under section 5 of the* Sexual Offences Act *1956 (intercourse with a girl under 13);*

    (g) *an offence under section 16 (possession of a firearm with intent to injure), section 17 (use of a firearm to resist arrest) or section 18 (carrying a firearm with criminal intent) of the* Firearms Act *1968; and*

    (h) *robbery where, at some time during the commission of the offence, the offender had in his possession a firearm or imitation firearm within the meaning of that Act.*

(6) *An offence committed in Scotland is a serious offence for the purposes of this section if the conviction for it was obtained on indictment in the High Court of Justiciary and it is any of the following, namely—*

    (a) *culpable homicide;*

    (b) *attempted murder, incitement to commit murder or conspiracy to commit murder;*

    (c) *rape or attempted rape;*

    (d) *clandestine injury to women or an attempt to cause such injury;*

    (e) *sodomy, or an attempt to commit sodomy, where the complainer, that is to say, the person against whom the offence was committed, did not consent;*

    (f) *assault where the assault—*

        (i) *is aggravated because it was carried out to the victim's severe injury or the danger of the victim's life; or*

        (ii) *was carried out with an intention to rape or to ravish the victim;*

    (g) *robbery where, at some time during the commission of the offence, the offender had in his possession a firearm or imitation firearm within the meaning of the* Firearms Act *1968;*

    (h) *an offence under section 16 (possession of a firearm with intent to injure), section 17 (use of a firearm to resist arrest) or section 18 (carrying a firearm with criminal intent) of that Act;*

    (i) *lewd, libidinous or indecent behaviour or practices; and*

    (j) *an offence under section 5(1) of the* Criminal Law (Consolidation) (Scotland) Act *1995 (unlawful intercourse with a girl under 13).*

(7) *An offence committed in Northern Ireland is a serious offence for the purposes of this section if it is any of the following, namely—*

    (a) *an offence falling within any of paragraphs (a) to (e) of subsection (5) above;*

    (b) *an offence under section 4 of the* Criminal Law Amendment Act *1885 (intercourse with a girl under 14);*

    (c) *an offence under Article 17 (possession of a firearm with intent to injure), Article 18(1) (use of a firearm to resist arrest) or Article 19 (carrying a firearm with criminal intent) of the* Firearms (Northern Ireland) Order *1981; and*

    (d) *robbery where, at some time during the commission of the offence, the offender had in his possession a firearm or imitation firearm within the meaning of that Order.*

[This section is printed as amended, as from a day to be appointed, by the *CJCSA* 2000, s.74, and Sched. 7, para. 189 (substitution of words in square brackets for paras (a) and (b) in subs. (2)). It is repealed, as from April 4, 2005 (*Criminal Justice Act 2003 (Commencement No. 8 and Transitional and Saving Provisions) Order* 2005 (S.I. 2005 No. 950), by the *CJA* 2003, s.332, and

Sched. 37 Pt 7. For the saving provisions in relation to an offence committed before April 4, 2005, see § 5–1a in the main work.]

Serious offences

The only attempts which are serious offences are those specifically mentioned: *R. v. Buckland*; *R. v. Newman* [2000] 1 Cr.App.R. 471, CA. Offences under the *Firearms Act* 1968, s.17(2) are serious offences: *ibid.*; as are offences under sections 16, 17 and 18 of that Act where the firearm was an imitation only: *ibid.*

An offence of robbery is a "serious offence" within section 109(2)(h) if the offence was committed as a joint enterprise where a firearm or imitation was used, even though the offender himself had never had possession of it, provided that there was joint possession of it; where, in relation to the alleged index offence, there is an issue as to whether this was established against the offender, the court must be satisfied that at the earlier hearing the offender admitted, or it was admitted on his behalf, that he was in joint possession of the firearm: *R. v. Flamson* [2002] 2 Cr.App.R.(S.) 48, CA. The court considered that *R. v. Eubank* [2002] 1 Cr.App.R.(S.) 4, CA (§ 24–49 in the main work) had no application to the facts of the case. In *R. v. Murphy* [2003] 1 Cr.App.R.(S.) 39, CA, however, it was held, without reference to *Flamson*, that where there was an issue as to whether the defendant had been in possession of a firearm, the proper way to resolve the issue was, in accordance with *Eubank*, for an appropriate count under the *Firearms Act* 1968 to be included in the indictment. Where this course had not been adopted, it was not open to the judge to conclude in relation to either the index offence or the fresh offence that it fell within section 109(1)(h); absent an unequivocal admission on the part of the defendant (see *R. v. Benjafield*; *R. v. Sobers* [2004] 1 Cr.App.R.(S.) 52, CA).

R. v. Benfield; *R. v. Sobers* was followed in *R. v. Hylands* [2005] Crim.L.R. 154, CA, where it was said that for an offence of robbery to fall within section 109(5)(h) of the 2000 Act, the qualifying condition relating to a firearm or imitation firearm had to be established either by means of an appropriate count under the *Firearms Act* 1968 being included in the indictment, or there had to be an unequivocal admission in relation thereto; and this applies where the only issue in relation to the robbery is identity (there being unchallenged evidence before the jury that the robber was in possession of a firearm at the time of the robbery); if there was any doubt about the matter, it was to be resolved in favour of the defendant.

As to whether a conviction at a court-martial in Germany for an offence of wounding with intent to cause grievous bodily harm committed whilst a serving member of the armed forces in Germany may qualify as a "serious offence" within the meaning of section 109(1)(a) of the *PCC(S)A* 2000, see *R. v. Sanders, post*, § 5–256.

"exceptional circumstances"

The meaning of "exceptional circumstances" (s.109(2)) was reconsidered in *R. v. Offen* [2001] 1 W.L.R. 253, CA. Lord Woolf C.J. said that quite apart from the impact of the *Human Rights Act* 1998, the rationale of the section should be highly relevant in deciding whether or not exceptional circumstances existed. The question whether circumstances were appropriately regarded as "exceptional" must be influenced by the context in which the question was being asked. The policy and intention of Parliament were to protect the public against a person who had committed two serious offences. It therefore could be assumed that the section was not intended to apply to someone in relation to whom it was established that there would be no need for protection in the future. In other words, if the facts showed the statutory assumption was misplaced, then this, in the statutory context, was not the normal situation and in consequence, for the purposes of the section, the position was exceptional. The time that elapsed between the two offences could, but would not necessarily, reflect on whether, after the second serious offence was committed, there was any danger against which the public would need protection. The same was true of two differing offences, and the age of the offender. These were all circumstances which could give rise to the conclusion that what could be normal and not exceptional in a different context was exceptional in this context. If this approach was not adopted, then in the case of the serious offences listed in the section, the gravity of which could vary greatly, the approach to "exceptional circumstances" could be unduly restrictive. The aim of section 2 was not to increase the time offenders spent in prison as a punishment for the offence they had committed, but to provide for an assessment to be made to see whether the offender posed a real risk to the public, in which event his release was deferred. Section 109 established a norm. The norm was that those who commit two serious offences were a danger or risk to the public. If in fact, taking into account all the circumstances relating to a particular offender, he did not create an unacceptable risk to the public, he was an exception to this norm.

Construing section 109 in accordance with the duty imposed on the court by section 3 of the 1998 Act, and taking into account the rationale of the section, gave content to "exceptional circumstances". In the court's judgment, section 109 would not contravene Convention rights if courts applied the section so that it did not result in offenders being sentenced to life imprisonment when they did not constitute a significant risk to the public. Whether there was a significant risk would depend on the evidence which was before the court. If the offender was a significant risk, the court could impose a life sentence under section 109 without contravening the Convention. It would be part of the responsibility of judges to assess the risk to the public that offenders constituted. In many cases the degree of risk that an offender constituted would be established by his record, with or without the assistance of assessments made in reports which were available to the court. If courts needed further assistance, they could call for it when deciding whether a discretionary life sentence should be imposed. There should be no undue difficulty in making a similar assessment when considering whether the court was required to impose an automatic life sentence, although the task would not be straightforward, because of the lack of information as to the first serious offence which will sometimes exist because of the passage of time. This did not mean that the court was approaching the passing of an automatic life sentence as if it was no different from the imposition of a discretionary life sentence. Notwithstanding the interpretation resulting from the application of section 3(1) of the 1998 Act suggested, section 109 would give effect to the intention of Parliament. It would do so, however, in a more just, less arbitrary and more proportionate manner. Section 109 would still mean that a judge was obliged to pass a life sentence in accordance with its terms unless, in all the circumstances, the offender posed no significant risk to the public. There was no such obligation in cases where section 109 did not apply. In addition, if the judge decided not to impose a life sentence under section 109, he would have to give reasons as required by section 109(3). Furthermore, the issue of dangerousness would have to be addressed in every case and a decision made as to whether or not to impose a life sentence.

Offen has since been applied in *R. v. McDonald* [2001] 2 Cr.App.R.(S.) 127,
CA (having regard, in particular, to the length of time since the appellant's
conviction for his previous "serious" offences (14 years) and to the fact that it
was not the appellant but a co-defendant who had produced an imitation
firearm in the course of the robbery, although it belonged to the appellant, it
would be wrong to conclude that the appellant presented a serious risk of
harm to the public so as to justify the imposition of an automatic life sentence);
and in *R. v. Kelly (No. 2)* [2002] 1 Cr.App.R.(S.) 85, CA, it was held that the
statutory presumption that arises under section 109(2), and which flows from
the existence of two qualifying offences remains in place, and has to be
displaced by the defendant in any given case; and such displacement may be
achieved in a number of ways, including scrutiny of the offending and behaviour pattern, or by positive psychiatric or similar evidence, such evidence being likely to be required if the court is to be persuaded that the presumption
cannot apply since the criterion to be established is that there is "no need to
protect the public in the future" or "no significant risk to the public".

In *R. v. Baff* [2003] 2 Cr.App.R.(S.) 37, CA, it was said that the use of imitation firearms for the purpose of robbery caused as much fear and alarm to
vulnerable members of the public as robbery with a real firearm; and that, if
the court were to rule that section 109 did not as a matter of principle apply
where the offender limited his offending to robberies with an imitation firearm,
it would be creating an exception to an express provision flatly contradicting
an aspect of sentencing policy laid down by Parliament.

In *R. v. Richards* [2002] 2 Cr.App.R.(S.) 26, CA, it was held that in considering whether a defendant who qualifies for an automatic life sentence under
section 109 presents a significant risk to the public, the judge may take account of a significant risk of the commission of serious offences other than
those listed as "serious" in the section itself, for example, burglaries of dwellings or a conspiracy to import hard drugs. For a criticism of this decision, see
the commentary in the *Criminal Law Review*. It is inconsistent with the view of
the court in *R. v. Fletcher*; *R. v. Smith* [2002] 1 Cr.App.R.(S.) 82, CA, to the effect that the "danger in point is that of violent or sexual offending."

Richards was not cited in *R. v. Stark* [2002] 2 Cr.App.R.(S.) 104, CA, where
there was a high risk of further offences being committed by the appellant,
but no significant risk of danger to the public by way of either violent or
sexual offences; accordingly, it was held that the case was to be regarded as an
exception to the norm, which was that those who committed two serious offences were a danger or risk to the public.

The approach in *R. v. Stark* and *R. v. Fletcher*; *R. v. Smith* was followed,
and that in *Richards* expressly disapproved in *R. v. Magalhaes* [2005] 2
Cr.App.R.(S.) 13, CA.

In *R. v. Frost* [2001] 2 Cr.App.R.(S.) 26, CA, the appellant had been found
guilty by a youth court in 1991 of wounding with intent to resist arrest. He
was later convicted of wounding with intent to cause grievous bodily harm.
The court held that the finding of guilt by the youth court amounted to a
"conviction" for the purposes of *PCC(S)A* 2000, s.109(1), by virtue of the
CYPA 1933, s.59. If the appellant had been older and had been subject to a
probation order, the "conviction" would have been deemed not to be a
conviction by virtue of the *PCCA* 1973, s.13(1) *(rep.)*, but this provision did
not apply to a supervision order. The anomaly which resulted from this
amounted to an "exceptional circumstance" for the purposes of section 109,
and the sentence of life imprisonment was quashed, even though it could not
be said that the offender presented no significant risk to the public.

The fact that the offender is mentally ill and eligible for a hospital order does not in itself amount to an "exceptional circumstance" for this purpose: see *R. v. Newman* [2000] 2 Cr.App.R.(S.) 227, CA; *R. v. Drew* [2003] 2 Cr.App.R. 24, HL (where a submission that an automatic life sentence on conviction of wounding with intent constituted inhuman or degrading treatment was rejected; having been transferred administratively to hospital within a few days of the passing of sentence, the appellant was receiving the same treatment as he would have received had he been made subject to a hospital order, and he could not complain of the stigma attaching to the sentence as he had been convicted by a jury, who must therefore have been satisfied as to his intent).

On appeal, the issue is whether the offender created an unacceptable risk to the public at the time when he was sentenced, not at the time when the Court of Appeal is considering the matter: see *R. v. Watkins* [2003] 1 Cr.App.R.(S.) 16, CA; *R. v. Noorkoiv* [2002] 2 Cr.App.R.(S.) 91, CA.

C. MINIMUM FIXED TERM SENTENCES

(1) Legislation

Powers of Criminal Courts (Sentencing) Act 2000, sss.112–115

Offences under service law

★**5-256**   The amendment of section 114 of the 2000 Act effected by the *AFA* 2006 comes into force on October 31, 2009: *Armed Forces Act 2006 (Commencement No. 5) Order* 2009 (S.I. 2009 No. 1167). In connection with that commencement, see the transitional provisions in the *Armed Forces Act 2006 (Transitional Provisions etc.) Order* 2009 (S.I. 2009 No. 1059), Sched. 1, para. 45(3) (interpretation of references to an "offence under section 42" of the 2006 Act and to "the corresponding offence under the law of England and Wales").

In *R. v. Sanders* [2007] 1 Cr.App.R.(S.) 74, CA, it was held that the effect of section 114 of the *PCC(S)A* 2000 was limited to deeming the conviction to have been in England and Wales; it did not deem the offence to have been committed in England and Wales; where, therefore, the appellant had previously been convicted of an offence under section 70 of the *Army Act* 1955 and the corresponding civil offence had been one of those listed in section 109(5), but the offence had been committed abroad, he was not to be regarded as having previously been convicted of a serious offence, since, under section 109(5), an offence would only be "serious" if committed in England and Wales; section 114 would bite only in relation to convictions under section 70 where the offence occurred in England and Wales. It should be noted that the repeal of the words "a serious offence" in section 114(1)(b) is of no effect where an offender is being dealt with for an offence committed prior to April 4, 2005.

D. Discretionary Custodial Sentences

(1) General restrictions

(c) *Legislation (offences committed before April 4, 2005)*

Powers of Criminal Courts (Sentencing) Act 2000, ss.79, 80

General restrictions on imposing discretionary custodial sentences

79.—(1) *This section applies where a person is convicted of an offence punishable with a*   **5–276a**
custodial sentence other than one—

   (a) *fixed by law; or*

   (b) *falling to be imposed under section 109(2), 110(2) or 111(2) below.*

  (2) *Subject to subsection (3) below, the court shall not pass a custodial sentence on the offender unless it is of the opinion—*

   (a) *that the offence, or the combination of the offence and one or more offences associated with it, was so serious that only such a sentence can be justified for the offence; or*

   (b) *where the offence is a violent or sexual offence, that only such a sentence would be adequate to protect the public from serious harm from him.*

  (3) *Nothing in subsection (2) above shall prevent the court from passing a custodial sentence on the offender if he fails to express his willingness to comply with—*

   (a) *a requirement which is proposed by the court to be included in a community rehabilitation order or supervision order and which requires an expression of such willingness; or*

   (b) *a requirement which is proposed by the court to be included in a drug treatment and testing order or an order under section 52(4) above (order to provide samples). In relation to an offence committed before 1st October 1997:*

  (4) *Where a court passes a custodial sentence, it shall—*

   (a) *in a case not falling within subsection (3) above, state in open court that it is of the opinion that either or both of paragraphs (a) and (b) of subsection (2) above apply and why it is of that opinion; and*

   (b) *in any case, explain to the offender in open court and in ordinary language why it is passing a custodial sentence on him.*

  (5) *A magistrates' court shall cause a reason stated by it under subsection (4) above to be specified in the warrant of commitment and to be entered in the register.*

[This section is printed as amended by the *CJCSA* 2000, s.74 and Sched. 7, para. 1. It is repealed, as from April 4, 2005 (*Criminal Justice Act 2003 (Commencement No. 8 and Transitional and Saving Provisions) Order* 2005 (S.I. 2005 No. 950)), by the *CJA* 2003, s.332, and Sched. 37, Pt 7. As to the saving provision in relation to offences committed before April 4, 2005, see § 5–1a in the main work.]

In relation to an offence committed before October 1, 1997, see the transitional provision in Sched. 11, para. 4(d).

Length of discretionary custodial sentences: general provision.

80.—(1) *This section applies where a court passes a custodial sentence other than one*   **5–276b**
fixed by law or falling to be imposed under section 109(2) below.

  (2) *Subject to sections 110(2) and 111(2) below, the custodial sentence shall be—*

   (a) *for such term (not exceeding the permitted maximum) as in the opinion of the court is commensurate with the seriousness of the offence, or the combination of the offence and one or more offences associated with it; or*

(b) *where the offence is a violent or sexual offence, for such longer term (not exceeding that maximum) as in the opinion of the court is necessary to protect the public from serious harm from the offender.*

(3) *Where the court passes a custodial sentence for a term longer than is commensurate with the seriousness of the offence, or the combination of the offence and one or more offences associated with it, the court shall—*

(a) *state in open court that it is of the opinion that subsection (2)(b) above applies and why it is of that opinion; and*

(b) *explain to the offender in open court and in ordinary language why the sentence is for such a term.*

(4) *A custodial sentence for an indeterminate period shall be regarded for the purposes of subsections (2) and (3) above as a custodial sentence for a term longer than any actual term.*

(5) *Subsection (3) above shall not apply in any case where the court passes a custodial sentence falling to be imposed under subsection (2) of section 110 or 111 below which is for the minimum term specified in that subsection.*

[This section is repealed, as from April 4, 2005 (*Criminal Justice Act 2003 (Commencement No. 8 and Transitional and Saving Provisions) Order* 2005 (S.I. 2005 No. 950)), by the *CJA* 2003, s.332, and Sched. 37, Pt 7. As to the saving provision in relation to offences committed before April 4, 2005, see § 5–1a in the main work.]

Powers of Criminal Courts (Sentencing) Act 2000, s.161

Meaning of "associated offence", "sexual offence", "violent offence" and "protecting the public from serious harm".

5–276c   **161.**—(1) [See § 5–2 in the main work.]

(2) *In this Act, "sexual offence" means any of the following—*

(f) *an offence under the* Protection of Children Act *1978;*

(fa) *an offence under section 3 of the* Sexual Offences (Amendment) Act *2000;*

(fa) *an offence under any provision of Part 1 of the* Sexual Offences Act *2003; except section 52, 53 or 71*

(g) *an offence under section 1 of the* Criminal Law Act *1977; of conspiracy to commit any of the offences in paragraphs (a) to (f) above;*

(h) *an offence under section 1 of the* Criminal Attempts Act *1981; of attempting to commit any of those offences;*

(i) *an offence of inciting another to commit any of those offences.*

(3) *In this Act, "violent offence" means an offence which leads, or is intended or likely to lead, to a person's death or to physical injury to a person, and includes an offence which is required to be charged as arson (whether or not it would otherwise fall within this definition).*

(4) *In this Act any reference, in relation to an offender convicted of a violent or sexual offence, to protecting the public from serious harm from him shall be construed as a reference to protecting members of the public from death or serious personal injury, whether physical or psychological, occasioned by further such offences committed by him.*

5–276d   [Subss. (2) to (4) are as amended and repealed in part, by the *Sexual Offences (Amendment) Act* 2000, s.6(1); and the *SOA* 2003, ss.139 and 140, and Sched. 6, para. 4 (insertion of second para. (fa) in subs. (2)), and Sched. 7 (repeal of subs. (2)(a)–(e), the failure to repeal the first para. (fa) being accounted for by the draftsman having overlooked the amendment made by the 2000 Act). The amendments effected by the 2003 Act took effect on May 1, 2004 (*Sexual Offences Act 2003 (Commencement) Order* 2004 (S.I. 2004 No. 874)). For the former provisions, which will continue to apply in relation to offences committed before that date (*Interpretation Act* 1978, s.16 (Appendix B–16)), see the 2004 edition of this work. Subss. (2) to (4) are repealed, as from April 4, 2005 (*Criminal Justice Act 2003 (Commencement No. 8 and*

Transitional and Saving Provisions) Order 2005 (S.I. 2005 No. 950)), by the *CJA* 2003, s.332, and Sched. 7. As to the saving provision in relation to offences committed before April 4, 2005, see § 5–1a in the main work.]

"Violent" and "sexual" offences

Whether any particular offence is a violent offence depends on the facts of the individual offence. An offence which leads to or is intended to lead only to psychological injury is not a "violent offence" but it is not necessary that serious harm should have been caused (see *R. v. Robinson* [1994] 1 W.L.R. 168, CA). Nor does it have to be established that physical injury was a probability: *R. v. Szczerba* [2002] 2 Cr.App.R.(S.) 86, CA.   **5–276e**

In *R. v. Cochrane*, 15 Cr.App.R.(S.) 708, CA, it was held that a robbery in which the victim was threatened with a knife was a "violent offence" as the incident could have resulted in injury, either accidentally or if the victim had resisted. See also *R. v. Bibby*, 16 Cr.App.R.(S.) 127, CA. For cases of robbery by persons armed with a firearm, see *R. v. Touriq Khan*, 16 Cr.App.R.(S.) 180, CA, *R. v. Palin*, 16 Cr.App.R.(S.) 888, CA, and *R. v. Baker* [2001] 1 Cr.App.R.(S.) 55, CA. An offence of threatening to kill which does not involve the infliction of physical injury will not normally be a "violent offence": see *R. v. Richart*, 16 Cr.App.R.(S.) 977, CA, *R. v. Ragg* [1996] 1 Cr.App.R.(S.) 176, CA and *R. v. Birch* [2002] 1 Cr.App.R.(S.) 129, CA; but see *R. v. Wilson* [1998] 1 Cr.App.R.(S.) 341, CA.

Attempted arson is "an offence which is required to be charged as arson" and is accordingly a "violent offence" within section 161(3): *R. v. Guirke* [1997] 1 Cr.App.R.(S.) 170, CA.

"Serious harm" (s.161(4) of the Act of 2000)

See § 5–292 in the main work.   **5–276f**

The criterion of seriousness

For discussion of the relevant authorities in relation to section 79(1), see § 5–272 in the main work.   **5–276g**

Sentences commensurate with the seriousness of the offence

For relevant considerations where a court is deciding what term of custody is commensurate with an offence or group of offences, see § 5–274 in the main work.   **5–276h**

Longer than normal sentences

For the definitions of "sexual offence" and "violent offence", see section 161(2) and (3) of the *PCC(S)A* 2000 (*ante*, § 5–275c); and for the authorities in relation thereto, see *ante*, § 5–275e. For the construction of references to "protecting the public from serious harm", see section 161(4) of the 2000 Act (*ante*, § 5–275c); and the authorities referred to at § 5–292 in the main work.   **5–276i**

An isolated offence, however serious, will rarely be sufficient to justify a longer than normal sentence under section 80(2)(b), whether the offence is violent or sexual, or both: *R. v. Walsh*, 16 Cr.App.R.(S.) 204, CA; *R. v. Mumtaz Ali*, 16 Cr.App.R.(S.) 692, CA. A longer than commensurate sentence may be passed on an offender with no previous convictions: *R. v. Thomas*, 16 Cr.App.R.(S.) 616, CA.

A court deciding whether to draw the inference that the offender is likely to commit further violent or sexual offences may need to examine the circumstances of the current offence in some detail, going beyond what would be necessary if only a commensurate sentence were in issue: *R. v. Oudkerk*, 16 Cr.App.R.(S.) 172, CA. Equally, if the inference is to be based on a previous conviction, the court may need to examine the circumstances of that offence in detail: *R. v. Samuels*, 16 Cr.App.R.(S.) 856, CA.

An offender may satisfy the requirements of section 80(2)(b) even though the members of the public who are at risk from him are a small group, or possibly an individual: *R. v. Hashi*, 16 Cr.App.R.(S.) 121, CA. Where the offender's behaviour is directed at a small group of people, who can be protected from him by other means, a longer than commensurate sentence may not be justified: *R. v. Nicholas*, 15 Cr.App.R.(S.) 381, CA; *R. v. Swain*, 15 Cr.App.R.(S.) 765, CA; *R. v. L.*, 15 Cr.App.R.(S.) 501, CA.

In many cases the inference of dangerousness will be based in part on psychiatric evidence: *R. v. Lyons*, 15 Cr.App.R.(S.) 460, CA; *R. v. Fawcett*, 16 Cr.App.R.(S.) 55, CA; *R. v. Etchells* [1996] 1 Cr.App.R.(S.) 163, CA.

The principles which should be applied in deciding the length of a longer than commensurate sentence were considered in *R. v. Mansell*, 15 Cr.App.R.(S.) 771, CA; and *R. v. Crow*; *R. v. Pennington*, 16 Cr.App.R.(S.) 409, CA. Lord Taylor C.J. said that some allowance should usually be made, even in the worst cases, for a plea of guilty. A sentence imposed under section 80(2)(b), whilst long enough to give necessary protection for the public, should still bear a reasonable relationship to the offence for which it was imposed.

This principle was not applied in *R. v. Chapman* [2000] 1 Cr.App.R. 77, CA, where it was said that there was no necessary ratio between the part of the sentence intended to punish and the part intended to protect. There was no objection in principle if the court regarded a sentence of two years as necessary to punish, but an additional term of six or eight years as necessary to protect, making a total term of eight or ten years. *Chapman* was followed in *R. v. Wilson* [2000] 2 Cr.App.R.(S.) 323, CA, but not apparently in *R. v. De Silva* [2000] 2 Cr.App.R.(S.) 408, CA.

5–276j   The question whether a longer than commensurate sentence may properly be imposed to run consecutively to a sentence of imprisonment was considered by the Court of Appeal in *R. v. Everleigh* [2002] 1 Cr.App.R.(S.) 32. The court considered *R. v. King*, 16 Cr.App.R.(S.) 987; *R. v. Walters* [1997] 2 Cr.App.R.(S.) 87; *R. v. Johnson* [1998] 1 Cr.App.R.(S.) 126; *R. v. Cuthbertson and Jenks* [2000] 1 Cr.App.R.(S.) 359; *R. v. Parsons* [2000] 1 Cr.App.R.(S.) 428; *R. v. Blades* [2000] 1 Cr.App.R.(S.) 463; *R. v. Sullivan* [2000] 2 Cr.App.R.(S.) 318; *R. v. Sowden* [2000] 2 Cr.App.R.(S.) 360; *R. v. Wilson* [2000] 2 Cr.App.R.(S.) 323; and *R. v. Ellis* [2001] 1 Cr.App.R.(S.) 43. Accepting that not all of these of authorities could be reconciled, the court held that they showed that it was inappropriate to pass a longer than the normal sentence to run consecutively to another sentence imposed on the same occasion, because a longer than normal sentence is intended in itself to protect the public from serious harm, without the need for any additional penalty in relation to other conduct punishable at the same time. Secondly, there was nothing inappropriate, but on the contrary it might be desirable, for a longer than normal sentence to be passed consecutively either to a sentence passed on an earlier occasion (*Wilson*) or to a period of return to custody ordered under the *PCC(S)A* 2000, s.116, which was a consequence of a sentence passed on an earlier occasion (*Blades*). As was pointed out in *Blades*, it was important that both the public and the defendant should know that a sentence once passed would have to be served (subject to any reduction which might be appropriate in accordance with *R. v. Taylor* [1998] 1 Cr.App.R.(S.) 312). It was desirable that the sentencing judge, if imposing a consecutive sentence, should make it plain what were the factors which he had taken into consideration in so passing the sentence under section 80(2)(b).

In *R. v. Christie*, 16 Cr.App.R.(S.) 469, CA, it was said to be wrong to add an additional period to the sentence under section 80(2)(b) if the commensurate sentence already incorporated an element for the protection of the public. In *R. v. Campbell* [1997] 1 Cr.App.R.(S.) 119, CA, it was held that if the sentencing guidelines for a particular offence included an element for the protection of the public, the sentencer should decide what was the appropriate sentence, leaving out of account any element for the protection of the public, and should then add the greater element needed for the protection of the public from serious harm under section 80(2)(b). This would avoid the risk of imposing an element of the sentence twice over. In *R. v. Gabbidon and Bramble* [1997] 2 Cr.App.R.(S.) 19, CA, this approach was described as too difficult an exercise in forensic archaeology; it was better that the sentencer simply applied the principle of balance stated by Lord Taylor C.J. in *R. v. Mansell*, 15 Cr.App.R.(S.) 771.

In a case where a longer than normal sentence is passed on one offender and a commensurate sentence on the other, it does not necessarily follow that there is any disparity of sentence, provided that there is evidence of continuing dangerousness on the part of one offender and not in the case of the other: *R. v. Bestwick and Huddlestone*, 16 Cr.App.R.(S.) 168, CA.

A longer than commensurate sentence may be imposed on an offender under section 80(2)(b) even though he does not qualify for a sentence of life imprisonment under the criteria established for that form of sentence: *R. v. Helm*, 16 Cr.App.R.(S.) 834, CA. The enactment of section 80(2)(b) has not reduced the requirements for a life sentence: *R. v. Roche*, 16 Cr.App.R.(S.) 849, CA.

Where a sentencer has in mind the possibility of passing a longer than commensurate sentence, he should warn counsel for the defendant of his intentions and invite submissions on the question: *R. v. Baverstock*, 96 Cr.App.R. 435, CA. This point has been repeated in many cases; it is particularly important when any question arises as to whether the offence is a "violent offence" for the purposes of the Act. Where a court passes a longer than commensurate sentence it is required by the *PCC(S)A* 2000, s.80(3) to state in open court that it is of the opinion that subsection (2)(b) applies and why it is of that opinion, and explain to the offender in open court and in ordinary language why the sentence is for such a term. Failure to comply with this obligation does not invalidate the sentence: *Baverstock, ante*; *R. v. Thomas*, 16 Cr.App.R.(S.) 616, CA. Even where the nature of the expected future harm is obvious, the sentencer should ensure that he has properly identified what the harm was before he proceeded to sentence, and should point out clearly and in straightforward terms what it was that he considered to be the serious harm in question: *R. v. Bacon*, 16 Cr.App.R.(S.) 1031, CA.

Where a court fails to pass a longer than commensurate sentence where such a sentence should be passed, the resulting sentence may be "unduly lenient" and may be the subject of a reference by the Attorney-General under the *CJA* 1988, s.36: *Att-Gen.'s Reference (No. 9 of 1994) (R. v. Groves)*, 16 Cr.App.R.(S.) 366, CA. Where a person sentenced to a longer than commensurate sentence persuades the Court of Appeal that the case is not one in which a longer than commensurate sentence should have been passed, the court is not bound to substitute a shorter sentence; its powers are at large, and it may approve the sentence passed as a commensurate sentence if it considers it appropriate to do so: *R. v. Palmer* [1996] 2 Cr.App.R.(S.) 68, CA; and see also *R. v. Henshaw* [1996] 2 Cr.App.R.(S.) 310, CA; and *R. v. Rai and Robinson* [2000] 2 Cr.App.R.(S.) 120, CA.

(2) Imprisonment

(b) *Maximum*

The most serious example of the offence

5–282   *R. v. Bright* is now reported at [2008] 2 Cr.App.R.(S.) 102.

A judge's view that the maximum sentence prescribed by Parliament for a particular offence is "woefully inadequate" is irrelevant to the determination of the proper sentence: *R. v. Sherif* [2009] 2 Cr.App.R.(S.) 33, CA.

(c) *Life sentences, sentences for public protection and extended sentences for dangerous offenders*

Extended sentences (offences committed before April 4, 2005)

5–288a   The *CJA* 2003 introduced a new scheme of custodial sentences for dangerous offenders. Offenders being sentenced after April 4, 2005, in respect of offences committed before that date will, however, continue to receive extended sentences under the former regime (*PCC(S)A* 2000, s.85 (*post*)) if appropriate. For the definitions of "sexual" and "violent" offence, see section 161 of the *PCC(S)A* 2000, *ante* § 5–275c.

Powers of Criminal Courts (Sentencing) Act 2000, s.85

Sexual or violent offences: extension of certain custodial sentences for licence purposes

5–288b   85.—(1) *This section applies where a court—*

    (a) *proposes to impose a custodial sentence for a sexual or violent offence committed on or after 30th September 1998; and*

    (b) *considers that the period (if any) for which the offender would, apart from this section, be subject to a licence would not be adequate for the purpose of preventing the commission by him of further offences and securing his rehabilitation.*

(2) *Subject to subsections (3) to (5) below, the court may pass on the offender an extended sentence, that is to say, a custodial sentence the term of which is equal to the aggregate of—*

    (a) *the term of the custodial sentence that the court would have imposed if it had passed a custodial sentence otherwise than under this section ("the custodial term"); and*

    (b) *a further period ("the extension period") for which the offender is to be subject to a licence and which is of such length as the court considers necessary for the purpose mentioned in* subsection (1) *above.*

(3) *Where the offence is a violent offence, the court shall not pass an extended sentence the custodial term of which is less than four years.*

(4) *The extension period shall not exceed—*

    (a) *ten years in the case of a sexual offence; and*

    (b) *five years in the case of a violent offence.*

(5) *The term of an extended sentence passed in respect of an offence shall not exceed the maximum term permitted for that offence.*

(6) *Subsection (2) of section 80 above (length of discretionary custodial sentences) shall apply as if the term of an extended sentence did not include the extension period.*

(7) *The Secretary of State may by order amend paragraph (b) of subsection (4) above by*

*substituting a different period, not exceeding ten years, for the period for the time being
specified in that paragraph.*

(8) *In this section "licence" means a licence under Part II of the* Criminal Justice Act
1991 *(early release of prisoners).*

[This section is repealed, as from April 4, 2005 (*Criminal Justice Act 2003
(Commencement No. 8 and Transitional and Saving Provisions) Order* 2005 (S.I.
2005 No. 950)), by the *CJA* 2003, s.332, and Sched. 37, Pt 7. As to the saving provision in relation to offences committed before April 4, 2005, see
§ 5–1a in the main work.]

General guidance on the use of the power to impose an extended sentence   **5–288c**
under section 85 was given in *R. v. Nelson* [2002] 1 Cr.App.R.(S.) 134, CA.
When dealing with a violent or sexual offence, the court should consider the
matter in three stages. The first stage was to decide on the sentence which
would be commensurate. The second stage was to consider whether a longer
period in custody was needed to protect the public from serious harm from
the offender. If so, a longer than commensurate custodial sentence would be
called for. The third stage, in relation to a sexual offence, or a violent offence
for which the appropriate custodial sentence was four years or longer, was to
consider whether that sentence was adequate to prevent the commission by
the offender of further offences and secure his rehabilitation. If not, an
extended sentence was called for. It was not appropriate to reduce the
custodial term because an extended licence period was being imposed.

The risk of further offences being committed by the offender did not justify
a longer than commensurate sentence unless those further offences might
cause death or some physical or psychological injury. There might be cases in
which, because of the power to impose an extended licence period, a longer
than commensurate sentence might not be necessary. One purpose of an
extended sentence was to reduce the likelihood of re-offending, and it was
therefore particularly suitable where a commensurate custodial term was too
short for this to be done in prison and where the normal licence period, if
any, would not be long enough to permit attendance at a treatment programme in the community. This would arise particularly in relation to less
serious sexual offences, where the likelihood of re-offending appeared high,
but where a longer than commensurate sentence could not be justified because
the offender does not present a risk of serious harm to the public. The use of
an extended sentence, with a relatively short custodial term, less than 12
months, had been endorsed in *R v. Ajaib* [2001] 1 Cr.App.R.(S.) 31, CA.

Extended sentences with longer than commensurate custodial terms would
be appropriate, at the other end of the spectrum, where a violent or sexual
offence is committed by a seriously dangerous offender, in relation to whom a
life sentence, if available, might well have been passed. There might also be
cases in which a discretionary life sentence was available for the offence but
the criteria which have to be established before such a sentence can be passed
may not all be present. Where a longer than commensurate sentence was
called for, it should usually be accompanied by an extension period because a
seriously dangerous offender, attracting a longer than commensurate
sentence, might well commit further offences.

In determining the length of an extended sentence, the court must decide   **5–288d**
what period would be adequate to secure the offender's rehabilitation and to
prevent re-offending. This would often be difficult. In some cases, involving
less serious sexual offences where the custodial term was relatively short, the
court might be able to take advice on the availability and length of treatment

programmes and tailor the extension period accordingly. In all cases the court should consider whether a particular extension period could be justified on the evidence available. A long extension period should usually be based on a clear implication from the offender's criminal record or on what was said in a pre-sentence report or a psychiatric report. The objective, where possible should be to fix the length of the extension period by reference to what could realistically be achieved within it. When the offender was clearly dangerous the custodial term would usually be longer than commensurate and a long period of extended licence would often be called for. It was clear from *R. v. Gould* [2000] 2 Cr.App.R.(S.) 173, CA, that a court imposing an extended sentence should bear in mind that the offender may ultimately serve the whole or part of the extension period in custody. But, as the legislature's intention in introducing extended sentences was clearly to place an offender at risk of recall for some considerable time, it would be illogical to require strict proportionality between the duration of the extension period and the seriousness of the offence. Proportionality with the seriousness of the offence was of central importance to a custodial term. It should not be a primary factor in determining the length of an extension period. It did, however, have some relevance and the implications of the overall sentence should be borne in mind.

There had been conflicting views as to whether the legislation permitted the imposition of consecutive extended sentences. The court was in no doubt that sensible practice required that extended sentences should not, generally, be imposed consecutively.

Where a sentencer was considering imposing an extended sentence, counsel should be warned of this, so that argument can be heard on the point. Judges should always take care to use the correct terminology when passing sentence. In particular, a longer than commensurate sentence should be so described: it was not an extended sentence. Judges should also seek to explain to a defendant the effect of the sentence passed.

Criminal Justice Act 2003, ss.224–229

Meaning of "specified offence" etc.

5–292   *R. v. B.* is now reported at [2009] 1 Cr.App.R.(S.) 6.

The assessment of dangerousness

★5–297   Section 376 of the *AFA* 2006 comes into force on October 31, 2009: *Armed Forces Act 2006 (Commencement No. 5) Order* 2009 (S.I. 2009 No. 1167).

Schedule 15A offences (ss.225(3A), 227(2A))

5–301   The *Sexual Offences (Northern Ireland Consequential Amendments) Order* 2008 (S.I. 2008 No. 1779) came into force on February 2, 2009: see the *Sexual Offences (Northern Ireland) Order 2008 (Commencement) Order* 2008 (S.R.N.I. 2008 No. 510).

Life sentences, sentences for public protection, extended sentences

(i) *General matters*

5–303   In *R. v. Stannard* [2009] 2 Cr.App.R.(S.) 21, CA, the court held that where a person aged 18 or over (at the date of conviction) fell to be sentenced before July 14, 2008 (*i.e.* the date on which the statutory assumption of dangerousness was abolished by the *CJIA* 2008, s.13) for a "serious offence" within the meaning of the dangerous offender provisions of the 2003 Act (see s.224 (§ 5–292 in the main work)) committed on or after April 4, 2005 (*i.e.* the date on which the dangerous offender provisions came into force), and for other offences committed before that date, and the court was satisfied on the basis of all the information before it (which would include evidence relating to the offences committed before April 4, 2005) of the significant risk described in section 225(1)(b), the sentence had to be either imprisonment for life or imprisonment for public protection. This requirement could not be avoided merely because the pre-April 4, 2005, offending was even more grave than the "serious offence".

In *Att.-Gen.'s Reference (No. 55 of 2008) (R. v. C.)* [2009] 2 Cr.App.R.(S.) 22, CA, the court discussed the effect of the amendments to the dangerous offender sentencing provisions made by the *CJIA* 2008. Its comments were that, first, the assessment of dangerousness can now be made untrammelled by artificial constraints; but the principles identified and explained in *R. v. Johnson* (see § 5–306 in the main work) (in particular, that the court is concerned with future risk and public protection), are unchanged. Secondly, the overarching consideration (*viz.* whether the court is of the opinion that there is a significant risk to members of the public of serious harm occasioned by the commission of further specified offences by the offender) is unchanged. Absent such risk, there is no question of a sentence under these provisions. Thirdly, in determining whether there is such a risk, the court should have in mind all the alternative and cumulative methods of providing the necessary public protection against the risk posed by the offender (*e.g.* a sexual offences prevention order with appropriate conditions could form part of the total protective sentencing package). Fourthly, as to the new subsection (3B) of section 225 (second alternative condition for imposing sentence of imprisonment for public protection is that the notional minimum term is at least two years), where the offender falls to be dealt with for two or more offences, this condition may be established notwithstanding the absence of an individual offence for which a two-year minimum term would be appropriate. The totality of the offending should be reflected in the assessment of the notional determinate term for this purpose. Fifthly, as to the choice between a sentence of imprisonment for public protection and an extended sentence, the latter should be selected if, taken together with any other appropriate orders that might be made, it would achieve appropriate public protection against the risk posed by the individual.

(ii) *Imposition of life imprisonment or detention for life*

Whilst *R. v. Kehoe* (see the main work, and now reported at [2009] 1 Cr.App.R.(S.) 9) is probably to be taken as the leading authority on this issue, for a further case to similar effect, see *R. v. Stanley* [2008] 2 Cr.App.R.(S.) 107, CA.   **5–304**

Whilst it was desirable, once it had been accepted that the dangerousness criteria applied, that a judge contemplating a discretionary life sentence should alert counsel to that fact in order to give counsel the opportunity to raise any matters of law concerning the approach to such a sentence, the lack of such warning could not in itself be a reason for allowing an appeal: *R. v. Cross* [2009] 1 Cr.App.R.(S.) 34, CA (see also *post*, § 19–205).   ★

(iv) *Assessment of significant risk*

R. v. Johnson (see the main work) was considered by the Court of Appeal in   **5–306**

91

Att.-Gen.'s Reference (No. 55 of 2008) (R. v. C.) in light of the amendments to the legislation effected by the *CJIA* 2008: see *ante*, § 5–303.

It was clear from section 229 of the *CJA* 2003 (see § 5–297 in the main work) that a court was entitled to take account of offences to be taken into consideration when assessing whether there was a significant risk to members of the public occasioned by the commission by the defendant of further specified offences: *R. v. Lavery,* 172 J.P. 561, CA.

Consecutive/concurrent sentences

5–307a   *R. v. Hills; R. v. Pomfret; R. v. Davies* is now reported at [2009] 1 Cr.App.R.(S.) 75, *sub nom. R. v. Hills.*

Fixing the minimum term (life sentences not fixed by law)

Powers of Criminal Courts (Sentencing) Act 2000, s.82A

Determination of tariffs

5–310   Section 22 of the *CJIA* 2008 came into force on November 3, 2008: *Criminal Justice and Immigration Act 2008 (Commencement No. 3 and Transitional Provisions) Order* 2008 (S.I. 2008 No. 2712).

★   The amendment of section 82A of the 2000 Act effected by the *AFA* 2006 comes into force on October 31, 2009: *Armed Forces Act 2006 (Commencement No. 5) Order* 2009 (S.I. 2009 No. 1167).

5–312   As to the commencement of section 22 of the *CJIA* 2008, see *ante*, § 5–310.

(e) *Prison sentences of less than 12 months*

Criminal Justice Act 2003, ss.181, 182

CHAPTER 3

PRISON SENTENCES OF LESS THAN 12 MONTHS

Prison sentences of less than twelve months

[Prison sentences of less than 12 months

5–314   **181.**—(1) Any power of a court to impose a sentence of imprisonment for a term of less than 12 months on an offender may be exercised only in accordance with the following provisions of this section unless the court makes an intermittent custody order (as defined by section 183).

(2) The term of the sentence—

    (a) must be expressed in weeks,

    (b) must be at least 28 weeks,

    (c) must not be more than 51 weeks in respect of any one offence, and

    (d) must not exceed the maximum term permitted for the offence.

(3) The court, when passing sentence, must—

    (a) specify a period (in this Chapter referred to as "the custodial period") at the end of which the offender is to be released on a licence, and

    (b) by order require the licence to be granted subject to conditions requiring the offender's compliance during the remainder of the term (in this Chapter

referred to as "the licence period") or any part of it with one or more
requirements falling within section 182(1) and specified in the order.

(4) In this Part "custody plus order" means an order under subsection (3)(b).

(5) The custodial period—

    (a) must be at least 2 weeks, and

    (b) in respect of any one offence, must not be more than 13 weeks.

(6) In determining the term of the sentence and the length of the custodial period, the court must ensure that the licence period is at least 26 weeks in length.

(7) Where a court imposes two or more terms of imprisonment in accordance
with this section to be served consecutively—

    (a) the aggregate length of the terms of imprisonment must not be more than
        65 weeks, and

    (b) the aggregate length of the custodial periods must not be more than 26
        weeks.

(7A) For the purposes of subsection (7)(a) the aggregate length of the terms of
imprisonment is not to be regarded as being more than 65 weeks if the aggregate of
all the custodial periods and the longest of the licence periods in relation to those
terms is not more than 65 weeks.

(8) A custody plus order which specifies two or more requirements may, in relation to any requirement, refer to compliance within such part of the licence period as
is specified in the order.

(9) Subsection (3)(b) does not apply where the sentence is a suspended sentence.]

This section comes into force on a day to be appointed. It is printed as
amended by the *CJIA* 2008, s.20(1) and (2). As from a day to be appointed,
the *AFA* 2006, s.196, provides that in sections 181 and 182, "court" includes
a relevant service court.

Licence conditions

182.—(1) The requirements falling within this subsection are—   **5-315**

    (a) an unpaid work requirement (as defined by section 199),

    (b) an activity requirement (as defined by section 201),

    (c) a programme requirement (as defined by section 202),

    (d) a prohibited activity requirement (as defined by section 203),

    (e) a curfew requirement (as defined by section 204),

    (f) an exclusion requirement (as defined by section 205),

    (g) a supervision requirement (as defined by section 213), and

    (h) in a case where the offender is aged under 25, an attendance centre require-
        ment (as defined by section 214).

[(2) The power under section 181(3)(b) to determine the conditions of the licence
has effect subject to section 218 and to the following provisions of Chapter 4 relating
to particular requirements—

    (a) section 199(3) (unpaid work requirement),

    (b) section 201(3) and (4) (activity requirement),

    (c) section 202(4) and (5) (programme requirement), and

    (d) section 203(2) (prohibited activity requirement).]

(3) Where the court makes a custody plus order requiring a licence to contain a
curfew requirement or an exclusion requirement, the court must also require the
licence to contain an electronic monitoring requirement (as defined by section 215)
unless—

    (a) the court is prevented from doing so by section 215(2) or 218(4), or

    (b) in the particular circumstances of the case, it considers it inappropriate to
        do so.

(4) Where the court makes a custody plus order requiring a licence to contain an
unpaid work requirement, an activity requirement, a programme requirement, a

prohibited activity requirement, a supervision requirement or an attendance centre requirement, the court may also require the licence to contain an electronic monitoring requirement unless the court is prevented from doing so by section 215(2) or 218(4).

(5) Before making a custody plus order requiring a licence to contain two or more different requirements falling within subsection (1), the court must consider whether, in the circumstances of the case, the requirements are compatible with each other.

Subsections (1) and (3) to (5) came into force on January 26, 2004, for the purposes of the passing of a sentence of imprisonment to which an intermittent custody order relates and the release on licence of a person serving such a sentence: *Criminal Justice Act 2003 (Commencement No. 1) Order* 2003 (S.I. 2003 No. 3282). See, however, §§ 5–313a, 5–313c in the main work.

As to the word "court", see *ante*, § 5–314.

Criminal Justice Act 2003, ss.183–185

Intermittent custody

Intermittent custody

5-316   **183.**—(1) A court may, when passing a sentence of imprisonment for a term complying with subsection (4)—

    (a) specify the number of days that the offender must serve in prison under the sentence before being released on licence for the remainder of the term, and

    (b) by order—

        (i) specify periods during which the offender is to be released temporarily on licence before he has served that number of days in prison, and

        (ii) require any licence to be granted subject to conditions requiring the offender's compliance during the licence periods with one or more requirements falling within section 182(1) and specified in the order.

(2) In this Part "intermittent custody order" means an order under subsection (1)(b).

(3) In this Chapter—

    "licence period", in relation to a term of imprisonment to which an intermittent custody order relates, means any period during which the offender is released on licence by virtue of subsection (1)(a) or (b)(i);

    "the number of custodial days", in relation to a term of imprisonment to which an intermittent custody order relates, means the number of days specified under subsection (1)(a).

(4) The term of the sentence—

    (a) must be expressed in weeks,

    (b) must be at least 28 weeks,

    (c) must not be more than 51 weeks in respect of any one offence, and

    (d) must not exceed the maximum term permitted for the offence.

(5) The number of custodial days—

    (a) must be at least 14, and

    (b) in respect of any one offence, must not be more than 90.

(6) A court may not exercise its powers under subsection (1) unless the offender has expressed his willingness to serve the custodial part of the proposed sentence intermittently, during the parts of the sentence that are not to be licence periods.

(7) Where a court exercises its powers under subsection (1) in respect of two or more terms of imprisonment that are to be served consecutively—

    (a) the aggregate length of the terms of imprisonment must not be more than 65 weeks, and

(b) the aggregate of the numbers of custodial days must not be more than 180.

(8) The Secretary of State may by order require a court, in specifying licence periods under subsection (1)(b)(i), to specify only—

(a) periods of a prescribed duration,

(b) periods beginning or ending at prescribed times, or

(c) periods including, or not including, specified parts of the week.

(9) An intermittent custody order which specifies two or more requirements may, in relation to any requirement, refer to compliance within such licence period or periods, or part of a licence period, as is specified in the order.

Subsection (8) came into force on Royal Assent (November 20, 2003): s.336(1). The remainder of the section came into force on January 26, 2004, for the purposes of the passing of a sentence of imprisonment to which an intermittent custody order relates and the release on licence of a person serving such a sentence: S.I. 2003 No. 3282 (*ante*, § 5–315). See, however, §§ 5–313a, 5–313c in the main work.

The *Intermittent Custody (Transitory Provisions) Order* 2003 (S.I. 2003 No. 3283) modifies section 183 (in relation to any time before the commencement of the repeal of section 78 of the *PCC(S)A* 2000 (*ante*, § 5–267)) by substituting "14" for "28", "26" for "51", "45" for "90", "52" for "65" and "90" for "180" in subsections (4)(b), (4)(c), (5)(b), (7)(a) and (7)(b) respectively.

Restrictions on power to make intermittent custody order

184.—(1) A court may not make an intermittent custody order unless it has   **5-317** been notified by the Secretary of State that arrangements for implementing such orders are available in the area proposed to be specified in the intermittent custody order and the notice has not been withdrawn.

(2) The court may not make an intermittent custody order in respect of any offender unless—

(a) it has consulted an officer of a local probation board or an officer of a provider of probation services,

(b) it has received from the Secretary of State notification that suitable prison accommodation is available for the offender during the custodial periods, and

(c) it appears to the court that the offender will have suitable accommodation available to him during the licence periods.

(3) In this section "custodial period", in relation to a sentence to which an intermittent custody order relates, means any part of the sentence that is not a licence period.

Intermittent custody: licence conditions

185.—(1) Section 183(1)(b) has effect subject to section 218 and to the following   **5-318** provisions of Chapter 4 limiting the power to require the licence to contain particular requirements—

(a) section 199(3) (unpaid work requirement),

(b) section 201(3) and (4) (activity requirement),

(c) section 202(4) and (5) (programme requirement), and

(d) section 203(2) (prohibited activity requirement).

(2) Subsections (3) to (5) of section 182 have effect in relation to an intermittent custody order as they have effect in relation to a custody plus order.

Sections 184 and 185 came into force on January 26, 2004, for the purposes of the passing of a sentence of imprisonment to which an intermittent custody order relates and the release on licence of a person serving such a sentence: S.I. 2003 No. 3282 (*ante*, § 5–315). See, however, §§ 5–313a, 5–313c in the main work. Section 184 is printed as amended by the *Offender Management Act 2007 (Consequential Amendments) Order* 2008 (S.I. 2008 No. 912), art. 3, and Sched. 1, para. 19(1) and (4).

Revocation or amendment

5–319   Section 187 gives effect to Schedule 10 (*post*, §§ 5–327b *et seq.*), which contains provisions relating to the revocation or amendment of custody plus orders and the amendment of intermittent custody orders.

Transfer of orders

5–320   Section 188 gives effect to Schedule 11 (not set out in this work), which makes provision for the transfer of custody plus orders and intermittent custody orders to Scotland or Northern Ireland.

Criminal Justice Act 2003, ss.189–192

Erratum

5–321   Owing to a fault in the production process, part of the text of the main work was omitted. The final sub-paragraph in the main work should be replaced by the following text.

The *Criminal Justice Act 2003 (Sentencing) (Transitory Provisions) Order* 2005 (S.I. 2005 No. 643) modifies section 189 (in relation to any time before the commencement of the repeal of the *PCC(S)A* 2000, s.78 (*ante*, § 5–267)), by substituting "at least 14 days but not more than twelve months, or in the case of a magistrates' court, at least 14 days but not more than six months" for "at least 28 weeks" to "section 181" in subsection (1) and the words "twelve months, or in the case of a magistrates', six months" for "65 weeks" in subsection (2). With effect from October 31, 2009, the references to "a magistrates' court" in the substituted provisions are to be taken to include "the Service Civilian Court": *Armed Forces Act 2006 (Transitional Provisions etc.) Order* 2009 (S.I. 2009 No. 1059), Sched. 2, para. 2(2).

★

The section is further modified (in relation to any time before the coming into force of the *CJCSA* 2000, s.61) (abolition of sentences of detention in a young offender institution, custody for life, etc.) by inserting the words "or in the case of a person aged at least 18 but under 21, detention in a young offender institution" after "sentence of imprisonment" in subsection (1), the words "or detention in a young offender institution" after "sentence of imprisonment" in subsection (1)(b), and the words "or in the case of a person aged at least 18 but under 21, a sentence of detention in a young offender institution" after "sentence of imprisonment" in subsection (6): *ibid.*

★

As from October 31, 2009 (*Armed Forces Act 2006 (Commencement No. 5) Order* 2009 (S.I. 2009 No. 1167)), the *AFA* 2006, s.196, provides that in sections 189 and 190, "court" includes a relevant service court.

In order lawfully to suspend a sentence of imprisonment under section 189, the court must order the offender to comply with one or more requirements falling within section 190(1) during a period specified as the supervision period (which may or may not be the same period as the operational period of the suspended sentence): *R. v. Lees-Wolfenden* [2007] 1 Cr.App.R.(S.) 119, CA.

It was held in *R. v. Waters and Young*, unreported, October 8, 2008, CA ([2008] EWCA Crim. 2538), that where the appropriate sentence is an immediate custodial sentence of such length that the offender would be entitled to immediate release by virtue of time in custody on remand, it was improper to impose a suspended sentence of equivalent length, under section 189 of the 2003 Act, on the basis that the imposition of an immediate sentence would be meaningless in such circumstances. The sentence would be a real sentence, notwithstanding that its custodial portion had already been served. As to this case, see also *post*, § 7–130.

Power to provide for review of suspended sentence order

Section 203 of the *AFA* 2006 comes into force on October 31, 2009: *Armed Forces Act 2006 (Commencement No. 5) Order* 2009 (S.I. 2009 No. 1167).   ★**5–323**

Criminal Justice Act 2003, Sched. 10

Section 187   SCHEDULE 10

REVOCATION OR AMENDMENT OF CUSTODY PLUS ORDERS AND AMENDMENT OF INTERMITTENT
CUSTODY ORDERS

Interpretation

1.—(1) In this Schedule—   **5–327b**
"the appropriate court" means —
  (a) where the custody plus order or intermittent custody order was made
    by the Crown Court, the Crown Court, and
  (b) in any other case, a magistrates' court acting in the local justice area
    concerned;
"the offender", in relation to a custody plus order or intermittent custody order,
  means the person in respect of whom the order is made;
"the local justice area concerned", in relation to a custody plus order or intermittent custody order, means the local justice area for the time being specified in
  the order;
"the responsible officer" has the meaning given by section 197.

(2) In this Schedule any reference to a requirement being imposed by, or included in, a custody plus order or intermittent custody order is to be read as a reference to compliance with the requirement being required by the order to be a condition of a licence.

Orders made on appeal

2. Where a custody plus order or intermittent custody order has been made on   **5–327c**
appeal, it is to be taken for the purposes of this Schedule to have been made by the Crown Court.

Revocation of custody plus order or removal from intermittent custody order
of requirements as to licence conditions

3.—(1) Where at any time while a custody plus order or intermittent custody or-   **5–327d**
der is in force, it appears to the appropriate court on the application of the offender or the responsible officer that, having regard to circumstances which have arisen since the order was made, it would be in the interests of justice to do so, the court may—
  (a) in the case of a custody plus order, revoke the order, and
  (b) in the case of an intermittent custody order, amend the order so that it
    contains only provision specifying periods for the purposes of section
    183(1)(b)(i).

(2) The revocation under this paragraph of a custody plus order does not affect

the sentence of imprisonment to which the order relates, except in relation to the conditions of the licence.

Amendment by reason of change of residence

5–327e
4.—(1) This paragraph applies where, at any time during the term of imprisonment to which a custody plus order or intermittent custody order relates, the appropriate court is satisfied that the offender proposes to change, or has changed, his residence during the licence period from the local justice area concerned to another local justice area.

(2) Subject to sub-paragraphs (3) and (4), the appropriate court may, and on the application of the Secretary of State or the responsible officer must, amend the custody plus order or intermittent custody order by substituting the other local justice area for the area specified in the order.

(3) The court may not amend under this paragraph a custody plus order or intermittent custody order which contains requirements which, in the opinion of the court, cannot be complied with unless the offender resides in the local justice area concerned unless, in accordance with paragraph 5, it either—

    (a) cancels those requirements, or

    (b) substitutes for those requirements other requirements which can be complied with if the offender does not reside in that area.

(4) The court may not amend under this paragraph any custody plus order or intermittent custody order imposing a programme requirement unless it appears to the court that the accredited programme specified in the requirement is available in the other local justice area.

Amendment of requirements of custody plus order or intermittent custody order

5–327f
5.—(1) At any time during the term of imprisonment to which a custody plus order or intermittent custody order relates, the appropriate court may, on the application of the offender, the Secretary of State or the responsible officer, by order amend any requirement of the custody plus order or intermittent custody order—

    (a) by cancelling the requirement, or

    (b) by replacing it with a requirement of the same kind imposing different obligations, which the court could include if it were then making the order.

(2) For the purposes of sub-paragraph (1)—

    (a) a requirement falling within any paragraph of section 182(1) is of the same kind as any other requirement falling within that paragraph, and

    (b) an electronic monitoring requirement is a requirement of the same kind as any requirement falling within section 182(1) to which it relates.

(3) Sub-paragraph (1)(b) has effect subject to the provisions mentioned in subsection (2) of section 182, and to subsections (3) and (5) of that section.

Alteration of pattern of temporary release

5–327g
6.—(1) At any time during the term of imprisonment to which an intermittent custody order relates, the appropriate court may, on the application of the offender, the Secretary of State or the responsible officer, amend the order—

    (a) so as to specify different periods for the purposes of section 183(1)(b)(i), or

    (b) so as to provide that he is to remain in prison until the number of days served by him in prison is equal to the number of custodial days.

(2) The appropriate court may not by virtue of sub-paragraph (1) amend an intermittent custody order unless it has received from the Secretary of State notification that suitable prison accommodation is available for the offender during the periods which, under the order as amended, will be custodial periods.

(3) In this paragraph "custodial period" has the same meaning as in section 184(3).

Supplementary

7. No application may be made under paragraph 3(1), 5(1) or 6(1) while an appeal against the sentence of which the custody plus or intermittent custody order forms part is pending.   **5–327h**

8.—(1) Subject to sub-paragraph (2), where a court proposes to exercise its powers under paragraph 5 or 6, otherwise than on the application of the offender, the court—

  (a) must summon him to appear before the court, and

  (b) if he does not appear in answer to the summons, may issue a warrant for his arrest.

(2) This paragraph does not apply to an order cancelling any requirement of a custody plus or intermittent custody order.

9.—(1) On the making under this Schedule of an order revoking or amending a custody plus order or amending an intermittent custody order, the proper officer of the court must—

  (a) provide copies of the revoking or amending order to the offender and the responsible officer,

  (b) in the case of an amending order which substitutes a new local justice area, provide a copy of the amending order to—

    (i) the local probation board acting for that area, or (as the case may be) a provider of probation services operating in that area, and

    (ii) the magistrates' court acting in that area,

  (c) in the case of an order which cancels or amends a requirement specified in the first column of Schedule 14, provide a copy of so much of the amending order as relates to that requirement to the person specified in relation to that requirement in the second column of that Schedule.

(2) Where under sub-paragraph (1)(b) the proper officer of the court provides a copy of an amending order to a magistrates' court acting in a different area, the officer must also provide to that court such documents and information relating to the case as it considers likely to be of assistance to a court acting in that area in the exercise of its functions in relation to the order.

[Sched. 10 is printed as amended by the *Courts Act 2003 (Consequential Provisions) Order* 2005 (S.I. 2005 No. 886), art. 2, and Sched., para. 108; and the *Offender Management Act 2007 (Consequential Amendments) Order* 2008 (S.I. 2008 No. 912), art. 3, Sched. 1, para. 19(1) and (18).]

Schedule 10 (and section 187, which gives effect to it) came into force on January 26, 2004, for the purposes of the passing of a sentence of imprisonment to which an intermittent custody order relates and the release on licence of a person serving such a sentence: S.I. 2003 No. 3282 (*ante*, § 5–315).

As from a day to be appointed, the *AFA* 2006, s.199(1) provides that in Schedule 10, as it applies to a custody plus order made by a relevant service court, "the appropriate court" means the Crown Court and the definition of the "appropriate court", in paragraph 1(1), and paragraph 2 are to be treated as omitted; and section 199(2) provides that paragraph 9(1)(b)(ii) and (2) do not apply in relation to a custody plus order made by a relevant service court.

Criminal Justice Act 2003, Sched. 12

Supplementary

Sections 205 and 206 of, and Schedule 7 to, the *AFA* 2006 come into force on October 31, 2009: *Armed Forces Act 2006 (Commencement No. 5) Order* 2009 (S.I. 2009 No. 1167). In connection with the commencement of those   **★5–334j** provisions, see the transitory provision in the *Armed Forces Act 2006 (Transitional Provisions etc.) Order* 2009 (S.I. 2009 No. 1059), Sched. 2, para. 3(d) (reference to "12 months" in para. 15(5A) to have effect as reference to "6 months" pending commencement of repeal of *CJCSA* 2000, s.78).

Authorities

★5–334k   It follows from paragraph 2.2.22 of the "New sentences: *Criminal Justice Act 2003*" guideline (*post*, Appendix K–60) (where new offence is not imprisonable, the sentencing court should consider whether it is appropriate to activate a previous suspended sentence at all) that it may be appropriate to activate a suspended sentence even though the new offence does not warrant custody: *Nobbs v. DPP* [2009] R.T.R. 9, DC.

★   Where a suspended sentence has been breached by the commission of a further offence, but an unpaid work requirement attached to that order has been met, since paragraph 8(3) of Schedule 12 to the 2003 Act (§ 5–333 in the main work) acknowledges that it may be unjust to order the term of imprisonment to be served at all in light of the degree to which the community requirements have been completed, it follows that the same consideration must apply to the decision whether, if the sentence suspended is activated, it should be activated in full or only in part: *R. v. Zeca*, *The Times*, March 17, 2009, CA.

(4) Detention and training orders

Powers of Criminal Courts (Sentencing) Act 2000, ss.101, 102

Term of order, consecutive terms and taking account of remands

5–349   Section 22 of the *CJIA* 2008 came into force on November 3, 2008: *Criminal Justice and Immigration Act 2008 (Commencement No. 3 and Transitional Provisions) Order* 2008 (S.I. 2008 No. 2712).

★   Sections 211 and 213 of the *AFA* 2006 come into force on October 31, 2009: *Armed Forces Act 2006 (Commencement No. 5) Order* 2009 (S.I. 2009 No. 1167).

Powers of Criminal Courts (Sentencing) Act 2000, ss.103, 104

Breach of supervision requirements

5–352   In *H. v. Doncaster Youth Court and Doncaster Youth Offending Service*, 173 J.P. 162, DC, it was held that the words "the remainder of the term of the detention and training order" in section 104(3) of the Act of 2000 means, on a natural reading, the period between (i) the occasion on which it is proved the offender has failed to comply with the requirements of the supervision element of the detention and training order, contrary to section 103(6)(b) (§ 5–351 in the main work), and (ii) the expiry of that order. The court found that if Parliament had intended otherwise, for instance, for the potential return period to be measured from the date of the breach, it would have adopted wording similar to that used in sections 105 and 116 of the Act (§ 5–353 in the main work and § 5–364r, *post*, respectively).

Interaction with sentences of detention in a young offender institution

★5–354   As from October 31, 2009, in section 106(1) of the Act of 2000, "court" includes a relevant service court within the meaning given by section 196(2) of the *AFA* 2006 and references to a detention and training order include an order under section 211 of the 2006 Act: *Armed Forces Act 2006 (Transitional Provisions etc.) Order* 2009 (S.I. 2009 No. 1059), Sched. 2, para. 10.

Interaction with sentences of detention

 The amendment of section 106A of the 2000 Act effected by the *AFA* 2006 comes into force on October 31, 2009: *Armed Forces Act 2006 (Commencement No. 5) Order* 2009 (S.I. 2009 No. 1167). In connection with that commencement, see the transitional provision in the *Armed Forces Act 2006 (Transitional Provisions etc.) Order* 2009 (S.I. 2009 No. 1059), Sched. 1, para. 45(2) (interpretation of references to "a sentence of detention").

  ★5–354a

E. Release on Licence

Saving and transitional provisions

 R. (Noone) v. Governor of H.M.P. Drake Hall (referred to in the main work) has been reversed in part: see *R. (Noone) v. Governor of Drake Hall Prison* [2009] 1 All E.R. 494, CA (Civ. Div.). It was held that where an offender was sentenced in respect of offences committed on or after April 4, 2005, to consecutive sentences of imprisonment totalling 12 months or more, with at least one of the sentences being for a term of less than 12 months, paragraph 14 of Schedule 2 to S.I. 2005 No. 950 (see the main work) applied, and this was so irrespective of the fact that other sentences were imposed of longer than 12-months' duration; and the effect of that paragraph was that separate release regimes applied, the release regime under the *CJA* 1991 applying to the sentence of less than 12 months, and the regime under the *CJA* 2003 to the sentence of 12 months or more, and that time spent on licence and eligibility for home detention curfew would be dependent on the order in which the sentences were pronounced in court.

  5–364b

Order for return to prison (offences committed before April 4, 2005/short sentences)

 The repeal of sections 116 and 117 of the *PCC(S)A* 2000 effected by the *CJA* 2003, "is of no effect in relation to a person in a case in which the sentence of imprisonment referred to in section 116(1)(a) … is imposed in respect of an offence committed before April 4, 2005 or is for a term of less than twelve months" (*Criminal Justice Act 2003 (Commencement No. 8 and Transitional and Saving Provisions) Order* 2005 (S.I. 2005 No. 950), Sched. 2, para. 29 (§ 5–364n in the main work). As those provisions will continue to apply for an indeterminate period, they are set out below.

  5–364q

Powers of Criminal Courts (Sentencing) Act 2000, s.116

Power to order return to prison etc. where offence committed during original sentence

 116.—(1) *This section applies to a person if—*

  (a) *he has been serving a determinate sentence of imprisonment which he began serving on or after 1st October 1992;*

  (b) *he is released under any provision of Part II of the* Criminal Justice Act *1991 (early release of prisoners) other than section 33(1A);*

  (c) *before the date on which he would (but for his release) have served his sentence in full, he commits an offence punishable with imprisonment ("the new offence"); and*

  5–364r

(d) *whether before or after that date, he is convicted of the new offence.*

(2) *Subject to subsection (3) below, the court by or before which a person to whom this section applies is convicted of the new offence may, whether or not it passes any other sentence on him, order him to be returned to prison for the whole or any part of the period which—*

    (a) *begins with the date of the order; and*

    (b) *is equal in length to the period between the date on which the new offence was committed and the date mentioned in subsection (1)(c) above.*

(3) *A magistrates' court—*

    (a) *shall not have power to order a person to whom this section applies to be returned to prison for a period of more than six months; but*

    (b) *subject to section 25 of the* Criminal Justice and Public Order Act *1994 (restrictions on granting bail), may commit him in custody or on bail to the Crown Court to be dealt with under subsection (4) below.*

(4) *Where a person is committed to the Crown Court under subsection (3) above, the Crown Court may order him to be returned to prison for the whole or any part of the period which—*

    (a) *begins with the date of the order; and*

    (b) *is equal in length to the period between the date on which the new offence was committed and the date mentioned in subsection (1)(c) above.*

(5) *Subsection (3)(b) above shall not be taken to confer on the magistrates' court a power to commit the person to the Crown Court for sentence for the new offence, but this is without prejudice to any such power conferred on the magistrates' court by any other provision of this Act.*

(6) *The period for which a person to whom this section applies is ordered under subsection (2) or (4) above to be returned to prison—*

    (a) *shall be taken to be a sentence of imprisonment for the purposes of Part II of the* Criminal Justice Act *1991 and this section;*

    (b) *shall, as the court may direct, either be served before and be followed by, or be served concurrently with, the sentence imposed for the new offence; and*

    (c) *in either case, shall be disregarded in determining the appropriate length of that sentence.*

(7) *As a consequence of subsection (6)(a) above, the court shall not be prevented by section 265 of the* Criminal Justice Act *2003 (restriction on consecutive sentences for released prisoners) from making any direction authorised by subsection (6)(b) above.*

(8) *Where the new offence is found to have been committed over a period of two or more days, or at some time during a period of two or more days, it shall be taken for the purposes of this section to have been committed on the last of those days.*

(9) *For the purposes of sections 9 and 10 of the* Criminal Appeal Act *1968 (rights of appeal), any order made in respect of a person by the Crown Court under subsection (2) or (4) above shall be treated as a sentence passed on him for the offence for which the sentence referred to in subsection (1) above was passed.*

(10) *This section and section 117 below apply to persons serving—*

    (a) *determinate sentences of detention under section 91 above, or*

    (b) *sentences of detention in a young offender institution,*

as they apply to persons serving equivalent sentences of imprisonment; and references in this section and section 117 to imprisonment or prison shall be construed accordingly.

(11) *In this section "sentence of imprisonment" does not include a committal for contempt of court or any kindred offence.*

[This section is printed as amended by the *CJIA* 2008, s.148(1), and Sched.26, paras 40 and 45. It is repealed, as from April 4, 2005, by the *CJA* 2003, s.332, and Sched. 37, Pt 7 (*Criminal Justice Act 2003 (Commencement No. 8 and Transitional and Saving Provisions) Order* 2005 (S.I. 2005 No. 950)). As to the saving and transitional provisions applicable to Chapter 6 of Part 12, see §§ 5–364b *et seq.* in the main work.]

*Treatment for purposes of section 116(1) of person serving two or more sentences or extended
sentence*

117.—(1) *For the purposes of any reference in section 116(1) above (however expressed)*   **5–364s**
*to the term of imprisonment to which a person has been sentenced, consecutive terms and
terms which are wholly or partly concurrent shall be treated as a single term if—*

    (a) *the sentences were passed on the same occasion; or*

    (b) *where they were passed on different occasions, the person has not been released
under Part II of the* Criminal Justice Act *1991 at any time during the period
beginning with the first and ending with the last of those occasions;*

but this is subject to subsection (4) below.

    (2) *Where a suspended sentence of imprisonment is ordered to take effect, with or without
any variation of the original term, the occasion on which that order is made shall be treated
for the purposes of subsection (1) above as the occasion on which the sentence is passed.*

    (3) *Where a person has been sentenced to two or more terms of imprisonment which are
wholly or partly concurrent and do not fall to be treated as a single term, the date mentioned
in section 116(1)(c) above shall be taken to be that on which he would (but for his release)
have served each of the sentences in full.*

    (4) *Subsections (1) to (3) above apply only where one or more of the sentences concerned
were passed on or after 30th September 1998; but where, by virtue of section 51(2) of the
Criminal Justice Act 1991 as enacted, the terms of two or more sentences passed before
30th September 1998 have been treated as a single term for the purposes of Part II of that
Act, they shall be treated as a single term for the purposes of section 116(1) above.*

    (5) *Section 116(1) and subsection (3) above shall each have effect as if the term of an
extended sentence (within the meaning of section 85 above) included the extension period
(within the meaning of that section).*

[This section is repealed, as from April 4, 2005, by the *CJA* 2003, s.332,
and Sched. 37, Pt 7 (*Criminal Justice Act 2003 (Commencement No. 8 and
Transitional and Saving Provisions) Order* 2005 (S.I. 2005 No. 950)). As to the
saving and transitional provisions applicable to Chapter 6 of Part 12, see
§§ 5–364b *et seq.* in the main work.]

    The power to order a return to custody applies only when the offender is   **5–364t**
convicted of an offence committed after his release from custody under Part
II of the 1991 Act. It accordingly does not apply to an offence committed by
an offender who is unlawfully at large following an escape from prison: *R. v.
Matthews and Jacobs* [2002] 1 W.L.R. 2583, CA; nor to an offence committed
by an offender while still in custody serving the custodial part of the sentence:
R. v. Qureshi [2002] 2 Cr.App.R.(S.) 11, CA. But an offender may be made the
subject of more than one order under section 116 in respect of the same
sentence, as where he is released after being made the subject of a section 116
order and then commits a further offence before the date on which the
sentence for the original offence would have expired: *R. v. Pick and Dillon*
[2006] 1 Cr.App.R.(S.) 61, CA.

    In *R. v. Taylor* [1998] 1 Cr.App.R.(S.) 312, the Court of Appeal considered
the principles on which a court should act in deciding whether to order a
return to custody under section 116. The sentencing tribunal should first
decide what was the appropriate sentence for the new offence, so that it
received the sentence it merited. The possibility of an order under section
116 should be disregarded at this stage, as section 116(6)(c) required. In
considering whether an order under section 116 should be made, it would
usually be appropriate to have regard to the nature and extent of any progress made by the defendant since his release and the nature and gravity of the
new offence and whether it called for a custodial sentence. It would also be

necessary to have regard to the totality, both in determining whether a return to prison should be ordered and whether such a period should be served before or concurrently with the sentence for the new offence, and in determining how long the return period should be. See also *R. v. Blades* [2000] 1 Cr.App.R.(S.) 463, CA; and *R. v. Martin* [2002] 2 Cr.App.R.(S.) 112, CA (order for return to prison for nearly three years in respect of previous sentence for robbery, consecutive to three-month sentence for theft, quashed and substituted by order for return for six months' consecutive).

Before making an order under section 116, the court should ascertain whether any time spent in custody on remand is to be deducted from the term of the original sentence under the *CJA* 1967, s.67 (§ 5–129 in the 2004 edition of this work), as this time will reduce the period which is relevant for the purposes of section 116. If there is any uncertainty about the relevant dates, the court should discount the period of return to allow for it: *R. v. Divers* [1999] 2 Cr.App.R.(S.) 421, CA.

A period which an offender is ordered to serve under section 116 must not be made to run consecutively to a new custodial sentence: *R. v. Jones* [1996] Crim.L.R. 524, CA; *R. v. Clerkenwell Magistrates' Court, ex p. Feely* [1996] 2 Cr.App.R.(S.) 309, DC. If orders are made under section 116 in respect of two different sentences, they must begin on the same day and run concurrently: *R. v. Divers, ante.*

In *R. v. Harrow JJ., ex p. Jordan* [1997] 1 W.L.R. 84, DC, it was held that where an offender was convicted summarily of an offence committed during the term of a sentence imposed by the Crown Court, the whole matter should be dealt with either in the magistrates' court or in the Crown Court. The magistrates' court should either deal with the sentence and the return, or commit both the question of sentence and the question of return to the Crown Court. The latter course should be adopted if there was a significant period of the whole term of the sentence unexpired and the new offence was of any gravity. *Ex p. Jordan* was followed in *R. v. Burton on Trent JJ. and Stafford Crown Court, ex p. Smith* [1998] 1 Cr.App.R.(S.) 223, DC.

Where an offender is committed to the Crown Court for sentence under the *PCC(S)A* 2000, s.3 (§ 5–24 in the main work), for an either way offence committed within the relevant period following his release from an earlier sentence, the Crown Court has power to make an order under section 116 by virtue of section 5, whether or not he is also committed to be dealt with under section 116(3): *R. v. Stephenson* [1999] 1 Cr.App.R.(S.) 177, CA. Where the offender is not committed for the later offence under section 3, but is committed to be dealt with under section 116, the Crown Court will have no power to sentence him for the later offence unless he is committed for that offence under section 6 (§ 5–27 in the main work).

The fact that an offender has been recalled to custody following the revocation of his licence does not prevent the court from making an order under section 116 in respect of the same sentence: *R. v. Sharkey* [2000] 1 Cr.App.R. 409, CA, disapproving *R. v. Governor of HMP Elmley, ex p. Moorton* [1999] 2 Cr.App.R.(S.) 165, DC.

The *PCC(S)A* 2000, s.84 (repealed and replaced by the *CJA* 2003, s.265 (to the same effect, and set out in the main work at § 5–388)) does not prevent the imposition of a sentence of imprisonment to run consecutively to a period of return to prison ordered under section 116: *R. v. Lowe; R. v. Leask* [1999] 2 Cr.App.R.(S.) 316, CA.

Where an offender who has been released on licence from a sentence of imprisonment commits an offence during the licence period, his licence may

ɔe revoked under the *CJA* 2003, s.254, before he comes before the court to
ɔe sentenced for the later offence. Any sentence imposed for the later offence must not be ordered to run consecutively to the original sentence
which the offender is still serving following the revocation of his licence; but
if the court makes an order under section 116 for his return to custody in
respect of the original sentence, the sentence for the new offence may be
ordered to run consecutively to the period of return so ordered: see *R. v.
Laurent* [2001] 1 Cr.App.R.(S.) 65, CA; *R. v. Cawthorn* [2001] 1 Cr.App.R.(S.)
136, CA; and *R. v. Jesson* [2008] 1 Cr.App.R.(S.) 36, CA. It should be
remembered that an offender ordered to return to custody under section 116
would normally serve half of the period ordered before release, unless it
forms part of a long term sentence when added to the term of the new
sentence, while an offender who has been recalled following the revocation of
his licence is liable to be detained until the end of the licence period, unless
he is released again on licence. See also *R. v. Stocker* [2003] 2 Cr.App.R.(S.)
54, CA; and *R. v. Teasdale* [2004] 1 Cr.App.R.(S.) 6, CA.

Criminal Justice Act 2003, s.237

Meaning of "fixed-term" prisoner etc.
    Section 21(1) and (3) of the *CJIA* 2008 came into force on November 3,   **5–365**
2008: *Criminal Justice and Immigration Act 2008 (Commencement No. 3 and
Transitional Provisions) Order* 2008 (S.I. 2008 No. 2712).
    The amendment of section 237 of the 2003 Act effected by the *AFA* 2006   ★
comes into force on October 31, 2009: *Armed Forces Act 2006 (Commencement
No. 5) Order* 2009 (S.I. 2009 No. 1167). In connection with that commencement, see the transitional provision in the *Armed Forces Act 2006 (Transitional
Provisions etc.) Order* 2009 (S.I. 2009 No. 1059), Sched. 1, para. 53(8) (interpretation of references to "a sentence of imprisonment passed by a service
court" and to "a sentence of detention under section 209" of the 2006 Act).

Criminal Justice Act 2003, s.240A

Crediting periods of remand on bail: terms of imprisonment and detention
    Section 21(1) and (4) of the *CJIA* 2008 came into force on November 3,   **5–368a**
2008: *Criminal Justice and Immigration Act 2008 (Commencement No. 3 and
Transitional Provisions) Order* 2008 (S.I. 2008 No. 2712).
    The *Remand on Bail (Disapplication of Credit Period) Rules* 2008 (S.I. 2008
No. 2793) disapply in certain circumstances the requirements relating to the
crediting of periods of remand on bail in the 2003 Act, s.240A(2) (in respect
of offences on or after April 4, 2005), and the 2008 Act, Sched. 6, para. 2(2)
(in respect of offences before April 4, 2005).
    Rule 2 effectively provides that where an offender receives concurrent or
consecutive sentences, the time spent on bail subject to an electronically
monitored curfew condition should not be credited more than once (if it is
credited against one of the sentences, then it should be ignored in relation to
the other). Rule 3 provides that time spent on bail subject to an electronically
monitored curfew condition shall not be credited where the offender is at the
same time subject to an electronically monitored curfew imposed as a consequence of early release or release on licence from prison (under Part 2 of the
CJA 1991 Act or Chapter 6 of Part 12 of the 2003 Act) or from a detention
and training order, or as part of a community order or a suspended
sentence order under the 2003 Act or a curfew order under the *PCC(S)A*
2000, s.37(1), or as part of any other requirement to remain at one or more

specified places for a specified number of hours in any given day, provided that the requirement was imposed by a court or the Secretary of State and arises as a result of a conviction. Rule 4 provides that time spent on bail subject to an electronically monitored curfew condition shall not be credited where the offender is at the same time on temporary release from prison (under the *Prison Rules* 1999 (S.I. 1999 No. 728), r.9), a young offender institution (under the *Young Offender Institution Rules* 2000 (S.I. 2000 No. 3371), r.5), or a secure training centre (under the *Secure Training Centre Rules* 1998 (S.I. 1998 No. 472), r.5).

In cases not covered by section 240A (*i.e.* because sentencing took place before its commencement), it was appropriate to make some modest adjustment in the final sentence where the defendant was effectively subject to house arrest (*i.e.* a 24 hour curfew), but not where he was subject only to a night-time curfew: *R. v. Sherif* [2009] 2 Cr.App.R.(S.) 33, CA (making an allowance of three months in the case of offenders who had been subject to house arrest for approximately 16 months).

Offences committed before April 4, 2005

5–368b   Section 23 of, and Schedule 6 to, the *CJIA* 2008 came into force on November 3, 2008: *Criminal Justice and Immigration Act 2008 (Commencement No. 3 and Transitional Provisions) Order* 2008 (S.I. 2008 No. 2712).

As to the disapplication of the requirements of Schedule 6 in certain circumstances, see S.I. 2008 No. 2793 (*ante*, § 5–368a).

Guidance

★5–368c   It was held in *R. v. Vaughan* [2009] 1 Cr.App.R.(S.) 63, CA, that the fact that a defendant continues, during the period in question, to maintain his denial or non-admission of guilt is not a factor which can in itself justify withholding a direction under section 240 of the *CJA* 2003 (§ 5–368 in the main work) in relation to that period. A defendant who maintains a denial of guilt right through to conviction is normally entitled to a full section 240 direction in respect of time spent in custody awaiting trial. The court said that the normal and proper way to reflect a failure to acknowledge guilt at the first opportunity is by withholding or reducing any discount for a plea.

★   Where the appellant had committed offences of dishonesty whilst on licence from a sentence for an offence of violence and the probation service had taken the considered decision not to recommend his recall, it was not open to the judge to refuse a direction under section 240 that time spent on remand should count towards his sentence on the basis that he had been on licence at the time of the fresh offences and "should still have been serving [his] sentence": *R. v. Metcalfe* [2009] 3 *Archbold News* 4, CA.

Warning to defence advocate

★5–368e   What was said in *R. v. Barber* (see the main work) was reiterated in *R. v. Metcalfe*, *ante* § 5–368c.

Errors and omissions

★5–368f   Given the significant problems that have arisen since the implementation of section 240 of the *CJA* 2003 in making an accurate calculation at the time of sentence of the number of days spent in custody on remand, judges should use the following formula (adapted from that suggested in *R. v. Gordon* (see the main work)) when imposing a custodial sentence in the hope that this will avoid the unnecessary costs incurred in the Court of Appeal if it transpires that mistakes have been made, *viz.* "The defendant will receive full credit for the full period of time spent in custody on remand and half the time spent under curfew if the curfew qualified under the provisions of section 240 [*sic*]. On the information before me, the total period is ... days but if this period is mistaken, this court will order an amendment of the record for the correct period to be recorded.": *R. v. Nnaji*; *R. v. Johnson* [2009] Crim.L.R. 541, CA.

Effect of direction under section 240 or 240A on release on licence

    Section 21(1) and (5) of the *CJIA* 2008 came into force on November 3, 2008: *Criminal Justice and Immigration Act 2008 (Commencement No. 3 and Transitional Provisions) Order* 2008 (S.I. 2008 No. 2712).   **5–369**

    The amendment of section 241 of the 2003 Act effected by the *AFA* 2006 comes into force on October 31, 2009: *Armed Forces Act 2006 (Commencement No. 5) Order* 2009 (S.I. 2009 No. 1167).   ★

Interpretation of sections 240, 240A and 241

    Section 21(1) and (6) of the *CJIA* 2008 came into force on November 3, 2008: *Criminal Justice and Immigration Act 2008 (Commencement No. 3 and Transitional Provisions) Order* 2008 (S.I. 2008 No. 2712).   **5–370**

Criminal Justice Act 2003, s.245

Restrictions on operation of section 244(1) in relation to intermittent custody prisoners

    245.—(1) Where an intermittent custody prisoner returns to custody after being unlawfully at large within the meaning of section 49 of the *Prison Act* at any time during the currency of his sentence, section 244(1) does not apply until—   **5–373**

    (a) the relevant time (as defined in subsection (2)), or

    (b) if earlier, the date on which he has served in prison the number of custodial days required by the intermittent custody order.

    (2) In subsection (1)(a) "the relevant time" means—

    (a) in a case where, within the period of 72 hours beginning with the return to custody of the intermittent custody prisoner, the Secretary of State or the responsible officer has applied to the court for the amendment of the intermittent custody order under paragraph 6(1)(b) of Schedule 10, the date on which the application is withdrawn or determined, and

    (b) in any other case, the end of that 72–hour period.

    (3) section 244(1) does not apply in relation to an intermittent custody prisoner at any time after he has been recalled under section 254, unless after his recall the Board has directed his further release on license

    This section came into force on January 26, 2004, for the purposes of intermittent custody only: S.I. 2003 No. 3282 (*ante*, § 5–364a). As to saving of the former legislation, see §§ 5–364b *et seq.* in the main work.

Criminal Justice Act 2003, ss.246–253

Power to release prisoners on licence before required to do so

    The amendment of section 246 of the 2003 Act effected by the *AFA* 2006 comes into force on October 31, 2009: *Armed Forces Act 2006 (Commencement No. 5) Order* 2009 (S.I. 2009 No. 1167).   ★**5–374**

Licence conditions

    The amendment of section 250 of the 2003 Act effected by the *AFA* 2006   ★**5–378**

Archbold
paragraph
numbers

comes into force on October 31, 2009: *Armed Forces Act 2006 (Commencement No. 5) Order* 2009 (S.I. 2009 No. 1167).

Licence conditions on re-release of prisoner serving sentence of less than 12 months

★5–379   The amendment of section 251 of the 2003 Act effected by the *AFA* 2006 comes into force on October 31, 2009: *Armed Forces Act 2006 (Commencement No. 5) Order* 2009 (S.I. 2009 No. 1167).

Duty to comply with licence conditions

★5–380   The amendment of section 252 of the 2003 Act effected by the *AFA* 2006 comes into force on October 31, 2009: *Armed Forces Act 2006 (Commencement No. 5) Order* 2009 (S.I. 2009 No. 1167).

Criminal Justice Act 2003, ss.263, 264, 264A

Concurrent terms

★5–386   The amendment of section 263 of the 2003 Act effected by the *AFA* 2006 comes into force on October 31, 2009: *Armed Forces Act 2006 (Commencement No. 5) Order* 2009 (S.I. 2009 No. 1167).

Criminal Justice Act 2003, s.265

Restriction on consecutive sentences for released prisoners

★5–389   Since section 265 of the 2003 Act prohibits a court from imposing a sentence that runs consecutively to an earlier sentence in respect of which the offender has been released on a licence which has subsequently been revoked, and since the power in section 116 of the *PCC(S)A* 2000 (*ante*, § 5–364r) to order an offender to return to prison to serve the appropriate proportion of the earlier sentence was removed by the 2003 Act (save for offences committed before April 4, 2005, and for sentences of less than 12 months), it would be wrong in principle and contrary to section 153(2) of the 2003 Act (§ 5–266 in the main work) for a judge to impose a sentence which would otherwise be disproportionate to the most recent offence merely so as to ensure that the offender serves a period in custody over and above the remainder of the licence period imposed for the previous offence; the court sentencing for the later offence may in effect be powerless to impose any additional period of custody to reflect the later criminality: *R. v. Whittles* [2009] Crim.L.R. 534, CA. This decision is in flat contradiction to the earlier decision of the court in *R. v. Booker* [2009] Crim.L.R. 458. Whilst the court in *Whittles* did not refer to *Booker*, it is submitted that the decision in *Whittles* is to be preferred. Most importantly, it is supported by authority (see *R. v. Drewett* [2007] 1 Cr.App.R.(S.) 32, CA (not referred to in *Booker*)); but see also the commentary to *Booker* in *Criminal Law Week* 2009/19/16.

Criminal Justice Act 2003, s.268

Interpretation of Chapter 6

★5–390   The amendment of section 268 of the 2003 *Act* effected by the *AFA* 2006 comes into force on October 31, 2009: *Armed Forces Act 2006 (Commencement No. 5) Order* 2009 (S.I. 2009 No. 1167).

VII. FINES

Determining the amount of the fine

5–405   *R. v. Southampton University N.H.S. Trust* (see the main work) was

considered in *R. v. Guy's and St Thomas N.H.S. Trust* [2008] 4 All E.R. 1174,
CA, where it was said that it was against the public interest to punish by a
large fine a not-for-profit organisation carrying out work for the public benefit, although a fine was still appropriate even where there had been no
management negligence in order to encourage them to re-double their efforts
to ensure that their staff were kept up to the mark.

VIII. COMPENSATION, RESTITUTION AND REPARATION

A. COMPENSATION ORDERS

"Personal injury, loss or damage"

    Revenue and Customs Prosecutions Office v. Duffy is now reported at [2008] 2   **5–415**
Cr.App.R.(S.) 103.

IX. DEPRIVATION AND CONFISCATION

B. CONFISCATION UNDER THE DRUG TRAFFICKING ACT 1994

Valuation of property

    Where a judge assessed the value of the defendant's proceeds of drug traf-   **5–449**
ficking at £3.2 million, he was correct in taking the view that he was required
by the *DTA* 1994 to make a confiscation order in that amount, unless the
defendant satisfied him (to the civil standard) that his realisable assets were
less than that amount; and where the defendant had failed to do so, there
was no obligation on the judge to assume that the defendant would have
incurred some expenses to be set against that figure, and to make some
discount in respect thereof; such approach was misconceived; his task
under the statute was to assess the value of the proceeds in accord with the
provisions of the statute (which was not the same as profit), and to make an
order in that amount unless the value of the realisable assets was less than
that amount, and the burden of proof in that regard was on the defendant:
R. v. Versluis [2005] 2 Cr.App.R.(S.) 26, CA.

"drug trafficking offence"

    Where the defendant was convicted of a conspiracy to convert the proceeds   **5–449a**
of drug trafficking "or" the proceeds of criminal conduct (the substantive offences being created by the *DTA* 1994, s.49, and the *CJA* 1988, s.93C,
respectively), this was to be construed as a finding that the agreement was
not restricted to the laundering of the proceeds of drug trafficking or to the
proceeds of criminal conduct other than drug trafficking, but was an agreement to launder money, whatever its provenance; it was, in effect, an agreement to launder both the proceeds of drug trafficking and the proceeds of
other criminal conduct; accordingly, the defendant was properly to be
regarded as having been convicted of a "drug trafficking offence" for the
purposes of the confiscation provisions of the 1994 Act as the definition of
that expression extended to a conspiracy to commit an offence contrary to
section 49; and the judge had, therefore, erred in declining to conduct
confiscation proceedings under the 1994 Act: *R. v. Suchedina (Att.-Gen.'s Reference (No. 4 of 2003))* [2005] 1 Cr.App.R. 2, CA.

Variation of realisable amount

★**5–449b**   Where, following the grant of a certificate of inadequacy by the High Court under section 17 of the 1994 Act, the Crown Court had, pursuant to subsection (4) of that section, substituted a nil amount as the amount to be recovered, it was possible, if the defendant thereafter came into funds, for the amount to be varied upwards again if the High Court issued a certificate under section 16(2) that the amount that might be realised was now more than the amount that had been substituted for the original amount; but the Crown Court had a discretion as to whether to accede to an application for the amount to be increased following such certification, and one factor to be taken into account by it in deciding how to exercise its discretion would be whether the state had sat on its hands after significant and clear evidence about the defendant's change in financial circumstances had come to its attention or had unreasonably delayed in re-opening the issue: *R. v. Griffin* [2009] Crim.L.R. 537, CA.

Restraint orders; payment of legal expenses out of restrained assets

5–449c   See *Revenue and Customs Prosecution Office v. Briggs-Price and O'Reilly, post,* § 5–453.

C. Confiscation under the Criminal Justice Act 1988

Postponement of determinations

5–450   In *R. v. Haisman* [2004] 1 Cr.App.R.(S) 63, CA, it was held that where prosecuting counsel had invited the judge to postpone confiscation proceedings and to proceed to sentence, and the judge responded by saying, "If everyone agrees to that, I will do that" and there was no dissent from any counsel to that course, the judge had "manifestly reached a decision"(*R. v. Ross* [2001] 2 Cr.App.R.(S.) 109, CA) to postpone the confiscation proceedings under section 72A of the *CJA* 1988, with the consequence that the confiscation orders made subsequent to the imposition of sentence were lawful.

Assessment of benefit/making of assumptions

5–450a   The assumption provided for in section 72AA(4)(a) of the 1988 Act (*viz.* that any property transferred to the defendant since the beginning of the relevant period was received by him "in connection with the commission of offences to which this Part of this Act applies") includes within its scope offences committed by persons other than the defendant; thus it is not sufficient to rebut the presumption to show that the property was obtained by the defendant as a result of somebody else's criminal conduct; but the defendant's knowledge or lack of knowledge would be highly material in deciding whether to apply the safety valve in subsection (5) (assumption not to be made if court is satisfied that there would be a serious risk of injustice): *R. v. Ilyas* [2009] 1 Cr.App.R.(S.) 59, CA. See the commentary by David Thomas Q.C. in the *Criminal Law Review* for the suggestion that this decision will not carry across to the *PCA* 2002 regime; and see the commentary in *Criminal Law Week* 2008/39/9 as to the limitations of the actual decision, and, in particular, for the suggestion that it is out of kilter with the decision of the House of Lords in *R. v. May* (§ 5–768 in the main work).

Amount that might be realised

5–451   In *R. v. Blee* [2004] 1 Cr.App.R.(S.) 33, CA, it was held that whereas section

74(3) of the *CJA* 1988 provides that "the amount that might be realised at the time a confiscation order is made"includes "the total of the values at that time of all gifts caught by this Part of this Act" and whereas section 74(10) provides that a gift is caught by that part of the Act if "(a) it was made by the defendant at any time after the commission of the offence ...; and (b) the court considers it appropriate in all the circumstances to take the gift into account" it follows that the fact that the property held by the donee at the time of the confiscation order is less than the value of the gift does not *per se* preclude the court from taking the full value of the gift into account; the court is given a discretion by section 74(10) and the question for it to decide is whether it is "appropriate" to take the gift into account; if it considers it appropriate to take it into account (in whole or in part), then to the extent that it does so, the value of the gift is to be included in the computation of the amount that might be realised; in exercising the discretion, the court may have regard to the timing of the gift (here, made when the defendant, having been on the run, had decided to surrender), to the fact that it was made to a person from whom the defendant would be likely to be able to receive an equivalent benefit in return, if he wished, and to the fact that whilst the donee currently had assets worth considerably less than the value of the gift, he was in highly paid employment and would be likely again to hold substantial assets; and, where it is said that the gift has been dissipated prior to the confiscation order, this is a matter to be considered under section 74(10), rather than on a subsequent application for a certificate of inadequacy.

Valuation of property

In *R. v. Hedges* (2004) 148 S.J. 974, CA, it was held that in making a   **5–452**
confiscation order against a defendant whose only realisable asset was the house which he owned jointly with his wife, the correct approach to valuation of his interest in the property had been to determine the market value of the property, then deduct the outstanding mortgage and the reasonable costs of sale before making a confiscation order in respect of half the remaining amount; such an approach properly reflected the intention of section 74(4) of the *CJA* 1988 and was to be preferred to that of dividing the value of the house and then deducting the remaining mortgage and costs of sale from the defendant's half share, on the basis that he was responsible for payment of the mortgage; whilst it was true that the defendant was in theory liable to repay the whole mortgage, being jointly and severally liable, the reality was that the mortgage and the costs of sale would be discharged out of the proceeds of sale, the net effect of which would be to reduce his share in the value of the house by half the amount of the mortgage and costs of sale.

In *R. v. Ahmed* [2005] 1 All E.R. 128, CA, it was held that where a court concludes that an offender has benefited from relevant criminal conduct (*CJA* 1988, s.71(1A)), the court has no discretion, in valuing the realisable assets for the purposes of determining the amount of the confiscation order, to exclude from the computation, the value of the defendant's share in the matrimonial home, notwithstanding the probability that the home would have to be sold to meet the confiscation order; the words "the amount appearing to the court" in subsection (6)(b) (" ... the sum which an order made by a court under this section requires an offender to pay shall be equal to (a) ...; or (b) the amount appearing to the court to be the amount that might be realised at the time the order is made, whichever is the less") did not give the court a discretion; it merely referred to the valuation process to be carried out under section 74, and section 3 of the *Human Rights*

Act 1998 (§ 16–15 in the main work) did not require it to be read as construing such a discretion on the court on account of the possible interference with innocent third parties' rights under Article 8 of the ECHR (*ibid.*, § 16–101); the court is merely concerned with the arithmetic exercise of computing what is, in effect, a statutory debt; such process does not involve any assessment of the way in which the debt may ultimately be paid; different considerations would apply if the debt is not met and the prosecution determine to take enforcement action; if a court is asked to make an order for the sale of the matrimonial home then the third party's rights under Article 8 would clearly be engaged; and it would be at that stage that the court would have to consider whether or not it would be proportionate to make an order for the sale of the home. In connection with this case, see *Webber v. Webber (CPS intervening)*, § 5–776 in the main work.

In the earlier case of *R. v. Goodenough* [2005] 1 Cr.App.R.(S.) 88, CA, it was held that where a defendant's only realisable asset was his equity in the matrimonial home, the making of a confiscation order in accordance with the requirements of the 1988 Act for the amount by which he had benefited from his offending (being an amount less than the value of his equity) did not infringe or interfere with his rights under Article 8 or under Article 1 of the First Protocol (right to peaceful enjoyment of possessions); the rights of the defendant's wife might be infringed if the house were to be sold in order to raise the money to pay the amount of the confiscation order, and it would be open to the wife to oppose any application to appoint a receiver to enforce the order.

Restraint orders; payment of legal expenses out of restrained assets

5–453   In *Revenue and Customs Prosecution Office v. Briggs-Price and O'Reilly* [2007] L.S. Gazette, June 28, 32, CA (Civ. Div.) ([2007] EWCA Civ. 568) it was held, in relation to the confiscation regimes under the *CJA* 1988 and the *DTA* 1994, that the principle in *Customs and Excise Commrs v. Norris* [1991] 2 Q.B. 293, CA (Civ. Div.) (defendant's legal expenses may be met from restrained assets), applies both to legal expenses incurred prior to conviction (and any appeal against conviction) and to legal expenses incurred in connection with the making of a confiscation order and an appeal against such order; there is a discretion in such cases, which will be exercised for a proper and legitimate purpose within the scope of the statutory regime where the released assets are to meet expenses for a prospective appeal which are neither excessive nor improperly incurred (such amount as is released being capable of control by assessment).

Certificate of inadequacy

5–454   It was held in *Escobar v. DPP* [2009] 1 W.L.R. 64, DC, that when making an order under section 83(4) of the *CJA* 1988 for the reduction of a sum payable under a confiscation order (following the issue of a certificate of inadequacy), the Crown Court has jurisdiction to fix a time for payment (by way of extension of the original date). The court said that although there is no express power to extend time in section 83, section 75(1) ("(1) Where the Crown Court orders the defendant to pay an amount under this Part ..., sections 139(1) to (4) ... of the *Powers of Criminal Courts (Sentencing) Act* 2000 (powers of Crown Court in relation to fines and enforcement of Crown Court fines) shall have effect as if that amount were a fine imposed on him by the Crown Court.") operates so as to incorporate section 139(1) of the 2000

Act (§ 5–396 in the main work), which in turn gives the court power to extend the time for payment when it substitutes a lesser sum under section 83. When read as a whole, section 75 is generally concerned to make provision for orders made under section 83 as well as those under other provisions in Part VI, and this is consistent with the natural and grammatical meaning of the relevant provisions, in that the Crown Court is making an order under section 83(4) and the effect of that order is that the defendant has to pay an amount due under Part VI. For the suggestion that the court's conclusion is out of kilter with the legislative structure, see *Criminal Law Week* 2009/02/5. For the relevant provisions of the *PCA* 2002, see sections 23 and 39 (§§ 5–584, 5–600), neither of which contain any provision for an extension of the time allowed to pay.

D. Confiscation under the Proceeds of Crime Act 2002

(1) Summary

Guidance to prosecutors

The CPS issued guidance to prosecutors on May 28, 2009, in order to assist them in deciding whether to institute confiscation proceedings against a defendant. The guidance does little more than summarise what has been said by the House of Lords and the Court of Appeal in a number of well-known cases. Apart from a short introduction, which acknowledges that confiscation proceedings may be stayed where they should not have been instigated, the guidance is in four sections, *viz.* (i) the principles to be applied when determining whether a case properly falls within the relevant statutory regime for confiscation; (ii) two examples of how the principles apply to particular facts; (iii) the exercise of the prosecutor's discretion; and (iv) some examples of when it may be inappropriate for prosecutors to decide to instigate confiscation proceedings. *As to (i)*, the guidance is based in large part on the House of Lords' decisions in *R. v. May* (§ 5–768 in the main work), *Jennings v. CPS* § 5–769 in the main work) and *R. v. Green* (§ 5–769 in the main work). It does, however, emphasise (a) that if it appears that a defendant has no assets with which to pay any confiscation order, the prosecutor will have to consider whether it would be in the public interest to seek a confiscation order, (b) that it is imperative that those responsible for the criminal investigation should be made aware of the importance of establishing the role of a particular defendant in a criminal enterprise, (c) that it is important that any basis of plea sets out the defendant's role and that the prosecutor makes clear to the court whether there are any assertions made by the defendant, which the prosecution are not in a position to dispute for the purposes of sentence, but that may be contradicted by information that subsequently becomes available in the confiscation proceedings, and (d) that as the evidence from the criminal investigation, the financial investigation and the trial itself emerges, the appropriateness of seeking a confiscation order should be kept under review. *As to (ii)*, the guidance summarises the cases of *R. v. Sivaraman* (§ 5–768 in the main work) and *R. v. Allpress* (*post*, § 5–768). *As to (iii)*, it is said that the prosecutor should consider in each case whether the statutory regime would operate in a way that would be oppressive. Prosecutors are reminded of their role as ministers of justice and that they should bear in mind what was said in *R. v. Benjafield*; *R. v. Rezvi* [2003] 1 A.C. 1099, HL, to be the three legitimate aims of confiscation, *viz.* punishment, deterrence and the reduction in profits

★**5–547**

available to fund further criminal enterprises (per Lord Steyn (at [14])). *As to (iv)*, four examples are given, *viz.* (a) where the prosecution is reneging on an earlier agreement not to seek a confiscation order; (b) in a simple benefit case, where the defendant has voluntarily paid full compensation to the victim or victims or is ready, willing and able immediately to repay all of the victims the full amount of their losses and has not otherwise profited from his crime; (c) where proper application of the statute would compel the court to conclude that property obtained for the most part legitimately, and to which the defendant would have been entitled but for his criminal conduct, must be treated as benefit and *R. v. Shabir* (§ 5–767a in the main work), is cited by way of example; and (d) where the defendant has obtained employment as a result of a deception if the link between the criminality and the receipt of his wages is too remote, as where, had the representation been corrected, the employment would have continued, or where, after many years of otherwise lawful employment, a relatively minor previous conviction is discovered. In connection with (d), see *R. v. Carter, Kulish (Viktoriya), Kulish (Ruslan) and Lyashkov, post,* § 5–772.

(2) Legislation

(a) *Statute*

Proceeds of Crime Act 2002, ss.6–91

Making of order

5–566   Where a defendant appears before the Crown Court to be dealt with in respect of two or more indictments, each indictment represents a separate set of proceedings for the purposes of section 6(2)(a) of the 2002 Act: *R. v. Moulden* [2009] 1 Cr.App.R. 27, CA. As to the consequences of this where one indictment charges pre-commencement offences and one charges post-commencement offences, see *post,* § 5–665.

★   Section 6(6) has no application where the victim takes, or intends to take, proceedings against a party other than the defendant, including against a company owned by the defendant: *R. v. Lowe* [2009] Crim.L.R. 452, CA.

Recoverable amount

5–567   See *Grayson v. U.K.; Barnham v. Same, post,* § 16–78.

Assumptions to be made in case of criminal lifestyle

5–570   See *Grayson v. U.K.; Barnham v. Same, post,* § 16–78.

Effect of order on court's other powers

5–573   As from June 18, 2009 (*Counter-Terrorism Act 2008 (Commencement No. 3) Order* 2009 (S.I. 2009 No. 1256)), "or 23A" is inserted after "section 23" in section 13(3)(d) of the 2002 Act: *Counter-Terrorism Act* 2008, s.39, and Sched. 3, para. 7(1).

Postponement

★**5–574**   As to the importance of a judge making it clear whether he is proceeding under section 6 of the 2002 Act (within section 14(1)(a)), in which case the power to order a statement of information under section 16 will be triggered,

or he is postponing proceedings under section 6, in which case the power to
proceed to sentence will be triggered, see *CPS, Swansea v. Gilleeney and
Gilleeney* [2009] Crim.L.R. 455, CA.

Inadequacy of available amount: variation of order

On an application by the defendant, under section 23 of the *PCA* 2002, for   **★5–584**
a confiscation order to be varied on account of the inadequacy of the available amount, it was not open to the defendant to challenge a finding of the
Crown Court when making the original order that he had hidden assets: *R.
v. Younis* [2009] 2 Cr.App.R.(S.) 34, CA.

See also *Escobar v. DPP, ante,* § 5–454, a decision in relation to the *CJA*
1988.

Restraint orders

In *Re B. (Restraint Order)* [2009] 1 Cr.App.R. 14, CA, it was said that before   **★5–602**
making a restraint order under section 41 of the 2002 Act, section 40(2) (§ 5–
601 in the main work) requires a judge to be satisfied that a criminal investigation has been started in regard to an offence and that there is reasonable
cause to believe that the alleged offender has benefited from criminal conduct
(as defined in s.76(1) (§ 5–637 in the main work)). In addition, the court said
that the judge must be satisfied that there is a real as opposed to a fanciful
risk that, if the order is not made, the assets in respect of which the order is
requested are liable to be dissipated. Since a restraint order is an interference
with the right to peaceful enjoyment of one's possessions under Article 1 of
the First Protocol to the ECHR, there can be no justification for such restraint
unless such a risk exists. The court stated that further authority for this proposition can be found in section 69(2)(a) (§ 5–630 in the main work), which
requires that the power to make a restraint order must be exercised with a
view to the value for the time being of realisable property being made available for satisfying any confiscation order, and also in *Jennings v. CPS* [2008] 1
A.C. 1046, HL (at [60], [65]). *Jennings* was also said to be authority for the
proposition (at [55]) that the prosecution may be entitled to rely as a feature
tending towards proof of a risk of dissipation on the very fact of the dishonesty which has founded the reasonable cause to believe that the applicant had
benefited from his criminal conduct. Where, however, the appellant had had
ample opportunity to dissipate his assets, but had not done so, and indeed
had actually disclosed the existence of further assets that the prosecution had
not been aware of, the court held that it was incumbent on both the prosecution and the judge to explain how it could be said that there was a real risk
that he would dissipate his assets when he had had every opportunity to do so
in the past. The making of a restraint order can have serious personal and
professional consequences on the citizen concerned and it is therefore
important to see that there are good reasons and a proper basis for making
such an order, particularly where the citizen has not been charged. The fact
that such applications must be dealt with without a hearing unless the Crown
Court orders otherwise (in accordance with rule 61.3 of the *Criminal Procedure Rules* 2005 (S.I. 2005 No. 384) (§ 5–712 in the main work)) does not in
any way obviate the need for careful scrutiny by the court of an *ex parte* application lest rights enshrined in the European human rights legislation be
infringed.

Where a firm of solicitors was instructed by its client to advise and act for
him in connection with a Revenue and Customs investigation, where he paid
money to the firm on account of their fees, where a restraint order (under the

2002 Act, s.41) was subsequently made against him preventing him from disposing of, or dealing with, or diminishing the value of, any of his assets and where, by the time the firm received notice of the order, their fees exceeded the amount paid on account, the restraint order did not prevent the firm, once it had complied with rule 19(2) of the Solicitors' Accounts Rules 1998 ("A solicitor who properly requires payment of his or her fees from money held for the client ... in a client account must first give or send a bill of costs, or other written notification of the costs incurred, to the client ..."), from transferring the money from the client account to the firm's office account in satisfaction of their fees, nor was it necessary for the firm to apply for a variation of the restraint order because, (i) the funds did not constitute "realisable property" (defined in the 2002 Act, s.83 (§ 5–644 in the main work) of the client within the scope of section 41, and, in any event, (ii) whereas a line of authority has established that where there is a restraint order, a third party may lay itself open to a charge of contempt in one of two ways, the firm here would neither be acting in contempt of court by aiding or abetting the client to act in breach of the restraint order, nor, independently, by deliberately interfering with the course of justice by frustrating the purposes for which the order was made; *as to (i),* as between the client and the firm there was both a contractual and fiduciary relationship; the funds placed by the client with the firm were subject to a trust (*Twinsectra Ltd v. Yardley* [2002] 2 A.C. 164, HL), with the terms of the contract determining the scope of the firm's fiduciary obligations (*viz.* to hold the sum paid on account on trust for the client until they had earned fees to that amount); as the remuneration to which the firm was entitled grew, so, however, the client's beneficial interest diminished; once the firm was entitled to payment of that sum in full, the client's interest in the relevant account became literally nominal and therefore constituted neither "property" (as defined in s.84 (§ 5–645 in the main work) nor, consequently, "realisable property" for the purposes of section 41; *as to (ii),* the purpose of the restraint order was to preserve the value and accessibility of assets held by the defendant for satisfying a confiscation order, not to prevent third parties from enforcing civil rights against a defendant if those rights would be unaffected by any order which may be made against the defendant at the end of the proceedings; here, the firm had a contractual right to payment of the fees, for which the money on account was paid, and, given that the money in the client account would not be used to satisfy any future confiscation order against the client because of the security of the solicitor's lien over those amounts, utilising the fund in payment of the firm's fees would neither breach the restraint order by depleting the true value of the client's assets nor frustrate its purpose: *Irwin Mitchell v. Revenue and Customs Prosecutions Office* [2009] 1 Cr.App.R. 22, CA.

★   In *Re M. (Restraint order: Reasonable living expenses), The Times,* June 16, 2009, CA, it was held that section 41(3) of the 2002 Act makes a distinction between living expenses and legal expenses, so that if an expense falls within the definition of the latter it cannot also fall within the definition of the former; and that, on any reasonable construction, a contribution to the Legal Services Commission as a condition of the grant of legal aid to institute judicial review proceedings in connection with an offence in respect of which a restraint order has been made is not an "ordinary living expense" within the standard-form wording of an exception to a restraint order, nor is it a "reasonable living expense" for the purposes of section 41; instead, it is a legal expense; and the payment of such a contribution out of an amount allowed for "ordinary living expenses" would therefore be in breach of a restraint order. In addition, the court said that a judge who discovered that such a contribution was being made would be likely to vary the restraint order so as to impose a condition that such contribution should not be made (because the payment would indicate that the subject of the order was being allowed too much money out of the restrained assets for his living expenses) if indeed he was not bound to do so by the terms of section 41(4) and 69 (powers of court and receiver (§ 5–630 in the main work)).

Free property

As from June 18, 2009 (*Counter-Terrorism Act 2008 (Commencement No. 3) Order* 2009 (S.I. 2009 No. 1256)), ", 23A" is inserted after "section 23" in section 82(e) of the 2002 Act: *Counter-Terrorism Act* 2008, s.39, and Sched. 3, para. 7(1).   ★5–643

(b) *Subordinate legislation*

Commmencement

Proceeds of Crime Act 2002 (Commencement No. 5, Transitional Provisions, Savings and Amendment) Order 2003 (S.I. 2003 No. 333)

Citation and interpretation

1.—(1) [*Citation.*]   **5–663**

(2) In this Order, "the Act" means the *Proceeds of Crime Act* 2002.

(3) Where an offence is found to have been committed over a period of two or more days, or at some time during a period of two or more days, it shall be taken for the purposes of this Order to have been committed on the earliest of those days.

Commencement of provisions

2.—(1) The provisions of the Act listed in column 1 of the Schedule to this Order shall come into force on 24th March 2003, subject to the transitional provisions and savings contained in this Order.   **5–664**

(2) But where a particular purpose is specified in relation to any such provision in column 2 of that Schedule, the provision concerned shall come into force only for that purpose.

Transitional provisions relating to confiscation orders—England and Wales

3.—(1) Section 6 of the Act (making of confiscation order) shall not have effect where the offence, or any of the offences, mentioned in section 6(2) was committed before 24th March 2003.   **5–665**

(2) Section 27 of the Act (defendant convicted or committed absconds) shall not have effect where the offence, or any of the offences, mentioned in section 27(2) was committed before 24th March 2003.

(3) Section 28 of the Act (defendant neither convicted nor acquitted absconds) shall not have effect where the offence, or any of the offences, in respect of which proceedings have been started but not concluded was committed before 24th March 2003.

4. [*Transitional provisions relating to confiscation orders—Northern Ireland*]

It was held in *R. v. Moulden* [2009] 1 Cr.App.R. 27, CA, that where the respondent appeared before the Crown Court to be dealt with in respect of two indictments, one alleging offences committed before March 24, 2003, and the other alleging offences committed after that date, each indictment represented a separate set of "proceedings" for the purposes of section 6(2)(a) of the 2002 Act (see § 5–566 in the main work) and accordingly, by virtue of article 3(1), the 2002 Act had no application to the pre-March 24, 2003, indictment, but did apply to the post-March 24, 2003, indictment. The judge had, therefore, been correct to apply the confiscation provisions of the *CJA* 1988 to the one indictment and the confiscation provisions of the 2002 Act to the other indictment, and to reject the prosecution submission that the effect of these provisions was to disapply the 2002 Act in relation to both indictments, thereby triggering the assumptions provided for by section 72AA of the 1988 Act.

Transitional provisions relating to restraint orders and enforcement abroad—England and Wales

5–666   **5.** Sections 41 (restraint orders) and 74 (enforcement abroad) of the Act shall not have effect where—

(a) the powers in those sections would otherwise be exercisable by virtue of a condition in section 40(2) or (3) of the Act being satisfied; and

(b) the offence mentioned in section 40(2)(a) or 40(3)(a), as the case may be, was committed before 24th March 2003.

6. [*Transitional provisions relating to restraint orders and enforcement abroad—Northern Ireland.*]

Transitional provisions relating to criminal lifestyle—England and Wales

5–667   **7.**—(1) This article applies where the court is determining under section 6(4)(a) of the Act whether the defendant has a criminal lifestyle.

(2) Conduct shall not form part of a course of criminal activity under section 75(3)(a) of the Act where any of the three or more offences mentioned in section 75(3)(a) was committed before 24th March 2003.

(3) Where the court is applying the rule in section 75(5) of the Act on the calculation of relevant benefit for the purposes of determining whether or not the test in section 75(2)(b) of the Act is satisfied by virtue of conduct forming part of a course of criminal activity under section 75(3)(a) of the Act, the court must not take into account benefit from conduct constituting an offence mentioned in section 75(5)(c) of the Act which was committed before 24th March 2003.

(4) Conduct shall form part of a course of criminal activity under section 75(3)(b) of the Act, notwithstanding that any of the offences of which the defendant was convicted on at least two separate occasions in the period mentioned in section 75(3)(b) were committed before 24th March 2003.

(5) Where the court is applying the rule in section 75(5) of the Act on the calculation of relevant benefit for the purposes of determining whether or not the test in section 75(2)(b) of the Act is satisfied by virtue of conduct forming part of a course of criminal activity under section 75(3)(b) of the Act, the court may take into account benefit from conduct constituting an offence committed before 24th March 2003.

(6) Where the court is applying the rule in section 75(6) of the Act on the calculation of relevant benefit for the purposes of determining whether or not the test in section 75(2)(c) of the Act is satisfied, the court must not take into account benefit from conduct constituting an offence mentioned in section 75(6)(b) of the Act which was committed before 24th March 2003.

[This article is printed as substituted by the *Proceeds of Crime Act 2002 (Commencement No. 5) (Amendment of Transitional Provisions) Order* 2003 (S.I. 2003 No. 531).]

8. [*Transitional provisions relating to criminal lifestyle—Northern Ireland.*]

Transitional provisions relating to particular criminal conduct

5–668   **9.** Conduct which constitutes an offence which was committed before 24th

118

March 2003 is not particular criminal conduct under section 76(3) or 224(3) of the Act.

Savings for England and Wales

10.—(1) Where, under article 3 or 5, a provision of the Act does not have effect, **5-669** the following provisions shall continue to have effect—

    (a) sections 71 to 89 (including Schedule 4) and 102 of the *Criminal Justice Act* 1988;

    (b) paragraphs 83 and 84 of Schedule 17 to the *Housing Act* 1988;

    (c) sections 21(3)(e) to (g), 27, 28 and 34 of the *Criminal Justice Act* 1993;

    (d) paragraph 36 of Schedule 9 to the *Criminal Justice and Public Order Act* 1994;

    (e) sections 1 to 36 and 41 of the *Drug Trafficking Act* 1994;

    (f) sections 1 to 10, 15(1) and (3) (including Schedule 1), 16(2), (5) and (6) of the *Proceeds of Crime Act* 1995;

    (g) section 4(3) of the *Private International Law (Miscellaneous Provisions) Act* 1995;

    (h) sections 35 to 38 of the *Proceeds of Crime (Scotland) Act* 1995;

    (i) the *Proceeds of Crime (Enforcement of Confiscation Orders made in England and Wales or Scotland) Order (Northern Ireland) 1997* and the *Proceeds of Crime (Northern Ireland) Order* 1996, so far as necessary for the continued operation of the Proceeds of Crime (Enforcement of Confiscation Orders made in England and Wales or Scotland) Order (Northern Ireland) 1997;

    (j) paragraphs 23 and 36 of Schedule 5 to the *Justices of the Peace Act* 1997;

    (k) section 83 of, paragraph 114 of Schedule 8 to and paragraph 8 of Schedule 9 to the *Crime and Disorder Act* 1998;

    (l) paragraphs 139 and 172 of Schedule 13 to the *Access to Justice Act* 1999;

    (m) paragraphs 105 to 113 and 163 to 173 of Schedule 9 to the *Powers of Criminal Courts (Sentencing) Act* 2000;

    (n) paragraphs 6(1) to (3) and 10 of Schedule 15 to the *Terrorism Act* 2000.

(2) Where under article 3 or 5, a provision of the Act does not have effect, the following provisions shall continue to have effect as if they had not been amended by Schedule 11 to the Act—

    (a) section 13(6) of the *Criminal Justice (International Co-operation) Act* 1990;

    (b) paragraph 17(3) of Schedule 8 to the *Terrorism Act* 2000.

11. [*Savings for Northern Ireland.*]

12. [*Savings for enforcement of Scottish orders in England, Wales and Northern Ireland.*]

13. [*Savings in relation to external orders.*]

14. [*Amendment of arts 3 and 5 of S.I. 2003 No. 120, post, §§ 26–4 et seq.*]

Article 2   THE SCHEDULE

Column 1	Column 2	**5-670**
Part 2 (sections 6 to 91, including Schedule 2) (Confiscation: England and Wales).	So far as not already in force.	
Part 4 (sections 156 to 239, including Schedule 5) (Confiscation: Northern Ireland).		
Part 9 (sections 417 to 434) (Insolvency etc.).		
Part 10 (sections 435 to 442) (Information).	So far as not already in force.	
Section 444 (External requests and orders).		

Column 1	Column 2
Section 445 (External investigations).	
Section 447 (Interpretation).	
Section 456 (Amendments).	Commenced for the purposes of the provisions of Schedule 11 to the Act commenced by this Order.
Section 457 (Repeals).	Commenced for the purposes of the provisions of Schedule 12 to the Act commenced by this Order.
In Schedule 11, paragraphs 1, 4, 5, 7, 8, 9, 11, 14(2) and (3), 15, 16, 17(2), (4) and (6), 19(2) and (3), 20, 21, 25(2)(a) and (h) to (j), 26, 27, 28(1) and (2)(e) and (g), 31(2) and (3)(a) to (c), 32, 37 and 39.	Paragraphs 7, 11, 15, 16, 20, 21 and 39 are commenced except to the extent that they relate to Part 3 of the Act. Paragraph 17(2) is commenced so far as it repeals sections 71 to 89, 94 and 99 to 102 of the *Criminal Justice Act* 1988. Paragraph 25(2)(a) is commenced so far as it repeals sections 1 to 38 and 41 of the *Drug Trafficking Act* 1994. Paragraph 27 is commenced so far as not already in force. Paragraph 31(2) is commenced so far as it repeals articles 4 to 41 of the *Proceeds of Crime (Northern Ireland) Order* 1996.
In Schedule 12, the following entries; the entry relating to the *Criminal Appeal (Northern Ireland) Act* 1980; the entry relating to the *Police and Criminal Evidence Act* 1984; the entry relating to the *Criminal Justice Act* 1988; the entry relating to the *Housing Act* 1988; the entry relating to the *Police and Criminal Evidence (Northern Ireland) Order* 1989; in the entry relating to the *Criminal Justice (International Co-operation) Act* 1990, the entry in the second column concerning section 13 of that Act; the entry relating to the *Criminal Justice (Confiscation) (Northern Ireland) Order* 1990; the entry relating to the *Criminal Justice Act* 1993; the entry relating to the *Drug Trafficking Act* 1994; the entry relating to the *Proceeds of Crime Act* 1995; in the entry relating to the *Criminal Procedure (Consequential Provisions) (Scotland) Act* 1995, the entry in the second column concerning Schedule 4 of that Act; the entry relating to the *Private International Law (Miscellaneous Provisions) Act* 1995; in the entry relating to the *Proceeds of Crime (Scotland) Act* 1995, the entry in the second column concerning sections 35 to 39 of that Act, the entry in the second column concerning section 40 of that Act and the entry in the second column concerning section 42 of that Act; the entry relating to the *Proceeds of Crime (Northern Ireland) Order* 1996; the entry relating to the *Justices of the Peace Act* 1997; in the entry relating to the *Crime*	second column concerning section 83 of that Act, the entry in the second column concerning The entry relating to sections 71 to 102 of the *Criminal Justice Act* 1988 is commenced so far as it repeals sections 71 to 89, 94 and 99 to 102 of that Act. The entries relating to the *Criminal Justice Act* 1993, the *Proceeds of Crime Act* 1995 and the *Access to Justice Act* 1999 are commenced so far as not already in force. The entry relating to sections 1 to 54 of the *Drug Trafficking Act* 1994 is commenced so far as it repeals sections 1 to 38 and 41 of that Act. The entry relating to Parts II and III of the *Proceeds of Crime (Northern Ireland) Order* 1996 is commenced so far as it repeals articles 4 to 41 of that Order. The entry relating to the *Terrorism Act* 2000 is commenced so far as it repeals paragraphs 6 and 10 of Schedule 15 to that Act.

Column 1

and Disorder Act 1998, the entry in the
Schedule 8 of that Act and the entry in
the second column concerning Schedule
9 of that Act; the entry relating to the
Access to Justice Act 1999; the entry relating to the *Powers of Criminal Courts
(Sentencing) Act* 2000; the entry relating
to the *Terrorism Act* 2000; and the entry
relating to the *Criminal Justice and Police
Act* 2001.

Column 2

(3) Authorities

Lack of discretion/abuse of process

R. v. Farquhar is now reported at [2008] 2 Cr.App.R.(S.) 104.

R. v. Morgan; *R. v. Bygrave* is now reported at [2008] 4 All E.R. 890.

R. v. Shabir is now reported at [2009] 1 Cr.App.R.(S.) 84.

As to the extremely limited scope of the jurisdiction to stay confiscation
proceedings as an abuse, see *R. v. Lowe* [2009] Crim.L.R. 452, CA.

5–767a

★

Factual basis for making order

It was held in *R. v. Sangha* [2009] 2 Cr.App.R.(S.) 17, CA, that whilst, when
making a confiscation order, a judge must act consistently with the jury's
verdict and the verdict's factual basis, it is nevertheless open to him, in the
light of the evidence as a whole (including any evidence given in the confiscation proceedings), to make additional and more extensive findings of fact than
those upon which the verdict was based and, where other misconduct is relevant, to consider evidence of that other misconduct, even where the
misconduct amounts to a criminal offence. Such a conclusion was not
precluded by the principle in *R. v. Canavan*; *R. v. Kidd*; *R. v. Shaw* (§ 5–68 in
the main work), *viz.* that the sentence of the court should be based solely on
the offences proved or admitted, which, as was identified in *R. v. Considine*; *R.
v. Davis* (see § 5–306 in the main work), in respect of the dangerous offender
provisions, is a principle that has important limits.

As to the making of factual assumptions, see § 5–773 in the main work.

As to the extent to which a judge must conduct a confiscation hearing in accordance with a written basis of plea, see *R. v. Lazarus* (§ 5–73 in the main
work).

5–767b

General approach

R. v. May is now reported at [2008] 1 A.C. 1028.

R. v. Newman is now reported at [2009] 1 Cr.App.R.(S.) 12.

R. v. Sivaraman is now reported at [2009] 1 Cr.App.R.(S.) 80.

Whilst what was said by the House of Lords in *R. v. May* (see the main
work) about the approach to be taken to the confiscation legislation may
technically have been *obiter* to the extent that it applied to the *PCA* 2002,
there could be no doubt that it was intended to apply as much to the 2002
Act as to the *CJA* 1988 and the *DTA* 1994: *R. v. Allpress* [2009] Crim.L.R.
363, CA. Applying that guidance in relation to the case of a person who acts

5–768

as a mere courier or custodian of criminal property, such a person does not "obtain" the property which he is delivering or minding within the meaning of the 2002 Act, nor does it constitute a "payment or other reward" within the 1994 Act; the courier or minder does not obtain ownership of the property which he is charged with delivering or minding, nor does he obtain a right to possession of the property within section 84(2)(h) of the 2002 Act (§ 5–645 in the main work), there being a significant difference between *de facto* possession and a right to possession; the fact that a bailee may maintain an action for the value of goods against a third party who wrongly interferes with his possession is far removed from the question of whether a mere custodian has a right to possession so as to have an interest in the property for the purposes of section 84(2). The court added that there still seemed to be two common misconceptions about the confiscation legislation, the first being that in assessing benefit in a conspiracy case each conspirator is to be taken as having jointly obtained the whole benefit obtained by the conspiracy, and the second being that anybody who has taken part in a conspiracy in more than a minor way is to be taken as having a joint share in all benefits obtained from the conspiracy.

Benefit

Property

5–769　　*R. v. Green* is now reported at [2008] 1 A.C. 1053.

Jennings v. CPS is now reported at [2008] 1 A.C. 1046.

As to whether a courier or minder "obtains" the property that he is charged with delivering or minding, see *R. v. Allpress, ante,* § 5–768.

★**5–770**　　*R. v. Abijade* (see the main work) was effectively overruled by the House of Lords in *R. v. Islam, The Times,* June 12, 2009. Their Lordships held (by a majority of 3:2) that it is consistent with both the language and spirit of the statutory confiscation scheme under the *PCA* 2002 to take account of the black market value of illegally-imported drugs when assessing the "recoverable amount" for the purposes of section 7(1) (§ 5–567 in the main work), but to leave that value out of account when calculating (in accordance with s.9) the "available amount" for the purposes of section 7(2); section 79 (*ibid.,* § 5–640) applies for the purpose of deciding the value at any time of property then held by a person, and provides (subs. (2)) that "its value is the market value of the property at that time"; to take account of black market value when calculating an offender's benefit (*i.e.* the value of the property obtained by him as a result of or in connection with his offending) but to leave it out of account when calculating the available amount is not to ascribe different meanings to "market value" within the same statute, but to recognise that at the time the offender obtains the property it may have a value to him because it can be sold, albeit only on the black market, whereas at the time of calculating the available amount, the drugs will not be available to him and could not possibly be sold with a view to raising cash to meet a confiscation order.

5–771　　*R. v. Waller* is now reported at [2009] 1 Cr.App.R.(S.) 76.

Pecuniary advantage

★**5–772**　　*R. v. Rowbotham* (see the main work) and other cases involving the smuggling of tobacco are currently (as at June 20, 2009) under review: see *R. v. Khan, Lockett and Carrington, The Times,* April 23, 2009, CA.

★　　In *R. v. Carter, Kulish (Viktoriya), Kulish (Ruslan) and Lyashkov,* unreported,

February 6, 2006, CA ([2006] EWCA Crim. 416), the court was concerned
with the *CJA* 1988, s.71(4) and (5) (in materially identical terms to s.76(4)
and (5) of the 2002 Act (§ 5–637 in the main work)). It was held that where
a person was convicted of obtaining a pecuniary advantage, *viz.* the opportunity to earn remuneration, by deception (*i.e.* that he was lawfully entitled
to work in this country), contrary to the *Theft Act* 1968, s.16(2)(c) (*rep.*), his
benefit was the full value of the wages paid to him. The question formulated
in *R. v. King and Stockwell* [1987] Q.B. 547, CA (in respect of obtaining property by deception), applied equally to section 71(4), so that the relevant question for the purposes of that subsection was "Was the deception an operative
cause of the obtaining of benefit?" Thus, the court found that where an opportunity to work had been obtained by a false representation, the false representation continued thereafter for the benefit of the offender who, by
permitting the representation to continue, was able to retain his employment.
Accordingly, the deception had been an operative cause of the obtaining of
the wages, and the wages could properly be regarded as having been obtained
by the deception so as to constitute the defendant's "benefit". For criticism of
this decision, see *Criminal Law Week* 2009/09/09/4.

Assumptions to be made in case of a criminal lifestyle
    In *R. v. Winters, The Times,* January 12, 2009, CA, it was held that to trigger   **5–773**
section 4(3)(b) ("(3) The required assumptions are— ... (b) that any expenditure of [the defendant's] since the beginning of that period was met out of
payments received by him in connection with drug trafficking carried on by
him; ... .") of the *DTA* 1994 (which closely corresponds to the *PCA* 2002,
s.10(4) (§ 5–570 in the main work)), the prosecution must prove to the civil
standard that the expenditure in question was incurred by the defendant.
Prima facie evidence of expenditure by the defendant since the beginning
of the relevant period is insufficient.

"Realisable property" (s.83) and "property" (s.84)

    Telli v. Revenue and Customs Prosecutions Office is now reported at [2008] 2   **5–775**
Cr.App.R.(S.) 48.
    Gibson v. Revenue and Customs Prosecutions Office is now reported at [2008] 2
F.L.R. 1672.
    In *R. v. Summers* [2008] 2 Cr.App.R.(S.) 101, CA, the court was concerned
with the provisions of the *CJA* 1988, as amended by the *PCA* 1995, but there
is no doubt that its conclusions apply equally to the 2002 Act. It was held
that the burden of establishing that the realisable amount is less than the
defendant's assessed benefit, so as to justify a lower figure for the confiscation order, is for the defendant to discharge on the balance of probabilities,
and would only be discharged by clear and cogent evidence. No distinction
was to be drawn when applying this principle as between the situation
where the defendant was unable to show what had become of some or all of
the proceeds of his criminal conduct and that in which it was asserted that
he had other undisclosed assets available to satisfy the confiscation order
that were not derived from his particular criminal conduct. The suggestion
that in the latter case, it was for the prosecution to adduce evidence as to
the amount and availability of such hidden assets was misconceived; it was
for the defendant to establish that he had no such assets. The court
observed, however, that the judgment of a judge at first instance would be
defective if it did not indicate "even if briefly" how the figures for benefit
and realisable assets were arrived at.

Procedure

★5–777   As to the need for the Crown Court to set out all its relevant findings of fact in its rulings, including any facts agreed before it: *R. v. Lowe* [2009] Crim.L.R. 452, CA.

X. *DISQUALIFICATION, RESTRICTION, EXCLUSION, ETC., ORDERS*

A. Banning Orders Under the Football Spectators Act 1989

Banning orders made on conviction of an offence

5–825   *R. (White) v. Crown Court at Blackfriars* is also reported at [2008] 2 Cr.App.R.(S.) 97, *sub nom. R. (White) v. Blackfriars Crown Court.*

Banning orders: general

5–829   *R. (White) v. Crown Court at Blackfriars* is also reported at [2008] 2 Cr.App.R.(S.) 97, *sub nom. R. (White) v. Blackfriars Crown Court.*

Football Spectators Act 1989, Sched. 1

5–839   *DPP v. Beaumont; DPP v. Dowling* is also reported at [2008] 1 W.L.R. 2186, *sub nom. DPP v. Beaumont.*

D. Disqualification from Driving

(2) Notes on disqualification from driving (s.146)

★5–846   In *R. v. Sofekun* [2009] 1 Cr.App.R.(S.) 78, CA, the court held that it is plain from the terms of section 146 of the *PCC(S)A* 2000 (see § 5–844 in the main work) and the decision in *R. v. Cliff* (see the main work), that the power conferred by section 146 is an additional punitive power, available to the court whether or not the defendant has committed a driving-related offence. The section makes disqualification available as part of the overall penalty and *Cliff* should not be taken to have created any restrictions on the exercise of the power, which cannot otherwise be found in the statutory provision itself.

(2) Notes on disqualification from driving (s.147)

★5–847   In *Sofekun* (*ante*, § 5–846), it was held that a car was undoubtedly being used for the purpose of "committing or facilitating" the offence of possession of cannabis with intent to supply within section 147 of the 2000 Act (§ 5–845 in the main work), where 58 bags each containing herbal cannabis were found in the offender's possession and where 30 of those bags were secreted in his car. The car was akin to a small mobile shop or warehouse.

F. Disqualification or Being Barred from Working with
Children or Vulnerable Adults

(2) Legislation

Criminal Justice and Court Services Act 2000, ss.26–31

Equivalent armed forces offences

The amendment of section 27 of the 2000 *Act* effected by the *AFA* 2006   **★5–856**
comes into force on October 31, 2009: *Armed Forces Act 2006 (Commencement
No. 5) Order* 2009 (S.I. 2009 No. 1167).

Sections 28 to 29B: supplemental

The amendment of section 30 of the 2000 Act effected by the *AFA* 2006   **★5–861**
comes into force on October 31, 2009: *Armed Forces Act 2006 (Commencement
No. 5) Order* 2009 (S.I. 2009 No. 1167).

Appeals

The amendment of section 31 of the 2000 Act effected by the *AFA* 2006   **★5–862**
comes into force on October 31, 2009: *Armed Forces Act 2006 (Commencement
No. 5) Order* 2009 (S.I. 2009 No. 1167).

Criminal Justice and Court Services Act 2000, s.42

Equivalent armed forces offences

The amendment of section 42 of the 2000 Act effected by the *AFA* 2006   **★5–863**
comes into force on October 31, 2009: *Armed Forces Act 2006 (Commencement
No. 5) Order* 2009 (S.I. 2009 No. 1167).

(4) Bars on working with children or vulnerable adults

The *Safeguarding Vulnerable Groups Act 2006 (Prescribed Criteria) (Foreign*   **5–865b**
Offences) Order 2008 (S.I. 2008 No. 3050) amends paragraph 24 of Schedule 3
to the 2006 Act to enable the Secretary of State to prescribe "foreign offences"
for the purposes of paragraphs 1, 2, 7 and 8 of that schedule. The conduct
which constitutes the offence must be such as to amount to an offence under
the law of England and Wales. Paragraph 25 is amended, in consequence, to
stipulate that it only applies to convictions by or before a court in England
and Wales.

The *Safeguarding Vulnerable Groups Act 2006 (Commencement No. 3) Order*
2009 (S.I. 2009 No. 39) brought various provisions of the Act into force on
January 20, 2009. Critical to the functions of the criminal courts was the commencement on this date of paragraph 25 of Schedule 3. The effect (see the
main work) is that where a person is convicted of a specified offence on or after that day, the court is obliged to inform him that the Independent Barring
Board will include him in the relevant list or lists. The specified offences are
to be found in the schedule to the *Safeguarding Vulnerable Groups Act 2006
(Prescribed Criteria and Miscellaneous Provisions) Regulations* 2009 (S.I. 2009
No. 37). There are four paragraphs to the schedule and they list respectively
offences which will result in automatic inclusion in the children's list with no
right to make representations, inclusion in the children's list with the right to
make representations, automatic inclusion in the adults' list with no right to
make representations and inclusion in the adults' list with a right to make

representations. The lists are extremely long, in consequence of which, Scottish offences, Northern Irish offences and armed forces offences have been omitted from the following summary of the listed offences.

List 1: (a) if committed against, or in respect of a child, offences contrary to the *SOA* 1956, s.1, the *MHA* 1959, s.128, or the *SOA* 2003, s.1, 2 or 30 to 41; (b) offences contrary to the 1956 Act, s.5, or the 2003 Act, ss.5 to 8.

List 2: (a) murder and kidnapping; (b) if the offence was committed against, or in respect of an adult, offences contrary to the 1956 Act, s.1, or the 2003 Act, s.1, 2 or 30 to 41; (c) if committed against a child, offences contrary to the 1956 Act, s.10 or 11; (d) if the person with whom the offence was committed was under the age of 16 or did not consent, the offences contrary to the 1956 Act, s.12 or 13; (e) an offence contrary to the *Misuse of Drugs Act* 1971, s.4(3), if the person to whom the drugs were supplied or offered was a child; (f) an offence contrary to the *CEMA* 1979, s.170, where the prohibition on importation breached was that established by the *Customs Consolidation Act* 1876, s.42; (g) offences contrary to section 62 or 63 of the 2003 Act where the relevant sexual offence was one specified in this schedule and was intended to be committed in relevant circumstances, if any, specified in the schedule in relation to that offence; (h) the offences contrary to section 66 or 67 of the 2003 Act if committed against a child under 16; and (i) offences contrary to the *Offences against the Person Act* 1861, s.21, the *CYPA* 1933, s.1, the *Infanticide Act* 1938, s.1, the 1956 Act, s.2 to 4, 6, 7, 9, 14 to 17 or 19 to 31, the *MHA* 1959, s.128, the *Indecency with Children Act* 1960, s.1, the *SOA* 1967, s.4 or 5, the *Theft Act* 1968, s.9(1)(a), the *CLA* 1977, s.54, the *Protection of Children Act* 1978, s.1, the *MHA* 1983, ss.126 to 129, the *Child Abduction Act* 1984, s.1, 2 or 6, the *CJA* 1988, s.160, the *Sexual Offences (Amendment) Act* 2000, s.3, the *Nationality, Immigration and Asylum Act* 2002, s.145, the 2003 Act, s.3, 4, 9 to 12, 14 to 20, 25, 26, 47 to 50, 52, 53, 57 to 59 or 61, the *Asylum and Immigration Act* 2004, s.4, the *Domestic Violence, Crime and Victims Act* 2004, s.5, the *Mental Capacity Act* 2005, s.44.

List 3: offences contrary to the 2003 Act, ss.30 to 41.

List 4: (a) murder and kidnapping; (b) if the offence was committed against a child, an offence contrary to the 1956 Act, s.1 or the 2003 Act, s.1; (c) if committed against a child or the other party did not consent, offences contrary to the 1956 Act, s.10 or 11; (d) if the person with whom the offence was committed was under the age of 16 or did not consent, the offences contrary to the 1956 Act, s.12 or 13; (e) & (f) as List 2; and (g) as (i) in List 2, plus the offences contrary to section 5 of the 1956 Act and sections 2, 5 to 8, 62, 63, 66 and 67 of the 2003 Act.

As to this legislation, three points should be noted. First, judges should beware saying anything more to the defendant beyond the fact that as a result of the conviction he will be put on the relevant list by the board. Any more detailed explanation runs the risk of creating confusion. This may be illustrated by the fact that whilst a person convicted of a specified offence on or after the commencement date will be put on the barred list as a result thereof, he will not actually be barred from working with children or adults as a result of being included on that list until section 3 of the 2006 Act is commenced in full (currently anticipated for October, 2009). In the meantime, the person will be barred from working with children or adults, if at all, as a result of the continued operation of the current legislation, including, most significantly, for the criminal courts, sections 26 to 31 of the *CJCSA* 2000 (§§ 5–855 *et seq.* in the main work), the prospective repeal of which has not yet been brought into force.

Secondly, the board has apparently abandoned the name given to it by the statute, and has chosen to operate under the name of the Independent Safeguarding Authority instead.

Thirdly, the lists contain a series of anomalies (both as to what is included and as to what is excluded). As to these, see the commentary in *Criminal Law Week* 2009/04/12.

J. Anti-Social Behaviour Orders

Crime and Disorder Act 1998, s.1C

Orders on conviction in criminal proceedings

Sections 123 and 124 of, and Schedule 27, paras 33 and 34, to, the *CJIA* 2008 came into force on February 1, 2009: *Criminal Justice and Immigration Act 2008 (Commencement No. 6 and Transitional Provisions) Order* 2009 (S.I. 2009 No. 140). **5–880**

Crime and Disorder Act 1998, ss.1A, 1B

Individual support orders

Section 124 of, and Schedule 27, para. 34, to, the *CJIA* 2008 came into force on February 1, 2009: S.I. 2009 No. 140 (*ante*, § 5–880). **5–882**

Individual support orders: explanation, breach, amendment etc.

Section 124 of, and Schedule 27, para. 34, to, the *CJIA* 2008 came into force on February 1, 2009: S.I. 2009 No. 140 (*ante*, § 5–880). **5–883**

Authorities

Evidence and procedure

With reference to the discussion in the penultimate paragraph in the main work, the Criminal Procedure Rule Committee has now made rules (see §§ 5–886h *et seq.* in the main work). As to the status of these rules, however, see the discussion at § 5–886g in the main work. **5–884**

Necessity for, and ambit of, order

Where it was not disputed that the claimant had, with others, engaged in anti-social behaviour over a period of 13 months which had involved intimidation of the public through language and gestures, where he and the others wore hooded tops to conceal their identity, and where the lower court was satisfied that the inclusion in an anti-social behaviour order of a prohibition on wearing hooded tops would reduce the menace and fear of anti-social behaviour resulting from the group's swagger, it met the test for inclusion of such a condition, *viz.* it was clear, necessary and proportionate (*R. v. Boness* (see the main work)); the wearing of hooded clothing was in effect a uniform which both contributed to the menace and fear and increased the confidence of the group that they would not be identified: *R. (B.) v. Greenwich Magistrates' Court*, 173 J.P. 52, DC. **5–884a**

It was held in *R. (Cooke) v. DPP*, 172 J.P. 596, DC, that it would be wrong in law to make an anti-social behaviour order in respect of an offender who, by reason of mental incapacity, was truly incapable of understanding or complying with its terms, since such an order would be incapable of protecting the public (as required by s.1C(2)(b) of the 1998 Act (§ 5–880 in the main work)). However, the fact that an offender would be likely (but not bound) to breach an order because he was suffering from a personality disorder was not of itself a good reason for not making an order where he did have the capacity to understand its terms and what behaviour it prohibited. Whether or not he had sufficient capacity to comply with an order's terms was a question of fact, to be decided on the basis of medical evidence from a psychiatrist.

Crime and Disorder Act 1998, ss.1CA, 1I

Variation and discharge of orders under section 1C

5–885   There is no right of appeal to the Crown Court against a variation of an anti-social behaviour order made by a magistrates' court under section 1CA of the 1998 Act: *R. (Langley) v. Preston Crown Court (West Lancashire D.C. and Secretary of State for Justice (interested parties))*, 172 J.P. 605, DC (but expressing the *obiter* view that there would be a right of appeal to the Court of Appeal against a variation made by the Crown Court, as to which, see *post*, § 7–119).

Review of anti-social behaviour orders

5–885b   Section 123 of the *CJIA* 2008 came into force on February 1, 2009: S.I. 2009 No. 140 (*ante*, § 5–880).

K. FINANCIAL REPORTING ORDERS

(2) Legislation

Serious Organised Crime and Police Act 2005, ss.76–81

Financial reporting orders: making

5–886a   As to whether section 76 is retrospective and the right of appeal against such an order, see *R. v. Adams, post*, §§ 7–119, 16–100.

★   It was held in *R. v. Wright* [2009] 2 Cr.App.R.(S.) 45, CA, that, by virtue of section 76(2), where a person has been convicted of an offence specified in subsection (3), a financial reporting order may be made in respect of him if the risk of him committing another (but not necessarily the same) specified offence is sufficiently high to justify it. The court added that it is clear that, while not constituting the paradigm case for which the section was intended, such an order could be made in the case of a defendant sentenced to a long custodial sentence, particularly a career "master" criminal who would be able to use his "loyal acolytes" outside prison to manipulate, conceal and deploy his substantial hidden assets despite his status as a category A prisoner. However, it was also said that such an order should not be imposed for the purpose of facilitating the enforcement of a confiscation order. Judges asked to make such orders should give careful consideration as to whether such an order will achieve anything where there are alternative powers available to financial investigators which would have much the same effect.

XI. ORDERS UNDER THE MENTAL HEALTH ACT 1983

(1) Hospital and guardianship orders

Mental Health Act 1983, s.37

Power of courts to order hospital admission or guardianship

★5–894   In *R. (D.B.) v. Nottinghamshire Healthcare N.H.S. Trust; R. (X.) v. An N.H.S.*

Trust [2009] 2 All E.R. 792, CA (Civ. Div.), it was held that a hospital order under section 37 of the 1983 Act ceases to have effect if the offender who is the subject of the order is not admitted to the hospital named in the order within a period of 28 days from the date of the making of the order; section 40 (§ 5–895 in the main work) expressly limits the authority conferred by an order made under section 37 to the period of 28 days from the date of the making of the order; and it follows that once the period of 28 days has expired, not only will the hospital order cease to have effect, but also any authority therein to convey a patient to the hospital named or to detain the patient in that hospital will lapse. The court added that the following practical considerations should also be observed: (i) whilst the standard form of hospital order (annexed to the judgment) correctly reflects the provisions of the Act (as does Home Office Circular 66/1980), it is preferable that it should also specify the date when the 28-day period expires and include a direction or recommendation on the lines of that set out in the circular (*viz.* that "if at any time it appears to the person in whose custody the defendant is detained in a place of safety that the defendant might not be admitted to hospital in pursuance of the order within 28 days of this date [the date on which the order is made], that person shall within 21 days of this date (or at once if it becomes apparent only after 21 days that the defendant might not be admitted to hospital) report the circumstances to the chief clerk of the court and unless otherwise directed by the chief clerk shall bring the defendant before the court forthwith so as to enable it within 28 days of this date to make such order as may be necessary"); (ii) all parties should bear in mind the power of the court under the *PCC(S)A* 2000, s.155 (§ 5–940 in the main work) to vary or, if necessary, rescind an order, but rescission should be a last resort; and (iii) since the exercise by the sentencing court of the power conferred by section 37(4) to direct conveyance to and detention in a place of safety pending admission to hospital is not automatic or mandatory, the court should, unless the offender is to be immediately conveyed from the court to the hospital, ensure that the power is expressly exercised.

(2) Restriction orders

Mental Health Act 1983, s.41

Power of higher courts to restrict discharge from hospital

Section 41(3)(b) of the *MHA* 1983 has been amended so as to substitute the words "the appropriate tribunal" for the words "a Mental Health Review Tribunal": *Transfer of Tribunal Functions Order* 2008 (S.I. 2008 No. 2833).   **5–898**

(3) Hospital and limitation directions

Crime (Sentences) Act 1997, s.47

Power to specify hospital units

The amendment of section 47 of the 1997 Act effected by the *AFA* 2006 comes into force on October 31, 2009: *Armed Forces Act 2006 (Commencement No. 5) Order* 2009 (S.I. 2009 No. 1167).   **★5–909**

XII. RECOMMENDATION FOR DEPORTATION

Immigration Act 1971, Sched. 3

In paragraph 2(1) of Schedule 3 to the 1971 Act, the words "not detained" are substituted for the words "neither detained" and the words "nor for the   **5–914** time being released on bail by any court having power so to release him" are omitted: *Asylum and Treatment of Claimants, etc.) Act* 2004, s.34(1).

In paragraph 2(1) of Schedule 3 to the 1971 Act, the words "or he is released on bail" are inserted at the end: *Immigration and Asylum Act* 1999, s.54(1) and (2).

In paragraph 2(2) of Schedule 3 to the 1971 Act, the words "105 of the *Nationality, Immigration and Asylum Act* 2002 (notice of decision)" are substituted for the words "18 of this Act", the words "not detained" are substituted for the words "neither detained" and the words "nor for the time being released on bail by a court having power so to release him" are omitted: *Nationality, Immigration and Asylum Act* 2002, s.114(3), and Sched. 7, para. 7, and the *Asylum and Immigration (Treatment of Claimants, etc.) Act* 2004, s.34(2).

In paragraph 2(3) of Schedule 3 to the 1971 Act, the words "he is released on bail or" are inserted after the words "detained unless": *Immigration and Asylum Act* 1999, s.54(1) and (3).

In paragraph 2(4) of Schedule 3 to the 1971 Act, the words "; and for that purpose the reference in paragraph 17(1) to a person liable to detention includes a reference to a person who would be liable to detention upon receipt of a notice which is ready to be given to him" are inserted at the end: *Immigration, Asylum and Nationality Act* 2006, s.53.

A new paragraph 2(4A) of Schedule 3 to the 1971 Act has been inserted by the *Immigration and Asylum Act* 1999, s.54(1) and (4), as follows—

> "(4A) Paragraphs 22 to 25 of Schedule 2 to this Act apply in relation to a person detained under sub-paragraph (1), (2) or (3) as they apply in relation to a person detained under paragraph 16 of that Schedule.".

★ As to the proper interpretation of paragraph 2 of Schedule 3 to the 1971 Act, see *R. (Sedrati) v. Secretary of State for the Home Department* (§ 5–923 in the main work), and *Abdi, Ashori, Madani, Mighty and Lumba v. Secretary of State for the Home Department* [2009] A.C.D. 22, QBD (Davis J.).

A new paragraph 3 of Schedule 3 to the 1971 Act has been substituted by the *Nationality, Immigration and Asylum Act* 2002, s.114(3), and Sched. 7, para. 8, as follows—

> "3. So far as they relate to an appeal under section 82(1) of the *Nationality, Immigration and Asylum Act* 2002 against a decision of the kind referred to in section 82(2)(j) or (k) of that Act (decision to make deportation order and refusal to revoke deportation order), paragraphs 29 to 33 of Schedule 2 to this Act shall apply for the purposes of this Schedule as if the reference in paragraph 29(1) to Part I of that Schedule were a reference to this Schedule.".

In paragraph 5(2)(a) of Schedule 3 to the 1971 Act, the word "any" should be inserted before the word "such" where it appears for the second time.

Criteria for exercise of power to make recommendation

★5–919   The *Immigration (European Economic Area) Regulations* 2006 (S.I. 2006 No. 1003) have been amended by the *Immigration (European Economic Area) (Amendment) Regulations* 2009 (S.I. 2009 No. 1117). The amendments include amendments to regulation 19, but they do not affect the thrust of what is said in the main work.

Persons in breach of immigration laws

★5–921   In *R. v. Okhotnikov* [2009] 1 Cr.App.R.(S.) 33, CA, it was said, considering

R. v. Banabbas (see the main work), and its application of the *R. v. Nazari* guidance (§ 5–919 in the main work), that it was undoubtedly the case that involvement in the production and dissemination of false driving documents and passports to foreign nationals could be viewed as undermining the good order of society.

Recommendations for deportation were upheld in respect of offenders ★ convicted of keeping a brothel (*SOA* 1956, s.33A) in *R. v. Shi and Yang* [2009] 1 Cr.App.R.(S.) 82, CA. The court said that the offenders had been involved in a commercial enterprise that encouraged the influx of illegal immigrants and thrived on their exploitation, extracting substantial profit for the organisers.

XIV. ORDERS AGAINST PARENTS OR GUARDIANS

(3) Parenting orders

Crime and Disorder Act 1998, ss.8–10

Appeals against parenting orders

For the words "the High Court" wherever they occur in section 10 of the   ★**5–935** 1998 Act there are substituted the words "a county court ": *Access to Justice Act 1999 (Destination of Appeals) (Family Proceedings) Order* 2009 (S.I. 2009 No. 871).

XV. MISCELLANEOUS MATTERS

B. Alteration of Sentence

Powers of Criminal Courts (Sentencing) Act 2000, s.155

Alteration of Crown Court sentence

In addition to being repealed in part by Schedule 28, Pt 3, to the *CJIA*   **5–940** 2008, as noted in the main work, section 155 of the 2000 Act was further amended by the 2008 Act, s.47, and Sched. 8, para. 28, with effect from July 14, 2008 (*Criminal Justice and Immigration Act 2008 (Commencement No. 2 and Transitional and Saving Provisions) Order* 2008 (S.I. 2008 No. 1586)), so as (i) to substitute "56" for "28" in subsection (1), (ii) to omit the words "within the time allowed by that subsection" at the end of that subsection, and (iii) to insert a new subsection (1A), as follows—

> "(1A) The power conferred by subsection (1) may not be exercised in relation to any sentence or order if an appeal, or an application for leave to appeal, against that sentence or order has been determined.".

Variation after expiration of relevant time limit

The sort of formal variation contemplated by *R. v. Saville* and *R. v. Norman*   ★**5–943** (see the main work) did not extend to the substitution of a confiscation order under the *PCA* 2002 where the original order had been erroneously made under the *CJA* 1988: *R. v. Bukhari* [2009] 2 Cr.App.R.(S.) 18, CA.

CHAPTER 6

COSTS AND CRIMINAL DEFENCE SERVICE

I. COSTS

B. PROSECUTION OF OFFENCES ACT 1985

(1) **Awards out of central funds**

(a) *Defence costs*

Principles governing exercise of discretion

6–14   Where a prosecution was stayed as an abuse of process, a court had been in error in refusing to make a defendant's costs order on the ground that the defendant had by his conduct brought the prosecution on itself where the prosecution's failure that had led to the grant of the stay was wholly unrelated to the conduct of the defendant: *R.E. Williams & Sons (Wholesale) Ltd v. Hereford Magistrates' Court*, 172 J.P. 571, DC (although it should be noted that the court did not hear full argument).

★   A refusal to make a defendant's costs order in favour of an acquitted defendant could not be justified on the ground that he (i) had accepted a caution and thus brought suspicion on himself (*Dowler v. Merseyrail*, unreported, March 4, 2009, DC ([2009] EWHC 558 (Admin.))), (ii) had been acquitted on an "unmeritorious technicality" when it was accepted by the prosecution that the breached procedural requirement was fundamental (*R. (Spiteri) v. Basildon Crown Court*, unreported, March 19, 2009, DC ([2009] EWHC 665 (Admin.))) or (iii) had brought his prosecution for assaulting a police officer on himself by his aggressive behaviour towards the police and had been fortunate not to be charged with a public order offence to which, in the view of the justices, he would have had no answer (*Emohare v. Thames Magistrates' Court*, 173 J.P. 303, DC). In the first two of these cases, the court drew particular attention to paragraph II.1.1 of *Practice Direction (Costs: Criminal Proceedings)* (§ 6–105 in the main work) and emphasised that it is not enough to justify a refusal of costs to an acquitted defendant that be brought suspicion on himself. The prosecution must also have been misled into thinking that the case against him was stronger than it was. In the second and third cases, the court emphasised that observations about technical acquittals or being fortunate not to have been charged with a different offence were inconsistent with the presumption of innocence.

Amount of award

★6–16   In *Brewer v. Secretary of State for Justice*, unreported, May 8, 2009, QBD (Holroyde J.) ([2009] EWHC 987 (Q.B.), it was held that where a defendant's costs order is made under the *Prosecution of Offences Act* 1985, s.16 (§ 6–3 in the main work), the fact that the solicitors instructed under a representation order have made their own claim for fees and disbursements does not neces-

sarily preclude the defendant from being awarded — pursuant to a separate
claim — sums to compensate him for expenses he has directly incurred in respect of professional services, including legal services, but that is likely to follow where the claim does relate to legal services; whether such costs are in fact
allowed will depend on whether in the circumstances of the particular case
the defendant can show the determining officer that the expenses claimed fall
within section 16 and regulation 7 of the *Costs in Criminal Cases (General)
Regulations* 1986 (S.I. 1986 No 1335) (§ 6–59 in the main work) as being
"properly incurred by him in the proceedings"; but such a claim is all the
more likely to fail when the subject matter of it is expenses incurred by him
during the currency of the representation order in respect of legal professional services, particularly where the solicitors were instructed under the representation order at the relevant time, but played no part in engaging or
instructing the person in respect of whose fees the claim is made. Apart from
listing various matters for a determining officer to take into account when
considering any such claim, his Lordship noted, *obiter*, that (i) an expense will
not be prevented from being an "out-of-pocket expense" within the definition
of "expenses" in regulation 4 of the 1986 regulations (§ 6–56 in the main
work) solely on the grounds of quantum, or solely because it covers professional expense, although a claim for the expense of "a second set of representation costs" is likely to be unsuccessful for other reasons, and (ii) advocates
applying for a defendant's costs order should (a) indicate at least the heads of
claim which will or may be made, (b) if possible, give a rough indication of the
expected quantum, and (c) alert the judge if a substantial or unusual claim is
anticipated, thereby reducing the possible need for two separate claims.

(2) Award of costs against accused

Investigation expenses

In *R. v. Balshaw* [2009] 4 *Archbold News* 3, CA ([2009] EWCA Crim. 470), it   **★6–33**
was held that an order under section 18 of the *Prosecution of Offences Act* 1985
(§ 6–27 in the main work) may be made against the accused in respect of fees
which the prosecution will pay to another body (*e.g.* the police) which has
itself incurred liability to pay those fees; in such a case the court need only be
satisfied that it is just and reasonable for the prosecutor to meet those fees.

(3) Provision for orders as to costs in other circumstances

Prosecution of Offences Act 1985, s.19

The amendments of section 19 of the 1985 Act effected by the *AFA* 2006   **★6–39**
come into force on October 31, 2009: *Armed Forces Act 2006 (Commencement
No. 5) Order* 2009 (S.I. 2009 No. 1167).

C. Costs in Criminal Cases (General) Regulations 1986 (S.I. 1986 No. 1335)

Part III - Costs out of central funds (regs 4-13)

Application and definitions

As to the definition of "expenses" in regulation 4 of the 1986 regulations,   **★6–56**
see *Brewer v. Secretary of State for Justice, ante*, § 6–16.

II. CRIMINAL DEFENCE SERVICE

B. PRIMARY LEGISLATION

Financial eligibility

★**6–149a** For regulations made under paragraph 6 of Schedule 3 to the 1999 Act (§ 6–147 in the main work), see the *Criminal Defence Service (Information Requests) Regulations* 2009 (S.I. 2009 No. 391). For regulations made under paragraph 8(2) of Schedule 3 to the 1999 Act (§ 6–147 in the main work), see the *Criminal Defence Service (Information Requests) (Prescribed Benefits) Regulations* 2009 (S.I. 2009 No. 212).

C. SECONDARY LEGISLATION

Criminal Defence Service (General) (No. 2) Regulations 2001 (S.I. 2001 No. 1437)

Advocates in the Crown Court and above

6–167 It was said in *R. v. Various defendants (including Z., W. and D.)*, unreported, October 9, 2008, Crown Court at Leeds (H.H.J. Peter Collier Q.C.), that when an advocate considers making an application to have his representation order in the Crown Court extended to cover representation by two junior advocates, the following guiding principles should be kept in mind: (i) the critical question is whether the case for the assisted person is one which involves substantial, novel or complex issues of law or fact which could not be adequately presented by a single advocate (reg. 14(4)(a) (§ 6–166 in the main work)); (ii) in a multi-handed case, equality of arms does not demand that any given defendant should have two counsel because the prosecution are represented by two counsel; (iii) the identity of the proposed advocate is irrelevant as the court has no power to grant a certificate to a particular advocate (this being a matter, first, for the instructing litigator who will be bound to achieve the most effective representation for the client, and, secondly, for funders and professional regulators concerned as to the proper exercise of that task and the proper acceptance of their role by second advocates); (iv) it will usually be inappropriate to deal with such applications before the prosecution case has been served (and in a complex case that should include a full summary) and the defence statement has been filed; this will enable the judge dealing with the application to understand the true nature of the case against each defendant and the defence case; (v) a two junior case is a two-headed train with both engines operating on full power; the role of a second junior includes case preparation, preparation of schedules, summarising and editing interviews, agreeing the draft of any admissions, full involvement at the trial, being involved in the crucial hour just before the court sits when negotiations will be taking place and the defendant may need to be seen, and making a full note of the evidence; any application for two juniors should identify with some precision what the work is that will be done by the second junior and why it needs a second junior to do that work rather than it being done by a sole junior or someone in the litigator's office; (vi) a certificate for a second junior counsel is no more designed to allow the leading junior to move between cases and commitments than it is for the second junior to act in a similar way; and (vii) many of the cases that properly fall within the criteria for the grant of a representation order for two juniors will equally qualify for representation by Queen's Counsel and junior; where the criteria for extending

the representation order to a Queen's Counsel may be met, the client should
be so informed (to avoid any potential conflict between junior counsel's
financial interest and the best interests of the defendant); the difference in
cost is not so great and cases in which the leaders are silks are often conducted
more expeditiously than those where the leaders are juniors.

CHAPTER 7

CRIMINAL APPEAL

II. HIGH COURT JURISDICTION IN CROWN COURT PROCEEDINGS

A. JURISDICTION

(1) Appeal by way of case stated

Supreme Court [Senior Courts] Act 1981, s.28

Appeals from Crown Court and inferior courts

    In *Brett v. DPP*, 173 J.P. 274, DC, it was observed, *obiter*, that where an ap-   ★**7–3**
peal by way of case stated results in a conviction being quashed, the default
position should be to remit any prosecution that remains viable back to the
originating court for retrial before a differently constituted bench.

(2) Judicial review

(a) *Statute*

Supreme Court [Senior Courts] Act 1981, ss.29, 31

Mandatory, prohibiting and quashing orders

    The amendment of section 29 of the 1981 Act effected by the *AFA* 2006   ★**7–4**
comes into force on October 31, 2009: *Armed Forces Act 2006 (Commencement
No. 5) Order* 2009 (S.I. 2009 No. 1167).

    In subsection (3A) of section 29 the reference to the Service Civilian Court   ★
includes a Standing Civilian Court and the reference to the jurisdiction of the
Court Martial in the matters mentioned there includes the jurisdiction of a
court-martial in matters relating to trial by court-martial for an offence and
appeals from a Standing Civilian Court: *Armed Forces Act 2006 (Transitional
Provisions etc.) Order* 2009 (S.I. 2009 No. 1059), art. 205, and Sched. 1, para.
21.

Application for judicial review

    Section 19 of the *Tribunals, Courts and Enforcement Act* 2007 came into force   **7–5**
on November 3, 2008: *Tribunals, Courts and Enforcement Act 2007 (Commencement No. 6 and Transitional Provisions) Order* 2008 (S.I. 2008 No. 2696).

(c) *Matters relating to trial on indictment*

Matters relating to trial on indictment

★7-12   (t) A challenge to the *vires* of the prosecutor, and taking place once the case had proceeded to the Crown Court and been the subject of a ruling by a Crown Court judge: *R. (Securiplan) v. Security Industry Authority* [2009] 2 All E.R. 211, DC (see also *ante*, § 1–263).

III. THE COURT OF APPEAL

C. PRACTICE AND PROCEDURE

Supreme Court [Senior Courts] Act 1981, ss.56, 56B, 59

Allocation of cases in criminal division

★7-31   The amendment of section 56B of the 1981 Act effected by the *Constitutional Reform Act* 2005 came into force on April 3, 2006: *Constitutional Reform Act 2005 (Commencement No. 5) Order* 2006 (S.I. 2006 No. 1014).

IV. APPEAL TO COURT OF APPEAL BY THE DEFENDANT

A. APPEAL AGAINST CONVICTION ON INDICTMENT

(3) Determination of appeals

Ancient convictions

7-51b   In *R. v. Stock* [2009] Crim.L.R. 188, CA, it was said that on an appeal against conviction following a reference by the Criminal Cases Review Commission where there has already been one or more unsuccessful appeals, the issue for the court is the safety of the conviction, not the guilt of the defendant; but, in making this assessment where there is no new evidence or argument (including argument that was not fully or properly developed previously), the court's power to depart from its previous reasoning or conclusion should be confined to "exceptional circumstances".

Right to a fair trial

7-51c   The decision of the House of Lords in *R. v. Davis* is now reported at [2008] 1 A.C. 1128.

(4) Grounds of appeal

Miscellaneous

(i) *Mistakes by, misconduct of, trial judge*

7-81   The defendant was denied a fair trial and his conviction was rendered unsafe where the judge had interrupted his evidence on numerous occasions to ask questions (*viz.* 60 during examination-in-chief and 50 during cross-examination), where the judge had given the clear impression to the jury that

he doubted the defendant's case and had taken on the role of cross-examining
in a way that was more suitable for prosecuting counsel than for the judge: *R.
v. Copsey and Copsey* [2008] 9 *Archbold News* 3, CA.

In *R. v. Cole, The Times*, March 16, 2009, CA, where a judge had intervened   ★
a number of times during the course of the evidence, seeking to aid prosecution witnesses and to belittle an independent witness who supported the
defence case, had showed hostility to the defendant, the (relatively junior)
defence counsel and the defence submissions, and at one point gave defence
counsel, in the presence of the defendant (but not the jury), a note that was
offensively critical, his conduct had rendered the trial unfair and the conviction unsafe. The court found that the note, in particular, had been wholly
inappropriate in that it subjected counsel to the sort of criticism (calculated to
undermine counsel's confidence) which should play no part in a trial,
particularly as the defendant was able to hear the criticism so as to engender
in him a feeling that he had not had "a fair crack of the whip".

(xvi) *Irregularity in relation to jury*
See also *R. v. Thakrar* [2009] Crim.L.R. 357, CA (jury discovering   ★7–95
defendant's previous convictions having researched defendant on internet).

(9) Retrials

Criminal Appeal Act 1968, s.7

Power to order a retrial
Panday v. Virgil (Senior Superintendent of Police) is now reported at [2008] 1   **7–112**
A.C. 1386.

Criminal Appeal Act 1968, Sched. 2

Sentence on conviction at retrial
Section 22 of the *CJIA* 2008 came into force on November 3, 2008: *Crimi-*   **7–117**
nal Justice and Immigration Act 2008 (Commencement No. 3 and Transitional Pro-
visions) Order 2008 (S.I. 2008 No. 2712).

B. APPEAL AGAINST SENTENCE

(1) Who can appeal

Criminal Appeal Act 1968, s.9

Appeal against sentence following conviction on indictment
Sections 179, 181, 203 and 205 of, and Schedule 5 to, the *AFA* 2006 come   ★7–118
into force on October 31, 2009: *Armed Forces Act 2006 (Commencement No. 5)
Order* 2009 (S.I. 2009 No. 1167).

It was held in *R. v. Hughes, The Times*, June 1, 2009, CA, that whilst the   ★
plain effect of section 9(1) was to restrict the defendant to a single appeal, the
court's power to entertain an appeal against sentence was not, as a matter
purely of jurisdiction, extinguished by an earlier reference of the sentence to
the Court of Appeal by the Attorney-General under section 36 of the *CJA*
1988 (§ 7–368 in the main work). In such a case, the defendant's right to
appeal remained extant and unexercised. However, the court emphasised

that this finding did not mean that the court would give leave to appeal. Leave would only be granted if there was good reason to do so and, ordinarily, where the defendant would otherwise suffer significant injustice.

Criminal Appeal Act 1968, s.50

Meaning of "sentence"

7–119   A financial reporting order made under section 76(1) of the *SOCPA* 2005 (§ 5–886a in the main work) is a "sentence" for the purposes of the right of appeal against sentence under the *CAA* 1968, s.9 (§ 7–118 in the main work); it is an order that can only be made after conviction (see *R. v. Hayden* (cited in the main work (at § 7–120))): *R. v. Adams* [2008] 4 All E.R. 574, CA.

The court expressed the *obiter* view in *R. (Langley) v. Preston Crown Court (West Lancashire D.C. and Secretary of State for Justice (interested parties))*, 172 J.P. 605, DC, that where, pursuant to section 1CA of the *CDA* 1998 (§ 5–885 in the main work), the Crown Court varies an anti-social behaviour order made on conviction, an appeal will lie to the Court of Appeal on the basis that the variation would be an "order made by a court when dealing with an offender" within the definition of "sentence" in section 50 of the 1968 Act.

Proper construction of section 11(3)

7–130   It was held in *R. v. Waters and Young*, unreported, October 8, 2008, CA ([2008] EWCA Crim. 2538), that where the appropriate sentence was a custodial sentence of such length that the offender would have been entitled to immediate release by virtue of time spent in custody on remand, but a suspended sentence under the *CJA* 2003, s.189, was inappropriately imposed (see *ante*, § 5–321), it was permissible to substitute the immediate custodial sentence that ought to have been imposed. Such a substitution would not be contrary to section 11(3) of the 1968 Act (appellant not to be more severely dealt with on appeal than he was dealt with by the court below (see § 7–126 in the main work)) because pre-2003 Act authority to the effect that immediate custodial sentences (even if of shorter duration) were more severe than suspended sentences no longer applied. The court said that section 189 provides for a new form of suspended sentence, one that has to be accompanied by specific community requirements, breach of which may trigger the suspended sentence and that the ordinary person would not consider that an offender had been more severely dealt with where an immediate custodial sentence that in reality had already been served was substituted.

★   In *R. v. Bukhari* [2009] 2 Cr.App.R.(S.) 18, the Court of Appeal held that where a confiscation order was made under the *CJA* 1988 when it should have been made by reference to the *PCA* 2002 (because of the date of the offences), whilst it was not open to the Crown Court to vary the order where the time allowed for variation under section 155(1) of the *PCC(S)A* 2000 (§ 5–940 in the main work) had expired, having regard to section 11(3) of 1968 Act, there was nothing to prevent the court from substituting an appropriate order under the 2002 Act, given that the appellant would have consented to such an order had the error been spotted at the time and that he would not be disadvantaged if the order were so substituted.

(3) Notes on appeal against sentence

Principles on which court acts

R. v. Bright is now reported at [2008] 2 Cr.App.R.(S.) 102.

F. Reference of Cases to Court of Appeal

Criminal Appeal Act 1995, s.9

For the purposes of deciding whether to refer a conviction to the Court of Appeal under the *CAA* 1995, s.9 (§ 7–154 in the main work), the Criminal Cases Review Commission is under no duty to investigate an allegation by the defendant that he was entrapped into committing the offence where there is no evidential basis for such a finding: *R. (Edwards) v. Criminal Cases Review Commission* [2009] A.C.D. 13(4), DC (leaving open the question whether it is permissible for a defendant to allege entrapment at the same time as running a substantive defence). ★7–155

I. Notification of Result of Appeal and Matters Depending Thereon

(4) Effect of appeal on sentence

Criminal Appeal Act 1968, s.29

Where an application for leave to appeal against conviction or sentence was renewed to the full court and was wholly without merit, the court would exercise its power (under the *CAA* 1968, s.29 (§ 7–225 in the main work)) to order that part of the time spent in custody pending the hearing of the application should not count towards the sentence to be served: *R. v. Fortean, The Times*, March 4, 2009, CA (making a loss of time order of six weeks). ★7–228

J. Supplementary Provisions

(2) Powers exercisable by a single judge

Criminal Appeal Act 1968, s.31

Errata

The words "live link" should appear before the word "direction" in section 31(2)(ca) of the 1968 Act. **7–231**

In the annotations to section 31, for "the *CJA* 2003, s.331, and Sched. 32, paras 86 and 87", read "the *CJA* 2003, s.331, and Sched. 36, paras 86 and 87".

(3) Powers exercisable by registrar

Criminal Appeal Act 1968, s.31A

Erratum

In the annotations to section 31A, for "the *CJA* 2003, s.331, and Sched. 32, **7–236** paras 86 and 88", read "the *CJA* 2003, s.331, and Sched. 36, paras 86 and 88".

V. APPEAL TO THE COURT OF APPEAL BY THE PROSECUTION

A. GENERAL

Criminal Justice Act 2003, s.57

Introduction

★**7–243**   *R. v. Al-Ali* is now reported at [2009] 1 Cr.App.R. 21.

B. TERMINATING RULINGS

Criminal Justice Act 2003, ss.58–61

General right of appeal in respect of rulings

7–244   For further consideration of *R. v. Y.* (see the main work), see *R. v. O., J. and S.* [2008] Crim.L.R. 892, CA, where it was held that the decision provided clear and binding authority that a ruling as to the admissibility of evidence may also be the subject of an appeal under sections 58 to 61 where the prosecution accept that the effect of the ruling, if not reversed, will be to bring the trial to an end, providing that the remaining conditions which apply to those sections are also fulfilled. This was the case whether or not the offence under consideration was a "qualifying offence" for the purposes of the right of appeal under section 62 (§ 7–248 in the main work).

E. RULES OF PROCEDURE

Criminal Procedure Rules 2005 (S.I. 2005 No. 384), Pt 67 (as substituted by the Criminal Procedure (Amendment No. 2) Rules 2007 (S.I. 2007 No. 2317))

Decision to appeal

7–259b   Whereas rule 67.2(1) of the 2005 rules requires the prosecution to inform the Crown Court of an intention to appeal "immediately" after the ruling, there was sufficient immediacy where the judge had adjourned for the day following the ruling so as to allow the prosecution time to consider it, and the prosecution informed the court of their wish to appeal the following morning, albeit after a short further adjournment: *R. v. O., J. and S.* [2008] Crim.L.R. 892, CA.

VI. RETRIAL FOR SERIOUS OFFENCES

A. CASES THAT MAY BE RETRIED

Criminal Justice Act 2003, s.75

7–260   It was held in *R. v. Andrews* [2009] 1 Cr.App.R. 26, CA, that whilst a person who has been acquitted may only be retried in relation to a "qualifying offence" (as to which, see § 7–261 in the main work), and whilst rape is a qualify-

ing offence but indecent assault is not, where the respondent had previously
been acquitted of two counts of indecent assault and one count of rape, and
where evidence relating to the non-qualifying offences was to be put to the
jury as evidence of the "grooming" process to which the complainant was
subjected before the alleged rape, the acquittals of indecent assault did not
render a retrial of the rape allegation unfair. The court said that it was well
established before the *CJA* 2003 came into force that a jury considering
sexual allegations against a defendant may hear allegations made by other
complainants, even if charges based on those allegations had resulted in
acquittals. Following an acquittal, evidence may be admissible, notwithstanding that to admit the evidence may suggest that the defendant was guilty of
the offence of which he was acquitted.

Qualifying offences (Sched. 5)

Whereas it is stated in the main work that the offences against the person   **7–261**
listed in Schedule 5 are the same as those listed in Schedule 4, it should be
noted that an offence contrary to section 18 of the *Offences against the Person
Act* 1861 is listed in Schedule 4, but is not listed in Schedule 5.

B. APPLICATION FOR RETRIAL

Criminal Justice Act 2003, ss.76–83

New and compelling evidence

When considering, on an application for a retrial, whether evidence is "new   **7–264**
and compelling", the question is not whether the form, type or nature of the
evidence can be said to be new or compelling, but whether it is indeed new
and compelling and highly probative of the allegation: *R. v. Andrews (ante,*
§ 7–260). Where, therefore, none of the new evidence relied on by the prosecution in their application for a retrial of an allegation of rape came from witnesses who provided "direct" evidence that the complainant was raped, the
section did not require that it should. What mattered was that the evidence
should have been admissible to prove that, in accordance with her complaint,
and contrary to the respondent's evidence at trial, he raped her. It followed
that similar fact evidence could be "new and compelling" evidence for this
purpose.

F. SUPPLEMENTARY

Criminal Justice Act 2003, ss.92–97

The amendment of section 94 of the 2003 Act effected by the *AFA* 2006   **★7–280**
comes into force on October 31, 2009: *Armed Forces Act 2006 (Commencement
No. 5) Order* 2009 (S.I. 2009 No. 1167).

X. APPEAL TO THE HOUSE OF LORDS [SUPREME COURT] FROM THE COURT OF APPEAL

B. Matters Preliminary to Hearing

Criminal Appeal Act 1968, s.36

Bail on appeal by defendant

★**7–327**   The amendment of section 36 of the 1968 Act effected by section 47 of the *CJA* 2003 came into force on July 24, 2006: *Criminal Justice Act 2003 (Commencement No. 13 and Transitional Provision) Order* 2006 (S.I. 2006 No. 1835).

XIII. REFERENCES TO THE COURT OF APPEAL BY THE ATTORNEY-GENERAL

B. Of Sentence

Plea of guilty following judicial indication as to sentence

★**7–369d**   Where prosecution counsel acquiesced in a judge's mistaken indication as to the appropriate starting point when fixing a minimum term for an offence of murder under Schedule 21 to the *CJA* 2003 (§§ 5–245 *et seq.*), it remained open to the Attorney-General to refer the sentence to the Court of Appeal as being unduly lenient where the offender had done nothing in reliance upon the acquiescence: *Att.-Gen.'s References (Nos 25 and 26 of 2008) (R. v. McCarry George and Waters)* [2009] 1 Cr.App.R.(S.) 116, CA (distinguishing *Att.-Gen.'s References (Nos 80 and 81 of 1999) (R. v. Thompson and Rodgers)* (see the main work)).

Criminal Procedure Rules 2005 (S.I. 2005 No. 384), Pt 70 (as substituted by the Criminal Procedure (Amendment No. 2) Rules 2007 (S.I. 2007 No. 2317))

Anonymity of defendant on reference of point of law

★**7–378a**   In *Re British Broadcasting Corporation: Att.-Gen.'s Reference (No. 3 of 1999)*, *The Times*, June 18, 2009, HL, doubt was expressed as to the *vires* of rule 70.8 of the 2005 rules, with a majority of their Lordships being of the view that its scope is limited to prohibiting identification of the respondent in court during the course of the reference proceedings, as well as in the reference itself. However, they were also of the opinion that the Court of Appeal or House of Lords would have power to grant an injunction *contra mundum* to protect the identity of a respondent where this was necessary to protect his right to privacy and where there was no conflicting interest, such as the freedom of the press, that outweighed that right.

CHAPTER 8

ORAL TESTIMONY OF WITNESSES

I. PRELIMINARIES

A. SECURING ATTENDANCE OF WITNESSES, PRODUCTION OF DOCUMENTS, ETC.

(7) Evidence given in Children Act 1989, wardship or family proceedings

Disclosure ordered to prosecution/police

Where, in the course of care proceedings relating to a mother's second   **8–21c**
child, she had confessed in the presence of two medical experts to causing
fatal head injuries to her first child, where the defendant's legal team had
agreed to the disclosure of the confession to the police on the presumption
that it was protected by section 98(2) of the *Children Act* 1989 (see the main
work), and where the police then sought to make the transcript of the confession available to medical experts instructed by them (all but one of whom had
been experts in the family proceedings and had reported before the confession was made that the injuries to the first child were non-accidental), on the
basis that it would assist them in detailing the mechanisms of the injury
(whilst accepting that the confession itself would not be admissible in any trial
as primary evidence), it was sufficient that precise details of the alleged mechanism in an agreed, summarised form be placed before them; it was appropriate that they should comment on the mother's version of events, but it was
not necessary for them to know of her express confession; it was important
for all parties to take into account that the operation of the family courts is assisted if parties are prepared to be open and frank; clearly, they will only be
so if they feel they have the protection of section 98(2), so that what is said
does not directly incriminate them so far as criminal proceedings are
concerned; here, it was clear that the mother made her confession on the
understanding that it would not be used against her in any future criminal
proceedings: *Re. M. (Care Disclosure to Police)* [2008] 2 F.L.R. 390, Fam D
(Baron J.).

IV. RULES OF EVIDENCE AND PRACTICE RELATING TO THE QUESTIONING OF WITNESSES

A. GENERAL

(1) Special measures directions

Youth Justice and Criminal Evidence Act 1999, ss.61–63

General interpretation etc. of Part II

The amendment of section 63 of the 1999 Act effected by the *AFA* 2006   **★8–55w**

143

comes into force on October 31, 2009: *Armed Forces Act 2006 (Commencement No. 5) Order* 2009 (S.I. 2009 No. 1167).

B. EXAMINATION-IN-CHIEF

(1) Introduction

(a) *Identification of witness*

Name

8–70   *R. v. Davis* is now reported at [2008] 1 A.C. 1128.

The *Criminal Evidence (Witness Anonymity) Act* 2008 was considered in *R. v. Mayers and other appeals*; *R. v. P.* [2009] 2 All E.R. 145, CA. *As to procedural issues*, the court said that, first, a witness anonymity order may be regarded as a special measure of last resort. Witness relocation could only be a practicable alternative in the rarest of circumstances as such a course, if in effect forced on a witness, would undoubtedly engage his right to a private life. Secondly, the principles which govern the use of special counsel in relation to public interest immunity should be adapted to their possible use in this context, but bearing in mind that there is one significant difference; the former is concerned with the circumstances in which non-disclosure to the defence may be appropriate, whereas the latter is concerned with whether sufficient and complete investigation and consequent disclosure have taken place. Since the obligations of the prosecution in this context go much further than their ordinary duties of disclosure, the services of special counsel may enable a judge to ensure that any investigative steps specific to the case, and not perhaps otherwise apparent, have been undertaken. But if the judge entertains reservations about the good faith of the efforts of the prosecution to investigate any relevant consideration, an application will be met with a point blank refusal.

As to disclosure, the court observed that whilst the defence statement must help to inform and focus the process, the process is not to be circumscribed by a minute analysis of the statement, not least because the very fact of the defence not knowing the identity of the proposed witness might be the reason for material being omitted from the statement. The prosecution must be pro-active, concentrating on the credibility of the witness and the interests of justice.

As to the statutory conditions set out in section 4 (§ 8–71c in the main work), first, all three conditions have to be met. Secondly, the most helpful approach would be to begin by addressing condition C (necessary in the interests of justice because it is important that the witness should testify and the witness would not testify without an order). The test is stark, so that it must be clear that, notwithstanding the contempt powers of the court, the witness will not testify. That the witness would prefer not to testify or is reluctant is insufficient, but the circumstances of the offence itself may justify an inference to this effect. There is also no requirement that the judge should be satisfied that any threat should come from the defendant personally. As to undercover police officers, a judge would normally be entitled to follow the unequivocal assertion by such an officer that without an anonymity order, he would not be prepared to testify. Thirdly, in relation to condition A (order must be necessary in order to protect safety of witness or another or to prevent serious damage to property or to prevent real harm to the public interest), different considerations may inform the decision of the court when deciding between different civilian witnesses (*e.g.* children and adults, vulnerable witnesses, *etc.*). As to investigators involved in covert operations, there is an obvious public interest in maintaining the anonymity of such witnesses, to which end there has been a regular practice for security, undercover and test purchase officers to give evidence anonymously. This is so much so that if an order is refused, the prosecution will often stay the proceedings rather than expose the witness to the risk of identification. Normally there will be no disadvantage to the defence in not knowing the officer's true identity, and whilst each case requires a fact-specific decision, none of these general considerations require specific evidence. Fourthly, condition B (making the order would be consistent with the defendant having a fair trial) is fact specific, but in the vast majority of cases, all the express considerations listed in section 5 (*post*), which bear on the proper protection of the interests of the defendant, will require attention, and only after each has been addressed will it be possible to conclude that condition B has been satisfied.

As to the statutory considerations set out in section 5 (§ 8–71d in the main work), first, these are to be taken into account when deciding whether the conditions in section 4 are met, but none outweighs any of the others and the order in which they appear does not represent an order of priority or importance. Nor are they exhaustive; their focus is the protection of the interests of the defendant. Secondly, the first restates the common law principle that the defendant is normally entitled to know the identity of any witness who incriminates him. Its promulgation acknowledges the potential disadvantage to the defendant if he is ignorant of the witness's identity, and reinforces the principle of open justice. It is linked with the last, which reinforces the view that a witness anonymity order does indeed represent the last practical resort. Thirdly, the second, fourth and fifth considerations (extent to which credibility in issue, whether evidence could be properly tested, whether there is any reason to believe the witness dishonest or has a motive to lie), whilst distinct, are linked in that they relate to the weight to be attached to the evidence of the anonymous witness and the safeguarding of the process by which his credibility may, so far as practicable, be objectively verified and then tested in cross-examination. Taken together, they are likely to require an overall view of the potential impact of the proposed witness on the trial. It is in this context that the process of investigation and disclosure is crucial, not simply in relation to previous occasions when the witness may have been dishonest in general, but also with regard to whether there may be any reason to question his honesty or motivation in the particular case. The responsibility of the prosecution to ensure a fair trial, and to reveal any material which may undermine their case or advance the defendant's case will be crucially engaged in addressing this group of considerations. Fourthly, as to the third consideration (whether the evidence might be the sole or decisive evidence), the fact that a witness might provide the sole or decisive evidence is not conclusive. Where, however, the evidence is both sole and decisive, condition B may be harder to fulfil. It follows that a court will have to examine whether there is independent support for the witness, as the more support there is, the safer it would be to admit the evidence. Where there is more than one witness, questions of possible collusion or contamination should be addressed. Suspicion is less likely to be engendered about the integrity of witnesses who immediately, or virtually immediately, are identified or identify themselves, before there would be an opportunity to engineer a sophisticated conspiracy, than it would be in the case of witnesses who turn up late or out of the blue.

As to the warning to be given to the jury as required by section 7 (§ 8–71f in the main work), the warning must be sufficient to ensure that the jury does not make any assumptions adverse to the defendant, or favourable to the witness, from the fact that an anonymity order has been made, and, in particular, must not infer guilt from this fact. A judge should further direct the jury about the obvious difficulties facing a defendant who is challenging either the credibility or the accuracy of an anonymous witness.

As to anonymous hearsay, neither the Act of 2008, nor the CJA 2003, nor the common law permits reading to the court a statement made by an unidentified and unidentifiable person.

★ *R. v. Powar (Harbinder) and Powar (Kulwinder), The Times,* April 24, 2009, CA, was an appeal against convictions obtained before the House of Lords' decision in *R. v. Davis* (cited in the main work). The Court of Appeal stated that whilst the calling of anonymous witnesses must not become a routine event in the prosecution of serious crime, witness anonymity orders are not to be confined to cases of terrorism or gangland killings. Furthermore, for the purposes of deciding whether condition A for the making of a witness anonymity order, as set out in section 4(3) of the 2008 Act (order necessary in order to protect safety of witness (§ 8–71c in the main work)), was satisfied, the court held that it was permissible to have regard not only to the witness's own reasonable fear (as provided for by subs. (6)), but also to the circumstances of the offence itself and to the background. In the circumstances of the particular case, anonymity orders had been made in respect of six witnesses (all neighbours of the defendants). Through inadvertence, the identity of some of them had been compromised and it was held that the judge had been right to refuse to lift the previous orders on the basis that they were no longer necessary as the "cat was out of the bag". It was one thing for the defendants to have a suspicion as to the identity of the witnesses, it was quite another thing to confirm their identity to them. Furthermore, it was said that stripping the witnesses of their protection would inform anyone in the public gallery, including associates of the defendants, of their true identities, which the judge correctly thought would heighten the risks.

C. Cross-Examination

(3) Restrictions

(b) *In proceedings for sexual offences*

Youth Justice and Criminal Evidence Act 1999, ss.41–43

★**8–123p** Where the defence sought leave to cross-examine the complainant about her previous sexual behaviour under section 41(3) (similarity of conduct could not reasonably be explained on the basis of coincidence), and where the source of their information were medical notes compiled during consultations by the complainant with two medical practitioners, the judge had been entitled to take into account that it was known (as a result of a further statement made by the complainant) that if what the complainant was recorded as having said to the medical practitioners were put to her, her explanation (which the defence were in no position to contradict) would have emphasised the dissimilarities between the conduct of which she spoke during those consultations and the conduct of which she complained: *R. v. Harris* [2009] 3 *Archbold News* 2, CA.

(7) Of the defendant

Criminal Evidence Act 1898, s.6

The amendments to section 6 of the 1898 Act effected by the *AFA* 2006   **★8–162**
come into force on October 31, 2009: *Armed Forces Act 2006 (Commencement
No. 5) Order* 2009 (S.I. 2009 No. 1167). In connection with that commencement, see the transitional provision in the *Armed Forces Act 2006 (Transitional
Provisions etc.) Order* 2009 (S.I. 2009 No. 1059), Sched. 1, para. 2 (interpretation of reference to "service offence").

CHAPTER 9

DOCUMENTARY AND REAL EVIDENCE

I. DOCUMENTS: GENERAL

B. ORIGINAL EVIDENCE OR HEARSAY

(1) Identifying purpose for which document tendered

As to whether the terms of a prisoner's licence were hearsay within the *CJA*   **9–3**
2003, see *West Midlands Probation Board v. French* (*post*, § 11–4).

II. PUBLIC DOCUMENTS

A. DEFINITION

As to a parole licence falling with the rule in *Sturla v. Freccia*, see *West*   **9–16**
Midlands Probation Board v. French (*post*, § 11–4).

D. CATEGORIES OF PUBLIC DOCUMENT

(1) Statutes and laws

Documentary Evidence Act 1868, s.2

As to a parole licence falling within section 2 of the 1868 Act, see *West*   **9–31**
Midlands Probation Board v. French (*post*, § 11–4).

Byelaws

Local Government Act 1972, s.238

As from February 9, 2009 (*Local Transport Act 2008 (Commencement No. 1*   **9–33**
and Transitional Provisions) Order 2009 (S.I. 2009 No. 107)), the *Local Transport
Act* 2008, s.77(5), and Sched. 4, para. 48(1) and (4), amend section 238 of the
1972 Act, so as to substitute the words "or an Integrated Transport Authority

for an integrated transport area in England" for the words "or a metropolitan county passenger transport authority".

(4) Public registers

Shareholders

9–55   Section 127 of the *Companies Act* 2006 comes into force on October 1, 2009: *Companies Act 2006 (Commencement No. 8, Transitional Provisions and Savings) Order* 2008 (S.I. 2008 No. 2860).

(6) Certificates given under public authority

Companies

9–68   Section 13 of the *Companies Act* 2006 comes into force on October 1, 2009: *Companies Act 2006 (Commencement No. 8, Transitional Provisions and Savings) Order* 2008 (S.I. 2008 No. 2860).

(8) Judicial documents

(g) *Convictions and acquittals*

Police and Criminal Evidence Act 1984, ss.74, 75

Provisions supplementary to section 74

★9–83   The amendments of section 75 of the 1984 Act effected by the *AFA* 2006 comes into force on October 31, 2009: *Armed Forces Act 2006 (Commencement No. 5) Order* 2009 (S.I. 2009 No. 1167).

Police and Criminal Evidence Act 1984, s.82

Part VIII—interpretation

★9–84   The amendments of section 82 of the 1984 Act effected by the *AFA* 2006 come into force on October 31, 2009: *Armed Forces Act 2006 (Commencement No. 5) Order* 2009 (S.I. 2009 No. 1167). In connection with that commencement, see the transitional provision in the *Armed Forces Act 2006 (Transitional Provisions etc.) Order* 2009 (S.I. 2009 No. 1059), Sched. 1, para. 28(1) (interpretation of references to "proceedings", "the Court Martial" and "the Service Civilian Court").

Proof of convictions in magistrates' courts

9–96   With effect from April 6, 2009, a new Part 37 is substituted for the existing Part 37 of the *Criminal Procedure Rules* 2005 (S.I. 2005 No. 384): *Criminal Procedure (Amendment No. 2) Rules* 2008 (S.I. 2008 No. 3269). The new Part 37 contains no rule corresponding to the former rule 37.5.

III. PRIVATE DOCUMENTS

A. PROOF OF CONTENTS

(1) Primary and secondary evidence

Police and Criminal Evidence Act 1984, ss.71, 72

Part VII—supplementary

The amendments of section 72 of the 1984 Act effected by the *AFA* 2006 come into force on October 31, 2009: *Armed Forces Act 2006 (Commencement No. 5) Order* 2009 (S.I. 2009 No. 1167).   ★9–102b

CHAPTER 10

MISCELLANEOUS SOURCES OF EVIDENCE

II. ADMISSIONS

Criminal Justice Act 1967, s.10

With effect from April 6, 2009, a new Part 37 is substituted for the existing Part 37 of the *Criminal Procedure Rules* 2005 (S.I. 2005 No. 384): *Criminal Procedure (Amendment No. 2) Rules* 2008 (S.I. 2008 No. 3269). The former rule 37.4 is replaced by new rule 37.6, which requires merely that, unless the court otherwise directs, a written record should be made of any admission.   10–7

VI. LETTERS OF REQUEST

Crime (International Co-operation) Act 2003, ss.9, 10

It was held in *R. v. I.* [2009] 2 *Archbold News* 3, CA, that evidence which had been obtained under a letter of request could not be used in relation to the prosecution of the defendant where the letter of request had not made an investigation into her, or a possible prosecution of her, part of the purpose for which the information and evidence was sought. Unless the consent of the requested state was given, section 9(2) of the 2003 Act (see the main work) prevented this.   ★10–60a

VII. EXPERT EVIDENCE

A. LEGISLATION

Criminal Procedure Rules 2005 (S.I. 2005 No. 384), Pt 24

Effect of failure to disclose

For an example of a decision to refuse permission to the defence to adduce expert evidence on account of a failure to comply with the provisions of rule   ★10–63

24.1 of the 2005 rules as to the giving of notice of such evidence being up-held, see *Writtle v. DPP*, 173 J.P. 224, DC (report served after conclusion of prosecution case and sought to raise an entirely new issue).

Chapter 11

HEARSAY EVIDENCE

II. STATUTE

A. Criminal Justice Act 2003

(2) The basic rules

Criminal Justice Act 2003, ss.114, 115, 133, 134

Admissibility of hearsay

11–3   As to the statements of absent witnesses and the "interests of justice", see *R. v. Pulley, post,* § 11–15.

Obiter observations were made in *R. v. Ali and Hussain,* 172 J.P. 516, CA, to the effect that, in making a ruling as to whether it was in the "interests of justice" within section 114(1)(d) of the 2003 Act for a hearsay statement to be admitted in evidence, a judge was not entitled to rely upon material he had been shown, or arguments that had been advanced, in the course of an *ex parte* public interest immunity hearing in the absence of the defence. The court said that it was wrong, and contrary to Article 6 of the ECHR (§ 16–57 in the main work) for the prosecution to have the advantage of relying on material unavailable to the defence.

In *R. v. Z.* [2009] 1 Cr.App.R. 34, CA, it was said that section 114(1)(d) is to be cautiously applied, since otherwise the conditions laid down by Parliament in section 116 (admissibility of hearsay where witness unavailable) (§ 11–15 in the main work) would be circumvented; however, the section should not be so narrowly applied that it has no effect; and it followed that there will be cases in which hearsay may be admitted under section 114(1)(d) in circumstances in which it could not be admitted under section 116; section 114(2) contains a list of matters which it is mandatory for the court to take account of when deciding whether to admit hearsay under subsection (1); a judge should therefore, when giving his ruling on an application under subsection (1)(d), make it clear that he has taken those matters into account, although that does not mean he must refer to and express a conclusion on each of them (*cf. R. v. Taylor* and *R. v. Y.* (cited in the main work)); and, while the Court of Appeal does not readily interfere with a judge's decision to admit evidence under section 114(1)(d), it will be more willing to do so where it can be shown that he has not taken into account relevant matters listed in subsection (2). Where, therefore, the appellant had been charged with counts of indecent assault and rape, contrary to the *SOA* 1956, and where the prosecution sought to adduce evidence, *inter alia*, of a woman (D) who claimed to have been sexually abused and raped by the appellant when a girl but who did not now wish to give evidence on the grounds that she wished to put the experience behind her, the court said that relevant matters for the judge to take into account

were those in section 114(2)(a) (probative value of statement), (g) (whether
oral evidence can be given, if not, why not), (h) (amount of difficulty involved
in challenging statement) and (i) (extent to which that difficulty would prejudice party facing it); in particular, it was to be noted that paragraph (g)
referred to the inability of the witness to give evidence, and not to the witness's
reluctance or unwillingness (however understandable that attitude may be),
and this was consistent with the restrictions contained in section 116; D's evidence was not only hearsay but bad character evidence of disputed serious
misconduct, and had the judge taken into account the relevant matters, he
could not have concluded that this was a case where the prosecution's application was "fairly conventional" and "straightforward"; it would be a rare case
indeed in which such significant, potentially prejudicial evidence should be
admitted as hearsay where the maker of the statement was alive and well and
able, although reluctant, to testify, if her reluctance was not due to fear (*i.e.*
the condition in s.116(2) was not satisfied).

Statements and matters stated

    It was held in *West Midlands Probation Board v. French* [2009] 1 Cr.App.R.   **11–4**
29, DC, that where a prisoner was released on licence, and where, in
subsequent proceedings for an alleged breach of the terms of the licence, it
was sought to prove the fact of the licence and its terms by production of a
copy thereof, the contents were hearsay within the 2003 Act because it
contained representations of fact and stated matters which were intended to
be acted upon by others (see s.115(2) and (3)) in that it recited that a licence
had been issued and the terms upon which it was issued and this was to be
acted upon by, *inter alios*, the prison staff and the probation service. However,
it was admissible for the purpose of proving the matters stated therein (i) as a
public document under the rule in *Sturla v. Freccia* (1880) 5 App.Cas. 623,
HL (§ 9–16 in the main work), in that it was made by a public officer for an
official purpose and for the public to make use of, "public" here meaning all
those who had a legitimate interest in the matter that was recorded in the
document; (ii) under section 2 of the *Documentary Evidence Act* 1868 (§ 9–30 in
the main work) as an "order" made by a government department, it having
been held (*R. v. Clarke (J.F.)* [1969] 2 Q.B. 91, CA), that "order" should be
given a wide meaning that would cover, at any rate, any executive act of
government performed by the bringing into existence of a public document
for the purpose of giving effect to an Act of Parliament; and (iii) under section
117 of the Act of 2003 (§ 11–26 in the main work) as a document created in
the course of a profession or other occupation and as one in relation to which
the additional admissibility requirements set out in subsection (5) did not apply by virtue of subsection (4), as it could not be said that the document was
one that had been prepared "for the purposes of pending or contemplated
criminal proceedings". The court also commented that there appeared to be
no reason why the document should not also have been admitted under section 114(1)(d) of the 2003 Act (§ 11–3 in the main work) as being in the
"interests of justice" and doubting whether it would be open to a defendant to
challenge the validity of the licence itself in breach proceedings, rather than
judicial review proceedings. For the suggestion that no issue of hearsay arose
at all, see *Criminal Law Week* 2009/01/2.

Limitations on the exclusionary rule

Implied assertions

    That part of a telephone conversation between a drug dealer and the re-   **11–13** spondent in which the dealer sought to ascertain the availability and cost of amphetamine paste contained no representation of fact or opinion for the purposes of section 115 of the *CJA* 2003 (§ 11–4 in the main work) and was a clear example of what was analysed in *R. v. Kearley* (see the main work), as an implied assertion by the dealer that the person to whom his comments were addressed (the respondent) was his supplier; given the decision in *R. v. Sukadave Singh* (§ 11–14 in the main work), that sections 115 and 118 (§ 11–70 in the main work), when read together, create a new rule against hearsay that does not extend to implied assertions, the evidence of the conversation was not hearsay and was admissible: *R. v. K. (M.)*, 172 J.P. 538, CA.

(3) Principal categories of admissibility

(a) *Absent witnesses*

Criminal Justice Act 2003, s.116

Cases where a witness is unavailable

11–15   The proposition that the presence of serious inconsistencies and lies in the statement of an absent witness necessarily operates in favour of admission, because inconsistencies favour the defence, could not be accepted; on that approach, the court was less likely to admit an apparently reliable statement than an apparently unreliable statement: *R. v. Pulley*, 72 J.C.L. 356, CA ([2008] EWCA Crim. 356).

★   As to a statement being admissible under section 116 of the 2003 Act notwithstanding that it is inadmissible under a statutory provision that is concerned with the particular type of statement, see *Brett v. DPP, post*, § 32–163.

As to the relationship between sections 114 and 116, see *R. v. Z., ante*, § 11–3.

Witness dead (s.116(2)(a))

★11–18a   As to *R. v. Al-Khawaja*, see *Al-Khawaja v. U.K.; Tahery v. U.K. (post*, §§ 16–58, 16–91); and the response of the Court of Appeal in *R. v. Horncastle and Blackmore; R. v. Marquis and Graham; R. v. Carter, post*, § 11–25.

Witness cannot be found (s.116(2)(d))

11–21   Where the witness was a retired public servant and no attempt had been made to discover his current address through his pension, the Court of Appeal described the steps taken to find him as "desultory" and ruled that the judge had been in error in permitting his statement to be admitted under this provision: *R. v. Kamuhuza*, 173 J.P. 55, CA.

The "interests of justice" (s.116(4))

★11–25   The Court of Appeal undertook a detailed re-examination of the background to, and the provisions of, Chapter 2 of Part 11 of the *CJA* 2003 in *R. v. Horncastle and Blackmore; R. v. Marquis and Graham; R. v. Carter, The Times*, June 3, 2009, CA, in light of the jurisprudence of the European Court of Human Rights up to and including *Al-Khawaja v. U.K.; Tahery v. U.K. (post*, §§ 16–58, 16–91). It concluded that, provided the terms of the Act are observed, the admission of the statement of an absent, but identified, witness

vill not involve a breach of Article 6(1) or (3)(d) of the ECHR (§ 16–57 in the
nain work) even if the evidence of the absent witness is the sole or decisive
·vidence against the accused. Where the hearsay is demonstrably reliable, or
ts reliability can be properly tested and assessed, the court held that there
·re, in the language of the European Court of Human Rights, sufficient
·ounter-balancing measures to make the trial fair; and, given that Article
·(3)(d) does not create an absolute right in an accused to have every witness
igainst him present to be examined, the balance struck by the statutory code
s a legitimate one and consistent with the Convention. In relation to wit-
iesses who are in fear, the court added that it matters not whether a witness's
·ear was brought about by or on behalf of the defendant; it is, however,
mportant that all possible efforts are made to get the witness to court and this
hould include making the witness understand the importance of a citizen's
luty and that the violent and intimidatory will only flourish the more if that
luty is not done, whilst they will normally back down in the face of a determi-
iation that it be performed; for this reason, the court said that it is of particu-
ar importance that assurances are never given to potential witnesses that
heir evidence will be read; whilst the Act requires fear to be construed broadly
see s.116(3) (§ 11–15 in the main work)), it is not expected that fear based on
nappropriate assurances by police officers will result in the evidence being
ead.

The Court of Appeal said (at [79]) that there was nothing in the judgment
n *Al-Khawaja v. U.K.*; *Tahery v. U.K.* that led it to conclude that "this court
vas wrong in the result it reached in a number of its decisions" in relation to
Article 6(1) and (3)(d). It does not list the cases it had in mind in making this
ibservation, and it does not indicate whether it even accepts that its decisions
n the two cases that were the subject of the Strasbourg judgment (as to one of
vhich, see § 11–18a in the main work) must now be regarded as wrongly
lecided. However, the court said nothing to impugn what the Strasbourg
·ourt said as to the inadequacy as counter-balancing measures of the op-
iortunity of the defendant to give evidence and of cautionary directions by
he judge in summing up.

The net effect of the Court of Appeal's judgment (particularly its require-
nent that hearsay that is the sole or decisive evidence be "manifestly reliable"
·r capable of being "properly tested and assessed") is to align the law in
:ngland and Wales more closely with that in Canada: see *R. v. Khelawon*
§ 11–3 in the main work) (where hearsay is shown to be necessary, it may be
idmitted if, because of the way in which it came about, its contents are shown
o be trustworthy, or if circumstances permit the ultimate trier of fact suf-
iciently to assess its worth).

(b) *Documents created or received in the course of a trade, business or
profession*

Criminal Justice Act 2003, s.117

3usiness and other documents

As to a parole licence falling within section 117, see *West Midlands Probation*   **11–26**
3oard v. French (ante, § 11–4).

(d) *Previous statements of witnesses*

Criminal Justice Act 2003, ss.119, 120

Previous inconsistent statements

11–35   Section 119 of the 2003 Act (previous inconsistent statements admissible a evidence of any matter stated) comes into play principally when a witnes maintains that the contents of a prior statement are not true; the big chang made by the section is that, in contrast to the former position, the jury ar now permitted to look at all the circumstances of the case and decide that prior statement is true even where the witness declines to adopt it or state that it is not true; however, where a witness adopts the statement after bein declared hostile, the court has no need to rely on section 119; any potentia unfairness to which that section might give rise is balanced by section 12 (§ 11–45 in the main work) and the general obligation on a judge to direct jury to disregard any evidence if of the opinion that no reasonable jury coul properly rely on it: *R. v. Gibbons* [2009] Crim.L.R. 197, CA.

★   In *R. v. Billingham and Billingham* [2009] Crim.L.R. 529, CA, the cour stated that, whereas the present Judicial Studies Board's direction on previou inconsistent statements is to the effect that if the jury are sure that one of th accounts is true, "then it is evidence you may consider when deciding upo your verdict", this requires modification where a witness has previously mad a statement that exculpates the accused. In such a case, the jury should b directed that they may act on the prior statement if they think it may be tru

Other prior statements (s.120)

Rebuttal of suggestion of fabrication (s.120(2))

★**11–36**   It was held in *R. v. Athwal* [2009] 5 *Archbold News* 2, CA, that where it sought to admit a statement for the purposes of rebutting a suggestion tha the witness's evidence is fabricated under section 120(2), compliance with th notice requirements in Part 34 of the *Criminal Procedure Rules* 2005 (S.I. 200 No. 384) (§§ 11–52 *et seq.* in the main work) will not always be possible (becaus it will generally not be until after a witness has been cross-examined that th need to rebut the allegation will be apparent) in which case it will then be fc the judge to satisfy himself that overall fairness can be achieved by the exercis of his discretion and by his powers of dispensation under rule 34.7. The cour further held that whereas section 120(2), unlike the common law rule, did nc require the suggestion to be one of "recent" fabrication, the mere fact that th witness had said substantially the same thing on a previous occasion woul not generally be sufficient. Something more would normally be required (*e.ε* the absence on the earlier occasion of a factor which was being advanced as possible explanation for the falsity of the evidence in court). However, whe circumstances had so changed, it may not matter when they changec provided that there was a qualitative difference in circumstances, bι substantial similarity between the two accounts. The court said that th touchstone was whether the evidence may fairly assist the jury in ascertainin where the truth lies. It was for the judge to preserve the balance of fairness I ensuring that unjustified excursions into self-corroboration were not permi ted, whether the witness was called by the prosecution or the defence.

(5) Rules of court

Criminal Procedure Rules 2005 (S.I. 2005 No. 384), Pt 34

As to the extent to which compliance with the rules will be possible where it   ★**11–52**
is sought to admit a statement for the purposes of rebutting a suggestion of
fabrication under section 120(2), see *ante*, § 11–36.

CHAPTER 12

PRIVILEGE, PUBLIC INTEREST IMMUNITY AND DISCLOSURE

I. PRIVILEGE

B. ANSWERS WHICH MAY INCRIMINATE A WITNESS

Privilege against self-incrimination

In *R. v. S. (F.) and A. (S.)* [2009] 1 Cr.App.R. 18, CA, encrypted files on the   **12–2**
appellants' computers were expected to provide incriminating evidence
against them in relation to terrorist offences. They had been served with notices, pursuant to section 49 of the *RIPA* 2000 (see § 25–367 in the main
work) obliging them to disclose full encryption keys to allow access to the
encrypted material. The appellants sought a stay of counts alleging failure
to comply with the notices, contrary to section 53 of the Act of 2000, on the
basis that the requirement to provide that information constituted an
impermissible infringement of the privilege against self-incrimination. It
was held that although the privilege against self-incrimination might be
engaged by a requirement of disclosure of knowledge of the means of access to protected data under compulsion of law, it would only be so engaged
if the data itself contained incriminating matters. If the material were
incriminatory it would be open to the judge in any subsequent trial to
exclude evidence of the underlying material, or of the means by which the
prosecution gained access to it or of the defendant's knowledge of the
means of access (under the *PACE Act* 1984, s.78); accordingly, the extent to
which the privilege may be engaged is strictly limited. Furthermore, the
court said that the principle that evidence existing independently of the
will of the subject does not normally engage the privilege against self-
incrimination is clearly established in domestic law, and the key which
provides access to protected data, like the data itself, exists separately from
a person's "will"; even if a person created his own key, once created, the
key to the data remains independent of his "will", albeit it is retained only
in his memory, at least until it is changed.

C. LEGAL PROFESSIONAL PRIVILEGE

(1) The nature of legal professional privilege

As to whether covert surveillance of privileged communications between   ★**12–7**
lawyers and their clients is permitted under Part II of the *RIPA* 2000, see

McE. v. Prison Service of Northern Ireland (Northern Ireland Human Rights Commission intervening); C. v. Chief Constable of the Police Service of Northern Ireland (Same intervening); M. v. Same (Same intervening) [2009] 2 W.L.R. 782, HL (*post*, § 15–252).

★   The presence of an appropriate adult during a conversation between an accused and his solicitor does not stop that conversation being subject to legal privilege. Part of the role of an appropriate adult is to facilitate communication between solicitor and client, and it could not be right either as a matter of principle or policy that vulnerable individuals should in practice be deprived of the opportunity of confidential legal advice. However, it is not that conversations with an appropriate adult are privileged but that the presence of an appropriate adult at a conversation that would otherwise attract legal privilege does not destroy that privilege. Where such a meeting takes place and the appropriate adult is a social worker, that does not prevent another social worker from interviewing the accused about the complaints against him and using information resulting from that meeting in the course of child protection procedures: *A Local Authority v. B.* [2009] 1 F.L.R. 289 (Fam D) (Hedley J.).

(5) Statutory extensions

★**12–20**   The amendment of section 33 of the *Administration of Justice Act* 1985 effected by the *Legal Services Act* 2007, s.182 and Sched. 17, para. 22, came into force on March 31, 2009: *Legal Services Act 2007 (Commencement No. 4, Transitory and Transitional Provisions and Appointed Day) Order* 2009 (S.I. 2009 No. 503).

III. DISCLOSURE

A. PRELIMINARY

European Convention on Human Rights

12–51b   While the ECHR requires the prosecution to disclose any material of which they are aware and which either materially weakens their case or materially strengthens the defence case, they are not under a duty to search for disclosable material to disclose. Whilst their duty requires them to be alert to examine and re-examine their case in the light of known and emerging lines of defence, they are under no duty to comb through all the material in their possession for the purposes of investigating all possible lines of defence. Equally at the appeal stage, there is no duty on them to re-investigate the entire position on disclosure, though their disclosure obligation does extend to material which should have been disclosed at an earlier stage, or which had become disclosable in the light of developments in the appeal, or which was disclosable but had only come to their attention since the trial. Where there had been a failure to comply with the Article 6 duty of disclosure at trial, it would be incompatible with the appellant's rights under that article for the prosecution to seek to support the conviction if the appellant were able to show that there was a reasonable possibility of unfairness as a result of the non-disclosure. The fact that no point had been taken at trial about non-disclosure when the issues were at the forefront of everyone's mind was a factor to be taken into account, as was the extent to which the grounds of appeal

have identified the issue at trial which was likely to have been affected by the
non-disclosure: *McDonald v. H.M. Advocate, The Times*, November 5, 2008,
PC.

B. LEGISLATION

(1) Criminal Procedure and Investigations Act 1996

Criminal Procedure and Investigations Act 1996, ss.1, 2

General interpretation
   R. *(Dacre and Associated Newspapers) v. City of Westminster Magistrates' Court*   **12–53**
is now reported at [2009] 1 Cr.App.R. 6, *sub nom. R. (Dacre) v. Westminster
Magistrates' Court.*

Criminal Procedure and Investigations Act 1996, ss.3, 4

Initial duty of prosecutor to disclose
   Failure by the prosecution to make proper disclosure is inherently unfair,   **12–54a**
creates unjustified pressure on the defence team struggling with the difficult
task of defending and may deprive the defendant of a proper opportunity of
presenting his case before the jury; and, since a jury might not appreciate the
importance of proper, timely advance disclosure, and might regard cross-
examination designed to elicit the defects and failures in disclosure as whinge-
ing in an effort to draw attention away from the real issues, where there has
been inadequate disclosure, the judge should explain these difficulties to the
jury and the importance to a fair trial of fulfilling the duty to disclose relevant
information and should explain that any difficulties or defects in the defence
case may have been aggravated and exacerbated by the prosecution's failure:
R. v. Kenedy, unreported, October 9, 2008, CA ([2008] EWCA Crim. 2817).

Criminal Procedure and Investigations Act 1996, ss. 5, 6

Compulsory disclosure by accused
   In *R. v. Essa* [2009] 5 *Archbold News* 2, CA ([2009] EWCA Crim. 43), it was   **★12–56**
said that no lawyer should advise a client not to serve a defence statement.
Section 5(5) of the 1996 Act requires the accused to give such a statement to
the court and the prosecutor. It is not open to those who advise defendants to
pick and choose which statutory rules applicable to the conduct of criminal
proceedings they obey and which they do not. (See also *post*, § 12–62.)

Criminal Procedure and Investigations Act 1996, ss.6A–6E

Contents of defence statement
   The amendment of section 6A (insertion of subs. (1)(ca)) of the 1996 Act ef-   **12–57a**
fected by the *CJIA* 2008, s.60(1), came into force on November 3, 2008:
*Criminal Justice and Immigration Act 2008 (Commencement No. 3 and Transitional
Provisions) Order* 2008 (2008 S.I. No. 2712). The amendment is of no effect either in relation to offences into which a criminal investigation within the
meaning of section 1(4) of the 1996 Act has begun, in England and Wales,
before April 4, 2005, or in relation to cases to which Part I of that Act applies
by virtue of section 1(1) or (2) before November 3, 2008.

Criminal Procedure and Investigations Act 1996, ss.10, 11

Faults in disclosure by accused
   The amendment of section 11 (insertion of words in square brackets into   **12–62**

subs. (2)(f)(ii)) of the 1996 Act effected by the *CJIA* 2008, s.60(2), came into force on November 3, 2008: *Criminal Justice and Immigration Act 2008 (Commencement No. 3 and Transitional Provisions) Order* 2008 (S.I. 2008 No. 2712). The amendment is of no effect either in relation to offences into which a criminal investigation within the meaning of section 1(4) of the 1996 Act has begun, in England and Wales, before April 4, 2005, or in relation to cases to which Part I of that Act applies by virtue of section 1(1) or (2) before November 3, 2008.

★ Section 11(5) of the 1996 Act, which entitles the prosecution to comment on the absence of a defence statement, is compatible with the right to a fair trial enshrined in Article 6 of the ECHR (§ 16–57 in the main work). Although the prosecution do not need to make a preliminary application to the judge for leave to cross-examine upon the topic, the use which can be made of this provision is not without judicial control. The judge is able to interfere and stop cross-examination if it is unfair and can decide, where such examination has been embarked upon, the terms in which he directs the jury. If the cross-examination was unfair it is open to the judge to tell the jury to disregard it: *R. v. Essa* [2009] 5 *Archbold News* 2, CA ([2009] EWCA Crim. 43). (See also *ante*, § 12–56.)

(2) Rules and regulations

12–80c As to whether a judge may rely on material shown to him in an *ex parte* public interest immunity application when deciding on an application to admit hearsay as being in "the interests of justice", see *R. v. Ali and Hussain ante*, § 11–3.

(3) Codes of practice

★12–100b As from October 31, 2009, the existing code of practice for the conduct of service investigations by service policemen is revoked and replaced: *Criminal Procedure and Investigations Act 1996 (Code of Practice) (Armed Forces) Order* 2009 (S.I. 2009 No. 989). The new code reflects changes in the structure of service courts made by the *AFA* 2006.

(5) Miscellaneous

Criminal Procedure Rules 2005 (S.I. 2005 No. 384), Pt 21

Advance information

12–114 As from April 6, 2009, a new Part 21 (initial details of prosecution case) is substituted for the existing Part 21 (advance information in magistrates courts) by the *Criminal Procedure (Amendment No. 2) Rules* 2008 (S.I. 2008 No. 3269), r.8, and Sched. 1. As to the application of the new Part 21, see rule 2.1(13) of the 2005 rules, *ante*, § 2–206.

Criminal Procedure Rules 2005 (S.I. 2005 No. 384), Pt 21 (as substituted by the Criminal Procedure (Amendment No. 2) Rules 2008 (S.I. 2008 No. 3269), r.8, and Sched. 1)

When this Part applies

12–115 21.1.—(1) This Part applies in a magistrates' court, where the offence is one that can be tried in a magistrates' court.

158

(2) The court may direct that, for a specified period, this Part will not apply—
  (a) to any case in that court; or
  (b) to any specified category of case.

Providing initial details of the prosecution case
21.2. The prosecutor must provide initial details of the prosecution case by—   **12–116**
  (a) serving those details on the court officer; and
  (b) making those details available to the defendant,
at, or before, the beginning of the day of the first hearing.

Content of initial details
21.3. Initial details of the prosecution case must include—   **12–117**
  (a) a summary of the evidence on which that case will be based; or
  (b) any statement, document or extract setting out facts or other matters on
    which that case will be based; or
  (c) any combination of such a summary, statement, document or extract; and
  (d) the defendant's previous convictions.

CHAPTER 13

EVIDENCE OF BAD CHARACTER

I. INTRODUCTION

C. INTERPRETATION

Criminal Justice Act 2003, s.112

Interpretation of Chapter 1
The amendment of section 112 of the 2003 Act effected by the *AFA* 2006   ★**13–8**
comes into force on October 31, 2009: *Armed Forces Act 2006 (Commencement
No. 5) Order* 2009 (S.I. 2009 No. 1167). In connection with that commencement, see the transitional provision in the *Armed Forces Act 2006 (Transitional
Provisions etc.) Order* 2009 (S.I. 2009 No. 1059), Sched. 1, para. 53(2) (interpretation of reference to "service offence").

D. ARMED FORCES

The amendments to Schedule 6 to the 2003 Act effected by the *AFA* 2006   ★**13–10**
come into force on October 31, 2009: *Armed Forces Act 2006 (Commencement
No. 5) Order* 2009 (S.I. 2009 No. 1167). For rules made under Schedule 6, see
the *Armed Forces (Service Civilian Court) Rules* 2009 (S.I. 2009 No. 1209) and
the *Armed Forces (Summary Appeal Court) Rules* 2009 (S.I. 2009 No. 1211).

III. DEFENDANTS

A. ADMISSIBILITY

Criminal Justice Act 2003, ss.101, 108

In *R. v. McAllister* [2009] 1 Cr.App.R. 10, CA, the court held: (i) that where   ★**13–25a** a trial judge rules that admission of bad character evidence would not have such an adverse effect on the fairness of the proceedings as to require exclusion (see s.101(3)), but fails to give reasons, it is open to the Court of Appeal to reach its own conclusion, and (ii) that where admission of the evidence would involve a risk of a satellite trial, this was a factor to be weighed in the scales against admission lest the jury should be diverted and deflected from their immediate task. As to this case see also *post*, § 13–42. As to the need to avoid satellite litigation, see also *R. v. O'Dowd* [2009] 5 *Archbold News* 1, CA (where it was emphasised that the risks are greater where there has been no conviction in relation to the conduct alleged, where it is ancient and where it is disputed).

B. The Seven Gateways

(4) Important matter in issue between defendant and prosecution (ss.101(1)(d), 103)

(a) *Matters in issue*

★**13–38**   *R. v. Freeman; R. v. Crawford* is now reported at [2009] 1 Cr.App.R. 15.

The unlikelihood of coincidence

★**13–42**   It was held in *R. v. McAllister* [2009] 1 Cr.App.R. 10, CA, that asking a jury to look at evidence relating to a number of allegations as a whole in order to cast light on the evidence relating to an individual offence is not the same as asking a jury to consider the defendant's propensity to commit an offence. The court found that, on the contrary, it is merely asking the jury to recognise that evidence in relation to a particular offence on an indictment may appear stronger and more compelling when all the evidence, including evidence relating to other offences, is looked at as a whole. In such cases, the evidence (which may loosely be described as "similar fact") is adduced not as evidence of a propensity, but rather to explain and augment other evidence (proof of guilt *via* the unlikelihood of coincidence). It was said that a true propensity case requires the prosecution to prove the defendant's guilt of another offence (which may or may not be the subject of another conviction). Once the jury are satisfied that a defendant is guilty of that other offence (or other disreputable conduct), they may deploy that conclusion as tending to show he is more likely to have committed the offence on the indictment. See also *ante*, § 13–25a.

Practical application

Identity
★**13–45**   See *R. v. Spittle, post*, § 13–67.

Particular topics

Directing the jury
★**13–63a**   *R. v. Freeman; R. v. Crawford* is now reported at [2009] 1 Cr.App.R. 15.

(c) Propensity evidence

Authorities

Resolution of factual disputes

In *R. v. K.* [2009] Crim.L.R. 517, CA, it was said that the course recom-   ★**13–66**
mended in *Ainscough* and *Humphris* (see the main work) need not be followed
where the defendant admits sufficient in relation to the circumstances of the
previous offence for the relevant propensity to be established.

Establishing a propensity (s.103(2)–(6))

Section 103(2) of the *CJA* 2003 (§ 13–37 in the main work) provides   ★**13–67**
permissive and simple ways of establishing propensity; where they do not
apply, propensity may be established by other means; thus a defendant's
propensity to conspire to commit burglary could be proved by evidence of
his having committed substantive burglaries notwithstanding that conspiracy to burgle and burglary were neither of the same description as each
other (see subs. (4)(a)) nor of the same category as each other (see subs.
(4)(b) and the *Criminal Justice Act 2003 (Categories of Offences) Order* 2004 (S.I.
2004 No. 3346) (referred to in the main work)): *R. v. Johnson* [2009] 4 *Archbold News* 1, CA.

In *R. v. Spittle* [2009] R.T.R. 14, CA, where the defendant was charged   ★
with, *inter alia*, dangerous driving (*RTA* 1988, s.2 (§ 32–27 in the main
work)), evidence of his previous convictions for driving whilst disqualified
was held to have been admissible within section 101(1) of the *CJA* 2003
(§ 13–25 in the main work) in that it supported the correctness of the
identification which was the only issue in the case (considering *R. v. Eastlake
(Nicky) and Eastlake (Kevin Scott)* (cited in the main work)). As to this case, see
also *post*, § 14–25.

(6) Correcting a false impression

Criminal Justice Act 2003, s.105

Misleading impression about the defendant

Where a prosecution application to adduce evidence of the defendant's bad   **13–76**
character under the *CJA* 2003, s.101(1)(f) (§ 13–25 in the main work), was
based on an answer given by the defendant in cross-examination, "I am not
that type of person.", the application should have been refused where the
question had had two parts, in consequence of which it was not possible to
be sure as to which part the answer related or what, therefore, the defendant was saying: *R. v. Good*, 173 J.P. 1, CA.

As to section 105(7) ("(7) Only prosecution evidence is admissible under   ★
section 101(1)(f).".), it was held in *R. v. Assani* [2009] Crim.L.R. 514, CA, that
the mere fact that the relevant material was contained in a statement made by
a prosecution witness did not make it "prosecution evidence".

Effect of previous convictions being "spent"

R. v. M. (Ian) (see the main work) was considered in *R. v. M. (C.P.) (Practice*   ★**13–77**
Note) [2009] 2 Cr.App.R. 54(3), CA. Without purporting to overrule it, the

161

court expressed the view that once a judge had decided that a defendant with previous convictions could be treated as a person of good character, it was inappropriate to give the good character direction in terms that left it open to the jury to disagree. It should be given in affirmative terms. For consideration as to how to balance these contrasting positions, see the commentary in *Criminal Law Week* 2009/23/7.

(7) Attack on another person's character (ss.101(1)(g), 106)

Attack on another person's character

★**13–78**   As to section 106(3) of the 2003 Act, see *R. v. Assani, ante,* § 13–76.

Evidence/ imputation that another has committed an offence/ behaved reprehensibly

The nature of the previous convictions as a factor in the exercise of discretion, scope of cross-examination and evidential significance of matters cross-examined to

★**13–97**   What was said in *R. v. McLeod* as to the primary purpose of cross-examination of the accused under this head being to show that his evidence is not worthy of belief was endorsed by the Court of Appeal in *R. v. Hearne,* 173 J.P. 97 (as to which, see also *post,* § 13–101).

Directing the jury

★**13–101**   In *R. v. Hearne, ante,* § 13–97, where evidence of the appellant's two old previous convictions for burglary was admitted under sections 101(1)(g) and 106 of the 2003 Act (§§ 13–25, 13–78 in the main work), it was found that the judge might have been wise to warn the jury that they should not deploy the previous convictions as any evidence of a propensity to commit burglary (the offence with which the appellant was charged), let alone a propensity for untruthfulness. However, no harm was done because it was made clear that the only reason the evidence was admitted was as background.

V. REHABILITATION OF OFFENDERS

(1) Introduction

13–120   The *Rehabilitation of Offenders Act 1974 (Exceptions) Order* 1975 (S.I. 1975 No. 1023) has been further amended by the *Tribunals Courts and Enforcement Act 2007 (Transitional and Consequential Provisions) Order* 2008 (S.I. 2008 No 2683), the *Rehabilitation of Offenders Act 1974 (Exceptions) (Amendment) (England and Wales) Order* 2008 (S.I. 2008 No. 3259); and the *Health Care and Associated Professions (Miscellaneous Amendments and Practitioner Psychologists) Order* 2009 (S.I. 2009 No. 1182), Sched. 4, Pts 1 and 6.

(3) Statute

Rehabilitation of Offenders Act 1974, s.1

Rehabilitated persons and spent convictions

★**13–123**   The amendment of section 1 of the 1974 Act effected by the *AFA* 2006 comes into force on October 31, 2009: *Armed Forces Act 2006 (Commencement No. 5) Order* 2009 (S.I. 2009 No. 1167).

Rehabilitation of Offenders Act 1974, s.2

Rehabilitation of persons dealt with in service disciplinary proceedings

The amendments of section 2 of the 1974 Act effected by the *AFA* 2006   **★13–124**
come into force on October 31, 2009: *Armed Forces Act 2006 (Commencement
No. 5) Order* 2009 (S.I. 2009 No. 1167).

Rehabilitation of Offenders Act 1974, s.5

Rehabilitated persons and spent convictions

The amendments of section 5 of the 1974 Act effected by the *AFA* 2006   **★13–131**
come into force on October 31, 2009: *Armed Forces Act 2006 (Commencement
No. 5) Order* 2009 (S.I. 2009 No. 1167).

Rehabilitation of Offenders Act 1974, s.6

The rehabilitation period applicable to a conviction

Section 49 of, and Schedule 10 to, the *CJIA* 2008 came into force on   **13–132**
December 19, 2008: *Criminal Justice and Immigration Act 2008 (Commencement
No. 5) Order* 2008 (S.I. 2008 No. 3260).

Cautions, etc.

As to the commencement of section 49 of, and Schedule 10 to, the *CJIA*   **13–135**
2008, see *ante*, § 13–132.

CHAPTER 14

EVIDENCE OF IDENTIFICATION

I. VISUAL IDENTIFICATION

B. THE TURNBULL GUIDELINES

(6) Application of the guidelines to specific circumstances

Identification by police officers

In *R. v. Spittle* [2009] R.T.R. 14, CA, a police officer being carried as a pas-   **★14–25**
senger in a police car saw the driver of a speeding vehicle for two or three
seconds. He immediately informed his colleague that he recognised the driver
though he could not put a name to him. After the incident, he returned to
the police station and identified the defendant from photographs as being the
driver. He later identified the defendant through a video identification procedure, as did his colleague. It was held that the judge had been correct to refuse to withdraw the case from the jury. Of particular importance was the fact
that the officer had been alerted to the fact that there was a dangerous driver
about. This was quite different from a case where a witness purports to identify
someone whom he has never seen before and who, in the context of an unexpected incident, is not alert to the need to observe particularly carefully with a
view to making an identification. The officer was alert and trained to carry out
observation. As to this case, see also *ante*, § 13–67.

E. Identification and the Use of Visual Aids

(2) Identification of the defendant

Identification by the jury

14–46   Where a jury have been invited to conclude that a defendant had committed an offence by looking at an image or images captured at the scene of the crime, there is a general and invariable requirement for the judge to warn them of the risk of mistaken identification and of the need to exercise particular care in any identification which they make for themselves. It was not sufficient to direct the jury not to leap to the conclusion that the person in the images was the defendant and that they had to consider the matter carefully without, at that point in the summing-up, a careful and full direction as to the dangers of possible misidentification: *R. v. Ali* [2009] Crim.L.R. 40, CA. Where a witness had given evidence that he recognised the defendant in the images, although recognition might be more reliable than identification by a stranger, the risk of mistaken identification remained, and it was incumbent on the judge to direct the jury in such a way that they fully understood that mistakes could be made, and had been made in the past, in purported recognition of those with whom a witness believed he was familiar: *ibid.*

Recognition by a witness

14–47   In *R. v. Chaney* [2009] 1 Cr.App.R. 35, CA, the court approved the guidance given in *R. v. Smith* (cited in the mainwork, and now reported at [2009] 1 Cr.App.R. 36, *sub nom. R. v. Smith (Dean Martin)*), on the issue of police officers being shown CCTV images, *etc.*, for the purpose of having an opportunity of recognising an offender, and subsequent police guidance to similar effect.

★   Neither Code D nor the safeguards referred to in *R. v. Smith, ante,* applied where a police officer was asked to view CCTV footage to see if he could recognise an offender, having been informed that it was thought that the appellant (whom he had last seen at least two years earlier) could be seen on the recording, when it was not proposed to call the officer to give evidence at trial. When the officer did in fact give evidence, the judge had given a clear warning that the officer had been expecting to see the appellant when he viewed the footage. The jury were entitled to look at the recording to make their own assessment as to the clarity of the image and, once they had reached the conclusion that it was sufficiently clear, to see whether the defendant resembled the man shown on the recording: *R. v. Tucker* [2009] Crim.L.R. 441, CA.

III. IDENTIFICATION BY OTHER EVIDENCE

Evidence as to patterns of criminal behaviour

14–70   Where the issue at a trial of seven counts of robbery was identity, and where evidence was admitted of a person responsible for monitoring crime in the area to the effect that no similar offences were reported following the defendant's arrest, such evidence had been relevant and probative; nor was it unfairly prejudicial as the defence were able to submit that it was of no value because, for example, the real robber might have died, moved area, stopped committing robberies or been arrested or imprisoned: *R. v. Wilson* [2009] Crim.L.R. 193, CA.

CHAPTER 15

INVESTIGATORY POWERS; CONFESSIONS; DISCRETION TO EXCLUDE EVIDENCE, ETC.

I. INVESTIGATORY POWERS

A. POLICE AND CRIMINAL EVIDENCE ACT 1984

(2) Codes of practice

(a) *Statute*

Police and Criminal Evidence Act 1984, ss.66, 67

Codes of practice

As from a day to be appointed, codes of practice under section 66 of the   **15–3**
PACE Act 1984 must make provision about the questioning of a person by a
constable in accordance with section 22 of the *Counter-Terrorism Act* 2008
(post-charge questioning in relation to terrorist offences): 2008 Act, s.22(7).

Codes of practice - supplementary

The amendment of section 67 of the 1984 Act effected by the *AFA* 2006   **★15–5**
comes into force on October 31, 2009: *Armed Forces Act 2006 (Commencement
No. 5) Order* 2009 (S.I. 2009 No. 1167).

(b) *Commencement*

As from January 1, 2009, the *Police and Criminal Evidence Act 1984 (Codes   **15–7**
of Practice) (Revisions to Code A) (No. 2) Order* 2008 (S.I. 2008 No. 3146) made
the following amendments to Code A: (1) paragraphs 2.2 and 2.3 (searches
requiring reasonable grounds for suspicion (*post*, Appendix A–5)) now make it
clear that reasonable suspicion should not be based on single factors alone; (2)
paragraph 4 (recording requirements (*post*, Appendix A–11)) is varied so as
(a) to amend paragraph 4.10A and insert a new paragraph 4.10B to clarify
the position regarding receipts for stops or stop and searches, and (b) to enable police officers in England and Wales, and community support officers, to
provide a receipt rather than a full record when undertaking an encounter in
accordance with paragraphs 4.12 to 4.19, the only recording requirement
now relating to the ethnicity of the person who is the subject of such an
encounter; (3) a new "Note for Guidance" numbered 25 is inserted in relation
to new paragraph 4.10B; (4) Annex D and Annex E are deleted (the latter
having been inserted as part of a pilot scheme in certain areas with effect from
October 27, 2008, by the *Police and Criminal Evidence Act 1984 (Codes of
Practice) (Revisions to Code A) Order* 2008 (S.I. 2008 No. 2638)). Code A (as
amended) is set out at Appendix A, post.

(3) "Reasonable grounds for suspicion"

15–24 *O'Hara* (cited in the main work) was followed in *Commr of Police of the Metropolis v. Raissi*: see *post*, § 25–81.

(7) Application of Act to Armed Forces

Police and Criminal Evidence Act 1984, s.113

★**15–30** The amendments to section 113 of the 1984 Act effected by the *AFA* 2006 came into force on March 28, 2009, so far as is necessary for the purpose of enabling the Secretary of State to make orders, regulations and rules: *Armed Forces Act 2006 (Commencement No. 4) Order* 2009 (S.I. 2009 No. 812)); and for all other purposes, they come into force on October 31, 2009: *Armed Forces Act 2006 (Commencement No. 5) Order* 2009 (S.I. 2009 No. 1167). In connection with these commencement provisions, see the transitional provisions in the *Armed Forces Act 2006 (Transitional Provisions etc.) Order* 2009 (S.I. 2009 No. 1059), Sched. 1, para. 28(2) and (3) (interpretation of references to "service offences", to "a power conferred by or under the *Armed Forces Act* 2006", and to "persons charged under that Act with service offences").

C. Entry, Search and Seizure

(2) Statute

Police and Criminal Evidence Act 1984, s.8

15–72 *Redknapp* (cited in the main work) is now reported at [2009] 1 All E.R. 229, *sub nom. Redknapp v. Commr of Police for City of London.*

Police and Criminal Evidence Act 1984, Sched. 1

Procedure

15–79 *Redknapp* (cited in the main work) is now reported at [2009] 1 All E.R. 229, *sub nom. Redknapp v. Commr of Police for City of London.*

In *R. (Faisaltex Ltd) v. Preston Crown Court* [2009] 1 Cr.App.R. 37, it was held that there was no basis for issuing a warrant under Schedule 1 to the 1984 Act in relation to material located in solicitors' offices, where the solicitors were reputable and were not under investigation. There was no reason to think that the solicitors would not comply with a production order, so the condition in paragraph 14(d) of Schedule 1 was not satisfied.

Privilege against self-incrimination

15–89 In *R. (Malik) v. Manchester Crown Court* [2008] 4 All E.R. 403, DC, judicial review proceedings were brought in relation to a production order issued pursuant to provisions in the *Terrorism Act* 2000 analogous to those in the *PACE Act* 1984. The court reviewed the authorities on whether the privilege against self-incrimination can be invoked in relation to pre-existing documents. The majority decision in *C. Plc v. P.* [2008] Ch. 1, CA (Civ. Div.), was to the effect that no such privilege exists, but the House of Lords have granted leave to appeal against this decision. Pending the House of Lords' ruling, the court in *Malik* recommended that circuit judges adopt the majority's approach in *R. (Bright) v. Central Criminal Court* (cited in the main work), that is to treat the privilege against self-incrimination as an important relevant factor to be taken into account when deciding how to exercise discretion in respect of the disclosure of pre-existing documents. The following non-exhaustive factors should be considered: (1) the true benefit to the investigation of the material in question, including the extent to which the material can be (a) obtained by other means, (b) disclosed in stages, the non-privileged material being disclosed first, and (c) redacted; (2) the importance of the privilege itself, convincing justification being needed to compel a person to forego its protection; (3) the gravity of the offence with which the person required to surrender the privilege might be charged, disclosure requiring greater justification for more serious offences; (4) the risk of prosecution, although in the absence of an offer of immunity the court should be slow to treat a prosecution as unlikely; and (5) the trial judge's power to exclude evidence under section 78 of the 1984 Act. As to this case, see also *post*, § 25–122.

Police and Criminal Evidence Act 1984, s.17

Entry for purpose of arrest, etc.

In *Baker v. CPS*, 173 J.P. 215, DC, the court considered the power of   ★**15-109**
search conferred by section 17(1)(e) of the 1984 Act. The following propositions, all *obiter*, are derived from the judgments: (i) the power is wide enough to cover saving a person from seriously harming himself, as well as seriously harming third parties; (ii) entry will be lawful provided that the officer reasonably believes that this is necessary to save life or limb or to prevent serious damage to property; (iii) there is no need for an officer to explain the reason for his entry to the occupier where this is impossible, impracticable or undesirable, as in cases of emergency; (iv) the power of search extends to a search of the person, provided that it is limited to the object of saving life and limb where the risk thereto is properly regarded as imminent; and (v) an officer who has entered lawfully under this power is entitled to remain on the premises until he is reasonably satisfied that life, limb or property are no longer in danger and, while he is thus lawfully on the premises, he may search for anything which he reasonably believes may be used to endanger life, limb or property.

Police and Criminal Evidence Act 1984, s.22

Retention

In *Scopelight Ltd v. Chief of Police for Northumbria and the Federation Against*   ★**15-119**
Copyright Theft Ltd, unreported, May 7, 2009, QBD (Sharp J.) ([2009] EWHC 958 (QB)), it was held that, once the CPS have decided not to prosecute, the police do not have power to retain private property under section 22 of the 1984 Act so that a private body can consider whether to bring a prosecution, or whilst that private prosecution is being brought; while section 22(2) specifies certain stated purposes for which anything seized for the purposes of a criminal investigation may be retained, which include use as evidence at a trial for an offence, it must be read subject to the statutory purposes for which the legislation contemplated that the police powers of retention might be exercised. For a criticism of this decision, see the commentary in *Criminal Law Week* 2009/22/10.

Criminal Justice and Police Act 2001, ss.53–58

Retention of seized items

15-135   As from a day to appointed, the reference in section 57(1)(k) of the 2001 Act to section 40(4) of the *Human Fertilisation and Embryology Act* 1990 is substituted by a reference to paragraph 7(4) of Schedule 3B to the 1990 Act: *Human Fertilisation and Embryology Act* 2008, s.65, and Sched. 7, para. 19.

Criminal Justice and Police Act 2001, ss.63–66

General interpretation of Part 2

★15-147   The amendment relating to the *Estate Agents Act* 1979, s.11, came into force on October 1, 2008: *Consumers, Estate Agents and Redress Act 2007 (Commencement No. 5 and Savings and Transitional Provisions) Order* 2008 (S.I. 2008 No. 2550).

As from a day to be appointed, the *Human Fertilisation and Embryology Act* 2008, s.65, and Sched. 7, para. 20, make the following amendments to section 66 of the 2001 Act: (i) after section 66(4)(j), there is inserted a paragraph (ja) referring to paragraph 5 of Schedule 3B to the *Human Fertilisation and Embryology Act* 1990; and (ii) section 66(5)(g) is repealed.

Powers of seizure (Schedule 1, Parts 1, 2 and 3)

Powers to which section 50 applies (list 1)

15-148   As from a day to appointed, in Schedule 1, paragraph 52, to the 2001 Act, the reference to section 40(2) of the *Human Fertilisation and Embryology Act* 1990 is substituted by a reference to paragraph 7(1) and (2) of Schedule 3B to the 1990 Act: *Human Fertilisation and Embryology Act* 2008, s.65, and Sched. 7, para. 21.

D. Arrest

(2) The Police and Criminal Evidence Act 1984

Preserved powers of arrest

★15-172   The repeals in Schedule 2 to the 1984 Act effected by the *AFA* 2006 come into force on October 31, 2009: *Armed Forces Act 2006 (Commencement No. 5) Order* 2009 (S.I. 2009 No. 1167).

E. Questioning and Treatment of Persons

(5) Access to legal advice

Police and Criminal Evidence Act 1984, s.58

Section 58 and drink driving cases

15-221   *Kennedy v. DPP* (see the main work) was considered in *Gearing v. DPP, post*, § 32–104.

(8) Fingerprints, photographs, intimate and other samples

Police and Criminal Evidence Act 1984, s.61

Fingerprinting

As from a day to be appointed, after section 61(6B) of the 1984 Act, the **15–232**
Counter-Terrorism Act 2008, s.10(1), inserts a new subsection (6BA), as follows—

> "(6BA) A constable may take a person's fingerprints without the appropriate consent if the person is subject to a control order.".

As from a day to be appointed, the *Counter-Terrorism Act* 2008, s.10(6)(a), makes the following consequential amendments to section 61 of the 1984 Act: (i) in subsection (6C), after "subsection (6A)", there are inserted the words "or (6BA)"; (ii) in subsection (7), for "or (6A)" there are substituted the words ", (6A) or (6BA)"; and (iii) in subsection (7A), after "subsection (6A)", in both places where it occurs, there are inserted the words "or (6BA)".

The amendments effected by section 10 of the 2008 Act have effect from the commencement of that section regardless of when the control order was made: 2008 Act, s.13.

Police and Criminal Evidence Act 1984, s.63

Other samples

As from a day to be appointed, after section 63(3C) of the 1984 Act, the **15–238**
Counter-Terrorism Act 2008, s.10(2), inserts a new subsection (3D), as follows—

> "(3D) A non-intimate sample may also be taken from a person without the appropriate consent if the person is subject to a control order.".

As from a day to be appointed, the *Counter-Terrorism Act* 2008, s.10(6)(b), makes the following consequential amendments to section 63 of the 1984 Act: (i) in subsection (8A) for "or (3C)" there are substituted the words ", (3C) or (3D)"; (ii) in the opening words of subsection (8B), after "police station", there are inserted the words "or by virtue of subsection (3D) at a place other than a police station"; and (iii) in paragraph (a) of that subsection, after "officer", there are inserted the words ", or, in a subsection (3D) case, a constable,".

The amendments effected by section 10 of the 2008 Act have effect from the commencement of that section regardless of when the control order was made: 2008 Act, s.13.

Police and Criminal Evidence Act 1984, s.63A

Fingerprints and samples: supplementary provisions

As from a day to be appointed, the *Counter-Terrorism Act* 2008, s.10(3), **15–241**
makes the following amendments to section 63A of the 1984 Act: (i) in subsection (1), after "reported for such an offence", there are inserted the words "or he is or has been subject to a control order"; and (ii) after subsection (6), there is inserted a new subsection (6A), as follows—

> "(6A) A constable may require a person who is subject to a control order to attend a police station in order to—
>> (a) have his fingerprints taken in accordance with section 61(6BA);
>> (b) have a non-intimate sample taken in accordance with section 63(3D).".

As from a day to be appointed, the *Counter-Terrorism Act* 2008, s.10(6)(c), amends section 63A(7) of the 1984 Act so that, after "subsection (4)", there are inserted the words "or (6A)".

The amendments effected by section 10 of the 2008 Act have effect from the commencement of that section regardless of when the control order was made: 2008 Act, s.13.

As from a day to be appointed, the *Counter-Terrorism Act* 2008, s.14(1) and (2), substitute new paragraphs (a) and (b) in section 63A(1) of the 1984 Act, as follows—

> "(a) other fingerprints, impressions of footwear or samples—
>> (i) to which the person seeking to check has access and which are held by or on behalf of any one or more relevant law-enforcement authorities or are held in connection with or as a result of an investigation of an offence, or
>> (ii) which are held by or on behalf of the Security Service or the Secret Intelligence Service;
> (b) information derived from other samples—
>> (i) which is contained in records to which the person seeking to check has access and which are held as mentioned in paragraph (a)(i) above, or
>> (ii) which is held by or on behalf of the Security Service or the Secret Intelligence Service".

As from a day to be appointed, the *Counter-Terrorism Act* 2008, s.14(1) and (3), substitute the following for the words from "other fingerprints" to the end of section 63A(1ZA) of the 1984 Act—

> "other fingerprints—
> (a) to which the person seeking to check has access and which are held by or on behalf of any one or more relevant law-enforcement authorities or which are held in connection with or as a result of an investigation of an offence, or
> (b) which are held by or on behalf of the Security Service or the Secret Intelligence Service.".

Police and Criminal Evidence Act 1984, s.64

Destruction of fingerprints and samples

15–246   As from a day to be appointed, after section 64(1A) of the 1984 Act, the *Counter-Terrorism Act* 2008, s.10(4), inserts a new subsection (1AA), as follows—

> "(1AA) Where fingerprints or samples are taken from a person who is subject to a control order the fingerprints or samples may be retained after they have fulfilled the purposes for which they were taken but shall not be used by any person except as described in subsection (1AB).".

As from a day to be appointed, the *Counter-Terrorism Act* 2008, s.10(6)(d) amends section 64(1B) of the 1984 Act so that, after "subsection (1A)", there is inserted ", (1AA)".

The amendments effected by section 10 of the 2008 Act have effect from the commencement of that section regardless of when the control order was made: 2008 Act, s.13.

As from a day to be appointed, the *Counter-Terrorism Act* 2008, s.14(1) and (4), amend section 64(1A) of the 1984 Act by substituting for "except for purposes" to the end the words "except as described in subsection (1AB)".

As from a day to be appointed, after section 64(1AA) (*ante*, inserted by the *Counter-Terrorism Act* 2008, s.10) of the 1984 Act, the *Counter-Terrorism Act* 2008, s.14(1) and (5), insert a new subsection (1AB), as follows—

> "(1AB) The fingerprints, impressions of footwear or samples may be used—
> (a) in the interests of national security,

(b) for purposes related to the prevention or detection of crime, the investigation of an offence or the conduct of a prosecution, or

(c) for purposes related to the identification of a deceased person or of the person from whom the material came.".

As from a day to be appointed, the *Counter-Terrorism Act* 2008, s.14(1) and (6), amend section 64(1B) of the 1984 Act by inserting, after "(1AA)" (inserted by the 2008 Act, s.10, *ante*), the words "or (1AB)".

Section 18 of the *Counter-Terrorism Act* 2008 provides a statutory framework **15–247** for the use and retention of DNA samples or profiles and fingerprints that are not held subject to other statutory provisions and there are limitations on their use (in subs. (2)) that match those in new section 64(1AB) of the 1984 Act (*ante*). However, section 18(3) contains a condition that the samples and fingerprints cannot be used for such purposes unless either they have been (i) obtained by the law enforcement authority that holds them pursuant to an authorisation under Part 3 of the *Police Act* 1997 or Part 2 of the *RIPA* 2000, (ii) supplied to the authority by another law enforcement authority, or (iii) otherwise lawfully obtained or acquired by the authority for any of the purposes set out in subsection (2).

In *S. v. U.K.* (2009) 48 E.H.R.R. 50, ECtHR, it was held, contrary to the **15–248** domestic courts' view (see the main work), that section 64(1A) of the 1984 Act is incompatible with Article 8(1) of the ECHR, in that the blanket and indiscriminate nature of the power fails to strike a fair balance between the competing public and private interests and oversteps any acceptable margin of appreciation in that regard; of particular concern is that unconvicted persons, entitled to the presumption of innocence, are to be treated in the same way as convicted persons; and the retention of an unconvicted person's data is especially harmful in the case of minors, given their special situation and the importance of their development and integration into society.

(9) Definitions

Police and Criminal Evidence Act 1984, s.65

Part V: supplementary

As from a day to be appointed, at the appropriate places in section 65(1) of **15–249** the 1984 Act, the following definitions are inserted by the *Counter-Terrorism Act* 2008, s.10(5)—

"' control order' has the same meaning as in the *Prevention of Terrorism Act* 2005;";

"' person subject to a control order' means a person who has become bound by a control order (see section 7(8) of the *Prevention of Terrorism Act* 2005) that remains in force;".

The amendments effected by section 10 of the 2008 Act have effect from the commencement of that section regardless of when the control order was made: 2008 Act, s.13.

F. Police Act 1997 and Regulation of Investigatory Powers Act 2000

In *McE. v. Prison Service of Northern Ireland (Northern Ireland Human Rights* ★**15–252** *Commission intervening); C. v. Chief Constable of the Police Service of Northern Ireland (Same intervening); M. v. Same (Same intervening)* [2009] 2 W.L.R. 782, the House of Lords considered the lawfulness of covert surveillance of privileged conversations (*i.e.* conversations between detainees and lawyers or medical advisers) in police stations and prisons. It was held that: (i) such conversations may be subject to covert surveillance under Part II of *RIPA* 2000, it being clear from the wording of the Act and the history of the legislation on the subject that Parliament intended that the covert surveillance provisions should extend to the type of lawyer/client and doctor/patient consultations that are ordinarily protected by legal professional privilege; but (ii) covert "directed surveillance" of lawyer/client or doctor/patient consultations carried out under section 28 of the 2000 Act, and in accordance with the code of practice on covert surveillance, would violate the rights of a client/patient under Article 8 of the ECHR (right to privacy and respect for family life (§ 16–101 in the main work)), because directed surveillance would not be proportionate in terms of the interference that such surveillance involved and the degree of protection that could be achieved; what was required was a level of authorisation comparable to that for "intrusive surveillance" under section 32; and whereas the Secretary of State had proposed making an order under section 47(1)(b) for such directed surveillance to be treated as intrusive surveillance, no such order had yet been made; until this was done, any directed surveillance of legal consultations in prisons or police stations would be unlawful. As to the admissibility of intelligence obtained by such covert surveillance at trial, see *post*, § 15–531.

II. CONFESSIONS AND RELATED TOPICS

A. CONFESSIONS

(1) Police and Criminal Evidence Act 1984

(a) *Words and phrases*

Police and Criminal Evidence Act 1984, ss.76, 76A

"likely ... to render unreliable any confession which might be made by him in consequence thereof"

15–365   In *R. v. Sherif, Ali (Siraj), Ali (Muhedin), Mohammed, Abdurahman and Abdullahi, The Times*, February 11, 2009, CA, the police justifiably treated a defendant as a potential witness when they started to interview him at a police station, but continued to treat him as such after the point had been reached when he should have been arrested and cautioned. He then made a witness statement which the prosecution sought to adduce as a confession. It was held on appeal that, as to section 76 of the 1984 Act, in deciding whether anything had been said or done that could undermine the reliability of the statement, the judge had been entitled to take into account the fact that, in the prepared statement made by the defendant after arrest and caution, he asserted that he was seeking to give assistance to the police and that he said nothing to suggest that the circumstances were such as to render it likely that what he said was not reliable. For a criticism of this decision, see the commentary in *Criminal Law Week* 2009/06/1.

B. Accusations Made in the Presence of the Defendant

(3) Criminal Justice and Public Order Act 1994

Adverse inferences from a failure to mention facts

Criminal Justice and Public Order Act 1994, s.34

Effect of accused's failure to mention facts when questioned or charged

As from a day to be appointed, the *Counter-Terrorism Act* 2008, s.22(9), inserts a new paragraph (c) after section 34(1)(b) of the 1994 Act, as follows— **15–414**

"; or
(c) at any time after being charged with the offence, on being questioned under section 22 of the *Counter-Terrorism Act* 2008 (post-charge questioning), failed to mention any such fact,".

Silence when questioned or charged

In *R. v. Essa* [2009] 5 *Archbold News* 2, CA ([2009] EWCA Crim. 43), the court said, in relation to section 34 of the 1994 Act , that counsel should use a measure of judgment as to whether it is wise to embark on cross-examination about it and, if cross-examination is embarked upon, the court should use a measure of judgment as to whether a direction as to the drawing of inferences will assist the jury, particularly in cases where the silence at interview has zero or marginal significance. **★15–417**

Criminal Justice and Public Order Act 1994, s.36

Effect of accused's failure or refusal to account for objects, substances or marks

Nothing in section 36 of the 1994 Act is to be read as excluding the operation of that section in relation to a request made in the course of post-charge questioning pursuant to section 22 of the *Counter-Terrorism Act* 2008 (in force as from a day to be appointed): 2008 Act, s.22(10). **15–433**

The Judicial Studies Board specimen direction on section 36 is available on the JSB website (*www.jsboard.co.uk*) and is set out below: **15–434**

"1. The prosecution's case is that:
(a) when the police officer arrested the defendant [he had on him/in or on his clothing or footwear/in his possession] [there was at the place where he was arrested] a (*specify the object , substance or mark concerned*);
(b) the officer reasonably believed that (*e.g. he may have used it to commit the burglary for which he is now being tried*);
(c) the officer told him of his belief, asked him to account for the presence of the [object/substance/mark] and told him that (*e.g. if he did not do so a court may later ask itself why not*); and
(d) the defendant [failed/refused] to account for the presence of [object/substance/mark].

2. If you are sure that the prosecution's case is right, you may draw the conclusion that [he had no innocent account to give at that time/he had no account that he believed would stand up to scrutiny at that time/he has invented his account since that time/he has tailored his account since that time to fit the prosecution's case/ (*here refer to any other reasonable inferences contended for*)]. If you do draw that conclusion, you must not convict him wholly or mainly on the strength of it; but you may take it into account as some additional support for the prosecution's case, and when deciding whether his [evidence/case] about the [object/substance/mark] is true.

3. However, you may draw such a conclusion against him only if you think it is a fair and proper conclusion, and you are satisfied about two things: first, that apart from his [failure/refusal] to account for the [object/substance/mark], the prosecution's case against him is so strong that it clearly calls for an answer by him; second, that the only sensible explanation for his [failure/refusal] is that he had no innocent account to give, or no account that would stand up to scrutiny.

4. (*Add, if appropriate:*) The defence invite you not to draw any conclusion from the defendant's [failure/refusal], on the basis of the following evidence (*here set out the evidence*). If you [accept the evidence and] think this amounts to a reason why you should not draw any conclusion from his [failure/refusal] , do not do so. Otherwise subject to what I have said, you may do so."

Criminal Justice and Public Order Act 1994, s.37

Effect of accused's failure or refusal to account for presence at a particular place

15–435 Nothing in section 37 of the 1994 Act is to be read as excluding the operation of that section in relation to a request made in the course of post-charge questioning pursuant to section 22 of the *Counter-Terrorism Act* 2008 (in force as from a day to be appointed): 2008 Act, s.22(10).

15–437 The Judicial Studies Board specimen direction on section 37 is available on the JSB website (*www.jsboard.co.uk*) and is set out below:

"1. The prosecution's case is that:
    (a) the officer who arrested the defendant found him (*e.g. outside a warehouse while it was being burgled*);
    (b) the officer reasonably believed that the defendant may have been there (*e.g. as a look-out*);
    (c) the officer told the defendant of his belief and asked him to account for his presence there; and
    (d) the defendant [failed/refused] to do so.

2. If you are sure that the prosecution's case is right, you may draw the conclusion that [he had no innocent account to give at that time/he had no account that he believed would stand up to scrutiny at that time/he has invented his account since that time/he has tailored his account since that time to fit the prosecution's case/ (*here refer to any other reasonable inferences contended for*)]. If you do draw that conclusion you must not convict him wholly or mainly on the strength of it; but you may take it into account as some additional support for the prosecution's case, and when deciding whether his [evidence/case] about his presence at the scene is true.

3. You may draw such a conclusion against him only if you think it is a fair and proper conclusion, and you are satisfied about two things: first, that apart from his [failure/refusal] to account for his presence, the prosecution's case against him is so strong that it clearly calls for an answer by him; second, that the only sensible explanation for his [failure/refusal] is that he had no innocent account to give, or no account that would stand up to scrutiny.

4. (*Add, if appropriate:*) The defence invite you not to draw any conclusion from the defendant's [failure/refusal], on the basis of the following evidence (*here set out the evidence*). If you [accept the evidence and] think this amounts to a reason why you should not draw any inference from his [failure/refusal] , do not do so. Otherwise subject to what I have said, you may do so."

Application to armed forces

★**15–439** As from October 31, 2009, S.I. 1997 No. 16 and S.I. 2006 No. 2326 (see the main work) are revoked and effectively replaced by the *Criminal Justice and Public Order Act 1994 (Application to the Armed Forces) Order* 2009 (S.I. 2009 No. 990). Article 4(1) provides that, in relation to any time before that date

references in the Act (as applied by the order) to an accused's being charged
with a service offence are to be read as references to an allegation of an offence being reported to the accused's commanding officer in the form of a
charge under section 76(1) of the *Army Act* 1955, section 76(1) of the *Air Force
Act* 1955 or section 52B(1) of the *Naval Discipline Act* 1957.

III. DISCRETION TO EXCLUDE EVIDENCE

A. UNDER STATUTE

(4) Appeal

(b) *The judge's discretion: Wednesbury principles*

The House of Lords' decision in *R. v. Davis* is now reported at [2008] 1   **15–473**
A.C. 1128.

(11) Evidence obtained through unlawful act or trickery

Eavesdropping

In *McE. v. Prison Service of Northern Ireland (Northern Ireland Human Rights   **★15–531**
Commission intervening); C. v. Chief Constable of the Police Service of Northern
Ireland (Same intervening); M. v. Same (Same intervening)* (*ante*, § 15–252), Lord
Hope said, *obiter*, that whilst their Lordships had not been asked to decide
whether intelligence obtained by covert surveillance of otherwise privileged
conversations could be used against a detainee in evidence at trial, basic rules
of fairness strongly indicated to the contrary (at [66]).

(13) Abuse of process

As to abuse of process in the context of evidence obtained abroad, see *R. v.*   **★15–534**
Redmond, *ante*, § 4–65.

CHAPTER 16

HUMAN RIGHTS

IV. THE RIGHTS GUARANTEED

A. RIGHT TO LIFE

Positive obligations

Van Colle v. Chief Constable of Hertfordshire Police; Smith Chief Constable of   **★16–38a**
Sussex Police (cited in the main work) is now reported at [2009] 1 A.C. 225, *sub
nom. Van Colle v. Chief Constable of the Hertfordshire Police (Secretary of State for
the Home Department intervening); Smith v. Chief Constable of Sussex Police (Secretary of State for the Home Department intervening)*.

As to the state's duty to address a defendant's mental condition, see *R. (Platts) v. H.M. Coroner for South Yorkshire (East District) (Chief Constable of South Yorkshire, interested party)*, 172 J.P. 632, QBD (Wilkie J.), where it was said to be arguable that the state, through the CPS, had breached its positive obligation under Article 2 when it withdrew proceedings in a magistrates' court against a defendant with an obvious mental condition when that decision gave the court no option but to release the defendant (who committed suicide 50 minutes later) unconstrained and unaided.

B. PROHIBITION OF TORTURE

Scope

16–40   The decision of the Divisional Court in *R. (Wellington) v. Secretary of State for the Home Department* has been upheld by the House of Lords: see [2009] 1 A.C. 335.

Positive obligations

16–40a   The Court of Appeal decision in *R. (L.) (a Patient) (by the Official Solicitor as litigation friend) v. Secretary of State for the Home Department* has been unanimously upheld by the House of Lords: see [2008] 3 W.L.R. 1325, *sub nom. R. (L. (A Patient)) v. Secretary of State for Justice (Equality and Human Rights Commission intervening)*.

Where medical evidence had stated that the applicant, the alleged victim of an offence of wounding with intent to cause grievous bodily harm, was suffering from a mental condition which might affect his perception and recollection of events so as to make his account of them unreliable, and where this led the prosecution to a decision not to prosecute, based on a belief that the applicant's mental disability would make his identification of the prospective defendant unreliable (in the absence of any other relevant evidence), that decision violated Article 3 of the ECHR: *R. (F.B.) v. DPP* [2009] 1 Cr.App.R. 38. The decision not to prosecute, taken as it was on the eve of the trial, was not reasonably defensible; it humiliated the applicant and caused him to feel that he was being treated as a second class citizen; far from serving the state's positive obligation to provide protection against serious assaults through the criminal justice system, the nature and manner of the abandonment of the prosecution increased the applicant's sense of vulnerability and of being beyond the protection of the law. See also *post*, E–12e.

D. RIGHT TO LIBERTY AND SECURITY

General

16–45   The decision of the Court of Appeal in *Austin v. Commr of Police of the Metropolis* has been upheld by the House of Lords: see [2009] 2 W.L.R. 372.

E. RIGHT TO A FAIR TRIAL

Application

16–58   The provisions of Article 6(3) of the ECHR constitute express guarantees and cannot be read, as they had been by the Court of Appeal in *R. v. Sellick*

and Sellick (§§ 11–23, 11–25 in the main work), as illustrations of matters to be
taken into account when considering whether a fair trial has been held; and
even where those minimum rights have been respected, the general right to a
fair trial guaranteed by Article 6(1) requires that the court should ascertain
whether the proceedings as a whole were fair: *Al-Khawaja v. U.K.*; *Tahery v.
U.K.* (2009) 49 E.H.R.R. 1, ECtHR.

Evidence

In connection with *Jalloh v. Germany* and the absolute prohibition on the   **16–67**
use of evidence obtained in consequence of a violation of Article 3, see *Gäfgen
v. Germany* (2009) 48 E.H.R.R. 13 (principle extends beyond confessions so as
to include incriminating real evidence recovered as a result of violation).

Anonymity of witnesses

R. v. Davis is now reported [2008] 1 A.C. 1128.   **16–68**

Doorson v. Netherlands (see the main work) was approved in *Al-Khawaja v.
U.K.*; *Tahery v. U.K.* (2009) 49 E.H.R.R. 1, ECtHR.

Trial in the absence of the accused

Spiers (Prosecutor Fiscal) v. Ruddy is now reported at [2008] 1 A.C. 873.   **16–72**

Trial within a reasonable time

In *Burns v. H.M. Advocate (Advocate General for Scotland intervening)* [2009]   **16–73**
2 W.L.R. 935, PC, a person was interviewed in England by police officers of
an English police force who told him that in their opinion there was sufficient
evidence to charge him with an offence and that they would be recommend-
ing such a course either in England or Scotland (where he lived). The Privy
Council held that time began to run for the purposes of the reasonable time
requirement in Article 6(1) of the ECHR (§ 16–57 in the main work) from the
date of the interview, and not from the later date when the Lord Advocate, as
the competent authority in Scotland, required the person to answer charges
on which he was indicted to stand trial in Scotland. It was said that to hold
otherwise would defeat one of the purposes of the requirement (*viz.* to protect
persons from the trauma of awaiting their fate for inordinate periods). Once
the individual had been told of the recommendation that would be made, he
would have been in a state of uncertainty, and to him, it was no more than a
legal technicality whether the charges were brought in England or Scotland.
Furthermore, it was the United Kingdom, not England or Scotland, that was
party to the convention, and the way that the United Kingdom chose to distribute its criminal jurisdiction could not impair an accused's right to trial
within a reasonable time. Accordingly, it was held to be appropriate to look at
the sum total of the actions of the competent authorities on both sides of the
border.

As to the period to be considered including any confiscation proceedings
and any appellate proceedings in relation thereto, see *Bullen and Soneji v.
U.K.*, *The Times*, February 2, 2009, ECtHR.

As to unacceptable delays in the enforcement of a confiscation order, see   ★
also *R. (Minshall) v. Marylebone Magistrates' Court (Revenue and Customs
Prosecutions Office interested party)* [2009] 2 All E.R. 806, QBD (Pitchford J.).

The presumption of innocence

R. (Harris) v. Secretary of State for the Home Department is now reported at   **16–77**

[2009] 1 Cr.App.R. 2, *sub nom. R. (Allen) (formerly Harris) v. Secretary of State for Justice.*

Ashley v. Chief Constable of Sussex Police (Sherwood intervening); *Ashley v. Same* is now reported at [2008] 1 A.C. 962.

16-78   In *Grayson v. U.K.* (2009) 48 E.H.R.R. 30, ECtHR, it was held, in relation to the confiscation provisions of the *DTA* 1994, that it was not incompatible with the concept of a fair trial under Article 6 of the ECHR (§ 16–57 in the main work), or with the right to peaceful enjoyment of possessions under Article 1 of the First Protocol thereto, to place the onus on the defendant, once he had been convicted of a major offence of drug dealing, of establishing that the source of money or assets which he had been shown to have possessed in the years preceding the offence was legitimate; nor was it incompatible with Article 6 to place the burden on the defendant of showing that the amount that might be realised was less than the amount assessed as his benefit; requiring him to prove these matters to the civil standard did not exceed reasonable limits. The court adopted the general approach in *Phillips v. U.K.* (see the main work), but stressed that what is important is how the domestic provisions are applied in the circumstances of the particular case.

The prosecution's duty of disclosure

16-83   See *McDonald v. H.M. Advocate, ante,* § 12–51b.

Public interest immunity

16-85   As to whether Article 6 is contravened where a judge rules on whether or not a hearsay statement can be admitted by relying upon material he has been shown, or arguments that have been advanced, in the course of an *ex parte* public interest immunity hearing, see *ante,* § 11–3.

The prohibition on hearsay

16-91   The approach to the use of the hearsay evidence of absent witnesses whose evidence has not been tested by cross-examination in *Luca v. Italy* (see the main work) was robustly reaffirmed in *Al-Khawaja v. U.K.*; *Tahery v. U.K.* (2009) 49 E.H.R.R. 1, ECtHR (as to which, see also *ante,* § 16–58). It was said that there was no authority for any general proposition that untested statements could be admitted consistently with Article 6(1) and (3)(d) where they were the sole or decisive evidence against a defendant (applying *Luca,* and distinguishing *R. v. Sellick* (witness fear induced by defendants (see § 11–25 in the main work))); and that it was doubtful whether any counter-balancing factors would be sufficient to justify the admission of such statements. Where, therefore, (i) the statement of the sole witness to an alleged crime who had died before trial, and (ii) the statement of a witness to a stabbing who was in genuine fear of giving evidence were admitted and those statements had been the sole or, at least, the decisive basis for each applicant's conviction, the applicants' rights under Article 6 had been violated; *as to (i),* the evidence of the witness had been the only evidence going directly to the commission of an indecent assault on her by the applicant, there were only minor inconsistencies between this statement and what was said by other witnesses which could have been explored in cross-examination, and it was difficult to see how the defence could have challenged the complainant's credibility given that her account corresponded in large part with that of another complainant; the absence of collusion, whilst being a factor in domestic law in favour of admissibility, could not be regarded as a counter-balancing factor for the purposes of Article 6; and no appropriate direction could effectively counter-balance the effect of an untested statement which was the decisive evidence against the applicant; *as to (ii)*, where the evidence of the witness had been the only evidence identifying the applicant as the person who had stabbed the victim in the back, the fact that alternative or special measures were found to be inappropriate did not absolve the domestic courts of their responsibility to ensure that there was no breach of Article 6 when they then allowed witness statements to be read; indeed, the rejection of less restrictive measures implied a greater duty to ensure respect for the rights of the defence; the right of an accused to give evidence in his defence could not be said to counter-balance the loss of opportunity to see and have examined and cross-examined the only prosecution eye-witness against him; and a warning by the judge to the jury, including a reminder that it was not the applicant who was responsible for the absence, however clearly expressed, would not be a sufficient counter-balance where that witness's untested statement was the only direct evidence against the applicant.

For the response of the Court of Appeal to this decision, see *R. v. Horncastle and Blackmore; R. v. Marquis and Graham; R. v. Carter, ante*, § 11–25. It should also be noted that the United Kingdom government has requested that the chamber decision be referred to the Grand Chamber. ★

F. Punishment Without Law

Retroactive offences

Norris v. Government of United States of America is now reported at [2008] 1 A.C. 920.   **16–99**

Retroactive penalties

A financial reporting order made under section 76(1) of the *SOCPA* 2005 (§ 5–886a in the main work) is not a penalty for the purposes of Article 7(1) of the ECHR (§ 16–97 in the main work); it is a preventative measure intended to enable the courts to keep control over those in respect of whom there is a risk that they will indulge in future criminal activity; accordingly, there is no question of a bar on the retrospective application of that section: *R. v. Adams* [2008] 4 All E.R. 574, CA. This expression of opinion was strictly *obiter* as was the approval of that opinion in *R. v. Wright* [2009] 2 Cr.App.R.(S.) 45, CA.   **16–100**

Where the offender had been party to an attack on the victim in 2003 ★ which had caused him to be in a permanent vegetative state and to die in 2006, and where the offender was sentenced to imprisonment for public protection under section 225 of the *CJA* 2003 (§ 5–293 in the main work), the fact that such sentence did not become available until after the date of the assault (s.225 coming into force on April 4, 2005) did not make it inconsistent with Article 7; the offence was not complete until the victim died; and even if the offence was to be taken to have been committed in 2003 for the purposes of Article 7, the sentence imposed was not heavier than the sentence that could have been imposed on him on that date, *viz.* imprisonment for life: *R. v. Gorman* [2009] 2 Cr.App.R.(S.) 36, CA.

G. RIGHT TO RESPECT FOR PRIVATE AND FAMILY LIFE

Interference

16-106 As to the incompatibility of the provisions of the *SOA* 2003 imposing sex offender notification requirements with Article 8 of the ECHR (§ 16-101 in the main work), see *post*, § 20-263.

As to *R. (S.) v. Chief Constable of South Yorkshire*; *R. (Marper) v. Same*, see *S. v. U.K.*, *post*, § 16-107.

Justification

16-107 In *S. v. U.K.* (2009) 48 E.H.R.R. 50, the European Court of Human Rights held (in disagreement with the House of Lords, as to which, see the main work) that the power under section 64(1A) of the *PACE Act* 1984 (§ 15-246 in the main work) to retain fingerprints or samples taken from a person in connection with the investigation of an offence, notwithstanding that he may have been acquitted of the offence or that proceedings against him were discontinued, was incompatible with Article 8(1).

Other issues

16-112a As to assisted suicide, see also *R. (Purdy) v. DPP* (*post*, § 18-6).

L. PROHIBITION OF DISCRIMINATION

16-140 As to *R. (S.) v. Chief Constable of South Yorkshire*; *R. (Marper) v. Same*, see *S. v. U.K.*, *ante*, § 16-107. In the light of the reasoning that led to its conclusion in relation to Article 8, the European Court of Human Rights did not consider it necessary to examine separately the applicants' complaint under Article 14.

CHAPTER 17

THE MENTAL ELEMENT IN CRIME

II. SPECIFIC REQUIREMENTS AS TO STATE OF MIND

G. "KNOWINGLY"

17-49 *Westminster City Council v. Croyalgrange Ltd* (see the main work) was referred to in *R. v. Sherif, Ali (Siraj), Ali (Muhedin), Mohammed, Abdurahman and Abdullahi, The Times*, February 11, 2009, CA, in which it was said that where an offence is defined in such a way that it has to be proved that the defendant did an act "knowing or believing" particular facts, it is not sufficient to prove that the defendant closed his eyes, but a jury are entitled to conclude, if satisfied that he deliberately closed his eyes to the obvious because he did not wish to be told the truth, that that fact was capable of being evidence in support of a conclusion that the defendant did indeed either know or believe the matter in question.

H. Suspects

In connection with *R. v. Da Silva* (see the main work), see *Shah v. HSBC*　★**17–49a**
Private Bank (U.K.) Ltd, post, § 26–12.

VI. DURESS

C. Onus of Proof and Evidence

As to the need for defence lawyers to be alert to the possibility of a defence　**17–125**
of duress, wherever there is credible material showing that the defendant
might have been a victim of human trafficking, see *R. v. O., post*, Appendix
E–12d.

CHAPTER 18

PRINCIPALS AND SECONDARY PARTIES

I. INTRODUCTION

B. Specific Statutory Provisions

Suicide Act 1961, s.2

Criminal liability for complicity in another's suicide

In *R. (Purdy) v. DPP* [2009] 1 Cr.App.R. 32, CA (Civ. Div.), it was held that　★**18–6**
the domestic courts remained bound by the decision of the House of Lords in
R. (Pretty) v. DPP, Secretary of State for the Home Department intervening (see
the main work) as to whether Article 8(1) was engaged by the prohibition on
assisted suicide in section 2 of the 1961 Act, but that, even if it were engaged,
the fact that the DPP had not provided case-specific policy guidance as to the
circumstances in which individuals would be prosecuted under section 2(1)
above and beyond that already provided by the Code for Crown Prosecutors
post, Appendix E–6) did not prevent the state's interference from being "in
accordance with the law", as required by Article 8(2); the director was under
no obligation to issue specific guidance; indeed, to do so in the terms sought
by the applicant would be in effect to recognise exceptional defences which
Parliament had chosen not to enact.

III. SECONDARY PARTIES

B. Aiders and Abettors

(6) Joint enterprise/ common design

In connection with the authorities cited in the main work, see *R. v. Mitchell*　★**18–15**
2009] Crim.L.R. 287, CA, also an appeal against conviction for murder by a
person convicted otherwise than as the principal, in which it was said that

there had been three issues for the jury: (i) whether the initial common enterprise (to which the appellant was undoubtedly party) was still in existence at the time of the infliction of the fatal injury; (ii) if it was, whether there had been an effective withdrawal (as to which, see *post*, § 18–26); and (iii) if not, whether the principal went beyond the scope of the enterprise by doing an act fundamentally or radically different from what was foreseen as a real possibility.

E. Countermand And Withdrawal

★**18–26**   In *R. v. Mitchell, ante*, § 18–15, it was said that the relevant principles were set out in *R. v. Mitchell and King*, *R. v. Robinson* and *R. v. O'Flaherty, Ryan and Toussaint* (as to which, see the main work).

Chapter 19

OFFENCES AGAINST THE PERSON

I. HOMICIDE

A. Murder

(2) Liability of secondary parties

Principle

★**19–24**   As to the liability of secondary parties, see also *R. v. Mitchell, ante*, §§ 18–15, 18–26.

★**19–26**   *R. v. Rahman* is now reported at [2009] 1 A.C. 129.

★   In connection with the authorities cited in the main work, and, in particular, *Gilmour* and *Gillard*, see also *R. v. Parsons* [2009] 2 *Archbold News* 3, CA (where a person charged as a secondary party to murder foresaw the act of the principal that caused the victim's death (use of a gun, knife, blunt instrument, boot, *etc.*), but did not realise that the principal might act with an intent to kill or to cause really serious harm, but did envisage that harm less than serious bodily harm might result, he would be guilty of manslaughter (*R. v. Day (M.)* [2001] Crim.L.R. 984, CA); but a judge would only be obliged to leave manslaughter to the jury as an alternative to murder on this basis where there was evidence to support such a conclusion).

(4) Defences

(b) *Diminished responsibility*

(iv) *Drink and mental abnormality*

19–72   *R. v. Wood* is also reported at [2008] 2 Cr.App.R. 34.

Sentence

★**19–81**   The general approach in *R. v. Chambers* and *R. v. Bryan* (see the main work) was approved in *R. v. Wood* [2009] Crim.L.R. 543, CA. It was said, first, that the mere fact that a case is one of manslaughter on the grounds of diminished responsibility does not preclude a sentence of imprisonment for life; however, in reality, that sentence will be rare and will usually be reserved for particularly grave cases where the defendant's responsibility for his actions, although diminished, remains high; secondly, that the assessment of the seriousness of an offence of manslaughter on the grounds of diminished responsibility should not be focused exclusively on the defendant's culpability without considering the harm consequent on his actions; and, thirdly, that whilst there is no express statutory link between the guidance in Schedule 21 to the *CJA* 2003 (determination of the minimum term in relation to mandatory life sentence for murder (§§ 5–245 *et seq.*)) and the principles to be applied in diminished responsibility cases, when assessing the seriousness of such an offence with a view to fixing the minimum custodial term, there is no logical reason why, subject to the specific element of reduced culpability inherent in the defence, the guidance should be ignored; a vast disproportion between sentences for murder and sentences for manslaughter bordering on murder would be inimical to the administration of justice; and thus, actual sentences imposed in cases decided before the 2003 Act came into force should be treated with the utmost caution.

B. Manslaughter

(2) Involuntary manslaughter

(b) *"Unlawful act" manslaughter*

Unlawful acts

It was held in *R. v. Byram*, 72 J.C.L. 353, CA ([2008] EWCA Crim. 516), that where the appellant had pleaded guilty to manslaughter and to administering a noxious substance, contrary to the *Offences against the Person Act* 1861, s.23, on the basis of the Court of Appeal's decision in *R. v. Kennedy (No. 2)* [2005] 1 W.L.R. 2159, before its reversal by the House of Lords in *R. v. Kennedy (No. 2)* (see the main work), his conviction should be quashed. The court found that his pleas were tendered and accepted, and the entire proceedings were conducted, on what had proved to be a fallacious basis. **19–100**

R. v. Kennedy (No. 2) (*ante*) was not followed by the House of Lords in relation to the Scottish offence of culpable homicide: see *Kane v. H.M. Advocate*; *MacAngus v. H.M. Advocate*, *The Times*, February 6, 2009, High Court of Justiciary. ★

(c) *Manslaughter by gross negligence*

The existence of the duty of care

In *R. v. Evans (Gemma)*, *The Times*, April 7, 2009, CA, it was held: (i) that in the context of an omission to act, it is an essential requirement of any potential conviction for gross negligence manslaughter that the defendant failed to act when he was under a duty to do so; a mere or pure omission is not sufficient; but a duty to act sufficient to found liability is not confined to cases of familial or professional relationships; where a person creates, or contributes to the creation of, a state of affairs that he knows or ought reasonably to know has ★**19–111** become life threatening, a consequent duty on him to act by taking reasonable steps to save the other's life will normally arise; and (ii) that, as to whether the judge, or jury, or a combination of both, should decide whether the defendant owed the deceased a duty of care, the existence, or otherwise, of a duty of care or a duty to act is a question of law for the judge, whereas the question of whether the facts establish the existence of the duty is for the jury once they have been directed as to the law; and, in so far as *R. v. Willoughby* (see the main work), has been interpreted to the contrary, it has been misunderstood; whilst in simple cases it may be proper for a judge to direct the jury that a duty of care exists, in any case where the issue is in dispute, and therefore in more complex cases, assuming that the judge has found that it would be open to the jury to find that there was a duty of care, or a duty to act, the jury should be directed that if the relevant facts are established, a duty arises in law; under this interpretation, there is no potential problem under Article 6 (right to a fair trial (§ 16–57 in the main work)) or 7 (no punishment without law (*ibid.*, § 16–97)) of the ECHR.

(6) Sentence

Maximum

★**19–116**   As to the liability of a person convicted of manslaughter to be sentenced as a dangerous offender under the provisions of Chapter 5 of Part 12 of the *CJA* 2003 (§§ 5–288 *et seq.* in the main work), notwithstanding that the assault that caused the death occurred before the commencement date of those provisions, see *R. v. Gorman, ante,* § 16–100.

D. Causing or Allowing the Death of a Child or Vulnerable Adult

(1) Statute

Domestic Violence, Crime and Victims Act 2004, s.5

The offence

19–118a   In *R. v. Khan, Naureen and Hussain* [2009] 1 Cr.App.R. 28, CA, it was held: (i) the state of vulnerability envisaged by subsections (1)(a) and (6) of section 5 of the 2004 Act does not need to be long-standing; it may be short, or temporary and a fit adult may become vulnerable as a result of accident, or injury, or illness; the anticipation of a full recovery does not necessarily diminish an individual's temporary vulnerability; (ii) whether or not contact between the defendant and the victim is "frequent" within subsection (1)(a)(ii) is a simple question of fact, which does not require further elucidation or definition; in particular, it does not need to be examined in the context of the risk against which the victim required protection, and the defendant's awareness of that risk, since to do so would be to import into that paragraph criteria more properly belonging to paragraph (1)(d); (iii) the requirement in subsection (1)(d)(ii) that a defendant has not taken such steps as he may reasonably have been expected to take is a precondition which requires close analysis of the defendant's personal position; without laying down principles of law, it may, in certain circumstances, be reasonable for a defendant not to have taken steps to protect the victim where the defendant was himself the subject of abuse from the victim's killer; (iv) there is no general rule that a judge should, in his direction to the jury, identify the steps which a defendant could reasonably have been expected to take; and (v) although, for the purposes of subsection (1)(d)(iii), the act resulting in death must occur in circumstances "of the kind" which were foreseen or ought to have been foreseen by the defendant, the circumstances need not be identical; whether or not circumstances are of the same kind is ultimately a question for the jury.

IV. COMMON ASSAULT AND BATTERY

A. DEFINITIONS

Examples–battery

Collins v. Wilcock (referred to in the main work) was applied in *McMillan v. CPS*, 172 J.P. 485, DC, where the appellant, who was in a drunken state, was seen shouting, being abusive and arguing in the garden of her daughter's house and where a police officer had taken her by the arm to steady her for her own safety whilst he led her (without any resistance from her) down some steep steps from the garden to the street in order to speak to her. It was held that the officer had been acting within the bounds of what were "generally acceptable standards of conduct" and he had not, therefore, committed an assault.

19–175

C. DEFENCES

Lawful correction

Section 548 of the *Education Act* 1996 is amended (as from a day to be appointed) by the *Education and Skills Act* 2008, s.169(1), and Sched. 1, para. 9, so as to substitute references to "a relevant institution" for the references to "a school", with "relevant institution" being defined as a school or independent educational institution other than a school in England ("independent educational institution" having the same meaning as in Chapter 1 of Part 4 of the 2008 Act).

19–185

IV. WOUNDING, CAUSING GRIEVOUS BODILY HARM

(5) Sentence

Guideline

See *R. v. Herbert* (*ante*, § 5–100).

Where, in practical terms, the victim's life was ended as a result of the offender's actions, neither authority nor the Sentencing Guideline Council's guideline on offences against the person (*post*, Appendix K–113 *et seq.*) supported the argument that the sentence for an offence contrary to section 18 of the *Offences against the Person Act* 1861 should bear some relation to what would have been imposed if the offender had been convicted of murder: *R. v. Cross* [2009] 1 Cr.App.R.(S.) 34, CA (see also *ante*, § 5–304).

19–205
★

IX. OFFENCES IN RELATION TO POLICE OFFICERS

A. ASSAULTS

In the execution of duty

Common law

19–271   In connection with *Collins v. Wilcock* (referred to in the main work), see *Mc-Millan v. CPS, ante,* § 19–175.

X. HARASSMENT

A. INTRODUCTION

★**19–277a**   In *Ferguson v. British Gas Trading Ltd* [2009] 3 *Archbold News* 2, CA (Civ. Div.), the defendant had sent the claimant, their former customer, bill after bill and threatening letter after threatening letter (to cut off her gas supply, to start legal proceedings and to report her to credit rating agencies). The court, whilst accepting that a course of conduct must be grave before the offence or tort of harassment (*Protection from Harassment Act* 1997, ss.1-3 (§§ 19–277b *et seq.* in the main work)) can be held to be made out, said it was strongly arguable that the impugned conduct was on the wrong side of the line as being "oppressive and unacceptable" (*Majrowski v. Guy's and St Thomas's N.H.S. Trust* (see the main work), *per* Lord Nicholls (at [30])). To argue, as the defendant had, that the claimant knew that the claims and threats were unjustified was absurd, as was their argument that the claimant must have known that the correspondence was computer generated.

B. STATUTE

Protection from Harassment Act 1997, ss.1, 2

Prohibition of harassment

19–277b   In *DPP v. Hardy*, 173 J.P. 10, DC, the court held that section 1(3)(c) of the 1997 Act does not place a burden of proof on a defendant such that evidence is required from him before he is entitled to rely on it. It was said that justices may legitimately form an opinion at the close of the prosecution case that a case is not made out by virtue of the reasonableness of the defendant's conduct. However, where the defendant had telephoned one of the directors of a small business to find out why his partner had been unsuccessful in a job application and, after she had hung up having explained that she could not discuss the matter on grounds related to data protection, had then telephoned again 95 times in approximately 90 minutes, set his phone to autodial, told her he was "set for the night", and made it clear that he knew her home address and date of birth, and where there was also evidence that the recipient felt intimated, but where no threats were made and where the defendant made no further contact after a long conversation with another director (the son of the original recipient), which ended amicably, the justices' conclusion that there was no case to answer was, on the facts, perverse. Conduct which begins with what is (or may be) a legitimate inquiry is capable of becoming harassment within the meaning of section 1 by reason of the manner of its be-

ing pursued and its persistence, and there was at least a prima facie case that
here it had in fact done so.

XIII. OFFENCES RELATING TO CHILDREN AND YOUNG PERSONS

A. OFFENCES RELATING TO THE TREATMENT, CONTROL AND MAINTEANCE OF CHILDREN AND YOUNG PERSONS

(2) Cruelty

(f) *Ingredients of the offence*

Wilfully

A failure to direct a jury as to the requirement that an assault be wilful or as   ★**19–300**
to the meaning of wilfulness did not render a conviction for an offence contrary to the *CYPA* 1933, s.1 (§ 19–291 in the main work), unsafe where the
defence had never suggested that the injuries were caused when the defendant had been acting in an innocent but misguided way: *R. v. D.* [2009]
Crim.L.R. 280, CA (see also *post*, § 19–305).

In a manner likely to cause unnecessary suffering or injury to health

A conviction for an offence contrary to the *CYPA* 1933, s.1 (§ 19–291 in the   ★**19–305**
main work), was not rendered unsafe by virtue of a failure to direct the
jury that if they were satisfied about the assault, they also had to be satisfied
that it was carried out in such a manner as was likely to cause the child unnecessary suffering or injury to health, where the injuries were such that
the jury must have been so satisfied once they were satisfied that they were
caused by an assault committed by the defendant: *R. v. D.* [2009] Crim.L.R.
280, CA (see also *post*, § 19–305).

XIV. FALSE IMPRISONMENT AND KIDNAPPING

(3) Sentence

In *R. v. Dzokamshure* [2009] 1 Cr.App.R.(S.) 112, CA, the appellant had   ★**19–337**
forced his way into the home of his former partner and dragged her out
violently before driving her off in his car, saying that he needed to teach her a
lesson for forming a new relationship. After an unknown time, he had let her
get out on a motorway slip road, and there had subsequently been fulsome
forgiveness of him by the victim. The court rejected an argument that this was
the sort of "family tiff" or "lovers' dispute" mentioned in *R. v. Spence and
Thomas* (see the main work). Upholding a sentence of 18 months' imprisonment on a plea of guilty, the court said that the Sentencing Guideline Council's
guideline on domestic violence (*post*, Appendix K–82) and, in particular, the
section entitled "wishes of the victim and effect on sentence" was relevant by
analogy although it did not apply with full force.

(5) Defences

Arrest under criminal process

(i) *By warrant*

★**19–341**   The amendment of section 125D of the *MCA* 1980 effected by the *AFA* 2006 comes into force on October 31, 2009: *Armed Forces Act 2006 (Commencement No. 5) Order* 2009 (S.I. 2009 No. 1167). In connection with that commencement, see the transitional provision in the *Armed Forces Act 2006 (Transitional Provisions etc.) Order* 2009 (S.I. 2009 No. 1059), Sched. 1, para. 18(2) (interpretation of reference to a "warrant").

CHAPTER 20

SEXUAL OFFENCES

I. INTRODUCTION

Sexual Offences Acts 1956 to 1992

Indecent assault as alternative to rape

20–1   In relation to conduct occurring prior to the commencement of the *SOA* 2003, the effect of the decision in *R. v. J.* [2005] 1 A.C. 562, HL (on a true construction of the 1956 Act, it was impermissible to prosecute a charge of indecent assault under section 14(1) in circumstances where the only conduct upon which that charge was based was an act of unlawful sexual intercourse with a girl under the age of 16 in respect of which no prosecution could be commenced under section 6(1) by virtue of the time bar of 12 months contained in section 37(2) of, and Schedule 2 to, the Act) was not such as to preclude a judge from leaving it to a jury to convict of indecent assault as an alternative to a charge of rape, under section 6(3) of the *CLA* 1967 (§ 4–455 in the main work), where they were satisfied as to the act of sexual intercourse and as to the fact that the girl was under 16 at the time, and where they acquitted of rape on the ground that they were not satisfied as to lack of consent, and this was so notwithstanding that the proceedings for rape had been begun over 12 months after the alleged offence; the decision in *J.* had turned on the words of Schedule 2 to the 1956 Act, which provided that "A prosecution may not be commenced more than 12 months after the offence charged."; leaving a possible alternative verdict to a jury could not be described as a "commencement" of proceedings for the offence; but it would be an abuse of process to bring a charge of rape against a person against whom there was no evidence whatever of rape (in particular as to lack of consent) in order to circumvent a time limit: *R. v. Timmins* [2006] 1 Cr.App.R. 18, CA.

In the earlier case of *R. v. Rabbitts* (2005) 149 S.J. 890, CA, it was held that, *R. v. J.* having decided that, as a matter of statutory construction, it was not open to the prosecution to bring a charge of indecent assault where the conduct on which the prosecution was based was an act of consensual sexual intercourse with a girl under 16, and where the purpose was to circumvent the statutory time limit of 12 months on prosecutions for unlawful sexual intercourse with a girl of that age, it made no difference that the count of

indecent assault was included in the indictment as an alternative to a charge
of rape to cater for the possibility that the jury would not be satisfied as to
lack of consent.

In *R. v. Cottrell*; *R. v. Fletcher* [2008] 1 Cr.App.R. 7, CA, it was said that to
the extent that *Timmins* and *Rabbitts* are inconsistent, they should be followed
as they apply to the facts of the individual case. As to the flawed nature of the
decision in *Timmins*, see *Criminal Law Week* 2005/43/4.

Indecent assault

Whilst *R. v. Court* [1989] A.C. 28, HL, is authority for the proposition that a   **20–1c**
doctor who obtained sexual satisfaction from a necessary medical examination
properly conducted was not guilty of indecent assault under the *SOA* 1956,
s.14, in a case where the prosecution case was limited to an allegation that
the defendant doctor had carried out a medical examination in appropriate
circumstances but in an inappropriate way and as a cloak for his own sexual
gratification, and where the issue had been as to the manner in which the
defendant had carried out the examination (*i.e.* in an appropriate way in the
presence of a chaperon or in an inappropriate way in the absence of a
chaperon), there had been no need to direct the jury as to the remote theo-
retical possibility suggested in *Court*: *R. v. Kumar* (2006) 150 S.J. 1053, CA.

Sentencing in historic cases

Sentences in historic cases of buggery of boys should now be determined as   **20–1d**
if the offence was one of rape in accordance with the guidelines in *R. v. Millberry*; *R. v. Morgan*; *R. v. Lackenby* (§ 20–23 in the main work), instead of in
accordance with the guidelines given in relation to buggery in *R. v. Willis*, 60
Cr.App.R. 146, CA; it is important that the sentence should reflect the gravity
of the offence, rather than the particular label attached to it; and since there is
no distinction in principle or in essential gravity made in the *Millberry*
guidelines between rape of a male and rape of a female, it would be wrong
for a sentence for buggery to be imposed on any other basis: *R. v. Patterson*
[2006] 2 Cr.App.R.(S.) 48, CA (not following *R. v. A. and W.* [2001] 2
Cr.App.R. 18, CA, to the extent that it had been suggested there that the
guidelines in *Willis* remained the starting point). This approach was taken   ★
further in *R. v. Kearns* [2009] 1 Cr.App.R.(S.) 107, CA, where it was applied
to what was seemingly a case of consensual buggery of a 15-year-old boy. For
the suggestion that there was no justification for equating such a case to
"rape", see *Criminal Law Week* 2009/16/8.

Where an offender falls to be sentenced for sexual offences committed long
ago, good conduct in the interim, the effect immediate imprisonment would
have on the offender and his family, and the fact that there is no risk to the
public, do not amount to "exceptional circumstances" within section 118(4)(b)
of the *PCC(S)A* 2000, and do not, therefore, justify the suspension of a
sentence of imprisonment; there is a need to maintain consistency when
sentencing for old and recent offences in this class of case: *Att.-Gen.'s Reference (No. 39 of 2006) (R. v. J. (Rodney Clive))* [2007] 1 Cr.App.R.(S.) 34, CA.

II. OFFENCES

A. General Interpretation

(1) Consent

Sexual Offences Act 2003, s.74

20–10   In *R. v. Kirk*, unreported, March 4, 2008, CA ([2008] EWCA Crim. 434), the complainant had been subjected to sexual abuse by the appellant's brother, and to a lesser extent, the appellant, from under the age of eight onwards. The appellant was convicted of raping her on an occasion when she had agreed to have sex with him in exchange for £3.25 for food when she was 15 and was homeless, tired, dirty and hungry. The judge, in directing the jury, drew a distinction between consent and submission, to the effect that there would have been no consent if the complainant had merely willingly submitted to sex because her will had been overborne. The Court of Appeal held that the judge's use of the expression "willing submission" was not an easy one, given that willingness is usually associated with consent. However, whilst it was not an expression that could be commended for use on other occasions, in the context of the full and detailed direction given by the judge, the jury would not have been misled or distracted. The court said that it was clear that the judge had used the word "willing" in the sense that submission had not been achieved by physical force.

B. Rape

(2) Indictment

★20–24   As to whether an indictment is bad for duplicity where it alleges rape by penetration either vaginally or anally, see *ante*, § 1–137; as to how a judge should direct a jury in such circumstances, see *ante*, § 4–391.

(8) Summing up

20–27a   A judge is entitled to make comments as to the way the evidence is to be approached, particularly in areas where there is a danger of a jury coming to an unjustified conclusion without an appropriate warning; the fact that the trauma of rape can cause feelings of shame and guilt which might inhibit a woman from making a complaint is sufficiently well known to justify a comment to that effect; and a judge would be entitled to refer, in an appropriate case, to the particular feelings of shame and embarrassment that may arise where the alleged offender is the complainant's partner; however, any comment must be uncontroversial: *R. v. Doody*, *The Times*, November 26, 2008, CA.

E. Rape and other Offences against Children under 13

(4) Sentence

★20–55   *Att.-Gen.'s Reference (No. 29 of 2008) (R. v. Dixon)* is now reported at [2009] 1 Cr.App.R.(S.) 86.

F. Child Sex Offences

(5) Child sex offences committed by persons under 18

(d) *Sentence*

R. v. B. is now reported at [2009] 1 Cr.App.R.(S.) 6.   **20–82**

(7) Meeting a child following sexual grooming

(a) *Statute*

Sexual Offences Act 2003, s.15

Meeting a child following sexual grooming, etc.
The amendments to section 15 of the 2003 Act effected by the *Sexual Of-*   **20–91**
fences (Northern Ireland Consequential Amendments) Order 2008 (S.I. 2008 No.
1779) came into force on February 2, 2009: see article 2(3) of that order and
the *Sexual Offences (Northern Ireland) Order 2008 (Commencement) Order* 2008
(S.R.N.I. 2008 No. 510).

G. Abuse of Position of Trust

(1) Statute

Sexual Offences Act 2003, ss.16–24

Abuse of position of trust: acts done in Scotland
The amendments to section 20 of the 2003 Act effected by the *Sexual Of-*   **20–100**
fences (Northern Ireland Consequential Amendments) Order 2008 (S.I. 2008 No.
1779) came into force on February 2, 2009: see article 2(3) of that order and
the *Sexual Offences (Northern Ireland) Order 2008 (Commencement) Order* 2008
(S.R.N.I. 2008 No. 510).

Positions of trust
The amendments to section 21 of the 2003 Act effected by the *Sexual Of-*   **20–101**
fences (Northern Ireland Consequential Amendments) Order 2008 (S.I. 2008 No.
1779) came into force on February 2, 2009: see article 2(3) of that order and
the *Sexual Offences (Northern Ireland) Order 2008 (Commencement) Order* 2008
(S.R.N.I. 2008 No. 510).
Subsection (3)(a) of section 21 of the 2003 Act is amended, as from a day to
be appointed, by the *CYPA* 2008, s.8(2), and Sched. 1, para. 15, so as to
substitute for the words "under section 23(2)", the words "in accordance
with section 22C(6)".
Subsection (7) of section 21 of the 2003 Act has been amended by the
Education and Skills Act 2008, s.169(1), and Sched. 1, para. 81, so as to
substitute a new paragraph (b), as follows—

"(b) section 68, 70(1)(b) or 74 of the *Education and Skills Act* 2008,".

Positions of trust: interpretation
The repeals in section 22 of the 2003 Act effected by the *Sexual Offences*   **20–102**

(Northern Ireland Consequential Amendments) Order 2008 (S.I. 2008 No. 1779) came into force on February 2, 2009: see article 2(3) of that order and the *Sexual Offences (Northern Ireland) Order 2008 (Commencement) Order* 2008 (S.R.N.I. 2008 No. 510).

H. Familial Child Sex Offences

(1) Statute

Sexual Offences Act 2003, ss.25–29

Family relationships

20–112 Subsection (5)(c) of section 27 of the 2003 Act is amended, as from a day to be appointed, by the *CYPA* 2008, s.8(2), and Sched. 1, para. 16, so as to substitute new sub-paragraphs (i) and (ia) for sub-paragraph (i), as follows—

> "(i) he is a person with whom the child has been placed under section 22C of the *Children Act* 1989 in a placement falling within subsection (6)(a) or (b) of that section (placement with local authority foster parent),
>
> (ia) he is a person with whom the child has been placed under section 59(1)(a) of that Act (placement by voluntary organisation),".

I. Offences against Person with a Mental Disorder Impeding Choice

(5) Elements of the offence

★20–132 *R. v. C. (Mental disorder: Sexual Activity)* is now reported at [2009] 1 Cr.App.R. 15, *sub nom. R. v. C.*

L. Abuse of Children Through Prostitution and Pornography

(1) Paying for sexual services of a child

(a) *Statute*

Sexual Offences Act 2003, s.47

Paying for sexual services of a child

20–155 The repeal of section 47(7) of the 2003 Act effected by the *Sexual Offences (Northern Ireland) Consequential Amendments) Order* 2008 (S.I. 2008 No. 1779) came into force on February 2, 2009: see article 2(3) of that order and the *Sexual Offences (Northern Ireland) Order 2008 (Commencement) Order* 2008 (S.R.N.I. 2008 No. 510).

Q. Other Statutory Offences

(2) Voyeurism

(e) *Elements of the offence*

20–217 *R. v. Bassett* is also reported at [2009] 1 Cr.App.R. 7.

III. ANONYMITY OF VICTIMS

Sexual Offences (Amendment) Act 1992, ss.1–4

Offences to which this Act applies

The amendment of section 2 of the 1992 Act effected by the *AFA* 2006   **★20–258**
comes into force on October 31, 2009: *Armed Forces Act 2006 (Commencement
No. 5) Order* 2009 (S.I. 2009 No. 1167).

Power to displace section 1

The amendment of section 3 of the 1992 Act effected by the *AFA* 2006   **★20–259**
comes into force on October 31, 2009: *Armed Forces Act 2006 (Commencement
No. 5) Order* 2009 (S.I. 2009 No. 1167).

Special rules for cases of incest or buggery

The repeal of section 4(9) of the 1992 Act effected by the *AFA* 2006 comes   **★20–260**
into force on October 31, 2009: *Armed Forces Act 2006 (Commencement No. 5)
Order* 2009 (S.I. 2009 No. 1167).

Sexual Offences (Amendment) Act 1992, s.6

Interpretation

The amendments of section 6 of the 1992 Act effected by the *AFA* 2006   **★20–261**
come into force on October 31, 2009: *Armed Forces Act 2006 (Commencement
No. 5) Order* 2009 (S.I. 2009 No. 1167). In connection with that commencement, see the transitional provision in the *Armed Forces Act 2006 (Transitional
Provisions etc.) Order* 2009 (S.I. 2009 No. 1059), Sched. 1, para. 32(3) (interpretation of references to "an offence under section 42 of the *Armed Forces
Act* 2006" and to "being charged under Part 5" of that Act).

IV. NOTIFICATION AND ORDERS

A. NOTIFICATION REQUIREMENTS

(1) Summary

It was held in *R. (F. and T.) v. Secretary of State for Justice* [2009] 2   **20–263**
Cr.App.R.(S.) 47, DC, that (a) the effect of subjecting young offenders to the
notification requirements of the *SOA* 2003 indefinitely and without any right
to review amounted to a breach of the right to respect for private and family life under Article 8 of the ECHR (§ 16–101 in the main work), and (b)
the failure to provide for a review scheme in relation to all offenders subject
to notification requirements rendered the statutory scheme incompatible
with Article 8. The court said that it was difficult to see how it could be justifiable in Article 8 terms to deny a person who believed himself to be in a
position where he could demonstrate that he presents no measurable risk
of re-offending an opportunity to establish that. As a matter of principle, an
offender was entitled to have the question of whether or not the notification
requirements continue to serve a legitimate purpose determined. See also
post, § 20–271.

In *R. v. F.* [2009] Crim.L.R. 462, CA, it was held that the disproportionate   **★**
consequences of a sentence of 30 months' detention on a young sex offender

highlighted by the decision in *R. (F. and T.) v. Secretary of State for Justice* (*ante*) did not compel a sentencer to reduce an otherwise appropriate sentence so as to achieve compliance with Article 8 of the ECHR.

(3) Legislation

Sexual Offences Act 2003, ss.83–86

Notification requirements: travel outside the United Kingdom

20–271   It was held in *R. (F. and T.) v. Secretary of State for Justice* [2009] 2 Cr.App.R.(S.) 47, DC, that the travel notification requirements in section 86 of the 2003 Act are not unlawful as being contrary to Parliament and Council Directive 2004/38/EC (on the right of families to move and reside freely within the territory of the member states), and they are, therefore, not contrary to European law. A person subject to such a requirement does not require permission to leave the country, and the requirements do not impose a restriction on doing so. The court held that they are not, therefore, a formality equivalent to an exit visa, but are a mechanism whereby the police can determine whether or not they wish to apply to a magistrates' court for a foreign travel order under section 114 of the Act, so as to prevent the offender from leaving the United Kingdom or to restrict the destinations to which he might go, where such an order is necessary for the purpose of protecting children generally, or any child, from serious sexual harm at the hands of the offender. Whilst the court acknowledged that such an order would clearly be a restriction on movement, it also said that it would equally clearly be permitted by article 27 of the Directive (restrictions permissible on grounds of public policy, public security and public health). See also *ante*, § 20–263.

Sexual Offences Act 2003, ss.87–91

Method of notification and related matters

★20–272   The *Sexual Offences Act 2003 (Prescribed Police Stations) Regulations* 2005 (S.I. 2005 No. 210) have been revoked and replaced by the *Sexual Offences Act 2003 (Prescribed Police Stations) Regulations* 2009 (S.I. 2009 No. 722).

Sexual Offences Act 2003, Sched. 3

20–312a   The insertion of paragraph 35A into Schedule 3 to the 2003 Act took effect on January 26, 2009: see *post*, § 20–320.

20–320   Paragraph 58 of Schedule 26 to the *CJIA* 2008 (inserting para. 35A into Schedule 3 to the 2003 Act) came into force on January 26, 2009: *Criminal Justice and Immigration Act 2008 (Commencement No. 4 and Saving Provision) Order* 2008 (S.I. 2008 No. 2993).

Interpretation of Schedule 3

20–321   In *R. v. Davison* [2009] 2 Cr.App.R.(S.) 13, CA, it was said that where an offender was sentenced to a community sentence comprising a community order with an unpaid work requirement to be completed before the anniversary of the day sentence was imposed, this was "a community sentence of at least 12 months" within Schedule 3 to the *SOA* 2003 (§§ 20–278 *et seq.* in the main work), so as to render him liable to the notification requirements of that Act upon his conviction of sexual assault. The court held that the length of a community sentence must be capable of being determined on the date it is made, and the period specified under section 177(5) of the *CJA* 2003 (§ 5–130 in the main work) by a court when imposing a community order is the relevant period for determining the duration of the order for the purposes of Schedule 3, however long it in fact takes the offender to carry out the requirements of the order. Observations to the contrary in *R. v. Odam* [2009] 1 Cr.App.R.(S.) 22, CA, were disapproved.

D. Sexual Offences Prevention Orders

(2) Legislation

Sexual Offences Act 2003, ss.104–113

Sexual offences prevention orders: applications and grounds

While it was made clear in *R. v. Terrell* (see the main work) that serious   ★**20–324**
harm of the level required to justify imprisonment for public protection could be made out where an offender risked progressing to physical contact offences or becoming a photographer or a commissioner of indecent images or playing a more significant role in a distribution network, it is not enough that there is a possibility of future offending that might occasion serious harm. The risk of such harm being occasioned by future offending must be significant. That requires some evidential basis from which it can be assessed that either serious harm caused in the past will be repeated, or that the offender will move on to more serious offences that give rise to a significant risk of serious harm: *R. v. Hicks* [2009] L.S. Gazette, May 7, 18, CA ([2009] EWCA Crim. 733).

Other offences for purposes of Part 2

The insertion of paragraph 172A of Schedule 5 to the *SOA* 2003 effected   ★**20–336**
by the *AFA* 2006 comes into force on October 31, 2009: *Armed Forces Act 2006 (Commencement No. 5) Order* 2009 (S.I. 2009 No. 1167).

G. Interpretation, etc. of Part 2

Sexual Offences Act 2003, ss.131–136

Young offenders: application

The amendment of section 131 of the 2003 Act effected by the *AFA* 2006   ★**20–339**
comes into force on October 31, 2009: *Armed Forces Act 2006 (Commencement No. 5) Order* 2009 (S.I. 2009 No. 1167).

Part 2: general interpretation

The amendments of section 133 of the 2003 Act effected by the *AFA* 2006   **20–341**
come into force on October 31, 2009: *Armed Forces Act 2006 (Commencement No. 5) Order* 2009 (S.I. 2009 No. 1167). In connection with that commencement, see the transitional provision in the *Armed Forces Act 2006 (Transitional Provisions etc.) Order* 2009 (S.I. 2009 No. 1059), Sched. 1, para. 52(1) (interpretation of definitions of "the period of conditional discharge" and "service detention").

Conditional discharges and probation orders

The amendment of section 134 of the 2003 Act effected by the *AFA* 2006   ★**20–342**
comes into force on October 31, 2009: *Armed Forces Act 2006 (Commencement No. 5) Order* 2009 (S.I. 2009 No. 1167).

CHAPTER 21

OFFENCES UNDER THE THEFT AND FRAUD ACTS

I. INTRODUCTION

Sentencing guidelines

21–4c The Sentencing Guidelines Council has issued a guideline on theft and burglary in a building other than a dwelling. The guideline applies only to the sentencing of offenders aged 18 and over, who are sentenced on or after January 5, 2009, and is based on first-time offenders convicted after trial. See *post*, Appendix K–209 *et seq.*

Theft in breach of trust

21–4d As to the non-applicability of the guidelines in *R. v. Barrick* (see the main work) and *R. v. Clark* (see § 21–4e in the main work) to sentencing in cases of corruption, see *R. v. Ozakpinar* [2009] 1 Cr.App.R.(S.) 8, CA.

II. THEFT

(3) Elements of the offence

(f) *"With the intention of permanently depriving the other of it"*

Theft Act 1968, s.6

21–76 Where a person dishonestly appropriated property belonging to another with the intention of returning it to the owner, but only if the owner met a demand for the payment of a sum of money, it was open to a court to find that he had the necessary intent for an offence of theft by virtue of the operation of section 6(1) of the 1968 Act: *R. v. Raphael* [2008] Crim.L.R. 995, CA.

III. ROBBERY AND ASSAULT WITH INTENT TO ROB

A. ROBBERY

(4) Sentence

Guideline cases

Robbery in the course of burglary

21–92 It was held in *Att.-Gen.'s Reference (No. 124 of 2008) (R. v. Doran)* [2009] 2 Cr.App.R.(S.) 29, CA, that a robbery in the victim's home was not intended by the Sentencing Guidelines Council's guideline (*post*, Appendix K–80) to be treated in the same way as a street robbery. The factor of invasion of a person's home is significant. The court said that while some regard needs to be had to the general level of sentencing for robberies that are covered by the guideline, it is not sensible to apply any arithmetical formula to such guidelines (as had been suggested in *Att.-Gen.'s References (Nos 38, 39 and 40 of 2007) (R. v. Crummack, Stell and Campbell)* (see the main work)). Having regard to the authorities and the recommendations in the guideline, sentence for a robbery involving the targeting of an elderly householder, but without weapons or significant violence, ought to be in the general range of five to six years after trial.

IV. BURGLARY AND AGGRAVATED BURGLARY

A. BURGLARY

(5) Sentence

Authorities (dwellings)

Having considered *R. v. McInerney*; *R. v. Keating* (see the main work), the Court of Appeal concluded in *R. v. Saw* [2009] 2 All E.R. 1138, that revised guidance was necessary. The court said that the starting point must always be that this is a serious offence, involving the violation of something precious; and that, since the disturbance and stress suffered by the home owner is not quantifiable in bare economic terms, particular focus is required on the impact of the offence on those living in the burgled home; whether or not the offender has any specific intention to cause harm, he runs the risk that the victim may suffer serious adverse consequences. The court then listed the following matters of aggravation, but stressed that the list was not exhaustive: trauma to the victim beyond the normal, inevitable consequence of intrusion and theft, pre-meditation and professional planning or organisation, vandalism, deliberate targeting of a vulnerable victim, or of any victim (*e.g.* out of spite or upon racial grounds), the particular vulnerability of the victim, whether targeted or not, the presence of the occupier at the time, theft of or damage to property of high economic or sentimental value, the commission of the offence whilst on bail, appearance before the court for two or more offences and the offender's previous record (including for offences of dishonesty short of dwelling house burglary). The court said that this list merely emphasises that what is required is that the sentencing court should address two specific features, *viz.* the overall criminality of the defendant in light of his record and the true impact of the offence on the victim.

As to mitigation, good character, the fact that only property of low economic or sentimental value was stolen, that the defendant played only a minor part or was exploited by others, that he committed the offence on impulse, that he is genuinely remorseful or cooperated with the police or has responded well to previous sentences are all relevant, but this list, the court said, is no more exhaustive than the list of aggravating factors.

As to disposal, whilst emphasising that the judge is not the prisoner of a tariff, following conviction (i) there will be low level burglaries, with minimal loss and damage, and without raised culpability or impact, which may be dealt with by some form of punishment in the community rather than an immediate custodial penalty; (ii) any offence which reflects any of the identified aggravating features should, subject to strong personal mitigation, normally attract a custodial sentence; cases of limited raised culpability and/or impact should ordinarily involve a custodial sentence, probably in the general range of nine to 18 months, with a longer sentence being indicated by a record of relevant offending or by a significant impact on the victim, or both, and a shorter sentence being indicated by an established (not merely asserted) subsidiary role or demonstrated exploitation by other offenders; in such cases, a community order may be appropriate if it provides the best prospect of preventing future offending; (iii) in cases of seriously raised culpability and/or serious impact, the starting point should be a custodial sentence, probably in the general range of two years and upwards; for a single offence, the range would ordinarily be 18 months to four years with possible sentences beyond that range where the culpability and/or impact is at an extreme level; longer sentences may be indicated, for example, by a record of relevant offending or where the hallmarks of professional crime are evident, and shorter ones by an established minor role or demonstrated exploitation, but all aggravating and mitigating features must be evaluated; a community order for this class of case would only begin to arise for consideration in the most extreme and exceptional circumstances.

The court also observed, in relation to cases attracting a minimum three-year term (*PCC(S)A* 2000, s.111 (§ 5–253 in the main work)), that it is to be remembered that that term is not a guideline, it is a minimum.

Non-dwellings

21–114a   See now the definitive guideline issued by the Sentencing Guidelines Council, *post*, Appendix K–209 *et seq.*

XVIII. FRAUD ACT 2006

(4) Sentence

Authorities

★**21–368**   In *R. v. Darwin (Anne) and Darwin (John)*, *The Times*, April 1, 2009, CA, the offenders (a married couple) were guilty of a fraudulent conspiracy pursuant to which they collected the insurance and pension money due to D1 on D2's death whilst he was still alive. They had led their sons to believe that they were bereaved and had used them to help launder the money (which the children had done entirely innocently). It was held that their sentences of six years and six months' (D1/ on conviction) and six years and three months' imprisonment (D2/ guilty plea) were severe but not manifestly excessive. The court said that the children were directly and unequivocally victims of their parents' dishonest scheme, and in every case where a court was passing sentence, it should reflect the nature and extent of the impact of the crime on the victims. Here, the insurance companies were the financial victims, but the children were the human victims. Whereas the financial aspect of the fraud and the draft guidelines issued by the Sentencing Guidelines Council on February 25, 2009, on sentencing for statutory fraud offences suggested a shorter sentence, this was a case with unique or virtually unique aggravating features and the sentence reflected the judge's view of the punishment appropriate to the culpability of the appellants, the harm they caused and the losses they inflicted. See also *ante*, § 5–77a.

CHAPTER 22

FORGERY, PERSONATION AND CHEATING

I. FORGERY

B. MISCELLANEOUS OFFENCES AKIN TO FORGERY

(2) Identity documents

(c) *Mode of trial and sentence*

Att.-Gen.'s References (Nos 1 and 6 of 2008) (R. v. Dziruni and Laby) is now **22–45e**
reported at [2008] 2 Cr.App.R.(S.) 99.

R. v. Adebayo (see the main work) was disapproved in *R. v. Ovieriakhi, The* ★
Times, March 10, 2009, CA, where it was said valid distinctions were to be
drawn according to the nature of the document involved and the use to which
it was put or intended to be put.

In *R. v. Velev* [2009] 1 Cr.App.R.(S.) 96, CA, it was said that when sentenc- ★
ing in respect of a major conspiracy to manufacture false identity documents,
a court had to attach substantial weight, first, to what the conspiracy was hop-
ing to achieve, secondly, to the role of the defendant and, thirdly, to what that
person had gained or was likely to gain from the conspiracy. The court added
that, whilst all such cases such were fact-sensitive, organisers could expect sentences of nine years after a trial, whilst those who were workers and lieuten-
ants could expect six-and-a-half years after trial.

(e) *Defences*

See section 31 of the *Immigration and Asylum Act* 1999 (§ 25–228d in the **22–45g**
main work).

As to the possibility of a defence of duress being available to a victim of human trafficking, see *R. v. O., post*, Appendix E–12d.

CHAPTER 24

FIREARMS AND OFFENSIVE WEAPONS

I. FIREARMS

A. FIREARMS ACT 1968

(4) Prohibited weapons and ammunition

Firearms Act 1968, s.5

Prohibited weapon

24-25   A stun gun disguised as a torch, in addition to coming within section 5(1)(b) of the 1968 Act (§ 24–19 in the main work), also comes within section 5(1A)(a) as a "firearm which is disguised as another object", having regard to the definition of firearm in section 57(1) of the 1968 Act (§ 24–57 in the main work): *R. v. Weaver*, unreported, October 10, 2007, CA ([2007] EWCA Crim. 3485).

(6) Prevention of crime and preservation of public safety

(a) *Possession with intent to endanger life*

Firearms Act 1968, s.16

Ingredients

24-38a   *R. v. Salih* is now reported at [2008] 1 W.L.R. 2627.

(g) *Possession of firearms by persons previously convicted of crime*

Firearms Act 1968, s.21

Sentence

★24-68   The court, in deciding on sentence under section 21 of the 1968 Act, takes into account the weapon's nature, how readily it can be fired, the presence of any ammunition, and any previous convictions for possessing such a weapon: *R. v. Gambah* [2009] 2 Cr.App.R.(S.) 16, CA.

II. OFFENSIVE WEAPONS

B. Prevention of Crime Act 1953

(4) Sentence

R. v. Povey is now reported at [2009] 1 Cr.App.R.(S.) 42.   ★**24–109**

(5) Ingredients of the offence

(a) *"has with him"*

Knowledge
  In *R. v. Tsap*, 173 J.P. 4, CA, it was held, following *Glidewell* (cited in the   **24–110**
main work) and *R. v. Ivey*, unreported, August 15, 2000, CA, that where the
matters relied on in support of a defence of reasonable excuse go beyond
mere forgetfulness, it should normally, and almost invariably, be left to the
jury to decide the issue.

(d) *"without lawful authority or reasonable excuse"*

Other excuses
  As to forgetfulness as a reasonable excuse, see *R. v. Tsap, ante,* § 24–110.   **24–123**

Chapter 25

OFFENCES AGAINST THE CROWN AND GOVERNMENT

V. TERRORISM

A. Terrorism Act 2000

Terrorism Act 2000, s.1

Terrorism: interpretation
  As from February 16, 2009 (*Counter-Terrorism Act 2008 (Commencement No.*   **25–56**
2) Order 2009 (S.I. 2009 No. 58)), ", racial" is inserted after "religious" in section 1(1)(c) of the Act of 2000: *Counter-Terrorism Act* 2008, s.75(1) and (2)(a).

Terrorism Act 2000, ss.15–23

Disclosure of information: duty
  As from February 16, 2009 (*Counter-Terrorism Act 2008 (Commencement No.*   **25–68**
2) Order 2009 (S.I. 2009 No. 58)), section 19(1)(b) of the Act of 2000 is
amended by the *Counter-Terrorism Act* 2008, s.77(1) and (2), so as to substitute
for the words "comes to his attention in the course of a trade, profession,
business or employment", the words—

"comes to his attention—

(i) in the course of a trade, profession or business, or

(ii) in the course of his employment (whether or not in the course of a trade, profession or business)".

Meaning of "employment"

25–73a   As from February 16, 2009 (*Counter-Terrorism Act 2008 (Commencement No. 2) Order* 2009 (S.I. 2009 No. 58)), the *Counter-Terrorism Act* 2008, s.77(1) and (3) insert a new section 22A into the Act of 2000.

Terrorism Act 2000, s.22A

Meaning of "employment"

22A.—(1) In sections 19 to 21B—

(a) "employment" means any employment (whether paid or unpaid) and includes—

(i) work under a contract for services or as an office-holder,

(ii) work experience provided pursuant to a training course or programme or in the course of training for employment, and

(iii) voluntary work;

(b) "employer" has a corresponding meaning.

Forfeiture

★**25–74**   As from June 18, 2009 (*Counter-Terrorism Act 2008 (Commencement No. 3) Order* 2009 (S.I. 2009 No. 1256)), the *Counter-Terrorism Act* 2008, s.34, substitutes a new section 23 in the Act of 2000.

Terrorism Act 2000, s.23

Forfeiture: terrorist property offences

23.—(1) The court by or before which a person is convicted of an offence under any of sections 15 to 18 may make a forfeiture order in accordance with the provisions of this section.

(2) Where a person is convicted of an offence under section 15(1) or (2) or 16, the court may order the forfeiture of any money or other property which, at the time of the offence, the person had in their possession or under their control and which—

(a) had been used for the purposes of terrorism, or

(b) they intended should be used, or had reasonable cause to suspect might be used, for those purposes.

(3) Where a person is convicted of an offence under section 15(3) the court may order the forfeiture of any money or other property which, at the time of the offence, the person had in their possession or under their control and which—

(a) had been used for the purposes of terrorism, or

(b) which, at that time, they knew or had reasonable cause to suspect would or might be used for those purposes.

(4) Where a person is convicted of an offence under section 17 or 18 the court may order the forfeiture of any money or other property which, at the time of the offence, the person had in their possession or under their control and which—

(a) had been used for the purposes of terrorism, or

(b) was, at that time, intended by them to be used for those purposes.

(5) Where a person is convicted of an offence under section 17 the court may order the forfeiture of the money or other property to which the arrangement in question related, and which—

    (a) had been used for the purposes of terrorism, or

    (b) at the time of the offence, the person knew or had reasonable cause to suspect would or might be used for those purposes.

(6) Where a person is convicted of an offence under section 18 the court may order the forfeiture of the money or other property to which the arrangement in question related.

(7) Where a person is convicted of an offence under any of sections 15 to 18, the court may order the forfeiture of any money or other property which wholly or partly, and directly or indirectly, is received by any person as a payment or other reward in connection with the commission of the offence.

Forfeiture: other terrorism offences and offences with a terrorist connection
    As from June 18, 2009 (*Counter-Terrorism Act 2008 (Commencement No. 3) Order* 2009 (S.I. 2009 No. 1256)), the *Counter-Terrorism Act* 2008, s.35(1), inserts a new section 23A into the Act of 2000.   ★**25-75**

Terrorism Act 2000, s.23A

Forfeiture: other terrorism offences and offences with a terrorist connection
    23A.—(1) The court by or before which a person is convicted of an offence to which this section applies may order the forfeiture of any money or other property in relation to which the following conditions are met—

    (a) that it was, at the time of the offence, in the possession or control of the person convicted; and

    (b) that—

        (i) it had been used for the purposes of terrorism,

        (ii) it was intended by that person that it should be used for the purposes of terrorism, or

        (iii) the court believes that it will be used for the purposes of terrorism unless forfeited.

(2) This section applies to an offence under—

    (a) any of the following provisions of this Act—

        section 54 (weapons training);

        section 57, 58 or 58A (possessing things and collecting information for the purposes of terrorism);

        section 59, 60 or 61 (inciting terrorism outside the United Kingdom);

    (b) any of the following provisions of Part 1 of the *Terrorism Act* 2006 —

        section 2 (dissemination of terrorist publications);

        section 5 (preparation of terrorist acts);

        section 6 (training for terrorism);

        sections 9 to 11 (offences involving radioactive devices or materials).

(3) This section applies to any ancillary offence (as defined in section 94 of the *Counter-Terrorism Act* 2008) in relation to an offence listed in subsection (2).

(4) This section also applies to an offence specified in Schedule 2 to the *Counter-Terrorism Act* 2008 (offences where terrorist connection to be considered) as to which—

    (a) in England and Wales, the court dealing with the offence has determined, in accordance with section 30 of that Act, that the offence has a terrorist connection;

    (b) [*Scotland*].

(5) The Secretary of State may by order amend subsection (2).

(6) An order adding an offence to subsection (2) applies only in relation to offences committed after the order comes into force.

For section 94 of the 2008 Act, see *post*, § 25–142v.

Forfeiture: supplementary provisions

★**25–76**   As from June 18, 2009 (*Counter-Terrorism Act 2008* (*Commencement No. 3,
Order* 2009 (S.I. 2009 No. 1256)), the *Counter-Terrorism Act* 2008, s.36, inserts
a new section 23B into the Act of 2000.

Terrorism Act 2000, s.23B

Forfeiture: supplementary provisions

23B.—(1) Before making an order under section 23 or 23A, a court must give
an opportunity to be heard to any person, other than the convicted person, who
claims to be the owner or otherwise interested in anything which can be forfeited
under that section.

(2) In considering whether to make an order under section 23 or 23A in respect
of any property, a court shall have regard to—

   (a) the value of the property, and
   (b) the likely financial and other effects on the convicted person of the making
       of the order (taken together with any other order that the court contem-
       plates making).

(3) [*Scotland.*]

(4) Schedule 4 makes further provision in relation to forfeiture orders under section 23 or 23A.

Terrorism Act 2000, ss.37–39

Information about acts of terrorism

25–82   In *R. v. Sherif* [2009] 2 Cr.App.R.(S.) 33, CA, it was said in relation to the
approach to sentencing for offences under section 38B of the Act of 2000 that
in many cases it will be the seriousness of the terrorist activity about which the
defendant has failed to give information that will determine the level of
criminality, rather than the extent of the information that could have been
provided; and that where a defendant is convicted of two offences, one of failing to give information that might prevent an act of terrorism (s.38B(1)(a))
and one of failing to give information that might lead to the arrest of a person
in respect of the same act of terrorism after it has taken place (s.38B(1)(b)),
consecutive sentences are not wrong in principle.

Terrorism Act 2000, ss.40–43

Arrest without warrant

25–85   Whereas the second element on which the power of arrest without warrant
under section 41 of the *Terrorism Act* 2000 depends is that there are reasonable grounds for the arresting officer's suspicion and whereas this is an objective requirement (*Castorina v. Chief Constable of Surrey, The Times,* June 15,
1988, CA (Civ. Div.)), in *O'Hara v. Chief Constable of the Royal Ulster Constabulary* [1997] A.C. 286, HL, it was unanimously decided that an order by a
superior officer to an arresting officer was not in itself sufficient to afford the
arresting officer a reasonable suspicion, that the executive discretion to arrest
vested in the arresting officer, not his superior officers, and that the only relevant matters were those present to the mind of the arresting officer and in existence to the knowledge of the officer at the time of the arrest (which might
include hearsay coming from other officers): *Raissi v. Commr of Police of the
Metropolis* [2009] 2 W.L.R. 1243, CA (Civ. Div.).

Search of persons

Section 1 of the *Counter-Terrorism Act* 2008 creates a new power for a constable to remove documents in the course of terrorist-related searches (*viz.* under the 2000 Act, s.43 or Sched. 5, para. 1, 3, 11, 15, 28 or 31 (§§ 25–120 *et seq.* in the main work), the *Anti-Terrorism, Crime and Security Act* 2001, s.52(1) or (3)(b) (§ 25–141f in the main work), the *Prevention of Terrorism Act* 2005, s.7A, 7B or 7C (searches in connection with control orders), or the *Terrorism Act* 2006, s.28 (search for terrorist publications)) for the purpose of ascertaining whether they may be seized and to retain them until the examination is completed. If the document (a) consists of information that is stored in electronic form, and (b) is accessible from the premises being searched, the constable may require the document to be produced in a form in which it can be taken away and in a form in which it is visible and legible. Section 1(4) provides that a constable has the same powers of seizure in relation to a document removed under this section as the constable would have had if it had not been removed (and if anything discovered on examination after removal had been discovered without it having been removed). It is a summary offence wilfully to obstruct a constable in the exercise of the power conferred by section 1 (s.2(1)). Section 1 does not apply to a document that is subject to legal privilege (s.3). Where a document is removed under section 1, the constable who removed it must make a written record of the removal (s.4). The document may not be retained for more than 48 hours without authorisation and then for no longer than 96 hours (s.5). Where a document has been retained by virtue of section 5, a person on whom the document was found in the course of a search of that person, the occupier of the premises in which the document was found, a person who had custody or control of the document when it was found, or a person acting on behalf of any such person, is entitled (a) to have access to that document under the supervision of a constable (s.6(1)), or (b) to be provided with a copy of it within a reasonable time from making a request (s.6(2)), unless the officer in charge of the investigation has reasonable grounds for believing that this would prejudice any investigation for the purposes of which the original search was carried out or the document was removed or detained, would prejudice the investigation of any offence, would prejudice any criminal proceedings that might be brought as the result of such investigations, or would facilitate an offence (s.6(4)). Section 7 relates to the photographing and copying of removed documents, section 8 relates to the return of such documents and section 9 contains supplementary provisions in relation to the power to remove documents.

Sections 1 to 8 of the 2008 Act come into force on a day to be appointed.

Terrorism Act 2000, ss.54–58

Weapons training

As from June 18, 2009 (*Counter-Terrorism Act 2008 (Commencement No. 3) Order* 2009 (S.I. 2009 No. 1256)), subsections (7) to (9) of section 54 of the Act of 2000 are repealed: *Counter-Terrorism Act* 2008, ss.39 and 99, and Sched. 3, para. 2, and Sched. 9, Pt 3.

Possession for terrorist purposes

As to the nature of the offence under section 57(1) of the Act of 2000, and as to the scope of the defence provided for by subsection (2), see *R. v. G.; R. v. J.*, *post*, § 25–98.

Collection of information

As from June 18, 2009 (*Counter-Terrorism Act 2008 (Commencement No. 3)*

25–87

★**25–94**

★**25–97**

★**25–98**

Order 2009 (S.I. 2009 No. 1256)), subsections (5) to (7) of section 58 of the Act of 2000 are repealed: *Counter-Terrorism Act* 2008, ss.39 and 99, and Sched. 3 para. 3, and Sched. 9, Pt 3.

★   The ingredients of the offences created by sections 57 (§ 25–97 in the main work) and 58, the relationship of those sections to each other and the nature of the defences specifically provided for by section 57(2) and 58(3) were given detailed consideration by the House of Lords in *R. v. G.; R. v. J.* [2009] 2 W.L.R. 724. It was held: (i) *as to the ingredients of the offence under section 58(1)* (a) Parliament cannot have intended to criminalise the possession of information of a kind which is useful to people for all sorts of everyday purposes and which many members of the public regularly obtain or use, simply because that information could also be useful to someone who was preparing an act of terrorism; to fall within the section the information must, of its very nature, be designed to provide practical assistance to a person committing or preparing an act of terrorism; it is not necessary, however, that the information should be useful only to a person committing, etc., an act of terrorism; for instance, information on where to obtain explosives is capable of falling within section 58(1), even though a bank robber might also find it useful; (b) the role of extrinsic evidence is limited; whilst it can be used to explain to the jury the significance of something in a document or the true nature of the information in a document, since the document must contain information which is, of its very nature, likely to be useful to a potential terrorist, evidence cannot be led with the aim of showing that a document, such as a timetable, containing everyday information, should be treated as falling within section 58(1); section 58(1) would, therefore, cover a training manual about making or planting bombs or explosives, or a document containing information about how to get unauthorised entry to military establishments, government offices, etc., and information, whether in the form of an electronic key or otherwise, which enabled a potential terrorist to obtain access to such information; (c) in relation to possession of such a document or record, the prosecution must prove that the defendant knew that he had the document or record and that he had control of it; (d) it is a requirement of section 58(1)(b) that the defendant not only possessed the document but was aware of the nature of the information which it contained; this does not mean that the prosecution have to show that the defendant knew everything that was in the document or record; it is enough that he knew the nature of the material it contained; but a defendant cannot keep a document in his possession and claim ignorance of its contents by deliberately choosing not to inquire into them; and (e) information will meet the description contained in section 58(1) irrespective of who might commit or prepare an act of terrorism and so be likely to find the information useful; it could be a third party, it could indeed be the defendant himself or it could be that the defendant has stored the information without having any clear idea of what he intends to do with it; (ii) *as to the ingredients of the offence under section 57*, it is immediately obvious that the section covers the possession of far more things than could ever fall within the scope of section 58, as section 57 extends to the possession of any "article", which includes "substance and any other thing" (s.121 (§ 25–108 in the main work)); also, in contrast to section 58(1), the circumstances of the defendant's possession form one of the crucial elements of the section 57(1) offence; (iii) *as to the overlap between sections 57(1) and 58(1)*, following *R. v. Rowe* (§ 25–97 in the main work), possession of a document or record could, in an appropriate case, fall within section 57 as well as section 58; (iv) *as to the operation of the defences under sections 58(3) and 57(2)*, it is only when the prosecution have already proved all the elements under section 58(1) or 57(1) that the defendant needs to rely on the defence in section 58(3) or 57(2); if, applying section 58(3), the jury accept that the defendant had a reasonable excuse for possessing the material, then he is entitled to be acquitted even though it remains the case that the prosecution have proved all the necessary elements of the offence in terms of section 58(1); the same applies in relation to section 57(1) and (2); when a defence is raised under either section, applying section 118(2) (§ 25–106 in the main work), the defence is satisfied unless the prosecution prove beyond reasonable doubt that it is not satisfied, *i.e.* there is an evidential burden on the defendant to raise a defence, which the prosecution must then disprove; there is no need for the prosecution to go further once the defence is raised by, for example, proving beyond reasonable doubt that the defendant's possession of the article was for a purpose connected with the commission, etc., of an act of terrorism (*i.e.* if the defence is, for example, that fertiliser was possessed for gardening purposes, all the prosecution have to do is prove that it was not possessed for those purposes); (v) *as to the scope of the defence under section 58(3)*, the Court of Appeal in *R. v. K.* (see the main work), erred in interpreting the defence as "... simply an explanation that the document or record is possessed for a purpose other than to assist in the commission or preparation of an act of terrorism", which would provide substantially the same defence as that in section 57(2); the language of the two defences is different and it is neither appropriate nor possible to interpret the two provisions as if they said substantially the same thing; the Court of Appeal's interpretation robbed the adjective "reasonable" of all its substance; neither the judge nor jury are left with any room to consider whether the excuse tendered by the accused is actually reasonable; Parliament could not have intended that "excuses" which infringed some other provision of the criminal or civil law and which the jury would rightly consider as outrageous rather than reasonable should nevertheless amount to a reasonable excuse and lead to an acquittal of an offence under section 58; the fact that a defence of this kind would show that the accused's purpose was not to commit an act of terrorism is not an issue under section 58; what the accused has to show is that he had an objectively reasonable excuse for possessing something which Parliament has made it, prima facie, a crime for him to possess because of its potential utility to a terrorist.

Offences relating to information about members of the armed forces, etc.

As from February 16, 2009 (*Counter-Terrorism Act 2008 (Commencement No. 2) Order* 2009 (S.I. 2009 No. 58)), the *Counter-Terrorism Act* 2008, s.76(1), inserts a new section 58A into the Act of 2000.   **25–98a**

Terrorism Act 2000, s.58A

Eliciting, publishing or communicating information about members of armed forces, etc.

58A.—(1) A person commits an offence who—

    (a) elicits or attempts to elicit information about an individual who is or has been—

        (i) a member of Her Majesty's forces,

        (ii) a member of any of the intelligence services, or

        (iii) a constable,

        which is of a kind likely to be useful to a person committing or preparing an act of terrorism, or

    (b) publishes or communicates any such information.

(2) It is a defence for a person charged with an offence under this section to prove that they had a reasonable excuse for their action.

(3) A person guilty of an offence under this section is liable—

(a) on conviction on indictment, to imprisonment for a term not exceeding 1(years or to a fine, or to both;

(b) on summary conviction—

(i) in England and Wales or Scotland, to imprisonment for a term no exceeding 12 months or to a fine not exceeding the statutory maximum, or to both;

(ii) [*Northern Ireland*].

(4) In this section "the intelligence services" means the Security Service, the Secret Intelligence Service and GCHQ (within the meaning of section 3 of the *Intelligence Services Act* 1994).

(5) Schedule 8A to this Act contains supplementary provisions relating to the offence under this section.

Section 76(2) of the 2008 Act provides that in the application of section 58A in relation to an offence committed before the commencement of section 154(1) of the *CJA* 2003, the reference in subsection (3)(b)(i) to "12 months" is to be read as a reference to "six months".

25–98b   Section 76(4) of the 2008 Act gives effect to Schedule 8 which sets out a new Schedule 8A (offence under s.58A: supplementary provisions) to be inserted into the 2000 Act. The purpose of Schedule 8A is to comply with European Parliament and Council Directive 2000/31/EC on certain legal aspects of information society services and to provide for various exceptions to the offence in relation to information service providers. Its effect broadly corresponds to that of the *Electronic Commerce Directive (Terrorism Act 2006) Regulations* 2007 (S.I. 2007 No. 1550), as to which, see § 25–141sa in the main work.

Terrorism Act 2000, ss.114–131

Consent to prosecution

25–105   As from February 16, 2009 (*Counter-Terrorism Act 2008 (Commencement No. 2) Order* 2009 (S.I. 2009 No. 58)), the words "outside the United Kingdom or" are inserted after the word "committed" in section 117(2A) of the Act of 2000: *Counter-Terrorism Act* 2008, s.29.

Defences

25–106   As from February 16, 2009 (*Counter-Terrorism Act 2008 (Commencement No. 2) Order* 2009 (S.I. 2009 No. 58)), "58A," is inserted after "58," in section 118(5)(a) of the Act of 2000: *Counter-Terrorism Act* 2008, s.76(3).

Supplemental powers of court in respect of forfeiture orders

★25–107a   As from June 18, 2009 (*Counter-Terrorism Act 2008 (Commencement No. 3) Order* 2009 (S.I. 2009 No. 1256)), the *Counter-Terrorism Act* 2008, s.38(1), substitutes a new section 120A in the Act of 2000.

Terrorism Act 2000, s.120A

Supplementary powers of forfeiture

120A.—(1) A court by or before which a person is convicted of an offence under a provision mentioned in column 1 of the following table may order the forfeiture of any item mentioned in column 2 in relation to that offence.

Offence   *Items liable to forfeiture*

Section 54 (weapons training)	Anything that the court considers to have been in the possession of the person for purposes connected with the offence.
Section 57 (possession for terrorist purposes)	Any article that is the subject matter of the offence.
Section 58 (collection of information)	Any document or record containing information of the kind mentioned in subsection (1)(a) of that section.
Section 58A (eliciting, publishing or communicating information about members of armed forces etc)	Any document or record containing information of the kind mentioned in subsection (1)(a) of that section.

(2) Before making an order under this section, a court must give an opportunity to be heard to any person, other than the convicted person, who claims to be the owner or otherwise interested in anything which can be forfeited under this section.

(3) An order under this section does not come into force until there is no further possibility of it being varied, or set aside, on appeal (disregarding any power of a court to grant leave to appeal out of time).

(4) Where a court makes an order under this section, it may also make such other provision as appears to it to be necessary for giving effect to the forfeiture, including, in particular, provision relating to the retention, handling, disposal or destruction of what is forfeited.

(5) Provision made by virtue of subsection (4) may be varied at any time by the court that made it.

(6) The power of forfeiture under this section is in addition to any power of forfeiture under section 23A.

Terrorism Act 2000, Sched. 2

Proscribed organisations

The *Proscribed Organisations (Name Change) Order* 2009 (S.I. 2009 No. 578) provides that the name "Jama'at ud Da'wa", not being a name specified in Schedule 2 to the 2000 Act, is to be treated as an additional name for the organisation listed in that schedule as "Lashkar e Tayyaba".

Terrorism Act 2000, Sched. 4

Forfeiture orders

Interpretation/implementation of forfeiture orders

As from June 18, 2009 (*Counter-Terrorism Act 2008 (Commencement No. 3) Order* 2009 (S.I. 2009 No. 1256)), the *Counter-Terrorism Act* 2008, s.39, and Sched. 3, para. 5(1) and (2), amend paragraph 1 of Schedule 4 to the Act of 2000, so as (i) to insert "or 23A" after "section 23" in the definition of "forfeiture order" and (ii) to insert the following definition after the definition of "forfeited property"—   ★**25–112**

"'relevant offence' means—

(a) an offence under any of sections 15 to 18,

(b) an offence to which section 23A applies, or

    (c) in relation to a restraint order, any offence specified in Schedule 2 to the *Counter-Terrorism Act* 2008 (offences where terrorist connection to be considered)".

★   As from June 18, 2009 (*Counter-Terrorism Act 2008 (Commencement No. 3) Order* 2009 (S.I. 2009 No. 1256)), the *Counter-Terrorism Act* 2008, s.39, and Sched. 3, para. 5(1) and (3), amend paragraphs 2(1)(d) and 4(2)(c) of Schedule 4 to the Act of 2000, so as to substitute "section 23B(1)" for "section 23(7)" in both places.

Application of proceeds to compensate victims

★**25–112a**   As from June 18, 2009 (*Counter-Terrorism Act 2008 (Commencement No. 3) Order* 2009 (S.I. 2009 No. 1256)), the *Counter-Terrorism Act* 2008, s.37(1), amends Schedule 4 to the Act of 2000, so as to insert a new paragraph 4A, as follows—

    "Application of proceeds to compensate victim

      4A.—(1) Where a court makes a forfeiture order in a case where—

        (a) the offender has been convicted of an offence that has resulted in a person suffering personal injury, loss or damage, or

        (b) any such offence is taken into consideration by the court in determining sentence,

    the court may also order that an amount not exceeding a sum specified by the court is to be paid to that person out of the proceeds of the forfeiture.

      (2) For this purpose the proceeds of the forfeiture means the aggregate amount of—

        (a) any forfeited money, and

        (b) the proceeds of the sale, disposal or realisation of any forfeited property, after deduction of the costs of the sale, disposal or realisation,

    reduced by the amount of any payment under paragraph 2(1)(d) or 3(1).

      (3) The court may make an order under this paragraph only if it is satisfied that but for the inadequacy of the offender's means it would have made a compensation order under section 130 of the *Powers of Criminal Courts (Sentencing) Act* 2000 under which the offender would have been required to pay compensation of an amount not less than the specified amount.".

Restraint orders

★**25–113**   As from June 18, 2009 (*Counter-Terrorism Act 2008 (Commencement No. 3) Order* 2009 (S.I. 2009 No. 1256)), paragraphs 5 and 6 of Schedule 4 to the Act of 2000 are subject to minor amendments (substituting references to "a relevant offence" for references to offences under sections 15 to 18 of the Act): see the *Counter-Terrorism Act* 2008, s.39, and Sched. 3, para. 5(1), (5) and (6).

Compensation

★**25–114**   As from June 18, 2009 (*Counter-Terrorism Act 2008 (Commencement No. 3) Order* 2009 (S.I. 2009 No. 1256)), paragraphs 9 and 10 of Schedule 4 to the Act of 2000 are subject to minor amendments (omission of the heading "Compensation" and substitution of references to "a relevant offence" for references to offences under sections 15 to 18 of the Act): see the *Counter-Terrorism Act* 2008, s.39, and Sched. 3, para. 5(1) and (7) to (9).

Enforcement of orders made elsewhere

★**25–116**   As from June 18, 2009 (*Counter-Terrorism Act 2008 (Commencement No. 3)*

Order 2009 (S.I. 2009 No. 1256)), paragraph 12 of Schedule 4 to the Act of 2000 is amended to include references to section 23A: see the *Counter-Terrorism Act* 2008, s.39, and Sched. 3, para. 5(1) and (10).

High Court proceedings

RSC, Ord. 115, Pt III, has been subject to a further minor amendment by the *Civil Procedure (Amendment No. 3) Rules* 2008 (S.I. 2008 No. 3327). **25–117**

Terrorism Act 2000, Sched. 5

Searches

In relation to searches under paragraphs 1 and 3 of Schedule 5 to the Act **25–120** of 2000, see *ante*, § 25–87, as to the effect of sections 1 to 8 of the *Counter-Terrorism Act* 2008.

Excluded and special procedure material: production & access

In relation to an application under paragraph 5 of Schedule 5 to the Act of **25–122** 2000 for access to excluded material consisting of journalistic material, (i) *as to freedom of expression*, the applicant had to provide a clear and compelling case in justification of it; in considering the application, there was a need to balance the gravity of the activities that were the subject of the investigation and the likely benefit to the investigation from making the order against the considerable weight attaching to the confidentiality of journalistic sources; the proportionality of any proposed order had to be measured and justified against the weight attaching to the interest in protecting such sources; (ii) *as to the privilege against self-incrimination*, see *ante*, § 15–89; (iii) *as to the appointment of a special advocate*, the power of the court to request such an appointment of its own motion should be exercised only in exceptional cases and as a last resort; in deciding whether to make such a request, the court should have regard to the seriousness of the issue that the court has to determine; even in a case which was conducted entirely *ex parte*, the court might consider that the absent party was afforded a sufficient measure of procedural protection by the obligation on the applicant to lay before the court any material that undermined or qualified his case; furthermore, the court itself could be expected to perform a role of testing the case for the applicant; those features alone might suffice to satisfy the court that the procedure was fair, but a further consideration was the extent to which a special advocate was likely to be able to assist the absent party's case: *R. (Malik) v. Manchester Crown Court and another* [2008] 4 All E.R. 403, DC.

Excluded or special procedure material: search

In relation to a search pursuant to a warrant issued under paragraph 11 of **25–123** Schedule 5 to the Act of 2000, see *ante*, § 25–87, as to the effect of sections 1 to 8 of the *Counter-Terrorism Act* 2008.

Urgent cases

In relation to a search under paragraph 15 of Schedule 5 to the Act of **25–125** 2000, see *ante*, § 25–87, as to the effect of sections 1 to 8 of the *Counter-Terrorism Act* 2008.

Terrorism Act 2000, Sched. 7

Modifications applicable to Channel Tunnel

Article 7 of the *Channel Tunnel (International Arrangements) Order* 1993 (S.I. **25–136a**

1993 No. 1813) (Appendix F–13a, *post*) provides that the enactments mentioned in Schedule 4 to that order shall (a) in their application to France by virtue of article 4(1) or (1B), and (b) in their application to the United Kingdom within the tunnel system and elsewhere for the authorised purposes (as to which, see article 2(2)), have effect with the modifications set out in Schedule 4. As a result of the amendment of that schedule by the *Channel Tunnel (International Arrangements) (Amendment) Order* 2001 (S.I. 2001 No. 178), Schedule 7 to the 2000 Act, being one of the enactments mentioned therein, has effect with the following modifications—

  (i) in paragraph 1(2) omit the references to "the border area", "captain", "ship" and "vehicle" and for the words "an airport or hoverport" are substituted the words—

  "a railway station or other place where
    (a) persons embark or disembark or
    (b) goods are loaded or unloaded,
      on or from a through train or shuttle train, as the case may be";

 (ii) in paragraph 1(3) for the words "ship or aircraft" wherever occurring, there are substituted the words "through train or shuttle train";

(iii) in paragraph 2(2), the words "or in the border area", "or in the area" and "or Northern Ireland" are omitted;

 (iv) in paragraph 2(3) for the words "ship or aircraft" there are substituted "through train or shuttle train" and there are omitted the words "or Northern Ireland";

  (v) after paragraph 2(3) there is inserted—

  "**3A.** An examination under sub-paragraph (1) may be commenced in a train during the period when it is a control area.";

 (vi) paragraphs 3 and 4 are omitted;

(vii) in paragraph 5 the words "or 3" are omitted;

(viii) in paragraph 6, in sub-paragraph (1), for the word "vehicle" there are substituted the words "through train or shuttle train" and, in sub-paragraph (2), for the words "ship, aircraft or vehicle" there are substituted the words "through train or shuttle train";

 (ix) in paragraph 7 for the words "ship or aircraft", wherever occurring, there are substituted the words "through train or shuttle train";

  (x) in paragraph 8 for the words "ship or aircraft", wherever occurring, there are substituted the words "through train or shuttle train", and sub-paragraph (2) is omitted;

 (xi) in paragraph 9, in sub-paragraph (2), the words "or in Northern Ireland" are omitted and for the words "ship, aircraft or vehicle" there are substituted the words "through train or shuttle train" and, in sub-paragraph (4), for the words "ship or aircraft or enter a vehicle" there are substituted the words "through train or shuttle train";

(xii) paragraph 12 is omitted;

(xiii) in paragraph 13 for the words "ships or aircraft" and the words

"ship or aircraft", wherever occurring, there are substituted the
words "a through train or shuttle train" and for the words "United
Kingdom" there are substituted the words "Tunnel System";
(xiv) for paragraph 14 there is substituted—

> **14.**—(1) The Secretary of State may from time to time give written notice to
> persons operating international services designating all or any through trains
> as control areas while they are within any area in the UK specified in the no-
> tice or while they constitute a control zone.
>
> (2) The Secretary of State may from time to time give written notice designat-
> ing a control area—
>> (i) to the Concessionaires as respects any part of the tunnel system in
>> the UK or of a control zone within the tunnel system in France or
>> Belgium, or
>> (ii) to any occupier or person concerned with the management of a
>> terminal control point in the UK.
>
> (3) A notice under sub-paragraph (1) or (2) above may specify facilities to be
> provided and conditions and restrictions to be observed in a control area,
> and any persons to whom such a notice is given shall take all reasonable
> steps to secure that any such facilities, conditions or restrictions are
> provided or observed.";

(xv) paragraphs 15, 16 and 17 are omitted, and
(xvi) the Table of Designated Ports is omitted.

Terrorism Act 2000, Sched. 8

Rights: England, Wales and Northern Ireland

As from June 18, 2009 (*Counter-Terrorism Act 2008 (Commencement No. 3)*   ★**25–140a**
Order 2009 (S.I. 2009 No. 1256)), "or 23A" is inserted after "section 23" in
paragraph 8(4)(d) of Schedule 8 to the Act of 2000: *Counter-Terrorism Act
2008*, s.39, and Sched. 3, para. 6.

As from February 16, 2009 (*Counter-Terrorism Act 2008 (Commencement No.
2) Order* 2009 (S.I. 2009 No. 58)), the *Counter-Terrorism Act* 2008, s.82(1),
substitutes a new sub-paragraph (3) in paragraph 9 of Schedule 8 to the Act
of 2000, as follows—

> "(3) A direction under this paragraph may be given only if the officer giving it has
> reasonable grounds for believing—
>> (a) that, unless the direction is given, the exercise of the right by the detained
>> person will have any of the consequences specified in paragraph 8(4), or
>> (b) that the detained person has benefited from his criminal conduct and that,
>> unless the direction is given, the exercise of the right by the detained
>> person will hinder the recovery of the value of the property constituting
>> the benefit.".

As from a day to be appointed, the *Counter-Terrorism Act* 2008, s.16(1) and
(2), amend paragraph 14(2) of Schedule 8 to the Act of 2000 by substituting
the words "or as mentioned in sub-paragraph (2A)" for the words from "or
for purposes related" to the end.

As from a day to be appointed, the *Counter-Terrorism Act* 2008, s.16(1) and
(3), amend paragraph 14 of Schedule 8 to the Act of 2000 by inserting a new
sub-paragraph (2A), as follows—

> "(2A) The fingerprints or samples may be used—
>> (a) in the interests of national security,

213

(b) for purposes related to the prevention or detection of crime, the investigation of an offence or the conduct of a prosecution, or

(c) for purposes related to the identification of a deceased person or of the person from whom the material came.".

As from a day to be appointed, paragraph 14(3) of Schedule 8 to the Act of 2000 is repealed: *Counter-Terrorism Act* 2008, ss.16(1) and (4), and 99, and Sched. 9, Pt 1.

As from a day to be appointed, the *Counter-Terrorism Act* 2008, s.16(1) and (5), amend paragraph 14(4) of Schedule 8 to the Act of 2000 by inserting a new sub-paragraph (ba), as follows—

"(ba) material to which section 18 of the *Counter-Terrorism Act* 2008 applies,".

Warrants of further detention

25–140i   As from February 16, 2009 (*Counter-Terrorism Act 2008 (Commencement No. 2) Order* 2009 (S.I. 2009 No. 58)), the words "after consulting the Lord Chancellor" are omitted from paragraph 29(4)(a) and (c) of Schedule 8 to the Act of 2000: *Counter-Terrorism Act* 2008, ss.82(2) and 99, and Sched. 9, Pt 6.

Information

★**25–140n**   As from June 18, 2009 (*Counter-Terrorism Act 2008 (Commencement No. 3) Order* 2009 (S.I. 2009 No. 1256)), "or 23A" is inserted after "section 23" in paragraph 34(2)(c) of Schedule 8 to the Act of 2000: *Counter-Terrorism Act* 2008, s.39, and Sched. 3, para. 6.

Terrorism Act 2000, Sched. 14

25–141   Article 7 of the *Channel Tunnel (International Arrangements) Order* 1993 (S.I. 1993 No. 1813) (Appendix F–13a, *post*) provides that the enactments mentioned in Schedule 4 to that order shall (a) in their application to France by virtue of article 4(1) or (1B), and (b) in their application to the United Kingdom within the tunnel system and elsewhere for the authorised purposes (as to which, see article 2(2)), have effect with the modifications set out in Schedule 4. As a result of the amendment of that schedule by the *Channel Tunnel (International Arrangements) (Amendment) Order* 2001 (S.I. 2001 No. 178), Schedule 14 to the 2000 Act, being one of the enactments mentioned therein, has effect with the following modifications: in paragraphs 5 and 6, after the words "this Act", in each place where they occur, there are inserted the words "or the *Channel Tunnel (International Arrangements) Order* 1993".

B. Anti-Terrorism, Crime and Security Act 2001

Anti-terrorism, Crime and Security Act 2001, ss.47–56

Powers of entry

25–141f   In relation to a search pursuant to a warrant issued under section 52 of the 2001 Act, see *ante*, § 25–87, as to the effect of sections 1 to 8 of the *Counter-Terrorism Act* 2008.

Anti-terrorism, Crime and Security Act 2001, ss.113–115

Application of section 113

25–141l   As from February 16, 2009 (*Counter-Terrorism Act 2008 (Commencement No. 2) Order* 2009 (S.I. 2009 No. 58)), ", racial" is inserted after "religious" in section 113A(2) of the 2001 Act: *Counter-Terrorism Act* 2008, s.75(1) and (2)(b).

C. Terrorism Act 2006

(1) Encouragement, etc., of terrorism

Terrorism Act 2006, ss.1, 2

Sentence

R. v. Rahman; *R. v. Mohammed* is now reported at [2009] 1 Cr.App.R.(S.)   ★**25–141s**
70.

(2) Preparation of terrorist acts and training

Terrorism Act 2006, ss.5–8

Powers of forfeiture in respect of offences under s.6
   As from June 18, 2009 (*Counter-Terrorism Act 2008 (Commencement No. 3)*   ★**25–142**
Order 2009 (S.I. 2009 No. 1256)), the *Counter-Terrorism Act* 2008, s.38(2),
inserts a new subsection (7) in section 7 of the 2006 Act, as follows—

   "(7) The power of forfeiture under this section is in addition to any power of forfeiture under section 23A of the *Terrorism Act* 2000.".

(3) Offences involving radioactive devices and material and nuclear facilities and sites

Forfeiture of devices, materials or facilities
   As from June 18, 2009 (*Counter-Terrorism Act 2008 (Commencement No. 3)*   ★**25–142h**
Order 2009 (S.I. 2009 No. 1256)), the *Counter-Terrorism Act* 2008, s.38(3),
inserts a new section 11A into the 2006 Act.

Terrorism Act 2006, s.11A

Forfeiture of devices, materials or facilities
   11A.—(1) A court by or before which a person is convicted of an offence under
section 9 or 10 may order the forfeiture of any radioactive device or radioactive
material, or any nuclear facility, made or used in committing the offence.
   (2) A court by or before which a person is convicted of an offence under section
11 may order the forfeiture of any radioactive device or radioactive material, or any
nuclear facility, which is the subject of—
      (a) a demand under subsection (1) of that section, or
      (b) a threat falling within subsection (3) of that section.
   (3) Before making an order under this section, a court must give an opportunity
to be heard to any person, other than the convicted person, who claims to be the
owner or otherwise interested in anything which can be forfeited under this section.
   (4) An order under this section does not come into force until there is no further
possibility of it being varied, or set aside, on appeal (disregarding any power of a
court to grant leave to appeal out of time).
   (5) Where a court makes an order under this section, it may also make such other
provision as appears to it to be necessary for giving effect to the forfeiture, including,
in particular, provision relating to the retention, handling, disposal or destruction of
what is forfeited.
   (6) Provision made by virtue of subsection (5) may be varied at any time by the
court that made it.
   (7) The power of forfeiture under this section is in addition to any power of forfeiture under section 23A of the *Terrorism Act* 2000.

Terrorism Act 2006, ss.17–19

Consents to prosecutions

25–142k   As from February 16, 2009 (*Counter-Terrorism Act 2008 (Commencement No. 2) Order* 2009 (S.I. 2009 No. 58)), the words "outside the United Kingdom or" are inserted after the word "committed" in section 19(2) of the 2006 Act: *Counter-Terrorism Act* 2008, s.29.

EA. COUNTER-TERRORISM ACT 2008

(1) Post-charge questioning of terrorist suspects

Counter-Terrorism Act 2008, s.22

25–142n   *[Post-charge questioning: England and Wales*
22.—(1) The following provisions apply in England and Wales.
(2) A judge of the Crown Court may authorise the questioning of a person about an offence—
> (a) after the person has been charged with the offence or been officially informed that they may be prosecuted for it, or
> (b) after the person has been sent for trial for the offence,
if the offence is a terrorism offence or it appears to the judge that the offence has a terrorist connection.
(3) The judge—
> (a) must specify the period during which questioning is authorised, and
> (b) may impose such conditions as appear to be necessary in the interests of justice, which may include conditions as to the place where the questioning is to be carried out.
(4) The period during which questioning is authorised—
> (a) begins when questioning pursuant to the authorisation begins and runs continuously from that time (whether or not questioning continues), and
> (b) must not exceed 48 hours.
This is without prejudice to any application for a further authorisation under this section.
(5) Where the person is in prison or otherwise lawfully detained, the judge may authorise the person's removal to another place and detention there for the purpose of being questioned.
(6) A judge must not authorise the questioning of a person under this section unless satisfied—
> (a) that further questioning of the person is necessary in the interests of justice,
> (b) that the investigation for the purposes of which the further questioning is proposed is being conducted diligently and expeditiously, and
> (c) that what is authorised will not interfere unduly with the preparation of the person's defence to the charge in question or any other criminal charge.
(7) Codes of practice under section 66 of the *Police and Criminal Evidence Act* 1984 must make provision about the questioning of a person by a constable in accordance with this section.
(8) Nothing in this section prevents codes of practice under that section making other provision for the questioning of a person by a constable about an offence—
> (a) after the person has been charged with the offence or been officially informed that they may be prosecuted for it, or
> (b) after the person has been sent for trial for the offence.
(9) [*Amends CJPOA 1994, s.34, ante, § 15–414.*]
(10) Nothing in section 36 or 37 of that Act (effect of accused's failure or refusal to account for certain matters) is to be read as excluding the operation of those sections in relation to a request made in the course of questioning under this section.]

Section 22 comes into force on a day to be appointed.

Section 25 provides for the compulsory video recording with sound of
interviews under section 22. The Secretary of State must issue a code of
practice in this regard (ss.25(3)–(5) and 26). Failure to observe a provision of
the code does not of itself render a constable liable to civil or criminal proceedings: s.26(7); and the code shall be admissible in evidence in criminal and civil
proceedings, and is to be taken into account by a court or tribunal in any case
in which it appears to the court to be relevant.

Counter-Terrorism Act 2008, s.27

[Meaning of "terrorism offence"
27.—(1) For the purposes of sections 22 to 24 (post-charge questioning) the fol-   **25–142c**
owing are terrorism offences—

    (a) an offence under any of the following provisions of the *Terrorism Act* 2000—

        sections 11 to 13 (offences relating to proscribed organisations),

        sections 15 to 19, 21A and 21D (offences relating to terrorist prop-
erty),

        sections 38B and 39 (disclosure of and failure to disclose informa-
tion about terrorism),

        section 54 (weapons training),

        sections 56 to 58A (directing terrorism, possessing things and col-
lecting information for the purposes of terrorism),

        sections 59 to 61 (inciting terrorism outside the United Kingdom),

        paragraph 14 of Schedule 5 (order for explanation of material:
false or misleading statements),

        paragraph 1 of Schedule 6 (failure to provide customer informa-
tion in connection with a terrorist investigation),

        paragraph 18 of Schedule 7 (offences in connection with port and
border controls);

    (b) an offence in respect of which there is jurisdiction by virtue of any of sec-
tions 62 to 63D of that Act (extra-territorial jurisdiction in respect of certain
offences committed outside the United Kingdom for the purposes of terrorism etc);

    (c) an offence under section 113 of the *Anti-Terrorism, Crime and Security Act*
2001 (use of noxious substances or things);

    (d) an offence under any of the following provisions of Part 1 of the *Terrorism
Act* 2006—

        sections 1 and 2 (encouragement of terrorism),

        sections 5, 6 and 8 (preparation and training for terrorism),

        sections 9, 10 and 11 (offences relating to radioactive devices and
material and nuclear facilities);

    (e) an offence in respect of which there is jurisdiction by virtue of section 17 of
that Act (extra-territorial jurisdiction in respect of certain offences committed outside the United Kingdom for the purposes of terrorism etc);

    (f) an offence under paragraph 8 or 9 of Schedule 3 to the *Justice and Security
(Northern Ireland) Act* 2007 (offences in connection with searches for muni-
tions and transmitters in Northern Ireland).

(2) Any ancillary offence in relation to an offence listed in subsection (1) is a terrorism offence for the purposes of sections 22 to 24.

(3) The Secretary of State may by order amend subsection (1).

(4) Any such order is subject to affirmative resolution procedure.]

Section 27 comes into force on a day to be appointed.

(2) Jurisdiction

Counter-Terrorism Act 2008, s.28

Jurisdiction to try offences committed in the UK

25–142p   28.—(1) Where an offence to which this section applies is committed in th United Kingdom—

    (a) proceedings for the offence may be taken at any place in the Unite Kingdom, and

    (b) the offence may for all incidental purposes be treated as having been con mitted at any such place.

(2) The section applies to—

    (a) an offence under any of the following provisions of the *Terrorism Act* 2000– sections 11 to 13 (offences relating to proscribed organisations), sections 15 to 19, 21A and 21D (offences relating to terrorist property), sections 38B and 39 (disclosure of and failure to disclose information abou terrorism), section 47 (offences relating to stop and search powers), section 51 (parking a vehicle in contravention of an authorisation or restric tion), section 54 (weapons training), sections 56 to 58A (directing terrorism and possessing things or collectin information for the purposes of terrorism), section 116 (failure to stop a vehicle when required to do so), paragraph 1 of Schedule 6 (failure to provide customer information in con nection with a terrorist investigation), paragraph 18 of Schedule 7 (offences in connection with port and borde controls);

    (b) an offence under section 113 of the *Anti-terrorism, Crime and Security A* 2001 (use of noxious substances or things to cause harm and intimidate);

    (c) an offence under any of the following provisions of the *Terrorism Act* 2006– sections 1 and 2 (encouragement of terrorism), sections 5, 6 and 8 (preparation and training for terrorism), sections 9, 10 and 11 (offences relating to radioactive devices etc).

(3) The Secretary of State may by order amend subsection (2).

(4) Any such order is subject to affirmative resolution procedure.

(5) The power conferred by subsection (3) may be exercised so as to add offenc to subsection (2) only if it appears to the Secretary of State necessary to do so for th purpose of dealing with terrorism.

(6) [*Amends* Justice and Security (Northern Ireland) Act *2007, s.1.*]

★   Section 28 came into force on June 18, 2009 (*Counter-Terrorism Act 200 (Commencement No. 3) Order* 2009 (S.I. 2009 No. 1256)).

(3) Sentence

Counter-Terrorism Act 2008, s.30

Sentences for offences with a terrorist connection: England and Wales

25–142q   30.—(1) This section applies where a court in England and Wales is considerin for the purposes of sentence the seriousness of an offence specified in Schedule (offences where terrorist connection to be considered).

(2) If having regard to the material before it for the purposes of sentencing it ap pears to the court that the offence has or may have a terrorist connection, the cou must determine whether that is the case.

(3) For that purpose the court may hear evidence, and must take account of any representations made by the prosecution and the defence, as in the case of any other matter relevant for the purposes of sentence.

(4) If the court determines that the offence has a terrorist connection, the court—

    (a) must treat that fact as an aggravating factor, and

    (b) must state in open court that the offence was so aggravated.

(5) In this section "sentence", in relation to an offence, includes any order made by a court when dealing with a person in respect of the offence.

(6) This section has effect in relation only to offences committed on or after the day it comes into force.

Section 30 came into force on June 18, 2009 (*Counter-Terrorism Act 2008*   ★
(Commencement No. 3) Order 2009 (S.I. 2009 No. 1256)).

The offences listed in Schedule 2 (in force as from a day to be appointed) as   **25–142r**
offences where a court has to consider whether there is a terrorist connection are: (i) the common law offences of murder, manslaughter, culpable homicide and abduction; (ii) the offences contrary to sections 4, 23, 28, 29, 30 and 64 of the *Offences against the Person Act* 1861; (iii) the offences contrary to sections 2 to 5 of the *Explosive Substances Act* 1883; (iv) the offence contrary to section 1 of the *Biological Weapons Act* 1974; (v) the offence contrary to section 1 of the *Taking of Hostages Act* 1982; (vi) the offences contrary to sections 1 to 4 and 6(2) of the *Aviation Security Act* 1982; (vii) the offences contrary to sections 1B, 1C and 2 (so far as relating to an offence specified in this schedule) of the *Nuclear Material (Offences) Act* 1983; (viii) the offences contrary to sections 1, 9, 10, 11 and 14(4) (so far as relating to an offence under section 9 or 11) of the *Aviation and Maritime Security Act* 1990; (ix) an offence under Part II of the *Channel Tunnel (Security) Order* 1994 (S.I. 1994 No. 570); (x) the offences contrary to sections 2 and 11 of the *Chemical Weapons Act* 1996; (xi) the offences contrary to sections 47 and 114 of the *Anti-terrorism, Crime and Security Act* 2001; and (xii) any "ancillary offence" (as to which, see *post*, § 25–142v) in relation to an offence specified in the schedule.

(4) Notification requirements

Part 4 of the 2008 Act (ss.40–61) imposes notification requirements on   **25–142s**
persons dealt with in respect of certain offences. The framework is similar to that for sex offenders which exists under the *SOA* 2003 (as to which, see §§ 20–263 *et seq.* in the main work). Sections 41 to 43 specify the offences to which Part 4 applies. Sections 44 to 46 set out the persons to whom the requirements apply and which sentences or orders trigger the requirements.

Section 47 provides that an offender to whom the requirements apply must, within three days of him being dealt with in respect of the offence in question (time in custody being disregarded in making this computation), notify certain personal information to the police. Section 48 provides that such a person, on the occurrence of certain events (*viz.* his use of an unnotified name, a change of address, his residing or staying at any unnotified premises, any prescribed change of circumstances or his release from custody) must within three days beginning on the day the event occurred, notify that event to the police. Section 49 provides that a person who has notified the police in accordance with section 47, 48 or 56 (*post*) or section 49 itself must, within a year after each notification, re-notify the information specified in section 47(2) to the police, unless he is in custody, serving a sentence of imprisonment or detention, detained in hospital or detained under the *Immigration Acts* (in which case he must notify it to the police upon being released in accordance with section 48(4) and (10)). Section 50 provides for the method of notification and related matters, including a requirement under subsection (6) that the person making the notification must, if requested to do so, allow the officer or person to whom the notification is made to take his fingerprints, photograph any part of him, or both, for the purpose of verifying his identity. Section 52 permits the Secretary of State to make provision by regulations requiring a person to whom the notification requirements apply and who intends to travel outside the United Kingdom to notify the police of his departure and return. Section 53 provides that the requirements will apply for a period of 30 years, 15 years or 10 years depending on the age of the offender and the nature of the penalty imposed.

A person commits an offence if (a) he fails without reasonable excuse to comply with section 47, 48, 49, 50(6) or 56 (*post*) or any regulations made under section 52(1), or (b) if he gives information in purported compliance with those sections that he knows to be false (s.54(1)). The offence is triable either way (maximum penalty on conviction on indictment, five years' imprisonment, or a fine, or both) (s.54(2)). A person commits an offence under section 54(1) on the day on which he first fails to comply, and continues to commit it throughout any period during which the failure continues; but a person must not be prosecuted for such an offence more than once in respect of the same failure (s.54(4)). Section 55 makes provision regarding the effect of absence abroad on the notification requirements. Section 56 provides that, where a person returns to the United Kingdom after a period of absence, where the person was not required to make a notification under section 47 before his departure from the United Kingdom, and where there has been a change to any information last notified to the police in accordance with section 47, 48, 49 or this section or the period after which re-notification was required under section 49(1) has expired, the person must notify or re-notify the police of the information in accordance with section 47(2).

Sections 57 to 59 give effect to Schedules 4 to 6 respectively. Schedule 4 makes provision for notification orders where the person has been dealt with outside the United Kingdom in respect of a corresponding foreign offence. Schedule 5 makes provision for foreign travel restriction orders which prohibit persons to whom the notification requirements apply from travelling outside the United Kingdom. Schedule 6 makes provision for the application of Part 4 to service offences and related matters. Sections 60 and 61 are definitional and interpretative provisions

★　　Part 4 (including Schedules 4 to 6) comes into force on October 1, 2009: *Counter-Terrorism Act 2008 (Commencement No. 4) Order* 2009 (S.I. 2009 No. 1493).

(5) Interpretation

Counter-Terrorism Act 2008, ss.92–94

Meaning of "terrorism"

25–142t　　**92.** In this Act "terrorism" has the same meaning as in the *Terrorism Act* 2000 (see section 1 of that Act).

For section 1 of the 2000 Act, see § 25–56 in the main work and, *ante, in* this supplement.

Meaning of offence having a "terrorist connection"

25–142u　　**93.** For the purposes of this Act an offence has a terrorist connection if the offence—

220

(a) is, or takes place in the course of, an act of terrorism, or

(b) is committed for the purposes of terrorism.

Meaning of "ancillary offence"

94.—(1) In this Act "ancillary offence", in relation to an offence, means any of the following—   **25-142v**

(a) aiding, abetting, counselling or procuring the commission of the offence (or, in Scotland, being art and part in the commission of the offence);

(b) an offence under Part 2 of the *Serious Crime Act* 2007 (encouraging or assisting crime) in relation to the offence (or, in Scotland, inciting a person to commit the offence);

(c) attempting or conspiring to commit the offence.

(2) In subsection (1)(b) the reference to an offence under Part 2 of the *Serious Crime Act* 2007 includes, in relation to times before the commencement of that Part, an offence of incitement under the law of England and Wales or Northern Ireland.

VI. IMMIGRATION

Immigration and Asylum Act 1999, s.31

Defences based on Article 31(1) of the Refugee Convention

R. v. Asfaw (United Nations High Commissioner for Refugees Intervening) is now reported at [2008] 1 A.C. 1061.   **25-228e**

Defences

As to the possibility of a defence of duress being available to a victim of human trafficking, see *R. v. O., post*, Appendix E–12d.   **25-228f**

X. INCITING TO DISAFFECTION

All of the provisions of the *AFA* 2006 mentioned in the main work come into force on October 31, 2009: *Armed Forces Act 2006 (Commencement No. 5) Order* 2009 (S.I. 2009 No. 1167).   **★25-282**

XIV. OFFENCES RELATING TO POSTS AND TELECOMMUNICATIONS

C. REGULATION OF INVESTIGATORY POWERS ACT 2000

Introduction

In *R. v. S. (F.) and A. (S.)* [2009] 1 Cr.App.R. 18, the Court of Appeal upheld the refusal of the trial judge to order that counts alleging that the appellants had committed offences under section 53 of the Act of 2000 should be stayed where encrypted files on their computers were expected to provide incriminating evidence against them in relation to terrorist offences (see *ante*, § 12–2).   **25-367**

Regulation of Investigatory Powers Act 2000, ss.15–19

Exceptions to section 17

The amendment of section 18 of the Act of 2000 effected by the *AFA* 2006   **★25-378**

comes into force on October 31, 2009: *Armed Forces Act 2006 (Commencement No. 5) Order* 2009 (S.I. 2009 No. 1167).

With effect from November 27, 2008, the *Counter-Terrorism Act* 2008, s.69(1) and (2) inserted a new paragraph (db) in section 18(1) of the Act of 2000, as follows—

> "(db) any financial restrictions proceedings as defined in section 65 of the *Counter-Terrorism Act* 2008, or any proceedings arising out of such proceedings;".

With effect from November 27, 2008, the *Counter-Terrorism Act* 2008, s.69(1) and (3) inserted a new paragraph (zb) in section 18(2) of the Act of 2000, as follows—

> "(zb) in the case of proceedings falling within paragraph (db), to—
>> (i) a person, other than the Treasury, who is or was a party to the proceedings, or
>> (ii) any person who for the purpose of the proceedings (but otherwise than by virtue of appointment as a special advocate) represents a person falling within sub-paragraph (i);".

As from February 16, 2009 (*Counter-Terrorism Act 2008 (Commencement No. 2) Order* 2009 (S.I. 2009 No. 58)), the *Counter-Terrorism Act* 2008, s.74(1) substitutes a new paragraph (c) in section 18(7) of the Act of 2000, as follows—

> "(c) a disclosure to the panel of an inquiry held under the *Inquiries Act* 2005 or to a person appointed as counsel to such an inquiry where, in the course of the inquiry, the panel has ordered the disclosure to be made to the panel alone or (as the case may be) to the panel and the person appointed as counsel to the inquiry; or".

XVII. REVENUE AND CUSTOMS OFFENCES

A. Cheating the Public Revenue

Sentence

25–385a   In *R. v. Mehta, Sharman, Reardon and Ratcliff, The Times*, October 3, 2008, CA, when considering the appropriate sentence for a missing trader/carousel fraud, the court emphasised that a distinction was to be drawn between the missing traders who withheld the VAT and the eventual reclaimers of VAT upon export on the one hand and those who were operators of genuine companies with legitimate trade and who lent themselves to the fraud as "buffer" companies, and through whose hands the actual or notional commodities passed, on the other. As to the latter, the court also noted an error in the judgment in *Att.-Gen.'s References (Nos 88, etc., of 2006) (R. v. Meehan* (see the main work), as identified in *R. v. Takkar* [2008] 2 Cr.App.R.(S.) 92 CA. Whereas the court had said (at [19]) that the appropriate bracket "after plea of guilty" would be six to eight years' imprisonment, it should have said that this was the bracket for such offenders "on conviction".

B. Customs and Excise Management Act 1979

(5) Illegal exportation

Customs and Excise Management Act 1979, s.68

Offences in relation to exportation of prohibited goods

As to the increase in penalty for certain offences under section 68 of the   **25–414**
1979 Act, see *post*, § 25–452.

(12) Untrue declarations and falsifying documents

For the most recent amendment to the *Statistics of Trade (Customs and*   **25–451**
Excise) Regulations 1992 (S.I. 1992 No. 2790), see the *Statistics of Trade (Customs
and Excise) (Amendment) (No. 2) Regulations* 2008 (S.I. 2008 No. 2847).

(13) Fraudulent evasion offences

Customs and Excise Management Act 1979, s.170

Penalty for fraudulent evasion of duty, etc.

Where an offence under section 68 (§ 25–414 in the main work) or 170 of   **25–452**
the 1979 Act relates to a breach of a prohibition or restriction on exportation
in Part 2 of the *Export Control Order* 2008 (S.I. 2008 No. 3231) (prohibitions
in relation to military goods, software and technology, additional dual-use
goods, etc.) or in either Council Regulation (EC) No. 1334/2000 ("the dual-
use regulation") or Council Regulation (EC) No. 1236/2005 ("the torture
regulation"), article 42 increases the maximum penalty on conviction on
indictment to 10 years' imprisonment.

Chapter 26

MONEY LAUNDERING OFFENCES

I. PROCEEDS OF CRIME ACT 2002

B. Offences

(4) Legislation

Proceeds of Crime Act 2002, s.327

Concealing etc.

In *R. v. F.* [2009] Crim.L.R. 45, CA, where the facts were that the appellant   **26–11**
was found with large amounts of cash in luggage which he was attempting to
smuggle out of the country for a friend, and had no idea where the money
came from, but "knew it was wrong", it was held that they came within proposition (b) in *R. v. Anwoir* (see the main work). The court said that it was not
necessary for the purposes of procedural fairness for at least some background

material to be available to enable the jury to conclude that criminality of some particular sort was involved, nor was there any procedural unfairness arising out of the fact that the prosecution were unable to point to any particular criminality (considering also *R. v. Craig* and *Prosecution Appeal (No. 11 of 2007)*; *R. v. W.* (both cited in the main work)).

Proceeds of Crime Act 2002, s.328

Arrangements

★**26–12**   *K. Ltd v. National Westminster Bank plc (Revenue and Customs Commrs intervening) (Practice Note)* (see the main work), together with the definition of suspicion provided in *R. v. Da Silva* (§ 17–49a in the main work), clearly establish that suspicion under Part 7 of the 2002 Act is a purely subjective matter, that it does not matter whether or not there are reasonable or rational grounds for that suspicion provided that it is genuinely held, and that, whilst to be a suspicion rather than a mere feeling of unease it must be thought to be based on possible facts, the sufficiency of those facts as a grounding for the suspicion is irrelevant unless good faith is in issue: *Shah v. HSBC Private Bank (U.K.) Ltd*, unreported, January 26, 2009, QBD (Hamblen J.) ([2009] EWHC 79 (Q.B.)). Whilst it may well be the case that a "mechanical suspicion" (*e.g.* a suspicion generated automatically by a computer programme) would not be a relevant suspicion for the purposes of the Act if there was no element of human-held suspicion, this is never realistically likely to be the case where a bank has made an authorised disclosure under section 338 (§ 26–36 in the main work), since human intervention and decision will always be an inevitable part of that process: *ibid.*

II. MONEY LAUNDERING REGULATIONS

26–45   The *Money Laundering Regulations* 2007 (S.I. 2007 No. 2157) have been subjected to minor consequential amendments by the *Transfer of Tribunal Functions and Revenue and Customs Appeals Order* 2009 (S.I. 2009 No. 56); and have been further amended by the *Payment Services Regulations* 2009 (S.I. 2009 No. 209) (including by the insertion of a new regulation 49A providing that Revenue and Customs Commissioners may disclose to the Financial Services Authority information held in connection with their functions under the regulations).

CHAPTER 27

HARMFUL OR DANGEROUS DRUGS

A. INTRODUCTION

(4) Classification of controlled drugs

Misuse of Drugs Act 1971, Sched. 2

Class B drugs

27–9   As from January 26, 2009, Part II, para. 1(a), of Schedule 2 to the 1971 Act is amended by the insertion after "Amphetamine" of "Cannabinol", "Cannabinol derivatives" and "Cannabis and cannabis resin": *Misuse of Drugs Act 1971 (Amendment) Order* 2008 (S.I. 2008 No. 3130).

As from January 26, 2009, after Part II, para. 2, of Schedule 2 to the 1971 Act, S.I. 2008 No. 3130 (*ante*) inserts a new paragraph 2A, as follows—

"2A. Any ester or ether of cannabinol or of a cannabinol derivative.".

As from January 26, 2009, Part II, para. 3, of Schedule 2 to the *Misuse of Drugs Act* 1971 is amended by the substitution of ", 2 or 2A" for "or 2": S.I. 2008 No. 3130 (*ante*).

Class C drugs

As from January 26, 2009, Part III, para. 1(a), of Schedule 2 to the 1971 **27–10** Act is amended by the deletion of "Cannabinol", "Cannabinol derivatives", and "Cannabis and cannabis resin": S.I. 2008 No. 3130 (*ante*, § 27–9).

As from January 26, 2009, Part III, para. 1(d), of Schedule 2 to the 1971 Act is amended by the deletion of "or of cannabinol or a cannabinol derivative": S.I. 2008 No. 3130 (*ante*).

G. OCCUPIERS OF PREMISES

Misuse of Drugs Act 1971, s. 8

Class of offence, mode of trial and sentence

Where a manager of a public house permitted the public house to be used ★**27–85** for the smoking of cannabis, that would normally be substantially more serious than permitting a private house to be used for the same purpose. One important reason for this is that it effectively involves drug-taking in public, in an environment which makes it seem an acceptable activity so that others may be encouraged to share in it and take it up. Further, and equally important, the use of drugs is frequently associated with dealing in drugs: *R. v. Lunn* [2009] 1 Cr.App.R.(S.) 93, CA (upholding a sentence of 30 months' imprisonment on conviction).

R. LAW ENFORCEMENT AND PUNISHMENT OF OFFENCES

(2) Procedure and penalties

Sentencing guidelines

Cannabinol, cannabinol derivatives, cannabis and cannabis resin have been **27–107a** reclassified as Class B drugs: see *ante*, §§ 27–9, 27–10.

Production/cultivation of cannabis

In *R. v. Wong* [2008] 2 Cr.App.R.(S.) 111, CA, a sentence of five-and-a-half **27–111** years' imprisonment after a guilty plea was held to be entirely appropriate in respect of an offender who was clearly more than just a "manager", though not an "organiser" (within the *R. v. Xu* categorisation of offenders (see the main work)), of a sophisticated factory in which 3,000 cannabis plants were found growing and where the potential yield was worth between £635,000 (wholesale) and £2 million (retail).

Chapter 28

OFFENCES AGAINST PUBLIC JUSTICE

I. PERVERTING THE COURSE OF PUBLIC JUSTICE

G. Sentence

28–28   In *R. v. Jones (Conrad Steven)* [2008] 2 Cr.App.R.(S.) 75, CA, 12 years' imprisonment, said to be the heaviest reported sentence for the offence, was upheld where the appellant, in a case "which exemplified all the worst features of professional crime", made a sustained and determined attempt to intimidate a prosecution witness who was to give evidence in a trial of five men for murder.

In *Att.-Gen.'s Ref. (No. 17 of 2008)* [2008] R.T.R. 29, CA, it was said that a sentence of immediate imprisonment should be imposed in all but the most exceptional cases of perverting the course of justice. 18 months' imprisonment was held to be the starting point on a guilty plea where the defendant over a 17-month period had taken numerous steps to avoid detection in relation to speeding offences.

★   Substantial sentences of imprisonment are appropriate for falsely alleging rape: *R. v. Beeton* [2009] 1 Cr.App.R.(S.) 46, CA (four years reduced to three years on late guilty plea for multiple false allegations), and *R. v. McKenning* [2009] 1 Cr.App.R.(S.) 106, CA (two years upheld on guilty plea at first opportunity).

III. CONTEMPT OF COURT

B. Common Law

(7) Contempt by jurors

Juries Act 1974, s.20

Offences

28–46   Where a juror gives an explanation for non-attendance which is at least capable of showing "reasonable cause", it is incumbent on the judge to address the explanation in determining whether an offence has been committed under section 20(1)(a) of the 1974 Act: *R. v. D.A.* [2009] Crim.L.R. 289, CA.

C. Contempt of Court Act 1981

(1) The strict liability rule

Contempt of Court Act 1981, Sched. 1

★**28–65**   The amendments to Schedule 1 to the 1981 Act effected by the *AFA* 2006

226

come into force on October 31, 2009: *Armed Forces Act 2006 (Commencement
No. 5) Order* 2009 (S.I. 2009 No. 1167). In connection with that commencement, see the transitional provision in the *Armed Forces Act 2006 (Transitional
Provisions etc.) Order* 2009 (S.I. 2009 No. 1059), Sched. 1, para. 20 (interpretation of reference to "a service offence").

(5) Restriction of publication of matters exempted from disclosure

Contempt of Court Act 1981, s.11

Publication of matters exempted from disclosure in court
  In *Re The Times Newspapers Ltd* [2009] 1 W.L.R. 1015, Ct-MAC, the court **28–97**
confirmed that section 11 does not confer a power to order that a defendant's
identity be withheld from the public; such an order can only be made pursuant to the court's inherent jurisdiction where, if anonymity were not granted,
the administration of justice would be seriously affected, or there is a "real
and immediate" risk to life.

(6) Magistrates' courts

  Haw v. City of Westminster Magistrates' Court is now reported at [2008] Q.B. **28–99**
888.

(8) Interpretation

Contempt of Court Act 1981, s.19

Interpretation
  The amendment of section 19 of the 1981 Act effected by the *AFA* 2006 **★28–104**
comes into force on October 31, 2009: *Armed Forces Act 2006 (Commencement
No. 5) Order* 2009 (S.I. 2009 No. 1167).

D. Summary Powers to Deal with Contempt

(1) The jurisdiction

  The Crown Court has jurisdiction to hear contempt proceedings arising **28–105**
out of an alleged breach of its own restraint order (made pursuant to the *PCA*
2002, s.41), and there is no reason why such proceedings should not be
entertained in the Crown Court, even though the Divisional Court has
concurrent jurisdiction: *R. v. M. (Contemopt of Court)* [2009] 1 Cr.App.R. 17,
CA.

F. Appeals

Administration of Justice Act 1960, s.13

  The amendments of section 13 of the 1960 Act effected by the *AFA* 2006 **★28–139**
come into force on October 31, 2009: *Armed Forces Act 2006 (Commencement
No. 5) Order* 2009 (S.I. 2009 No. 1167).
  Haw v. City of Westminster Magistrates' Court is now reported at [2008] Q.B. **28–140**
888.

VII. OFFENCES AKIN TO PERJURY

D. FALSE WRITTEN STATEMENTS TENDERED IN EVIDENCE

Criminal Justice Act 1967, s.89

★**28–189**   The partial repeal of section 89(1) of the 1967 Act effected by the *AFA* 2006 comes into force on October 31, 2009: *Armed Forces Act 2006 (Commencement No. 5) Order* 2009 (S.I. 2009 No. 1167).

VIII. PRISON SECURITY

A. ESCAPE

(2) Statute

Prison Act 1952, ss.13(2), 39

Assisting a prisoner to escape

★**28–198**   As from October 31, 2009, section 39 of the 1952 Act is applied to service custody premises and detainees in such premises, subject to modifications: *Service Custody and Service of Relevant Sentences Rules* 2009 (S.I. 2009 No. 1096), r.71(1).

Criminal Justice Act 1961, s.22(2), (2A)

Harbouring escaped prisoners

28–200   The amendment to section 22 of the 1961 Act effected by the *AFA* 2006 comes into force on October 31, 2009: *Armed Forces Act 2006 (Commencement No. 5) Order* 2009 (S.I. 2009 No. 1167). In connection with that commencement, see the transitional provision in the *Armed Forces Act 2006 (Transitional Provisions etc.) Order* 2009 (S.I. 2009 No. 1059), Sched. 1, para. 8 (extension of reference to a person who has been sentenced as mentioned in subs. (2) to include persons receiving custodial sentences under the former armed forces legislation).

★   As from October 31, 2009, section 22(2) is applied to service custody premises and detainees in such premises, subject to modifications: *Service Custody and Service of Relevant Sentences Rules* 2009 (S.I. 2009 No. 1096), r.71(1), (2).

E. SMUGGLING OF PROHIBITED ARTICLES INTO OR OUT OF PRISON

Prison Act 1952, ss. 40A–40C

★**28–222c**   As from October 31, 2009, sections 40A to 40C of the 1952 Act are applied to service custody premises and detainees in such premises, subject to modifications: *Service Custody and Service of Relevant Sentences Rules* 2009 (S.I. 2009 No. 1096), r.71(1).

F. UNAUTHORISED PHOTOGRAPHY, RECORDINGS INSIDE PRISON

Prison Act 1952, ss. 40D, 40E

★**28–222d**   As from October 31, 2009, sections 40D and 40E of the 1952 Act are applied to service custody premises and detainees in such premises, subject to modifications: *Service Custody and Service of Relevant Sentences Rules* 2009 (S.I. 2009 No. 1096), r.71(1).

CHAPTER 29

PUBLIC ORDER OFFENCES

I. *PUBLIC ORDER ACT 1986*

B. NEW OFFENCES (PT I (SS.1–10))

(9) Racially or religiously aggravated offences

Crime and Disorder Act 1998, s.31

See *Kendall v. South East Magistrates' Court*, ante, § 5–88. **29–38b**

III. *MAKING OF THREATS*

B. BOMB HOAXES

Sentencing

The public and the emergency services need protection from those who **29–70** potentially cause fear and disruption by bomb hoaxes. Deterrence is of critical importance and it will, accordingly, be rare, if ever, that such an offence results in a non-custodial sentence, regardless of personal mitigation: *R. v. Philipson* [2008] 2 Cr.App.R.(S.) 110, CA.

CHAPTER 30

COMMERCE, FINANCIAL MARKETS AND INSOLVENCY

I. *INVESTIGATIVE POWERS*

B. INSOLVENCY ACT 1986

(6) Investigation of a bankrupt's affairs

Insolvency Act 1986, s.366

Public examination

The first instance decision in *Re Rottmann* (see the main work) has been up- **★30–71** held on appeal: see *Re Rottmann (a Bankrupt)*, *The Times*, March, 27, 2009, CA (Civ. Div.).

C. FINANCIAL SERVICES AND MARKETS ACT 2000

(2) General enquiries by the Financial Services Authority

Financial Services and Markets Act 2000, ss.165–177

Appointment of persons to carry out investigations in particular cases

30–80   As from November 27, 2008, the *Counter-Terrorism Act* 2008, s.62, and Sched. 7, para. 33, insert, after section 168(4)(b) of the *FSMA* 2000, a new paragraph (ba), as follows—

> "(ba) a person may be guilty of an offence under Schedule 7 to the *Counter-Terrorism Act* 2008 (terrorist financing or money laundering);".

The provisions of section 168 have been modified by the *Payment Services Regulations* 2009 (S.I. 2009 No. 209), reg. 95, and Sched. 5, in relation to the Financial Services Authority's functions under those regulations.

II. OFFENCES IN RELATION TO COMMERCE, FINANCIAL MARKETS AND INSOLVENCY

A. COMPANIES ACTS 1985 AND 2006

(4) Table of indictable offences

30–112   The following offence-creating sections in the table at § 30–114 in the main work are brought into force on October 1, 2009, by the *Companies Act 2006 (Commencement No. 8, Transitional Provisions and Savings) Order* 2008 (S.I. 2008 No. 2860): sections 542(4), 549(4), 557(1), 572(2), 590(1), 597(3), 607(1), 627(7), 647(1), 656(4), 658(2), 680(1), 707(6), 715(1), 728(4), 732(1), 860(4), 862(4), 876(3), 1004(5), 1005(4), 1006(4) (both offences), 1007(4) (both offences), 1009(5), 1112(1) and 1153(2).

(7) Consequential and transitional provisions

30–125   There have been two further commencement orders made in relation to the *Companies Act* 2006: the *Companies Act 2006 (Commencement No. 7, Transitional Provisions and Savings) Order* 2008 (S.I. 2008 No. 1886) and the *Companies Act 2006 (Commencement No. 8, Transitional Provisions and Savings) Order* 2008 (S.I. 2008 No. 2860).

C. INSOLVENCY ACT 1986

(4) Offences in connection with debt relief orders

★30–193   The *Tribunals, Courts and Enforcement Act* 2007, s.108, and Scheds 17 to 20, were brought into force on February 24, 2009, for the purpose of making rules, regulations and orders, and, for all other purposes, on April 6, 2009: *Tribunals, Courts and Enforcement Act 2007 (Commencement No. 7) Order* 2009 (S.I. 2009 No. 382).

E. Financial Services and Markets Act 2000

(2) General provision as to offences and interpretation

Financial Services and Markets Act 2000, ss.400-403

Power of the Authority to institute proceedings for certain other offences
As to section 402(1)(a) of the 2000 Act, see *R. (Uberoi) v. City of Westminster*   ★**30–204**
Magistrates' Court (Financial Services and H.M. Treasury as interested parties),
post, § 30–240.

(3) Carrying on unauthorised investment business

Financial Services and Markets Act 2000, ss.19, 21-25

Contravention of section 21
In *R. v. Powell and Hinkson* [2009] 1 Cr.App.R.(S.) 30, the appellants were   ★**30–211**
convicted of offences contrary to section 21 of the 2000 Act. On appeal, their
sentences of 15 months' imprisonment were upheld. Although there was no
finding of dishonesty, the sentences were justified given that: (i) they were not
authorised by the Financial Services Authority; (ii) their conduct was carried
out over a significant period of time, on a large scale, with a complete lack of
integrity, and was motivated by greed; (iii) they caused serious loss to those
that trusted them; and (iv) they carried on even though they had been warned
by a bank manager that they needed authorisation. In assessing culpability,
their grossly reckless behaviour was plainly relevant.

The *Financial Services and Markets Act 2000 (Exemption) Order* 2001 (S.I.   **30–212**
2001 No. 1201) has been further amended by the *Financial Services and
Markets Act 2000 (Exemption) (Amendment) Order* 2009 (S.I. 2009 No. 118) and
the *Financial Services and Markets Act 2000 (Exemption) (Amendment) Order*
2009 (S.I. 2009 No. 264).

The *Financial Services and Markets Act 2000 (Regulated Activities) Order* 2001
(S.I. 2001 No. 544) has been further amended by the *Payment Services Regula-
tions* 2009 (S.I. 2009 No. 209); the *Financial Services and Markets Act 2000
(Regulated Activities) (Amendment) Order* 2009 (S.I. 2009 No. 1342); and the   ★
*Financial Services and Markets Act 2000 (Regulated Activities) (Amendment) (No.
2) Order* 2009 (S.I. 2009 No. 1389).

F. Enterprise Act 2002

(2) Cartel offence

Enterprise Act 2002, ss.188–190

Cartel offence
In *R. v. Whittle, Allison and Brammar, The Times*, November 27, 2008, CA, it   **30–217**
was said that the following non-exhaustive factors are relevant in sentencing
cartel offences: (i) the offence's gravity and nature; (ii) its duration; (iii) the
defendant's degree of culpability in implementing the cartel agreement; (iv)
the defendant's degree of culpability in enforcing the agreement; (v) whether
the defendant's conduct was contrary to guidelines laid down in a company
compliance manual; (vi) mitigating factors, such as any co-operation the defendant may have provided in respect of the enquiry; whether or not the de-

fendant was compelled to participate in the cartel under duress; whether the offence was a first offence; and any personal circumstances of the defendant suggesting leniency.

G. Insider Dealing

Criminal Justice Act 1993, ss.52-64, Scheds 1, 2

Penalties and prosecution

★30–240   Despite the wording of section 61(2) of the 1993 Act (proceedings under this part not to be instituted except by or with the consent of the Secretary of State or the DPP), it was held in *R. (Uberoi) v. City of Westminster Magistrates' Court (Financial Services and H.M. Treasury as interested parties)* [2009] Crim.L.R. 445, DC, that proceedings for insider dealing were validly instituted by the FSA pursuant to section 402(1) of the *FSMA* 2000 (§ 30–204 in the main work), without obtaining the prior consent of the Secretary of State or the DPP, because Parliament must have intended the FSA to have such powers notwithstanding the failure to amend or address section 61(2) of the 1993 Act.

CHAPTER 31

OFFENCES AGAINST PUBLIC MORALS AND POLICY

II. PUBLIC NUISANCE

A. Common Law

(6) Unlawful treatment of dead bodies

Leaving corpse unburied/preventing burial of a corpse

31–55   Where an undertaker realised that the body of a baby had inadvertently not been put into the coffin before the burial and had, without informing the parents, put the body into the coffin of an elderly lady who was cremated later the same day, the case was clearly covered by the common law offence of preventing the burial of a corpse. The fact that the appellant had acted in panic rather than from some dishonest motive did not mean that the offence had not been committed: *R. v. Skidmore* [2009] Crim.L.R. 42, CA.

III. OBSCENE OR INDECENT PUBLICATIONS AND DISPLAYS, ETC.

B. Statute

(1) Obscene Publications Acts 1959 and 1964

(c) *Offences*

Obscene Publications Act 1959, s.2

31–74   The amendment to section 2 of the 1959 Act effected by the *CJIA* 2008 increase in maximum penalty from three to five years) came into force on anuary 26, 2009: *Criminal Justice and Immigration Act 2008 (Commencement No. 4 and Saving Provision) Order* 2008 (S.I. 2008 No. 2993).

(5) Criminal Justice Act 1988

Criminal Justice Act 1988, ss.160, 160A

Possession

The principle that a person only possesses indecent images which have **31–118** been deleted from a computer if he has the skill and the computer software to allow him to retrieve them (see *R. v. Porter* in the main work), applies equally to cases where the images were stored on floppy disks rather than on a computer's hard disk drive. In such a case, the issue of possession is for the jury to determine having regard to all the factors in the case, including the defendant's knowledge and the particular circumstances: *R. v. Rowe*, 172 J.P. 685, CA.

(6) Criminal Justice and Immigration Act 2008

Criminal Justice and Immigration Act 2008, ss.63–68

Sections 63 to 68 of the *CJIA* 2008 came into force on January 26, 2009: **31–126** *Criminal Justice and Immigration Act 2008 (Commencement No. 4 and Saving Provision) Order* 2008 (S.I. 2008 No. 2993).

Schedule 14 to the *CJIA* 2008 came into force on January 26, 2009: S.I. **31–127** 2008 No. 2993 (*ante*).

IV. CORRUPTION

B. STATUTE

(2) Public Bodies Corrupt Practices Act 1889

Public Bodies Corrupt Practices Act 1889, ss.1, 2

Penalty for offences

The guidelines for theft in breach of trust cases do not provide the yardstick **31–132** for sentence in cases of corruption, which contain elements of criminality which go beyond and are quite different from the dishonesty involved in such cases: *R. Ozakpinar* [2009] 1 Cr.App.R.(S.) 8, CA.

CHAPTER 32

MOTOR VEHICLE OFFENCES

II. DRIVING OFFENCES

A. CAUSING DEATH BY DANGEROUS DRIVING

(5) Sentence

Guidelines

★**32-7**   In *R. v. Curtis (Att.-Gen.'s Reference No. 17 of 2009), The Times*, May 12
2009, CA, it was said that an immediate custodial sentence for causing death
by dangerous driving was inevitable where the offender deliberately
disregarded the law, in this instance by sending and receiving text message
while driving. In determining the sentence's length, a significant factor was
whether the phoning or texting happened at the moment of, or in the immediate few seconds before, impact, or whether the earlier phoning or texting
may have played some part in the driver's lack of proper attention to the road
ahead. On the particular facts, the court made no ruling as to whether the
case was to be treated as falling within level 2 or level 3 of the Sentencing
Guidelines Council's guideline (*post*, Appendix K-192).

(6) Ingredients of the offence

"road or other public place"

★**32-18**   A tarmac roadway in a privately-owned caravan park, following a route
with defined edges, road markings and signs, and to which the public had unrestricted access, was both a road and a highway within the meaning of section 192(1) of the RTA 1988: *Barrett v. DPP* [2009] 3 *Archbold News* 3, DC.

B. DANGEROUS DRIVING

(2) Indictment

Order of trials where there is an excess alcohol charge

32-29   *R. v. Arnold* is now reported at [2008] 2 Cr.App.R. 37.

H. DRIVING, BEING IN CHARGE, WHILST ABOVE THE PRESCRIBED LIMIT

(5) Ingredients of the offence

"breath"

★**32-80a**   *McNeil v. DPP* is now reported at [2008] R.T.R. 27.

J. Failing to Provide Evidential Specimen

(5) Procedure

Warning of consequence of non-compliance

The police are not obliged to retain CCTV footage or audio tapes record-   **32-98**
ing any warning given under section 7(7) of the *RTA* 1988: *Morris v. DPP*,
173 J.P. 41, QBD (Slade J.).

Blood and urine samples

In *Hussain v. DPP* [2008] R.T.R. 30, DC, the court preferred the reasoning   **32-99**
in *Stewart v. DPP* to that of McCombe J. in *Jubb v. DPP* (both cited in the
main work). The appellant's conviction for refusing to supply a specimen contrary to section 7(6) of the *RTA* 1988 was upheld where, having supplied
two specimens as initially requested, he then refused to comply with a
requirement to supply two further specimens on a different machine. It was
held that the initial specimens provided by the appellant were not valid, by
reason of the malfunction of the first machine, and therefore the appellant
had not provided two specimens of breath, having regard to section 11(3)
of the 1988 Act (as to which, see § 32–91 in the main work). For a criticism
of this decision, see the commentary in *Criminal Law Week* 2008/34/9.

"without reasonable excuse"

Kennedy v. DPP (see the main work) was followed in *Gearing v. DPP* [2009]   **32-104**
R.T.R. 7, DC, where it was held that the police were in breach of section 58 of
the *PACE Act* 1984 (§ 15–221 in the main work) in making no attempt to
give effect to the appellant's request for legal advice until immediately after
she had refused to comply with the requirement to provide two specimens
of breath, but that nonetheless there was no reason for excluding the evidence of the procedure under section 78 of the 1984 Act.

M. Driving Without a Licence

(4) Interpretation

Road Traffic Act 1988, s.108

In *Criminal Proceedings Against Weber* [2009] R.T.R. 6, ECJ, it was held that   **★32-111**
a member state was entitled to refuse to recognise, in its territory, a driving
licence issued by another member state, where the motorist's right to drive in
the first member state had been withdrawn, even though the withdrawal was
ordered after the issue of that driving licence, provided that the licence was
obtained during a period in which a licence issued in the first member state
was suspended, and both the suspension and the withdrawal were based on
grounds existing at the date of issue of the second driving licence.

(5) Grant and form of licences

Grant of licences

As from March 30, 2009, S.I. 1999 No. 2864 (see the main work) has been   **★32-112** further amended by the *Motor Vehicles (Driving Licences) (Amendment) Regulations* 2009 (S.I. 2009 No. 788).

Road Traffic Act 1988, s.97A

Meaning of "driving record"

32–112a   Section 97A came into force on April 1, 2009: *Road Safety Act 2006 (Commencement No. 5) Order* 2008 (S.I. 2008 No. 3164).

N. Obtaining a Licence, or Driving, While Disqualified

(5) Evidence

★32–118   The importance of admissible evidence of disqualification on a charge of driving while disqualified, in the absence of a formal or informal admission to that effect, was emphasised in *Mills v. DPP* [2009] R.T.R. 12, DC, where the justices wrongly drew an inference (pursuant to the *CJPOA* 1994, s.34), from the defendant's "no comment" interview, that he was disqualified.

R. Police Powers

(2) Power to require production of licence

(a) Statute

Road Traffic Act 1988, s.164

Power of constables to require production of driving licence and in certain cases statement of date of birth

32–141   The remainder of paragraph 27(a) of Schedule 5 to the *Crime (International Co-operation) Act* 2003 (insertion of words in square brackets in section 164(3) of the 1988 Act) is brought into force 90 days after the date on which the United Kingdom and Ireland make declarations under Article 15(4) of the convention drawn up on the basis of Article K.3 of the Treaty of European Union on Driving Disqualifications signed on June 17, 1998 or, if they are not made on the same date, 90 days after the later of the dates on which those declarations are made: *Crime International Co-operation Act 2003 (Commencement No. 4) Order* 2008 (S.I. 2008 No. 3009).

S. Procedure and Evidence

(5) Evidence

Road Traffic Offenders Act 1988, ss.13, 15, 16

Documentary evidence as to specimens in such proceedings

★32–163   Justices had been entitled to admit a certificate of analysis of a blood specimen through the mechanism provided by the *CJA* 2003, s.116 (hearsay where witness is unavailable (§ 11–15 in the main work)), notwithstanding that the certificate had originally been served under section 16 of the *RTOA* 1988 and notice had been given pursuant to section 16(4) requiring the analyst (who was then living in Bulgaria) to attend; section 16 does not provide an xhaustive process for proving the proportion of alcohol in a specimen of reath, blood or urine: *Brett v. DPP*, 173 J.P.274, DC.

T. DISQUALIFICATION AND ENDORSEMENT

(5) Statutory provisions — general

Road Traffic Offenders Act 1988, ss.27, 28

Penalty points to be attributed to an offence

The new subsections (3) to (3B) in section 28 of the *RTOA* 1988 came into   **32–175**
orce on March 31, 2009; and the amendment to the new subsection (3) (effected by Sched. 2 to the *RSA* 2006), as noted in the main work, comes into orce on April 1, 2009: *Road Safety Act 2006 (Commencement No. 5) Order* '008 (S.I. 2008 No. 3164).

Road Traffic Offenders Act 1988, s.29

Penalty points to be taken into account on conviction

The amendment to section 29(1)(b) of the *RTOA* 1988 effected by the *RSA*   **32–176**
'006, s.9(6), and Sched. 2, paras 2 and 4, came into force on April 1, 2009: *Road Safety Act 2006 (Commencement No. 5) Order* 2008 (S.I. 2008 No. 3164).

Road Traffic Offenders Act 1988, s.30

Penalty points: modification where fixed penalty also in question

The amendments to section 30(1)(b) and (2)(b) of the *RTOA* 1988 effected   **32–177**
ŋy the *RSA* 2006, s.9(6), and Sched. 2, paras 2 and 5, came into force on ᴀpril 1, 2009: *Road Safety Act 2006 (Commencement No. 5) Order* 2008 (S.I. ⸰008 No. 3164).

Road Traffic Offenders Act 1988, s.31

Court may take particulars endorsed on licence into consideration

The repeal of the words "on licence" in the heading to section 31 of the   **32–178**
ᴿTOA 1988 and the substitution of subsection (1) came into force on April , 2009: *Road Safety Act 2006 (Commencement No. 5) Order* 2008 (S.I. 2008 No. ·164).

(14) Removal of disqualification

Road Traffic Offenders Act 1988, s.42

Removal of disqualification

The omission of the italicised words and the insertion of the words in   **32–207**
quare brackets in section 42 of the *RTOA* 1988 effected by the *RSA* 2006, .9(6), and Sched. 2, paras 2 and 8, came into force on April 1, 2009: *Road 'afety Act 2006 (Commencement No. 5) Order* 2008 (S.I. 2008 No. 3164).

(15) Endorsement

Road Traffic Offenders Act 1988, s.44

Orders for endorsement

The amendment of the heading to, and the insertion of subsection (3A) in,   **32–210**

section 44 of the *RTOA* 1988 effected by the *RSA* 2006, s.9(1) and (2), came
into force on April 1, 2009: *Road Safety Act 2006 (Commencement No. 5) Order*
2008 (S.I. 2008 No. 3164).

Road Traffic Offenders Act 1988, s.44A

Endorsement of driving record in accordance with order
32–210a   Section 44A came into force on April 1, 2009: *Road Safety Act 2006 (Commencement No. 5) Order* 2008 (S.I. 2008 No. 3164).

Road Traffic Offenders Act 1988, s.45

Effect of endorsement of counterparts
32–211   The amendments to section 45 of the *RTOA* 1988 effected by the *RSA*
2006, s.58 (insertion of words in double square brackets in subs. (6) in
substitution for the italicised words that precede them and insertion of
word in double square brackets in subs. (7)(a)) came into force on Royal Assent (*i.e.* November 8, 2006).

The amendments to section 45 of the *RTOA* 1988 effected by the *RSA*
2006, ss.9(6) and 59, Sched. 2, paras 2 and 9, and Sched. 7(3) (insertion of
words in square brackets in the heading and omission of italicised words in
subs. (1)), came into force on April 1, 2009: *Road Safety Act 2006 (Commencement No. 5) Order* 2008 (S.I. 2008 No. 3164).

Road Traffic Offenders Act 1988, s.45A

Effect of endorsement on driving records
32–211a   Section 45A of the *RTOA* 1988 came into force on April 1, 2009: *Road Safety Act 2006 (Commencement No. 5) Order* 2008 (S.I. 2008 No. 3164).

(16) New drivers

Road Traffic (New Drivers) Act 1995, ss.1–3

Surrender of licences
32–214   The amendments to section 2 of the 1995 Act effected by the *RSA* 2006,
ss.5 and 59, Sched. 1, paras 24 and 25, and Sched. 7(2), came into force on
March 31, 2009: *Road Safety Act 2006 (Commencement No. 5) Order* 2008 (S.I.
2008 No. 3164).

Revocation of licences
32–215   The amendments to section 3 of the 1995 Act effected by the *RSA* 2006, s.5
and Sched. 1, paras 24 and 26, came into force on March 31, 2009: *Road
Safety Act 2006 (Commencement No. 5) Order* 2008 (S.I. 2008 No. 3164).

(17) Miscellaneous and general

Road Traffic Offenders Act 1988, ss.46, 47, 49

*Combination of disqualification and endorsement with probation orders and orders
for discharge*
32–216   The amendments to section 46 of the *RTOA* 1988 effected by the *RSA*

2006, s.9(6), and Sched. 2, paras 2 and 11, came into force on April 1,
2009: *Road Safety Act 2006 (Commencement No. 5) Order* 2008 (S.I. 2008 No.
3164).

Supplementary provisions as to disqualifications and endorsements
   The amendments to section 47 of the *RTOA* 1988 effected by the *RSA*   **32–217**
2006, s.9(6), and Sched. 2, paras 2 and 12, came into force on April 1,
2009: *Road Safety Act 2006 (Commencement No. 5) Order* 2008 (S.I. 2008 No.
3164).

E. Motor Vehicles (E.C. Type Approval) Regulations 1998

   As from April 29, 2009, the 1998 regulations (and the subsequent series of   **★32–231**
amending regulations) were revoked and effectively replaced by the *Road
Vehicles (Approval) Regulations* 2009 (S.I. 2009 No. 717). Regulation 33 of the
2009 regulations creates offences that correspond to those created by regulation 14 of the 1998 regulations.

Chapter 33

CONSPIRACY, ENCOURAGEMENT AND ATTEMPT TO COMMIT CRIME

I. CONSPIRACY

B. Statutory Offence of Conspiracy

The offence of conspiracy
   Sections 42 and 45 of the *AFA* 2006 come into force on October 31, 2009:   **★33–3**
Armed Forces Act 2006 (Commencement No. 5) Order 2009 (S.I. 2009 No. 1167).

(3) Jurisdiction

(b) *Conspiracy to commit a crime abroad*

Criminal Law Act 1977, s.1A

Conspiracy to commit offences outside the United Kingdom
   Having regard to section 1A(6) of the 1977 Act, the maximum penalty for a   **★33–22**
section 1A offence is the same as for section 1, and is provided by section 3
(§ 33–32 in the main work), *i.e.* the same as the maximum for the substantive
English offence, and not the maximum available in the relevant foreign jurisdiction; however, where the foreign maximum is less than the English
maximum, the judge in his discretion can moderate sentence if fairness so
requires: *R. v. Patel* [2009] 3 *Archbold News* 4, CA.

C. SAVING OF CERTAIN CONSPIRACIES AT COMMON LAW, ETC.

(2) Conspiracy to defraud

Limitations

33–37   *Norris v. Government of the United States of America* is now reported at [2008] 1 A.C. 920.

II. SOLICITING OR INCITING A CRIME

(1) Common law

(a) *Introduction*

Definition

33–78   To solicit or incite another to commit a crime was indictable at common law. A person was guilty of incitement to commit an offence or offences if (a) he incited another to do or cause to be done an act or acts which, if done, would involve the commission of an offence or offences by the other; and (b) he intended or believed that the other, if he acted as incited, should or would do so with the fault required for the offence or offences: *DPP v. Armstrong (Andrew)* [2000] Crim.L.R. 379, DC; *R. v. Claydon* [2006] 1 Cr.App.R. 20, CA (approving, in both cases, the Law Commissions's definition (*Criminal Law: A Criminal Code*, Law Com. No. 177, 1989)). In *Invicta Plastics Ltd v. Clare* [1976] R.T.R. 251, the Divisional Court adopted *dicta* of Lord Denning M.R. in *Race Relations Board v. Applin* [1973] 1 Q.B. 815 at 825, CA (Civ. Div.), to the effect that "to incite" was not limited to urging or spurring on by advice, encouragement or persuasion but included inciting another to do an act by threats or by pressure. Incitement also included an offer of a bribe to a person to commit an offence: *Wade v. Broughton* (1814) 3 V. & B. 172.

It was irrelevant whether the solicitation or incitement was effective: *Armstrong, ante*; or whether the principal offence existed under the common law or was created by statute: see 1 Russ.Cr. 12th ed., 176. However, the offence had to be one which was capable of being committed by the person incited: *R. v. Claydon, ante*.

Agents provocateurs

33–79   See §§ 15–514 *et seq.* in the main work, and see *R. v. Anderson* [1986] 1 A.C. 27 at 38, HL.

Mens rea

33–80   A person accused of incitement must be shown to have intended or believed that the person incited would, if he acted as incited to do, do so with the *mens rea* appropriate to the offence (*ante*, § 33–78). As with conspiracy (§ 33–15 in the main work), it is submitted that laudable ulterior motives are irrelevant. To the extent that *R. v. Shaw* [1994] Crim.L.R. 365, CA (93 05976 W2) is authority to the contrary, it is submitted that it is wrong (see the commentary in the *Criminal Law Review*); and it was disapproved in *Claydon, ante*, § 33–78. The explanation for the decision (that a person charged with inciting an offence of dishonesty had to be proved to have been dishonest himself) may lie in the fact that the prosecution had so put their case (transcript p.7F).

In *R. v. Curr*, 51 Cr.App.R. 113, CA, it was held that a person could only
be convicted of incitement if the person incited knew that the conduct incited
amounted to an offence. This was also disapproved of in *R. v. Claydon, ante,*
where it was said that the actual knowledge or state of mind of the person
incited was irrelevant. Albeit that this was *obiter*, it is submitted that this view is
to be preferred, the offence being concerned with the state of mind of the in-
itor, not of the incitee.

(b) *Jurisdiction*

The common law jurisdiction in respect of incitement appears to be the   **33–81**
same as that for conspiracy, as to which see §§ 33–21 *et seq.* in the main work.
In *R. v. Tompkins* [2007] Crim.L.R. 235, CA, it was assumed that the courts of
England and Wales have jurisdiction to try an allegation of incitement where
the incitor was at all material times within the jurisdiction and the incitee was
at all material times without the jurisdiction, provided that the *actus reus* of
the offence was to occur, at least in part, within the jurisdiction.

As to the extended jurisdiction of the courts in relation to allegations of
incitement to commit certain sexual acts outside the United Kingdom, see the
Sexual Offences (Conspiracy and Incitement) Act 1996, s.2 (§ 2–36b in the main
work); and as to their extended jurisdiction in relation to incitement to
commit fraud and related offences, see Part I of the *CJA* 1993 (§§ 2–37 *et
seq.* in the main work).

(c) *Indictment*

STATEMENT OF OFFENCE

Incitement to steal.   **33–82**

PARTICULARS OF OFFENCE

*A B, on the —— day of ——, 20—, unlawfully incited J N to steal property belonging
to Y Z.*

Penalty—fine and/or imprisonment: *R. v. Higgins*, 2 East 5.

(d) *Particular offences*

To conspire or to incite

Section 5(7) of the *CLA* 1977 (§ 33–34 in the main work) abolished the of-   **33–83**
fence of incitement to conspire.

In the course of giving the Court of Appeal's judgment in *R. v. Sirat*, 83
Cr.App.R. 41, Parker L.J. said:

> "There is no doubt that at common law incitement to commit a crime is an
> offence. This being so, it follows logically that if A incites B to incite C to commit a
> crime, *e.g.* to wound D, A is guilty of incitement to commit a crime, namely, incite-
> ment" (at p. 43).

Later in the judgment, however, his Lordship said, having read out the
terms of section 5(7) of the 1977 Act:

"If, therefore, A incites B to agree with C that C will wound D, A's incitement of B is by statute not an offence.... Where however the facts are that the accused's incitement of B is actually to enter into an agreement with C for the commission of a crime, it would in our judgment be impossible to hold that the accused can be guilty of incitement, on the ground that B must of necessity propose the crime to C on the way to making the agreement. Whether other forms of incitement to incite survive will fall for decision when the question arises. It may appear to be absurd that, where a person is inciting actual agreement to be made for the commission of a crime, he should be guilty of no offence, but that where he does not seek actual agreement but mere encouragement he should be guilty. This however is not necessarily absurd, for there may well be circumstances where there is no question of an agreement being sought but where the particular form of incitement is more effective than any attempt to secure agreement" (at pp. 44–45).

To attempt, and attempt to incite

33–84   On an indictment charging the defendants with inciting, counselling and procuring a pregnant woman to administer to herself a noxious thing, namely an abortifacient, with intent to procure a miscarriage (see the *Offences against the Person Act* 1861, s.58 (§ 19–149 in the main work)), and with conspiracy to incite her to do the same, it was held (a) that if the woman, believing that she was taking a noxious thing within the meaning of the statute, did, with intent to procure her own abortion, take a thing in fact harmless, she was guilty of an attempt to commit an offence against section 58; but (b) that if the defendants in supplying the drug to the woman, though they well knew that she would take it in the belief that it was an abortifacient did not themselves believe that it was capable of procuring her own abortion, they could not be convicted of *inciting* her to commit the said offence, although if they had so believed it would have been otherwise: *R. v. Brown*, 63 J.P. 790.

In logic, it would seem that an incitement to attempt to commit an offence must necessarily be an incitement to commit that offence.

Where a letter was sent soliciting and inciting the addressee to commit a crime, but was not proved to have reached the intended recipient, the sender could properly be convicted of an attempt to incite the commission of the crime: *R. v. Banks* (1873) 12 Cox 393; *R. v. Ransford* (1874) 13 Cox 9; *R. v. Krause*, 66 J.P. 121; *R. v. Cope*, 16 Cr.App.R. 77, which may be distinguished from *R. v. Woods*, 22 Cr.App.R. 41, because in the former case the intended recipient of the letter would, if he had received it, have understood that he was being instigated to the commission of a crime, whereas in the latter case he would not; and *R. v. Goldman* [2001] Crim.L.R. 822, CA (defendant guilty of attempt to incite addressee to distribute indecent photographs of children even where he was responding to an offer made by the addressee).

To do the impossible

33–85   A person cannot be convicted of incitement to commit a particular offence if the person incited was incapable as a matter of law of committing the offence: *R. v. Claydon* [2006] 1 Cr.App.R. 20, CA. Nor can a person be convicted of incitement to commit a particular offence if its commission is factually impossible: see *R. v. Fitzmaurice* [1983] Q.B. 1083, 76 Cr.App.R. 17, CA (giving as an example incitement to murder a person who turned out to have been dead at the time of the incitement). Where it is contended that the offence incited was factually impossible, it is necessary to analyse the evidence with care to decide the precise offence which the defendant is alleged to have incited: *ibid.* At common law, the position was the same for conspiracy and at tempts, but see now the *CLA* 1977, s.1(1)(b) (§ 33–2 in the main work), and the *Criminal Attempts Act* 1981, s.1(2) (§ 33–120 in the main work).

To commit a summary offence

Incitement to commit a summary offence was a summary offence, punishable as for the offence incited: *MCA* 1980, s.45(1), (3). **33–86**

To commit an offence triable either way

See the *MCA* 1980, s.17(1), and Sched. 1, paras 33 and 35. The effect is **33–87** that incitement to commit an offence triable either way is generally itself triable either way. Note that whilst paragraph 35 of Schedule 1 to the 1980 Act was repealed by the *SCA* 2007, ss.63(2) and 92, Sched. 6, para. 55(1) and (4), and Sched. 14, its effect has been preserved in relation to pre-commencement offences by the 2007 Act, s.91(1), and Sched. 13, para. 5(1)(b) (§ 33–118 in the main work).

(e) *Evidence*

Prove the soliciting or inciting as alleged in the indictment. Prove it in the **33–88** same manner as the offence of being a counsellor and procurer would be proved, except that this offence is committed even though the offence solicited was not in fact committed. It is no defence to the above indictment that the person incited purposely submitted himself to the incitement with intent to betray the inciter: *R. v. Quail* (1866) 4 F. & F. 1076.

On a charge of inciting a person to receive stolen goods it is no defence that at the time of the incitement there did not exist stolen goods of the type mentioned: *R. v. McDonough*, 47 Cr.App.R. 37, CCA.

A charge of incitement to distribute indecent photographs of children could be founded on the defendant's entering the website of a commercial child pornography business and paying the required entrance fee with his credit card; it mattered not that the process was entirely automated by the computer; the computer merely facilitated the business, and it was irrelevant to say that only the computer was incited; someone lay behind the computer: *R. (O.) v. Coventry Magistrates' Court* [2004] Crim.L.R. 948, DC.

IV. ATTEMPT TO COMMIT CRIME

D. Pleading and Practice

Sentence

In *R. v. Knight* [2009] 1 Cr.App.R.(S.) 57, CA, a 30-year term of imprison- **★33–138** ment imposed for attempted murder (poisoning husband with anti-freeze for financial gain) was upheld on appeal; the judge had been entitled to adopt by analogy the 30-year starting point for murder for gain; that the appellant's offence was less serious than murder was reflected in her eligibility for early release on licence, in contrast to a mandatory life sentence for murder with a minimum term.

APPENDIX A

Codes of Practice and Attorney General's Guidelines

I. CODES OF PRACTICE

A. UNDER THE POLICE AND CRIMINAL EVIDENCE ACT 1984

(1) Introduction

The *Police and Criminal Evidence Act* 1984 makes provision for the issuing   **A–1**
by the Secretary of State of codes of practice in connection with the tape-
recording of interviews (s.60, § 15–223 in the main work), the visual recording of interviews (s.60A, § 15–231 in the main work), the exercise by police officers of statutory powers of "stop and search" (s.66(1)(a)(i) and (ii), § 15–3 in
the main work), the exercise by police officers of statutory powers to arrest a
person (s.66(1)(a)(iii), § 15–3 in the main work) the detention, treatment,
questioning and identification of persons by police officers (s.66(1)(b), § 15–3
in the main work), and searches of premises and seizure of property (s.66(1)(c)
and (d), § 15–3 in the main work).

As at October 27, 2008, there were eight extant codes: Code A (stop and
search); Code B (search and seizure); Code C (detention, treatment and
questioning of persons), Code D (identification), Code E (tape-recording of
interviews), Code F (visual recording of interviews), Code G (arrest) and Code
H (detention, treatment and questioning of persons under section 41 of, and
Schedule 8 to, the *Terrorism Act* 2000).

Code F and Code G (which was new) came into force on January 1, 2006:
Police and Criminal Evidence Act 1984 (Codes of Practice) Order 2005 (S.I. 2005
No. 3503). Code H came into force on July 25, 2006: *Police and Criminal Evidence Act 1984 (Code of Practice C and Code of Practice H) Order* 2006 (S.I.
2006 No. 1938). The current codes A to E came into force on February 1,
2008: *Police and Criminal Evidence Act 1984 (Codes of Practice) Order* 2008 (S.I.
2008 No. 167). A revision to Code A took effect on October 27, 2008 (*Police
and Criminal Evidence Act 1984 (Codes of Practice) (Revisions to Code A) Order*
2008 (S.I. 2008 No. 2638)); and a further revision took effect on January 1,
2009 (*Police and Criminal Evidence Act 1984 (Codes of Practice) (Revisions to
Code A) (No. 2) Order* 2008 (S.I. 2008 No. 3146)). For a summary, see *ante*,
§ 15–7.

It should be noted that the new Code A (as revised, *ante*) applies only in re lation to a search commencing after midnight on December 31, 2008; Code I applies only to applications for warrants made after midnight on January 31 2008; and to searches and seizures made after midnight on January 31, 2008 Code C applies only to people in police detention after midnight on Januar 31, 2008; Code D applies only to an identification procedure carried out afte midnight on January 31, 2008; Code E applies only to interviews carried ou after midnight on January 31, 2008; and Code H applies only to people i police detention, following their arrest under the *Terrorism Act* 2000, s.41, af ter midnight on July 24, 2006.

In relation to searches, *etc.*, taking place before the specified dates, th previous versions of the codes will be the applicable provisions.

For further details in relation to the codes generally, see the main work a §§ 15–3 *et seq.* (primary legislation), § 15–7 (commencement), § 15–8 (status o codes), § 15–10 (who is bound by the codes), § 15–12 (admissibility), anc § 15–13 (breaches).

It should be noted that the original text of the codes (as published by Th Stationery Office and available on the Home Office website) is littered with er rors of grammar and punctuation. No change has been made to the word used, however obviously inappropriate, but limited changes have been mad to the punctuation, use of case, use of italics and paragraphing. This has beer done with a view to injecting some consistency and intelligibility.

(2) Stop and search

A.   Code of Practice for the Exercise by:

**Police Officers of Statutory Powers of Stop and Search
Police Officers and Police Staff of Requirements to Record Public Encounters**

Commencement—Transitional arrangements

A–2   This code applies to any search by a police officer and the requirement to record public encounters taking place after midnight on 31 December, 2008.

General

This code of practice must be readily available at all police stations for consultatio by police officers, detained persons and members of the public.

The notes for guidance included are not provisions of this code, but are guidanc to police officers and others about its application and interpretation. Provisions in th annexes to the code are provisions of this code.

This code governs the exercise by police officers of statutory powers to search person or a vehicle without first making an arrest. The main stop and search power to which this code applies are set out in Annex A, but that list should not be regardec as definitive. [See *Note 1*.] In addition, it covers requirements on police officers an police staff to record encounters not governed by statutory powers.

This code does not apply to:

(a) the powers of stop and search under;

    (i) *Aviation Security Act* 1982, section 27(2);

    (ii) *Police and Criminal Evidence Act* 1984, section 6(1) (which relates specifi cally to powers of constables employed by statutory undertakers on th premises of the statutory undertakers);

(b) searches carried out for the purposes of examination under Schedule 7 to th *Terrorism Act* 2000 and to which the Code of Practice issued under paragrap 6 of Schedule 14 to the *Terrorism Act* 2000 applies.

A:1 Principles governing stop and search

A:1.1 Powers to stop and search must be used fairly, responsibly, with respect   **A–3** for people being searched and without unlawful discrimination. The *Race Relations (Amendment) Act* 2000 makes it unlawful for police officers to discriminate on the grounds of race, colour, ethnic origin, nationality or national origins when using their powers.

A:1.2 The intrusion on the liberty of the person stopped or searched must be brief and detention for the purposes of a search must take place at or near the location of the stop.

A:1.3 If these fundamental principles are not observed the use of powers to stop and search may be drawn into question. Failure to use the powers in the proper manner reduces their effectiveness. Stop and search can play an important role in the detection and prevention of crime, and using the powers fairly makes them more effective.

A:1.4 The primary purpose of stop and search powers is to enable officers to allay or confirm suspicions about individuals without exercising their power of arrest. Officers may be required to justify the use or authorisation of such powers, in relation both to individual searches and the overall pattern of their activity in this regard, to their supervisory officers or in court. Any misuse of the powers is likely to be harmful to policing and lead to mistrust of the police. Officers must also be able to explain their actions to the member of the public searched. The misuse of these powers can lead to disciplinary action.

A:1.5 An officer must not search a person, even with his or her consent, where no power to search is applicable. Even where a person is prepared to submit to a search voluntarily, the person must not be searched unless the necessary legal power exists, and the search must be in accordance with the relevant power and the provisions of this Code. The only exception, where an officer does not require a specific power, applies to searches of persons entering sports grounds or other premises carried out with their consent given as a condition of entry.

A:2 Explanation of powers to stop and search

A:2.1 This code applies to powers of stop and search as follows: **A–4**

   (a) powers which require reasonable grounds for suspicion, before they may be exercised; that articles unlawfully obtained or possessed are being carried, or under section 43 of the *Terrorism Act* 2000 that a person is a terrorist;

   (b) authorised under section 60 of the *Criminal Justice and Public Order Act* 1994, based upon a reasonable belief that incidents involving serious violence may take place or that people are carrying dangerous instruments or offensive weapons within any locality in the police area;

   (c) authorised under section 44(1) and (2) of the *Terrorism Act* 2000 based upon a consideration that the exercise of one or both powers is expedient for the prevention of acts of terrorism;

   (d) powers to search a person who has not been arrested in the exercise of a power to search premises (see Code B paragraph 2.4).

Searches requiring reasonable grounds for suspicion

A:2.2 Reasonable grounds for suspicion depend on the circumstances in each   **A–5** case. There must be an objective basis for that suspicion based on facts, information, and/or intelligence which are relevant to the likelihood of finding an article of a certain kind or, in the case of searches under section 43 of the *Terrorism Act* 2000, to the likelihood that the person is a terrorist. Reasonable suspicion can never be supported on the basis of personal factors. It must rely on intelligence or information about, or some specific behaviour by the person concerned. For example, other than a witness description of a suspect, a person's race, age, appearance, or the fact that the person is known to have a previous conviction, cannot be used alone or in combination with each other, or in combination with any other factor, as the reason for searching that person. Reasonable suspicion cannot be based on generalisations or stereotypical images of certain groups or categories of people as more likely to be involved in criminal activity. A person's religion cannot be considered as reasonable grounds for suspicion and should never be considered as a reason to stop or stop and search an individual.

A:2.3 Reasonable suspicion can sometimes exist without specific information or intelligence and on the basis of the behaviour of a person. For example, if an officer encounters someone on the street at night who is obviously trying to hide something, the officer may (depending on the other surrounding circumstances) base such suspicion on the fact that this kind of behaviour is often linked to stolen or prohibited articles being carried. Similarly, for the purposes of section 43 of the *Terrorism Act* 2000, suspicion that a person is a terrorist may arise from the person's behaviour at or near a location which has been identified as a potential target for terrorists.

A:2.4 However, reasonable suspicion should normally be linked to accurate and current intelligence or information, such as information describing an article being carried, a suspected offender, or a person who has been seen carrying a type of article known to have been stolen recently from premises in the area. Searches based on accurate and current intelligence or information are more likely to be effective. Targeting searches in a particular area at specified crime problems increases their effectiveness and minimises inconvenience to law-abiding members of the public. It also helps in justifying the use of searches both to those who are searched and to the public. This does not however prevent stop and search powers being exercised in other locations where such powers may be exercised and reasonable suspicion exists.

A:2.5 Searches are more likely to be effective, legitimate, and secure public confidence when reasonable suspicion is based on a range of factors. The overall use of these powers is more likely to be effective when up to date and accurate intelligence or information is communicated to officers and they are well-informed about local crime patterns.

A:2.6 Where there is reliable information or intelligence that members of a group or gang habitually carry knives unlawfully or weapons or controlled drugs, and wear a distinctive item of clothing or other means of identification to indicate their membership of the group or gang, that distinctive item of clothing or other means of identification may provide reasonable grounds to stop and search a person. [See *Note 9*]

A:2.7 A police officer may have reasonable grounds to suspect that a person is in innocent possession of a stolen or prohibited article or other item for which he or she is empowered to search. In that case the officer may stop and search the person even though there would be no power of arrest.

A:2.8 Under section 43(1) of the *Terrorism Act* 2000 a constable may stop and search a person whom the officer reasonably suspects to be a terrorist to discover whether the person is in possession of anything which may constitute evidence that the person is a terrorist. These searches may only be carried out by an officer of the same sex as the person searched.

A:2.9 An officer who has reasonable grounds for suspicion may detain the person concerned in order to carry out a search. Before carrying out a search the officer may ask questions about the person's behaviour or presence in circumstances which gave rise to the suspicion. As a result of questioning the detained person, the reasonable grounds for suspicion necessary to detain that person may be confirmed or, because of a satisfactory explanation, be eliminated. [See *Notes 2* and *3*.] Questioning may also reveal reasonable grounds to suspect the possession of a different kind of unlawful article from that originally suspected. Reasonable grounds for suspicion however cannot be provided retrospectively by such questioning during a person's detention or by refusal to answer any questions put.

A:2.10 If, as a result of questioning before a search, or other circumstances which come to the attention of the officer, there cease to be reasonable grounds for suspecting that an article is being carried of a kind for which there is a power to stop and search, no search may take place. [See *Note 3*.] In the absence of any other lawful power to detain, the person is free to leave at will and must be so informed.

A:2.11 There is no power to stop or detain a person in order to find grounds for a search. Police officers have many encounters with members of the public which do not involve detaining people against their will. If reasonable grounds for suspicion emerge during such an encounter, the officer may search the person, even though no grounds existed when the encounter began. If an officer is detaining someone for the purpose of a search, he or she should inform the person as soon as detention begins.

Searches authorised under section 60 of the Criminal Justice and Public Order Act 1994

A:2.12 Authority for a constable in uniform to stop and search under section 60 of the *Criminal Justice and Public Order Act* 1994 may be given if the authorising officer reasonably believes:

    (a) that incidents involving serious violence may take place in any locality in the officer's police area, and it is expedient to use these powers to prevent their occurrence, or

    (b) that persons are carrying dangerous instruments or offensive weapons without good reason in any locality in the officer's police area.

A:2.13 An authorisation under section 60 may only be given by an officer of the rank of inspector or above, in writing, specifying the grounds on which it was given, the locality in which the powers may be exercised and the period of time for which they are in force. The period authorised shall be no longer than appears reasonably necessary to prevent, or seek to prevent incidents of serious violence, or to deal with the problem of carrying dangerous instruments or offensive weapons. It may not exceed 24 hours. [See *Notes 10–13*.]

A:2.14 If an inspector gives an authorisation, he or she must, as soon as practicable, inform an officer of or above the rank of superintendent. This officer may direct that the authorisation shall be extended for a further 24 hours, if violence or the carrying of dangerous instruments or offensive weapons has occurred, or is suspected to have occurred, and the continued use of the powers is considered necessary to prevent or deal with further such activity. That direction must also be given in writing at the time or as soon as practicable afterwards. [See *Note 12*.]

Powers to require removal of face coverings

A:2.15 Section 60AA of the *Criminal Justice and Public Order Act* 1994 also **A–6** provides a power to demand the removal of disguises. The officer exercising the power must reasonably believe that someone is wearing an item wholly or mainly for the purpose of concealing identity. There is also a power to seize such items where the officer believes that a person intends to wear them for this purpose. There is no power to stop and search for disguises. An officer may seize any such item which is discovered when exercising a power of search for something else, or which is being carried, and which the officer reasonably believes is intended to be used for concealing anyone's identity. This power can only be used if an authorisation under section 60 or an authorisation under section 60AA is in force.

A:2.16 Authority for a constable in uniform to require the removal of disguises and to seize them under section 60AA may be given if the authorising officer reasonably believes that activities may take place in any locality in the officer's police area that are likely to involve the commission of offences and it is expedient to use these powers to prevent or control these activities.

A:2.17 An authorisation under section 60AA may only be given by an officer of the rank of inspector or above, in writing, specifying the grounds on which it was given, the locality in which the powers may be exercised and the period of time for which they are in force. The period authorised shall be no longer than appears reasonably necessary to prevent, or seek to prevent the commission of offences. It may not exceed 24 hours. [See *Notes 10–13.*]

A:2.18 If an inspector gives an authorisation, he or she must, as soon as practicable, inform an officer of or above the rank of superintendent. This officer may direct that the authorisation shall be extended for a further 24 hours, if crimes have been committed, or is [*sic*] suspected to have been committed, and the continued use of the powers is considered necessary to prevent or deal with further such activity. This direction must also be given in writing at the time or as soon as practicable afterwards. [See *Note 12.*]

Searches authorised under section 44 of the Terrorism Act 2000

A:2.19 An officer of the rank of assistant chief constable (or equivalent) or above, may give authority for the following powers of stop and search under section 44 of the *Terrorism Act* 2000 to be exercised in the whole or part of his or her police area if the officer considers it is expedient for the prevention of acts of terrorism:

    (a) under section 44(1) of the *Terrorism Act* 2000, to give a constable in uniform power to stop and search any vehicle, its driver, any passenger in the vehicle and anything in or on the vehicle or carried by the driver or any passenger; and

    (b) under section 44(2) of the *Terrorism Act* 2000, to give a constable in uniform power to stop and search any pedestrian and anything carried by the pedestrian.

An authorisation under section 44(1) may be combined with one under section 44(2).

A:2.20 If an authorisation is given orally at first, it must be confirmed in writing by the officer who gave it as soon as reasonably practicable.

A:2.21 When giving an authorisation, the officer must specify the geographical area in which the power may be used, and the time and date that the authorisation ends (up to a maximum of 28 days from the time the authorisation was given). [See *Notes 12* and *13.*]

A:2.22 The officer giving an authorisation under section 44(1) or (2) must cause the Secretary of State to be informed, as soon as reasonably practicable, that such an authorisation has been given. An authorisation which is not confirmed by the Secretary of State within 48 hours of its having been given, shall have effect up until the end of that 48 hour period or the end of the period specified in the authorisation (whichever is the earlier). [See *Note 14.*]

A:2.23 Following notification of the authorisation, the Secretary of State may:

    (i) cancel the authorisation with immediate effect or with effect from such other time as he or she may direct;

    (ii) confirm it but for a shorter period than that specified in the authorisation; or

    (iii) confirm the authorisation as given.

A:2.24 When an authorisation under section 44 is given, a constable in uniform may exercise the powers:

    (a) only for the purpose of searching for articles of a kind which could be used in connection with terrorism (see paragraph 2.25);

    (b) whether or not there are any grounds for suspecting the presence of such articles.

A:2.24A When a community support officer on duty and in uniform has been conferred powers under section 44 of the *Terrorism Act* 2000 by a chief officer of their force, the exercise of this power must comply with the requirements of this code of practice, including the recording requirements.

A:2.25 The selection of persons stopped under section 44 of *Terrorism Act* 2000 should reflect an objective assessment of the threat posed by the various terrorist groups active in Great Britain. The powers must not be used to stop and search for reasons unconnected with terrorism. Officers must take particular care not to discriminate against members of minority ethnic groups in the exercise of these powers. There may be circumstances, however, where it is appropriate for officers to take account of a person's ethnic origin in selecting persons to be stopped in response to a specific terrorist threat (for example, some international terrorist groups are associated with particular ethnic identities). [See *Notes 12* and *13*.]

A:2.26 The powers under sections 43 and 44 of the *Terrorism Act* 2000 allow a constable to search only for articles which could be used for terrorist purposes. However, this would not prevent a search being carried out under other powers if, in the course of exercising these powers, the officer formed reasonable grounds for suspicion.

Powers to search in the exercise of a power to search premises

A:2.27 The following powers to search premises also authorise the search of a **A–8**
person, not under arrest, who is found on the premises during the course of the search:

> (a) section 139B of the *Criminal Justice Act* 1988 under which a constable may enter school premises and search the premises and any person on those premises for any bladed or pointed article or offensive weapon; and

> (b) under a warrant issued under section 23(3) of the *Misuse of Drugs Act* 1971 to search premises for drugs or documents but only if the warrant specifically authorises the search of persons found on the premises.

A:2.28 Before the power under section 139B of the *Criminal Justice Act* 1988 may be exercised, the constable must have reasonable grounds to believe that an offence under section 139A of the *Criminal Justice Act* 1988 (having a bladed or pointed article or offensive weapon on school premises) has been or is being committed. A warrant to search premises and persons found therein may be issued under section 23(3) of the *Misuse of Drugs Act* 1971 if there are reasonable grounds to suspect that controlled drugs or certain documents are in the possession of a person on the premises.

A:2.29 The powers in paragraph 2.27(a) or (b) do not require prior specific grounds to suspect that the person to be searched is in possession of an item for which there is an existing power to search. However, it is still necessary to ensure that the selection and treatment of those searched under these powers is based upon objective factors connected with the search of the premises, and not upon personal prejudice.

A:3 Conduct of searches

A:3.1 All stops and searches must be carried out with courtesy, consideration **A–9**
and respect for the person concerned. This has a significant impact on public confidence in the police. Every reasonable effort must be made to minimise the embarrassment that a person being searched may experience. [See *Note 4*.]

A:3.2 The co-operation of the person to be searched must be sought in every case, even if the person initially objects to the search. A forcible search may be made only if it has been established that the person is unwilling to co-operate or resists. Reasonable force may be used as a last resort if necessary to conduct a search or to detain a person or vehicle for the purposes of a search.

A:3.3 The length of time for which a person or vehicle may be detained must be reasonable and kept to a minimum. Where the exercise of the power requires reasonable suspicion, the thoroughness and extent of a search must depend on what is suspected of being carried, and by whom. If the suspicion relates to a particular article which is seen to be slipped into a person's pocket, then, in the absence of other grounds for suspicion or an opportunity for the article to be moved elsewhere, the search must be confined to that pocket. In the case of a small article which can readily be concealed, such as a drug, and which might be concealed anywhere on the person, a more extensive search may be necessary. In the case of searches mentioned in paragraph 2.1(b), (c) and (d), which do not require reasonable grounds for suspicion, officers may make any reasonable search to look for items for which they are empowered to search. [See *Note 5.*]

A:3.4 The search must be carried out at or near the place where the person or vehicle was first detained. [See *Note 6.*]

A:3.5 There is no power to require a person to remove any clothing in public other than an outer coat, jacket or gloves except under section 45(3) of the *Terrorism Act* 2000 (which empowers a constable conducting a search under section 44(1) or 44(2) of that Act to require a person to remove headgear and footwear in public) and under section 60AA of the *Criminal Justice and Public Order Act* 1994 (which empowers a constable to require a person to remove any item worn to conceal identity). [See *Notes 4* and *6.*] A search in public of a person's clothing which has not been removed must be restricted to superficial examination of outer garments. This does not, however, prevent an officer from placing his or her hand inside the pockets of the outer clothing, or feeling round the inside of collars, socks and shoes if this is reasonably necessary in the circumstances to look for the object of the search or to remove and examine any item reasonably suspected to be the object of the search. For the same reasons, subject to the restrictions on the removal of headgear, a person's hair may also be searched in public (see paragraphs 3.1 and 3.3).

A:3.6 Where on reasonable grounds it is considered necessary to conduct a more thorough search (*e.g.* by requiring a person to take off a T-shirt), this must be done out of public view, for example, in a police van unless paragraph 3.7 applies, or police station if there is one nearby. [See *Note 6.*] Any search involving the removal of more than an outer coat, jacket, gloves, headgear or footwear, or any other item concealing identity, may only be made by an officer of the same sex as the person searched and may not be made in the presence of anyone of the opposite sex unless the person being searched specifically requests it. [See *Notes 4, 7* and *8.*]

A:3.7 Searches involving exposure of intimate parts of the body must not be conducted as a routine extension of a less thorough search, simply because nothing is found in the course of the initial search. Searches involving exposure of intimate parts of the body may be carried out only at a nearby police station or other nearby location which is out of public view (but not a police vehicle). These searches must be conducted in accordance with paragraph 11 of Annex A to Code C except that an intimate search mentioned in paragraph 11(f) of Annex A to Code C may not be authorised or carried out under any stop and search powers. The other provisions of Code C do not apply to the conduct and recording of searches of persons detained at police stations in the exercise of stop and search powers. [See *Note 7.*]

Steps to be taken prior to a search

A–10 **A:3.8** Before any search of a detained person or attended vehicle takes place the officer must take reasonable steps to give the person to be searched or in charge of the vehicle the following information:

    (a) that they are being detained for the purposes of a search;

    (b) the officer's name (except in the case of enquiries linked to the investigation of terrorism, or otherwise where the officer reasonably believes that giving his or her name might put him or her in danger, in which case a warrant or other identification number shall be given) and the name of the police station to which the officer is attached;

    (c) the legal search power which is being exercised; and

    (d) a clear explanation of;

        (i) the purpose of the search in terms of the article or articles for which there is a power to search; and

        (ii) in the case of powers requiring reasonable suspicion (see paragraph 2.1(a)), the grounds for that suspicion; or

        (iii) in the case of powers which do not require reasonable suspicion (see paragraph 2.1(b), and (c)), the nature of the power and of any necessary authorisation and the fact that it has been given.

A:3.9 Officers not in uniform must show their warrant cards. Stops and searches under the powers mentioned in paragraphs 2.1(b) and (c) may be undertaken only by a constable in uniform.

A:3.10 Before the search takes place the officer must inform the person (or the owner or person in charge of the vehicle that is to be searched) of his or her entitlement to a copy of the record of the search, including his entitlement to a record of the search if an application is made within 12 months, if it is wholly impracticable to make a record at the time. If a record is not made at the time the person should also be told how a copy can be obtained (see section 4). The person should also be given information about police powers to stop and search and the individual's rights in these circumstances.

A:3.11 If the person to be searched, or in charge of a vehicle to be searched, does not appear to understand what is being said, or there is any doubt about the person's ability to understand English, the officer must take reasonable steps to bring information regarding the person's rights and any relevant provisions of this code to his or her attention. If the person is deaf or cannot understand English and is accompanied by someone, then the officer must try to establish whether that person can interpret or otherwise help the officer to give the required information.

A:4 Recording requirements

A:4.1 An officer who has carried out a search in the exercise of any power to which this code applies, must make a record of it at the time, unless there are exceptional circumstances which would make this wholly impracticable (*e.g.* in situations involving public disorder or when the officer's presence is urgently required elsewhere). If a record is not made at the time, the officer must do so as soon as practicable afterwards. There may be situations in which it is not practicable to obtain the information necessary to complete a record, but the officer should make every reasonable effort to do so. [See *Note 21*.]

A–11

A:4.2 A copy of a record made at the time must be given immediately to the person who has been searched. In all cases the officer must ask for the name, address and date of birth of the person searched, but there is no obligation on a person to provide these details and no power of detention if the person is unwilling to do so.

A:4.2A A receipt of the record rather than a copy of the record may be given immediately to the person who has been searched provided it is produced by electronic means and states how the full record can be accessed. When providing such a receipt, the officer must inform the person that the receipt is in place of a full written record, that the full record is available in electronic or in hard copy format and how the full record can be accessed. The person may request a copy in either format but not both. The full record must comply with paragraph 4.3 of this code. [See *Note 22*.]

A:4.3 The following information must always be included in the record of a search even if the person does not wish to provide any personal details:

(i) the name of the person searched, or (if it is withheld) a description;

(ii) a note of the person's self-defined ethnic background; [see *Note 18*];

(iii) when a vehicle is searched, its registration number; [see *Note 16*];

(iv) the date, time, and place that the person or vehicle was first detained;

(v) the date, time and place the person or vehicle was searched (if different from (iv));

(vi) the purpose of the search;

(vii) the grounds for making it, or in the case of those searches mentioned in paragraph 2.1(b) and (c), the nature of the power and of any necessary authorisation and the fact that it has been given; [see *Note 17*];

(viii) its outcome (*e.g.* arrest or no further action);

    (ix) a note of any injury or damage to property resulting from it;

    (x) subject to paragraph 3.8(b), the identity of the officer making the search. [See *Note 15*.]

A:4.4 Nothing in paragraph 4.3 or 4.10A requires the names of police officers to be shown on the search record or any other record required to be made under this code in the case of enquiries linked to the investigation of terrorism or otherwise where an officer reasonably believes that recording names might endanger the officers. In such cases the record must show the officer's warrant or other identification number and duty station.

A:4.5 A record is required for each person and each vehicle searched. However, if a person is in a vehicle and both are searched, and the object and grounds of the search are the same, only one record need be completed. If more than one person in a vehicle is searched, separate records for each search of a person must be made. If only a vehicle is searched, the name of the driver and his or her self-defined ethnic background must be recorded, unless the vehicle is unattended.

A:4.6 The record of the grounds for making a search must, briefly but informatively, explain the reason for suspecting the person concerned, by reference to the person's behaviour and/or other circumstances.

A:4.7 Where officers detain an individual with a view to performing a search, but the search is not carried out due to the grounds for suspicion being eliminated as a result of questioning the person detained, a record must still be made in accordance with the procedure outlined in paragraph 4.12.

A:4.8 After searching an unattended vehicle, or anything in or on it, an officer must leave a notice in it (or on it, if things on it have been searched without opening it) recording the fact that it has been searched.

A:4.9 The notice must include the name of the police station to which the officer concerned is attached and state where a copy of the record of the search may be obtained and where any application for compensation should be directed.

A:4.10 The vehicle must if practicable be left secure.

A:4.10A When an officer makes a record of the stop electronically and if the officer is able to provide a copy of the record at the time of the stop or stop and search, he or she must do so. This means that if the officer has or has access to a portable printer for use with the electronic recording equipment, then a copy of the record must be provided.

A:4.10B If the officer is carrying a paper version of the form, then a record must be provided at the time of the incident [see *Note 25*]. An officer would not be required to produce anything other than a receipt if neither of these two scenarios (4.10A and 4.10B) are met, nor would they be required to provide a full record at the scene in the event that he or she was called to respond to an incident of higher priority. Where the person has been searched, the officer must explain how the person can obtain a full copy of the record of the stop or search and give the person a receipt which contains:

- a unique reference number and guidance on how to obtain a full copy of the stop or search;
- the name of the officer who carried out the stop or search (unless paragraph 4.4 applies); and
- the power used to stop and search them. [See *Note 21*.]

Recording of encounters not governed by statutory powers

A:4.11 *Not used.*

A:4.12 When an officer requests a person in a public place to account for themselves, *i.e.* their actions, behaviour, presence in an area or possession of anything, a record of the encounter as set out in paragraph 4.17 must be completed at the time and a receipt given to the person in accordance with paragraphs 4.12A and 4.17 below. The record must identify the name of the officer who has made the stop and conducted the encounter. This does not apply under the exceptional circumstances outlined in paragraph 4.1 of this code.

A:4.12A A receipt can be provided in place of the record of the encounter as set out in paragraph 4.17. The officer conducting the encounter is required to record only the person's self-defined ethnic background. [See *Notes 18 and 24*.]

A:4.13 The requirements in paragraph 4.12 and 4.12A do not apply to general conversations such as when giving directions to a place, or when seeking witnesses. It also does not include occasions on which an officer is seeking general information or questioning people to establish background to incidents which have required officers to intervene to keep the peace or resolve a dispute.

A:4.14 A separate record or receipt need not be completed when:

- stopping a person in a vehicle when an HORT/1 form, a Vehicle Defect Rectification Scheme Notice, or a fixed penalty notice is issued. It also does not apply when a specimen of breath is required under section 6 of the *Road Traffic Act* 1988;
- stopping a person when a penalty notice is issued for an offence.

A:4.15 Officers must inform the person of their entitlement to a receipt of the encounter.

A:4.16 The provisions of paragraph 4.4 of this code apply equally when the encounters described in 4.12, 4.12A and 4.13 are recorded.

A:4.17 The following information must be included in the record:

(i) a note of the person's self-defined ethnic background. [See *Note 18*.]

A:4.18 There is no power to require the person questioned to provide personal details. If a person refuses to give their self-defined ethnic background, the record should provide a description of the person's ethnic background. [See *Note 18*.]

A:4.19 A receipt of an encounter must always be made when the criteria set out in 4.12 have been met. If the criteria are not met but the person requests a receipt, the officer should provide a receipt but record on it that the encounter did not meet the criteria. The officer can refuse to issue the receipt if he or she reasonably believes that the purpose of the request is deliberately aimed at frustrating or delaying legitimate police activity. [See *Note 20*.]

A:4.20 All references to officers in this section include police staff designated as community support officers under section 38 of the *Police Reform Act* 2002.

A:5 Monitoring and supervising the use of stop and search powers

A:5.1 Supervising officers must monitor the use of stop and search powers and **A–12** should consider in particular whether there is any evidence that they are being exercised on the basis of stereotyped images or inappropriate generalisations. Supervising officers should satisfy themselves that the practice of officers under their supervision in stopping, searching and recording is fully in accordance with this code. Supervisors must also examine whether the records reveal any trends or patterns which give cause for concern, and if so take appropriate action to address this.

A:5.2 Senior officers with area or force-wide responsibilities must also monitor the broader use of stop and search powers and, where necessary, take action at the relevant level.

A:5.3 Supervision and monitoring must be supported by the compilation of comprehensive statistical records of stops and searches at force, area and local level. Any apparently disproportionate use of the powers by particular officers or groups of officers or in relation to specific sections of the community should be identified and investigated.

A:5.4 In order to promote public confidence in the use of the powers, forces in consultation with police authorities must make arrangements for the records to be scrutinised by representatives of the community, and to explain the use of the powers at a local level. [See *Note 19*.]

Notes for Guidance

Officers exercising stop and search powers

A–13

A:1 *This code does not affect the ability of an officer to speak to or question a person in the ordinary course of the officer's duties without detaining the person or exercising any element of compulsion. It is not the purpose of the code to prohibit such encounters between the police and the community with the co-operation of the person concerned and neither does it affect the principle that all citizens have a duty to help police officers to prevent crime and discover offenders. This is a civic rather than a legal duty; but when a police officer is trying to discover whether, or by whom, an offence has been committed he or she may question any person from whom useful information might be obtained, subject to the restrictions imposed by Code C. A person's unwillingness to reply does not alter this entitlement, but in the absence of a power to arrest, or to detain in order to search, the person is free to leave at will and cannot be compelled to remain with the officer.*

A:2 *In some circumstances preparatory questioning may be unnecessary, but in general a brief conversation or exchange will be desirable not only as a means of avoiding unsuccessful searches, but to explain the grounds for the stop/search, to gain co-operation and reduce any tension there might be surrounding the stop/search.*

A:3 *Where a person is lawfully detained for the purpose of a search, but no search in the event takes place, the detention will not thereby have been rendered unlawful.*

A:4 *Many people customarily cover their heads or faces for religious reasons – for example, Muslim women, Sikh men, Sikh or Hindu women, or Rastarfarian men or women. A police officer cannot order the removal of a head or face covering except where there is reason to believe that the item is being worn by the individual wholly or mainly for the purpose of disguising identity, not simply because it disguises identity. Where there may be religious sensitivities about ordering the removal of such an item, the officer should permit the item to be removed out of public view. Where practicable, the item should be removed in the presence of an officer of the same sex as the person and out of sight of anyone of the opposite sex.*

A:5 *A search of a person in public should be completed as soon as possible.*

A:6 *A person may be detained under a stop and search power at a place other than where the person was first detained, only if that place, be it a police station or elsewhere, is nearby. Such a place should be located within a reasonable travelling distance using whatever mode of travel (on foot or by car) is appropriate. This applies to all searches under stop and search powers, whether or not they involve the removal of clothing or exposure of intimate parts of the body (see paragraphs 3.6 and 3.7) or take place in or out of public view. It means, for example, that a search under the stop and search power in section 23 of the Misuse of Drugs Act 1971 which involves the compulsory removal of more than a person's outer coat, jacket or gloves cannot be carried out unless a place which is both nearby the place they were first detained and out of public view, is available. If a search involves exposure of intimate parts of the body and a police station is not nearby, particular care must be taken to ensure that the location is suitable in that it enables the search to be conducted in accordance with the requirements of paragraph 11 of Annex A to Code C.*

A:7 *A search in the street itself should be regarded as being in public for the purposes of paragraphs 3.6 and 3.7 above, even though it may be empty at the time a search begins. Although there is no power to require a person to do so, there is nothing to prevent an officer from asking a person voluntarily to remove more than an outer coat, jacket or gloves (and headgear or footwear under section 45(3) of the Terrorism Act 2000) in public.*

A:8 *Where there may be religious sensitivities about asking someone to remove headgear using a power under section 45(3) of the Terrorism Act 2000, the police officer should offer to carry out the search out of public view (for example, in a police van or police station if there is one nearby).*

A:9 *Other means of identification might include jewellery, insignias, tattoos or other features which are known to identify members of the particular gang or group.*

Authorising officers

A–14

A:10 *The powers under section 60 are separate from and additional to the normal stop and search powers which require reasonable grounds to suspect an individual of carrying an offensive weapon (or other article). Their overall purpose is to prevent serious violence and the widespread carrying of weapons which might lead to persons being seriously injured by disarming potential offenders in circumstances where other powers would not be sufficient. They should not therefore be used to replace or circumvent the normal powers for dealing* *with routine crime problems. The purpose of the powers under section 60AA is to prevent those involved in intimidatory or violent protests using face coverings to disguise identity.*

A:11 *Authorisations under section 60 require a reasonable belief on the part of the authorising officer. This must have an objective basis, for example: intelligence or relevant information such as a history of antagonism and violence between particular groups; previous incidents of violence at, or connected with, particular events or locations; a significant increase in knife-point robberies in a limited area; reports that individuals are regularly carrying weapons in a particular locality; or in the case of section 60AA previous incidents of crimes being committed while wearing face coverings to conceal identity.*

A:12 *It is for the authorising officer to determine the period of time during which the powers mentioned in paragraph 2.1 (b) and (c) may be exercised. The officer should set the minimum period he or she considers necessary to deal with the risk of violence, the carrying of knives or offensive weapons, or terrorism. A direction to extend the period authorised under the powers mentioned in paragraph 2.1(b) may be given only once. Thereafter further use of the powers requires a new authorisation. There is no provision to extend an authorisation of the powers mentioned in paragraph 2.1(c); further use of the powers requires a new authorisation.*

A:13 *It is for the authorising officer to determine the geographical area in which the use of the powers is to be authorised. In doing so the officer may wish to take into account factors such as the nature and venue of the anticipated incident, the number of people who may be in the immediate area of any possible incident, their access to surrounding areas and the anticipated level of violence. The officer should not set a geographical area which is wider than that he or she believes necessary for the purpose of preventing anticipated violence, the carrying of knives or offensive weapons, acts of terrorism, or, in the case of section 60AA, the prevention of commission of offences. It is particularly important to ensure that constables exercising such powers are fully aware of where they may be used. If the area specified is smaller than the whole force area, the officer giving the authorisation should specify either the streets which form the boundary of the area or a divisional boundary within the force area. If the power is to be used in response to a threat or incident that straddles police force areas, an officer from each of the forces concerned will need to give an authorisation.*

A:14 *An officer who has authorised the use of powers under section 44 of the* Terrorism Act 2000 *must take immediate steps to send a copy of the authorisation to the National Joint Unit, Metropolitan Police Special Branch, who will forward it to the Secretary of State. The Secretary of State should be informed of the reasons for the authorisation. The National Joint Unit will inform the force concerned, within 48 hours of the authorisation being made, whether the Secretary of State has confirmed or cancelled or altered the authorisation.*

Recording

A:15 *Where a stop and search is conducted by more than one officer the identity of all the officers engaged in the search must be recorded on the record. Nothing prevents an officer who is present but not directly involved in searching from completing the record during the course of the encounter.*   **A–15**

A:16 *Where a vehicle has not been allocated a registration number (e.g. a rally car or a trials motorbike) that part of the requirement under 4.3(iii) does not apply.*

A:17 *It is important for monitoring purposes to specify whether the authority for exercising a stop and search power was given under section 60 of the* Criminal Justice and Public Order Act 1994, *or under section 44(1) or 44(2) of the* Terrorism Act 2000.

A:18 *Officers should record the self-defined ethnicity of every person stopped according to the categories used in the 2001 census question listed in Annex B. Respondents should be asked to select one of the five main categories representing broad ethnic groups and then a more specific cultural background from within this group. The ethnic classification should be coded for recording purposes using the coding system in Annex B. An additional "Not stated" box is available but should not be offered to respondents explicitly. Officers should be aware and explain to members of the public, especially where concerns are raised, that this information is required to obtain a true picture of stop and search activity and to help improve ethnic monitoring, tackle discriminatory practice, and promote effective use of the powers. If the person gives what appears to the officer to be an "incorrect" answer (e.g. a person who appears to be white states that they are black), the officer should record the response that has been given. Officers should also record their own perception of the ethnic* *background of every person stopped and this must be done by using the PNC/Phoenix classification system. If the "Not stated" category is used the reason for this must be recorded on the form.*

A:19 *Arrangements for public scrutiny of records should take account of the right to confidentiality of those stopped and searched. Anonymised forms and/or statistics generated from records should be the focus of the examinations by members of the public.*

A:20 *Where an officer engages in conversation which is not pertinent to the actions or whereabouts of the individual (e.g. does not relate to why the person is there, what they are doing or where they have been or are going) then issuing a form would not meet the criteria set out in paragraph 4.12. Situations designed to impede police activity may arise, for example, in public order situations where individuals engage in dialogue with the officer but the officer does not initiate or engage in contact about the person's individual circumstances.*

A:21 *In situations where it is not practicable to provide a written record or a full copy of an electronic record or an electronic receipt (in accordance with paragraphs 4.2A and 4.13A above) of the stop or stop and search at that time, the officer should consider providing the person with details of the station to which the person may attend for a record. This may take the form of a simple business card, adding the date of the stop or stop and search.*

A:22 *The ability to provide an electronic receipt for a stop or stop and search is limited to officers from those British Transport Police (BTP) designated areas set out in Annex D to this code and to a limited pilot period. The operational nature of BTP policing means that officers from these locations may provide electronic receipts in the course of their duties throughout England and Wales.*

Definition of offensive weapon

A:23 *"Offensive weapon" is defined as any article made or adapted for use for causing injury to the person, or intended by the person having it with him for such use or by someone else. There are three categories of offensive weapons: those made for causing injury to the person; those adapted for such a purpose; and those not so made or adapted, but carried with the intention of causing injury to the person. A firearm, as defined by section 57 of the Firearms Act 1968, would fall within the definition of offensive weapon if any of the criteria above.*

A:24 *Under paragraph 4.12A, the officer carrying out the encounter may consider recording the date, time and location of the encounter when the encounter is not recorded electronically. This information is in support of section 5 of this code and is not required to be provided to the person subject to the encounter.*

A:25 *Under 4.10B, an officer with an electronic recording device may be carrying a paper version of the record for use as a contingency in the event of a technical breakdown. In these circumstances, where the officer is able to make an electronic record, there would be no requirement to provide a written record.*

ANNEX A

Summary of main stop and search powers

This table relates to stop and search powers only. Individual statutes below may contain other police powers of entry, search and seizure.

POWER	Object of search	Extent of Search	Where Exercisable
Unlawful articles general			
1. *Public Stores Act* 1875, s.6	HM Stores stolen or unlawfully obtained	Persons, vehicles and vessels	Anywhere where the constabulary powers are exercisable
2. *Firearms Act* 1968, s.47	Firearms	Persons and vehicles	A public place, or anywhere in the case of reasonable suspicion of offences of carrying firearms with criminal intent or trespassing with firearms
3. *Misuse of Drugs Act* 1971, s.23	Controlled drugs	Persons and vehicles	Anywhere
4. *Customs and Excise Management Act* 1979, s.163	Goods: (a) on which duty has not been paid; (b) being unlawfully removed, imported or exported; (c) otherwise liable to forfeiture to HM Customs and Excise	Vehicles and vessels only	Anywhere
5. *Aviation Security Act* 1982, s.27(1)	Stolen or unlawfully obtained goods	Airport employees and vehicles carrying airport employees or aircraft or any vehicle in a cargo area whether or not carrying an employee	Any designated airport

Provision	Articles / goods	Persons/vehicles	Location
6. *Police and Criminal Evidence Act* 1984, s.1	Stolen goods; articles for use in certain *Theft Act* offences; offensive weapons, including bladed or sharply-pointed articles (except folding pocket knives with a bladed cutting edge not exceeding 3 inches); prohibited possession of a category 4 (display grade) firework, any person under 18 in possession of an adult firework in a public place.	Persons and vehicles	Where there is public access
	Criminal damage: articles made, adapted or intended for use in destroying or damaging property	Persons and vehicles	Where there is public access
Police and Criminal Evidence Act 1984, s.6(3) (by a constable of the United Kingdom Atomic Energy Authority Constabulary in respect of property owned or controlled by British Nuclear Fuels plc)	HM Stores (in the form of goods and chattels belonging to British Nuclear Fuels plc)	Persons, vehicles and vessels	Anywhere where the constabulary powers are exercisable
7. *Sporting Events (Control of Alcohol etc.) Act* 1985, s.7	Intoxicating liquor	Persons, coaches and trains	Designated sports grounds or coaches and trains travelling to or from a designated sporting event.
8. *Crossbows Act* 1987, s.4	Crossbows or parts of crossbows (except crossbows with a draw weight of less than 1.4 kilograms)	Persons and vehicles	Anywhere except dwellings
9. *Criminal Justice Act* 1988 s.139B	Offensive weapons, bladed or sharply pointed article	Persons	School premises

Evidence of game and wildlife offences			
10. *Poaching Prevention Act* 1862, s.2	Game or poaching equipment	Persons and vehicles	A public place
11. *Deer Act* 1991, s.12	Evidence of offences under the Act	Persons and vehicles	Anywhere except dwellings
12. *Conservation of Seals Act* 1970, s.4	Seals or hunting equipment	Vehicles only	Anywhere
13. *Badgers Act* 1992, s.11	Evidence of offences under the Act	Persons and vehicles	Anywhere
14. *Wildlife and Countryside Act* 1981, s.19	Evidence of wildlife offences	Persons and vehicles	Anywhere except dwellings
Other			
15. *Terrorism Act* 2000, s.43	Evidence of liability to arrest under section 41 of the Act	Persons	Anywhere
16. *Terrorism Act* 2000, s.44(1)	Articles which could be used for a purpose connected with the commission, preparation or instigation of acts of terrorism	Vehicles, driver and passengers	Anywhere within the area or locality authorised under subsection (1)
17. *Terrorism Act* 2000, s.44(2)	Articles which could be used for a purpose connected with the commission, preparation or instigation of acts of terrorism	Pedestrians	Anywhere within the area of locality authorised
18. Paragraphs 7 and 8 of Schedule 7 to the *Terrorism Act* 2000	Anything relevant to determining if a person being examined falls within paragraph 2(1)(a) to (c) of Schedule 5	Persons, vehicles, vessels etc.	Ports and airports
19. Section 60 *Criminal Justice and Public Order Act* 1994, as amended by s.8 of the *Knives Act* 1997	Offensive weapons or dangerous instruments to prevent incidents of serious violence or to deal with the carrying of such items	Persons and vehicles	Anywhere within a locality authorised under subsection (1)

ANNEX B

Self-Defined ethnic classification categories

A–17

White	**W**
A.	W1
White—British	
B.	W2
White—Irish	
C.	W9
Any other White background	
Mixed	**M**
D.	M1
White and Black Caribbean	
E.	M2
White and Black African	
F.	M3
White and Asian	
G.	M9
Any other Mixed Background	
Asian/ Asian—British	**A**
H.	A1
Asian—Indian	
I.	A2
Asian—Pakistani	
J.	A3
Asian—Bangladeshi	
K.	A9
Any other Asian background	
Black / Black—British	**B**
L.	B1
Black—Caribbean	
M.	B2
Black African	
N.	B9
Any other Black background	
Other	**O**
O.	O1
Chinese	
P.	O9
Any other	
Not stated	**NS**

ANNEX C

Summary of powers of community support officers to search and seize

A–17a

The following is a summary of the search and seizure powers that may be exercised by a community support officer (CSO) who has been designated with the relevant powers in accordance with Part 4 of the *Police Reform Act* 2002.

When exercising any of these powers, a CSO must have regard to any relevant provisions of this code, including section 3 governing the conduct of searches and the steps to be taken prior to a search.

1. Power to stop and search not requiring consent

Designation	Power conferred	Object of Search	Extent of Search	Where Exercisable
Police Reform Act 2002, Schedule 4, paragraph 15	(a) *Terrorism Act 2000*, s.44(1)(a) and (d) and 45(2);	Items intended to be used in connection with terrorism	(a) Vehicles or anything carried in or on the vehicle and anything carried by driver or passenger.	Anywhere within area of locality authorised and in the company and under the supervision of a constable.
	(b) *Terrorism Act 2000*, s.44(2)(b) and 45(2)		(b) Anything carried by a pedestrian.	

2. Powers to search requiring the consent of the person and seizure

A CSO may detain a person using reasonable force where necessary as set out in Part 1 of Schedule 4 to the *Police Reform Act 2002*. If the person has been lawfully detained, the CSO may search the person provided that person gives consent to such a search in relation to the following:

Designation	Powers conferred	Object of Search	Extent of Search	Where Exercisable
Police Reform Act 2002, Schedule 4, paragraph 7A	(a) *Criminal Justice and Police Act 2001*, s.12(2)	(a) Alcohol or a container for alcohol	(a) Persons	(a) Designated public place
	(b) *Confiscation of Alcohol (Young Persons) Act 1997*, s.1	(b) Alcohol	(b) Persons under 18 years old	(b) Public place
	(c) *Children and Young Persons Act 1933*, s.7(3)	(c) Tobacco or cigarette papers	(c) Persons under 16 years old found smoking	(c) Public place

3. Powers to search not requiring the consent of the person and seizure

A CSO may detain a person using reasonable force where necessary as set out in Part 1 of Schedule 4 to the *Police Reform Act 2002*. If the person has been lawfully detained, the CSO may search the person without the need for that person's consent in relation to the following:

Designation	Power conferred	Object of Search	Extent of Search	Where Exercisable
Police Reform Act 2002, Schedule 4, paragraph 2A	*Police and Criminal Evidence Act 1984*, s.32	(a) Objects that might be used to cause physical injury to the person or the CSO.	Persons made subject to a requirement to wait.	Any place where the requirement to wait has been made.
		(b) Items that might be used to assist escape.		

4. Powers to seize without consent

This power applies when drugs are found in the course of any search mentioned above.

Designation	Power conferred	Object of Seizure	Where Exercisable
Police Reform Act 2002, Schedule 4, paragraph 7B	*Police Reform Act 2002*, Schedule 4, paragraph 7B	Controlled drugs in a person's possession.	Any place where the person is in possession of the drug.

(3) Search and seizure

The text that follows is of the version of the code that came into force on ꞌebruary 1, 2008: see *ante*, Appendix A–1.   **A–18**
For authorities in relation to Code B, see, in particular, §§ 15–104 and 15–⎿51 in the main work.

B. Code of Practice for Searches of Premises by Police Officers and the Seizure of Property Found by Police Officers on Persons or Premises

Commencement—transitional arrangements

This code applies to applications for warrants made after midnight 31 January   **A–19** 2008 and to searches and seizures taking place after midnight on 31 January 2008.

B:1 Introduction

B:1.1 This code of practice deals with police powers to: **A–20**
- search premises
- seize and retain property found on premises and persons.

B:1.1A These powers may be used to find:
- property and material relating to a crime
- wanted persons
- children who abscond from local authority accommodation where they have been remanded or committed by a court.

B:1.2 A justice of the peace may issue a search warrant granting powers of entry, search and seizure, *e.g.* warrants to search for stolen property, drugs, firearms and evidence of serious offences. Police also have powers without a search warrant. The main ones provided by the *Police and Criminal Evidence Act* 1984 (*PACE*) include powers to search premises:
- to make an arrest
- after an arrest.

B:1.3 The right to privacy and respect for personal property are key principles of the *Human Rights Act* 1998. Powers of entry, search and seizure should be fully and clearly justified before use because they may significantly interfere with the occupier's privacy. Officers should consider if the necessary objectives can be met by less intrusive means.

B:1.4 In all cases, police should:
- exercise their powers courteously and with respect for persons and property
- only use reasonable force when this is considered necessary and proportionate to the circumstances.

B:1.5 If the provisions of *PACE* and this code are not observed, evidence obtained from a search may be open to question.

B:2 General

B:2.1 This code must be readily available at all police stations for consultation by: **A–21**
- police officers
- police staff

- detained persons
- members of the public.

B:2.2 The *Notes for Guidance* included are not provisions of this code.

B:2.3 This code applies to searches of premises:

    (a) by police for the purposes of an investigation into an alleged offence, with the occupier's consent, other than:

- routine scene of crime searches;
- calls to a fire or burglary made by or on behalf of an occupier or searches following the activation of fire or burglar alarms or discovery of insecure premises;
- searches when paragraph 5.4 applies;
- bomb threat calls;

    (b) under powers conferred on police officers by *PACE*, sections 17, 18 and 32;

    (c) undertaken in pursuance of search warrants issued to and executed by constables in accordance with *PACE*, sections 15 and 16; [see *Note* 2A];

    (d) subject to paragraph 2.6, under any other power given to police to enter premises with or without a search warrant for any purpose connected with the investigation into an alleged or suspected offence. [See *Note 2B*]

For the purposes of this code, "premises" as defined in *PACE*, section 23, includes any place, vehicle, vessel, aircraft, hovercraft, tent or movable structure and any offshore installation as defined in the *Mineral Workings (Offshore Installations) Act* 1971, section 1. See *Note 2D*.

B:2.4 A person who has not been arrested but is searched during a search of premises should be searched in accordance with Code A. See *Note 2C*.

B:2.5 This code does not apply to the exercise of a statutory power to enter premises or to inspect goods, equipment or procedures if the exercise of that power is not dependent on the existence of grounds for suspecting that an offence may have been committed and the person exercising the power has no reasonable grounds for such suspicion.

B:2.6 This code does not affect any directions of a search warrant or order lawfully executed in England or Wales that any item or evidence seized under that warrant or order be handed over to a police force, court, tribunal, or other authority outside England or Wales. For example, warrants and orders issued in Scotland or Northern Ireland, see *Note 2B(f)* and search warrants issued under the *Criminal Justice (International Co-operation) Act* 1990, section 7.

B:2.7 When this code requires the prior authority or agreement of an officer of at least inspector or superintendent rank, that authority may be given by a sergeant or chief inspector authorised to perform the functions of the higher rank under *PACE*, section 107.

B:2.8 Written records required under this code not made in the search record shall, unless otherwise specified, be made:

- in the recording officer's pocket book ("pocket book" includes any official report book issued to police officers) or
- on forms provided for the purpose.

B:2.9 Nothing in this code requires the identity of officers, or anyone accompanying them during a search of premises, to be recorded or disclosed:

    (a) in the case of enquiries linked to the investigation of terrorism; or

    (b) if officers reasonably believe recording or disclosing their names might put them in danger.

In these cases officers should use warrant or other identification numbers and the name of their police station. Police staff should use any identification number provided to them by the police force. See *Note 2E*.

B:2.10 The "officer in charge of the search" means the officer assigned specific duties and responsibilities under this code. Whenever there is a search of premises to which this code applies one officer must act as the officer in charge of the search. See *Note 2F.*

B:2.11 In this code:

(a) "designated person" means a person other than a police officer, designated under the *Police Reform Act* 2002, Part 4 who has specified powers and duties of police officers conferred or imposed on them; [see *Note 2G*];

(b) any reference to a police officer includes a designated person acting in the exercise or performance of the powers and duties conferred or imposed on them by their designation;

(c) a person authorised to accompany police officers or designated persons in the execution of a warrant has the same powers as a constable in the execution of the warrant and the search and seizure of anything related to the warrant. These powers must be exercised in the company and under the supervision of a police officer. See *Note 3C.*

B:2.12 If a power conferred on a designated person:

(a) allows reasonable force to be used when exercised by a police officer, a designated person exercising that power has the same entitlement to use force;

(b) includes power to use force to enter any premises, that power is not exercisable by that designated person except:

  (i) in the company and under the supervision of a police officer; or

  (ii) for the purpose of:

- saving life or limb; or
- preventing serious damage to property.

B:2.13 Designated persons must have regard to any relevant provisions of the codes of practice.

Notes for guidance

B:2A PACE *sections 15 and 16 apply to all search warrants issued to and executed by*   **A–22**
constables under any enactment, e.g. search warrants issued by a:

(a) *justice of the peace under the*:

Theft Act *1968, section 26—stolen property*;

Misuse of Drugs Act *1971, section 23—controlled drugs*;

PACE, *section 8—evidence of an indictable offence*;

Terrorism Act *2000, Schedule 5, paragraph 1*;

(b) *circuit judge under*:

PACE, *Schedule 1*;

Terrorism Act *2000, Schedule 5, paragraph 11.*

B:2B *Examples of the other powers in paragraph 2.3(d) include*:

(a) Road Traffic Act *1988, section 6E(1) giving police power to enter premises under section 6E(1) to*:

- *require a person to provide a specimen of breath; or*
- *arrest a person following*:
  - *a positive breath test*;
  - *failure to provide a specimen of breath*;

(b) Transport and Works Act *1992, section 30(4) giving police powers to enter premises mirroring the powers in (a) in relation to specified persons working on transport systems to which the Act applies*;

(c) Criminal Justice Act *1988, section 139B giving police power to enter and search school premises for offensive weapons, bladed or pointed articles*;

(d) Terrorism Act *2000, Schedule 5, paragraphs 3 and 15 empowering a superintendent in urgent cases to give written authority for police to enter and search premises for the purposes of a terrorist investigation*;

(e) Explosives Act *1875, section 73(b) empowering a superintendent to give writ ten authority for police to enter premises, examine and search them for explosives*

(f) *search warrants and production orders or the equivalent issued in Scotland or Northern Ireland endorsed under the* Summary Jurisdiction (Process) Ac *1881 or the* Petty Sessions (Ireland) Act *1851 respectively for execution in England and Wales.*

B:2C *The* Criminal Justice Act *1988, section 139B provides that a constable who ha reasonable grounds to believe an offence under the* Criminal Justice Act *1988, section 139A has or is being committed may enter school premises and search the premises and any persons on the premises for any bladed or pointed article or offensive weapon. Persons ma be searched under a warrant issued under the* Misuse of Drugs Act *1971, section 23(3) t search premises for drugs or documents only if the warrant specifically authorises the searcl of persons on the premises.*

B:2D *The* Immigration Act *1971, Part III and Schedule 2 gives immigration officer powers to enter and search premises, seize and retain property, with and without a searcl warrant. These are similar to the powers available to police under search warrants issued b a justice of the peace and without a warrant under* PACE, *sections 17, 18, 19 and 32 except they only apply to specified offences under the* Immigration Act *1971 and immigra tion control powers. For certain types of investigations and enquiries these powers avoid th need for the Immigration Service to rely on police officers becoming directly involved. When exercising these powers, immigration officers are required by the* Immigration and Asylum Act *1999, section 145 to have regard to this code's corresponding provisions. When im migration officers are dealing with persons or property at police stations, police officers should give appropriate assistance to help them discharge their specific duties and responsibilities.*

B:2E *The purpose of paragraph 2.9(b) is to protect those involved in serious organised crime investigations or arrests of particularly violent suspects when there is reliable informa tion that those arrested or their associates may threaten or cause harm to the officers or anyone accompanying them during a search of premises. In cases of doubt, an officer o inspector rank or above should be consulted.*

B:2F *For the purposes of paragraph 2.10, the officer in charge of the search shoula normally be the most senior officer present. Some exceptions are:*

(a) *a supervising officer who attends or assists at the scene of a premises search ma appoint an officer of lower rank as officer in charge of the search if that officer i*

- *more conversant with the facts;*
- *a more appropriate officer to be in charge of the search;*

(b) *when all officers in a premises search are the same rank. The supervising office if available must make sure one of them is appointed officer in charge of the search, otherwise the officers themselves must nominate one of their number a the officer in charge;*

(c) *a senior officer assisting in a specialist role. This officer need not be regarded a having a general supervisory role over the conduct of the search or be appointer or expected to act as the officer in charge of the search.*

Except in (c), nothing in this note diminishes the role and responsibilities of a supervisor officer who is present at the search or knows of a search taking place.

B:2G *An officer of the rank of inspector or above may direct a designated investigating officer not to wear a uniform for the purposes of a specific operation.*

B:3 Search warrants and production orders

(a) Before making an application

B:3.1 When information appears to justify an application, the officer must take reasonable steps to check the information is accurate, recent and not provided maliciously or irresponsibly. An application may not be made on the basis of in formation from an anonymous source if corroboration has not been sought. See *Note 3A.*

B:3.2 The officer shall ascertain as specifically as possible the nature of the articles concerned and their location.

B:3.3 The officer shall make reasonable enquiries to:

(i) establish if:

- anything is known about the likely occupier of the premises and the nature of the premises themselves;
- the premises have been searched previously and how recently;

(ii) obtain any other relevant information.

B:3.4 An application:

(a) to a justice of the peace for a search warrant or to a circuit judge for a search warrant or production order under *PACE*, Schedule 1 must be supported by a signed written authority from an officer of inspector rank or above; [Note: if the case is an urgent application to a justice of the peace and an inspector or above is not readily available, the next most senior officer on duty can give the written authority];

(b) to a circuit judge under the *Terrorism Act* 2000, Schedule 5 for

- a production order;
- search warrant; or
- an order requiring an explanation of material seized or produced under such a warrant or production order

must be supported by a signed written authority from an officer of superintendent rank or above.

B:3.5 Except in a case of urgency, if there is reason to believe a search might have an adverse effect on relations between the police and the community, the officer in charge shall consult the local police/community liaison officer:

- before the search; or
- in urgent cases, as soon as practicable after the search.

(b) *Making an application*

B:3.6 A search warrant application must be supported in writing, specifying:

(a) the enactment under which the application is made, see *Note 2A*;

(b) (i) whether the warrant is to authorise entry and search of:

- one set of premises; or
- if the application is under *PACE* section 8, or Schedule 1, paragraph 12, more than one set of specified premises or all premises occupied or controlled by a specified person, and

(ii) the premises to be searched;

(c) the object of the search, see *Note 3B*;

(d) the grounds for the application, including, when the purpose of the proposed search is to find evidence of an alleged offence, an indication of how the evidence relates to the investigation;

(da) where the application is under *PACE* section 8, or Schedule 1, paragraph 12 for a single warrant to enter and search:

(i) more than one set of specified premises, the officer must specify each set of premises which it is desired to enter and search;

(ii) all premises occupied or controlled by a specified person, the officer must specify:

- as many sets of premises which it is desired to enter and search as it is reasonably practicable to specify;
- the person who is in occupation or control of those premises and any others which it is desired to search;
- why it is necessary to search more premises than those which can be specified;
- why it is not reasonably practicable to specify all the premises which it is desired to enter and search;

271

Archbold
paragraph
numbers

   (db) whether an application under *PACE* section 8 is for a warrant authoris ing entry and search on more than one occasion, and if so, the officer must state the grounds for this and whether the desired number of entries authorised is unlimited or a specified maximum;

   (e) there are no reasonable grounds to believe the material to be sought when making application to a:

      (i) justice of the peace or a circuit judge consists of or includes items subject to legal privilege;

      (ii) justice of the peace, consists of or includes excluded material or special procedure material;

      [Note: this does not affect the additional powers of seizure in the *Criminal Justice and Police Act* 2001, Part 2 covered in paragraph 7.7, see *Note 3B*]:

   (f) if applicable, a request for the warrant to authorise a person or persons to accompany the officer who executes the warrant, see *Note 3C*.

B:3.7 A search warrant application under *PACE*, Schedule 1, paragraph 12(a) shall if appropriate indicate why it is believed service of notice of an application for a production order may seriously prejudice the investigation. Applications for search warrants under the *Terrorism Act* 2000, Schedule 5, paragraph 11 must indicate why a production order would not be appropriate.

B:3.8 If a search warrant application is refused, a further application may not be made for those premises unless supported by additional grounds.

Notes for guidance

A–24

B:3A *The identity of an informant need not be disclosed when making an application, but the officer should be prepared to answer any questions the magistrate or judge may have about:*

    ● *the accuracy of previous information from that source*

    ● *any other related matters.*

B:3B *The information supporting a search warrant application should be as specific as possible, particularly in relation to the articles or persons being sought and where in the premises it is suspected they may be found. The meaning of "items subject to legal privilege", "excluded material" and "special procedure material" are defined by* PACE, *sections 10, 11 and 14 respectively.*

B:3C *Under* PACE, *section 16(2), a search warrant may authorise persons other than police officers to accompany the constable who executes the warrant. This includes, e.g. any suitably qualified or skilled person or an expert in a particular field whose presence is needed to help accurately identify the material sought or to advise where certain evidence is most likely to be found and how it should be dealt with. It does not give them any right to force entry, but it gives them the right to be on the premises during the search and to search for or seize property without the occupier's permission.*

B:4 Entry without warrant—particular powers

(a) *Making an arrest etc*

A–25

B:4.1 The conditions under which an officer may enter and search premises without a warrant are set out in *PACE*, section 17. It should be noted that this section does not create or confer any powers of arrest. See other powers in *Note 2B(a)*.

(b) *Search of premises where arrest takes place or the arrested person was immediately before arrest*

B:4.2 When a person has been arrested for an indictable offence, a police officer has power under *PACE*, section 32 to search the premises where the person was arrested or where the person was immediately before being arrested.

(c) *Search of premises occupied or controlled by the arrested person*

B:4.3 The specific powers to search premises occupied or controlled by a person arrested for an indictable offence are set out in *PACE*, section 18. They may not be exercised, except if section 18 (5) applies, unless an officer of inspector rank or above has given written authority. That authority should only be given when the authorising officer is satisfied the necessary grounds exist. If possible the authorising officer should record the authority on the Notice of Powers and Rights and, subject to paragraph 2.9, sign the notice. The record of the grounds for the search and the nature of the evidence sought as required by section 18(7) of the Act should be made in:

- the custody record if there is one, otherwise
- the officer's pocket book, or
- the search record.

B:5 Search with consent

B:5.1 Subject to paragraph 5.4, if it is proposed to search premises with the consent of a person entitled to grant entry the consent must, if practicable, be given in writing on the Notice of Powers and Rights before the search. The officer must make any necessary enquiries to be satisfied the person is in a position to give such consent. See *Notes 5A* and *5B*. **A–26**

B:5.2 Before seeking consent the officer in charge of the search shall state the purpose of the proposed search and its extent. This information must be as specific as possible, particularly regarding the articles or persons being sought and the parts of the premises to be searched. The person concerned must be clearly informed they are not obliged to consent and anything seized may be produced in evidence. If at the time the person is not suspected of an offence, the officer shall say this when stating the purpose of the search.

B:5.3 An officer cannot enter and search or continue to search premises under paragraph 5.1 if consent is given under duress or withdrawn before the search is completed.

B:5.4 It is unnecessary to seek consent under paragraphs 5.1 and 5.2 if this would cause disproportionate inconvenience to the person concerned. See *Note 5C*.

Notes for guidance

B:5A *In a lodging house or similar accommodation, every reasonable effort should be made to obtain the consent of the tenant, lodger or occupier. A search should not be made solely on the basis of the landlord's consent unless the tenant, lodger or occupier is unavailable and the matter is urgent.* **A–27**

B:5B *If the intention is to search premises under the authority of a warrant or a power of entry and search without warrant, and the occupier of the premises co-operates in accordance with paragraph 6.4, there is no need to obtain written consent.*

B:5C *Paragraph 5.4 is intended to apply when it is reasonable to assume innocent occupiers would agree to, and expect, police to take the proposed action, e.g. if:*

- *a suspect has fled the scene of a crime or to evade arrest and it is necessary quickly to check surrounding gardens and readily accessible places to see if the suspect is hiding*
- *police have arrested someone in the night after a pursuit and it is necessary to make a brief check of gardens along the pursuit route to see if stolen or incriminating articles have been discarded.*

B:6 Searching premises—general considerations

(a) *Time of searches*

B:6.1 Searches made under warrant must be made within three calendar months of the date of the warrant's issue. **A–28**

B:6.2 Searches must be made at a reasonable hour unless this might frustrate the purpose of the search.

B:6.3 When the extent or complexity of a search mean it is likely to take a long time, the officer in charge of the search may consider using the seize and sift powers referred to in section 7.

B:6.3A A warrant under *PACE*, section 8 may authorise entry to and search of premises on more than one occasion if, on the application, the justice of the peace is satisfied that it is necessary to authorise multiple entries in order to achieve the purpose for which the warrant is issued. No premises may be entered or searched on any subsequent occasions without the prior written authority of an officer of the rank of inspector who is not involved in the investigation. All other warrants authorise entry on one occasion only.

B:6.3B Where a warrant under *PACE*, section 8, or Schedule 1, paragraph 12 authorises entry to and search of all premises occupied or controlled by a specified person, no premises which are not specified in the warrant may be entered and searched without the prior written authority of an officer of the rank of inspector who is not involved in the investigation.

(b) *Entry other than with consent*

B:6.4 The officer in charge of the search shall first try to communicate with the occupier, or any other person entitled to grant access to the premises, explain the authority under which entry is sought and ask the occupier to allow entry, unless:

  (i) the search premises are unoccupied;

  (ii) the occupier and any other person entitled to grant access are absent;

  (iii) there are reasonable grounds for believing that alerting the occupier or any other person entitled to grant access would frustrate the object of the search or endanger officers or other people.

B:6.5 Unless sub-paragraph 6.4(iii) applies, if the premises are occupied the officer, subject to paragraph 2.9, shall, before the search begins:

  (i) identify him or herself, show their warrant card (if not in uniform) and state the purpose of and grounds for the search;

  (ii) identify and introduce any person accompanying the officer on the search (such persons should carry identification for production on request) and briefly describe that person's role in the process.

B:6.6 Reasonable and proportionate force may be used if necessary to enter premises if the officer in charge of the search is satisfied the premises are those specified in any warrant, or in exercise of the powers described in paragraph 4.1 to 4.3, and if:

  (i) the occupier or any other person entitled to grant access has refused entry;

  (ii) it is impossible to communicate with the occupier or any other person entitled to grant access; or

  (iii) any of the provisions of paragraph 6.4 apply.

(c) *Notice of powers and rights*

A–29   **B:6.7** If an officer conducts a search to which this code applies the officer shall, unless it is impracticable to do so, provide the occupier with a copy of a notice in a standard format:

  (i) specifying if the search is made under warrant, with consent, or in the exercise of the powers described in paragraphs 4.1 to 4.3; [Note: the notice format shall provide for authority or consent to be indicated, see paragraphs 4.3 and 5.1];

  (ii) summarising the extent of the powers of search and seizure conferred by *PACE*;

  (iii) explaining the rights of the occupier, and the owner of the property seized;

  (iv) explaining compensation may be payable in appropriate cases for damages [*sic*] caused entering and searching premises, and giving the address to send a compensation application, see *Note 6A*;

    (v) stating this code is available at any police station.

B:6.8 If the occupier is:

- present, copies of the notice and warrant shall, if practicable, be given to them before the search begins, unless the officer in charge of the search reasonably believes this would frustrate the object of the search or endanger officers or other people;

- not present, copies of the notice and warrant shall be left in a prominent place on the premises or appropriate part of the premises and endorsed, subject to paragraph 2.9 with the name of the officer in charge of the search, the date and time of the search.

The warrant shall be endorsed to show this has been done.

(d) *Conduct of searches*

B:6.9 Premises may be searched only to the extent necessary to achieve the object of the search, having regard to the size and nature of whatever is sought.

B:6.9A A search may not continue under:

- a warrant's authority once all the things specified in that warrant have been found;

- any other power once the object of that search has been achieved.

B:6.9B No search may continue once the officer in charge of the search is satisfied whatever is being sought is not on the premises. See *Note 6B*. This does not prevent a further search of the same premises if additional grounds come to light supporting a further application for a search warrant or exercise or further exercise of another power. For example, when, as a result of new information, it is believed articles previously not found or additional articles are on the premises.

B:6.10 Searches must be conducted with due consideration for the property and privacy of the occupier and with no more disturbance than necessary. Reasonable force may be used only when necessary and proportionate because the co-operation of the occupier cannot be obtained or is insufficient for the purpose. See *Note 6C*.

B:6.11 A friend, neighbour or other person must be allowed to witness the search if the occupier wishes unless the officer in charge of the search has reasonable grounds for believing the presence of the person asked for would seriously hinder the investigation or endanger officers or other people. A search need not be unreasonably delayed for this purpose. A record of the action taken should be made on the premises search record including the grounds for refusing the occupier's request.

B:6.12 A person is not required to be cautioned prior to being asked questions that are solely necessary for the purpose of furthering the proper and effective conduct of a search, see Code C, paragraph 10.1(c). For example, questions to discover the occupier of specified premises, to find a key to open a locked drawer or cupboard or to otherwise seek co-operation during the search or to determine if a particular item is liable to be seized.

B:6.12A If questioning goes beyond what is necessary for the purpose of the exemption in Code C, the exchange is likely to constitute an interview as defined by Code C, paragraph 11.1A and would require the associated safeguards included in Code C, section 10.

(e) *Leaving premises*

B:6.13 If premises have been entered by force, before leaving the officer in charge of the search must make sure they are secure by: **A–30**

- arranging for the occupier or their agent to be present;

- any other appropriate means.

(f) *Searches under PACE Schedule 1 or the Terrorism Act 2000, Schedule 5*

B:6.14 An officer shall be appointed as the officer in charge of the search, see paragraph 2.10, in respect of any search made under a warrant issued under

PACE Act 1984, Schedule 1 or the *Terrorism Act* 2000, Schedule 5. They are responsible for making sure the search is conducted with discretion and in a manner that causes the least possible disruption to any business or other activities carried out on the premises.

B:6.15 Once the officer in charge of the search is satisfied material may not be taken from the premises without their knowledge, they shall ask for the documents or other records concerned. The officer in charge of the search may also ask to see the index to files held on the premises, and the officers conducting the search may inspect any files which, according to the index, appear to contain the material sought. A more extensive search of the premises may be made only if:

- the person responsible for them refuses to:
  - produce the material sought, or
  - allow access to the index;
- it appears the index is:
  - inaccurate, or
  - incomplete;
- for any other reason the officer in charge of the search has reasonable grounds for believing such a search is necessary in order to find the material sought.

Notes for guidance

B:6A *Whether compensation is appropriate depends on the circumstances in each case. Compensation for damage caused when effecting entry is unlikely to be appropriate if the search was lawful, and the force used can be shown to be reasonable, proportionate and necessary to effect entry. If the wrong premises are searched by mistake everything possible should be done at the earliest opportunity to allay any sense of grievance and there should normally be a strong presumption in favour of paying compensation.*

B:6B *It is important that, when possible, all those involved in a search are fully briefed about any powers to be exercised and the extent and limits within which it should be conducted.*

B:6C *In all cases the number of officers and other persons involved in executing the warrant should be determined by what is reasonable and necessary according to the particular circumstances.*

B:7 Seizure and retention of property

(a) *Seizure*

B:7.1 Subject to paragraph 7.2, an officer who is searching any person or premises under any statutory power or with the consent of the occupier may seize anything:

(a) covered by a warrant;

(b) the officer has reasonable grounds for believing is evidence of an offence or has been obtained in consequence of the commission of an offence but only if seizure is necessary to prevent the items being concealed, lost, disposed of, altered, damaged, destroyed or tampered with;

(c) covered by the powers in the *Criminal Justice and Police Act* 2001, Part 2 allowing an officer to seize property from persons or premises and retain it for sifting or examination elsewhere.

See *Note 7B.*

B:7.2 No item may be seized which an officer has reasonable grounds for believing to be subject to legal privilege, as defined in *PACE*, section 10, other than under the *Criminal Justice and Police Act* 2001, Part 2.

B:7.3 Officers must be aware of the provisions in the *Criminal Justice and Police Act* 2001, section 59, allowing for applications to a judicial authority for the return of property seized and the subsequent duty to secure in section 60, see paragraph 7.12(iii).

B:7.4 An officer may decide it is not appropriate to seize property because of an explanation from the person holding it but may nevertheless have reasonable grounds for believing it was obtained in consequence of an offence by some person. In these circumstances, the officer should identify the property to the holder, inform the holder of their suspicions and explain the holder may be liable to civil or criminal proceedings if they dispose of, alter or destroy the property.

B:7.5 An officer may arrange to photograph, image or copy, any document or other article they have the power to seize in accordance with paragraph 7.1. This is subject to specific restrictions on the examination, imaging or copying of certain property seized under the *Criminal Justice and Police Act* 2001, Part 2. An officer must have regard to their statutory obligation to retain an original document or other article only when a photograph or copy is not sufficient.

B:7.6 If an officer considers information stored in any electronic form and accessible from the premises could be used in evidence, they may require the information to be produced in a form:

- which can be taken away and in which it is visible and legible; or
- from which it can readily be produced in a visible and legible form.

(b) *Criminal Justice and Police Act 2001: specific procedures for seize and sift powers*

B:7.7 The *Criminal Justice and Police Act* 2001, Part 2 gives officers limited powers **A–33** to seize property from premises or persons so they can sift or examine it elsewhere. Officers must be careful they only exercise these powers when it is essential and they do not remove any more material than necessary. The removal of large volumes of material, much of which may not ultimately be retainable, may have serious implications for the owners, particularly when they are involved in business or activities such as journalism or the provision of medical services. Officers must carefully consider if removing copies or images of relevant material or data would be a satisfactory alternative to removing originals. When originals are taken, officers must be prepared to facilitate the provision of copies or images for the owners when reasonably practicable. See *Note 7C*.

B:7.8 Property seized under the *Criminal Justice and Police Act* 2001, sections 50 or 51 must be kept securely and separately from any material seized under other powers. An examination under section 53 to determine which elements may be retained must be carried out at the earliest practicable time, having due regard to the desirability of allowing the person from whom the property was seized, or a person with an interest in the property, an opportunity of being present or represented at the examination.

B:7.8A All reasonable steps should be taken to accommodate an interested person's request to be present, provided the request is reasonable and subject to the need to prevent harm to, interference with, or unreasonable delay to the investigatory process. If an examination proceeds in the absence of an interested person who asked to attend or their representative, the officer who exercised the relevant seizure power must give that person a written notice of why the examination was carried out in those circumstances. If it is necessary for security reasons or to maintain confidentiality officers may exclude interested persons from decryption or other processes which facilitate the examination but do not form part of it. See *Note 7D*.

B:7.9 It is the responsibility of the officer in charge of the investigation to make sure property is returned in accordance with sections 53 to 55. Material which there is no power to retain must be:

- separated from the rest of the seized property;
- returned as soon as reasonably practicable after examination of all the seized property.

B:7.9A Delay is only warranted if very clear and compelling reasons exist, *e.g.* the:

- unavailability of the person to whom the material is to be returned;
- need to agree a convenient time to return a large volume of material.

B:7.9B Legally privileged, excluded or special procedure material which cannot be retained must be returned:

- as soon as reasonably practicable;
- without waiting for the whole examination.

B:7.9C As set out in section 58, material must be returned to the person from whom it was seized, except when it is clear some other person has a better right to it. See *Note 7E.*

B:7.10 When an officer involved in the investigation has reasonable grounds to believe a person with a relevant interest in property seized under section 50 or 51 intends to make an application under section 59 for the return of any legally privileged, special procedure or excluded material, the officer in charge of the investigation should be informed as soon as practicable and the material seized should be kept secure in accordance with section 61. See *Note 7C.*

B:7.11 The officer in charge of the investigation is responsible for making sure property is properly secured. Securing involves making sure the property is not examined, copied, imaged or put to any other use except at the request, or with the consent, of the applicant or in accordance with the directions of the appropriate judicial authority. Any request, consent or directions must be recorded in writing and signed by both the initiator and the officer in charge of the investigation. See *Notes 7F* and *7G.*

B:7.12 When an officer exercises a power of seizure conferred by sections 50 or 51 they shall provide the occupier of the premises or the person from whom the property is being seized with a written notice:

- (i) specifying what has been seized under the powers conferred by that section;
- (ii) specifying the grounds for those powers;
- (iii) setting out the effect of sections 59 to 61 covering the grounds for a person with a relevant interest in seized property to apply to a judicial authority for its return and the duty of officers to secure property in certain circumstances when an application is made;
- (iv) specifying the name and address of the person to whom:
  - notice of an application to the appropriate judicial authority in respect of any of the seized property must be given;
  - an application may be made to allow attendance at the initial examination of the property.

B:7.13 If the occupier is not present but there is someone in charge of the premises, the notice shall be given to them. If no suitable person is available, so the notice will easily be found it should either be:

- left in a prominent place on the premises;
- attached to the exterior of the premises.

(c) *Retention*

B:7.14 Subject to paragraph 7.15, anything seized in accordance with the above provisions may be retained only for as long as is necessary. It may be retained, among other purposes:

- (i) for use as evidence at a trial for an offence;
- (ii) to facilitate the use in any investigation or proceedings of anything to which it is inextricably linked, see *Note 7H;*
- (iii) for forensic examination or other investigation in connection with an offence;
- (iv) in order to establish its lawful owner when there are reasonable grounds for believing it has been stolen or obtained by the commission of an offence.

B:7.15 Property shall not be retained under paragraph 7.14(i), (ii) or (iii) if a copy or image would be sufficient.

(d) *Rights of owners etc*

B:7.16 If property is retained, the person who had custody or control of it immediately before seizure must, on request, be provided with a list or description of the property within a reasonable time.

B:7.17 That person or their representative must be allowed supervised access to the property to examine it or have it photographed or copied, or must be provided with a photograph or copy, in either case within a reasonable time of any request and at their own expense, unless the officer in charge of an investigation has reasonable grounds for believing this would:

    (i) prejudice the investigation of any offence or criminal proceedings; or

    (ii) lead to the commission of an offence by providing access to unlawful material such as pornography.

A record of the grounds shall be made when access is denied.

Notes for guidance

B:7A *Any person claiming property seized by the police may apply to a magistrates' court* **A–35** *under the* Police (Property) Act *1897 for its possession and should, if appropriate, be advised of this procedure.*

B:7B *The powers of seizure conferred by* PACE, *sections 18(2) and 19(3) extend to the seizure of the whole premises when it is physically possible to seize and retain the premises in their totality and practical considerations make seizure desirable. For example, police may remove premises such as tents, vehicles or caravans to a police station for the purpose of preserving evidence.*

B:7C *Officers should consider reaching agreement with owners and/or other interested parties on the procedures for examining a specific set of property, rather than awaiting the judicial authority's determination. Agreement can sometimes give a quicker and more satisfactory route for all concerned and minimise costs and legal complexities.*

B:7D *What constitutes a relevant interest in specific material may depend on the nature of that material and the circumstances in which it is seized. Anyone with a reasonable claim to ownership of the material and anyone entrusted with its safe keeping by the owner should be considered.*

B:7E *Requirements to secure and return property apply equally to all copies, images or other material created because of seizure of the original property.*

B:7F *The mechanics of securing property vary according to the circumstances; "bagging up", i.e. placing material in sealed bags or containers and strict subsequent control of access is the appropriate procedure in many cases.*

B:7G *When material is seized under the powers of seizure conferred by* PACE, *the duty to retain it under the code of practice issued under the* Criminal Procedure and Investigations Act *1996 is subject to the provisions on retention of seized material in* PACE, *section 22.*

B:7H *Paragraph 7.14(ii) applies if inextricably linked material is seized under the* Criminal Justice and Police Act *2001, sections 50 or 51. Inextricably linked material is material it is not reasonably practicable to separate from other linked material without prejudicing the use of that other material in any investigation or proceedings. For example, it may not be possible to separate items of data held on computer disk without damaging their evidential integrity. Inextricably linked material must not be examined, imaged, copied or used for any purpose other than for proving the source and/or integrity of the linked material.*

B:8 Action after searches

B:8.1 If premises are searched in circumstances where this code applies, unless **A–36** the exceptions in paragraph 2.3(a) apply, on arrival at a police station the officer in charge of the search shall make or have made a record of the search, to include:

    (i) the address of the searched premises;

    (ii) the date, time and duration of the search;

    (iii) the authority used for the search:

- if the search was made in exercise of a statutory power to search premises without warrant, the power which was used for the search:
- if the search was made under a warrant or with written consent;
  - a copy of the warrant and the written authority to apply for it, see paragraph 3.4; or
  - the written consent;

  shall be appended to the record or the record shall show the location of the copy warrant or consent;

(iv) subject to paragraph 2.9, the names of:
  - the officer(s) in charge of the search;
  - all other officers and any authorised persons who conducted the search;

(v) the names of any people on the premises if they are known;

(vi) any grounds for refusing the occupier's request to have someone present during the search, see paragraph 6.11;

(vii) a list of any articles seized or the location of a list and, if not covered by a warrant, the grounds for their seizure;

(viii) whether force was used, and the reason;

(ix) details of any damage caused during the search, and the circumstances;

(x) if applicable, the reason it was not practicable:
  (a) to give the occupier a copy of the notice of powers and rights, see paragraph 6.7;
  (b) before the search to give the occupier a copy of the notice, see paragraph 6.8;

(xi) when the occupier was not present, the place where copies of the notice of powers and rights and search warrant were left on the premises, see paragraph 6.8.

B:8.2 On each occasion when premises are searched under warrant, the warrant authorising the search on that occasion shall be endorsed to show:

(i) if any articles specified in the warrant were found and the address where found;

(ii) if any other articles were seized;

(iii) the date and time it was executed and if present, the name of the occupier or if the occupier is not present the name of the person in charge of the premises;

(iv) subject to paragraph 2.9, the names of the officers who executed it and any authorised persons who accompanied them;

(v) if a copy, together with a copy of the notice of powers and rights was:
  - handed to the occupier;
  - or endorsed as required by paragraph 6.8; and left on the premises and where.

B:8.3 Any warrant shall be returned within three calendar months of its issue or sooner on completion of the search(es) authorised by that warrant, if it was issued by a:

- justice of the peace, to the designated officer for the local justice area in which the justice was acting when issuing the warrant; or
- judge, to the appropriate officer of the court concerned.

B:9 Search registers

A–37   **B:**9.1 A search register will be maintained at each sub-divisional or equivalent police station. All search records required under paragraph 8.1 shall be made, copied, or referred to in the register. See *Note 9A.*

Note for guidance

B:9A *Paragraph 9.1 also applies to search records made by immigration officers. In these cases, a search register must also be maintained at an immigration office. See also Note 2D.*

(4) Detention, treatment and questioning of persons

The text that follows is of the version of the code that came into force on February 1, 2008: see *ante*, Appendix A–1.

For authorities in relation to Code C, see, in particular, §§ 15–210 *et seq.* (right of access to solicitor), § 15–251 (general), § 15–352 (confessions), § 15–425 (sufficient evidence for prosecution to succeed), §§ 15–452 *et seq.* (discretionary exclusion of evidence) in the main work.

C. Code of Practice for the Detention, Treatment and Questioning of Persons by Police Officers

Commencement—Transitional arrangements

This code applies to people in police detention after midnight on January 31, 2008, notwithstanding that their period of detention may have commenced before that time.

C:1 General

C:1.1 All persons in custody must be dealt with expeditiously, and released as soon as the need for detention no longer applies.

C:1.1A A custody officer must perform the functions in this code as soon as practicable. A custody officer will not be in breach of this code if delay is justifiable and reasonable steps are taken to prevent unnecessary delay. The custody record shall show when a delay has occurred and the reason. See *Note 1H*.

C:1.2 This code of practice must be readily available at all police stations for consultation by:

- police officers;
- police staff;
- detained persons;
- members of the public.

C:1.3 The provisions of this code:

- include the *Annexes*;
- do not include the *Notes for Guidance*.

C:1.4 If an officer has any suspicion, or is told in good faith, that a person of any age may be mentally disordered or otherwise mentally vulnerable, in the absence of clear evidence to dispel that suspicion, the person shall be treated as such for the purposes of this code. See *Note 1G*.

C:1.5 If anyone appears to be under 17, they shall be treated as a juvenile for the purposes of this code in the absence of clear evidence that they are older.

C:1.6 If a person appears to be blind, seriously visually impaired, deaf, unable to read or speak or has difficulty orally because of a speech impediment, they shall be treated as such for the purposes of this code in the absence of clear evidence to the contrary.

C:1.7 "The appropriate adult" means, in the case of a:

    (a) juvenile:

        (i) the parent, guardian or, if the juvenile is in local authority or voluntary organisation care, or is otherwise being looked after

A–38

A–39

A–40

A–41

> > under the *Children Act* 1989, a person representing that authorit
> > or organisation;
> > (ii) a social worker of a local authority;
> > (iii) failing these, some other responsible adult aged 18 or over who i
> > not a police officer or employed by the police;
> >
> > (b) person who is mentally disordered or mentally vulnerable: see *Note 1D*;
> > (iv) a relative, guardian or other person responsible for their care o
> > custody;
> > (v) someone experienced in dealing with mentally disordered o
> > mentally vulnerable people but who is not a police officer o
> > employed by the police;
> > (vi) failing these, some other responsible adult aged 18 or over who i
> > not a police officer or employed by the police.

C:1.8 If this code requires a person be given certain information, they do no
have to be given it if at the time they are incapable of understanding what is said
are violent or may become violent or in urgent need of medical attention, bu
they must be given it as soon as practicable.

C:1.9 References to a custody officer include any:—

- police officer; or
- designated staff custody officer acting in the exercise or performance o
  the powers and duties conferred or imposed on them by their designa
  tion,

performing the functions of a custody officer. See *Note 1J*.

C:1.9A When this code requires the prior authority or agreement of an office
of at least inspector or superintendent rank, that authority may be given by
sergeant or chief inspector authorised to perform the functions of the higher ranl
under the *Police and Criminal Evidence Act* 1984 (*PACE*), section 107.

C:1.10 Subject to paragraph 1.12, this Code applies to people in custody at po
lice stations in England and Wales, whether or not they have been arrested, an
to those removed to a police station as a place of safety under the *Mental Healt
Act* 1983, sections 135 and 136. Section 15 applies solely to people in police deten
tion, *e.g.* those brought to a police station under arrest or arrested at a police statio
for an offence after going there voluntarily.

C:1.11 People detained under the *Terrorism Act* 2000, Schedule 8 and section 4
and other provisions of that Act are not subject to any part of this code. Such person
are subject to the code of practice for detention, treatment and questioning o
persons by police officers detained [*sic*] under that Act.

C:1.12 This code's provisions do not apply to people in custody:

> (i) arrested on warrants issued in Scotland by officers under the *Crimina
> Justice and Public Order Act* 1994, section 136(2), or arrested or detaine
> without warrant by officers from a police force in Scotland under sectio
> 137(2); in these cases, police powers and duties and the person's right
> and entitlements whilst at a police station in England or Wales are th
> same as those in Scotland;
>
> (ii) arrested under the *Immigration and Asylum Act* 1999, section 142(3) in o
> der to have their fingerprints taken;
>
> (iii) whose detention is authorised by an immigration officer under the *Im
> migration Act* 1971;
>
> (iv) who are convicted or remanded prisoners held in police cells on behalf o
> the Prison Service under the *Imprisonment (Temporary Provisions) Ac
> 1980;
>
> (v) [*not used*];
>
> (vi) detained for searches under stop and search powers except as require
> by Code A.

The provisions on conditions of detention and treatment in sections 8 and 9 must b
considered as the minimum standards of treatment for such detainees.

C:1.13 In this Code:

    (a) "designated person" means a person other than a police officer, designated under the *Police Reform Act* 2002, Part 4 who has specified powers and duties of police officers conferred or imposed on them;

    (b) reference to a police officer includes a designated person acting in the exercise or performance of the powers and duties conferred or imposed on them by their designation.

C:1.14 Designated persons are entitled to use reasonable force as follows:— **A–42**

    (a) when exercising a power conferred on them which allows a police officer exercising that power to use reasonable force, a designated person has the same entitlement to use force; and

    (b) at other times when carrying out duties conferred or imposed on them that also entitle them to use reasonable force, for example:

- when at a police station carrying out the duty to keep detainees for whom they are responsible under control and to assist any other police officer or designated person to keep any detainee under control and to prevent their escape;
- when securing, or assisting any other police officer or designated person in securing, the detention of a person at a police station;
- when escorting, or assisting any other police officer or designated person in escorting, a detainee within a police station;
- for the purpose of saving life or limb; or
- preventing serious damage to property.

C:1.15 Nothing in this code prevents the custody officer, or other officer given custody of the detainee, from allowing police staff who are not designated persons to carry out individual procedures or tasks at the police station if the law allows. However, the officer remains responsible for making sure the procedures and tasks are carried out correctly in accordance with the codes of practice. Any such person must be:

    (a) a person employed by a police authority maintaining a police force and under the control and direction of the chief officer of that force;

    (b) employed by a person with whom a police authority has a contract for the provision of services relating to persons arrested or otherwise in custody.

C:1.16 Designated persons and other police staff must have regard to any relevant provisions of the codes of practice.

C:1.17 References to pocket books include any official report book issued to police officers or other police staff.

Notes for guidance

C:1A *Although certain sections of this code apply specifically to people in custody at police stations, those there voluntarily to assist with an investigation should be treated with no less consideration, e.g. offered refreshments at appropriate times, and enjoy an absolute right to obtain legal advice or communicate with anyone outside the police station.* **A–43**

C:1B *A person, including a parent or guardian, should not be an appropriate adult if they:*

- *are*
  - *suspected of involvement in the offence;*
  - *the victim;*
  - *a witness;*
  - *involved in the investigation;*
- *received admissions prior to attending to act as the appropriate adult.*

    Note: If a juvenile's parent is estranged from the juvenile, they should not be asked to act as the appropriate adult if the juvenile expressly and specifically objects to their presence.

C:1C *If a juvenile admits an offence to, or in the presence of, a social worker or member* *of a youth offending team other than during the time that person is acting as the juvenile's appropriate adult, another appropriate adult should be appointed in the interest of fairness.*

C:1D *In the case of people who are mentally disordered or otherwise mentally vulnerable, it may be more satisfactory if the appropriate adult is someone experienced or trained in their care rather than a relative lacking such qualifications. But if the detainee prefers a relative to a better qualified stranger or objects to a particular person their wishes should, if practicable, be respected.*

C:1E *A detainee should always be given an opportunity, when an appropriate adult is called to the police station, to consult privately with a solicitor in the appropriate adult's absence if they want. An appropriate adult is not subject to legal privilege.*

C:1F *A solicitor or independent custody visitor (formerly a lay visitor) present at the police station in that capacity may not be the appropriate adult.*

C:1G *"Mentally vulnerable" applies to any detainee who, because of their mental state or capacity, may not understand the significance of what is said, of questions or of their replies. "Mental disorder" is defined in the* Mental Health Act 1983, *section 1(2) as "mental illness, arrested or incomplete development of mind, psychopathic disorder and any other disorder or disability of mind". When the custody officer has any doubt about the mental state or capacity of a detainee, that detainee should be treated as mentally vulnerable and an appropriate adult called.*

C:1H *Paragraph 1.1A is intended to cover delays which may occur in processing detainees* e.g. *if:*

- *a large number of suspects are brought into the station simultaneously to be placed in custody;*
- *interview rooms are all being used;*
- *there are difficulties contacting an appropriate adult, solicitor or interpreter.*

C:1I *The custody officer must remind the appropriate adult and detainee about the right to legal advice and record any reasons for waiving it in accordance with section 6.*

C:1J *The designation of police staff custody officers applies only in police areas where an order commencing the provisions of the* Police Reform Act 2002, *section 38 and Schedule 4A, for designating police staff custody officers is in effect.*

C:1K *This code does not affect the principle that all citizens have a duty to help police officers to prevent crime and discover offenders. This is a civic rather than a legal duty; but when a police officer is trying to discover whether, or by whom, an offence has been committed he is entitled to question any person from whom he thinks useful information can be obtained, subject to the restrictions imposed by this code. A person's declaration that he is unwilling to reply does not alter this entitlement.*

C:2 Custody records

A–44

C:2.1A When a person is brought to a police station:

- under arrest;
- is arrested [*sic*] at the police station having attended there voluntarily; or
- attends [*sic*] a police station to answer bail,

they should be brought before the custody officer as soon as practicable after their arrival at the station or, if appropriate, following arrest after attending the police station voluntarily. This applies to designated and non-designated police stations. A person is deemed to be "at a police station" for these purposes if they are within the boundary of any building or enclosed yard which forms part of that police station.

C:2.1 A separate custody record must be opened as soon as practicable for each person brought to a police station under arrest or arrested at the station having gone there voluntarily or attending a police station in answer to street bail. All information recorded under this code must be recorded as soon as practicable in the custody record unless otherwise specified. Any audio or video recording made in the custody area is not part of the custody record.

C:2.2 If any action requires the authority of an officer of a specified rank, subject to paragraph 2.6A, their name and rank must be noted in the custody record.

C:2.3 The custody officer is responsible for the custody record's accuracy and completeness and for making sure the record or copy of the record accompanies a detainee if they are transferred to another police station. The record shall show the:

- time and reason for transfer;
- time a person is released from detention.

C:2.4 A solicitor or appropriate adult must be permitted to consult a detainee's custody record as soon as practicable after their arrival at the station and at any other time whilst the person is detained. Arrangements for this access must be agreed with the custody officer and may not unreasonably interfere with the custody officer's duties.

C:2.4A When a detainee leaves police detention or is taken before a court they, their legal representative or appropriate adult shall be given, on request, a copy of the custody record as soon as practicable. This entitlement lasts for 12 months after release.

C:2.5 The detainee, appropriate adult or legal representative shall be permitted to inspect the original custody record after the detainee has left police detention provided they give reasonable notice of their request. Any such inspection shall be noted in the custody record.

C:2.6 Subject to paragraph 2.6A, all entries in custody records must be timed and signed by the maker. Records entered on computer shall be timed and contain the operator's identification.

C:2.6A Nothing in this code requires the identity of officers or other police staff to be recorded or disclosed:

(a) [*not used*]
(b) if the officer or police staff reasonably believe recording or disclosing their name might put them in danger.

In these cases, they shall use their warrant or other identification numbers and the name of their police station. See *Note 2A.*

C:2.7 The fact and time of any detainee's refusal to sign a custody record, when asked in accordance with this code, must be recorded.

Note for guidance

C:2A *The purpose of paragraph 2.6A(b) is to protect those involved in serious organised crime investigations or arrests of particularly violent suspects when there is reliable information that those arrested or their associates may threaten or cause harm to those involved. In cases of doubt, an officer of inspector rank or above should be consulted.* **A–45**

C:3 Initial action

(a) *Detained persons—normal procedure*

C:3.1 When a person is brought to a police station under arrest or arrested at **A–46** the station having gone there voluntarily, the custody officer must make sure the person is told clearly about the following continuing rights which may be exercised at any stage during the period in custody:

(i) the right to have someone informed of their arrest as in section 5;
(ii) the right to consult privately with a solicitor and that free independent legal advice is available;
(iii) the right to consult these codes of practice. See *Note 3D.*

C:3.2 The detainee must also be given:

- a written notice setting out:
  - the above three rights;
  - the arrangements for obtaining legal advice;
  - the right to a copy of the custody record as in paragraph 2.4A;

    – the caution in the terms prescribed in section 10;

    ● an additional written notice briefly setting out their entitlements while in custody, see *Notes 3A* and *3B*.

Note: the detainee shall be asked to sign the custody record to acknowledge receipt of these notices. Any refusal must be recorded on the custody record.

C:3.3 A citizen of an independent Commonwealth country or a national of a foreign country, including the Republic of Ireland, must be informed as soon a practicable about their rights of communication with their High Commission embassy or consulate; see *section 7*;

C:3.4 The custody officer shall:

    ● record the offence(s) that the detainee has been arrested for and the reason(s) for the arrest on the custody record; see paragraph 10.3 and Code G paragraphs 2.2 and 4.3;

    ● note on the custody record any comment the detainee makes in relation to the arresting officer's account but shall not invite comment. If the arresting officer is not physically present when the detainee is brought to a police station, the arresting officer's account must be made available to the custody officer remotely or by a third party on the arresting officer's behalf. If the custody officer authorises a person's detention the detainee must be informed of the grounds as soon as practicable and before they are questioned about any offence;

    ● note any comment the detainee makes in respect of the decision to detain them but shall not invite comment;

    ● not put specific questions to the detainee regarding their involvement in any offence, nor in respect of any comments they may make in response to the arresting officer's account or the decision to place them in detention. Such an exchange is likely to constitute an interview as in paragraph 11.1A and require the associated safeguards in section 11.

See paragraph 11.13 in respect of unsolicited comments.

C:3.5 The custody officer shall:

    (a) ask the detainee, whether at this time, they:

        (i) would like legal advice, see paragraph 6.5;

        (ii) want someone informed of their detention, see section 5;

    (b) ask the detainee to sign the custody record to confirm their decisions in respect of (a);

    (c) determine whether the detainee:

        (i) is, or might be, in need of medical treatment or attention, see section 9;

        (ii) requires:

            ● an appropriate adult;

            ● help to check documentation;

            ● an interpreter;

    (d) record the decision in respect of (c).

C:3.6 When determining these needs the custody officer is responsible for initiating an assessment to consider whether the detainee is likely to present specific risks to custody staff or themselves. Such assessments should always include a check on the Police National Computer, to be carried out as soon as practicable, to identify any risks highlighted in relation to the detainee. Although such assessments are primarily the custody officer's responsibility, it may be necessary for them to consult and involve others, *e.g.* the arresting officer or an appropriate health care professional, see paragraph 9.13. Reasons for delaying the initiation or completion of the assessment must be recorded.

C:3.7 Chief officers should ensure that arrangements for proper and effective risk assessments required by paragraph 3.6 are implemented in respect of all detainees at police stations in their area.

C:3.8 Risk assessments must follow a structured process which clearly defines the categories of risk to be considered and the results must be incorporated in the detainee's custody record. The custody officer is responsible for making sure those responsible for the detainee's custody are appropriately briefed about the risks. If no specific risks are identified by the assessment, that should be noted in the custody record. See *Note 3E* and paragraph 9.14.

C:3.9 The custody officer is responsible for implementing the response to any specific risk assessment, *e.g.*:

- reducing opportunities for self harm;
- calling a health care professional;
- increasing levels of monitoring or observation.

C:3.10 Risk assessment is an ongoing process and assessments must always be subject to review if circumstances change.

C:3.11 If video cameras are installed in the custody area, notices shall be prominently displayed showing cameras are in use. Any request to have video cameras switched off shall be refused.

(b) *Detained persons—special groups*

C:3.12 If the detainee appears deaf or there is doubt about their hearing or **A-47** speaking ability or ability to understand English, and the custody officer cannot establish effective communication, the custody officer must, as soon as practicable, call an interpreter for assistance in the action under paragraphs 3.1–3.5. See section 13.

C:3.13 If the detainee is a juvenile, the custody officer must, if it is practicable, ascertain the identity of a person responsible for their welfare. That person:

- may be:
  - the parent or guardian;
  - if the juvenile is in local authority or voluntary organisation care, or is otherwise being looked after under the *Children Act* 1989, a person appointed by that authority or organisation to have responsibility for the juvenile's welfare;
  - any other person who has, for the time being, assumed responsibility for the juvenile's welfare;
- must be informed as soon as practicable that the juvenile has been arrested, why they have been arrested and where they are detained. This right is in addition to the juvenile's right in section 5 not to be held incommunicado. See *Note 3C*.

C:3.14 If a juvenile is known to be subject to a court order under which a person or organisation is given any degree of statutory responsibility to supervise or otherwise monitor them, reasonable steps must also be taken to notify that person or organisation (the "responsible officer"). The responsible officer will normally be a member of a youth offending team, except for a curfew order which involves electronic monitoring when the contractor providing the monitoring will normally be the responsible officer.

C:3.15 If the detainee is a juvenile, mentally disordered or otherwise mentally vulnerable, the custody officer must, as soon as practicable:

- inform the appropriate adult, who in the case of a juvenile may or may not be a person responsible for their welfare, as in paragraph 3.13, of:
  - the grounds for their detention;
  - their whereabouts;
- ask the adult to come to the police station to see the detainee.

C:3.16 It is imperative that a mentally disordered or otherwise mentally vulnerable person, detained under the *Mental Health Act* 1983, section 136, be assessed as soon as possible. If that assessment is to take place at the police station, an approved social worker and a registered medical practitioner shall be called to the station as soon as possible in order to interview and examine the detainee. Once the detainee has been interviewed, examined and suitable arrangements made for their treatment or care, they can no longer be detained under section 136. A detainee must be immediately discharged from detention under section 136 if a registered medical practitioner, having examined them, concludes they are not mentally disordered within the meaning of the Act.

C:3.17 If the appropriate adult is:

- already at the police station, the provisions of paragraphs 3.1 to 3.5 must be complied with in the appropriate adult's presence;
- not at the station when these provisions are complied with, they must be complied with again in the presence of the appropriate adult when they arrive.

C:3.18 The detainee shall be advised that:

- the duties of the appropriate adult include giving advice and assistance;
- they can consult privately with the appropriate adult at any time.

C:3.19 If the detainee, or appropriate adult on the detainee's behalf, asks for a solicitor to be called to give legal advice, the provisions of section 6 apply.

C:3.20 If the detainee is blind, seriously visually impaired or unable to read the custody officer shall make sure their solicitor, relative, appropriate adult or some other person likely to take an interest in them and not involved in the investigation is available to help check any documentation. When this code requires written consent or signing the person assisting may be asked to sign instead, if the detainee prefers. This paragraph does not require an appropriate adult to be called solely to assist in checking and signing documentation for a person who is not a juvenile, or mentally disordered or otherwise mentally vulnerable (see paragraph 3.15).

(c) Persons attending a police station voluntarily

A–48

C:3.21 Anybody attending a police station voluntarily to assist with an investigation may leave at will unless arrested. See *Note 1K.* If it is decided they shall not be allowed to leave, they must be informed at once that they are under arrest and brought before the custody officer, who is responsible for making sure they are notified of their rights in the same way as other detainees. If they are not arrested but are cautioned as in section 10, the person who gives the caution must, at the same time, inform them they are not under arrest, they are not obliged to remain at the station but if they remain at the station they may obtain free and independent legal advice if they want. They shall be told the right to legal advice includes the right to speak with a solicitor on the telephone and be asked if they want to do so.

C:3.22 If a person attending the police station voluntarily asks about their entitlement to legal advice, they shall be given a copy of the notice explaining the arrangements for obtaining legal advice. See paragraph 3.2.

(d) Documentation

C:3.23 The grounds for a person's detention shall be recorded, in the person's presence if practicable.

C:3.24 Action taken under paragraphs 3.12 to 3.20 shall be recorded.

(e) Persons answering street bail

C:3.25 When a person is answering street bail, the custody officer should link any documentation held in relation to arrest with the custody record. Any further action shall be recorded on the custody record in accordance with paragraphs 3.23 and 3.24 above.

Notes for guidance

A–49

C:3A *The notice of entitlements should:*

- *list the entitlements in this code, including:*
  - *visits and contact with outside parties, including special provisions for Commonwealth citizens and foreign nationals;*

  – *reasonable standards of physical comfort;*
  – *adequate food and drink;*
  – *access to toilets and washing facilities, clothing, medical attention, and exercise when practicable;*
 ● *mention the:*
  – *provisions relating to the conduct of interviews;*
  – *circumstances in which an appropriate adult should be available to assist the detainee and their statutory rights to make representation whenever the period of their detention is reviewed.*

C:3B *In addition to notices in English, translations should be available in Welsh, the main minority ethnic languages and the principal European languages, whenever they are likely to be helpful. Audio versions of the notice should also be made available.*

C:3C *If the juvenile is in local authority or voluntary organisation care but living with their parents or other adults responsible for their welfare, although there is no legal obligation to inform them, they should normally be contacted, as well as the authority or organisation unless suspected of involvement in the offence concerned. Even if the juvenile is not living with their parents, consideration should be given to informing them.*

C:3D *The right to consult the codes of practice does not entitle the person concerned to delay unreasonably any necessary investigative or administrative action whilst they do so. Examples of action which need not be delayed unreasonably include:*

 ● *procedures requiring the provision of breath, blood or urine specimens under the* Road Traffic Act *1988 or the* Transport and Works Act *1992;*
 ● *searching detainees at the police station;*
 ● *taking fingerprints, footwear impressions or non-intimate samples without consent for evidential purposes.*

C:3E *Home Office Circular 32/2000 provides more detailed guidance on risk assessments and identifies key risk areas which should always be considered.*

C:4 Detainee's property

(a) *Action*

C:4.1 The custody officer is responsible for: **A–50**
  (a) ascertaining what property a detainee:
  (i) has with them when they come to the police station, whether on:
   ● arrest or re-detention on answering to bail;
   ● commitment to prison custody on the order or sentence of a court;
   ● lodgement at the police station with a view to their production in court from prison custody;
   ● transfer from detention at another station or hospital;
   ● detention under the *Mental Health Act* 1983, section 135 or 136;
   ● remand into police custody on the authority of a court;
  (ii) might have acquired for an unlawful or harmful purpose while in custody;
  (b) the safekeeping of any property taken from a detainee which remains at the police station.

The custody officer may search the detainee or authorise their being searched to the extent they consider necessary, provided a search of intimate parts of the body or involving the removal of more than outer clothing is only made as in Annex A. A search may only be carried out by an officer of the same sex as the detainee. See *Note 4A.*

C:4.2 Detainees may retain clothing and personal effects at their own risk unless the custody officer considers they may use them to cause harm to themselves or others, interfere with evidence, damage property, effect an escape or they are needed as evidence. In this event the custody officer may withhold such articles as they consider necessary and must tell the detainee why.

C:4.3 Personal effects are those items a detainee may lawfully need, use or refer to while in detention but do not include cash and other items of value.

(b) *Documentation*

C:4.4 It is a matter for the custody officer to determine whether a record should be made of the property a detained person has with him or had taken from him on arrest. Any record made is not required to be kept as part of the custody record but the custody record should be noted as to where such a record exists. Whenever a record is made the detainee shall be allowed to check and sign the record of property as correct. Any refusal to sign shall be recorded.

C:4.5 If a detainee is not allowed to keep any article of clothing or personal effects, the reason must be recorded.

Notes for guidance

A–51   C:4A PACE, *section 54(1) and paragraph 4.1 require a detainee to be searched when it is clear the custody officer will have continuing duties in relation to that detainee or when that detainee's behaviour or offence makes an inventory appropriate. They do not require every detainee to be searched, e.g. if it is clear a person will only be detained for a short period and is not to be placed in a cell, the custody officer may decide not to search them. In such a case the custody record will be endorsed "not searched", paragraph 4.4 will not apply, and the detainee will be invited to sign the entry. If the detainee refuses, the custody officer will be obliged to ascertain what property they have in accordance with paragraph 4.1.*

C:4B *Paragraph 4.4 does not require the custody officer to record on the custody record property in the detainee's possession on arrest if, by virtue of its nature, quantity or size, it is not practicable to remove it to the police station.*

C:4C *Paragraph 4.4 does not require items of clothing worn by the person be recorded unless withheld by the custody officer as in paragraph 4.2.*

C:5 Right not to be held incommunicado

(a) *Action*

A–52   C:5.1 Any person arrested and held in custody at a police station or other premises may, on request, have one person known to them or likely to take an interest in their welfare informed at public expense of their whereabouts as soon as practicable. If the person cannot be contacted the detainee may choose up to two alternatives. If they cannot be contacted, the person in charge of detention or the investigation has discretion to allow further attempts until the information has been conveyed. See *Notes 5C* and *5D*.

C:5.2 The exercise of the above right in respect of each person nominated may be delayed only in accordance with Annex B.

C:5.3 The above right may be exercised each time a detainee is taken to another police station.

C:5.4 The detainee may receive visits at the custody officer's discretion. See *Note 5B*.

C:5.5 If a friend, relative or person with an interest in the detainee's welfare enquires about their whereabouts, this information shall be given if the suspect agrees and Annex B does not apply. See *Note 5D*.

C:5.6 The detainee shall be given writing materials, on request, and allowed to telephone one person for a reasonable time, see *Notes 5A* and *5E*. Either or both these privileges may be denied or delayed if an officer of inspector rank or above considers sending a letter or making a telephone call may result in any of the consequences in:

    (a) Annex B, paragraphs 1 and 2 and the person is detained in connection with an indictable offence; or

    (b) [*not used*].

Nothing in this paragraph permits the restriction or denial of the rights in paragraphs 5.1 and 6.1.

C:5.7 Before any letter or message is sent, or telephone call made, the detainee shall be informed that what they say in any letter, call or message (other than in a communication to a solicitor) may be read or listened to and may be given in evidence. A telephone call may be terminated if it is being abused. The costs can be at public expense at the custody officer's discretion.

C:5.7A Any delay or denial of the rights in this section should be proportionate and should last no longer than necessary.

(b) *Documentation*

C:5.8 A record must be kept of any:

    (a) request made under this section and the action taken;

    (b) letters, messages or telephone calls made or received or visit received;

    (c) refusal by the detainee to have information about them given to an outside enquirer. The detainee must be asked to countersign the record accordingly and any refusal recorded.

Notes for guidance

C:5A *A person may request an interpreter to interpret a telephone call or translate a*   **A–53**
letter.

C:5B *At the custody officer's discretion, visits should be allowed when possible, subject to having sufficient personnel to supervise a visit and any possible hindrance to the investigation.*

C:5C *If the detainee does not know anyone to contact for advice or support or cannot contact a friend or relative, the custody officer should bear in mind any local voluntary bodies or other organisations who might be able to help. Paragraph 6.1 applies if legal advice is required.*

C:5D *In some circumstances it may not be appropriate to use the telephone to disclose information under paragraphs 5.1 and 5.5.*

C:5E *The telephone call at paragraph 5.6 is in addition to any communication under paragraphs 5.1 and 6.1.*

C:6 Right to legal advice

(a) *Action*

C:6.1 Unless Annex B applies, all detainees must be informed that they may at   **A–54**
any time consult and communicate privately with a solicitor, whether in person, in writing or by telephone, and that free independent legal advice is available. See paragraph 3.1, *Note 6B* and *Note 6J*.

C:6.2 *Not Used*

C:6.3 A poster advertising the right to legal advice must be prominently displayed in the charging area of every police station. See *Note 6H*.

C:6.4 No police officer should, at any time, do or say anything with the intention of dissuading a detainee from obtaining legal advice.

C:6.5 The exercise of the right of access to legal advice may be delayed only as in Annex B. Whenever legal advice is requested, and unless Annex B applies, the custody officer must act without delay to secure the provision of such advice. If, on being informed or reminded of this right, the detainee declines to speak to a solicitor in person, the officer should point out that the right includes the right to speak with a solicitor on the telephone. If the detainee continues to waive this right the officer should ask them why and any reasons should be recorded on the custody record or the interview record as appropriate. Reminders of the right to legal advice must be given as in paragraphs 3.5, 11.2, 15.4, 16.4, 2B of Annex A, 3 of Annex K and 16.5 and Code D, paragraphs 3.17(ii) and 6.3. Once it is clear a detainee does not want to speak to a solicitor in person or by telephone they should cease to be asked their reasons. See *Note 6K*.

C:6.5A In the case of a juvenile, an appropriate adult should consider whether legal advice from a solicitor is required. If the juvenile indicates that they do not want legal advice, the appropriate adult has the right to ask for a solicitor to attend if this would be in the best interests of the person. However, the detained person cannot be forced to see the solicitor if he is adamant that he does not wish to do so.

C:6.6 A detainee who wants legal advice may not be interviewed or continue to be interviewed until they have received such advice unless:

    (a) Annex B applies, when the restriction on drawing adverse inferences from silence in Annex C will apply because the detainee is not allowed an opportunity to consult a solicitor; or

    (b) an officer of superintendent rank or above has reasonable grounds for believing that:

        (i) the consequent delay might:

- lead to interference with, or harm to, evidence connected with an offence;
- lead to interference with, or physical harm to, other people;
- lead to serious loss of, or damage to, property;
- lead to alerting other people suspected of having committed an offence but not yet arrested for it;
- hinder the recovery of property obtained in consequence of the commission of an offence;

        (ii) when a solicitor, including a duty solicitor, has been contacted and has agreed to attend, awaiting their arrival would cause unreasonable delay to the process of investigation;

        [Note: in these cases the restriction on drawing adverse inferences from silence in Annex C will apply because the detainee is not allowed an opportunity to consult a solicitor];

    (c) the solicitor the detainee has nominated or selected from a list:

        (i) cannot be contacted;

        (ii) has previously indicated they do not wish to be contacted; or

        (iii) having been contacted, has declined to attend; and

    the detainee has been advised of the Duty Solicitor Scheme but has declined to ask for the duty solicitor; in these circumstances the interview may be started or continued without further delay provided an officer of inspector rank or above has agreed to the interview proceeding; [Note: the restriction on drawing adverse inferences from silence in *Annex C* will not apply because the detainee is allowed an opportunity to consult the duty solicitor];

    (d) the detainee changes their mind, about wanting legal advice. In these circumstances the interview may be started or continued without delay provided that:

        (i) the detainee agrees to do so, in writing or on the interview record made in accordance wtih Code E or F; and

        (ii) an officer of inspector rank or above has inquired about the detainee's reasons for their change of mind and gives authority for the interview to proceed.

    Confirmation of the detainee's agreement, their change of mind, the reasons for it if given and, subject to paragraph 2.6A, the name of the authorising officer shall be recorded in the written interview record or the interview record made in accordance with Code E or F. See *Note 6I.* [Note: In these circumstances the restriction on drawing adverse inferences from silence in Annex C will not apply because the detainee is allowed an opportunity to consult a solicitor if they wish.]

A–55   **C:**6.7 If paragraph 6.6(b)(i) applies, once sufficient information has been obtained to avert the risk, questioning must cease until the detainee has received legal advice unless paragraph 6.6(a), (b)(ii), (c) or (d) applies.

C:6.8 A detainee who has been permitted to consult a solicitor shall be entitled on request to have the solicitor present when they are interviewed unless one of the exceptions in paragraph 6.6 applies.

C:6.9 The solicitor may only be required to leave the interview if their conduct is such that the interviewer is unable properly to put questions to the suspect. See *Notes 6D* and *6E*.

C:6.10 If the interviewer considers a solicitor is acting in such a way, they will stop the interview and consult an officer not below superintendent rank, if one is readily available, and otherwise an officer not below inspector rank not connected with the investigation. After speaking to the solicitor, the officer consulted will decide if the interview should continue in the presence of that solicitor. If they decide it should not, the suspect will be given the opportunity to consult another solicitor before the interview continues and that solicitor given an opportunity to be present at the interview. See *Note 6E*.

C:6.11 The removal of a solicitor from an interview is a serious step and, if it occurs, the officer of superintendent rank or above who took the decision will consider if the incident should be reported to the Law Society. If the decision to remove the solicitor has been taken by an officer below superintendent rank, the facts must be reported to an officer of superintendent rank or above who will similarly consider whether a report to the Law Society would be appropriate. When the solicitor concerned is a duty solicitor, the report should be both to the Law Society and to the Legal Services Commission.

C:6.12 "Solicitor" in this code means:

- a solicitor who holds a current practising certificate;
- an accredited or probationary representative included on the register of representatives maintained by the Legal Services Commission.

C:6.12A An accredited or probationary representative sent to provide advice by, and on behalf of, a solicitor shall be admitted to the police station for this purpose unless an officer of inspector rank or above considers such a visit will hinder the investigation and directs otherwise. Hindering the investigation does not include giving proper legal advice to a detainee as in *Note 6D*. Once admitted to the police station, paragraphs 6.6 to 6.10 apply.

C:6.13 In exercising their discretion under paragraph 6.12A, the officer should take into account in particular:

- whether:
  - the identity and status of an accredited or probationary representative have been satisfactorily established;
  - they are of suitable character to provide legal advice, *e.g.* a person with a criminal record is unlikely to be suitable unless the conviction was for a minor offence and not recent;
- any other matters in any written letter of authorisation provided by the solicitor on whose behalf the person is attending the police station. See *Note 6F*.

C:6.14 If the inspector refuses access to an accredited or probationary representative or a decision is taken that such a person should not be permitted to remain at an interview, the inspector must notify the solicitor on whose behalf the representative was acting and give them an opportunity to make alternative arrangements. The detainee must be informed and the custody record noted.

C:6.15 If a solicitor arrives at the station to see a particular person, that person must, unless Annex B applies, be so informed whether or not they are being interviewed and asked if they would like to see the solicitor. This applies even if the detainee has declined legal advice or, having requested it, subsequently agreed to be interviewed without receiving advice. The solicitor's attendance and the detainee's decision must be noted in the custody record.

(b) *Documentation*

C:6.16 Any request for legal advice and the action taken shall be recorded.

C:6.17 A record shall be made in the interview record if a detainee asks for legal advice and an interview is begun either in the absence of a solicitor or their representative, or they have been required to leave an interview.

Notes for guidance

A–56　　**C:6A** *In considering if paragraph 6.6(b) applies, the officer should, if practicable, ask the solicitor for an estimate of how long it will take to come to the station and relate this to the time detention is permitted, the time of day (i.e. whether the rest period under paragraph 12.2 is imminent) and the requirements of other investigations. If the solicitor is on their way or is to set off immediately, it will not normally be appropriate to begin an interview before they arrive. If it appears necessary to begin an interview before the solicitor's arrival, they should be given an indication of how long the police would be able to wait before 6.6(b) applies so there is an opportunity to make arrangements for someone else to provide legal advice.*

C:6B [See note C:6B2, *post.*]

C:6B1 [See note C:6B2, *post.*]

C:6B2 ***With effect from 21 April 2008****, the contents of Notes for Guidance 6B and 6B1 above will be superseded by this paragraph in all police forces areas in England and Wales by the following. A detainee who asks for legal advice to be paid for by himself should be given an opportunity to consult a specific solicitor or another solicitor from that solicitor's firm. If this solicitor is unavailable by these means, they may choose up to two alternatives. If these attempts are unsuccessful, the custody officer has discretion to allow further attempts until a solicitor has been contacted and agrees to provide legal advice. Otherwise, publicly funded legal advice shall in the first instance be accessed by telephoning a call centre authorised by the Legal Services Commission (LSC) to deal with calls from the police station. The Defence Solicitor Call Centre will determine whether legal advice should be limited to telephone advice or whether a solicitor should attend. Legal advice will be by telephone if a detainee is:*

- *detained for a non-imprisonable offence,*
- *arrested on a bench warrant for failing to appear and being held for production before the court (except where the solicitor has clear documentary evidence available that would result in the client being released from custody),*
- *arrested on suspicion of driving with excess alcohol (failure to provide a specimen, driving whilst unfit/drunk in charge of a motor vehicle), or*
- *detained in relation to breach of police or court bail conditions.*

An attendance by a solicitor for an offence suitable for telephone advice will depend on whether limited exceptions apply, such as:

- *whether the police are going to carry out an interview or an identification parade,*
- *whether the detainee is eligible for assistance from an appropriate adult,*
- *whether the detainee is unable to communicate over the telephone,*
- *whether the detainee alleges serious maltreatment by the police.*

Apart from carrying out these duties, an officer must not advise the suspect about any particular firm of solicitors.

C:6C *Not Used*

C:6D *A detainee has a right to free legal advice and to be represented by a solicitor. Legal advice by telephone advice may be provided in respect of those offences listed in Note for Guidance 6B1 and 6B2 above. The Defence Solicitor Call Centre will determine whether attendance is required by a solicitor. The solicitor's only role in the police station is to protect and advance the legal rights of their client. On occasions this may require the solicitor to give advice which has the effect of the client avoiding giving evidence which strengthens a prosecution case. The solicitor may intervene in order to seek clarification, challenge an improper question to their client or the manner in which it is put, advise their client not to reply to particular questions, or if they wish to give their client further legal advice. Paragraph 6.9 only applies if the solicitor's approach or conduct prevents or unreasonably obstructs proper questions being put to the suspect or the suspect's response being recorded. Examples of unacceptable conduct include answering questions on a suspect's behalf or providing written replies for the suspect to quote.*

C:6E *An officer who takes the decision to exclude a solicitor must be in a position to satisfy the court the decision was properly made. In order to do this they may need to witness what is happening.*

C:6F *If an officer of at least inspector rank considers a particular solicitor or firm of solicitors is persistently sending probationary representatives who are unsuited to provide legal advice, they should inform an officer of at least superintendent rank, who may wish to take the matter up with the Law Society.*

C:6G *Subject to the constraints of Annex B, a solicitor may advise more than one client in an investigation if they wish. Any question of a conflict of interest is for the solicitor under their professional code of conduct. If, however, waiting for a solicitor to give advice to one client may lead to unreasonable delay to the interview with another, the provisions of paragraph 6.6(b) may apply.* **A–57**

C:6H *In addition to a poster in English, a poster or posters containing translations into Welsh, the main minority ethnic languages and the principal European languages should be displayed wherever they are likely to be helpful and it is practicable to do so.*

C:6I *Paragraph 6.6(d) requires the authorisation of an officer of inspector rank or above to the continuation of an interview when a detainee who wanted legal advice changes their mind. It is permissible for such authorisation to be given over the telephone, if the authorising officer is able to satisfy themselves about the reason for the detainee's change of mind and is satisfied it is proper to continue the interview in those circumstances.*

C:6J *Whenever a detainee exercises their right to legal advice by consulting or communicating with a solicitor, they must be allowed to do so in private. This right to consult or communicate in private is fundamental. If the requirement for privacy is compromised because what is said or written by the detainee or solicitor for the purpose of giving and receiving legal advice is overheard, listened to, or read by others without the informed consent of the detainee, the right will effectively have been denied. When a detainee chooses to speak to a solicitor on the telephone, they should be allowed to do so in private unless this is impractical because of the design and layout of the custody area or the location of telephones. However, the normal expectation should be that facilities will be available, unless they are being used, at all police stations to enable detainees to speak in private to a solicitor either face to face or over the telephone.*

C:6K *A detainee is not obliged to give reasons for declining legal advice and should not be pressed to do so.*

C:7 Citizens of independent Commonwealth countries or foreign nationals

(a) *Action*

C:7.1 Any citizen of an independent Commonwealth country or a national of a foreign country, including the Republic of Ireland, may communicate at any time with the appropriate High Commission, embassy or consulate. The detainee must be informed as soon as practicable of: **A–58**

- this right;
- their right, upon request, to have their High Commission, embassy or consulate told of their whereabouts and the grounds for their detention. Such a request should be acted upon as soon as practicable.

C:7.2 If a detainee is a citizen of a country with which a bilateral consular convention or agreement is in force requiring notification of arrest, the appropriate High Commission, embassy or consulate shall be informed as soon as practicable, subject to paragraph 7.4. The countries to which this applies as at 1 April 2003 are listed in Annex F.

C:7.3 Consular officers may visit one of their nationals in police detention to talk to them and, if required, to arrange for legal advice. Such visits shall take place out of the hearing of a police officer.

C:7.4 Notwithstanding the provisions of consular conventions, if the detainee is a political refugee whether for reasons of race, nationality, political opinion or religion, or is seeking political asylum, consular officers shall not be informed of the arrest of one of their nationals or given access or information about them except at the detainee's express request.

(b) *Documentation*

A–59   **C:**7.5 A record shall be made when a detainee is informed of their rights under this section and of any communications with a High Commission, embassy or consulate.

Note for guidance

A–60   **C:**7A *The exercise of the rights in this section may not be interfered with even though Annex B applies.*

C:8 Conditions of detention

(a) *Action*

A–61   **C:**8.1 So far as it is practicable, not more than one detainee should be detained in each cell.

C:8.2 Cells in use must be adequately heated, cleaned and ventilated. They must be adequately lit, subject to such dimming as is compatible with safety and security to allow people detained overnight to sleep. No additional restraints shall be used within a locked cell unless absolutely necessary and then only restraint equipment, approved for use in that force by the chief officer, which is reasonable and necessary in the circumstances having regard to the detainee's demeanour and with a view to ensuring their safety and the safety of others. If a detainee is deaf, mentally disordered or otherwise mentally vulnerable, particular care must be taken when deciding whether to use any form of approved restraints.

C:8.3 Blankets, mattresses, pillows and other bedding supplied shall be of a reasonable standard and in a clean and sanitary condition. See *Note 8A.*

C:8.4 Access to toilet and washing facilities must be provided.

C:8.5 If it is necessary to remove a detainee's clothes for the purposes of investigation, for hygiene, health reasons or cleaning, replacement clothing of a reasonable standard of comfort and cleanliness shall be provided. A detainee may not be interviewed unless adequate clothing has been offered.

C:8.6 At least two light meals and one main meal should be offered in any 24 hour period. See *Note 8B.* Drinks should be provided at meal times and upon reasonable request between meals. Whenever necessary, advice shall be sought from the appropriate health care professional, see *Note 9A,* on medical and dietary matters. As far as practicable, meals provided shall offer a varied diet and meet any specific dietary needs or religious beliefs the detainee may have. The detainee may, at the custody officer's discretion, have meals supplied by their family or friends at their expense. See *Note 8A.*

C:8.7 Brief outdoor exercise shall be offered daily if practicable.

C:8.8 A juvenile shall not be placed in a police cell unless no other secure accommodation is available and the custody officer considers it is not practicable to supervise them if they are not placed in a cell or that a cell provides more comfortable accommodation than other secure accommodation in the station. A juvenile may not be placed in a cell with a detained adult.

(b) *Documentation*

A–62   **C:**8.9 A record must be kept of replacement clothing and meals offered.

C:8.10 If a juvenile is placed in a cell, the reason must be recorded.

C:8.11 The use of any restraints on a detainee whilst in a cell, the reasons for it and, if appropriate, the arrangements for enhanced supervision of the detainee whilst so restrained, shall be recorded. See paragraph 3.9.

Notes for guidance

A–63   **C:**8A *The provisions in paragraph 8.3 and 8.6 respectively are of particular importance in the case of a person likely to be detained for an extended period. In deciding whether to allow meals to be supplied by family or friends, the custody officer is entitled to take account* *of the risk of items being concealed in any food or package and the officer's duties and responsibilities under food handling legislation.*

C:8B *Meals should, so far as practicable, be offered at recognised meal times, or at other times that take account of when the detainee last had a meal.*

C:9 Care and treatment of detained persons

(a) *General*

C:9.1 Nothing in this section prevents the police from calling the police surgeon or, if appropriate, some other health care professional, to examine a detainee for the purposes of obtaining evidence relating to any offence in which the detainee is suspected of being involved. See *Note 9A.* **A–64**

C:9.2 If a complaint is made by, or on behalf of, a detainee about their treatment since their arrest, or it comes to notice that a detainee may have been treated improperly, a report must be made as soon as practicable to an officer of inspector rank or above not connected with the investigation. If the matter concerns a possible assault or the possibility of the unnecessary or unreasonable use of force, an appropriate health care professional must also be called as soon as practicable.

C:9.3 Detainees should be visited at least every hour. If no reasonably foreseeable risk was identified in a risk assessment, see paragraphs 3.6–3.10, there is no need to wake a sleeping detainee. Those suspected of being intoxicated through drink or drugs or having swallowed drugs, see *Note 9CA,* or whose level of consciousness causes concern must, subject to any clinical directions given by the appropriate health care professional, see paragraph 9.13:

- be visited and roused at least every half hour;
- have their condition assessed as in Annex H;
- and clinical treatment arranged if appropriate.

See *Notes 9B, 9C* and *9H.*

C:9.4 When arrangements are made to secure clinical attention for a detainee, the custody officer must make sure all relevant information which might assist in the treatment of the detainee's condition is made available to the responsible health care professional. This applies whether or not the health care professional asks for such information. Any officer or police staff with relevant information must inform the custody officer as soon as practicable.

(b) *Clinical treatment and attention*

C:9.5 The custody officer must make sure a detainee receives appropriate clinical attention as soon as reasonably practicable if the person: **A–65**

    (a) appears to be suffering from physical illness; or

    (b) is injured; or

    (c) appears to be suffering from a mental disorder; or

    (d) appears to need clinical attention.

C:9.5A This applies even if the detainee makes no request for clinical attention and whether or not they have already received clinical attention elsewhere. If the need for attention appears urgent, *e.g.* when indicated as in Annex H, the nearest available health care professional or an ambulance must be called immediately.

C:9.5B The custody officer must also consider the need for clinical attention as set out in Note for Guidance 9C in relation to those suffering the effects of alcohol or drugs.

C:9.6 Paragraph 9.5 is not meant to prevent or delay the transfer to a hospital if necessary of a person detained under the *Mental Health Act* 1983, section 136. See *Note 9D.* When an assessment under that Act takes place at a police station, see paragraph 3.16, the custody officer must consider whether an appropriate health care professional should be called to conduct an initial clinical check on the detainee.

This applies particularly when there is likely to be any significant delay in the arrival of a suitably qualified medical practitioner.

C:9.7 If it appears to the custody officer, or they are told, that a person brought to a station under arrest may be suffering from an infectious disease or condition, the custody officer must take reasonable steps to safeguard the health of the detainee and others at the station. In deciding what action to take, advice must be sought from an appropriate health care professional. See *Note 9E*. The custody officer has discretion to isolate the person and their property until clinical directions have been obtained.

A–66

C:9.8 If a detainee requests a clinical examination, an appropriate health care professional must be called as soon as practicable to assess the detainee's clinical needs. If a safe and appropriate care plan cannot be provided, the police surgeon's advice must be sought. The detainee may also be examined by a medical practitioner of their choice at their expense.

C:9.9 If a detainee is required to take or apply any medication in compliance with clinical directions prescribed before their detention, the custody officer must consult the appropriate health care professional before the use of the medication. Subject to the restrictions in paragraph 9.10, the custody officer is responsible for the safekeeping of any medication and for making sure the detainee is given the opportunity to take or apply prescribed or approved medication. Any such consultation and its outcome shall be noted in the custody record.

C:9.10 No police officer may administer or supervise the self-administration of medically prescribed controlled drugs of the types and forms listed in the *Misuse of Drugs Regulations* 2001, Schedule 2 or 3. A detainee may only self-administer such drugs under the personal supervision of the registered medical practitioner authorising their use. Drugs listed in Schedule 4 or 5 may be distributed by the custody officer for self-administration if they have consulted the registered medical practitioner authorising their use, this may be done by telephone, and both parties are satisfied self-administration will not expose the detainee, police officers or anyone else to the risk of harm or injury.

C:9.11 When appropriate health care professionals administer drugs or other medications, or supervise their self-administration, it must be within current medicines legislation and the scope of practice as determined by their relevant professional body.

C:9.12 If a detainee has in their possession, or claims to need, medication relating to a heart condition, diabetes, epilepsy or a condition of comparable potential seriousness then, even though paragraph 9.5 may not apply, the advice of the appropriate health care professional must be obtained.

C:9.13 Whenever the appropriate health care professional is called in accordance with this section to examine or treat a detainee, the custody officer shall ask for their opinion about:

- any risks or problems which police need to take into account when making decisions about the detainee's continued detention;
- when to carry out an interview if applicable; and
- the need for safeguards.

C:9.14 When clinical directions are given by the appropriate health care professional, whether orally or in writing, and the custody officer has any doubts or is in any way uncertain about any aspect of the directions, the custody officer shall ask for clarification. It is particularly important that directions concerning the frequency of visits are clear, precise and capable of being implemented. See *Note 9F*.

(c) *Documentation*

A–67

C:9.15 A record must be made in the custody record of:

(a) the arrangements made for an examination by an appropriate health care professional under paragraph 9.2 and of any complaint reported under that paragraph together with any relevant remarks by the custody officer;

(b) any arrangements made in accordance with paragraph 9.5;

(c) any request for a clinical examination under paragraph 9.8 and any arrangements made in response;

(d) the injury, ailment, condition or other reason which made it necessary to make the arrangements in (a) to (c), see *Note 9G*;

(e) any clinical directions and advice, including any further clarifications, given to police by a health care professional concerning the care and treatment of the detainee in connection with any of the arrangements made in (a) to (c), see *Note 9F*;

(f) if applicable, the responses received when attempting to rouse a person using the procedure in Annex H, see *Note 9H*.

C:9.16 If a health care professional does not record their clinical findings in the custody record, the record must show where they are recorded. See *Note 9G*. However, information which is necessary to custody staff to ensure the effective ongoing care and well being of the detainee must be recorded openly in the custody record, see paragraph 3.8 and Annex G, paragraph 7.

C:9.17 Subject to the requirements of section 4, the custody record shall include:

● a record of all medication a detainee has in their possession on arrival at the police station;

● a note of any such medication they claim to need but do not have with them.

Notes for guidance

C:9A *A "health care professional" means a clinically qualified person working within the*   **A–68**
scope of practice as determined by their relevant professional body. Whether a health care professional is "appropriate" depends on the circumstances of the duties they carry out at the time.

C:9B *Whenever possible juveniles and mentally vulnerable detainees should be visited more frequently.*

C:9C *A detainee who appears drunk or behaves abnormally may be suffering from illness, the effects of drugs or may have sustained injury, particularly a head injury which is not apparent. A detainee needing or dependent on certain drugs, including alcohol, may experience harmful effects within a short time of being deprived of their supply. In these circumstances, when there is any doubt, police should always act urgently to call an appropriate health care professional or an ambulance. Paragraph 9.5 does not apply to minor ailments or injuries which do not need attention. However, all such ailments or injuries must be recorded in the custody record and any doubt must be resolved in favour of calling the appropriate health care professional.*

C:9CA *Paragraph 9.3 would apply to a person in police custody by order of a magistrates' court under the* Criminal Justice Act *1988, section 152 (as amended by the* Drugs Act *2005, section 8) to facilitate the recovery of evidence after being charged with drug possession or drug trafficking and suspected of having swallowed drugs. In the case of the healthcare needs of a person who has swallowed the drugs, the custody officer subject to any clinical directions, should consider the necessity for rousing every half hour. This does not negate the need for regular visiting of the suspect in the cell.*

C:9D *Whenever practicable, arrangements should be made for persons detained for assessment under the* Mental Health Act *1983, section 136 to be taken to a hospital. There is no power under that Act to transfer a person detained under section 136 from one place of safety to another place of safety for assessment.*

C:9E *It is important to respect a person's right to privacy and information about their health must be kept confidential and only disclosed with their consent or in accordance with clinical advice when it is necessary to protect the detainee's health or that of others who come into contact with them.*

C:9F *The custody officer should always seek to clarify directions that the detainee requires constant observation or supervision and should ask the appropriate health care professional to explain precisely what action needs to be taken to implement such directions.*

C:9G *Paragraphs 9.15 and 9.16 do not require any information about the cause of an injury, ailment or condition to be recorded on the custody record if it appears capable of providing evidence of an offence.*

C:9H *The purpose of recording a person's responses when attempting to rouse them using the procedure in Annex H is to enable any change in the individual's consciousness level to be noted and clinical treatment arranged if appropriate.*

C:10 Cautions

(a) *When a caution must be given*

A–69 **C:**10.1 A person whom there are grounds to suspect of an offence, see *Note 10A*, must be cautioned before any questions about an offence, or further questions if the answers provide the grounds for suspicion, are put to them if either the suspect's answers or silence (*i.e.* failure or refusal to answer or answer satisfactorily) may be given in evidence to a court in a prosecution. A person need not be cautioned if questions are for other necessary purposes, *e.g.*:

(a) solely to establish their identity or ownership of any vehicle;
(b) to obtain information in accordance with any relevant statutory requirement, see paragraph 10.9;
(c) in furtherance of the proper and effective conduct of a search, *e.g.* to determine the need to search in the exercise of powers of stop and search or to seek co-operation while carrying out a search;
(d) to seek verification of a written record as in paragraph 11.13.

C:10.2 Whenever a person not under arrest is initially cautioned, or reminded they are under caution, that person must at the same time be told they are not under arrest and are free to leave if they want to. See *Note 10C*.

C:10.3 A person who is arrested, or further arrested, must be informed at the time, or as soon as practicable thereafter, that they are under arrest and the grounds for their arrest, see paragraph 3.4, *Note 10B* and Code G, paragraphs 2.2 and 4.3.

C:10.4 As per Code G, section 3, a person who is arrested, or further arrested, must also be cautioned unless:

(a) it is impracticable to do so by reason of their condition or behaviour at the time;
(b) they have already been cautioned immediately prior to arrest as in paragraph 10.1.

(b) *Terms of the cautions*

C:10.5 The caution which must be given on:

(a) arrest;
(b) all other occasions before a person is charged or informed they may be prosecuted, see section 16,

should, unless the restriction on drawing adverse inferences from silence applies, see Annex C, be in the following terms:

> "You do not have to say anything. But it may harm your defence if you do not mention when questioned something which you later rely on in court. Anything you do say may be given in evidence."

Where the use of the Welsh Language is appropriate, a constable may provide the caution directly in Welsh in the following terms:

> "Does dim rhaid i chi ddweud dim byd. Ond gall niweidio eich amddiffyniad os na fyddwch chi'n sôn, wrth gael eich holi, am rywbeth y byddwch chi'n dibynnu arno nes ymlaen yn y Llys. Gall unrhyw beth yr ydych yn ei ddweud gael ei roi fel tystiolaeth."

See *Note 10G.*

A–70 **C:**10.6 Annex C, paragraph 2 sets out the alternative terms of the caution to be used when the restriction on drawing adverse inferences from silence applies.

C:10.7 Minor deviations from the words of any caution given in accordance with this code do not constitute a breach of this code, provided the sense of the relevant caution is preserved. See *Note 10D*.

C:10.8 After any break in questioning under caution, the person being questioned must be made aware they remain under caution. If there is any doubt the relevant caution should be given again in full when the interview resumes. See *Note 10E*.

C:10.9 When, despite being cautioned, a person fails to co-operate or to answer particular questions which may affect their immediate treatment, the person should be informed of any relevant consequences and that those consequences are not affected by the caution. Examples are when a person's refusal to provide:

- their name and address when charged may make them liable to detention;
- particulars and information in accordance with a statutory requirement, *e.g.* under the *Road Traffic Act* 1988, may amount to an offence or may make the person liable to a further arrest.

(c) *Special warnings under the Criminal Justice and Public Order Act 1994, sections 36 and 37*

C:10.10 When a suspect interviewed at a police station or authorised place of   **A–71** detention after arrest fails or refuses to answer certain questions, or to answer satisfactorily, after due warning, see *Note 10F*, a court or jury may draw such inferences as appear proper under the *Criminal Justice and Public Order Act* 1994, sections 36 and 37. Such inferences may only be drawn when:

(a) the restriction on drawing adverse inferences from silence, see Annex C, does not apply; and

(b) the suspect is arrested by a constable and fails or refuses to account for any objects, marks or substances, or marks on such objects found:

- on their person;
- in or on their clothing or footwear;
- otherwise in their possession; or
- in the place they were arrested;

(c) the arrested suspect was found by a constable at a place at or about the time the offence for which that officer has arrested them is alleged to have been committed, and the suspect fails or refuses to account for their presence there.

When the restriction on drawing adverse inferences from silence applies, the suspect may still be asked to account for any of the matters in (b) or (c) but the special warning described in paragraph 10.11 will not apply and must not be given.

C:10.11 For an inference to be drawn when a suspect fails or refuses to answer a question about one of these matters or to answer it satisfactorily, the suspect must first be told in ordinary language:

(a) what offence is being investigated;

(b) what fact they are being asked to account for;

(c) this fact may be due to them taking part in the commission of the offence;

(d) a court may draw a proper inference if they fail or refuse to account for this fact;

(e) a record is being made of the interview and it may be given in evidence if they are brought to trial.

(d) *Juveniles and persons who are mentally disordered or otherwise mentally vulnerable*

C:10.12 If a juvenile or a person who is mentally disordered or otherwise mentally vulnerable is cautioned in the absence of the appropriate adult, the caution must be repeated in the adult's presence.

(e) *Documentation*

C:10.13 A record shall be made when a caution is given under this section, either in the interviewer's pocket book or in the interview record.

Notes for guidance

C:10A *There must be some reasonable, objective grounds for the suspicion, based on known facts or information which are relevant to the likelihood the offence has been committed and the person to be questioned committed it.*

C:10B *An arrested person must be given sufficient information to enable them to understand they have been deprived of their liberty and the reason they have been arrested e.g. when a person is arrested on suspicion of committing an offence they must be informed of the suspected offence's nature, when and where it was committed. The suspect must also be informed of the reason or reasons why the arrest is considered necessary. Vague or technical language should be avoided.*

C:10C *The restriction on drawing inferences from silence, see Annex C, paragraph 1 does not apply to a person who has not been detained and who therefore cannot be prevented from seeking legal advice if they want, see paragraph 3.21.*

C:10D *If it appears a person does not understand the caution, the person giving it should explain it in their own words.*

C:10E *It may be necessary to show to the court that nothing occurred during an interview break or between interviews which influenced the suspect's recorded evidence. After a break in an interview or at the beginning of a subsequent interview, the interviewing officer should summarise the reason for the break and confirm this with the suspect.*

C:10F *The* Criminal Justice and Public Order Act *1994, sections 36 and 37 apply only to suspects who have been arrested by a constable or Customs and Excise officer and are given the relevant warning by the police or customs officer who made the arrest or who is investigating the offence. They do not apply to any interviews with suspects who have not been arrested.*

C:10G *Nothing in this code requires a caution to be given or repeated when informing a person not under arrest they may be prosecuted for an offence. However, a court will not be able to draw any inferences under the* Criminal Justice and Public Order Act *1994, section 34, if the person was not cautioned.*

C:11 Interviews—general

(a) *Action*

C:11.1A An interview is the questioning of a person regarding their involvement or suspected involvement in a criminal offence or offences which, under paragraph 10.1, must be carried out under caution. Whenever a person is interviewed they must be informed of the nature of the offence, or further offence. Procedures under the *Road Traffic Act* 1988, section 7 or the *Transport and Work Act* 1992, section 31 do not constitute interviewing for the purpose of this code.

C:11.1 Following a decision to arrest a suspect, they must not be interviewed about the relevant offence except at a police station or other authorised place of detention, unless the consequent delay would be likely to:

    (a) lead to:

- interference with, or harm to, evidence connected with an offence;
- interference with, or physical harm to, other people; or
- serious loss of, or damage to, property;

    (b) lead to alerting other people suspected of committing an offence but not yet arrested for it; or

    (c) hinder the recovery of property obtained in consequence of the commission of an offence.

Interviewing in any of these circumstances shall cease once the relevant risk has been averted or the necessary questions have been put in order to attempt to avert that risk.

C:11.2 Immediately prior to the commencement or re-commencement of any interview at a police station or other authorised place of detention, the interviewer should remind the suspect of their entitlement to free legal advice and that the interview can be delayed for legal advice to be obtained, unless one of the exceptions in paragraph 6.6 applies. It is the interviewer's responsibility to make sure all reminders are recorded in the interview record.

C:11.3 [*Not Used.*]

C:11.4 At the beginning of an interview the interviewer, after cautioning the suspect, see section 10, shall put to them any significant statement or silence which occurred in the presence and hearing of a police officer or other police staff before the start of the interview and which have not been put to the suspect in the course of a previous interview. See *Note 11A*. The interviewer shall ask the suspect whether they confirm or deny that earlier statement or silence and if they want to add anything.

C:11.4A A significant statement is one which appears capable of being used in evidence against the suspect, in particular a direct admission of guilt. A significant silence is a failure or refusal to answer a question or answer satisfactorily when under caution, which might, allowing for the restriction on drawing adverse inferences from silence, see Annex C, give rise to an inference under the *Criminal Justice and Public Order Act* 1994, Part III.

C:11.5 No interviewer may try to obtain answers or elicit a statement by the use of oppression. Except as in paragraph 10.9, no interviewer shall indicate, except to answer a direct question, what action will be taken by the police if the person being questioned answers questions, makes a statement or refuses to do either. If the person asks directly what action will be taken if they answer questions, make a statement or refuse to do either, the interviewer may inform them what action the police propose to take provided that action is itself proper and warranted.

C:11.6 The interview or further interview of a person about an offence with which that person has not been charged or for which they have not been informed they may be prosecuted, must cease when:

   (a) the officer in charge of the investigation is satisfied all the questions they consider relevant to obtaining accurate and reliable information about the offence have been put to the suspect, this includes allowing the suspect an opportunity to give an innocent explanation and asking questions to test if the explanation is accurate and reliable, *e.g.* to clear up ambiguities or clarify what the suspect said;

   (b) the officer in charge of the investigation has taken account of any other available evidence; and

   (c) the officer in charge of the investigation, or in the case of a detained suspect, the custody officer, see paragraph 16.1, reasonably believes there is sufficient evidence to provide a realistic prospect of conviction for that offence. See *Note 11B*.

This paragraph does not prevent officers in revenue cases or acting under the confiscation provisions of the *Criminal Justice Act* 1988 or the *Drug Trafficking Act* 1994 from inviting suspects to complete a formal question and answer record after the interview is concluded.

(b) *Interview records*

   C:11.7 (a) An accurate record must be made of each interview, whether or not **A–74** the interview takes place at a police station.

   (b) The record must state the place of interview, the time it begins and ends, any interview breaks and, subject to paragraph 2.6A, the names of all those present; and must be made on the forms provided for this purpose or in the interviewer's pocket book or in accordance with the Codes of Practice E or F.

   (c) Any written record must be made and completed during the interview, unless this would not be practicable or would interfere with the conduct of the interview, and must constitute either a verbatim record of what has been said or, failing this, an account of the interview which adequately and accurately summarises it.

C:11.8 If a written record is not made during the interview it must be made as soon as practicable after its completion.

C:11.9 Written interview records must be timed and signed by the maker.

C:11.10 If a written record is not completed during the interview the reason must be recorded in the interview record.

C:11.11 Unless it is impracticable, the person interviewed shall be given the opportunity to read the interview record and to sign it as correct or to indicate how they consider it inaccurate. If the person interviewed cannot read or refuses to read the record or sign it, the senior interviewer present shall read it to them and ask whether they would like to sign it as correct or make their mark or to indicate how they consider it inaccurate. The interviewer shall certify on the interview record itself what has occurred. See *Note 11E.*

C:11.12 If the appropriate adult or the person's solicitor is present during the interview, they should also be given an opportunity to read and sign the interview record or any written statement taken down during the interview.

C:11.13 A written record shall be made of any comments made by a suspect, including unsolicited comments, which are outside the context of an interview but which might be relevant to the offence. Any such record must be timed and signed by the maker. When practicable the suspect shall be given the opportunity to read that record and to sign it as correct or to indicate how they consider it inaccurate. See *Note 11E.*

C:11.14 Any refusal by a person to sign an interview record when asked in accordance with this code must itself be recorded.

(c) *Juveniles and mentally disordered or otherwise mentally vulnerable people*

A–75

C:11.15 A juvenile or person who is mentally disordered or otherwise mentally vulnerable must not be interviewed regarding their involvement or suspected involvement in a criminal offence or offences, or asked to provide or sign a written statement under caution or record of interview, in the absence of the appropriate adult unless paragraphs 11.1, 11.18 to 11.20 apply. See *Note 11C.*

C:11.16 Juveniles may only be interviewed at their place of education in exceptional circumstances and only when the principal or their nominee agrees. Every effort should be made to notify the parent(s) or other person responsible for the juvenile's welfare and the appropriate adult, if this is a different person, that the police want to interview the juvenile and reasonable time should be allowed to enable the appropriate adult to be present at the interview. If awaiting the appropriate adult would cause unreasonable delay, and unless the juvenile is suspected of an offence against the educational establishment, the principal or their nominee can act as the appropriate adult for the purposes of the interview.

C:11.17 If an appropriate adult is present at an interview, they shall be informed:

- they are not expected to act simply as an observer; and
- the purpose of their presence is to:
  - advise the person being interviewed;
  - observe whether the interview is being conducted properly and fairly;
  - facilitate communication with the person being interviewed.

(d) *Vulnerable suspects–urgent interviews at police stations*

C:11.18. The following persons may not be interviewed unless an officer of superintendent rank or above considers delay will lead to the consequences in paragraph 11.1(a) to (c), and is satisfied the interview would not significantly harm the person's physical or mental state (see Annex G):

(a) a juvenile or person who is mentally disordered or otherwise mentally vulnerable if at the time of the interview the appropriate adult is not present;

(b) anyone other than in (a) who at the time of the interview appears unable to:
- appreciate the significance of questions and their answers; or
- understand what is happening because of the effects of drink, drugs or any illness, ailment or condition;

(c) a person who has difficulty understanding English or has a hearing disability, if at the time of the interview an interpreter is not present.

C:11.19 These interviews may not continue once sufficient information has been obtained to avert the consequences in paragraph 11.1(a) to (c).

C:11.20. A record shall be made of the grounds for any decision to interview a person under paragraph 11.18.

Notes for guidance

C:11A *Paragraph 11.4 does not prevent the interviewer from putting significant statements and silences to a suspect again at a later stage or a further interview.*   **A–76**

C:11B *The* Criminal Procedure and Investigations Act *1996 code of practice, paragraph 3.4 states "In conducting an investigation, the investigator should pursue all reasonable lines of enquiry, whether these point towards or away from the suspect. What is reasonable will depend on the particular circumstances." Interviewers should keep this in mind when deciding what questions to ask in an interview.*

C:11C *Although juveniles or people who are mentally disordered or otherwise mentally vulnerable are often capable of providing reliable evidence, they may, without knowing or wishing to do so, be particularly prone in certain circumstances to provide information that may be unreliable, misleading or self-incriminating. Special care should always be taken when questioning such a person, and the appropriate adult should be involved if there is any doubt about a person's age, mental state or capacity. Because of the risk of unreliable evidence it is also important to obtain corroboration of any facts admitted whenever possible.*

C:11D *Juveniles should not be arrested at their place of education unless this is unavoidable. When a juvenile is arrested at their place of education, the principal or their nominee must be informed.*

C:11E *Significant statements described in paragraph 11.4 will always be relevant to the offence and must be recorded. When a suspect agrees to read records of interviews and other comments and sign them as correct, they should be asked to endorse the record with, e.g. "I agree that this is a correct record of what was said" and add their signature. If the suspect does not agree with the record, the interviewer should record the details of any disagreement and ask the suspect to read these details and sign them to the effect that they accurately reflect their disagreement. Any refusal to sign should be recorded.*

C:12 Interviews in police stations

(a) Action

C:12.1 If a police officer wants to interview or conduct enquiries which require   **A–77** the presence of a detainee, the custody officer is responsible for deciding whether to deliver the detainee into the officer's custody.

C:12.2 Except as below, in any period of 24 hours a detainee must be allowed a continuous period of at least 8 hours for rest, free from questioning, travel or any interruption in connection with the investigation concerned. This period should normally be at night or other appropriate time which takes account of when the detainee last slept or rested. If a detainee is arrested at a police station after going there voluntarily, the period of 24 hours runs from the time of their arrest and not the time of arrival at the police station. The period may not be interrupted or delayed, except:

(a) when there are reasonable grounds for believing not delaying or interrupting the period would:

> (i) involve a risk of harm to people or serious loss of, or damage to, property;
>
> (ii) delay unnecessarily the person's release from custody;
>
> (iii) otherwise prejudice the outcome of the investigation;
>
> (b) at the request of the detainee, their appropriate adult or legal representative;
>
> (c) when a delay or interruption is necessary in order to:
>
> (i) comply with the legal obligations and duties arising under section 15;
>
> (ii) to take action required under section 9 or in accordance with medical advice.

If the period is interrupted in accordance with (a), a fresh period must be allowed. Interruptions under (b) and (c), do not require a fresh period to be allowed.

C:12.3 Before a detainee is interviewed the custody officer, in consultation with the officer in charge of the investigation and appropriate health care professionals as necessary, shall assess whether the detainee is fit enough to be interviewed. This means determining and considering the risks to the detainee's physical and mental state if the interview took place and determining what safeguards are needed to allow the interview to take place. See *Annex G.* The custody officer shall not allow a detainee to be interviewed if the custody officer considers it would cause significant harm to the detainee's physical or mental state. Vulnerable suspects listed at paragraph 11.18 shall be treated as always being at some risk during an interview and these persons may not be interviewed except in accordance with paragraphs 11.18 to 11.20.

C:12.4 As far as practicable interviews shall take place in interview rooms which are adequately heated, lit and ventilated.

C:12.5 A suspect whose detention without charge has been authorised under *PACE*, because the detention is necessary for an interview to obtain evidence of the offence for which they have been arrested, may choose not to answer questions but police do not require the suspect's consent or agreement to interview them for this purpose. If a suspect takes steps to prevent themselves being questioned or further questioned, *e.g.* by refusing to leave their cell to go to a suitable interview room or by trying to leave the interview room, they shall be advised their consent or agreement to interview is not required. The suspect shall be cautioned as in section 10, and informed if they fail or refuse to co-operate, the interview may take place in the cell and that their failure or refusal to co-operate may be given in evidence. The suspect shall then be invited to co-operate and go into the interview room.

C:12.6 People being questioned or making statements shall not be required to stand.

A–78   **C:12.7** Before the interview commences each interviewer shall, subject to paragraph 2.6A, identify themselves and any other persons present to the interviewee.

C:12.8 Breaks from interviewing should be made at recognised meal times or at other times that take account of when an interviewee last had a meal. Short refreshment breaks shall be provided at approximately two hour intervals, subject to the interviewer's discretion to delay a break if there are reasonable grounds for believing it would:

> (i) involve a:
>
> • risk of harm to people;
>
> • serious loss of, or damage to, property;
>
> (ii) unnecessarily delay the detainee's release;
>
> (iii) otherwise prejudice the outcome of the investigation.

See *Note 12B.*

C:12.9 If during the interview a complaint is made by or on behalf of the interviewee concerning the provisions of this code, the interviewer should:

> (i) record it in the interview record;

(ii) inform the custody officer, who is then responsible for dealing with it as in section 9.

(b) *Documentation*

C:12.10 A record must be made of the:

- time a detainee is not in the custody of the custody officer, and why;
- reason for any refusal to deliver the detainee out of that custody.

C:12.11 A record shall be made of:

(a) the reasons it was not practicable to use an interview room; and

(b) any action taken as in paragraph 12.5.

The record shall be made on the custody record or in the interview record for action taken whilst an interview record is being kept, with a brief reference to this effect in the custody record.

C:12.12 Any decision to delay a break in an interview must be recorded, with reasons, in the interview record.

C:12.13 All written statements made at police stations under caution shall be written on forms provided for the purpose.

C:12.14 All written statements made under caution shall be taken in accordance with Annex D. Before a person makes a written statement under caution at a police station they shall be reminded about the right to legal advice. See *Note 12A.*

Notes for guidance

C:12A *It is not normally necessary to ask for a written statement if the interview was re-*   *corded in writing and the record signed in accordance with paragraph 11.11 or audibly or visually recorded in accordance with Code E or F. Statements under caution should normally be taken in these circumstances only at the person's express wish. A person may however be asked if they want to make such a statement.*

C:12B *Meal breaks should normally last at least 45 minutes and shorter breaks after two hours should last at least 15 minutes. If the interviewer delays a break in accordance with paragraph 12.8 and prolongs the interview, a longer break should be provided. If there is a short interview, and another short interview is contemplated, the length of the break may be reduced if there are reasonable grounds to believe this is necessary to avoid any of the consequences in paragraph 12.8(i) to (iii).*

C:13 Interpreters

(a) *General*

C:13.1 Chief officers are responsible for making sure appropriate arrange-   ments are in place for provision of suitably qualified interpreters for people who:

- are deaf;
- do not understand English.

Whenever possible, interpreters should be drawn from the National Register of Public Service Interpreters (NRPSI) or the Council for the Advancement of Communication with Deaf People (CACDP) Directory of British Sign Language/English Interpreters.

(b) *Foreign languages*

C:13.2 Unless paragraphs 11.1, 11.18 to 11.20 apply, a person must not be interviewed in the absence of a person capable of interpreting if:

(a) they have difficulty understanding English;

(b) the interviewer cannot speak the person's own language;

(c) the person wants an interpreter present.

C:13.3 The interviewer shall make sure the interpreter makes a note of the interview at the time in the person's language for use in the event of the interpreter being called to give evidence, and certifies its accuracy. The interviewer should allow sufficient time for the interpreter to note each question and answer after each is put, given and interpreted. The person should be allowed to read the record or have it read to them and sign it as correct or indicate the respects in which they consider it inaccurate. If the interview is audibly recorded or visually recorded, the arrangements in Code E or F apply.

C:13.4 In the case of a person making a statement to a police officer or other police staff other than in English:

> (a) the interpreter shall record the statement in the language it is made;
> (b) the person shall be invited to sign it;
> (c) an official English translation shall be made in due course.

(c) *Deaf people and people with speech difficulties*

C:13.5 If a person appears to be deaf or there is doubt about their hearing or speaking ability, they must not be interviewed in the absence of an interpreter unless they agree in writing to being interviewed without one or paragraphs 11.1, 11.18 to 11.20 apply.

C:13.6 An interpreter should also be called if a juvenile is interviewed and the parent or guardian present as the appropriate adult appears to be deaf or there is doubt about their hearing or speaking ability, unless they agree in writing to the interview proceeding without one or paragraphs 11.1, 11.18 to 11.20 apply.

C:13.7 The interviewer shall make sure the interpreter is allowed to read the interview record and certify its accuracy in the event of the interpreter being called to give evidence. If the interview is audibly recorded or visually recorded, the arrangements in Code E or F apply.

(d) *Additional rules for detained persons*

C:13.8 All reasonable attempts should be made to make the detainee understand that interpreters will be provided at public expense.

C:13.9 If paragraph 6.1 applies and the detainee cannot communicate with the solicitor because of language, hearing or speech difficulties, an interpreter must be called. The interpreter may not be a police officer or any other police staff when interpretation is needed for the purposes of obtaining legal advice. In all other cases a police officer or other police staff may only interpret if the detainee and the appropriate adult, if applicable, give their agreement in writing or if the interview is audibly recorded or visually recorded as in Code E or F.

C:13.10 When the custody officer cannot establish effective communication with a person charged with an offence who appears deaf or there is doubt about their ability to hear, speak or to understand English, arrangements must be made as soon as practicable for an interpreter to explain the offence and any other information given by the custody officer.

(e) *Documentation*

C:13.11 Action taken to call an interpreter under this section and any agreement to be interviewed in the absence of an interpreter must be recorded.

C:14 Questioning—special restrictions

C:14.1 If a person is arrested by one police force on behalf of another and the lawful period of detention in respect of that offence has not yet commenced in accordance with *PACE*, section 41 no questions may be put to them about the offence while they are in transit between the forces except to clarify any voluntary statement they make.

C:14.2 If a person is in police detention at a hospital they may not be questioned without the agreement of a responsible doctor. See *Note 14A*.

Note for guidance

C:14A *If questioning takes place at a hospital under paragraph 14.2, or on the way to*

*or from a hospital, the period of questioning concerned counts towards the total period of
detention permitted.*

C:15 Reviews and extensions of detention

(a) *Persons detained under PACE*

C:15.1 The review officer is responsible under *PACE*, section 40 for periodically   **A–85**
determining if a person's detention, before or after charge, continues to be necessary.
This requirement continues throughout the detention period and except as in
paragraph 15.10, the review officer must be present at the police station holding the
detainee. See *Notes 15A* and *15B*.

C:15.2 Under *PACE*, section 42, an officer of superintendent rank or above who
is responsible for the station holding the detainee may give authority any time after
the second review to extend the maximum period the person may be detained
without charge by up to 12 hours. Further detention without charge may be authorised only by a magistrates' court in accordance with *PACE*, sections 43 and 44. See
Notes 15C, 15D and *15E*.

C:15.2A Section 42(1) of *PACE* as amended extends the maximum period of
detention for indictable offences from 24 hours to 36 hours. Detaining a juvenile or
mentally vulnerable person for longer than 24 hours will be dependent on the circumstances of the case and with regard to the person's:

    (a) special vulnerability;

    (b) the legal obligation to provide an opportunity for representations to be
made prior to a decision about extending detention;

    (c) the need to consult and consider the views of any appropriate adult; and

    (d) any alternatives to police custody.

C:15.3 Before deciding whether to authorise continued detention the officer
responsible under paragraphs 15.1 or 15.2 shall give an opportunity to make
representations about the detention to:

    (a) the detainee, unless in the case of a review as in paragraph 15.1, the
detainee is asleep;

    (b) the detainee's solicitor if available at the time; and

    (c) the appropriate adult if available at the time.

C:15.3A Other people having an interest in the detainee's welfare may also
make representations at the authorising officer's discretion.

C:15.3B Subject to paragraph 15.10, the representations may be made orally
in person or by telephone or in writing. The authorising officer may, however, refuse to hear oral representations from the detainee if the officer considers them
unfit to make representations because of their condition or behaviour. See *Note
15C*.

C:15.3C The decision on whether the review takes place in person or by
telephone or by video conferencing (see *Note 15G*) is a matter for the review officer.
In determining the form the review may take, the review officer must always take full
account of the needs of the person in custody. The benefits of carrying out a review
in person should always be considered, based on the individual circumstances of
each case with specific additional consideration if the person is:

    (a) a juvenile (and the age of the juvenile); or

    (b) mentally vulnerable; or

    (c) has [*sic*] been subject to medical attention for other than routine minor
ailments; or

    (d) there are presentational or community issues around the person's
detention.

C:15.4 Before conducting a review or determining whether to extend the   **A–86**
maximum period of detention without charge, the officer responsible must make

sure the detainee is reminded of their entitlement to free legal advice, see paragraph 6.5, unless in the case of a review the person is asleep.

C:15.5 If, after considering any representations, the officer decides to keep the detainee in detention or extend the maximum period they may be detained without charge, any comment made by the detainee shall be recorded. If applicable, the officer responsible under paragraph 15.1 or 15.2 shall be informed of the comment as soon as practicable. See also paragraphs 11.4 and 11.13.

C:15.6 No officer shall put specific questions to the detainee:

- regarding their involvement in any offence; or
- in respect of any comments they may make;
  - when given the opportunity to make representations; or
  - in response to a decision to keep them in detention or extend the maximum period of detention.

Such an exchange could constitute an interview as in paragraph 11.1A and would be subject to the associated safeguards in section 11 and, in respect of a person who has been charged, paragraph 16.5. See also paragraph 11.13.

C:15.7 A detainee who is asleep at a review, see paragraph 15.1, and whose continued detention is authorised must be informed about the decision and reason as soon as practicable after waking.

C:15.8 [*Not used.*]

(b) *Telephone review of detention*

A–87   **C:15.9** *PACE*, section 40A provides that the officer responsible under section 40 for reviewing the detention of a person who has not been charged, need not attend the police station holding the detainee and may carry out the review by telephone.

C:15.9A *PACE*, section 45A(2) provides that the officer responsible under section 40 for reviewing the detention of a person who has not been charged, need not attend the police station holding the detainee and may carry out the review by video conferencing facilities. (See *Note 15G*.)

C:15.9B A telephone review is not permitted where facilities for review by video conferencing exist and it is practicable to use them.

C:15.9C The review officer can decide at any stage that a telephone review or review by video conferencing should be terminated and that the review will be conducted in person. The reasons for doing so should be noted in the custody record. See *Note 15F*.

C:15.10 When a telephone review is carried out, an officer at the station holding the detainee shall be required by the review officer to fulfil that officer's obligations under *PACE* section 40 or this code by:

(a) making any record connected with the review in the detainee's custody record;

(b) if applicable, making a record in (a) in the presence of the detainee; and

(c) giving the detainee information about the review.

C:15.11 When a telephone review is carried out, the requirement in paragraph 15.3 will be satisfied:

(a) if facilities exist for the immediate transmission of written representations to the review officer, *e.g.* fax or email message, by giving the detainee an opportunity to make representations:

(i) orally by telephone; or

(ii) in writing using those facilities; and

(b) in all other cases, by giving the detainee an opportunity to make their representations orally by telephone.

(d) *Documentation*

C:15.12 It is the officer's responsibility to make sure all reminders given under paragraph 15.4 are noted in the custody record.

C:15.13 The grounds for, and extent of, any delay in conducting a review shall be recorded.

C:15.14 When a telephone review is carried out, a record shall be made of:

(a) the reason the review officer did not attend the station holding the detainee;

(b) the place the review officer was;

(c) the method representations, oral or written, were made to the review officer, see paragraph 15.11.

C:15.15 Any written representations shall be retained.

C:15.16 A record shall be made as soon as practicable about the outcome of each review or determination whether to extend the maximum detention period without charge or an application for a warrant of further detention or its extension. If paragraph 15.7 applies, a record shall also be made of when the person was informed and by whom. If an authorisation is given under *PACE*, section 42, the record shall state the number of hours and minutes by which the detention period is extended or further extended. If a warrant for further detention, or extension, is granted under section 43 or 44, the record shall state the detention period authorised by the warrant and the date and time it was granted.

Notes for guidance

C:15A *Review officer for the purposes of*:   **A–88**

- PACE, *sections 40 and 40A means, in the case of a person arrested but not charged, an officer of at least inspector rank not directly involved in the investigation and, if a person has been arrested and charged, the custody officer.*

C:15B *The detention of persons in police custody not subject to the statutory review requirement in paragraph 15.1 should still be reviewed periodically as a matter of good practice. Such reviews can be carried out by an officer of the rank of sergeant or above. The purpose of such reviews is to check the particular power under which a detainee is held continues to apply, any associated conditions are complied with and to make sure appropriate action is taken to deal with any changes. This includes the detainee's prompt release when the power no longer applies, or their transfer if the power requires the detainee be taken elsewhere as soon as the necessary arrangements are made. Examples include persons*:

(a) *arrested on warrant because they failed to answer bail to appear at court;*

(b) *arrested under the* Bail Act *1976, section 7(3) for breaching a condition of bail granted after charge;*

(c) *in police custody for specific purposes and periods under the* Crime (Sentences) Act *1997, Schedule 1;*

(d) *convicted, or remand prisoners, held in police stations on behalf of the Prison Service under the* Imprisonment (Temporary Provisions) Act *1980, section 6;*

(e) *being detained to prevent them causing a breach of the peace;*

(f) *detained at police stations on behalf of the Immigration Service.*

(g) *detained by order of a magistrates' court under the* Criminal Justice Act *1988, section 152 (as amended by the* Drugs Act *2005, section 8) to facilitate the recovery of evidence after being charged with drug possession or drug trafficking and suspected of having swallowed drugs.*

The detention of persons remanded into police detention by order of a court under the Magistrates' Courts Act *1980, section 128 is subject to a statutory requirement to review that detention. This is to make sure the detainee is taken back to court no later than the end of the period authorised by the court or when the need for their detention by police ceases, whichever is the sooner.*

C:15C *In the case of a review of detention, but not an extension, the detainee need not be woken for the review. However, if the detainee is likely to be asleep, e.g. during a period of rest allowed as in paragraph 12.2, at the latest time a review or authorisation to extend detention may take place, the officer should, if the legal obligations and time constraints permit, bring forward the procedure to allow the detainee to make representations. A* *detainee not asleep during the review must be present when the grounds for their continued detention are recorded and must at the same time be informed of those grounds unless the review officer considers the person is incapable of understanding what is said, violent or likely to become violent or in urgent need of medical attention.*

C:15D *An application to a magistrates' court under PACE, sections 43 or 44 for a warrant of further detention or its extension should be made between 10am and 9pm, and if possible during normal court hours. It will not usually be practicable to arrange for a court to sit specially outside the hours of 10am to 9pm. If it appears a special sitting may be needed outside normal court hours but between 10am and 9pm, the clerk to the justices should be given notice and informed of this possibility, while the court is sitting if possible.*

C:15E *In paragraph 15.2, the officer responsible for the station holding the detainee includes a superintendent or above who, in accordance with their force operational policy or police regulations, is given that responsibility on a temporary basis whilst the appointed long-term holder is off duty or otherwise unavailable.*

C:15F *The provisions of PACE, section 40A allowing telephone reviews do not apply to reviews of detention after charge by the custody officer. When video conferencing is not required, they allow the use of a telephone to carry out a review of detention before charge. The procedure under PACE, section 42 must be done in person.*

C:15G *The use of video conferencing facilities for decisions about detention under section 45A of PACE is subject to the introduction of regulations by the Secretary of State.*

C:16 Charging detained persons

(a) *Action*

C:16.1 When the officer in charge of the investigation reasonably believes there is sufficient evidence to provide a realistic prospect of the detainee's conviction for the offence (see paragraph 11.6) they shall without delay, and subject to the following qualification, inform the custody officer who will be responsible for considering whether the detainee should be charged. See *Notes 11B* and *16A*. When a person is detained in respect of more than one offence it is permissible to delay informing the custody officer until the above conditions are satisfied in respect of all the offences, but see paragraph 11.6. If the detainee is a juvenile, mentally disordered or otherwise mentally vulnerable, any resulting action shall be taken in the presence of the appropriate adult if they are present at the time. See *Notes 16B* and *16C*.

C:16.1A Where guidance issued by the Director of Public Prosecutions under section 37A is in force the custody officer must comply with that guidance in deciding how to act in dealing with the detainee. See *Notes 16AA* and *16AB*.

C:16.1B Where in compliance with the DPP's Guidance the custody officer decides that the case should be immediately referred to the CPS to make the charging decision, consultation should take place with a Crown Prosecutor as soon as is reasonably practicable. Where the Crown Prosecutor is unable to make the charging decision on the information available at that time, the detainee may be released without charge and on bail (with conditions if necessary) under section 37(7)(a). In such circumstances, the detainee should be informed that they are being released to enable the Director of Public Prosecutions to make a decision under section 37B.

C:16.2 When a detainee is charged with or informed they may be prosecuted for an offence, see *Note 16B*, they shall, unless the restriction on drawing adverse inferences from silence applies, see Annex C, be cautioned as follows:

> *"You do not have to say anything. But it may harm your defence if you do not mention now something which you later rely on in court. Anything you do say may be given in evidence.".*

Where the use of the Welsh Language is appropriate, a constable may provide the caution directly in Welsh in the following terms:

> *"Does dim rhaid i chi ddweud dim byd. Ond gall niweidio eich amddiffyniad os na fy-*

ddwch chi'n sôn, yn awr, am rywbeth y byddwch chi'n dibynnu arno nes ymlaen yn y llys.
Gall unrhyw beth yr ydych yn ei ddweud gael ei roi fel tystiolaeth."

Annex C, paragraph 2 sets out the alternative terms of the caution to be used when the restriction on drawing adverse inferences from silence applies.

C:16.3 When a detainee is charged they shall be given a written notice showing particulars of the offence and, subject to paragraph 2.6A, the officer's name and the case reference number. As far as possible the particulars of the charge shall be stated in simple terms, but they shall also show the precise offence in law with which the detainee is charged. The notice shall begin:

"You are charged with the offence(s) shown below." Followed by the caution.

If the detainee is a juvenile, mentally disordered or otherwise mentally vulnerable, the notice should be given to the appropriate adult.

C:16.4 If, after a detainee has been charged with or informed they may be prosecuted for an offence, an officer wants to tell them about any written statement or interview with another person relating to such an offence, the detainee shall either be handed a true copy of the written statement or the content of the interview record brought to their attention [*sic*]. Nothing shall be done to invite any reply or comment except to:

(a) caution the detainee, *"You do not have to say anything, but anything you do say may be given in evidence."*; where the use of the Welsh Language is appropriate, caution the detainee in the following terms: *"Does dim rhaid i chi ddweud dim byd, ond gall unrhyw beth yr ydych yn ei ddweud gael ei roi fel tystiolaeth."*; and

(b) remind the detainee about their right to legal advice.

C:16.4A If the detainee:

• cannot read, the document may be read to them;

• is a juvenile, mentally disordered or otherwise mentally vulnerable, the appropriate adult shall also be given a copy, or the interview record shall be brought to their attention.

C:16.5 A detainee may not be interviewed about an offence after they have **A–90** been charged with, or informed they may be prosecuted for it, unless the interview is necessary:

• to prevent or minimise harm or loss to some other person, or the public;

• to clear up an ambiguity in a previous answer or statement;

• in the interests of justice for the detainee to have put to them, and have an opportunity to comment on, information concerning the offence which has come to light since they were charged or informed they might be prosecuted.

Before any such interview, the interviewer shall:

(a) caution the detainee, *"You do not have to say anything, but anything you do say may be given in evidence."*; where the use of the Welsh Language is appropriate, the interviewer shall caution the detainee, *"Does dim rhaid i chi ddweud dim byd, ond gall unrhyw beth yr ydych yn ei ddweud gael ei roi fel tystiolaeth."*;

(b) remind the detainee about their right to legal advice.

See *Note 16B.*

C:16.6 The provisions of paragraphs 16.2 to 16.5 must be complied with in the appropriate adult's presence if they are already at the police station. If they are not at the police station then these provisions must be complied with again in their presence when they arrive unless the detainee has been released. See *Note 16C.*

C:16.7 When a juvenile is charged with an offence and the custody officer authorises their continued detention after charge, the custody officer must try to make arrangements for the juvenile to be taken into the care of a local authority to be detained pending appearance in court unless the custody officer certifies it is impracticable to do so or, in the case of a juvenile of at least 12 years old [*sic*], no secure accommodation is available and there is a risk to the public of serious harm from that juvenile, in accordance with *PACE*, section 38(6). See *Note 16D*.

(b) *Documentation*

C:16.8 A record shall be made of anything a detainee says when charged.

C:16.9 Any questions put in an interview after charge and answers given relating to the offence shall be recorded in full during the interview on forms for that purpose and the record signed by the detainee or, if they refuse, by the interviewer and any third parties present. If the questions are audibly recorded or visually recorded the arrangements in Code E or F apply.

C:16.10 If it is not practicable to make arrangements for a juvenile's transfer into local authority care as in paragraph 16.7, the custody officer must record the reasons and complete a certificate to be produced before the court with the juvenile. See *Note 16D*.

Notes for guidance

A-91

C:16A *The custody officer must take into account alternatives to prosecution under the Crime and Disorder Act 1998, reprimands and warning applicable to persons under 18, and in national guidance on the cautioning of offenders, for persons aged 18 and over.*

C:16AA *When a person is arrested under the provisions of the Criminal Justice Act 2003 which allow a person to be re-tried after being acquitted of a serious offence which is a qualifying offence specified in Schedule 5 to that Act and not precluded from further prosecution by virtue of section 75(3) of that Act the detention provisions of PACE are modified and make an officer of the rank of superintendant or above who has not been directly involved in the investigation responsible for determining whether the evidence is sufficient to charge.*

C:16AB *Where guidance issued by the Director of Public Prosecutions under section 37B is in force, a custody officer who determines in accordance with that guidance that there is sufficient evidence to charge the detainee, may detain that person for no longer than is reasonably necessary to decide how that person is to be dealt with under PACE section 37(7)(a) to (d), including, where appropriate, consultation with the duty prosecutor. The period is subject to the maximum period of detention before charge determined by PACE, sections 41 to 44. Where in accordance with the guidance the case is referred to the CPS for decision, the custody officer should ensure that an officer involved in the investigation sends to the CPS such information as is specified in the guidance.*

C:16B *The giving of a warning or the service of the Notice of Intended Prosecution required by the Road Traffic Offenders Act 1988, section 1 does not amount to informing a detainee they may be prosecuted for an offence and so does not preclude further questioning in relation to that offence.*

C:16C *There is no power under PACE to detain a person and delay action under paragraphs 16.2 to 16.5 solely to await the arrival of the appropriate adult. After charge, bail cannot be refused, or release on bail delayed, simply because an appropriate adult is not available, unless the absence of that adult provides the custody officer with the necessary grounds to authorise detention after charge under PACE, section 38.*

C:16D *Except as in paragraph 16.7, neither a juvenile's behaviour nor the nature of the offence provides grounds for the custody officer to decide it is impracticable to arrange the juvenile's transfer to local authority care. Similarly, the lack of secure local authority accommodation does not make it impracticable to transfer the juvenile. The availability of secure accommodation is only a factor in relation to a juvenile aged 12 or over when the local authority accommodation would not be adequate to protect the public from serious harm from them. The obligation to transfer a juvenile to local authority accommodation applies as much to a juvenile charged during the daytime as to a juvenile to be held overnight, subject to a requirement to bring the juvenile before a court under PACE, section 46.*

C:17 Testing persons for the presence of specified Class A drugs

(a) *Action*

A-91a

C:17.1 This section of Code C applies only in selected police stations in police areas where the provisions for drug testing under section 63B of *PACE* (as amended by section 5 of the *Criminal Justice Act* 2003 and section 7 of the *Drugs Act* 2005) are in force and in respect of which the Secretary of State has given a notification to the relevant chief officer of police that arrangements for the taking of samples have been made. Such a notificiation will cover either a police area as a whole or particular stations within a police area. The notification indicates whether the testing applies to those arrested or charged or under the age of 18 as the case may be and testing can only take place in respect of the persons so indicated in the notification. Testing cannot be carried out unless the relevant notification has been given and has not been withdrawn. See *Note 17F*.

C:17.2 A sample of urine or a non-intimate sample may be taken from a person in police detention for the purpose of ascertaining whether he has any specified Class A drug in his body only where they have been brought before the custody officer and;

    (a) either the arrest condition, see paragraph 17.3, or the charge condition, see paragraph 17.4, is met;

    (b) the age condition, see paragraph 17.5, is met;

    (c) the notification condition is met in relation to the arrest condition, the charge condition, or the age condition, as the case may be; (testing on charge and/or arrest must be specifically provided for in the notification for the power to apply; in addition, the fact that testing of under 18s is authorised must be expressly provided for in the notification before the power to test such persons applies); see paragraph 17.1; and

    (d) a police officer has requested the person concerned to give the sample (the request condition).

C:17.3 The arrest condition is met where the detainee:

    (a) has been arrested for a trigger offence, see *Note 17E*, but not charged with that offence; or

    (b) has been arrested for any other offence but not charged with that offence and a police officer of inspector rank or above, who has reasonable grounds for suspecting that their misuse of any specified Class A drug caused or contributed to the offence, has authorised the sample to be taken.

C:17.4 The charge condition is met where the detainee:

    (a) has been charged with a trigger offence, or

    (b) has been charged with any other offence and a police officer of inspector rank or above, who has reasonable grounds for suspecting that the detainee's misuse of any specified Class A drug caused or contributed to the offence, has authorised the sample to be taken.

C:17.5 The age condition is met where:

    (a) in the case of a detainee who has been arrested but not charged as in paragraph 17.3, they are aged 18 or over;

    (b) in the case of a detainee who has been charged as in paragraph 17.4, they are aged 14 or over.

C:17.6 Before requesting a sample from the person concerned, an officer must:

    (a) inform them that the purpose of taking the sample is for drug testing under *PACE*; this is to ascertain whether they have a specified Class A drug present in their body;

    (b) warn them that if, when so requested, they fail without good cause to provide a sample they may be liable to prosecution;

    (c) where the taking of the sample has been authorised by an inspector or above in accordance with paragraph 17.3(b) or 17.4(b) above, inform them that the authorisation has been given and the grounds for giving it;

    (d) remind them of the following rights, which may be exercised at any stage during the period in custody:

    (i) the right to have someone informed of their arrest [see section 5];

    (ii) the right to consult privately with a solicitor and that free independent legal advice is available [see section 6]; and

    (iii) the right to consult these codes of practice [see section 3].

C:17.7 In the case of a person who has not attained the age of 17—

    (a) the making of the request for a sample under paragraph 17.2(d) above;

    (b) the giving of the warning and the information under paragraph 17.6 above; and

    (c) the taking of the sample,

may not take place except in the presence of an appropriate adult. (See *Note 17G*.)

C:17.8 Authorisation by an officer of the rank of inspector or above within paragraph 17.3(b) or 17.4(b) may be given orally or in writing but, if it is given orally, it must be confirmed in writing as soon as practicable.

C:17.9 If a sample is taken from a detainee who has been arrested for an offence but not charged with that offence as in paragraph 17.3, no further sample may be taken during the same continuous period of detention. If during that same period the charge condition is also met in respect of that detainee, the sample which has been taken shall be treated as being taken by virtue of the charge condition, see paragraph 17.4, being met.

C:17.10 A detainee from whom a sample may be taken may be detained for up to six hours from the time of the charge if the custody officer reasonably believes the detention is necessary to enable a sample to be taken. Where the arrest condition is met, a detainee whom the custody officer has decided to release on bail without charge may continue to be detained, but not beyond 24 hours from the relevant time (as defined in section 41(2) of *PACE*), to enable a sample to be taken.

C:17.11 A detainee in respect of whom the arrest condition is met, but not the charge condition, see paragraphs 17.3 and 17.4, and whose release would be required before a sample can be taken had they not continued to be detained as a result of being arrested for a further offence which does not satisfy the arrest condition, may have a sample taken at any time within 24 hours after the arrest for the offence that satisfies the arrest condition.

(b) *Documentation*

C:17.12 The following must be recorded in the custody record:

    (a) if a sample is taken following authorisation by an officer of the rank of inspector or above, the authorisation and the grounds for suspicion;

    (b) the giving of a warning of the consequences of failure to provide a sample;

    (c) the time at which the sample was given; and

    (d) the time of charge or, where the arrest condition is being relied upon, the time of arrest and, where applicable, the fact that a sample taken after arrest but before charge is to be treated as being taken by virtue of the charge condition, where that is met in the same period of continuous detention. See paragraph 17.9.

(c) *General*

C:17.13 A sample may only be taken by a prescribed person. See *Note 17C*.

C:17.14 Force may not be used to take any sample for the purpose of drug testing.

C:17.15 The terms "Class A drug" and "misuse" have the same meanings as in the *Misuse of Drugs Act* 1971. "Specified" (in relation to a Class A drug) and "trigger offence" have the same meanings as in Part III of the *Criminal Justice and Court Services Act* 2000.

C:17.16 Any sample taken:

    (a) may not be used for any purpose other than to ascertain whether the person concerned has a specified Class A drug present in his body; and

(b) can be disposed of as clinical waste unless it is to be sent for further analysis in cases where the test result is disputed at the point when the result is known, or where medication has been taken, or for quality assurance purposes.

(d) *Assessment of misuse of drugs*

C:17.17 Under the provisions of Part 3 of the *Drugs Act* 2005, where a detainee has tested positive for a specified Class A drug under section 63B of *PACE* a police officer may, at any time before the person's release from the police station, impose a requirement on the detainee for them to attend an initial assessment of their drug misuse by a suitably qualified person and to remain for its duration. Where such a requirement is imposed, the officer must, at the same time, impose a second requirement on the detainee to attend and remain for a follow-up assessment. The officer must inform the detainee that the second requirement will cease to have effect if, at the initial assessment they are informed that a follow-up assessment is not necessary. These requirements may only be imposed on a person if:

(a) they have reached the age of 18;

(b) notification has been given by the Secretary of State to the relevant chief officer of police that arrangements for conducting initial and follow-up assessments have been made for those from whom samples for testing have been taken at the police station where the detainee is in custody.

C:17.18 When imposing a requirement to attend an initial assessment and a follow-up assessment the police officer must:

(a) inform the person of the time and place at which the initial assessment is to take place;

(b) explain that this information will be confirmed in writing; and

(c) warn the person that they may be liable to prosecution if they fail without good cause to attend the initial assessment and remain for its duration and if they fail to attend the follow-up assessment and remain for its duration (if so required).

C:17.19 Where a police officer has imposed a requirement to attend an initial assessment and a follow-up assessment in accordance with paragraph 17.17, he must, before the person is released from detention, give the person notice in writing which:

(a) confirms their requirement to attend and remain for the duration of the assessments; and

(b) confirms the information and repeats the warning referred to in paragraph 17.18.

C:17.20 The following must be recorded in the custody record:

(a) that the requirement to attend an initial assessment and a follow-up assessment has been imposed; and

(b) the information, explanation, warning and notice given in accordance with paragraphs 17.17 and 17.19.

C:17.21 Where a notice is given in accordance with paragraph 17.19, a police officer can give the person a further notice in writing which informs the person of any change to the time or place at which the initial assessment is to take place and which repeats the warning referred to in paragraph 17.18(c).

C:17.22 Part 3 of the *Drugs Act* 2005 also requires police officers to have regard to any guidance issued by the Secretary of State in respect of the assessment provisions.

Notes for Guidance

C:17A *When warning a person who is asked to provide a urine or non-intimate sample in accordance with paragraph 17.6(b), the following form of words may be used:*

"*You do not have to provide a sample, but I must warn you that if you fail or refuse without good cause to do so, you will commit an offence for which you may be imprisoned, or fined, or both.".*

Where the Welsh language is appropriate, the following form of words may be used:

"*Does dim rhaid i chi roi sampl, ond mae'n rhaid i mi eich rhybuddio y byddwch chi'n cyflawni trosedd os byddwch chi'n methu neu yn gwrthod gwneud hynny heb reswm da, ac y gellir, oherwydd hynny, eich carcharu, eich dirwyo, neu'r ddau.*"

C:17B *A sample has to be sufficient and suitable. A sufficient sample is sufficient in quantity and quality to enable drug testing analysis to take place. A suitable sample is one which, by its nature, is suitable for a particular form of drug analysis.*

C:17C *A prescribed person in paragraph 17.13 is one who is prescribed in regulations made by the Secretary of State under section 63B(6) of the* Police and Criminal Evidence Act 1984. [*The regulations are currently contained in regulation S.I. 2001 No. 2645, the* Police and Criminal Evidence Act 1984 (Drug Testing Persons in Police Detention) (Prescribed Persons) Regulations 2001.]

C:17D *Samples, and the information derived from them, may not be subsequently used in the investigation of any offence or in evidence against the persons from whom they were taken.*

C:17E *Trigger offences are:*

1. *Offences under the following provisions of the* Theft Act 1968:

section 1	*(theft)*
section 8	*(robbery)*
section 9	*(burglary)*
section 10	*(aggravated burglary)*
section 12	*(taking a motor vehicle or other conveyance without authority)*
section 12A	*(aggravated vehicle-taking)*
section 22	*(handling stolen goods)*
section 25	*(going equipped for stealing, etc.)*

2. *Offences under the following provisions of the* Misuse of Drugs Act 1971, *if committed in respect of a specified Class A drug:—*

section 4	*(restriction on production and supply of controlled drugs)*
section 5(2)	*(possession of a controlled drug)*
section 5(3)	*(possession of a controlled drug with intent to supply)*

3. *Offences under the following provisions of the* Fraud Act 2006:

section 1	*(fraud)*
section 6	*(possession etc. of articles for use in frauds)*
section 7	*(making or supplying articles for use in frauds)*

3A. *An offence under section 1(1) of the* Criminal Attempts Act 1981 *if committed in respect of an offence under—*

(a) *any of the following provisions of the* Theft Act 1968

section 1	*(theft)*
section 8	*(robbery)*
section 9	*(burglary)*
section 22	*(handling stolen goods)*

(b) *section 1 of the* Fraud Act 2006

4. *Offences under the following provisions of the* Vagrancy Act 1824:

section 3	*(begging)*
section 4	*(persistent begging)*

C:17F *The power to take samples is subject to notification by the Secretary of State that appropriate arrangements for the taking of samples have been made for the police area as a whole or for the particular police station concerned for whichever of the following is specified in the notification:*

(a) *persons in respect of whom the arrest condition is met;*

(b) *persons in respect of whom the charge condition is met;*

(c) *persons who have not attained the age of 18.*

Note: Notification is treated as having been given for the purposes of the charge condition in relation to a police area, if testing (on charge) under section 63B(2) of PACE was in force immediately before section 7 of the Drugs Act 2005 *was brought into force; and for the purposes of the age condition, in relation to a police area or police station, if immediately before that day, notification that arrangements had been made for the taking of samples from persons under the age of 18 (those aged 14–17) had been given and had not been withdrawn.*

C:17G *Appropriate adult in paragraph 17.7 means the person's—*

(a) *parent or guardian or, if they are in the care of a local authority or voluntary organisation, a person representing that authority or organisation; or*

(b) *a social worker of a local authority; or*

(c) *if no person falling within (a) or (b) above is available, any responsible person aged 18 or over who is not a police officer or a person employed by the police.*

ANNEX A

Intimate and strip searches

A *Intimate search*

C:1. An intimate search consists of the physical examination of a person's body orifices other than the mouth. The intrusive nature of such searches means the actual and potential risks associated with intimate searches must never be underestimated.   **A–92**

(a) *Action*

C:2. Body orifices other than the mouth may be searched only: **A–93**

(a) if authorised by an officer of inspector rank or above who has reasonable grounds for believing that the person may have concealed on themselves:

(i) anything which they could and might use to cause physical injury to themselves or others at the station; or

(ii) a Class A drug which they intended to supply to another or to export;

and the officer has reasonable grounds for believing that an intimate search is the only means of removing those items; and

(b) if the search is under paragraph 2(a)(ii) (a drug offence search), the detainee's appropriate consent has been given in writing.

C:2A. Before the search begins, a police officer, designated detention officer or staff custody officer, must tell the detainee:—

(a) that the authority to carry out the search has been given;

(b) the grounds for giving the authorisation and for believing that the article cannot be removed without an intimate search.

C:2B Before a detainee is asked to give appropriate consent to a search under paragraph 2(a)(ii) (a drug offence search) they must be warned that if they refuse without good cause their refusal may harm their case if it comes to trial, see *Note A6*. This warning may be given by a police officer or member of police staff. A detainee who is not legally represented must be reminded of their entitlement to have free legal advice, see Code C, paragraph 6.5, and the reminder noted in the custody record.

C:3. An intimate search may only be carried out by a registered medical practitioner or registered nurse, unless an officer of at least inspector rank considers this is not practicable and the search is to take place under paragraph 2(a)(i), in which case a police officer may carry out the search. See *Notes A1* to *A5*.

C:3A. Any proposal for a search under paragraph 2(a)(i) to be carried out by someone other than a registered medical practitioner or registered nurse must only be considered as a last resort and when the authorising officer is satisfied the risks associated with allowing the item to remain with the detainee outweigh the risks associated with removing it. See *Notes A1* to *A5*.

C:4. An intimate search under:

- paragraph 2(a)(i) may take place only at a hospital, surgery, other medical premises or police station;
- paragraph 2(a)(ii) may take place only at a hospital, surgery or other medical premises and must be carried out by a registered medical practitioner or a registered nurse.

C:5. An intimate search at a police station of a juvenile or mentally disordered or otherwise mentally vulnerable person may take place only in the presence of an appropriate adult of the same sex, unless the detainee specifically requests a particular adult of the opposite sex who is readily available. In the case of a juvenile the search may take place in the absence of the appropriate adult only if the juvenile signifies in the presence of the appropriate adult they do not want the adult present during the search and the adult agrees. A record shall be made of the juvenile's decision and signed by the appropriate adult.

C:6. When an intimate search under paragraph 2(a)(i) is carried out by a police officer, the officer must be of the same sex as the detainee. A minimum of two people, other than the detainee, must be present during the search. Subject to paragraph 5, no person of the opposite sex who is not a medical practitioner or nurse shall be present, nor shall anyone whose presence is unnecessary. The search shall be conducted with proper regard to the sensitivity and vulnerability of the detainee.

(b) *Documentation*

A–94

C:7. In the case of an intimate search the following shall be recorded as soon as practicable, in the detainee's custody record:

(a) for searches under paragraphs 2(a)(i) and (ii);

- the authorisation to carry out the search;
- the grounds for giving the authorisation;
- the grounds for believing the article could not be removed without an intimate search;
- which parts of the detainee's body were searched;
- who carried out the search;
- who was present;
- the result;

(b) for searches under paragraph 2(a)(ii):

- the giving of the warning required by paragraph 2B;
- the fact that the appropriate consent was given or (as the case may be) refused, and if refused, the reason given for the refusal (if any).

C:8. If an intimate search is carried out by a police officer, the reason why it was impracticable for a registered medical practitioner or registered nurse to conduct it must be recorded.

B *Strip search*

A–95

C:9. A strip search is a search involving the removal of more than outer clothing. In this code, outer clothing includes shoes and socks.

(a) *Action*

A–96

C:10. A strip search may take place only if it is considered necessary to remove an article which a detainee would not be allowed to keep, and the officer reasonably considers the detainee might have concealed such an article. Strip searches shall not be routinely carried out if there is no reason to consider that articles are concealed.

The conduct of strip searches

C:11. When strip searches are conducted:

    (a) a police officer carrying out a strip search must be the same sex as the detainee;

    (b) the search shall take place in an area where the detainee cannot be seen by anyone who does not need to be present, nor by a member of the opposite sex except an appropriate adult who has been specifically requested by the detainee;

    (c) except in cases of urgency, where there is risk of serious harm to the detainee or to others, whenever a strip search involves exposure of intimate body parts, there must be at least two people present other than the detainee, and if the search is of a juvenile or mentally disordered or otherwise mentally vulnerable person, one of the people must be the appropriate adult. Except in urgent cases as above, a search of a juvenile may take place in the absence of the appropriate adult only if the juvenile signifies in the presence of the appropriate adult that they do not want the adult to be present during the search and the adult agrees. A record shall be made of the juvenile's decision and signed by the appropriate adult. The presence of more than two people, other than an appropriate adult, shall be permitted only in the most exceptional circumstances;

    (d) the search shall be conducted with proper regard to the sensitivity and vulnerability of the detainee in these circumstances and every reasonable effort shall be made to secure the detainee's co-operation and minimise embarrassment. Detainees who are searched shall not normally be required to remove all their clothes at the same time, *e.g.* a person should be allowed to remove clothing above the waist and redress before removing further clothing;

    (e) if necessary to assist the search, the detainee may be required to hold their arms in the air or to stand with their legs apart and bend forward so a visual examination may be made of the genital and anal areas provided no physical contact is made with any body orifice;

    (f) if articles are found, the detainee shall be asked to hand them over. If articles are found within any body orifice other than the mouth, and the detainee refuses to hand them over, their removal would constitute an intimate search, which must be carried out as in Part A;

    (g) a strip search shall be conducted as quickly as possible, and the detainee allowed to dress as soon as the procedure is complete.

(b) *Documentation*

C:12. A record shall be made on the custody record of a strip search including **A–97** the reason it was considered necessary, those present and any result.

Notes for guidance

C:A1 *Before authorising any intimate search, the authorising officer must make every* **A–98** *reasonable effort to persuade the detainee to hand the article over without a search. If the detainee agrees, a registered medical practitioner or registered nurse should whenever possible be asked to assess the risks involved and, if necessary, attend to assist the detainee.*

C:A2 *If the detainee does not agree to hand the article over without a search, the authorising officer must carefully review all the relevant factors before authorising an intimate search. In particular, the officer must consider whether the grounds for believing an article may be concealed are reasonable.*

C:A3 *If authority is given for a search under paragraph 2(a)(i), a registered medical practitioner or registered nurse shall be consulted whenever possible. The presumption should be that the search will be conducted by the registered medical practitioner or registered nurse and the authorising officer must make every reasonable effort to persuade the detainee to allow the medical practitioner or nurse to conduct the search.*

C:A4 *A constable should only be authorised to carry out a search as a last resort and when all other approaches have failed. In these circumstances, the authorising officer must be satisfied the detainee might use the article for one or more of the purposes in paragraph 2(a)(i) and the physical injury likely to be caused is sufficiently severe to justify authorising a constable to carry out the search.*

C:A5 *If an officer has any doubts whether to authorise an intimate search by a constable, the officer should seek advice from an officer of superintendent rank or above.*

C:A6 *In warning a detainee who is asked to consent to an intimate drug offence search, as in paragraph 2B, the following form of words may be used:*

"You do not have to allow yourself to be searched, but I must warn you that if you refuse without good cause, your refusal may harm your case if it comes to trial.".

Where the use of the Welsh Language is appropriate, the following form of words may be used:

"Nid oes rhaid i chi roi caniatâd i gael eich archwilio, ond mae'n rhaid i mi eich rhybuddio os gwrthodwch heb reswm da, y gallai eich penderfyniad i wrthod wneud niwed i'ch achos pe bai'n dod gerbron llys."

ANNEX B

Delay in notifying arrest or allowing access to legal advice

A *Persons detained under PACE*

　　C:1. The exercise of the rights in section 5 or section 6, or both, may be delayed if the person is in police detention, as in *PACE*, section 118(2), in connection with an indictable offence, has not yet been charged with an offence and an officer of superintendent rank or above, or inspector rank or above only for the rights in section 5, has reasonable grounds for believing their exercise will:

(i) lead to:

- interference with, or harm to, evidence connected with an indictable offence; or
- interference with, or physical harm to, other people; or

(ii) lead to alerting other people suspected of having committed an indictable offence but not yet arrested for it; or

(iii) hinder the recovery of property obtained in consequence of the commission of such an offence.

C:2. These rights may also be delayed if the officer has reasonable grounds to believe that:

(i) the person detained for an indictable offence has benefited from their criminal conduct (decided in accordance with Part 2 of the *Proceeds of Crime Act* 2002); and

(ii) the recovery of the value of the property constituting that benefit will be hindered by the exercise of either right.

C:3. Authority to delay a detainee's right to consult privately with a solicitor may be given only if the authorising officer has reasonable grounds to believe the solicitor the detainee wants to consult will, inadvertently or otherwise, pass on a message from the detainee or act in some other way which will have any of the consequences specified under paragraphs 1 or 2. In these circumstances the detainee must be allowed to choose another solicitor. See *Note B3.*

C:4. If the detainee wishes to see a solicitor, access to that solicitor may not be delayed on the grounds they might advise the detainee not to answer questions or the solicitor was initially asked to attend the police station by someone else. In the latter case the detainee must be told the solicitor has come to the police station at another person's request, and must be asked to sign the custody record to signify whether they want to see the solicitor.

C:5. The fact the grounds for delaying notification of arrest may be satisfied does not automatically mean the grounds for delaying access to legal advice will also be satisfied.

C:6. These rights may be delayed only for as long as grounds exist and in no case beyond 36 hours after the relevant time as in *PACE*, section 41. If the grounds cease to apply within this time, the detainee must, as soon as practicable, be asked if they want to exercise either right, the custody record must be noted accordingly, and action taken in accordance with the relevant section of the code.

C:7. A detained person must be permitted to consult a solicitor for a reasonable time before any court hearing.

B [*Not used.*]

C *Documentation*

C:13. The grounds for action under this annex shall be recorded and the **A–100** detainee informed of them as soon as practicable.

C:14. Any reply given by a detainee under paragraphs 6 or 11 must be recorded and the detainee asked to endorse the record in relation to whether they want to receive legal advice at this point.

D *Cautions and special warnings*

C:15. When a suspect detained at a police station is interviewed during any period for which access to legal advice has been delayed under this annex, the court or jury may not draw adverse inferences from their silence.

Notes for guidance

C:B1 *Even if Annex B applies in the case of a juvenile, or a person who is mentally* **A–101** *disordered or otherwise mentally vulnerable, action to inform the appropriate adult and the person responsible for a juvenile's welfare if that is a different person, must nevertheless be taken as in paragraph 3.13 and 3.15.*

C:B2 *In the case of Commonwealth citizens and foreign nationals, see Note 7A.*

C:B3 *A decision to delay access to a specific solicitor is likely to be a rare occurrence and only when it can be shown the suspect is capable of misleading that particular solicitor and there is more than a substantial risk that the suspect will succeed in causing information to be conveyed which will lead to one or more of the specified consequences.*

ANNEX C

Restriction on drawing adverse inferences from silence and terms of the caution when the restriction applies

(a) *The restriction on drawing adverse inferences from silence*

C:1. The *Criminal Justice and Public Order Act* 1994, sections 34, 36 and 37 as **A–102** amended by the *Youth Justice and Criminal Evidence Act* 1999, section 58 describe the conditions under which adverse inferences may be drawn from a person's failure or refusal to say anything about their involvement in the offence when interviewed, after being charged or informed they may be prosecuted. These provisions are subject to an overriding restriction on the ability of a court or jury to draw adverse inferences from a person's silence. This restriction applies:

    (a) to any detainee at a police station, see *Note 10C*, who, before being interviewed, see section 11, or being charged or informed they may be prosecuted, see section 16, has:

        (i) asked for legal advice, see section 6, paragraph 6.1;

        (ii) not been allowed an opportunity to consult a solicitor, including the duty solicitor, as in this code; and

        (iii) not changed their mind about wanting legal advice, see section 6, paragraph 6.6(d);

           – [note the condition in (ii) will

                – apply when a detainee who has asked for legal advice is interviewed before speaking to a solicitor as in section 6, paragraph 6.6(a) or (b);

                – not apply if the detained person declines to ask for the duty solicitor, see section 6, paragraphs 6.6(c) and (d)];

    (b) to any person charged with, or informed they may be prosecuted for, an offence who:

        (i) has had brought to their notice a written statement made by another person or the content of an interview with another person which relates to that offence, see section 16, paragraph 16.4;

        (ii) is interviewed about that offence, see section 16, paragraph 16.5; or

        (iii) makes a written statement about that offence, see Annex D paragraphs 4 and 9.

(b) Terms of the caution when the restriction applies

C:2. When a requirement to caution arises at a time when the restriction on drawing adverse inferences from silence applies, the caution shall be:

    "You do not have to say anything, but anything you do say may be given in evidence.".

Where the use of the Welsh Language is appropriate, the caution may be used directly in Welsh in the following terms:

    "Does dim rhaid i chi ddweud dim byd, ond gall unrhyw beth yr ydych chi'n ei ddweud gael ei roi fel tystiolaeth."

C:3. Whenever the restriction either begins to apply or ceases to apply after a caution has already been given, the person shall be re-cautioned in the appropriate terms. The changed position on drawing inferences and that the previous caution no longer applies shall also be explained to the detainee in ordinary language. See *Note C2*.

Notes for guidance

C:C1 *The restriction on drawing inferences from silence does not apply to a person who has not been detained and who therefore cannot be prevented from seeking legal advice if they want to, see paragraphs 10.2 and 3.15.*

C:C2 *The following is suggested as a framework to help explain changes in the position on drawing adverse inferences if the restriction on drawing adverse inferences from silence:*
(a) begins to apply:

    "The caution you were previously given no longer applies. This is because after that caution:

    (i) you asked to speak to a solicitor but have not yet been allowed an opportunity to speak to a solicitor;" see paragraph 1(a); or

    "(ii) you have been charged with/informed you may be prosecuted." See paragraph 1(b).

    "This means that from now on, adverse inferences cannot be drawn at court and your defence will not be harmed just because you choose to say nothing. Please listen carefully

*to the caution I am about to give you because it will apply from now on. You will see that
it does not say anything about your defence being harmed.";*

*(b) ceases to apply before or at the time the person is charged or informed they may be
prosecuted, see paragraph 1(a);*

*"The caution you were previously given no longer applies. This is because after that
caution you have been allowed an opportunity to speak to a solicitor. Please listen carefully to the caution I am about to give you because it will apply from now on. It explains
how your defence at court may be affected if you choose to say nothing.".*

ANNEX D

Written statements under caution

(a) *Written by a person under caution*

C:1. A person shall always be invited to write down what they want to say.   **A–103**

C:2. A person who has not been charged with, or informed they may be prosecuted for, any offence to which the statement they want to write relates, shall:

    (a) unless the statement is made at a time when the restriction on drawing
adverse inferences from silence applies, see Annex C, be asked to write
out and sign the following before writing what they want to say:

        *"I make this statement of my own free will. I understand that I do not have
to say anything but that it may harm my defence if I do not mention
when questioned something which I later rely on in court. This statement
may be given in evidence.";*

    (b) if the statement is made at a time when the restriction on drawing adverse
inferences from silence applies, be asked to write out and sign the following before writing what they want to say;

        *"I make this statement of my own free will. I understand that I do not have
to say anything. This statement may be given in evidence.".*

C:3. When a person, on the occasion of being charged with or informed they
may be prosecuted for any offence, asks to make a statement which relates to any
such offence and wants to write it they shall:

    (a) unless the restriction on drawing adverse inferences from silence, see An-
nex C, applied when they were so charged or informed they may be
prosecuted, be asked to write out and sign the following before writing
what they want to say:

        *"I make this statement of my own free will. I understand that I do not have
to say anything but that it may harm my defence if I do not mention
when questioned something which I later rely on in court. This statement
may be given in evidence.";*

    (b) if the restriction on drawing adverse inferences from silence applied
when they were so charged or informed they may be prosecuted, be
asked to write out and sign the following before writing what they want
to say:

        *"I make this statement of my own free will. I understand that I do not have
to say anything. This statement may be given in evidence.".*

C:4. When a person, who has already been charged with or informed they may
be prosecuted for any offence, asks to make a statement which relates to any such
offence and wants to write it they shall be asked to write out and sign the following before writing what they want to say:

    *"I make this statement of my own free will. I understand that I do not have to say
anything. This statement may be given in evidence.".*

C:5. Any person writing their own statement shall be allowed to do so without
any prompting except a police officer or police staff may indicate to them which
matters are material or question any ambiguity in the statement.

(b) Written by a police officer or other police staff

C:6. If a person says they would like someone to write the statement for them, a police officer, or other police staff shall write the statement.

C:7. If the person has not been charged with, or informed they may be prosecuted for, any offence to which the statement they want to make relates they shall, before starting, be asked to sign, or make their mark, to the following:

> (a) unless the statement is made at a time when the restriction on drawing adverse inferences from silence applies, see Annex C:
>
>> "*I,...................., wish to make a statement. I want someone to write down what I say. I understand that I do not have to say anything but that it may harm my defence if I do not mention when questioned something which I later rely on in court. This statement may be given in evidence.*";
>
> (b) if the statement is made at a time when the restriction on drawing adverse inferences from silence applies:
>
>> "*I,...................., wish to make a statement. I want someone to write down what I say. I understand that I do not have to say anything. This statement may be given in evidence.*".

C:8. If, on the occasion of being charged with or informed they may be prosecuted for any offence, the person asks to make a statement which relates to any such offence they shall before starting be asked to sign, or make their mark to, the following:

> (a) unless the restriction on drawing adverse inferences from silence applied, see Annex C, when they were so charged or informed they may be prosecuted:
>
>> "*I,...................., wish to make a statement. I want someone to write down what I say. I understand that I do not have to say anything but that it may harm my defence if I do not mention when questioned something which I later rely on in court. This statement may be given in evidence.*";
>
> (b) if the restriction on drawing adverse inferences from silence applied when they were so charged or informed they may be prosecuted:
>
>> "*I,...................., wish to make a statement. I want someone to write down what I say. I understand that I do not have to say anything. This statement may be given in evidence.*".

C:9. If, having already been charged with or informed they may be prosecuted for any offence, a person asks to make a statement which relates to any such offence they shall before starting, be asked to sign, or make their mark to:

> "*I,...................., wish to make a statement. I want someone to write down what I say. I understand that I do not have to say anything. This statement may be given in evidence.*".

C:10. The person writing the statement must take down the exact words spoken by the person making it and must not edit or paraphrase it. Any questions that are necessary, *e.g.* to make it more intelligible, and the answers given must be recorded at the same time on the statement form.

C:11. When the writing of a statement is finished the person making it shall be asked to read it and to make any corrections, alterations or additions they want. When they have finished reading they shall be asked to write and sign or make their mark on the following certificate at the end of the statement:

> "*I have read the above statement, and I have been able to correct, alter or add anything I wish. This statement is true. I have made it of my own free will.*".

C:12. If the person making the statement cannot read, or refuses to read it, or to write the above mentioned certificate at the end of it or to sign it, the person taking the statement shall read it to them and ask them if they would like to correct, alter or add anything and to put their signature or make their mark at the end. The person taking the statement shall certify on the statement itself what has occurred.

ANNEX E

Summary of provisions relating to mentally disordered and otherwise mentally vulnerable people

C:1. If an officer has any suspicion, or is told in good faith, that a person of any   **A–105**
age may be mentally disordered or otherwise mentally vulnerable, or mentally
incapable of understanding the significance of questions or their replies that
person shall be treated as mentally disordered or otherwise mentally vulnerable
for the purposes of this code. See paragraph 1.4.

C:2. In the case of a person who is mentally disordered or otherwise mentally
vulnerable, "the appropriate adult" means:

    (a) a relative, guardian or other person responsible for their care or custody;

    (b) someone experienced in dealing with mentally disordered or mentally
        vulnerable people but who is not a police officer or employed by the po-
        lice;

    (c) failing these, some other responsible adult aged 18 or over who is not a
        police officer or employed by the police.

See paragraph 1.7(b) and Note 1D.

C:3. If the custody officer authorises the detention of a person who is mentally
vulnerable or appears to be suffering from a mental disorder, the custody officer
must as soon as practicable inform the appropriate adult of the grounds for
detention and the person's whereabouts, and ask the adult to come to the police
station to see them. If the appropriate adult:

    • is already at the station when information is given as in paragraphs 3.1 to
      3.5 the information must be given in their presence;

    • is not at the station when the provisions of paragraph 3.1 to 3.5 are
      complied with these provisions must be complied with again in their
      presence once they arrive.

See paragraphs 3.15 to 3.17.

C:4. If the appropriate adult, having been informed of the right to legal advice,
considers legal advice should be taken, the provisions of section 6 apply as if the
mentally disordered or otherwise mentally vulnerable person had requested access to legal advice. See paragraph 3.19 and *Note E1*.

C:5. The custody officer must make sure a person receives appropriate clinical
attention as soon as reasonably practicable if the person appears to be suffering
from a mental disorder or in urgent cases immediately call the nearest health care
professional or an ambulance. It is not intended these provisions delay the transfer
of a detainee to a place of safety under the *Mental Health Act* 1983, section 136 if
that is applicable. If an assessment under that Act is to take place at a police station,
the custody officer must consider whether an appropriate health care professional
should be called to conduct an initial clinical check on the detainee. See paragraph
9.5 and 9.6.

C:6. It is imperative a mentally disordered or otherwise mentally vulnerable
person detained under the *Mental Health Act* 1983, section 136 be assessed as soon
as possible. If that assessment is to take place at the police station, an approved social
worker and registered medical practitioner shall be called to the station as soon as
possible in order to interview and examine the detainee. Once the detainee has been
interviewed, examined and suitable arrangements been made for their treatment or
care, they can no longer be detained under section 136. A detainee should be immediately discharged from detention if a registered medical practitioner having
examined them, concludes they are not mentally disordered within the meaning of
the Act. See paragraph 3.16.

C:7. If a mentally disordered or otherwise mentally vulnerable person is
cautioned in the absence of the appropriate adult, the caution must be repeated
in the appropriate adult's presence. See paragraph 10.12.

C:8. A mentally disordered or otherwise mentally vulnerable person must not
be interviewed or asked to provide or sign a written statement in the absence of

the appropriate adult unless the provisions of paragraphs 11.1 or 11.18 to 11.20 apply. Questioning in these circumstances may not continue in the absence of the appropriate adult once sufficient information to avert the risk has been obtained A record shall be made of the grounds for any decision to begin an interview in these circumstances. See paragraphs 11.1, 11.15 and 11.18 to 11.20.

C:9. If the appropriate adult is present at an interview, they shall be informed they are not expected to act simply as an observer and the purposes of their presence are to:

- advise the interviewee;
- observe whether or not the interview is being conducted properly and fairly;
- facilitate communication with the interviewee.

See paragraph 11.17.

A-106   C:10. If the detention of a mentally disordered or otherwise mentally vulnerable person is reviewed by a review officer or a superintendent, the appropriate adult must, if available at the time, be given an opportunity to make representations to the officer about the need for continuing detention. See paragraph 15.3.

C:11. If the custody officer charges a mentally disordered or otherwise mentally vulnerable person with an offence or takes such other action as is appropriate when there is sufficient evidence for a prosecution this must be done in the presence of the appropriate adult. The written notice embodying any charge must be given to the appropriate adult. See paragraphs 16.1 to 16.4A.

C:12. An intimate or strip search of a mentally disordered or otherwise mentally vulnerable person may take place only in the presence of the appropriate adult of the same sex, unless the detainee specifically requests the presence of a particular adult of the opposite sex. A strip search may take place in the absence of an appropriate adult only in cases of urgency when there is a risk of serious harm to the detainee or others. See Annex A, paragraphs 5 and 11(c).

C:13. Particular care must be taken when deciding whether to use any form of approved restraints on a mentally disordered or otherwise mentally vulnerable person in a locked cell. See paragraph 8.2.

Notes for guidance

A-107   C:E1 *The purpose of the provision at paragraph 3.19 is to protect the rights of a mentally disordered or otherwise mentally vulnerable detained person who does not understand the significance of what is said to them. If the detained person wants to exercise the right to legal advice, the appropriate action should be taken and not delayed until the appropriate adult arrives. A mentally disordered or otherwise mentally vulnerable detained person should always be given an opportunity, when an appropriate adult is called to the police station, to consult privately with a solicitor in the absence of the appropriate adult if they want.*

C:E2 *Although people who are mentally disordered or otherwise mentally vulnerable are often capable of providing reliable evidence, they may, without knowing or wanting to do so be particularly prone in certain circumstances to provide information that may be unreliable, misleading or self-incriminating. Special care should always be taken when questioning such a person, and the appropriate adult should be involved if there is any doubt about a person's mental state or capacity. Because of the risk of unreliable evidence, it is important to obtain corroboration of any facts admitted whenever possible.*

C:E3 *Because of the risks referred to in Note E2, which the presence of the appropriate adult is intended to minimise, officers of superintendent rank or above should exercise their discretion to authorise the commencement of an interview in the appropriate adult's absence only in exceptional cases, if it is necessary to avert an immediate risk of serious harm. See paragraphs 11.1, 11.18 to 11.20.*

ANNEX F

**Countries with which bilateral consular conventions or agreements requiring
notification of the arrest and detention of their nationals are in force as at 1
April 2003**

A–108

Armenia	Kazakhstan
Austria	Macedonia
Azerbaijan	Mexico
Belarus	Moldova
Belgium	Mongolia
Bosnia-Herzegovina	Norway
Bulgaria	Poland
China*	Romania
Croatia	Russia
Cuba	Slovak Republic
Czech Republic	Slovenia
Denmark	Spain
Egypt	Sweden
France	Tajikistan
Georgia	Turkmenistan
German Federal Republic	Ukraine
Greece	USA
Hungary	Uzbekistan
Italy	Yugoslavia
Japan	

* Police are required to inform Chinese officials of arrest/detention in the Manchester consular district only. This comprises Derbyshire, Durham, Greater Manchester, Lancashire, Merseyside, North South and West Yorkshire, and Tyne and Wear.

ANNEX G

Fitness to be interviewed

C:1. This annex contains general guidance to help police officers and health care professionals assess whether a detainee might be at risk in an interview.

A–109

C:2. A detainee may be at risk in an interview if it is considered that:

    (a) conducting the interview could significantly harm the detainee's physical or mental state;

    (b) anything the detainee says in the interview about their involvement or suspected involvement in the offence about which they are being interviewed **might** be considered unreliable in subsequent court proceedings because of their physical or mental state.

C:3. In assessing whether the detainee should be interviewed, the following must be considered:

    (a) how the detainee's physical or mental state might affect their ability to understand the nature and purpose of the interview, to comprehend what is being asked and to appreciate the significance of any answers given and make rational decisions about whether they want to say anything;

    (b) the extent to which the detainee's replies may be affected by their physical or mental condition rather than representing a rational and accurate explanation of their involvement in the offence;

(c) how the nature of the interview, which could include particularly probing questions, might affect the detainee.

A–110 **C:4.** It is essential health care professionals who are consulted consider the functional ability of the detainee rather than simply relying on a medical diagnosis, *e.g.* it is possible for a person with severe mental illness to be fit for interview.

C:5. Health care professionals should advise on the need for an appropriate adult to be present, whether reassessment of the person's fitness for interview may be necessary if the interview lasts beyond a specified time, and whether a further specialist opinion may be required.

C:6. When health care professionals identify risks they should be asked to quantify the risks. They should inform the custody officer:

- whether the person's condition:
  – is likely to improve;
  – will require or be amenable to treatment; and
- indicate how long it may take for such improvement to take effect.

C:7. The role of the health care professional is to consider the risks and advise the custody officer of the outcome of that consideration. The health care professional's determination and any advice or recommendations should be made in writing and form part of the custody record.

C:8. Once the health care professional has provided that information, it is a matter for the custody officer to decide whether or not to allow the interview to go ahead and if the interview is to proceed, to determine what safeguards are needed. Nothing prevents safeguards being provided in addition to those required under the code. An example might be to have an appropriate health care professional present during the interview, in addition to an appropriate adult, in order constantly to monitor the person's condition and how it is being affected by the interview.

ANNEX H

Detained person: observation list

A–111 **C:1.** If any detainee fails to meet any of the following criteria, an appropriate health care professional or an ambulance must be called.

C:2. When assessing the level of rousability, consider:

Rousability—can they be woken?
- go into the cell
- call their name
- shake gently

Response to questions—can they give appropriate answers to questions such as:
- What's your name?
- Where do you live?
- Where do you think you are?

Response to commands—can they respond appropriately to commands such as:
- Open your eyes!
- Lift one arm, now the other arm!

C:3. Remember to take into account the possibility or presence of other illnesses, injury, or mental condition, a person who is drowsy and smells of alcohol may also have the following:

- Diabetes
- Epilepsy
- Head injury
- Drug intoxication or overdose
- Stroke

ANNEX I
[*Not used*]

ANNEX J
[*Not used*]

ANNEX K

X-rays and ultrasound scans

(a) *Action*

C:1. *PACE*, section 55A allows a person who has been arrested and is in police   **A–111a**
detention to have an x-ray taken of them or an ultrasound scan to be carried out on
them (or both) if:

   (a) authorised by an officer of inspector rank or above who has reasonably
   grounds for believing that the detainee:
      (i) may have swallowed a Class A drug; and
      (ii) was in possession of that Class A drug with the intention of supplying
      it to another or to export; and
   (b) the detainee's appropriate consent has been given in writing.

C:2. Before an x-ray is taken or an ultrasound scan carried out, a police officer,
designated detention officer or staff custody officer must tell the detainee:—

   (a) that the authority has been given; and
   (b) the grounds for giving the authorisation.

C:3. Before a detainee is asked to give appropriate consent to an x-ray or an
ultrasound scan, they must be warned that if they refuse without good cause their
refusal may harm their case if it comes to trial, see *Notes K1* and *K2*. This warning
may be given by a police officer or member of police staff. A detainee who is not
legally represented must be reminded of their entitlement to have free legal advice,
see Code C, paragraph 6.5, and the reminder noted in the custody record.

C:4. An x-ray may be taken, or an ultrasound scan may be carried out, only by
a registered medical practitioner or registered nurse, and only at a hospital,
surgery or other medical premises.

(b) *Documentation*

C:5. The following shall be recorded as soon as practicable in the detainee's
custody record:

   (a) the authorisation to take the x-ray or carry out the ultrasound scan (or
   both);
   (b) the grounds for giving the authorisation;
   (c) the giving of the warning required by paragraph 3; and
   (d) the fact that the appropriate consent was given or (as the case may be)
   refused, and if refused, the reason given for the refusal (if any); and
   (e) if an x-ray is taken or an ultrasound scan carried out:
      - where it was taken or carried out;

- who took it or carried it out;
- who was present;
- the result.

Paragraphs 1.4–1.7 of this code apply and an appropriate adult should be presen
when consent is sought to any procedure under this annex.

Notes for guidance

A–111b   **C:**K1 *If authority is given for an x-ray to be taken or an ultrasound scan to be carried
out (or both), consideration should be given to asking a registered medical practitioner o
registered nurse to explain to the detainee what is involved and to allay any concerns th
detainee might have about the effect which taking an x-ray or carrying out an ultrasoun
scan might have on them. If appropriate consent is not given, evidence of the explanatio
may, if the case comes to trial, be relevant to determining whether the detainee had a goo
cause for refusing.*

C:K2 *In warning a detainee who is asked to consent to an x-ray being taken or a
ultrasound scan being carried out (or both), as in paragraph 3, the following form of word
may be used:*

"You do not have to allow an x-ray of you to be taken or an ultrasound scan to be car
ried out on you, but I must warn you that if you refuse without good cause, your refusa
may harm your case if it comes to trial.".

Where the use of the Welsh Language is appropriate, the following form of word
may be provided in Welsh:

*"Does dim rhaid i chi ganiatáu cymryd sgan uwchsain neu belydr-x (neu'r ddau) ar
noch, ond mae'n rhaid i mi eich rhybuddio os byddwch chi'n gwrthod gwneud hynny he
reswm da, fe allai hynny niweidio eich achos pe bai'n dod gerbron llys."*

(5) Identification

A–112   The text that follows is of the version of the code that came into force or
February 1, 2008 see *ante*, Appendix A–1.

In connection with Code D, see also §§ 14–29 *et seq.* (application of code)
§§ 14–33 *et seq.* (identification parades), § 14–39 (group identification
confrontation and video identification), §§ 14–40 *et seq.* (effect of breaches)
§§ 14–43 *et seq.* (photographs), §§ 14–46 *et seq.* (video recordings), and § 15-
234 (photographs) in the main work.

D. Code of Practice for the Identification of Persons by Police Officers

Commencement—Transitional arrangements

A–112a   This code has effect in relation to any identification procedure carried out afte
midnight on 31 December 2005.

D:1 Introduction

A–113   **D:**1.1 This code of practice concerns the principal methods used by police t
identify people in connection with the investigation of offences and the keeping o
accurate and reliable criminal records.

D:1.2 Identification by witnesses arises, *e.g.*, if the offender is seen committin
the crime and a witness is given an opportunity to identify the suspect in a vide
identification, identification parade or similar procedure. The procedures ar
designed to:

- test the witness's ability to identify the person they saw on a previous o
casion;

- provide safeguards against mistaken identification.

While this code concentrates on visual identification procedures, it does not preclude the police making use of aural identification procedures such as a "voice identification parade", where they judge that appropriate.

D:1.3 Identification by fingerprints applies when a person's fingerprints are taken to:

- compare with fingerprints found at the scene of a crime;
- check and prove convictions;
- help to ascertain a person's identity.

D:1.3A Identification using footwear impressions applies when a person's footwear impressions are taken to compare with impressions found at the scene of a crime.

D:1.4 Identification by body samples and impressions includes taking samples such as blood or hair to generate a DNA profile for comparison with material obtained from the scene of a crime, or a victim.

D:1.5 Taking photographs of arrested people applies to recording and checking identity and locating and tracing persons who: **A–114**

- are wanted for offences;
- fail to answer their bail.

D:1.6 Another method of identification involves searching and examining detained suspects to find, *e.g.*, marks such as tattoos or scars which may help establish their identity or whether they have been involved in committing an offence.

D:1.7 The provisions of the *Police and Criminal Evidence Act* 1984 (*PACE*) and this code are designed to make sure fingerprints, samples, impressions and photographs are taken, used and retained, and identification procedures carried out, only when justified and necessary for preventing, detecting or investigating crime. If these provisions are not observed, the application of the relevant procedures in particular cases may be open to question.

D:2 General

D:2.1 This code must be readily available at all police stations for consultation by: **A–115**

- police officers and police staff;
- detained persons;
- members of the public.

D:2.2 The provisions of this code:

- include the *Annexes*;
- do not include the *Notes for guidance*.

D:2.3 Code C, paragraph 1.4, regarding a person who may be mentally disordered or otherwise mentally vulnerable and the *Notes for guidance* applicable to those provisions apply to this Code.

D:2.4 Code C, paragraph 1.5, regarding a person who appears to be under the age of 17 applies to this code.

D:2.5 Code C, paragraph 1.6, regarding a person who appears blind, seriously visually impaired, deaf, unable to read or speak or has difficulty orally because of a speech impediment applies to this code.

D:2.6 In this code: **A–116**

- "appropriate adult" means the same as in Code C, paragraph 1.7,
- "solicitor" means the same as in Code C, paragraph 6.12,
- and the *Notes for guidance* applicable to those provisions apply to this code.

D:2.7 References to custody officers include those performing the functions of custody officer, see paragraph 1.9 of Code C.

D:2.8 When a record of any action requiring the authority of an officer of a specified rank is made under this code, subject to paragraph 2.18, the officer's name and rank must be recorded,

D:2.9 When this code requires the prior authority or agreement of an officer of at least inspector or superintendent rank, that authority may be given by a sergeant or chief inspector who has been authorised to perform the functions of the higher rank under *PACE*, section 107.

D:2.10 Subject to paragraph 2.18, all records must be timed and signed by the maker.

D:2.11 Records must be made in the custody record, unless otherwise specified. References to "pocket book" include any official report book issued to police officers or police staff.

D:2.12 If any procedure in this code requires a person's consent, the consent of a:

- mentally disordered or otherwise mentally vulnerable person is only valid if given in the presence of the appropriate adult;
- juvenile, is only valid if their parent's or guardian's consent is also obtained unless the juvenile is under 14, when their parent's or guardian's consent is sufficient in its own right. If the only obstacle to an identification procedure in section 3 is that a juvenile's parent or guardian refuses consent or reasonable efforts to obtain it have failed, the identification officer may apply the provisions of paragraph 3.21. See *Note 2A*.

D:2.13 If a person is blind, seriously visually impaired or unable to read, the custody officer or identification officer shall make sure their solicitor, relative, appropriate adult or some other person likely to take an interest in them and not involved in the investigation is available to help check any documentation. When this code requires written consent or signing, the person assisting may be asked to sign instead, if the detainee prefers. This paragraph does not require an appropriate adult to be called solely to assist in checking and signing documentation for a person who is not a juvenile, or mentally disordered or otherwise mentally vulnerable (see *Note 2B* and Code C, paragraph 3.15).

D:2.14 If any procedure in this code requires information to be given to or sought from a suspect, it must be given or sought in the appropriate adult's presence if the suspect is mentally disordered, otherwise mentally vulnerable or a juvenile. If the appropriate adult is not present when the information is first given or sought, the procedure must be repeated in the presence of the appropriate adult when they arrive. If the suspect appears deaf or there is doubt about their hearing or speaking ability or ability to understand English, and effective communication cannot be established, the information must be given or sought through an interpreter.

D:2.15 Any procedure in this code involving the participation of a suspect who is mentally disordered, otherwise mentally vulnerable or a juvenile must take place in the presence of the appropriate adult. See Code C, paragraph 1.4.

D:2.15A Any procedure in this code involving the participation of a witness who is or appears to be mentally disordered, otherwise mentally vulnerable or a juvenile should take place in the presence of a pre-trial support person. However the support-person must not be allowed to prompt any identification of a suspect by a witness. See *Note 2AB*.

D:2.16 References to:

- "taking a photograph", include the use of any process to produce a single still or moving, visual image;
- "photographing a person", should be construed accordingly;
- "photographs", "films", "negatives" and "copies" include relevant visual images recorded, stored, or reproduced through any medium;
- "destruction" includes the deletion of computer data relating to such images or making access to that data impossible.

D:2.17 Except as described, nothing in this code affects the powers and procedures:

   (i) for requiring and taking samples of breath, blood and urine in relation to driving offences, etc, when under the influence of drink, drugs or excess alcohol under the:

- *Road Traffic Act* 1988, sections 4 to 11;
- *Road Traffic Offenders Act* 1988, sections 15 and 16;
- *Transport and Works Act* 1992, sections 26 to 38;

   (ii) under the *Immigration Act* 1971, Schedule 2, paragraph 18, for taking photographs and fingerprints from persons detained under that Act, Schedule 2, paragraph 16 (Administrative Controls as to Control on Entry etc.); for taking fingerprints in accordance with the *Immigration and Asylum Act* 1999, sections 141 and 142(3), or other methods for collecting information about a person's external physical characteristics provided for by regulations made under that Act, section 144;

   (iii) under the *Terrorism Act* 2000, Schedule 8, for taking photographs, fingerprints, skin impressions, body samples or impressions from people:

- arrested under that Act, section 41,
- detained for the purposes of examination under that Act, Schedule 7, and to whom the code of practice issued under that Act, Schedule 14, paragraph 6, applies ("the terrorism provisions"); see *Note 2C*;

   (iv) for taking photographs, fingerprints, skin impressions, body samples or impressions from people who have been:

- arrested on warrants issued in Scotland, by officers exercising powers under the *Criminal Justice and Public Order Act* 1994, section 136(2);
- arrested or detained without warrant by officers from a police force in Scotland exercising their powers of arrest or detention under the *Criminal Justice and Public Order Act* 1994, section 137(2) (cross border powers of arrest, etc.).

Note: In these cases, police powers and duties and the person's rights and entitlements whilst at a police station in England and Wales are the same as if the person had been arrested in Scotland by a Scottish police officer.

D:2.18 Nothing in this code requires the identity of officers or police staff to be recorded or disclosed:

   (a) in the case of enquiries linked to the investigation of terrorism;

   (b) if the officers or police staff reasonably believe recording or disclosing their names might put them in danger.

In these cases, they shall use warrant or other identification numbers and the name of their police station. *See Note 2D.*

D:2.19 In this code: **A–118**

   (a) "designated person" means a person other than a police officer, designated under the *Police Reform Act* 2002, Part 4, who has specified powers and duties of police officers conferred or imposed on them;

   (b) any reference to a police officer includes a designated person acting in the exercise or performance of the powers and duties conferred or imposed on them by their designation.

D:2.20 If a power conferred on a designated person:

   (a) allows reasonable force to be used when exercised by a police officer, a designated person exercising that power has the same entitlement to use force;

   (b) includes power to use force to enter any premises, that power is not exercisable by that designated person except:

      (i) in the company, and under the supervision, of a police officer; or

(ii) for the purpose of:

- saving life or limb; or
- preventing serious damage to property.

D:2.21 Nothing in this code prevents the custody officer, or other officer given custody of the detainee, from allowing police staff who are not designated persons to carry out individual procedures or tasks at the police station if the law allows. However, the officer remains responsible for making sure the procedures and tasks are carried out correctly in accordance with the codes of practice. Any such person must be:

(a) a person employed by a police authority maintaining a police force and under the control and direction of the chief officer of that force;

(b) employed by a person with whom a police authority has a contract for the provision of services relating to persons arrested or otherwise in custody.

D:2.22 Designated persons and other police staff must have regard to any relevant provisions of the codes of practice.

Notes for guidance

A-119

D:2A *For the purposes of paragraph 2.12, the consent required from a parent or guardian may, for a juvenile in the care of a local authority or voluntary organisation, be given by that authority or organisation. In the case of a juvenile, nothing in paragraph 2.12 requires the parent, guardian or representative of a local authority or voluntary organisation to be present to give their consent, unless they are acting as the appropriate adult under paragraphs 2.14 or 2.15. However, it is important that a parent or guardian not present is fully informed before being asked to consent. They must be given the same information about the procedure and the juvenile's suspected involvement in the offence as the juvenile and appropriate adult. The parent or guardian must also be allowed to speak to the juvenile and the appropriate adult if they wish. Provided the consent is fully informed and is not withdrawn, it may be obtained at any time before the procedure takes place.*

D:2AB *The* Youth Justice and Criminal Evidence Act *1999 guidance "Achieving Best Evidence in Criminal Proceedings" indicates that a pre-trial support person should accompany a vulnerable witness during any identification procedure. It states that this support person should not be (or not be likely to be) a witness in the investigation.*

D:2B *People who are seriously visually impaired or unable to read may be unwilling to sign police documents. The alternative, i.e. their representative signing on their behalf, seeks to protect the interests of both police and suspects.*

D:2C *Photographs, fingerprints, samples and impressions may be taken from a person detained under the terrorism provisions to help determine whether they are, or have been, involved in terrorism, as well as when there are reasonable grounds for suspecting their involvement in a particular offence.*

D:2D *The purpose of paragraph 2.18(b) is to protect those involved in serious organised crime investigations or arrests of particularly violent suspects when there is reliable information that those arrested or their associates may threaten or cause harm to the officers. In cases of doubt, an officer of inspector rank or above should be consulted.*

D:3 Identification by witnesses

A-120

D:3.1 A record shall be made of the suspect's description as first given by a potential witness. This record must:

(a) be made and kept in a form which enables details of that description to be accurately produced from it, in a visible and legible form, which can be given to the suspect or the suspect's solicitor in accordance with this code; and

(b) unless otherwise specified, be made before the witness takes part in any identification procedures under paragraphs 3.5 to 3.10, 3.21 or 3.23.

A copy of the record shall where practicable, be given to the suspect or their solicitor before any procedures under paragraphs 3.5 to 3.10, 3.21 or 3.23 are carried out. See *Note 3E.*

(a) *Cases when the suspect's identity is not known*

D:3.2 In cases when the suspect's identity is not known, a witness may be taken to a particular neighbourhood or place to see whether they can identify the person they saw. Although the number, age, sex, race, general description and style of clothing of other people present at the location and the way in which any identification is made cannot be controlled, the principles applicable to the formal procedures under paragraphs 3.5 to 3.10 shall be followed as far as practicable. For example:

(a) where it is practicable to do so, a record should be made of the witness's description of the suspect, as in paragraph 3.1(a), before asking the witness to make an identification;

(b) care must be taken not to direct the witness's attention to any individual unless, taking into account all the circumstances, this cannot be avoided; however, this does not prevent a witness being asked to look carefully at the people around at the time or to look towards a group or in a particular direction, if this appears necessary to make sure that the witness does not overlook a possible suspect simply because the witness is looking in the opposite direction and also to enable the witness to make comparisons between any suspect and others who are in the area; see *Note 3F*;

(c) where there is more than one witness, every effort should be made to keep them separate and witnesses should be taken to see whether they can identify a person independently;

(d) once there is sufficient information to justify the arrest of a particular individual for suspected involvement in the offence, *e.g.*, after a witness makes a positive identification, the provisions set out from paragraph 3.4 onwards shall apply for any other witnesses in relation to that individual; subject to paragraphs 3.12 and 3.13, it is not necessary for the witness who makes such a positive identification to take part in a further procedure;

(e) the officer or police staff accompanying the witness must record, in their pocket book, the action taken as soon as, and in as much detail, as possible. The record should include: the date, time and place of the relevant occasion the witness claims to have previously seen the suspect; where any identification was made; how it was made and the conditions at the time (*e.g.*, the distance the witness was from the suspect, the weather and light); if the witness's attention was drawn to the suspect; the reason for this; and anything said by the witness or the suspect about the identification or the conduct of the procedure.

D:3.3 A witness must not be shown photographs, computerised or artist's composite likenesses or similar likenesses or pictures (including "E-fit" images) if the identity of the suspect is known to the police and the suspect is available to take part in a video identification, an identification parade or a group identification. If the suspect's identity is not known, the showing of such images to a witness to obtain identification evidence must be done in accordance with Annex E.

(b) *Cases when the suspect is known and available*

D:3.4 If the suspect's identity is known to the police and they are available, the identification procedures set out in paragraphs 3.5 to 3.10 may be used. References in this section to a suspect being "known" mean there is sufficient information known to the police to justify the arrest of a particular person for suspected involvement in the offence. A suspect being "available" means they are immediately available or will be within a reasonably short time and willing to take an effective part in at least one of the following which it is practicable to arrange: **A–121**

- video identification;
- identification parade; or
- group identification.

Video identification

D:3.5 A "video identification" is when the witness is shown moving images of a known suspect, together with similar images of others who resemble the suspect. Moving images must be used unless:

- the suspect is known but not available (see paragraph 3.21 of this code); or
- in accordance with paragraph 2A of Annex A of this code, the identification officer does not consider that replication of a physical feature can be achieved or that it is not possible to conceal the location of the feature on the image of the suspect.

The identification officer may then decide to make use of video identification but using still images.

D:3.6 Video identifications must be carried out in accordance with Annex A.

Identification parade

D:3.7 An "identification parade" is when the witness sees the suspect in a line of others who resemble the suspect.

D:3.8 Identification parades must be carried out in accordance with Annex B.

Group identification

D:3.9 A "group identification" is when the witness sees the suspect in an informal group of people.

D:3.10 Group identifications must be carried out in accordance with Annex C.

Arranging identification procedures

D:3.11 Except for the provisions in paragraph 3.19, the arrangements for, and conduct of, the identification procedures in paragraphs 3.5 to 3.10 and circumstances in which an identification procedure must be held shall be the responsibility of an officer not below inspector rank who is not involved with the investigation, "the identification officer". Unless otherwise specified, the identification officer may allow another officer or police staff, see paragraph 2.21, to make arrangements for, and conduct, any of these identification procedures. In delegating these procedures, the identification officer must be able to supervise effectively and either intervene or be contacted for advice. No officer or any other person involved with the investigation of the case against the suspect, beyond the extent required by these procedures, may take any part in these procedures or act as the identification officer. This does not prevent the identification officer from consulting the officer in charge of the investigation to determine which procedure to use. When an identification procedure is required, in the interest of fairness to suspects and witnesses, it must be held as soon as practicable.

Circumstances in which an identification procedure must be held

A–122   **D:3.12** Whenever:

  (i) a witness has identified a suspect or purported to have identified them prior to any identification procedure set out in paragraphs 3.5 to 3.10 having been held; or

  (ii) there is a witness available, who expresses an ability to identify the suspect, or where there is a reasonable chance of the witness being able to do so, and they have not been given an opportunity to identify the suspect in any of the procedures set out in paragraphs 3.5 to 3.10,

and the suspect disputes being the person the witness claims to have seen, an identification procedure shall be held unless it is not practicable or it would serve no useful purpose in proving or disproving whether the suspect was involved in committing the offence. For example, when it is not disputed that the suspect is already well known to the witness who claims to have seen them commit the crime.

D:3.13 Such a procedure may also be held if the officer in charge of the investigation considers it would be useful.

Selecting an identification procedure

D:3.14 If, because of paragraph 3.12, an identification procedure is to be held, the suspect shall initially be offered a video identification unless:

(a) a video identification is not practicable; or

(b) an identification parade is both practicable and more suitable than a video identification; or

(c) paragraph 3.16 applies.

The identification officer and the officer in charge of the investigation shall consult each other to determine which option is to be offered. An identification parade may not be practicable because of factors relating to the witnesses, such as their number, state of health, availability and travelling requirements. A video identification would normally be more suitable if it could be arranged and completed sooner than an identification parade.

D:3.15 A suspect who refuses the identification procedure first offered shall be asked to state their reason for refusing and may get advice from their solicitor and/or if present, their appropriate adult. The suspect, solicitor and/or appropriate adult shall be allowed to make representations about why another procedure should be used. A record should be made of the reasons for refusal and any representations made. After considering any reasons given, and representations made, the identification officer shall, if appropriate, arrange for the suspect to be offered an alternative which the officer considers suitable and practicable. If the officer decides it is not suitable and practicable to offer an alternative identification procedure, the reasons for that decision shall be recorded.

D:3.16 A group identification may initially be offered if the officer in charge of the investigation considers it is more suitable than a video identification or an identification parade and the identification officer considers it practicable to arrange.

Notice to suspect

D:3.17 Unless paragraph 3.20 applies, before a video identification, an **A–123** identification parade or group identification is arranged, the following shall be explained to the suspect:

(i) the purposes of the video identification, identification parade or group identification;

(ii) their entitlement to free legal advice; see Code C, paragraph 6.5;

(iii) the procedures for holding it, including their right to have a solicitor or friend present;

(iv) that they do not have to consent to or co-operate in a video identification, identification parade or group identification;

(v) that if they do not consent to, and co-operate in, a video identification, identification parade or group identification, their refusal may be given in evidence in any subsequent trial and police may proceed covertly without their consent or make other arrangements to test whether a witness can identify them, see paragraph 3.21;

(vi) whether, for the purposes of the video identification procedure, images of them have previously been obtained, see paragraph 3.20, and if so, that they may co-operate in providing further, suitable images to be used instead;

(vii) if appropriate, the special arrangements for juveniles;

(viii) if appropriate, the special arrangements for mentally disordered or otherwise mentally vulnerable people;

(ix) that if they significantly alter their appearance between being offered an identification procedure and any attempt to hold an identification procedure, this may be given in evidence if the case comes to trial, and the identification officer may then consider other forms of identification, see paragraph 3.21 and *Note 3C*;

(x) that a moving image or photograph may be taken of them when they attend for any identification procedure;

(xi) whether, before their identity became known, the witness was shown photographs, a computerised or artist's composite likeness or similar likeness or image by the police; see *Note 3B*;

(xii) that if they change their appearance before an identification parade, it may not be practicable to arrange one on the day or subsequently and, because of the appearance change, the identification officer may consider alternative methods of identification; see *Note 3C*;

(xiii) that they or their solicitor will be provided with details of the description of the suspect as first given by any witnesses who are to attend the video identification, identification parade, group identification or confrontation, see paragraph 3.1.

D:3.18 This information must also be recorded in a written notice handed to the suspect. The suspect must be given a reasonable opportunity to read the notice, after which, they should be asked to sign a second copy to indicate if they are willing to co-operate with the making of a video or take part in the identification parade or group identification. The signed copy shall be retained by the identification officer.

D:3.19 The duties of the identification officer under paragraphs 3.17 and 3.18 may be performed by the custody officer or other officer not involved in the investigation if:

(a) it is proposed to release the suspect in order that an identification procedure can be arranged and carried out and an inspector is not available to act as the identification officer, see paragraph 3.11, before the suspect leaves the station; or

(b) it is proposed to keep the suspect in police detention whilst the procedure is arranged and carried out and waiting for an inspector to act as the identification officer, see paragraph 3.11, would cause unreasonable delay to the investigation.

The officer concerned shall inform the identification officer of the action taken and give them the signed copy of the notice. See *Note 3C*.

D:3.20 If the identification officer and officer in charge of the investigation suspect, on reasonable grounds that if the suspect was given the information and notice as in paragraphs 3.17 and 3.18, they would then take steps to avoid being seen by a witness in any identification procedure, the identification officer may arrange for images of the suspect suitable for use in a video identification procedure to be obtained before giving the information and notice. If suspect's [*sic*] images are obtained in these circumstances, the suspect may, for the purposes of a video identification procedure, co-operate in providing new images which if suitable would be used instead, see paragraph 3.17(vi).

(c) *Cases when the suspect is known but not available*

D:3.21 When a known suspect is not available or has ceased to be available, see paragraph 3.4, the identification officer may make arrangements for a video identification (see Annex A). If necessary, the identification officer may follow the video identification procedures but using **still** images. Any suitable moving or still images may be used and these may be obtained covertly if necessary. Alternatively, the identification officer may make arrangements for a group identification. See *Note 3D*. These provisions may also be applied to juveniles where the consent of their parent or guardian is either refused or reasonable efforts to obtain that consent have failed (see paragraph 2.12).

D:3.22 Any covert activity should be strictly limited to that necessary to test the ability of the witness to identify the suspect.

D:3.23 The identification officer may arrange for the suspect to be confronted by the witness if none of the options referred to in paragraphs 3.5 to 3.10 or 3.21 are practicable. A "confrontation" is when the suspect is directly confronted by the witness. A confrontation does not require the suspect's consent. Confrontations must be carried out in accordance with Annex D.

D:3.24 Requirements for information to be given to, or sought from, a suspect or for the suspect to be given an opportunity to view images before they are shown to a witness, do not apply if the suspect's lack of co-operation prevents the necessary action.

(d) *Documentation*

D:3.25 A record shall be made of the video identification, identification parade, group identification or confrontation on forms provided for the purpose.   **A–125**

D:3.26 If the identification officer considers it is not practicable to hold a video identification or identification parade requested by the suspect, the reasons shall be recorded and explained to the suspect.

D:3.27 A record shall be made of a person's failure or refusal to co-operate in a video identification, identification parade or group identification and, if applicable, of the grounds for obtaining images in accordance with paragraph 3.20.

(e) *Showing films and photographs of incidents and information released to the media*

D:3.28 Nothing in this code inhibits showing films or photographs to the public through the national or local media, or to police officers for the purposes of recognition and tracing suspects. However, when such material is shown to potential witnesses, including police officers, see *Note 3A*, to obtain identification evidence, it shall be shown on an individual basis to avoid any possibility of collusion, and, as far as possible, the showing shall follow the principles for video identification if the suspect is known, see Annex A, or identification by photographs if the suspect is not known, see Annex E.   **A–126**

D:3.29 When a broadcast or publication is made, see paragraph 3.28, a copy of the relevant material released to the media for the purposes of recognising or tracing the suspect, shall be kept. The suspect or their solicitor shall be allowed to view such material before any procedures under paragraphs 3.5 to 3.10, 3.21 or 3.23 are carried out, provided it is practicable and would not unreasonably delay the investigation. Each witness involved in the procedure shall be asked, after they have taken part, whether they have seen any broadcast or published films or photographs relating to the offence or any description of the suspect and their replies shall be recorded. This paragraph does not affect any separate requirement under the *Criminal Procedure and Investigations Act* 1996 to retain material in connection with criminal investigations.

(f) *Destruction and retention of photographs taken or used in identification procedures*

D:3.30 *PACE*, section 64A, see paragraph 5.12, provides powers to take photographs of suspects and allows these photographs to be used or disclosed only for purposes related to the prevention or detection of crime, the investigation of offences or the conduct of prosecutions by, or on behalf of, police or other law enforcement and prosecuting authorities inside and outside the United Kingdom or the enforcement of a sentence. After being so used or disclosed, they may be retained but can only be used or disclosed for the same purposes.

D:3.31 Subject to paragraph 3.33, the photographs (and all negatives and copies), of suspects not taken in accordance with the provisions in paragraph 5.12 which are taken for the purposes of, or in connection with, the identification procedures in paragraphs 3.5 to 3.10, 3.21 or 3.23 must be destroyed unless the suspect:

    (a) is charged with, or informed they may be prosecuted for, a recordable offence;

    (b) is prosecuted for a recordable offence;

    (c) is cautioned for a recordable offence or given a warning or reprimand in accordance with the *Crime and Disorder Act* 1998 for a recordable offence; or

    (d) gives informed consent, in writing, for the photograph or images to be retained for purposes described in paragraph 3.30.

D:3.32 When paragraph 3.31 requires the destruction of any photograph, the person must be given an opportunity to witness the destruction or to have a certificate confirming the destruction if they request one within five days of being informed that the destruction is required.

D:3.33 Nothing in paragraph 3.31 affects any separate requirement under the *Criminal Procedure and Investigations Act* 1996 to retain material in connection with criminal investigations.

Notes for guidance

D:3A *Except for the provisions of Annex E, paragraph 1, a police officer who is a witness for the purposes of this part of the code is subject to the same principles and procedures as a civilian witness.*

D:3B *When a witness attending an identification procedure has previously been shown photographs, or been shown or provided with computerised or artist's composite likenesses, or similar likenesses or pictures, it is the officer in charge of the investigation's responsibility to make the identification officer aware of this.*

D:3C *The purpose of paragraph 3.19 is to avoid or reduce delay in arranging identification procedures by enabling the required information and warnings, see sub-paragraphs 3.17(ix) and 3.17(xii), to be given at the earliest opportunity.*

D:3D *Paragraph 3.21 would apply when a known suspect deliberately makes themself "unavailable" in order to delay or frustrate arrangements for obtaining identification evidence. It also applies when a suspect refuses or fails to take part in a video identification, an identification parade or a group identification, or refuses or fails to take part in the only practicable options from that list. It enables any suitable images of the suspect, moving or still, which are available or can be obtained, to be used in an identification procedure. Examples include images from custody and other CCTV systems and from visually recorded interview records, see Code F, Note for Guidance 2D.*

D:3E *When it is proposed to show photographs to a witness in accordance with Annex E, it is the responsibility of the officer in charge of the investigation to confirm to the officer responsible for supervising and directing the showing, that the first description of the suspect given by that witness has been recorded. If this description has not been recorded, the procedure under Annex E must be postponed. See Annex E, paragraph 2.*

D:3F *The admissibility and value of identification evidence obtained when carrying out the procedure under paragraph 3.2 may be compromised if:*

(a) *before a person is identified, the witness's attention is specifically drawn to that person;*
 or

(b) *the suspect's identity becomes known before the procedure.*

D:4 Identification by fingerprints and footwear impressions

(A) *Taking fingerprints in connection with a criminal investigation*

(a) *General*

D:4.1 References to "fingerprints" means [*sic*] any record, produced by any method, of the skin pattern and other physical characteristics or features of a person's:

(i) fingers; or
(ii) palms.

(b) *Action*

D:4.2 A person's fingerprints may be taken in connection with the investigation of an offence only with their consent or if paragraph 4.3 applies. If the person is at a police station consent must be in writing.

D:4.3 *PACE*, section 61, provides powers to take fingerprints without consent from any person over the age of ten years:

(a) under section 61(3), from a person detained at a police station in consequence of being arrested for a recordable offence, see *Note 4A*, if they have not had their fingerprints taken in the course of the investigation of the offence unless those previously taken fingerprints are not a complete set or some or all of those fingerprints are not of sufficient quality to allow satisfactory analysis, comparison or matching;

(b) under section 61(4), from a person detained at a police station who has been charged with a recordable offence, see *Note 4A*, or informed they will be reported for such an offence if they have not had their fingerprints taken in the course of the investigation of the offence unless those previously taken fingerprints are not a complete set or some or all of those fingerprints are not of sufficient quality to allow satisfactory analysis, comparison or matching;

(c) under section 61(4A), from a person who has been bailed to appear at a court or police station if the person:

(i) has answered to bail for a person whose fingerprints were taken previously and there are reasonable grounds for believing they are not the same person; or

(ii) who has answered to bail claims to be a different person from a person whose fingerprints were previously taken;

and in either case, the court or an officer of inspector rank or above, authorises the fingerprints to be taken at the court or police station;

(d) under section 61(6), from a person who has been:

(i) convicted of a recordable offence;

(ii) given a caution in respect of a recordable offence which, at the time of the caution, the person admitted; or

(iii) warned or reprimanded under the *Crime and Disorder Act* 1998, section 65, for a recordable offence.

D:4.4 *PACE*, section 27, provides power to:

(a) require the person as in paragraph 4.3(d) to attend a police station to have their fingerprints taken if the:

(i) person has not been in police detention for the offence and has not had their fingerprints taken in the course of the investigation of that offence; or

(ii) fingerprints that were taken from the person in the course of the investigation of that offence, do not constitute a complete set or some, or all, of the fingerprints are not of sufficient quality to allow satisfactory analysis, comparison or matching; and

(b) arrest, without warrant, a person who fails to comply with the requirement.

Note: the requirement must be made within one month of the date the person is convicted, cautioned, warned or reprimanded and the person must be given a period of at least 7 days within which to attend. This 7 day period need not fall during the month allowed for making the requirement.

D:4.5 A person's fingerprints may be taken, as above, electronically.

D:4.6 Reasonable force may be used, if necessary, to take a person's fingerprints without their consent under the powers as in paragraphs 4.3 and 4.4.

D:4.7 Before any fingerprints are taken with, or without, consent as above, the person must be informed:

(a) of the reason their fingerprints are to be taken;

(b) of the grounds on which the relevant authority has been given if the power mentioned in paragraph 4.3(c) applies;

(c) that their fingerprints may be retained and may be subject of a speculative search against other fingerprints, see *Note 4B*, unless destruction of the fingerprints is required in accordance with Annex F, Part (a); and

(d) that if their fingerprints are required to be destroyed, they may witness their destruction as provided for in Annex F, Part (a).

(c) *Documentation*

D:4.8 A record must be made as soon as possible, of the reason for taking a person's fingerprints without consent. If force is used, a record shall be made of the circumstances and those present.

D:4.9 A record shall be made when a person has been informed under the terms of paragraph 4.7(c), of the possibility that their fingerprints may be subject of a speculative search.

(B) *Taking fingerprints in connection with immigration enquiries*

Action

A–129   **D:**4.10 A person's fingerprints may be taken for the purposes of Immigration Service enquiries in accordance with powers and procedures other than under *PACE* and for which the Immigration Service (not the police) are responsible, only with the person's consent in writing or if paragraph 4.11 applies.

D:4.11 Powers to take fingerprints for these purposes without consent are given to police and immigration officers under the:

   (a) *Immigration Act* 1971, Schedule 2, paragraph 18(2), when it is reasonably necessary for the purposes of identifying a person detained under the *Immigration Act* 1971, Schedule 2, paragraph 16 (detention of person liable to examination or removal);

   (b) *Immigration and Asylum Act* 1999, section 141(7)(a), from a person who fails to produce, on arrival, a valid passport with a photograph or some other document satisfactorily establishing their identity and nationality if an immigration officer does not consider the person has a reasonable excuse for the failure;

   (c) *Immigration and Asylum Act* 1999, section 141(7)(b), from a person who has been refused entry to the UK but has been temporarily admitted if an immigration officer reasonably suspects the person might break a condition imposed on them relating to residence or reporting to a police or immigration officer, and their decision is confirmed by a chief immigration officer;

   (d) *Immigration and Asylum Act* 1999, section 141(7)(c), when directions are given to remove a person:

      • as an illegal entrant,

      • liable to removal under the *Immigration and Asylum Act* 1999, section 10,

      • who is the subject of a deportation order from the UK;

   (e) *Immigration and Asylum Act* 1999, section 141(7)(d), from a person arrested under UK immigration laws under the *Immigration Act* 1971, Schedule 2, paragraph 17;

   (f) *Immigration and Asylum Act* 1999, section 141(7)(e), from a person who has made a claim:

      • for asylum;

      • under Article 3 of the European Convention on Human Rights; or

   (g) *Immigration and Asylum Act* 1999, section 141(7)(f), from a person who is a dependant of someone who falls into (b) to (f) above.

D:4.12 The *Immigration and Asylum Act* 1999, section 142(3), gives a police and immigration officer power to arrest, without warrant, a person who fails to comply with a requirement imposed by the Secretary of State to attend a specified place for fingerprinting.

D:4.13 Before any fingerprints are taken, with or without consent, the person must be informed:

   (a) of the reason their fingerprints are to be taken;

   (b) the fingerprints, and all copies of them, will be destroyed in accordance with Annex F, Part B.

D:4.14 Reasonable force may be used, if necessary, to take a person's fingerprints without their consent under powers as in paragraph 4.11.

D:4.15 Paragraphs 4.1 and 4.8 apply.

(C) *Taking footwear impressions in connection with a criminal investigation*

(a) *Action*

D:4.16 Impressions of a person's footwear may be taken in connection with the investigation of an offence only with their consent or if paragraph 4.17 applies. If the person is at a police station consent must be in writing.

D:4.17 *PACE*, section 61A, provides power for a police officer to take footwear impressions without consent from any person over the age of 10 years who is detained at a police station:

- (a) in consequence of being arrested for a recordable offence, see *Note 4A*; or if the detainee has been charged with a recordable offence, or informed they will be reported for such an offence; and
- (b) the detainee has not had an impression of their footwear taken in the course of the investigation of the offence unless the previously taken impression is not complete or is not of sufficient quality to allow satisfactory analysis, comparison or matching (whether in the case in question or generally).

D:4.18 Reasonable force may be used, if necessary, to take a footwear impression from a detainee without consent under the power in paragraph 4.17.

D:4.19 Before any footwear impression is taken with, or without, consent as above, the person must be informed:

- (a) of the reason the impression is to be taken;
- (b) that the impression may be retained and may be subject of a speculative search against other impressions, see *Note 4B*, unless destruction of the impression is required in accordance with Annex F, Part (a); and
- (c) that if their footwear impressions are required to be destroyed, they may witness their destruction as provided for in Annex F, Part (a).

(b) *Documentation*

D:4.20 A record must be made as soon as possible, of the reason for taking a person's footwear impressions without consent. If force is used, a record shall be made of the circumstances and those present.

D:4.21 A record shall be made when a person has been informed under the terms of paragraph 4.19(b), of the possibility that their footwear impressions may be subject of a speculative search.

Notes for guidance

D:4A *References to "recordable offences" in this code relate to those offences for which convictions, cautions, reprimands and warnings may be recorded in national police records. See PACE, section 27(4). The recordable offences current at the time when this code was prepared, are any offences which carry a sentence of imprisonment on conviction (irrespective of the period, or the age of the offender or actual sentence passed) as well as the non-imprisonable offences under the* Vagrancy Act *1824, sections 3 and 4 (begging and persistent begging), the* Street Offences Act *1959, section 1 (loitering or soliciting for purposes of prostitution), the* Road Traffic Act *1988, section 25 (tampering with motor vehicles), the* Criminal Justice and Public Order Act *1994, section 167 (touting for car hire services) and others listed in the* National Police Records (Recordable Offences) Regulations *2000 as amended.*

D:4B *Fingerprints, footwear impressions or a DNA sample (and the information derived from it) taken from a person arrested on suspicion of being involved in a recordable offence, or charged with such an offence, or informed they will be reported for such an offence, may be subject of a speculative search. This means the fingerprints, footwear impressions or DNA sample may be checked against other fingerprints, footwear impressions and DNA records* *held by, or on behalf of, the police and other law enforcement authorities in, or outside, the UK, or held in connection with, or as a result of, an investigation of an offence inside or outside the UK. Fingerprints, footwear impressions and samples taken from a person suspected of committing a recordable offence but not arrested, charged or informed they will be reported for it, may be subject to a speculative search only if the person consents in writing. The following is an example of a basic form of words:*

> *"I consent to my fingerprints, footwear impressions and DNA sample and information derived from it being retained and used only for purposes related to the prevention and detection of a crime, the investigation of an offence or the conduct of a prosecution either nationally or internationally.*
>
> *I understand that my fingerprints, footwear impressions or DNA sample may be checked against other fingerprint, footwear impressions and DNA records held by or on behalf of relevant law enforcement authorities, either nationally or internationally.*
>
> *I understand that once I have given my consent for my fingerprints, footwear impressions or DNA sample to be retained and used I cannot withdraw this consent.".*

See Annex F regarding the retention and use of fingerprints and footwear impressions taken with consent for elimination purposes.

D:5 Examinations to establish identity and the taking of photographs

(A) *Detainees at police stations*

(a) *Searching or examination of detainees at police stations*

A–130 **D:5.1** *PACE*, section 54A(1), allows a detainee at a police station to be searched or examined or both, to establish:

  (a) whether they have any marks, features or injuries that would tend to identify them as a person involved in the commission of an offence and to photograph any identifying marks, see paragraph 5.5; or

  (b) their identity, see *Note 5A*.

A person detained at a police station to be searched under a stop and search power, see Code A, is not a detainee for the purposes of these powers.

D:5.2 A search and/or examination to find marks under section 54A(1)(a) may be carried out without the detainee's consent, see paragraph 2.12, only if authorised by an officer of at least inspector rank when consent has been withheld or it is not practicable to obtain consent, see *Note 5D*.

D:5.3 A search or examination to establish a suspect's identity under section 54A(1)(b) may be carried out without the detainee's consent, see paragraph 2.12, only if authorised by an officer of at least inspector rank when the detainee has refused to identify themselves or the authorising officer has reasonable grounds for suspecting the person is not who they claim to be.

D:5.4 Any marks that assist in establishing the detainee's identity, or their identification as a person involved in the commission of an offence, are identifying marks. Such marks may be photographed with the detainee's consent, see paragraph 2.12; or without their consent if it is withheld or it is not practicable to obtain it, see *Note 5D*.

D:5.5 A detainee may only be searched, examined and photographed under section 54A, by a police officer of the same sex.

D:5.6 Any photographs of identifying marks, taken under section 54A, may be used or disclosed only for purposes related to the prevention or detection of crime, the investigation of offences or the conduct of prosecutions by, or on behalf of, police or other law enforcement and prosecuting authorities inside, and outside, the UK. After being so used or disclosed, the photograph may be retained but must not be used or disclosed except for these purposes, see *Note 5B*.

D:5.7 The powers, as in paragraph 5.1, do not affect any separate requirement under the *Criminal Procedure and Investigations Act* 1996 to retain material in connection with criminal investigations.

D:5.8 Authority for the search and/or examination for the purposes of paragraphs 5.2 and 5.3 may be given orally or in writing. If given orally, the authorising officer must confirm it in writing as soon as practicable. A separate authority is required for each purpose which applies.

D:5.9 If it is established a person is unwilling to co-operate sufficiently to enable a search and/or examination to take place or a suitable photograph to be taken, an officer may use reasonable force to:

(a) search and/or examine a detainee without their consent; and

(b) photograph any identifying marks without their consent.

D:5.10 The thoroughness and extent of any search or examination carried out in accordance with the powers in section 54A must be no more than the officer considers necessary to achieve the required purpose. Any search or examination which involves the removal of more than the person's outer clothing shall be conducted in accordance with Code C, Annex A, paragraph 11.

D:5.11 An intimate search may not be carried out under the powers in section 54A.

(b) *Photographing detainees at police stations and other persons elsewhere than at a police station*

D:5.12 Under *PACE*, section 64A, an officer may photograph:

(a) any person whilst they are detained at a police station; and

(b) any person who is elsewhere than at a police station and who has been:—

(i) arrested by a constable for an offence;

(ii) taken into custody by a constable after being arrested for an offence by a person other than a constable;

(iii) made subject to a requirement to wait with a community support officer under paragraph 2(3) or (3B) of Schedule 4 to the *Police Reform Act* 2002;

(iv) given a penalty notice by a constable in uniform under Chapter 1 of Part 1 of the *Criminal Justice and Police Act* 2001, a penalty notice by a constable under section 444A of the *Education Act* 1996, or a fixed penalty notice by a constable in uniform under section 54 of the *Road Traffic Offenders Act* 1988;

(v) given a notice in relation to a relevant fixed penalty offence (within the meaning of paragraph 1 of Schedule 4 to the *Police Reform Act* 2002) by a community support officer by virtue of a designation applying that paragraph to him;

(vi) given a notice in relation to a relevant fixed penalty offence (within the meaning of paragraph 1 of Schedule 5 to the *Police Reform Act* 2002) by an accredited person by virtue of accreditation specifying that that paragraph applies to him; or

(vii) given a direction to leave and not return to a specified location for up to 48 hours by a police constable (under section 27 of the *Violent Crime Reduction Act* 2006).

D:5.12A Photographs taken under *PACE*, section 64A:

(a) may be taken with the person's consent, or without their consent if consent is withheld or it is not practicable to obtain their consent, see *Note 5E*; and

(b) may be used or disclosed only for purposes related to the prevention or detection of crime, the investigation of offences or the conduct of prosecutions by, or on behalf of, police or other law enforcement and prosecuting authorities inside and outside the United Kingdom or the enforcement of any sentence or order made by a court when dealing with an offence. After being so used or disclosed, they may be retained but can only be used or disclosed for the same purposes. See *Note 5B*.

D:5.13 The officer proposing to take a detainee's photograph may, for this purpose, require the person to remove any item or substance worn on, or over, all, or any part of, their head or face. If they do not comply with such a requirement, the officer may remove the item or substance.

D:5.14 If it is established the detainee is unwilling to co-operate sufficiently to enable a suitable photograph to be taken and it is not reasonably practicable to take the photograph covertly, an officer may use reasonable force, see *Note 5F*:

    (a) to take their photograph without their consent; and

    (b) for the purpose of taking the photograph, remove any item or substance worn on, or over, all, or any part of, the person's head or face which they have failed to remove when asked.

D:5.15 For the purposes of this code, a photograph may be obtained without the person's consent by making a copy of an image of them taken at any time on a camera system installed anywhere in the police station.

(c) *Information to be given*

A–132   **D:**5.16 When a person is searched, examined or photographed under the provisions as in paragraph 5.1 and 5.12, or their photograph obtained as in paragraph 5.15, they must be informed of the:

    (a) purpose of the search, examination or photograph;

    (b) grounds on which the relevant authority, if applicable, has been given; and

    (c) purposes for which the photograph may be used, disclosed or retained.

This information must be given before the search or examination commences or the photograph is taken, except if the photograph is:

    (i) to be taken covertly;

    (ii) obtained as in paragraph 5.15, in which case the person must be informed as soon as practicable after the photograph is taken or obtained.

(d) *Documentation*

D:5.17 A record must be made when a detainee is searched, examined, or a photograph of the person, or any identifying marks found on them, are taken. The record must include the:

    (a) identity, subject to paragraph 2.18, of the officer carrying out the search, examination or taking the photograph;

    (b) purpose of the search, examination or photograph and the outcome;

    (c) detainee's consent to the search, examination or photograph, or the reason the person was searched, examined or photographed without consent;

    (d) giving of any authority as in paragraphs 5.2 and 5.3, the grounds for giving it and the authorising officer.

D:5.18 If force is used when searching, examining or taking a photograph in accordance with this section, a record shall be made of the circumstances and those present.

(B) *Persons at police stations not detained*

A–133   **D:**5.19 When there are reasonable grounds for suspecting the involvement of a person in a criminal offence, but that person is at a police station **voluntarily** and not detained, the provisions of paragraphs 5.1 to 5.18 should apply, subject to the modifications in the following paragraphs.

D:5.20 References to the "person being detained" and to the powers mentioned in paragraph 5.1 which apply only to detainees at police stations shall be omitted

D:5.21 Force may not be used to:

    (a) search and/or examine the person to:

        (i) discover whether they have any marks that would tend to identify them as a person involved in the commission of an offence; or

(ii) establish their identity, see *Note 5A*;

(b) take photographs of any identifying marks, see paragraph 5.4; or

(c) take a photograph of the person.

D:5.22 Subject to paragraph 5.24, the photographs of persons or of their identifying marks which are not taken in accordance with the provisions mentioned in paragraphs 5.1 or 5.12, must be destroyed (together with any negatives and copies) unless the person:

(a) is charged with, or informed they may be prosecuted for, a recordable offence;

(b) is prosecuted for a recordable offence;

(c) is cautioned for a recordable offence or given a warning or reprimand in accordance with the *Crime and Disorder Act* 1998 for a recordable offence; or

(d) gives informed consent, in writing, for the photograph or image to be retained as in paragraph 5.6.

D:5.23 When paragraph 5.22 requires the destruction of any photograph, the person must be given an opportunity to witness the destruction or to have a certificate confirming the destruction provided they so request the certificate within five days of being informed the destruction is required.

D:5.24 Nothing in paragraph 5.22 affects any separate requirement under the *Criminal Procedure and Investigations Act* 1996 to retain material in connection with criminal investigations.

Notes for guidance

D:5A *The conditions under which fingerprints may be taken to assist in establishing a*   **A–134**
person's identity, are described in section 4.

D:5B *Examples of purposes related to the prevention or detection of crime, the investigation of offences or the conduct of prosecutions include:*

(a) *checking the photograph against other photographs held in records or in connection with, or as a result of, an investigation of an offence to establish whether the person is liable to arrest for other offences;*

(b) *when the person is arrested at the same time as other people, or at a time when it is likely that other people will be arrested, using the photograph to help establish who was arrested, at what time and where;*

(c) *when the real identity of the person is not known and cannot be readily ascertained or there are reasonable grounds for doubting a name and other personal details given by the person, are their real name and personal details; in these circumstances, using or disclosing the photograph to help to establish or verify their real identity or determine whether they are liable to arrest for some other offence, e.g. by checking it against other photographs held in records or in connection with, or as a result of, an investigation of an offence;*

(d) *when it appears any identification procedure in section 3 may need to be arranged for which the person's photograph would assist;*

(e) *when the person's release without charge may be required, and if the release is:*

(i) *on bail to appear at a police station, using the photograph to help verify the person's identity when they answer their bail and if the person does not answer their bail, to assist in arresting them; or*

(ii) *without bail, using the photograph to help verify their identity or assist in locating them for the purposes of serving them with a summons to appear at court in criminal proceedings;*

(f) *when the person has answered to bail at a police station and there are reasonable grounds for doubting they are the person who was previously granted bail, using the photograph to help establish or verify their identity;*

(g) *when the person arrested on a warrant claims to be a different person from the person named on the warrant and a photograph would help to confirm or disprove their claim;*

(h) *when the person has been charged with, reported for, or convicted of, a recordable offence and their photograph is not already on record as a result of (a) to (f) or their photograph is on record but their appearance has changed since it was taken and the person has not yet been released or brought before a court.*

D:5C *There is no power to arrest a person convicted of a recordable offence solely to take their photograph. The power to take photographs in this section applies only where the person is in custody as a result of the exercise of another power,* e.g. *arrest for fingerprinting under* PACE, *section 27.*

D:5D *Examples of when it would not be practicable to obtain a detainee's consent, see paragraph 2.12, to a search, examination or the taking of a photograph of an identifying mark include:*

(a) *when the person is drunk or otherwise unfit to give consent;*

(b) *when there are reasonable grounds to suspect that if the person became aware a search or examination was to take place or an identifying mark was to be photographed, they would take steps to prevent this happening,* e.g. *by violently resisting, covering or concealing the mark etc and it would not otherwise be possible to carry out the search or examination or to photograph any identifying mark;*

(c) *in the case of a juvenile, if the parent or guardian cannot be contacted in sufficient time to allow the search or examination to be carried out or the photograph to be taken.*

D:5E *Examples of when it would not be practicable to obtain the person's consent, see paragraph 2.12, to a photograph being taken include:*

(a) *when the person is drunk or otherwise unfit to give consent;*

(b) *when there are reasonable grounds to suspect that if the person became aware a photograph, suitable to be used or disclosed for the use and disclosure described in paragraph 5.6, was to be taken, they would take steps to prevent it being taken,* e.g. *by violently resisting, covering or distorting their face etc, and it would not otherwise be possible to take a suitable photograph;*

(c) *when, in order to obtain a suitable photograph, it is necessary to take it covertly; and*

(d) *in the case of a juvenile, if the parent or guardian cannot be contacted in sufficient time to allow the photograph to be taken*

D:5F *The use of reasonable force to take the photograph of a suspect elsewhere than at a police station must be carefully considered. In order to obtain a suspect's consent and co-operation to remove an item of religious headwear to take their photograph, a constable should consider whether in the circumstances of the situation the removal of the headwear and the taking of the photograph should be by an officer of the same sex as the person. It would be appropriate for these actions to be conducted out of public view.*

D:6 Identification by body samples and impressions

(A) *General*

D:6.1 References to:

(a) an "intimate sample" mean a dental impression or sample of blood, semen or any other tissue fluid, urine, or pubic hair, or a swab taken from any part of a person's genitals or from a person's body orifice other than the mouth;

(b) a "non-intimate sample" means [*sic*]:

(i) a sample of hair, other than pubic hair, which includes hair plucked with the root, see *Note 6A*;

(ii) a sample taken from a nail or from under a nail;

(iii) a swab taken from any part of a person's body other than a part from which a swab taken would be an intimate sample;

(iv) saliva;

(v) a skin impression which means any record, other than a fingerprint, which is a record, in any form and produced by any method, of the skin pattern and other physical characteristics or features of the whole, or any part of, a person's foot or of any other part of their body.

(B) *Action*

(a) *Intimate samples*

D:6.2 *PACE*, section 62, provides that intimate samples may be taken under: **A–136**

(a) section 62(1), from a person in police detention only:

(i) if a police officer of inspector rank or above has reasonable grounds to believe such an impression or sample will tend to confirm or disprove the suspect's involvement in a recordable offence, see *Note 4A*, and gives authorisation for a sample to be taken; and

(ii) with the suspect's written consent;

(b) section 62(1A), from a person not in police detention but from whom two or more non-intimate samples have been taken in the course of an investigation of an offence and the samples, though suitable, have proved insufficient if:

(i) a police officer of inspector rank or above authorises it to be taken; and

(ii) the person concerned gives their written consent. See *Notes 6B* and *6C*.

D:6.3 Before a suspect is asked to provide an intimate sample, they must be warned that if they refuse without good cause their refusal may harm their case if it comes to trial, see *Note 6D*. If the suspect is in police detention and not legally represented, they must also be reminded of their entitlement to have free legal advice, see Code C, paragraph 6.5, and the reminder noted in the custody record. If paragraph 6.2(b) applies and the person is attending a station voluntarily, their entitlement to free legal advice as in Code C, paragraph 3.21 shall be explained to them.

D:6.4 Dental impressions may only be taken by a registered dentist. Other intimate samples, except for samples of urine, may only be taken by a registered medical practitioner or registered nurse or registered paramedic.

(b) *Non-intimate samples*

D:6.5 A non-intimate sample may be taken from a detainee only with their **A–137** written consent or if paragraph 6.6 applies.

D:6.6 (a) Under section 63, a non-intimate sample may not be taken from a person without consent and the consent must be in writing.

(aa) A non-intimate sample may be taken from a person without the appropriate consent in the following circumstances:

(i) under section 63(2A) where the person is in police detention as a consequence of his arrest for a recordable offence and he has not had a non-intimate sample of the same type and from the same part of the body taken in the course of the investigation of the offence by the police or he has had such a sample taken but it proved insufficient;

(ii) under section 63(3)(a) where he is being held in custody by the police on the authority of a court and an officer of at least the rank of inspector authorises it to be taken;

(b) under section 63(3A), from a person charged with a recordable offence or informed they will be reported for such an offence; and

(i) that person has not had a non-intimate sample taken from them in the course of the investigation; or

(ii) if they have had a sample taken, it proved unsuitable or insufficient for the same form of analysis, see *Note 6B*; or

(c) under section 63(3B), from a person convicted of a recordable offence af
ter the date on which that provision came into effect. *PACE*, section 63A
describes the circumstances in which a police officer may require a person
convicted of a recordable offence to attend a police station for a non
intimate sample to be taken.

D:6.7 Reasonable force may be used, if necessary, to take a non-intimate sample
from a person without their consent under the powers mentioned in paragraph
6.6.

D:6.8 Before any intimate sample is taken with consent or non-intimate sample
is taken with, or without, consent, the person must be informed:

  (a) of the reason for taking the sample;

  (b) of the grounds on which the relevant authority has been given;

  (c) that the sample or information derived from the sample may be retained
  and subject of a speculative search, see *Note 6E*, unless their destruction
  is required as in Annex F, Part A.

D:6.9 When clothing needs to be removed in circumstances likely to cause
embarrassment to the person, no person of the opposite sex who is not a
registered medical practitioner or registered health care professional shall be
present (unless in the case of a juvenile, mentally disordered or mentally vulner
able person, that person specifically requests the presence of an appropriate adult
of the opposite sex who is readily available), nor shall anyone whose presence i
unnecessary. However, in the case of a juvenile, this is subject to the overriding
proviso that such a removal of clothing may take place in the absence of the ap
propriate adult only if the juvenile signifies, in their presence, that they prefer the
adult's absence and they agree.

(c) *Documentation*

D:6.10 A record of the reasons for taking a sample or impression and, if ap
plicable, of its destruction must be made as soon as practicable. If force is used, a
record shall be made of the circumstances and those present. If written consent i
given to the taking of a sample or impression, the fact must be recorded in
writing.

D:6.11 A record must be made of a warning given as required by paragraph
6.3.

D:6.12 A record shall be made of the fact that a person has been informed a
in paragraph 6.8(c) that samples may be subject of a speculative search.

Notes for guidance

D:6A *When hair samples are taken for the purpose of DNA analysis (rather than fo
other purposes such as making a visual match), the suspect should be permitted a reasonabl
choice as to what part of the body the hairs are taken from. When hairs are plucked, they
should be plucked individually, unless the suspect prefers otherwise and no more should b
plucked than the person taking them reasonably considers necessary for a sufficient sample.*

D:6B *(a) An insufficient sample is one which is not sufficient either in quantity or qualit
to provide information for a particular form of analysis, such as DNA analysis. A sampl
may also be insufficient if enough information cannot be obtained from it by analysis becaus
of loss, destruction, damage or contamination of the sample or as a result of an earlier
unsuccessful attempt at analysis.*

*(b) An unsuitable sample is one which, by its nature, is not suitable for a particular form
of analysis.*

D:6C *Nothing in paragraph 6.2 prevents intimate samples being taken for elimination
purposes with the consent of the person concerned but the provisions of paragraph 2.12 re
lating to the role of the appropriate adult, should be applied. Paragraph 6.2(b) does not
however, apply where the non-intimate samples were previously taken under the* Terroris
Act 2000, Schedule 8, paragraph 10.

D:6D *In warning a person who is asked to provide an intimate sample as in paragrap
6.3, the following form of words may be used:*

"You do not have to provide this sample/allow this swab or impression to be taken, but I must warn you that if you refuse without good cause, your refusal may harm your case if it comes to trial.".

D:6E *Fingerprints or a DNA sample and the information derived from it taken from a person arrested on suspicion of being involved in a recordable offence, or charged with such an offence, or informed they will be reported for such an offence, may be subject of a speculative search. This means they may be checked against other fingerprints and DNA records held by, or on behalf of, the police and other law enforcement authorities in or outside the UK or held in connection with, or as a result of, an investigation of an offence inside or outside the UK. Fingerprints and samples taken from any other person, e.g. a person suspected of committing a recordable offence but who has not been arrested, charged or informed they will be reported for it, may be subject to a speculative search only if the person consents in writing to their fingerprints being subject of such a search. The following is an example of a basic form of words:*

"I consent to my fingerprints/DNA sample and information derived from it being retained and used only for purposes related to the prevention and detection of a crime, the investigation of an offence or the conduct of a prosecution either nationally or internationally.

I understand that this sample may be checked against other fingerprint/DNA records held by or on behalf of relevant law enforcement authorities, either nationally or internationally.

I understand that once I have given my consent for the sample to be retained and used I cannot withdraw this consent.".

See Annex F regarding the retention and use of fingerprints and samples taken with consent for elimination purposes.

D:6F *Samples of urine and non-intimate samples taken in accordance with sections 63B and 63C of PACE may not be used for identification purposes in accordance with this code. See Code C, note for guidance 17D.*

ANNEX A

Video identification

(a) *General*

D:1 The arrangements for obtaining and ensuring the availability of a suitable   **A–139**
set of images to be used in a video identification must be the responsibility of an
identification officer, who has no direct involvement with the case.

D:2 The set of images must include the suspect and at least eight other people
who, so far as possible, resemble the suspect in age, general appearance and position in life. Only one suspect shall appear in any set unless there are two suspects
of roughly similar appearance, in which case they may be shown together with at
least twelve other people.

D:2A If the suspect has an unusual physical feature, *e.g.* a facial scar, tattoo or
distinctive hairstyle or hair colour which does not appear on the images of the other
people that are available to be used, steps may be taken to:

(a) conceal the location of the feature on the images of the suspect and the
other people; or

(b) replicate that feature on the images of the other people.

For these purposes, the feature may be concealed or replicated electronically or by
any other method which it is practicable to use to ensure that the images of the
suspect and other people resemble each other. The identification officer has discretion to choose whether to conceal or replicate the feature and the method to be used.
If an unusual physical feature has been described by the witness, the identification officer should, if practicable, have that feature replicated. If it has not been described,
concealment may be more appropriate.

D:2B If the identification officer decides that a feature should be concealed or replicated, the reason for the decision and whether the feature was concealed or replicated in the images shown to any witness shall be recorded.

D:2C If the witness requests to view an image where an unusual physical feature has been concealed or replicated without the feature being concealed or replicated, the witness may be allowed to do so.

D:3 The images used to conduct a video identification shall, as far as possible, show the suspect and other people in the same positions or carrying out the same sequence of movements. They shall also show the suspect and other people under identical conditions unless the identification officer reasonably believes:

(a) because of the suspect's failure or refusal to co-operate or other reasons, it is not practicable for the conditions to be identical; and

(b) any difference in the conditions would not direct a witness's attention to any individual image.

D:4 The reasons identical conditions are not practicable shall be recorded on forms provided for the purpose.

D:5 Provision must be made for each person shown to be identified by number.

D:6 If police officers are shown, any numerals or other identifying badges must be concealed. If a prison inmate is shown, either as a suspect or not, then either all, or none of, the people shown should be in prison clothing.

D:7 The suspect or their solicitor, friend, or appropriate adult must be given a reasonable opportunity to see the complete set of images before it is shown to any witness. If the suspect has a reasonable objection to the set of images or any of the participants, the suspect shall be asked to state the reasons for the objection. Steps shall, if practicable, be taken to remove the grounds for objection. If this is not practicable, the suspect and/or their representative shall be told why their objections cannot be met and the objection, the reason given for it and why it cannot be met shall be recorded on forms provided for the purpose.

D:8 Before the images are shown in accordance with paragraph 7, the suspect or their solicitor shall be provided with details of the first description of the suspect by any witnesses who are to attend the video identification. When a broadcast or publication is made, as in paragraph 3.28, the suspect or their solicitor must also be allowed to view any material released to the media by the police for the purpose of recognising or tracing the suspect, provided it is practicable and would not unreasonably delay the investigation.

D:9 The suspect's solicitor, if practicable, shall be given reasonable notification of the time and place the video identification is to be conducted so a representative may attend on behalf of the suspect. If a solicitor has not been instructed, this information shall be given to the suspect. The suspect may not be present when the images are shown to the witness(es). In the absence of the suspect's representative, the viewing itself shall be recorded on video. No unauthorised people may be present.

(b) *Conducting the video identification*

D:10 The identification officer is responsible for making the appropriate arrangements to make sure, before they see the set of images, witnesses are not able to communicate with each other about the case, see any of the images which are to be shown, see, or be reminded of, any photograph or description of the suspect or be given any other indication as to the suspect's identity, or overhear a witness who has already seen the material. There must be no discussion with the witness about the composition of the set of images and they must not be told whether a previous witness has made any identification.

D:11 Only one witness may see the set of images at a time. Immediately before the images are shown, the witness shall be told that the person they saw on a specified earlier occasion may, or may not, appear in the images they are shown and that if they cannot make a positive identification, they should say so. The witness shall be advised that at any point, they may ask to see a particular part of the set of images or to have a particular image frozen for them to study. Furthermore, it should be pointed out to the witness that there is no limit on how many times they can view the whole set of images or any part of them. However, they should be asked not to make any decision as to whether the person they saw is on the set of images until they have seen the whole set at least twice.

D:12 Once the witness has seen the whole set of images at least twice and has indicated that they do not want to view the images, or any part of them, again, the witness shall be asked to say whether the individual they saw in person on a specified earlier occasion has been shown and, if so, to identify them by number of the image. The witness will then be shown that image to confirm the identification, see paragraph 17.

D:13 Care must be taken not to direct the witness's attention to any one individual image or give any indication of the suspect's identity. Where a witness has previously made an identification by photographs, or a computerised or artist's composite or similar likeness, the witness must not be reminded of such a photograph or composite likeness once a suspect is available for identification by other means in accordance with this code. Nor must the witness be reminded of any description of the suspect.

D:14 After the procedure, each witness shall be asked whether they have seen any broadcast or published films or photographs, or any descriptions of suspects relating to the offence and their reply shall be recorded.

(c) *Image security and destruction*

D:15 Arrangements shall be made for all relevant material containing sets of images used for specific identification procedures to be kept securely and their movements accounted for. In particular, no-one involved in the investigation shall be permitted to view the material prior to it being shown to any witness.

D:16 As appropriate, paragraph 3.30 or 3.31 applies to the destruction or retention of relevant sets of images.

(d) *Documentation*

D:17 A record must be made of all those participating in, or seeing, the set of images whose names are known to the police.

D:18 A record of the conduct of the video identification must be made on forms provided for the purpose. This shall include anything said by the witness about any identifications or the conduct of the procedure and any reasons it was not practicable to comply with any of the provisions of this code governing the conduct of video identifications.

ANNEX B

Identification parades

(a) *General*

D:1 A suspect must be given a reasonable opportunity to have a solicitor or friend present, and the suspect shall be asked to indicate on a second copy of the notice whether or not they wish to do so.　　**A–142**

D:2 An identification parade may take place either in a normal room or one equipped with a screen permitting witnesses to see members of the identification parade without being seen. The procedures for the composition and conduct of the identification parade are the same in both cases, subject to paragraph 8 (except that an identification parade involving a screen may take place only when the suspect's solicitor, friend or appropriate adult is present or the identification parade is recorded on video).

D:3 Before the identification parade takes place, the suspect or their solicitor shall be provided with details of the first description of the suspect by any witnesses who are attending the identification parade. When a broadcast or publication is made as in paragraph 3.28, the suspect or their solicitor should also be allowed to view any material released to the media by the police for the purpose of recognising or tracing the suspect, provided it is practicable to do so and would not unreasonably delay the investigation.

(b) *Identification parades involving prison inmates*

D:4 If a prison inmate is required for identification, and there are no security problems about the person leaving the establishment, they may be asked to participate in an identification parade or video identification.

D:5 An identification parade may be held in a Prison Department establishment but shall be conducted, as far as practicable under normal identification parade rules. Members of the public shall make up the identification parade unless there are serious security, or control, objections to their admission to the establishment. In such cases, or if a group or video identification is arranged within the establishment, other inmates may participate. If an inmate is the suspect, they are not required to wear prison clothing for the identification parade unless the other people taking part are other inmates in similar clothing, or are members of the public who are prepared to wear prison clothing for the occasion.

(c) *Conduct of the identification parade*

A-143   **D:**6 Immediately before the identification parade, the suspect must be reminded of the procedures governing its conduct and cautioned in the terms of Code C, paragraphs 10.5 or 10.6, as appropriate.

D:7 All unauthorised people must be excluded from the place where the identification parade is held.

D:8 Once the identification parade has been formed, everything afterwards, in respect of it, shall take place in the presence and hearing of the suspect and any interpreter, solicitor, friend or appropriate adult who is present (unless the identification parade involves a screen, in which case everything said to, or by, any witness at the place where the identification parade is held, must be said in the hearing and presence of the suspect's solicitor, friend or appropriate adult or be recorded on video).

D:9 The identification parade shall consist of at least eight people (in addition to the suspect) who, so far as possible, resemble the suspect in age, height, general appearance and position in life. Only one suspect shall be included in an identification parade unless there are two suspects of roughly similar appearance, in which case they may be paraded together with at least twelve other people. In no circumstances shall more than two suspects be included in one identification parade and where there are separate identification parades, they shall be made up of different people.

D:10 If the suspect has an unusual physical feature, *e.g.*, a facial scar, tattoo or distinctive hairstyle or hair colour which cannot be replicated on other members of the identification parade, steps may be taken to conceal the location of that feature on the suspect and the other members of the identification parade if the suspect and their solicitor, or appropriate adult, agree. For example, by use of a plaster or a hat, so that all members of the identification parade resemble each other in general appearance.

D:11 When all members of a similar group are possible suspects, separate identification parades shall be held for each unless there are two suspects of similar appearance when they may appear on the same identification parade with at least twelve other members of the group who are not suspects. When police officers in uniform form an identification parade any numerals or other identifying badges shall be concealed.

D:12 When the suspect is brought to the place where the identification parade is to be held, they shall be asked if they have any objection to the arrangements for the identification parade or to any of the other participants in it and to state the reasons for the objection. The suspect may obtain advice from their solicitor or friend, if present, before the identification parade proceeds. If the suspect has a reasonable objection to the arrangements or any of the participants, steps shall, if practicable, be taken to remove the grounds for objection. When it is not practicable to do so, the suspect shall be told why their objections cannot be met and the objection, the reason given for it and why it cannot be met, shall be recorded on forms provided for the purpose.

D:13 The suspect may select their own position in the line, but may not otherwise interfere with the order of the people forming the line. When there is more than one witness, the suspect must be told, after each witness has left the room, that they can, if they wish, change position in the line. Each position in the line must be clearly numbered, whether by means of a number laid on the floor in front of each identification parade member or by other means.

D:14 Appropriate arrangements must be made to make sure, before witnesses **A–144** attend the identification parade, they are not able to:

    (i) communicate with each other about the case or overhear a witness who has already seen the identification parade;

    (ii) see any member of the identification parade;

    (iii) see, or be reminded of, any photograph or description of the suspect or be given any other indication as to the suspect's identity; or

    (iv) see the suspect before or after the identification parade.

D:15 The person conducting a witness to an identification parade must not discuss with them the composition of the identification parade and, in particular, must not disclose whether a previous witness has made any identification.

D:16 Witnesses shall be brought in one at a time. Immediately before the witness inspects the identification parade, they shall be told the person they saw on a specified earlier occasion may, or may not, be present and if they cannot make a positive identification, they should say so. The witness must also be told they should not make any decision about whether the person they saw is on the identification parade until they have looked at each member at least twice.

D:17 When the officer or police staff (see paragraph 3.11) conducting the identification procedure is satisfied the witness has properly looked at each member of the identification parade, they shall ask the witness whether the person they saw on a specified earlier occasion is on the identification parade and, if so, to indicate the number of the person concerned, see paragraph 28.

D:18 If the witness wishes to hear any identification parade member speak, adopt any specified posture or move, they shall first be asked whether they can identify any person(s) on the identification parade on the basis of appearance only. When the request is to hear members of the identification parade speak, the witness shall be reminded that the participants in the identification parade have been chosen on the basis of physical appearance only. Members of the identification parade may then be asked to comply with the witness's request to hear them speak, see them move or adopt any specified posture.

D:19 If the witness requests that the person they have indicated remove **A–145** anything used for the purposes of paragraph 10 to conceal the location of an unusual physical feature, that person may be asked to remove it.

D:20 If the witness makes an identification after the identification parade has ended, the suspect and, if present, their solicitor, interpreter or friend shall be informed. When this occurs, consideration should be given to allowing the witness a second opportunity to identify the suspect.

D:21 After the procedure, each witness shall be asked whether they have seen any broadcast or published films or photographs or any descriptions of suspects relating to the offence and their reply shall be recorded.

D:22 When the last witness has left, the suspect shall be asked whether they wish to make any comments on the conduct of the identification parade.

(d) *Documentation*

D:23 A video recording must normally be taken of the identification parade. If that is impracticable, a colour photograph must be taken. A copy of the video recording or photograph shall be supplied, on request, to the suspect or their solicitor within a reasonable time.

D:24 As appropriate, paragraph 3.30 or 3.31, should apply to any photograph or video taken as in paragraph 23.

D:25 If any person is asked to leave an identification parade because they are interfering with its conduct, the circumstances shall be recorded.

D:26 A record must be made of all those present at an identification parade whose names are known to the police.

D:27 If prison inmates make up an identification parade, the circumstances must be recorded.

D:28 A record of the conduct of any identification parade must be made on forms provided for the purpose. This shall include anything said by the witness or the suspect about any identifications or the conduct of the procedure, and any reasons it was not practicable to comply with any of this code's provisions.

ANNEX C

Group identification

(a) *General*

A–146   **D:1** The purpose of this annex is to make sure, as far as possible, group identifications follow the principles and procedures for identification parades so the conditions are fair to the suspect in the way they test the witness's ability to make an identification.

D:2 Group identifications may take place either with the suspect's consent and co-operation or covertly without their consent.

D:3 The location of the group identification is a matter for the identification officer, although the officer may take into account any representations made by the suspect, appropriate adult, their solicitor or friend.

D:4 The place where the group identification is held should be one where other people are either passing by or waiting around informally, in groups such that the suspect is able to join them and be capable of being seen by the witness at the same time as others in the group. For example people leaving an escalator, pedestrians walking through a shopping centre, passengers on railway and bus stations, waiting in queues or groups or where people are standing or sitting in groups in other public places.

D:5 If the group identification is to be held covertly, the choice of locations will be limited by the places where the suspect can be found and the number of other people present at that time. In these cases, suitable locations might be along regular routes travelled by the suspect, including buses or trains or public places frequented by the suspect.

A–147   **D:6** Although the number, age, sex, race and general description and style of clothing of other people present at the location cannot be controlled by the identification officer, in selecting the location the officer must consider the general appearance and numbers of people likely to be present. In particular, the officer must reasonably expect that over the period the witness observes the group, they will be able to see, from time to time, a number of others whose appearance is broadly similar to that of the suspect.

D:7 A group identification need not be held if the identification officer believes, because of the unusual appearance of the suspect, none of the locations it would be practicable to use, satisfy the requirements of paragraph 6 necessary to make the identification fair.

D:8 Immediately after a group identification procedure has taken place (with or without the suspect's consent), a colour photograph or video should be taken of the general scene, if practicable, to give a general impression of the scene and the number of people present. Alternatively, if it is practicable, the group identification may be video recorded.

D:9 If it is not practicable to take the photograph or video in accordance with paragraph 8, a photograph or film of the scene should be taken later at a time determined by the identification officer if the officer considers it practicable to do so.

D:10 An identification carried out in accordance with this code remains a group identification even though, at the time of being seen by the witness, the suspect was on their own rather than in a group.

D:11 Before the group identification takes place, the suspect or their solicitor shall be provided with details of the first description of the suspect by any witnesses who are to attend the identification. When a broadcast or publication is made, as in paragraph 3.28, the suspect or their solicitor should also be allowed to view any material released by the police to the media for the purposes of recognising or tracing the suspect, provided that it is practicable and would not unreasonably delay the investigation.

D:12 After the procedure, each witness shall be asked whether they have seen any broadcast or published films or photographs or any descriptions of suspects relating to the offence and their reply recorded.

(b) *Identification with the consent of the suspect*

D:13 A suspect must be given a reasonable opportunity to have a solicitor or   **A–148**
friend present. They shall be asked to indicate on a second copy of the notice whether or not they wish to do so.

D:14 The witness, the person carrying out the procedure and the suspect's solicitor, appropriate adult, friend or any interpreter for the witness, may be concealed from the sight of the individuals in the group they are observing, if the person carrying out the procedure considers this assists the conduct of the identification.

D:15 The person conducting a witness to a group identification must not discuss with them the forthcoming group identification and, in particular, must not disclose whether a previous witness has made any identification.

D:16 Anything said to, or by, the witness during the procedure about the identification should be said in the presence and hearing of those present at the procedure.

D:17 Appropriate arrangements must be made to make sure, before witnesses attend the group identification, they are not able to:

    (i) communicate with each other about the case or overhear a witness who has already been given an opportunity to see the suspect in the group;

    (ii) see the suspect; or

    (iii) see, or be reminded of, any photographs or description of the suspect or be given any other indication of the suspect's identity.

D:18 Witnesses shall be brought one at a time to the place where they are to observe the group. Immediately before the witness is asked to look at the group, the person conducting the procedure shall tell them that the person they saw may, or may not, be in the group and that if they cannot make a positive identification, they should say so. The witness shall be asked to observe the group in which the suspect is to appear. The way in which the witness should do this will depend on whether the group is moving or stationary.

Moving group

D:19 When the group in which the suspect is to appear is moving, *e.g.* leaving   **A–149**
an escalator, the provisions of paragraphs 20 to 24 should be followed.

D:20 If two or more suspects consent to a group identification, each should be the subject of separate identification procedures. These may be conducted consecutively on the same occasion.

D:21 The person conducting the procedure shall tell the witness to observe the group and ask them to point out any person they think they saw on the specified earlier occasion.

D:22 Once the witness has been informed as in paragraph 21 the suspect should be allowed to take whatever position in the group they wish.

D:23 When the witness points out a person as in paragraph 21 they shall, if practicable, be asked to take a closer look at the person to confirm the identification. If this is not practicable, or they cannot confirm the identification, they shall be asked how sure they are that the person they have indicated is the relevant person.

D:24 The witness should continue to observe the group for the period which the person conducting the procedure reasonably believes is necessary in the circumstances for them to be able to make comparisons between the suspect and other individuals of broadly similar appearance to the suspect as in paragraph 6.

Stationary groups

A–150

D:25 When the group in which the suspect is to appear is stationary, *e.g.* people waiting in a queue, the provisions of paragraphs 26 to 29 should be followed.

D:26 If two or more suspects consent to a group identification, each should be subject to separate identification procedures unless they are of broadly similar appearance when they may appear in the same group. When separate group identifications are held, the groups must be made up of different people.

D:27 The suspect may take whatever position in the group they wish. If there is more than one witness, the suspect must be told, out of the sight and hearing of any witness, that they can, if they wish, change their position in the group.

D:28 The witness shall be asked to pass along, or amongst, the group and to look at each person in the group at least twice, taking as much care and time as possible according to the circumstances, before making an identification. Once the witness has done this, they shall be asked whether the person they saw on the specified earlier occasion is in the group and to indicate any such person by whatever means the person conducting the procedure considers appropriate in the circumstances. If this is not practicable, the witness shall be asked to point out any person they think they saw on the earlier occasion.

D:29 When the witness makes an indication as in paragraph 28, arrangements shall be made, if practicable, for the witness to take a closer look at the person to confirm the identification. If this is not practicable, or the witness is unable to confirm the identification, they shall be asked how sure they are that the person they have indicated is the relevant person.

All cases

A–151

D:30 If the suspect unreasonably delays joining the group, or having joined the group, deliberately conceals themselves [*sic*] from the sight of the witness, this may be treated as a refusal to co-operate in a group identification.

D:31 If the witness identifies a person other than the suspect, that person should be informed what has happened and asked if they are prepared to give their name and address. There is no obligation upon any member of the public to give these details. There shall be no duty to record any details of any other member of the public present in the group or at the place where the procedure is conducted.

D:32 When the group identification has been completed, the suspect shall be asked whether they wish to make any comments on the conduct of the procedure.

D:33 If the suspect has not been previously informed, they shall be told of any identifications made by the witnesses.

(c) *Identification without the suspect's consent*

D:34 Group identifications held covertly without the suspect's consent should, as far as practicable, follow the rules for conduct of group identification by consent.

D:35 A suspect has no right to have a solicitor, appropriate adult or friend present as the identification will take place without the knowledge of the suspect.

D:36 Any number of suspects may be identified at the same time.

(d) *Identifications in police stations*

D:37 Group identifications should only take place in police stations for reasons of safety, security or because it is not practicable to hold them elsewhere.

D:38 The group identification may take place either in a room equipped with a screen permitting witnesses to see members of the group without being seen, or anywhere else in the police station that the identification officer considers appropriate.

D:39 Any of the additional safeguards applicable to identification parades should be followed if the identification officer considers it is practicable to do so in the circumstances.

(e) *Identifications involving prison inmates*

D:40 A group identification involving a prison inmate may only be arranged in the prison or at a police station.

D:41 When a group identification takes place involving a prison inmate, whether in a prison or in a police station, the arrangements should follow those in paragraphs 37 to 39. If a group identification takes place within a prison, other inmates may participate. If an inmate is the suspect, they do not have to wear prison clothing for the group identification unless the other participants are wearing the same clothing.

(f) *Documentation*

D:42 When a photograph or video is taken as in paragraph 8 or 9, a copy of the photograph or video shall be supplied on request to the suspect or their solicitor within a reasonable time.

D:43 Paragraph 3.30 or 3.31, as appropriate, shall apply when the photograph or film taken in accordance with paragraph 8 or 9 includes the suspect.

D:44 A record of the conduct of any group identification must be made on forms provided for the purpose. This shall include anything said by the witness or suspect about any identifications or the conduct of the procedure and any reasons why it was not practicable to comply with any of the provisions of this code governing the conduct of group identifications.

ANNEX D

Confrontation by a witness

D:1 Before the confrontation takes place, the witness must be told that the person they saw may, or may not, be the person they are to confront and that if they are not that person, then the witness should say so.

D:2 Before the confrontation takes place the suspect or their solicitor shall be provided with details of the first description of the suspect given by any witness who is to attend. When a broadcast or publication is made, as in paragraph 3.28, the suspect or their solicitor should also be allowed to view any material released to the media for the purposes of recognising or tracing the suspect, provided it is practicable to do so and would not unreasonably delay the investigation.

D:3 Force may not be used to make the suspect's face visible to the witness.

D:4 Confrontation must take place in the presence of the suspect's solicitor, interpreter or friend unless this would cause unreasonable delay.

D:5 The suspect shall be confronted independently by each witness, who shall be asked "Is this the person?". If the witness identifies the person but is unable to confirm the identification, they shall be asked how sure they are that the person is the one they saw on the earlier occasion.

D:6 The confrontation should normally take place in the police station, either in a normal room or one equipped with a screen permitting a witness to see the suspect without being seen. In both cases, the procedures are the same except that a room equipped with a screen may be used only when the suspect's solicitor, friend or appropriate adult is present or the confrontation is recorded on video.

D:7 After the procedure, each witness shall be asked whether they have seen any broadcast or published films or photographs or any descriptions of suspects relating to the offence and their reply shall be recorded.

ANNEX E

Showing photographs

(a) *Action*

A–155   **D:1** An officer of sergeant rank or above shall be responsible for supervising and directing the showing of photographs. The actual showing may be done by another officer or police staff, see paragraph 3.11.

D:2 The supervising officer must confirm the first description of the suspect given by the witness has been recorded before they are shown the photographs. If the supervising officer is unable to confirm the description has been recorded they shall postpone showing the photographs.

D:3 Only one witness shall be shown photographs at any one time. Each witness shall be given as much privacy as practicable and shall not be allowed to communicate with any other witness in the case.

D:4 The witness shall be shown not less than twelve photographs at a time, which shall, as far as possible, all be of a similar type.

D:5 When the witness is shown the photographs, they shall be told the photograph of the person they saw may, or may not, be amongst them and if they cannot make a positive identification, they should say so. The witness shall also be told they should not make a decision until they have viewed at least twelve photographs. The witness shall not be prompted or guided in any way but shall be left to make any selection without help.

D:6 If a witness makes a positive identification from photographs, unless the person identified is otherwise eliminated from enquiries or is not available, other witnesses shall not be shown photographs. But both they, and the witness who has made the identification, shall be asked to attend a video identification, an identification parade or group identification unless there is no dispute about the suspect's identification.

A–156   **D:7** If the witness makes a selection but is unable to confirm the identification, the person showing the photographs shall ask them how sure they are that the photograph they have indicated is the person they saw on the specified earlier occasion.

D:8 When the use of a computerised or artist's composite or similar likeness has led to there being a known suspect who can be asked to participate in a video identification, appear on an identification parade or participate in a group identification, that likeness shall not be shown to other potential witnesses.

D:9 When a witness attending a video identification, an identification parade or group identification has previously been shown photographs or computerised or artist's composite or similar likeness (and it is the responsibility of the officer in charge of the investigation to make the identification officer aware that this is the case), the suspect and their solicitor must be informed of this fact before the identification procedure takes place.

D:10 None of the photographs shown shall be destroyed, whether or not an identification is made, since they may be required for production in court. The photographs shall be numbered and a separate photograph taken of the frame or part of the album from which the witness made an identification as an aid to reconstituting it.

(b) *Documentation*

D:11. Whether or not an identification is made, a record shall be kept of the **A–157** showing of photographs on forms provided for the purpose. This shall include anything said by the witness about any identification or the conduct of the procedure, any reasons it was not practicable to comply with any of the provisions of this code governing the showing of photographs and the name and rank of the supervising officer.

D:12 The supervising officer shall inspect and sign the record as soon as practicable.

ANNEX F

Fingerprints, footwear impressions and samples—destruction and speculative searches

(a) *Fingerprints, footwear impressions and samples taken in connection with a criminal investigation*

D:1 When fingerprints, footwear impressions or DNA samples are taken from a **A–158** person in connection with an investigation and the person is not suspected of having committed the offence, see *Note F1*, they must be destroyed as soon as they have fulfilled the purpose for which they were taken unless:

    (a) they were taken for the purposes of an investigation of an offence for which a person has been convicted; and

    (b) fingerprints, footwear impressions or samples were also taken from the convicted person for the purposes of that investigation.

However, subject to paragraph 2, the fingerprints, footwear impressions and samples, and the information derived from samples, may not be used in the investigation of any offence or in evidence against the person who is, or would be, entitled to the destruction of the fingerprints, footwear impressions and samples, see *Note F2*.

D:2 The requirement to destroy fingerprints, footwear impressions and DNA samples, and information derived from samples, and restrictions on their retention and use in paragraph 1 do not apply if the person gives their written consent for their fingerprints, footwear impressions or sample to be retained and used after they have fulfilled the purpose for which they were taken, see *Note F1*.

D:3 When a person's fingerprints, footwear impressions or sample are to be destroyed:

    (a) any copies of the fingerprints and footwear impressions must also be destroyed;

    (b) the person may witness the destruction of their fingerprints, footwear impressions or copies if they ask to do so within five days of being informed destruction is required;

    (c) access to relevant computer fingerprint data shall be made impossible as soon as it is practicable to do so and the person shall be given a certificate to this effect within three months of asking; and

(d) neither the fingerprints, footwear impressions, the sample, or any information derived from the sample, may be used in the investigation of any offence or in evidence against the person who is, or would be, entitled to its destruction.

D:4 Fingerprints, footwear impressions or samples, and the information derived from samples, taken in connection with the investigation of an offence which are not required to be destroyed, may be retained after they have fulfilled the purposes for which they were taken but may be used only for purposes related to the prevention or detection of crime, the investigation of an offence or the conduct of a prosecution in, as well as outside, the UK and may also be subject to a speculative search. This includes checking them against other fingerprints, footwear impressions and DNA records held by, or on behalf of, the police and other law enforcement authorities in, as well as outside, the UK.

(b) Fingerprints taken in connection with Immigration Service enquiries

D:5 Fingerprints taken for Immigration Service enquiries in accordance with powers and procedures other than under *PACE* and for which the Immigration Service, not the police, are responsible, must be destroyed as follows:

(a) fingerprints and all copies must be destroyed as soon as practicable if the person from whom they were taken proves they are a British or Commonwealth citizen who has the right of abode in the UK under the *Immigration Act* 1971, section 2(1)(b);

(b) fingerprints taken under the power as in paragraph 4.11(g) from a dependant of a person in 4.11(b) to (f) must be destroyed when that person's fingerprints are to be destroyed;

(c) fingerprints taken from a person under any power as in paragraph 4.11 or with the person's consent which have not already been destroyed as above, must be destroyed within ten years of being taken or within such period specified by the Secretary of State under the *Immigration and Asylum Act* 1999, section 143(5).

Notes for guidance

D:F1 *Fingerprints, footwear impressions and samples given voluntarily for the purpose of elimination play an important part in many police investigations. It is, therefore, important to make sure innocent volunteers are not deterred from participating and their consent to their fingerprints, footwear impressions and DNA being used for the purposes of a specific investigation is fully informed and voluntary. If the police or volunteer seek to have the fingerprints, footwear impressions or samples retained for use after the specific investigation ends, it is important the volunteer's consent to this is also fully informed and voluntary.*

Examples of consent for:

● *DNA/fingerprints/footwear impressions—to be used only for the purposes of a specific investigation;*

● *DNA/fingerprints/footwear impressions—to be used in the specific investigation **and** retained by the police for future use.*

*To minimise the risk of confusion, each consent should be physically separate and the volunteer should be asked to sign **each consent**.*

(a) DNA:

(i) DNA sample taken for the purposes of elimination or as part of an intelligence-led screening and to be used only for the purposes of that investigation and destroyed afterwards:

"*I consent to my DNA/mouth swab being taken for forensic analysis. I understand that the sample will be destroyed at the end of the case and that my profile will only be compared to the crime stain profile from this enquiry. I have been advised that the person taking the sample may be required to give evidence and/or provide a written statement to the police in relation to the taking of it.*".

(ii) DNA sample to be retained on the National DNA database and used in the future:

"I consent to my DNA sample and information derived from it being retained and used only for purposes related to the prevention and detection of a crime, the investigation of an offence or the conduct of a prosecution either nationally or internationally.

I understand that this sample may be checked against other DNA records held by, or on behalf of, relevant law enforcement authorities, either nationally or internationally.

I understand that once I have given my consent for the sample to be retained and used I cannot withdraw this consent.".

(b) Fingerprints:

(i) Fingerprints taken for the purposes of elimination or as part of an intelligence-led screening and to be used only for the purposes of that investigation and destroyed afterwards:

"I consent to my fingerprints being taken for elimination purposes. I understand that the fingerprints will be destroyed at the end of the case and that my fingerprints will only be compared to the fingerprints from this enquiry. I have been advised that the person taking the fingerprints may be required to give evidence and/or provide a written statement to the police in relation to the taking of it.".

(ii) Fingerprints to be retained for future use:

"I consent to my fingerprints being retained and used only for purposes related to the prevention and detection of a crime, the investigation of an offence or the conduct of a prosecution either nationally or internationally.

I understand that my fingerprints may be checked against other records held by, or on behalf of, relevant law enforcement authorities, either nationally or internationally.

I understand that once I have given my consent for my fingerprints to be retained and used I cannot withdraw this consent.".

(c) Footwear impressions:

(i) Footwear impressions taken for the purposes of elimination or as part of an intelligence-led screening and to be used only for the purposes of that investigation and destroyed afterwards:

"I consent to my footwear impressions being taken for elimination purposes. I understand that the footwear impressions will be destroyed at the end of the case and that my footwear impressions will only be compared to the footwear impressions from this enquiry. I have been advised that the person taking the footwear impressions may be required to give evidence and/or provide a writtens statement to the police in relation to the taking of it.".

(ii) Footwear impressions to be retained for future use:

"I consent to my footwear impressions being retained and used only for purposes related to the prevention and detection of a crime, the investigation of an offence or the conduct of a prosecution, either nationally or internationally.

I understand that my footwear impressions may be checked against other records held by, or on behalf of, relevant law enforcement authorities, either nationally or internationally.

I understand that once I have given my consent for my footwear impressions to be retained and used I cannot withdraw this consent.".

D:F2 *The provisions for the retention of fingerprints, footwear impressions and samples in paragraph 1 allow for all fingerprints, footwear impressions and samples in a case to be available for any subsequent miscarriage of justice investigation.*   **A–161**

(6) Tape-recording of interviews

The text that follows is of the version of the code that came into force on February 1, 2008: see *ante*, Appendix A–1.   **A–162**

For further details of the application of the code, and as to commencement of the governing legislation, see § 15–224, *ante*.

E.   Code of Practice on Audio Recording Interviews with Suspects

Commencement—Transitional arrangements

A–162a   This code applies to interviews carried out after midnight on 31 January, 2008, notwithstanding that the interview may have commenced before that time.

E:1 General

A–163   E:1.1 This code of practice must be readily available for consultation by:
- police officers;
- police staff;
- detained persons;
- members of the public.

E:1.2 The *Notes for Guidance* included are not provisions of this code.

E:1.3 Nothing in this code shall detract from the requirements of Code C, the code of practice for the detention, treatment and questioning of persons by police officers.

E:1.4 This code does not apply to those people listed in Code C, paragraph 1.12.

E:1.5 The term:
- "appropriate adult" has the same meaning as in Code C, paragraph 1.7;
- "solicitor" has the same meaning as in Code C, paragraph 6.12.

A–164   E:1.6 In this code:
- (aa) "recording media" means any removable, physical audio recording medium (such as magnetic type, optical disc or solid state memory) which can be played and copied;
- (a) "designated person" means a person other than a police officer, designated under the *Police Reform Act* 2002, Part 4 who has specified powers and duties of police officers conferred or imposed on them;
- (b) any reference to a police officer includes a designated person acting in the exercise or performance of the powers and duties conferred or imposed on them by their designation;
- (c) "digital network solution" means the use of platform architecture that secures a network by providing each user with a digital identity and is managed by a central digital certificate authority (see section 7 of this code).

E:1.7 If a power conferred on a designated person:
- (a) allows reasonable force to be used when exercised by a police officer, a designated person exercising that power has the same entitlement to use force;
- (b) includes power to use force to enter any premises, that power is not exercisable by that designated person except:
  - (i) in the company, and under the supervision, of a police officer; or
  - (ii) for the purpose of:
    - saving life or limb; or
    - preventing serious damage to property.

A–165   E:1.8 Nothing in this code prevents the custody officer, or other officer given custody of the detainee, from allowing police staff who are not designated persons to carry out individual procedures or tasks at the police station if the law allows. However, the officer remains responsible for making sure the procedures and tasks are carried out correctly in accordance with these codes. Any such police staff must be:

(a) a person employed by a police authority maintaining a police force and under the control and direction of the chief officer of that force; or

(b) employed by a person with whom a police authority has a contract for the provision of services relating to persons arrested or otherwise in custody.

E:1.9 Designated persons and other police staff must have regard to any relevant provisions of the codes of practice.

E:1.10 References to pocket book [*sic*] include any official report book issued to police officers or police staff.

E:1.11 References to a custody officer include those performing the functions of a custody officer as in paragraph 1.9 of Code C.

E:2 Recording and sealing master recordings

E:2.1 Recording of interviews shall be carried out openly to instil confidence in its reliability as an impartial and accurate record of the interview.   **A–166**

E:2.2 One recording, the master recording, will be sealed in the suspect's presence. A second recording will be used as a working copy. The master recording is either of the two recordings used in a twin deck/drive machine or the only recording in a single deck/drive machine. The working copy is either the second/third recording used in a twin/triple deck/drive machine or a copy of the master recording made by a single deck/drive machine. See *Notes 2A* and *2B*.

E:2.3 Nothing in this code requires the identity of officers or police staff conducting interviews to be recorded or disclosed:

(a) in the case of enquiries linked to the investigation of terrorism; or

(b) if the interviewer reasonably believes recording or disclosing their name might put them in danger.

In these cases interviewers should use warrant or other identification numbers and the name of their police station. See *Note 2C*.

Notes for guidance

E:2A *The purpose of sealing the master recording in the suspect's presence is to show the recording's integrity is preserved. If a single deck/drive machine is used the working copy of the master recording must be made in the suspect's presence and without the master recording leaving their sight. The working copy shall be used for making further copies if needed.*   **A–167**

E:2B *[Not used.]*

E:2C *The purpose of paragraph 2.3(b) is to protect those involved in serious organised crime investigations or arrests of particularly violent suspects when there is reliable information that those arrested or their associates may threaten or cause harm to those involved. In cases of doubt, an officer of inspector rank or above should be consulted.*

E:3 Interviews to be audio recorded

E:3.1 Subject to paragraphs 3.3 and 3.4, audio recording shall be used at police stations for any interview: **A–168**

(a) with a person cautioned under Code C, section 10 in respect of any indictable offence, including an offence triable either way, see *Note 3A*;

(b) which takes place as a result of an interviewer exceptionally putting further questions to a suspect about an offence described in paragraph 3.1(a) after they have been charged with, or told they may be prosecuted for, that offence, see Code C, paragraph 16.5;

(c) when an interviewer wants to tell a person, after they have been charged with, or informed they may be prosecuted for, an offence described in paragraph 3.1(a), about any written statement or interview with another person, see Code C, paragraph 16.4.

E:3.2 The *Terrorism Act* 2000 makes separate provision for a code of practice for the audio recording of interviews of those arrested under section 41 or detained under Schedule 7 of [*sic*] the Act. The provisions of this code do not apply to such interviews.

E:3.3 The custody officer may authorise the interviewer not to audio record the interview when it is:

      (a) not reasonably practicable because of equipment failure or the unavail-ability of a suitable interview room or recording equipment and the au-thorising officer considers, on reasonable grounds, that the interview should not be delayed; or

      (b) clear from the outset there will not be a prosecution.

Note: in these cases the interview should be recorded in writing in accordance with Code C, section 11. In all cases the custody officer shall record the specific reasons for not audio recording. See *Note 3B*.

E:3.4 If a person refuses to go into or remain in a suitable interview room, see Code C, paragraph 12.5, and the custody officer considers, on reasonable grounds, that the interview should not be delayed the interview may, at the custody officer's discretion, be conducted in a cell using portable recording equipment or, if none is available, recorded in writing as in Code C, section 11. The reasons for this shall be recorded.

E:3.5 The whole of each interview shall be audio recorded, including the taking and reading back of any statement.

Notes for guidance

A–169   **E:3A** *Nothing in this code is intended to preclude audio recording at police discretion of interviews at police stations with people cautioned in respect of offences not covered by paragraph 3.1, or responses made by persons after they have been charged with, or told they may be prosecuted for, an offence, provided this code is complied with.*

E:3B *A decision not to audio record an interview for any reason may be the subject of comment in court. The authorising officer should be prepared to justify that decision.*

E:4 The interview

(a) *General*

A–170   **E:4.1** The provisions of Code C:

      • sections 10 and 11, and the applicable *Notes for Guidance* apply to the conduct of interviews to which this code applies;

      • paragraphs 11.7 to 11.14 apply only when a written record is needed.

E:4.2 Code C, paragraphs 10.10, 10.11 and Annex C describe the restriction on drawing adverse inferences from a suspect's failure or refusal to say anything about their involvement in the offence when interviewed or after being charged or informed they may be prosecuted, and how it affects the terms of the caution and determines if and by whom a special warning under sections 36 and 37 can be given.

(b) *Commencement of interviews*

E:4.3 When the suspect is brought into the interview room the interviewer shall, without delay but in the suspect's sight, load the recorder with new recording media and set it to record. The recording media must be unwrapped or opened in the suspect's presence.

E:4.4 The interviewer should tell the suspect about the recording process. The interviewer shall:

      (a) say the interview is being audibly recorded;

      (b) subject to paragraph 2.3, give their name and rank and that of any other interviewer present;

      (c) ask the suspect and any other party present, *e.g.* a solicitor, to identify themselves;

(d) state the date, time of commencement and place of the interview;

(e) state the suspect will be given a notice about what will happen to the copies of the recording.

See *Note 4A.*

E:4.5 The interviewer shall:

- caution the suspect, see Code C, section 10;
- remind the suspect of their entitlement to free legal advice, see Code C, paragraph 11.2.

E:4.6 The interviewer shall put to the suspect any significant statement or silence, see Code C, paragraph 11.4.

(c) *Interviews with deaf persons*

E:4.7 If the suspect is deaf or is suspected of having impaired hearing, the interviewer shall make a written note of the interview in accordance with Code C, at the same time as audio recording it in accordance with this code. See *Notes 4B* and *4C.* **A–171**

(d) *Objections and complaints by the suspect*

E:4.8 If the suspect objects to the interview being audibly recorded at the outset, during the interview or during a break, the interviewer shall explain that the interview is being audibly recorded and that this code requires the suspect's objections to be recorded on the audio recording. When any objections have been audibly recorded or the suspect has refused to have their objections recorded, the interviewer shall say they are turning off the recorder, give their reasons and turn it off. The interviewer shall then make a written record of the interview as in Code C, section 11. If, however, the interviewer reasonably considers they may proceed to question the suspect with the audio recording still on, the interviewer may do so. This procedure also applies in cases where the suspect has previously objected to the interview being visually recorded, see Code F 4.8, and the investigating officer has decided to audibly record the interview. See *Note 4D.*

E:4.9 If in the course of an interview a complaint is made by or on behalf of the person being questioned concerning the provisions of this code or Code C, the interviewer shall act as in Code C, paragraph 12.9. See *Notes 4E* and *4F.*

E:4.10 If the suspect indicates they want to tell the interviewer about matters not directly connected with the offence and they are unwilling for these matters to be audio recorded, the suspect should be given the opportunity to tell the interviewer at the end of the formal interview.

(e) *Changing recording media*

E:4.11 When the recorder shows the recording media only has a short time left, the interviewer shall tell the suspect the recording media are coming to an end and round off that part of the interview. If the interviewer leaves the room for a second set of recording media, the suspect shall not be left unattended. The interviewer will remove the recording media from the recorder and insert the new recording media which shall be unwrapped or opened in the suspect's presence. The recorder should be set to record on the new media. To avoid confusion between the recording media, the interviewer shall mark the media with an identification number immediately after they are removed from the recorder.

(f) *Taking a break during interview*

E:4.12 When a break is taken, the fact that a break is to be taken, the reason for it and the time shall be recorded on the audio recording. **A–172**

E:4.12A When the break is taken and the interview room vacated by the suspect, the recording media shall be removed from the recorder and the procedures for the conclusion of an interview followed, see paragraph 4.18.

E:4.13 When a break is a short one and both the suspect and an interviewer remain in the interview room, the recording may be stopped. There is no need to remove the recording media and when the interview recommences the recording should continue on the same recording media. The time the interview recommences shall be recorded on the audio recording.

E:4.14 After any break in the interview the interviewer must, before resuming the interview, remind the person being questioned that they remain under caution or, if there is any doubt, give the caution in full again. See *Note 4G.*

(g) *Failure of recording equipment*

E:4.15 If there is an equipment failure which can be rectified quickly, *e.g.* by inserting new recording media, the interviewer shall follow the appropriate procedures as in paragraph 4.11. When the recording is resumed the interviewer shall explain what happened and record the time the interview recommences. If, however, it will not be possible to continue recording on that recorder and no replacement recorder is readily available, the interview may continue without being audibly recorded. If this happens, the interviewer shall seek the custody officer's authority as in paragraph 3.3. See *Note 4H.*

(h) *Removing recording media from the recorder*

E:4.16 When recording media is removed from the recorder during the interview, they shall be retained and the procedures in paragraph 4.18 followed.

(i) *Conclusion of interview*

E:4.17 At the conclusion of the interview, the suspect shall be offered the opportunity to clarify anything he or she has said and asked if there is anything they want to add.

E:4.18 At the conclusion of the interview, including the taking and reading back of any written statement, the time shall be recorded and the recording shall be stopped. The interviewer shall seal the master recording with a master recording label and treat it as an exhibit in accordance with force standing orders. The interviewer shall sign the label and ask the suspect and any third party present during the interview to sign it. If the suspect or third party refuse to sign the label an officer of at least inspector rank, or if not available the custody officer, shall be called into the interview room and asked, subject to paragraph 2.3, to sign it.

E:4.19 The suspect shall be handed a notice which explains:
- how the audio recording will be used;
- the arrangements for access to it;
- that if the person is charged or informed they will be prosecuted, a copy of the audio recording will be supplied as soon as practicable or as otherwise agreed between the suspect and the police.

Notes for guidance

E:4A *For the purpose of voice identification the interviewer should ask the suspect and any other people present to identify themselves.*

E:4B *This provision is to give a person who is deaf or has impaired hearing equivalent rights of access to the full interview record as far as this is possible using audio recording.*

E:4C *The provisions of Code C, section 13 on interpreters for deaf persons or for interviews with suspects who have difficulty understanding English continue to apply. However, in an audibly recorded interview the requirement on the interviewer to make sure the interpreter makes a separate note of the interview applies only to paragraph 4.7 (interviews with deaf persons).*

E:4D *The interviewer should remember that a decision to continue recording against the wishes of the suspect may be the subject of comment in court.*

E:4E *If the custody officer is called to deal with the complaint, the recorder should, if possible, be left on until the custody officer has entered the room and spoken to the person being interviewed. Continuation or termination of the interview should be at the interviewer's discretion pending action by an inspector under Code C, paragraph 9.2.*

E:4F *If the complaint is about a matter not connected with this code or Code C, the deci-*

sion to continue is at the interviewer's discretion. When the interviewer decides to continue the interview, they shall tell the suspect the complaint will be brought to the custody officer's attention at the conclusion of the interview. When the interview is concluded the interviewer must, as soon as practicable, inform the custody officer about the existence and nature of the complaint made.

E:4G *The interviewer should remember that it may be necessary to show to the court that nothing occurred during a break or between interviews which influenced the suspect's recorded evidence. After a break or at the beginning of a subsequent interview, the interviewer should consider summarising on the record the reason for the break and confirming this with the suspect.*

E:4H *Where the interview is being recorded and the media or the recording equipment fails the officer conducting the interview should stop the interview immediately. Where part of the interview is unaffected by the error and is still accessible on the media, that media shall be copied and sealed in the suspect's presence and the interview recommenced using new equipment/media as required. Where the content of the interview has been lost in its entirety the media should be sealed in the suspect's presence and the interview begun again. If the recording equipment cannot be fixed or no replacement is immediately available the interview should be recorded in accordance with Code C, section 11.*

E:5 After the interview

E:5.1 The interviewer shall make a note in their pocket book that the interview has taken place, was audibly recorded, its time, duration and date and the master recording's identification number. **A–175**

E:5.2 If no proceedings follow in respect of the person whose interview was recorded, the recording media must be kept securely as in paragraph 6.1 and *Note 6A*.

Note for guidance

E:5A *Any written record of an audibly recorded interview should be made in accordance with national guidelines approved by the Secretary of State.* **A–176**

E:6 Media security

E:6.1 The officer in charge of each police station at which interviews with suspects are recorded shall make arrangements for master recordings to be kept securely and their movements accounted for on the same basis as material which may be used for evidential purposes, in accordance with force standing orders. See *Note 6A*. **A–177**

E:6.2 A police officer has no authority to break the seal on a master recording required for criminal trial or appeal proceedings. If it is necessary to gain access to the master recording, the police officer shall arrange for its seal to be broken in the presence of a representative of the Crown Prosecution Service. The defendant or their legal adviser should be informed and given a reasonable opportunity to be present. If the defendant or their legal representative is present they shall be invited to reseal and sign the master recording. If either refuses or neither is present this should be done by the representative of the Crown Prosecution Service. See *Notes 6B* and *6C*.

E:6.3 If no criminal proceedings result or the criminal trial and, if applicable, appeal proceedings to which the interview relates have been concluded, the chief officer of police is responsible for establishing arrangements for breaking the seal on the master recording, if necessary.

E:6.4 When the master recording seal is broken, a record must be made of the procedure followed, including the date, time, place and persons present.

Notes for guidance

E:6A *This section is concerned with the security of the master recording sealed at the conclusion of the interview. Care must be taken of working copies of recordings because their loss or destruction may lead to the need to access master recordings.* **A–178**

E:6B *If the recording has been delivered to the Crown Court for their keeping after com mittal for trial the crown prosecutor will apply to the chief clerk of the Crown Court centr for the release of the recording for unsealing by the crown prosecutor.*

E:6C *Reference to the Crown Prosecution Service or to the crown prosecutor in this par of the code should be taken to include any other body or person with a statutory responsibilit for prosecution for whom the police conduct any audibly recorded interviews.*

E:7 Recording of interviews by secure digital network

E:7.1 This section of the code applies only in the following area

- Lancashire Constabulary, Eastern Division as defined at 1 September 2007.

E:7.2 This section of the code does not extend to the audio recording o interviews with suspects by secure digital network (SDN) to any other Division o the Lancashire Constabulary nor to any other police force area in England an Wales. Any interviews with suspects subject to recording by secure digital networl in an area other than that listed in paragraph 7.1 above must be simultaneously recorded, and any recordings used, in accordance with sections 1 to 6 above.

E:7.3 The following requirements are solely applicable to the use of a secure digital network for the recording of interviews.

Application of sections 1 to 6 of Code E
E:7.4 Sections 1 to 6 of Code E above apply except for the following paragraphs:

- paragraph 2.2
- paragraph 4.3
- paragraph 4.4 (e)
- paragraphs 4.11 – 4.19
- paragraphs 6.1 – 6.4.

Commencement of interview
E:7.5 When the suspect is brought into the interview room, the interviewe shall without delay and in the sight of the suspect, switch on the recording equip ment and enter his or her digital identifier.

E:7.6 The interviewer must then provide the appropriate case reference fo the interview and inform the suspect that the interview is being recorded via secure digital network and that recording commenced when the interviewe inserted the digital identifier.

E:7.7 In addition to the requirements of paragraph 4.4(a) – (d) above, th interviewer must inform the person that the recording of the interview can onl be accessed on the order of a court; that copies of the recording will be mad available in the event that he or she is charged or informed that they will prose cuted; and that a written notice will be provided to them at the end of th interview setting out their access rights and what will happen to the recording.

Taking a break during interview
E:7.8 When a break is taken and the interview room vacated by the suspect the recording shall be stopped and the procedures for the conclusion of a interview followed.

E:7.9 When a break is a short one and either the suspect or the interviewer o both remain in the interview room, the recording must be stopped. There is n need to create a new secure digital network file. When the interview recommence the recording should continue on the same secure network file. The time th interview recommences shall be recorded on the audio recording.

E:7.10 After any break in the interview the interviewer must, before resumin the interview, remind the person being questioned that they remain under cau

tion or, if there is any doubt, give the caution in full again. See *Note for Guidance
4G.*

Failure of recording equipment

E:7.11 If there is an equipment failure which can be rectified quickly, *e.g.* by
commencing a new secure digital network recording, the interviewer shall follow the
appropriate procedures as in paragraph 7.8. When the recording is resumed the
interviewer shall explain what happened and record the time the interview
recommences. If, however, it is not possible to continue recording on the secure
digital network the interview should be recorded on removable media as in
paragraph 4.3 unless the necessary equipment is not available. If this happens the
interview may continue without being audibly recorded and the interviewer shall
seek the custody officer's authority as in paragraph 3.3. See *Note for Guidance 4H.*

Conclusion of interview

E:7.12 At the conclusion of the interview, the suspect shall be offered the opportunity to clarify anything he or she has said and asked if there is anything they
want to add.

E:7.13 At the conclusion of the interview, including the taking and reading
back of any written statement:

(a) the time shall be orally recorded;

(b) the suspect shall be handed a notice which explains:

- how the audio recording will be used,
- the arrangements for access to it,
- that if the person is charged or informed they will be prosecuted, a
  copy of the audio recording will be supplied as soon as practicable or
  as otherwise agreed between the suspect and the police; see *Note for
  Guidance 7A*;

(c) the suspect must be asked to confirm that he or she has received a copy
of the notice at paragraph 7.13(b) above; if the suspect fails to accept or
to acknowledge receipt of the notice, the interviewer will state for the recording that a copy of the notice has been provided to the suspect and
that he or she has refused to take a copy of the notice or has refused to
acknowledge receipt;

(d) the time shall be recorded and the interviewer shall notify the suspect
that the recording is being saved to the secure network. The interviewer
must save the recording in the presence of the suspect. The suspect
should then be informed that the interview is terminated.

Note for guidance

E:7A *The notice at paragraph 7.13 above should provide a brief explanation on the
secure digital network and how access is strictly limited to the recording. The notice should
also explain the access rights of the suspect, his or her legal representative, the police and the
prosecutor to copies of the recording of the interview. Space should be provided on the form
to insert the date and the file reference number for the interview.*

(7) Visual recording of interviews

The text that follows is of the version of the code that came into force on
January 1, 2006: see *ante,* Appendix A–1.

The *Police and Criminal Evidence Act 1984 (Visual Recording of Interviews)
(Certain Police Areas) Order* 2002 (S.I. 2002 No. 1069) (made under
s.60A(1)(b) and (2)) required the visual recording of interviews held by police officers at Basingstoke, Portsmouth, Southampton, Chatham,
Gravesend, Tonbridge, Bromley, Colindale, Edmonton, Redditch, Telford
and Worcester police stations and commencing after midnight on May 7,
2002.

The *Police and Criminal Evidence Act 1984 (Visual Recording of Interviews) (Certain Police Areas) (No. 2) Order* 2002 (S.I. 2002 No. 2527) (made under s.60A(1)(b) and (2)) required the visual recording of interviews held by police officers at Harlow, Colchester, and Southend police stations and commencing after midnight on October 29, 2002.

The *Police and Criminal Evidence Act 1984 (Visual Recording of Interviews) (Certain Police Areas) Order* 2003 (S.I. 2003 No. 2463) revoked S.I. 2002 No. 1069 and S.I. 2002 No. 2527 (*ante*) as from November 1, 2003, so that visual recording of interviews in the police areas specified in those orders was no longer mandatory.

As at June 22, 2009, there was no requirement on any police force to make visual recordings of interviews, but police officers who choose to make such recordings will still be required to have regard to the provisions of this code.

F.   Code of Practice on Visual Recordings With Sound Of Interviews With Suspects

Commencement—Transitional arrangements

A–180a   The contents of this code should be considered if an interviewing officer decides to make a visual recording with sound of an interview with a suspect after midnight on 31 December 2005. There is no statutory requirement to visually record interviews.

F:1. General

A–181   **F:1.1** This code of practice must be readily available for consultation by police officers and other police staff, detained persons and members of the public.

F:1.2 The notes for guidance included are not provisions of this code. They form guidance to police officers and others about its application and interpretation

F:1.3 Nothing in this code shall be taken as detracting in any way from the requirements of the Code of Practice for the Detention, Treatment and Questioning of Persons by Police Officers (Code C). [See *Note 1A*.]

F:1.4 The interviews to which this code applies are set out in paragraphs 3.1–3.3.

F:1.5 In this code, the term "appropriate adult", "solicitor" and "interview" have the same meaning as those set out in Code C. The corresponding provisions and Notes for Guidance in Code C applicable to those terms shall also apply where appropriate.

F:1.6 Any reference in this code to visual recording shall be taken to mean visual recording with sound.

F:1.7 References to "pocket book" in this code include any official report book issued to police officers.

Note for guidance

F:1A *As in paragraph 1.9 of Code C, references to custody officers include those carrying out the functions of a custody officer.*

F:2. Recording and sealing of master tapes

A–182   **F:2.1** The visual recording of interviews shall be carried out openly to instil confidence in its reliability as an impartial and accurate record of the interview [See *Note 2A*.]

F:2.2 The camera(s) shall be placed in the interview room so as to ensure coverage of as much of the room as is practicably possible whilst the interviews are taking place.

F:2.3 The certified recording medium will be of a high quality, new and previ ously unused. When the certified recording medium is placed in the recorder and switched on to record, the correct date and time, in hours, minutes and seconds will be superimposed automatically, second by second, during the whole recording. [See *Note 2B*.]

F:2.4 One copy of the certified recording medium, referred to in this code as the master copy, will be sealed before it leaves the presence of the suspect. A second copy will be used as a working copy. [See *Note 2C* and *2D*.]

F:2.5 Nothing in this code requires the identity of an officer to be recorded or disclosed if:

    (a) the interview or record relates to a person detained under the *Terrorism Act* 2000; or

    (b) otherwise where the officer reasonably believes that recording or disclosing their name might put them in danger.

In these cases, the officer will have their back to the camera and shall use their warrant or other identification number and the name of the police station to which they are attached. Such instances and the reasons for them shall be recorded in the custody record. [See *Note 2E*.]

Notes for guidance

F:2A *Interviewing officers will wish to arrange that, as far as possible, visual recording   **A–183** arrangements are unobtrusive. It must be clear to the suspect, however, that there is no opportunity to interfere with the recording equipment or the recording media.*

F:2B *In this context, the certified recording media will be of either a VHS or digital CD format and should be capable of having an image of the date and time superimposed upon them as they record the interview.*

F:2C *The purpose of sealing the master copy before it leaves the presence of the suspect is to establish their confidence that the integrity of the copy is preserved.*

F:2D *The recording of the interview may be used for identification procedures in accordance with paragraph 3.21 or Annex E of Code D.*

F:2E *The purpose of the [sic] paragraph 2.5 is to protect police officers and others involved in the investigation of serious organised crime or the arrest of particularly violent suspects when there is reliable information that those arrested or their associates may threaten or cause harm to the officers, their families or their personal property.*

F:3. Interviews to be visually recorded

F:3.1 Subject to paragraph 3.2 below, if an interviewing officer decides to make   **A–184** a visual recording, these are the areas where it might be appropriate:

    (a) with a suspect in respect of an indictable offence (including an offence triable either way) [see *Notes 3A* and *3B*];

    (b) which takes place as a result of an interviewer exceptionally putting further questions to a suspect about an offence described in sub-paragraph (a) above after they have been charged with, or informed they may be prosecuted for, that offence [see *Note 3C*];

    (c) in which an interviewer wishes to bring to the notice of a person, after that person has been charged with, or informed they may be prosecuted for an offence described in sub-paragraph (a) above, any written statement made by another person, or the content of an interview with another person [see *Note 3D*];

    (d) with, or in the presence of, a deaf or deaf/blind or speech impaired person who uses sign language to communicate;

    (e) with, or in the presence of anyone who requires an "appropriate adult"; or

    (f) in any case where the suspect or their representative requests that the interview be recorded visually.

F:3.2 The *Terrorism Act* 2000 makes separate provision for a code of practice for   **A–185**

375

the video recording of interviews in a police station of those detained under Schedule 7 or section 41 of the Act. The provisions of this code do not therefore apply to such interviews [see *Note 3E*].

F:3.3 The custody officer may authorise the interviewing officer not to record the interview visually:

(a) where it is not reasonably practicable to do so because of failure of the equipment, or the non-availability of a suitable interview room, or recorder and the authorising officer considers on reasonable grounds that the interview should not be delayed until the failure has been rectified or a suitable room or recorder becomes available; in such cases the custody officer may authorise the interviewing officer to audio record the interview in accordance with the guidance set out in Code E;

(b) where it is clear from the outset that no prosecution will ensue; or

(c) where it is not practicable to do so because at the time the person resists being taken to a suitable interview room or other location which would enable the interview to be recorded, or otherwise fails or refuses to go into such a room or location, and the authorising officer considers on reasonable grounds that the interview should not be delayed until these conditions cease to apply.

In all cases the custody officer shall make a note in the custody records [*sic*] of the reasons for not taking a visual record. [See *Note 3F*.]

F:3.4 When a person who is voluntarily attending the police station is required to be cautioned in accordance with Code C prior to being interviewed, the subsequent interview shall be recorded, unless the custody officer gives authority in accordance with the provisions of paragraph 3.3 above for the interview not to be so recorded.

F:3.5 The whole of each interview shall be recorded visually, including the taking and reading back of any statement.

F:3.6 A visible illuminated sign or indicator will light and remain on at all times when the recording equipment is activated or capable of recording or transmitting any signal or information.

Notes for guidance

A–186

F:3A *Nothing in the code is intended to preclude visual recording at police discretion of interviews at police stations with people cautioned in respect of offences not covered by paragraph 3.1, or responses made by interviewees after they have been charged with or informed they may be prosecuted for, an offence, provided that this code is complied with.*

F:3B *Attention is drawn to the provisions set out in Code C about the matters to be considered when deciding whether a detained person is fit to be interviewed.*

F:3C *Code C sets out the circumstances in which a suspect may be questioned about an offence after being charged with it.*

F:3D *Code C sets out the procedures to be followed when a person's attention is drawn after charge, to a statement made by another person. One method of bringing the content of an interview with another person to the notice of a suspect may be to play him a recording of that interview.*

F:3E *When it only becomes clear during the course of an interview which is being visually recorded that the interviewee may have committed an offence to which paragraph 3.2 applies, the interviewing officer should turn off the recording equipment and the interview should continue in accordance with the provisions of the* Terrorism Act 2000.

F:3F *A decision not to record an interview visually for any reason may be the subject of comment in court. The authorising officer should therefore be prepared to justify their decision in each case.*

F:4. The interview

(a) *General*

F:4.1 The provisions of Code C in relation to cautions and interviews and the   **A–187**
Notes for Guidance applicable to those provisions shall apply to the conduct of
interviews to which this code applies.

F:4.2 Particular attention is drawn to those parts of Code C that describe the
restrictions on drawing adverse inferences from a suspect's failure or refusal to
say anything about their involvement in the offence when interviewed, or after being charged or informed they may be prosecuted and how those restrictions affect
the terms of the caution and determine 'whether a special warning under sections
36 and 37 of the *Criminal Justice and Public Order Act* 1994 can be given.

(b) *Commencement of interviews*

F:4.3 When the suspect is brought into the interview room the interviewer   **A–188**
shall without delay, but in sight of the suspect, load the recording equipment and
set it to record. The recording media must be unwrapped or otherwise opened in
the presence of the suspect. [See *Note 4A*].

F:4.4 The interviewer shall then tell the suspect formally about the visual
recording. The interviewer shall:

    (a) explain the interview is being visually recorded;

    (b) subject to paragraph 2.5, give his or her name and rank, and that of any
    other interviewer present;

    (c) ask the suspect and any other party present (*e.g.* his solicitor) to identify
    themselves;

    (d) state the date, time of commencement and place of the interview; and

    (e) state that the suspect will be given a notice about what will happen to the
    recording.

F:4.5 The interviewer shall then caution the suspect, which should follow that
set out in Code C, and remind the suspect of their entitlement to free and independent legal advice and that they can speak to a solicitor on the telephone.

F:4.6 The interviewer shall then put to the suspect any significant statement or
silence (*i.e.* failure or refusal to answer a question or to answer it satisfactorily) which
occurred before the start of the interview, and shall ask the suspect whether they
wish to confirm or deny that earlier statement or silence or whether they wish to add
anything. The definition of a "significant" statement or silence is the same as that set
out in Code C.

(c) *Interviews with the deaf*

F:4.7 If the suspect is deaf or there is doubt about their hearing ability, the   **A–189**
provisions of Code C on interpreters for the deaf or for interviews with suspects
who have difficulty in understanding English continue to apply.

(d) *Objections and complaints by the suspect*

F:4.8 If the suspect raises objections to the interview being visually recorded ei-   **A–190**
ther at the outset or during the interview or during a break in the interview, the
interviewer shall explain the fact that the interview is being visually recorded and
that the provisions of this code require that the suspect's objections shall be recorded on the visual recording. When any objections have been visually recorded
or the suspect has refused to have their objections recorded, the interviewer shall
say that they are turning off the recording equipment, give their reasons and turn
it off. If a separate audio recording is being maintained, the officer shall ask the
person to record the reasons for refusing to agree to visual recording of the
interview. Paragraph 4.8 of Code E will apply if the person objects to audio recording of the interview. The officer shall then make a written record of the
interview. If the interviewer reasonably considers they may proceed to question
the suspect with the visual recording still on, the interviewer may do so. See *Note
4G*.

F:4.9 If in the course of an interview a complaint is made by the person being questioned, or on their behalf, concerning the provisions of this code or of Code C, then the interviewer shall act in accordance with Code C, record it in the interview record and inform the custody officer. [See *4B* and *4C.*]

F:4.10 If the suspect indicates that they wish to tell the interviewer about matters not directly connected with the offence of which they are suspected and that they are unwilling for these matters to be recorded, the suspect shall be given the opportunity to tell the interviewer about these matters after the conclusion of the formal interview.

(e) *Changing the recording media*

A–191　　F:4.11 In instances where the recording medium is not of sufficient length to record all of the interview with the suspect, further certified recording medium will be used. When the recording equipment indicates that the recording medium has only a short time left to run, the interviewer shall advise the suspect and round off that part of the interview. If the interviewer wishes to continue the interview but does not already have further certified recording media with him, they shall obtain a set. The suspect should not be left unattended in the interview room. The interviewer will remove the recording media from the recording equipment and insert the new ones which have been unwrapped or otherwise opened in the suspect's presence. The recording equipment shall then be set to record. Care must be taken, particularly when a number of sets of recording media have been used, to ensure that there is no confusion between them. This could be achieved by marking the sets of recording media with consecutive identification numbers.

(f) *Taking a break during the interview*

A–192　　F:4.12 When a break is to be taken during the course of an interview and the interview room is to be vacated by the suspect, the fact that a break is to be taken, the reason for it and the time shall be recorded. The recording equipment must be turned off and the recording media removed. The procedures for the conclusion of an interview set out in paragraph 4.19, below, should be followed.

F:4.13 When a break is to be a short one, and both the suspect and a police officer are to remain in the interview room, the fact that a break is to be taken, the reasons for it and the time shall be recorded on the recording media. The recording equipment may be turned off, but there is no need to remove the recording media. When the interview is recommenced the recording shall continue on the same recording media and the time at which the interview recommences shall be recorded.

F:4.14 When there is a break in questioning under caution, the interviewing officer must ensure that the person being questioned is aware that they remain under caution. If there is any doubt the caution must be given again in full when the interview resumes. [See *Notes 4D* and *4E.*]

(g) *Failure of recording equipment*

A–193　　F:4.15 If there is a failure of equipment which can be rectified quickly, the appropriate procedures set out in paragraph 4.12 shall be followed. When the recording is resumed the interviewer shall explain what has happened and record the time the interview recommences. If, however, it is not possible to continue recording on that particular recorder and no alternative equipment is readily available, the interview may continue without being recorded visually. In such circumstances, the procedures set out in paragraph 3.3 of this code for seeking the authority of the custody officer will be followed. [See *Note 4F.*]

(h) *Removing used recording media from recording equipment*

A–194　　F:4.16 Where used recording media are removed from the recording equipment during the course of an interview, they shall be retained and the procedures set out in paragraph 4.18 below followed.

(i) *Conclusion of interview*

F:4.17 Before the conclusion of the interview, the suspect shall be offered the opportunity to clarify anything he or she has said and asked if there is anything that they wish to add.

F:4.18 At the conclusion of the interview, including the taking and reading back of any written statement, the time shall be recorded and the recording equipment switched off. The master tape or CD shall be removed from the recording equipment, sealed with a master copy label and treated as an exhibit in accordance with the force standing orders. The interviewer shall sign the label and also ask the suspect and any appropriate adults or other third party present during the interview to sign it. If the suspect or third party refuses to sign the label, an officer of at least the rank of inspector, or if one is not available, the custody officer, shall be called into the interview room and asked to sign it.

F:4.19 The suspect shall be handed a notice which explains the use which will be made of the recording and the arrangements for access to it. The notice will also advise the suspect that a copy of the tape shall be supplied as soon as practicable if the person is charged or informed that he will be prosecuted.

Notes for guidance

F:4A *The interviewer should attempt to estimate the likely length of the interview and ensure that an appropriate quantity of certified recording media and labels with which to seal the master copies are available in the interview room.*

F:4B *Where the custody officer is called immediately to deal with the complaint, wherever possible the recording equipment should be left to run until the custody officer has entered the interview room and spoken to the person being interviewed. Continuation or termination of the interview should be at the discretion of the interviewing officer pending action by an inspector as set out in Code C.*

F:4C *Where the complaint is about a matter not connected with this code of practice or Code C, the decision to continue with the interview is at the discretion of the interviewing officer. Where the interviewing officer decides to continue with the interview, the person being interviewed shall be told that the complaint will be brought to the attention of the custody officer at the conclusion of the interview. When the interview is concluded, the interviewing officer must, as soon as practicable, inform the custody officer of the existence and nature of the complaint made.*

F:4D *In considering whether to caution again after a break, the officer should bear in mind that he may have to satisfy a court that the person understood that he was still under caution when the interview resumed.*

F:4E *The officer should bear in mind that it may be necessary to satisfy the court that nothing occurred during a break in an interview or between interviews which influenced the suspect's recorded evidence. On the re-commencement of an interview, the officer should consider summarising on the tape or CD the reason for the break and confirming this with the suspect.*

F:4F *If any part of the recording media breaks or is otherwise damaged during the interview, it should be sealed as a master copy in the presence of the suspect and the interview resumed where it left off. The undamaged part should be copied and the original sealed as a master tape in the suspect's presence, if necessary after the interview. If equipment for copying is not readily available, both parts should be sealed in the suspect's presence and the interview begun again.*

F:4G *The interviewer should be aware that a decision to continue recording against the wishes of the suspect may be the subject of comment in court.*

F:5. After the interview

F:5.1 The interviewer shall make a note in his or her pocket book of the fact that the interview has taken place and has been recorded, its time, duration and date and the identification number of the master copy of the recording media.

F:5.2 Where no proceedings follow in respect of the person whose interview was recorded, the recording media must nevertheless be kept securely in accordance with paragraph 6.1 and Note 6A.

Note for guidance

F:5A *Any written record of a recorded interview shall be made in accordance with national guidelines approved by the Secretary of State, and with regard to the advice contained in the Manual of Guidance for the preparation, processing and submission of files.*

F:6. Master copy security

(a) *General*

A–198   **F:6.1** The officer in charge of the police station at which interviews with suspects are recorded shall make arrangements for the master copies to be kept securely and their movements accounted for on the same basis as other material which may be used for evidential purposes, in accordance with force standing orders. [See *Note 6A*.]

(b) *Breaking master copy seal for criminal proceedings*

A–199   **F:6.2** A police officer has no authority to break the seal on a master copy which is required for criminal trial or appeal proceedings. If it is necessary to gain access to the master copy, the police officer shall arrange for its seal to be broken in the presence of a representative of the Crown Prosecution Service. The defendant or their legal adviser shall be informed and given a reasonable opportunity to be present. If the defendant or their legal representative is present they shall be invited to reseal and sign the master copy. If either refuses or neither is present, this shall be done by the representative of the Crown Prosecution Service. [See *Notes 6B* and *6C*.]

(c) *Breaking master copy seal: other cases*

A–200   **F:6.3** The chief officer of police is responsible for establishing arrangements for breaking the seal of the master copy where no criminal proceedings result, or the criminal proceedings, to which the interview relates, have been concluded and it becomes necessary to break the seal. These arrangements should be those which the chief officer considers are reasonably necessary to demonstrate to the person interviewed and any other party who may wish to use or refer to the interview record that the master copy has not been tampered with and that the interview record remains accurate. [See *Note 6D*.]

F:6.4 Subject to paragraph 6.6, a representative of each party must be given a reasonable opportunity to be present when the seal is broken, the master copy copied and re-sealed.

F:6.5 If one or more of the parties is not present when the master copy seal is broken because they cannot be contacted or refuse to attend or paragraph 6.6 applies, arrangements should be made for an independent person such as a custody visitor, to be present. Alternatively, or as an additional safeguard, arrangement should be made for a film or photographs to be taken of the procedure.

F:6.6 Paragraph 6.5 does not require a person to be given an opportunity to be present when:

> (a) it is necessary to break the master copy seal for the proper and effective further investigation of the original offence or the investigation of some other offence; and

> (b) the officer in charge of the investigation has reasonable grounds to suspect that allowing an opportunity might prejudice any such an investigation or criminal proceedings which may be brought as a result or endanger any person. [See *Note 6E*.]

(e) *Documentation*

A–201   **F:6.7** When the master copy seal is broken, copied and re-sealed, a record must be made of the procedure followed, including the date time and place and persons present.

Notes for guidance

A–202   **F:6A** *This section is concerned with the security of the master copy which will have been* sealed at the conclusion of the interview. Care should, however, be taken of working copies since their loss or destruction may lead unnecessarily to the need to have access to master copies.

F:6B *If the master copy has been delivered to the Crown Court for their keeping after committal for trial the crown prosecutor will apply to the chief clerk of the Crown Court centre for its release for unsealing by the crown prosecutor.*

F:6C *Reference to the Crown Prosecution Service or to the crown prosecutor in this part of the code shall be taken to include any other body or person with a statutory responsibility for prosecution for whom the police conduct any recorded interviews.*

F:6D *The most common reasons for needing access to master copies that are not required for criminal proceedings arise from civil actions and complaints against police and civil actions between individuals arising out of allegations of crime investigated by police.*

F:6E *Paragraph 6.6 could apply, for example, when one or more of the outcomes or likely outcomes of the investigation might be: (i) the prosecution of one or more of the original suspects; (ii) the prosecution of someone previously not suspected, including someone who was originally a witness; and (iii) any original suspect being treated as a prosecution witness and when premature disclosure of any police action, particularly through contact with any parties involved, could lead to a real risk of compromising the investigation and endangering witnesses.*

(8) Statutory power of arrest

The first version of Code G came into force on January 1, 2006, to coincide with the commencement of the substantial changes to the provisions of the *PACE Act* 1984 relating to the powers of arrest of police constables. As from that date, all offences became arrestable offences, but the lawfulness of an arrest by a constable for an offence became dependent on the constable having "reasonable grounds for believing that for any of the reasons mentioned in subsection (5) [of section 24] it is necessary to arrest the person in question". For the substituted section 24, see § 15–163 in the main work.   **A–203**

As to the content of this code, paragraph 2.1 significantly over-simplifies the requirements of a lawful arrest, and there is an error in paragraph 2.3. This states that a constable may arrest without warrant "in relation to any offence, except for the single exception [*sic*] listed in Note for Guidance 1". That note recites the powers of arrest for offences under the *CLA* 1967, ss.4(1) and 5(1) (assisting offenders/ concealment of evidence) require that the offences to which they relate must carry a maximum term of at least five years' imprisonment. This, however, is to confuse the ingredients of the offence and the power of arrest.

G. Code of Practice for the Statutory Power of Arrest by Police Officers
Commencement
This code applies to any arrest made by a police officer after midnight on 31 December 2005.   **A–203a**

G:1 Introduction

G:1.1 This code of practice deals with statutory power of police to arrest persons suspected of involvement in a criminal offence.   **A–204**

G:1.2 The right to liberty is a key principle of the *Human Rights Act* 1998. The exercise of the power of arrest represents an obvious and significant interference with that right.

G:1.3 The use of the power must be fully justified and officers exercising the power should consider if the necessary objectives can be met by other, less intrusive means. Arrest must never be used simply because it can be used. Absence of justification for exercising the powers of arrest may lead to challenges should the case proceed to court. When the power of arrest is exercised it is essential that it is exercised in a non-discriminatory and proportionate manner.

G:1.4 Section 24 of the *Police and Criminal Evidence Act* 1984 (as substituted by section 110 of the *Serious Organised Crime and Police Act* 2005) provides the statutory power of arrest. If the provisions of the Act and this code are not observed, both the arrest and the conduct of any subsequent investigation may be open to question.

G:1.5 This code of practice must be readily available at all police stations for consultation by police officers and police staff, detained persons and members of the public.

G:1.6 The notes for guidance are not provisions of this code.

G:2 Elements of arrest under section 24 PACE

A–205   **G:**2.1 A lawful arrest requires two elements:

> A person's involvement or suspected involvement or attempted involvement in the commission of a criminal offence;

AND

> reasonable grounds for believing that the person's arrest is necessary.

G:2.2 Arresting officers are required to inform the person arrested that they have been arrested, even if this fact is obvious, and of the relevant circumstances of the arrest in relation to both elements and to inform the custody officer of these on arrival at the police station. See Code C, paragraph 3.4.

Involvement in the commision of an offence

A–206   **G:**2.3 A constable may arrest without warrant in relation to any offence, except for the single exception listed in *Note for Guidance* 1. A constable may arrest anyone:

- who is about to commit an offence or is in the act of committing an offence;
- whom the officer has reasonable grounds for suspecting is about to commit an offence or to be committing an offence;
- whom the officer has reasonable grounds to suspect of being guilty of an offence which he or she has reasonable grounds for suspecting has been committed;
- anyone [*sic*] who is guilty of an offence which has been committed or anyone whom the officer has reasonable grounds for suspecting to be guilty of that offence.

Necessity criteria

A–207   **G:**2.4 The power of arrest is only exercisable if the constable has reasonable grounds for believing that it is necessary to arrest the person. The criteria for what may constitute necessity are set out in paragraph 2.9. It remains an operational decision at the discretion of the arresting officer as to:

- what action he or she may take at the point of contact with the individual;
- the necessity criterion or criteria (if any) which applies to the individual; and
- whether to arrest, report for summons, grant street bail, issue a fixed penalty notice or take any other action that is open to the officer.

G:2.5 In applying the criteria, the arresting officer has to be satisfied that at least one of the reasons supporting the need for arrest is satisfied.

G:2.6 Extending the power of arrest to all offences provides a constable with the ability to use that power to deal with any situation. However, applying the necessity criteria requires the constable to examine and justify the reason or reasons why a person needs to be taken to a police station for the custody officer to decide whether the person should be placed in police detention.

G:2.7 The criteria below are set out in section 24 of *PACE* as substituted by section 110 of the *Serious Organised Crime and Police Act* 2005. The criteria are exhaustive. However, the circumstances that may satisfy those criteria remain a matter for the operational discretion of individual officers. Some examples are given below of what those circumstances may be.

G:2.8 In considering the individual circumstances, the constable must take into account the situation of the victim, the nature of the offence, the circumstances of the suspect and the needs of the investigative process.

G:2.9 The criteria are that the arrest is necessary: **A–208**

(a) to enable the name of the person in question to be ascertained (in the case where the constable does not know, and cannot readily ascertain, the person's name, or has reasonable grounds for doubting whether a name given by the person as his name is his real name);

(b) correspondingly as regards the person's address;

   an address is a satisfactory address for service of summons if the person will be at it for a sufficiently long period for it to be possible to serve him or her with a summons; or, that some other person at that address specified by the person will accept service of the summons on their behalf;

(c) to prevent the person in question—

  (i) causing physical injury to himself or any other person;

  (ii) suffering physical injury;

  (iii) causing loss or damage to property;

  (iv) committing an offence against public decency (only applies where members of the public going about their normal business cannot reasonably be expected to avoid the person in question); or

  (v) causing an unlawful obstruction of the highway;

(d) to protect a child or other vulnerable person from the person in question;

(e) to allow the prompt and effective investigation of the offence or of the conduct of the person in question;

   this may include cases such as:

  (i) where there are reasonable grounds to believe that the person:

- has made false statements;
- has made statements which cannot be readily verified;
- has presented false evidence;
- may steal or destroy evidence;
- may make contact with co-suspects or conspirators;
- may intimidate or threaten or make contact with witnesses;
- where it is necessary to obtain evidence by questioning [*sic*]; or

  (ii) when considering arrest in connection with an indictable offence, there is a need to:

- enter and search any premises occupied or controlled by a person;
- search the person;
- prevent contact with others;
- take fingerprints, footwear impressions, samples or photographs of the suspect;

  (iii) ensuring compliance with statutory drug testing requirements;

(f) to prevent any prosecution for the offence from being hindered by the disappearance of the person in question;

this may arise if there are reasonable grounds for believing that:

- if the person is not arrested he or she will fail to attend court;
- street bail after arrest would be insufficient to deter the suspect from trying to evade prosecution.

G:3 Information to be given on arrest

(a) Cautions—when a caution must be given (taken from Code C section 10)

A–209   **G:3.1** A person whom there are grounds to suspect of an offence (see *Note 2*) must be cautioned before any questions about an offence, or further questions if the answers provide the grounds for suspicion, are put to them if either the suspect's answers or silence (*i.e.* failure or refusal to answer or answer satisfactorily) may be given in evidence to a court in a prosecution. A person need not be cautioned if questions are for other necessary purposes *e.g.*:

(a) solely to establish their identify or ownership of any vehicle;

(b) to obtain information in accordance with any relevant statutory requirement;

(c) in furtherance of the proper and effective conduct of a search, *e.g.* to determine the need to search in the exercise of powers to stop and search or to seek co-operation while carrying out a search;

(d) to seek verification of a written record as in Code C, paragraph 11.13;

(e) when examining a person in accordance with the *Terrorism Act* 2000, Schedule 7 and the Code of Practice for Examining Officers issued under that Act, Schedule 14, paragraph 6.

G:3.2 Whenever a person not under arrest is initally cautioned, or reminded they are under caution, that person must at the same time be told they are not under arrest and are free to leave if they want to.

G:3.3 A person who is arrested, or further arrested, must be informed at the time, or as soon as practicable thereafter, that they are under arrest and the grounds for their arrest, see *Note 3*.

G:3.4 A person who is arrested, or further arrested, must also be cautioned unless:

(a) it is impracticable to do so by reason of their condition or behaviour at the time;

(b) they have already been cautioned immediately prior to arrest as in paragraph 3.1.

(c) [sic] Terms of the caution (taken from Code C section 10)

A–210   **G:3.5** The caution, which must be given on arrest, should be in the following terms:

"You do not have to say anything. But it may harm your defence if you do not mention when questioned something which you later rely on in court. Anything you do say may be given in evidence.".

See *Note 5*.

G:3.6 Minor deviations from the words of any caution given in accordance with this code do not constitute a breach of this code, provided the sense of the relevant caution is preserved. See *Note 6*.

G:3.7 When, despite being cautioned, a person fails to co-operate or to answer particular questions which may affect their immediate treatment, the person should be informed of any relevant consequences and that those consequences are not affected by the caution. Examples are when a person's refusal to provide:

- their name and address when charged may make them liable to detention;
- particulars and information in accordance with a statutory requirement,

e.g. under the *Road Traffic Act* 1988, may amount to an offence or may
make the person liable to a further arrest.

G:4 Records of arrest

(a) *General*

G:4.1 The arresting officer is required to record in his pocket book or by other   **A–211**
methods used for recording information:

- the nature and cirumstances of the offence leading to the arrest;
- the reason or reasons why arrest was necessary;
- the giving of the caution;
- anything said by the person at the time of the arrest.

G:4.2 Such a record should be made at the time of the arrest unless
impracticable to do. If not made at that time, the record should then be completed
as soon as possible thereafter.

G:4.3 On arrival at the police station, the custody officer shall open the custody
record (see paragraph 1.1A and section 2 of Code C). The information given by
the arresting officer on the circumstances and reason or reasons for arrest shall be
recorded as part of the custody record. Alternatively, a copy of the record made
by the officer in accordance with paragraph 4.1 above shall be attached as part of
the custody record. See paragraph 2.2 and Code C, paragraphs 3.4 and 10.3.

G:4.4 The custody record will serve as a record of the arrest. Copies of the
custody record will be provided in accordance with paragraphs 2.4 and 2.4A of
Code C and access for inspection of the original record in accordance with
paragraph 2.5 of Code C.

(b) *Interviews and arrests*

G:4.5 Records of interviews, significant statements or silences will be treated in
the same way as set out in sections 10 and 11 of Code C and in Code E (audio recording of interviews).

Notes for guidance

G:1 *The powers of arrest for offences under section 4(1) and 5(1) of the* Criminal Law   **A–212**
*Act 1967 require that the offences to which they relate must carry a sentence fixed by law or
one which a first time offender aged 18 or over could be sentenced to 5 years or more
imprisonment.*

G:2 *There must be some reasonable, objective grounds for the suspicion, based on known
facts or information which are relevant to the likelihood the offence has been committed and
the person to be questioned committed it.*

G:3 *An arrested person must be given sufficient information to enable them to understand
they have been deprived of their liberty and the reason they have been arrested, e.g. when a
person is arrested on suspicion of committing an offence they must be informed of the
suspected offence's nature, when and where it was committed. The suspect must also be
informed of the reason or reasons why arrest is considered necessary. Vague or technical
language should be avoided.*

G:4 *Nothing in this code requires a caution to be given or repeated when informing a
person not under arrest they may be prosecuted for an offence. However, a court will not be
able to draw any inferences under the* Criminal Justice and Public Order Act *1994, section 34, if the person was not cautioned.*

G:5 *If it appears a person does not understand the caution, the people giving it should
explain it in their own words.*

G:6 *The powers available to an officer as the result of an arrest – for example, entry and
search of premises, holding a person incommunicado, setting up road blocks – are only
available in respect of indictable offences and are subject to the specific requirements on authorisation as set out in the 1984 Act and relevant PACE code of practice.*

(9) Detention treatment and questioning of terrorist suspects

The *Police and Criminal Evidence Act 1984 (Code of Practice C and Code of*   **A–213**

Practice H) Order 2006 (S.I. 2006 No. 1938) provided for a revised Code C (*ante*, A–38 *et seq.*), and for a new Code H (on detention, treatment and questioning by police officers of persons under section 41 of, and Schedule 8 to, the *Terrorism Act* 2000), to come into operation on July 25, 2006. The new codes are consequential upon the commencement of the provisions of the *Terrorism Act* 2006, which are concerned with the 28-day detention of those arrested under section 41 of the 2000 Act. Whereas Code C had previously regulated those detained following arrest under section 41, this is now regulated by Code H. Code C was revised so as to remove references to detention under the 2000 Act. The new Code H largely mirrors the provisions of Code C, but with various differences. Principally, these are: (i) that less detail as to the grounds of arrest is required; (ii) that the detainee is to be transferred to prison and dealt with under the *Prison Rules* 1999 (S.I. 1999 No. 728) where a warrant has been issued providing for detention beyond 14 days; (iii) that there is more detailed provision as to visiting rights and exercise, and a clear demarcation is made between visits from friends and family, and official visits; (iv) that moving a detainee from a police station for medical treatment or any other reason does not "stop the clock" as it would in the case of a non-terrorism detainee; (v) there is specific provision as to the allocation of reading material; (vi) there is a requirement that the detainee is to receive daily healthcare visits; and (vii) there are notes for guidance concerning applications to extend the period of detention. Code H applies to any person arrested under section 41 who is in police detention after midnight on July 24, 2006, notwithstanding that he may have been arrested before that time.

H.   Code of Practice in Connection with the Detention, Treatment and Questioning by Police Officers of Persons under Section 41 of, and Schedule 8 to, the Terrorism Act 2000

Commencement—Transitional Arrangements

A–214   This code applies to people in police detention following their arrest under section 41 of the *Terrorism Act* 2000, after midnight (on 24 July 2006), notwithstanding that they may have been arrested before that time.

H:1 General

A–214a   **H:1.1** This code of practice applies to, and only to, persons arrested under section 41 of the *Terrorism Act* 2000 (TACT) and detained in police custody under those provisions and Schedule 8 of the Act. References to detention under this provision that were previously included in *PACE* Code C—Code for the Detention, Treatment, and Questioning of Persons by Police Officers, no longer apply.

H:1.2 The code ceases to apply at any point that a detainee is:

    (a) charged with an offence

    (b) released without charge, or

    (c) transferred to a prison see *section 14.5*.

H:1.3 References to an offence in this code include being concerned in the commission, preparation or instigation of acts of terrorism.

H:1.4 This code's provisions do not apply to detention of individuals under any other terrorism legislation. This code does not apply to people:

    (i) detained under section 5(1) of the *Prevention of Terrorism Act* 2005;

    (ii) detained for examination under TACT, Schedule 7, and to whom the code of practice issued under that Act, Schedule 14, paragraph 6, applies;

    (iii) detained for searches under stop and search powers.

The provisions for the detention, treatment and questioning by police officers of persons other than those in police detention following arrest under section 41 of TACT, are set out in Code C issued under section 66(1) of the *Police & Criminal Evidence Act (PACE)* 1984 (*PACE* Code C).

H:1.5 All persons in custody must be dealt with expeditiously, and released as soon as the need for detention no longer applies.

H:1.6 There is no provision for bail under TACT prior to charge.

H:1.7 An officer must perform the assigned duties in this code as soon as practicable. An officer will not be in breach of this code if delay is justifiable and reasonable steps are taken to prevent unnecessary delay. The custody record shall show when a delay has occurred and the reason. *See Note 1H.*

H:1.8–1.10 [*Identical to C:1.2 to C:1.4, respectively.*]

H:1.11 For the purposes of this code, a juvenile is any person under the age of 17. If anyone appears to be under 17, and there is no clear evidence that they are 17 or over, they shall be treated as a juvenile for the purposes of this code.

H:1.12–1.15 [*Identical to C:1.6 to C:1.9, respectively.*]

H:1.16 When this code requires the prior authority or agreement of an officer of at least inspector or superintendent rank, that authority may be given by a sergeant or chief inspector authorised by section 107 of *PACE* to perform the functions of the higher rank under TACT.

H:1.17–1.19 [*Identical to C:1.13 to C:1.15, respectively.*]

H:1.20 Designated persons and other police staff must have regard to any relevant provisions of this code.

H:1.21 [*Identical to C:1.17.*]

Notes for guidance

H:1A [*Identical to C:1A.*] **A–214b**

H:1B *A person, including a parent or guardian, should not be an appropriate adult if they:*

- *are*
  - *suspected of involvement in the offence or involvement in the commission, preparation or instigation of acts of terrorism*
  - *the victim*
  - *a witness*
  - *involved in the investigation*
- *received admissions prior to attending to act as the appropriate adult.*

Note: If a juvenile's parent is estranged from the juvenile, they should not be asked to act as the appropriate adult if the juvenile expressly and specifically objects to their presence.

H:1C–1G [*Identical to C:1C to C:1G, respectively.*]

H:1H *Paragraph 1.7 is intended to cover delays which may occur in processing detainees e.g if:*

- *a large number of suspects are brought into the station simultaneously to be placed in custody;*
- *interview rooms are all being used;*
- *there are difficulties contacting an appropriate adult, solicitor or interpreter.*

H:1I–1K [*Identical to C:1I to C:1K, respectively.*]

H:1L *If a person is moved from a police station to receive medical treatment, or for any other reason, the period of detention is still calculated from the time of arrest under section 41 of TACT (or, if a person was being detained under TACT, Schedule 7, when arrested, from the time at which the examination under Schedule 7 began).*

H:1M *Under paragraph 1 of Schedule 8 to TACT, all police stations are designated for detention of persons arrested under section 41 of TACT. Paragraph 4 of Schedule 8 requires that the constable who arrests a person under section 41 takes him as soon as practicable to the police station which he considers is "most appropriate".*

H:2 Custody records

A–215   **H:2.1** When a person is brought to a police station:

- under TACT section 41 arrest, or
- is arrested under TACT section 41 at the police station having attended there voluntarily,

they should be brought before the custody officer as soon as practicable after their arrival at the station or, if appropriate, following arrest after attending the police station voluntarily *see Note 3H*. A person is deemed to be "at a police station" for these purposes if they are within the boundary of any building or enclosed yard which forms part of that police station.

H:2.2 A separate custody record must be opened as soon as practicable for each person brought to a police station under arrest or arrested at the station having gone there voluntarily. All information recorded under this code must be recorded as soon as practicable in the custody record unless otherwise specified. Any audio or video recording made in the custody area is not part of the custody record.

H:2.3 If any action requires the authority of an officer of a specified rank, this must be noted in the custody record, subject to paragraph 2.8.

H:2.4 [*Identical to C:2.3.*]

H:2.5 A solicitor or appropriate adult must be permitted to consult a detainee's custody record as soon as practicable after their arrival at the station and at any other time whilst the person is detained. Arrangements for this access must be agreed with the custody officer and may not unreasonably interfere with the custody officer's duties or the justifiable needs of the investigation.

H:2.6 [*Identical to C:2.4A.*]

H:2.7 The detainee, appropriate adult or legal representative shall be permitted to inspect the original custody record once the detained person is no longer held under the provisions of TACT section 41 and Schedule 8, provided they give reasonable notice of their request. Any such inspection shall be noted in the custody record.

H:2.8 All entries in custody records must be timed and identified by the maker. Nothing in this code requires the identity of officers or other police staff to be recorded or disclosed in the case of enquiries linked to the investigation of terrorism. In these cases, they shall use their warrant or other identification numbers and the name of their police station *see Note 2A*. If records are entered on computer these shall also be timed and contain the operator's identification.

H:2.9 [*Identical to C:2.7.*]

Note for guidance

A–215a   **H:2A** *The purpose of paragraph 2.8 is to protect those involved in terrorist investigations or arrests of terrorist suspects from the possibility that those arrested, their associates or other individuals or groups may threaten or cause harm to those involved.*

H:3 Initial action

(a) *Detained persons—normal procedure*

A–215b   **H:3.1** When a person is brought to a police station under arrest or arrested at the station having gone there voluntarily, the custody officer must make sure the person is told clearly about the following continuing rights which may be exercised at any stage during the period in custody:

(i) the right to have someone informed of their arrest as in section 5;

(ii) the right to consult privately with a solicitor and that free independent legal advice is available;

(iii) the right to consult this code of practice. *See Note 3D.*

H:3.2 [*Identical to C:3.2, save for reference to "paragraph 2.6" in lieu of reference to "paragraph 2.4A".*]

H:3.3 [*Identical to C:3.3.*]

H:3.4 The custody officer shall:

- record that the person was arrested under section 41 of TACT and the reason(s) for the arrest on the custody record [see paragraph 10.2 and *Note for Guidance 3G*];
- note on the custody record any comment the detainee makes in relation to the arresting officer's account but shall not invite comment; if the arresting officer is not physically present when the detainee is brought to a police station, the arresting officer's account must be made available to the custody officer remotely or by a third party on the arresting officer's behalf;
- note any comment the detainee makes in respect of the decision to detain them but shall not invite comment;
- not put specific questions to the detainee regarding their involvement in any offence, nor in respect of any comments they may make in response to the arresting officer's account or the decision to place them in detention [see paragraphs 14.1 and 14.2 and *Notes for Guidance 3H, 14A* and *14B*]. Such an exchange is likely to constitute an interview as in paragraph 11.1 and require the associated safeguards in section 11.

See paragraph 5.9 of the code of practice issued under TACT, Schedule 8, paragraph 3, in respect of unsolicited comments.

If the first review of detention is carried out at this time, see paragraphs 14.1 and 14.2, and Part II of Schedule 8 to the *Terrorism Act* 2000 in respect of action by the review officer.

H:3.5 [*Identical to C:3.5.*]

H:3.6 When determining these needs the custody officer is responsible for initiating an assessment to consider whether the detainee is likely to present specific risks to custody staff, any individual who may have contact with detainee (*e.g.* legal advisers, medical staff), or themselves. Such assessments should always include a check on the Police National Computer, to be carried out as soon as practicable, to identify any risks highlighted in relation to the detainee. Although such assessments are primarily the custody officer's responsibility, it will be necessary to obtain information from other sources, especially the investigation team [see *Note 3E*], the arresting officer or an appropriate health care professional, see *paragraph 9.15*. Reasons for delaying the initiation or completion of the assessment must be recorded.

H:3.7 [*Identical to C:3.7.*]

H:3.8 Risk assessments must follow a structured process which clearly defines the categories of risk to be considered and the results must be incorporated in the detainee's custody record. The custody officer is responsible for making sure those responsible for the detainee's custody are appropriately briefed about the risks. The content of any risk assessment and any analysis of the level of risk relating to the person's detention is not required to be shown or provided to the detainee or any person acting on behalf of the detainee. If no specific risks are identified by the assessment, that should be noted in the custody record. *See Note 3F* and paragraph 9.15.

H:3.9 Custody officers are responsible for implementing the response to any specific risk assessment, which should include for example:

- reducing opportunities for self harm;
- calling a health care professional;
- increasing levels of monitoring or observation;
- reducing the risk to those who come into contact with the detainee.

See Note for Guidance 3F.

H:3.10, 3.11 [*Identical to C:3.10 and C:3.11, respectively.*]

H:3.12 A constable, prison officer or other person authorised by the Secretary of State may take any steps which are reasonably necessary for—

    (a) photographing the detained person,

    (b) measuring him, or

    (c) identifying him.

H:3.13 Paragraph 3.12 concerns the power in TACT, Schedule 8, paragraph 2. The power in TACT, Schedule 8, paragraph 2, does not cover the taking of fingerprints, intimate samples or non-intimate samples, which is covered in TACT, Schedule 8, paragraphs 10–15.

(b) *Detained persons—special groups*

H:3.14–3.16 [*Identical to C:3.12 to C:3.14, respectively.*]

H:3.17 [*Identical to C:3.15, save for reference to "paragraph 3.15" in lieu of reference to "paragraph 3.13".*]

H:3.18–3.20 [*Identical to C:3.17 to C:3.19, respectively.*]

H:3.21 [*Identical to C:3.20, save for reference to "paragraph 3.17" in lieu of reference to "paragraph 3.15".*]

(c) *Documentation*

H:3.22 [*Identical to C:3.23.*]

H:3.23 Action taken under paragraphs 3.14 to 3.22 shall be recorded.

Notes for guidance

H:3A *The notice of entitlements should:*

- *list the entitlements in this code, including:*
  - *visits and contact with outside parties where practicable, including special provisions for Commonwealth citizens and foreign nationals;*
  - *reasonable standards of physical comfort;*
  - *adequate food and drink;*
  - *access to toilets and washing facilities, clothing, medical attention, and exercise when practicable;*
- *mention the:*
  - *provisions relating to the conduct of interviews;*
  - *circumstances in which an appropriate adult should be available to assist the detainee and their statutory rights to make representation whenever the period of their detention is reviewed.*

H:3B, 3C [*Identical to C:3B and C:3C, respectively.*]

H:3D *The right to consult this or other relevant codes of practice does not entitle the person concerned to delay unreasonably any necessary investigative or administrative action whilst they do so. Examples of action which need not be delayed unreasonably include:*

- *searching detainees at the police station;*
- *taking fingerprints or non-intimate samples without consent for evidential purposes.*

H:3E *The investigation team will include any officer involved in questioning a suspect, gathering or analysing evidence in relation to the offences of which the detainee is suspected of having committed. Should a custody officer require information from the investigation team, the first point of contact should be the officer in charge of the investigation.*

H:3F *Home Office Circular 32/2000 provides more detailed guidance on risk assessments and identifies key risk areas which should always be considered. This should be read with the Guidance on Safer Detention & Handling of Persons in Police Custody issued by the National Centre for Policing Excellence in conjunction with the Home Office and Association of Chief Police Officers.*

H:3G *Arrests under TACT section 41 can only be made where an officer has reasonable grounds to suspect that the individual concerned is a "terrorist". This differs from the PACE* *power of arrest in that it need not be linked to a specific offence. There may also be circumstances where an arrest under TACT is made on the grounds of sensitive information which cannot be disclosed. In such circumstances, the grounds for arrest may be given in terms of the interpretation of a "terrorist" set out in TACT sections 40(1)(a) or 40(1)(b).*

H:3H *For the purpose of arrests under TACT section 41, the review officer is responsible for authorising detention (see paragraphs 14.1 and 14.2, and Notes for Guidance 14A and 14B). The review officer's role is explained in TACT Schedule 8 Part II. A person may be detained after arrest pending the first review, which must take place as soon as practicable after the person's arrest.*

H:4 Detainee's property

(a) *Action*

H:4.1 The custody officer is responsible for: **A–216a**

   (a) ascertaining what property a detainee:

      (i) has with them when they come to the police station, either on first arrival at the police station or any subsequent arrivals at a police station in connection with that detention;

      (ii) might have acquired for an unlawful or harmful purpose while in custody;

   (b) the safekeeping of any property taken from a detainee which remains at the police station.

The custody officer may search the detainee or authorise their being searched to the extent they consider necessary, provided a search of intimate parts of the body or involving the removal of more than outer clothing is only made as in Annex A. A search may only be carried out by an officer of the same sex as the detainee. See *Note 4A.*

H:4.2, 4.3 [*Identical to C:4.2 and C:4.3, respectively.*]

(b) *Documentation*

H:4.4 It is a matter for the custody officer to determine whether a record should be made of the property a detained person has with him or had taken from him on arrest [see *Note for Guidance 4D*]. Any record made is not required to be kept as part of the custody record but the custody record should be noted as to where such a record exists. Whenever a record is made the detainee shall be allowed to check and sign the record of property as correct. Any refusal to sign shall be recorded.

H:4.5 [*Identical to C:4.5.*]

Notes for guidance

H:4A–4C [*Identical to C:4A to C:4C, respectively.*] **A–216b**

H:4D *Section 43(2) of TACT allows a constable to search a person who has been arrested under section 41 to discover whether he has anything in his possession that may constitute evidence that he is a terrorist.*

H:5 Right not to be held incommunicado

(a) *Action*

H:5.1 Any person arrested and held in custody at a police station or other **A–217** premises may, on request, have one named person who is a friend, relative or a person known to them who is likely to take an interest in their welfare informed at public expense of their whereabouts as soon as practicable. If the person cannot be contacted the detainee may choose up to two alternatives. If they cannot be contacted, the person in charge of detention or the investigation has discretion to allow further attempts until the information has been conveyed. See *Notes 5D* and *5E.*

H:5.2 [*Identical to C:5.2.*]

H:5.3 The above right may be exercised each time a detainee is taken to another police station or returned to a police station having been previously transferred to prison. This code does not afford such a right to a person on transfer to a prison, where a detainee's rights will be governed by prison rules [see paragraph 14.8].

H:5.4 If the detainee agrees, they may receive visits from friends, family or others likely to take an interest in their welfare, at the custody officer's discretion. Custody officers should liaise closely with the investigation team [see *Note 3E*] to allow risk assessments to be made where particular visitors have been requested by the detainee or identified themselves to police. In circumstances where the nature of the investigation means that such requests cannot be met, consideration should be given, in conjunction with a representative of the relevant scheme, to increasing the frequency of visits from independent visitor schemes. See *Notes 5B* and *5C*.

H:5.5 [*Identical to C:5.5, save for reference to "Note 5E" in lieu of reference to "Note 5D".*]

H:5.6 The detainee shall be given writing materials, on request, and allowed to telephone one person for a reasonable time, see *Notes 5A* and *5F*. Either or both these privileges may be denied or delayed if an officer of inspector rank or above considers sending a letter or making a telephone call may result in any of the consequences in Annex B, paragraphs 1 and 2, particularly in relation to the making of a telephone call in a language which an officer listening to the call [see paragraph 5.7] does not understand. See *Note 5G*.

Nothing in this paragraph permits the restriction or denial of the rights in paragraphs 5.1 and 6.1.

H:5.7 Before any letter or message is sent, or telephone call made, the detainee shall be informed that what they say in any letter, call or message (other than in a communication to a solicitor) may be read or listened to and may be given in evidence. A telephone call may be terminated if it is being abused [see *Note 5G*]. The costs can be at public expense at the custody officer's discretion.

H:5.8 [*Identical to C:5.7A.*]

(b) *Documentation*

H:5.9 A record must be kept of any:

(a) request made under this section and the action taken;

(b) letters, messages or telephone calls made or received or visit received;

(c) refusal by the detainee to have information about them given to an outside enquirer, or any refusal to see a visitor. The detainee must be asked to countersign the record accordingly and any refusal recorded.

Notes for guidance

A–217a

H:5A *A person may request an interpreter to interpret a telephone call or translate a letter.*

H:5B *At the custody officer's discretion (and subject to the detainee's consent), visits from friends, family or others likely to take an interest in the detainee's welfare, should be allowed when possible, subject to sufficient personnel being available to supervise a visit and any possible hindrance to the investigation. Custody officers should bear in mind the exceptional nature of prolonged TACT detention and consider the potential benefits that visits may bring to the health and welfare of detainees who are held for extended periods.*

H:5C *Official visitors should be given access following consultation with the officer who has overall responsibility for the investigation provided the detainee consents, and they do not compromise safety or security or unduly delay or interfere with the progress of an investigation. Official visitors should still be required to provide appropriate identification and subject to any screening process in place at the place of detention. Official visitors may include:*

- *an accredited faith representative*
- *Members of either House of Parliament*

- *public officials needing to interview the prisoner in the course of their duties*
- *other persons visiting with the approval of the officer who has overall responsibility for the investigation*
- *consular officials visiting a detainee who is a national of the country they represent subject to Annex F.*

Visits from appropriate members of the Independent Custody Visitors Scheme should be dealt with in accordance with the separate Code of Practice on Independent Custody Visiting.

H:5D *If the detainee does not know anyone to contact for advice or support or cannot contact a friend or relative, the custody officer should bear in mind any local voluntary bodies or other organisations that might be able to help. Paragraph 6.1 applies if legal advice is required.*

H:5E *In some circumstances it may not be appropriate to use the telephone to disclose information under paragraphs 5.1 and 5.5.*

H:5F *The telephone call at paragraph 5.6 is in addition to any communication under paragraphs 5.1 and 6.1. Further calls may be made at the custody officer's discretion.*

H:5G *The nature of terrorism investigations means that officers should have particular regard to the possibility of suspects attempting to pass information which may be detrimental to public safety, or to an investigation.*

H:6 Right to legal advice

(a) *Action*

H:6.1 Unless Annex B applies, all detainees must be informed that they may at any time consult and communicate privately with a solicitor, whether in person, in writing or by telephone, and that free independent legal advice is available from the duty solicitor. Where an appropriate adult is in attendance, they must also be informed of this right. See paragraph 3.1, *Note 11*, *Note 6B* and *Note 6I*   **A–217b**

H:6.2 A poster advertising the right to legal advice must be prominently displayed in the charging area of every police station. See *Note 6G*.

H:6.3 [*Identical to C:6.4.*]

H:6.4 The exercise of the right of access to legal advice may be delayed exceptionally only as in Annex B. Whenever legal advice is requested, and unless Annex B applies, the custody officer must act without delay to secure the provision of such advice. If, on being informed or reminded of this right, the detainee declines to speak to a solicitor in person, the officer should point out that the right includes the right to speak with a solicitor on the telephone [see paragraph 5.6]. If the detainee continues to waive this right the officer should ask them why and any reasons should be recorded on the custody record or the interview record as appropriate. Reminders of the right to legal advice must be given as in paragraphs 3.5, 11.3, and the *PACE* Code D on the Identification of Persons by Police Officers (*PACE* Code D), paragraphs 3.19(ii) and 6.2. Once it is clear a detainee does not want to speak to a solicitor in person or by telephone they should cease to be asked their reasons. See *Note 6J*.

H:6.5 An officer of the rank of Commander or Assistant Chief Constable may give a direction under TACT, Schedule 8, paragraph 9, that a detainee may only consult a solicitor within the sight and hearing of a qualified officer. Such a direction may only be given if the officer has reasonable grounds to believe that if it were not, it may result in one of the consequences set out in TACT, Schedule 8, paragraphs 8(4) or 8(5)(c). See Annex B, paragraph 3 and *Note 6I*. A "qualified officer" means a police officer who:

(a) is at least the rank of inspector;

(b) is of the uniformed branch of the force of which the officer giving the direction is a member, and

(c) in the opinion of the officer giving the direction, has no connection with the detained person's case.

Officers considering the use of this power should first refer to Home Office Circular 40/2003.

H:6.6 [*Identical to C:6.5A.*]

H:6.7 A detainee who wants legal advice may not be interviewed or continue to be interviewed until they have received such advice unless:

   (a) [*identical to C:6.6(a)*],

   (b) [*identical to C:6.6(b)*],

   (c) [*identical to C:6.6(c)*],

   (d) the detainee changes their mind, about wanting legal advice.

In these circumstances the interview may be started or continued without delay provided that:

    (i) the detainee agrees to do so, in writing or on the interview record made in accordance with the code of practice issued under TACT Schedule 8, paragraph 3; and

    (ii) an officer of inspector rank or above has inquired about the detainee's reasons for their change of mind and gives authority for the interview to proceed.

Confirmation of the detainee's agreement, their change of mind, the reasons for it if given and, subject to paragraph 2.8, the name of the authorising officer shall be recorded in the written interview record or the interview record made in accordance with the code of practice issued under paragraph 3 of Schedule 8 to the *Terrorism Act*. See *Note 6H*. Note: in these circumstances the restriction on drawing adverse inferences from silence in Annex C will not apply because the detainee is allowed an opportunity to consult a solicitor if they wish.

H:6.8 If paragraph 6.7(a) applies, where the reason for authorising the delay ceases to apply, there may be no further delay in permitting the exercise of the right in the absence of a further authorisation unless paragraph 6.7(b), (c) or (d) applies.

H:6.9 [*Identical to C:6.8, save for reference to "paragraph 6.7" in lieu of reference to "paragraph 6.6".*]

H:6.10 The solicitor may only be required to leave the interview if their conduct is such that the interviewer is unable properly to put questions to the suspect. See *Notes 6C* and *6D*.

H:6.11 [*Identical to C:6.10, save for reference to "Note 6D" in lieu of reference to "Note 6E".*]

H:6.12 [*Identical to C:6.11.*]

H:6.13 [*Identical to C:6.12.*]

H:6.14 [*Identical to C:6.12A, save for references to "Note 6C" and to "paragraphs 6.7 to 6.11" in lieu of references to "Note 6D" and "paragraphs 6.6. to 6.10".*]

H:6.15 In exercising their discretion under paragraph 6.14, the officer should take into account in particular:

   • whether:

    – the identity and status of an accredited or probationary representative have been satisfactorily established;

    – they are of suitable character to provide legal advice,

    – any other matters in any written letter of authorisation provided by the solicitor on whose behalf the person is attending the police station See *Note 6E*.

H:6.16 If the inspector refuses access to an accredited or probationary representative or a decision is taken that such a person should not be permitted to remain at an interview, the inspector must notify the solicitor on whose behalf the representative was acting and give them an opportunity to make alternative arrangements. The detainee must be informed and the custody record noted.

H:6.17 If a solicitor arrives at the station to see a particular person, that person

must, unless Annex B applies, be so informed whether or not they are being
interviewed and asked if they would like to see the solicitor. This applies even if
the detainee has declined legal advice or, having requested it, subsequently agreed
to be interviewed without receiving advice. The solicitor's attendance and the
detainee's decision must be noted in the custody record.

(b) *Documentation*

    H:6.18, 6.19 [*Identical to C:6.16 and C:6.17, respectively.*]

Notes for guidance

    H:6A *If paragraph 6.7(b) applies, the officer should, if practicable, ask the solicitor for*   **A–218**
*an estimate of how long it will take to come to the station and relate this to the time detention
is permitted, the time of day (i.e. whether the rest period under paragraph 12.2 is imminent)
and the requirements of other investigations. If the solicitor is on their way or is to set off immediately, it will not normally be appropriate to begin an interview before they arrive. If it
appears necessary to begin an interview before the solicitor's arrival, they should be given an
indication of how long the police would be able to wait so there is an opportunity to make
arrangements for someone else to provide legal advice. Nothing within this section is
intended to prevent police from ascertaining immediately after the arrest of an individual
whether a threat to public safety exists (see paragraph 11.2).*

    H:6B [*Identical to C:6B.*]

    H:6C [*Identical to C:6D.*]

    H:6D [*Identical to C:6E.*]

    H:6E [*Identical to C:6F.*]

    H:6F [*Identical to C:6G, save for reference to "paragraph 6.7(b)" in lieu of reference to
"paragraph 6.6(b)".*]

    H:6G [*Identical to C:6H.*]

    H:6H [*Identical to C:6I, save for reference to "Paragraph 6.7(d)" in lieu of reference
to "Paragraph 6.6(d)".*]

    H:6I *Whenever a detainee exercises their right to legal advice by consulting or com-
municating with a solicitor, they must be allowed to do so in private. This right to consult or
communicate in private is fundamental. Except as allowed by the* Terrorism Act 2000,
*Schedule 8, paragraph 9, if the requirement for privacy is compromised because what is said
or written by the detainee or solicitor for the purpose of giving and receiving legal advice is
overheard, listened to, or read by others without the informed consent of the detainee, the
right will effectively have been denied. When a detainee chooses to speak to a solicitor on the
telephone, they should be allowed to do so in private unless a direction under Schedule 8,
paragraph 9 of the* Terrorism Act 2000 *has been given or this is impractical because of the
design and layout of the custody area, or the location of telephones. However, the normal
expectation should be that facilities will be available, unless they are being used, at all police
stations to enable detainees to speak in private to a solicitor either face to face or over the
telephone.*

    H:6J [*Identical to C:6K.*]

H:7 Citizens of independent Commonwealth countries or foreign nationals

[*Identical to C:7.*]   **A–218a**

H:8 Conditions of detention

(a) *Action*

    H:8.1, 8.2 [*Identical to C:8.1 and C:8.2, respectively.*]   **A–218b**

    H:8.3 [*Identical to C:8.3, save for omission of reference to Note 8A.*]

    H:8.4, 8.5 [*Identical to C:8.4 and C:8.5, respectively.*]

    H:8.6 At least two light meals and one main meal should be offered in any 24 hour period. See *Note 8B*. Drinks should be provided at meal times and upon reasonable request between meals. Whenever necessary, advice shall be sought from the appropriate health care professional, see *Note 9A*, on medical and dietary matters. As far as practicable, meals provided shall offer a varied diet and meet any specific dietary needs or religious beliefs the detainee may have. Detainees should also be made aware that the meals offered meet such needs. The detainee may, at the custody officer's discretion, have meals supplied by their family or friends at their expense. See *Note 8A*.

H:8.7 Brief outdoor exercise shall be offered daily if practicable. Where facilities exist, indoor exercise shall be offered as an alternative if outside conditions are such that a detainee cannot be reasonably expected to take outdoor exercise (*e.g.*, in cold or wet weather) or if requested by the detainee or for reasons of security, see *Note 8C*.

H:8.8 Where practicable, provision should be made for detainees to practice [*sic*] religious observance. Consideration should be given to providing a separate room which can be used as a prayer room. The supply of appropriate food and clothing, and suitable provision for prayer facilities, such as uncontaminated copies of religious books, should also be considered. See *Note 8D*.

H:8.9 [*Identical to C:8.8.*]

H:8.10 Police stations should keep a reasonable supply of reading material available for detainees, including but not limited to, the main religious texts. See *Note 8D*. Detainees should be made aware that such material is available and reasonable requests for such material should be met as soon as practicable unless to do so would:

> (i) interfere with the investigation; or
>
> (ii) prevent or delay an officer from discharging his statutory duties, or those in this code.

If such a request is refused on the grounds of (i) or (ii) above, this should be noted in the custody record and met as soon as possible after those grounds cease to apply.

(b) *Documentation*

H:8.11, 8.12 [*Identical to C:8.9 and C:8.11, respectively.*]

Notes for guidance

H:8A *In deciding whether to allow meals to be supplied by family or friends, the custody officer is entitled to take account of the risk of items being concealed in any food or package, and the officer's duties and responsibilities under food handling legislation. If an officer needs to examine food or other items supplied by family and friends before deciding whether they can be given to the detainee, he should inform the person who has brought the item to the police station of this and the reasons for doing so.*

H:8B [*Identical to C:8B.*]

H:8C *In light of the potential for detaining individuals for extended periods of time, the overriding principle should be to accommodate a period of exercise, except where to do so would hinder the investigation, delay the detainee's release or charge, or it is declined by the detainee.*

H:8D *Police forces should consult with representatives of the main religious communities to ensure the provision for religious observance is adequate, and to seek advice on the appropriate storage and handling of religious texts or other religious items.*

H:9 Care and treatment of detained persons

(a) *General*

H:9.1 Notwithstanding other requirements for medical attention as set out in this section, detainees who are held for more than 96 hours must be visited by a healthcare professional at least once every 24 hours.

H:9.2, 9.3 [*Identical to C:9.1 and C:9.2, respectively.*]

H:9.4 [*Identical to C:9.3, save for references to "Note 9C", "paragraph 9.15" and
"Note 9G" in lieu of references to "Note 9CA", "paragraph 9.13" and "Note 9H",
respectively.*]

H:9.5 [*Identical to C:9.4.*]

(b) *Clinical treatment and attention*

H:9.6, 9.7, 9.8 [*Identical to C:9.5, C:9.5A and C: 9.5B, respectively.*]

H:9.9 [*Identical to C:9.7, save for reference to "Note 9D" in lieu of reference to "Note
9E".*]

H:9.10 [*Identical to C:9.8.*]

H:9.11 [*Identical to C:9.7, save for reference to "paragraph 9.12" in lieu of reference
to "paragraph 9.10".*]

H:9.12, 9.13 [*Identical to C:9.10 and C:9.11, respectively.*]

H:9.14 [*Identical to C:9.12, save for reference to "paragraph 9.6" in lieu of reference
to "paragraph 9.5".*]

H:9.15 [*Identical to C:9.13.*]

H:9.16 [*Identical to C:9.14, save for reference to "Note 9E" in lieu of reference to
"Note 9F".*]

(c) *Documentation*

H:9.17 [*Identical to C:9.15, save for references to "paragraph 9.3", "paragraph 9.6",
"paragraph 9.10", "Note 9F", "Note 9E" and "Note 9G" in lieu of references to "paragraph
9.2", "paragraph 9.5", "paragraph 9.8", "Note 9G", Note 9F" and "Note 9H",
respectively.*]

H:9.18 [*Identical to C.9.16, save for reference to "Note 9F" in lieu of reference to
"Note 9G".*]

H:9.19 [*Identical to C.9.17.*]

Notes for guidance

H:9A, 9B [*Identical to C:9A and C:9B, respectively.*]   **A-219b**

H:9C [*Identical to C:9C, save for reference to "Paragraph 9.6" in lieu of reference to
"Paragraph 9.5".*]

H:9D, 9E [*Identical to C:9E and C:9F, respectively.*]

H:9F [*Identical to C:9G, save for reference to "Paragraphs 9.17 and 9.18" in lieu of
reference to "Paragraphs 9.15 and 9.16".*]

H:9G [*Identical to C:9H.*]

H:10 Cautions

(a) *When a caution must be given*

H:10.1 A person whom there are grounds to suspect of an offence, see *Note*   **A-220**
10A, must be cautioned before any questions about an offence, or further questions if
the answers provide the grounds for suspicion, are put to them if either the suspect's
answers or silence (*i.e.* failure or refusal to answer or answer satisfactorily) may be
given in evidence to a court in a prosecution.

H:10.2 A person who is arrested, or further arrested, must be informed at the
time, or as soon as practicable thereafter, that they are under arrest and the
grounds for their arrest, see paragraph 3.4, *Note 3G* and *Note 10B.*

H:10.3 [*Effectively identical to C:10.4.*]

(b) *Terms of the cautions*

H:10.4 The caution which must be given on:

    (a) arrest;

    (b) all other occasions before a person is charged or informed they may be
        prosecuted, see *PACE* Code C, section 16.

should, unless the restriction on drawing adverse inferences from silence applies, see Annex C, be in the following terms:

> *"You do not have to say anything. But it may harm your defence if you do not men tion when questioned something which you later rely on in Court. Anything you d say may be given in evidence."*

See *Note 10F*

H:10.5 [*Identical to C:10.6.*]

H:10.6 [*Identical to C:10.7, save for reference to "Note 10C" in lieu of reference to "Note 10D".*]

H:10.7 [*Identical to C:10.8, save for reference to "Note 10D" in lieu of reference to "Note 10E".*]

H:10.8 [*Intended to be identical to C.10.9, but there is a drafting error in that the words following "statutory requirement" have been omitted.*]

(c) *Special warnings under the Criminal Justice and Public Order Act 1994, sections 36 and 37*

H:10.9 [*Identical to C.10.10, save for references to "Note 10E" and "paragraph 10.10" in lieu of references to "Note 10F" and "paragraph 10.11", respectively.*]

H:10.10 [*Identical to C.10.11.*]

(d) *Juveniles and persons who are mentally disordered or otherwise mentally vulnerable*

H:10.11 [*Identical to C.10.12.*]

(e) *Documentation*

H:10.12 [*Identical to C.10.13.*]

Notes for guidance

A-220a

H:10A [*Identical to C:10A.*]

H:10B [*Identical to C:10B, save for inclusion of reference to "Note 3G" after the word "committed".*]

H:10C–10F [*Identical to C:10D to C:10G.*]

Interviews—general

(a) *Action*

A-220b

H:11.1 An interview in this code is the questioning of a person arrested on suspicion of being a terrorist which, under paragraph 10.1, must be carried out under caution. Whenever a person is interviewed they must be informed of the grounds for arrest [see *Note 3G*].

H:11.2 Following a decision to arrest a suspect, they must not be interviewed about the relevant offence except at a place designated for detention under Schedule 8, paragraph 1, of the *Terrorism Act* 2000, unless the consequent delay would be likely to:

(a) lead to:
- interference with, or harm to, evidence connected with an offence;
- interference with, or physical harm to, other people; or
- serious loss of, or damage to, property;

(b) lead to alerting other people suspected of committing an offence but not yet arrested for it; or

(c) hinder the recovery of property obtained in consequence of the commission of an offence.

Interviewing in any of these circumstances shall cease once the relevant risk has been averted or the necessary questions have been put in order to attempt to avert that risk.

H:11.3 Immediately prior to the commencement or re-commencement of an

interview at a designated place of detention, the interviewer should remind the
suspect of their entitlement to free legal advice and that the interview can be
delayed for legal advice to be obtained, unless one of the exceptions in paragraph
6.7 applies. It is the interviewer's responsibility to make sure all reminders are recorded in the interview record.

H:11.4, 11.5 [*Identical to C:11.4 and C:11.4A.*]

H:11.6 [*Identical to C.11.5, save for reference "paragraph 10.8" in lieu of reference to
"paragraph 10.9".*]

H:11.7 [*Identical to C.11.6, but with the omission of the final sub-paragraph of that
paragraph.*]

(b) *Interview records*

H:11.8 Interview records should be made in accordance with the code of
practice issued under Schedule 8, paragraph 3, to the *Terrorism Act* where the
interview takes place at a designated place of detention.

(c) *Juveniles and mentally disordered or otherwise mentally vulnerable people*

H:11.9 [*Identical to C:11.15, save for reference to "paragraphs 11.2, 11.11 to 11.13"
in lieu of reference to "paragraphs 11.1, 11.18 to 11.20".*]

H:11.10 If an appropriate adult is present at an interview, they shall be
informed:

● they are not expected to act simply as an observer; and
● the purpose of their presence is to:
  – advise the person being interviewed;
  – observe whether the interview is being conducted properly and fairly;
  – facilitate communication with the person being interviewed.

The appropriate adult may be required to leave the interview if their conduct is such
that the interviewer is unable properly to put questions to the suspect. This will
include situations where the appropriate adult's approach or conduct prevents or
unreasonably obstructs proper questions being put to the suspect or the suspect's responses being recorded. If the interviewer considers an appropriate adult is acting in
such a way, they will stop the interview and consult an officer not below superintendent rank, if one is readily available, and otherwise an officer not below inspector
rank not connected with the investigation. After speaking to the appropriate adult,
the officer consulted will decide if the interview should continue without the attendance of that appropriate adult. If they decide it should not, another appropriate
adult should be obtained before the interview continues, unless the provisions of
paragraph 11.11 below apply.

(d) *Vulnerable suspects—urgent interviews at police stations*

H:11.11–11.13 [*Identical to C:11.18 to C:11.20, save for references to "paragraph
11.2(a) to (c)" and "paragraph 11.11" in lieu of references to "paragraph 11.1(a) to (c)"
and "paragraph 11.18", respectively.*]

Notes for guidance

H:11A–11C [*Identical to C:11A to C:11C, respectively.*] **A–221**

H:11D *Consideration should be given to the effect of extended detention on a detainee
and any subsequent information they provide, especially if it relates to information on matters that they have failed to provide previously in response to similar questioning see Annex
G.*

H:11E [*Identical to C:11E.*]

H:12 Interviews in police stations

(a) *Action*

H:12.1 [*Identical to C:12.1.*] **A–221a**

H:12.2 Except as below, in any period of 24 hours a detainee must be allowed a continuous period of at least 8 hours for rest, free from questioning, travel or any interruption in connection with the investigation concerned. This period should normally be at night or other appropriate time which takes account of when the detainee last slept or rested. If a detainee is arrested at a police station after going there voluntarily, the period of 24 hours runs from the time of their arrest (or, if a person was being detained under TACT Schedule 7 when arrested from the time at which the examination under Schedule 7 began) and not the time of arrival at the police station. The period may not be interrupted or delayed except:

    (a) when there are reasonable grounds for believing not delaying or interrupting the period would:

        (i) involve a risk of harm to people or serious loss of, or damage to property;

        (ii) delay unnecessarily the person's release from custody;

        (iii) otherwise prejudice the outcome of the investigation;

    (b) at the request of the detainee, their appropriate adult or legal representative;

    (c) when a delay or interruption is necessary in order to:

        (i) comply with the legal obligations and duties arising under section 14;

        (ii) to take action required under section 9 or in accordance with medical advice.

If the period is interrupted in accordance with (a), a fresh period must be allowed. Interruptions under (b) and (c), do not require a fresh period to be allowed.

H:12.3 [*Identical to C:12.3, save that there is no reference to "Annex G" and the references to "paragraph 11.18" and "paragraphs 11.18 to 11.20" are replaced by references to "paragraph 11.11" and "paragraphs 11.11 to 11.13".*]

H:12.4 [*Identical to C:12.4.*]

H:12.5 A suspect whose detention without charge has been authorised under TACT Schedule 8, because the detention is necessary for an interview to obtain evidence of the offence for which they have been arrested, may choose not to answer questions but police do not require the suspect's consent or agreement to interview them for this purpose. If a suspect takes steps to prevent themselves being questioned or further questioned, *e.g.* by refusing to leave their cell to go to a suitable interview room or by trying to leave the interview room, they shall be advised their consent or agreement to interview is not required. The suspect shall be cautioned as in section 10, and informed if they fail or refuse to co-operate, the interview may take place in the cell and that their failure or refusal to co-operate may be given in evidence. The suspect shall then be invited to co-operate and go into the interview room.

H:12.6 People being questioned or making statements shall not be required to stand.

H:12.7 Before the interview commences each interviewer shall, subject to the qualification at paragraph 2.8, identify themselves and any other persons present to the interviewee.

H:12.8 [*Identical to C:12.8.*]

H:12.9 During extended periods where no interviews take place, because of the need to gather further evidence or analyse existing evidence, detainees and their legal representative shall be informed that the investigation into the relevant offence remains ongoing. If practicable, the detainee and legal representative should also be made aware in general terms of any reasons for long gaps between interviews. Consideration should be given to allowing visits, more frequent exercise, or for reading or writing materials to be offered: see paragraph 5.4, section 8 and *Note 12C.*

H:12.10 [*Identical to C:12.9.*]

(b) *Documentation*
   H:12.11–12.15 [*Identical to C:12.10 to C:12.14, respectively.*]

Notes for guidance
   H:12A *It is not normally necessary to ask for a written statement if the interview was re-* **A–221b**
corded in writing and the record signed in accordance with the code of practice issued under
TACT, Schedule 8, paragraph 3. Statements under caution should normally be taken in
these circumstances only at the person's express wish. A person may however be asked if they
want to make such a statement.
   H:12B [*Identical to C:12B.*]
   H:12C *Consideration should be given to the matters referred to in paragraph 12.9 after*
a period of over 24 hours without questioning. This is to ensure that extended periods of
detention without an indication that the investigation remains ongoing do not contribute to a
deterioration of the detainee's well-being.

H:13 Interpreters

(a) *General*
   H:13.1 [*Identical to C:13.1.*]

(b) *Foreign languages*
   H:13.2 [*Identical to C:13.2, save for reference to "paragraphs 11.2, 11.11 to 11.13"*
in lieu of reference to "paragraph 11.1, 11.18 to 11.20".]
   H:13.3 The interviewer shall make sure the interpreter makes a note of the
interview at the time in the person's language for use in the event of the
interpreter being called to give evidence, and certifies its accuracy. The interviewer
should allow sufficient time for the interpreter to note each question and answer
after each is put, given and interpreted. The person should be allowed to read
the record or have it read to them and sign it as correct or indicate the respects in
which they consider it inaccurate. If the interview is audibly recorded or visually
recorded with sound, the code of practice issued under paragraph 3 of Schedule
8 to the *Terrorism Act* 2000 will apply.
   H:13.4 [*Identical to C:13.4.*]

(c) *Deaf people and people with speech difficulties*
   H:13.5, 13.6 [*Identical to C:13.5 and C:13.6, respectively, save for references to*
"paragraphs 11.2, 11.11 to 11.13" in lieu of references to "paragraph 11.1, 11.18 to
11.20".]
   H:13.7 The interviewer shall make sure the interpreter is allowed to read the
interview record and certify its accuracy in the event of the interpreter being
called to give evidence. If the interview is audibly recorded or visually recorded,
the code of practice issued under TACT, Schedule 8, paragraph 3 will apply.

(d) *Additional rules for detained persons*
   H:13.8 All reasonable attempts should be made to make the detainee
understand that interpreters will be provided at public expense.
   H:13.9 If paragraph 6.1 applies and the detainee cannot communicate with
the solicitor because of language, hearing or speech difficulties, an interpreter
must be called. The interpreter may not be a police officer or any other police
staff when interpretation is needed for the purposes of obtaining legal advice. In
all other cases a police officer or other police staff may only interpret if the
detainee and the appropriate adult, if applicable, give their agreement in writing
or if the interview is audibly recorded or visually recorded as in the code of
practice issued under TACT, Schedule 8, paragraph 3.
   H:13.10 [*Identical to C:13.10.*]

(e) *Documentation*
   H:13.11 [*Identical to C:13.11.*]

H:14 Reviews and extensions of detention

(a) *Reviews and extensions of detention*

A–222   **H:14.1** The powers and duties of the review officer are in the *Terrorism Act* 2000, Schedule 8, Part II. See *Notes 14A* and *14B*. A review officer should carry out his duties at the police station where the detainee is held, and be allowed such access to the detainee as is necessary for him to exercise those duties.

H:14.2 For the purposes of reviewing a person's detention, no officer shall put specific questions to the detainee:

- regarding their involvement in any offence; or
- in respect of any comments they may make:
  - when given the opportunity to make representations; or
  - in response to a decision to keep them in detention or extend the maximum period of detention.

Such an exchange could constitute an interview as in paragraph 11.1 and would be subject to the associated safeguards in section 11 and, in respect of a person who has been charged, see *PACE* Code C, section 16.8.

H:14.3 If detention is necessary for longer than 48 hours, a police officer of at least superintendent rank, or a Crown Prosecutor may apply for warrants of further detention under the *Terrorism Act* 2000, Schedule 8, Part III.

H:14.4 When an application for a warrant of further or extended detention is sought under paragraph 29 or 36 of Schedule 8, the detained person and their representative must be informed of their rights in respect of the application. These include:

(a) the right to a written or oral notice of the warrant [see *Note 14G*];

(b) the right to make oral or written representations to the judicial authority about the application;

(c) the right to be present and legally represented at the hearing of the application, unless specifically excluded by the judicial authority;

(d) their right to free legal advice (see section 6 of this code).

(b) *Transfer of detained persons to prison*

H:14.5 Where a warrant is issued which authorises detention beyond a period of 14 days from the time of arrest (or if a person was being detained under TACT, Schedule 7, from the time at which the examination under Schedule 7 began), the detainee must be transferred from detention in a police station to detention in a designated prison as soon as is practicable, unless:

(a) the detainee specifically requests to remain in detention at a police station and that request can be accommodated, or

(b) there are reasonable grounds to believe that transferring a person to a prison would:

(i) significantly hinder a terrorism investigation;

(ii) delay charging of the detainee or his release from custody, or

(iii) otherwise prevent the investigation from being conducted diligently and expeditiously.

If any of the grounds in (b)(i) to (iii) above are relied upon, these must be presented to the judicial authority as part of the application for the warrant that would extend detention beyond a period of 14 days from the time of arrest (or if a person was being detained under TACT, Schedule 7, from the time at which the examination under Schedule 7 began. See *Note 14J*.

H:14.6 If a person remains in detention at a police station under a warrant of further detention as described at section 14.5, they must be transferred to a prison as soon as practicable after the grounds at (b)(i) to (iii) of that section cease to apply.

H:14.7 Police should maintain an agreement with the National Offender

Management Service (NOMS) that stipulates named prisons to which individuals
may be transferred under this section. This should be made with regard to ensuring detainees are moved to the most suitable prison for the purposes of the
investigation and their welfare, and should include provision for the transfer of
male, female and juvenile detainees. Police should ensure that the governor of a
prison to which they intend to transfer a detainee is given reasonable notice of
this. Where practicable, this should be no later than the point at which a warrant
is applied for that would take the period of detention beyond 14 days.

H:14.8 Following a detained person's transfer to a designated prison, their
detention will be governed by the terms of Schedule 8 and prison rules, and this
code of practice will not apply during any period that the person remains in
prison detention. The code will once more apply if a detained person is
transferred back from prison detention to police detention. In order to enable the
governor to arrange for the production of the detainee back into police custody,
police should give notice to the governor of the relevant prison as soon as possible
of any decision to transfer a detainee from prison back to a police station. Any
transfer between a prison and a police station should be conducted by police, and
this code will be applicable during the period of transit. See *Note 14K*. A detainee
should only remain in police custody having been transferred back from a prison,
for as long as is necessary for the purpose of the investigation.

H:14.9 The investigating team and custody officer should provide as much information as necessary to enable the relevant prison authorities to provide appropriate facilities to detain an individual. This should include, but not be limited
to:

    (i) medical assessments;

   (ii) security and risk assessments;

  (iii) details of the detained person's legal representatives;

  (iv) details of any individuals from whom the detained person has requested
visits, or who have requested to visit the detained person.

H:14.10 Where a detainee is to be transferred to prison, the custody officer
should inform the detainee's legal adviser beforehand that the transfer is to take
place (including the name of the prison). The custody officer should also make all
reasonable attempts to inform:

    ● family or friends who have been informed previously of the detainee's
detention; and

    ● the person who was initially informed of the detainee's detention as at
paragraph 5.1.

(c) *Documentation*

H:14.11 It is the responsibility of the officer who gives any reminders as at
paragraph 14.4, to ensure that these are noted in the custody record, as well any
comments made by the detained person upon being told of those rights.

H:14.12 The grounds for, and extent of, any delay in conducting a review shall
be recorded.

H:14.13 Any written representations shall be retained.

H:14.14 A record shall be made as soon as practicable about the outcome of
each review or determination whether to extend the maximum detention period
without charge or an application for a warrant of further detention or its
extension.

H:14.15 Any decision not to transfer a detained person to a designated prison
under paragraph 14.5, must be recorded, along with the reasons for this decision.
If a request under paragraph 14.5(a) is not accommodated, the reasons for this
should also be recorded.

Notes for guidance

  H:14A *TACT, Schedule 8, Part II sets out the procedures for review of detention up to*   **A–222a**

48 hours from the time of arrest under TACT, section 41 (or if a person was being detained under TACT, Schedule 7, from the time at which the examination under Schedule 7 began). These include provisions for the requirement to review detention, postponing a review, grounds for continued detention, designating a review officer, representations, rights of the detained person and keeping a record. The review officer's role ends after a warrant has been issued for extension of detention under Part III of Schedule 8.

H:14B *Section 24(1) of the Terrorism Act 2006, amended the grounds contained within the 2000 Act on which a review officer may authorise continued detention. Continued detention may be authorised if it is necessary—*

    (a) *to obtain relevant evidence whether by questioning him or otherwise;*

    (b) *to preserve relevant evidence;*

    (c) *while awaiting the result of an examination or analysis of relevant evidence;*

    (d) *for the examination or analysis of anything with a view to obtaining relevant evidence;*

    (e) *pending a decision to apply to the Secretary of State for a deportation notice to be served on the detainee, the making of any such application, or the consideration of any such application by the Secretary of State;*

    (f) *pending a decision to charge the detainee with an offence.*

H:14C *Applications for warrants to extend detention beyond 48 hours, may be made for periods of 7 days at a time (initially under TACT, Schedule 8, paragraph 29, and extensions thereafter under TACT, Schedule 8, paragraph 36), up to a maximum period of 28 days from the time of arrest (or if a person was being detained under TACT, Schedule 7, from the time at which the examination under Schedule 7 began). Applications may be made for shorter periods than 7 days, which must be specifi ed. The judicial authority may also substitute a shorter period if he feels a period of 7 days is inappropriate.*

H:14D *Unless Note 14F applies, applications for warrants that would take the total period of detention up to 14 days or less should be made to a judicial authority, meaning a District Judge (Magistrates' Court) designated by the Lord Chancellor to hear such applications.*

H:14E *Any application for a warrant which would take the period of detention beyond 14 days from the time of arrest (or if a person was being detained under TACT, Schedule 7, from the time at which the examination under Schedule 7 began), must be made to a High Court judge.*

H:14F *If an application has been made to a High Court judge for a warrant which would take detention beyond 14 days, and the High Court judge instead issues a warrant for a period of time which would not take detention beyond 14 days, further applications for extension of detention must also be made to a High Court judge, regardless of the period of time to which they refer.*

H:14G *TACT, Schedule 8, paragraph 31, requires a notice to be given to the detained person if a warrant is sought for further detention. This must be provided before the judicial hearing of the application for that warrant and must include:*

    (a) *notification that the application for a warrant has been made;*

    (b) *the time at which the application was made;*

    (c) *the time at which the application is to be heard;*

    (d) *the grounds on which further detention is sought.*

A notice must also be provided each time an application is made to extend an existing warrant

H:14H *An officer applying for an order under TACT, Schedule 8, paragraph 34, to withhold specified information on which he intends to rely when applying for a warrant of further detention, may make the application for the order orally or in writing. The most appropriate method of application will depend on the circumstances of the case and the need to ensure fairness to the detainee.*

H:14I *Where facilities exist, hearings relating to extension of detention under Part II of Schedule 8 may take place using video conferencing facilities provided that the requirements set out in Schedule 8 are still met. However, if the judicial authority requires the detained person to be physically present at any hearing, this should be complied with as soon as practicable. Paragraphs 33(4) to 33(9) of TACT, Schedule 8, govern the relevant conduct of hearings.*

H:14J *Transfer to prison is intended to ensure that individuals who are detained for extended periods of time are held in a place designed for longer periods of detention than police stations. Prison will provide detainees with a greater range of facilities more appropriate to longer detention periods.*

H:14K *The code will only apply as is appropriate to the conditions of detention during the period of transit. There is obviously no requirement to provide such things as bed linen or reading materials for the journey between prison and police station.*

H:15 Charging

H:15.1 Charging of detained persons is covered by *PACE* and guidance issued   **A–222b**
under *PACE* by the Director of Public Prosecutions. General guidance on charging can be found in section 16 of *PACE* Code C.

H:16 Testing persons for the presence of specified Class A drugs

H:16.1 The provisions for drug testing under section 63B of PACE (as   **A–223**
amended by section 5 of the *Criminal Justice Act* 2003 and section 7 of the *Drugs Act* 2005), do not apply to detention under TACT, section 41 and Schedule 8. Guidance on these provisions can be found in section 17 of *PACE* Code C.

ANNEX A

Intimate and strip searches

A *Intimate search*

H:1. [*Identical to Code C, Annex A, para. 1.*]   **A–223a**

(a) *Action*
H:2. Body orifices other than the mouth may be searched only if authorised by an officer of inspector rank or above who has reasonable grounds for believing that the person may have concealed on themselves anything which they could and might use to cause physical injury to themselves or others at the station and the officer has reasonable grounds for believing that an intimate search is the only means of removing those items.

H:3. [*Identical to Code C, Annex A, para. 2A.*]
H:4. [*Identical to Code C, Annex A, para. 3.*]
H:5. [*Identical to Code C, Annex A, para. 4, save for reference to "paragraph 2" in lieu of reference to "paragraph 2(a)(i)".*]
H:6. [*Identical to Code C, Annex A, para. 5.*]
H:7. [*Identical to Code C, Annex A, para. 4, save for references to "paragraph 2" and "paragraph 6" in lieu of references to "paragraph 2(a)(i)" and "paragraph 5".*]

(b) *Documentation*
H:8. In the case of an intimate search under paragraph 2, the following shall be recorded as soon as practicable, in the detainee's custody record:

- the authorisation to carry out the search;
- the grounds for giving the authorisation;
- the grounds for believing the article could not be removed without an intimate search;
- which parts of the detainee's body were searched;
- who carried out the search;
- who was present;

● the result.

H:9. [*Identical to Code C, Annex A, para. 8.*]

B *Strip search*

H:10. [*Identical to Code C, Annex A, para. 9.*]

(a) *Action*

H:11. [*Identical to Code C, Annex A, para. 10.*]

The conduct of strip searches

H:12. [*Identical to Code C, Annex A, para. 11.*]

(b) *Documentation*

H:13. [*Identical to Code C, Annex A, para. 12.*]

Notes for guidance

A-223b

H:A1 [*Identical to Code C, Annex A, A1.*]

H:A2 [*Identical to Code C, Annex A, A2.*]

H:A3 [*Identical to Code C, Annex A, A3, save for reference to "paragraph 2" in lieu of reference to "paragraph 2(a)(i)".*]

H:A4 [*Identical to Code C, Annex A, A4, save for reference to "paragraph 2" in lieu of reference to "paragraph 2(a)(i)".*]

H:A5 [*Identical to Code C, Annex A, A5.*]

ANNEX B

Delay in notifying arrest or allowing access to legal advice for persons detained under the Terrorism Act 2000

A *Delays under TACT, Schedule 8*

A-224

H:1. The rights as in sections 5 or 6, may be delayed if the person is detained under the *Terrorism Act* 2000, section 41, has not yet been charged with an offence and an officer of superintendent rank or above has reasonable grounds for believing the exercise of either right will have one of the following consequences:

(a) interference with or harm to evidence of a serious offence,

(b) interference with or physical injury to any person,

(c) the alerting of persons who are suspected of having committed a serious offence but who have not been arrested for it,

(d) the hindering of the recovery of property obtained as a result of a serious offence or in respect of which a forfeiture order could be made under section 23,

(e) interference with the gathering of information about the commission, preparation or instigation of acts of terrorism,

(f) the alerting of a person and thereby making it more difficult to prevent an act of terrorism, or

(g) the alerting of a person and thereby making it more difficult to secure a person's apprehension, prosecution or conviction in connection with the commission, preparation or instigation of an act of terrorism.

H:2. These rights may also be delayed if the officer has reasonable grounds for believing that:

(a) the detained person has benefited from his criminal conduct (to be decided in accordance with Part 2 of the *Proceeds of Crime Act* 2002), and

    (b) the recovery of the value of the property constituting the benefit will be hindered by—

        (i) informing the named person of the detained person's detention (in the case of an authorisation under paragraph 8(1)(a) of Schedule 8 to TACT), or

        (ii) the exercise of the right under paragraph 7 (in the case of an authorisation under paragraph 8(1)(b) of Schedule 8 to TACT).

H:3. Authority to delay a detainee's right to consult privately with a solicitor may be given only if the authorising officer has reasonable grounds to believe the solicitor the detainee wants to consult will, inadvertently or otherwise, pass on a message from the detainee or act in some other way which will have any of the consequences specified under paragraph 8 of Schedule 8 to the *Terrorism Act* 2000. In these circumstances the detainee must be allowed to choose another solicitor. See *Note B3.*

H:4. [*Identical to Code C, Annex B, para. 4.*]

H:5. [*Identical to Code C, Annex B, para. 5.*]

H:6. These rights may be delayed only for as long as is necessary but not beyond 48 hours from the time of arrest (or if a person was being detained under TACT, Schedule 7, from the time at which the examination under Schedule 7 began). If the above grounds cease to apply within this time the detainee must as soon as practicable be asked if they wish to exercise either right, the custody record noted accordingly, and action taken in accordance with the relevant section of this code.

H:7. A person must be allowed to consult a solicitor for a reasonable time before any court hearing.

B *Documentation*

H:8. [*Identical to Code C, Annex B, para. 13.*]

H:9. [*Identical to Code C, Annex B, para. 14, save for reference to "paragraph 6" in lieu of reference to "paragraphs 6 or 11".*]

C *Cautions and special warnings*

H:10. [*Identical to Code C, Annex B, para. 15.*]

Notes for guidance

H:B1 [*Identical to Code C, Annex B, B1, save for reference to "paragraph 3.15 and 3.17" in lieu of reference to "paragraph 3.13 and 3.15".*]   **A–224a**

H:B2 [*Identical to Code C, Annex B, B2.*]

H:B3 [*Identical to Code C, Annex B, B3.*]

ANNEX C

Restriction on drawing adverse inferences from silence and terms of the caution when the restriction applies

(a) *The restriction on drawing adverse inferences from silence*

H:1. The *Criminal Justice and Public Order Act* 1994, sections 34, 36 and 37 as   **A–224b**
amended by the *Youth Justice and Criminal Evidence Act* 1999, section 58 describe the conditions under which adverse inferences may be drawn from a person's failure or refusal to say anything about their involvement in the offence when interviewed, after being charged or informed they may be prosecuted. These provisions are subject to an overriding restriction on the ability of a court or jury to draw adverse inferences from a person's silence. This restriction applies:

(a) to any detainee at a police station who, before being interviewed, see section 11 or being charged or informed they may be prosecuted, see section 15, has:

(i) asked for legal advice, see section 6, paragraph 6.1;

(ii) not been allowed an opportunity to consult a solicitor, including the duty solicitor, as in this code; and

(iii) not changed their mind about wanting legal advice, see section 6, paragraph 6.7(c);

Note the condition in (ii) will

– apply when a detainee who has asked for legal advice is interviewed before speaking to a solicitor as in section 6, paragraph 6.6(a) or (b);

– not apply if the detained person declines to ask for the duty solicitor, see section 6, paragraphs 6.7(b) and (c);

(b) to any person charged with, or informed they may be prosecuted for, an offence who:

(i) has had brought to their notice a written statement made by another person or the content of an interview with another person which relates to that offence, see *PACE* Code C, section 16, paragraph 16.6;

(ii) is interviewed about that offence, see *PACE* Code C, section 16, paragraph 16.8; or

(iii) makes a written statement about that offence, see Annex D, paragraphs 4 and 9.

(b) *Terms of the caution when the restriction applies*

H:2. [*Identical to Code C, Annex C, para. 2.*]

H:3. [*Identical to Code C, Annex C, para. 3, save for reference to "Note C1" in lieu of reference to "Note C2".*]

Notes for guidance

A–225   **H:**C1 [*Identical to Code C, Annex C, C2.*]

ANNEX D

Written statements under caution

A–225a   [*Identical to Annex D to Code C.*]

ANNEX E

Summary of provisions relating to mentally disordered and otherwise mentally vulnerable people

A–225b   **H:**1. [*Identical to Code C, Annex E, para. 1, save for reference to "paragraph 1.10" in lieu of reference to "paragraph 1.4".*]

H:2. [*Identical to Code C, Annex E, para. 2, save for reference to "paragraph 1.13(b)" in lieu of reference to "paragraph 1.7(b)".*]

H:3. If the detention of a person who is mentally vulnerable or appears to be suffering from a mental disorder is authorised by the review officer (see paragraphs 14.1 and 14.2 and *Notes for Guidance 14A* and *14B*), the custody officer must as soon as practicable inform the appropriate adult of the grounds for detention and the person's whereabouts, and ask the adult to come to the police station to see them. If the appropriate adult:

● is already at the station when information is given as in paragraphs 3.1 to 3.5 the information must be given in their presence

• is not at the station when the provisions of paragraph 3.1 to 3.5 are complied with these provisions must be complied with again in their presence once they arrive.

See paragraphs 3.15 to 3.16.

H:4. [*Identical to Code C, Annex E, para. 4, save for reference to "paragraph 3.20" in lieu of reference to "paragraph 3.19".*]

H:5. [*Identical to Code C, Annex E, para. 5, save for reference to "paragraph 9.6 and 9.8" in lieu of reference to "paragraph 9.5 and 9.6".*]

H:6. [*Identical to Code C, Annex E, para. 7, save for reference to "paragraph 10.11" in lieu of reference to "paragraph 10.12".*]

H:7. [*Identical to Code C, Annex E, para. 8, save for references to "paragraphs 11.2 or 11.11 to 11.13" and "paragraphs 11.2, 11.9 and 11.11 to 11.13" in lieu of references to "paragraphs 11.1 or 11.18 to 11.20" and "paragraphs 11.1, 11.15 and 11.18 to 11.20", respectively.*]

H:8. [*Identical to Code C, Annex E, para. 9, save for reference to "paragraph 11.10" in lieu of reference to "paragraph 11.17".*]

H:9. [*Identical to Code C, Annex E, para. 11, save for reference to "PACE Code C, section 16" in lieu of reference to "paragraphs 16.1 to 16.4A".*]

H:10. [*Identical to Code C, Annex E, para. 12, save for reference to "paragraphs 6 and 12(c)" in lieu of reference to "paragraphs 5 and 11(c)".*]

H:11. [*Identical to Code C, Annex E, para. 13.*]

Notes for guidance

H:E1 [*Identical to Code C, Annex E, E1, save for reference to "paragraph 3.20" in lieu of reference to "paragraph 3.19".*]   **A–226**

H:E2 [*Identical to Code C, Annex E, E2.*]

H:E3 [*Identical to Code C, Annex E, E3, save for reference to "paragraphs 11.2, 11.11 to 11.13" in lieu of reference to "paragraphs 11.1, 11.18 to 11.20".*]

ANNEX F

Countries with which bilateral consular conventions or agreements requiring notification of the arrest and detention of their nationals are in force
[*Identical to Annex F to Code C.*]   **A–226a**

ANNEX G

Fitness to be interviewed
[*Identical to Annex G to Code C.*]   **A–226b**

ANNEX H

Detained person: observation list
[*Identical to Annex H to Code C.*]   **A–227**

B. UNDER THE CRIMINAL PROCEDURE AND INVESTIGATIONS ACT 1996

Introduction

Pursuant to sections 23 and 25 of the 1996 Act (§§ 12–73, 12–74 in the main work), the Secretary of State has prepared and published two codes of   **A–231** practice governing the action the police must take in recording and retaining material obtained in the course of a criminal investigation and regulating its supply to the prosecutor for a decision on disclosure.

The first code came into force on the day appointed for the purpose of Part I of the 1996 Act, namely April 1, 1997 (S.I. 1997 No. 1033). The revised code (set out *post*) came into force on April 4, 2005: *Criminal Procedure and Investigations Act 1996 (Code of Practice) Order* 2005 (S.I. 2005 No. 985).

In connection with this code, see also § 12–72 in the main work (meaning of "investigation").

CRIMINAL PROCEDURE AND INVESTIGATIONS ACT 1996 CODE OF PRACTICE UNDER PART II

Preamble

A–232   This code of practice is issued under Part II of the *Criminal Procedure and Investigations Act* 1996 ('the Act'). It sets out the manner in which police officers are to record, retain and reveal to the prosecutor material obtained in a criminal investigation and which may be relevant to the investigation, and related matters.

Introduction

A–232a   1.1 This code of practice applies in respect of criminal investigations conducted by police officers which begin on or after the day on which this code comes into effect. Persons other than police officers who are charged with the duty of conducting an investigation as defined in the Act are to have regard to the relevant provisions of the code, and should take these into account in applying their own operating procedures.

1.2 This code does not apply to persons who are not charged with the duty of conducting an investigation as defined in the Act.

1.3 Nothing in this code applies to material intercepted in obedience to a warrant issued under section 2 of the *Interception of Communications Act* 1985 or section 5 of the *Regulation of Investigatory Powers Act* 2000, or to any copy of that material as defined in section 10 of the 1985 Act or section 15 of the 2000 Act.

1.4 This code extends only to England and Wales.

Definitions

A–233   2.1 In this code:

— a *criminal investigation* is an investigation conducted by police officers with a view to it being ascertained whether a person should be charged with an offence, or whether a person charged with an offence is guilty of it. This will include:

— investigations into crimes that have been committed;

— investigations whose purpose is to ascertain whether a crime has been committed, with a view to the possible institution of criminal proceedings; and

— investigations which begin in the belief that a crime may be committed, for example when the police keep premises or individuals under observation for a period of time, with a view to the possible institution of criminal proceedings;

— charging a person with an offence includes prosecution by way of summons;

— an *investigator* is any police officer involved in the conduct of a criminal investigation. All investigators have a responsibility for carrying out the duties imposed on them under this code, including in particular recording information, and retaining records of information and other material;

— the *officer in charge of an investigation* is the police officer responsible for directing a criminal investigation. He is also responsible for ensuring that proper procedures are in place for recording information, and retaining records of information and other material, in the investigation;

— the *disclosure officer* is the person responsible for examining material retained by the police during the investigation; revealing material to the prosecutor during the investigation and any criminal proceedings resulting from it, and certifying that he has done this; and disclosing material to the accused at the request of the prosecutor;

— the *prosecutor* is the authority responsible for the conduct, on behalf of the Crown, of criminal proceedings resulting from a specific criminal investigation;

— *material* is material of any kind, including information and objects, which is obtained in the course of a criminal investigation and which may be relevant to the investigation. This includes not only material coming into the possession of the investigator (such as documents seized in the course of searching premises) but also material generated by him (such as interview records);

— material may be *relevant to the investigation* if it appears to an investigator, or to the officer in charge of an investigation, or to the disclosure officer, that it has some bearing on any offence under investigation or any person being investigated, or on the surrounding circumstances of the case, unless it is incapable of having any impact on the case;

— *sensitive material* is material, the disclosure of which, the disclosure officer believes, would give rise to a real risk of serious prejudice to an important public interest;

— references to *prosecution disclosure* are to the duty of the prosecutor under sections 3 and 7A of the Act to disclose material which is in his possession or which he has inspected in pursuance of this code, and which might reasonably be considered capable of undermining the case against the accused, or of assisting the case for the accused;

— references to the disclosure of material to a person accused of an offence include references to the disclosure of material to his legal representative;

— references to police officers and to the chief officer of police include those employed in a police force as defined in section 3(3) of the *Prosecution of Offences Act* 1985.

As to the meaning of "criminal investigation", see *DPP v. Metten*, unreported, January 22, 1999, DC (§ 12–72 in the main work).

General responsibilities

3.1 The functions of the investigator, the officer in charge of an investigation and the disclosure officer are separate. Whether they are undertaken by one, two or more persons will depend on the complexity of the case and the administrative arrangements within each police force. Where they are undertaken by more than one person, close consultation between them is essential to the effective performance of the duties imposed by this code.   **A–234**

3.2 In any criminal investigation, one or more deputy disclosure officers may be appointed to assist the disclosure officer, and a deputy disclosure officer may perform any function of a disclosure officer as defined in paragraph 2.1.

3.3 The chief officer of police for each police force is responsible for putting in place arrangements to ensure that in every investigation the identity of the officer in charge of an investigation and the disclosure officer is recorded. The chief officer of police for each police force shall ensure that disclosure officers and deputy disclosure officers have sufficient skills and authority, commensurate with the complexity of the investigation, to discharge their functions effectively. An individual must not be appointed as disclosure officer, or continue in that role, if that is likely to result in a conflict of interest, for instance, if the disclosure officer is the victim of the alleged crime which is the subject of the investigation. The advice of a more senior officer must always be sought if there is doubt as to whether a conflict of interest precludes an individual acting as disclosure officer. If thereafter the doubt remains, the advice of a prosecutor should be sought.

3.4 The officer in charge of an investigation may delegate tasks to another investigator, to civilians employed by the police force, or to other persons participating in the investigation under arrangements for joint investigations, but he remains responsible for ensuring that these have been carried out and for accounting for any general policies followed in the investigation. In particular, it is an essential part of his duties to ensure that all material which may be relevant to an investigation is retained, and either made available to the disclosure officer or (in exceptional circumstances) revealed directly to the prosecutor.

3.5 In conducting an investigation, the investigator should pursue all reasonable lines of inquiry, whether these point towards or away from the suspect. What is reasonable in each case will depend on the particular circumstances. For example, where material is held on computer, it is a matter for the investigator to decide which material on the computer it is reasonable to inquire into, and in what manner.

3.6 If the officer in charge of an investigation believes that other persons may be in possession of material that may be relevant to the investigation, and if this has not been obtained under paragraph 3.5 above, he should ask the disclosure officer to inform them of the existence of the investigation and to invite them to retain the material in case they receive a request for its disclosure. The disclosure officer should inform the prosecutor that they may have such material. However, the officer in charge of an investigation is not required to make speculative enquiries of other persons; there must be some reason to believe that they may have relevant material. That reason may come from information provided to the police by the accused or from other inquiries made or from some other source.

3.7 If, during a criminal investigation, the officer in charge of an investigation or disclosure officer for any reason no longer has responsibility for the functions falling to him, either his supervisor or the police officer in charge of criminal investigations for the police force concerned must assign someone else to assume that responsibility. That person's identity must be recorded, as with those initially responsible for these functions in each investigation.

As to the meaning of "criminal investigation", see *DPP v. Metten*, unreported, January 22, 1999, DC (§ 12–72 in the main work).

Recording of information

A–235   4.1 If material which may be relevant to the investigation consists of information which is not recorded in any form, the officer in charge of an investigation must ensure that it is recorded in a durable or retrievable form (whether in writing, on video or audio tape, or on computer disk).

4.2 Where it is not practicable to retain the initial record of information because it forms part of a larger record which is to be destroyed, its contents should be transferred as a true record to a durable and more easily-stored form before that happens.

4.3 Negative information is often relevant to an investigation. If it may be relevant it must be recorded. An example might be a number of people present in a particular place at a particular time who state that they saw nothing unusual.

4.4 Where information which may be relevant is obtained, it must be recorded at the time it is obtained or as soon as practicable after that time. This includes, for example, information obtained in house-to-house enquiries, although the requirement to record information promptly does not require an investigator to take a statement from a potential witness where it would not otherwise be taken.

Retention of material

(a) *Duty to retain material*

5.1 The investigator must retain material obtained in a criminal investigation   **A–236**
which may be relevant to the investigation. Material may be photographed, video-recorded, captured digitally or otherwise retained in the form of a copy rather than the original at any time, if the original is perishable; the original was supplied to the investigator rather than generated by him and is to be returned to its owner; or the retention of a copy rather than the original is reasonable in all the circumstances.

5.2 Where material has been seized in the exercise of the powers of seizure conferred by the *Police and Criminal Evidence Act* 1984, the duty to retain it under this code is subject to the provisions on the retention of seized material in section 22 of that Act.

5.3 If the officer in charge of an investigation becomes aware as a result of developments in the case that material previously examined but not retained (because it was not thought to be relevant) may now be relevant to the investigation, he should, wherever practicable, take steps to obtain it or ensure that it is retained for further inspection or for production in court if required.

5.4 The duty to retain material includes in particular the duty to retain material falling into the following categories, where it may be relevant to the investigation:

— crime reports (including crime report forms, relevant parts of incident report books or police officer's notebooks);

— custody records;

— records which are derived from tapes of telephone messages (for example, 999 calls) containing descriptions of an alleged offence or offender;

— final versions of witness statements (and draft versions where their content differs from the final version), including any exhibits mentioned (unless these have been returned to their owner on the understanding that they will be produced in court if required);

— interview records (written records, or audio or video tapes, of interviews with actual or potential witnesses or suspects);

— communications between the police and experts such as forensic scientists, reports of work carried out by experts, and schedules of scientific material prepared by the expert for the investigator, for the purposes of criminal proceedings;

— records of the first description of a suspect by each potential witness who purports to identify or describe the suspect, whether or not the description differs from that of subsequent descriptions by that or other witnesses;

— any material casting doubt on the reliability of a witness.

5.5 The duty to retain material, where it may be relevant to the investigation, also includes in particular the duty to retain material which may satisfy the test for prosecution disclosure in the Act, such as:

— information provided by an accused person which indicates an explanation for the offence with which he has been charged;

— any material casting doubt on the reliability of a confession;

— any material casting doubt on the reliability of a prosecution witness.

413

5.6 The duty to retain material falling into these categories does not extend to items which are purely ancillary to such material and possess no independent significance (for example, duplicate copies of records or reports).

(b) *Length of time for which material is to be retained*

5.7 All material which may be relevant to the investigation must be retained until a decision is taken whether to institute proceedings against a person for an offence.

5.8 If a criminal investigation results in proceedings being instituted, all material which may be relevant must be retained at least until the accused is acquitted or convicted or the prosecutor decides not to proceed with the case.

5.9 Where the accused is convicted, all material which may be relevant must be retained at least until:

— the convicted person is released from custody, or discharged from hospital, in cases where the court imposes a custodial sentence or a hospital order;

— six months from the date of conviction, in all other cases.

If the court imposes a custodial sentence or hospital order and the convicted person is released from custody or discharged from hospital earlier than six months from the date of conviction, all material which may be relevant must be retained at least until six months from the date of conviction.

5.10 If an appeal against conviction is in progress when the release or discharge occurs, or at the end of the period of six months specified in paragraph 5.9, all material which may be relevant must be retained until the appeal is determined. Similarly, if the Criminal Cases Review Commission is considering an application at that point in time, all material which may be relevant must be retained at least until the Commission decides not to refer the case to the Court.

Preparation of material for prosecutor

(a) *Introduction*

A–237   6.1 The officer in charge of the investigation, the disclosure officer or an investigator may seek advice from the prosecutor about whether any particular item of material may be relevant to the investigation.

6.2 Material which may be relevant to an investigation, which has been retained in accordance with this code, and which the disclosure officer believes will not form part of the prosecution case, must be listed on a schedule.

6.3 Material which the disclosure officer does not believe is sensitive must be listed on a schedule of non-sensitive material. The schedule must include a statement that the disclosure officer does not believe the material is sensitive.

6.4 Any material which is believed to be sensitive must be either listed on a schedule of sensitive material or, in exceptional circumstances, revealed to the prosecutor separately. If there is no sensitive material, the disclosure officer must record this fact on a schedule of sensitive material.

6.5 Paragraphs 6.6 to 6.11 below apply to both sensitive and non-sensitive material. Paragraphs 6.12 to 6.14 apply to sensitive material only.

(b) *Circumstances in which a schedule is to be prepared*

6.6 The disclosure officer must ensure that a schedule is prepared in the following circumstances:

— the accused is charged with an offence which is triable only on indictment;

— the accused is charged with an offence which is triable either way, and it is considered either that the case is likely to be tried on indictment or that the accused is likely to plead not guilty at a summary trial;

— the accused is charged with a summary offence, and it is considered that he is likely to plead not guilty.

6.7 In respect of either way and summary offences, a schedule may not be needed if a person has admitted the offence, or if a police officer witnessed the offence and that person has not denied it.

6.8 If it is believed that the accused is likely to plead guilty at a summary trial, it is not necessary to prepare a schedule in advance. If, contrary to this belief, the accused pleads not guilty at a summary trial, or the offence is to be tried on indictment, the disclosure officer must ensure that a schedule is prepared as soon as is reasonably practicable after that happens.

(c) *Way in which material is to be listed on schedule*

6.9 The disclosure officer should ensure that each item of material is listed separately on the schedule, and is numbered consecutively. The description of each item should make clear the nature of the item and should contain sufficient detail to enable the prosecutor to decide whether he needs to inspect the material before deciding whether or not it should be disclosed.

6.10 In some enquiries it may not be practicable to list each item of material separately. For example, there may be many items of a similar or repetitive nature. These may be listed in a block and described by quantity and generic title.

6.11 Even if some material is listed in a block, the disclosure officer must ensure that any items among that material which might satisfy the test for prosecution disclosure are listed and described individually.

(d) *Treatment of sensitive material*

6.12 Subject to paragraph 6.13 below, the disclosure officer must list on a sensitive schedule any material, the disclosure of which he believes would give rise to a real risk of serious prejudice to an important public interest, and the reason for that belief. The schedule must include a statement that the disclosure officer believes the material is sensitive. Depending on the circumstances, examples of such material may include the following among others:

— material relating to national security;

— material received from the intelligence and security agencies;

— material relating to intelligence from foreign sources which reveals sensitive intelligence gathering methods;

— material given in confidence;

— material relating to the identity or activities of informants, or undercover police officers, or witnesses, or other persons supplying information to the police who may be in danger if their identities are revealed;

— material revealing the location of any premises or other place used for police surveillance, or the identity of any person allowing a police officer to use them for surveillance;

— material revealing, either directly or indirectly, techniques and methods relied upon by a police officer in the course of a criminal investigation, for example covert surveillance techniques, or other methods of detecting crime;

— material whose disclosure might facilitate the commission of other offences or hinder the prevention and detection of crime;

— material upon the strength of which search warrants were obtained;

— material containing details of persons taking part in identification parades;

— material supplied to an investigator during a criminal investigation which has been generated by an official of a body concerned with the regulation or supervision of bodies corporate or of persons engaged in financial activities, or which has been generated by a person retained by such a body;

— material supplied to an investigator during a criminal investigation which relates to a child or young person and which has been generated by a local authority social services department, an Area Child Protection Committee or other party contacted by an investigator during the investigation;

— material relating to the private life of a witness.

6.13 In exceptional circumstances, where an investigator considers that material is so sensitive that its revelation to the prosecutor by means of an entry on the sensitive schedule is inappropriate, the existence of the material must be revealed to the prosecutor separately. This will apply only where compromising the material would be likely to lead directly to the loss of life, or directly threaten national security.

6.14 In such circumstances, the responsibility for informing the prosecutor lies with the investigator who knows the detail of the sensitive material. The investigator should act as soon as is reasonably practicable after the file containing the prosecution case is sent to the prosecutor. The investigator must also ensure that the prosecutor is able to inspect the material so that he can assess whether it is disclosable and, if so, whether it needs to be brought before a court for a ruling on disclosure.

Revelation of material to prosecutor

A–238
7.1 The disclosure officer must give the schedules to the prosecutor. Wherever practicable this should be at the same time as he gives him the file containing the material for the prosecution case (or as soon as is reasonably practicable after the decision on mode of trial or the plea, in cases to which paragraph 6.8 applies).

7.2 The disclosure officer should draw the attention of the prosecutor to any material an investigator has retained (including material to which paragraph 6.13 applies) which may satisfy the test for prosecution disclosure in the Act, and should explain why he has come to that view.

7.3 At the same time as complying with the duties in paragraphs 7.1 and 7.2, the disclosure officer must give the prosecutor a copy of any material which falls into the following categories (unless such material has already been given to the prosecutor as part of the file containing the material for the prosecution case):

— information provided by an accused person which indicates an explanation for the offence with which he has been charged;

— any material casting doubt on the reliability of a confession;

— any material casting doubt on the reliability of a prosecution witness;

— any other material which the investigator believes may satisfy the test for prosecution disclosure in the Act.

— any other material which the investigator believes may fall within the test for primary prosecution disclosure in the Act.

7.4 If the prosecutor asks to inspect material which has not already been copied to him, the disclosure officer must allow him to inspect it. If the prosecutor asks for a copy of material which has not already been copied to him, the disclosure officer must give him a copy. However, this does not apply where the disclosure officer believes, having consulted the officer in charge of the investigation, that the material is too sensitive to be copied and can only be inspected.

7.5 If material consists of information which is recorded other than in writing, whether it should be given to the prosecutor in its original form as a whole, or by way of relevant extracts recorded in the same form, or in the form of a transcript, is a matter for agreement between the disclosure officer and the prosecutor.

Subsequent action by disclosure officer

A–239
8.1 At the time a schedule of non-sensitive material is prepared, the disclosure officer may not know exactly what material will form the case against the accused, and the prosecutor may not have given advice about the likely relevance of particular items of material. Once these matters have been determined, the disclosure officer must give the prosecutor, where necessary, an amended schedule listing any additional material:

    — which may be relevant to the investigation,

    — which does not form part of the case against the accused,

    — which is not already listed on the schedule, and

    — which he believes is not sensitive,

unless he is informed in writing by the prosecutor that the prosecutor intends to disclose the material to the defence.

8.2 Section 7A of the Act imposes a continuing duty on the prosecutor, for the duration of criminal proceedings against the accused, to disclose material which satisfies the test for disclosure (subject to public interest considerations). To enable him to do this, any new material coming to light should be treated in the same way as the earlier material.

8.3 In particular, after a defence statement has been given, the disclosure officer must look again at the material which has been retained and must draw the attention of the prosecutor to any material which might reasonably be considered capable of undermining the case for the prosecution against the accused or of assisting the case for the accused; and he must reveal it to him in accordance with paragraphs 7.4 and 7.5 above.

Certification by disclosure officer

9.1 The disclosure officer must certify to the prosecutor that to the best of his **A–240** knowledge and belief, all relevant material which has been retained and made available to him has been revealed to the prosecutor in accordance with this code. He must sign and date the certificate. It will be necessary to certify not only at the time when the schedule and accompanying material is submitted to the prosecutor, and when relevant material which has been retained is reconsidered after the accused has given a defence statement, but also whenever a schedule is otherwise given or material is otherwise revealed to the prosecutor.

Disclosure of material to accused

10.1 If material has not already been copied to the prosecutor, and he requests its **A–241** disclosure to the accused on the ground that:

    — it satisfies the test for prosecution disclosure, or

    — it satisfies the test for prosecution disclosure, or

the disclosure officer must disclose it to the accused.

10.2 If material has been copied to the prosecutor, and it is to be disclosed, whether it is disclosed by the prosecutor or the disclosure officer is a matter of agreement between the two of them.

10.3 The disclosure officer must disclose material to the accused either by giving him a copy or by allowing him to inspect it. If the accused person asks for a copy of any material which he has been allowed to inspect, the disclosure officer must give it to him, unless in the opinion of the disclosure officer that is either not practicable (for example because the material consists of an object which cannot be copied, or because the volume of material is so great), or not desirable (for example because the material is a statement by a child witness in relation to a sexual offence).

10.4 If material which the accused has been allowed to inspect consists of information which is recorded other than in writing, whether it should be given to the accused in its original form or in the form of a transcript is matter for the discretion of the disclosure officer. If the material is transcribed, the disclosure officer must ensure that the transcript is certified to the accused as a true record of the material which has been transcribed.

10.5 If a court concludes that an item of sensitive material satisfies the prosecution disclosure test and that the interests of the defence outweigh the public interest in withholding disclosure, it will be necessary to disclose the material if the case is to proceed. This does not mean that sensitive documents must always be disclosed in their original form: for example, the court may agree that sensitive details still requiring protection should be blocked out, or that documents may be summarised or that the prosecutor may make an admission about the substance of the material under section 10 of the *Criminal Justice Act* 1967.

II. ATTORNEY GENERAL'S GUIDELINES

A. Disclosure

Introduction

A–242   In April, 2005, the Attorney-General issued new guidelines on the disclosure of unused material in criminal proceedings in light of the abolition of the distinction between primary and secondary disclosure, and the introduction of a single test for disclosure of material that "might reasonably be considered capable of undermining the prosecution case or assisting the case for the accused". Much of the content follows the 2000 guidelines (see the previous supplement) closely; but there is a strong emphasis on the need for all concerned in the criminal process to apply the provisions of the 1996 Act in a rigorous fashion. The new guidelines were to be adopted with immediate effect in relation to all cases submitted to prosecuting authorities in receipt of the guidelines, save where they specifically refer to provisions of the *CJA* 2003 or the new code of practice on disclosure (*ante*, § A–231 *et seq.*) that do not yet apply to the particular case.

Foreword

A–242a   Disclosure is one of the most important issues in the criminal justice system and the application of proper and fair disclosure is a vital component of a fair criminal justice system. The "golden rule" is that fairness requires full disclosure should be made of all material held by the prosecution that weakens its case or strengthens that of the defence.

This amounts to no more and no less than a proper application of the *Criminal Procedure and Investigations Act* 1996 (CPIA) recently amended by the *Criminal Justice Act* 2003. The amendments in the *Criminal Justice Act* 2003 abolished the concept of "primary" and "secondary" disclosure, and introduced an amalgamated test for disclosure of material that "might reasonably be considered capable of undermining the prosecution case or assisting the case for accused". It also introduced a new Code of Practice. In the light of these, other new provisions and case law I conducted a review of the Attorney General's Guidelines issued in November 2000.

Concerns had previously been expressed about the operation of the then existing provisions by judges, prosecutors, and defence practitioners. It seems to me that we must all make a concerted effort to comply with the CPIA disclosure regime robustly in a consistent way in order to regain the trust and confidence of all those involved in the criminal justice system. The House of Lords in *R v H & C* made it clear that so long as the current disclosure system was operated with scrupulous attention, in accordance with the law and with proper regard to the interests of the defendant, it was entirely compatible with Article 6 of the European Convention on Human Rights (ECHR).

It is vital that everybody in the criminal justice system operates these procedures properly and fairly to ensure we protect the integrity of the criminal justice system whilst at the same time ensuring that a just and fair disclosure process is not abused so that it becomes unwieldy, bureaucratic and effectively unworkable. This means that all those involved must play their role.

Investigators must provide detailed and proper schedules. Prosecutors must not abrogate their duties under the CPIA by making wholesale disclosure in order to avoid carrying out the disclosure exercise themselves. Likewise, defence practitioners should avoid fishing expeditions and where disclosure is not provided using this as an excuse for an abuse of process application. I hope also that the courts will apply the legal regime set out under the CPIA rather than ordering disclosure because either it is easier or it would not "do any harm".

This disclosure regime must be made to work and it can only work if there is trust and confidence in the system and everyone plays their role in it. If this is achieved applications for a stay of proceedings on the grounds of non disclosure will only be made exceedingly sparingly and never on a speculative basis. Likewise such applications are only likely to succeed in extreme cases and certainly not where the alleged disclosure is in relation to speculative requests for material.

I have therefore revised the Guidelines to take account of developments and to start the process of ensuring that everyone works to achieve consistency of approach to CPIA disclosure. The amalgamated test should introduce a more streamlined process which is more objective and should therefore deal with some of the concerns about inconsistency in the application of the disclosure regime by prosecutors.

A draft set of these revised Guidelines went out for consultation, and resulted in many thoughtful and detailed responses from practitioners, including members of the judiciary, who have to work with the scheme on a daily basis. The Group that was established to advise me on the revision of the Guidelines has taken account of the results of the consultation exercise. I give my warm thanks to all who have offered responses on the consultation and assisted in the revision of these Guidelines.

I am publishing today the revised Guidelines that, if properly, applied will contribute to ensuring that the disclosure regime operates effectively, fairly and justly - which is vitally important to the integrity of the criminal justice system and the way in which it is perceived by the general public.

Disclosure of information in criminal proceedings

Introduction

1. Every accused person has a right to a fair trial, a right long embodied in our **A-243** law and guaranteed under Article 6 of the European Convention on Human Rights (ECHR). A fair trial is the proper object and expectation of all participants in the trial process. Fair disclosure to an accused is an inseparable part of a fair trial.

2. What must be clear is that a fair trial consists of an examination not just of all the evidence the parties wish to rely on but also all other relevant subject matter. A fair trial should not require consideration of irrelevant material and should not involve spurious applications or arguments which serve to divert the trial process from examining the real issues before the court.

3. The scheme set out in the *Criminal Procedure and Investigations Act* 1996 (as amended by the *Criminal Justice Act* 2003) (the Act) is designed to ensure that there is fair disclosure of material which may be relevant to an investigation and which does not form part of the prosecution case. Disclosure under the Act should assist the accused in the timely preparation and presentation of their case and assist the court to focus on all the relevant issues in the trial. Disclosure which does not meet these objectives risks preventing a fair trial taking place.

4. This means that the disclosure regime set out in the Act must be scrupulously followed. These Guidelines build upon the existing law to help to ensure that the legislation is operated more effectively, consistently and fairly.

5. Disclosure must not be an open ended trawl of unused material. A critical element to fair and proper disclosure is that the defence play their role to ensure that the prosecution are directed to material which might reasonably be considered capable of undermining the prosecution case or assisting the case for the accused. This process is key to ensuring prosecutors make informed determinations about disclosure of unused material.

6. Fairness does recognise that there are other interests that need to be protected, including those of victims and witnesses who might otherwise be exposed to harm.

The scheme of the Act protects those interests. It should also ensure that material is not disclosed which overburdens the participants in the trial process, diverts attention from the relevant issues, leads to unjustifiable delay, and is wasteful of resources.

7. Whilst it is acknowledged that these Guidelines have been drafted with a focus on Crown Court proceedings the spirit of the Guidelines must be followed where they apply to proceedings in the magistrates' court.

General principles

A–244
8. Disclosure refers to providing the defence with copies of, or access to, any material which might reasonably be considered capable of undermining the case for the prosecution against the accused, or of assisting the case for the accused, and which has not previously been disclosed.

9. Prosecutors will only be expected to anticipate what material might weaken their case or strengthen the defence in the light of information available at the time of the disclosure decision, and this may include information revealed during questioning.

10. Generally, material which can reasonably be considered capable of undermining the prosecution case against the accused or assisting the defence case will include anything that tends to show a fact inconsistent with the elements of the case that must be proved by the prosecution. Material can fulfil the disclosure test:

(a) by the use to be made of it in cross-examination; or
(b) by its capacity to support submissions that could lead to:
   (i) the exclusion of evidence; or
   (ii) a stay of proceedings; or
   (iii) a court or tribunal finding that any public authority had acted incompatibly with the accused 's rights under the ECHR, or
(c) by its capacity to suggest an explanation or partial explanation of the accused's actions.

11. In deciding whether material may fall to be disclosed under paragraph 10, especially (b)(ii), prosecutors must consider whether disclosure is required in order for a proper application to be made. The purpose of this paragraph is not to allow enquiries to support speculative arguments or for the manufacture of defences.

12. Examples of material that might reasonably be considered capable of undermining the prosecution case or of assisting the case for the accused are:

i. Any material casting doubt upon the accuracy of any prosecution evidence.
ii. Any material which may point to another person, whether charged or not (including a co-accused) having involvement in the commission of the offence.
iii. Any material which may cast doubt upon the reliability of a confession.
iv. Any material that might go to the credibility of a prosecution witness.
v. Any material that might support a defence that is either raised by the defence or apparent from the prosecution papers.
vi. Any material which may have a bearing on the admissibility of any prosecution evidence.

13. It should also be borne in mind that while items of material viewed in isolation may not be reasonably considered to be capable of undermining the prosecution case or assisting the accused, several items together can have that effect.

14. Material relating to the accused's mental or physical health, intellectual capacity, or to any ill treatment which the accused may have suffered when in the investigator's custody is likely to fall within the test for disclosure set out in paragraph 8 above.

Defence statements

A–245
15. A defence statement must comply with the requirements of section 6A of the Act. A comprehensive defence statement assists the participants in the trial to ensure that it is fair. The trial process is not well served if the defence make general and unspecified allegations and then seek far-reaching disclosure in the hope that material may turn up to make them good. The more detail a defence statement contains the

more likely it is that the prosecutor will make an informed decision about whether any remaining undisclosed material might reasonably be considered capable of undermining the prosecution case or of assisting the case for the accused, or whether to advise the investigator to undertake further enquiries. It also helps in the management of the trial by narrowing down and focussing on the issues in dispute. It may result in the prosecution discontinuing the case. Defence practitioners should be aware of these considerations when advising their clients.

16. Whenever a defence solicitor provides a defence statement on behalf of the accused it will be deemed to be given with the authority of the solicitor's client.

Continuing duty of prosecutor to disclose

17. Section 7A of the Act imposes a continuing duty upon the prosecutor to keep under review at all times the question of whether there is any unused material which might reasonably be considered capable of undermining the prosecution case against the accused or assisting the case for the accused and which has not previously been disclosed. This duty arises after the prosecutor has complied with the duty of initial disclosure or purported to comply with it and before the accused is acquitted or convicted or the prosecutor decides not to proceed with the case. If such material is identified, then the prosecutor must disclose it to the accused as soon as is reasonably practicable. **A–246**

18. As part of their continuing duty of disclosure, prosecutors should be open, alert and promptly responsive to requests for disclosure of material supported by a comprehensive defence statement. Conversely, if no defence statement has been served or if the prosecutor considers that the defence statement is lacking specificity or otherwise does not meet the requirements of section 6A of the Act, a letter should be sent to the defence indicating this. If the position is not resolved satisfactorily, the prosecutor should consider raising the issue at a hearing for directions to enable the court to give a warning or appropriate directions.

19. When defence practitioners are dissatisfied with disclosure decisions by the prosecution and consider that they are entitled to further disclosure, applications to the court should be made pursuant to section 8 of the Act and in accordance with the procedures set out in the Criminal Procedure Rules. Applications for further disclosure should not be made as ad hoc applications but dealt with under the proper procedures.

Applications for non-disclosure in the public interest

20. Before making an application to the court to withhold material which would otherwise fall to be disclosed, on the basis that to disclose would give rise to a real risk of serious prejudice to an important public interest, prosecutors should aim to disclose as much of the material as they properly can (for example, by giving the defence redacted or edited copies or summaries). Neutral material or material damaging to the defendant need not be disclosed and must not be brought to the attention of the court. It is only in truly borderline cases that the prosecution should seek a judicial ruling on the disclosability of material in its possession. **A–247**

21. Prior to or at the hearing, the court must be provided with full and accurate information. Prior to the hearing the prosecutor and the prosecution advocate must examine all material, which is the subject matter of the application and make any necessary enquiries of the investigator. The prosecutor (or representative) and/or investigator should attend such applications.

22. The principles set out at paragraph 36 of *R v H & C* should be rigorously applied firstly by the prosecutor and then by the court considering the material. It is essential that these principles are scrupulously attended to to ensure that the procedure for examination of material in the absence of the accused is compliant with Article 6 of ECHR.

Responsibilities

Investigators and disclosure officers

23. Investigators and disclosure officers must be fair and objective and must work **A–248**

together with prosecutors to ensure that disclosure obligations are met. A failure to take action leading to inadequate disclosure may result in a wrongful conviction. It may alternatively lead to a successful abuse of process argument, an acquittal against the weight of the evidence or the appellate courts may find that a conviction is unsafe and quash it.

24. Officers appointed as disclosure officers must have the requisite experience, skills, competence and resources to undertake their vital role. In discharging their obligations under the Act, code, common law and any operational instructions, investigators should always err on the side of recording and retaining material where they have any doubt as to whether it may be relevant.

25. An individual must not be appointed as disclosure officer, or continue in that role, if that is likely to result in a conflict of interest, for instance, if the disclosure officer is the victim of the alleged crime which is the subject of investigation. The advice of a more senior investigator must always be sought if there is doubt as to whether a conflict of interest precludes an individual acting as the disclosure officer. If thereafter a doubt remains, the advice of a prosecutor should be sought.

26. There may be a number of disclosure officers, especially in large and complex cases. However, there must be a lead disclosure officer who is the focus for enquiries and whose responsibility it is to ensure that the investigator's disclosure obligations are complied with. Disclosure officers, or their deputies, must inspect, view or listen to all relevant material that has been retained by the investigator, and the disclosure officer must provide a personal declaration to the effect that this task has been undertaken.

27. Generally this will mean that such material must be examined in detail by the disclosure officer or the deputy, but exceptionally the extent and manner of inspecting, viewing or listening will depend on the nature of material and its form. For example, it might be reasonable to examine digital material by using software search tools, or to establish the contents of large volumes of material by dip sampling. If such material is not examined in detail, it must nonetheless be described on the disclosure schedules accurately and as clearly as possible. The extent and manner of its examination must also be described together with justification for such action.

28. Investigators must retain material that may be relevant to the investigation. However, it may become apparent to the investigator that some material obtained in the course of an investigation because it was considered potentially relevant, is in fact incapable of impact. It need not then be retained or dealt with in accordance with these Guidelines, although the investigator should err on the side of caution in coming to this conclusion and seek the advice of the prosecutor as appropriate.

29. In meeting the obligations in paragraph 6.9 and 8.1 of the Code, it is crucial that descriptions by disclosure officers in non-sensitive schedules are detailed, clear and accurate. The descriptions may require a summary of the contents of the retained material to assist the prosecutor to make an informed decision on disclosure. Sensitive schedules must contain sufficient information to enable the prosecutor to make an informed decision as to whether or not the material itself should be viewed, to the extent possible without compromising the confidentiality of the information.

30. Disclosure officers must specifically draw material to the attention of the prosecutor for consideration where they have any doubt as to whether it might reasonably be considered capable of undermining the prosecution case or of assisting the case for the accused.

31. Disclosure officers must seek the advice and assistance of prosecutors when in doubt as to their responsibility as early as possible. They must deal expeditiously with requests by the prosecutor for further information on material, which may lead to disclosure.

Prosecutors

A–249   32. Prosecutors must do all that they can to facilitate proper disclosure, as part of their general and personal professional responsibility to act fairly and impartially, in the interests of justice and in accordance with the law. Prosecutors must also be alert to the need to provide advice to, and where necessary probe actions taken by, disclosure officers to ensure that disclosure obligations are met.

Supplement No. 3—July, 2009 **A–250**

33. Prosecutors must review schedules prepared by disclosure officers thoroughly and must be alert to the possibility that relevant material may exist which has not been revealed to them or material included which should not have been. If no schedules have been provided, or there are apparent omissions from the schedules, or documents or other items are inadequately described or are unclear, the prosecutor must at once take action to obtain properly completed schedules. Likewise schedules should be returned for amendment if irrelevant items are included. If prosecutors remain dissatisfied with the quality or content of the schedules they must raise the matter with a senior investigator, and if necessary, persist, with a view to resolving the matter satisfactorily.

34. Where prosecutors have reason to believe that the disclosure officer has not discharged the obligation in paragraph 26 to inspect, view or listen to relevant material, they must at once raise the matter with the disclosure officer and, if it is believed that the officer has not inspected, viewed or listened to the material, request that it be done.

35. When prosecutors or disclosure officers believe that material might reasonably be considered capable of undermining the prosecution case or assisting the case for the accused, prosecutors must always inspect, view or listen to the material and satisfy themselves that the prosecution can properly be continued having regard to the disclosability of the material reviewed. Their judgement as to what other material to inspect, view or listen to will depend on the circumstances of each case.

36. Prosecutors should copy the defence statement to the disclosure officer and investigator as soon as reasonably practicable and prosecutors should advise the investigator if, in their view, reasonable and relevant lines of further enquiry should be pursued.

37. Prosecutors cannot comment upon, or invite inferences to be drawn from, failures in defence disclosure otherwise than in accordance with section 11 of the Act. Prosecutors may cross-examine the accused on differences between the defence case put at trial and that set out in his or her defence statement. In doing so, it may be appropriate to apply to the judge under section 6E of the Act for copies of the statement to be given to a jury, edited if necessary to remove inadmissible material. Prosecutors should examine the defence statement to see whether it points to other lines of enquiry. If the defence statement does point to other reasonable lines of inquiry further investigation is required and evidence obtained as a result of these enquiries may be used as part of the prosecution case or to rebut the defence.

38. Once initial disclosure is completed and a defence statement has been served requests for disclosure should ordinarily only be answered if the request is in accordance with and relevant to the defence statement. If it is not, then a further or amended defence statement should be sought and obtained before considering the request for further disclosure.

39. Prosecutors must ensure that they record in writing all actions and decisions they make in discharging their disclosure responsibilities, and this information is to be made available to the prosecution advocate if requested or if relevant to an issue.

40. If the material does not fulfil the disclosure test there is no requirement to disclose it. For this purpose, the parties' respective cases should not be restrictively analysed but must be carefully analysed to ascertain the specific facts the prosecution seek to establish and the specific grounds on which the charges are resisted. Neutral material or material damaging to the defendant need not be disclosed and must not be brought to the attention of the court. Only in truly borderline cases should the prosecution seek a judicial ruling on the disclosability of material in its hands.

41. If prosecutors are satisfied that a fair trial cannot take place where material which satisfies the disclosure test cannot be disclosed, and that this cannot or will not be remedied including by, for example, making formal admissions, amending the charges or presenting the case in a different way so as to ensure fairness or in other ways, they must not continue with the case.

Prosecution advocates

42. Prosecution advocates should ensure that all material that ought to be disclosed **A–250**

under the Act is disclosed to the defence. However, prosecution advocates cannot be expected to disclose material if they are not aware of its existence. As far as is possible, prosecution advocates must place themselves in a fully informed position to enable them to make decisions on disclosure.

43. Upon receipt of instructions, prosecution advocates should consider as a priority all the information provided regarding disclosure of material. Prosecution advocates should consider, in every case, whether they can be satisfied that they are in possession of all relevant documentation and that they have been instructed fully regarding disclosure matters. Decisions already made regarding disclosure should be reviewed. If as a result, the advocate considers that further information or action is required, written advice should be promptly provided setting out the aspects that need clarification or action. Prosecution advocates must advise on disclosure in accordance with the Act. If necessary and where appropriate a conference should be held to determine what is required.

44. The prosecution advocate must keep decisions regarding disclosure under review until the conclusion of the trial. The prosecution advocate must in every case specifically consider whether he or she can satisfactorily discharge the duty of continuing review on the basis of the material supplied already, or whether it is necessary to inspect further material or to reconsider material already inspected. Prosecution advocates must not abrogate their responsibility under the Act by disclosing material which could not be considered capable of undermining the prosecution case or of assisting the case for the accused.

45. Prior to the commencement of a trial, the prosecuting advocate should always make decisions on disclosure in consultation with those instructing him or her and the disclosure officer. After a trial has started, it is recognised that in practice consultation on disclosure issues may not be practicable; it continues to be desirable, however, whenever this can be achieved without affecting unduly the conduct of the trial.

46. There is no basis in law or practice for disclosure on a "counsel to counsel" basis.

Involvement of other agencies

Material held by government departments or other Crown bodies

A–251   47. Where it appears to an investigator, disclosure officer or prosecutor that a Government department or other Crown body has material that may be relevant to an issue in the case, reasonable steps should be taken to identify and consider such material. Although what is reasonable will vary from case to case, the prosecution should inform the department or other body of the nature of its case and of relevant issues in the case in respect of which the department or body might possess material, and ask whether it has any such material.

48. It should be remembered that investigators, disclosure officers and prosecutors cannot be regarded to be in constructive possession of material held by Government departments or Crown bodies simply by virtue of their status as Government departments or Crown bodies.

49. Departments in England and Wales should have identified personnel as established Enquiry Points to deal with issues concerning the disclosure of information in criminal proceedings.

50. Where, after reasonable steps have been taken to secure access to such material, access is denied the investigator, disclosure officer or prosecutor should consider what if any further steps might be taken to obtain the material or inform the defence.

Material held by other agencies

A–252   51. There may be cases where the investigator, disclosure officer or prosecutor believes that a third party (for example, a local authority, a social services department, a hospital, a doctor, a school, a provider of forensic services) has material or information which might be relevant to the prosecution case. In such cases, if the material or information might reasonably be considered capable of undermining the prosecution case or of assisting the case for the accused prosecutors should take what steps they regard as appropriate in the particular case to obtain it.

52. If the investigator, disclosure officer or prosecutor seeks access to the material or information but the third party declines or refuses to allow access to it, the matter should not be left. If despite any reasons offered by the third party it is still believed that it is reasonable to seek production of the material or information, and the requirements of section 2 of the *Criminal Procedure (Attendance of Witnesses) Act* 1965 or as appropriate section 97 of the *Magistrates Courts Act* 1980 are satisfied, then the prosecutor or investigator should apply for a witness summons causing a representative of the third party to produce the material to the Court.

53. Relevant information which comes to the knowledge of investigators or prosecutors as a result of liaison with third parties should be recorded by the investigator or prosecutor in a durable or retrievable form (for example potentially relevant information revealed in discussions at a child protection conference attended by police officers).

54. Where information comes into the possession of the prosecution in the circumstances set out in paragraphs 51–53 above, consultation with the other agency should take place before disclosure is made: there may be public interest reasons which justify withholding disclosure and which would require the issue of disclosure of the information to be placed before the court.

Other disclosure

Disclosure prior to initial disclosure

55. Investigators must always be alive to the potential need to reveal and prosecutors to the potential need to disclose material, in the interests of justice and fairness in the particular circumstances of any case, after the commencement of proceedings but before their duty arises under the Act. For instance, disclosure ought to be made of significant information that might affect a bail decision or that might enable the defence to contest the committal proceedings.

A–253

56. Where the need for such disclosure is not apparent to the prosecutor, any disclosure will depend on what the accused chooses to reveal about the defence. Clearly, such disclosure will not exceed that which is obtainable after the statutory duties of disclosure arise

Summary trial

57. The prosecutor should, in addition to complying with the obligations under the Act, provide to the defence all evidence upon which the Crown proposes to rely in a summary trial. Such provision should allow the accused and their legal advisers sufficient time properly to consider the evidence before it is called.

A–254

Material relevant to sentence

58. In all cases the prosecutor must consider disclosing in the interests of justice any material, which is relevant to sentence (*e.g.* information which might mitigate the seriousness of the offence or assist the accused to lay blame in part upon a co-accused or another person).

A–255

Post conviction

59. The interests of justice will also mean that where material comes to light after the conclusion of the proceedings, which might cast doubt upon the safety of the conviction, there is a duty to consider disclosure. Any such material should be brought immediately to the attention of line management.

A–256

60. Disclosure of any material that is made outside the ambit of Act will attract confidentiality by virtue of *Taylor v SFO* [1998].

Applicability of these guidelines

61. Although the relevant obligations in relation to unused material and disclosure imposed on the prosecutor and the accused are determined by the date on which the investigation began, these Guidelines should be adopted with immediate effect in re-

A–257

lation to all cases submitted to the prosecuting authorities in receipt of these Guidelines save where they specifically refer to the statutory or Code provisions of the *Criminal Justice Act* 2003 that do not yet apply to the particular case.

B. ACCEPTANCE OF PLEAS

Introduction

A-258   On October 21, 2005, the Attorney General issued the following guidelines on the acceptance of pleas. They replace guidelines issued in December, 2000, as an apparent response to the comments of the Court of Appeal in *Att.-Gen.'s Reference (No. 44 of 2000) (R. v. Peverett)* [2001] 1 Cr.App.R. 27.

The Attorney-General revised the guidelines in June, 2007, by issuing a replacement paragraph C.6 (*post*, A–261). His covering letter to prosecutors suggests that in most cases all the information required of the prosecution to comply with their new obligations will be in one document, which he refers to as "the plea and sentence document". It advises that this document should be lodged with the court and served on the defence at least seven days before the plea and case management hearing and at an equivalent point in a magistrates' court. The letter also states that where a case goes to trial, the prosecution advocate should review the document prior to sentence to reflect any changes in the way the case was presented to the court and to ensure that the document is up-to-date and reflects the verdict of the court.

Attorney-General's Guidelines on the Acceptance of Pleas and the Prosecutor's Role in the Sentencing Exercise

A. Foreword

A-259   **A:1.** Prosecutors have an important role in protecting the victim's interests in the criminal justice process, not least in the acceptance of pleas and the sentencing exercise. The basis of plea, particularly in a case that is not contested, is the vehicle through which the victim's voice is heard. Factual inaccuracies in pleas in mitigation cause distress and offence to victims, the families of victims and witnesses. This can take many forms but may be most acutely felt when the victim is dead and the family hears inaccurate assertions about the victim's character or lifestyle. Prosecution advocates are reminded that they are required to adhere to the standards set out in the Victim's Charter, which places the needs of the victim at the heart of the criminal justice process, and that they will be subject to a similar obligation in respect of the Code of Practice for Victims of Crime when it comes into force.

A:2. The principle of fairness is central to the administration of justice. The implementation of *Human Rights Act* 1998 [*sic*] in October 2000 incorporated into domestic law the principle of fairness to the accused articulated in the European Convention on Human Rights. Accuracy and reasonableness of plea plays an important part in ensuring fairness both to the accused and to the victim.

A:3. The Attorney General's Guidelines on the Acceptance of Pleas issued on December 7, 2000 highlighted the importance of transparency in the conduct of justice. The basis of plea agreed by the parties in a criminal trial is central to the sentencing process. An illogical or unsupported basis of plea can lead to the passing of an unduly lenient sentence and has a consequential effect where consideration arises as to whether to refer the sentence to the Court of Appeal under section 36 of the *Criminal Justice Act* 1988.

A:4. These Guidelines, which expand upon and now replace the Guidelines issued on the 7 December 2000 [*sic*], give guidance on how prosecutors should meet these objectives of protection of victims' interests and of securing fairness and transparency in the process. They take into account the guidance issued by the Court of Appeal (Criminal) Division [*sic*] in *R. v. Beswick* [1996] 1 Cr.App.R. 343, *R. v. Tolera* [1999] 1 Cr.App.R. 25 and *R. v. Underwood* [2005] 1 Cr.App.R 13. They complement the Bar Council Guidance on Written Standards for the Conduct of Professional Work issued with the 7th edition of the Code of Conduct for the Bar of England and Wales and the Law Society's Professional Conduct Rules. When considering the acceptance of a guilty plea prosecution advocates are also reminded of the need to apply "The Farquharson Guidelines on The Role and Responsibilities of the Prosecution Advocate".

A:5. The Guidelines should be followed by all prosecutors and those persons designated under section 7 of the *Prosecution of Offences Act* 1985 (designated caseworkers) and apply to prosecutions conducted in England and Wales.

B.　General Principles

B:1. Justice in this jurisdiction, save in the most exceptional circumstances, is conducted in public. This includes the acceptance of pleas by the prosecution and sentencing.　　**A–260**

B:2. The Code for Crown Prosecutors governs the prosecutor's decision-making prior to the commencement of the trial hearing and sets out the circumstances in which pleas to a reduced number of charges, or less serious charges, can be accepted.

B:3. When a case is listed for trial and the prosecution form the view that the appropriate course is to accept a plea before the proceedings commence or continue, or to offer no evidence on the indictment or any part of it, the prosecution should whenever practicable speak to the victim or the victim's family, so that the position can be explained. The views of the victim or the family may assist in informing the prosecutor's decision as to whether it is the [*sic*] public interest, as defined by the Code for Crown Prosecutors, to accept or reject the plea. The victim or victim's family should then be kept informed and decisions explained once they are made at court.

B:4. The appropriate disposal of a criminal case after conviction is as much a part of the criminal justice process as the trial of guilt or innocence. The prosecution advocate represents the public interest, and should be ready to assist the court to reach its decision as to the appropriate sentence. This will include drawing the court's attention to:

— any victim personal statement or other information available to the prosecution advocate as to the impact of the offence on the victim;

— where appropriate, to any evidence of the impact of the offending on a community;

— any statutory provisions relevant to the offender and the offences under consideration;

— any relevant sentencing guidelines and guideline cases; and

— the aggravating and mitigating factors of the offence under consideration;

The prosecution advocate may also offer assistance to the court by making submissions, in the light of all these factors, as to the appropriate sentencing range.

In all cases, it is the prosecution advocate's duty to apply for appropriate ancillary orders, such as anti-social behaviour orders and confiscation orders. When considering which ancillary orders to apply for, prosecution advocates must always have regard to the victim's needs, including the question of his or her future protection.

C.　The Basis of Plea

C:1. The basis of a guilty plea must not be agreed on a misleading or untrue set of facts and must take proper account of the victim's interests. An illogical or insupportable basis of plea will inevitably result in the imposition of an inappropriate sentence and is capable of damaging public confidence in the criminal justice system.　　**A–261**

C:2. When the defendant indicates an acceptable plea, the defence advocate should reduce the basis of the plea to writing. This should be done in all cases save for those in which the issue is simple or where the defendant has indicated that the guilty plea has been or will be tendered on the basis of the prosecution case.

C:3. The written basis of plea must be considered with great care, taking account of the position of any other relevant defendant where appropriate. The prosecution should not lend itself to any agreement whereby a case is presented to the sentencing judge on a misleading or untrue set of facts or on a basis that is detrimental to the victim's interests. There will be cases where a defendant seeks to mitigate on the basis of assertions of fact which are outside the scope of the prosecution's knowledge. A typical example concerns the defendant's state of mind. If a defendant wishes to be sentenced on this basis, the prosecution advocate should invite the judge not to accept the defendant's version unless he or she gives evidence on oath to be tested in cross-examination.

C:4. The prosecution advocate should show the prosecuting authority any written record relating to the plea and agree with them the basis on which the case will be opened to the court.

C:5. It is the responsibility of the prosecution advocate thereafter to ensure that the defence advocate is aware of the basis on which the plea is accepted by the prosecution and the way in which the prosecution case will be opened to the court.

C:6. (1) In all cases before the Crown Court, and in cases before the magistrates' court where the issues are complex or there is scope for misunderstanding, the prosecution must commit to writing the aggravating and mitigating factors that will form the opening of the prosecution case as well any statutory limitations on sentencing. The prosecution will address, where relevant, the factors outlined at B4 including the matters set out in the next sub-paragraph.

(2) The matters to be dealt with are:

- the aggravating and mitigating factors of the offence (not personal mitigation);
- any statutory provisions relevant to the offender and the offence under consideration so that the judge is made aware of any statutory limitations on sentencing;
- any relevant sentencing guidelines and guideline cases;
- identifying any victim personal statement or other information available to the prosecution advocate as to the impact of the offence on the victim;
- where appropriate, any evidence of the impact of the offending on a community;
- an indication, where applicable, of an intention to apply for any ancillary orders such as anti-social behaviour orders and confiscation orders, and so far as possible, indicating the nature of the order to be sought.

C:7. When the prosecution advocate has agreed the written basis of plea submitted by the defence advocate, he or she should endorse the document accordingly. If the prosecution advocate takes issue with all or part of the written basis of plea, he or she should set out in writing what is accepted and what is rejected or not accepted. Where there is a dispute about a particular fact which the defence advocate believes to be effectively immaterial to the sentencing decision, the difference should be recorded so that the judge can make up his or her own mind. The signed original document should be made available to the trial judge and thereafter lodged with the court papers, as it will form part of the record of the hearing.

C:8. Where a defendant declines to admit an offence that he or she previously indicated should be taken into consideration, the prosecution advocate should indicate to the defence advocate and the court that, subject to further review, the offence may now form the basis of a new prosecution.

C:9. Where the basis of plea cannot be agreed and the discrepancy between the two accounts is such as to have a potentially significant effect on the level of sentence, it is the duty of the defence advocate so to inform the court before the sentencing process begins. There remains an overriding duty on the prosecution advocate to ensure that the sentencing judge is made aware of the discrepancy and of the consideration which must be given to the holding of a *Newton* hearing to resolve the issue. The court should be told where a derogatory reference to a victim, witness or third party is not accepted, even though there may be no effect on sentence.

C:10. Whenever an agreement as to the basis of plea is made between the prosecution and defence, any such agreement will be subject to the approval of the trial judge, who may of his or her own motion disregard the agreement and direct that a *Newton* hearing should be held to determine the proper basis on which sentence should be passed.

D. Sentence Indications

D:1. Only in the Crown Court may sentence indications be sought. Advocates   **A–262** there are reminded that indications as to sentence should not be sought from the trial judge unless issues between the prosecution and defence have been addressed and resolved. Therefore, in difficult or complicated cases, no less than seven days notice in writing of an intention to seek an indication should normally be given to the prosecution and the court. When deciding whether the circumstances of a case require such notice to be given, defence advocates are reminded that prosecutors should not agree a basis of plea unless and until the necessary consultation has taken place first with the victim and/or the victim's family and second, in the case of an independent prosecution advocate, with the prosecuting authority.

D:2. If there is no final agreement about the plea to the indictment, or the basis of plea, and the defence nevertheless proceeds to seek an indication of sentence, which the judge appears minded to give, the prosecution advocate should remind him or her of the guidance given in *R. v. Goodyear (Karl)* [2005] EWCA 888 [*sic*] that normally speaking an indication of sentence should not be given until the basis of the plea has been agreed or the judge has concluded that he or she can properly deal with the case without the need for a trial of the issue.

D:3. If an indication is sought, the prosecution advocate should normally enquire whether the judge is in possession of or has access to all the evidence relied on by the prosecution, including any victim personal statement, as well as any information about relevant previous convictions recorded against the defendant.

D:4. Before the judge gives the indication, the prosecution advocate should draw the judge's attention to any minimum or mandatory statutory sentencing requirements. Where the prosecution advocate would be expected to offer the judge assistance with relevant guideline cases or the views of the Sentencing Guidelines Council, he or she should invite the judge to allow them to do so. Where it applies, the prosecution advocate should remind the judge that the position [*sic*] of the Attorney General to refer any sentencing decision as unduly lenient is unaffected. In any event, the prosecution advocate should not say anything which may create the impression that the sentence indication has the support or approval of the Crown.

E. Pleas in Mitigation

E:1. The prosecution advocate must challenge any assertion by the defence in   **A–263** mitigation which is derogatory to a person's character (for instance, because it suggests that his or her conduct is or has been criminal, immoral or improper) and which is either false or irrelevant to proper sentencing considerations. If the defence advocate persists in that assertion, the prosecution advocate should invite the court to consider holding a *Newton* hearing to determine the issue.

E:2. The defence advocate must not submit in mitigation anything that is derogatory to a person's character without giving advance notice in writing so as to afford the prosecution advocate the opportunity to consider their position under paragraph E:1. When the prosecution advocate is so notified they must take all reasonable steps to establish whether the assertions are true. Reasonable steps will include seeking the views of the victim. This will involve seeking the views of the victim's family if the victim is deceased, and the victim's parents or legal guardian where the victim is a child. Reasonable steps may also include seeking the views of the police or other law enforcement authority, as appropriate. An assertion which is derogatory to a person's character will rarely amount to mitigation unless it has a causal connection to the circumstances of the offence or is otherwise relevant to proper sentencing considerations.

E:3. Where notice has not been given in accordance with paragraph E:2, the prosecution advocate must not acquiesce in permitting mitigation which is derogatory to a person's character. In such circumstances, the prosecution advocate should draw the attention of the court to the failure to give advance notice and seek time, and if necessary, an adjournment to investigate the assertion in the same way as if proper notice had been given. Where, in the opinion of the prosecution advocate, there are substantial grounds for believing that such an assertion is false or irrelevant to sentence, he or she should inform the court of their opinion and invite the court to consider making an order under section 58(8) of the *Criminal Procedure and Investigations Act* 1996, preventing publication of the assertion.

E:4. Where the prosecution advocate considers that the assertion is, if true, relevant to sentence, or the court has so indicated, he or she should seek time, and if necessary an adjournment, to establish whether the assertion is true. If the matter cannot be resolved to the satisfaction of the parties, the prosecution advocate should invite the court to consider holding a *Newton* hearing to determine the issue.

C. JURY CHECKS

Introduction

A-264   For the background to these guidelines, see §§ 4–212, 4–213 in the main work.

Attorney-General's Guidelines: Jury checks, 88 Cr.App.R. 123 at 124

A-265   1. The principles which are generally to be observed are:
   (a) that members of a jury should be selected at random from the panel;
   (b) the *Juries Act* 1974 together with the *Juries Disqualification Act* 1984 identified those classes of persons who alone are disqualified from or ineligible for service on a jury. No other class of person may be treated as disqualified or ineligible;
   (c) the correct way for the Crown to seek to exclude a member of the panel from sitting as a juror is by the exercise in open court of the right to request a stand by or, if necessary, to challenge for cause.

   2. Parliament has provided safeguards against jurors who may be corrupt or biased. In addition to the provision for majority verdicts, there is the sanction of a criminal offence for a disqualified person to serve on a jury. The omission of a disqualified person from the panel is a matter for the police as the only authority able to carry out such a search as part of their usual function of preventing the commission of offences. The recommendations of the Association of Chief Police Officer respecting checks on criminal records for disqualified persons are annexed to these guidelines.

A-266   3. There are however certain exceptional types of case of public importance for which the provisions as to majority verdicts and the disqualification of jurors may not be sufficient to ensure the proper administration of justice. In such cases it is in the interests both of justice and the public that there should be further safeguards against the possibility of bias and in such cases checks which go beyond the investigation of criminal records may be necessary.

4. These classes of case may be defined broadly as:

    (a) cases in which national security is involved and part of the evidence is likely to be heard *in camera*;

    (b) terrorist cases.

5. The particular aspects of these cases which may make it desirable to seek extra precautions are:

    (a) in security cases a danger that a juror, either voluntarily or under pressure, may make an improper use of evidence which, because of its sensitivity has been given *in camera*;

    (b) in both security and terrorist cases the danger that a juror's political beliefs are so biased as to go beyond normally reflecting the broad spectrum of views and interests in the community to reflect the extreme views of sectarian interest or pressure group to a degree which might interfere with his fair assessment of the facts of the case or lead him to exert improper pressure on his fellow jurors.

6. In order to ascertain whether in exceptional cases of the above nature either of   **A–267** these factors might seriously influence a potential juror's impartial performance of his duties or his respecting the secrecy of evidence given *in camera*, it may be necessary to conduct a limited investigation of the panel. In general, such further investigation beyond one of criminal records made for disqualifications may only be made with the records of Police Special Branches. However, in cases falling under paragraph 4(a) above, (security cases), the investigation may, additionally, involve the security services. No checks other than on these sources and no general enquiries are to be made save to the limited extent that they may be needed to confirm the identity of a juror about whom the initial check has raised serious doubts.

7. No further investigation, as described in paragraph 6 above, should be made save with the personal authority of the Attorney-General on the application of the Director of Public Prosecutions and such checks are hereafter referred to as "authorised checks." When a Chief Officer of Police has reason to believe that it is likely that an authorised check may be desirable and proper in accordance with these guidelines he should refer the matter to the Director of Public Prosecutions with a view to his having the conduct of the prosecution from an early stage. The Director will make any appropriate application to the Attorney-General.

8. The result of any authorised check will be sent to the Director of Public Prosecutions. The Director will then decide, having regard to the matters set out in paragraph 5 above, what information ought to be brought to the attention of prosecuting counsel.

9. No right of stand by should be exercised by Counsel for the Crown on the basis of information obtained as a result of an authorised check save with the personal authority of the Attorney-General and unless the information is such as, having regard to the facts of the case and the offences charged, to afford strong reason for believing that a particular juror might be a security risk, be susceptible to improper approaches or be influenced in arriving at a verdict for the reasons given above.

10. Where a potential juror is asked to stand by for the Crown, there is no duty to   **A–268** disclose to the defence the information upon which it was founded; but counsel may use his discretion to disclose it if its nature and source permit it.

11. When information revealed in the course of an authorised check is not such as to cause counsel for the Crown to ask for a juror to stand by, but does give reason to believe that he may be biased against the accused, the defence should be given, at least, an indication of why that potential juror may be inimical to their interests; but because of its nature and source it may not be possible to give the defence more than a general indication.

12. A record is to be kept by the Director of Public Prosecutions of the use made by counsel of the information passed to him and of the jurors stood by or challenged by the parties to the proceedings. A copy of this record is to be forwarded to the

Attorney-General for the sole purpose of enabling him to monitor the operation of these guidelines.

13. No use of the information obtained as a result of an authorised check is to be made except as may be necessary in direct relation to or arising out of the trial for which the check was authorised.

Annex to the Attorney-General's Guidelines on Jury Checks; Recommendations of the Association of Chief Police Officers, 88 Cr.App.R. 123 at 125

A-269   1. The Association of Chief Police Officers recommends that in the light of observations made in *Mason*, 71 Cr.App.R. 157 the police should undertake a check of the names of potential jurors against records of previous convictions in any case when the Director of Public Prosecutions or a chief constable considers that in all the circumstances it would be in the interests of justice so to do, namely:

(i) in any case in which there is reason to believe that attempts are being made to circumvent the statutory provisions excluding disqualified persons from service on a jury, including any case when there is reason to believe that a particular juror may be disqualified;

(ii) in any case in which it is believed that in a previous related abortive trial an attempt was made to interfere with a juror or jurors;

(iii) in any other case in which in the opinion of the Director of Public Prosecutions or the chief constable it is particularly important to ensure that no disqualified person serves on the jury.

2. The association also recommends that no further checks should be made unless authorised by the Attorney-General under his guidelines and no inquiries carried out save to the limited extent that they may be needed to confirm the identity of a juror about whom the initial check has raised serious doubts.

3. The Association of Chief Police Officers further recommends that chief constables should agree to undertake checks of jurors, on behalf of the defence only if requested to do so by the Director of Public Prosecutions acting on behalf of the Attorney-General. Accordingly if the police are approached directly with such a request they will refer it to the Director.

4. When, as a result of any checks of criminal records, information is obtained which suggests that, although not disqualified under the terms of the *Juries Act* 1974 a person may be unsuitable to sit as a member of a particular jury the police or the Director may pass the relevant information to prosecuting counsel, who will decide what use to make of it.

D. PROSECUTION'S RIGHT OF STAND BY

A-270   For the background to these guidelines, see §§ 4-249, 4-250 in the main work.

Attorney-General's Guidelines on the Exercise by the Crown of its Right of Stand By, 88 Cr.App.R. 123

A-271   1. Although the law has long recognised the right of the Crown to exclude a member of a jury panel from sitting as a juror by the exercise in open court of the right to request a stand by or, if necessary, by challenge for cause, it has been customary for those instructed to prosecute on behalf of the Crown to assert that right only sparingly and in exceptional circumstances. It is generally accepted that the prosecution should not use its right in order to influence the overall composition of a jury or with a view to tactical advantage.

2. The approach outlined above is founded on the principles that:

(a) the members of a jury should be selected at random from the panel subject to any rule of law as to right of challenge by the defence; and

(b) the *Juries Act* 1974 together with the *Juries Disqualification Act* 1984 identified those classes of persons who alone are disqualified from or inelig-
ble for service on a jury. No other class of person may be treated as disqualified or ineligible.

3. The enactment by Parliament of section 118 of the *Criminal Justice Act* 1988
abolishing the right of defendants to remove jurors by means of peremptory challenge makes it appropriate that the Crown should assert its right to stand by only on
the basis of clearly defined and restrictive criteria. Derogation from the principle that
members of a jury should be selected at random should be permitted only where it is
essential.

4. Primary responsibility for ensuring that an individual does not serve on a jury
if he is not competent to discharge properly the duties of a juror rests with the appropriate court officer and, ultimately, the trial judge. Current legislation provides,
in sections 9 and 10 of the *Juries Act* 1974, fairly wide discretions to excuse or discharge jurors either at the person's own request, where he offers "good reason why
he should be excused," or where the judge determines that "on account of physical
For "disability"substitute infirmity or insufficient understanding of English there is
doubt as to his capacity to act effectively as a juror. ..."

5. The circumstances in which it would be proper for the Crown to exercise its
right to stand by a member of a jury panel are:

(a) where a jury check authorised in accordance with the Attorney-General's
Guidelines on Jury Checks reveals information justifying exercise of the
right to stand by in accordance with paragraph 9 of the guidelines and the
Attorney-General personally authorises the exercise of the right to stand
by; or

(b) where a person is about to be sworn as a juror who is manifestly unsuitable and the defence agree that, accordingly, the exercise by the prosecution of the right to stand by would be appropriate. An example of the sort
of *exceptional* circumstances which might justify stand by is where it
becomes apparent that, despite the provisions mentioned in paragraph 4
above, a juror selected for service to try a complex case is in fact illiterate.

E. Conspiracy To Defraud

The Attorney-General has issued guidance to prosecuting authorities in re-   **A–272**
lation to charging a common law conspiracy to defraud instead of a substantive offence, contrary to the *Fraud Act* 2006, or a statutory conspiracy to commit a substantive offence, contrary to section 1 of the *CLA* 1977 (§ 34–2 in the
main work); the prosecutor should consider (i) whether the conduct alleged
falls within the ambit of a statutory offence, and (ii) whether such a charge
or charges would adequately reflect the gravity of the alleged offending; as
to (i), non-exhaustive examples of circumstances falling outside of the range
of statutory offences, but within the ambit of the common law offence, are:
(a) the dishonest obtaining of land or other property which cannot be
stolen; (b) the dishonest infringement of another's right (*e.g.* the dishonest
exploitation of another's patent); (c) an agreement involving an intention that
the final offence be committed by someone outside the conspiracy; and (d) an
agreement where the conspirators cannot be proved to have had the necessary degree of knowledge for the substantive offence to be perpetrated; as to
(ii), prosecution for the common law offence may be more effective where the
interests of justice can only be served by presenting an overall picture which
could not be achieved by charging a series of substantive offences or statutory
conspiracies (because of a large number of counts and/or the possibility of
severed trials and evidence on one count being deemed inadmissible on another); where a case lawyer proposes to charge the common law offence, he
must consider, and set out in the review note, how much such a charge would

add to the amount of evidence likely to be called by the parties, the justification for using the charge, and why specific statutory offences are inadequate or otherwise inappropriate; a supervising lawyer experienced in fraud cases must also specifically approve the charge: *Attorney-General's guidance on the use of the common law offence of conspiracy to defraud*, unreported, January 9, 2007.

F. Prosecutor's Role in Applications for Witness Anonymity Orders

A–273   On July 21, 2008, the Attorney-General issued guidelines on the overarching principles which a prosecutor must consider when deciding whether to apply for witness anonymity orders under the *Criminal Evidence (Witness Anonymity) Act* 2008 (§§ 8–71 *et seq.* in the main work).

The guidance is in four parts (Part A (foreword), Part B (prosecutor's duties), Part C (applications by defendants) and Part D (appointment and role of special counsel)), and, to a large extent, highlights various provisions of the Act and restates elementary aspects of fairness at trial. Paragraph A2 makes clear that, given that the defendant's right to confront and challenge those who accuse him is an important aspect of a fair trial, making a witness anonymity order is a serious step which must only be taken where there are genuine grounds to believe that the conditions set out in the Act have been satisfied, which must be evaluated with care on the facts of each case. Paragraph B3 sets out the prosecutor's role, which prosecutors must approach in light of their overriding duties to be fair, independent and objective, and which includes a duty: (a) to examine with care and probe where appropriate, the material provided in support of the application and the evidential basis for it, and (b) to put before the court and to disclose to the defendant all material relevant to the application and the defence, including material which may undermine or qualify the prosecution case. Any such material is particularly relevant if credibility is in issue, for example, if there is a known link between the witness and defendant or a co-accused. Paragraph B4 explains that applications should only be authorised by prosecutors of an appropriately senior level. Paragraph D5 explains that a prosecutor making an application for an order must always be prepared to assist the court to consider whether the circumstances are such that exceptionally the appointment of special counsel may be called for, and, where appropriate, should draw to the attention of the court any aspect of the application which may be relevant to such appointment. Where the court decides to invite the Attorney-General to appoint special counsel, the prosecutor should (regardless of any steps taken by the court or any defendant) ensure that the Attorney-General's office is promptly notified and receives all information needed to take a decision as to whether to make such appointment. If special counsel is appointed, the prosecutor should then provide special counsel with open material made available to the accused regarding the application, and any other open material requested by special counsel. Closed or unredacted material which has been provided to the court should only be given to special counsel after open material has been provided and after special counsel has subsequently sought instructions from the defendant and his legal representative.

G. Plea Discussions in Cases of Serious or Complex Fraud

(1) Guidelines

★**A–274**   On March 18, 2009, the Attorney-General issued guidelines setting out the process by which a prosecutor may discuss allegations of serious or complex fraud with a person whom he is prosecuting or expecting to prosecute.

Attorney General's Guidelines on Plea Discussions in Cases of Serious or Complex Fraud

A. Foreword

A:1 These guidelines set out a process by which a prosecutor may discuss an allegation of serious or complex fraud with a person who he or she is prosecuting or expects to prosecute, or with that person's legal representative. They come into force on the 5th day of May 2009 and apply to plea discussions initiated on or after that date. ★A–275

A:2 The guidelines will be followed by all prosecutors in England and Wales when conducting plea discussions in cases of serious or complex fraud. For the purposes of the guidelines, fraud means any financial, fiscal or commercial misconduct or corruption which is contrary to the criminal law. Fraud may be serious or complex if at least two of the following factors are present:

- the amount obtained or intended to be obtained is alleged to exceed £500,000;
- there is a significant international dimension;
- the case requires specialised knowledge of financial, commercial, fiscal or regulatory matters such as the operation of markets, banking systems, trusts or tax regimes;
- the case involves allegations of fraudulent activity against numerous victims;
- the case involves an allegation of substantial and significant fraud on a public body;
- the case is likely to be of widespread public concern;
- the alleged misconduct endangered the economic well-being of the United Kingdom, for example by undermining confidence in financial markets.

Taking account of these matters, it is for the prosecutor to decide whether or not a case is one of fraud, and whether or not it is serious or complex.

A:3 The decision whether a person should be charged with a criminal offence rests with the prosecutor. In selecting the appropriate charge or charges, the prosecutor applies principles set out in the Code for Crown Prosecutors ("the code"). Charges should reflect the seriousness and extent of the offending, give the court adequate sentencing powers and enable the case to be presented in a clear and simple way. The code also states that prosecutors should not go ahead with more charges to encourage a defendant to plead guilty to a few; equally, prosecutors should not charge a more serious offence to encourage a defendant to plead to a less serious one.

A:4 Once proceedings are instituted, the accused may plead guilty to all of the charges selected. If the defendant will plead guilty to some, but not all, of the charges or to a different, possibly less serious charge, the code states that a prosecutor is entitled to accept such pleas if he or she assesses that the court could still pass an adequate sentence. In taking these decisions the prosecutor also applies the Attorney General's Guidelines on the Acceptance of Pleas and the Prosecutor's Role in the Sentencing Exercise ("the acceptance of pleas guidelines") [*ante*, A–259 *et seq.*].

A:5 The purpose of plea discussions is to narrow the issues in the case with a view to reaching a just outcome at the earliest possible time, including the possibility of reaching an agreement about acceptable pleas of guilty and preparing a joint submission as to sentence.

A:6 The potential benefits of plea discussions are that:

- early resolution of the case may reduce the anxiety and uncertainty fo victims and witnesses, and provide earlier clarity for accused persons wh admit their guilt (subject to the court's power to reject the agreement);
- the issues in dispute may be narrowed so that even if the case proceeds t trial, it can be managed more efficiently in accordance with rule 3.2 o the *Criminal Procedure Rules* 2005. If pleas are agreed, litigation can b kept to a minimum.

A:7 Where plea discussions take place prior to the commencement of proceed ings, the charges brought by the prosecutor will reflect those agreed, rather tha those that the prosecutor would necessarily have preferred if no agreement ha been reached. Also, any criminal investigation may not be complete when thes discussions take place. For these reasons it is important that the procedures fol lowed should command public and judicial confidence; that any agreemen reached is reasonable, fair and just; that there are safeguards to ensure tha defendants are not under improper pressure to make admissions; and that ther are proper records of discussions that have taken place.

A:8 The guidelines are not intended to prevent or discourage existing prac tices by which prosecutors and prosecuting advocates discuss cases with defenc legal representatives after charge, in order to narrow the issues or to agree a basi of plea. Neither do they affect the existing practice of judicial sentence indication at the plea and case management hearing or later in accordance with the guid ance in *R. v. Goodyear* [2005] 2 Cr.App.R. 20 (§ 5–79b in the main work) (see als the acceptance of pleas guidelines). They complement, and do not detract from o replace, the code and the acceptance of pleas guidelines, or any other relevant guid ance such as the Prosecutor's Pledge, the Victim's Charter and the Code of Practic for Victims of Crime.

A:9 Where a plea agreement is reached, it remains entirely a matter for th court to decide how to deal with the case.

B. General Principles

★**A-276**   **B:1** In conducting plea discussions and presenting a plea agreement to th court, the prosecutor must act openly, fairly and in the interests of justice.

B:2 Acting in the interests of justice means ensuring that the plea agreemen reflects the seriousness and extent of the offending, gives the court adequat sentencing powers, and enables the court, the public and the victims to hav confidence in the outcome. The prosecutor must consider carefully the impact o a proposed plea or basis of plea on the community and the victim, and on th prospects of successfully prosecuting any other person implicated in the offending The prosecutor must not agree to a reduced basis of plea which is misleading untrue or illogical.

B:3 Acting fairly means respecting the rights of the defendant and of any othe person who is being or may be prosecuted in relation to the offending. Th prosecutor must not put improper pressure on a defendant in the course of ple discussions, for example by exaggerating the strength of the case in order t persuade the defendant to plead guilty, or to plead guilty on a particular basis.

B:4 Acting openly means being transparent with the defendant, the victim an the court. The prosecutor must:

- ensure that a full and accurate record of the plea discussions is prepare and retained;
- ensure that the defendant has sufficient information to enable him or he to play an informed part in the plea discussions;
- communicate with the victim before accepting a reduced basis of ple wherever it is practicable to do so, so that the position can be explaine and
- ensure that the plea agreement placed before the court fully and fairl reflects the matters agreed. The prosecutor must not agree additiona matters with the defendant which are not recorded in the plea agreemen and made known to the court.

C. Initiating Plea Discussions

When and with whom discussions should be initiated and conducted

C:1 Where he or she believes it advantageous to do so, the prosecutor may initiate plea discussions with any person who is being prosecuted or investigated
with a view to prosecution in connection with a serious or complex fraud, and
who is legally represented. The prosecutor will not initiate plea discussions with a
defendant who is not legally represented. If the prosecutor receives an approach
from such a defendant, he or she may enter into discussions if satisfied that it is
appropriate to do so.

C:2 Where proceedings have not yet been instituted, the prosecutor should not
initiate plea discussions until he or she and the investigating officer are satisfied
that the suspect's criminality is known. This will not usually be the case until after
the suspect has been interviewed under caution.

C:3 The prosecutor should be alert to any attempt by the defendant to use
plea discussions as a means of delaying the investigation or prosecution, and
should not initiate or continue discussions where the defendant's commitment to
the process is in doubt. The prosecutor should ensure that the position is
preserved during plea discussions by, for example, restraining assets in anticipation of the making of a confiscation order. Where a defendant declines to take
part in plea discussions, the prosecutor should not make a second approach unless there is a material change in circumstances.

Invitation letter

C:4 In order to initiate the plea discussions, the prosecutor will send the
defendant's representatives a letter which:

- asks whether the defence wish to enter into discussions in accordance
  with these guidelines; and
- sets a deadline for a response from the defence.

Terms and conditions letter

C:5 Where the defence agree to engage in plea discussions, the prosecutor
should send them a letter setting out the way in which the discussions will be
conducted. This letter should deal with:

- the confidentiality of information provided by the prosecutor and defendant in the course of the plea discussions;
- the use which may be made by the prosecutor of information provided
  by the defendant; and
- the practical means by which the discussions will be conducted.

Confidentiality and use of information

C:6 In relation to confidentiality, the prosecutor will indicate that he or she
intends to provide an undertaking to the effect that the fact that the defendant
has taken part in the plea discussions, and any information provided by the
defence in the course of the plea discussions will be treated as confidential and
will not be disclosed to any other party other than for the purposes of the plea
discussions and plea agreement (applying these guidelines), or as required by law.
The undertaking will make it clear that the law in relation to the disclosure of
unused material may require the prosecutor to provide information about the
plea discussions to another defendant in criminal proceedings.

C:7 The prosecutor will require the defendant's legal representative to provide
an undertaking to the effect that information provided by the prosecutor in the
course of the plea discussions will be treated as confidential and will not be
disclosed to any other party, other than for the purposes of the plea discussion
and plea agreement or as required by law.

C:8 In relation to the use of information, the prosecutor will indicate that he or she intends to undertake not to rely upon the fact that the defendant has taken part in the plea discussions, or any information provided by the defendant in the course of the discussions, as evidence in any prosecution of that defendant for the offences under investigation, should the discussions fail. However, this undertaking will make it clear that the prosecutor is not prevented from:

- relying upon a concluded and signed plea agreement as confession evidence or as admissions;

- relying upon any evidence obtained from enquiries made as a result of the provision of information by the defendant;

- relying upon information provided by the defendant as evidence against him or her in any prosecution for an offence other than the fraud which is the subject of the plea discussion and any offence which is consequent upon it, such as money laundering; and

- relying upon information provided by the defendant in a prosecution of any other person for any offence (so far as the rules of evidence allow).

C:9 In exceptional circumstances the prosecutor may agree to different terms regarding the confidentiality and use of information. However, the prosecutor must not surrender the ability to rely upon a concluded and signed plea agreement as evidence against the defendant. The prosecutor may reserve the right to bring other charges (additional to those to which the defendant has indicated a willingness to plead guilty) in specific circumstances, for example if substantial new information comes to light at a later stage, the plea agreement is rejected by the court, or the defendant fails to honour the agreement.

C:10 Until the issues of confidentiality and use of information have been agreed to the satisfaction of both parties, and the agreement reflected in signed undertakings, the prosecutor must not continue with the substantive plea discussions.

D. Conducting Plea Discussions

Statement of case

★A–278

D:1 Where plea discussions take place prior to proceedings being instituted the prosecutor will provide a statement of case to the defence. This is a written summary of the nature of the allegation against the suspect and the evidence which has been obtained, or is expected to be obtained, to support it. The statement of case should include a list of the proposed charges. Material in support of the statement of case may also be provided, whether or not in the form of admissible evidence. However, the prosecutor is not obliged to reveal to the suspect all of the information or evidence supporting his case, provided that this does not mislead the suspect to his or her prejudice.

D:2 Where plea discussions are initiated after proceedings have been commenced, but before the prosecutor has provided the defence with a case summary or opening note, the prosecutor may provide a statement of case to assist the defendant in understanding the evidence and identifying the issues.

Unused material

D:3 These guidelines do not affect the prosecutor's existing duties in relation to the disclosure of unused material. Where plea discussions take place prior to the institution of proceedings, the prosecutor should ensure that the suspect is not misled as to the strength of the prosecution case. It will not usually be necessary to provide copies of unused material in order to do this.

Conducting and recording the discussions

D:4 Having provided the defence with the statement of case and supporting material, the parties will then be in a position to conduct the plea discussions proper. Whether this is done by correspondence, by face-to-face meetings or by a combination of the two is a matter for the parties to decide in the individual case.

D:5 It is essential that a full written record is kept of every key action and event in the discussion process, including details of every offer or concession made by each party, and the reasons for every decision taken by the prosecutor. Meetings between the parties should be minuted and the minutes agreed and signed. Particular care should be taken where the defendant is not legally represented. The prosecutor should only meet with a defendant who is not legally represented if the defendant agrees to the meeting being recorded, or to the presence of an independent third party.

Queen's evidence

D:6 If the defendant offers at any stage to provide information, or to give evidence about the criminal activities of others, any such offer will be dealt with in accordance with sections 71 to 75 of the *Serious Organised Crime and Police Act* 2005 ("*SOCPA*"), the judgment of the Court of Appeal in *R v P*; *R v Blackburn* [2008] 2 Cr.App.R.(S.) 5 (§ 5–94e in the main work) and the guidance agreed and issued by the Director of Public Prosecutions, the Director of the Serious Fraud Office and the Director of Revenue and Customs Prosecutions.

Discussion of pleas

D:7 In deciding whether or not to accept an offer by the defendant to plead guilty, the prosecutor will follow sections 7 and 10 of the code relating to the selection of charges and the acceptance of guilty pleas. The prosecutor should ensure that:

- the charges reflect the seriousness and extent of the offending;
- they give the court adequate powers to sentence and impose appropriate post-conviction orders;
- they enable the case to be presented in a clear and simple way (bearing in mind that many cases of fraud are necessarily complex);
- the basis of plea enables the court to pass a sentence that matches the seriousness of the offending, particularly if there are aggravating features;
- the interests of the victim, and where possible any views expressed by the victim, are taken into account when deciding whether it is in the public interest to accept the plea; and
- the investigating officer is fully appraised of developments in the plea discussions and his or her views are taken into account.

D:8 In reaching an agreement on pleas, the parties should resolve any factual issues necessary to allow the court to sentence the defendant on a clear, fair and accurate basis. Before agreeing to proposed pleas, the prosecutor should satisfy him or herself that the full code test as set out in the code will be made out in respect of each charge. In considering whether the evidential stage of the test will be met, the prosecutor should assume that the offender will sign a plea agreement amounting to an admission to the charge.

Discussion of sentence

D:9 Where agreement is reached as to pleas, the parties should discuss the appropriate sentence with a view to presenting a joint written submission to the court. This document should list the aggravating and mitigating features arising from the agreed facts, set out any personal mitigation available to the defendant, and refer to any relevant sentencing guidelines or authorities. In the light of all of these factors, it should make submissions as to the applicable sentencing range in the relevant guideline. The prosecutor must ensure that the submissions are realistic, taking full account of all relevant material and considerations.

D:10 The prosecutor should bear in mind all of the powers of the court, and seek to include in the joint submission any relevant ancillary orders. It is particularly desirable that measures should be included that achieve redress for victims (such as compensation orders) and protection for the public (such as directors' disqualification orders, serious crime prevention orders or financial reporting orders).

D:11 Due regard should be had to the court's asset recovery powers and the desirability of using these powers both as a deterrent to others and as a means of preventing the defendant from benefiting from the proceeds of crime or funding future offending. The *Proceeds of Crime Act* 2002 requires the Crown Court to proceed to the making of a confiscation order against a convicted defendant who has benefited from his criminal conduct where the prosecutor asks the court to do so, or the court believes that it is appropriate to do so. Fraud is an acquisitive crime, and the expectation in a fraud case should be that a confiscation order will be sought by the prosecutor reflecting the full benefit to the defendant. However, in doing so it is open to the prosecutor to take a realistic view of the likely approach of the court to the determination of any points in dispute (such as the interest of a third party in any property).

D:12 In the course of the plea discussions the prosecutor must make it clear to the defence that the joint submission as to sentence (including confiscation) is not binding on the court.

Liaison with another prosecutor or regulator

D:13 The prosecutor may become aware that another prosecuting authority or regulatory body (either in England and Wales or elsewhere) has an interest in the defendant. The prosecutor should liaise with the other agency, in accordance with the Prosecutors' Convention and any other relevant agreement or guidance. The other agency may wish to take part in the plea discussions, or they may authorise the prosecutor to discuss with the defendant the matters which they are interested in, with a view to resolving all matters in one plea agreement. The prosecutor should warn the defendant that a plea agreement will not bind any other agency which is not a party to it.

E. The Written Plea Agreement

★**A-279**

E:1 All matters agreed between the prosecutor and the defence must be reduced to writing as a plea agreement and signed by both parties. The plea agreement will include:

- a list of the charges;
- a statement of the facts; and
- a declaration, signed by the defendant personally, to the effect that he or she accepts the stated facts and admits he or she is guilty of the agreed charges.

E:2 Any agreement under the *SOCPA* regarding the giving of assistance to the prosecutor by the defendant should be in a separate document accompanying the plea agreement.

E:3 Once a plea agreement is signed in a case where proceedings have not yet been commenced, the prosecutor will review the case in accordance with the code and, assuming the evidential stage of the full code test is satisfied on the basis of the signed plea agreement and the other available evidence, will arrange for proceedings to be instituted by summons or charge.

E:4 In advance of the defendant's first appearance in the Crown Court, the prosecutor should send the court sufficient material to allow the judge to understand the facts of the case and the history of the plea discussions, to assess whether the plea agreement is fair and in the interests of justice, and to decide the appropriate sentence. This will include:

- the signed plea agreement;
- a joint submission as to sentence and sentencing considerations;

- any relevant sentencing guidelines or authorities;
- all of the material provided by the prosecution to the defendant in the course of the plea discussions;
- any material provided by the defendant to the prosecution, such as documents relating to personal mitigation; and
- the minutes of any meetings between the parties and any correspondence generated in the plea discussions.

E:5 It will then be for the court to decide how to deal with the plea agreement. In particular, the court retains an absolute discretion as to whether or not it sentences in accordance with the joint submission from the parties.

F. Failure of Plea Discussions

F:1 There are several circumstances in which plea discussions may result in an outcome other than the defendant pleading guilty in accordance with a plea agreement. The prosecutor or the defendant may break off the discussions. They may be unable to reach an agreement. They may reach an agreement, but intervening events may lead the prosecutor to decide that proceedings should not be instituted. Proceedings may be instituted but the court may reject the plea agreement. The defendant may decline to plead guilty in accordance with the plea agreement, either as a result of a sentence indication given under the procedure set out in *R. v. Goodyear*, or for some other reason. **★A–280**

F:2 If any of these situations arises, the prosecutor may wish for further enquiries to be made with a view to bringing or completing proceedings against the defendant. If proceedings have already been instituted, the prosecutor will use the appropriate means to delay them – either discontinuing under section 23 or 23A of the *Prosecution of Offences Act* 1985 or (if the indictment has already been preferred) applying for an adjournment or stay of the proceedings. Theprosecutor and the defendant's representatives will continue to be bound by the preliminary undertakings made in relation to the confidentiality and use of information provided in the course of the plea discussions.

F:3 Where plea discussions have broken down for any reason, it will be rare that the prosecutor will wish to re-open them, but he or she may do so if there is a material change in circumstances which warrants it.

(2) Practice

Paragraphs IV.45.18 to IV.45.28 of the consolidated criminal practice direction, as inserted by *Practice Direction (Criminal proceedings: victim personal statements; pleas of guilty in the Crown Court; forms)*, *The Times*, May 19, 2009, Supreme Court, with effect from May 14, 2009, make provision as to the practice to be followed where a plea agreement has been reached and a joint sentencing submission is to be placed before the court. **★A–281**

Practice Direction (Criminal Proceedings: Consolidation), paras IV.45.18–IV.45.28 (as inserted by Practice Direction (Criminal proceedings: victim personal statements; pleas of guilty in the Crown Court; forms), The Times, May 19, 2009)

IV.45.18 In this part— **★A–282**
  (a) "a plea agreement" means a written basis of plea agreed between the prosecution and defendant(s) in accordance with the principles set out in *R v Underwood* [see § 5–73 in the main work and *ante*], supported by admissible documentary evidence or admissions under section 10 of the *Criminal Justice Act* 1967;
  (b) "a sentencing submission" means sentencing submissions made jointly by the

prosecution and defence as to the appropriate sentencing authorities and applicable sentencing range in the relevant sentencing guideline relating to the plea agreement;

(c) "serious or complex fraud" includes, but is not limited to, allegations of fraud where two or more of the following are present [list as per the guidelines, *ante*, A–275]:

Procedure

★**A–283**   **IV.45.19** The procedure regarding agreed bases of plea outlined in paragraphs IV.45.10 to IV.45.12, above [*ante*, § 5–73], applies with equal rigour to the acceptance of pleas under this procedure. However, because under this procedure the parties will have been discussing the plea agreement and the charges from a much earlier stage, it is vital that the judge is fully informed of all relevant background to the discussions, charges and the eventual basis of plea.

IV.45.20 Where the defendant has not yet appeared before the Crown Court, the prosecutor must send full details of the plea agreement and sentencing submission(s) to the court, at least 7 days in advance of the defendant's first appearance. Where the defendant has already appeared before the Crown Court, the prosecutor must notify the court as soon as is reasonably practicable that a plea agreement and sentencing submissions under the Attorney-General's Plea Discussion Guidelines are to be submitted. The court should set a date for the matter to be heard, and the prosecutor must send full details of the plea agreement and sentencing submission(s) to the court as soon as practicable, or in accordance with the directions of the court.

IV.45.21 The provision to the judge of full details of the plea agreement requires sufficient information to be provided to allow the judge to understand the facts of the case and the history of the plea discussions, to assess whether the plea agreement is fair and in the interests of justice, and to decide the appropriate sentence. This will include, but is not limited to: (i) the plea agreement; (ii) the sentencing submission(s); (iii) all of the material provided by the prosecution to the defendant in the course of the plea discussions; (iv) relevant material provided by the defendant, for example documents relating to personal mitigation; and (v) the minutes of any meetings between the parties and any correspondence generated in the plea discussions. The parties should be prepared to provide additional material at the request of the court.

IV.45.22 The court should at all times have regard to the length of time that has elapsed since the date of the occurrence of the events giving rise to the plea discussions, the time taken to interview the defendant, the date of charge and the prospective trial date (if the matter were to proceed to trial) so as to ensure that its consideration of the plea agreement and sentencing submissions does not cause any unnecessary further delay.

Status of plea agreement and joint sentencing submissions

★**A–284**   **IV.45.23** Where a plea agreement and joint sentencing submissions are submitted, it remains entirely a matter for the court to decide how to deal with the case. The judge retains the absolute discretion to refuse to accept the plea agreement and to sentence otherwise than in accordance with the sentencing submissions made under the Attorney-General's Plea Discussion Guidelines.

IV.45.24 Sentencing submissions should draw the court's attention to any applicable range in any relevant guideline, and to any ancillary orders that may be applicable. Sentencing submissions should not include a specific sentence or agreed range other than the ranges set out in sentencing guidelines or authorities.

IV.45.25 Prior to pleading guilty in accordance with the plea agreement, the defendant(s) may apply to the court for an indication of the likely maximum sentence [in accordance with *R. v. Gooodyear*, as to which, see § 5–79b in the main work].

IV.45.26 In the event that the judge indicates a sentence or passes a sentence which is not within the submissions made on sentencing, the plea agreement remains binding.

IV.45.27 If the defendant does not plead guilty in accordance with the plea agreement or if a defendant who has pleaded guilty in accordance with a plea agreement successfully applies to withdraw his plea under rule 39.3 of the *Criminal Proce-dure Rules*, the signed plea agreement may be treated as confession evidence, and may be used against the defendant at a later stage in these or any other proceedings. Any credit for a timely guilty plea may be lost. The court may exercise its discretion under section 78 of the *Police and Criminal Evidence Act* 1984 to exclude any such evidence ... .

IV.45.28   Where a defendant has failed to plead guilty in accordance with a plea agreement, for example in the circumstances set out in paragraph IV.45.27, above, the case is unlikely to be ready for trial immediately. The prosecution may have been commenced earlier than it otherwise would have been, in reliance upon the defendant's agreement to plead guilty. This is likely to be a relevant consideration for the court in deciding whether or not to grant an application to adjourn or stay the proceedings to allow the matter to be prepared for trial in accordance with the protocol on the Control and Management of Heavy Fraud and other Complex Criminal Cases, or as required.

In the case of life imprisonment, a plea would be the most that can happen... Where the plea of guilty would entitle... the plea of guilty would be... may be duly entered to delincum rights prejudices or unlawful proceedings in any court or a guilty plea may before the court in writing made known in a section 7A of the Sentencing Act 1991, as set out by section 6 above.

IV 47.9% — Where a defendant has failed to plead guilty is a defendant with a plea successfully carried in the circumstances cannot in paragraph IV 47.7% above in the case concluded under rights for trial provisions but the... prosecution must be for a committed offence that it still means would give rise in relation... where the defendant's are entitled to enter guilty. This is likely to be a relevant consideration in matters for the court in relation to whether or not to grant the application for a discount in any case if the court may allow the accused to be released in a matter accordance with the provisions of the control and Mental Health of Herin, if... and other complexity to the... this case as are required.

APPENDIX B

Interpretation Act 1978

General provisions as to enactment and operation

Words of enactment

1. Every section of an Act takes effect as a substantive enactment without introductory words.   **B–1**

Amendment or repeal in same Session

2. Any Act may be amended or repealed in the Session of Parliament in which it is passed.   **B–2**

Judicial notice

3. Every Act is a public Act to be judicially noticed as such, unless the contrary is expressly provided by the Act.   **B–3**

Time of commencement

4. An Act or provision of an Act comes into force—   **B–4**

    (a) where provision is made for it to come into force on a particular day, at the beginning of that day;

    (b) where no provision is made for its coming into force, at the beginning of the day on which the Act receives the Royal Assent.

Interpretation and construction

Definitions

5. In any Act, unless the contrary intention appears, words and expressions listed in Schedule 1 to this Act are to be construed according to that Schedule.   **B–5**

Gender and number

6. In any Act, unless the contrary intention appears,—   **B–6**

    (a) words importing the masculine gender include the feminine;

    (b) words importing the feminine gender include the masculine;

    (c) words in the singular include the plural and words in the plural include the singular.

References to service by post

7. Where an Act authorises or requires any document to be served by post (whether the expression "serve" or the expression "give" or "send" or any other expression is used) then, unless the contrary intention appears, the service is deemed to be effected by properly addressing, prepaying and posting a letter containing the document and, unless the contrary is proved, to have been effected at the time at which the letter would be delivered in the ordinary course of post.   **B–7**

References to distance

8. In the measurement of any distance for the purposes of an Act, that distance shall, unless the contrary intention appears, be measured in a straight line on a horizontal plane.   **B–8**

References to time of day

9. Subject to section 3 of the *Summer Time Act* 1972 (construction of references to points of time during the period of summer time), whenever an expression of time occurs in an Act, the time referred to shall, unless it is otherwise specifically stated, be held to be Greenwich mean time.   **B–9**

References to Sovereign

10. In any Act a reference to the Sovereign reigning at the time of the passing   **B–10**

447

of the Act is to be construed, unless the contrary intention appears, as a reference to the Sovereign for the time being.

Construction of subordinate legislation

B–11   **11.** Where an Act confers power to make subordinate legislation, expressions used in that legislation have, unless the contrary intention appears, the meaning which they bear in the Act.

Statutory powers and duties

Continuity of powers and duties

B–12   **12.**—(1) Where an Act confers a power or imposes a duty it is implied, unless the contrary intention appears, that the power may be exercised, or the duty is to be performed, from time to time as occasion requires.

(2) Where an Act confers a power or imposes a duty on the holder of an office as such, it is implied, unless the contrary intention appears, that the power may be exercised, or the duty is to be performed, by the holder for the time being of the office.

Anticipatory exercise of powers

B–13   **13.** Where an Act which (or any provision of which) does not come into force immediately on its passing confers power to make subordinate legislation, or to make appointments, give notices, prescribe forms or do any other thing for the purposes of the Act, then, unless the contrary intention appears, the power may be exercised, and any instrument made thereunder may be made so as to come into force, at any time after the passing of the Act so far as may be necessary or expedient for the purpose—

(a) of bringing the Act or any provision of the Act into force; or

(b) of giving full effect to that Act or any such provision at or after the time when it comes into force.

Implied power to amend

B–14   **14.** Where an Act confers power to make—

(a) rules, regulations or byelaws; or

(b) Orders in Council, orders or other subordinate legislation to be made by statutory instrument,

it implies, unless the contrary intention appears, a power exercisable in the same manner and subject to the same conditions or limitations, to revoke, amend or re enact any instrument made under the power.

Repealing enactments

Repeal of repeal

B–15   **15.** Where an Act repeals a repealing enactment, the repeal does not revive any enactment previously repealed unless words are added reviving it.

General savings

B–16   **16.**—(1) Without prejudice to section 15, where an Act repeals an enactment the repeal does not, unless the contrary intention appears,—

(a) revive anything not in force or existing at the time at which the repeal takes effect;

(b) affect the previous operation of the enactment repealed or anything duly done or suffered under that enactment;

(c) affect any right, privilege, obligation or liability acquired, accrued or incurred under that enactment;

(d) affect any penalty, forfeiture or punishment incurred in respect of any of fence committed against that enactment;

448

(e) affect any investigation, legal proceeding or remedy in respect of any such right, privilege, obligation, liability, penalty, forfeiture or punishment;

and any such investigation, legal proceeding or remedy may be instituted, continued or enforced, and any such penalty, forfeiture or punishment may be imposed, as if the repealing Act had not been passed.

(2) This section applies to the expiry of a temporary enactment as if it were repealed by an Act.

[Considered in *R. v. West London Stipendiary Magistrate, ex p. Simeon* [1983] A.C. 234, HL. See also *Hough v. Windus* (1884)12 Q.B.D. 224, and *R. v. Fisher (Charles)* [1969] 1 W.L.R. 8, CA.]

Repeal and re-enactment

17.—(1) Where an Act repeals a previous enactment and substitutes provisions **B–17** for the enactment repealed, the repealed enactment remains in force until the substitute provisions come into force.

(2) Where an Act repeals and re-enacts, with or without modification, a previous enactment then, unless the contrary intention appears,—

    (a) any reference in any other enactment to the enactment so repealed shall be construed as a reference to the provision re-enacted;

    (b) in so far as any subordinate legislation made or other thing done under the enactment so repealed, or having effect as if so made or done, could have been made or done under the provision re-enacted, it shall have effect as if made or done under that provision.

Miscellaneous

Duplicated offences

18. Where an act or omission constitutes an offence under two or more Acts, or **B–18** both under an Act and at common law, the offender shall, unless the contrary intention appears, be liable to be prosecuted and punished under either or any of those Acts or at common law, but shall not be liable to be punished more than once for the same offence.

See in the main work, § 4–123.

Citation of other Acts

19. Where an Act cites another Act by year, statute, session or chapter, or a sec- **B–19** tion or other portion of another Act by number or letter, the reference shall, unless the contrary intention appears, be read as referring—

    (a) in the case of Acts included in any revised edition of the statutes printed by authority, to that edition;

    (b) in the case of Acts not so included but included in the edition prepared under the direction of the Record Commission, to that edition;

    (c) in any other case, to the Acts printed by the Queen's Printer, or under the superintendence or authority of Her Majesty's Stationery Office.

(2) An Act may continue to be cited by the short title authorised by any enactment notwithstanding the repeal of that enactment.

References to other enactments

20.—(1) Where an Act describes or cites a portion of an enactment by referring **B–20** to words, sections or other parts from or to which or from and to which the portion extends, the portion described or cited includes the words, sections or other parts referred to unless the contrary intention appears.

(2) Where an Act refers to an enactment, the reference unless the contrary intention appears, is a reference to that enactment as amended, and includes a reference thereto as extended or applied, by or under any other enactment, including any other provision of that Act.

References to Community instruments

B–20a   **20A.** Where an Act passed after the commencement of this section refers to a Community instrument that has been amended, extended or applied by another such instrument, the reference, unless the contrary intention appears, is a reference to that instrument as so amended, extended or applied.

[This section was inserted by the *Legislative and Regulatory Reform Act* 2006, s.25(1).]

Supplementary

Interpretation, etc.

B–21   **21.**—(1) In this Act "Act" includes a local and personal or private Act; and "subordinate legislation" means Orders in Council, orders, rules, regulations, schemes, warrants, byelaws and other instruments made or to be made under any Act.

(2) This Act binds the Crown.

Application to Acts and Measures

B–22   **22.**—(1) This Act applies to itself, to any Act passed after the commencement of this Act (subject, in the case of section 20A, to the provision made in that section) and, to the extent specified in Part I of Schedule 2, to Acts passed before the commencement of this Act.

(2) In any of the foregoing provisions of this Act a reference to an Act is a reference to an Act to which that provision applies; but this does not affect the generality of references to enactments or of the references in section 19(1) to other Acts.

(3) This Act applies to Measures of the General Synod of the Church of England (and, so far as it relates to Acts passed before the commencement of this Act, to Measures of the Church Assembly passed after May 28, 1925) as it applies to Acts.

[This section is printed as amended by the *Legislative and Regulatory Reform Act* 2006, s.25(2).]

Application to other instruments

B–23   **23.**—(1) The provisions of this Act, except sections 1 to 3 and 4(b), apply, so far as applicable and unless the contrary intention appears, to subordinate legislation made after the commencement of this Act and, to the extent specified in Part II of Schedule 2, to subordinate legislation made before the commencement of this Act, as they apply to Acts.

(2) In the application of this Act to Acts passed or subordinate legislation made after the commencement of this Act, all references to an enactment include an enactment comprised in subordinate legislation whenever made, and references to the passing or repeal of an enactment are to be construed accordingly.

(3) Sections 9 and 19(1) also apply to deeds and other instruments and documents as they apply to Acts and subordinate legislation; and in the application of section 17(2)(a) to Acts passed or subordinate legislation made after the commencement of this Act, the reference to any other enactment includes any deed or other instrument or document.

(4) Subsections (1) and (2) of this section do not apply to Orders in Council made under section 5 of the *Statutory Instruments Act* 1946, section 1(3) of the *Northern*

Ireland (Temporary Provisions) Act 1972 or Schedule 1 to the *Northern Ireland Act* 1974.

23A. [*Acts of the Scottish Parliament, etc.*] **B–23a**
23B. [*Measures and Acts of the National Assembly for Wales, etc.*] **B–23b**
24. [*Application to Northern Ireland.*] **B–24**

Repeals and savings

25.—(1) The enactments described in Schedule 3 are repealed to the extent **B–25**
specified in the third column of that Schedule.

(2) Without prejudice to section 17(2)(a), a reference to the *Interpretation Act* 1889, to any provision of that Act or to any other enactment repealed by this Act whether occurring in another Act, in subordinate legislation, in Northern Ireland legislation or in any deed or other instrument or document, shall be construed as referring to this Act, or to the corresponding provision of this Act, as it applies to Acts passed at the time of the reference.

(3) The provisions of this Act relating to Acts passed after any particular time do not affect the construction of Acts passed before that time, though continued or amended by Acts passed thereafter.

26. [*Commencement.*] **B–26**
27. [*Short title.*] **B–27**

SCHEDULES

SCHEDULE 1

WORDS AND EXPRESSIONS DEFINED

Note: The years or dates which follow certain entries in this Schedule are relevant **B–28**
for the purposes of paragraph 4 of Schedule 2 (application to existing enactments).

Definitions

... .

"Bank of England" means, as the context requires, the Governor and Company of the Bank of England or the bank of the Governor and Company of the Bank of England.

... .

"British Islands" means the United Kingdom, the Channel Islands and the Isle of Man. [1889]

"British possession" means any part of Her Majesty's dominions outside the United Kingdom; and where parts of such dominions are under both a central and local legislature, all parts under the central legislature are deemed, for the purposes of this definition, to be one British possession. [1889]

... .

"Central funds", in an enactment providing in relation to England and Wales for the payment of costs out of central funds, means money provided by Parliament.

... .

"Civil partnership" means a civil partnership which exists under or by virtue of the *Civil Partnership Act* 2004 (and any reference to a civil partner is to be read accordingly).

[This definition is inserted by the *Civil Partnership Act* 2004, s.261(1), and Sched. 27, para. 59.]

"Colonial legislature", and "legislature" in relation to a British possession, mean the authority, other than the Parliament of the United Kingdom or Her Majesty in Council, competent to make laws for the possession. [1889]

"Colony" means any part of Her Majesty's dominions outside the British Islands except—

451

> (a) countries having fully responsible status within the Commonwealth;
>
> (b) territories for whose external relations a country other than the United Kingdom is responsible;
>
> (c) associated states; and where parts of such dominions are under both a central and a local legislature, all parts under the central legislature are deemed for the purposes of this definition to be one colony. [1889]

"Commencement", in relation to an Act or enactment, means the time when the Act or enactment comes into force.

"Committed for trial" means—

> (a) *in relation to England and Wales, committed in custody or on bail by a magistrates' court pursuant to section 6 of the* Magistrates' Courts Act *1980, or by any judge or other authority having power to do so, with a view to trial before a judge and jury;* [1989]
>
> (b) [*Northern Ireland*].

[This definition is printed as amended by the *MCA* 1980, s.154 and Sched. 7, para. 169. Paragraph (a) is repealed as from a day to be appointed: *CJA* 2003, ss.41 and 332, Sched. 3, para.49(a), and Sched. 37, Pt 4.]

"The Communities", "the Treaties" or "the Community Treaties" and other expressions defined by section 1 of and Schedule 1 to the *European Communities Act* 1972 have the meanings prescribed by that Act.

.... .

"Consular officer" has the meaning assigned by Article 1 of the Vienna Convention set out in Schedule 1 to the *Consular Relations Act* 1968.

.... .

"County Court" means—

> (a) in relation to England and Wales, a court held for a district under the *County Courts Act* 1984;
>
> (b) [*Northern Ireland*].

[This definition is printed as amended by the *County Courts Act* 1984, Sched. 2.]

"Court of Appeal" means—

> (a) in relation to England and Wales, Her Majesty's Court of Appeal in England;
>
> (b) in relation to Northern Ireland, Her Majesty's Court of Appeal in Northern Ireland.

"Court of summary jurisdiction", "summary conviction" and "Summary Jurisdiction Acts", in relation to Northern Ireland, have the same meanings as in Measures of the Northern Ireland Assembly and Acts of the Parliament of Northern Ireland.

"Crown Court" means—

> (a) in relation to England and Wales, the Crown Court constituted by section 4 of the *Courts Act* 1971;
>
> (b) [*Northern Ireland*].

.... .

"EEA agreement" means the agreement on the European Economic Area signed at Oporto on 2nd May 1992, together with the Protocol adjusting that Agreement signed at Brussels on 17th March 1993, as modified or supplemented from time to time. [The date of the coming into force of this paragraph.]

"EEA state", in relation to any time, means—

> (a) a state which at that time is a member State; or

    (b) any other state which at that time is a party to the EEA agreement. [The date of the coming into force of this paragraph.]

[These two definitions were inserted, as from January 8, 2007, by the *Legislative and Regulatory Reform Act* 2006, s.26(1).]

    "England" means, subject to any alteration of boundaries under Part IV of the *Local Government Act* 1972, the area consisting of the counties established by section 1 of that Act, Greater London and the Isles of Scilly. [1st April 1974]

    .... .

    "Governor-General" includes any person who for the time being has the powers of the Governor-General, and "Governor", in relation to any British possession, includes the officer for the time being administering the government of that possession. [1889]

    "Her Majesty's Revenue and Customs" has the meaning given by section 4 of the *Commissioners for Revenue and Customs Act* 2005.

[This definition was inserted by the *Commissioners for Revenue and Customs Act* 2005, s.4(3).]

    "High Court" means—

        (a) in relation to England and Wales, Her Majesty's High Court of Justice in England;

        (b) in relation to Northern Ireland, Her Majesty's High Court of Justice in Northern Ireland.

    .... .

    "Land" includes buildings and other structures, land covered with water, and any estate, interest, easement, servitude or right in or over land. [1st January 1979]

    .... .

    "London borough" means a borough described in Schedule 1 to the *London Government Act* 1963, "inner London borough" means one of the boroughs so described and numbered from 1 to 12 and "outer London borough" means one of the boroughs so described and numbered 13 to 32, subject (in each case) to any alterations made under Part IV of the *Local Government Act* 1972 or Part II of the *Local Government Act* 1992.

[This definition is printed as amended by the *Local Government Act* 1992, s.27(1), and Sched. 3, para. 21.]

    "Lord Chancellor" means the Lord High Chancellor of Great Britain.

    "Magistrates' court" has the meaning assigned to it—

        (a) in relation to England and Wales, by section 148 of the *Magistrates' Courts Act* 1980;

        (b) [*Northern Ireland*].

[This definition is printed as amended by the *MCA* 1980, s.154, and Sched. 7, para. 169.]

    "Month" means calendar month. [1850]

    .... .

    "Oath" and "affidavit" include affirmation and declaration, and "swear" includes affirm and declare.

    "Officer of Revenue and Customs" has the meaning given by section 2(1) of the *Commissioners for Revenue and Customs Act* 2005.

[This definition was inserted by the *Commissioners for Revenue and Customs Act* 2005, s.2(7).]

"Ordnance Map" means a map made under powers conferred by the *Ordnance Survey Act* 1841 or the *Boundary Survey (Ireland) Act* 1854.

"Parliamentary Election" means the election of a Member to serve in Parliament for a constituency. [1889]

"Person" includes a body of persons corporate or unincorporate. [1889]

"Police area", "police authority" and other expressions relating to the police have the meaning or effect described—

    (a) in relation to England and Wales, by section 101(1) of the *Police Act* 1996;

    (b) [*Scotland*].

[This definition is printed as amended by the *Police Act* 1996, Sched. 7, para. 32.]

"The Privy Council" means the Lords and others of Her Majesty's Most Honourable Privy Council.

"Registered" in relation to nurses, midwives and health visitors, means registered in the register maintained by the United Kingdom Central Council for Nursing, Midwifery and Health Visiting by virtue of qualifications in nursing, midwifery or health visiting, as the case may be.

[This definition was inserted by the *Nurses, Midwives and Health Visitors Act* 1979, s.23(4), and Sched. 7, para. 30.]

"Registered medical practitioner" means a fully registered person within the meaning of the *Medical Act* 1983 who holds a licence to practise under that Act. [1st January 1979]

[This definition is printed as amended by the *Medical Act* 1983, s.56(1), and Sched. 5, para. 18; and the *Medical Act 1983 (Amendment) Order* 2002 (S.I 2002 No. 3135), Sched.1, para. 10.]

"Rules of Court" in relation to any court means rules made by the authority having power to make rules or orders regulating the practice and procedure of that court, and in Scotland includes Acts of Adjournal and Acts of Sederunt; and the power of the authority to make rules of court (as above defined) includes power to make such rules for the purpose of any Act which directs or authorises anything to be done by rules of court. [1889]

"Secretary of State" means one of Her Majesty's Principal Secretaries of State.

["Senior Courts" means the Senior Courts of England and Wales.]

[This definition is inserted, as from a day to be appointed, by the *Constitutional Reform Act* 2005, s.59(5), and Sched. 11, para. 24.]

["Sent for trial" means, in relation to England and Wales, sent by a magistrates'court to the Crown Court for trial pursuant to section 51 or 51A of the *Crime and Disorder Act* 1998.]

[This definition is inserted, as from a day to be appointed, by the *CJA* 2003, s.41, and Sched. 3, para. 49(b).]

    .... .

"Sheriff", in relation to Scotland, includes sheriff principal. [1889]

"The standard scale", with reference to a fine or penalty for an offence triable only summarily,—

    (a) in relation to England and Wales, has the meaning given by section 37 of the *Criminal Justice Act* 1982;

(b) [*Scotland*];

(c) [*Northern Ireland*].

[This definition was inserted by the *CJA* 1988, s.170(1), and Sched. 15,
para. 58(a). (For s.37 of the 1982 Act, see the main work, § 5–403.)]

"Statutory declaration" means a declaration made by virtue of the *Statutory Declarations Act* 1835.

"Statutory maximum", with reference to a fine or penalty on summary conviction for an offence—

(a) in relation to England and Wales, means the prescribed sum within
the meaning of section 32 of the *Magistrates' Courts Act* 1980;

(b) [*Scotland*]; and

(c) [*Northern Ireland*].

[This definition was inserted by the *CJA* 1988, s.170(1), and Sched. 15,
para. 58(b). (For s.32 of the 1980 Act, see the main work, § 1–75aa.)]

"Supreme Court" means [the Supreme Court of the United Kingdon]—

(a) *in relation to England and Wales, the Court of Appeal and the High
Court together with the Crown Court*;

(b) *in relation to Northern Ireland, the Supreme Court of Judicature of
Northern Ireland.*

.... .

[Paras (a) and (b) are repealed, and the words in square brackets are
inserted, as from a day to be appointed, by the *Constitutional Reform Act* 2005,
s.59(5), and Sched. 11, para. 24.]

"The Treasury" means the Commissioners of Her Majesty's Treasury.

"United Kingdom" means Great Britain and Northern Ireland. [12th April
1927]

"Wales" means the combined area of the counties which were created by section
20 of the *Local Government Act* 1972, as originally enacted, but subject to any
alteration made under section 73 of that Act (consequential alteration of
boundary following alteration of watercourse) [1st April 1974]

[This definition was substituted by the *Local Government (Wales) Act* 1994,
Sched. 2, para. 9.]

.... .

"Writing" includes typing, printing, lithography, photography and other modes
of representing or reproducing words in avisible form, and expressions
referring to writing are construed accordingly.

Construction of certain expressions relating to offences

In relation to England and Wales—

(a) "indictable offence" means an offence which, if committed by an adult, is
triable on indictment, whether it is exclusively so triable or triable either
way;

(b) "summary offence" means an offence which, if committed by an adult, is
triable only summarily;

(c) "offence triable either way" means an offence, other than an offence triable on indictment only by virtue of Part V of the *Criminal Justice Act*
1988 which, if committed by an adult, is triable either on indictment or
summarily;

and the terms "indictable", "summary" and "triable either way", in their application to offences are to be construed accordingly.

In the above definitions references to the way or ways in which an offence is triable are to be construed without regard to the effect, if any, of section 22 of the *Magistrates' Courts Act* 1980 on the mode of trial in a particular case.

[This para. is printed as amended by the *MCA* 1980, Sched. 7; and the *CJA* 1988, Sched. 15, para. 59.]

Construction of certain references to relationships

In relation to England and Wales—

    (a) references (however expressed) to any relationship between two persons;

    (b) references to a person whose father and mother were or were not married to each other at the time of his birth; and

    (c) references cognate with references falling within paragraph (b) above,

shall be construed in accordance with section 1 of the *Family Law Reform Act* 1987. [The date of the coming into force of that section.]

[This para. was added by Schedule 2 to the *Family Law Reform Act* 1987.]

NOTE: the definitions of the following expressions have been omitted: "Associated state", "Bank of Ireland", "Building regulations", "Charity Commissioners", "Comptroller and Auditor General", "Consular officer", "The Corporation Tax Acts", "Crown Estate Commissioners", "Financial year", "The Income Tax Acts", "Lands Clauses Act", "National Debt Commissioners", "Northern Ireland legislation", "Sewerage undertaker", "The Tax Acts" and "Water undertaker".

SCHEDULE 2

APPLICATION OF ACT TO EXISTING ENACTMENTS

PART I

ACTS

B-29   1. The following provisions of this Act apply to Acts whenever passed:—

        Section 6(a) and (c) so far as applicable to enactments relating to offences punishable on indictment or on summary conviction

        Section 9

        Section 10

        Section 11 so far as it relates to subordinate legislation made after the year 1889

        Section 18

        Section 19(2).

    2. The following apply to Acts passed after the year 1850:—

        Section 1

        Section 2

        Section 3

        Section 6(a) and (c) so far as not applicable to such Acts by virtue of paragraph 1

        Section 15

        Section 17(1).

    3. The following apply to Acts passed after the year 1889:—

        Section 4

        Section 7

        Section 8

Section 12
Section 13
Section 14 so far as it relates to rules, regulations or byelaws
Section 16(1)
Section 17(2)(a)
Section 19(1)
Section 20(1).

4.—(1) Subject to the following provisions of this paragraph—

(a) paragraphs of Schedule 1 at the end of which a year or date is specified or described apply, so far as applicable, to Acts passed on or after the date, or after the year, so specified or described; and

(b) paragraphs of that Schedule at the end of which no year or date is specified or described apply, so far as applicable, to Acts passed at any time.

(2) The definition of "British Islands", in its application to Acts passed after the establishment of the Irish Free State but before the commencement of this Act, includes the Republic of Ireland.

(3) The definition of "colony", in its application to an Act passed at any time before the commencement of this Act, includes—

(a) any colony within the meaning of section 18(3) of the *Interpretation Act* 1889 which was excluded, but in relation only to Acts passed at a later time, by any enactment repealed by this Act;

(b) any country or territory which ceased after that time to be part of Her Majesty's dominions but subject to a provision for the continuation of existing law as if it had not so ceased;

and paragraph (b) of the definition does not apply.

(4) The definition of "Lord Chancellor" does not apply to Acts passed before 1st October 1921 in which that expression was used in relation to Ireland only.

(5) The definition of "person", so far as it includes bodies corporate, applies to any provision of an Act whenever passed relating to an offence punishable on indictment or on summary conviction.

(6) This paragraph applies to the *National Health Service Reorganisation Act* 1973 and the *Water Act* 1973 as if they were passed after 1st April 1974.

[Para. 4 is printed as amended by the *Family Law Reform Act* 1987, Scheds 2 and 4.]

5. The following definitions shall be treated as included in Schedule 1 for the purposes specified in this paragraph—

(a) in any Act passed before 1st April 1974, a reference to England includes Berwick upon Tweed and Monmouthshire and, in the case of an Act passed before the *Welsh Language Act* 1967, Wales;

(b) in any Act passed before the commencement of this Act and after the year 1850, "land" includes messuages, tenements and hereditaments, houses and buildings of any tenure;

(c) [*Scotland*].

Part II
Subordinate Legislation

6. Sections 4(a), 9 and 19(1), and so much of Schedule 1 as defines the following   **B–30** expressions, namely—

England;
Local land charges register and appropriate local land charges register;
Police area (and related expressions) in relation to Scotland;
United Kingdom;
Wales;

apply to subordinate legislation made at any time before the commencement of this

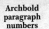

Act as they apply to Acts passed at that time.

[Para. 6 is printed as repealed in part by the *British Nationality Act* 1981, Sched. 9.]

7. The definition in Schedule 1 of "county court", in relation to England and Wales, applies to Orders in Council made after the year 1846.

APPENDIX C

The Duties of Advocates

I. CODE OF CONDUCT

The eighth edition of the *Code of Conduct for the Bar of England and Wales*   **C–1**
came into force on October 31, 2004.

CODE OF CONDUCT FOR THE BAR OF ENGLAND AND WALES

Table of contents

Those provisions marked with an asterisk (*) are set out in full below.   **C–2**

Table of Annexes

PART I—PRELIMINARY

C–3   **101** The Eighth Edition of the Code was adopted by the Bar Council on 18 September 2004 and came into force on 31st October 2004.

102 This Code includes the Annexes.

103 Amendments and additions to this Code may be made by Resolution of the Bar Council which shall be operative upon such date as the Resolution shall appoint or if no such date is appointed on the later of:

(a) the date of the Resolution; and

(b) the date when approval of the amendment or addition, if required, is given under Schedule 4 of the Act.

Amendments and additions will be published from time to time in such manner as the Bar Council may determine.

General purpose of the Code

104 The general purpose of this Code is to provide the requirements for practice   **C–4**
as a barrister and the rules and standards of conduct applicable to barristers which
are appropriate in the interests of justice and in particular:

(a) in relation to self-employed barristers to provide common and enforceable rules and standards which require them:

(i) to be completely independent in conduct and in professional standing
as sole practitioners;

(ii) to act only as consultants instructed by solicitors and other approved
persons (save where instructions can properly be dispensed with);

(iii) to acknowledge a public obligation based on the paramount need for
access to justice to act for any client in cases within their field of
practice;

(b) to make appropriate provision for employed barristers taking into account the fact that such barristers are employed to provide legal services
to or on behalf of their employer.

PART III—FUNDAMENTAL PRINCIPLES

Applicable to all barristers

301 A barrister must have regard to paragraph 104 and must not: **C–5**

(a) engage in conduct whether in pursuit of his profession or otherwise
which is:

(i) dishonest or otherwise discreditable to a barrister;

(ii) prejudicial to the administration of justice; or

(iii) likely to diminish public confidence in the legal profession or the
administration of justice or otherwise bring the legal profession into
disrepute;

(b) engage directly or indirectly in any occupation if his association with that
occupation may adversely affect the reputation of the Bar or in the case
of a practising barrister prejudice his ability to attend properly to his
practice.

Applicable to practising barristers

302 A barrister has an overriding duty to the Court to act with independence in   **C–6**
the interests of justice: he must assist the Court in the administration of justice and
must not deceive or knowingly or recklessly mislead the Court.

303 A barrister:

(a) must promote and protect fearlessly and by all proper and lawful means
the lay client's best interests and do so without regard to his own interests
or to any consequences to himself or to any other person (including any
professional client or other intermediary or another barrister);

(b) owes his primary duty as between the lay client and any professional client or other intermediary to the lay client and must not permit the
intermediary to limit his discretion as to how the interests of the lay client
can best be served;

(c) when supplying legal services funded by the Legal Services Commission
as part of the Community Legal Service or the Criminal Defence Service
owes his primary duty to the lay client subject only to compliance with
paragraph 304.

304 A barrister who supplies legal services funded by the Legal Services Commission as part of the Community Legal Service or the Criminal Defence Service must in
connection with the supply of such services comply with any duty imposed on him by

or under the *Access to Justice Act* 1999 or any regulations or code in effect under that Act and in particular with the duties set out in Annex E.

305.1 A barrister must not in relation to any other person (including a client or another barrister or a pupil or a student member of an Inn of Court) discriminate directly or indirectly or victimise because of race, colour, ethnic or national origin, nationality, citizenship, sex, sexual orientation, marital status, disability, religion or political persuasion.

305.2 A barrister must not in relation to any offer of a pupillage or tenancy discriminate directly or indirectly against a person on grounds of age, save where such discrimination can be shown to be objectively and reasonably justifiable.

306 A barrister is individually and personally responsible for his own conduct and for his professional work: he must exercise his own personal judgment in all his professional activities.

307 A barrister must not:

    (a) permit his absolute independence integrity and freedom from external pressures to be compromised;

    (b) do anything (for example accept a present) in such circumstances as may lead to any inference that his independence may be compromised;

    (c) compromise his professional standards in order to please his client the Court or a third party, including any mediator;

    (d) give a commission or present or lend any money for any professional purpose to or (save as a remuneration in accordance with the provisions of this Code) accept any money by way of loan or otherwise from any client or any person entitled to instruct him as an intermediary;

    (e) make any payment (other than a payment for advertising or publicity permitted by this Code or in the case of a barrister in independent practice remuneration paid to any clerk or other employee or staff of his chambers) to any person for the purpose of procuring professional instructions;

    (f) receive or handle client money securities or other assets other than by receiving payment of remuneration or (in the case of an employed barrister) where the money or other asset belongs to his employer.

PART IV—SELF-EMPLOYED BARRISTERS

Instructions

     401 A self-employed barrister whether or not he is acting for a fee:

    (a) may supply legal services only if appointed by the Court or is instructed:

        (i) by a professional client;

        (ii) by a licensed access client, in which case he must comply with the Licensed Access Rules (reproduced in Annex F1); or

        (iii) subject to paragraph 204(c), by or on behalf of any other lay client, in which cased he must comply with the Public Access Rules (reproduced in Annex F2); or

    (b) must not in the course of his practice:

        (i) undertake the management administration or general conduct of a lay client's affairs;

        (ii) conduct litigation or *inter-partes* work (for example the conduct of correspondence with an opposite party, instructing any expert witness or other person on behalf of his lay client or accepting personal liability for the payment of any such person);

        (iii) investigate or collect evidence for use in any Court;

        (iv) except as permitted by paragraph 707, or by the Public Access Rules take any proof of evidence in any criminal case;

(v) attend at a police station without the presence of a solicitor to advise a suspect or interviewee as to the handling and conduct of police interviews;

(vi) act as a supervisor for the purposes of section 84(2) of the *Immigration and Asylum Act* 1999.

Fees and remuneration

405 Subject to paragraph 307 a barrister in independent practice may charge for any work undertaken by him (whether or not it involves an appearance in Court) on any basis or by any method he thinks fit provided that such basis or method:

    (a) is permitted by law;

    (b) does not involve the payment of a wage or salary.

406.1 A self-employed barrister who receives fees in respect of work done by another barrister must himself and without delegating the responsibility to anyone else pay forthwith the whole of the fee in respect of that work to that other barrister.

406.2 Subject to paragraph 805 a self-employed barrister who arranges for another barrister to undertake work for him (other than a pupil or a person who has asked to do the work in order to increase his own skill or experience) must himself and without delegating the responsibility to anyone else:

    (a) pay proper financial remuneration for the work done;

    (b) make payment within a reasonable time and in any event within three months after the work has been done unless otherwise agreed in advance with the other barrister.

PART VI—ACCEPTANCE AND RETURN OF INSTRUCTIONS

Acceptance of instructions and the "Cab-rank rule"

601 A barrister who supplies advocacy services must not withhold those services:

    (a) on the ground that the nature of the case is objectionable to him or to any section of the public;

    (b) on the ground that the conduct opinions or beliefs of the prospective client are unacceptable to him or to any section of the public;

    (c) on any ground relating to the source of any financial support which may properly be given to the prospective client for the proceedings in question (for example, on the ground that such support will be available as part of the Community Legal Service or Criminal Defence Service).

602 A self-employed barrister must comply with the "Cab-rank rule" and accordingly except only as otherwise provided in paragraphs 603, 604, 605 and 606 he must in any field in which he professes to practise in relation to work appropriate to his experience and seniority and irrespective of whether his client is paying privately or is publicly funded:

    (a) accept any brief to appear before a Court in which he professes to practise;

    (b) accept any instructions;

    (c) act for any person on whose behalf he is instructed;

and do so irrespective of (i) the party on whose behalf he is instructed (ii) the nature of the case and (iii) any belief or opinion which he may have formed as to the character reputation cause conduct guilt or innocence of that person.

603 A barrister must not accept any instructions if to do so would cause him to be professionally embarrassed and for this purpose a barrister will be professionally embarrassed:

    (a) if he lacks sufficient experience or competence to handle the matter;

    (b) if having regard to his other professional commitments he will be unable to do or will not have adequate time and opportunity to prepare that which he is required to do;

(c) if the instructions seek to limit the ordinary authority or discretion of a barrister in the conduct of proceedings in Court or to require a barrister to act otherwise than in conformity with law or with the provisions of this Code;

(d) if the matter is one in which he has reason to believe that he is likely to be a witness or in which whether by reason of any connection with the client or with the Court or a member of it or otherwise it will be difficult for him to maintain professional independence or the administration of justice might be or appear to be prejudiced;

(e) if there is or appears to be a conflict or risk of conflict either between the interests of the barrister and some other person or between the interests of any one or more clients (unless all relevant persons consent to the barrister accepting the instructions);

(f) if there is a significant risk that information confidential to another client or former client might be communicated to or used for the benefit of anyone other than that client or former client without their consent;

(g) if he is a self-employed barrister where the instructions are delivered by a solicitor or firm of solicitors in respect of whom a Withdrawal of Credit Direction has been issued by the Chairman of the Bar pursuant to the Terms of Work on which Barristers Offer their Services to Solicitors and the Withdrawal of Credit Scheme 1988 as amended and in force from time to time (reproduced in Annex G1) unless his fees are paid directly by the Legal Services Commission or the instructions are accompanied by payment of an agreed fee or the barrister agrees in advance to accept no fee for such work or has obtained the consent of the Chairman of the Bar;

(h) if the barrister is instructed by or on behalf of a lay client who has not also instructed a solicitor or other professional client, and if the barrister is satisfied that it is in the interests of the client or in the interests of justice for the lay client to instruct a solicitor or other professional client.

604 Subject to paragraph 601 a self-employed barrister is not obliged to accept instructions:

(a) requiring him to do anything other than during the course of his ordinary working year;

(b) other than at a fee which is proper having regard to:

   (i) the complexity length and difficulty of the case;

   (ii) his ability experience and seniority; and

  (iii) the expenses which he will incur;

   and any instructions in a matter funded by the Legal Services Commission as part of the Community Legal Service or the Criminal Defence Service for which the amount or rate of the barrister's remuneration is prescribed by regulation or subject to assessment shall for this purpose unless the Bar Council or the Bar in general meeting otherwise determines (either in a particular case or in any class or classes of case or generally) be deemed to be at a proper professional fee;

(c) to do any work under a conditional fee agreement;

(d) save in a matter funded by the Legal Services Commission as part of the Community Legal Service or the Criminal Defence Service:

   (i) unless and until his fees are agreed;

   (ii) if having required his fees to be paid before he accepts the instructions those fees are not paid;

(e) from anyone other than a professional client who accepts liability for the barrister's fees;

(f) in a matter where the lay client is also the professional client;

(g) to do any work under the Contractual Terms on which Barristers offer their Services to Solicitors 2001 as amended and in force from time to time (reproduced in Appendix G2) or on any other contractual terms.

605 A self-employed Queen's Counsel is not obliged to accept instructions:

(a) to settle alone any document of a kind generally settled only by or in conjunction with a junior;

(b) to act without a junior if he considers that the interests of the lay client require that a junior should also be instructed.

606.1 A barrister (whether he is instructed on his own or with another advocate) must in the case of all instructions consider whether consistently with the proper and efficient administration of justice and having regard to:

(a) the circumstances (including in particular the gravity complexity and likely cost) of the case;

(b) the nature of his practice;

(c) his ability experience and seniority; and

(d) his relationship with the client;

the best interests of the client would be served by instructing or continuing to instruct him in that matter.

606.2 Where a barrister is instructed in any matter with another advocate or advocates the barrister must in particular consider whether it would be in the best interests of the client to instruct only one advocate or fewer advocates.

606.3 A barrister who in any matter is instructed either directly by the lay client or by an intermediary who is not a solicitor or other authorised litigator should consider whether it would be in the interests of the lay client or the interests of justice to instruct a solicitor or other authorised litigator or other appropriate intermediary either together with or in place of the barrister.

606.4 In cases involving several parties, a barrister must on receipt of instructions and further in the event of any change of circumstances consider whether, having regard to all the circumstances including any actual or potential conflict of interest, any client ought to be separately represented or advised or whether it would be in the best interests of any client to be jointly represented or advised with another party.

607 If at any time in any matter a barrister considers that it would be in the best interests of any client to have different representation, he must immediately so advise the client.

Withdrawal from a case and return to instructions

608 A barrister must cease to act and if he is a self-employed barrister must   **C–10**
return any instructions:

(a) if continuing to act would cause him to be professionally embarrassed within the meaning of paragraph 603 provided that if he would be professionally embarrassed only because it appears to him that he is likely to be a witness on a material question of fact he may retire or withdraw only if he can do so without jeopardising the client's interests;

(b) if having accepted instructions on behalf of more than one client there is or appears to be:

(i) a conflict or risk of conflict between the interests of any one or more of such clients; or

(ii) risk of a breach of confidence;

and the clients do not all consent to him continuing to act;

(c) if in any case funded by the Legal Services Commission as part of the Community Legal Service or Criminal Defence Service it has become apparent to him that such funding has been wrongly obtained by false or inaccurate information and action to remedy the situation is not immediately taken by the client;

(d) if the client refuses to authorise him to make some disclosure to the Court which his duty to the Court requires him to make;

(e) if having become aware during the course of a case of the existence of a document which should have been but has not been disclosed or discovery the client fails forthwith to disclose it;

(f) if having come into possession of a document belonging to another party by some means other than the normal and proper channels and having read it before he realises that it ought to have been returned unread to the person entitled to possession of it he would thereby be embarrassed in the discharge of his duties by his knowledge of the contents of the document provided that he may retire or withdraw only if he can do so without jeopardising the client's interests.

609 Subject to paragraph 610 a barrister may withdraw from a case where he is satisfied that:

(a) his instructions have been withdrawn;

(b) his professional conduct is being impugned;

(c) advice which he has given in accordance with paragraph 607 or 703 had not been heeded; or

(d) there is some other substantial reason for so doing.

610 A barrister must not:

(a) cease to act or return instructions without having first explained to the client his reasons for doing so;

(b) return instructions to another barrister without the consent of the client;

(c) return a brief which he has accepted and for which a fixed date has been obtained or (except with the consent of the lay client and where appropriate the Court) break any other engagement to supply legal services in the course of his practice so as to enable him to attend or fulfil an engagement (including a social or non-professional engagement) of any other kind;

(d) except as provided in paragraph 608 return any instructions or withdraw from a case in such a way or in such circumstances that the client may be unable to find other legal assistance in time to prevent prejudice being suffered by the client.

PART VII—CONDUCT OF WORK BY PRACTISING BARRISTERS

General

   701 A barrister:

(a) must in all his professional activities be courteous and act promptly conscientiously diligently and with reasonable competence and take all reasonable and practicable steps to avoid unnecessary expense or waste of the Court's time and to ensure that professional engagements are fulfilled;

(b) must not undertake any task which:

(i) he knows or ought to know he is not competent to handle;

(ii) he does not have adequate time and opportunity to prepare for or perform; or

(iii) he cannot discharge within the time requested or otherwise within a reasonable time having regard to the pressure of other work.

(c) must read all instructions delivered to him expeditiously;

(d) must have regard to any relevant Written Standards for the conduct of Professional Work issued by the Bar Council;

(e) must inform his client forthwith and subject to paragraph 610 return the instructions to the client or to another barrister acceptable to the client:

(i) if it becomes apparent to him that he will not be able to do the work within the time requested or within a reasonable time after receipt of instructions;

  (ii) if there is an appreciable risk that he may not be able to undertake a brief or fulfil any other professional engagement which he has accepted;

 (f) must ensure that adequate records supporting the fees charged or claimed in a case are kept at least until the last of the following: his fees have been paid, any taxation or determination or assessment of costs in the case has been completed, or the time for lodging an appeal against assessment or the determination of that appeal, has expired, and must provide his professional or licensed access client or other intermediary or the lay client with such records or details of the work done as may reasonably be required.

Confidentiality

702 Whether or not the relation of counsel and client continues a barrister must **C-12** preserve the confidentiality of the lay client's affairs and must not without the prior consent of the lay client or as permitted by law lend or reveal the contents of the papers in any instructions to or communicate to any third person (other than another barrister, a pupil, in the case of a Registered European Lawyer, the person with whom he is acting in conjunction for the purposes of paragraph 5(3) of the Registered European Lawyers Rules or any other person who needs to know it for the performance of their duties) information which has been entrusted to him in confidence or use such information to the lay client's detriment or to his own or another client's advantage.

Conflicts between lay clients and intermediaries

703 If a self-employed barrister forms the view that there is a conflict of interest **C-13** between his lay client and a professional client or other intermediary (for example because he considers that the intermediary may have been negligent) he must consider whether it would be in the lay client's interest to instruct another professional adviser or representative and, if he considers that it would be, the barrister must so advise and take such steps as he considers necessary to ensure that his advice is communicated to the lay client (if necessary by sending a copy of his advice in writing directly to the lay client as well as to the intermediary).

Drafting documents

704 A barrister must not devise facts which will assist in advancing the lay client's **C-14** case and must not draft any statement of case, witness statement, affidavit, notice of appeal or other document containing:

 (a) any statement of fact or contention which is not supported by the lay client or by his instructions;

 (b) any contention which he does not consider to be properly arguable;

 (c) any allegation of fraud unless he has clear instructions to make such allegation and has before him reasonably credible material which as it stands establishes a prima facie case of fraud;

 (d) in the case of a witness statement or affidavit any statement of fact other than the evidence which in substance according to his instructions the barrister reasonably believes the witness would give if the evidence contained in the witness statement or affidavit were being given in oral examination;

provided that nothing in this paragraph shall prevent a barrister drafting a document containing specific factual statements or contentions included by the barrister subject to confirmation of their accuracy by the lay client or witness.

Contact with witnesses

705 A barrister must not: **C-15**

    (a) rehearse practise or coach a witness in relation to his evidence;

    (b) encourage a witness to give evidence which is untruthful or which is not the whole truth;

    (c) except with the consent of the representative for the opposing side or of the Court, communicate directly or indirectly about a case with any witness, whether or not the witness is his lay client, once that witness has begun to give evidence until the evidence of that witness has been concluded.

Attendance of professional client

C–16

706 A self-employed barrister who is instructed by a professional client should not conduct a case in Court in the absence of his professional client or a representative of his professional client unless the Court rules that it is appropriate or he is satisfied that the interests of the lay client and the interests of justice will not be prejudiced.

707 A self-employed barrister who attends Court in order to conduct a case in circumstances where no professional client or representative of a professional client is present may if necessary interview witnesses and take proofs of evidence.

Conduct in Court

C–17

708 A barrister when conducting proceedings in Court:

    (a) is personally responsible for the conduct and presentation of his case and must exercise personal judgment upon the substance and purpose of statements made and questions asked;

    (b) must not unless invited to do so by the Court or when appearing before a tribunal where it is his duty to do so assert a personal opinion of the facts or the law;

    (c) must ensure that the Court is informed of all relevant decisions and legislative provisions of which he is aware whether the effect is favourable or unfavourable towards the contention for which he argues;

    (d) must bring any procedural irregularity to the attention of the Court during the hearing and not reserve such matter to be raised on appeal;

    (e) must not adduce evidence obtained otherwise than from or through the client or devise facts which will assist in advancing the lay client's case;

    (f) must not make a submission which he does not consider to be properly arguable;

    (g) must not make statements or ask questions which are merely scandalous or intended or calculated only to vilify insult or annoy either a witness or some other person;

    (h) must if possible avoid the naming in open Court of third parties whose character would thereby be impugned;

    (i) must not by assertion in a speech impugn a witness whom he has had an opportunity to cross-examine unless in cross-examination he has given the witness an opportunity to answer the allegation;

    (j) must not suggest that a victim, witness or other person is guilty of crime, fraud or misconduct or make any defamatory aspersion on the conduct of any other person or attribute to another person the crime or conduct of which his lay client is accused unless such allegations go to a matter in issue (including the credibility of the witness) which is material to the lay client's case and appear to him to be supported by reasonable grounds.

Media comment

C–18

709.1 A barrister must not in relation to any anticipated or current proceedings or mediation in which he is briefed or expects to appear or has appeared as an advocate express a personal opinion to or in the press or other media upon the facts of or the issues arising in the proceedings.

709.2 Paragraph 709.1 shall not prevent the expression of such an opinion on an issue in an educational or academic context.

Advertising and publicity

710.1 Subject to paragraph 710.2 a barrister may engage in any advertising or promotion in connection with his practice which conforms to the British Codes of Advertising and Sales Promotion and such advertising or promotion may include: **C–19**

  (a) photographs or other illustrations of the barrister;

  (b) statements of rates and methods of charging;

  (c) statements about the nature and extent of the barrister's services;

  (d) information about any case in which the barrister has appeared (including the name of any client for whom the barrister acted) where such information has already become publicly available or, where it has not already become publicly available, with the express prior written consent of the lay client.

710.2 Advertising or promotion must not:

  (a) be inaccurate or likely to mislead;

  (b) be likely to diminish public confidence in the legal profession or the administration of justice or otherwise bring the legal profession into disrepute;

  (c) make direct comparisons in terms of quality with or criticisms of other identifiable person (whether they be barristers or members of any other profession);

  (d) include statements about the barrister's success rate;

  (e) indicate or imply any willingness to accept instructions or any intention to restrict the persons from whom instructions may be accepted otherwise than in accordance with this Code;

  (f) be so frequent or obtrusive as to cause annoyance to those to whom it is directed.

II. BAR COUNCIL GUIDANCE

Written standards of work

The following standards have been issued by the Bar Council together with the eighth edition of the *Code of Conduct*. They do not form part of the code. Paragraph 701(d) of the code (*ante*, C–11) does, however, oblige a barrister to "have regard to any relevant Written Standards". **C–20**

WRITTEN STANDARDS FOR THE CONDUCT OF PROFESSIONAL WORK

GENERAL STANDARDS

1 Introduction

1.1 These Standards are intended as a guide to the way in which a barrister should carry out his work. They consist in part of matters which are dealt with expressly in the Code of Conduct and in part of statements of good practice. They must therefore be read in conjunction with the Code of Conduct, and are to be taken into account in determining whether or not a barrister has committed a disciplinary offence. They apply to employed barristers as well as to barristers in in- **C–21**

dependent practice, except where this would be inappropriate. In addition to these General Standards, there are Standards which apply specifically to the conduct of criminal cases.

2 General

C–22   **2.1** The work which is within the ordinary scope of a barrister's practice consists of advocacy, drafting pleadings and other legal documents and advising on questions of law. A barrister acts only on the instructions of a professional client, and does not carry out any work by way of the management, administration or general conduct of a lay client's affairs, nor the management, administration or general conduct of litigation nor the receipt or handling of clients' money.

2.2 It is a fundamental principle which applies to all work undertaken by a barrister that a barrister is under a duty to act for any client (whether legally aided or not) in cases within his field of practice. The rules which embody this principle and the exceptions to it are set out in paragraphs 303, 601, 602, 603, 604 and 605 of the Code of Conduct.

3 Acceptance of work

C–23   **3.1** As soon as practicable after receipt of any brief or instructions a barrister should satisfy himself that there is no reason why he ought to decline to accept it.

3.2 A barrister is not considered to have accepted a brief or instructions unless he has had an opportunity to consider it and has expressly accepted it.

3.3 A barrister should always be alert to the possibility of a conflict of interests. If the conflict is between the interests of his lay client and his professional client, the conflict must be resolved in favour of the lay client. Where there is a conflict between the lay client and the Legal Aid Fund, the conflict must be resolved in favour of the lay client, subject only to compliance with the provisions of the Legal Aid Regulations.

3.4 If after a barrister has accepted a brief or instructions on behalf of more than one lay client, there is or appears to be a conflict or a significant risk of a conflict between the interests of any one or more of such clients, he must not continue to act for any client unless all such clients give their consent to his so acting.

3.5 Even if there is no conflict of interest, when a barrister has accepted a brief or instructions for any party in any proceedings, he should not accept a brief or instructions in respect of an appeal or further stage of the proceedings for any other party without obtaining the prior consent of the original client.

3.6 A barrister must not accept any brief or instructions if the matter is one in which he has reason to believe that he is likely to be a witness. If, however, having accepted a brief or instructions, it later appears that he is likely to be a witness in the case on a material question of fact, he may retire or withdraw only if he can do so without jeopardising his client's interests.

3.7 A barrister should not appear as a barrister:

    (a) in any matter in which he is a party or has a significant pecuniary interest;

    (b) either for or against any local authority, firm or organisation of which he is a member or in which he has directly or indirectly a significant pecuniary interest;

    (c) either for or against any company of which he is a director, secretary or officer or in which he has directly or indirectly a significant pecuniary interest.

3.8 Apart from cases in which there is a conflict of interests, a barrister must not accept any brief or instructions if to do so would cause him to be otherwise professionally embarrassed: paragraph 603 of the Code of Conduct sets out the general principles applicable to such situations.

4 Withdrawal from a case and return of brief or instructions

C–24   **4.1** When a barrister has accepted a brief for the defence of a person charged

with a serious criminal offence, he should so far as reasonably practicable ensure that
the risk of a conflicting professional engagement does not arise.

4.2 The circumstances in which a barrister must withdraw from a case or return
his brief or instructions are set out in paragraph 608 of the Code of Conduct; the circumstances in which he is permitted to do so are set out in paragraph 609 the circumstances in which he must not do so are set out in paragraph 610.

5 Conduct of work

5.1 A barrister must at all times promote and protect fearlessly and by all proper
and lawful means his lay client's best interests.

5.2 A barrister must assist the Court in the administration of justice and, as part
of this obligation and the obligation to use only proper and lawful means to promote
and protect the interests of his client, must not deceive or knowingly or recklessly
mislead the Court.

5.3 A barrister is at all times individually and personally responsible for his own
conduct and for his professional work both in Court and out of Court.

5.4 A barrister must in all his professional activities act promptly, conscientiously,
diligently and with reasonable competence and must take all reasonable and
practicable steps to ensure that professional engagements are fulfilled. He must not
undertake any task which:

    (a) he knows or ought to know he is not competent to handle;

    (b) he does not have adequate time and opportunity to prepare for or
        perform; or

    (c) he cannot discharge within a reasonable time having regard to the pressure of other work.

5.5 A barrister must at all times be courteous to the Court and to all those with
whom he has professional dealings.

5.6 In relation to instructions to advise or draft documents, a barrister should
ensure that the advice or document is provided within such time as has been agreed
with the professional client, or otherwise within a reasonable time after receipt of the
relevant instructions. If it becomes apparent to the barrister that he will not be able
to do the work within that time, he must inform his professional client forthwith.

5.7 Generally, a barrister should ensure that advice which he gives is practical, appropriate to the needs and circumstances of the particular client, and clearly and
comprehensibly expressed.

5.8 A barrister must exercise his own personal judgment upon the substance and
purpose of any advice he gives or any document he drafts. He must not devise facts
which will assist in advancing his lay client's case and must not draft any originating
process, pleading, affidavit, witness statement or notice of appeal containing:

    (a) any statement of fact or contention (as the case may be) which is not supported by his lay client or by his brief or instructions;

    (b) any contention which he does not consider to be properly arguable;

    (c) any allegation of fraud unless he has clear instructions to make such an
        allegation and has before him reasonably credible material which as it
        stands establishes a prima facia case of fraud; or

    (d) in the case of an affidavit or witness statement, any statement of fact other
        than the evidence which in substance according to his instructions, the
        barrister reasonably believes the witness would give if the evidence
        contained in the affidavit or witness statement were being given *viva voce*.

5.9 A barrister should be available on reasonable notice for a conference prior to
the day of hearing of any case in which he is briefed; and if no such conference takes
place then the barrister should be available for a conference on the day of the
hearing. The venue of a conference is a matter for agreement between the barrister
and his professional clients.

5.10 A barrister when conducting proceedings at Court:

(a) is personally responsible for the conduct and presentation of his case and must exercise personal judgment upon the substance and purpose of statements made and questions asked;

(b) must not, unless asked to do so by the Court or when appearing before a tribunal where it his duty to do so, assert a personal opinion of the fact or the law;

(c) must ensure that the Court is informed of all relevant decisions and legislative provisions of which he is aware, whether the effect is favourable or unfavourable towards the contention for which he argues, and must bring any procedural irregularity to the attention of the Court during the hearing and not reserve such matter to be raised on appeal;

(d) must not adduce evidence obtained otherwise than from or through his professional client or devise facts which will assist in advancing his lay client's case;

(e) must not make statements or ask questions which are merely scandalous or intended or calculated only to vilify, insult or annoy either a witness or some other person;

(f) must if possible avoid the naming in open Court of third parties whose character would thereby be impugned;

(g) must not by assertion in a speech impugn a witness whom he has had an opportunity to cross-examine unless in cross-examination he has given the witness an opportunity to answer the allegation;

(h) must not suggest that a victim, witness or other person is guilty of crime, fraud or misconduct or make any defamatory aspersion on the conduct of any other person or attribute to another person the crime or conduct of which his lay client is accused unless such allegations go to a matter in issue (including the credibility of the witness) which is material to his lay client's case, and which appear to him to be supported by reasonable grounds.

5.11 A barrister must take all reasonable and practicable steps to avoid unnecessary expense or waste of the Court's time. He should, when asked, inform the Court of the probable length of his case; and he should also inform the Court of any developments which affect information already provided.

5.12 In Court a barrister's personal appearance should be decorous, and his dress, when robes are worn, should be compatible with them.

6.1 Witnesses

6.1.1 The rules which define and regulate the barrister's functions in relation to the preparation of evidence and contact with witnesses are set out in paragraph 704, 705, 706, 707 and 708 of the Code of Conduct.

6.1.2 There is no longer any rule which prevents a barrister from having contact with any witness.

6.1.3 In particular, there is no longer any rule in any case (including contested cases in the Crown Court) which prevents a barrister from having contact with a witness whom he may expect to call and examine in chief, with a view to introducing himself to the witness, explaining the court's procedure (and in particular the procedure for giving evidence), and answering any questions on procedure which the witness may have.

6.1.4 It is a responsibility of a barrister, especially when the witness is nervous, vulnerable or apparently the victim of criminal or similar conduct, to ensure that those facing unfamiliar court procedures are put as much at ease as possible.

6.1.5 Unless otherwise directed by the Court or with the consent of the representative for the opposing side or of the Court, a barrister should not communicate directly or indirectly about the case with any witness, whether or not the witness is his lay client, once that witness has begun to give evidence until it has been concluded.

6.2 Discussing the evidence with witnesses

6.2.1 Different considerations apply in relation to contact with witnesses for the   **C–27** purpose of interviewing them or discussing with them (either individually or together) the substance of their evidence or the evidence of other witnesses.

6.2.2 Although there is no longer any rule which prevents a barrister from having contact with witnesses for such purposes a barrister should exercise his discretion and consider very carefully whether and to what extent such contact is appropriate, bearing in mind in particular that it is not the barrister's function (but that of his professional client) to investigate and collect evidence.

6.2.3 The guiding principle must be the obligation of counsel to promote and protect his lay client's best interests so far as that is consistent with the law and with counsel's overriding duty to the court (Code of Conduct paragraphs 302, 303).

6.2.4 A barrister should be alert to the risks that any discussion of the substance of a case with a witness may lead to suspicions of coaching, and thus tend to diminish the value of the witness's evidence in the eyes of the court, or may place the barrister in a position of professional embarrassment, for example if he thereby becomes himself a witness in the case. These dangers are most likely to occur if such discussion takes place:

    (a) before the barrister has been supplied with a proof of the witness's evidence; or

    (b) in the absence of the barrister's professional client or his representative.

A barrister should also be alert to the fact that, even in the absence of any wish or intention to do so, authority figures do subconsciously influence lay witnesses. Discussion of the substance of the case may unwittingly contaminate the witness's evidence.

6.2.5 There is particular danger where such discussions:

    (a) take place in the presence of more than one witness of fact; or

    (b) involve the disclosure to one witness of fact of the factual evidence of another witness.

These practices have been strongly deprecated by the courts as tending inevitably to encourage the rehearsal or coaching of witnesses and to increase the risk of fabrication or contamination of evidence: *R. v. Arif* (1993) May 26; *Smith New Court Securities Ltd v. Scrimgeour Vickers (Asset Management) Ltd* [1992] B.C.L.C. 1104, [1994] 1 W.L.R. 1271.

That is not to suggest that it is always inappropriate to disclose one witness' evidence to another. If the witness is one to be called by the other party, it is almost inevitable that a witness' attention must be drawn to discrepancies between the two statements. Discretion is, however, required, especially where the evidence of independent witnesses is involved.

6.2.6 Whilst there is no rule that any longer prevents a barrister from taking a witness statement in civil cases (for cases in the Crown Court see below), there is a distinction between the settling of a witness statement and taking a witness statement. It is not appropriate for a barrister who has taken witness statements, as opposed to settling witness statements prepared by others, to act as counsel unless he is a junior member of the team of counsel and will not be examining the witness or there are exceptional circumstances, because it risks undermining the independence of the barrister as an advocate. Exceptional circumstances would include:

    (a) the witness is a minor one;

    (b) counsel has no choice but to take a proof and this is the only practical course in the interests of justice—this would apply, for instance, where a witness appears unexpectedly at Court and there is no one else competent to take the statement.

The Cab-rank Rule does not require a barrister to agree to undertake the task of taking witness statements.

6.2.7 There is no rule which prevents a barrister from exchanging common courtesies with the other side's witnesses. However, a barrister should not discuss the substance of the case or any evidence with the other side's witnesses except in rare and exceptional circumstances and then only with the prior knowledge of his opponent.

6.3 Criminal cases in the Crown Court

C-28
6.3.1 Contested criminal cases in the Crown Court present peculiar difficulties and may expose both barristers and witnesses to special pressures. As a general principle, therefore, with the exception of the lay client, character and expert witnesses, subject to 6.3.2 it is wholly inappropriate for a barrister in such a case to interview any potential witness. Interviewing includes discussing with any such witness the substance of his evidence or the evidence of other such witnesses.

6.3.2 Prosecution counsel may, if instructed to do so, interview potential witnesses for the purposes of, and in accordance with, the practice set out in the Code for Pre-Trial Witness Interviews.

6.3.3 There may be extraordinary circumstances in which a departure from the general principles set out in paragraphs 6.3.1 and 6.3.2 is unavoidable. An example of such circumstances is afforded by the decision in *Fergus* (1994) 98 Cr.App.R. 313.

6.3.4 Where any barrister has interviewed any potential witness or any such witness has been interviewed by another barrister, that fact shall be disclosed to all other parties in the case before the witness is called. A written record must also be made of the substance of the interview and the reason for it.

7 Documents

C-29
7.1 A barrister should not obtain or seek to obtain a document, or knowledge of the contents of a document, belonging to another party other than by means of the normal and proper channels for obtaining such documents or such knowledge.

7.2 If a barrister comes into possession of a document belonging to another party by some means other than the normal and proper channels (for example, if the document has come into his possession in consequence of a mistake or inadvertence by another person or if the document appears to belong to another party, or to be a copy of such a document, and to be privileged from discovery or otherwise to be one which ought not to be in the possession of his professional or lay client) he should:

    (a) where appropriate make enquiries of his professional client in order to ascertain the circumstances in which the document was obtained by his professional or lay client; and

    (b) unless satisfied that the document has been properly obtained in the ordinary course of events at once return the document unread to the person entitled to possession of it.

7.3.1 If having come into possession of such document the barrister reads it before he realises that he ought not to, and would be embarrassed in the discharge of his duties by his knowledge of the contents of the document, then provided he can do so without prejudice to his lay client he must return his brief or instructions and explain to his professional client why he has done so.

7.3.2 If, however, to return his brief or instructions would prejudice his lay client (for example, by reason of the proximity of the trial) he should not return his brief or instructions and should, unless the Court otherwise orders, make such use of the document as will be in his client's interests. He should inform his opponent of his knowledge of the document and of the circumstances, so far as known to him, in which the document was obtained and of his intention to use it. In the event of objection to the use of such document it is for the Court to determine what use, if any, may be made of it.

7.4 If during the course of a case a barrister becomes aware of the existence of a document which should have been but has not been disclosed on discovery he should advise his professional client to disclose it forthwith; and if it is not then disclosed, he must withdraw from the case.

8 Administration of practice

C-30
8.1 A barrister must ensure that his practice is properly and efficiently

administered in accordance with the provisions of paragraph 304 of the Code of Conduct.

8.2 A barrister should ensure that he is able to provide his professional client with full and proper details of and appropriate justification for fees which have been incurred, and a proper assessment of any work to be done, so that both the lay client and the professional client are able to determine the level of any financial commitment which has been incurred or may be incurred.

[The next paragraph is C–32.]

STANDARDS APPLICABLE TO CRIMINAL CASES

9 Introduction

9.1 These standards are to be read together with the General Standards and the Code of Conduct. They are intended as a guide to those matters which specifically relate to practice in the criminal Courts. They are not an alternative to the General Standards, which apply to all work carried out by a barrister. Particular reference is made to those paragraphs in the General Standards relating to the general conduct of a case (5.8), conduct in Court (5.10), discussion with witnesses (6.1, 6.2) and the use of documents belonging to other parties (7.1, 7.2, 7.3), which are not repeated in these standards.   **C–32**

10 Responsibilities of prosecuting counsel

10A The Standards and principles contained in this paragraph apply as appropriate to all practising barristers, whether in independent practice or employed and whether appearing as counsel in any given case or exercising any other professional capacity in connection with it.   **C–33**

10.1 Prosecuting counsel should not attempt to obtain a conviction by all means at his command. He should not regard himself as appearing for a party. He should lay before the Court fairly and impartially the whole of the facts which comprise the case for the prosecution and should assist the Court on all matters of law applicable to the case.

10.2 Prosecuting counsel should bear in mind at all times whilst he is instructed:

(i) that he is responsible for the presentation and general conduct of the case;

(ii) that he should use his best endeavours to ensure that all evidence or material that ought properly to be made available is either presented by the prosecution or disclosed to the defence.

10.3 Prosecuting counsel should, when instructions are delivered to him, read them expeditiously and, where instructed to do so, advise or confer on all aspects of the case well before its commencement.

10.4 In relation to cases tried in the Crown Court, prosecuting counsel:

(a) should ensure, if he is instructed to settle an indictment, that he does so promptly and within due time, and should bear in mind the desirability of not overloading an indictment with either too many defendants or too many counts, in order to present the prosecution case as simply and as concisely as possible;

(b) should ask, if the indictment is being settled by some other person, to see a copy of the indictment and should then check it;

(c) should decide whether any additional evidence is required and, if it is, should advise in writing and set out precisely what additional evidence is required with a view to serving it on the defence as soon as possible;

    (d) should consider whether all witness statements in the possession of the prosecution have been properly served on the defendant in accordance with the Attorney-General's Guidelines;

    (e) should eliminate all unnecessary material in the case so as to ensure an efficient and fair trial, and in particular should consider the need for particular witnesses and exhibits and draft appropriate admissions for service on the defence;

    (f) should in all Class 1 and Class 2 cases and in other cases of complexity draft a case summary for transmission to the Court.

10.5 Paragraphs 6 to 6.3.4 of the Written Standards for the Conduct of Professional Work refer.

10.6 Prosecuting counsel should at all times have regard to the report of Mr Justice Farquharson's Committee on the role of Prosecuting Counsel which is set out in *Archbold*. In particular, he should have regard to the following recommendations of the Farquharson Committee:

    (a) where counsel has taken a decision on a matter of policy with which his professional client has not agreed, it would be appropriate for him to submit to the Attorney-General a written report of all the circumstances, including his reasons for disagreeing with those who instructed him;

    (b) when counsel has had an opportunity to prepare his brief and to confer with those instructing him, but at the last moment before trial unexpectedly advises that the case should not proceed or that pleas to lesser offences should be accepted, and his professional client does not accept such advice, counsel should apply for an adjournment if instructed to do so;

    (c) subject to the above, it is for prosecuting counsel to decide whether to offer no evidence on a particular count or on the indictment as a whole and whether to accept pleas to a lesser count or counts.

10.7 It is the duty of prosecuting counsel to assist the Court at the conclusion of the summing-up by drawing attention to any apparent errors or omissions of fact or law.

10.8 In relation to sentence, prosecuting counsel:

    (a) should not attempt by advocacy to influence the Court with regard to sentence: if, however, a defendant is unrepresented it is proper to inform the Court of any mitigating circumstances about which counsel is instructed;

    (b) should be in a position to assist the Court if requested as to any statutory provisions relevant to the offence or the offender and as to any relevant guidelines as to sentence laid down by the Court of Appeal;

    (c) should bring any such matters as are referred to in (b) above to the attention of the Court if in the opinion of prosecuting counsel the Court has erred;

    (d) should bring to the attention of the Court any appropriate compensation, forfeiture and restitution matters which may arise on conviction, for example pursuant to sections 35–42 of the *Powers of Criminal Courts Act* 1973 and the *Drug Trafficking Offences Act* 1986;

    (e) should draw the attention of the defence to any assertion of material fact made in mitigation which the prosecution believes to be untrue: if the defence persist in that assertion, prosecuting counsel should invite the Court to consider requiring the issue to be determined by the calling of evidence in accordance with the decision of the Court of Appeal in *R. v. Newton* (1983) 77 Crim.App.R. 13.

11 Responsibilities of defence counsel

11.1 When defending a client on a criminal charge, a barrister must endeavour to protect his client from conviction except by a competent tribunal and upon legally admissible evidence sufficient to support a conviction for the offence charged.

11.2 A barrister acting for the defence:

(a) should satisfy himself, if he is briefed to represent more than one defendant, that no conflict of interest is likely to arise;

(b) should arrange a conference and if necessary a series of conferences with his professional and lay clients;

(c) should consider whether any enquiries or further enquiries are necessary and, if so, should advise in writing as soon as possible;

(d) should consider whether any witnesses for the defence are required and, if so, which;

(e) should consider whether a Notice of Alibi is required and, if so, should draft an appropriate notice;

(f) should consider whether it would be appropriate to call expert evidence for the defence and, if so, have regard to the rules of the Crown Court in relation to notifying the prosecution of the contents of the evidence to be given;

(g) should ensure that he has sufficient instructions for the purpose of deciding which prosecution witnesses should be cross-examined, and should then ensure that no other witnesses remain fully bound at the request of the defendant and request his professional client to inform the Crown Prosecution Service of those who can be conditionally bound;

(h) should consider whether any admissions can be made with a view to saving time and expense at trial, with the aim of admitting as much evidence as can properly be admitted in accordance with the barrister's duty to his client;

(i) should consider what admissions can properly be requested from the prosecution;

(j) should decide what exhibits, if any, which have not been or cannot be copied he wishes to examine, and should ensure that appropriate arrangements are made to examine them as promptly as possible so that there is no undue delay in the trial.

(k) should as to anything which he is instructed to submit in mitigation which casts aspersions on the conduct or character of a victim or witness in the case, notify the prosecution in advance so as to give prosecuting Counsel sufficient opportunity to consider his position under paragraph 10.8(e).

11.3 A barrister acting for a defendant should advise his lay client generally about his plea. In doing so he may, if necessary, express his advice in strong terms. He must, however, make it clear that the client has complete freedom of choice and that the responsibility for the plea is the client's.

11.4 A barrister acting for a defendant should advise his client as to whether or not to give evidence in his own defence but the decision must be taken by the client himself.

11.5.1 Where a defendant tells his counsel that he did not commit the offence with which he is charged but nevertheless insists on pleading guilty to it for reasons of his own, counsel should:

(a) advise the defendant that, if he is not guilty, he should plead not guilty but that the decision is one for the defendant; counsel must continue to represent him but only after he has advised what the consequences will be and that what can be submitted in mitigation can only be on the basis that the client is guilty;

(b) explore with the defendant why he wishes to plead guilty to a charge which he says he did not commit and whether any steps could be taken which would enable him to enter a plea of not guilty in accordance with his profession of innocence.

11.5.2 If the client maintains his wish to plead guilty, he should be further advised:

(a) what the consequences will be, in particular in gaining or adding to a criminal record and that it is unlikely that a conviction based on such a plea would be overturned on appeal;

(b) that what can be submitted on his behalf in mitigation can only be on the basis that he is guilty and will otherwise be strictly limited so that, for instance, counsel will not be able to assert that the defendant has shown remorse through his guilty plea.

11.5.3 If, following all of the above advice, the defendant persists in his decision to plead guilty

(a) counsel may continue to represent him if he is satisfied that it is proper to do so;

(b) before a plea of guilty is entered counsel or a representative of his professional client who is present should record in writing the reasons for the plea;

(c) the defendant should be invited to endorse a declaration that he has given unequivocal instructions of his own free will that he intends to plead guilty even though he maintains that he did not commit the offence(s) and that he understands the advice given by counsel and in particular the restrictions placed on counsel in mitigating and the consequences to himself; the defendant should also be advised that he is under no obligation to sign; and

(d) if no such declaration is signed, counsel should make a contemporaneous note of his advice.

12 Confessions of guilt

C–35   **12.1** In considering the duty of counsel retained to defend a person charged with an offence who confesses to his counsel that he did commit the offence charged, it is essential to bear the following points clearly in mind:

(a) that every punishable crime is a breach of common or statute law committed by a person of sound mind and understanding;

(b) that the issue in a criminal trial is always whether the defendant is guilty of the offence charged, never whether he is innocent;

(c) that the burden of proof rests on the prosecution.

12.2 It follows that the mere fact that a person charged with a crime has confessed to his counsel that he did commit the offence charged is no bar to that barrister appearing or continuing to appear in his defence, nor indeed does such a confession release the barrister from his imperative duty to do all that he honourably can for his client.

12.3 Such a confession, however, imposes very strict limitations on the conduct of the defence, a barrister must not assert as true that which he knows to be false. He must not connive at, much less attempt to substantiate, a fraud.

12.4 While, therefore, it would be right to take any objections to the competency of the Court, to the form of the indictment, to the admissibility of any evidence or to the evidence admitted, it would be wrong to suggest that some other person had committed the offence charged, or to call any evidence which the barrister must know to be false having regard to the confession, such, for instance, as evidence in support of an alibi. In other words, a barrister must not (whether by calling the defendant or otherwise) set up an affirmative case inconsistent with the confession made to him.

12.5 A more difficult question is within what limits may counsel attack the evidence for the prosecution either by cross-examination or in his speech to the tribunal charged with the decision of the facts. No clearer rule can be laid down than this that he is entitled to test the evidence given by each individual witness and to argue that the evidence taken as a whole is insufficient to amount to proof that the defendant is guilty of the offence charged. Further than this he ought not to go.

12.6 The foregoing is based on the assumption that the defendant has made a clear confession that he did commit the offence charged, and does not profess to deal with the very difficult questions which may present themselves to a barrister when a series of inconsistent statements are made to him by the defendant before or during the proceedings; nor does it deal with the questions which may arise where statements are made by the defendant which point almost irresistibly to the conclusion that the defendant is guilty but do not amount to a clear confession. Statements of this kind may inhibit the defence, but questions arising on them can only be answered after careful consideration of the actual circumstances of the particular case.

13 General

13.1 Both prosecuting and defence counsel: **C–36**

(a) should ensure that the listing officer receives in good time their best estimate of the likely length of the trial (including whether or not there is to be a plea of guilty) and should ensure that the listing officer is given early notice of any change of such estimate or possible adjournment;

(b) should take all reasonable and practicable steps to ensure that the case is properly prepared and ready for trial by the time that it is first listed;

(c) should ensure that arrangements have been made in adequate time for witnesses to attend Court as and when required and should plan, so far as possible, for sufficient witnesses to be available to occupy the full Court day;

(d) should, if a witness (for example a doctor) can only attend Court at a certain time during the trial without great inconvenience to himself, try to arrange for that witness to be accommodated by raising the matter with the trial Judge and with his opponent;

(e) should take all necessary steps to comply with the *Practice Direction (Crime: Tape Recording of Police Interviews)* [1989] 1 W.L.R. 631.

13.2 If properly remunerated (paragraph 502 of the Code), the barrister originally briefed in a case should attend all plea and directions hearings. If this is not possible, he must take all reasonable steps to ensure that the barrister who does appear is conversant with the case and is prepared to make informed decisions affecting the trial.

14 Video recordings

14.1 When a barrister instructed and acting for the prosecution or the defence of   **C–37** an accused has in his possession a copy of a video recording of a child witness which has been identified as having been prepared to be admitted in evidence at a criminal trial in accordance with section 54 of the *Criminal Justice Act* 1991, he must have regard to the following duties and obligations:

(a) Upon receipt of the recording, a written record of the date and time and from whom the recording was received must be made and a receipt must be given.

(b) The recording and its contents must be used only for the proper preparation of the prosecution or defence case or of an appeal against conviction and/or sentence, as the case may be, and the barrister must not make or permit any disclosure of the recording or its contents to any person except when, in his opinion, it is in the interests of his proper preparation of that case.

(c) The barrister must not make or permit any other person to make a copy of the recording, nor release the recording to the accused, and must ensure that:

(i) when not in transit or in use, the recording is always kept in a locked or secure place, and;

481

    (ii) when in transit, the recording is kept safe and secure at all times and is not left unattended, especially in vehicles or otherwise.

(d) Proper preparation of the case may involve viewing the recording in the presence of the accused. If this is the case, viewing should be done:

    (i) if the accused is in custody, only in the prison or other custodial institution where he is being held, in the presence of the barrister and/or his instructing solicitor;

    (ii) if the accused is on bail, at the solicitor's office or in counsel's chambers or elsewhere in the presence of the barrister and/or his instructing solicitor.

(e) The recording must be returned to the solicitor as soon as practicable after the conclusion of the barrister's role in the case. A written record of the date and time despatched and to whom the recording was delivered for despatch must be made.

15 Attendance of counsel at court

15.1 Prosecuting counsel should be present throughout the trial, including the summing-up and the return of the jury. He may not absent himself without leave of the Court; but, if two or more barristers appear for the prosecution, the attendance of one is sufficient.

15.2.1 Defence counsel should ensure that the defendant is never left unrepresented at any stage of his trial.

15.2.2 Where a defendant is represented by one barrister, that barrister should normally be present throughout the trial and should only absent himself in exceptional circumstances which he could not reasonably be expected to foresee and provided that:

(a) he has obtained the consent of the professional client (or his representative) and the lay client; and

(b) a competent deputy takes his place.

15.2.3 Where a defendant is represented by two barristers, neither may absent himself except for good reason and then only when the consent of the professional client (or his representative) and of the lay client has been obtained, or when the case is legally aided and the barrister thinks it necessary to do so in order to avoid unnecessary public expense.

15.2.4 These rules are subject to modification in respect of lengthy trials involving numerous defendants. In such trials, where after the conclusion of the opening speech by the prosecution defending counsel is satisfied that during a specific part of the trial there is no serious possibility that events will occur which will relate to his client, he may with the consent of the professional client (or his representative) and of the lay client absent himself for that part of the trial. He should also inform the judge. In this event it is his duty:

(a) to arrange for other defending counsel to guard the interests of his client;

(b) to keep himself informed throughout of the progress of the trial and in particular of any development which could affect his client; and

(c) not to accept any other commitment which would render it impracticable for him to make himself available at reasonable notice if the interests of his client so require.

15.3.1 If during the course of a criminal trial and prior to final sentence the defendant voluntarily absconds and the barrister's professional client, in accordance with the ruling of the Law Society, withdraws from the case, then the barrister too should withdraw. If the trial judge requests the barrister to remain to assist the Court, the barrister has an absolute discretion whether to do so or not. If he does remain, he should act on the basis that his instructions are withdrawn and he will not be entitled to use any material contained in this brief save for such part as has already been established in evidence before the Court. He should request the trial judge to instruct the jury that this is the basis on which he is prepared to assist the Court.

15.3.2 If for any reason the barrister's professional client does not withdraw from the case, the barrister retains an absolute discretion whether to continue to act. If he does continue, he should conduct the case as if his client were still present in Court but had decided not to give evidence and on the basis of any instruction he has received. He will be free to use any material contained in his brief and may cross-examine witnesses called for the prosecution and call witnesses for the defence.

16 Appeals

16.1.1 Attention is drawn to the Guide to Proceedings in the Court of Appeal Criminal Division ("the Guide") which is set out in full [in Appendix J, *post*].

16.1.2 In particular when advising after a client pleads guilty or is convicted, defence counsel is encouraged to follow the procedures set out at paragraphs 1.2 and 1.4 of the Guide.

16.2 If his client pleads guilty or is convicted, defence counsel should see his client after he has been sentenced in the presence of his professional client or his representative. He should then proceed as follows:

(a) if he is satisfied that there are no reasonable grounds of appeal he should so advise orally and certify in writing. Counsel is encouraged to certify using the form set out in Appendix 1 to the Guide. No further advice is necessary unless it is reasonable for a written advice to be given because the client reasonably requires it or because it is necessary e.g. in the light of the circumstances of the conviction, any particular difficulties at trial, the length and nature of the sentence passed, the effect thereof on the defendant or the lack of impact which oral advice given immediately after the trial may have on the particular defendant's mind.

(b) If he is satisfied that there are more reasonable grounds of appeal or if his view is a provisional one or if he requires more time to consider the prospects of a successful appeal he should so advise orally and certify in writing. Counsel is encouraged to certify using the form set out in Appendix 1 to the Guide. Counsel should then furnish written advice to the professional client as soon as he can and in any event within 14 days.

16.3 Counsel should not settle grounds of appeal unless he considers that such grounds are properly arguable, and in that event he should provide a reasoned written opinion in support of such grounds.

16.4 In certain cases counsel may not be able to perfect grounds of appeal without a transcript or other further information. In this event the grounds of appeal should be accompanied by a note to the Registrar setting out the matters on which assistance is required. Once such transcript or other information is available, counsel should ensure that the grounds of appeal are perfected by the inclusion of all necessary references.

16.5 Grounds of Appeal must be settled with sufficient particularity to enable the Registrar and subsequently the Court to identify clearly the matters relied upon.

16.6 If at any stage counsel is of the view that the appeal should be abandoned, he should at once set out his reasons in writing and send them to his professional client.

Service standards on returned briefs agreed with the CPS

The following standards agreed in 1996 have been issued by the Bar Council. They do not form part of the *Code of Conduct*.

SERVICE STANDARDS ON RETURNED BRIEFS AGREED WITH THE CPS

SERVICE STANDARD ON RETURNED BRIEFS

1 PRINCIPLE

C–41   **1.1** This Standard applies to all advocates instructed to prosecute on behalf of the CPS.

1.2 The fundamental principle upon which the Standard is based is that the advocate initially instructed should conduct the case.

1.3 This applies to all cases irrespective of whether or not they are contested.

1.4 For the purpose of this Standard a return means a brief which is passed to another advocate because the advocate instructed is unable to appear to represent the prosecution at any hearing, subject to the exceptions for interlocutory hearings referred to in paragraphs 1.13–1.15 below.

1.5 There is a need for positive action to be taken by all advocates, acting in conjunction with the CPS, to minimise the level of returns in order to ensure that the best possible service is provided. Such action will include ensuring that the advocate's availability is considered when cases are being fixed and that efforts are made to take this into account.

1.6 Whatever positive action is taken to reduce the level of returns, it is recognised that there will always be some briefs which are returned.

1.7 The impact of a return is dependent upon the nature of the case and the timing of its return.

1.8 There will be some degree of flexibility in uncontested cases in that the acceptability of the return will be influenced by the nature, complexity and seriousness of the case and the degree of involvement of the advocate before committal or transfer.

1.9 Where a return is unavoidable, the advocate will be responsible for ensuring that immediate notice is given to enable the CPS to choose and instruct another advocate and for that advocate fully to prepare the case.

1.10 Special attention must be paid to retrials, sensitive cases or those involving vulnerable witnesses, especially children, and those cases in which the advocate has settled the indictment, provided a substantive advice, attended a conference or been present at an *ex parte* hearing.

1.11 The advocate prosecuting a case in which the brief has been returned should not, without good reason and prior consultation with the CPS, reverse a decision previously taken by the advocate originally instructed. This is especially important in cases involving child witnesses and video evidence.

1.12 Whenever a brief is returned, the choice of an alternative advocate will always be a matter for the CPS. Where counsel has been instructed, the availability of alternative counsel in the chambers holding the brief will not be the determining factor in selecting a new advocate. Counsel's clerk will be expected to make realistic proposals as to an alternative advocate, whether or not within the same chambers, and consideration will be given to them.

1.13 When the CPS instructs an advocate to appear at an interlocutory hearing, including plea and directions hearings (PDH), bail applications, applications to make or break fixtures and mentions, the advocate instructed in the case will, wherever practicable, be expected to attend. If the advocate instructed is not available, an alternative advocate may be instructed provided that advocate is acceptable to the CPS and following consultation with the CPS.

1.14 If an advocate is unable to attend a PDH as a result of work commitments elsewhere, a returned brief will not be treated as a return for the purpose of monitoring compliance with this Standard, unless the advocate's clerk was consulted

484

about, and had confirmed, the advocate's availability for the PDH before the brief was delivered.

1.15 In the case of other interlocutory hearings, which may be potentially difficult or sensitive, the CPS will, whenever possible, consult the advocate's clerk about the advocate's availability before the date of hearing is arranged. Unless such consultation has taken place, a returned brief will not be counted as a return for the purpose of monitoring compliance with this Standard.

1.16 Following any interlocutory hearing, the brief will revert to the advocate originally instructed, subject to the CPS exercising its discretion to depart from this practice in any particular case.

1.17 In any case in which a brief is returned, and whatever the nature of the hearing, it will be the responsibility of the advocate holding the brief to ensure that the advocate to whom the brief is returned is fully informed of all matters relating to that hearing and, *where practicable*, to endorse the brief accordingly.

1.18 Notwithstanding the responsibility resting with the advocate returning the brief, the advocate accepting the brief also has a duty to be fully prepared to deal with any matter likely to arise at the hearing.

1.19 Subject to any other agreement negotiated with the CPS on the transfer of papers between advocates, whenever a brief is returned it will be the responsibility of the advocate or the advocate's clerk holding the brief to make arrangements to transfer the brief promptly to the agreed alternative advocate.

1.20 Neither the advocate nor the advocate's clerk should permit the number of briefs held by a single advocate to reach a point where returns are inevitable. The CPS must be informed if it appears that this situation might arise.

1.21 The CPS will make arrangements for the distribution of work to individual advocates so as to minimise the possibility of this happening.

2 GUIDANCE

2.1 Recommendations and guidance on counsel's responsibilities in relation to returned briefs have been given in the following reports: **C–42**

Seabrook Report on the Efficient Disposal of Business in the Crown Court—June 1992.
- Counsel should ensure that the CPS is notified as soon as he or his clerk knows he might have to return a brief due to other professional commitments.
- Counsel should ensure that immediate steps are taken to return a brief to another barrister acceptable to the CPS as soon as he or his clerk becomes aware that he will not be able to conduct the case.

Bar Standards Review Body Report—Blueprint for the Bar—September 1994.
- Counsel should provide written reasons upon request as to why a brief is returned.
- Counsel returning a brief should do so with as little disruption to the conduct of the case as practicable. This involves the provision of information to counsel taking on the case.

2.2 It is against this background that the procedures which follow have been developed.

3 PROCEDURE

Categorisation of cases

3.1 For the purpose of setting standards aimed at reducing the level of returns cases will fall within 3 categories.   **C–43**

3.2 Category A will comprise the following:
- cases in which the fees will be assessed *ex post facto*;
- pre-marked cases in which a Grade 4 Advocate or Special List Advocate (London and South Eastern Circuit) is instructed;

- cases in which Leading Counsel (including a Leading Junior) has been instructed by the CPS;
- cases falling within classes 1 and 2 of the Lord Chief Justice's Practice Direction classifying business within the Crown Court.

3.3 In category A cases no return of the brief is acceptable save where the following applies:

- the advocate is unable to attend court because of illness, accident, childbirth or unexpected incapacity;
- attending court would cause the advocate grave personal hardship as, for example, following a bereavement;
- subject to paragraph 3.8 below, circumstances have arisen outside the advocate's, or the advocate's clerk's, control which are such as to make a return inevitable;
- the case has been fixed for trial by the court in the knowledge that the advocate instructed will not be available.

3.4 Where a case has been so fixed, the CPS will decide whether to apply to the court to change the fixed date or to instruct a different advocate.

3.5 Category B will comprise cases in which the brief has been pre-marked and which do not fall within category A, and standard fee cases in which a fixed trial date has been allocated.

3.6 If a trial date has been fixed, no return of the trial brief is acceptable except as in 3.3 above.

3.7 If a trial date has been fixed before the brief is delivered, or has been fixed regardless of the advocate's availability, immediate steps will be taken by the CPS in liaison with the advocate or the advocate's clerk, to identify an appropriate advocate who will be available on the fixed date. Once the brief has been delivered or reallocated, no return is acceptable.

3.8 The advocate's involvement in a part-heard trial will not in itself justify a return in a category A or B case, unless the part-heard trial has been prolonged by unforeseeable circumstances. Where the advocate is involved in a part-heard trial, the position must be kept under constant review, and the CPS kept fully informed, so that an early decision can be made by the CPS as to whether to require a brief to be returned.

3.9 If a brief in a category A or B case is returned, the advocate will, upon CPS request, provide a written explanation as to why the return was unavoidable.

3.10 Category C will comprise standard fee cases which have not been given fixed trial dates.

3.11 It is recognised that, for cases which attract standard fees, a higher return rate is more difficult to avoid.

3.12 Subject to the requirements of Bar/CPS Standard 2 on pre-trial preparation having been carried out, if the advocate originally instructed in a category C case is not available, the CPS will agree to the brief being returned to another advocate of appropriate experience, who has adequate time to prepare for the hearing.

General procedural matters

C–44   **3.13** If a case appears in a warned list or firm date list and the advocate instructed will not be available, the advocate or the advocate's clerk must notify the CPS immediately.

3.14 The CPS will then decide whether to make representations to the court to take the case out of the list, or to allow the brief to be returned to another advocate.

3.15 Where a case has appeared in a reserve list, or where a system of overnight listing operates within the warned list, it is accepted that some returns will be inevitable.

3.16 The advocate or the advocate's clerk should give as much notice as possible of returns in these instances and should aim to give the CPS **two working days notice**. This situation could apply, for example, when an advocate becomes committed part way through the week to a case expected to last several days.

3.17 Where a system of firm dates operates within the warned list period, the CPS must be notified if it appears likely that the advocate may be unavailable, so that an early decision can be made on whether to instruct another advocate or whether to defer the decision.

3.18 The timing of the decision whether to instruct another advocate will always be a matter for the CPS and will be influenced by the nature of the case as well as the information provided by the advocate or the advocate's clerk.

August 1996

Criticism of previous counsel

In consequence of observations made by the Court of Appeal in *R. v. Clarke* **C–45** *and Jones, The Times,* August 19, 1994, and *R. v. Bowler, The Times,* May 9, 1995, the following guidance has been approved by Lord Taylor C.J. and the Bar Council.

1. Allegations against former counsel may receive substantial publicity whether accepted or rejected by the court. Counsel should not settle or sign grounds of appeal unless he is satisfied that they are reasonable, have some real prospect of success and are such that he is prepared to argue before the court (Guide to Proceedings in the Court of Appeal Criminal Division, para. 2.4 [§ 7–165 in the mainwork]). When such allegations are properly made however, in accordance with the Code of Conduct counsel newly instructed must promote and protect fearlessly by all proper and lawful means his lay client's best interests without regard to others, including fellow members of the legal profession (Code, para. 303(a)).

2. When counsel newly instructed is satisfied that such allegations are made, and a waiver of privilege is necessary, he should advise the lay client fully about the consequences of waiver and should obtain a waiver of privilege in writing signed by the lay client relating to communications with, instructions given to and advice given by former counsel. The allegations should be set out in the Grounds of Application for Leave of Appeal. Both waiver and grounds should be lodged without delay; the grounds may be perfected if necessary in due course.

3. On receipt of the waiver and grounds, the registrar of Criminal Appeals will send both to former counsel with an invitation on behalf of the court to respond to the allegations made.

4. If former counsel wishes to respond and considers the time for doing so insufficient, he should ask the Registrar for further time. The court will be anxious to have full information and to give counsel adequate time to respond.

5. The response should be sent to the Registrar. On receipt, he will send it to counsel newly instructed who may reply to it. The grounds and the responses will go before the single judge.

6. The Registrar may have received grounds of appeal direct from the applicant, and obtained a waiver of privilege before fresh counsel is assigned. In those circumstances, when assigning counsel, the Registrar will provide copies of the waiver, the grounds of appeal and any response from former counsel.

7. This guidance covers the formal procedures to be followed. It is perfectly proper for counsel newly instructed to speak to former counsel as a matter of courtesy before grounds are lodged to inform him of the position.

As to the need to follow the Bar Council's guidance, see *R. v. Nasser, The Times*, February 19, 1998, CA.

Preparation of defence statements

C–46   On September 24, 1997, the Professional Conduct and Complaints Committee of the Bar Council approved guidance as to the duties of counsel in relation to the preparation of defence statements pursuant to the *CPIA* 1996. The guidance is set out in full in the main work at §§ 12–99a, 12–99b.

III. MISCELLANEOUS AUTHORITIES ON DUTIES OF ADVOCATES

(1) Return of brief or instructions

C–47   Members of the criminal bar have a personal responsibility for compliance with provisions of the Code of Conduct relating to the return of instructions, of which their clerks should be aware. It is open to a court concerned with a problem caused by a late return of a brief to send a complaint to the Professional Conduct Committee of the Bar Council: *R. v. Sutton JJ., ex p. DPP*, 95 Cr.App.R. 180, DC, *per* Brooke J., at p. 186 (decided in relation to paragraphs 507 and 508 of the fifth edition of the Code of Conduct).

The absence of what counsel would regard as sufficient time for preparation does not constitute an exception to the cab-rank rule requiring him to act for his client: see *R. v. Ulcay* (§ 4–41 in the main work).

(2) Duty not to accept certain instructions

C–48   Counsel should not appear for the prosecution in a case where the defendant is a person he has previously represented; para. 501(f) of the Code of Conduct for the Bar (6th ed.) referred to the risk that the barrister might have considential information or special knowledge disadvantageous to the defendant, his former client; it is contrary to the spirit of the code that a barrister should put himself in a position where such a risk might be perceived: *R. v. Dann* [1997] Crim.L.R. 46, CA. As to *Dann*, see further *Re T. and A. (Children) (Risk of Disclosure)* [2002] 1 F.L.R. 859, CA (Civ.Div.).

(3) Duty of counsel to acquaint themselves with the terms of the indictment

C–49   See *R. v. Peckham*, 25 Cr.App.R. 125, CCA (prosecution), and *R. v. Olivo*, 28 Cr.App.R. 173, CCA (defence).

(4) Duty concerning recent legislation

C–50   In *R. v. Isaacs, The Times*, February 9, 1990, the Court of Appeal said that when presenting cases at first instance or in appellate courts, counsel have a positive duty to inform the court of all relevant commencement dates of recent legislation

(5) Duty of counsel to inform themselves of the sentencing powers of the court

C–51   The Court of Appeal has repeatedly emphasised the duty of both counsel to inform themselves before the commencement of proceedings in the Crown

Court of the sentencing powers of the court, including powers in relation to ancillary orders, such as costs, compensation, etc. The starting point is *R. v. Clarke (R.W.W.)*, 59 Cr.App.R. 298, CA. Lawton L.J. concluded the judgment of the court with the following general observations and guidance. His Lordship's remarks are even more apposite today than when they were made: legislation in relation to sentence has become ever more complex. Sections 28 and 29 of the *MCA* 1952 were replaced by sections 37 and 38 respectively of the *MCA* 1980, which have themselves since been subject to extensive amendment. Section 37 was eventually repealed by the *CDA* 1998, and section 38 was repealed and replaced by section 3 of the *PCC(S)A* 2000.

"We adjudge that counsel as a matter of professional duty to the Court, and in the case of defending counsel to their client, should always before starting a criminal case satisfy themselves as to what the maximum sentence is. There can be no excuse for counsel not doing this and they should remember that the performance of this duty is particularly important in a case where a man has been committed to the Crown Court for sentencing pursuant to the provisions of sections 28 and 29 of the *Magistrates' Courts Act* 1952, and section 56 of the *Criminal Justice Act* 1967. Those statutory provisions are pregnant with dangers for court and for counsel and above all for accused persons...

Secondly, those who administer the Crown Court should act as follows. Before the Crown Court came into existence..., it was the practice of many clerks of assize and many clerks of the peace to make a note on the documents put before the trial judge of the maximum sentence which could be passed and of the paragraphs in *Archbold's Criminal Pleading, Evidence and Practice* which dealt with the offence. In some Crown Courts this former practice has been followed. On the other hand it is clear from this case and from inquiries which we have made that it is not always followed. It should be; and it is particularly important that it should be when judges are asked to deal with cases committed for sentence under the statutory provisions to which I have already referred" (at pp. 301–302).

A reminder of the duty of counsel for both sides to ensure that sentences imposed, and orders made, are within the powers of the court, and to invite the court to vary a sentece if on subsequent consideration it appears to be unlawful, was given in *R. v. Komsta and Murphy*, 12 Cr.App.R.(S) 63. Turner J. commented that it could not be too clearly understood that there was positive obligation on counsel, both for the prosecution and the defence, to ensure that no order was made that the court had no power to make. The *PCC(S)A* 2000, s.155(1) (see § 5–940 in the main work) allowed the Crown Court to alter or vary any sentence or order, within the period of 28 days of the making of the order. If it appeared to either counsel that the order was one which the court had no power to make, counsel should not hesitate to invite the court to exercise such powers.

See also *R. v. Richards*, *The Times*, April 1, 1993, CA, *R. v. Hartrey* [1993] Crim.L.R. 230, CA, *R. v. Johnstone (D.)*, *The Times*, June 18, 1996, CA, *R. v. Bruley* [1996] Crim.L.R. 913, CA, *R. v. McDonnell* [1996] Crim.L.R. 914, CA, *R. v. Street*, 161 J.P. 28, CA, *R. v. Blight* [1999] Crim.L.R. 426, CA and, most recently, *R. v. Cain* [2007] 2 Cr.App.R.(S.) 25, CA. In *Blight*, it was said that counsel do not discharge their duty simply by having a copy of *Archbold* "to hand"; it is the duty of both counsel to be aware in advance of the powers of the court so that any error may be recited immediately; as to the defence counsel, it was said to be very difficult to see how mitigation can be done properly without having in the very front of the mind the powers within which the judge must exercise his duty. In *R. v. Cain*, it was said that defence advocates should ascertain and be prepared to assist the judge with any relevant legal restrictions on sentence, and the prosecution advocate should ensure that the sentencer does not, through inadvertence, impose an unlawful sentence; in particular, prosecution advocates should always be ready to assist the court by drawing attention to any statutory provisions that govern the court's sentencing powers and to any sentencing guidelines or guideline decisions of the Court of Appeal.

C–52 In *R. v. Reynolds* [2007] 2 Cr.App.R.(S.) 87, CA, it was said that prosecuting and defence advocates must ensure that they are fully aware of the potential impact of the provisions of the dangerous offender provisions in Chapter 5 of Part 12 of the *CJA* 2003 (§§ 5–291 *et seq.* in the main work), that they are able to assist the sentencer in that respect and are alert to any mistakes made in passing sentence so that any problem can be resolved before it is too late.

(6) Defendant absconding

C–53 See *R. v. Shaw*, 70 Cr.App.R. 313, CA, see § 3–200 in the main work, and for relevant provisions of the 8th edition of the Code of Conduct, see *ante*, C–1 in this supplement.

(7) Defendant not giving evidence

C–54 In *R. v. Bevan*, 98 Cr.App.R. 354, CA, it was held that where a defendant decides not to give evidence, it should be the invariable practice of counsel to record that decision and to cause the defendant to sign that record, indicating clearly first, that he has, of his own free will, decided not to give evidence and, secondly, that he has so decided bearing in mind the advice given to him by counsel. In the light of section 35 of the *CJPOA* 1994 (§ 4–305 in the main work), the advice of the Court of Appeal in *Bevan* is likely to become of greater importance than at the time of the decision. As to this, see also *Ebanks (Kurt) v. The Queen* [2006] 1 W.L.R. 1827, PC (§ 4–308 in the mainwork).

(8) Duties in relation to cross-examination

C–55 See §§ 8–113, 8–118 *et seq.* in the main work and, in relation to defence counsel's duty when cross-examining a co-defendant, see *R. v. Fenlon*, 71 Cr.App.R. 307, CA, see § 8–164 in the main work.

(9) Duties in relation to the summing up

C–56 See §§ 4–371 *et seq.* in the main work

(10) Duties in relation to appeal

C–57 As to the duty to advise in relation to the possibility of an appeal against conviction or sentence, see §§ 7–163 *et seq.* in the main work, and *ante*, C–39, C–45.

As to counsel's general duty in relation to the drafting of grounds of appeal, see § 7–179 in the main work. As to criticism of former counsel, see § 7–82 in the main work, and § C–45, *ante*.

As to the duty of counsel for the prosecution, see § 7–206 in the main work.

The duty of a barrister to present his client's case before the Court of Appeal could not extend to advancing the client's assertion, unsubstantiated by any evidence, that the trial judge was corrupt or biased. A barrister's duty in such circumstances is either to decline to comply with the instructions or to withdraw from the case: *Thatcher v. Douglas*, *The Times*, January 8, 1996, CA (Civ. Div.).

(11) Duties of prosecuting counsel

Apart from the matters mentioned above, see also (a) *The Role and Respon-*   **C–58**
sibilities of the Prosecution Advocate, post, E–15 *et seq.*; (b) *R. v. Herbert*, 94
Cr.App.R. 230, CA (§ 4–105 in the main work) and *R. v. Richards and Stober*,
96 Cr.App.R. 258, CA (§ 19–87 in the main work), in relation to "plea–bar-
gaining" and the acceptance of pleas, with particular reference to cases where
there are two or more defendants; (c) §§ 4–268 *et seq.* in the main work, in relation to the opening of a case generally, and *R. v. Hobstaff*, 14 Cr.App.R.(S.)
605, CA, in relation to opening the facts on a plea of guilty; and (d) the
Attorney-General's guidelines on the acceptance of pleas and the prosecutor's
role in the sentencing exercise (*ante*, Appendix A–258 *et seq.*).

(12) Advocate as witness

In *R. v. Jacquith (or Jaquith) and Emode* [1989] Crim.L.R. 508 and 563, CA,   **C–59**
junior counsel for one defendant has been called on his behalf to rebut a suggestion of recent invention made against him. The Court of Appeal said that
the evidence on this point was admissible but it was very undesirable for
counsel to give evidence on this point in court. In addition to the effect on the
jury it caused embarrassment and difficulty to other members of the Bar who
had to set about cross-examining a colleague.

May L.J. said that the suggestion had been made that the court givesome
indication of its views concerning evidence given by counsel and also where a
client alleged an attempt to pervert the court of justice by a co-defendant.
their Lordships considered, however, that the right course would be to list
points for consideration by the Bar Council and the Law Society. It was not
sought to lay these maters down as ones of principle; their Lordships merely
thought they deserved consideration.

1. No advocate should ever give evidence if that could possibly be avoided.
2. Where it was not possible for an advocate to avoid giving evidence, he
should take no further part in the case. It necessarily followed that, if he was
not being led, the trial must stop and a retrial be ordered. 3. There was a
duty on counsel to anticipate circumstances in which he might be called upon
to give evidence. Experienced counsel ought to be able to anticipate whether
such a situation might arise. Where such a situation was anticipated, or envisaged even as a possibility, he should withdraw from the case. 4. Where it
came to the notice of a legal adviser, through an accused person, that one of
his co-defendants had attempted to pervert the court of justice, there was a
duty on the legal adviser, usually the instructing solicitor, to take a detailed
proof at once to provide a record and for further investigation. 5. Where the
giving of evidence by an advocate caused real embarrassment or inhibition or
difficulty regarding cross-examination by other advocates, the judge should
exercise his discretion to discharge the jury and order a retrial.

For relevant provisions of the 8th edition of the Code of Conduct, see *ante*,
in this supplement.

(13) Co-habiting counsel

It is generally undesirable for husband and wife, or other partners living   **C–60**
together, to appear as counsel on opposite sides in the same criminal matter
since it might give rise to an apprehension that the proper conduct of the case
had been in some way affected by that personal relationship: *R. v. Batt, The
Times*, May 30, 1996, CA. See also *Re L. (Minors) (Care Proceedings: Solicitors)*
[2001] 1 W.L.R. 100, Fam D. (Wilson J.).

APPENDIX D

Forms for use at Preliminary Hearings and Plea and Case Management Hearings

CROWN COURT

CASE PROGRESSION

PRELIMINARY HEARING

Date of hearing: / /   Judge: **D–1**

Prosecution advocate:		
D1	[bail][custody] represented by:	
D2	[bail][custody] represented by:	
D3	[bail][custody] represented by:	
D4	[bail][custody] represented by:	
D5	[bail][custody] represented by:	

No. of case in Crown Court: URN:

	D1	D2	D3	D4	D5
Has the defendant been advised about credit for pleading guilty?					
Has the defendant been warned that if he is on bail and fails to attend, the proceedings may continue in his absence?					

1) TRIAL JUDGE

Should the future management of the case be under the supervision of the trial judge or a nominated judge?   YES/NO

2) PLEA

		D1	D2	D3	D4	D5
a.	**Is it likely that the case can be concluded by the defendant pleading guilty?**					

     b.   If yes and if the defendant cannot be sentenced at the preliminary hearing, go to 3) and/or 4) as appropriate

3) LIKELY GUILTY PLEA

     a.   *The defendant will be sentenced on:*   / /   *or at the plea and case management hearing*

     b.   *The directions made by the magistrates' court when the case was sent shall apply subject to the following amendments:*

     c.   *The pre-sentence report (if required) to be received by the Crown Court and made available to the defence and the prosecution by:*

     d.   *The defence to serve any material which it wishes the court to consider when sentencing by:*

		D1	D2	D3	D4	D5
e.	**Does the defence intend to make "derogatory assertions" against a person's character in the course of mitigation?**					

     f.   *If yes, the court orders:*

g. Are there any other matters against a defendant which should be dealt with at the same time as the proceedings in this case (other offences/TIC's)?

D1	D2	D3	D4	D5

h. If yes, give brief details:

i. *If there are other matters, the court orders:*

j. *Further orders (e.g. orders re medical, psychiatric reports, confiscation proceedings or Newton hearings):*

4) DIRECTIONS FOR PLEA AND CASE MANAGEMENT HEARING
  a. *The directions made by the Magistrates' Court when the case was sent shall apply subject to the following amendments:*

  b. *Further orders:*

5) EXPERT EVIDENCE
  a. Is this a case in which the parties will rely on expert evidence?

P	D1	D2	D3	D4	D5

  b. *If yes, the court orders:*

6) TRIAL
  a. Can the date of the trial or the period during which the trial will take place be fixed now?   YES/NO

  b. *If yes, the trial will take place on:*
     or within the period of :
     and it is estimated that it will last:

CROWN COURT

CASE PROGRESSION

PRELIMINARY HEARING

<u>**GUIDANCE NOTES**</u>

General notes

These notes accompany the preliminary hearing form.

The parties must ensure that the Court has a copy of the "CASE SENT TO THE CROWN COURT UNDER SECTION 51 OF THE CRIME AND DISORDER ACT 1998" form completed in the Magistrates' Court.

The answers to the questions in bold must be filled in before the hearing. The proposed italicised orders should be filled in before the hearing, if possible (if there are more than five defendants, a further form should be filled in only so far as necessary).

Except where otherwise required, a direction in the form to "serve" material means serve on the other party(ies) and file with the Crown Court.

Notes relevant to specific sections

1) TRIAL JUDGE OR NOMINATED JUDGE

If the case is due to last for more than 4 weeks or if it seems likely that a preparatory hearing will be ordered, the future case management should normally be under the supervision of the trial judge or a nominated judge. It may also be desirable for the future case management to be under the supervision of the trial judge or a nominated judge in other cases where, for example there are difficult issues of law to be considered or where the prosecution intends to make a public interest immunity application.

If the case fits into this category, the court should normally make the necessary directions for the plea and case management hearing and then direct that the case be considered by the Resident Judge.

2) PLEA

If it is likely that the case can be concluded by all the defendants pleading guilty then 3) should be completed and there should be no need to make any orders under 4). Otherwise any appropriate orders under 3) should be made in respect of those defendants likely to plead guilty and 4) should be completed.

3) LIKELY GUILTY PLEA

3b. The Crown Court has a greater power to vary the time limits than the magistrates' court.

3c. A pre-sentence report will not be required in every case.

3e. Advance notice of the fact that such an assertion is going to be made should be given to the prosecution to enable it to decide whether to challenge the assertion and to enable the sentencing court to consider whether to make an order restricting the publication of the assertion under sections 58-61 of the Criminal Procedure and Investigations Act 1996 ("CPIA").

3i. If the defendant is facing charges in other courts give brief details of offence, court and court number.

4) DIRECTIONS FOR PLEA AND CASE MANAGEMENT HEARING

4a. The Crown Court has a greater power to vary the time limits than the Magistrates' Court.

5) EXPERT EVIDENCE

The court should identify any issues in relation to which it is appropriate to call expert evidence and set a timetable for obtaining, serving, and (if possible) agreeing such evidence or identifying the issues in dispute. See also paragraph 15 of the guidance notes to the PCMH form.

The parties should consider whether orders being considered by the court will involve costs being incurred which may not be met by the Legal Services Commission.

7) TRIAL

The court should consider whether it is possible and desirable to set the trial date or period because, for example, of the health, vulnerability or availability of a witness or the defendant or because the defendant falls within the definition of a persistent young offender, or because experts and/or leading counsel may have to be instructed and, before any such instructions can be expected, it is necessary to know the date.

The Crown Court

Case No	D1
Date of trial	
Fixed	☐
Warned	☐

Plea and Case Management Hearing

D–2

Advocates Questionnaire

■ Parties must complete this form.
■ This form is to be used at all Crown Court Centres, without local variation.
There is an electronic version of the form which contains answer boxes that expand. The form is at:
http://www.hmcourts-service.gov.uk/HMCSCourtFinder

1

Date of PCMH	PTI URN
Judge	Estimated length of trial

2   **Parties' details**

	Parties name	Age	Remand status	CTL expires	Advocate at PCMH	Trial advocate (if known)
P						
D1			C ☐ B ☐			

3   **Contact details**

3.1   Parties

P	Office	Name		Phone	
		Email			
	Advocate	Name		Phone	
		Email			
D1	Solicitor	Name		Phone	
		Email			
	Advocate	Name		Phone	
		Email			

3.2

Case progression officers

P

Name	Phone
Email	

D1

Name	Phone
Email	

Court

Name	Phone
Email	

4   Which orders made at the magistrates' court have not been complied with?

5

D1   Has the defendant been advised that he or she will receive credit for a guilty plea?   ☐ No ☐ Yes

6

D1   Has the defendant been warned that the case may proceed in his or her absence?   ☐ No ☐ Yes

7   What plea(s) is/are the defendant(s) offering?

D1

8   Should the case be referred to the Resident Judge for a trial judge to be allocated?   ☐ No ☐ Yes

9   Give details of any issues relating to the fitness to plead or to stand trial.

D1

10

10.1   Has the prosecution made statutory disclosure?

P

D1

10.2   Has a defence statement been served?

D1	

10.3 Does it comply with the statutory requirements?

P	

10.4 If not clear from the defence statement, what are the real issues?

D1	

10.5
   D1   Has/will the defence made/make an application in writing under
section 8 of the Criminal Procedure and Investigations Act 1996?   ☐ No ☐ Yes

11   What further evidence is to be served by the prosecution?
By when is it reasonably practicable to serve this?

P	

12
12.1   Give details of any expert evidence likely to be relied upon, including
why it is required and by when it is reasonably practicable to serve this.

P	

D1	

12.2   Is a note of agreement/disagreement required?

13
13.1
   D1   Has the defence completed the Witness List (see **36**)?   ☐ No ☐ Yes

5122 Plea and Case Management Hearing, Criminal Procedure Rules 2006 (12.06)   HMCS

13.2   Is any witness summons necessary?

13.3
   D1   Is a timetable for the calling of witnesses required (see **30**)?   ☐ No ☐ Yes

14
14.1
   D1   Is a certificate for a litigator sought?   ☐ No ☐ Yes

14.2   If **Yes**, why and for how long?
   D1

For 15 to 35, answer the relevant questions only

15   **Admissions, schedules etc.**
    What matters can usefully be admitted or put into schedules, diagrams, visual aids etc.?

16   **Case summary**

   P   Is it proposed to serve a case summary or note of opening?   ☐ No ☐ Yes

17   **Special measures**
17.1   Give details of any special measures application to be made.

17.2
    Can any order be made now?   ☐ No ☐ Yes

17.3   What other arrangements are needed for any young/vulnerable/intimidated witness?

18 Young defendants

Are any arrangements needed for any young defendant?

D1

19 Reporting restrictions

State type and grounds of any reporting restriction sought.

P

D1

20 Third party material

20.1 What third party material is sought, from whom, and why?

P

D1

20.2 If the material can be obtained without a court order, by whom and by when?

P

D1

20.3 Should any person adversely affected by an order be notified?

21 Defendant's interview(s)

21.1 Is there an issue in relation to the accuracy of
the transcript/admissibility of the defendant's interview?

5122 Plea and Case Management Hearing, Criminal Procedure Rules 2006 (12.06)   HMCS

D1

21.2   What proposals are made for any editing required?

D1

21.3   What proposals are made to summarise the interview(s)?

D1

22   Video Evidence

22.1   Is there video evidence of any young/vulnerable/intimidated witness yet to be served?

22.2   Has each video been transcribed?

22.3   Is there an issue in relation to the accuracy/admissibility/quality of any video or transcript?

23   Witness interview(s)

23.1   Are there any videos/audio tapes of witness interviews which,
if they meet the disclosure test, are yet to be disclosed as unused material?

23.2   If so, is any application made for that video/audio tape to be
transcribed and, if so, why?

24   **CCTV evidence**

24.1   Are there any outstanding issues in relation to service disclosure of CCTV footage?
If the material is in the possession of a third party, complete 20 instead.

24.2   Is an edited version to be served/used?

25   **Electronic equipment**

25.1   Give details of any special equipment (e.g. CCTV, live link, audio recordings, DVD)
required in the trial courtroom.

P

D1

25.2   Is the evidence in its present form compatible with the equipment in court?

26   **Cross-examination on sexual history**

If an application has not already been made, does the defence intend to make
an application under section 41 of the Youth Justice and Criminal Evidence Act 1999
to cross-examine a witness about his or her sexual history?

D1

27   **Bad character**

Are any directions necessary in relation to bad character applications?
Are there any further applications?

P

D1

_____

28   Hearsay

Are any directions necessary in relation to hearsay applications?
Are there to be any further applications?

P

_____

D1

_____

29   Admissibility and legal issues

What points on admissibility/other legal issues are to be taken?
Is it necessary for any to be resolved before trial?

P

_____

D1

_____

30   Timetable of trial

Are there matters which need to be determined on the day of trial, which
may affect the timetable of trial?
If so, when will (1) the jury and (2) the witnesses be required?

P

_____

31   Public interest immunity

Is any 'on notice' public interest immunity application to be made?

P

32　Jury bundle

What proposals do the prosecution make for a jury bundle?

P

33　Concurrent family proceedings

Give details of any concurrent family proceedings.

34　Other special arrangements

Give details of any special arrangements (e.g., interpreter, intermediary,
wheelchair access, hearing loop system) needed for anyone attending the trial.

35　Linked criminal proceedings

Are there other criminal proceedings against the defendant or otherwise linked?

36   **Witness List**

The defence should indicate here which prosecution witnesses are required to give evidence at trial. The attendance of any witness is subject to the judge's direction.

Name of witness	Page No.	Type of witness: Provide specific details of the type of witness. For example: eye witness, police officer, firearms expert, continuity	Required by

PCMH form: Guidance

How to use the form

The parties should complete only one form for each case. **The form should be used in every Crown Court centre, without any local exception or variation.**

The form may be completed in manuscript or electronically.

Questions 1 to 14 must be answered in every case. Questions 15–35 need only be answered if they are relevant.

The advocate may be asked by the court to expand upon or explain an entry, or to account for the absence of an entry, where one is required. The judge will record on the template any orders made and, if practicable, issue a copy to the parties before the hearing ends. The parties must obtain a copy of that record and comply with the orders made by the date given.

Accessing the form

The current version of the form is available on the Court Service web-site at http://www.hmcourts-service.gov.uk/HMCSCourtFinder. Please note that the form will be updated from time to time. When you open the file, a box will appear with the options of disabling or enabling macros. Choosing "enable macros" will produce a fully operational e-form. Choosing "disable macros" may cause some of the functions to be lost, including the option of altering the number of defendants or using a screen reader.

Next will appear the box giving the option of a screen reader. This is software which translates text into speech.

The next box asks for the number of defendants in the case. This can be altered later by clicking on "Add Def" in the toolbar at the top of the screen.

Once this question has been answered, the form that is produced is ready for completion.

The space available to answer any question expands to accommodate the text inserted. The Tab button can be used to jump to the next box. Alternatively, the arrow keys will move the cursor backwards or forwards.

Transmitting the form

If you complete the form on the screen, it can still be printed off and used in hard copy. Alternatively, it can be emailed; the process for this differs depending on whether Outlook is available.

In order to send the form by email, click on the "e-mail" button on the toolbar at the top of the screen and follow the instructions. If the document is to be emailed using Outlook, that programme must be open at the time. Following the instructions will produce an e-mail window with the form attached. If Outlook is not used, the file must be saved and can then be attached in the usual way.

The need for an effective PCMH

The public, and all those concerned in or affected by a criminal case, have a right to expect that the business of the courts will be conducted fairly but also efficiently and effectively. Delays cost money and adversely impact on the quality of justice. The Plea and Case Management Hearing offers the best, and often the only, opportunity for the judge properly and effectively to manage the case before it is listed for trial. Other hearings – formerly called 'mentions'– are expensive and should actively be discouraged; nearly everything formerly done at a 'mention' can – and should – be done in some other way (usually by telephone or on paper or by an exchange of email, as permitted by CrimPR 3.5(2)(d)). An effective PCMH is therefore vital.

Advocates should attend the hearing fully prepared to deal with the issues that are likely to arise, and the listing officer should consider reasonable requests to list the PCMH to enable trial counsel to attend.

Since an effective PCMH can only take place after the defence have had a proper opportunity to consider the papers, it is suggested that at least four weeks should elapse between the service and listing of the PCMH.

The short guidance given here is intended to be followed in every case but, of course, it is not possible to cover exhaustively all the situations which may be relevant to achieving an effective PCMH. See also Consolidated Criminal Practice Direction (CCPD) IV.41, Management of Cases to be Heard in the Crown Court; V.56 Case Management in Magistrates' Courts and Criminal Case Management Framework (available on-line at www.cjsonline.gov.uk/framework).

Contents of the form

Date of trial and custody time limits

The date of trial should normally be fixed at the PCMH (or before). Any application to extend the Custody Time Limit is best dealt with at the PCMH, when the reasons for fixing a case beyond the time limits will be clear; otherwise there will be the avoidable expense of another hearing.

1,2 and 3 details of case and parties

This section must be fully completed. The parties must be able to contact one another as must case progression officers and the court. Any change in the details must immediately be notified to the other parties and to the court. See CrimPR 3.4.

4 Compliance with the directions given by magistrates' courts

The standard/specific directions given by magistrates' courts should be complied with (CrimPR 3.5(3)). The court will need to know which orders have not been complied with, and why.

5 Credit for guilty plea

Defendants are entitled to be given the advice that credit is given for guilty pleas and the earlier the plea is entered, the greater is the credit given. The judge needs to know that this advice has been given.

6 Trial in absence

Defendants need to be warned that if they waive their right to attend, the trial may proceed in their absence. No one can engineer an adjournment simply by absconding. Those who claim to be ill must support that claim by medical evidence to the effect that they are unfit to attend their trial; it is unlikely that a medical certificate merely suggesting that they are unfit to work will be sufficient. See CCPD , I.13; CrimPR 3.8(2)(a).

7 The pleas which the defendant is offering

Recording in writing pleas offered to alternative offences which the prosecution are initially unwilling to accept will be advantageous to the defendant if the prosecution subsequently changes its position. In such circumstances, it will be easier for a defendant to claim maximum credit if that offer has been recorded. Pleas offered to counts on the indictment must similarly be recorded before credit is claimed.

8 Allocation of the case

Most courts have a system to identify before the PCMH those cases which require allocation to a particular judge; this question is intended to seek out those cases which have been missed.

9 Fitness to plead

This is self explanatory but the judge will need assistance to fix a timetable for the service of experts' reports and for the issue to be tried.

10 Disclosure and defence statement

The parties must identify any outstanding disclosure points. The defence must serve a detailed defence statement setting out the issues in the trial; any failure to do so may be the subject of adverse comment at the trial and the judge may issue a warning to this effect, under section 11(3) of the Criminal Procedure and Investigations Act 1996. Pending service of a defence statement, question 10.4 allows the defence to give some notification of the defence. The practice of appending long 'shopping lists' to vague and unspecific defence statements has no legal foundation; any application for further disclosure should be made by way of formal application under section 8 of the Criminal Procedure and Investigations Act 1996 (as amended). The judge will expect reference to and compliance with the Disclosure Protocol: A Protocol for the Control and Management of Unused Material in the Crown Court.

11 and 12 Timetable of further evidence and expert evidence

Advocates should have available proper information as to what remains to be served, together with a realistic timetable for compliance. Parties should be prepared to provide realistic time estimates and not rely on a standard time period of, for example, 28 days if this has little bearing on the true amount of time likely to be required. The court needs detailed and accurate information as to when the evidence will be available. These enquiries should be made before the hearing. Failure to do so is likely to cause unnecessary adjournments. Consideration should be given to CrimPR 33.5 and whether (now or later) the experts should be asked to confer to identify the real areas of dispute.

13 Witness list (see also 36)

The mere fact of warning a witness to attend may cause him or her anxiety. Furthermore, the warning of witnesses is time consuming and expensive. The court may decline to order the attendance of witnesses unless their presence is really necessary. Consideration should therefore also be given to those witnesses in respect of whom a summons is required. See CrimPR Part 28 for rules on witness summonses. Thought should always be given to the staggering of witnesses to eliminate or reduce waiting times. The witnesses' availability must be known at the PCMH to ensure that the trial date is convenient.

14 Certificate for a litigator

Attendance by a litigator is not a matter of right and should always be justified by reference to the facts of the particular case.

15 Admissions

Properly drafted admissions can save a great deal of court time and proposals should be made in most cases.

16 Case summary

Case summaries should have been provided before the PCMH in all Class 1 cases and in any other case of complexity, but they may be needed in other cases as well.

17 Special measures

In accordance with CrimPR Part 29, special measures applications should have been made by the parties and considered by the court before the PCMH, but this question serves to remind advocates and judges of any outstanding applications.

18 Young and other vulnerable defendants

The needs of young and other vulnerable defendants must be identified in advance of the trial so that the necessary arrangements can be made. See CCPD III.30.

19 Reporting restrictions

Reporting restrictions need to be carefully considered and balanced against the rights of
the press and other interested parties. The judge is likely to require assistance before
making any order. See CCPD I.3.

20 Third party material and applications to produce documents

Such applications must comply with CrimPR Part 28. Careful thought needs to go into
identifying the witness to be served, the material sought and the reason that it is said to be
relevant to an issue in the case. Any person whose right of confidentiality might be
adversely affected must also be identified and information provided as to how and by
whom they are to be notified, how they are to be permitted to make representations and
when and by whom any rulings are to be made. It is important that such applications are
made no later than the PCMH to avoid adjournments at a later stage arising out of
delayed applications.

21 Defendant's interviews

Inaccuracies within transcriptions and likely submissions as to admissibility must be
identified. Furthermore, the police may interview suspects at length, producing bundles
of transcripts, the volume of which may make them unsuitable to put before a jury. The
parties must consider producing summaries. The production of the first draft is primarily
the responsibility of the advocate for the prosecution. If practicable, interviews should be
available in electronic form, so that editing, pagination and copying can be done without
delay. Further guidance is given in CCPD IV.43.

22 Video evidence

These four questions, each of which raises a separate point, are self explanatory but
failure to address them is a frequent source of adjournments. Accuracy, admissibility and
quality are not the same. Errors of transcription or material on the tape that is indistinct or
unclear, or which is alleged to be inadmissible, must be dealt with at PCMH. Editing
takes time. It should not be done on the morning of the trial or the day beforehand. Only
if these issues are addressed in advance can child witnesses be called as soon as they
arrive at court. It is unacceptable to prolong the anxiety of vulnerable witnesses simply
because these issues have not been resolved at PCMH. These matters are already
addressed in the Supplementary Pre-trial Checklist for Cases Involving Young Witnesses.
See also CrimPR Part 29 for rules on special measures directions; and CCPD IV.40.

23 Witness interviews

The issues raised in this question differ from those raised in question 22. There is a
growing practice of recording interviews with witnesses before setting out their evidence
in a written witness statement. If this is done, then, subject to the disclosure test, the
video or audio recording should be disclosed as unused material. The prosecution
advocate therefore needs to know if any witness was interviewed in this way (which may
not be clear from the papers served). It will normally suffice for the video or audio
recording itself to be disclosed. Transcripts are expensive and any claim for a transcript
needs to be justified.

24 and 25 CCTV and electronic equipment

The prosecution only have duties to consider disclosure of CCTV footage in their possession. If the defence seek footage from third parties, it is for them to do so, rather than the prosecution. Furthermore, much CCTV footage is in a format (e.g. multiplex) which is unsuitable for showing in court without adaptation or editing. This must be sorted out before the trial. Many courts have simple VHS video and DVD playback facilities and the parties must ensure that the material which they want to play is compatible with the court equipment (if not, they must provide their own).

26 Cross-examination on sexual history

Section 41 of the Youth Justice and Criminal Evidence Act 1999 enacts an important principle and compliance with its requirements is vital to ensure that those who complain that they are victims of rape (and other sexual offences) receive the protection which the law affords to them. In accordance with CrimPR Part 36, applications should be made and considered – by the trial judge if possible – at or before the PCMH. Applications made on the day of the trial are strongly to be discouraged.

27 and 28 Bad character and hearsay

CrimPR 34.5 and 35.6 provide for detailed applications to be made in the prescribed forms. Questions 27 and 28 therefore only seek to identify any outstanding issues (or potential future applications).

29 Admissibility and legal issues

Issues of admissibility and legal issues should, where possible, be identified before the trial, so that the parties can exchange skeleton arguments and the judge can properly prepare for the hearing. See also section 7 of the Criminal Justice Act 1987; and sections 31 and 40 of the Criminal Procedure and Investigations Act 1996.

30 Timetable of the trial

If there are to be preliminary points taken, then consideration must be given to when a jury will be required and arrangements made to stagger the attendance of witnesses. No one should be asked to attend for a 10.30am start only to find that there is a lengthy legal argument before the case can even be opened. See CrimPR 3.10, which deals with, amongst other things, timetabling and witness arrangements.

31 PII claims

If a claim is to be made on notice, then the necessary arrangements must be made. See CrimPR Part 25.

32 Jury bundle

If a jury bundle will be needed at the trial, then its content will need to be agreed before the trial. Any outstanding issues need to be identified.

33 Concurrent family proceedings

It is important to identify those cases where there are concurrent family proceedings, so that the Designated Family Judge can be alerted.

34 Special arrangements

Any requirements for an interpreter or for those with a disability must be identified in advance, so that proper arrangements can be made. See CrimPR 10.5(1)(h) and 12.1(1)(e).

35 Linked criminal proceedings

These need to be identified, if possible with the court reference numbers.

TEMPLATE FOR ORDERS MADE AT PCMH
*delete as appropriate

PCMH question	Description of order/ work required	Order made
	Trial date [*fixed for] [*warned for week commencing]	
1	Estimated length of hearing	
9	The defence to serve expert evidence (fitness to plead)	
9	The prosecution to serve expert evidence in response (fitness to plead)	
10	The defence to serve any Defence Statement by	
10	Was a warning given that inferences may be drawn from failure to comply?	
10	The prosecution to make further disclosure by	
10	The defence to make any application under section 8 CPIA for disclosure by	
11	The prosecution to serve further evidence by	
12	The prosecution to serve expert evidence by	
12	The defence to serve any expert evidence on which they rely by	
13	Defence to serve a list of witnesses required at trial by	
13	Record any ruling that the judge has made that the attendance of any witness on that list is not required'.	
14	Certificate for litigator granted for [*the first day] [*the whole trial]	
15	Prosecution to serve schedule of facts for agreement by	
16	Prosecution to serve case summary or note of opening by	
17	Prosecution to apply for special measures directions by	
17	Defence to apply for special measures directions by	
19	Reporting restrictions made in terms attached	
20	Prosecution to seek disclosure of third party material by	
20	Defence to seek disclosure of third party material by	
20	Person adversely affected [being] to be notified by	
21	Defence to notify editing required of defendant's interview by	
21	Prosecution to respond to same by	
21	Prosecution to prepare summaries for agreement by	
22	Prosecution to serve video tape of vulnerable witness by	
22	Prosecution to serve [*transcript][*summary] of evidence by	
22	Defence to notify editing required of defendant's interview by	
22	Prosecution to respond to same by	
23	Prosecution to serve tapes of witness interviews by	
23	Prosecution to transcribe tapes of witness interviews by	
24	Prosecution to serve or disclose CCTV footage by	
24	Prosecution to serve edited version of CCTV footage by	
25	Prosecution to confirm that court equipment compatible with tape by	
26	Defence to serve application to cross-examine on sexual history by	
27	Prosecution to serve further bad character application by	
27	Defence to serve further bad character application by	
28	Prosecution to serve further hearsay application by	
28	Defence to serve further hearsay application by	
29	Defence to serve skeleton argument on legal points to be taken by	
29	Prosecution to respond by	
	*Other orders	
	*	
	*	

Judge's signature ....Date............................

APPENDIX E

Crown Prosecution Service

I. CODE FOR CROWN PROSECUTORS

A. INTRODUCTION

The Crown Prosecution Service is the principal public prosecuting author-   **E–1**
ity for England and Wales and is headed by the Director of Public Prosecutions, who is to discharge his functions under the superintendence of the
Attorney-General (*Prosecution of Offences Act* 1985, s.3(1)). The Attorney-
General is accountable to Parliament for the Service.

The Crown Prosecution Service is a national organisation consisting of 42
areas. Each area is headed by a Chief Crown Prosecutor and corresponds to a
single police force area, with one for London. It was set up in 1986 to prosecute cases investigated by the police.

Although the Crown Prosecution Service works closely with the police, it is
independent of them. The independence of crown prosecutors is of
fundamental constitutional importance. Casework decisions taken with fairness, impartiality and integrity help deliver justice for victims, witnesses,
defendants and the public.

The Crown Prosecution Service co-operates with the investigating and
prosecuting agencies of other jurisdictions.

The Director of Public Prosecutions is responsible for issuing a Code for
Crown Prosecutors under section 10 of the *Prosecution of Offences Act* 1985,
giving guidance on the general principles to be applied when making decisions about prosecutions. This is the fifth edition of the code and replaces all
earlier versions. For the purpose of this code, "Crown Prosecutor" includes
members of staff in the Crown Prosecution Service who are designated by the
Director of Public Prosecutions under section 7A of the Act and are exercising
powers under that section.

B. THE CODE

1. INTRODUCTION

1.1 The decision to prosecute an individual is a serious step. Fair and effective   **E–2**
prosecution is essential to the maintenance of law and order. Even in a small case a
prosecution has serious implications for all involved – victims, witnesses and
defendants. The Crown Prosecution Service applies the Code for Crown Prosecutors
so that it can make fair and consistent decisions about prosecutions.

1.2 The Code helps the Crown Prosecution Service to play its part in making sure
that justice is done. It contains information that is important to police officers and

others who work in the criminal justice system and to the general public. Police officers should apply the provisions of this Code whenever they are responsible for deciding whether to charge a person with an offence.

1.3 The Code is also designed to make sure that everyone knows the principles that the Crown Prosecution Service applies when carrying out its work. By applying the same principles, everyone involved in the system is helping to treat victims, witnesses and defendants fairly, while prosecuting cases effectively.

2. General Principles

E–3   2.1 Each case is unique and must be considered on its own facts and merits. However, there are general principles that apply to the way in which Crown Prosecutors must approach every case.

2.2 Crown Prosecutors must be fair, independent and objective. They must not let any personal views about ethnic or national origin, disability, sex, religious beliefs, political views or the sexual orientation of the suspect, victim or witness influence their decisions. They must not be affected by improper or undue pressure from any source.

2.3 It is the duty of Crown Prosecutors to make sure that the right person is prosecuted for the right offence. In doing so, Crown Prosecutors must always act in the interests of justice and not solely for the purpose of obtaining a conviction.

2.4 Crown Prosecutors should provide guidance and advice to investigators throughout the investigative and prosecuting process. This may include lines of inquiry, evidential requirements and assistance in any pre-charge procedures. Crown Prosecutors will be proactive in identifying and, where possible, rectifying evidential deficiencies and in bringing to an early conclusion those cases that cannot be strengthened by further investigation.

2.5 It is the duty of Crown Prosecutors to review, advise on and prosecute cases, ensuring that the law is properly applied, that all relevant evidence is put before the court and that obligations of disclosure are complied with, in accordance with the principles set out in this Code.

2.6 The Crown Prosecution Service is a public authority for the purposes of the *Human Rights Act* 1998. Crown Prosecutors must apply the principles of the European Convention on Human Rights in accordance with the Act.

3. The Decision to Prosecute

E–4   3.1 In most cases, Crown Prosecutors are responsible for deciding whether a person should be charged with a criminal offence, and if so, what that offence should be. Crown Prosecutors make these decisions in accordance with this Code and the Director's Guidance on Charging. In those cases where the police determine the charge, which are usually more minor and routine cases, they apply the same provisions.

3.2 Crown Prosecutors make charging decisions in accordance with the Full Code Test (see section 5 below), other than in those limited circumstances where the Threshold Test applies (see section 6 below).

3.3 The Threshold Test applies where the case is one in which it is proposed to keep the suspect in custody after charge, but the evidence required to apply the Full Code Test is not yet available.

3.4 Where a Crown Prosecutor makes a charging decision in accordance with the Threshold Test, the case must be reviewed in accordance with the Full Code Test as soon as reasonably practicable, taking into account the progress of the investigation.

4. Review

E–5   4.1 Each case the Crown Prosecution Service receives from the police is reviewed to make sure that it is right to proceed with a prosecution. Unless the Threshold

Test applies, the Crown Prosecution Service will only start or continue with a prosecution when the case has passed both stages of the Full Code Test.

4.2 Review is a continuing process and Crown Prosecutors must take account of any change in circumstances. Wherever possible, they should talk to the police first if they are thinking about changing the charges or stopping the case. Crown Prosecutors should also tell the police if they believe that some additional evidence may strengthen the case. This gives the police the chance to provide more information that may affect the decision.

4.3 The Crown Prosecution Service and the police work closely together, but the final responsibility for the decision whether or not a charge or a case should go ahead rests with the Crown Prosecution Service.

5. THE FULL CODE TEST

5.1 The Full Code Test has two stages. The first stage is consideration of the evidence. If the case does not pass the evidential stage it must not go ahead no matter how important or serious it may be. If the case does pass the evidential stage, Crown Prosecutors must proceed to the second stage and decide if a prosecution is needed in the public interest. The evidential and public interest stages are explained below.

The evidential stage

5.2 Crown Prosecutors must be satisfied that there is enough evidence to provide a 'realistic prospect of conviction' against each defendant on each charge. They must consider what the defence case may be, and how that is likely to affect the prosecution case.

5.3 A realistic prospect of conviction is an objective test. It means that a jury or bench of magistrates or judge hearing a case alone, properly directed in accordance with the law, is more likely than not to convict the defendant of the charge alleged. This is a separate test from the one that the criminal courts themselves must apply. A court should only convict if satisfied so that it is sure of a defendant's guilt.

5.4 When deciding whether there is enough evidence to prosecute, Crown Prosecutors must consider whether the evidence can be used and is reliable. There will be many cases in which the evidence does not give any cause for concern. But there will also be cases in which the evidence may not be as strong as it first appears. Crown Prosecutors must ask themselves the following questions:

Can the evidence be used in court?

(a) Is it likely that the evidence will be excluded by the court? There are certain legal rules which might mean that evidence which seems relevant cannot be given at a trial. For example, is it likely that the evidence will be excluded because of the way in which it was gathered? If so, is there enough other evidence for a realistic prospect of conviction?

Is the evidence reliable?

(b) Is there evidence which might support or detract from the reliability of a confession? Is the reliability affected by factors such as the defendant's age, intelligence or level of understanding?

(c) What explanation has the defendant given? Is a court likely to find it credible in the light of the evidence as a whole? Does it support an innocent explanation?

(d) If the identity of the defendant is likely to be questioned, is the evidence about this strong enough?

(e) Is the witness's background likely to weaken the prosecution case? For example, does the witness have any motive that may affect his or her attitude to the case, or a relevant previous conviction?

(f) Are there concerns over the accuracy or credibility of a witness? Are these concerns based on evidence or simply information with nothing to support it? Is there further evidence which the police should be asked to seek out which may support or detract from the account of the witness?

5.5 Crown Prosecutors should not ignore evidence because they are not sure that it can be used or is reliable. But they should look closely at it when deciding if there is a realistic prospect of conviction.

The public interest stage

E-7   5.6 In 1951, Lord Shawcross, who was Attorney General, made the classic statement on public interest, which has been supported by Attorneys General ever since: "It has never been the rule in this country - I hope it never will be - that suspected criminal offences must automatically be the subject of prosecution". (House of Commons Debates, volume 483, column 681, 29 January 1951.)

5.7 The public interest must be considered in each case where there is enough evidence to provide a realistic prospect of conviction. Although there may be public interest factors against prosecution in a particular case, often the prosecution should go ahead and those factors should be put to the court for consideration when sentence is being passed. A prosecution will usually take place unless there are public interest factors tending against prosecution which clearly outweigh those tending in favour, or it appears more appropriate in all the circumstances of the case to divert the person from prosecution (see section 8 below).

5.8 Crown Prosecutors must balance factors for and against prosecution carefully and fairly. Public interest factors that can affect the decision to prosecute usually depend on the seriousness of the offence or the circumstances of the suspect. Some factors may increase the need to prosecute but others may suggest that another course of action would be better.

The following lists of some common public interest factors, both for and against prosecution, are not exhaustive. The factors that apply will depend on the facts in each case.

Some common public interest factors in favour of prosecution

5.9 The more serious the offence, the more likely it is that a prosecution will be needed in the public interest. A prosecution is likely to be needed if:

(a) a conviction is likely to result in a significant sentence;

(b) a conviction is likely to result in a confiscation or any other order;

(c) a weapon was used or violence was threatened during the commission of the offence;

(d) the offence was committed against a person serving the public (for example, a police or prison officer, or a nurse);

(e) the defendant was in a position of authority or trust;

(f) the evidence shows that the defendant was a ringleader or an organiser of the offence;

(g) there is evidence that the offence was premeditated;

(h) there is evidence that the offence was carried out by a group;

(i) the victim of the offence was vulnerable, has been put in considerable fear, or suffered personal attack, damage or disturbance;

(j) the offence was committed in the presence of, or in close proximity to, a child;

(k) the offence was motivated by any form of discrimination against the victim's ethnic or national origin, disability, sex, religious beliefs, political views or sexual orientation, or the suspect demonstrated hostility towards the victim based on any of those characteristics;

(l) there is a marked difference between the actual or mental ages of the defendant and the victim, or if there is any element of corruption;

(m) the defendant's previous convictions or cautions are relevant to the present offence;

(n) the defendant is alleged to have committed the offence while under an order of the court;

(o) there are grounds for believing that the offence is likely to be continued or repeated, for example, by a history of recurring conduct;

(p) the offence, although not serious in itself, is widespread in the area where it was committed; or

(q) a prosecution would have a significant positive impact on maintaining community confidence.

Some common public interest factors against prosecution

5.10 A prosecution is less likely to be needed if:

(a) the court is likely to impose a nominal penalty;

(b) the defendant has already been made the subject of a sentence and any further conviction would be unlikely to result in the imposition of an additional sentence or order, unless the nature of the particular offence requires a prosecution or the defendant withdraws consent to have an offence taken into consideration during sentencing;

(c) the offence was committed as a result of a genuine mistake or misunderstanding (these factors must be balanced against the seriousness of the offence);

(d) the loss or harm can be described as minor and was the result of a single incident, particularly if it was caused by a misjudgment;

(e) there has been a long delay between the offence taking place and the date of the trial, unless:

- the offence is serious;
- the delay has been caused in part by the defendant;
- the offence has only recently come to light; or
- the complexity of the offence has meant that there has been a long investigation;

(f) a prosecution is likely to have a bad effect on the victim's physical or mental health, always bearing in mind the seriousness of the offence;

(g) the defendant is elderly or is, or was at the time of the offence, suffering from significant mental or physical ill health, unless the offence is serious or there is real possibility that it may be repeated. The Crown Prosecution Service, where necessary, applies Home Office guidelines about how to deal with mentally disordered offenders. Crown Prosecutors must balance the desirability of diverting a defendant who is suffering from significant mental or physical ill health with the need to safeguard the general public;

(h) the defendant has put right the loss or harm that was caused (but defendants must not avoid prosecution or diversion solely because they pay compensation); or

(i) details may be made public that could harm sources of information, international relations or national security;

5.11 Deciding on the public interest is not simply a matter of adding up the number of factors on each side. Crown Prosecutors must decide how important each factor is in the circumstances of each case and go on to make an overall assessment.

The relationship between the victim and the public interest

5.12 The Crown Prosecution Service prosecutes cases on behalf of the public at large and not just in the interests of any particular individual. However, when considering the public interest test Crown Prosecutors should always take into account the consequences for the victim of the decision whether or not to prosecute, and any views expressed by the victim or the victim's family.

5.13 It is important that a victim is told about a decision which makes a significant difference to the case in which they are involved. Crown Prosecutors should ensure that they follow any agreed procedures.

6 THE THRESHOLD TEST

E–8   6.1 The Threshold Test requires Crown Prosecutors to decide whether there is at least a reasonable suspicion that the suspect has committed an offence, and if there is, whether it is in the public interest to charge that suspect.

6.2 The Threshold Test is applied to those cases in which it would not be appropriate to release a suspect on bail after charge, but the evidence to apply the Full Code Test is not yet available.

6.3 There are statutory limits that restrict the time a suspect may remain in police custody before a decision has to be made whether to charge or release the suspect. There will be cases 12 where the suspect in custody presents a substantial bail risk if released, but much of the evidence may not be available at the time the charging decision has to be made. Crown Prosecutors will apply the Threshold Test to such cases for a limited period.

6.4 The evidential decision in each case will require consideration of a number of factors including:
- the evidence available at the time;
- the likelihood and nature of further evidence being obtained;
- the reasonableness for believing that evidence will become available;
- the time it will take to gather that evidence and the steps being taken to do so;
- the impact the expected evidence will have on the case;
- the charges that the evidence will support.

6.5 The public interest means the same as under the Full Code Test, but will be based on the information available at the time of charge which will often be limited.

6.6 A decision to charge and withhold bail must be kept under review. The evidence gathered must be regularly assessed to ensure the charge is still appropriate and that continued objection to bail is justified. The Full Code Test must be applied as soon as reasonably practicable.

7 SELECTION OF CHARGES

E–9   7.1 Crown Prosecutors should select charges which:
   (a) reflect the seriousness and extent of the offending;
   (b) give the court adequate powers to sentence and impose appropriate post conviction orders; and
   (c) enable the case to be presented in a clear and simple way.

This means that Crown Prosecutors may not always choose or continue with the most serious charge where there is a choice.

7.2 Crown Prosecutors should never go ahead with more charges than are necessary just to encourage a defendant to plead guilty to a few. In the same way, they should never go ahead with a more serious charge just to encourage a defendant to plead guilty to a less serious one.

7.3 Crown Prosecutors should not change the charge simply because of the decision made by the court or the defendant about where the case will be heard.

8 DIVERSION FROM PROSECUTION

Adults

E–10   8.1 When deciding whether a case should be prosecuted in the courts, Crown

Prosecutors should consider the alternatives to prosecution. Where appropriate, the availability of suitable rehabilitative, reparative or restorative justice processes can be considered.

8.2 Alternatives to prosecution for adult suspects include a simple caution and a conditional caution.

Simple caution

8.3 A simple caution should only be given if the public interest justifies it and in accordance with Home Office guidelines. Where it is felt that such a caution is appropriate, Crown Prosecutors must inform the police so they can caution the suspect. If the caution is not administered, because the suspect refuses to accept it, a Crown Prosecutor may review the case again.

Conditional caution

8.4 A conditional caution may be appropriate where a Crown Prosecutor considers that while the public interest justifies a prosecution, the interests of the suspect, victim and community may be better served by the suspect complying with suitable conditions aimed at rehabilitation or reparation. These may include restorative processes.

8.5 Crown Prosecutors must be satisfied that there is sufficient evidence for a realistic prospect of conviction and that the public interest would justify a prosecution should the offer of a conditional caution be refused or the offender fail to comply with the agreed conditions of the caution.

8.6 In reaching their decision, Crown Prosecutors should follow the Conditional Cautions Code of Practice and any guidance on conditional cautioning issued or approved by the Director of Public Prosecutions.

8.7 Where Crown Prosecutors consider a conditional caution to be appropriate, they must inform the police, or other authority responsible for administering the conditional caution, as well as providing an indication of the appropriate conditions so that the conditional caution can be administered.

Youths

8.8 Crown Prosecutors must consider the interests of a youth when deciding whether it is in the public interest to prosecute. However Crown Prosecutors should not avoid prosecuting simply because of the defendant's age. The seriousness of the offence or the youth's past behaviour is very important.

8.9 Cases involving youths are usually only referred to the Crown Prosecution Service for prosecution if the youth has already received a reprimand and final warning, unless the offence is so serious that neither of these were appropriate or the youth does not admit committing the offence. Reprimands and final warnings are intended to prevent re-offending and the fact that a further offence has occurred indicates that attempts to divert the youth from the court system have not been effective. So the public interest will usually require a prosecution in such cases, unless there are clear public interest factors against prosecution.

9. MODE OF TRIAL

9.1 The Crown Prosecution Service applies the current guidelines for magistrates **E–11** who have to decide whether cases should be tried in the Crown Court when the offence gives the option and the defendant does not indicate a guilty plea. Crown Prosecutors should recommend Crown Court trial when they are satisfied that the guidelines require them to do so.

9.2 Speed must never be the only reason for asking for a case to stay in the magistrates' courts. But Crown Prosecutors should consider the effect of any likely delay if they send a case to the Crown Court, and any possible stress on victims and witnesses if the case is delayed.

10. ACCEPTING GUILTY PLEAS

E–12

10.1 Defendants may want to plead guilty to some, but not all, of the charges Alternatively, they may want to plead guilty to a different, possibly less serious charge because they are admitting only part of the crime. Crown Prosecutors should only accept the defendant's plea if they think the court is able to pass a sentence that matches the seriousness of the offending, particularly where there are aggravating features. Crown Prosecutors must never accept a guilty plea just because it is convenient.

10.2 In considering whether the pleas offered are acceptable, Crown Prosecutors should ensure that the interests of the victim and, where possible, any views expressed by the victim or victim's family, are taken into account when deciding whether it is in the public interest to accept the plea. However, the decision rests with the Crown Prosecutor.

10.3 It must be made clear to the court on what basis any plea is advanced and accepted. In cases where a defendant pleads guilty to the charges but on the basis of facts that are different from the prosecution case, and where this may significantly affect sentence, the court should be invited to hear evidence to determine what happened, and then sentence on that basis.

10.4 Where a defendant has previously indicated that he or she will ask the court to take an offence into consideration when sentencing, but then declines to admit that offence at court, Crown Prosecutors will consider whether a prosecution is required for that offence. Crown Prosecutors should explain to the defence advocate and the court that the prosecution of that offence may be subject to further review.

10.5 Particular care must be taken when considering pleas which would enable the defendant to avoid the imposition of a mandatory minimum sentence. When pleas are offered, Crown Prosecutors must bear in mind the fact that ancillary orders can be made with some offences but not with others.

11 PROSECUTORS' ROLE IN SENTENCING

E–12a

11.1 Crown Prosecutors should draw the court's attention to:

- any aggravating or mitigating factors disclosed by the prosecution case;
- any victim personal statement;
- where appropriate, evidence of the impact of the offending on a community;
- any statutory provisions or sentencing guidelines which may assist;
- any relevant statutory provisions relating to ancillary orders (such as anti-social behaviour orders).

11.2 The Crown Prosecutor should challenge any assertion made by the defence in mitigation that is inaccurate, misleading or derogatory. If the defence persist in the assertion, and it appears relevant to the sentence, the court should be invited to hear evidence to determine the facts and sentence accordingly.

12 RE-STARTING A PROSECUTION

E–12b

12.1 People should be able to rely on decisions taken by the Crown Prosecution Service. Normally, if the Crown Prosecution Service tells a suspect or defendant that there will not be a prosecution, or that the prosecution has been stopped, that is the end of the matter and the case will not start again. But occasionally there are special reasons why the Crown Prosecution Service will re-start the prosecution, particularly if the case is serious.

12.2 These reasons include:

(a) rare cases where a new look at the original decision shows that it was clearly wrong and should not be allowed to stand;

(b) cases which are stopped so that more evidence which is likely to become

available in the fairly near future can be collected and prepared. In these
cases, the Crown Prosecutor will tell the defendant that the prosecution
may well start again; and

(c) cases which are stopped because of a lack of evidence but where more
significant evidence is discovered later.

12.3 There may also be exceptional cases in which, following an acquittal of a serious offence, the Crown Prosecutor may, with the written consent of the Director of
Public Prosecutions, apply to the Court of Appeal for an order quashing the acquittal
and requiring the defendant to be retried, in accordance with Part 10 of the *Criminal
Justice Act* 2003.

The Code is a public document. It is available on the CPS Website: www.cps.gov.uk
Further copies may be obtained from:
Crown Prosecution Service
Communications Branch
50 Ludgate Hill
London
EC4M 7EX
Telephone: 020 7273 8442
Fax: 020 7329 8030
Email: publicity.branch@cps.gsi.gov.uk

© Crown Copyright 2004

C. Authorities

Charging of youths

Whereas the code for crown prosecutors requires consideration to be given   **E–12c**
to the interests of a child or young person when deciding whether it is in the
public interest to prosecute (see para. 8.8, *ante*, E–10), there is no requirement that a crown prosecutor should obtain a risk assessment from the youth
offending services or that he should contact the potential defendant's school:
R. (A.) v. South Yorkshire Police and CPS, 171 J.P. 465, DC.

In *D. and B. v. Commr of Police for the Metropolis, CPS, Croydon JJ.* [2008]
A.C.D. 47, DC, it was held that it was permissible for a crown prosecutor to
decide that the combination of the seriousness of an offence and the public
interest warranted prosecution, despite the fact that the particular circumstances of the offence would normally, in accordance with the guidance issued
under section 65 of the *CDA* 1998, be such as to justify only a final warning.
As to this case, see also § 4–62 in the main work.

Charging victims of human trafficking

Where it is possible that a defendant or potential defendant is a victim of   **E–12d**
human trafficking, a prosecutor should take cognisance of the CPS guidance
on (i) the prosecution of defendants charged with immigration offences
(including that of possessing a false identity document with intent, contrary to
the *Identity Cards Act* 2006, s.25(1) (§ 22–45a in the main work)) who might be
victims of trafficking, and (ii) the prosecution of young offenders charged with
offences who might be such victims; in particular, under (i), when deciding
whether to prosecute, or to continue to prosecute, a "credible trafficked victim"
for immigration offences, prosecutors should consider whether this would
serve the public interest; and under (ii), a case should be discontinued on
evidential grounds where there is clear evidence that a youth has a credible
defence of duress, but, if the evidence is less certain, further details should be

sought from the police and youth offender teams; the defence, on the other hand, should make inquiries wherever there is credible material showing that the defendant might have been a trafficked victim, especially if the client is young; as a signatory to the Council of Europe Convention on Action against Trafficking in Human Beings, the United Kingdom is required to identify and protect victims of trafficking, and, whereas the CPS guidance supports the purpose of the convention, a trial which had failed to have proper regard to it was not fair, either under the principles of the common law or under the principles enshrined in the ECHR: *R. v. O.*, *The Times*, October 2, 2008, CA.

The transcript of the judgment is not available and due caution is thus required. On the basis of the report published in *The Times*, however, the judgment is confusing. The court "identifies" two protocols as being the measures taken by the United Kingdom government in support of the purpose of the convention to which it refers (which was signed by the government on March 23, 2007), the first of which deals with the matters set out in (i), *ante*, and the second in (ii), *ante*. The court, according to the report, then goes on to say that these two protocols have been incorporated into the code for crown prosecutors. Yet, the protocols supposedly issued by the United Kingdom do not appear to exist (the only protocols in point being an informal CPS protocol, as to which, see *post*, and the United Nations Protocol to Prevent, Suppress and Punish Trafficking in Persons, especially Women and Children supplementing the United Nations Convention Against Transnational Organised Crime, signed by the United Kingdom on December 14, 2000, and ratified on February 9, 2006), and the current code contains no reference to either "human trafficking" or to any such protocols.

What the court appears to have done is to confuse the code (which was only ever intended to deal with general principles) with the various pieces of internal "legal guidance" issued by the CPS in respect of specific categories of offences (as to which, see *post*). Under a number of these, the information highlighted in the judgment in respect of defendants who might be trafficked victims is set out in detail, based on an internal CPS Policy Bulletin (PB 126 2007 – Human Trafficking – where victims of human trafficking may be charged with criminal offences). In particular, the Immigration and Offences Protocol legal guidance (http://www.cps.gov.uk/legal/h_to_k/ immigration_offences_and_protocol/) contains two sections with the same titles as (i) and (ii), *ante*. As to the status of such guidance, see *post*, E–13.

The full code test/evidential stage

E–12e   When applying the "realistic prospect of conviction" test, a prosecutor should adopt a "merits based" approach, imagining himself to be the fact finder and asking himself, whether, on balance, the evidence is sufficient to merit a conviction, taking into account what he knows about the defence case, rather than a predictive "bookmaker's" approach, based on past experience of similar cases; questions of how a jury are likely to see a case are not relevant at this stage but at a later stage, under the public interest test in paragraphs 5.6 to 5.13 of the code: *R. (F.B.) v. DPP* [2009] 1 Cr.App.R. 38, DC. As to this case, see also ante, §§ 1–263, 16–40a.

II. LEGAL GUIDANCE AND CHARGING STANDARDS

E–13   Apart from the code for crown prosecutors, the CPS has prepared legal guidance to prosecutors and caseworkers in relation to many criminal offences

and procedural issues. It has never been suggested that such guidance has the
force of law, or even parity of standing with the code. It is merely, in the
words of the CPS website (where it is available to the public), "an aid to guide
crown prosecutors and associate prosecutors in the use of their discretion in
making decisions in cases", which "does not create any rights enforceable at
law, in any legal proceedings", and is subject to the principles as set out in the
code for crown prosecutors.

Incorporated within the guidance are various "charging standards" for   **E–14**
various offences or groups of offences, such as offences against the person,
driving offences, public order offences and theft. They contain a mixture of
propositions of law (as to the ingredients of the various offences, maximum
penalties, available alternative verdicts, *etc.*) and guidance as to the various
factors that should be taken into consideration in deciding which offence to
charge. The standards emphasise that they:

   (a) are not to be used in the determination of any pre-charge decision,
such as the decision to arrest;

   (b) do not override any guidance issued on the use of appropriate alternative forms of disposal short of charge, such as cautioning;

   (c) do not override the principles set out in the code for crown prosecutors;

   (d) do not override the need for consideration to be given in every case as
to whether a charge or prosecution is in the public interest;

   (e) do not override particular policy guidance involving hate crimes; and

   (f) do not remove the need for each case to be considered on its individual merits or fetter the discretion of the police to charge and the CPS
to prosecute the most appropriate offence depending on the particular
facts of the case in question.

The following recitation of general charging principles is common to all the
standards:

   (a) the charge or charges preferred should accurately reflect the extent of
the defendant's involvement and responsibility, thereby allowing the
courts the discretion to sentence appropriately;

   (b) the choice of charges should ensure the clear and simple presentation
of the case, particularly where there is more than one defendant;

   (c) it is wrong to encourage a defendant to plead guilty to a few charges
by selecting more charges than are necessary;

   (d) it is wrong to select a more serious charge which is not supported by
the evidence in order to encourage a plea of guilty to a lesser allegation.

III. THE ROLE AND RESPONSIBILITIES OF THE PROSECUTION ADVOCATE

FOREWORD

The Prosecution Advocate plays an important public role and as such may be   **E–15**
considered a cornerstone of an open and fair criminal justice system. The principles
so well articulated by Farquharson L.J. and his committee as to the role of the prosecution advocate have served us well since they were published in 1986. However,
the time has come for new guidance which, whilst building on the established

principles, reflects the changes that have occurred in the criminal courts, at the Bar and within the Crown Prosecution Service over recent years.

I welcome and commend the new Guidelines which, whilst not legally binding unless expressly approved by the Court of Appeal, nonetheless provide important practical guidance for practitioners involved in the prosecution process.

Lord Woolf C.J.

INTRODUCTION

E-16   The work undertaken in 1986 by the committee chaired by Farquharson L.J. has, for over 15 years, provided valuable guidance as to role [*sic*] of the prosecution advocate and their relationship with the Crown Prosecution Service (CPS).

However, the ever-evolving criminal justice system, changes at the Bar and developments in the CPS brought about by the implementation of Sir Iain Glidewell's Review, mean that the environment in whcih we all operate has radically changed since the original report was published.

Whilst the principles established by Farquharson L.J.'s committee have been enormously helpful and will continue to apply, the time has come for new guidance that reflects the changes and emphasises the new relationship that is developing between CPS Areas and the local Bar.

The new Guidelines have therefore been developed to take account of the changes and are the result of the Bar and CPS working in partnership and in consultation with the judiciary, Bar Council and Law Society.

We commend the Guidelines as providing valuable guidance and a framework within which the Bar and the CPS can work effectively together.

Lord Goldsmith Q.C., Attorney General
David Calvert-Cmith Q.C., Director of Public Prosecutions

1. Pre-trial preparation

Farquharson

E-17   *(a) It is the duty of prosecution counsel to read the Instructions delivered to him expeditiously and to advise or confer with those instructing him on all aspects of the case well before its commencement.*

E-18   1.1 The Crown Prosecution Service (CPS) will deliver instructions at a stage in the proceedings that allows sufficient time for the prosecution advocate adequately to consider, prepare and advise on the evidence before the court hearing or draft/agree the indictment.

1.2 Where a CPS higher court advocate represents the prosecution at a Plea and Directions Hearing (PDH), the CPS will deliver instructions to the trial advocate no later than 10 working days after the date of the PDH.

1.3 The CPS will deliver instructions which:

   i. address the issues in the case including any strategic decisions that have been or may need to be made;

   ii. identify relevant case law;

   iii. explain the basis and rationale of any decision made in relation to the disclosure of unused material;

   iv. where practical, provide specific guidance or indicate parameters on acceptable plea(s); and

   v. where a case is an appeal either to the Crown Court from the magistrates' court or is before the Court of Appeal, Divisional Court or House of Lords, address the issues raised in the notice of appeal, case stated, application for judicial review or petition.

Action on receipt of instructions

1.4 On receipt of instructions the prosecution advocate will consider the papers   **E–19**
and advise the CPS, ordinarily in writing, or orally in cases of urgency where:

    i. the prosecution advocate forms a different view to that expressed by the
CPS (or where applicable a previous prosecution advocate) on acceptability of plea;

    ii. the indictment as preferred requires amendment;

    iii. additional evidence is required;

    iv. there is an evidential deficiency (which cannot be addressed by the obtain-
ing of further evidence) and, applying the Code for Crown Prosecutors,
there is no longer a realistic prospect of conviction; or the prosecution
advocate believes that it is not in the public interest to continue the prosecution;

    v. in order to expedite and simplify proceedings certain formal admissions
should be made;

    vi. the prosecution advocate, having reviewed previous disclosure decisions,
disagrees with a decision that has been made; or is not satisfied that he or
she is in possession of all relevant documentation; or considers that he or
she has not been fully instructed regarding disclosure matters;

    vii. a case conference is required (particularly where there is a sensitive issue,
e.g. informant/ PII/ disclosure etc);

    viii. the presentation of the case to the court requires special preparation of
material for the jury or presentational aids.

1.5 The prosecution advocate will endeavour to respond within five working days   **E–20**
of receiving instructions, or within such period as may be specified or agreed where
the case is substantial or the issues complex.

1.6 Where the prosecution advocate is to advise on a specific aspect of the case
other than 1.4 (i–viii), the advocate should contact the CPS and agree a realistic timescale within which advice is to be provided.

1.7 The prosecution advocate will inform the CPS without delay where the
advocate is unlikely to be available to undertake the prosecution or advise within the
relevant timescale.

1.8 When returning a brief, the advocate originally instructed must ensure that
the case is in good order and should discuss outstanding issues or potential difficulties with the advocate receiving the brief. Where the newly instructed advocate
disagrees with a decision or opinion reached by the original advocate, the CPS
should be informed so that the matter can be discussed.

Case summaries

1.9 When a draft case summary is prepared by the CPS, the prosecution advocate   **E–21**
will consider the summary and either agree the contents or advise the CPS of any
proposed amendment.

1.10 In cases where the prosecution advocate is instructed to settle the case summary or schedules, the document(s) will be prepared and submitted to the CPS
without delay.

Case management plan

1.11 On receipt of a case management plan the prosecution advocate, having   **E–22**
considered the papers, will contact the Crown Prosecutor within seven days, or such
period as may be specified or agreed where the case is substantial or the issues
complex, to discuss and agree the plan. The plan will be maintained and regularly
reviewed to reflect the progress of the case.

Keeping the prosecution advocate informed

1.12 The CPS will inform the prosecution advocate of developments in the case   **E–23** without delay and, where a decision is required which may materially affect the conduct and presentation of the case, will consult with the prosecution advocate prior to that decision.

1.13 Where the CPS is advised by the defence of a plea(s) of guilty or there are developments which suggest that offering no evidence on an indictment or count therein is an appropriate course, the matter should always be discussed with the prosecution advocate without delay unless to do so would be wholly impracticable.

Victims and witnesses

E–24

1.14 When a decision whether or not to prosecute is based on the public interest, the CPS will always consider the consequences of that decision for the victim and will take into account any views expressed by the victim or the victim's family.

1.15 The prosecution advocate will follow agreed procedures and guidance on the care and treatment of victims and witnesses, particularly those who may be vulnerable or have special needs.

Appeals

E–25

1.16 Where the prosecution advocate forms a different view to that expressed by the CPS on the conduct/approach to the appeal, the advocate should advise the CPS within FIVE working days of receiving instructions or such period as may be specified or agreed where the case is substantial or the issues complex.

PDH and other preliminary hearings

E–26

1.17 The principles and procedures applying to trials as set out in the following paragraphs will be equally applicable where the prosecution advocate is conducting a PDH or other preliminary hearing.

2. Withdrawal of instructions

Farquharson

E–27

(b) A solicitor who has briefed counsel to prosecute may withdraw his instructions before the commencement of the trial up to the point when it becomes impracticable to do so, if he disagrees with the advice given by Counsel or for any other proper professional reason.

2.1 The CPS will consult and take all reasonable steps to resolve any issue or disagreement and will only consider withdrawing instructions from a prosecution advocate as a last resort.

2.2 If the prosecution advocate disagrees with any part of his or her instructions the advocate should contact the responsible Crown Prosecutor to discuss the matter. Until the disagreement has been resolved the matter will remain confidential and must not be discussed by the prosecution advocate with any other party to the proceedings.

"Proper professional reason"

E–28

2.3 The prosecution advocate will keep the CPS informed of any personal concerns, reservations or ethical issues that the advocate considers have the potential to lead to possible conflict with his or her instructions.

2.4 Where the CPS identifies the potential for professional embarrassment or has concerns about the prosecution advocate's ability or experience to present the case effectively to the court, the CPS reserves the right to withdraw instructions.

Timing

E–29

2.5 It is often difficult to define when, in the course of a prosecution it becomes impracticable to withdraw instructions as circumstances will vary according to the case. The nature of the case, its complexity, witness availability and the view of the court will often be factors that will influence the decision.

2.6 In the majority of prosecutions it will not be practicable to withdraw instructions once the judge has called the case before the court as a preliminary step to the swearing of the jury.

2.7 If instructions are withdrawn, the prosecution advocate will be informed in writing and reasons will be given.

2.8 Instructions may only be withdrawn by or with the consent of the Chief Crown Prosecutor, Assistant Chief Crown Prosecutor, Head of a CPS Trials Unit or, in appropriate cases, Head of a CPS Criminal Justice Unit.

2.9 In relation to cases prosecuted by the CPS Casework Directorate, the decision may only be taken by the Director Casework or Head of Division.

3. Presentation and conduct

Farquharson

(c) *While he remains instructed it is for counsel to take all necessary decisions in the presentation and general conduct of the prosecution.* **E–30**

3.1 The statement at 3(c) applies when the prosecution advocate is conducting the trial, PDH or any other preliminary hearing, but is subject to the principles and procedures relating to matters of policy set out in section 4 below.

Disclosure of material

3.2 Until the conclusion of the trial the prosecution advocate and CPS have a **E–31** continuing duty to keep under review decisions regarding disclosure. The prosecution advocate should in every case specifically consider whether he or she can satisfactorily discharge the duty of continuing review on the basis of the material supplied already, or whether it is necessary to inspect further material or to reconsider material already inspected.

3.3 Disclosure of material must always follow the established law and procedure. Unless consultation is impracticable or cannot be achieved without a delay to the hearing, it is desirable that the CPS, and where appropriate the disclosure officer are consulted over disclosure decisions.

4. Policy decisions

Farquharson

(d) *Where matters of policy[1] fall to be decided after the point indicated in (b) above* **E–32** *(including offering no evidence on the indictment or on a particular count, or on the acceptance of pleas to lesser counts), it is the duty of Counsel to consult his Instructing Solicitor/ Crown Prosecutor whose views at this stage are of crucial importance.*

(e) *In the rare case where counsel and his instructing solicitor are unable to agree on a matter of policy, it is, subject to (g) below, for prosecution counsel to make the necessary decisions.*

Policy issues arising at trial

4.1 The prosecution advocate should alert the CPS at the first opportunity if a **E–33** matter of policy is likely to arise.

4.2 The prosecution advocate must not give an indication or undertaking which binds the prosecution without first discussing the issue with the CPS.

CPS representation at Crown Court

4.3 Whenever possible, an experienced Crown Prosecutor will be available at the **E–34** Crown Court to discuss and agree any issue involving the conduct or progress of the case.

4.4 When it is not possible to provide a Crown Prosecutor at court, an experienced caseworker will attend and facilitate communication between the prosecution advocate and the Crown Prosecutor having responsibility for the case.

4.5 In exceptional circumstances where it is not possible to contact a Crown Prosecutor, the prosecution advocate should ask the court to adjourn the hearing for a realistic period in order to consult with the CPS. Where an adjournment is refused, the prosecution advocate may make the decision but should record his or her reasons in writing.

Referral to senior CPS representative

4.6 Where an issue remains unresolved following consultation with a Crown Prosecutor; or where the case/issue under consideration is substantial, sensitive or complex; or the prosecution advocate disagrees with the advice of the Crown Prosecutor, the matter may be referred to the Chief Crown Prosecutor, the Director Casework or to a senior Crown Prosecutor with delegated authority to act on their behalf.

4.7 In order to ensure consultation takes place at the highest level appropriate to the circumstances and nature of the case, the court should be asked to adjourn if necessary. When an adjournment is sought, the facts leading to the application should be placed before the court only in so far as they are relevant to that application.

4.8 Where a Chief Crown Prosecutor has been directly involved in the decision making process and the issue remains unresolved, the matter may be referred to the Director of Public Prosecutions.

Farquharson

(f) Where counsel has taken a decision on a matter of policy with which his Instructing Solicitor has not agreed, then it would be appropriate for the Attorney General to require Counsel to submit to him a written report of all the circumstances, including his reasons for disagreeing with those who instruct him.

4.9 It will only be in exceptional circumstances that the Attorney General will require a written report. The prosecution advocate will first discuss the decision with the Chief Crown Prosecutor or the Director, Casework. Where, by agreement, the issue remains one that either party considers should be drawn to the attention of the Director of Public Prosecutions the prosecution advocate will, on request, provide a written report for submission to the Director of Public Prosecutions. If he considers it appropriate to do so, the Director of Public Prosecutions may refer the matter to the Attorney General.

4.10 Where there has been a disagreement on a matter of policy, provided that the CPS is satisfied that the prosecution advocate followed the principles set out in this document, the professional codes of conduct and was not *Wednesbury* unreasonable, the CPS will not apply sanctions in respect of any future work solely as a result of the decision in a particular case.

5. Change of advice

Farquharson

(g) When counsel has had the opportunity to prepare his brief and to confer with those instructing him, but at the last moment before trial unexpectedly advises that the case should not proceed or that pleas to lesser offences should be accepted, and his Instructing Solicitor does not accept such advice, counsel should apply for an adjournment if instructed so to do.

5.1 The CPS and the prosecution advocate should agree a period of adjournment that would allow a newly instructed advocate to prepare for trial. The period should be realistic and acknowledge that in such circumstances a case conference will usually be required.

5.2 The facts leading to the application for the adjournment should be placed before the court only in so far as they are relevant to that application.

6. Prosecution advocate's role in decision making at trial

Farquharson

(h) *Subject to the above, it is for prosecution counsel to decide whether to offer no evidence* **E–39**
on a particular count or on the indictment as a whole and whether to accept pleas to a lesser
count or counts.

6.1 The prosecution advocate may ask the defence advocate as to whether a plea
will be forthcoming but at this initial stage should not suggest or indicate a plea that
might be considered acceptable to the prosecution before a plea is offered.

6.2 Where the defence advocate subsequently offers details of a plea, the prosecution advocate may discuss the matter with a view to establishing an acceptable plea
that reflects the defendant's criminality and provides the court with sufficient powers
to sentence appropriately.

Responsibility of prosecution advocate to consult

6.3 Where the prosecution advocate forms the view that the appropriate course is **E–40**
to accept a plea before proceedings commence or continue, or to offer no evidence
on the indictment or any part of it, the prosecution advocate should:

    i. whenever practicable, speak with the victim or victim's family attending
       court to explain the position;

    ii. ensure that the interests of the victim or any views expressed by the
       victim or victim's family are taken into account as part of the decision
       making process; and

    iii. keep the victim or victim's family attending court informed and explain
       decisions as they are made.

6.4 Where appropriate the prosecution advocate may seek an adjournment of the
court hearing in order to facilitate discussion with the victim or victim's family.

6.5 The prosecution advocate should always comply with paragraph 6.3 and,
where practicable, discuss the matter with the CPS before informing the defence
advocate or the court that a plea is acceptable.

6.6 Where the defendant indicates an acceptable plea, unless the issue is simple,
the defence should reduce the basis of the plea to writing. The prosecution advocate
should show the CPS any written record relating to the plea and agree with the CPS
the basis on which the case will be opened to the court.

6.7 It is the responsibility of the prosecution advocate to ensure that the defence
advocate is aware of the basis on which the plea is accepted by the prosecution and
the way in which the prosecution case will be opened to the court.

6.8 It will not be necessary for the prosecution advocate to consult the CPS where
the plea or course of action accords with the written instructions received from the
CPS, although paragraph 6.3 may still apply.

Prosecution advocate's role in sentencing

6.9 The prosecution advocate should always draw the court's attention to any **E–41**
matters, including aggravating or mitigating features, that might affect sentence. Additionally, the advocate should be in a position to assist the court, if requested, with
any statutory provisions or sentencing guidelines and should always draw attention
to potential sentencing errors.

6.10 Where a discussion on plea and sentence takes place, the prosecution
advocate must adhere to the Attorney General's Guidelines on the Acceptance of
Pleas published on 7 December 2000.

7. Seeking judicial approval

Farquharson

(i) *If prosecution counsel invites the Judge to approve the course he is proposing to take,* **E–42**
then he must abide by the judge's decision.

7.1 A discussion with the judge about the acceptability of a plea or conduct of the case should be held in the presence of the defendant unless exceptional circumstances apply.[2]

7.2 In exceptional circumstances, where the prosecution advocate considers it appropriate to communicate with the judge or seek the judge's view in chambers, the CPS should be consulted before such a step is taken.

7.3 Where discussions take place in chambers it is the responsibility of the prosecution advocate to remind the judge, if necessary, that an independent record must always be kept.

7.4 The prosecution advocate should also make a full note of such an event, recording all decisions and comments. This note should be made available to the CPS.

Farquharson

(j) If prosecution counsel does not invite the judge's approval of his decision it is open to the judge to express his dissent with the course proposed and invite counsel to reconsider the matter with those instructing him, but having done so, the final decision remains with counsel.

7.5 Where a judge expresses a view based on the evidence or public interest, the CPS will carry out a further review of the case.

7.6 The prosecution advocate will inform the CPS in a case where the judge has expressed a dissenting view and will agree the action to be taken. Where there is no CPS representative at court, the prosecution advocate will provide a note of the judge's comments.

7.7 The prosecution advocate will ensure that the judge is aware of all factors that have a bearing on the prosecution decision to adopt a particular course. Where there is a difference of opinion between the prosecution advocate and the CPS the judge will be informed as to the nature of the disagreement.

Farquharson

(k) In an extreme case where the judge is of the opinion that the course proposed by counsel would lead to serious injustice, he may decline to proceed with the case until counsel has consulted with either the Director or the Attorney General as may be appropriate.

7.8 As a preliminary step, the prosecution advocate will discuss the judge's observations with the Chief Crown Prosecutor in an attempt to resolve the issue. Where the issue remains unresolved the Director of Public Prosecutions will be consulted. In exceptional circumstances the Director of Public Prosecutions may consult the Attorney General.

Note: These Guidelines are subject to the Code of Conduct of the Bar of England and Wales (barrister advocates) and The Law Society's The Guide to the Professional Conduct of Solicitors (solicitor advocates). Whilst reference is made in the guidelines to the CPS and levels of authority within the Service, the guidelines may be adopted as best practice, with consequential amendments to levels of authority, by other prosecuting authorities.

These Guidelines may be amended at any time and copyright is waived.

These Guidelines are also available on the CPS Website: www.cps.gov.uk.

Footnotes

1. (See Farquharson (d)), "'policy' decisions should be understood as referring to non-evidential decisions on: the acceptance of pleas of guilty to lesser counts or groups of counts or available alternatives; offering no evidence on particular counts; consideration of a retrial; whether to lodge an appeal; certification of a point of law; and the withdrawal of the prosecution as a whole."

2. (See para. 7.1.), "For the purposes of these guidelines, 'exceptional circumstances' would include the following:

(i) Where there is material or information which should not be made public,
e.g. a police text, or for some other compelling reason such as a defendant
or witness suffering, unkown to them, from a serious or terminal illness;
or

(ii) There are sensitivities surrounding a prosecution decision or proposed action which need to be explained in chambers with a view to obtaining
judicial approval. Such approval may be given in open court where it is
necessary to explain a prosecution decision or action in order to maintain
public confidence in the criminal justice system."

APPENDIX F

The Channel Tunnel

Introduction

The starting point is the Treaty between the United Kingdom of Great   **F–1**
Britain and Northern Ireland and the French Republic concerning the
Construction and Operation by Private Concessionaires of a Channel Fixed
Link (the "Treaty of Canterbury") (T.S. No. 15 (1992) (Cm 1827)). It is only
necessary to set out Article 1 thereof, which contains definitions. These are
incorporated in Article 1(1) of Schedule 2 to the *Channel Tunnel (International
Arrangements) Order* 1993 (S.I. 1993 No. 1813) (*post*).

The *Channel Tunnel Act* 1987 provided, *inter alia*, for the construction and
operation of the tunnel system, for the incorporation of part of the tunnel
system into the United Kingdom and for the application and enforcement of
law in relation to, and otherwise for the regulation of, that system and matters
connected with it.

S.I. 1993 No. 1813, *ante*, is made under section 11 of the 1987 Act. It
makes detailed provision in relation, *inter alia*, to the application of the criminal law outside the United Kingdom and in relation to the powers of
constables and other officers. Article 1 provides for it to come into force on a
date to be notified in the London, Edinburgh and Belfast *Gazettes*. The date
notified was August 2, 1993 (*London Gazette*, August 6, 1993).

In relation to rail traffic between the United Kingdom and Belgium, there
is a further agreement and a further order. The agreement is the Agreement
between the Government of the Kingdom of Belgium, the Government of the
French Republic and the Government of the United Kingdom of Great Britain and Northern Ireland Concerning Rail Traffic between Belgium and the
United Kingdom Using the Channel Fixed Link. This agreement came into
force on December 1, 1997.

The further order is the *Channel Tunnel (Miscellaneous Provisions) Order*
1994 (S.I. 1994 No. 1405). Apart from certain amending provisions, which
came into force on July 1, 1994, this order came into force simultaneously
with the agreement.

S.I. 1994 No. 1405 is made under section 11 of the *Channel Tunnel Act*
1987. It gives qualified effect in United Kingdom law to material provisions
(the "tripartite articles" set out in Schedule 2) of the agreement.

The tripartite articles are by article 3(1) given the force of law within, and
for the purposes specified in article 2(2) outside, the control zones accorded to
Belgium ("the Belgian control zone") and to France by the tripartite articles;
article 3(2) affirms that Belgian, and French, officers may to the extent specified in the tripartite articles go about their business in the United Kingdom,
and article 3(3) ensures that Belgian officers can be provided with the required
facilities. Article 4(1) performs the corresponding operation for British officers
working in Belgium or France.

Article 5(1) to (3) extends English criminal jurisdiction to conduct in a
United Kingdom control zone which, if taking place in England, would constitute an offence under a frontier control enactment as defined in Schedule 1.
Article 5(4) creates a presumption as to jurisdiction where it is uncertain in
which of the three states an offence not of that kind was committed.

Treaty between the United Kingdom of Great Britain and Northern Ireland and the French Republic Concerning The Construction and Operation by Private Concessionaires of a Channel Fixed Link
(T.S. No. 15 (1992) (Cm. 1827))

ARTICLE 1

Object and Definitions

F-2   (1) The High Contracting Parties undertake to permit the construction and operation by private concessionaires (hereinafter referred to as "the Concessionaires") of a Channel fixed link in accordance with the provisions of this Treaty, of its supplementary Protocols and arrangements and of a concession between the two Governments and the Concessionaires (hereinafter referred to as "the Concession"). The Channel fixed link shall be financed without recourse to government funds or to government guarantees of a financial or commercial nature.

(2) The Channel fixed link (hereinafter referred to as "the Fixed Link"), which shall be more particularly described in the Concession, means a twin bored tunnel rail link, with associated service tunnel under the English Channel between Cheriton in Kent and Fréthun in the Pas-de-Calais, together with the terminal areas for control of access to, and egress from, the tunnels, and shall include any freight or other facility, and any road link between the United Kingdom and France, which may hereafter be agreed between the High Contracting Parties to form part of the Fixed Link.

Channel Tunnel Act 1987, s.1(1), (3)–(10)

Construction and operation of a tunnel rail link between the United Kingdom and France

F-3   **1.**—(1) The primary purpose of this Act is to provide for the construction and operation of a tunnel rail link (together with associated works, facilities and installations) under the English Channel between the United Kingdom and France, in accordance with—

(a) the Treaty between the United Kingdom of Great Britain and Northern Ireland and the French Republic concerning the Construction and Operation by Private Concessionaires of a Channel Fixed Link, signed at Canterbury on 12th February 1986, together with its supplementary protocols and arrangements; and

(b) the Concession between Her Majesty's Government in the United Kingdom and the Government of the French Republic on the one hand and private Concessionaires on the other hand which, in accordance with Article 1 of that Treaty, regulates, together with that Treaty, the construction and operation of the Channel fixed link referred to in that Article.

(3) Subject to section 3 of this Act, the expressions defined below in this section have the meanings there given for the purposes of this Act.

(4) "The Treaty" means the Treaty mentioned in paragraph (a) of subsection (1) above, including its supplementary protocols and arrangements, and "the Concession" means the Concession mentioned in paragraph (b) of that subsection.

(5) "Concession agreement" means any agreement or arrangement which for the time being constitutes, or is included among the agreements or arrangements which together for the time being constitute, the Concession.

(6) "Concession lease" means any lease granted by the Secretary of State to the Concessionaires in pursuance of the Concession, and references to a Concession lease include any provisions of a Concession agreement providing for the grant of a lease of any land by the Secretary of State to the Concessionaires.

(7) "The tunnel system" means the tunnel rail link, together with its associated works, facilities and installations, to be constructed in pursuance of the Treaty, and incorporating—

(a) tunnels under the English Channel between Cheriton, Folkestone, in

Kent and Fréthun in the Pas de Calais, comprising two main tunnels
capable of carrying both road traffic on shuttle trains and rail traffic, and
an associated service tunnel;

(b) two terminal areas, for controlling access to and egress from the tunnels,
located at the portals of the tunnels in the vicinity of Cheriton, Folkestone and Fréthun respectively;

(c) a service and maintenance area at the Old Dover Colliery site;

(d) an inland clearance depot at Ashford, in Kent, for the accommodation, in
connection with the application to them of customs and other controls, of
freight vehicles which have been or are to be conveyed through the tunnels on shuttle services;

(e) necessary links with the road and rail networks of each country; and

(f) the fixed and movable equipment needed for the operation of the tunnels and the associated works, facilities and installations mentioned in
paragraphs (b) to (e) above or for the operation of shuttle services using
the tunnels.

(8) "The Concessionaires" means the person or persons who, under the Concession, have for the time being the function of constructing and operating or (as the
case may be) of operating the tunnel system.

(9) "Shuttle train" means a train designed for the purpose of carrying road traffic
between Cheriton, Folkestone and Fréthun by way of the tunnels and "shuttle service" means a service operated by means of a shuttle train.

(10) Where the Concessionaires for the time being are two or more persons, any
provision of this Act conferring or imposing upon them any right, power, liability or
duty shall have effect (except where the context otherwise requires) so as to confer or
impose it upon them jointly; but anything done by or in relation to any one of them
which purports to be done by or in relation to both or all of them shall have effect
for the purposes of this Act as if done by or in relation to them jointly.

Channel Tunnel Act 1987, s.10(1)

Incorporation of part of the tunnel into the United Kingdom and general application of law

10.—(1) The land compromising the tunnel system as far as the frontier, so far   **F–4**
as not forming part of the United Kingdom before the passing of this Act, shall, as
it becomes occupied by or on behalf of the Concessionaires working from England,
together with so much of the surrounding subsoil as is necessary for the security
of the part of the system so occupied, be incorporated into England and form
part of the district of Dover in the county of Kent, and the law of England shall
apply accordingly.

Channel Tunnel Act 1987, s.11(1), (3), (4)

Regulation of the tunnel system: application and enforcement of law, etc.

11.—(1) The appropriate Minister may by order make such provision as ap-   **F–5**
pears to him to be necessary or expedient—

(a) for the purpose of implementing the international arrangements, or enabling those arrangements to be implemented.

(b) [*transfer of property*];

(c) in relation to the construction, operation or use of the tunnel system or any
part of the tunnel system, so far as relates to activities carried on, persons
employed or engaged in work, things done or omitted or other matters
arising anywhere within the system (whether in England or in France),
including in particular (without prejudice to the generality of the preceding
provision) provision with respect to controls in relation to persons or goods
within the system;

(d) for the purpose of applying any provisions of the law of England (with or without modifications), or excluding or modifying any of those provisions in relation to things done or omitted or other matters arising anywhere within the tunnel system (whether in England or France);

(e) with respect to controls in relation to persons or goods—

    (i) on trains engaged on international services; or

    (ii) at authorised terminal control points for such services; outside the tunnel system (whether in the United Kingdom or elsewhere);

(f) in relation to persons employed or engaged on work outside the tunnel system (whether in the United Kingdom or elsewhere)—

    (i) on any train engaged on an international service, in or for the purpose of or in connection with the operation of that service; or

    (ii) in or for the purposes of or in connection with the exercise, on any such train or at any authorised terminal control point for such service of any controls in relation to persons or goods as are mentioned in paragraph (e) above;

(g) for the purpose of dealing with any matters arising out of or connected with any provision within the powers conferred by any of paragraphs (a) to (f) above (whether or not those matters arise within the tunnel system, or any such train or at any such control point); or

(h) otherwise in relation to, or for regulating any matters arising out of or connected with, the tunnel system.

(3) Without prejudice to the generality of subsection (1) above, the kind of provision that may be made by an order under this section includes the following—

(a) provision creating new criminal offences punishable as may be provided by the order or imposing penalties otherwise than in respect of criminal offences;

(b) [*fees and charges*];

(c) provision conferring power on any Minister of the Crown or Government department to make orders, rules, regulations or other subordinate instruments of a legislative character;

(d) provision for, or authorising any such order, rule, regulation or other subordinate instrument to provide for, the delegation of any function conferred or imposed by or in pursuance of any order under this section or by any enactment;

(e) provision, subject to subsection (4) below, for or in connection with the enforcement or execution outside the United Kingdom of any provision of the law of England or within the United Kingdom of any provision of the law of any other country, including in particular—

    (i) provision conferring powers on any officer belonging to the United Kingdom to arrest and detain outside the United Kingdom persons suspected of having committed offences under the law of England and bring them to lawful custody in England;

    (ii) provision conferring powers on any such officer to arrest and detain within the United Kingdom persons suspected of having committed offences under the law of any other country and surrender them to the custody of officers belonging to that country without the authority of any order or a court in any part of the United Kingdom; and

    (iii) provision for or in connection with the exercise in the United Kingdom by officers belonging to any other country of powers corresponding to those mentioned in sub-paragraph (i) above; and

(f) provision conferring jurisdiction on courts or tribunals in any part of the United Kingdom or limiting the jurisdiction otherwise exercisable by any such courts or tribunals.

(4) An order under this section may not make provision for or in connection with the exercise of powers by officers belonging to one country in any other country except—

(a) within the tunnel system;

(b) on trains engaged on international services; or

(c) at authorised terminal control points for such services.

Channel Tunnel Act 1987, s.12

Controls on board trains engaged on international services

12.—(1) It shall be duty of the appropriate Minister to secure that, where this   **F–6**
subsection applies, controls exercisable in relation to—

(a) passengers carried on a train engaged on an international service on a journey beginning or intended to end at a place in Great Britain other than London or Cheriton, Folkestone or any place between those places; or

(b) things contained in the baggage of such passengers;

shall be exercised on the train.

(2) Subject to subsection (3) below, subsection (1) above applies where—

(a) the person operating the service has made a request to the appropriate Minister that the controls in question should be exercised on trains engaged on the service in question;

(b) the appropriate Minister has approved as satisfactory arrangements made by that person for the provision of facilities to enable the controls in question to be exercised on such trains;

(c) facilities enabling the exercise of the controls in question are provided on the train in question in accordance with such approved arrangements; and

(d) the controls are exercised by customs officers or immigration officers.

(3) Subsection (1) above does not apply—

(a) in the case of passengers carried on a particular train or part of a particular train, or things contained in the baggage of such passengers, if in the opinion of a customs officer or immigration officer exercising the controls it is not reasonably practicable effectively to exercise the controls in question on the train or part of a train; and

(b) in the case of any particular passenger or things contained in the baggage of any particular passenger, if in the opinion of any such officer it is not reasonably practicable effectively to exercise the controls in question in relation to the passenger or his baggage on the train.

(4) [*Fees and charges.*]

(5) In this section—

"customs officer" means an officer or other person acting under the authority of the Commissioners of Customs and Excise; and

"immigration officer" means an immigration officer appointed for the purposes of the *Immigration Act* 1971.

Channel Tunnel Act 1987, s.13

Provisions supplementary to sections 11 and 12

13.—(1) Subject to subsection (2) below, in sections 11 and 12 of this Act "the   **F–7**
appropriate Minister" means, in relation to any matter, the Minister in charge of any Government department concerned with that matter or, where more than one such department is concerned with that matter, the Ministers in charge of those departments, acting jointly.

(2) Where the Commissioners of Customs and Excise or the Forestry Commissioners are concerned with any matter (whether alone or together with any other Government department) subsection (1) above shall apply as if the references to the Minister or Ministers in charge of any Government department or departments concerned with that matter were or included references to those Commissioners.

(3) The validity of any order purporting to be made under section 11 of this Act shall not be affected by any question whether or not the order fell by virtue of subsection (1) above to be made by the Minister or department (or any of the Ministers or departments) purporting to make it.

(4) In sections 11 and 12 of this Act "controls" means prohibitions, restrictions or requirements of any descriptions, and any reference to the exercise of controls is a reference to the exercise or performance of any functions conferred or imposed by any enactment, or otherwise under any lawful authority, for or in connection with the enforcement of prohibitions, restrictions or requirements of any description.

(5) For the purposes of those sections a train is engaged on an international service at any time when the whole or any part of the train is being used in the operation of such a service and a place is an authorised terminal control point for international services if it is designated as such in accordance with the international arrangements.

(6) In those sections and this section—

"the international arrangements" includes any agreements or arrangements between Her Majesty's Government in the United Kingdom and the Government of any country on the Continent of Europe other than France which for the time being apply for regulating any matters arising out of or connected with the operation of international services; and

"international service" means any service (including a shuttle service) for the carriage of passengers or goods by way of the tunnel system.

Policing of tunnel system

F–8   This is to be undertaken by constables under the direction of the Chief Constable of Kent constabulary: *Channel Tunnel Act* 1987, s.14(1). The Railways Board may, on the application of the Chief Constable, provide constables or other assistance for the policing of the tunnel system.

Channel Tunnel Act 1987, s.23

Control of traffic within the tunnel system

F–9   **23.**—(1) Subject to the following provisions of this section, the enactments relating to road traffic shall apply in relation to any tunnel system road to which the public does not have access as they apply in relation to a road which the public does have access.

(2) Those enactments shall apply in relation to any tunnel system road subject to such exceptions and modifications as the Secretary of State may by order specify.

(3) An order under subsection (2) above may, in particular, confer on the Concessionaires functions exercisable under those enactments by a highway authority or a local authority.

(4) The Secretary of State may by order provide that those enactments shall not apply in relation to any tunnel system road specified in the order and may require the Concessionaires to indicate any such road in a manner so specified.

(5) Those enactments shall not, in the case of any tunnel system road, apply in relation to it until such date as the Secretary of State may by order specify.

(6) Before making an order under this section, the Secretary of State shall consult the Concessionaires.

(7) In this section, "tunnel system road" means any length of road comprised in the tunnel system.

Channel Tunnel Act 1987, s.49(1)

Interpretation

F–10   **49.**—(1) In this Act, except where the context otherwise requires—

"enactment" includes an enactment contained in this Act or in any Act passed on or after the date on which this Act is passed, and any subordinate legislation within meaning of the *Interpretation Act* 1978;

"footpath" has the same meaning as in the *Highways Act* 1980;

"frontier" means the frontier between the United Kingdom and France fixed by the Treaty;

"functions" includes powers, duties and obligations;

"goods" includes vehicles (notwithstanding that they may be being used for the carriage of other goods or of persons), animals, plants and any other creature, substance or thing capable of being transported;

"the Intergovernmental Commission" means the Intergovernmental Commission established by the Treaty;

"the international arrangements" means—

    (a) the Treaty and the Concession; and

    (b) any other agreements or arrangements between Her Majesty's Government in the United Kingdom and the Government of the French Republic which for the time being apply for regulating any matters arising out of or connected with the tunnel system;

"land" includes buildings and other structures, land covered with water, and any estate, interest, easement, servitude or right in or over land;

"modification" includes addition, omission and alteration, and related expressions shall be construed accordingly;

"the Railways Board" has the meaning given by section 5(3);

"the Safety Authority" means the Safety Authority established by the Treaty;

"shuttle service" and "shuttle train" have the meanings given by section 1(9);

"substance" means any natural or artificial substance, whether in solid or liquid form or in the form of a gas or vapour;

"train" includes any locomotive and railway rolling stock of any description;

"the Treaty" has the meaning given by section 1(4);

"the tunnel system" has the meaning given by section 1(7); and

"vehicle" includes a railway vehicle.

The definitions of the following words and expressions have been omitted   **F–11**
from this subsection: "A20 improvement works", "the appropriate authority", "the arbitral tribunal", "bridleway", "deposited plans", "deposited sections", "Dover Harbour", "limits of deviation" and "nature conservation". Subsections (2) to (9) contain further interpretative provisions.

S.I. 1993 No. 1813, art. 1

Citation and commencement

1. This Order may be cited as the *Channel Tunnel (International Arrangements) Or-*   **F–12**
der 1993 and shall come into force on the date on which the Protocol between the Government of the United Kingdom of Great Britain and Northern Ireland and the Government of the French Republic Concerning Frontier Controls and Policing, Co-operation in Criminal Justice, Public Safety and Mutual Assistance Relating to the Channel Fixed Link enters into force. That date will be notified in the London, Edinburgh and Belfast *Gazettes*.

[The commencement date was August 2, 1993: see *ante*, Appendix F–1.]

S.I. 1993 No. 1813, arts 2–7

Interpretation

2.—(1) In this Order, except for the purpose of construing the international   **F–13**
articles or the supplementary articles, and in any enactment as applied by it with modifications, any expression for which there is an entry in the first column of Schedule 1 has the meaning given against it in the second column.

    (2) In this Order "the authorised purposes" means—

547

(a) purposes for which provision is authorised by any of paragraphs (a), (d) and (g), and

(b) purposes connected with any matter in relation to or with respect to or for regulating which provision is authorised by any of paragraphs (c), (e), (f) and (h), of section 11(1) of the *Channel Tunnel Act* 1987.

(3) In this Order "the international articles" means the provisions set out in Schedule 2 (being Articles or parts of Articles of the Protocol mentioned in article 1 above); and in the international articles the expression "the Fixed Link" shall for the purposes of this Order be taken to have the same meaning as is given to "the tunnel system" by section 1(7) of the *Channel Tunnel Act* 1987.

(4) In this Order "the supplementary articles" means the provisions set out in Schedule 2A (being Articles of the Additional Protocol between the Government of the United Kingdom of Great Britain and Nothern Ireland and the Government of the French Republic and amendments to those Articles made by the amending instrument), and in the supplementary articles "the Protocol signed at Sangatte" and "the Sangatte Protocol" mean the Protocol mentioned in article 1 above.

(5) In paragraph (4) and in the supplementary articles, "Additional Protocol" means the Additional Protocol to the Sangatte Protocol on the Establishment of Bureaux Responsible for Controls on Persons Travelling by Train between France and the United Kingdom, signed at Brussels on 29th May 2000.

(6) In paragraph (4) "the amending instrument" means the Agreement between the Government of the United Kingdom of Great Britain and Northern Ireland and the Government of the French Republic making amendments to the Additional Protocol to the Sangatte Protocol on the Establishment of Bureaux responsible for controls on persons travelling by train between the United Kingdom and France, and to the Agreement concerning the carrying of service weapons by French officers on the territory of the United Kingdom of Great Britain and Northern Ireland, signed in Paris on 18th June 2007.

[This article is printed as amended by the *Channel Tunnel (International Arrangements) (Amendment No. 3) Order* 2001 (S.I. 2001 No. 1544); and the *Channel Tunnel (International Arrangements) (Amendment) Order* 2007 (S.I. 2007 No. 2907).]

Application of international articles

3.—(1) The international articles shall have the force of law in the United Kingdom—

(a) within the tunnel system,

(b) within a control zone, and

(c) elsewhere for the authorised purposes only.

(2) Without prejudice to paragraph (1) officers belonging to the French Republic shall to the extent specified in the international articles have rights and obligations and powers to carry out functions in the United Kingdom.

(3) For the purpose of giving full effect to Article 34 of the international articles (accommodation etc., for authorities of adjoining State) the appropriate Minister may by written notice require any occupier or person concerned with the management of a terminal control point to provide free of charge such accommodation, installations and equipment as may be necessary to satisfy requirements determined under Article 33 of the Protocol mentioned in article 1 above (which requires the competent authorities of the two States to determine their respective requirements in consultation with one another).

[This article is printed as amended by the *Channel Tunnel (International Arrangements) (Amendment No. 4) Order* 2001 (S.I. 2001 No. 3707).]

Application of supplementary articles

3A.—(1) The supplementary articles shall have the force of law in the United Kingdom within a supplementary control zone.

(2) Subject to paragraph (4), without prejudice to paragraph (1), officers belonging to the French Republic who are responsible for immigration controls shall to the extent specified in the supplementary articles have rights and obligations and powers to carry out functions in the United Kingdom.

(3) Subject to paragraph (4), for the purpose of enabling the authorities of the French Republic to make use in the United Kingdom of the accommodation, installations and equipment necessary for the performance of their functions under the supplementary articles, the Secretary of State for the Home Department may by written notice require any occupier or person concerned with the management of a terminal control point to provide free of charge such accommodation, installations and equipment as may be necessary to satisfy requirements determined by the authorities of the French Republic in consultation with the authorities of the United Kingdom.

(4) Nothing in this article implies the existence of a supplementary control zone in the station of London-Waterloo on British Territory.

[This article was inserted by the *Channel Tunnel (International Arrangements) (Amendment No. 3) Order* 2001 (S.I. 2001 No. 1544. It is printed as amended by the *Channel Tunnel (International Arrangements) (Amendment No. 4) Order* 2001 (S.I. 2001 No. 3707); and the *Channel Tunnel (International Arrangements) (Amendment) Order* 2007 (S.I. 2007 No. 2907).]

Application of enactments

4.—(1) All frontier control enactments except those relating to transport and road traffic controls shall for the purpose of enabling officers belonging to the United Kingdom to carry out frontier controls extend to France within a control zone.

(1A) All frontier control enactments relating to transport and road traffic controls shall for the purpose of enabling officers belonging to the United Kingdom to carry out such controls extend to France within the control zone in France within the tunnel system.

(1B) All immigration control enactments shall, for the purpose of enabling immigration officers to carry out immigration controls, extend to France within a supplementary control zone.

(1C) The *Race Relations Act* 1976 shall apply to the carrying out by immigration officers of their functions in a control zone or a supplementary control zone outside the United Kingdom as it applies to the carrying out of their functions within the United Kingdom.

(2), (3) [*Application of Data Protection Act* 1984.]

[This article is printed as amended by the *Channel Tunnel (International Arrangements) (Amendment) Order* 1996 (S.I. 1996 No. 2283); the *Channel Tunnel (International Arrangements) (Amendment No. 3) Order* 2001 (S.I. 2001 No. 1544); and the *Channel Tunnel (International Arrangements) (Amendment No. 4) Order* 2001 (S.I. 2001 No. 3707).]

The *Data Protection Act* 1984 is repealed and replaced by the *Data Protection Act* 1998.

Application of criminal law

5.—(1) Any act or omission which—

    (a) takes place outside the United Kingdom in a control zone, and

    (b) would, if taking place in England, constitute an offence under a frontier control enactment,

or any act or omission which—

    (c) takes place outside the United Kingdom in a supplementary control zone, and

(d) would, if taking place in England, constitute an offence under an immigration control enactment

shall be treated for the purposes of that enactment as taking place in England.

(1A) Summary proceedings for anything that is by virtue of paragraph (1) an offence triable summarily or triable either way may be taken, and the offence may for all incidental purposes be treated as having been committed, in the county of Kent or in the inner London area as defined in section 2(1)(a) of the *Justices of the Peace Act* 1979.

(2) Any jurisdiction conferred by virtue of paragraphs (1) and (1A) on any court is without prejudice to any jurisdiction exercisable apart from this article by that or any other court.

(3) Where it is proposed to institute proceedings in respect of an alleged offence in any court and a question as to the court's jurisdiction arises under Article 38(2)(a) of the international articles, it shall be presumed, unless the contrary is proved, that the court has jurisdiction by virtue of that Article.

[This article is printed as amended by the *Channel Tunnel (Miscellaneous Provisions) Order* 1994 (S.I. 1994 No. 1405); and the *Channel Tunnel (International Arrangements) (Amendment No. 3) Order* 2001 (S.I. 2001 No. 1544).]

Persons boarding a through train

5A. For the purposes of the exercise of any power of an immigration officer in a supplementary control zone in France, any person who seeks to board a through train shall be deemed to be seeking to arrive in the United Kingdom through the tunnel system.

[This article was inserted by the *Channel Tunnel (International Arrangements) (Amendment No. 3) Order* 2001 (S.I. 2001 No. 1544).]

Powers of officers and supplementary controls

F–13a
6. Schedule 3 (which contains in Part I provision as to powers exercisable by constables and other officers and in Part II provision for meeting obligations under Article 25 of the Protocol mentioned in article 1 above concerning the prevention of animals from straying into the Fixed Link) shall have effect.

Enactments modified

7.—(1) Without prejudice to the generality of articles 4(1), 4(1B) and 5(1), the frontier control enactments mentioned in Schedule 4 shall—

(a) in their application to France by virtue of article 4(1) or article 4(1B), and

(b) in their application to the United Kingdom—

(i) within the tunnel system, and

(ii) elsewhere for the authorised purposes,

have effect with the modifications set out in Schedule 4.

(1A) Nothing in paragraph (1)(b)(ii) implies the existence of a supplementary control zone in the station of London-Waterloo on British Territory.

(2) Subject to paragraph (3), within a control zone or a supplementary control zone and on trains within the tunnel system section 54(3) of the *Firearms Act* 1968 (application to Crown Servants) shall have effect as if the reference to a member of a police force included a reference to an officer belonging to the French Republic exercising functions as mentioned in Article 28(2) of the international articles or functions under Article 3 of the supplementary articles.

(3) As respects officers exercising their functions in a control zone paragraph (2) applies only to the agreed number of specified officers mentioned in Article 28(2)(b) of the international articles.

(4) The frontier control enactments relating to transport and road traffic controls

in their application to France within the control zone in France within the tunnel system by virtue of Article 4(1A) shall have effect as if any reference therein to a "public road" or "road" were a reference to any part of that control zone.

[This paragraph is printed as amended by S.I. 1996 No. 2283, *ante*; S.I. 2001 No. 1544, *ante*; and S.I. 2007 No. 2907, *ante*.]

Amendment and repeals

Articles 8 and 9 give effect to Schedules 5 and 6, amendments and repeals   **F–14**
respectively.

S.I. 1993 No. 1813, Sched. 1

Article 2(1)   SCHEDULE 1

EXPRESSIONS DEFINED

Expression	*Meaning*	**5–15**
"The Concessionaires"	The meaning given by section 1(8) (read with section 3(3)) of the *Channel Tunnel Act* 1987.	
"Control zone"	A control zone within the meaning of the international articles.	
"Frontier controls"	So far as they constitute frontier controls within the meaning of the international articles and are controls in relation to persons or goods, police, immigration, customs, health, veterinary and phytosanitary, and transport and road traffic controls.	
"Frontier control enactment"	An Act, or an instrument made under an Act, for the time being in force, which contains provision relating to frontier controls.	
"Immigration control enactment"	An Act, or an instrument made under an Act, for the time being in force, which contains provision relating to immigration controls.	
"Immigration officer"	The same meaning as in the *Immigration Act* 1971.	
"The international articles"	The meaning given by article 2(3) above.	
"International service"	The meaning given in section 13(6) of the *Channel Tunnel Act* 1987.	
"Shuttle train"	The meaning given in section 1(9) of the *Channel Tunnel Act* 1987.	
"State of arrival"	The meaning given by the supplementary articles.	
"State of departure"	The meaning given by the supplementary articles.	
"The supplementary articles"	The meaning given by article 2(4) above.	
"Supplementary control zone"	The part of the territory of the State of departure, determined by mutual agreement between the Governments of the State of departure and the State of arrival but excluding the station of London–Waterloo on British territory, within which the officers of the State of arrival are empowered to effect controls under the supplementary articles.	

Expression	Meaning
"Terminal control point"	A place which is an authorised terminal control point for international services for the purposes of sections 11 and 12 of the *Channel Tunnel Act* 1987.
"Through train"	A train, other than a shuttle train, which for the purposes of sections 11 and 12 of the *Channel Tunnel Act* 1987 is engaged on an international service.
"Train manager"	In relation to a through train or shuttle train, the person designated as train manager by the person operating the international service on which the train is engaged.
"The tunnel system"	The meaning given by section 1(7) of the *Channel Tunnel Act* 1987.

[This Schedule is printed as amended by S.I. 1996 No. 2283; S.I. 2001 No. 1544; S.I. 2001 No. 3707; and S.I. 2007 No. 2907 (*ante*, F–13).]

S.I. 1993 No. 1813, Sched. 2

Article 2(3)   SCHEDULE 2

INTERNATIONAL ARTICLES

ARTICLE 1

Definitions

F–16   (1) Any term defined in the Treaty shall have the same meaning in this Protocol.

(2) Otherwise for the purposes of this Protocol the expression:

(a) "frontier controls" means police, immigration, customs, health, veterinary and phytosanitary, consumer protection, and transport and road traffic controls, as well as any other controls provided for in national or European Community laws and regulations;

(b) "host State" means the State in whose territory the controls of the other State are effected;

(c) "adjoining State" means the other State;

(d) "officers" means persons responsible for policing and frontier controls who are under the command of the persons or authorities designated in accordance with Article 2(1);

(e) "rescue services" means the authorities and organisations whose functions are provided for in the emergency arrangements referred to in Part VII of this Protocol who are under the command of the persons or authorities designated in accordance with Article 2(1);

(f) [...]

(g) "control zone" means the part of the territory of the host State determined by the mutual agreement between the two Governments within which the officers of the adjoining State are empowered to effect controls;

(h) "restricted zone" means the part of the Fixed Link situated in each State subject to special protective security measures;

(i) "through trains" means trains travelling the Fixed Link but originating and terminating outside it, as opposed to "shuttle trains" which are trains travelling solely within the Fixed Link.

PART I

AUTHORITIES AND GENERAL PRINCIPLES OF CO-OPERATION

ARTICLE 2

(1) Each of the Governments shall designate the authorities or the persons having **F–16a** charge of the services which in its territory have responsibility for the exercise of frontier controls, the maintenance of law and order and fire fighting and rescue within the Fixed Link.

....

PART II

FRONTIER CONTROLS AND POLICE: GENERAL

ARTICLE 5

(1) In order to simplify and speed up the formalities relating to entry into the **F–16b** State of arrival and exit from the State of departure, the two Governments agree to establish juxtaposed national control bureaux in the terminal installations situated at Fréthun in French territory and at Folkestone in British territory. These bureaux shall be so arranged that, for each direction of travel, the frontier controls shall be carried out in the terminal in the State of departure.

(2) Supplementary frontier controls may exceptionally be carried out in the Fixed Link by officers of the State of arrival on its own territory.

ARTICLE 6

The competence of those juxtaposed national control bureaux shall extend to all cross-frontier movements with the exception of customs clearance of commercial traffic.

ARTICLE 7

(1) For through trains, each state may carry out its frontier controls during the journey and may authorise the officers of the other State to carry out their frontier controls in its territory.

(2) The two States may agree to an extension of the control zones for through trains, as far as London and Paris, respectively.

ARTICLE 8

Within the Fixed Link, each Government shall permit officers of the other State to carry out their functions in its own territory in application of their powers relating to frontier controls.

ARTICLE 9

The laws and regulations to frontier controls of the adjoining State shall be applicable in the control zone situated in the host State and shall be put into effect by the officers of the adjoining State in the same way as in their own territory.

ARTICLE 10

(1) The officers of the adjoining State shall, in exercise of their national powers, be permitted in the control zone situated in the host State to detain or arrest persons in accordance with the laws and regulations relating to frontier controls of the adjoining State or persons sought by the authorities of the adjoining State. These officers shall also be permitted to conduct such persons to the territory of the adjoining State.

(2) However, except in exceptional circumstances, no person may be held more than 24 hours in the areas reserved, in the host State, for the frontier controls of the adjoining State. Any such detention shall be subject to the requirements and procedures laid down by the legislation of the adjoining State.

(3) In exceptional circumstances the 24 hour period of detention may be extended for a further period of 24 hours in accordance with the legislation of the adjoining State. The extension of the period of detention shall be notified to the authorities of the host State.

ARTICLE 11

Breaches of the laws and regulations relating to frontier controls of the adjoining State which are detected in the control zone situated in the host State shall be subject to the laws and regulations of the adjoining State, as if the breaches had occurred in the latter's own territory.

ARTICLE 12

(1) The frontier controls of the State of departure shall normally be effected before those of the State of arrival.

(2) The officers of the State of arrival are not authorised to carry out such controls before the end of controls of the State of departure. Any form of relinquishment of such controls shall be considered as a control.

(3) The officers of the State of departure may no longer carry out their controls when the officers of the State of arrival have begun their own operations except with the consent of the competent officers of the State of arrival.

(4) If exceptionally, in the course of the frontier controls, the sequence of operations provided for inparagraph (1) of this Article is modified, the officers of the State of arrival may not proceed to detentions, arrests or seizures until the frontier controls of the State of departure are completed. In such a case, these officers shall escort the persons, vehicles, merchandise, animals or other goods, for which the frontier controls of the State of departure are not yet completed, to the officers of that State. If these latter then wish to proceed to detentions, arrests or seizures, they shall have priority.

ARTICLE 14

The detailed plans for the Fixed Link and its means of access, shall, in accordance with the relevant provisions of the Concession, delimit among other things:

  (a) the control zones;
  (b) the restricted zones and their sub-divisions;
  (c) railway lines and their means of access included in the control zones;
  (d) the area of the frontier control installations and their means of access.

....

ARTICLE 16

Where investigations and proceedings concern offences committed in the Fixed Link or having a connection with the Fixed Link, the authorities of the host State shall, at the request of the authorities of the adjoining State, undertake official enquiries, the examination of witnesses and experts and the notification to accused persons of summonses and administrative decisions.

ARTICLE 17

The assistance provided for in Article 16 shall be furnished in accordance with the laws, regulations and procedures in force in the State providing the assistance, and with international agreements to which that State is a party.

ARTICLE 18

If the State of arrival refuses admission to persons, vehicles, animals or goods, or if persons decide not to pass through the frontier controls of the State of arrival, or send or take back any vehicles, animals or goods which are accompanying them, the authorities of the State of departure may not refuse to accept back such persons, vehicles, animals or goods. However, the authorities of the State of departure may take any measures to deal with them in accordance with national law and in a way which does not impose obligations on the other State.

554

ARTICLE 19

(2) In an emergency, the local representatives of the authorities concerned may by mutual agreement, provisionally bring into effect alterations to the delimitation of the control zones which may prove necessary. Any arrangement so reached shall come into effect immediately.

PART III

HEALTH, VETERINARY AND PHYTOSANITARY CONTROLS

[*Articles 20–24*]

PART IV

OFFICERS

ARTICLE 26

Officers of both States shall be permitted to circulate freely in the whole of the   **F–16c**
Fixed Link for official purposes. In carrying out their functions they shall be autho-rised to pass through the frontier controls simply by producing appropriate evidence of their identity and status.

ARTICLE 28

(1) Officers of the adjoining State may wear their national uniform or visible distinctive insignia in the host State.

(2) In accordance with the laws, regulations and procedures governing the car-riage and use of firearms in the host State, the competent authorities of that State will issue permanent licences to carry arms:

    (a) to officers of the adjoining State exercising their official functions on board trains within the Fixed Link; and

    (b) to an agreed number of specified officers of the adjoining State exercising their functions within the control zone of the host State.

ARTICLE 29

(1) The authorities of the host State shall grant the same protection and assistance to officers of the adjoining State, in the exercise of their functions, as they grant to their own officers.

(2) The provisions of the criminal law in force in the host State for the protection of officers in the exercise of their functions shall be equally applicable to the punish-ment of offences committed against officers of the adjoining State in the exercise of their functions.

ARTICLE 30

(1) Without prejudice to the application of the provisions of Article 46, claims for compensation for loss, injury or damage caused by or to officers of the adjoining State in the exercise of their functions in the host State shall be subject to the law and jurisdiction of the adjoining State as if the circumstances giving rise to the claim had occurred in that State.

(2) Officers of the adjoining State may not be prosecuted by authorities of the host State for any acts performed in the control zone or within the Fixed Link whilst in the exercise of their functions. In such a case, they shall come under the jurisdiction of the adjoining State, as if the act had been committed in that State.

(3) The judicial authorities or the police of the host State, having taken steps to record the complaint and to assemble the facts relating thereto, shall communicate all the particulars and evidence thereof to the competent authorities of the other State for the purposes of a possible prosecution according to the laws in force in the latter.

ARTICLE 31

(1) Officers of the adjoining State shall be permitted freely to transfer to that State sums of money levied on behalf of their Government in the control zone situated in the host State, as well as merchandise and other goods seized there.

(2) They may equally sell such merchandise and other goods in the host State in conformity with the provisions in force in the host State, and transfer the proceeds to the adjoining State.

PART V

FACILITIES

ARTICLE 34

F–16d   The authorities of the adjoining State shall be able to make use in the host State of the accommodation, installations and equipment necessary for the performance of their functions.

ARTICLE 35

(1) The officers of the adjoining State are empowered to keep order within the accommodation appointed for their exclusive use in the host State.

(2) The officers of the host State shall not have access to such accommodation, except at the request of the officers of the adjoining State or in accordance with the laws of the host State applicable to entry into and searches of private premises.

ARTICLE 36

All goods which are necessary to enable the officers of the adjoining State to carry out their functions in the host State shall be exempt from all taxes and dues on entry and exit.

ARTICLE 37

(1) The officers of the adjoining State whilst exercising their functions in the host State shall be authorised to communicate with their national authorities.

. . . .

PART VI

CO-OPERATION IN CRIMINAL JUSTICE

ARTICLE 38

F–16e   (1) Without prejudice to the provisions of Articles 11 and 30(2), when an offence is committed in the territory of one of the two States, including that lying within the Fixed Link up to its frontier, that State shall have jurisdiction.

(2) (a) Within the Fixed Link, each State shall have jurisdiction and shall apply its own law:

> (i) when it cannot be ascertained with certainty where an offence has been committed; or
>
> (ii) when an offence committed in the territory of one State is related to an offence committed on the territory of the other State; or
>
> (iii) when an offence has begun in or has been continued into its own territory;

> (b) however, the State which first receives the person suspected of having committed such an offence (in this Article referred to as "the receiving State") shall have priority in exercising jurisdiction.

(3) When the receiving State decides not to exercise its priority jurisdiction under paragraph (2) of this Article it shall inform the other State without delay. If the latter decides not to exercise its jurisdiction, the receiving State shall be obliged to exercise its jurisdiction in accordance with its own national law.

ARTICLE 39

Where an arrest has been made for an offence in respect of which a State has jurisdiction under Article 38, that arrest shall not be affected by the fact that it continues in the territory of the other State.

ARTICLE 40

Without prejudice to the application of Article 3 of the Treaty and Part II of this Protocol, the police and customs officers of one State may in accordance with their own national laws make arrests on the territory of the other State in cases where a person is found committing, attempting to commit, or just having committed an offence:

(a) on board any train which has commenced its journey from one State to the other and is within the Fixed Link; or

(b) within any tunnel described in Article 1(2) of the Treaty.

ARTICLE 41

In the case of arrests covered by Articles 39 and 40:

(a) the person arrested shall be presented without delay to the competent authorities of the State of arrival for that State to be responsible for determining the exercise of jurisdiction as required by Article 38; and

(b) where jurisdiction shall be exercised by the other State in accordance with Article 38, the person arrested may be transferred to the territory of that State. However, any such transfer shall take place within 48 hours of the presentation under paragraph (a) of this Article. Moreover, each State reserves the right not to transfer its nationals.

PART VII

PUBLIC SAFETY AND RESCUE

[*Articles 42–44*]

PART VIII

FINAL CLAUSES

[*Articles 46, 47*]

S.I. 1993 No. 1813, Sched. 2A

Article 2(4)   SCHEDULE 2A

SUPPLEMENTARY ARTICLES

ARTICLE 1

Any terms defined in Article 1 of the Protocol signed at Sangatte have the same   **F–16f** meaning in this Additional Protocol. For the purposes of this Additional Protocol, the following definitions shall be added:

"State of departure" means the State in which the persons boards the train;

"State of arrival" means the State in which the persons alight from the train.

ARTICLE 2

The authorities of the two States shall jointly put in place control bureaux, for persons using through trains and wishing to travel to the State of arrival, in the stations of London-Waterloo, London-St Pancras and Ashford on British territory, and the stations of Paris-Gare du Nord, Calais and Lille-Europe on French territory.

The provisions of the Protocol signed at Sangatte concerning the officers of the adjoining State shall be applicable, under the same conditions, to the officers of the

State of arrival who are on duty in the stations mentioned in the preceeding paragraph.

Amendments to Article 2

In addition to the stations referred to in Article 2, control bureaux shall also be established at the station of Ebbsfleet International on British Territory.

The provisions of the Additional Protocol apply to the station of Ebbsfleet International under the same conditions and in accordance with the same procedures as they apply to the stations referred to in the said Article 2.

ARTICLE 3

The purpose of the controls carried out by the authorities of the State of departure shall be to check whether the person can leave its territory.

The purpose of the controls carried out by the authorities of the State of arrival shall be to check whether the person is in possession of the necessary travel documents and fulfils the other conditions for entry to its territory. If this is not the case, the person shall be immediately handed over to the authorities of the State of departure who shall apply their domestic law procedures.

The authorities of the State of departure and of the State of arrival shall carry out their controls in accordance with this Additional Protocol, with their laws and regulations and with their international obligations.

The controls mentioned in the preceeding paragraphs are without prejudice to customs and security controls.

ARTICLE 4

Notwithstanding the third paragraph of Article 3 of this Additional Protocol, when a person submits a request for refugee status or any other kind of protection provided for in international law or in the domestic law of the State of departure during a control carried out at the station of the State of departure by the officers of the State of arrival, this request shall be examined by the authorities of the State of departure in accordance with the rules and procedures of its domestic law.

The same provisions shall be applicable when the request is submitted after the person has passed through this control and before the train doors close at the last scheduled stop at a station located in the territory of the State of departure. If such a request is made after the train doors have closed, it shall be processed by the State of arrival in accordance with the rules and procedures of its domestic law.

ARTICLE 5

The controls referred to in Article 3 of this Additional Protocol shall be carried out in accordance with Article 12 of the Sangatte Protocol.

ARTICLE 6

The procedures for the implementation of this Additional Protocol may, as far as necessary, be the subject of technical or administrative arrangements between the competent authorities of the two States.

[Sched. 2A was inserted by S.I. 2001 No. 1544 (*ante*, F–13). It is printed as amended by the *Channel Tunnel (International Arrangements) (Amendment) Order* 2007 (S.I. 2007 No. 2907).]

S.I. 1993 No. 1813, Sched. 3

Article 6   SCHEDULE 3

PART I

POWERS OF OFFICERS

Power to assist French authorities

F–17   1.—(1) Where—

(a) an officer belonging to the French Republic has in a control zone in the United Kingdom or in a supplementary control zone in the United Kingdom arrested or detained a person as permitted by Article 10(1) of the international articles and Article 2 of the supplementary articles, and

(b) such an officer so requests,

a constable or an officer commissioned by the Commissioners of Customs and Excise under section 6(3) of the *Customs and Excise Management Act* 1979 (in this Schedule referred to as a "customs officer") may make arrangements for the person to be taken into temporary custody.

(2) A person taken into temporary custody under sub-paragraph (1)—

(a) shall be treated for all purposes as being in lawful custody, and

(b) may be taken to a police station or such other place as may be appropriate in the circumstances, and shall in that case be treated as being a person in whose case sections 36(7) and (8), 54 to 56 and 58 of the *Police and Criminal Evidence Act* 1984 (in this Schedule referred to as "the 1984 Act"), and in the case of a child or young person section 34(2) to (7), (8) and (9) of the *Children and Young Persons Act* 1933, apply, and

(c) must be returned, before the end of the period for which he could in the circumstances be detained in the United Kingdom under Article 10 of the international articles or Article 2 of the supplementary articles, to a place where detention under that Article could be resumed.

(3) Where a person falls to be treated as mentioned in sub-paragraph (2)(b) section 56 of the 1984 Act shall be taken to apply as if he were detained for a serious arrestable offence.

[This paragraph is printed as amended by the *Channel Tunnel (Miscellaneous Provisions) Order* 1994 (S.I. 1994 No. 1405); and the *Channel Tunnel (International Arrangements) (Amendment No. 3) Order* 2001 (S.I. 2001 No. 1544).]

Powers of arrest outside United Kingdom

2.—(1) A constable may in a control zone in France—   **F–17a**

(a) exercise any power of arrest conferred by a frontier control enactment or conferred by the 1984 Act in respect of an offence under such an enactment,

(b) make any arrest authorised by a warrant issued by a court in the United Kingdom, and

(c) arrest any person whose name or description or both, together with particulars of an indictable offence of which there are reasonable grounds for suspecting him to be guilty, have been made available by a chief officer of police to other such officers.

(2) For the purposes of sub-paragraph (1)(a) the reference in sub-paragraph (1) to a constable shall be construed—

(a) in relation to the powers of arrest conferred by section 28A(1) and (3) of and paragraph 17(1) of Schedule 2 to the *Immigration Act* 1971, as including a reference both—

(i) to an immigration officer appointed for the purposes of that Act under paragraph 1 of that Schedule, and

(ii) to an officer of customs and excise who is the subject of arrangements for the employment of such officers as immigration officers made under that paragraph by the Secretary of State,

and where this sub-paragraph applies, the reference in sub-paragraph (1) [*sic*] to a control zone in France shall be construed as including a reference to a supplementary control zone in France.

(b) in relation to the power of arrest conferred by paragraph 6(4) of Schedule 5 to the *Prevention of Terrorism (Temporary Provisions) Act* 1989, as including a reference to any person who by virtue of paragraph 1(1) of that Schedule is an examining officer for the purposes of that Act, and

(c) in relation to any arrest that may be made by a customs officer by virtue of section 138 of the *Customs and Excise Management Act* 1979 and an arrest for a drug trafficking offence as defined in section 38(1) of the *Drug Trafficking Offences Act* 1986, as including a reference to a customs officer.

(3) A customs officer may in a control zone in France arrest any person whose name or description or both, together with particulars of an arrestable offence (within the meaning of section 24 of the 1984 Act) which is an offence in relation to an assigned matter as defined in section 1(1) of the *Customs and Excise Management Act* 1979 and of which there are reasonable grounds for suspecting him to be guilty, have been made available to customs officers generally under the authority of the Commissioners of Customs and Excise.

(4) For the purpose of enabling constables to make arrests in France in the cases described in Article 40 of the international articles sections 24 and 25 of the 1984 Act shall extend to France.

(5) Where—

(a) an arrest has been made for an offence of the kind mentioned in Article 39 of the international articles, and

(b) it falls to the competent authorities in France to determine the exercise of jurisdiction in accordance with Article 38,

the person arrested shall be treated as continuing to be under arrest while in France until he is presented to those authorities as required by Article 41(a).

(6) Where—

(a) an arrest falling within sub-paragraph (4) or (5) above has been made, and

(b) the competent authorities in France determine under Article 41 of the international articles that jurisdiction is to be exercised by the United Kingdom,

the person arrested shall be treated as having continued to be under arrest throughout, even if he was for some period in the custody of those authorities, and sections 30 and 41 of the 1984 Act shall apply accordingly.

(7) Any power conferred by an enactment to search an arrested person may be exercised following an arrest authorised by this paragraph as if the person had been arrested in the United Kingdom.

[This paragraph is printed as amended by the *Channel Tunnel (International Arrangements) (Amendment No. 3) Order* 2001 (S.I. 2001 No. 1544); and the *Serious Organised Crime and Police Act 2005 (Powers of Arrest) (Consequential Amendments) Order* 2005 (S.I. 2005 No. 3389).]

Arrested persons held in France

F–17b   3.—(1) Where—

(a) an arrest of any kind authorised by paragraph 2 above has been made in a control zone in France or in a supplementary control zone in France; or

(b) an arrest of any such kind has been made in the United Kingdom and the person arrested enters such a control zone while under arrest,

the person arrested may be held in France for a period of not more than 24 hours and, if there are exceptional circumstances and an officer belonging to the French Republic is notified of the extension, for a further period.

(2) Subject to sub-paragraphs (3) and (4), the person arrested shall be treated as if the place where he is held were for the purposes of the provisions mentioned in paragraph 1(2)(b) above and those of sections 61 to 63 of the 1984 Act a police station, or where the arrest was made by a customs officer, a customs office, in England, not being a police station or customs office designated under section 35 of the 1984 Act.

(3) Where—

(a) an arrest falling within paragraph 2(1)(a) or (3) above has been made by a customs officer, and

(b) the person arrested is held in France in a place within the tunnel system which would if it were in England be a customs office within the meaning of the 1984 Act, sections 34(1) to (5), 36, 37, 39 to 42, 50, 54, 55, 56(1) to (9), 58(1) to (11), 62, 63 and 64(1) to (6) of the 1984 Act and in the case of a child or young person section 34(2) to (7), (8) and (9) of the *Children and Young Persons Act* 1933, shall apply as if the place where he is held were a customs office in England designated under section 35 of the 1984 Act.

(4) Where the power of arrest mentioned in paragraph 2(2)(b) has been exercised any detention in France of the person arrested shall be treated for all purposes as being detention under paragraph 6(1) of Schedule 5 to the *Prevention of Terrorism (Temporary Provisions) Act* 1989, and section 16(2) of that Act, sections 51(b), 56 and 58 of the 1984 Act and section 34 of the *Children and Young Persons Act* 1933 as applying accordingly.

[This paragraph is printed as amended by the *Channel Tunnel (International Arrangements) (Amendment No. 3) Order* 2001 (S.I. 2001 No. 1544).]

Arrested persons arriving in the United Kingdom

F–17c

4.—(1) Where—
  (a) an arrest falling within Article 39 or 40 of the international articles has been made, and
  (b) the person arrested enters the United Kingdom while under arrest,
the person arrested shall be taken to a police station.

(2) The custody officer at the police station to which the person is taken shall determine—
  (a) whether the offence is one over which the United Kingdom has jurisdiction by virtue of Article 38(1), and
  (b) if he determines that it is not, whether it is one over which the United Kingdom may exercise jurisdiction by virtue of Article 38(2) and if so whether jurisdiction is to be exercised,
and may for the purpose of determining those questions detain the person at the police station for not longer than the permitted period.

(3) The permitted period is the period of 48 hours beginning at the time at which the person arrives at the police station.

(4) Subject to sub-paragraph (6), the person shall be treated—
  (a) as not being detained at the police station for the purposes of section 37 of the 1984 Act, and
  (b) as not being in police detention for the purposes of sections 40 to 43 of the 1984 Act.

(5) Where the custody officer determines that the United Kingdom does not have jurisdiction by virtue of Article 38(1) and—
  (a) that jurisdiction is not exercisable by virtue of Article 38(2), or
  (b) that jurisdiction is exercisable by virtue of Article 38(2) but is not to be exercised,
he shall immediately inform the competent French authorities of his determination and shall arrange for the person to be transferred to France within the permitted period.

(6) Where the custody officer determines that the United Kingdom has jurisdiction by virtue of Article 38(1) or that jurisdiction is exercisable by virtue of Article 38(2) and is to be exercised—
  (a) he shall immediately inform the person of his determination,
  (b) the person shall be treated as being in police detention for all purposes of Part IV of the 1984 Act, and
  (c) that Part shall have effect in relation to him as if the relevant time mentioned in section 41(1) were the time at which he is informed of the determination.

(7) Where the police station to which the person is taken is not a police station designated under section 35 of the 1984 Act, references in this paragraph to the custody officer are to be construed as references to an officer not below the rank of sergeant.

[The heading of paragraph 4 and sub-paragraph (1) were substituted by the *Channel Tunnel (Miscellaneous Provisions) Order* 1994: S.I. 1994 No. 1405, art. 8 and Sched. 4, with effect from July 1, 1994: *ibid.*, art. 1(2).]

Arrests of French officers

F–17d   5.—(1) This paragraph applies where an officer belonging to the French Republic ("the officer") is arrested for an act performed in the United Kingdom in the tunnel system or a control zone or supplementary control zone.

(2) If the officer enters France while under arrest—

    (a) he shall without delay be handed over for custody to the competent French authorities and shall be treated as continuing to be under arrest until he has been handed over, and

    (b) if after consultation with those authorities it is then determined that the act was not performed by the officer whilst in the exercise of his functions and he accordingly does not by virtue of Article 30(2) of the international articles come under French jurisdiction, he shall be treated as having continued to be under arrest until sub-paragraph (3) has been complied with.

(3) Where—

    (a) sub-paragraph (2)(b) applies, or

    (b) the officer does not enter France while under arrest,

he shall be taken to a police station designated under section 35 of the 1984 Act.

(4) Sub-paragraphs (5) to (9) apply in a case falling within sub-paragraph (3)(b).

(5) The custody officer at the police station to which the officer is taken shall after consultation with the competent French authorities determine whether the act was performed by the officer whilst in the exercise of his functions, and may for the purpose of determining that question detain the officer at the police station for not longer than the permitted period.

(6) The permitted period is the period of 48 hours beginning at the time at which the officer arrives at the police station.

(7) Subject to sub-paragraph (9), the officer shall be treated—

    (a) as not being detained at the police station for the purposes of section 37 of the 1984 Act, and

    (b) as not being in police detention for the purposes of sections 40 to 43 of the 1984 Act.

(8) Where the custody officer determines that the act was performed by the officer whilst in the exercise of his functions and the officer accordingly comes under French jurisdiction by virtue of Article 30(2), he shall immediately inform the competent French authorities and shall arrange for the officer to be transferred to France within the permitted period.

(9) In any other case—

    (a) the custody officer shall immediately inform the officer of his determination,

    (b) the officer shall be treated as being in police detention for all purposes of Part IV of the 1984 Act, and

    (c) that Part shall have effect in relation to him as if the relevant time mentioned in section 41(1) were the time at which he is informed of the determination.

[This paragraph is printed as amended by the *Channel Tunnel (International Arrangements) (Amendment No. 3) Order* 2001 (S.I. 2001 No. 1544).]

Arrests of United Kingdom officers

F–17e   6.—(1) This paragraph applies where an officer belonging to the United Kingdom ("the officer") is arrested for an act performed in France in the tunnel system or a control zone or supplementary control zone.

(2) If—

    (a) the officer does not enter the United Kingdom while under arrest, and

    (b) the competent French authorities determine that the act was performed
        by the officer whilst in the exercise of his functions and he accordingly
        comes under United Kingdom jurisdiction by virtue of Article 30(2) of the
        international articles,
he shall on being handed over by those authorities to a constable be treated as
having been arrested by the constable.

    (3) Where—

        (a) sub-paragraph (2)(b) applies, or

        (b) the officer enters the United Kingdom while under the original arrest,
he shall be taken to a police station designated under section 35 of the 1984 Act.

    (4) Sub-paragraphs (5) to (9) apply in a case falling within sub-paragraph (3)(b).

    (5) The custody officer at the police station to which the officer is taken shall—

        (a) immediately invite the competent French authorities to determine whether
        the act was performed by the officer whilst in the exercise of his functions,
        and

        (b) afford those authorities any assistance they may require in determining
        that question,
and may for the purpose of enabling that question to be determined detain the
officer at the police station for not longer than the permitted period.

    (6) The permitted period is the period of 48 hours beginning at the time at which
the officer arrives at the police station.

    (7) Subject to sub-paragraph (9), the officer shall be treated—

        (a) as not being detained at the police station for the purposes of section 37 of
        the 1984 Act, and

        (b) as not being in police detention for the purposes of sections 40 to 43 of
        the 1984 Act.

    (8) Where the competent French authorities determine that the act was not
performed by the officer whilst in the exercise of his functions and the officer accordingly does not by virtue of Article 30(2) come under United Kingdom jurisdiction,
the custody officer shall arrange for the officer to be transferred to France within the
permitted period.

    (9) In any other case—

        (a) the custody officer shall immediately inform the officer of the determina-
        tion,

        (b) the officer shall be treated as being in police detention for all purposes of
        Part IV of the 1984 Act, and

        (c) that Part shall have effect in relation to him as if the relevant time
        mentioned in section 41(1) were the time at which he is informed of the
        determination.

[This paragraph is printed as amended by the *Channel Tunnel (International
Arrangements) (Amendment No. 3) Order* 2001 (S.I. 2001 No. 1544).]

Supplementary controls over animals

Part II, consisting of eight paragraphs, imposes controls for the purpose of **F–18**
preventing the spread of the rabies virus through the tunnel to the United
Kingdom. Failure by the Concessionaires to carry out the duties imposed is
made an offence triable either way (maximum penalty on conviction on indictment is a fine). It is also an offence, punishable in the same way, for any
person to interfere with any anti-rabies installation, or to do any act which
might impair the effectiveness of any anti-rabies measure, or to obstruct a
person authorised to enforce the provisions of this Part.

Enactments modified

As to Schedule 4, see article 7, *ante*, F–13a. The enactments modified which **F–19** fall within the compass of this work are the *Immigration Act* 1971 (as to which, see § 25–233 in the main work) and the *Terrorism Act* 2000 (as to which, see *ante*, §§ 25–136a, 25–141).

Amendments, repeals, revocations

F–20   Relevant entries in Schedules 5 (amendments) and 6 (repeals and revocations) are noted at the appropriate place elsewhere in this work.

S.I. 1994 No. 1405, art. 1

Citation and commencement

F–21   1.—(1) This Order may be cited as the *Channel Tunnel (Miscellaneous Provisions) Order* 1994 and, except as provided in paragraphs (2) and (3) below, shall come into force on the date on which the Agreement between the Government of the Kingdom of Belgium, the Government of the French Republic and the Government of the United Kingdom and Great Britain and Northern Ireland Concerning Rail Traffic between Belgium and the United Kingdom Using the Channel Fixed Link enters into force. That date will be notified in the London, Edinburgh and Belfast *Gazettes*.

(2) Article 8 shall, to the extent necessary to give effect to those of the amendments specified in Schedule 4 that are mentioned in paragraph (3) below, come into force on 1st July 1994.

(3) The amendments are—

    (a) those specified in paragraphs 6, 8(b), 9, 10 and 12 of Schedule 4, and

    (b) those specified in paragraph 11 of Schedule 4 except the amendments to paragraphs 1(11)(d) and 3(b) of Schedule 4 to the 1993 Order.

S.I. 1994 No. 1405, arts 2–8

Interpretation

F–22   2.—(1) In this Order, except for the purpose of construing the tripartite articles and in any enactment as applied by it with modifications, any expression for which there is an entry in the first column of Schedule 1 has the meaning given against it in the second column.

(2) In this Order "the authorised purposes" means—

    (a) purposes for which provision is authorised by any of paragraphs (a), (d) and (g), and

    (b) purposes connected with any matter in relation to or with respect to or for regulating which provision is authorised by any of paragraphs (c), (e), (f) and (h),

of section 11(1) of the *Channel Tunnel Act* 1987.

(3) In this Order "the tripartite articles" means the provisions set out—

    (a) in Part I of Schedule 2 (being Articles or parts of Articles of the Agreement mentioned in article 1 above), and

    (b) in Part II of Schedule 2 (being Articles or parts of Articles of the Protocol attached to and forming part of that Agreement);

    (c) in Part III of Schedule 2 (being Articles or parts of Articles of the Protocol attached to and forming part of the Agreement, as applied by the Administrative Arrangement to immigration controls upon person travelling on international trains making a commercial stop);

and in the tripartite articles the expression "the Fixed Link" shall for the purpose of this Order be taken to have the same meaning as is given to "the tunnel system" by section 1(7) of the *Channel Tunnel Act* 1987.

[This article is printed as amended by the *Channel Tunnel (Miscellaneous Provisions) (Amendment) Order* 2004 (S.I. 2004 No. 2589).]

Application of tripartite articles

3.—(1) The tripartite articles shall have the force of law in the United Kingdom—

(a) within a control zone, and

(b) elsewhere for the authorised purposes only.

(2) Subject to paragraph (4), without prejudice to paragraph (1) officers belonging to the Kingdom of Belgium and officers belonging to the French Republic shall to the extent specified in the tripartite articles have rights and obligations and powers to carry out functions in the United Kingdom.

(3) Subject to paragraph (4), for the purpose of giving full effect to Article 17 of the Part II provisions and to Article 17 of the Part III provisions (accommodation, etc., for Belgian authorities) the appropriate Minister may by written notice require any occupier or person concerned with the management of a terminal control point to provide such accommodation, installations and equipment as may be necessary to satisfy requirements determined under Article 16 of the Protocol mentioned in article 2(3)(b) above and under that Article as applied by Article 3 of the Administrative Arrangement (which requires the competent authorities of the Kingdom of Belgium and of the United Kingdom to determine their respective requirements in consultation with one another).

(4) Nothing in this article implies the existence of a control zone in the station of London-Waterloo on British Territory.

[This article is printed as amended by the *Channel Tunnel (Miscellaneous Provisions) (Amendment) Order* 2004 (S.I. 2004 No. 2589); and the *Channel Tunnel (Miscellaneous Provisions) (Amendment) Order* 2007 (S.I. 2007 No. 2908).]

Application of enactments

4.—(1) All frontier enactments shall for the purpose of enabling officers belonging to the United Kingdom to carry out frontier controls extend—

(a) to France within a control zone, and

(b) to Belgium within a control zone.

(1A) The *Race Relations Act* 1976 shall apply to the carrying out by immigration officers of their functions in a control zone outside the United Kingdom as it applies to the carrying out of their functions within the United Kingdom.

(2), (3) [*Application of Data Protection Act* 1984.]

[This article is printed as amended by S.I. 2007 No. 2908 (*ante*).]

Application of criminal law

5.—(1) Any act or omission which—

(a) takes place outside the United Kingdom in a control zone, and

(b) would, if taking place in England, constitute an offence under a frontier control enactment,

shall be treated for the purposes of that enactment as taking place in England.

(2) Summary proceedings for anything that is by virtue of paragraph (1) an offence triable summarily or triable either way may be taken, and the offence may for all incidental purposes be treated as having been committed, in the county of Kent or in the inner London area as defined in section 2(1)(a) of the *Justices of the Peace Act* 1979.

(3) Any jurisdiction conferred by virtue of paragraphs (1) and (2) on any court is without prejudice to any jurisdiction exercisable apart from this article by that or any other court.

(4) Where it is proposed to institute proceedings in respect of an alleged offence in any court and a question as to the court's jurisdiction arises under Article 11(2) of the Part I provisions, it shall be presumed, unless the contrary is proved, that the court has jurisdiction by virtue of that Article.

Powers of officers

6. Schedule 3 (which contains provision as to powers exercisable by constables and other officers) shall have effect.

Enactments modified

7.—(1) Without prejudice to the generality of articles 4(1) and 5(1), the enactments specified in paragraph (2) shall—

(a) in their application to France and Belgium by virtue of article 4(1), and

(b) in their application to the United Kingdom for the authorised purposes,

have effect with modifications the same as those set out in Schedule 4 to the 1993 Order.

(2) Nothing in paragraph (1)(b) implies the existence of a control zone in the station of London-Waterloo on British Territory.

(2) The enactments are—

(a) *Immigration Act* 1971;

(b) *Public Health (Control of Disease) Act* 1984;

(c) *Immigration and Asylum Act* 1999;

(d) *Terrorism Act* 2000; and

(e) *Immigration, Asylum and Nationality Act* 2006.

[This article is printed as amended by the *Channel Tunnel (Miscellaneous Provisions) (Amendment) Order* 2006 (S.I. 2006 No. 2627); S.I. 2007 No. 2908 (*ante*); and the *Channel Tunnel (International Arrangements and Miscellaneous Provisions) (Amendment) Order* 2007 (S.I. 2007 No. 3579) (insertion of second para. (2)).]

Amendments of instruments

8. The instruments mentioned in Schedule 4 shall have effect with the amendments there specified.

S.I. 1994 No. 1405, Sched. 1

Article 2(1)   SCHEDULE 1

EXPRESSIONS DEFINED

F–23 *Expression*   *Meaning*

"Administrative arrangement"   The Administrative Arrangement made between the Secretary of State for the Home Department of the United Kingdom of Great Britain and Northern Ireland, the Vice Prime Minister, Minister of Home Affairs of the Kingdom of Belgium, and the Minister of the Interior, of Internal Security and Local Freedoms of the French Republic, concerning the exercise of Immigration Controls by British Officials at the Gare du Midi in Brussels and by Belgian Officials at Waterloo International Staton in London and Ashford International dated 1st October 2004.

"Control zone"   A control zone defined under Article 1(6) of the Part I provisions but excluding the station of London-Waterloo on British territory.

Expression	*Meaning*
"Frontier controls"	So far as they constitute frontier controls as defined in Article 1(1) of the Part I provisions and are controls in relation to persons or goods, police, immigration, customs, health, veterinary and phytosanitary controls.
"Immigration controls"	The controls carried out by the authorities of the State of arrival to check whether passengers making a journey between Belgium and the United Kingdom are in possession of the necessary travel documents and fulfil the other conditions for entry to its territory.
"International service"	The meaning given in section 13(6) of the *Channel Tunnel Act* 1987.
"Officers"	Persons responsible for authorising departure from or entry to the State of arrival.
"The 1993 Order"	The *Channel Tunnel (International Arrangements) Order* 1993.
"The Part I provisions"	The provisions set out in Part I of Schedule 2.
"The Part II provisions"	The provisions set out inPart II of Schedule 2.
"The Part III provisions"	The Provisions set out in Part III of Schedule 2.
"Through train"	A train, other than a shuttle train as defined in section 1(9) of the *Channel Tunnel Act* 1987, which for the purposes of sections 11 and 12 of that Act is engaged on an international service.

[The definitions of "Administrative arrangement", "Immigration controls", "Officers", and "The Part III provisions" were inserted by the *Channel Tunnel (Miscellaneous Provisions) (Amendment) Order* 2004 (S.I. 2004 No. 2589). In addition to the above definitions, the Schedule also contains definitions of the following expressions, which are identical to those contained in Schedule 1 to the 1993 Order (*ante*, F–15): "Frontier control enactment", "Terminal control point", "Train manager" and "The tunnel system". The definition of "control zone" is printed as amended by the *Channel Tunnel (Miscellaneous Provisions) (Amendment) Order* 2007 (S.I. 2007 No. 2908).]

S.I. 1994 No. 1405, Sched. 2

Article 2(3)   SCHEDULE 2

TRIPARTITE ARTICLES

PART I

AGREEMENT

PART I

General provisions

ARTICLE 1

Definitions

F–24   (1) "Frontier controls" means police, immigration, customs, health, veterinary and
phytosanitary, consumer protection, and transport controls, as well as any other
controls provided for in national or European Community laws and regulations.

(2) "Fixed Link" means the Channel Fixed Link defined in Article 1 of the Treaty
done at Canterbury on 12 February 1986.

(3) "Trains" means international trains travelling between Belgium and British
territory, using the Fixed Link and passing through French territory.

(4) "Non-stop trains" means international trains travelling between Belgian and
British territory, using the Fixed Link and crossing French territory without making
a commercial stop, except for technical stops.

(5) "Officers" means persons responsible for policing and frontier controls who are
under the command of the persons or authorities designated in accordance with
Article 3(2).

(6) "Control Zone" means that part of the territory of the host State and the non-
stop trains, within which the officers of the other States are empowered to effect
controls. Each control zone shall be defined by mutual agreement between the host
State and the State whose officers will be operating in the said zone; however, in the
case of non-stop trains, the control zone in French territory shall be determined
jointly by the three Governments.

(7) "Host State" means the State in whose territory the controls of the other States
are effected.

ARTICLE 2

Scope

(1) This Agreement shall apply to rail traffic between the United Kingdom and
Belgium travelling via the Fixed Link and passing through French territory.

. . . .

(3) A Protocol concerning frontier controls and policing on non-stop trains between the United Kingdom and Belgium via the Fixed Link is attached as an annex
to this Agreement and shall form an integral part thereof.

PART II

Authorities and General Principles of Co-operation

ARTICLE 3

F–24a   . . . .

(2) Each of the Governments shall designate the authorities or persons having
charge of the services which in its territory have responsibility for the exercise of
frontier controls and the maintenance of law and order.

ARTICLE 4

On non-stop trains, British officers may exercise frontier controls in Belgian and French territory, and Belgian officers in British and French territory.

ARTICLE 5

It is agreed that the frontier controls relating to non-stop trains shall in principle be effected under the exclusive responsibility of the British and Belgian authorities.

ARTICLE 9

The officers of the three States shall be authorised to circulate freely over the whole of the route between London and Brussels for official purposes simply by producing appropriate evidence of their identity and status.

PART III

Co-operation in Criminal Justice

ARTICLE 11

(1) Without prejudice to the provisions of Articles 4 and 14(2) of the Protocol attached as an annex to this Agreement, when an offence is committed on the territory of one of the three States that State shall have jurisdiction.   **F–24b**

(2) When it cannot be ascertained where such an offence has been committed, the State of arrival shall have jurisdiction.

ARTICLE 12

Where an arrest is made for an offence in respect of which one State has jurisdiction under Article 11, that arrest shall not be affected by the fact that its effects continue in the territory of the other States.

ARTICLE 13

Persons who are found committing, attempting to commit, or just having committed an offence and who are apprehended on the train during the journey shall be handed over as soon as possible to the empowered officers of the State which has jurisdiction under Article 11.

ARTICLE 14

(1) In the event that a person is found committing, attempting to commit or just having committed on board a train in the territory of a State one of the following offences: homicide, rape, arson, armed robbery, kidnapping and hostage taking, or use of explosives, the train must be stopped in order to enable the competent authorities of that State to take any measures relevant to their investigations and, where appropriate, detain the person suspected of having committed the offence.

(2) If the train cannot be stopped because it is within the Fixed Link or because it is about to leave the territory of the State in which one of the offences referred to in the preceding paragraph has been committed, authorised officers who are present must take all appropriate interim measures to ensure that, when the train arrives, the officers of the State which has jurisdiction under Article 11 are able to interview witnesses, take evidence or receive information relevant to their investigations and, where appropriate, take charge of the person suspected of having committed the offence.

ARTICLE 15

(1) When a person is arrested in a manner covered by Articles 6, 12, 13 and 14(2) of this Agreement, the arrest shall be notified without delay to the authorities of the

State of arrival. The person arrested may be transferred to the territory of the State which has jurisdiction under Article 11.

(2) However, any such transfer shall take place within no more than 24 hours of the notification under the preceding paragraph. Moreover, each State reserves the right not to authorise the transfer of its nationals.

PART V

Co-operation Between the Competent Authorities

ARTICLE 23

F–24c   (1) Each State shall waive any claim which it may have against the other States for compensation in respect of damage caused to its officers or its property.

(2) The provisions of this Article shall not affect in any way the rights of third parties under the laws of each State.

PART VI

Final Clauses

ARTICLE 24

F–24d   In addition to the arrangements provided for under Article 20, the procedures for the implementation of this Agreement and its Protocol may, as far as necessary, be the subject of technical or administrative arrangements between the competent authorities of the three States.

PART II

Protocol

ARTICLE 1

F–24e   This Protocol shall apply to non-stop rail traffic between the United Kingdom and Belgium travelling via the Fixed Link and passing through French territory.

ARTICLE 2

(1) The laws and regulations relating to frontier controls of one State shall be applicable in the control zone situated in the other States and shall be put into effect by the officers of that State in the same way as in their own territory.

(2) The officers of each State shall be subject to the legislation of that State on the protection of individuals with regard to automated processing of personal data when using their automated data files and equipment in the control zone situated in either of the other States.

ARTICLE 3

(1) The officers of the other States shall, in exercise of their national powers, be permitted in the control zone situated in the host State to detain or arrest persons in accordance with the laws and regulations relating to frontier controls of their own State or persons sought by the authorities of their own State. These officers shall also be permitted to conduct such persons to the territory of their own State.

(2) However, no person may be held for more than 24 hours in the areas reserved for frontier controls in the host State. Any such detention shall be subject to the requirements and procedures laid down by the legislation of the State of the officers who have made the detention or arrest.

ARTICLE 4

Breaches of the laws and regulations relating to frontier controls of other States which are detected in the control zone situated in the host State shall be subject to the laws and regulations of those other States, as if the breaches had occurred in the territory of the latter.

ARTICLE 5

(1) The frontier controls of the State of departure shall normally be effected before those of the State of arrival.

(2) The officers of the State of arrival are not authorised to begin to carry out such controls before the end of the controls of the State of departure. Any form of relinquishment of such controls shall be considered as a control.

(3) The officers of the State of departure may no longer carry out their controls when the officers of the State of arrival have begun their own operations, except with the consent of the competent officers of the State of arrival.

(4) If exceptionally, in the course of the frontier controls, the sequence of operations provided for in paragraph (1) of this Article is modified, the officers of the State of arrival may not proceed to detentions, arrests or seizures until the frontier controls of the State of departure are completed. In such a case, these officers shall escort the persons, vehicles, merchandise, animals or other goods, for which the frontier controls of the State of departure are not yet completed, to the officers of that State. If these latter then wish to proceed to detentions, arrests or seizure, they shall have priority.

ARTICLE 6

If the State of arrival refuses admission to persons, vehicles, animals or goods, or if persons refuse to submit to the frontier controls of the State of arrival, or send or take back any vehicles, animals or goods which are accompanying them, the authorities of the State of departure may not refuse to accept back such persons, vehicles, animals or goods. However, the authorities of the State of departure may take any measures to deal with them in accordance with the law applicable in that State and in a way which does not impose obligations either on the State of transit or on the State of arrival.

ARTICLE 7

. . . .

(2) In an emergency, the local representatives of the authorities concerned may by mutual agreement provisionally bring into effect alterations to the delimitation of the control zones which may prove necessary. Any arrangements so reached shall come into effect immediately.

ARTICLES 8–11

[Health, veterinary and phytosanitary controls]

ARTICLES 12

Officers of the other States may wear their national uniform or visible distinctive insignia in the host State.

ARTICLE 13

(1) The authorities of the host State shall grant the same protection and assistance to officers of the other States, in the exercise of their functions, as they grant to their own officers.

(2) The provisions of the criminal law in force in the host State for the protection of officers in the exercise of their functions shall be equally applicable to the punishment of offences committed against officers of the other States in the exercise of their functions.

ARTICLE 14

(1) Without prejudice to the application of the provisions of Article 23 of the

Agreement, claims for compensation for loss, injury or damage caused by or to officers of the other States in the exercise of their functions in the host State shall be subject to the law and jurisdiction of the State to which those officers belong as if the circumstance giving rise to the claim had occurred in that State.

(2) Officers of the other States may not be prosecuted by authorities of the host State for any acts performed in the control zone whilst in the exercise of their functions. In such a case, they shall come under the jurisdiction of their own State as if the act had been committed in that State.

(3) The judicial authorities or police of the host State who take steps to record the complaint and assemble the facts relating thereto shall communicate all the particulars and evidence thereof to the competent authorities of the State to which the accused officer belongs for the purposes of a possible prosecution according to the laws in force in that State.

ARTICLE 15

(1) Officers of the other States shall be permitted freely to transfer to their own States sums of money levied on behalf of their Governments in the control zone situated in the host State, as well as merchandise and other goods seized there.

(2) They may equally sell such merchandise and other goods in the host State in conformity with the provisions in force in the host State and transfer the proceeds to their own State.

ARTICLE 17

The authorities of the Kingdom of Belgium and of the United Kingdom shall use their best endeavours to ensure that the authorities of the other Party are able to make use in the host State of the accommodation, installations and equipment necessary for the performance of their functions.

ARTICLE 18

(1) The officers of the other States are empowered to keep order within the accommodation appointed for their exclusive use in the host State.

(2) The officers of the host State shall not have access to such accommodation, except at the request of the officers of the State concerned or in accordance with the laws of the host State applicable to entry into and searches of private premises.

ARTICLE 19

All goods which are necessary to enable the officers of the other States to carry out their functions in the host State shall be exempt from all taxes and dues on entry and exit.

ARTICLE 20

(1) The officers of the other States whilst exercising their functions in the host State shall be authorised to communicate with their national authorities.

....

PART III

**Articles or parts of Articles of the Protocol attached to and forming part of the
Agreement, as applied by the Administrative Arrangement to immigration
controls upon passengers travelling on international trains making a
commercial stop**

ARTICLE 1

F–24f   This Protocol shall apply to rail traffic between the United Kingdom and Belgium travelling via the Fixed Link and making a commercial stop in French territory.

ARTICLE 2

(1) The laws and regulations relating to immigration controls of one State shall be applicable in the control zone situated in the other States and shall be put into effect by the officers of that State in the same way as in their own territory.

(2) The officers of each State shall be subject to the legislation of that State on the protection of individuals with regard to automated processing of personal data when using their automated data files and equipment in the control zone situated in either of the other States.

ARTICLE 3

(1) The officers of the other States shall, in exercise of their national powers, be permitted in the control zone situated in the host state to detain or arrest persons in accordance with the laws relating to immigration control of their own State. These officers shall also be permitted to conduct such persons to the territory of their own State.

(2) However, no person may be held for more than 24 hours in the areas reserved for immigration controls in the host State. Any such detention shall be subject to the requirements and procedures laid down by the legislation of the State of the officers who have made the detention or arrest.

ARTICLE 4

Breaches of the laws and regulations relating to immigration controls of the other States which are detected in the control zone situated in the host State shall be subject to the laws and regulations of those other States, as if the breaches had occurred in the territory of the latter.

ARTICLE 5

(1) The immigration controls of the State of departure shall normally be effected before those of the state of arrival.

(2) The officers of the State of arrival are not authorised to begin to carry out such controls before the end of the controls of the State of departure. Any form of relinquishment of such controls shall be considered as a control.

(3) The officers of the State of departure may no longer carry out their immigration controls when the officers of the State of arrival have begun their own operations, except with the consent of the competent officers of the State of arrival.

(4) If exceptionally, in the course of the immigration controls, the sequence of operations provided for in paragraph (1) of this Article is modified, the officers of the State of arrival may not proceed to detentions, arrests or seizures until the immigration controls of the State of departure are completed. In such a case, these officers shall escort any persons and goods for which the immigration controls of the State of departure are not yet completed, to the officers of that State. If these latter then wish to proceed to detentions, arrests or seizures, they shall have priority.

ARTICLE 6

If the state of arrival refuses admission to persons or goods or if the persons refuse to submit to the immigration controls of the State of arrival, or send or take back any goods which are accompanying them, the authorities of the State of departure may not refuse to accept back such persons or goods. However, the authorities of the State of departure may take any measures to deal with them in accordance with the law applicable in that State and in a way which does not impose obligations either on the State of transit or on the State of arrival.

ARTICLE 7

In an emergency, the local representatives of the authorities concerned may by mutual agreement provisionally bring into effect alterations to the delimitation of the control zones which may prove necessary. Any arrangements so reached shall come into effect immediately.

ARTICLE 8

Immigration controls on persons for the purpose of safeguarding public health shall be carried out in the control zones situated in the host State by the competent authorities of the State of arrival in conformity with the regulations applicable in that State.

ARTICLE 12

Officers of the other States may wear their national uniform or visible distinctive insignia in the host State.

ARTICLE 13

(1) The authorities of the host State shall grant the same protection and assistance to officers of the other States, in the exercise of their functions, as they grant to their own officers.

(2) The provisions of the criminal law in force in the host State for the protection of officers in the exercise of their functions shall be equally applicable to the punishment of offences committed against officers of the other States in the exercise of their functions.

ARTICLE 14

(1) Without prejudice to the application of the provisions of Article 23 of the Agreement, claims for compensation for loss, injury or damage caused by or to officers of the other States in the exercise of their functions in the host State shall be subject to the law and jurisdiction of the State to which those officers belong as if the circumstance giving rise to the claim had occurred there.

(2) Officers of the other States may not be prosecuted by the authorities of the host State for any acts performed in the control zone whilst in the exercise of their functions. In such a case, they shall come under the jurisdiction of their own State as if the act had been committed there.

(3) The judicial authorities or police of the host State who take steps to record the complaint and assemble the facts relating thereto shall communicate all the particulars and evidence thereof to the competent authorities of the State to which the officer belongs for the purposes of a possible prosecution according to the laws in force in that State.

ARTICLE 17

The authorities of the Kingdom of Belgium and of the United Kingdom shall use their best endeavours to ensure that the authorities of the other party are able to make use in the host State of the accommodation, installations and equipment necessary for the performance of their functions.

ARTICLE 18

(1) The officers of the other State are empowered to keep order within the accommodation appointed for their exclusive use in the host State.

(2) The officers of the host State shall not have access to such accommodation except at the request of the officers of the State concerned or in accordance with the laws of the host State applicable to entry into and searches of private premises.

ARTICLE 19

All goods which are necessary to enable the officers of the other State to carry out their functions in the host State shall be exempt from all taxes and duty on entry and exit.

The officers of the other State whilst exercising their functions in the host State shall be authorised to communicate with their national authorities.

[Part III of this schedule was inserted by the *Channel Tunnel (Miscellaneous Provisions) Order* 2004 (S.I. 2004 No. 2589).]

Powers of officers

Paragraph 1 of Schedule 3 to S.I. 1994 No. 1405 provides that Part I of **F–25** Schedule 3 to the 1993 Order (*ante*, F–17) shall, with the variations set out in paragraphs 2 to 7, be taken to apply as if it were contained in the 1994 Order. Part I of Schedule 3 to the 1993 Order, *as so varied*, is set out below.

S.I. 1993 No. 1813, Sched. 3, Pt I (as varied by S.I. 1994 No. 1405, Sched. 3)

SCHEDULE 3

PART I

POWERS OF OFFICERS

Powers of arrest outside United Kingdom

2.—(1) A constable may in a control zone in France or Belgium—   **F–26**

    (a) exercise any power of arrest conferred by a frontier control enactment or conferred by the *Police and Criminal Evidence Act* 1984 (in this Schedule referred to as "the 1984 Act") in respect of an offence under such an enactment,

    (b) make any arrest authorised by a warrant issued by a court in the United Kingdom, and

    (c) arrest any person whose name or description or both, together with particulars of an arrestable offence (within the meaning of section 24 of the 1984 Act) of which there are reasonable grounds for suspecting him to be guilty, have been made available by a chief officer of police to other such officers.

(2) For the purposes of sub-paragraph (1)(a) the reference in sub-paragraph (1) to a constable shall be construed—

    (a) in relation to the powers of arrest conferred by section 25(3) of and paragraph 17(1) of Schedule 2 to the *Immigration Act* 1971, as including a reference both—

        (i) to an immigration officer appointed for the purposes of that Act under paragraph 1 of that Schedule, and

        (ii) to an officer of customs and excise who is the subject of arrangements for the employment of such officers as immigration officers made under that paragraph by the Secretary of State.

    (b) in relation to the power of arrest conferred by paragraph 6(4) of Schedule 5 to the *Prevention of Terrorism (Temporary Provisions) Act* 1989, as including a reference to any person who by virtue of paragraph 1(1) of that Schedule is an examining officer for the purposes of that Act, and

    (c) in relation to any arrest that may be made by a customs officer by virtue of section 138 of the *Customs and Excise Management Act* 1979 and an arrest for a drug trafficking offence as defined in section 38(1) of the *Drug Trafficking Offences Act* 1986, as including a reference to a customs officer.

(3) A customs officer may in a control zone in France or Belgium arrest any person whose name or description or both, together with particulars of an arrestable offence (within the meaning of section 24 of the 1984 Act) which is an offence in re-

lation to an assigned matter as defined in section 1(1) of the *Customs and Excise Management Act* 1979 and of which there are reasonable grounds for suspecting him to be guilty, have been made available to customs officers generally under the authority of the Commissioners of Customs and Excise.

(4) Sub-paragraph (5) applies where—

> (a) an arrest has been made for an offence of the kind mentioned in Article 12 of the Part I provisions, and
>
> (b) the person arrested enters France or Belgium ("the State of arrival") while under arrest.

(5) If jurisdiction is not asserted by the State of arrival, the person arrested shall be treated as having continued to be under arrest throughout, notwithstanding any intervening transfer of Custody to a person other than the person who arrested him, and sections 30 and 41 of the 1984 Act shall apply accordingly.

(6) [*Not printed in this work.*]

(7) Any power conferred by an enactment to search an arrested person may be exercised following an arrest authorised by this paragraph as if the person had been arrested in the United Kingdom.

3.—(1) Where—

> (a) an arrest of any kind authorised by paragraph 2 above has been made in a control zone in France or Belgium; or
>
> (b) an arrest of any such kind has been made in the United Kingdom and the person arrested enters such a control zone while under arrest,

the person arrested may be held in France or, as the case may be, Belgium for a period of not more than 24 hours.

(2) Subject to sub-paragraph (4), the person arrested shall be treated as if the place where he is held were for the purposes of sections 36(7) and (8), 54 to 56, 58 and 61 to 63 of the 1984 Act and in the case of a child or young person section 34(2) to (7), (8) and (9) of the *Children and Young Persons Act* 1933 a police station, or where the arrest was made by a customs officer, a customs office, in England, not being a police station or customs office designated under section 35 of the 1984 Act.

(4) Where the power of arrest mentioned in paragraph 2(2)(b) has been exercised any detention in France or Belgium of the persons arrested shall be treated for all purposes as being detention under paragraph 6(1) of Schedule 5 to the *Prevention of Terrorism (Temporary Provisions) Act* 1989, and section 16(2) of that Act, sections 51(b), 56 and 58 of the 1984 Act and section 34 of the *Children and Young Persons Act* 1933 as applying accordingly.

Arrested persons arriving in the United Kingdom

4.—(1) Where a constable is satisfied that an arrest made outside the United Kingdom on a through train was one falling within Article 13 or 14 of the Part I provisions (persons found committing, attempting to commit or just having committed an offence) he may arrange for the person arrested to be taken into temporary custody.

(2) A person taken into temporary custody under sub-paragraph (1)—

> (a) shall be treated for all purposes as being in lawful custody, and
>
> (b) may be taken to a police station or such other place as may be appropriate in the circumstances, and shall in that case be treated as being a person in whose case sections 36(7) and (8), 54 to 56 and 58 of the 1984 Act, and in the case of a child or young person section 34(2) to (7), (8) and (9) of the *Children and Young Persons Act* 1933, apply;

and arrangements must be made for him to be transferred within 24 hours from the time at which he was taken into custody to the State having jurisdiction by virtue of Article 11(1) of the Part I provisions.

(2A) Where an arrest has been made for an offence in respect of which the United Kingdom may have jurisdiction as the State of arrival by virtue of Article 11(2) of the Part I provisions the person arrested shall be taken to a police station.

(2B) The custody officer at the police station to which the person is taken shall consider whether the offence is one in respect of which the United Kingdom has jurisdiction by virtue of Article 11(2) of the Part I provisions and may for that purpose detain the person at the police station for not longer than the permitted period.

(3) The permitted period is the period of 24 hours beginning at the time at which the person arrives at the police station.

(4) Subject to sub-paragraph (6), the person shall be treated—

    (a) as not being detained at the police station for the purposes of section 37 of the 1984 Act, and

    (b) as not being in police detention for the purposes of sections 40 to 43 of the 1984 Act.

(5) Where the custody officer reaches the conclusion that the United Kingdom does not have jurisdiction by virtue of Article 11(2) he shall immediately inform the competent authorities of the State appearing to him to have jurisdiction by virtue of Article 11(1) that he has reached that conclusion and shall arrange for the person to be transferred to that State within the permitted period.

(6) Where the custody officer reaches the conclusion that the United Kingdom has jurisdiction by virtue of Article 11(2)—

    (a) he shall immediately inform the person of his conclusion,

    (b) the person shall be treated as being in police detention for all purposes of Part IV of the 1984 Act, and

    (c) that Part shall have effect in relation to him as if the relevant time mentioned in section 41(1) were the time at which he is informed of the conclusion.

(7) Where the police station to which the person is taken is not a police station designated under section 34 of the 1984 Act, references in this paragraph to the custody officer are to be construed as references to an officer not below the rank of sergeant.

Arrests of French officers

5.—(1) This paragraph applies where an officer belonging to the French Republic **F–26b** or to the Kingdom of Belgium ("the officer") is arrested for an act performed in the United Kingdom in a control zone.

(2) If the officer enters the State to which he belongs ("the home State") while under arrest—

    (a) he shall without delay be handed over for custody to the competent authorities of the home State and shall be treated as continuing to be under arrest until he has been handed over, and

    (b) if after consultation with those authorities it is then determined that the act was not performed by the officer whilst in the exercise of his functions and he accordingly does not by virtue of Article 14(2) of the Part II provisions come under the jurisdiction of the home State, he shall be treated as having continued to be under arrest until sub-paragraph (3) has been complied with.

(3) Where—

    (a) sub-paragraph (2)(b) applies, or

    (b) the officer does not leave the United Kingdom whilst under arrest,

he shall be taken to a police station designated under section 35 of the 1984 Act.

(4) Sub-paragraphs (5) to (9) apply in a case falling within sub-paragraph (3)(b).

(5) The custody officer at the police station to which the officer is taken shall after consultation with the competent authorities of the home State determine whether the act was performed by the officer whilst in the exercise of his functions, and may for the purpose of determining that question detain the officer at the police station for not longer than the permitted period.

(6) The permitted period is the period of 24 hours beginning at the time at which the officer arrives at the police station.

(7) Subject to sub-paragraph (9), the officer shall be treated—

    (a) as not being detained at the police station for the purposes of section 37 of the 1984 Act, and

    (b) as not being in police detention for the purposes of sections 40 to 43 of the 1984 Act.

(8) Where the custody officer determines that the act was performed by the officer whilst in the exercise of his functions and the officer accordingly comes under the jurisdiction of the home State by virtue of Article 14(2), he shall immediately inform the competent authorities of the home State and shall arrange for the officer to be transferred to the home State within the permitted period.

(9) In any other case—

> (a) the custody officer shall immediately inform the officer of his determination,
>
> (b) the officer shall be treated as being in police detention for all purposes of Part IV of the 1984 Act, and
>
> (c) that Part shall have effect in relation to him as if the relevant time mentioned in section 41(1) were the time at which he is informed of the determination.

Arrests of United Kingdom officers

F–26c 6.—(1) This paragraph applies where an officer belonging to the United Kingdom ("the officer") is arrested for an act performed in France or Belgium in a control zone.

(2) If—

> (a) the officer does not enter the United Kingdom while under arrest, and
>
> (b) the competent authorities of the State in which the act was performed ("the State concerned") determine that the act was performed by the officer whilst in the exercise of his functions and he accordingly comes under United Kingdom jurisdiction by virtue of Article 14(2) of the Part II provisions,

he shall on being handed over by those authorities to a constable be treated as having been arrested by the constable.

(3) Where—

> (a) sub-paragraph (2)(b) applies, or
>
> (b) the officer enters the United Kingdom while under the original arrest,

he shall be taken to a police station designated under section 35 of the 1984 Act.

(4) Sub-paragraphs (5) to (9) apply in a case falling within sub-paragraph (3)(b).

(5) The custody officer at the police station to which the officer is taken shall—

> (a) immediately invite the competent authorities of the State concerned to determine whether the act was performed by the officer whilst in the exercise of his functions, and
>
> (b) afford those authorities any assistance they may require in determining that question

and may for the purpose of enabling that question to be determined detain the officer at the police station for not longer than the permitted period.

(6) The permitted period is the period of 24 hours beginning at the time at which the officer arrives at the police station.

(7) Subject to sub-paragraph (9), the officer shall be treated—

> (a) as not being detained at the police station for the purposes of section 37 of the 1984 Act, and
>
> (b) as not being in police detention for the purposes of sections 40 to 43 of the 1984 Act.

(8) Where the competent authorities of the State concerned determine that the act was not performed by the officer whilst in the exercise of his functions and the officer accordingly does not by virtue of Article 14(2) come under United Kingdom jurisdiction, the custody officer shall arrange for the officer to be transferred to the State concerned within the permitted period.

(9) In any other case—

> (a) the custody officer shall immediately inform the officer of the determination,
>
> (b) the officer shall be treated as being in police detention for all purposes of Part IV of the 1984 Act, and
>
> (c) that Part shall have effect in relation to him as if the relevant time

mentioned in section 41(1) were the time at which he is informed of the determination.

Amendments

Relevant entries in Schedule 4 are noted at the appropriate place elsewhere   **F–27**
in this work.

APPENDIX G

Guidelines on Claims for Fees under a Crown Court Representation Order

A. Summary of Source Material

Legislation

As from April 2, 2001 the relevant provisions of the *Legal Aid in Criminal*   **G–1**
and Care Proceedings (Costs) Regulations 1989 (S.I. 1989 No. 343), as amended,
were superseded, virtually unamended, by the *Criminal Defence Service (Funding) Order* 2001 (S.I. 2001 No. 855) ("the *Funding Order* 2001"). This was
significantly amended by the *Criminal Defence Service (Funding) (Amendment)
(No. 3) Order* 2001 (S.I. 2001 No. 3341) which came into force on October
29, 2001, the *Criminal Defence Service (Funding) (Amendment) Order* 2004 (S.I.
2004 No. 2045) which came into force on August 2, 2004, and the *Criminal
Defence Service (Funding) (Amendment) Order* 2005 (S.I. 2005 No. 2621) which
came into effect on October 3, 2005, and applied in respect of proceedings in
which a representation order was made on or after that date and to appeals to
a costs judge made on or after that date. The amendments modified and
extended graduated fees to cover trials estimated to last up to 30 days, and
introduced and later amended a new regime for Very High Cost Cases. In relation to representation orders granted on or after April 30, 2007, the *Funding Order* 2001 was revoked and replaced by the *Criminal Defence Service
(Funding) Order* 2007 (S.I. 2007 No. 1174) ("the *Funding Order* 2007") (see
art. 4 of the 2007 order for the transitional provisions).

The 2007 order was first amended by the *Criminal Defence Service (Funding)
(Amendment) Order* 2007 (S.I. 2007 No. 3352). This makes minor changes to
Schedule 1 (the advocates' graduated fee scheme), disapplies the principal order to very high costs cases and introduces a graduated fee scheme for litigators in the Crown Court. The amendments apply to proceedings in which a
representation order is granted on or after January 14, 2008, and to proceedings which the Legal Services Commission classifies as a very high costs case
on or after that date. A "very high costs case" is given the same definition in
his order as in the new definition inserted into regulation 2 of the general
regulations (*ante*, § 6–153). The principal order continues to apply in its
unamended form to proceedings to which the amendments do not apply. For
he unamended text, see the first supplement to this edition of this work.

The 2007 order was further amended by the *Criminal Defence Service (Funding) (Amendment) Order* 2008 (S.I. 2008 No. 957) with effect from April 24,
2008. The effect of the amendments is: (i) that the principal order will apply
o a Very High Cost Case where a litigator instructs an advocate who is not a

member of a Very High Cost Case (Crime) Panel in accordance with the Very High Cost Case contract for panel members dated April 2, 2008, (ii) that in such a case the litigator may claim payment from the Legal Services Commission in respect of work undertaken by the advocate and authorised in accordance with the contract, and (iii) that where such a claim is made, the Legal Services Commission must pay the litigator at rates no higher than the rates specified.

The third set of amendments to the 2007 order was made by the *Criminal Defence Service (Funding) (Amendment No. 2) Order* 2008 (S.I. 2008 No. 2930). The effect was (i) to increase the maximum payments which the Legal Services Commission may make in very high cost criminal cases in which an advocate is instructed who is not a member of a panel for such cases, and (ii) in such cases, to provide for the payment of travelling and accommodation expenses incurred by the advocate where it considers there are exceptional circumstances. See *post*, G-81b.

The relevant provisions of the *Legal Aid in Criminal and Care Proceedings (General) Regulations* 1989 (S.I. 1989 No. 344) have also been replaced, again with little amendment, by the *Criminal Defence Service (General) (No. 2) Regulations* (S.I. 2001 No. 1437) (the "General Regulations"). Any reference hereafter to a regulation is a reference to the General Regulations. Any reference to an article or a Schedule, is a reference to the *Funding Order* 2001 or the *Funding Order* 2007. The General Regulations together with details of all amendments are set out *in extenso* in the main work at §§ 6–152 *et seq*. The *Funding Order* 2007 is set out in full, *post*, G–6 *et seq*.

The current regimes

G-2   Advocates' fees in the Crown Court effectively fall into one of three regimes:

(i) *Graduated fees*. These were introduced in 1997 for trials lasting up to 10 days, appeals and other minor Crown Court business: *Legal Aid in Criminal and Care Proceedings (Costs) Regulations* 1989 (S.I. 1989 No 343), Sched. 3. The scheme was then extended to cover trials of up to 25 days and, as from 2005, of trials up to 40 days. As from April 30, 2007, it is intended that the scheme will cover all Crown Court work save for those cases contracted under the Very High Costs Case provisions: *Funding Order* 2007, Sched. 1, para. 2(1). The new scheme is sometimes referred to as the Revised Advocacy Graduated Fee Scheme (RAGFS). The details are now contained in Schedule 1 to the *Funding Order* 2007, which replaces Schedule 4 to the *Funding Order* 2001.

(ii) *Very High Cost Cases (VHCC)*. This regime came into effect on October 29, 2001. All cases estimated to last more than 40 days are capable of being subject to a VHCC contract. As to the current VHCC regime, see *post*, G–181 *et seq*.

(iii) *Ex post facto cases*: art. 15(6). These broadly cover trials estimated to last more than 25 days where the representation order was granted on or before October 29, 2001, and those which are not remunerated under the VHCC or graduated fee schemes. However, circumstances can arise where the same counsel can be remunerated under both the *ex post facto* and the graduated fee regimes: see *post*, G–116. Where a representation order is made on or after April 30, 2007, a trial on indictment must be remunerated either as a graduated fee or under a VHCC contract. *Ex post facto* payments have effectively been abolished in relation to such orders.

Notes for guidance

(a) *Graduated fees*

The Ministry of Justice's *Graduated Fee Scheme Guidance (GFSG)* is updated   **G–3**
at regular intervals. In addition, guidance notes in respect of the *Funding Order* 2007, and RAGFS have been issued by the Criminal Bar Association,
and are available on both the Criminal Bar Association's and the Courts
Service's National Taxing Team's websites. The *GFSG* includes references to
costs judges' decisions which are given and commonly referred to and indexed
by their "X" references. For convenience these references are used hereafter.
The guidance may be cited by advocates when asking for a re-determination:
GFSG, Preface. However, while interesting and instructive, it is simply the
department's gloss on the wording of the regulations, and does not bind costs
judges: *R. v. Phillips*, X1, SCTO 594/97.

The Bar Council has also introduced a *Graduated Fee Payment Protocol*. This
is an essential part of the mechanism by which advocates will be remunerated
in future, and sets out arrangements to ensure that substitute advocates are
paid by instructed advocates. The protocol falls outside the immediate scope
of this work. It is available on both the Bar Council's and the Criminal Bar
Association's websites.

(b) *Very High Cost Cases*

Very High Cost Cases are governed by the *Very High Cost Criminal Cases
Arrangement 2002* (*Legal Services Commission Manual* Vol. 4, Part 4 B) and a
narrative and guidance may be found in Part D5 of the *Manual*. Some material decisions of the Appeal Committee are reported on the Department's
website.

(c) *Ex post facto*

Notes for guidance on the main principles of *ex post facto* taxation are
contained in the current edition of the *Taxing Officers' Notes for Guidance
(TONG)* which was issued in July 1995 by the Chief Taxing Master. *TONG*
does not bind any taxing authority or limit discretion in any way save where it
accurately reflects a decision of the High Court or a statutory provision. As
each case must be considered on its own facts, *TONG* does not bind a taxing
authority to take any decision which it does not consider to be justified:
TONG, para. 1.2.

TONG is supplemented by the *Directions for Determining Officers (DDO)*   **G–4**
which were issued on April 1, 1989, by the Lord Chancellor's Department
and later amended to reflect the changes effected by the *Legal Aid in Criminal
and Care Proceedings (Costs) (Amendment) Regulations* 1990 (S.I. 1990 No. 488).
These *Directions* represent the department's view of the interpretation and application of the regulations and may be amended or supplemented from time
to time by further directions from headquarters and circuit offices: *DDO*,
para. 1.

Taxing masters' and cost judges' decisions

Decisions of taxing masters have been collated in the Digest of Taxing   **G–5**
Master's Decisions (DTMD) and the Taxing Compendium (TC). The latter
work was published by the Legal Services Branch of the Lord Chancellor's
Department and up-dated on an *ad hoc* basis. It comprises summaries which
have been certified by taxing masters as containing matters of principle. It is

intended for the use of appropriate officers when assessing claims for fee under the *Legal Aid in Criminal and Care Proceedings (Costs) Regulations* 198 (S.I. 1989 No. 343) (see *ante*, G–1), and should be used in conjunction with *TONG* and *DDO*. The preface states that "it should be made available to solici tors and counsel for inspection on request." The DTMD was issued on March 31, 1980 and was made available to the Bar Council and the Law Society. I was last up-dated in July, 1987. Most important decisions are now reported in the Costs Law Reports. Some costs cases are also available from the Court Service's National Taxing Team website.

Contract Appeals Committee decisions

G–5a   Summaries of decisions of the Appeals Committee in respect of dispute arising under VHCC contracts have been collated and appear at the Lega Services Commission's website as Contract Appeals Committee Decision (*CACD*). These are meant to be updated regularly.

B. THE FUNDING ORDER (2007)

Criminal Defence Service (Funding) Order 2007
(S.I. 2007 No. 1174)

Citation and commencement

G–6   **1.** This Order may be cited as the *Criminal Defence Service (Funding) Order 200* and shall come into force on 30th April 2007.

Interpretation

G–7   **2.** In this Order—

"the Act" means the *Access to Justice Act* 1999;

"advocate" means a barrister, a solicitor advocate or a solicitor who is exercising their automatic rights of audience in the Crown Court;

"appropriate officer" means —

(a) in the case of proceedings in the civil division of the Court of Appeal the head of the civil appeals office;

(b) in the case of proceedings in the criminal division of the Court of Ap peal, the registrar;

(c) in the case of proceedings in the Crown Court, the Commission;

(d) in respect of advice or assistance as to an appeal from the Crow Court to the Court of Appeal (except in the case of an appeal unde section 9(11) of the *Criminal Justice Act* 1987 (preparatory hearings) where, on the advice of any representative instructed, notice of ap peal is given, or application for leave to appeal is made, whether o not such appeal is later abandoned, the registrar;

(e) in respect of advice or assistance as to an appeal to the Courts-Martia Appeal Court, the registrar;

(f) in respect of advice or assistance as to an appeal from the Court c Appeal to the House of Lords, where the appeal is not lodged wit the House of Lords, the registrar; and

(g) in any other case, the Commission,

and, in any case, includes an officer designated by the appropriate officer t act on his behalf for the purposes of this Order;

"assisted person" means a person in receipt of funded services;

"CDS Regulations" means the *Criminal Defence Service (General) (No.2) Regula tions* 2001;

"class 1 offence", "class 2 offence" and "class 3 offence" have the meanings give in paragraph III.21.1 of the *Practice Direction (Criminal Proceedings: Consolidation)*;

"the Commission" means the Legal Services Commission established under section 1 of the Act;

"fee earner" means a litigator, or person employed by a litigator, who undertakes work on a case;

"funded services" means services which are provided directly for an individual and funded for that individual as part of the Criminal Defence Service under sections 12 to 18 of the Act;

"instructed advocate" means

    (a) where a representation order provides for a single advocate, the first barrister or solicitor advocate instructed in the case, who has primary responsibility for the case; or

    (b) where a representation order provides for more than one advocate, each of—

        (i) the leading instructed advocate; and

        (ii) the led instructed advocate;

"leading instructed advocate" means the first leading barrister or solicitor advocate instructed in the case, who has primary responsibility for those aspects of a case undertaken by a leading advocate;

"led instructed advocate" means the first led barrister or solicitor advocate instructed in the case, who has primary responsibility for those aspects of the case undertaken by a led advocate;

"litigator" means the person named on the representation order as representing an assisted person, being a solicitor, firm of solicitors or other appropriately qualified person;

"registrar" means the registrar of criminal appeals;

"related proceedings" means —

    (a) two or more sets of proceedings involving the same defendant which are prepared, heard or dealt with together; or

    (b) proceedings involving more than one defendant which arise out of the same incident, so that the defendants are charged, tried or disposed of together;

"representation order" means a document granting a right to representation;

"representative" means a litigator or an advocate, including, where appropriate, an instructed advocate;

"senior solicitor" means a solicitor who, in the judgement of the appropriate officer, has the skill, knowledge and experience to deal with the most difficult and complex cases;

"solicitor advocate" means a solicitor who has obtained a higher courts advocacy qualification in accordance with regulations and rules of conduct of the Law Society;

"solicitor, legal executive or fee earner of equivalent experience" means a solicitor, Fellow of the Institute of Legal Executives or equivalent senior fee earner who, in the judgement of the appropriate officer, has good knowledge and experience of the conduct of criminal cases;

"trainee solicitor or fee earner of equivalent experience" means a trainee solicitor or other fee earner who is not a Fellow of the Institute of Legal Executives, who, in the judgement of the appropriate officer, carries out the routine work on a case; and

"Very High Cost Case" means a case in which a representation order has been granted and which the Commission classifies as a Very High Cost Case on the grounds that—

    (a) if the case were to proceed to trial, the trial would in the opinion of the Commission be likely to last for more than 40 days, and the Commission considers that there are no exceptional circumstances which make it unsuitable to be dealt with under its contractual arrangements for Very High Cost Cases; or

   (b) if the case were to proceed to trial, the trial would in the opinion o
        the Commission be likely to last no fewer than 25 and no more than
        40 days, and the Commission considers that there are circumstance
        which make it suitable to be dealt with under its contractual arrange
        ments for Very High Cost Cases;

   "Very High Cost Case (Crime) Panel" means a panel set up by the Commission
        from which representatives may be chosen to provide representation in Very
        High Cost Cases.

[This article is printed as amended by S.I. 2007 No. 3552 (*ante*, G–1).]

Scope

G–8   **3.**—(1) Article 10 of this Order applies to proceedings in magistrates' courts
only.

   (2) Article 12 of this Order applies to proceedings in magistrates' courts and to
proceedings in the Crown Court.

   (3) Articles 5, 6, 14 to 24, and 29 to 31 of, and Schedules 1 and 2 to, this Order
apply to proceedings in the Crown Court only.

   (4) Articles 4, 11, 13, 25 to 28 and 32 of this Order apply to proceedings in the
Crown Court and to proceedings in the Court of Appeal.

   (5) Article 8 of, and Schedule 4 to, this Order apply to proceedings in the Court
of Appeal only.

   (6) Article 9 of this Order applies to proceedings in the House of Lords only.

   (6A) This order does not apply to Very High Costs Cases, except as provided in
paragraph 25 of Schedule 2.

   (7) For the purpose of this Order any reference to the Court of Appeal includes a
reference to—

   (a) the criminal division of the Court of Appeal;

   (b) the civil division of the Court of Appeal;

   (c) the Courts-Martial Appeal Court; and

   (d) a Divisional Court of the High Court.

[This article is printed as amended by S.I. 2007 No. 3552; and S.I. 2008
No. 957 (*ante*, G–1).]

Funding of Services

G–9   **4.**—(1) Where a representation order is granted on or after 30th April 2007 for
proceedings in the Crown Court or Court of Appeal—

   (a) the Commission must fund representation in accordance with its duty
        under section 14(1) of the Act; and

   (b) the provisions of this Order apply.

   (2) Where a representation order is granted on or after 1st April 2003, but before
30th April 2007 for proceedings in the Crown Court or the Court of Appeal—

   (a) the Commission must fund representation in accordance with its duty
        under section 14(1) of the Act; and

   (b) the provisions of the *Criminal Defence Service (Funding) Order* 2001 apply.

   (3) Where a representation order is granted before 1st April 2003 for—

   (a) criminal proceedings in the House of Lords;

   (b) proceedings in the Court of Appeal; or

   (c) proceedings in the Crown Court,

the duty of the Commission under section 14(1) of the Act has effect as a duty o
the Lord Chancellor and the provisions of the *Criminal Defence Service (Funding)
Order* 2001 apply.

   (4) Where a representation order is granted before 1st April 2003 for—

   (a) any proceedings in the Crown Court which are prescribed under section
        12(2)(g) of the Act;

   (b) any Very High Cost Case which is the subject of an individual contract for
        the provision of funded services; or

(c) any proceedings in which representation is provided by a person employed
by the Commission for that purpose,

the Commission must fund representation in accordance with its duty under section 14(1) of the Act and the provisions of the *Criminal Defence Service (Funding)
Order* 2001 apply.

Claims for fees by advocates—Crown Court

5.—(1) Claims for fees by an instructed advocate in proceedings in the Crown   **G–10**
Court must be made and determined in accordance with the provisions of Schedule 1 to this Order.

(2) A claim for fees under this article and Schedule 1 must be made by each
instructed advocate.

(3) Subject to article 32, a claim by an instructed advocate for fees in respect of
work done under a representation order must not be entertained unless he submits
it within three months of the conclusion of the proceedings to which it relates.

(4) An instructed advocate must submit a claim for fees to the appropriate officer
in such form and manner as he may direct.

(5) An instructed advocate must supply such further information and documents
as the appropriate officer may require.

(6) Where a confiscation hearing under Part 2 of the *Proceeds of Crime Act* 2002
(Confiscation: England and Wales), section 2 of the *Drug Trafficking Act* 1994
(confiscation orders) or section 71 of the *Criminal Justice Act* 1988 (confiscation
orders) is to be held more than 28 days after—

(a) the conclusion of the trial to which the representation order relates; or

(b) the entering of a guilty plea,

an instructed advocate may submit any claim for fees in respect of the trial or
guilty plea as soon as the trial has concluded or the guilty plea has been entered.

(7) Where a representation order provides for representation by—

(a) a single advocate other than a QC, and a QC agrees to appear as the single
advocate; or

(b) two or more advocates other than QC, and a QC agrees to appear as a
leading junior,

that QC must be treated for all the purposes of this Order as having been
instructed under that representation order, and his remuneration must be
determined as if he were not a QC.

[This article is printed as amended by S.I. 2007 No. 3552 (*ante*, G–1).]

Claims for fees and disbursements by litigators—Crown Court

6.—(1) Claims for fees by litigators in proceedings in the Crown Court must be   **G–11**
made and determined in accordance with the provisions of Schedule 2 to this
Order.

(2) Claims for disbursements by litigators in proceedings in the Crown Court
must be made and determined in accordance with the provisions of articles 14 to 16.

(3) Subject to article 32, a claim by a litigator for fees in respect of work done
under a representation order must not be entertained unless he submits it within
three months of the conclusion of the proceedings to which it relates.

(4) Subject to paragraph (5), a claim for fees in proceedings in the Crown Court
must be submitted to the appropriate officer in such form and manner as he may
direct and must be accompanied by the representation order and any receipts or
other documents in support of any disbursement claimed.

(5) A claim under paragraph 15 or 22 of Schedule 2 to this order must—

(a) summarise the items of work done by a fee earner in respect of which fees
are claimed according to the classes specified in paragraph 2(1) of Schedule
2;

(b) state, where appropriate, the dates on which the items of work were done,
the time taken, the sums claimed and whether the work was done for more
than one assisted person;

(c) specify, where appropriate, the level of fee earner who undertook each of the items of work claimed; and

(d) give particulars of any work done in relation to more than one indictment or a retrial.

(6) Where the litigator claims that paragraph 25 of Schedule 2 applies in relation to an item of work, he must give full particulars in support of his claim.

(7) The litigator must specify any special circumstances which the litigator considers should be drawn to the attention of the appropriate officer.

(8) The litigator must supply such further information and documents as the appropriate officer may require.

[This article is printed as amended by S.I. 2007 No. 3552 (*ante*, G–1).]

Very High Cost Cases

G–12   **7.** [*Revoked by S.I. 2007 No. 3552, ante, G–1.*]

Proceedings in the Court of Appeal

G–13   **8.** Claims for fees by representatives in proceedings in the Court of Appeal must be made and determined in accordance with the provisions of Schedule 4 to this Order.

Proceedings in the House of Lords

G–14   **9.**—(1) In proceedings in the House of Lords, the fees payable to a representative under sections 13 or 14 of the Act must be determined by such officer as may be prescribed by order of the House of Lords.

(2) Subject to paragraph (1), this Order does not apply to proceedings in the House of Lords.

The General Criminal Contract

G–15   **10.**—(1) Where the Commission funds services as part of the Criminal Defence Service under section 13(2)(a) or 14(2)(a) of the Act, remuneration must be at rates no higher than those set out in Part E of the Specification to the General Criminal Contract, published by the Commission in February 2001, as amended.

[This article is printed as amended by S.I. 2007 No. 3552 (*ante*, G–1).]

Payments from other sources

G–16   **11.** Where a representation order has been made in respect of any proceedings, the representative, whether acting under a representation order or otherwise, must not receive or be a party to the making of any payment for work done in connection with those proceedings, except such payments as may be made—

(a) by the Lord Chancellor or the Commission; or

(b) in respect of any expenses or fees incurred in—

    (i) preparing, obtaining or considering any report, opinion or further evidence, whether provided by an expert witness or otherwise; or

    (ii) obtaining any transcripts or recordings,

where an application under CDS Regulations for an authority to incur such fees or expenses has been refused by a committee appointed under arrangements made by the Commission to deal with, amongst other things, appeals of, or review of, assessment of costs.

Indictable-only offences

G–17   **12.**—(1) Where a case is sent for trial to the Crown Court under section 51 of the *Crime and Disorder Act* 1998 (No committal proceedings for indictable-only offences), the payment in relation to work carried out in the magistrates' court is included within the applicable fee payable under Schedule 1 or Schedule 2.

(2) Paragraph (1) does not apply where the case is remitted to a magistrates' court.

[This article is printed as amended by S.I. 2007 No. 3552 (*ante*, G–1).]

13. Where representation is provided in proceedings referred to in section   **G–18**
12(2)(f) of the Act (proceedings for contempt in the face of a court), the Commission may only fund services as part of the Criminal Defence Service under section
13(2)(b) or 14(2)(b) of the Act in accordance with Schedules 1, 2 and 4.

[This article is printed as substituted by S.I. 2007 No. 3552.]

Interim payment of disbursements
14.—(1) A litigator may submit a claim to the appropriate officer for payment of   **G–19**
a disbursement for which he has incurred liability in proceedings in the Crown
Court in accordance with the provisions of this article.
(2) A claim for payment under paragraph (1) may be made where—
   (a) a litigator has obtained prior authority to incur expenditure of £100 or
       more under CDS Regulations; and
   (b) he has incurred such a liability.
(3) Without prejudice to articles 16(4) and 16(5) a claim for payment under
paragraph (1) must not exceed the maximum amount authorised under the prior
authority.
(4) A claim for payment under paragraph (1) may be made at any time before the
litigator submits a claim for fees under article 6.
(5) A claim for payment under paragraph (1) must be submitted to the appropriate officer in such form and manner as he may direct and must be accompanied by
the authority to incur expenditure and any invoices or other documents in support
of the claim.
(6) The appropriate officer must allow the disbursement subject to the limit in
paragraph (3) if it appears to have been reasonably incurred in accordance with the
prior authority.
(6A) The appropriate officer must notify the litigator and, where the disbursement claimed includes the fees or charges of any person, that person, of his decision.
(7) Where the appropriate officer allows the disbursement, he must notify the
litigator and, where the disbursement includes the fees or charges of any person,
that person, of the amount payable, and must authorise payment to the litigator
accordingly.
(8) Articles 29 to 31 do not apply to a payment under this article.

[This article is printed as amended by S.I. 2007 No. 3552 (*ante*, G–1).]

Interim disbursements and final determination of fees
15.—(1) On a final determination of fees, articles 6(2) and 16 apply notwith-   **G–20**
standing that a payment has been made under article 14.
(2) Where the amount found to be due under article 16 in respect of a disbursement is less than the amount paid under article 14 ("the interim payment"), the appropriate officer must deduct the difference from the sum otherwise payable to the
litigator on the determination of fees, and where the amount due under article 16
exceeds the interim payment, the appropriate officer must add the difference to the
amount otherwise payable to the litigator.

Determination of litigators' disbursements
16.—(1) Subject to paragraphs (2) to (5), the appropriate officer must allow   **G–21**
such disbursements claimed under article 6(2) as appear to him to have been reasonably incurred.
(2) If the disbursements claimed are abnormally large by reason of the distance of
the court or the assisted person's residence or both from the litigator's place of business, the appropriate officer may limit reimbursement of the disbursements to what
otherwise would, having regard to all the circumstances, be a reasonable amount.
(3) No question as to the propriety of any step or act in relation to which prior
authority has been obtained under CDS Regulations may be raised on any determi-

nation of disbursements, unless the litigator knew or ought reasonably to have known that the purpose for which the authority was given had failed or had become irrelevant or unnecessary before the disbursements were incurred.

(4) Where disbursements are reasonably incurred in accordance with and subject to the limit imposed by a prior authority given under CDS Regulations, no question may be raised on any determination of fees as to the amount of the payment to be allowed for the step or act in relation to which the authority was given.

(5) Where disbursements are incurred in taking any steps or doing any act for which authority may be given under CDS Regulations, without such authority having been given or in excess of any fee so authorised, payment in respect of those disbursements may nevertheless be allowed on a determination of disbursements payable under article 6.

Interim payments in cases awaiting determination of fees

G–22   **17.**—(1) The appropriate officer must make an interim payment in respect of a claim for fees in proceedings in the Crown Court in accordance with this article.

(2) Entitlement to a payment arises in respect of a claim for fees by an instructed advocate, where—

> (a) the graduated fee claimed in accordance with Schedule 1 is £4,000 or more (exclusive of VAT); and
>
> (c) the claim for fees is for less than the amounts mentioned in (a) but is related to any claim for fees falling under (a).

(3) For the purposes of this article, the following claims for fees are related to each other—

> (a) the claims of instructed advocates acting in the same proceedings for a defendant; and
>
> (b) the claims of any instructed advocate acting for any assisted person in related proceedings.

(4) Entitlement to a payment under paragraph (1) does not arise until three months have elapsed from the earlier of—

> (a) the date on which the claim for fees is received by the appropriate officer for determination, except that where there are related claims for fees, the date on which the last claim is received by the appropriate officer; or
>
> (b) three months after the conclusion of the last of any related proceedings.

(5) ... an instructed advocate may submit a claim for an interim payment under this article where—

> (a) no payment has been made under paragraph (1); and
>
> (b) six months have elapsed from the conclusion of the proceedings against the assisted person.

(6) Subject to article 32, payment must not be made under this article unless the instructed advocate has submitted a claim for fees in accordance with article 5(3).

[This article is printed as amended by S.I. 2007 No. 3552 (*ante*, G–1).]

Amount of interim payments in cases awaiting determination of fees

G–23   **18.**—(1) Where entitlement to an interim payment arises under article 17, the amount payable is 40 per cent of the total claim for fees, less any sum already paid.

(2) Articles 29 to 31 do not apply to an interim payment under this article.

Staged payments in long Crown Court proceedings

G–24   **19.**—(1) ... an instructed advocate may submit a claim to the appropriate officer for a staged payment of his fees in relation to proceedings in the Crown Court.

(2) Where a claim is submitted in accordance with this article, a staged payment must be allowed where the appropriate officer is satisfied—

> (a) that the claim relates to fees for a period of preparation of 100 hours or more, for which the ... instructed advocate will, subject to final determination of the fees payable, be entitled to be paid in accordance with Schedule 1; and

(b) that the period from committal, transfer or sending for trial (or from the date of the representation order, if later) to the conclusion of the Crown Court proceedings is likely to exceed 12 months, having regard, amongst other matters, to the number of defendants, the anticipated pleas and the weight and complexity of the case.

(3) In this article "preparation" means—

(a) reading the papers in the case;

(b) contact with prosecutors;

(c) written or oral advice on plea;

(d) researching the law, preparation for examination of witnesses and preparation of oral submissions;

(e) viewing exhibits or undisclosed material at police stations;

(f) written advice on evidence;

(g) preparation of written submissions, notices or other documents for use at the trial; and

(h) attendance at views at the scene of the alleged offence;

and is limited to preparation done before the trial, except in proceedings in which a preparatory hearing has been ordered under section 8 of the *Criminal Justice Act* 1987 (commencement of trial and arraignment), in which case it is limited to preparation done before the date on which the jury is sworn (or on which it became certain, by reason of pleas of guilty or otherwise, that the matter would not proceed to trial).

(4) The amount allowed for preparation falling within paragraph (3) must be computed by reference to the number of hours of preparation which it appears to the appropriate officer, without prejudice to the final determination of the fees payable, has been reasonably done, multiplied by the hourly rate for special preparation as set out in the table following paragraph 19 of Schedule 1, as appropriate to the category of advocate.

(6) A claim for staged payment of fees under this article must be made to the appropriate officer in such form and manner as he may direct, including such case plan as he may require for the purposes of paragraph (2)(a).

(7) An instructed advocate may claim further staged payments in accordance with this article in respect of further periods of preparation exceeding 100 hours which were not included in an earlier claim.

(8) Articles 29 to 31 do not apply to a payment under this article.

[This article is printed as amended by S.I. 2007 No. 3552 (*ante*, G–1).]

20. [*Revoked by S.I. 2007 No. 3552*, ante, *G–1*.]   **G–25**

Hardship payments

21.—(1) Subject to paragraphs (4) and (5), the appropriate officer may allow a   **G–26** hardship payment to a representative in the circumstances set out in paragraph (2).

(2) Those circumstances are that the representative—

(a) represents the assisted person in proceedings in the Crown Court;

(b) applies for such payment, in such form and manner as the appropriate officer may direct, not less than six months after he was first instructed in those proceedings, or in related proceedings if he was instructed in those proceedings earlier than in the proceedings to which the application relates;

(c) is unlikely to receive final payment in respect of the proceedings, as determined under Schedules 1 or 2, within the three months following the application for the hardship payment; and

(d) satisfies the appropriate officer that, by reason of the circumstance in subparagraph (c), he is likely to suffer financial hardship.

(3) Every application for a hardship payment by an advocate must be accompanied by such information and documents as the appropriate officer may require as evidence of—

(a) the work done by the advocate in relation to the proceedings up to the date of the application; and

(b) the likelihood of financial hardship.

(3A) Every application for a hardship payment by a litigator must be accompanied by such information and documents as the appropriate officer may require as evidence of—

(a) the Class of Offence with which the assisted person is charged, in accordance with Part 6 of Schedule 1;

(b) the length of trial, where appropriate;

(c) the number of pages of prosecution evidence, calculated in accordance with paragraph 1(2) of Schedule 2;

(d) the total number of defendants in the proceedings who are represented by the litigator;

(e) the likelihood of financial hardship.

(4) The amount of any hardship payment is at the discretion of the appropriate officer, but must not exceed such sum as would be reasonable remuneration for the work done by the representative in the proceedings up to the date of the application.

(5) A hardship payment must not be made if it appears to the appropriate officer that the sum which would be reasonable remuneration for the representative, or the sum required to relieve his financial hardship, is less than £5,000 (excluding VAT).

(6) Where the appropriate officer allows a hardship payment under paragraph (1), he must authorise payment accordingly.

(7) Where the application for a hardship payment is made by an advocate other than an instructed advocate, and the appropriate officer allows a hardship payment under paragraph (1)—

(a) payment must be made to the leading instructed advocate or the led instructed advocate, as appropriate; and

(b) the appropriate officer must notify the advocate who made the application that payment has been made to the instructed advocate.

[This article is printed as amended by S.I. 2007 No. 3552 (*ante*, G–1).]

Computation of final claim where an interim payment has been made

G–27   22.—(1) At the conclusion of a case in which one or more payments have been made to an instructed advocate or a litigator under articles 17 to 21, he must submit a claim under article 5 or 6 for the determination of his overall remuneration, whether or not such a claim will result in any payment additional to those already made.

(2) In the determination of the amount payable to an instructed advocate or litigator under article 5 or 6—

(a) the appropriate officer must deduct the amount of any payment made under articles 17 to 21 in respect of the same case from the amount that would otherwise be payable; and

(b) if the amount of the interim payment is greater than the amount that would otherwise be payable, the appropriate officer may recover the amount of the difference, either by way of repayment by the instructed advocate or litigator or by way of deduction from any other amount that may be due to him.

Payment of fees to advocates—Crown Court

G–28   23.—(1) Having determined the fees payable to each instructed advocate, in accordance with Schedule 1, the appropriate officer must notify each instructed advocate of the fees payable and authorise payment accordingly.

(2) Where, as a result of any redetermination or appeal made or brought pursuant to articles 29 to 31—

(a) the fees payable under paragraph (1) are increased, the appropriate officer must authorise payment of the increase; or

(b) the fees payable under paragraph (1) are decreased, the instructed advocate must repay the amount of such decrease.

(3) Where the payment of any fees of an instructed advocate is ordered under article 30(12) or article 31(8), the appropriate officer must authorise payment.

[This article is printed as amended by S.I. 2007 No. 3552 (*ante*, G–1).]

Payment of fees to litigators—Crown Court

24.—(1) Having determined the fees payable to a litigator in accordance with Schedule 2, the appropriate officer must authorise payment accordingly. **G–29**

(1A) Where the appropriate officer determines that the fees payable under paragraph (1) are greater than or less than the amount claimed by the litigator under article 6(1), he must notify the litigator of the amount he has determined to be payable.

(2) Where, as a result of any redetermination or appeal made or brought pursuant to articles 29 to 31—

 (a) the fees payable under paragraph (1) are increased, the appropriate officer must authorise payment of the increase; or

 (b) the fees payable under paragraph (1) are decreased, the litigator must repay the amount of such decrease.

(3) Where the payment of any fees of the litigator is ordered under article 30(12) or article 31(8), the appropriate officer must authorise payment.

[This article is printed as amended by S.I. 2007 No. 3552 (*ante*, G–1).]

Notification of fees

25. For the purposes of an order which is made under section 17 of the Act, except where the proceedings are in a magistrates' court only, having determined the fees payable to a representative in accordance with this Order, the appropriate officer must notify the court before which the proceedings are heard of the amount determined. **G–30**

Recovery of overpayments

26.—(1) This article applies where a representative is entitled to be paid a certain sum ("the amount due") by virtue of the provisions of Schedules 1, 2 or 4 and, for whatever reason, he is paid an amount greater than that sum. **G–31**

(2) Where this article applies, the appropriate officer may—

 (a) require immediate repayment of the amount in excess of the amount due ("the excess amount") and the representative must repay the excess amount to the appropriate officer; or

 (b) deduct the excess amount from any other sum which is or becomes payable to the representative by virtue of the provisions of Schedules 1, 2 or 4.

(3) The appropriate officer may proceed under paragraph (2)(b) without first proceeding under paragraph (2)(a).

(4) Paragraph (2) applies notwithstanding that the representative to whom the excess amount was paid is exercising, or may exercise, a right under articles 29 to 31.

Adverse observations

27.—(1) Where in any proceedings to which Schedule 1, 2 or 4 applies, the court makes adverse observations concerning a representative's conduct of the proceedings, the appropriate officer may reduce any fee which would otherwise be payable in accordance with Schedule 1, 2 or 4 by such proportion as he considers reasonable. **G–32**

(2) Before reducing the fee payable to a representative in accordance with the provisions of paragraph (1), the appropriate officer must give the representative the opportunity to make representations about whether it is appropriate to reduce the fee and the extent to which the fee should be reduced.

[This article is printed as amended by S.I. 2007 No. 3552 (*ante*, G–1).]

Wasted costs orders

28.—(1) Subject to paragraph (2), where the court has disallowed the whole or **G–33**

any part of any wasted costs under section 19A of the *Prosecution of Offences Act* 1985 (costs against legal representatives etc.), the appropriate officer, in determining fees in respect of work done by the representative against whom the wasted costs order was made, may deduct the amount in the wasted costs order from the amount otherwise payable in accordance with this Order.

(2) Where the appropriate officer, in accordance with this article, is minded to disallow any amount of a claim for work done to which the wasted costs order relates, he must disallow that amount or the amount of the wasted costs order, whichever is the greater.

Redetermination of fees by appropriate officer

G–34   **29.**—(1) Where—

    (a) an advocate in proceedings in the Crown Court is dissatisfied with the decision not to allow any of the following fees, or with the number of hours allowed in the calculation of such a fee, namely—

        (i) a special preparation fee under paragraph 14 of Schedule 1; or

        (ii) a wasted preparation fee under paragraph 15 of Schedule 1; or

    (b) an instructed advocate in proceedings in the Crown Court is dissatisfied with—

        (i) the decision not to allow an hourly fee in respect of attendance at conferences or views at the scene of the alleged offence under paragraph 16 of Schedule 1, or with the number of hours allowed in the calculation of such a fee;

        (ii) the calculation by the appropriate officer of the fee payable to the instructed advocate in accordance with Schedule 1; or

        (iii) the decision of the appropriate officer under paragraph 3(3) of Schedule 1 (reclassification of an offence not specifically listed in the relevant Table of Offences and so deemed to fall within Class H); or

    (c) a litigator is dissatisfied with—

        (i) the calculation by the appropriate officer of the fee payable to the litigator in accordance with Schedule 2; or

        (ii) the decision of the appropriate officer under paragraph 3(3) of Schedule 2 (reclassification of an offence not specifically listed in the relevant Table of Offences and so deemed to fall within Class H);

the advocate, instructed advocate or litigator, as the case may be, may apply to the appropriate officer to redetermine those fees, to review that decision or to reclassify the offence, as appropriate.

(2) An application under paragraph (1) may not challenge the quantum of any of the fees set out in Schedule 1 and Schedule 2.

(3) Subject to article 32, an application under paragraph (1), or paragraph 15(1) of Schedule 4, must be made—

    (a) within 21 days of the receipt of the fees payable under article 23, article 24 or paragraph 15 of Schedule 4, as appropriate;

    (b) by giving notice in writing to the appropriate officer, specifying the matters in respect of which the application is made and the grounds of objection and

    (c) in such form and manner as the appropriate officer may direct.

(4) The notice of application must be accompanied by the information and documents supplied under article 5, article 6 or Schedule 4, as appropriate.

(5) The notice of application must state whether the applicant wishes to appear or to be represented and, if the applicant so wishes, the appropriate officer must notify the applicant of the hearing date and time.

(6) The applicant must supply such further information and documents as the appropriate officer may require.

(7) The appropriate officer must, in the light of the objections made by the applicant or on his behalf—

    (a) redetermine the fees, whether by way of confirmation, or increase or decrease in the amount previously determined;

(c) confirm the classification of the offence within Class H; or

(d) reclassify the offence,

as the case may be, and must notify the applicant of his decision.

(8) Where the applicant so requests, the appropriate officer must give reasons in writing for his decision.

(9) Subject to article 32, any request under paragraph (8) must be made within 21 days of receiving notification of the appropriate officer's decision under paragraph (7).

[This article is printed as amended by S.I. 2007 No. 3552 (*ante*, G–1).]

Appeals to a Costs Judge

30.—(1) Where the appropriate officer has given his reasons for his decision   **G–35**
under article 29(8), a representative who is dissatisfied with that decision may appeal to a Costs Judge.

(2) Subject to article 32, an appeal under paragraph (1) or paragraph 15(2) of Schedule 4 must be instituted within 21 days of the receipt of the appropriate officer's reasons, by giving notice in writing to the Senior Costs Judge.

(3) The appellant must send a copy of any notice of appeal given under paragraph (2) to the appropriate officer.

(4) The notice of appeal must be accompanied by—

(a) a copy of any written representations given under article 29(3);

(b) the appropriate officer's reasons for his decision given under article 29(8); and

(c) the information and documents supplied to the appropriate officer under article 29.

(5) The notice of appeal must—

(a) be in such form as the Senior Costs Judge may direct—

(b) specify separately each item appealed against, showing (where appropriate) the amount claimed for the item, the amount determined and the grounds of the objection to the determination; and

(c) state whether the appellant wishes to appear or to be represented or whether he will accept a decision given in his absence.

(6) The Senior Costs Judge may, and if so directed by the Lord Chancellor either generally or in a particular case must, send to the Lord Chancellor a copy of the notice of appeal together with copies of such other documents as the Lord Chancellor may require.

(7) With a view to ensuring that the public interest is taken into account, the Lord Chancellor may arrange for written or oral representations to be made on his behalf and, if he intends to do so, he must inform the Senior Costs Judge and the appellant.

(8) Any written representations made on behalf of the Lord Chancellor under paragraph (7) must be sent to the Senior Costs Judge and the appellant and, in the case of oral representations, the Senior Costs Judge and the appellant must be informed of the grounds on which such representations will be made.

(9) The appellant must be permitted a reasonable opportunity to make representations in reply.

(10) The Costs Judge must inform the appellant (or the person representing him) and the Lord Chancellor, where representations have been or are to be made on his behalf, of the date of any hearing and, subject to the provisions of this article, may give directions as to the conduct of the appeal.

(11) The Costs Judge may consult the trial judge or the appropriate officer and may require the appellant to provide any further information which he requires for the purpose of the appeal and, unless the Costs Judge otherwise directs, no further evidence may be received on the hearing of the appeal and no ground of objection may be raised which was not raised under article 29.

(12) The Costs Judge has the same powers as the appropriate officer under this Order and, in the exercise of such powers, may alter the redetermination of the appropriate officer in respect of any sum allowed, whether by increase or decrease, as he thinks fit.

(13) The Costs Judge must communicate his decision and the reasons for it in writing to the appellant, the Lord Chancellor and the appropriate officer.

(14) Where he increases the sums redetermined under article 29, the Costs Judge may allow the appellant a sum in respect of part or all of any reasonable costs incurred by him in connection with the appeal (including any fee payable in respect of an appeal).

[This article is printed as amended by S.I. 2007 No. 3552 (*ante*, G–1).]

Appeals to the High Court

G–36

31.—(1) A representative who is dissatisfied with the decision of a Costs Judge on an appeal under article 30 may apply to a Costs Judge to certify a point of principle of general importance.

(2) Subject to article 32, an application under paragraph (1) or paragraph 15(3) of Schedule 4 must be made within 21 days of receiving notification of a Costs Judge's decision under article 30(13).

(3) Where a Costs Judge certifies a point of principle of general importance the appellant may appeal to the High Court against the decision of a Costs Judge on an appeal under article 30, and the Lord Chancellor must be a respondent to such an appeal.

(4) Subject to article 32, an appeal under paragraph (3) must be instituted within 21 days of receiving notification of a Costs Judge's certificate under paragraph (1).

(5) Where the Lord Chancellor is dissatisfied with the decision of a Costs Judge on an appeal under article 30, he may, if no appeal has been made by an appellant under paragraph (3), appeal to the High Court against that decision, and the appellant must be a respondent to the appeal.

(6) Subject to article 32, an appeal under paragraph (5) must be instituted within 21 days of receiving notification of the Costs Judge's decision under article 30(13).

(7) An appeal under paragraph (3) or (5) must—

    (a) be brought in the Queen's Bench Division;

    (b) subject to paragraph (4), follow the procedure set out in Part 52 of the *Civil Procedure Rules* 1998; and

    (c) be heard and determined by a single judge whose decision will be final.

(8) The judge has the same powers as the appropriate officer and a Costs Judge under this Order and may reverse, affirm or amend the decision appealed against or make such other order as he thinks fit.

Time limits

G–37

32.—(1) Subject to paragraph (2), the time limit within which any act is required or authorised to be done under this Order may, for good reason, be extended—

    (a) in the case of acts required or authorised to be done under article 30 or 31 by a Costs Judge or the High Court as the case may be; and

    (b) in the case of acts required or authorised to be done by a representative under any other article, by the appropriate officer.

(2) Where a representative without good reason has failed (or, if an extension were not granted, would fail) to comply with a time limit, the appropriate officer, a Costs Judge or the High Court, as the case may be, may, in exceptional circumstances, extend the time limit and must consider whether it is reasonable in the circumstances to reduce the fees payable to the representative under articles 5, 6 or 8 provided that the fees must not be reduced unless the representative has been allowed a reasonable opportunity to show cause orally or in writing why the fees should not be reduced.

(3) A representative may appeal to a Costs Judge against a decision made under this article by an appropriate officer and such an appeal must be instituted within 21 days of the decision being given by giving notice in writing to the Senior Costs Judge specifying the grounds of appeal.

In connection with this article, see *post*, G–269.

Revocation

33. Subject to article 4, the *Criminal Defence Service (Funding) Order* 2001 is revoked. **G-38**

Article 5(1)

SCHEDULE 1

A<small>DVOCATES'</small> G<small>RADUATED</small> F<small>EE</small> S<small>CHEME</small>

P<small>ART</small> 1

D<small>EFINITIONS AND</small> S<small>COPE</small>

Interpretation

1.—(1) In this Schedule— **G-39**

"case" means proceedings in the Crown Court against any one assisted person—

    (a) on one or more counts of a single indictment;

    (b) arising out of a single notice of appeal against conviction or sentence, or a single committal for sentence, whether on one or more charges; or

    (c) arising out of a single alleged breach of an order of the Crown Court,

and a case falling within paragraph (c) must be treated as a separate case from the proceedings in which the order was made;

"cracked trial" means a case on indictment in which—

    (a) a plea and case management hearing takes place and—

        (i) the case does not proceed to trial (whether by reason of pleas of guilty or for other reasons) or the prosecution offers no evidence; and

        (ii) either—

            (aa) in respect of one or more counts to which the assisted person pleaded guilty, he did not so plead at the plea and case management hearing; or

            (bb) in respect of one or more counts which did not proceed, the prosecution did not, before or at the plea and case management hearing, declare an intention of not proceeding with them; or

    (b) the case is listed for trial without a plea and case management hearing taking place;

"guilty plea" means a case on indictment which—

    (a) is disposed of without a trial because the assisted person pleaded guilty to one or more counts; and

    (b) is not a cracked trial;

"main hearing" means —

    (a) in relation to a case which goes to trial, the trial;

    (b) in relation to a guilty plea, the hearing at which pleas are taken or, where there is more than one such hearing, the last such hearing;

    (c) in relation to a cracked trial, the hearing at which—

        (i) the case becomes a cracked trial by meeting the conditions in the definition of a cracked trial, whether or not any pleas were taken at that hearing; or

        (ii) a formal verdict of not guilty was entered as a result of the prosecution offering no evidence, whether or not the parties attended the hearing;

    (d) in relation to an appeal against conviction or sentence in the Crown Court, the hearing of the appeal;

    (e) in relation to proceedings arising out of a committal for sentence in the Crown Court, the sentencing hearing; and

    (f) in relation to proceedings arising out of an alleged breach of an order of the Crown Court, the hearing at which those proceedings are determined;

"*Newton* Hearing" means a hearing at which evidence is heard for the purpose of determining the sentence of a convicted person in accordance with the principles of *R. v. Newton* (1982) 77 Cr.App.R. 13;

"standard appearance" means an appearance by the trial advocate or substitute advocate in any of the following hearings which do not form part of the main hearing—

> (a) a plea and case management hearing, except the first plea and case management hearing;
>
> (b) a pre-trial review;
>
> (c) the hearing of a case listed for plea which is adjourned for trial;
>
> (d) any hearing (except a trial, a plea and case management hearing, a pre-trial review or a hearing referred to in paragraph 2(1)(b)) which is listed but cannot proceed because of the failure of the assisted person or a witness to attend, the unavailability of a pre-sentence report or other good reason;
>
> (e) custody time limit applications;
>
> (f) bail and other applications (except where any such applications take place in the course of a hearing referred to in paragraph 2(1)(b)); or
>
> (g) the hearing of the case listed for mention only, including applications relating to the date of the trial (except where an application takes place in the course of a hearing referred to in paragraph 2(1)(b)),

provided that a fee is not payable elsewhere under this Schedule in respect of the hearing;

"substitute advocate" means an advocate who is not an instructed advocate or the trial advocate but who undertakes work on the case; and

"trial advocate" means an advocate instructed in accordance with a representation order to represent the assisted person at the main hearing in any case, including a QC or a leading junior advocate so instructed after the hearing at which pleas are taken.

(2) For the purposes of this Schedule, the number of pages of prosecution evidence served on the court includes all—

> (a) witness statements;
>
> (b) documentary and pictorial exhibits;
>
> (c) records of interviews with the assisted person; and
>
> (d) records of interviews with other defendants,

which form part of the committal or served prosecution documents or which are included in any notice of additional evidence, but does not include any document provided on CD-ROM or by other means of electronic communication.

(3) In proceedings on indictment in the Crown Court initiated otherwise than by committal for trial, the appropriate officer must determine the number of pages of prosecution evidence in accordance with sub-paragraph (2) or as nearly in accordance with sub-paragraph (2) as possible as the nature of the case permits.

(4) A reference to the Table of Offences in this Schedule is to the Table of Offences in Part 6 and a reference to a Class of Offence in this Schedule is to the Class in which that offence is listed in the Table of Offences.

[This paragraph is printed as amended by S.I. 2007 No. 3552 (*ante*, G–1).]

Application

G–40   2.—(1) Subject to sub-paragraphs (3) to (8), this Schedule applies to—

> (a) every case on indictment; and
>
> (b) the following proceedings in the Crown Court—
>
> > (i) an appeal against conviction or sentence;
> >
> > (ii) a sentencing hearing following a committal for sentence to the Crown Court; and
> >
> > (iii) proceedings arising out of an alleged breach of an order of the Crown Court (whether or not this Schedule applies to the proceedings in which the order was made).

(3) Sub-paragraph (4) applies where, following a trial, an order is made for a new trial and the same trial advocate appears at both trials where—

      (i) the defendant is an assisted person at both trials; or

      (ii) the defendant is an assisted person at the new trial only; or

      (iii) the new trial is a cracked trial or guilty plea.

(4) In respect of a new trial, or if he so elects, in respect of the first trial, the trial advocate will receive a graduated fee calculated in accordance with Part 2 or Part 3, as appropriate, except that the fee will be reduced by—

    (a) 30 percent, where the new trial started within one month of the conclusion of the first trial;

    (b) 20 percent, where the new trial did not start within one month of the conclusion of the first trial;

    (c) 40 percent where the new trial becomes a cracked trial or guilty plea within one month of the conclusion of the first trial; or

    (d) 25 percent where the new trial becomes a cracked trial or guilty plea more than one month after the conclusion of the first trial.

(5) Where a different trial advocate appears for the assisted person at each trial then, in respect of each trial, the trial advocate will receive a graduated fee calculated in accordance with Part 2 or Part 3, as appropriate.

(6) Where following a case on indictment a *Newton* hearing takes place—

    (a) for the purposes of this Schedule the case will be treated as having gone to trial;

    (b) the length of the trial will be taken to be the combined length of the main hearing and the *Newton* hearing;

    (c) the provisions of this Schedule relating to cracked trials and guilty pleas will not apply; and

    (d) no fee will be payable under paragraph 12 in respect of the *Newton* hearing.

(7) Sub-paragraph (8) applies where proceedings are—

    (a) sent for trial to the Crown Court under section 51 of the *Crime and Disorder Act* 1998 (no committal proceedings for indictable-only offences); or

    (b) transferred to the Crown Court under—

      (i) section 4 of the *Criminal Justice Act* 1987 (transfer of serious fraud cases); or

      (ii) section 53 of the *Criminal Justice Act* 1991 (transfer of certain cases involving children).

(8) Where, at any time after proceedings are sent or transferred to the Crown Court under the provisions referred to in sub-paragraph (7), they are—

    (a) discontinued by a notice served under section 23A of the *Prosecution of Offences Act* 1985 (discontinuance of proceedings after accused has been sent for trial); or

    (b) dismissed pursuant to—

      (i) paragraph 2 of Schedule 3 to the *Crime and Disorder Act* 1998 (applications for dismissal);

      (ii) section 6 of the *Criminal Justice Act* 1987 (applications for dismissal); or

      (iii) paragraph 5 of Schedule 6 to the *Criminal Justice Act* 1991 (applications for dismissal),

the provisions of paragraph 18 apply.

(9) For the purposes of this Schedule, a case on indictment which discontinues at or before the plea and case management hearing otherwise than—

    (a) by reason of a plea of guilty being entered, or

    (b) in accordance with paragraph 2 (8),

must be treated as a guilty plea.

[This paragraph is printed as amended by S.I. 2007 No. 3552 (*ante*, G–1).]

Class of offences

    3.—(1) For the purposes of this Schedule—   **G–41**

(a) every indictable offence falls within the Class under which it is listed in the Table of Offences and, subject to sub-paragraph (2), indictable offences not specifically so listed will be deemed to fall within Class H;

(b) conspiracy to commit an indictable offence contrary to section 1 of the *Criminal Law Act* 1977 (the offence of conspiracy), incitement to commit an indictable offence and attempts to commit an indictable offence contrary to section 1 of the *Criminal Attempts Act* 1981 (attempting to commit an offence), fall within the same Class as the substantive offence to which they relate;

(c) where the Table of Offences specifies that the Class within which an offence falls depends on whether the value involved exceeds a stated limit, the value must be presumed not to exceed that limit unless the advocate making the claim under article 5 proves otherwise to the satisfaction of the appropriate officer;

(d) where more than one count of the indictment is for an offence in relation to which the Class depends on the value involved, that value must be taken to be the total value involved in all those offences, but where two or more counts relate to the same property, the value of that property must be taken into account once only;

(e) where an entry in the Table of Offences specifies an offence as being contrary to a statutory provision, then subject to any express limitation in the entry that entry will include every offence contrary to that statutory provision whether or not the words of description in the entry are appropriate to cover all such offences;

(f) where in a case on indictment there is a hearing to determine the question of whether an assisted person is unfit to plead or unfit to stand trial, the trial advocate must elect whether that hearing falls within the same Class as the indictable offence to which it relates or within Class D; and

(g) where in a case on indictment a restriction order is made under section 41 of the *Mental Health Act* 1983 (power of higher courts to restrict discharge from hospital), the offence falls within Class A, regardless of the Class under which the offence would be listed in the Table of Offences but for this paragraph.

(2) Where an advocate in proceedings in the Crown Court is dissatisfied with the classification within Class H of an indictable offence not listed in the Table of Offences, he may apply to the appropriate officer when lodging his claim for fees to reclassify the offence.

(3) The appropriate officer must, in light of the objections made by the advocate—

(a) confirm the classification of the offence within Class H; or

(b) reclassify the offence,

and must notify the advocate of his decision.

PART 2

GRADUATED FEES FOR TRIAL

Calculation of Graduated Fees

G–42   4.—(1) The amount of the graduated fee for a single trial advocate representing one assisted person being tried on one indictment in the Crown Court in a trial lasting one to 40 days must be calculated in accordance with the following formula—

$$G = B + (d \times D) + (e \times E) + (w \times W)$$

(2) In the formula in sub-paragraph (1)—

G is the amount of the graduated fee;

B is the basic fee specified in the Table following paragraph 5 as appropriate to the offence for which the assisted person is tried and the category of trial advocate;

d is the number of days or parts of a day on which the advocate attended

at court by which the trial exceeds 2 days but does not exceed 40
days;

D is the fee payable in respect of daily attendance at court for the
number of days by which the trial exceeds two days but does not
exceed 40 days, as appropriate to the offence for which the assisted
person is tried and the category of trial advocate;

e is the number of pages of prosecution evidence excluding the first 50,
up to a maximum of 10,000;

E is the evidence uplift specified in the Table following paragraph 5 as
appropriate to the offence for which the assisted person is tried and
the category of trial advocate;

w is the number of prosecution witnesses excluding the first 10;

W is the witness uplift specified in the Table following paragraph 5 as
appropriate to the offence for which the assisted person is tried and
the category of trial advocate.

Table of fees

5. For the purposes of paragraph 4 the basic fee (B), the daily attendance fee (D),   **G–43**
the evidence uplift (E) and the witness uplift (W) appropriate to any offence will be
those specified in the Table following this paragraph in accordance with the Class
within which that offence falls.

TABLE OF FEES AND UPLIFTS

Class of Offence	Basic Fee (B)	Daily attendance fee (D)	Evidence uplift (E)	Witness uplift (W)
QC				
A	£4,434	£1,321	£1.89	£7.55
B	£2,924	£991	£1.89	£7.55
C	£2,275	£943	£1.89	£7.55
D	£2,641	£943	£1.89	£7.55
E	£1,750	£708	£1.89	£7.55
F	£1,750	£708	£1.89	£7.55
G	£2,200	£943	£1.89	£7.55
H	£2,200	£943	£1.89	£7.55
I	£2,453	£943	£1.89	£7.55
J	£3,302	£1,132	£1.89	£7.55
K	£3,302	£1,132	£1.89	£7.55
Leading Junior				
A	£3,325	£991	£1.42	£5.66
B	£2,193	£743	£1.42	£5.66
C	£1,706	£708	£1.42	£5.66
D	£1,981	£708	£1.42	£5.66
E	£1,313	£531	£1.42	£5.66
F	£1,313	£531	£1.42	£5.66
G	£1,650	£708	£1.42	£5.66
H	£1,650	£708	£1.42	£5.66
I	£1,840	£708	£1.42	£5.66
J	£2,476	£849	£1.42	£5.66
K	£2,476	£849	£1.42	£5.66

Class of Offence	Basic Fee (B)	Daily attendance fee (D)	Evidence uplift (E)	Witness uplift (W)
Led Junior				
A	£2,217	£660	£0.94	£3.77
B	£1,462	£495	£0.94	£3.77
C	£1,038	£472	£0.94	£3.77
D	£1,300	£472	£0.94	£3.77
E	£802	£354	£0.94	£3.77
F	£802	£354	£0.94	£3.77
G	£1,100	£472	£0.94	£3.77
H	£943	£472	£0.94	£3.77
I	£1,132	£472	£0.94	£3.77
J	£1,887	£566	£0.94	£3.77
K	£1,651	£566	£0.94	£3.77
Junior alone				
A	£2,547	£778	£1.13	£5.66
B	£1,509	£542	£1.13	£5.66
C	£1,038	£472	£1.13	£5.66
D	£1,300	£472	£1.13	£5.66
E	£755	£377	£1.13	£5.66
F	£802	£377	£1.13	£5.66
G	£1,415	£472	£1.13	£5.66
H	£943	£472	£1.13	£5.66
I	£1,132	£472	£1.13	£5.66
J	£1,887	£613	£1.13	£5.66
K	£1,887	£613	£1.13	£5.66

PART 3

GRADUATED FEES FOR GUILTY PLEAS AND CRACKED TRIALS

Calculation of graduated fees in guilty pleas and cracked trials—

G–44   6. The amount of the graduated fee for a single trial advocate representing one assisted person in a guilty plea or cracked trial is—

(a) the basic fee specified in the table following paragraph 7 as appropriate to the offence with which the assisted person is charged, the category of trial advocate and whether the case is a guilty plea or a cracked trial; and

(b) the evidence uplift, as appropriate to the number of pages of prosecution evidence, calculated in accordance with the table following paragraph 7.

Tables of fees

G–45   7.—(1) Subject to sub-paragraphs (2) and (3), for the purposes of paragraph 6 the basic fee and evidence uplift appropriate to any offence are specified in the Table following this paragraph in accordance with the class within which that offence falls.

(2) Where—

(a) the trial of a case does not commence on the date first fixed; or

(b) the case is not taken and disposed of from the first warned list in which it is entered,

the basic fee and evidence uplift for the offence are specified for the last third in the Table referred to in sub-paragraph (1).

(3) In this paragraph, and in the Tables following this paragraph, references to the first, second and last third are references to the first, second and last third—

(a) where a case is first listed for trial on a fixed date, of the period of time beginning after the date on which the case is so listed and ending before the date so fixed,

(b) where the case is first placed in a warned list, of the period of time beginning after the date on which the case is so placed and ending before the date of the start of that warned list, and

where the number of days in this period of time cannot be divided by three equally, any days remaining after such division must be added to the last third.

(4) Where a graduated fee is calculated in accordance with this Part for the purposes of paragraph 2(4), the fee must be calculated as if the trial had cracked in the final third.

TABLE A

FEES AND UPLIFTS IN GUILTY PLEAS AND TRIALS WHICH CRACK IN THE FIRST THIRD

Class of Offence	Basic fee	Evidence uplift per page of prosecution evidence (pages 1 to 1,000)	Evidence uplift per page of prosecution evidence (1,001 to 10,000)
QC			
A	£2,358.00	£2.53	£1.17
B	£1,509.00	£2.08	£1.04
C	£1,415.00	£1.48	£0.74
D	£1,509.00	£3.30	£1.65
E	£1,250.00	£1.06	£0.53
F	£1,250.00	£1.39	£0.70
G	£1,415.00	£1.84	£0.92
H	£1,415.00	£1.91	£0.95
I	£1,415.00	£1.86	£0.92
J	£1,981.00	£3.30	£1.65
K	£1,981.00	£1.84	£0.92
Leading Junior			
A	£1,768.50	£1.90	£0.88
B	£1,131.75	£1.56	£0.78
C	£1,061.25	£1.11	£0.56
D	£1,131.75	£2.48	£1.24
E	£937.50	£0.80	£0.40
F	£937.50	£1.04	£0.53
G	£1,061.25	£1.38	£0.69
H	£1,061.25	£1.43	£0.71
I	£1,061.25	£1.40	£0.69
J	£1,485.75	£2.48	£1.24
K	£1,485.75	£1.38	£0.69
Led Junior			
A	£1,179.00	£1.27	£0.59
B	£754.50	£1.04	£0.52
C	£707.50	£0.74	£0.37
D	£754.50	£1.65	£0.83
E	£625.00	£0.53	£0.27
F	£625.00	£0.70	£0.35
G	£707.50	£0.92	£0.46

Class of Offence	Basic fee	Evidence uplift per page of prosecution evidence (pages 1 to 1,000)	Evidence uplift per page of prosecution evidence (1,001 to 10,000)
H	£707.50	£0.96	£0.48
I	£707.50	£0.93	£0.46
J	£990.50	£1.65	£0.83
K	£990.50	£0.92	£0.46
Junior alone			
A	£1,312.00	£1.08	£0.54
B	£802.00	£0.94	£0.47
C	£519.00	£0.69	£0.35
D	£802.00	£1.37	£0.68
E	£472.00	£0.41	£0.20
F	£472.00	£0.63	£0.31
G	£755.00	£1.18	£0.59
H	£566.00	£0.63	£0.32
I	£660.00	£0.49	£0.25
J	£1,132.00	£1.37	£0.68
K	£1,132.00	£1.18	£0.59

TABLE B

FEES AND UPLIFTS IN TRIALS WHICH CRACK IN THE SECOND OR FINAL THIRD

Class of Offence	Basic Fee	Evidence uplift per page of prosecution evidence (pages 1 to 250)	Evidence uplift per page of prosecution evidence (pages 251 to 1,000)	A case that cracks in the second third — Evidence uplift per page of prosecution evidence (pages 1,001 to 10,000)	A case that cracks in the final third — Evidence uplift per page of prosecution evidence (pages 1,001 to 10,000)
QC					
A	£3,585.00	£4.70	£1.17	£1.55	£4.70
B	£2,264.00	£4.16	£1.04	£1.38	£4.16
C	£1,975.00	£2.95	£0.74	£0.97	£2.95
D	£2,264.00	£6.59	£1.65	£2.18	£6.59
E	£1,600.00	£2.11	£0.53	£0.70	£2.11
F	£1,600.00	£2.77	£0.70	£0.92	£2.77
G	£2,000.00	£3.68	£0.92	£1.22	£3.68
H	£2,000.00	£3.80	£0.95	£1.25	£3.80
I	£2,075.00	£3.72	£0.92	£1.23	£3.72
J	£3,019.00	£6.59	£1.65	£2.18	£6.59
K	£3,019.00	£3.68	£0.92	£1.22	£3.68

Class of Offence	Basic Fee	Evidence uplift per page of prosecution evidence (pages 1 to 250)	Evidence uplift per page of prosecution evidence (pages 251 to 1,000)	A case that cracks in the second third Evidence uplift per page of prosecution evidence (pages 1,001 to 10,000)	A case that cracks in the final third Evidence uplift per page of prosecution evidence (pages 1,001 to 10,000)
Leading Junior					
A	£2,688.75	£3.53	£0.88	£1.16	£3.53
B	£1,698.00	£3.12	£0.78	£1.04	£3.12
C	£1,481.25	£2.21	£0.56	£0.73	£2.21
D	£1,698.00	£4.94	£1.24	£1.64	£4.94
E	£1,200.00	£1.58	£0.40	£0.53	£1.58
F	£1,200.00	£2.08	£0.53	£0.69	£2.08
G	£1,500.00	£2.76	£0.69	£0.92	£2.76
H	£1,500.00	£2.85	£0.71	£0.94	£2.85
I	£1,556.25	£2.79	£0.69	£0.92	£2.79
J	£2,264.25	£4.94	£1.24	£1.64	£4.94
K	£2,264.25	£2.76	£0.69	£0.92	£2.76
Led Junior					
A	£1,792.50	£2.35	£0.59	£0.78	£2.35
B	£1,132.00	£2.08	£0.52	£0.69	£2.08
C	£987.50	£1.48	£0.37	£0.49	£1.48
D	£1,132.00	£3.30	£0.83	£1.09	£3.30
E	£800.00	£1.06	£0.27	£0.35	£1.06
F	£800.00	£1.39	£0.35	£0.46	£1.39
G	£1,000.00	£1.84	£0.46	£0.61	£1.84
H	£1,000.00	£1.90	£0.48	£0.63	£1.90
I	£1,037.50	£1.86	£0.46	£0.62	£1.86
J	£1,509.50	£3.30	£0.83	£1.09	£3.30
K	£1,509.50	£1.84	£0.46	£0.61	£1.84
Junior alone					
A	£1,981.00	£4.63	£2.15	£0.71	£2.15
B	£1,179.00	£4.03	£1.88	£0.62	£1.88
C	£755.00	£2.99	£1.39	£0.46	£1.39
D	£1,050.00	£5.87	£2.73	£0.90	£2.73
E	£660.00	£1.75	£0.82	£0.27	£0.82
F	£660.00	£2.70	£1.25	£0.42	£1.25
G	£1,132.00	£5.08	£2.37	£0.78	£2.37
H	£802.00	£2.71	£1.26	£0.42	£1.26
I	£943.00	£2.11	£0.98	£0.32	£0.98
J	£1,698.00	£5.87	£2.73	£0.90	£2.73
K	£1,604.00	£5.08	£2.37	£0.78	£2.37

PART 4

FIXED FEES

General provisions

G–46 8. Except as provided under this Part, all work undertaken by an advocate is included within the basic fee (B) specified in the Table following paragraph 5 as appropriate to—

(a) the offence for which the assisted person is tried;

(b) the category of advocate; and

(c) whether the case is a cracked trial, guilty plea or trial.

Fees for plea and case management hearings and standard appearances

G–47 9.—(1) The fee payable in respect of—

(a) an appearance by the trial advocate or substitute advocate at the first plea and case management hearing or pre-trial review; and

(b) up to four standard appearances by the trial advocate or substitute advocate,

is included within the basic fee (B) specified in paragraph 5 as appropriate to the offence for which the assisted person is tried and the category of trial advocate.

(2) The fee payable in respect of an appearance by the trial advocate or substitute advocate at a plea and case management hearing or standard appearance not included in sub-paragraph (1) is specified in the Table following paragraph 19 as appropriate to the category of trial advocate or substitute advocate.

(3) The fee payable for preparing and filing the plea and case management questionnaire where no oral hearing takes place is specified in the Table following paragraph 19 as appropriate to the category of trial advocate or substitute advocate.

(4) This paragraph does not apply to a standard appearance which is or forms part of the main hearing in a case or to a hearing for which a fee is payable elsewhere under this Schedule.

Fees for abuse of process, disclosure, admissibility and withdrawal of plea hearings

G–48 10.—(1) This paragraph applies to—

(a) the hearing of an application to stay the case on indictment or any count on the ground that the proceedings constitute an abuse of the process of the court;

(b) any hearing relating to the question of whether any material should be disclosed by the prosecution to the defence or the defence to the prosecution (whether or not any claim to public interest immunity is made);

(c) the hearing of an application under section 2(1) of the *Criminal Procedure (Attendance of Witnesses) Act* 1965 (issue of witness summons on application to Crown Court) for disclosure of material held by third parties;

(d) any hearing relating to the question of the admissibility as evidence of any material; and

(e) the hearing of an application to withdraw a plea of guilty where the application is—

(i) made by an advocate other than the advocate who appeared at the hearing at which the plea of guilty was entered; and

(ii) unsuccessful.

(2) Where a hearing to which this paragraph applies is held on any day of the main hearing of a case on indictment, no separate fee is payable in respect of attendance at the hearing, but the hearing is included in the length of the main hearing for the purpose of calculating the fees payable.

(3) Where a hearing to which this paragraph applies is held prior to the first or only day of the main hearing, it is not included in the length of the main hearing for the purpose of calculating the fees payable and the trial advocate or substitute advocate must be remunerated for attendance at such a hearing—

(a) in respect of any day where the hearing begins before and ends after the

608

luncheon adjournment, at the daily rate set out in the Table following
paragraph 19 as appropriate to the category of trial advocate or substitute
advocate; or

(b) in respect of any day where the hearing begins and ends before the luncheon adjournment, or begins after the luncheon adjournment, at the
half-daily rate set out in the Table following paragraph 19 as appropriate
to the category of trial advocate or substitute advocate.

Fees for confiscation hearings

11.—(1) This paragraph applies to—

G–49

(a) a hearing under Part 2 of the *Proceeds of Crime Act* 2002 (confiscation:
England and Wales);

(b) a hearing under section 2 of the *Drug Trafficking Act* 1994 (confiscation
orders); and

(c) a hearing under section 71 of the *Criminal Justice Act* 1988 (confiscation
orders).

(2) A hearing to which this paragraph applies is not included in the length of the
main hearing or of any sentencing hearing for the purpose of calculating the fees
payable, and the trial advocate or substitute advocate must be remunerated for attendance at such a hearing—

(a) in respect of any day where the hearing begins before and ends after the
luncheon adjournment, at the daily rate set out in the Table following
paragraph 19 as appropriate to the category of trial advocate or substitute
advocate; or

(b) in respect of any day where the hearing begins and ends before the luncheon adjournment, or begins after the luncheon adjournment, at the
half-daily rate set out in the Table following paragraph 19 as appropriate
to the category of trial advocate or substitute advocate.

Fees for sentencing hearings

12.—(1) This paragraph applies to—

G–50

(a) a sentencing hearing following a case on indictment to which this Schedule applies, where sentence has been deferred under section 1 of the *Powers of Criminal Courts (Sentencing) Act* 2000 (deferment of sentence); or

(b) a sentencing hearing following a case on indictment to which this Schedule applies, other than a hearing within paragraph (a) or a sentencing
hearing forming part of the main hearing.

(2) The fee payable to an advocate for appearing at a hearing to which this
paragraph applies is that set out in the Table following paragraph 19 as appropriate
to the category of trial advocate or substitute advocate and the circumstances of the
hearing.

Fees for ineffective trials

13. The fee set out in the Table following paragraph 19 as appropriate to the category of trial advocate will be payable in respect of each day on which the case was
listed for trial but did not proceed on the day for which it was listed, for whatever
reason.

G–51

Fees for special preparation

14.—(1) This paragraph applies where, in any case on indictment in the Crown
Court in respect of which a graduated fee is payable under Part 2 or Part 3—

G–52

(a) it has been necessary for an advocate to do work by way of preparation
substantially in excess of the amount normally done for cases of the same
type because the case involves a very unusual or novel point of law or
factual issue;

(b) the number of pages of prosecution evidence, as defined in paragraph
1(2), exceeds 10,000 and the appropriate officer considers it reasonable to
make a payment in excess of the graduated fee payable under this Schedule; or

(c) any or all of the prosecution evidence, as defined in paragraph 1(2), is served in electronic form only, and the appropriate officer considers it reasonable to make a payment in excess of the graduated fee payable under this Schedule.

(2) Where this paragraph applies, a special preparation fee may be paid, in addition to the graduated fee payable under Part 2 or Part 3.

(3) The amount of the special preparation fee must be calculated—

(a) where sub-paragraph (1)(a) applies, from the number of hours preparation in excess of the amount the appropriate officer considers reasonable for cases of the same type;

(b) where sub-paragraph (1)(b) applies, from the number of hours which the appropriate officer considers reasonable to read the excess pages; and

(c) where sub-paragraph (1)(c) applies, from the number of hours which the appropriate officer considers reasonable to view the prosecution evidence,

and in each case using the rates of hourly fees set out in the table following paragraph 19 as appropriate to the category of trial advocate.

(4) Any claim for a special preparation fee under this paragraph must be made by an instructed advocate, whether or not he did the work claimed for.

(5) An instructed advocate claiming a special preparation fee must supply such information and documents as may be required by the appropriate officer in support of the claim.

(6) In determining a claim under this paragraph, the appropriate officer must take into account all the relevant circumstances of the case, including, where special preparation work has been undertaken by more than one advocate, the benefit of such work to the trial advocate.

Fees for wasted preparation

G–53   15.—(1) A wasted preparation fee may be claimed where a trial advocate in any case to which this paragraph applies is prevented from representing the assisted person in the main hearing by any of the following circumstances—

(a) the trial advocate is instructed to appear in other proceedings at the same time as the main hearing in the case and has been unable to secure a change of date for either the main hearing or the other proceedings;

(b) the date fixed for the main hearing is changed by the court despite the trial advocate's objection;

(c) the trial advocate has withdrawn from the case with the leave of the court because of his professional code of conduct or to avoid embarrassment in the exercise of his profession;

(d) the trial advocate has been dismissed by the assisted person or the litigator; or

(e) the trial advocate is obliged to attend at any place by reason of a judicial office held by him or other public duty.

(2) This paragraph applies to every case on indictment to which this Schedule applies provided that—

(a) the case goes to trial, and the trial lasts for five days or more; or

(b) the case is a cracked trial, and the number of pages of prosecution evidence exceeds 150.

(3) The amount of the wasted preparation fee must be calculated from the number of hours of preparation reasonably carried out by the trial advocate, using the rate for hourly fees set out in the Table following paragraph 19 as appropriate to the category of trial advocate, but no such fee is payable unless the number of hours of preparation is eight or more.

(4) Any claim for a wasted preparation fee under this paragraph must be made by an instructed advocate, whether or not he did the work claimed for.

(5) An instructed advocate claiming a wasted preparation fee must supply such information and documents as may be required by the appropriate officer as proof of the circumstances in which he was prevented from representing the assisted person and of the number of hours of preparation.

Fees for conferences and views

G–54   16.—(1) This paragraph applies to the following types of work—

    (a) attendance by the trial advocate at pre-trial conferences with prospective or actual expert witnesses not held at court;

    (b) attendance by the trial advocate at views at the scene of the alleged offence;

    (c) attendance by the trial advocate at pre-trial conferences with the assisted person not held at court;

    (d) reasonable travelling time by the trial advocate for the purpose of attending a view at the scene of the alleged offence; or

    (e) reasonable travelling time by the trial advocate for the purpose of attending a pre-trial conference with the assisted person or prospective or actual expert witness, where the appropriate officer is satisfied that the assisted person or prospective or actual expert witness was unable or could not reasonably have been expected to attend a conference at the trial advocate's chambers or office.

(2) The fees payable in respect of attendance at the first three pre-trial conferences or views, as set out in sub-paragraph (1)(a) to (c), are included in the basic fee (B) specified in the Table following paragraph 5 or paragraph 7, as appropriate to the offence for which the assisted person is tried, the category of trial advocate and whether the case is a guilty plea, cracked trial or trial, provided that the trial advocate satisfies the appropriate officer that the work was reasonably necessary.

(3) The fee specified in the Table following paragraph 19 as appropriate to the category of trial advocate will be payable in the following circumstances, provided that the trial advocate satisfies the appropriate officer that the work was reasonably necessary—

    (a) for trials lasting not less than 21 and not more than 25 days, and cracked trials where it was accepted by the court at the plea and case management hearing that the trial would last not less than 21 days and not more than 25 days, one further pre-trial conference or view not exceeding two hours;

    (b) for trials lasting not less than 26 and not more than 35 days, and cracked trials where it was accepted by the court at the plea and case management hearing that the trial would last not less than 26 days and not more than 35 days, two further pre-trial conferences or views each not exceeding two hours; and

    (c) for trials lasting not less than 36 days, and cracked trials where it was accepted by the court at the plea and case management hearing that the trial would last not less than 36 days and not more than 40 days, three further pre-trial conferences or views each not exceeding two hours.

(4) Travel expenses must be paid for all conferences and views set out in sub-paragraph (1)(a) to (c), provided that the trial advocate satisfies the appropriate officer that they were reasonably incurred.

(5) Travelling time must be paid for all conferences and views set out in sub-paragraph (1)(a) to (c), provided that the trial advocate satisfies the appropriate officer that it was reasonable.

Fees for appeals, committals for sentence and breach hearings

17.—(1) Subject to sub-paragraphs (4) and (5) and paragraph 21 the fee payable **G–55** to a trial advocate in any of the hearings referred to in paragraph 2(1)(b) is the fixed fee specified in the Table following paragraph 19.

(2) Where a hearing referred to in paragraph 2(1)(b) is listed but cannot proceed because of the failure of the assisted person or a witness to attend, the unavailability of a pre-sentence report, or other good reason, the fee payable to the advocate is the fixed fee specified in the Table following paragraph 19.

(3) Where—

    (a) a bail application;

    (b) a mention hearing; or

    (c) any other application

takes place in the course of a hearing referred to in paragraph 2(1)(b), the fee payable to the advocate is the fixed fee specified in the Table following paragraph 19.

(4) Where it appears to the appropriate officer that the fixed fee allowed under sub-paragraph (1) would be inappropriate taking into account all of the relevant circumstances of the case he may instead allow fees in such amounts as appear to him to be reasonable remuneration for the relevant work in accordance with sub-paragraph (5).

(5) The appropriate officer may allow any of the following classes of fees to an advocate in respect of work allowed by him under this paragraph—

    (a) a fee for preparation including, where appropriate, the first day of the hearing including, where they took place on that day—

        (i) short conferences;

        (ii) consultations;

        (iii) applications and appearances (including bail applications);

        (iv) views at the scene of the alleged offence; and

        (v) any other preparation;

    (b) a refresher fee for any day or part of a day for which a hearing continued, including, where they took place on that day—

        (i) short conferences;

        (ii) consultations;

        (iii) applications and appearances (including bail applications);

        (iv) views at the scene of the alleged offence; and

        (v) any other preparation; and

    (c) subsidiary fees for—

        (i) attendance at conferences, consultations and views at the scene of the alleged offence not covered by paragraph (a) or (b);

        (ii) written advice on evidence, plea, appeal, case stated or other written work; and

        (iii) attendance at applications and appearances (including bail applications and adjournments for sentence) not covered by paragraph (a) or (b).

Fees for contempt proceedings

G-55a   17A.—(1) Subject to sub-paragraph (2), remuneration for advocates in proceedings referred to in section 12(2)(f) of the Act in the Crown Court must be at the rates specified in the table following this sub-paragraph.

Category of advocate	Payment rates (£ per day)
QC	300
Leading junior	225
Led junior or junior acting alone	150

(2) Where an advocate and a litigator are instructed in proceedings referred to in section 12(2)(f) of the Act, remuneration must be at the rates specified in the table following this sub-paragraph, as appropriate to the category of advocate.

Category of advocate	Payment rates (£ per day)
QC	175
Leading junior	125
Led junior or junior acting alone	100

[This paragraph was inserted by S.I. 2007 No. 3552 (*ante*, G-1).]

Discontinuance or dismissal of sent or transferred proceedings

G-56   18.—(1) This paragraph applies to proceedings which are—

    (a) sent for trial to the Crown Court under section 51 of the *Crime and Disorder Act* 1998 (no committal proceedings for indictable-only offences); or

    (b) transferred to the Crown Court under—

        (i) section 4 of the *Criminal Justice Act* 1987 (transfer of serious fraud cases); or

        (ii) section 53 of the *Criminal Justice Act* 1991 (transfer of certain cases involving children).

(2) Where proceedings referred to in sub-paragraph (1) are discontinued by a no-tice served under section 23A of the *Prosecution of Offences Act* 1985 (discontinuance of proceedings after accused has been sent for trial) at any time before the prosecu-tion serves its evidence in accordance with the *Crime and Disorder Act 1998 (Service of Prosecution Evidence) Regulations* 2005 the advocate must be paid 50 per cent of the basic fee (B) for a guilty plea, as specified in the Table following paragraph 7 as ap-propriate to the offence for which the assisted person is charged and the category of advocate.

(3) Where proceedings referred to in sub-paragraph (1) are discontinued by a no-tice served under section 23A of the *Prosecution of Offences Act* 1985 (discontinuance of proceedings after accused has been sent for trial) at any time after the prosecution serves its evidence in accordance with the *Crime and Disorder Act 1998 (Service of Prosecution Evidence) Regulations* 2005, the advocate must be paid a graduated fee calculated in accordance with paragraph 6, as appropriate for representing an as-sisted person in a guilty plea.

(4) Sub-paragraph (4A) applies to—

    (a) a plea and case management hearing that takes place after the prosecution serves its evidence; and

    (b) any other hearing that takes place before a plea and case management hearing has taken place but after the prosecution has served its evidence.

(4A) Where, at a hearing to which this sub-paragraph applies—

    (a) the prosecution offers no evidence and the assisted person is discharged; or

    (b) the assisted person is charged on an indictment which includes no offence that is triable only on indictment and the case is remitted to the magis-trates' court in accordance with paragraph 10(3)(a) of Schedule 3 to the *Crime and Disorder Act* 1998 (procedure where no indictable offence remains),

the advocate instructed in the proceedings must be paid a graduated fee calculated in accordance with paragraph 6, as appropriate for representing an assisted person in a guilty plea.

(5) Where an application for dismissal is made under paragraph 2 of Schedule 3 to the *Crime and Disorder Act* 1998 (applications for dismissal), section 6 of the *Crimi-nal Justice Act* 1987 (applications for dismissal) or paragraph 5 of Schedule 6 to the *Criminal Justice Act* 1991 (applications for dismissal), the advocate must be remuner-ated for attendance at the hearing of the application for dismissal—

    (a) in respect of any day where the hearing begins before and ends after the luncheon adjournment, at the daily rate set out in the Table following paragraph 19 as appropriate to the category of advocate; or

    (b) in respect of any day where the hearing begins and ends before the lun-cheon adjournment, or begins after the luncheon adjournment, at the half-daily rate set out in that Table as appropriate to the category of advocate,

provided that a fee is not payable elsewhere under this Schedule in respect of any day of the hearing.

(6) Where an application for dismissal is made under paragraph 2 of Schedule 3 to the *Crime and Disorder Act* 1998, section 6 of the *Criminal Justice Act* 1987 or paragraph 5 of Schedule 6 to the *Criminal Justice Act* 1991, and—

    (a) the charge, or charges, are dismissed and the assisted person is discharged; or

    (b) the charge, or charges, of an offence triable only on indictment are dismissed and the case is remitted to the magistrates' court in accordance with paragraph 10(3)(a) of Schedule 3 to the *Crime and Disorder Act* 1998,

in respect of the first day of the hearing of the application to dismiss, the advocate instructed in the proceedings must be paid a graduated fee calculated in accor-dance with paragraph 6, as appropriate for representing an assisted person in a guilty plea.

(7) Where an advocate represents more than one assisted person in proceedings

referred to in sub-paragraph (1), the advocate must be paid a fixed fee of 20 per cent of—

    (a) the fee specified in sub-paragraph (2) where that sub-paragraph applies; or

    (b) the basic fee (B) specified in the Table following paragraph 7 where sub-paragraph (3), (4) or (5) applies, as appropriate for the circumstances set out in the relevant sub-paragraph,

in respect of each additional assisted person he represents.

[This paragraph is printed as amended by S.I. 2007 No. 3552 (*ante*, G–1).]

Noting brief fees

G–57   19. The fee payable to an advocate retained solely for the purpose of making a note of any hearing must be the daily fee set out in the table following this paragraph.

FIXED FEES

Category of work	Paragraph providing for fee	Fee for QC	Fee for leading junior	Fee for led junior or junior alone
Standard appearance	9(2)	£200 per day	£150 per day	£100 per day
Paper plea and case management hearing	9(3)	£30 per case	£30 per case	£30 per case
Abuse of process hearing	10(1)(a)	Half day £300 Full day £575	Half day £225 Full day £400	Half day £150 Full day £275
Hearings relating to disclosure	10(1)(b) and (c)	Half day £300 Full day £575	Half day £225 Full day £400	Half day £150 Full day £275
Hearings relating to the admissibility of evidence	10(1)(d)	Half day £300 Full day £575	Half day £225 Full day £400	Half day £150 Full day £275
Hearings on withdrawal of a plea of guilty	10(1)(e)	Half day £300 Full day £575	Half day £225 Full day £400	Half day £150 Full day £275
Confiscation hearings	11	Half day £300 Full day £575	Half day £225 Full day £400	Half day £150 Full day £275

Category of work	Paragraph providing for fee	Fee for QC	Fee for leading junior	Fee for led junior or junior alone
Deferred sentencing hearing	12(1)(a)	£375 per day	£275 per day	£200 per day
Sentencing hearing	12(1)(b)	£300 per day	£200 per day	£125 per day
Ineffective trial payment	13	£325 per day	£225 per day	£150 per day
Special preparation	14	£85 per hour	£65 per hour	£45 per hour
Wasted preparation	15	£85 per hour	£65 per hour	£45 per hour
Conferences and views	16	£85 per hour	£65 per hour	£45 per hour
Appeals to the Crown Court against conviction	17(1)	£300 per day	£225 per day	£150 per day
Appeals to the Crown Court against sentence	17(1)	£250 per day	£175 per day	£125 per day
Proceedings relating to breach of an order of the Crown Court	17(1)	£250 per day	£175 per day	£125 per day
Committal for sentence	17(1)	£300 per day	£225 per day	£150 per day
Adjourned appeals, committals for sentence and breach hearings	17(2)	£200 per day	£150 per day	£100 per day
Bail applications, mentions and other applications in appeals, committals for sentence and breach hearings	17(3)	£200 per day	£150 per day	£100 per day
Second and subsequent days of an application to dismiss	18(6)	Half day £300 Full day £575	Half day £225 Full day £400	Half day £150 Full day £275
Noting brief	19	—	—	£125 per day

PART 5

MISCELLANEOUS

Identity of instructed advocate

    20.—(1) Where an instructed advocate is appointed before the plea and case   **G–58**
management hearing, he must notify the Court in writing as soon as he is appointed

and, where appropriate, he must confirm whether he is the leading instructed advocate or the led instructed advocate.

(2) Where the representation order provides for a single advocate and no instructed advocate has been notified to the Court in accordance with sub-paragraph (1)—

    (a) the barrister or solicitor advocate who attends the plea and case management hearing will be deemed to be the instructed advocate; and

    (b) the Court will make a written record of this fact.

(3) Where the representation order provides for a single advocate and no barrister or solicitor advocate attends the plea and case management hearing—

    (a) the barrister or solicitor advocate who attends the next hearing in the case will be deemed to be the instructed advocate; and

    (b) the Court will make a written record of this fact.

(4) Where the representation order provides for more than one advocate, and no leading instructed advocate has been notified to the Court in accordance with sub-paragraph (1), the leading advocate who attends—

    (a) the plea and case management hearing; or

    (b) where no leading advocate attends the plea and case management hearing, the next hearing in the case attended by a leading advocate

will be deemed to be the leading instructed advocate, and the Court will make a written record of this fact.

(5) Where the representation order provides for more than one advocate, and no led instructed advocate has been notified to the Court in accordance with sub-paragraph (1), the led advocate who attends—

    (a) the plea and case management hearing; or

    (b) where no led advocate attends the plea and case management hearing, the next hearing in the case attended by a led advocate

will be deemed to be the led instructed advocate, the Court will make a written record of this fact.

(6) Where a representation order is amended after the plea and case management hearing to provide for more than one advocate—

    (a) the additional instructed advocate must notify the Court in writing of his appointment within 7 days of the date on which the representation order is amended; and

    (b) each instructed advocate must notify the Court whether he is the leading instructed advocate or the led instructed advocate.

(7) Where no additional instructed advocate has been notified to the Court in accordance with sub-paragraph (6)(a), the advocate who attends the next hearing in the case will be deemed to be an instructed advocate and the Court will record in writing whether he is the leading instructed advocate or the led instructed advocate, as appropriate to the circumstances of the case.

(8) The Court will attach—

    (a) any notice received under sub-paragraph (1) or sub-paragraph (6); and

    (b) any record made by it under sub-paragraph (2), (3), (4), (5) or (7)

to the representation order.

(9) An instructed advocate must remain as instructed advocate at all times, except where—

    (a) a date for trial is fixed at or before the plea and case management hearing and the instructed advocate is unable to conduct the trial due to his other pre-existing commitments;

    (b) he is dismissed by the assisted person or the litigator; or

    (c) he is required to withdraw because of his professional code of conduct.

(10) Where, in accordance with sub-paragraph (9), an instructed advocate withdraws, he must—

    (a) immediately notify the court of his withdrawal—

        (i) in writing; or

        (ii) where the withdrawal takes place at a plea and case management hearing, orally; and

(b) within 7 days of the date of his withdrawal, notify the court in writing of the identity of a replacement instructed advocate, who must fulfil all the functions of an instructed advocate in accordance with this Order.

(11) This paragraph does not apply to a claim for fees under paragraph 27, 28 or 29.

Payment of fees to instructed advocate

21.—(1) In accordance with article 23 the appropriate officer must notify each instructed advocate of the total fees payable and authorise payment to him accordingly. **G–59**

(2) Payment of the fees in accordance with sub-paragraph (1) must be made to each instructed advocate.

(3) Where the representation order provides for a single advocate, the instructed advocate is responsible for arranging payment of fees to the trial advocate and any substitute advocate who has undertaken work on the case.

(4) Where there are two instructed advocates for an assisted person, payment must be made to each instructed advocate individually, and—

(a) the leading instructed advocate is responsible for arranging payment of fees to the trial advocate and any substitute advocate who have undertaken work on the case of a type for which a leading advocate is responsible; and

(b) the led instructed advocate is responsible for arranging payment of fees to the trial advocate and any substitute advocate who have undertaken work on the case of a type for which a led advocate is responsible.

(5) This paragraph does not apply to a claim for fees under paragraph 27, 28 or 29.

Additional charges and additional cases

22.—(1) Where an assisted person is charged with more than one offence on one indictment, the graduated fee payable to the trial advocate under this Schedule will be based on whichever of those offences the trial advocate selects. **G–60**

(2) Where two or more cases to which this Schedule applies involving the same trial advocate are heard concurrently (whether involving the same or different assisted persons)—

(a) the trial advocate must select one case ("the principal case"), which must be treated for the purposes of remuneration in accordance with this Schedule;

(b) in respect of the main hearing in each of the other cases the trial advocate must be paid a fixed fee of 20 per cent of—

(i) the basic fee (B) specified in the Table following paragraph 5 or paragraph 7, as appropriate, for the principal case, where that is a case falling within paragraph 2(1)(a), or

(ii) the fixed fee for the principal case, where that is a case falling within paragraph 2 (1)(b).

(3) Where a trial advocate or substitute advocate appears at a hearing specified in paragraph 9, 10, 11, 12 or 13, forming part of two or more cases involving different assisted persons, he must be paid—

(a) in respect of the first such case, the fixed fee for that hearing specified in the Table following paragraph 19; and

(b) in respect of each of the other cases, 20 per cent of that fee.

(4) Subject to sub-paragraphs (1) to (3), where a trial advocate or substitute advocate appears at a hearing forming part of two or more cases, he must be paid the fixed fee for that hearing specified in the Table following paragraph 19 in respect of one such case, without any increase in respect of the other cases.

(5) Where a trial advocate selects—

(a) one offence, in preference to another offence, under sub-paragraph (1); or

(b) one case as the principal case, in preference to another case, under sub-paragraph (2), that selection does not affect his right to claim any of the fees set out in the Table following paragraph 19 to which he would otherwise have been entitled.

Multiple advocates

G–61   23.—(1) Where a representation order provides for three advocates in a case the provisions of this Schedule will apply, and the fees payable to the led juniors in accordance with Part 2 or Part 3 will be payable to each led junior who is instructed in the case.

[This paragraph is printed as amended by S.I. 2007 No. 3552 (*ante*, G–1).]

Non-local appearances

G–62   24. Where an advocate is instructed to appear in a court which is not within 40 kilometres of his office or chambers, the appropriate officer may allow an amount for travelling and other expenses incidental to that appearance, provided that the amount must not be greater than the amount, if any, which would be payable to a trial advocate from the nearest local Bar or the nearest advocate's office (whichever is the nearer) unless the advocate instructed to appear has obtained prior approval under CDS Regulations for the incurring of such expenses or can justify his attendance having regard to all the relevant circumstances of the case.

Trials lasting over 40 days

G–63   25. Where a trial exceeds 40 days, the trial advocate must be paid a fee as set out in the Table following this paragraph, as appropriate to the category of trial advocate and the class of offence, for each day by which the trial exceeds 40 days on which the trial advocate attends court.

[This paragraph is printed as amended by S.I. 2007 No. 3552 (*ante*, G–1).]

DAILY RATES PAYABLE WHERE A TRIAL LASTS OVER 40 DAYS

Class of Offence	Daily rate payable for days 41 to 50	Daily rate payable for days 51 and over
QC		
A	£635	£680
B	£447	£479
C	£447	£479
D	£447	£479
E	£447	£479
F	£447	£479
G	£447	£479
H	£447	£479
I	£447	£479
J	£447	£479
K	£447	£479
Leading Junior		
A	£544	£583
B	£383	£411
C	£383	£411
D	£383	£411
E	£383	£411
F	£383	£411
G	£383	£411

Class of Offence	Daily rate payable for days 41 to 50	Daily rate payable for days 51 and over
H	£383	£411
I	£383	£411
J	£383	£411
K	£383	£411
Led Junior		
A	£363	£389
B	£256	£274
C	£256	£274
D	£256	£274
E	£256	£274
F	£256	£274
G	£256	£274
H	£256	£274
I	£256	£274
J	£256	£274
K	£256	£274
Junior acting alone		
A	£435	£467
B	£286	£306
C	£286	£306
D	£307	£329
E	£260	£279
F	£260	£279
G	£307	£329
H	£286	£306
I	£286	£306
J	£307	£329
K	£307	£329

Assisted person unfit to plead or stand trial

26. Where in any case a hearing is held to determine the question of whether the **G–64** assisted person is unfit to plead or to stand trial (a "fitness hearing")—

    (a) if a trial on indictment is held, or continues, at any time thereafter, the length of the fitness hearing is included in determining the length of the trial for the calculation of the graduated fee in accordance with Part 2 or Part 3;

    (b) if a trial on indictment is not held, or does not continue, thereafter by reason of the assisted person being found unfit to plead or to stand trial, the trial advocate must be paid—

        (i) a graduated fee calculated in accordance with paragraph 4 as appropriate to the combined length of—

            (aa) the fitness hearing; and

            (bb) any hearing under section 4A of the *Criminal Procedure (Insanity) Act* 1964 (finding that the accused did the act or made the omission charged against him); or

        (ii) a graduated fee calculated in accordance with paragraph 6 as appropriate for representing an assisted person in a cracked trial, whichever the trial advocate elects; and

(c) if at any time the assisted person pleads guilty to the indictable offence the trial advocate must be paid either—

    (i) a graduated fee calculated in accordance with paragraph 4 as appropriate to the length of the fitness hearing; or

    (ii) a graduated fee calculated in accordance with paragraph 6 as appropriate for representing an assisted person in a guilty plea,

whichever the trial advocate elects.

Cross examination of witness

G–65

27.—(1) Where in any case on indictment an advocate is retained solely for the purpose of cross-examining a witness under section 38 of the *Youth Justice and Criminal Evidence Act* 1999 (defence representation for purposes of cross-examination) he must be paid a graduated fee calculated in accordance with paragraph 4.

(2) For the purposes of this paragraph the daily attendance fee (D) is as set out in the Table following paragraph 5 as appropriate to the number of days of attendance at court by the advocate.

Provision of written or oral advice

G–66

28.—(1) Where in any case on indictment an advocate is assigned under a representation order solely for the purpose of providing written or oral advice, he will be paid for the reasonable number of hours of preparation for that advice using the rates of hourly fees for special preparation set out in the table following paragraph 19 as appropriate to the category of trial advocate.

(2) An advocate claiming a fee for advice under this paragraph may apply to the appropriate officer to redetermine the fee under article 29 and he must supply such information and documents as may be required by the appropriate officer as proof of the number of hours of preparation.

Mitigation of sentence

G–67

29.—(1) Where in any case on indictment an advocate is assigned under a representation order to appear at a sentencing hearing solely for the purpose of applying to the court to mitigate the assisted person's sentence, he must be paid in respect of that appearance the fee payable under paragraph 12 together with a fee calculated from the reasonable number of hours of preparation for that appearance using the rates of hourly fees for special preparation set out in the table following paragraph 19 as appropriate to the category of trial advocate.

(2) An advocate claiming an hourly preparation fee under this paragraph may apply to the appropriate officer to redetermine such hourly fee under article 29 and he must supply such information and documents as may be required by the appropriate officer as proof of the number of hours of preparation.

Table of offences

G–68

At the end of Schedule 1 to the 2007 order, there is a table of offences. For the effect thereof, see *post*, G–168 *et seq.*

Article 6(1)   SCHEDULE 2

LITIGATORS' GRADUATED FEE SCHEME

PART 1

DEFINITION AND SCOPE

Interpretation

G–69

1.—(1) In this Schedule—

"case" means proceedings in the Crown Court against any one assisted person—

    (a) on one or more counts of a single indictment;

    (b) arising out of a single notice of appeal against conviction or sentence or a single committal for sentence, whether on one or more charges or

(c) arising out of a single alleged breach of an order of the Crown Court,

and a case falling within paragraph (c) must be treated as a separate case from the proceedings in which the order was made;

"cracked trial" means a case on indictment in which—

(a) a plea and case management hearing takes place and—

(i) the case does not proceed to trial (whether by reason of pleas of guilty or for other reasons) or the prosecution offers no evidence; and

(ii) either—

(aa) in respect of one or more counts to which the assisted person pleaded guilty, he did not so plead at the plea and case management hearing; or

(bb) in respect of one or more counts which did not proceed, the prosecution did not, before or at the plea and case management hearing, declare an intention of not proceeding with them; or

(b) the case is listed for trial without a plea and case management hearing taking place;

"guilty plea" means a case on indictment which—

(a) is disposed of without a trial because the assisted person pleaded guilty to one or more counts; and

(b) is not a cracked trial;

"main hearing" means —

(a) in relation to a case which goes to trial, the trial;

(b) in relation to a guilty plea, the hearing at which pleas are taken or, where there is more than one such hearing, the last such hearing;

(c) in relation to a cracked trial, the hearing at which—

(i) the case becomes a cracked trial by meeting the conditions in the definition of a cracked trial, whether or not any pleas were taken at that hearing; or

(ii) a formal verdict of not guilty was entered as a result of the prosecution offering no evidence, whether or not the parties attended the hearing;

(d) in relation to an appeal against conviction or sentence in the Crown Court, the hearing of the appeal;

(e) in relation to proceedings arising out of a committal for sentence in the Crown Court, the sentencing hearing;

(f) in relation to proceedings arising out of an alleged breach of an order of the Crown Court, the hearing at which those proceedings are determined;

"*Newton* hearing" means a hearing at which evidence is heard for the purpose of determining the sentence of a convicted person in accordance with the principles of *R. v. Newton* (1982) 77 Cr.App.R. 13;

"PPE Cut-off" means the minimum number of pages of prosecution evidence for use in calculating the fee payable to a litigator under this Schedule, as set out in the tables following paragraphs 4(1) and 4(2).

(2) For the purpose of this Schedule, the number of pages of prosecution evidence served on the court includes all—

(a) witness statements;

(b) documentary and pictorial exhibits;

(c) records of interviews with the assisted person; and

(d) records of interviews with other defendants

which form part of the committal or served prosecution documents or which are included in any notice of additional evidence, but does not include any document provided on CD-ROM or by other means of electronic communication.

(3) In proceedings on indictment in the Crown Court initiated otherwise than by committal for trial, the appropriate officer must determine the number of pages of

prosecution evidence in accordance with sub-paragraph (2) or as nearly in accordance with sub-paragraph (2) as possible as the nature of the case permits.

(4) A reference to the Table of Offences in this Schedule is to the Table in Part 6 of Schedule 1 and a reference to a Class of Offence in this Schedule refers to the Class in which that offence is listed in the Table of Offences.

Application

G–69a

2.—(1) Subject to sub-paragraphs (2) to (3), this Schedule applies to—

(a) every case on indictment;

(b) the following proceedings in the Crown Court—

    (i) an appeal against conviction or sentence from the magistrates' court;

    (ii) a sentencing hearing following a committal for sentence to the Crown Court;

    (iii) proceedings arising out of an alleged breach of an order of the Crown Court (whether or not this Schedule applies to the proceedings in which the order was made);

(c) those proceedings listed in regulation 3(2) of the CDS Regulations, in so far as they are Crown Court proceedings;

(d) a sentencing hearing following a case on indictment to which this Schedule applies, where sentence has been deferred under section 1 of the *Powers of Criminal Courts (Sentencing) Act* 2000 (deferment of sentence);

(e) any other post-sentence hearing.

(2) Sub-paragraph (3) applies where proceedings are—

(a) sent for trial to the Crown Court under section 51 of the *Crime and Disorder Act* 1998 (no committal proceedings for indictable only offences); or

(b) transferred to the Crown Court under—

    (i) section 4 of the *Criminal Justice Act* 1987 (transfer of serious fraud cases); or

    (ii) section 53 of the *Criminal Justice Act* 1991 (transfer of certain cases involving children).

(3) Where, at any time after proceedings are sent or transferred to the Crown Court under the provisions referred to in sub-paragraph (2), they are—

(a) discontinued by a notice served under section 23A of the *Prosecution of Offences Act* 1985 (discontinuance of proceedings after accused has been sent for trial); or

(b) dismissed pursuant to—

    (i) paragraph 2 of Schedule 3 to the *Crime and Disorder Act* 1998 (applications for dismissal);

    (ii) section 6 of the *Criminal Justice Act* 1987 (applications for dismissal); or

    (iii) paragraph 5 of Schedule 6 to the *Criminal Justice Act* 1991 (applications for dismissal,

the provisions of paragraphs 16 and 17 apply.

(4) Where, following a case on indictment, a *Newton* hearing takes place—

(a) for the purposes of this Schedule the case will be treated as having gone to trial;

(b) the length of the trial will be taken to be the combined length of the main hearing and the *Newton* hearing;

(c) the provisions of this Schedule relating to cracked trials and guilty pleas will not apply.

(5) For the purposes of this Schedule, a case on indictment which discontinues at or before the plea and case management hearing otherwise than—

(a) by reason of a plea of guilty being entered, or

(b) in accordance with sub-paragraph (3) of this paragraph,

must be treated as a guilty plea.

(6) For the purposes of this Schedule, where a trial that is not a Very High Cost Case lasts over 200 days, it must be treated as if it had lasted 200 days.

(7) For the purposes of this Schedule, where a case that is not a Very High Cost Case has more than 99,999 pages of prosecution evidence, it must be treated as if it had 99,999 pages of prosecution evidence.

Class of offences

3.—(1) For the purposes of this Schedule— **G–70**

    (a) every indictable offence falls within the Class under which it is listed in the Table of Offences and, subject to sub-paragraph (2), indictable offences not specifically so listed will be deemed to fall within Class H;

    (b) conspiracy to commit an indictable offence contrary to section 1 of the *Criminal Law Act* 1977 (the offence of conspiracy), incitement to commit an indictable offence and attempts to commit an indictable offence contrary to section 1 of the *Criminal Attempts Act* 1981 (attempting to commit an offence), fall within the same Class as the substantive offence to which they relate;

    (c) where the Table of Offences specifies that the Class within which an offence falls depends on whether the value involved exceeds a stated limit, the value must be presumed not to exceed that limit unless the litigator making the claim under article 6 proves otherwise to the satisfaction of the appropriate officer;

    (d) where more than one count of the indictment is for an offence in relation to which the Class depends on the value involved, that value must be taken to be the total value involved in all those offences, but where two or more counts relate to the same property, the value of that property must be taken into account once only;

    (e) where an entry in the Table of Offences specifies an offence as being contrary to a statutory provision, then subject to any express limitation in the entry that entry will include every offence contrary to that statutory provision whether or not the words of description in the entry are appropriate to cover all such offences;

    (f) where in a case on indictment there is a hearing to determine the question of whether an assisted person is unfit to plead or unfit to stand trial, the litigator must elect whether that hearing falls within the same Class as the indictable offence to which it relates or within Class D;

    (g) where in a case on indictment a restriction order is made under section 41 of the *Mental Health Act* 1983 (power of higher courts to restrict discharge from hospital), the offence falls within Class A, regardless of the Class under which the offence would be listed in the Table of Offences, but for this paragraph.

(2) Where a litigator in proceedings in the Crown Court is dissatisfied with the classification within Class H of an indictable offence not listed in the Table of Offences, he may apply to the appropriate officer, when lodging his claim for fees, to reclassify the offence.

(3) The appropriate officer must, in light of the objections made by the litigator—

    (a) confirm the classification of the offence within Class H; or

    (b) reclassify the offence

and must notify the litigator of his decision.

PART 2

GRADUATED FEES FOR GUILTY PLEAS, CRACKED TRIALS AND TRIALS

Pages of prosecution evidence

4.—(1) For the purposes of this Part, the PPE Cut-off figures in a cracked trial or **G–70a** guilty plea are specified in the table following this sub-paragraph, as appropriate to the offence with which the assisted person is charged.

PPE Cut-off Figures in Cracked Trials and Guilty Pleas

	Class of offence										
Type of case	*A*	*B*	*C*	*D*	*E*	*F*	*G*	*H*	*I*	*J*	*K*
Cracked trial or guilty plea	150	70	40	80	40	50	120	40	40	80	120

(2) For the purposes of this Part, the PPE Cut-off figures in a trial are specified in the table following this sub-paragraph, as appropriate to the offence for which the assisted person is tried, and the length of trial.

PPE Cut-off figures in trials

Trial length in days	PPE Cut off A	PPE Cut off B	PPE Cut off C	PPE Cut off D	PPE Cut off E	PPE Cut off F	PPE Cut off G	PPE Cut off H	PPE Cut off I	PPE Cut off J	PPE Cut off K
1	150	70	40	80	40	50	120	40	40	80	120
2	150	70	40	80	40	50	120	40	40	80	120
3	246	105	81	95	120	138	186	122	134	95	186
4	341	139	120	126	158	173	252	157	185	126	252
5	431	170	157	156	195	206	314	191	232	156	314
6	523	203	193	186	229	240	372	225	281	186	372
7	615	238	230	218	265	276	433	260	329	218	433
8	716	274	267	257	301	310	495	301	376	257	495
9	807	306	301	293	333	342	550	338	420	293	550
10	898	338	339	330	365	373	606	374	464	330	606
11	991	370	378	367	399	405	663	412	509	367	663
12	1,084	402	417	404	433	437	721	449	554	404	721
13	1,184	434	455	440	467	470	779	486	598	440	779
14	1,286	465	493	477	500	501	836	523	642	477	836
15	1,389	497	531	514	532	533	894	559	686	514	894
16	1,491	535	569	551	565	564	951	596	730	551	951
17	1,594	573	607	587	598	596	1,007	637	774	587	1,007
18	1,696	611	646	624	646	627	1,063	687	818	624	1,063
19	1,798	649	684	661	696	659	1,119	736	862	661	1,119
20	1,901	687	722	697	746	690	1,174	786	907	697	1,174
21	2,017	722	753	742	787	720	1,230	826	943	742	1,230
22	2,132	757	785	786	828	752	1,286	867	980	786	1,286
23	2,247	792	819	830	868	784	1,341	908	1,017	830	1,341

Trial length in days	PPE Cut off A	PPE Cut off B	PPE Cut off C	PPE Cut off D	PPE Cut off E	PPE Cut off F	PPE Cut off G	PPE Cut off H	PPE Cut off I	PPE Cut off J	PPE Cut off K
24	2,362	826	857	874	908	816	1,396	948	1,053	874	1,396
25	2,477	860	894	917	948	848	1,451	988	1,088	917	1,451
26	2,593	895	931	961	988	880	1,505	1,028	1,124	961	1,505
27	2,708	935	967	1,005	1,028	912	1,560	1,068	1,160	1,005	1,560
28	2,823	975	1,004	1,049	1,068	944	1,615	1,107	1,196	1,049	1,615
29	2,938	1,016	1,041	1,099	1,108	976	1,670	1,147	1,231	1,099	1,670
30	3,053	1,057	1,077	1,150	1,148	1,007	1,725	1,187	1,267	1,150	1,725
31	3,168	1,098	1,114	1,200	1,188	1,039	1,780	1,226	1,303	1,200	1,780
32	3,284	1,138	1,151	1,251	1,228	1,070	1,835	1,266	1,349	1,251	1,835
33	3,399	1,179	1,187	1,301	1,268	1,102	1,889	1,307	1,394	1,301	1,889
34	3,514	1,220	1,224	1,352	1,308	1,133	1,944	1,357	1,439	1,352	1,944
35	3,629	1,261	1,262	1,402	1,347	1,165	1,999	1,407	1,485	1,402	1,999
36	3,744	1,302	1,303	1,453	1,435	1,196	2,054	1,457	1,530	1,453	2,054
37	3,859	1,348	1,345	1,503	1,526	1,228	2,109	1,507	1,575	1,503	2,109
38	3,975	1,395	1,386	1,554	1,617	1,259	2,164	1,557	1,621	1,554	2,164
39	4,090	1,441	1,428	1,604	1,708	1,291	2,219	1,607	1,666	1,604	2,219
40	4,178	1,484	1,444	1,652	1,745	1,314	2,271	1,629	1,704	1,652	2,271
41	4,266	1,527	1,461	1,700	1,782	1,338	2,324	1,651	1,742	1,700	2,324
42	4,355	1,570	1,477	1,748	1,820	1,361	2,377	1,673	1,780	1,748	2,377
43	4,443	1,613	1,494	1,796	1,857	1,384	2,430	1,695	1,818	1,796	2,430
44	4,532	1,656	1,511	1,844	1,895	1,410	2,483	1,716	1,856	1,844	2,483
45	4,621	1,699	1,527	1,892	1,932	1,440	2,536	1,738	1,894	1,892	2,536
46	4,709	1,742	1,544	1,939	1,970	1,470	2,589	1,760	1,932	1,939	2,589
47	4,798	1,785	1,560	1,987	2,007	1,501	2,642	1,782	1,970	1,987	2,642

Trial length in days	PPE Cut off A	PPE Cut off B	PPE Cut off C	PPE Cut off D	PPE Cut off E	PPE Cut off F	PPE Cut off G	PPE Cut off H	PPE Cut off I	PPE Cut off J	PPE Cut off K
48	4,887	1,828	1,577	2,039	2,045	1,531	2,695	1,804	2,008	2,039	2,695
49	4,975	1,871	1,594	2,091	2,082	1,561	2,749	1,826	2,046	2,091	2,749
50	5,064	1,914	1,610	2,144	2,120	1,591	2,802	1,848	2,084	2,144	2,802
51	5,153	1,957	1,627	2,196	2,158	1,622	2,855	1,870	2,122	2,196	2,855
52	5,242	2,000	1,644	2,249	2,195	1,652	2,908	1,892	2,160	2,249	2,908
53	5,330	2,043	1,660	2,301	2,233	1,682	2,962	1,914	2,198	2,301	2,962
54	5,419	2,086	1,677	2,354	2,271	1,712	3,015	1,936	2,236	2,354	3,015
55	5,508	2,129	1,694	2,406	2,308	1,743	3,068	1,958	2,275	2,406	3,068
56	5,597	2,172	1,710	2,459	2,346	1,773	3,121	1,980	2,313	2,459	3,121
57	5,686	2,215	1,727	2,512	2,384	1,803	3,175	2,002	2,351	2,512	3,175
58	5,775	2,258	1,744	2,564	2,422	1,833	3,228	2,024	2,389	2,564	3,228
59	5,863	2,301	1,760	2,617	2,459	1,864	3,281	2,046	2,427	2,617	3,281
60	5,952	2,345	1,777	2,669	2,497	1,894	3,335	2,068	2,465	2,669	3,335
61	6,041	2,388	1,794	2,722	2,535	1,924	3,388	2,090	2,503	2,722	3,388
62	6,130	2,431	1,811	2,775	2,572	1,959	3,442	2,112	2,542	2,775	3,442
63	6,219	2,474	1,827	2,827	2,610	2,020	3,495	2,134	2,580	2,827	3,495
64	6,308	2,517	1,844	2,880	2,648	2,081	3,549	2,156	2,618	2,880	3,549
65	6,397	2,561	1,861	2,933	2,686	2,141	3,602	2,178	2,656	2,933	3,602
66	6,486	2,604	1,877	2,985	2,723	2,202	3,656	2,200	2,694	2,985	3,656
67	6,575	2,647	1,894	3,038	2,761	2,263	3,709	2,222	2,776	3,038	3,709
68	6,664	2,690	1,911	3,091	2,799	2,323	3,763	2,244	2,865	3,091	3,763
69	6,754	2,734	1,927	3,144	2,836	2,384	3,816	2,266	2,954	3,144	3,816
70	6,843	2,777	1,944	3,196	2,874	2,445	3,870	2,288	3,043	3,196	3,870
71	6,932	2,820	1,961	3,249	2,912	2,506	3,923	2,310	3,132	3,249	3,923

Trial length in days	PPE Cut off A	PPE Cut off B	PPE Cut off C	PPE Cut off D	PPE Cut off E	PPE Cut off F	PPE Cut off G	PPE Cut off H	PPE Cut off I	PPE Cut off J	PPE Cut off K
72	7,021	2,864	1,978	3,302	2,950	2,566	3,977	2,332	3,221	3,302	3,977
73	7,110	2,907	1,994	3,355	2,987	2,627	4,031	2,354	3,310	3,355	4,031
74	7,199	2,950	2,016	3,407	3,025	2,688	4,084	2,376	3,399	3,407	4,084
75	7,289	2,994	2,040	3,460	3,063	2,749	4,138	2,398	3,488	3,460	4,138
76	7,378	3,037	2,064	3,513	3,101	2,809	4,192	2,420	3,577	3,513	4,192
77	7,467	3,080	2,089	3,566	3,138	2,870	4,245	2,442	3,666	3,566	4,245
78	7,556	3,124	2,113	3,619	3,176	2,931	4,299	2,464	3,755	3,619	4,299
79	7,646	3,167	2,137	3,672	3,214	2,992	4,353	2,486	3,844	3,672	4,353
80	7,735	3,211	2,161	3,724	3,251	3,052	4,406	2,508	3,933	3,724	4,406
81	7,824	3,254	2,185	3,777	3,289	3,113	4,460	2,530	4,023	3,777	4,460
82	7,914	3,297	2,210	3,830	3,327	3,174	4,514	2,552	4,112	3,830	4,514
83	8,003	3,341	2,234	3,883	3,365	3,235	4,568	2,575	4,201	3,883	4,568
84	8,093	3,384	2,258	3,936	3,402	3,295	4,622	2,597	4,290	3,936	4,622
85	8,182	3,428	2,282	3,989	3,440	3,356	4,675	2,619	4,379	3,989	4,675
86	8,271	3,471	2,307	4,042	3,478	3,417	4,729	2,641	4,469	4,042	4,729
87	8,361	3,515	2,331	4,095	3,516	3,478	4,783	2,663	4,558	4,095	4,783
88	8,450	3,558	2,355	4,148	3,553	3,539	4,837	2,685	4,647	4,148	4,837
89	8,540	3,602	2,379	4,201	3,591	3,599	4,891	2,707	4,737	4,201	4,891
90	8,629	3,645	2,404	4,254	3,629	3,660	4,945	2,729	4,826	4,254	4,945
91	8,719	3,689	2,428	4,307	3,666	3,721	4,999	2,751	4,915	4,307	4,999
92	8,809	3,733	2,452	4,360	3,704	3,782	5,053	2,774	5,005	4,360	5,053
93	8,898	3,776	2,477	4,413	3,742	3,843	5,107	2,796	5,094	4,413	5,107
94	8,988	3,820	2,501	4,466	3,780	3,903	5,161	2,818	5,183	4,466	5,161
95	9,077	3,863	2,525	4,519	3,817	3,964	5,215	2,840	5,273	4,519	5,215

Trial length in days	PPE Cut off A	PPE Cut off B	PPE Cut off C	PPE Cut off D	PPE Cut off E	PPE Cut off F	PPE Cut off G	PPE Cut off H	PPE Cut off I	PPE Cut off J	PPE Cut off K
96	9,167	3,907	2,549	4,572	3,855	4,025	5,269	2,862	5,362	4,572	5,269
97	9,257	3,951	2,574	4,625	3,893	4,086	5,323	2,884	5,452	4,625	5,323
98	9,346	3,994	2,598	4,679	3,930	4,147	5,377	2,906	5,541	4,679	5,377
99	9,436	4,038	2,622	4,732	3,968	4,207	5,431	2,929	5,631	4,732	5,431
100	9,526	4,082	2,647	4,785	4,006	4,268	5,485	2,951	5,720	4,785	5,485
101	9,616	4,125	2,671	4,838	4,044	4,329	5,539	2,973	5,810	4,838	5,539
102	9,705	4,169	2,695	4,891	4,081	4,390	5,593	2,995	5,899	4,891	5,593
103	9,795	4,213	2,720	4,944	4,119	4,451	5,647	3,032	5,989	4,944	5,647
104	9,885	4,257	2,744	4,997	4,157	4,512	5,702	3,073	6,079	4,997	5,702
105	9,975	4,300	2,768	5,051	4,195	4,573	5,756	3,114	6,168	5,051	5,756
106	10,065	4,344	2,793	5,104	4,232	4,633	5,810	3,155	6,258	5,104	5,810
107	10,155	4,388	2,817	5,157	4,270	4,694	5,864	3,196	6,348	5,157	5,864
108	10,245	4,432	2,841	5,210	4,308	4,755	5,918	3,237	6,437	5,210	5,918
109	10,334	4,475	2,866	5,264	4,345	4,816	5,973	3,278	6,527	5,264	5,973
110	10,424	4,519	2,890	5,317	4,383	4,877	6,027	3,319	6,617	5,317	6,027
111	10,514	4,563	2,914	5,370	4,421	4,938	6,081	3,361	6,706	5,370	6,081
112	10,604	4,607	2,939	5,423	4,459	4,999	6,135	3,402	6,796	5,423	6,135
113	10,694	4,650	2,963	5,477	4,496	5,059	6,189	3,443	6,886	5,477	6,189
114	10,784	4,694	2,987	5,530	4,534	5,120	6,244	3,484	6,976	5,530	6,244
115	10,874	4,738	3,012	5,583	4,572	5,181	6,298	3,525	7,066	5,583	6,298
116	10,964	4,782	3,036	5,637	4,610	5,242	6,352	3,566	7,155	5,637	6,352
117	11,054	4,826	3,060	5,690	4,647	5,303	6,406	3,607	7,245	5,690	6,406
118	11,145	4,869	3,085	5,743	4,685	5,364	6,460	3,648	7,335	5,743	6,460
119	11,235	4,913	3,109	5,797	4,723	5,425	6,514	3,689	7,425	5,797	6,514

Trial length in days	PPE Cut off A	PPE Cut off B	PPE Cut off C	PPE Cut off D	PPE Cut off E	PPE Cut off F	PPE Cut off G	PPE Cut off H	PPE Cut off I	PPE Cut off J	PPE Cut off K
120	11,325	4,957	3,133	5,850	4,760	5,486	6,569	3,730	7,515	5,850	6,569
121	11,415	5,001	3,158	5,904	4,798	5,547	6,623	3,771	7,605	5,904	6,623
122	11,504	5,044	3,182	5,956	4,836	5,607	6,677	3,812	7,693	5,956	6,677
123	11,593	5,088	3,206	6,009	4,874	5,668	6,731	3,853	7,782	6,009	6,731
124	11,681	5,131	3,230	6,061	4,911	5,729	6,785	3,895	7,871	6,061	6,785
125	11,770	5,175	3,254	6,114	4,949	5,789	6,839	3,936	7,959	6,114	6,839
126	11,859	5,218	3,278	6,167	4,987	5,850	6,892	3,977	8,048	6,167	6,892
127	11,948	5,261	3,302	6,219	5,025	5,911	6,945	4,017	8,137	6,219	6,945
128	12,037	5,304	3,326	6,272	5,062	5,971	6,999	4,058	8,225	6,272	6,999
129	12,125	5,347	3,350	6,324	5,100	6,032	7,052	4,098	8,314	6,324	7,052
130	12,214	5,390	3,374	6,377	5,138	6,093	7,106	4,139	8,403	6,377	7,106
131	12,303	5,433	3,398	6,430	5,175	6,153	7,159	4,179	8,491	6,430	7,159
132	12,392	5,476	3,422	6,482	5,213	6,214	7,212	4,219	8,580	6,482	7,212
133	12,481	5,520	3,446	6,535	5,251	6,274	7,266	4,260	8,669	6,535	7,266
134	12,570	5,563	3,470	6,588	5,289	6,335	7,319	4,300	8,757	6,588	7,319
135	12,658	5,606	3,494	6,640	5,326	6,396	7,373	4,341	8,846	6,640	7,373
136	12,747	5,649	3,518	6,693	5,364	6,456	7,426	4,381	8,935	6,693	7,426
137	12,836	5,692	3,542	6,745	5,402	6,517	7,479	4,422	9,023	6,745	7,479
138	12,925	5,735	3,566	6,798	5,439	6,578	7,533	4,462	9,112	6,798	7,533
139	13,014	5,778	3,590	6,851	5,477	6,638	7,586	4,503	9,201	6,851	7,586
140	13,102	5,821	3,614	6,903	5,515	6,699	7,639	4,543	9,289	6,903	7,639
141	13,191	5,864	3,638	6,956	5,553	6,760	7,693	4,584	9,378	6,956	7,693
142	13,280	5,908	3,662	7,008	5,590	6,820	7,746	4,624	9,467	7,008	7,746
143	13,369	5,951	3,686	7,061	5,628	6,881	7,800	4,664	9,555	7,061	7,800

Trial length in days	PPE Cut off A	PPE Cut off B	PPE Cut off C	PPE Cut off D	PPE Cut off E	PPE Cut off F	PPE Cut off G	PPE Cut off H	PPE Cut off I	PPE Cut off J	PPE Cut off K
144	13,458	5,994	3,709	7,114	5,666	6,942	7,853	4,705	9,644	7,114	7,853
145	13,546	6,037	3,733	7,166	5,704	7,002	7,906	4,745	9,733	7,166	7,906
146	13,635	6,080	3,757	7,219	5,741	7,063	7,960	4,786	9,821	7,219	7,960
147	13,724	6,123	3,781	7,272	5,779	7,124	8,013	4,826	9,910	7,272	8,013
148	13,813	6,166	3,805	7,324	5,817	7,184	8,067	4,867	9,999	7,324	8,067
149	13,902	6,209	3,829	7,377	5,854	7,245	8,120	4,907	10,087	7,377	8,120
150	13,990	6,252	3,853	7,429	5,892	7,305	8,173	4,948	10,176	7,429	8,173
151	14,079	6,296	3,877	7,482	5,930	7,366	8,227	4,988	10,265	7,482	8,227
152	14,168	6,339	3,901	7,535	5,968	7,427	8,280	5,029	10,353	7,535	8,280
153	14,257	6,382	3,925	7,587	6,005	7,487	8,333	5,069	10,442	7,587	8,333
154	14,346	6,425	3,949	7,640	6,043	7,548	8,387	5,110	10,531	7,640	8,387
155	14,435	6,468	3,973	7,692	6,081	7,609	8,440	5,150	10,619	7,692	8,440
156	14,523	6,511	3,997	7,745	6,119	7,669	8,494	5,190	10,708	7,745	8,494
157	14,612	6,554	4,021	7,798	6,156	7,730	8,547	5,231	10,797	7,798	8,547
158	14,701	6,597	4,045	7,850	6,194	7,791	8,600	5,271	10,885	7,850	8,600
159	14,790	6,641	4,069	7,903	6,232	7,851	8,654	5,312	10,974	7,903	8,654
160	14,879	6,684	4,093	7,956	6,269	7,912	8,707	5,352	11,063	7,956	8,707
161	14,967	6,727	4,117	8,008	6,307	7,973	8,760	5,393	11,151	8,008	8,760
162	15,056	6,770	4,141	8,061	6,345	8,033	8,814	5,433	11,240	8,061	8,814
163	15,145	6,813	4,165	8,113	6,383	8,094	8,867	5,474	11,329	8,113	8,867
164	15,234	6,856	4,189	8,166	6,420	8,155	8,921	5,514	11,417	8,166	8,921
165	15,323	6,899	4,213	8,219	6,458	8,215	8,974	5,555	11,506	8,219	8,974
166	15,411	6,942	4,237	8,271	6,496	8,276	9,027	5,595	11,595	8,271	9,027
167	15,500	6,985	4,261	8,324	6,534	8,337	9,081	5,636	11,683	8,324	9,081

Trial length in days	PPE Cut off A	PPE Cut off B	PPE Cut off C	PPE Cut off D	PPE Cut off E	PPE Cut off F	PPE Cut off G	PPE Cut off H	PPE Cut off I	PPE Cut off J	PPE Cut off K
168	15,589	7,029	4,285	8,376	6,571	8,397	9,134	5,676	11,772	8,376	9,134
169	15,678	7,072	4,309	8,429	6,609	8,458	9,188	5,716	11,861	8,429	9,188
170	15,767	7,115	4,333	8,482	6,647	8,518	9,241	5,757	11,949	8,482	9,241
171	15,855	7,158	4,357	8,534	6,684	8,579	9,294	5,797	12,038	8,534	9,294
172	15,944	7,201	4,380	8,587	6,722	8,640	9,348	5,838	12,127	8,587	9,348
173	16,033	7,244	4,404	8,639	6,760	8,700	9,401	5,878	12,215	8,639	9,401
174	16,122	7,287	4,428	8,692	6,798	8,761	9,454	5,919	12,304	8,692	9,454
175	16,211	7,330	4,452	8,745	6,835	8,822	9,508	5,959	12,393	8,745	9,508
176	16,300	7,373	4,476	8,797	6,873	8,882	9,561	6,000	12,481	8,797	9,561
177	16,388	7,417	4,500	8,850	6,911	8,943	9,615	6,040	12,570	8,850	9,615
178	16,477	7,460	4,524	8,903	6,948	9,004	9,668	6,081	12,659	8,903	9,668
179	16,566	7,503	4,548	8,955	6,986	9,064	9,721	6,121	12,747	8,955	9,721
180	16,655	7,546	4,572	9,008	7,024	9,125	9,775	6,162	12,836	9,008	9,775
181	16,744	7,589	4,596	9,060	7,062	9,186	9,828	6,202	12,925	9,060	9,828
182	16,832	7,632	4,620	9,113	7,099	9,246	9,881	6,242	13,013	9,113	9,881
183	16,921	7,675	4,644	9,166	7,137	9,307	9,935	6,283	13,102	9,166	9,935
184	17,010	7,718	4,668	9,218	7,174	9,368	9,988	6,323	13,191	9,218	9,988
185	17,099	7,762	4,692	9,271	7,211	9,428	10,042	6,364	13,279	9,271	10,042
186	17,188	7,805	4,716	9,323	7,248	9,489	10,095	6,404	13,368	9,323	10,095
187	17,276	7,848	4,740	9,376	7,285	9,549	10,148	6,445	13,457	9,376	10,148
188	17,365	7,891	4,764	9,429	7,322	9,610	10,202	6,485	13,545	9,429	10,202
189	17,454	7,934	4,788	9,481	7,360	9,671	10,255	6,526	13,634	9,481	10,255
190	17,543	7,977	4,812	9,534	7,397	9,731	10,309	6,566	13,723	9,534	10,309
191	17,632	8,020	4,836	9,587	7,434	9,792	10,362	6,607	13,811	9,587	10,362

Trial length in days	PPE Cut off A	PPE Cut off B	PPE Cut off C	PPE Cut off D	PPE Cut off E	PPE Cut off F	PPE Cut off G	PPE Cut off H	PPE Cut off I	PPE Cut off J	PPE Cut off K
192	17,720	8,063	4,860	9,639	7,471	9,853	10,415	6,647	13,900	9,639	10,415
193	17,809	8,106	4,884	9,692	7,508	9,913	10,469	6,687	13,988	9,692	10,469
194	17,898	8,150	4,908	9,744	7,545	9,974	10,522	6,728	14,077	9,744	10,522
195	17,987	8,193	4,932	9,797	7,582	10,035	10,575	6,768	14,166	9,797	10,575
196	18,076	8,236	4,956	9,850	7,620	10,095	10,629	6,809	14,254	9,850	10,629
197	18,165	8,279	4,980	9,902	7,657	10,156	10,682	6,849	14,343	9,902	10,682
198	18,253	8,322	5,004	9,955	7,694	10,217	10,736	6,890	14,432	9,955	10,736
199	18,342	8,365	5,028	10,007	7,731	10,277	10,789	6,930	14,520	10,007	10,789
200	18,431	8,408	5,051	10,060	7,768	10,338	10,842	6,971	14,609	10,060	10,842

Cracked trial or guilty plea where the number of pages of prosecution evidence is less than or equal to the PPE Cut-off

G–71 5.—(1) Where in a cracked trial or guilty plea the number of pages of prosecution evidence is less than or equal to the PPE Cut-off specified in the table following paragraph 4(1) as appropriate to the class of offence with which the assisted person is charged, the total fee payable to the litigator will be—

    (a) the basic fee, calculated in accordance with the table following sub-paragraph (2) of this paragraph;

    (b) the defendant uplift, if any, calculated in accordance with the table following paragraph 9; and

    (c) the adjustment for transfers and retrials, if any, calculated in accordance with paragraph 10.

(2) For the purposes of sub-paragraph (1), the basic fee appropriate to a cracked trial or a guilty plea is specified in the table following this sub-paragraph, in accordance with the type of case and Class of offence with which the assisted person is charged.

Type of case	Class of Offence										
	A	B	C	D	E	F	G	H	I	J	K
Cracked trial	2785.18	1036.20	766.89	1255.67	340.50	327.63	1074.22	346.31	370.66	1321.76	1130.76
Guilty plea	1907.11	609.44	485.38	708.34	202.41	214.59	667.17	209.28	191.34	745.63	702.29

Trial where the number of pages of prosecution evidence is less than or equal to the PPE Cut-off

G–71a 6.—(1) Where in a trial the number of pages of prosecution evidence is less than or equal to the PPE Cut-off specified in the table following paragraph 4(2) as appropriate to the offence for which the assisted person is tried and the length of trial, the total fee payable to the litigator will be—

    (a) the basic fee, calculated in accordance with the table following sub-paragraph (2) of this paragraph;

    (b) the length of trial proxy, if any, calculated in accordance with the table following sub-paragraph (3);

    (c) the defendant uplift, if any, calculated in accordance with the table following paragraph 9; and

    (d) the adjustment for transfers and retrials, if any, calculated in accordance with paragraph 10.

(2) For the purposes of sub-paragraph (1), the basic fee appropriate to a trial is specified in the table following this sub-paragraph, in accordance with the offence for which the assisted person is tried.

BASIC FEES FOR TRIALS (£)

Type of case	Class of Offence										
	A	B	C	D	E	F	G	H	I	J	K
Trial	2785.18	1202.92	810.51	1527.89	386.54	391.89	1074.22	392.05	391.72	1608.31	1130.76

(3) For the purposes of sub-paragraph (1), the length of trial proxy is specified in the table below, in accordance with the offence for which the assisted person is tried and the length of trial.

LENGTH OF TRIAL PROXY

Trial Length in Days	Trial length proxy A	Trial length proxy B	Trial length proxy C	Trial length proxy D	Trial length proxy E	Trial length proxy F	Trial length proxy G	Trial length proxy H	Trial length proxy I	Trial length proxy J	Trial length proxy K
1	0.00	0.00	0.00	0.00	0.00	0.00	0.00	0.00	0.00	0.00	0.00
2	0.00	0.00	0.00	0.00	0.00	0.00	0.00	0.00	0.00	0.00	0.00
3	1,567.39	496.31	473.98	262.93	785.29	706.78	597.73	771.17	945.08	276.76	629.18
4	3,125.99	964.00	924.20	801.42	1,132.77	984.95	1,187.50	1,106.66	1,447.59	843.60	1,250.00
5	4,606.67	1,408.31	1,351.90	1,312.99	1,462.86	1,249.21	1,747.80	1,425.36	1,924.97	1,382.09	1,839.79
6	6,102.89	1,858.61	1,776.66	1,833.56	1,772.17	1,519.38	2,270.67	1,741.43	2,411.61	1,930.05	2,390.18
7	7,586.15	2,303.80	2,203.87	2,346.50	2,099.12	1,789.40	2,824.77	2,059.74	2,890.57	2,469.99	2,973.44
8	9,069.42	2,748.97	2,631.09	2,859.44	2,426.07	2,055.07	3,378.86	2,378.05	3,369.53	3,009.93	3,556.69
9	10,404.37	3,149.63	3,015.57	3,342.88	2,720.32	2,294.19	3,877.54	2,664.53	3,806.50	3,518.82	4,081.63
10	11,739.31	3,550.30	3,400.07	3,826.32	3,014.59	2,533.30	4,376.22	2,951.00	4,243.47	4,027.71	4,606.55
11	13,101.98	3,951.50	3,794.99	4,313.36	3,322.37	2,779.24	4,897.29	3,245.35	4,689.34	4,540.38	5,155.06
12	14,465.79	4,352.20	4,190.10	4,797.10	3,630.24	3,025.17	5,418.70	3,539.33	5,135.58	5,049.58	5,703.89
13	15,805.12	4,752.90	4,576.22	5,280.84	3,937.70	3,270.12	5,940.11	3,826.93	5,574.00	5,558.78	6,252.75
14	17,144.46	5,153.61	4,962.33	5,764.59	4,235.69	3,510.51	6,461.49	4,114.53	6,012.41	6,067.98	6,801.57
15	18,483.80	5,554.31	5,348.45	6,248.32	4,532.77	3,750.89	6,982.85	4,402.14	6,450.82	6,577.18	7,350.37
16	19,823.13	5,955.02	5,734.56	6,732.06	4,829.87	3,991.29	7,503.38	4,689.74	6,889.23	7,086.38	7,898.30
17	21,162.47	6,355.73	6,120.68	7,215.80	5,126.96	4,231.68	8,010.04	4,977.34	7,327.64	7,595.57	8,431.63
18	22,501.80	6,756.43	6,506.79	7,699.54	5,424.05	4,472.07	8,516.70	5,264.94	7,766.05	8,104.77	8,964.95
19	23,841.14	7,157.13	6,892.90	8,183.28	5,721.14	4,712.46	9,023.36	5,552.54	8,204.46	8,613.97	9,498.27
20	25,180.48	7,557.84	7,279.02	8,667.02	6,018.23	4,952.85	9,530.02	5,840.14	8,642.88	9,123.17	10,031.60
21	26,528.83	7,927.97	7,596.29	9,159.97	6,263.74	5,149.52	10,036.68	6,076.67	9,003.14	9,642.08	10,564.93
22	27,868.58	8,298.07	7,913.63	9,652.84	6,509.26	5,346.28	10,543.34	6,313.31	9,363.42	10,160.89	11,098.26

Trial Length in Days	Trial length proxy A	Trial length proxy B	Trial length proxy C	Trial length proxy D	Trial length proxy E	Trial length proxy F	Trial length proxy G	Trial length proxy H	Trial length proxy I	Trial length proxy J	Trial length proxy K
23	29,208.32	8,668.15	8,231.00	10,137.38	6,747.46	5,543.04	11,050.01	6,549.95	9,723.73	10,670.92	11,631.58
24	30,548.08	9,029.83	8,548.37	10,621.91	6,985.68	5,739.80	11,556.66	6,786.59	10,080.08	11,180.95	12,164.91
25	31,887.82	9,391.50	8,864.09	11,106.44	7,223.89	5,936.55	12,063.32	7,019.41	10,431.95	11,691.00	12,698.24
26	33,227.57	9,753.17	9,174.28	11,590.99	7,462.10	6,133.31	12,569.98	7,250.40	10,783.83	12,201.03	13,231.57
27	34,567.32	10,114.85	9,484.49	12,075.51	7,700.31	6,330.07	13,076.64	7,481.38	11,135.70	12,711.06	13,764.89
28	35,907.06	10,476.53	9,794.68	12,560.05	7,938.53	6,526.83	13,583.31	7,712.37	11,487.57	13,221.10	14,298.22
29	37,246.82	10,838.20	10,104.88	13,044.58	8,176.73	6,721.29	14,089.97	7,943.34	11,839.46	13,731.14	14,831.54
30	38,586.56	11,199.87	10,415.07	13,529.11	8,414.94	6,914.62	14,596.63	8,174.32	12,191.33	14,241.17	15,364.87
31	39,926.31	11,561.55	10,725.27	14,013.65	8,653.16	7,107.96	15,103.29	8,405.31	12,543.20	14,751.21	15,898.20
32	41,266.06	11,923.23	11,035.47	14,498.18	8,891.37	7,301.29	15,609.95	8,636.29	12,895.08	15,261.24	16,431.52
33	42,605.81	12,284.90	11,345.67	14,982.72	9,129.58	7,494.62	16,116.60	8,867.28	13,246.95	15,771.29	16,964.85
34	43,945.56	12,646.57	11,655.86	15,467.26	9,367.79	7,687.96	16,623.27	9,098.26	13,598.83	16,281.32	17,498.18
35	45,285.31	13,008.25	11,966.06	15,951.79	9,606.00	7,881.29	17,129.93	9,329.24	13,950.71	16,791.35	18,031.51
36	46,625.06	13,369.92	12,276.26	16,436.32	9,844.21	8,074.63	17,636.59	9,560.22	14,302.58	17,301.39	18,564.83
37	47,964.81	13,731.60	12,586.46	16,920.86	10,082.43	8,267.96	18,143.25	9,791.21	14,654.45	17,811.43	19,098.16
38	49,304.55	14,093.27	12,896.66	17,405.39	10,320.64	8,461.29	18,649.91	10,022.19	15,006.33	18,321.46	19,631.49
39	50,644.31	14,454.94	13,206.85	17,889.92	10,558.84	8,654.63	19,156.57	10,253.17	15,358.20	18,831.50	20,164.82
40	51,667.89	14,785.90	13,329.94	18,346.59	10,654.34	8,797.55	19,641.20	10,353.05	15,651.51	19,312.20	20,674.95
41	52,697.86	15,119.38	13,454.39	18,805.74	10,752.37	8,940.76	20,129.41	10,454.14	15,946.54	19,795.51	21,188.86
42	53,728.06	15,452.95	13,578.88	19,265.01	10,850.45	9,083.97	20,617.80	10,555.27	16,241.65	20,278.95	21,702.94
43	54,758.50	15,786.64	13,703.38	19,724.39	10,948.58	9,227.20	21,106.33	10,656.41	16,536.81	20,762.51	22,217.20
44	55,789.17	16,120.43	13,827.90	20,183.88	11,046.75	9,370.43	21,595.04	10,757.57	16,832.03	21,246.19	22,731.63
45	56,820.09	16,454.31	13,952.45	20,643.48	11,144.95	9,513.67	22,083.91	10,858.77	17,127.33	21,729.98	23,246.22

Trial Length in Days	Trial length proxy A	Trial length proxy B	Trial length proxy C	Trial length proxy D	Trial length proxy E	Trial length proxy F	Trial length proxy G	Trial length proxy H	Trial length proxy I	Trial length proxy J	Trial length proxy K
46	57,851.23	16,788.30	14,077.02	21,103.21	11,243.21	9,656.92	22,572.94	10,959.97	17,422.67	22,213.90	23,761.00
47	58,882.61	17,122.39	14,201.62	21,563.03	11,341.51	9,800.18	23,062.14	11,061.21	17,718.09	22,697.92	24,275.94
48	59,914.23	17,456.59	14,326.24	22,022.98	11,439.86	9,943.44	23,551.50	11,162.47	18,013.57	23,182.08	24,791.06
49	60,946.09	17,790.89	14,450.89	22,483.03	11,538.24	10,086.71	24,041.02	11,263.74	18,309.10	23,666.34	25,306.34
50	61,978.18	18,125.29	14,575.55	22,943.19	11,636.66	10,230.00	24,530.71	11,365.05	18,604.70	24,150.72	25,821.80
51	63,010.50	18,459.79	14,700.25	23,403.47	11,735.14	10,373.29	25,020.57	11,466.37	18,900.37	24,635.23	26,337.44
52	64,043.06	18,794.39	14,824.96	23,863.86	11,833.66	10,516.60	25,510.58	11,567.72	19,196.09	25,119.85	26,853.24
53	65,075.86	19,129.10	14,949.70	24,324.37	11,932.22	10,659.90	26,000.76	11,669.09	19,491.87	25,604.59	27,369.22
54	66,108.89	19,463.91	15,074.46	24,784.97	12,030.83	10,803.22	26,491.11	11,770.48	19,787.72	26,089.45	27,885.37
55	67,142.16	19,798.82	15,199.24	25,245.69	12,129.47	10,946.54	26,981.61	11,871.89	20,083.63	26,574.42	28,401.69
56	68,175.66	20,133.84	15,324.06	25,706.54	12,228.16	11,089.88	27,472.28	11,973.33	20,379.61	27,059.51	28,918.19
57	69,209.40	20,468.95	15,448.89	26,167.49	12,326.89	11,233.23	27,963.11	12,074.78	20,675.64	27,544.72	29,434.86
58	70,243.38	20,804.17	15,573.74	26,628.55	12,425.63	11,376.58	28,454.11	12,176.26	20,971.74	28,030.05	29,951.69
59	71,277.59	21,139.50	15,698.63	27,089.73	12,524.37	11,519.94	28,945.28	12,277.77	21,267.90	28,515.50	30,468.71
60	72,312.03	21,474.92	15,823.53	27,551.00	12,623.11	11,663.31	29,436.60	12,379.29	21,564.12	29,001.06	30,985.90
61	73,346.71	21,810.44	15,948.46	28,012.41	12,721.86	11,806.69	29,928.09	12,480.84	21,860.41	29,486.75	31,503.25
62	74,381.63	22,146.08	16,073.41	28,473.92	12,820.60	11,950.07	30,419.74	12,582.42	22,156.76	29,972.54	32,020.78
63	75,416.78	22,481.80	16,198.38	28,935.55	12,919.34	12,093.46	30,911.56	12,684.01	22,453.17	30,458.47	32,538.49
64	76,452.18	22,817.64	16,323.39	29,397.28	13,018.08	12,236.87	31,403.54	12,785.63	22,749.63	30,944.50	33,056.36
65	77,487.80	23,153.57	16,448.41	29,859.12	13,116.82	12,380.28	31,895.69	12,887.26	23,046.17	31,430.66	33,574.41
66	78,523.66	23,489.62	16,573.46	30,321.09	13,215.56	12,523.70	32,387.99	12,988.92	23,342.77	31,916.93	34,092.62
67	79,559.75	23,825.76	16,698.52	30,783.16	13,314.30	12,667.13	32,880.47	13,090.60	23,639.42	32,403.32	34,611.01
68	80,596.09	24,162.01	16,823.62	31,245.34	13,413.04	12,810.57	33,373.11	13,192.31	23,936.14	32,889.83	35,129.58

Trial Length in Days	Trial length proxy A	Trial length proxy B	Trial length proxy C	Trial length proxy D	Trial length proxy E	Trial length proxy F	Trial length proxy G	Trial length proxy H	Trial length proxy I	Trial length proxy J	Trial length proxy K
69	81,632.66	24,498.35	16,948.73	31,707.63	13,511.78	12,954.02	33,865.90	13,294.04	24,232.93	33,376.46	35,648.31
70	82,669.46	24,834.80	17,073.87	32,170.04	13,610.52	13,097.48	34,358.87	13,395.79	24,529.77	33,863.20	36,167.23
71	83,706.49	25,171.35	17,199.04	32,632.57	13,709.26	13,240.94	34,851.99	13,497.57	24,826.68	34,350.07	36,686.31
72	84,743.77	25,508.01	17,324.22	33,095.20	13,808.00	13,384.42	35,345.28	13,599.36	25,123.65	34,837.05	37,205.57
73	85,781.29	25,844.77	17,449.44	33,557.95	13,906.74	13,527.90	35,838.74	13,701.17	25,420.68	35,324.14	37,724.99
74	86,819.03	26,181.63	17,574.67	34,020.80	14,005.48	13,671.39	36,332.36	13,803.02	25,717.78	35,811.36	38,244.59
75	87,857.00	26,518.59	17,699.93	34,483.76	14,104.22	13,814.89	36,826.14	13,904.89	26,014.94	36,298.70	38,764.36
76	88,895.23	26,855.65	17,825.21	34,946.85	14,202.96	13,958.39	37,320.09	14,006.77	26,312.15	36,786.15	39,284.30
77	89,933.68	27,192.82	17,950.52	35,410.04	14,301.70	14,101.91	37,814.19	14,108.67	26,609.43	37,273.73	39,804.42
78	90,972.37	27,530.09	18,075.85	35,873.35	14,400.44	14,245.43	38,308.47	14,210.60	26,906.77	37,761.41	40,324.71
79	92,011.29	27,867.46	18,201.20	36,336.77	14,499.18	14,388.97	38,802.91	14,312.56	27,204.19	38,249.23	40,845.17
80	93,050.45	28,204.93	18,326.58	36,800.29	14,597.92	14,532.51	39,297.51	14,414.54	27,501.65	38,737.15	41,365.80
81	94,089.85	28,542.51	18,451.97	37,263.94	14,696.66	14,676.06	39,792.27	14,516.54	27,799.18	39,225.19	41,886.60
82	95,129.47	28,880.19	18,577.40	37,727.69	14,795.40	14,819.62	40,287.21	14,618.55	28,096.77	39,713.35	42,407.58
83	96,169.34	29,217.97	18,702.85	38,191.56	14,894.14	14,963.18	40,782.29	14,720.60	28,394.43	40,201.63	42,928.73
84	97,209.45	29,555.86	18,828.31	38,655.53	14,992.89	15,106.77	41,277.55	14,822.66	28,692.14	40,690.03	43,450.06
85	98,249.78	29,893.84	18,953.81	39,119.62	15,091.63	15,250.35	41,772.98	14,924.75	28,989.92	41,178.54	43,971.55
86	99,290.36	30,231.93	19,079.34	39,583.83	15,190.37	15,393.94	42,268.55	15,026.86	29,287.77	41,667.18	44,493.22
87	100,331.17	30,570.12	19,204.88	40,048.14	15,289.11	15,537.54	42,764.31	15,129.00	29,585.68	42,155.93	45,015.06
88	101,372.21	30,908.42	19,330.44	40,512.57	15,387.85	15,681.16	43,260.22	15,231.15	29,883.64	42,644.81	45,537.07
89	102,413.49	31,246.81	19,456.03	40,977.11	15,486.59	15,824.77	43,756.29	15,333.33	30,181.67	43,133.80	46,059.26
90	103,455.00	31,585.31	19,581.64	41,441.75	15,585.33	15,968.40	44,252.53	15,435.52	30,479.76	43,622.90	46,581.62
91	104,496.76	31,923.91	19,707.28	41,906.52	15,684.07	16,112.04	44,748.94	15,537.75	30,777.91	44,112.13	47,104.14

Trial Length in Days	Trial length proxy A	Trial length proxy B	Trial length proxy C	Trial length proxy D	Trial length proxy E	Trial length proxy F	Trial length proxy G	Trial length proxy H	Trial length proxy I	Trial length proxy J	Trial length proxy K
92	105,538.75	32,262.61	19,832.94	42,371.40	15,782.81	16,255.69	45,245.50	15,639.99	31,076.13	44,601.46	47,626.84
93	106,580.97	32,601.42	19,958.62	42,836.38	15,881.55	16,399.34	45,742.23	15,742.26	31,374.41	45,090.93	48,149.72
94	107,623.43	32,940.33	20,084.33	43,301.48	15,980.29	16,543.00	46,239.13	15,844.55	31,672.75	45,580.50	48,672.77
95	108,666.13	33,279.34	20,210.06	43,766.69	16,079.03	16,686.67	46,736.19	15,946.87	31,971.15	46,070.20	49,195.98
96	109,709.06	33,618.46	20,335.82	44,232.02	16,177.77	16,830.35	47,233.40	16,049.19	32,269.62	46,560.02	49,719.38
97	110,752.22	33,957.68	20,461.60	44,697.46	16,276.51	16,974.04	47,730.79	16,151.51	32,568.14	47,049.95	50,242.94
98	111,795.63	34,297.00	20,587.40	45,163.00	16,375.25	17,117.74	48,228.34	16,253.84	32,866.73	47,540.00	50,766.68
99	112,839.26	34,636.42	20,713.23	45,628.66	16,473.99	17,261.45	48,726.06	16,356.16	33,165.39	48,030.17	51,290.59
100	113,883.13	34,975.94	20,839.07	46,094.43	16,572.73	17,405.16	49,223.93	16,458.49	33,464.09	48,520.45	51,814.66
101	114,927.24	35,315.57	20,964.94	46,560.32	16,671.47	17,548.89	49,721.97	16,560.81	33,762.88	49,010.86	52,338.92
102	115,971.58	35,655.29	21,090.84	47,026.31	16,770.21	17,692.61	50,220.18	16,663.13	34,061.71	49,501.38	52,863.34
103	117,016.17	35,995.12	21,216.77	47,492.43	16,868.95	17,836.35	50,718.54	16,765.46	34,360.61	49,992.03	53,387.95
104	118,060.98	36,335.06	21,342.70	47,958.65	16,967.69	17,980.10	51,217.08	16,867.78	34,659.57	50,482.78	53,912.71
105	119,106.03	36,675.10	21,468.63	48,424.97	17,066.43	18,123.86	51,715.78	16,970.10	34,958.60	50,973.66	54,437.66
106	120,151.32	37,015.23	21,594.56	48,891.42	17,165.17	18,267.63	52,214.52	17,072.43	35,257.69	51,464.66	54,962.66
107	121,196.84	37,355.44	21,720.49	49,357.97	17,263.91	18,411.40	52,713.27	17,174.75	35,556.84	51,955.77	55,487.65
108	122,242.60	37,695.64	21,846.43	49,824.66	17,362.66	18,555.18	53,212.02	17,277.07	35,856.05	52,447.00	56,012.65
109	123,288.60	38,035.85	21,972.36	50,291.43	17,461.40	18,698.98	53,710.76	17,379.40	36,155.33	52,938.35	56,537.64
110	124,334.83	38,376.05	22,098.29	50,758.32	17,560.14	18,842.77	54,209.51	17,481.72	36,454.66	53,429.81	57,062.64
111	125,381.29	38,716.26	22,224.22	51,225.34	17,658.88	18,986.59	54,708.26	17,584.04	36,754.06	53,921.40	57,587.63
112	126,427.99	39,056.46	22,350.15	51,692.45	17,757.62	19,130.40	55,207.00	17,686.37	37,053.52	54,413.10	58,112.63
113	127,474.93	39,396.66	22,476.09	52,159.69	17,856.36	19,274.23	55,705.74	17,788.69	37,353.05	54,904.92	58,637.63
114	128,522.10	39,736.87	22,602.02	52,627.02	17,955.10	19,418.07	56,204.49	17,891.01	37,652.64	55,396.86	59,162.62

Trial Length in Days	Trial length proxy A	Trial length proxy B	Trial length proxy C	Trial length proxy D	Trial length proxy E	Trial length proxy F	Trial length proxy G	Trial length proxy H	Trial length proxy I	Trial length proxy J	Trial length proxy K
115	129,569.51	40,077.07	22,727.95	53,094.47	18,053.84	19,561.91	56,703.23	17,993.34	37,952.28	55,888.92	59,687.62
116	130,617.15	40,417.28	22,853.88	53,562.04	18,152.58	19,705.76	57,201.98	18,095.66	38,251.99	56,381.10	60,212.61
117	131,665.03	40,757.48	22,979.81	54,029.72	18,251.32	19,849.62	57,700.72	18,197.98	38,551.77	56,873.39	60,737.61
118	132,713.15	41,097.69	23,105.74	54,497.51	18,350.06	19,993.49	58,199.47	18,300.31	38,851.60	57,365.80	61,262.60
119	133,761.50	41,437.89	23,231.68	54,965.41	18,448.80	20,137.37	58,698.22	18,402.63	39,151.50	57,858.33	61,787.60
120	134,810.09	41,778.09	23,357.61	55,433.43	18,547.54	20,281.26	59,196.96	18,504.95	39,451.46	58,350.98	62,312.60
121	135,858.91	42,118.30	23,483.54	55,901.56	18,646.28	20,425.15	59,695.71	18,607.28	39,751.48	58,843.74	62,837.59
122	136,892.03	42,458.50	23,609.47	56,362.76	18,745.02	20,568.43	60,194.46	18,709.60	40,047.31	59,329.22	63,362.59
123	137,925.16	42,798.71	23,735.40	56,823.97	18,843.76	20,711.70	60,693.20	18,811.92	40,343.13	59,814.69	63,887.58
124	138,958.29	43,134.92	23,859.50	57,285.16	18,942.50	20,854.97	61,190.98	18,914.25	40,638.96	60,300.17	64,411.56
125	139,991.41	43,470.02	23,983.54	57,746.36	19,041.24	20,998.25	61,682.25	19,016.57	40,934.79	60,785.64	64,928.68
126	141,024.54	43,805.11	24,107.58	58,207.57	19,139.98	21,141.51	62,173.51	19,118.83	41,230.61	61,271.11	65,445.80
127	142,057.67	44,140.22	24,231.63	58,668.77	19,238.72	21,284.79	62,664.77	19,219.63	41,526.44	61,756.60	65,962.93
128	143,090.79	44,475.32	24,355.67	59,129.97	19,337.46	21,428.07	63,156.04	19,320.42	41,822.27	62,242.07	66,480.04
129	144,123.92	44,810.42	24,479.71	59,591.17	19,436.20	21,571.34	63,647.30	19,421.20	42,118.09	62,727.54	66,997.17
130	145,157.05	45,145.52	24,603.75	60,052.37	19,534.94	21,714.61	64,138.57	19,521.99	42,413.92	63,213.02	67,514.29
131	146,190.17	45,480.62	24,727.80	60,513.57	19,633.69	21,857.89	64,629.84	19,622.78	42,709.75	63,698.49	68,031.40
132	147,223.30	45,815.73	24,851.84	60,974.77	19,732.43	22,001.16	65,121.10	19,723.57	43,005.57	64,183.97	68,548.53
133	148,256.43	46,150.83	24,975.88	61,435.97	19,831.17	22,144.43	65,612.37	19,824.36	43,301.40	64,669.45	69,065.65
134	149,289.56	46,485.92	25,099.92	61,897.17	19,929.91	22,287.70	66,103.63	19,925.15	43,597.23	65,154.92	69,582.77
135	150,322.68	46,821.03	25,223.97	62,358.37	20,028.65	22,430.98	66,594.89	20,025.93	43,893.06	65,640.39	70,099.89
136	151,355.80	47,156.13	25,348.02	62,819.57	20,127.39	22,574.26	67,086.16	20,126.72	44,188.89	66,125.87	70,617.01
137	152,388.94	47,491.23	25,472.06	63,280.77	20,226.13	22,717.52	67,577.42	20,227.51	44,484.71	66,611.34	71,134.14

Trial Length in Days	Trial length proxy A	Trial length proxy B	Trial length proxy C	Trial length proxy D	Trial length proxy E	Trial length proxy F	Trial length proxy G	Trial length proxy H	Trial length proxy I	Trial length proxy J	Trial length proxy K
138	153,422.06	47,826.33	25,596.10	63,741.98	20,324.87	22,860.80	68,068.69	20,328.30	44,780.54	67,096.82	71,651.25
139	154,455.18	48,161.43	25,720.14	64,203.18	20,423.61	23,004.08	68,559.96	20,429.09	45,076.37	67,582.29	72,168.37
140	155,488.31	48,496.54	25,844.19	64,664.38	20,522.35	23,147.34	69,051.22	20,529.88	45,372.20	68,067.77	72,685.50
141	156,521.44	48,831.63	25,968.23	65,125.58	20,621.09	23,290.62	69,542.49	20,630.66	45,668.02	68,553.24	73,202.61
142	157,554.57	49,166.74	26,092.27	65,586.78	20,719.83	23,433.90	70,033.75	20,731.46	45,963.85	69,038.71	73,719.74
143	158,587.69	49,501.84	26,216.31	66,047.99	20,818.57	23,577.17	70,525.01	20,832.25	46,259.68	69,524.20	74,236.86
144	159,620.82	49,836.94	26,340.36	66,509.19	20,917.31	23,720.44	71,016.28	20,933.03	46,555.50	70,009.67	74,753.97
145	160,653.95	50,172.04	26,464.40	66,970.38	21,016.05	23,863.71	71,507.55	21,033.82	46,851.33	70,495.14	75,271.10
146	161,687.07	50,507.14	26,588.44	67,431.59	21,114.79	24,006.99	71,998.81	21,134.60	47,147.16	70,980.62	75,788.22
147	162,720.20	50,842.25	26,712.49	67,892.79	21,213.53	24,150.26	72,490.07	21,235.40	47,442.98	71,466.09	76,305.34
148	163,753.33	51,177.34	26,836.53	68,354.00	21,312.27	24,293.53	72,981.34	21,336.19	47,738.81	71,951.57	76,822.46
149	164,786.45	51,512.44	26,960.57	68,815.19	21,411.01	24,436.81	73,472.60	21,436.97	48,034.64	72,437.05	77,339.58
150	165,819.58	51,847.55	27,084.61	69,276.39	21,509.75	24,580.09	73,963.86	21,537.76	48,330.46	72,922.52	77,856.71
151	166,852.71	52,182.65	27,208.66	69,737.60	21,608.49	24,723.35	74,455.13	21,638.55	48,626.29	73,407.99	78,373.82
152	167,885.84	52,517.74	27,332.70	70,198.80	21,707.23	24,866.63	74,946.39	21,739.34	48,922.12	73,893.47	78,890.94
153	168,918.96	52,852.85	27,456.74	70,660.00	21,805.97	25,009.91	75,437.66	21,840.13	49,217.94	74,378.94	79,408.07
154	169,952.09	53,187.95	27,580.78	71,121.20	21,904.71	25,153.17	75,928.92	21,940.92	49,513.77	74,864.42	79,925.18
155	170,985.22	53,523.06	27,704.83	71,582.40	22,003.46	25,296.45	76,420.19	22,041.70	49,809.60	75,349.90	80,442.31
156	172,018.34	53,858.15	27,828.87	72,043.61	22,102.20	25,439.72	76,911.46	22,142.49	50,105.42	75,835.37	80,959.43
157	173,051.46	54,193.25	27,952.91	72,504.80	22,200.94	25,583.00	77,402.71	22,243.29	50,401.25	76,320.84	81,476.54
158	174,084.60	54,528.36	28,076.95	72,966.01	22,299.68	25,726.27	77,893.98	22,344.07	50,697.08	76,806.32	81,993.67
159	175,117.72	54,863.46	28,201.00	73,427.21	22,398.42	25,869.54	78,385.25	22,444.86	50,992.90	77,291.80	82,510.79
160	176,150.85	55,198.56	28,325.05	73,888.41	22,497.16	26,012.82	78,876.51	22,545.65	51,288.73	77,777.27	83,027.91

Trial Length in Days	Trial length proxy A	Trial length proxy B	Trial length proxy C	Trial length proxy D	Trial length proxy E	Trial length proxy F	Trial length proxy G	Trial length proxy H	Trial length proxy I	Trial length proxy J	Trial length proxy K
161	177,183.97	55,533.66	28,449.09	74,349.61	22,595.90	26,156.09	79,367.78	22,646.43	51,584.56	78,262.75	83,545.03
162	178,217.10	55,868.76	28,573.13	74,810.81	22,694.64	26,299.36	79,859.05	22,747.23	51,880.38	78,748.22	84,062.15
163	179,250.23	56,203.86	28,697.17	75,272.02	22,793.38	26,442.64	80,350.31	22,848.02	52,176.21	79,233.69	84,579.28
164	180,283.35	56,538.96	28,821.22	75,733.22	22,892.12	26,585.91	80,841.57	22,948.80	52,472.04	79,719.17	85,096.39
165	181,316.49	56,874.07	28,945.26	76,194.41	22,990.86	26,729.18	81,332.84	23,049.59	52,767.86	80,204.65	85,613.51
166	182,349.61	57,209.17	29,069.30	76,655.62	23,089.60	26,872.46	81,824.10	23,150.38	53,063.69	80,690.12	86,130.64
167	183,382.73	57,544.26	29,193.34	77,116.82	23,188.34	27,015.73	82,315.37	23,251.17	53,359.52	81,175.59	86,647.75
168	184,415.86	57,879.37	29,317.39	77,578.03	23,287.08	27,159.00	82,806.64	23,351.96	53,655.34	81,661.07	87,164.88
169	185,448.99	58,214.47	29,441.43	78,039.22	23,385.82	27,302.28	83,297.90	23,452.75	53,951.17	82,146.54	87,682.00
170	186,482.11	58,549.57	29,565.47	78,500.42	23,484.56	27,445.55	83,789.17	23,553.53	54,247.00	82,632.02	88,199.11
171	187,515.24	58,884.67	29,689.51	78,961.63	23,583.30	27,588.83	84,280.43	23,654.32	54,542.83	83,117.50	88,716.24
172	188,548.37	59,219.77	29,813.56	79,422.83	23,682.04	27,732.10	84,771.69	23,755.11	54,838.66	83,602.97	89,233.36
173	189,581.50	59,554.88	29,937.60	79,884.03	23,780.78	27,875.37	85,262.95	23,855.90	55,134.49	84,088.44	89,750.49
174	190,614.62	59,889.97	30,061.64	80,345.23	23,879.52	28,018.65	85,754.22	23,956.69	55,430.31	84,573.92	90,267.60
175	191,647.74	60,225.07	30,185.69	80,806.43	23,978.26	28,161.92	86,245.48	24,057.47	55,726.14	85,059.40	90,784.72
176	192,680.88	60,560.18	30,309.73	81,267.63	24,077.00	28,305.19	86,736.75	24,158.26	56,021.97	85,544.87	91,301.85
177	193,714.00	60,895.28	30,433.77	81,728.83	24,175.74	28,448.47	87,228.01	24,259.06	56,317.79	86,030.35	91,818.96
178	194,747.13	61,230.38	30,557.81	82,190.03	24,274.49	28,591.74	87,719.28	24,359.84	56,613.62	86,515.82	92,336.09
179	195,780.26	61,565.48	30,681.86	82,651.23	24,373.23	28,735.01	88,210.54	24,460.63	56,909.45	87,001.29	92,853.21
180	196,813.38	61,900.58	30,805.90	83,112.43	24,471.97	28,878.29	88,701.80	24,561.42	57,205.27	87,486.77	93,370.32
181	197,846.51	62,235.69	30,929.95	83,573.63	24,570.71	29,021.56	89,193.07	24,662.20	57,501.10	87,972.25	93,887.45
182	198,879.63	62,570.78	31,053.99	84,034.83	24,669.45	29,164.83	89,684.34	24,763.00	57,796.93	88,457.72	94,404.57
183	199,912.76	62,905.89	31,178.03	84,496.04	24,766.77	29,308.11	90,175.60	24,863.79	58,092.75	88,943.20	94,921.69

Trial Length in Days	Trial length proxy A	Trial length proxy B	Trial length proxy C	Trial length proxy D	Trial length proxy E	Trial length proxy F	Trial length proxy G	Trial length proxy H	Trial length proxy I	Trial length proxy J	Trial length proxy K
184	200,945.89	63,240.99	31,302.08	84,957.24	24,864.03	29,451.38	90,666.87	24,964.57	58,388.58	89,428.67	95,438.81
185	201,979.01	63,576.09	31,426.12	85,418.43	24,961.29	29,594.66	91,158.14	25,065.36	58,684.41	89,914.14	95,955.93
186	203,012.14	63,911.19	31,550.16	85,879.64	25,058.55	29,737.93	91,649.40	25,166.15	58,980.23	90,399.63	96,473.06
187	204,045.27	64,246.29	31,674.20	86,340.84	25,155.81	29,881.20	92,140.66	25,266.94	59,276.06	90,885.10	96,990.17
188	205,078.39	64,581.39	31,798.25	86,802.05	25,253.07	30,024.48	92,631.93	25,367.73	59,571.89	91,370.57	97,507.29
189	206,111.52	64,916.49	31,922.29	87,263.24	25,350.33	30,167.74	93,123.19	25,468.52	59,867.71	91,856.04	98,024.42
190	207,144.65	65,251.59	32,046.33	87,724.44	25,447.59	30,311.02	93,614.46	25,569.30	60,163.54	92,341.52	98,541.53
191	208,177.78	65,586.70	32,170.37	88,185.65	25,544.85	30,454.30	94,105.73	25,670.09	60,459.37	92,827.00	99,058.66
192	209,210.90	65,921.80	32,294.42	88,646.85	25,642.11	30,597.57	94,596.99	25,770.89	60,755.19	93,312.47	99,575.78
193	210,244.03	66,256.89	32,418.46	89,108.05	25,739.37	30,740.84	95,088.26	25,871.67	61,051.02	93,797.95	100,092.89
194	211,277.16	66,592.00	32,542.50	89,569.25	25,836.63	30,884.12	95,579.52	25,972.46	61,346.85	94,283.42	100,610.02
195	212,310.28	66,927.10	32,666.54	90,030.45	25,933.89	31,027.39	96,070.78	26,073.25	61,642.67	94,768.89	101,127.14
196	213,343.40	67,262.20	32,790.59	90,491.66	26,031.15	31,170.66	96,562.05	26,174.03	61,938.50	95,254.37	101,644.26
197	214,376.54	67,597.30	32,914.63	90,952.85	26,128.41	31,313.93	97,053.30	26,274.83	62,234.33	95,739.85	102,161.38
198	215,409.66	67,932.40	33,038.67	91,414.06	26,225.67	31,457.21	97,544.57	26,375.62	62,530.15	96,225.32	102,678.50
199	216,442.79	68,267.51	33,162.71	91,875.26	26,322.93	31,600.49	98,035.84	26,476.40	62,825.98	96,710.80	103,195.63
200	217,475.91	68,602.60	33,286.76	92,336.46	26,420.19	31,743.75	98,527.10	26,577.19	63,121.81	97,196.27	103,712.74

Cracked trials and guilty pleas where the number of pages of prosecution evidence exceeds the PPE Cut-off

G-72

7.—(1) Where in a cracked trial or guilty plea the number of pages of prosecution evidence exceeds the PPE Cut-off specified in the tables following paragraph 4(1) as appropriate to the offence with which the assisted person is charged, the total fee payable to the litigator will be—

    (a) the final fee, calculated in accordance with sub-paragraph (2) of this paragraph;

    (b) the defendant uplift, if any, calculated in accordance with the table following paragraph 9; and

    (c) the adjustment for transfers and retrials, if any, calculated in accordance with paragraph 10.

(2) For the purposes of sub-paragraph (1), the final fee payable to a litigator in a cracked trial or guilty plea will be calculated in accordance with the following formula—

$$F = I + (D \times i)$$

(3) In the formula in sub-paragraph (2)—

    F is the amount of the final fee;

    I is the initial fee specified in the tables following this paragraph, as appropriate to the type of case, the offence with which the assisted person is charged and the number of pages of prosecution evidence;

    D is the difference between—

    (a) the number of pages of prosecution evidence in the case; and

    (b) the lower number in the PPE range as specified in the tables following this paragraph, as appropriate to the type of case, the offence with which the assisted person is charged and the number of pages of prosecution evidence in the case;

    i is the incremental fee per page of prosecution evidence specified in the tables following this paragraph, as appropriate to the type of case, the offence with which the assisted person is charged and the number of pages of prosecution evidence in the case.

TABLE OF FINAL FEES IN CRACKED TRIALS

Class of Offence	PPE Range	Initial Fee (£)	Incremental fee per page of prosecution evidence (£)
A	0–149	2,785.18	0
A	150–249	2,785.18	16.5771
A	250–499	4,442.89	16.2953
A	500–999	8,516.71	8.9555
A	1000–2799	12,994.44	5.7143
A	2800–4599	23,280.20	5.7143
A	4600–6399	33,565.95	5.7143
A	6400–8199	43,851.70	5.7143

Class of Offence	PPE Range	Initial Fee (£)	Incremental fee per page of prosecution evidence (£)
A	8200–9998	54,137.46	5.7143
A	9999–99999	64,417.49	5.7143
B	0–69	1,036.20	0
B	70–249	1,036.20	11.4339
B	250–999	3,094.31	5.3516
B	1000–2799	7,108.03	3.5644
B	2800–4599	13,524.03	3.5644
B	4600–6399	19,940.03	2.9971
B	6400–8199	25,334.77	2.9971
B	8200–9998	30,729.49	2.9971
B	9999–99999	36,121.23	2.9971
C	0–39	766.89	0
C	40–249	766.89	5.7329
C	250–999	1,970.80	3.2814
C	1000–2799	4,431.86	2.0898
C	2800–4599	8,193.57	2.0898
C	4600–6399	11,955.28	2.0898
C	6400–8199	15,716.99	2.0898
C	8200–9998	19,478.70	2.0898
C	9999–99999	23,238.32	2.0899
D	0–79	1,255.67	0
D	80–249	1,255.67	14.8109
D	250–999	3,773.52	8.9254
D	1000–2799	10,467.60	5.2700
D	2800–4599	19,953.59	5.2700
D	4600–6399	29,439.57	4.3244
D	6400–8199	37,223.44	4.3244
D	8200–9998	45,007.29	4.3244

Class of Offence	PPE Range	Initial Fee (£)	Incremental fee per page of prosecution evidence (£)
D	9999–99999	52,786.83	4.3243
E	0–39	340.50	0
E	40–249	340.50	6.7242
E	250–999	1,752.59	2.1277
E	1000–2799	3,348.37	0.8919
E	2800–4599	4,953.80	0.8919
E	4600–6399	6,559.23	0.8919
E	6400–8199	8,164.66	0.8919
E	8200–9998	9,770.09	0.8919
E	9999–99999	11,374.63	0.8919
F	0–49	327.63	0
F	50–249	327.63	6.4534
F	250–999	1,618.30	2.6162
F	1000–2799	3,580.48	1.0182
F	2800–4599	5,413.21	1.0182
F	4600–6399	7,245.94	1.0182
F	6400–8199	9,078.67	1.0182
F	8200–9998	10,911.40	1.0182
F	9999–99999	12,743.11	1.0182
G	0–119	1,074.22	0
G	120–249	1,074.22	9.0709
G	250–999	2,253.44	6.8647
G	1000–2799	7,401.94	6.0530
G	2800–4599	18,297.33	6.0530
G	4600–6399	29,192.73	5.2019
G	6400–8199	38,556.20	5.2019
G	8200–9998	47,919.68	5.2019

Class of Offence	PPE Range	Initial Fee (£)	Incremental fee per page of prosecution evidence (£)
G	9999–99999	57,277.96	5.2020
H	0–39	346.31	0
H	40–249	346.31	6.2247
H	250–999	1,653.49	2.2728
H	1000–2799	3,358.10	1.0168
H	2800–4599	5,188.37	1.0168
H	4600–6399	7,018.63	1.0168
H	6400–8199	8,848.89	1.0168
H	8200–9998	10,679.16	1.0168
H	9999–99999	12,508.40	1.0168
I	0–39	370.66	0
I	40–249	370.66	8.6497
I	250–999	2,187.10	3.3804
I	1000–2799	4,722.43	1.3114
I	2800–4599	7,082.89	1.3114
I	4600–6399	9,443.34	1.3114
I	6400–8199	11,803.80	1.3114
I	8200–9998	14,164.26	1.3114
I	9999–99999	16,523.40	1.3114
J	0–79	1,321.76	0
J	80–249	1,321.76	15.6288
J	250–999	3,978.65	9.8095
J	1000–2799	11,335.74	5.7334
J	2800–4599	21,655.89	5.7334
J	4600–6399	31,976.05	4.5514
J	6400–8199	40,168.54	4.5514
J	8200–9998	48,361.04	4.5514
J	9999–99999	56,548.99	4.5514

Class of Offence	PPE Range	Initial Fee (£)	Incremental fee per page of prosecution evidence (£)
K	0–119	1,130.76	0
K	120–249	1,130.76	9.5650
K	250–999	2,374.21	7.3335
K	1000–2799	7,874.30	6.4212
K	2800–4599	19,432.39	6.4212
K	4600–6399	30,990.49	5.4755
K	6400–8199	40,846.45	5.4755
K	8200–9998	50,702.41	5.4755
K	9999–99999	60,552.89	5.4756

TABLE OF FINAL FEES IN GUILTY PLEAS

Class of offence	PPE Range	Initial fee (£)	Incremental fee per page of prosecution evidence (£)
A	0–149	1,907.11	0
A	150–399	1,907.11	9.2742
A	400–999	4,225.66	5.3634
A	1000–2799	7,443.69	3.8000
A	2800–4599	14,283.77	3.8001
A	4600–6399	21,123.86	3.8001
A	6400–8199	27,963.96	3.8001
A	8200–9998	34,804.05	3.8001
A	9999–99999	41,640.34	3.8001
B	0–69	609.44	0
B	70–399	609.44	4.9497
B	400–999	2,242.84	2.4934
B	1000–2799	3,738.90	1.5916
B	2800–4599	6,603.75	1.5916
B	4600–6399	9,468.61	1.1661

Class of offence	PPE Range	Initial fee (£)	Incremental fee per page of prosecution evidence (£)
B	6400–8199	11,567.51	1.1661
B	8200–9998	13,666.41	1.1661
B	9999–99999	15,764.14	1.1661
C	0–39	485.38	0
C	40–399	485.38	2.9193
C	400–999	1,536.31	1.5971
C	1000–2799	2,494.54	0.8668
C	2800–4599	4,054.72	0.8668
C	4600–6399	5,614.91	0.8668
C	6400–8199	7,175.10	0.8668
C	8200–9998	8,735.29	0.8668
C	9999–99999	10,294.60	0.8668
D	0–79	708.34	0
D	80–399	708.34	5.7339
D	400–999	2,543.19	3.0095
D	1000–2799	4,348.90	1.8739
D	2800–4599	7,721.86	1.8739
D	4600–6399	11,094.83	1.1647
D	6400–8199	13,191.21	1.1646
D	8200–9998	15,287.57	1.1647
D	9999–99999	17,382.78	1.1647
E	0–39	202.41	0
E	40–399	202.41	3.2041
E	400–999	1,355.88	1.3732
E	1000–2799	2,179.80	0.5057
E	2800–4599	3,090.08	0.5057
E	4600–6399	4,000.36	0.5057
E	6400–8199	4,910.64	0.5057

Class of offence	PPE Range	Initial fee (£)	Incremental fee per page of prosecution evidence (£)
E	8200–9998	5,820.92	0.5057
E	9999–99999	6,730.69	0.5057
F	0–49	214.59	0
F	50–399	214.59	3.1058
F	400–999	1,301.62	1.0840
F	1000–2799	1,952.01	0.3488
F	2800–4599	2,579.80	0.3488
F	4600–6399	3,207.59	0.3488
F	6400–8199	3,835.38	0.3488
F	8200–9998	4,463.17	0.3488
F	9999–99999	5,090.61	0.3488
G	0–119	667.17	0
G	120–399	667.17	4.7216
G	400–999	1,989.23	3.0953
G	1000–2799	3,846.43	2.7317
G	2800–4599	8,763.51	2.7317
G	4600–6399	13,680.59	2.1643
G	6400–8199	17,576.39	2.1643
G	8200–9998	21,472.20	2.1643
G	9999–99999	25,365.84	2.1643
H	0–39	209.28	0
H	40–399	209.28	3.0613
H	400–999	1,311.33	1.0852
H	1000–2799	1,962.46	0.3465
H	2800–4599	2,586.14	0.3465
H	4600–6399	3,209.84	0.3465
H	6400–8199	3,833.53	0.3465

Class of offence	PPE Range	Initial fee (£)	Incremental fee per page of prosecution evidence (£)
H	8200–9998	4,457.23	0.3465
H	9999–99999	5,080.55	0.3465
I	0–39	191.34	0
I	40–399	191.34	3.4214
I	400–999	1,423.04	1.4936
I	1000–2799	2,319.22	0.5581
I	2800–4599	3,323.86	0.5581
I	4600–6399	4,328.49	0.5581
I	6400–8199	5,333.13	0.5581
I	8200–9998	6,337.78	0.5581
I	9999–99999	7,341.86	0.5581
J	0–79	745.63	0
J	80–399	745.63	6.1572
J	400–999	2,715.93	3.2471
J	1000–2799	4,664.21	2.0766
J	2800–4599	8,402.07	2.0766
J	4600–6399	12,139.92	1.2255
J	6400–8199	14,345.86	1.2255
J	8200–9998	16,551.81	1.2255
J	9999–99999	18,756.53	1.2255
K	0–119	702.29	0
K	120–399	702.29	5.7624
K	400–999	2,315.76	3.2075
K	1000–2799	4,240.26	2.9871
K	2800–4599	9,617.04	2.9871
K	4600–6399	14,993.82	2.2779
K	6400–8199	19,094.01	2.2779

Class of offence	PPE Range	Initial fee (£)	Incremental fee per page of prosecution evidence (£)
K	8200–9998	23,194.20	2.2779
K	9999–99999	27,292.10	2.2779

Trials where the number of pages of prosecution evidence exceeds the PPE Cut-off

G–72a

8.—(1) Where in a trial the number of pages of prosecution evidence exceeds the PPE Cut-off figure specified in the table following paragraph 4(2) as appropriate t the offence for which the assisted person is tried and the length of trial, the total fe payable to the litigator will be—

    (a) the final fee, calculated in accordance with sub-paragraph (2) of th paragraph;

    (b) the defendant uplift, if any, calculated in accordance with the table follow ing paragraph 9; and

    (c) the adjustment for transfers and retrials, if any, calculated in accordanc with paragraph 10.

(2) For the purposes of sub-paragraph (1), the final fee will be calculated in accor dance with the following formula—

$$F = I + (D \times i)$$

(3) In the formula in sub-paragraph (2)—

    F is the amount of the final fee;

    I is the initial fee specified in the table following this paragraph, as ap propriate to the offence for which the assisted person is tried and th number of pages of prosecution evidence;

    D is the difference between—

    (a) the number of pages of prosecution evidence in the case; and

    (b) the lower number in the PPE range as specified in the table followin this paragraph, as appropriate to the offence for which the assiste person is tried and the number of pages of prosecution evidence i the case;

    i is the incremental fee per page of prosecution evidence specified i the table following this paragraph, as appropriate to the offence fc which the assisted person is tried and the number of pages of prose cution evidence in the case.

TABLE OF FINAL FEES IN TRIALS

Offence Class	PPE Range	Initial Fee	Incremental fee per page
A	0–149	2,785.18	0
A	150–599	2,785.18	16.3759
A	600–1099	10,154.34	14.6753
A	1100–1899	17,491.98	13.0799
A	1900–3299	27,955.92	11.6330
A	3300–4999	44,242.16	11.6330
A	5000–5999	64,018.33	11.6331
A	6000–6999	75,651.38	11.6330
A	7000–7999	87,284.42	11.6330
A	8000–8999	98,917.44	11.6330

Offence Class	PPE Range	Initial Fee	Incremental fee per page
A	9000–9998	110,550.46	11.6330
A	9999–99999	122,171.85	11.6330
B	0–69	1,202.92	0
B	70–199	1,202.92	14.0353
B	200–499	3,027.51	12.5398
B	500–899	6,789.46	10.5557
B	900–1299	11,011.74	8.8680
B	1300–1999	14,558.94	7.7722
B	2000–3299	19,999.46	7.7722
B	3300–4999	30,103.28	7.7722
B	5000–5999	43,315.97	7.7722
B	6000–7999	51,088.14	7.7722
B	8000–8999	66,632.48	7.7722
B	9000–9998	74,404.65	7.7722
B	9999–99999	82,169.05	7.7722
C	0–39	810.51	0
C	40–299	810.51	11.5783
C	300–799	3,820.87	10.1155
C	800–1249	8,878.62	8.4660
C	1250–1999	12,688.32	7.4854
C	2000–3199	18,302.39	5.1761
C	3200–4559	24,513.74	5.1761
C	4560–5919	31,553.29	5.1761
C	5920–7279	38,592.83	5.1761
C	7280–8639	45,632.37	5.1761
C	8640–9998	52,671.91	5.1762
C	9999–99999	59,706.30	5.1762
D	0–79	1,527.89	0
D	80–209	1,527.89	17.2578
D	210–699	3,771.41	13.1781
D	700–1049	10,228.68	11.0609
D	1050–1999	14,100.00	9.5912
D	2000–3599	23,211.67	8.7658
D	3600–5199	37,236.90	8.7658
D	5200–6799	51,262.14	8.7658
D	6800–8399	65,287.39	8.7658
D	8400–9998	79,312.63	8.7658
D	9999–99999	93,329.10	8.7658
E	0–39	386.54	0
E	40–69	386.54	10.4287
E	70–129	699.40	9.3950
E	130–599	1,263.10	9.0869
E	600–1349	5,533.96	5.9649
E	1350–2999	10,007.63	2.6174
E	3000–4749	14,326.32	2.6174
E	4750–6499	18,906.75	2.6174

Offence Class	PPE Range	Initial Fee	Incremental fee per page
E	6500–8249	23,487.17	2.6174
E	8250–9998	28,067.60	2.6174
E	9999–99999	32,645.40	2.6174
F	0–49	391.89	0
F	50–229	391.89	8.0098
F	230–699	1,833.66	7.6326
F	700–1399	5,420.98	6.1357
F	1400–1949	9,715.95	4.7354
F	1950–3549	12,320.41	2.3624
F	3550–5149	16,100.18	2.3624
F	5150–6749	19,879.95	2.3624
F	6750–8349	23,659.72	2.3624
F	8350–9998	27,439.49	2.3624
F	9999–99999	31,335.02	2.3624
G	0–119	1,074.22	0
G	120–734	1,074.22	9.0131
G	735–1289	6,617.28	9.0746
G	1290–2399	11,653.69	9.2375
G	2400–4499	21,907.31	9.2029
G	4500–7999	41,233.37	9.2029
G	8000–8399	73,443.48	9.2029
G	8400–8799	77,124.64	9.2029
G	8800–9199	80,805.79	9.2029
G	9200–9599	84,486.95	9.2029
G	9600–9998	88,168.10	9.2029
G	9999–99999	91,840.06	9.2029
H	0–39	392.05	0
H	40–249	392.05	9.4203
H	250–619	2,370.32	7.8338
H	620–1299	5,268.81	5.8194
H	1300–2999	9,226.02	4.6188
H	3000–4999	17,077.91	2.4911
H	5000–5999	22,060.10	2.4910
H	6000–6999	24,551.12	2.4911
H	7000–7999	27,042.22	2.4911
H	8000–8999	29,533.32	2.4911
H	9000–9998	32,024.42	2.4911
H	9999–99999	34,513.02	2.4910
I	0–39	391.72	0
I	40–369	391.72	10.0165
I	370–799	3,697.16	9.9618
I	800–1299	7,980.75	9.8555
I	1300–2699	12,908.52	7.7641
I	2700–4199	23,778.23	3.3365
I	4200–5359	28,783.04	3.3365
I	5360–6519	32,653.42	3.3365

Offence Class	PPE Range	Initial Fee	Incremental fee per page
I	6520–7679	36,523.80	3.3366
I	7680–8839	40,394.20	3.3365
I	8840–9998	44,264.58	3.3365
I	9999–99999	48,131.63	3.3365
J	0–79	1,608.31	0
J	80–209	1,608.31	18.1662
J	210–699	3,969.91	13.8717
J	700–1049	10,767.03	11.6431
J	1050–1999	14,842.10	10.0960
J	2000–3599	24,433.34	9.2271
J	3600–5199	39,196.75	9.2271
J	5200–6799	53,960.15	9.2271
J	6800–8399	68,723.57	9.2271
J	8400–9998	83,486.98	9.2271
J	9999–99999	98,241.16	9.2272
K	0–119	1,130.76	0
K	120–734	1,130.76	9.4875
K	735–1289	6,965.55	9.5522
K	1290–2399	12,267.04	9.7237
K	2400–4499	23,060.31	9.6873
K	4500–7999	43,403.55	9.6873
K	8000–8399	77,308.93	9.6872
K	8400–8799	81,183.82	9.6872
K	8800–9199	85,058.72	9.6873
K	9200–9599	88,933.63	9.6872
K	9600–9998	92,808.53	9.6872
K	9999–99999	96,673.74	9.6872

Defendant uplifts

9.—(1) The defendant uplift payable to a litigator will be calculated in accordance **G–73** with the table following sub-paragraph (3).

(2) Only one defendant uplift will be payable in each case.

(3) In the table following this paragraph, the total fee means—

    (a) in a cracked trial or guilty plea where the number of pages of prosecution evidence does not exceed the PPE Cut-off specified in the table following paragraph 4(1), the basic fee specified in the table following paragraph 5(2);

    (b) in a trial where the number of pages of prosecution evidence does not exceed the PPE Cut-off specified in the table following paragraph 4(2), the basic fee specified in the table following paragraph 6(2) plus the length of trial proxy specified in the table following paragraph 6(3);

    (c) in a cracked trial or guilty plea where the number of pages of prosecution evidence exceeds the PPE Cut-off specified in the table following paragraph 4(1), the final fee, as calculated in accordance with paragraph 7(2); and

    (d) in a trial where the number of pages of prosecution evidence exceeds the PPE Cut-off specified in the table following paragraph 4(2), the final fee, as calculated in accordance with paragraph 8(2).

DEFENDANT UPLIFTS

Total number of defendants represented by litigator	Percentage uplift to total fee
2–4	20%
5+	30%

Retrials and transfers

G–73a   10.—(1) Where following a trial an order is made for a retrial and the same litigator acts for the assisted person at both trials that litigator will receive—

(a) in respect of the first trial, a fee calculated in accordance with the provisions of this Schedule; and

(b) in respect of the retrial, 25% of the fee, as appropriate to the circumstances and timing of the retrial, in accordance with the provisions of this Schedule.

(2) Where—

(a) a case is transferred to a new litigator; or

(b) a retrial is ordered and a new litigator acts for the assisted person at the retrial;

the original litigator and the new litigator must receive a percentage of the total fee, in accordance with the table following sub-paragraph (6), as appropriate to the circumstances and timing of the retrial, transfer or withdrawal of the representation order.

(3) Where a representation order is withdrawn before the case ends, a litigator must receive a percentage of the total fee, in accordance with the table following sub-paragraph (6), as appropriate to the circumstances and timing of a transfer.

(4) In the table following this paragraph, the total fee means—

(a) in a cracked trial or guilty plea where the number of pages of prosecution evidence is less than or equal to the PPE Cut-off specified in the table following paragraph 4(1), the basic fee as set out in the table following paragraph 5(2);

(b) in a trial where the number of pages of prosecution evidence is less than or equal to the PPE Cut-off specified in the table following paragraph 4(2) the basic fee specified in the table following paragraph 6(2) plus the length of trial proxy specified in the table following paragraph 6(3);

(c) in a cracked trial or guilty plea where the number of pages of prosecution evidence exceeds the PPE Cut-off specified in the table following paragraph 4(1), the final fee, as calculated in accordance with paragraph 7(2); and

(d) in a trial where the number of pages of prosecution evidence exceeds the PPE Cut-off specified in the table following paragraph 4(2), the final fee, as calculated in accordance with paragraph 8(2).

(5) Where a case becomes a Very High Cost Case after a representation order has been granted and is transferred from the litigator named on the representation order to a new litigator—

(a) the original litigator will be remunerated in accordance with the table following this paragraph; and

(b) the new litigator will be remunerated in accordance with the individual contract which applies to the case.

(6) Where a case becomes a Very High Cost Case after a representation order has been granted and the representation order is withdrawn before the end of the case, the litigator will be remunerated in accordance with the table following this paragraph as appropriate to the circumstances and timing of the withdrawal.

RETRIALS AND TRANSFERS

Scenario	Percent-age of the total fee	Case type used to determine total fee	Claim period
Cracked trial before retrial, where there is no change of litigator	25%	Cracked trial	—
Retrial, where there is no change of litigator	25%	Trial	—
Up to and including plea and case management hearing transfer (original litigator)	25%	Cracked trial	—
Up to and including plea and case management hearing transfer — guilty plea (new litigator)	100%	Guilty plea	—
Up to and including plea and case management hearing transfer — cracked trial (new litigator)	100%	Cracked trial	—
Up to and including plea and case management hearing transfer — trial (new litigator)	100%	Trial	—
Before trial transfer (original litigator)	75%	Cracked trial	—
Before trial transfer — cracked trial (new litigator)	100%	Cracked trial	—
Before trial transfer — trial (new litigator)	100%	Trial	—
During trial transfer (original litigator)	100%	Trial	Claim up to and including the day before the transfer
During trial transfer (new litigator)	50%	Trial	Claim for the full trial length
During trial transfer - retrial (new litigator)	25%	Trial	Claim for the full retrial length
Transfer before retrial (original litigator)	25%	Cracked trial	—
Transfer before cracked retrial (new litigator)	50%	Cracked trial	
Transfer before retrial (new litigator)	50%	Trial	Claim for the full retrial length
Transfer during or after retrial (original litigator)	25%	Trial	Claim up to and including the day before the transfer
Transfer during or after retrial (new litigator)	50%	Trial	Claim for the full retrial length

PART 3

FIXED FEES

General provisions

G–74   11. Except as provided under this Part, remuneration for all work undertaken by a litigator is included within the fee set out in Part 2 of this Schedule as appropriate to—

    (a) the offence for which the assisted person is charged or tried;

    (b) whether the case is a cracked trial, guilty plea or trial; and

    (c) the number of pages of prosecution evidence.

Fees for appeals and committals for sentence hearings

G–74a   12. The fee payable to a litigator instructed in—

    (a) an appeal against conviction from a magistrates' court;

    (b) an appeal against sentence from a magistrates' court;

    (c) a sentencing hearing following a committal for sentence to the Crown Court.

is that set out in the table following paragraph 14.

Fees for contempt proceedings

G–75   13. This paragraph applies to proceedings referred to in section 12(2)(f) of the Act in the Crown Court.

(2) Where, in proceedings to which this paragraph applies, the contempt is alleged to have been committed by a person other than a defendant in a case to which this Schedule applies, remuneration for litigators must be at the rate set out in the table following paragraph 14.

(3) Where, in proceedings to which this paragraph applies, the contempt is alleged to have been committed by the defendant in a case to which this Schedule applies, all work undertaken by the litigator is included within—

    (a) the fee payable under Part 2 of this Schedule, or

    (b) in proceedings under paragraph 12 or 14, the fixed fee set out in the table following paragraph 14.

Fees for alleged breaches of a Crown Court order

G–75a   14.—(1) This paragraph applies to proceedings in the Crown Court against one assisted person arising out of a single alleged breach of an order of the Crown Court.

(2) Where the litigator instructed in proceedings to which this paragraph applies was also instructed in the proceedings in which the Crown Court order was made, all work undertaken by the litigator is included within—

    (a) the fee payable under Part 2 of this Schedule, for the original case; or

    (b) in proceedings under paragraph 12, the fixed fee set out in the table following this paragraph for the original case.

(3) Where the litigator instructed in proceedings to which this paragraph applies was not instructed in the proceedings in which the Crown Court order was made, the fee payable to the litigator in respect of the proceedings to which this paragraph applies is that set out in the table following this sub-paragraph.

FIXED FEES

Type of proceedings	Paragraph providing for fee	Fee payable (£ per proceedings)
Appeal against sentence from a magistrates' Court	12	127.66
Appeal against conviction from a magistrates' Court	12	340.43
Committal for sentence	12	212.77
Contempt proceedings (where contempt is alleged to have been committed by a person other than the defendant)	13(2)	127.66
Alleged breach of a Crown Court order	14(3)	85.11

Fees for special preparation

15.—(1) This paragraph applies where, in any case on indictment in the Crown **G–76**
Court in respect of which a fee is payable under part 2, any or all of the prosecution
evidence, as defined in paragraph 1(2), is served in electronic form only, and the appropriate officer considers it reasonable to make a payment in excess of the fee payable under Part 2.

(2) Where this paragraph applies, a special preparation fee may be paid, in addition to the fee payable under Part 2.

(3) The amount of the special preparation fee must be calculated from the number of hours which the appropriate officer considers reasonable to view the prosecution evidence, and using the rates specified in the table following paragraph 22.

(4) A litigator claiming a special preparation fee must supply such information and documents as may be required by the appropriate officer in support of the claim.

(5) In determining a claim under this paragraph, the appropriate officer must take into account all the relevant circumstances of the case.

Discontinuance or dismissal of sent or transferred proceedings

16.—(1) This paragraph applies to proceedings which are— **G–76a**

    (a) sent for trial to the Crown Court under section 51 of the *Crime and Disorder Act* 1998 (no committal proceedings for indictable-only offences); or

    (b) transferred to the Crown Court under—

        (i) section 4 of the *Criminal Justice Act* 1987 (transfer of serious fraud cases); or

        (ii) section 53 of the *Criminal Justice Act* 1991 (transfer of certain cases involving children).

(2) Where proceedings to which this paragraph applies are discontinued by a notice served under section 23A of the *Prosecution of Offences Act* 1985 (discontinuance of proceedings after accused has been sent for trial) at any time before the prosecution serves its evidence in accordance with the *Crime and Disorder Act 1998 (Service of Prosecution Evidence) Regulations* 2005 the litigator must be paid 50 percent of the Basic fee for a guilty plea, as specified in the table following paragraph 5, as appropriate to the offence for which the assisted person is charged.

(3) Where proceedings to which this paragraph applies are discontinued by a notice served under section 23A of the *Prosecution of Offences Act* 1985 (discontinuance of proceedings after accused has been sent for trial) at any time after the prosecution serves its evidence in accordance with the *Crime and Disorder Act 1998 (Service of Prosecution Evidence) Regulations* 2005, the litigator must be paid a fee calculated in accordance with paragraph 5, or, where appropriate, paragraph 7, as appropriate for representing an assisted person in a guilty plea.

(4) Where an application for dismissal is made under paragraph 2 of Schedule 3 to the *Crime and Disorder Act* 1998, section 6 of the *Criminal Justice Act* 1987 or paragraph 5 of Schedule 6 to the *Criminal Justice Act* 1991, and—

(a) the charge, or charges are dismissed and the assisted person is discharged or

(b) the charge, or charges, of an offence triable only on indictment are dismissed and the case is remitted to the magistrates' court in accordance with paragraph 10(3)(a) of Schedule 3 to the *Crime and Disorder Act* 1998 (procedure where no indictable offence remains),

the litigator instructed in the proceedings must be paid a fee calculated in accordance with paragraph 5, or where appropriate, paragraph 7, as appropriate for representing an assisted person in a guilty plea.

(5) Sub-paragraph (6) applies to—

(a) a plea and case management hearing that takes place after the prosecution serves its evidence; and

(b) any other hearing that takes place before a plea and case management hearing has taken place, but after the prosecution has served its evidence

(6) Where, at a hearing to which this paragraph applies—

(a) the prosecution offers no evidence and the assisted person is discharged or

(b) the assisted person is charged on an indictment which includes no offence that is triable only on indictment, and the case is remitted to the magistrates' court in accordance with paragraph 10(3)(a) of Schedule 3 to the *Crime and Disorder Act* 1998,

the litigator must be paid a fee calculated in accordance with paragraph 5 or where appropriate paragraph 7, as appropriate for representing an assisted person in a guilty plea.

Defendant uplifts

G–77   17.—(1) Where a litigator represents more than one assisted person in proceedings referred to in paragraph 16(2), (3), (4) or (5), a defendant uplift will be payable

(2) The defendant uplift will be calculated in accordance with the table following this paragraph.

(3) In the table following this paragraph, the total fee means—

(a) the fee specified in sub-paragraph (2) where that sub-paragraph applies or

(b) the basic fee (B) specified in the table following paragraph 5, or, where appropriate, the initial fee specified in paragraph 7, where paragraph 16(3), (4) or (5) applies, as appropriate for the circumstances set out in that sub-paragraph.

DEFENDANT UPLIFTS

Total number of defendants represented by litigator	Percentage uplift to total fee
2–4	20%
5+	30%

Warrant for arrest

G–77a   18.—(1) This paragraph applies where—

(a) the assisted person fails to attend a hearing;

(b) at that hearing the court issues a warrant for the arrest of the assisted person, pursuant to section 7(1) of the *Bail Act* 1976 ("the warrant");

(c) the case does not proceed in the absence of the assisted person.

(2) Where in a case on indictment the warrant is not executed within three months of the date on which it was issued, the fee payable to the litigator is—

(a) where the warrant is issued at or before the plea and case management hearing, the fee payable for a guilty plea in accordance with paragraph 5 or where appropriate, paragraph 7;

(b) where the warrant is issued after the plea and case management hearing

but before the trial, the fee payable for a cracked trial in accordance with
paragraph 5 or where appropriate paragraph 7, as appropriate to the
class of offence with which the assisted person is charged;

(c) where the warrant is issued during the trial, and the trial is aborted as a
result, the fee payable for a trial as if the trial had ended on the day the
warrant was issued.

(3) Where the warrant is issued during the course of proceedings referred to in
paragraph 12 or 14 the fee payable to the litigator is the fee set out in the table following paragraph 14, as appropriate to the type of proceedings.

(4) Sub-paragraph (5) applies where—

(a) a fee has been paid, or is payable, to the litigator in accordance with sub-
paragraph (2);

(b) the warrant is executed within 15 months of the date on which it was issued;

(c) the case proceeds after the warrant has been executed; and

(d) the litigator submits a claim for fees for the determination of his overall
remuneration in the case, in accordance with article 6.

(5) Where this sub-paragraph applies—

(a) the appropriate officer must deduct the amount paid or payable in accordance with sub-paragraph (2) from the amount payable to the litigator on
the final determination of fees in the case;

(b) if the fee paid or payable in accordance with sub-paragraph (2) is greater
than the amount payable to the litigator on the final determination of fees
in the case, the appropriate officer may recover the amount of the difference by way of repayment by the litigator.

PART 4

MISCELLANEOUS

Additional charges

19.—(1) Where an assisted person is charged with more than one offence on one **G–78**
indictment, the fee payable to the litigator under this Schedule will be based on
whichever of those offences the litigator selects.

(2) Where a litigator selects one offence, in preference to another offence, under
sub-paragraph (1) that selection does not affect his right to claim any of the fees
provided for in Part 3 of this Schedule to which he would otherwise have been
entitled.

Assisted person unfit to plead or stand trial

20. Where in any case a hearing is held to determine the question of whether the **G–78a**
assisted person is unfit to plead or to stand trial (a "fitness hearing")—

(a) if a trial on indictment is held, or continues, at any time thereafter, the
length of the fitness hearing is included in determining the length of the
trial for the calculation of the fee in accordance with Part 2;

(b) if a trial on indictment is not held, or does not continue, thereafter by reason of the assisted person being found unfit to plead or to stand trial, the
litigator must be paid—

(i) a fee calculated in accordance with paragraph 6 or where appropriate paragraph 8, as appropriate to the combined length of—

(aa) the fitness hearing; and

(bb) any hearing under section 4A of the *Criminal Procedure
(Insanity) Act* 1964 (finding that the accused did the act or
made the omission charged against him); or

(ii) a fee calculated in accordance with paragraph 5, or where appropriate paragraph 7, as appropriate, for representing an assisted person
in a cracked trial,

whichever the litigator elects; and

(c) if at any time the assisted person pleads guilty to the indictable offence,
the litigator must be paid either—

661

     (i) a fee calculated in accordance with paragraph 6 or, where appropri ate, paragraph 8, as appropriate to the length of the fitness hearing or

     (ii) a fee calculated in accordance with paragraph 5 or, where appropri ate, paragraph 7, as appropriate for representing an assisted person in a guilty plea,

whichever the litigator elects.

Fees for confiscation proceedings

G–79   21.—(1) This paragraph applies to—

     (a) proceedings under Part 2 of the *Proceeds of Crime Act* 2002 (confiscation England and Wales);

     (b) proceedings under section 2 of the *Drug Trafficking Act* 1994 (confiscation orders) and

     (c) proceedings under section 71 of the *Criminal Justice Act* 1988 (confiscation orders).

(2) Where this paragraph applies, the appropriate officer may allow work done in the following classes by a litigator—

     (a) preparation, including taking instructions, interviewing witnesses ascertaining the prosecution case, preparing and perusing documents dealing with letters and telephone calls, instructing an advocate and expert witnesses, conferences, consultations and work done in connection with advice on appeal;

     (b) attending at court where an advocate is instructed, including conference with the advocate at court;

     (c) travelling and waiting;

     (d) writing routine letters and dealing with routine telephone calls.

(3) The appropriate officer must consider the claim, any further particulars, infor mation or documents submitted by the litigator under article 6 and any other rele vant information and must allow such work as appears to him to have been reason ably done in the proceedings.

(4) Subject to sub-paragraph (3), the appropriate officer must allow fees under this paragraph in accordance with paragraph 22.

(5) The appropriate officer must allow fees in accordance with paragraphs 22–2 as appropriate to such of the following grades of fee earner as he considers reason able—

     (a) senior solicitor;

     (b) solicitor, legal executive or fee earner of equivalent experience; or

     (c) trainee or fee earner of equivalent experience.

Prescribed fee rates

G–80   22. Subject to paragraphs 23 and 24, for proceedings in the Crown Court to which paragraph 21 applies the appropriate officer must allow fees for work under paragraph 21(2) at the following prescribed rates—

TABLE 1

Class of work	Grade of fee earner	Rate	Variations
Preparation	Senior solicitor	£53.00 per hour	£55.75 per hour for a fee earner whose office is situated within the London region of the Commission
	Solicitor, legal executive or fee earner of equiva-lent experience	£45.00 per hour	£47.25 per hour for a fee earner whose office is situated within the London region of the Commission

Class of work	Grade of fee earner	Rate	Variations
	Trainee or fee earner of equivalent experience	£29.75 per hour	£34.00 per hour for a fee earner whose office is situated within the London region of the Commission
Attendance at court where more than one representative instructed	Senior solicitor	£42.25 per hour	—
	Solicitor, legal executive or fee earner of equivalent experience	£34.00 per hour	—
	Trainee or fee earner of equivalent experience	£20.50 per hour	—
Travelling and waiting	Senior solicitor	£24.75 per hour	—
	Solicitor, legal executive or fee earner of equivalent experience	£24.75 per hour	—
	Trainee or fee earner of equivalent experience	£12.50 per hour	—
Writing routine letters and dealing with routine telephone calls		£3.45 per item	£3.60 per item for a fee earner whose office is situated within the London region of the Commission

Allowing fees at less than the prescribed rates

23. In respect of any item of work, the appropriate officer may allow fees at less **G–81** than the relevant prescribed rate specified in paragraph 22 where it appears to him reasonable to do so having regard to the competence and despatch with which the work was done.

Allowing fees at more than the prescribed rates

24.—(1) Upon a determination the appropriate officer may, subject to the provi- **G–81a** sions of this paragraph, allow fees at more than the relevant prescribed rate specified in paragraph 22 for preparation, attendance at court where more than one representative is instructed, routine letters written and routine telephone calls, in respect of offences in Class A, B, C, D, G, I, J or K in the Table of Offences.

(2) The appropriate officer may allow fees at more than the prescribed rate where it appears to him, taking into account all the relevant circumstances of the case, that—

    (a) the work was done with exceptional competence, skill or expertise;

    (b) the work was done with exceptional despatch; or

    (c) the case involved exceptional complexity or other exceptional circumstances.

(3) Paragraph 3 of Schedule 1 applies to litigators in respect of proceedings in the Crown Court as it applies to advocates.

(4) Where the appropriate officer considers that any item or class of work should be allowed at more than the prescribed rate, he must apply to that item or class of work a percentage enhancement in accordance with the following provisions of this paragraph.

(5) In determining the percentage by which fees should be enhanced above the prescribed rate the appropriate officer must have regard to—

(a) the degree of responsibility accepted by the fee earner;

(b) the care, speed and economy with which the case was prepared; and

(c) the novelty, weight and complexity of the case.

(6) The percentage above the relevant prescribed rate by which fees for work may be enhanced must not exceed 100 per cent.

(7) The appropriate officer may have regard to the generality of proceedings to which this Order applies in determining what is exceptional within the meaning of this paragraph.

Very High Cost Cases

G–81b   25.—(1) This paragraph applies where, in a Very High Cost Case, a litigator instructs an advocate who is not a member of a Very High Cost Case (Crime) Panel, in accordance with the contract.

(2) The litigator may claim payment from the Commission in respect of work undertaken by the advocate and authorised in accordance with the contract.

(3) Where such a claim is made, the Commission—

(a) must pay the litigator at rates no higher than the rates set out in the tables following this paragraph; and

(b) where it considers that there are exceptional circumstances, may pay the litigator such fees as it considers reasonable and has agreed in advance with the litigator in respect of—

(i) travelling (in excess of four hours in one day);

(ii) accommodation; and

(iii) subsistence, up to a maximum of £20 per day.

(4) In this paragraph "the contract" means the Very High Cost Case contract for panel members, made between the Commission and panel members and dated 2nd April 2008.

(5) In the tables following this paragraph—

(a) a reference in the first table to a category is a reference to that category as defined in the contract;

(b) a reference in the first table to a level A or B solicitor-advocate is a reference to a level A or B solicitor-advocate as defined in the contract;

(c) a reference in the second table to a junior includes a solicitor-advocate.

Preparation (hourly rates)	Category 1 £	Category 2 £	Category 3 £	Category 4 £
Counsel				
QC	152.50	119	95.50	95.50
Leading junior	133	104.50	83.50	83.50
Led junior	95.50	76	65	65
Junior alone	104.50	85.50	74	74
2nd led junior	67	53	46	46
Solicitor-advocate				
Leading level A	152.50	119	95.50	95.50
Led level A	133	104.50	83.50	83.50

Preparation (hourly rates)	Category 1 £	Category 2 £	Category 3 £	Category 4 £
Leading level B	133	104.50	83.50	83.50
Led level B	110	90.50	69	69
Level A alone	138	115	93.50	93.50
Level B alone	116	99.50	78.50	78.50
Second advocate	67	53	46	46

Advocacy	Preliminary hearing £	Half day £	Full day £
QC	119	250	500
Leading junior	90.50	205.25	410.50
Led junior	61	132.75	265.50
Junior alone	70	150	300
Second led junior	35.50	67.50	135
Noter	30.50	57.50	115

Travelling, waiting and mileage
£25 per hour for travelling (up to a maximum of four hours in one day) or waiting
£0.45 per mile for mileage

[This paragraph was inserted by S.I. 2008 No. 957 (*ante*, G–1). It is printed as amended, in relation to work done on or after November 13, 2008, by S.I. 2008 No. 2930 (*ante*, G–1).]

In *R. v. Farrell and Selby* [2007] Costs L.R. 495, SCCO (Costs Judge Campbell) it was held in relation to the provisions of paragraph 4 of Part 1 of Schedule 2 to the *Criminal Defence Service (Funding) Order* 2001 (S.I. 2001 No. 855) for paying enhanced rates to solicitors, (i) it was open to a determining officer to apply different rates of enhancement to different items of work; since a determining officer was required, in deciding on the rate of enhancement, to have regard, *inter alia*, to the "degree of responsibility accepted by the solicitor and his staff", it was permissible for a determining officer to apply a lesser rate of enhancement to work of a routine nature done by Grade B fee earners than that applied to the senior fee earners to whom they reported; (ii) when enhancement was appropriate, a determining officer should first assess what enhanced rate would have been applied if legal aid had been granted prior to October 1, 1994 (the date of commencement of the revised rules as to enhancement introduced by the *Legal Aid in Criminal and Care Proceedings Costs) (Amendment) (No. 3) Regulations* 1994 (S.I. 1994 No. 2218)), *viz.* the hourly broad average direct cost rate plus an appropriate uplift for care and conduct, and then he should adjust the resulting figure upwards to allow for subsequent inflation; he should then decide on a rate of enhancement such as

G–81c

665

would match this figure; where, however, the figure exceeded the maximum enhanced rate under the 2001 order, then the determining officer should apply the maximum enhanced rate. Since the provisions under consideration corresponded to those of paragraph 6 of Schedule 2 to the 2007 order (prior to amendment), it could safely be taken that this decision carried across to the current order (prior to amendment) with the effect—as in this case—that wherever enhanced rates are appropriate, the rate of enhancement is always going to be 100 per cent because the 1994 hourly direct cost plus uplift for care and attention, plus uplift for inflation is always going to exceed twice the current hourly rates, which have remained unchanged for many years. This was confirmed by the same costs judge in *R. v. Bowles* [2007] Costs L.R. 514 SCCO. Whilst the provision for payment at enhanced rates under the 2007 order (as amended) relates only to fees payable under paragraph 21, the provisions of paragraph 24 correspond to paragraph 6 of the unamended Schedule 2, and it would appear that the decision in *Farrell and Selby* will carry across to this paragraph in the same way that it carried across to paragraph 6.

Article 8	SCHEDULE 4

PROCEEDINGS IN THE COURT OF APPEAL

General provisions

G–82   1.—(1) The provisions of this Schedule apply to proceedings in the Court of Appeal.

(2) In determining fees the appropriate officer must, subject to the provisions of this Schedule—

   (a) take into account all the relevant circumstances of the case including the nature, importance, complexity or difficulty of the work and the time involved; and

   (b) allow a reasonable amount in respect of all work actually and reasonably done.

Claims for fees and disbursements by litigators

2.—(1) Subject to article 32, no claim by a litigator for fees and disbursements in respect of work done in proceedings in the Court of Appeal under a representation order must be entertained unless he submits it within three months of the conclusion of the proceedings to which it relates.

(2) Subject to sub-paragraph (3), a claim for fees in proceedings in the Court of Appeal must be submitted to the appropriate officer in such form and manner as he may direct and must be accompanied by the representation order and any receipts or other documents in support of any disbursement claimed.

(3) A claim must—

   (a) summarise the items of work done by a fee earner in respect of which fees are claimed according to the classes specified in paragraph 3(1);

   (b) state, where appropriate, the dates on which the items of work were done, the time taken, the sums claimed and whether the work was done for more than one assisted person;

   (c) specify, where appropriate, the level of fee earner who undertook each of the items of work claimed;

(d) give particulars of any work done in relation to more than one indictment or a retrial; and

(e) specify any disbursements claimed, the circumstances in which they were incurred and the amounts claimed in respect of them.

(4) Where the litigator claims that paragraph 9(1) applies in relation to an item of work, he must give full particulars in support of his claim.

(5) The litigator must specify any special circumstances which the litigator considers should be drawn to the attention of the appropriate officer.

(6) The litigator must supply such further information and documents as the appropriate officer may require.

(7) Where a retrospective representation order has been made under regulation 10(6) of the *Criminal Defence Service (General) (No. 2) Regulations* 2001 in respect of any proceedings where an appellant has been successful on appeal and granted a defendant's costs order under section 16(4) of the *Prosecution of Offences Act* 1985 (defence costs), the litigator must certify that no claim for fees incurred before the retrospective representation order was made has been or will be made from central funds in relation to that work.

Determination of litigators' fees

3.—(1) The appropriate officer may allow work done in the following classes by fee **G–83** earners—

(a) preparation, including taking instructions, interviewing witnesses, ascertaining the prosecution case, advising on plea and mode of trial, preparing and perusing documents, dealing with letters and telephone calls which are not routine, preparing for advocacy, instructing an advocate and expert witnesses, conferences, consultations, views and work done in connection with advice on appeal;

(b) advocacy, including applications for bail and other applications to the court;

(c) attending at court where an advocate is assigned, including conferences with the advocate at court;

(d) travelling and waiting; and

(e) writing routine letters and dealing with routine telephone calls.

(2) The appropriate officer must consider the claim, any further information or documents submitted by the fee earner under paragraph 2 and any other relevant information and must allow—

(a) such work as appears to him to have been reasonably done under the representation order (including any representation or advice which is deemed to be work done under that order) by a fee earner, classifying such work according to the classes specified in sub-paragraph (1) as he considers appropriate; and

(b) such time in each class of work allowed by him (other than routine letters written and routine telephone calls) as he considers reasonable.

(3) The fees allowed in accordance with this Schedule are those appropriate to such of the following grades of litigator as the appropriate officer considers reasonable—

(a) senior solicitor;

(b) solicitor, legal executive or fee earner of equivalent experience; or

(c) trainee or fee earner of equivalent experience.

Determination of litigators' disbursements

4. The appropriate officer must allow such disbursements claimed under **G–84** paragraph 2 as appear to him to have been reasonably incurred, provided that—

(a) if they are abnormally large by reason of the distance of the court or the assisted person's residence or both from the litigator's place of business, the appropriate officer may limit reimbursement of the disbursements to what otherwise would, having regard to all the circumstances, be a reasonable amount; and

(b) the cost of a transcript, or any part thereof, of the proceedings in the court from which the appeal lies obtained otherwise than through the registrar must not be allowed except where the appropriate officer considers that it is reasonable in all the circumstances for such disbursement to be allowed.

Claims for fees by advocates

5.—(1) Subject to article 32, a claim by an advocate for fees for work done in proceedings in the Court of Appeal under a representation order must not be entertained unless he submits it within three months of the conclusion of the proceedings to which the representation order relates.

(2) Where the advocate claims that paragraph 13 applies in relation to an item of work he must give full particulars in support of his claim.

(3) Subject to sub-paragraph (4), a claim for fees by an advocate in proceedings in the Court of Appeal must be submitted to the appropriate officer in such form and manner as he may direct.

(4) A claim must—

(a) summarise the items of work done by an advocate in respect of which fees are claimed according to the classes specified in paragraph 6(2);

(b) state, where appropriate, the dates on which the items of work were done, the time taken, the sums claimed and whether the work was done for more than one assisted person;

(c) give particulars of any work done in relation to more than one indictment or a retrial.

(5) The advocate must specify any special circumstances which the advocate considers should be drawn to the attention of the appropriate officer.

(6) The advocate must supply such further information and documents as the appropriate officer may require.

Determination of advocate's fees

G–85

6.—(1) The appropriate officer must consider the claim, any further particulars and information submitted by an advocate under paragraph 5 and any other relevant information and must allow such work as appears to him to have been reasonably done.

(2) The appropriate officer may allow any of the following classes of fee to an advocate in respect of work allowed by him under this paragraph—

(a) a basic fee for preparation including preparation for a pre-trial review and, where appropriate, the first day's hearing including, where they took place on that day, short conferences, consultations, applications and appearances (including bail applications), views and any other preparation;

(b) a refresher fee for any day or part of a day during which a hearing continued, including, where they took place on that day, short conferences, consultations, applications and appearances (including bail applications), views at the scene of the alleged offence and any other preparation;

(c) subsidiary fees for—

(i) attendance at conferences, consultations and views at the scene of the alleged offence not covered by paragraph (a) or (b);

(ii) written advice on evidence, plea or appeal or other written work; and

(iii) attendance at pre-trial reviews, applications and appearances (including bail applications and adjournments for sentence) not covered by paragraph (a) or (b).

(3) Where a representation order provides for representation by—

(a) a single advocate other than a QC and a QC agrees to appear as the single advocate; or

(b) two advocates other than QC, and a QC agrees to appear as a leading junior,

that QC must be treated for all the purposes of this Schedule as having been instructed under that representation order, and his remuneration must be determined as if he were not a QC.

Litigators' fees for proceedings in the Court of Appeal

7. For proceedings in the Court of Appeal the appropriate officer must allow fees **G–86** for work by litigators at the following prescribed rates—

Class of work	Grade of fee earner	Rate	Variations
Preparation	Senior solicitor	£53.00 per hour	£55.75 per hour for a litigator whose office is situated within the London region of the Commission
	Solicitor, legal executive or fee earner of equivalent experience	£45.00 per hour	£47.25 per hour for a litigator whose office is situated within the London region of the Commission
	Trainee or fee earner of equivalent experience	£29.75 per hour	£34.00 per hour for a litigator whose office is situated within the London region of the Commission
Advocacy	Senior solicitor	£64.00 per hour	
	Solicitor	£56.00 per hour	
Attendance at court where more than one representative assigned	Senior solicitor	£42.25 per hour	
	Solicitor, legal executive or fee earner of equivalent experience	£34.00 per hour	
	Trainee or fee earner of equivalent experience	£20.50 per hour	
Travelling and waiting	Senior solicitor	£24.75 per hour	
	Solicitor, legal executive or fee earner of equivalent experience	£24. 75 per hour	

Class of work	Grade of fee earner	Rate	Variations
	Trainee or fee earner of equivalent experience	£12.50 per hour	
Routine letters written and routine telephone calls		£3.45 per item	£3.60 per item for a fee earner whose office is situated within the London region of the Commission

G-87   8. In respect of any item of work, the appropriate officer may allow fees at less than the relevant prescribed rate specified in paragraph 7 where it appears to him reasonable to do so having regard to the competence and despatch with which the work was done.

9.—(1) Upon a determination of fees the appropriate officer may, subject to the provisions of this paragraph, allow fees at more than the relevant prescribed rate specified in paragraph 7 for preparation, advocacy, attendance at court where more than one representative is assigned, routine letters written and routine telephone calls, in respect of offences in Class A, B, C, D, G, I, J or K in the Table of Offences in Part 6 of Schedule 1.

(2) The appropriate officer may allow fees at more than the prescribed rate where it appears to him, taking into account all the relevant circumstances of the case, that—

(a) the work was done with exceptional competence, skill or expertise;

(b) the work was done with exceptional despatch; or

(c) the case involved exceptional complexity or other exceptional circumstances.

(3) Paragraph 3 of Schedule 1 applies to litigators in respect of proceedings in the Court of Appeal as it applies to advocates.

(4) Where the appropriate officer considers that any item or class of work should be allowed at more than the prescribed rate, he must apply to that item or class of work a percentage enhancement in accordance with the following provisions of this paragraph.

(5) In determining the percentage by which fees should be enhanced above the prescribed rate the appropriate officer may have regard to—

(a) the degree of responsibility accepted by the fee earner;

(b) the care, speed and economy with which the case was prepared; and

(c) the novelty, weight and complexity of the case.

(6) The percentage above the relevant prescribed rate by which fees for work may be enhanced must not exceed 100 per cent.

(7) The appropriate officer may have regard to the generality of proceedings to which this Order applies in determining what is exceptional within the meaning of this paragraph.

Advocates' fees for proceedings in the Court of Appeal

G-88   10. Subject to paragraph 13, for proceedings in the Court of Appeal the appropriate officer must allow fees for work by advocates at the following prescribed rates—

JUNIOR COUNSEL

Type of proceedings	Basic fee	Full day refresher	Subsidiary fees		
			Attendance at consultation, conferences and views	Written work	Attendance at pre-trial reviews, applications and other appearances
All appeals	Maximum amount: £545.00 per case	Maximum amount: £178.75 per day	£33.50 per hour, minimum amount: £16.75	Maximum amount: £58.25 per item	Maximum amount: £110 per appearance

QC

Type of proceedings	Basic fee	Full day refresher	Subsidiary fees		
			Attendance at consultation, conferences and views	Written work	Attendance at pre-trial reviews, applications and other appearances
All appeals	Maximum amount: £5,400.00 per case	Maximum amount: £330.50 per day	£62.50 per hour, minimum amount: £32.00	Maximum amount: £119.50 per item	Maximum amount: £257.50 per appearance

11. Where an hourly rate is specified in the Table following paragraph 10, the appropriate officer must determine any fee for such work in accordance with that hourly rate; provided that the fee determined must not be less than the minimum amount specified.   **G–89**

12. Where a refresher fee is claimed in respect of less than a full day, the appropriate officer must allow such fee as appears to him reasonable having regard to the fee which would be allowable for a full day.

13. Where it appears to the appropriate officer, taking into account all the relevant circumstances of the case, that owing to the exceptional circumstances of the case the amount payable by way of fees in accordance with the Table following paragraph 10 would not provide reasonable remuneration for some or all of the work he has allowed, he may allow such amounts as appear to him to be reasonable remuneration for the relevant work.   **G–90**

Payment of fees

14.—(1) Having determined the fees payable to a representative in accordance with the terms of this Schedule, the appropriate officer must notify the representative of the fees payable and authorise payment accordingly.   **G–91**

(2) Where, as a result of any redetermination or appeal made or brought pursuant to paragraph 15—

    (a) the fees payable under sub-paragraph (1) are increased, the appropriate officer must authorise payment of the increase; and

(b) the fees payable under sub-paragraph (1) are decreased, the representative must repay the amount of such decrease.

(3) Where the payment of any fees of the representative is ordered under article 30(12) or article 31(8), the appropriate officer must authorise payment.

[This paragraph is printed as amended by S.I. 2007 No. 3552 (*ante*, G–1).]

Redeterminations and appeals

G–92   15.—(1) Where a representative is dissatisfied with—

(a) the fees determined in accordance with the provisions of this Schedule; or

(b) the decision of the appropriate officer under paragraph 3(3) of Schedule 1

he may apply to the appropriate officer to redetermine those fees or reclassify the offence, in accordance with the provisions of article 29(3) to (9).

(2) Where—

(a) a representative has made an application to the appropriate officer under sub-paragraph (1); and

(b) the appropriate officer has given his reasons for a decision under article 29(7)

a representative who is dissatisfied with that decision may appeal to a Costs Judge, in accordance with the provisions of article 30(2) to (14).

(3) A representative who is dissatisfied with the decision of a Costs Judge on an appeal under sub-paragraph (2) may apply to a Costs Judge to certify a point of principle of general importance, and the provisions of article 31(2) to (8) will apply.

C. The Representation Order

G–93   Advocates are entitled to claim and be remunerated only for work done in respect of Crown Court proceedings in accordance with the provisions of the schedules to the funding orders: *Funding Order* 2001, arts 3(1)(c) and 5; *Funding Order* 2007, arts 4, 5 and 11. No entitlement arises unless, (a) a valid representation order exists for counsel who makes a claim; (b) work has been done under the order; and (c) the work done has been reasonably done. A claim to be recompensed for work done for a funded person will fail unless counsel has been properly instructed or assigned under the representation order.

Existence of a valid representation order

G–94   Payment can only be made for work done under a representation order There is no power under the Act or the Regulations to make a payment in respect of work actually and reasonably undertaken by counsel in the genuine but mistaken belief that the appropriate order was in existence.

Solicitors are obliged to enclose a copy of the representation order with counsel's instructions, and to inform counsel of any subsequent amendments *General Criminal Contract: Contract Specification*, Part B, para. 5.4. It is however, incumbent upon counsel to check whether the appropriate order exists. If it is not with his instructions, then it is his duty, if he seeks to look to the Criminal Defence Service (CDS) thereafter for remuneration, to see that the appropriate authority is obtained and supplied to him: *Hunt v. East Dorset Health Authority* [1992] 1 W.L.R. 785 at 788 (Hobhouse J.); and *R. v. Welsby* [1998] 1 Cr.App.R. 197, Crown Court (Ebsworth J.) (counsel has a professional duty to ensure that he is covered by appropriate certificate).

Determining the effective date of a representation order

G–95   The effective date of a representation order for the purposes of determin

ing which regulations apply is the date upon which representation was first
granted to counsel's instructing solicitors and not the date of the later representation order under which they instructed counsel: *R. v. Hadley* [2005]
Costs L.R. 548.

Orders made ultra vires

Representation orders assigning solicitors or counsel which are made *ultra*   **G–96**
vires are invalid, and work done under such an order cannot be remunerated.
However, where it is possible to construe an order as *intra vires*, that construction should be adopted: *R. v. O'Brien and Oliffe*, 81 Cr.App.R. 25 at 30 (Hobhouse J.). There is no power to backdate a representation order: *R. v. Welsby*,
ante; followed in *R. v. Conroy* [2004] Costs L.R. 182 in respect of the current
regulations.

Orders for two or more advocates

The instruction of more than one advocate must be specifically authorised   **G–97**
by the court. A representation order may provide for the services of: (i) either
junior or Queen's Counsel; (ii) two advocates, one of whom must be a Queen's
Counsel or junior counsel and the other of whom must be a junior counsel or
noting junior; or (iii) in the case of a Serious Fraud Office prosecution, three
advocates, the additional advocate being a junior or noting junior: reg. 14(2),
(6). Regulation 14 (wherein "junior counsel" means any advocate other than
Queen's Counsel: reg. 14(1)) provides the criteria for making the appropriate
representation order. A two counsel order or an order for Queen's Counsel
can only be made in the course of a trial, preliminary hearing, or pleas and
directions hearing by a specified judge: reg. 14(13). As to orders made by
magistrates, see *post*, G–98.

It is submitted that a leading junior would not be entitled to any remuneration where he acts under a certificate granted for Queen's Counsel. A leading junior who acted under an unamended legal aid certificate granted to
cover Queen's Counsel was not covered by the certificate and could not be
remunerated under the order or by a defendant's costs order under section
16 of the *Prosecution of Offences Act* 1985: *R. v. Liverpool Crown Court, ex p. The
Lord Chancellor, The Times*, April 22, 1993, DC. However, a Queen's Counsel
must be remunerated at the appropriate rate for junior counsel where he
agrees to act as a sole advocate or as a leading junior: *Funding Order* 2001,
Sched. 1, para. 15(9); *Funding Order* 2007, art. 5(7).

In every case where the services of more than one advocate are provided, it
is the duty of each legal representative to keep under review the need for the
number of advocates provided for in the representation order, and for
Queen's Counsel to keep under review whether he could act alone. Where
the legal representative is of the opinion that the representation order should
be amended to reduce the number of advocates instructed, he is under a duty
so to notify the court and the other legal representatives in writing: reg.
14(16), (17).

Queen's Counsel and magistrates' courts

A representation order may be granted for the provision of the services of   **G–98**
Queen's Counsel in a magistrates' court only in cases of murder and only
upon committal, transfer or sending for trial to the Crown Court: reg.
14(14)(a). A magistrates' court may only order provision of the services of

Queen's Counsel and junior counsel where the prosecution is brought by the Serious Fraud Office and upon receipt of notice of transfer: reg. 14(14)(b).

Orders for advocate acting without a solicitor

G–99   A representation order may be granted by a court for an advocate alone, without a solicitor, in respect of contempt proceedings, appeals to the Court of Appeal, or in cases or urgency where it appears to the court that there is no time to instruct a solicitor: reg. 15.

Orders for Queen's Counsel acting alone

G–100   Where prior authority has been obtained to instruct a Queen's Counsel alone, the propriety of the order may not be challenged on the determination of Queen's Counsel's fees unless the solicitor knew or ought reasonably to have known that the purpose for which the authority had been given had failed or become irrelevant or unnecessary before the fees were incurred: *Funding Order* 2001, Sched. 1, para. 15(8); *Funding Order* 2007, art. 16(3).

Work done under the order

G–101   The work claimed for must have been done under the order. Work done before the date of commencement of the representation order cannot be claimed or allowed: *R. v. Clarke* (1991) Costs L.R. 496. An order cannot be backdated in respect of proceedings in the Crown Court: *R. v. North Stafford-shire JJ., ex p. O'Hara* [1994] C.O.D. 248, DC; *R. v. Welsby* [1998] 1 Cr.App.R. 197, Crown Court (Ebsworth J.).

"Topping up"

G–102   An assisted person's solicitor or advocate is prohibited from receiving or being party to the making of any payment for work done in connection with the proceedings in respect of which the representation order was made other than payments by the Lord Chancellor or the Legal Services Commission or in respect of various specified disbursements: reg. 22 (§ 6–176 in the main work). These provisions are designed to prevent "topping" up of fees, rather than to prevent counsel from receiving payment for private fees incurred before the representation order was granted or *ex gratia* payments from solicitors who wrongly instructed counsel in the mistaken belief that he was covered by a representation order. However, once a representation order has been granted, the prohibition applies to all solicitors and advocates and not merely those persons acting under the representation order: *R. v. Grant* [2006] Cost L.R. 173.

D. Reasonable Remuneration

G–103   The basic principle of remuneration under the *ex post facto* regime is that counsel should receive reasonable remuneration for work actually and reasonably undertaken by him. Assessment of the work undertaken and the remuneration claimed is made in each case after the event by experienced officers appointed by the Lord Chancellor's department and subject to the appellate and expert supervision of costs judges and the High Court.

G–104   Graduated Fees are calculated by reference to pre-determined fixed fees. Although allowances are made for different classes of case and for the length and size of each case, the scheme necessarily embraces a "swings and round-abouts" principle. Save in exceptional cases, Graduated Fees draw no distinction between straightforward and complex cases of the same length, class and size.

When they were introduced in 1997, it was intended that they would be cost neutral. The extension of fees to cover 25 to 40 day cases represented a diminution in fees for defence work, balanced by an increase in the fees of prosecution counsel who are now subject to a similar scheme. The further extension of the scheme under the *Funding Order* 2007 to all trials on indictment save for those covered by VHCC contracts is a far remove from its original ambit, and may give rise to some serious underfunding of cases or aspects of cases.

Very High Cost Cases are remunerated by an hourly preparation fee and refreshers which fall within prescribed bands. The categorisation of the class of case, rates of remuneration, refresher and the number of hours of preparation allowed to counsel must be agreed before the work is undertaken. The Very High Costs Cases regime represents a significant diminution in the individual fees considered to be reasonable under the *ex post facto* regime.

E. Interim Fees and other Pre-assessment Payments

(1) Staged payments for preparation in long cases

Where the period from committal or transfer to the Crown Court and the   **G–105** conclusion of the proceedings is likely to exceed 12 months, a legal representative may apply for staged payments (*i.e.* interim fees for the preparation of a case) in respect of each period of preparation of 100 hours or more undertaken before trial or, in serious fraud cases, before the empanelling of a jury. Preparation in this context is widely defined and includes, *inter alia*, conferences with the defendant, written advice on evidence or plea, legal research and preparation for oral or written submissions: *Funding Order* 2001. Sched. 4, para. 1(1); *Funding Order* 2007, art. 19.

(2) Advance payments

Under the *Funding Order* 2001, advance payments are payable in all cases   **G–106** where pleas and directions hearings have been held and the advocate satisfies the appropriate authority that at least five days before the hearing, he has read the papers in the case, conferred with the defendant, contacted the prosecution and advised on plea: Sched. 1, para. 8(1). In such circumstances, the advocate is entitled to an advance payment, with an uplift of one–fifth for each additional defendant represented: Sched. 1, para. 8(3). The appropriate fee is set out in Sched. 1, para. 8(2). There are no provisions for advance payments under the *Funding Order* 2007.

(3) Interim payments for attendance at trial

Funding Order 2001

Application for interim payments for "attendance at court or refreshers"   **G–107** may be made where counsel has undertaken 26 or more days of court attendances during the main hearing, in non-graduated fee cases: Sched. 1, para. 7(2)(b) and (3)(b). The days need not be continuous, and any period less than a full day may be counted as a whole day: Sched. 1, para. 7(3). The daily rate for Queen's Counsel and junior counsel is the maximum refresher prescribed in Table 2 in Schedule 3; for leading junior counsel, 75 per cent of the rate for Queen's Counsel; and for a noting brief, one-half of junior counsel's fee: Sched. 1, para. 7(4). Interim payments are not subject to re-determination: Sched. 1, para. 7(9).

Funding Order 2007

G–108   There are similar provisions under the *Funding Order* 2007 for litigators, but not for advocates: see art. 20.

(4) Interim payments of expenses

Funding Order 2001

G–109   A legal representative may claim travel and accommodation expenses incurred in order to attend the trial or other main hearing when applying for interim payments under Sched. 1, para. 7, provided prior approval for incurring such expenses has been obtained under *CDS Regulations*: Sched.1, para. 7(7). The claim must be submitted in the form and manner directed by the appropriate authority: Sched. 1, para. 7(8).

Funding Order 2007

G–110   There are similar provisions under the *Funding Order* 2007 for litigators, but not for advocates: see art. 20.

(5) Interim payments pending determination

Entitlement

G–111   In certain circumstances, an advocate may claim an interim payment of 40 per cent of the total claim less any sum already paid: *Funding Order* 2001, Sched. 1, para. 5(1); *Funding Order* 2007, art. 18(1). Such payments may only be made where, (a) the basic fee claimed by counsel, or the total costs claimed by a solicitor in a related claim, or the basic fee claimed by counsel in a related claim, exceeds £4,000 (exclusive of VAT); and (b) three months have elapsed from either the date on which the bill is ready to tax or, if earlier, three months after the conclusion of the last of any related proceedings. A bill is deemed to be ready to tax on the date of receipt of the last bill in a related claim. Related claims are claims for costs of solicitors and counsel in the same proceedings acting for the same defendant or acting in related proceedings. Related proceedings are those involving the same defendant which are prepared, heard, or dealt with together, or proceedings involving more than one defendant arising out of the same incident so that the defendants are charged, tried, or disposed of together: *Funding Order* 2001, Sched. 1, para. 4; *Funding Order* 2007, art. 17.

There is no right of re-determination or appeal against the interim award: *Funding Order* 2001, Sched. 1, para. 5(2); *Funding Order* 2007, art. 18(2).

Claims

G–112   An advocate may submit a claim for interim payment where, (a) he is entitled to such payment; (b) no payment has been made; (c) six months have elapsed since the conclusion of the proceedings against the defendant he represented; and (d) counsel has submitted a proper claim under regulation 8(1) (three-month time limit for the submission of claims): *Funding Order* 2001, Sched. 1, para. 4(5) and (9); *Funding Order* 2007, art. 17(2)(a), (4)–(6).

(6) Hardship payments

A discretionary hardship payment may be made on proof of the likelihood   **G–113**
of financial hardship. The proof required is left to the discretion of taxing officers. Counsel are advised to contact their circuit representative, before submitting a claim, to determine the form of proof likely to be acceptable. The sum paid cannot exceed the amount which is likely to be eventually paid, but payment will not be made for sums less than £5,000. Claims may only be made, (a) at least six months after the legal representative was first instructed, (b) where no outstanding entitlement to interim or staged payments under *Funding Order* 2001, Sched. 1, para. 4, 6 or 7 exists, and (c) where final payment is unlikely to be made within the next three months by reason of which the applicant is likely to suffer financial hardship: *ibid.*, para. 9. There are similar provisions in the *Funding Order* 2007 (see art. 21).

(7) Obligations to submit claims

Any person who has received an advance, interim, staged or hardship pay-   **G–114**
ment must submit a final claim under the appropriate regulation for final determination of his overall remuneration: *Funding Order* 2001, Sched. 1, para. 10(1). Any such payment will be set off against the overall remuneration on final determination and excess payments can be recovered: *ibid.*, para. 10(2). There are similar provisions in the *Funding Order* 2007 (see art. 22).

F. GRADUATED FEES

(1) Introduction

Graduated fees were introduced into the *Legal Aid in Criminal and Care*   **G–115**
Proceedings (Costs) Regulations 1989 (S.I. 1989 No. 343) (see *ante*, G–1) by the *Legal Aid in Criminal and Care Proceedings (Costs) (Amendment) (No. 2) Regulations* 1996 (S.I. 1996 No. 2655) which came into effect on January 1, 1997: reg. 3(1). Those provisions were incorporated *seriatim* as Schedule 4 to the *Funding Order* 2001 although amendments were introduced by the *Criminal Defence Service (Funding) (Amendment) (No. 3) Order* (S.I. 2001 No. 3341) and the *Criminal Defence Service (Funding) (Amendment) Order* 2004 (S.I. 2004 No. 2045) which came into force on October 29, 2001, and August 2, 2004, respectively. Those amendments extended the ambit of graduated fees to cover trials estimated to last up to 25 days and then to 40 days. The *Funding Order* 2007 applied a new scheme, the *Revised Advocacy Graduated Fee Scheme* (RAGFS) in respect of representation orders made on or after April 30, 2007. The RAGFS applies to all trials on indictment save for those contracted under the VHCC scheme: *Funding Order* 2007, Sched. 1, para. 2.

The scheme determines the taxation and payment of fees for advocacy and preparation in something of a mechanistic or formulaic way: *Meeke and Taylor v. Secretary of State for Constitutional Affairs* [2006] Costs L.R. 1. It is a comprehensive scheme which must be applied by examining the particular wording of the legislation: *R. v. Kemp*, X15 363/99. There is no "equity" in the regulations; they have to be construed and given effect however hard the result might be: *R. v. Riddell*, X3, SCCO 319/98, even where payment is morally due: see *R. v. Dhaliwal* [2004] Costs L.R. 689. Conversely, as was pointed out in *R. v. Chubb* [2002] Costs L.R. 333:

> "As has often been said, when the graduated fee system was introduced, it was on a principle which was expressed as being 'swings and roundabouts'. It is perfectly reasonable where the system operates against the Lord Chancellor's Department, that an appeal should be launched. There are many occasions, in my experience, when the graduated fee system has operated very much to the disadvantage of members of the bar and there is no reason why the bar should not take advantage when it operates in their favour."

References within this section to paragraphs are references to paragraphs in Schedule 4 to the *Funding Order* 2001, as amended, or in Schedule 1 to the *Funding Order* 2007.

(2) Cases generally falling outside the graduated fee scheme

(a) *Representation orders made before April 30, 2007*

G–116   Cases fall outside the scheme where:

(a) the representation order provides for the services of more than two advocates: *Funding Order* 2001, Sched. 4, para. 4(a); or

(b) the trial or main hearing exceeds 40 days, unless it was accepted by the court at the pleas and directions hearing, or, after notification by the Commission, that the trial would not exceed 40 days: *ibid.*, para. 4(b); or

(c) the indictment otherwise falls outside the scheme because the page, witness or time limits for contested trials (*post*, G–122) guilty pleas (*post*, G–135) or cracked trials (*post*, G–136) are exceeded.

Very High Cost Cases (VHCC) also fall outside the scheme. It should be noted that where a representation order had been made before July 1, 2004 in a case which fell within the VHCC criteria then existing (*i.e.* the case was anticipated to last more than 25 days and defence costs were likely to exceed £150,000) the Commission may elect to treat the whole or any part of an advocate's claim under the graduated fee provisions: *Funding Order* 2001, arts 9 and 9A, and Sched. 4, para. 4(b)(iii). The fees in Very High Costs Cases are to be determined under Schedule 5: see *post*, G–181.

Under the original *Funding Order*, cases fell outside the scheme where, at the pleas and directions hearing, it was accepted that the trial would exceed 10 days: *Funding Order* 2001, Sched. 4, para. 2(2). When the scheme was revised to cover longer trials, the regulation was changed to reflect the "actual length of the trial" rather than its anticipated length: *Criminal Defence Service (Funding) (Amendment) (No. 3) Order* 2001 (S.I. 2001 No. 3341), art. 10. The (possibly unintended) effect of the change was to bring into the graduated fee scheme some trials which had been properly prepared on an *ex post facto* basis and which unexpectedly went short: see *R. v. Syed* [2004] Costs L.R. 686; *R. v. Hadley* [2005] Costs L.R. 548.

All things being equal, it is better that there should not be two separate assessments on different bases of the same case. However, circumstances can arise where it is legitimate for graduated fee and *ex post facto* payments to be made under the same representation order: *R. v. Gill* [2006] Costs L.R. 837. In *Gill*, the jury were discharged without reaching a verdict. That part of the case clearly fell within the graduated fee scheme. However, when the trial was relisted, the defendant pleaded guilty, and the case became a cracked trial. Under the regime then existing, as the case papers exceeded 250 pages, that part of the claim then fell to be remunerated *ex post facto*. For an example of a

case which fell under three different remuneration regimes, see *R. v. Russell*
[2006] Costs L.R. 841. As to hearings under the *Crime and Disorder Act* 1998,
s. 51, see *post*, G–118.

(b) *Representation orders made on or after April 30, 2007*

Every case on indictment falls within the scheme save for those contracted   **G–117**
as a Very High Costs Case: *Funding Order* 2007, Sched. 1, para. 2.

(3) Cases on indictment

Scheduled offences

A "case" includes proceedings in the Crown Court against any one assisted   **G–118**
person on one or more counts of a single indictment: *Funding Order* 2001,
Sched. 4, para. 1(1); *Funding Order* 2007, Sched. 1, para. 1(1). Where counts
or defendants are severed and dealt with separately, then each separate
indictment is a separate case. Conversely, indictments which are joined
should be treated as one case: *GFSG*: A1, A2: *R. v. Chubb* [2002] Costs L.R.
333. A "case" should not be confused with a trial; there may be two trials in
one case: *R. v. Bond* [2005] Costs L.R. 533.

All cases on indictment now fall within the scheme unless specifically
excluded: *Funding Order* 2001, Sched. 4, para. 2(1); *Funding Order* 2007,
Sched. 1, para. 2. For those cases which were specifically excluded, see *ante*,
G–116. Indictments are unlikely to have been preferred by the time of hearings under section 51 of the *CDA* 1998 (transfers to the Crown Court: see
§ 1–12c in the main work). Although the *CDA* 1998 is referred to in the
Funding Order 2001, "preliminary hearings" were not defined; accordingly,
fees for section 51 hearings were outwith the scheme and had to be
determined *ex post facto*: *R. v. Smith* [2004] Costs L.R. 348; and *R. v. Davies
(Benjamin)* [2007] Costs L.R. 116. Where such hearings fell within the scheme,
they should be remunerated under the *Funding Order* 2001, Schedule 4,
para. 11, rather than para. 16: see *Smith, ante*. Under the *Funding Order*
2007, such fees are paid as standard appearance or fixed fees: Sched 1,
para. 9. As to cases sent or transferred for trial, see also *post*, G–127.

Table of offences

The Table of Offences in Schedule 4 to the *Funding Order* 2001 and in   **G–119**
Schedule 1 to the *Funding Order* 2007 contains offences listed by statute with
a description set out only for convenience. The statutory reference includes
every offence contrary to that reference, whether or not the description of
the offence is apt to describe the offence actually charged: *Funding Order*
2001, para. 5(2)(e); *Funding Order* 2007, Sched. 1, para. 3(1)(e). Cases which
do not appear in the Table of Offences are deemed to fall within Class H:
Funding Order 2001, Sched. 4, para. 5(2)(a); *Funding Order* 2007, Sched. 1,
para. 3 (1)(a). An advocate who is dissatisfied with that deemed classification
may apply to the appropriate officer to reclassify the offence: *Funding Order*
2001, Sched. 4, para. 5(3); *Funding Order* 2007, Sched. 1, para. 3(2). The
Funding Order 2007 updated the Table of Offences and added a number of
offences including those under the *SOA* 2003 and the *Fraud Act* 2006. It also
created two new classes. The amendments effected by the *Funding Order* 2007
appear in italics.

The offences are divided into the following classes:

Class A	Homicide and related grave offences
Class B	Offences involving serious damage and serious drug offences
Class C	Lesser offences involving violence or damage, and less serious drug offences
Class D	Serious sexual offences and offences against children
Class E	Burglary and going equipped
Class F	Other offences of dishonesty including those where the value does not exceed £30,000
Class G	Other more serious offences of dishonesty including those where the value exceeds £30,000 *but does not exceed £100,000*
Class H	Miscellaneous lesser offences
Class I	Offences against public justice and similar offences
Class J	*Serious sexual offences*
Class K	*The most serious offences of dishonesty and other offences where the value exceeds £100,000*

Where counts of differing classes appear in the same indictment, the fee is based upon the class selected by the advocate: *Funding Order* 2001, Sched. 4, para. 23(1); *Funding Order* 2007, Sched. 1, para. 22(1). Once counsel has chosen which count to use as the basis of a claim, that choice is irrevocable: *R. v. Buoniauto*, X25, SCCO 483/2000. Where two or more advocates appear for the same defendant, the grounds of each claim must be the same: *R. v. Powell*, X8, SCTO 336/98.

The offences are summarised and listed alphabetically by statute: *post*, G–168 *et seq.*

G–120   Conspiracy, incitement or attempt to commit an offence fall within the same class as the substantive offence: *Funding Order* 2001, Sched. 4, para. 5(2)(b); *Funding Order* 2007, Sched. 1, para. 3 (1)(b). Conspiracy to defraud at common law does not appear in the table of offences. However, as a matter of practice, the offence was treated under the *Funding Order* 2001 as falling within Class F or G. Under the 2007 order, conspiracy to defraud will fall within Class F, G or K depending on the value of the fraud. Where the appropriate class depends upon a value, the lower value is presumed unless the claimant "proves otherwise to the satisfaction of the appropriate authority": *Funding Order* 2001, Sched. 4, para. 5(2)(c); *Funding Order* 2007, Sched. 1, para. 3(1)(c). This may be done by extracts from the indictment or witness statements. Values relating to offences taken into consideration should be excluded from the computation: *GFSG*: E10.

The calculation of values

G–121   The property values of each count falling within the same class may be aggregated, provided the same property is not counted twice: *Funding Order* 2001, Sched. 4, para. 5(2)(d); *Funding Order* 2007, Sched. 1, para. 3(1)(d). However, offences taken into consideration are excluded from the calculation, even where it is agreed that the counts on the indictment are to be treated merely as sample counts: *R. v. Knight*, X35, SCCO 34/2003.

Pleas and directions hearings and pre-trial reviews

Pleas and directions hearings are not defined under the *Funding Orders*. Ac-　**G–122**
cordingly if a matter is listed as a pleas and directions hearing, it will be so
treated. There is nothing to prevent a pleas and directions hearing from being adjourned, or there being more than one or even a series of such hearings: *R. v. Beecham*, X11, QBD (Ebsworth J., sitting with assessors). However,
the listing of the case is not necessarily determinative. For example, although
a case may be listed as a pleas and directions hearing, if a defendant pleads at
that hearing and is sentenced, it cannot be said that a pleas and directions
hearing has taken place: *R. v. Johnson*, SCCO 51/06. Pleas and directions
hearings (other than those which form part of the main hearing) and pre-trial
reviews are payable at a fixed rate. The enhanced rates and uplifts which apply to trial advocates who attend the pre-trial reviews or pleas and directions
hearings were abolished in respect of all such hearings which occurred on or
after June 1, 1998: *Legal Aid in Criminal and Care Proceedings (Costs) (Amendment) Regulations* 1998 (S.I. 1998 No. 1191). *Ex post facto* claims should be
made where a case is disposed of before such a hearing, *i.e.* where the defendant dies after committal but before the hearing: *GFSB*: B16. Any pre-trial
hearings to determine, for example, the admissibility of evidence, fall outside
the main hearing and are remunerated as standard appearance fees: *R. v.
Rahman*, X21, SCCO 119/2000; *R. v. Carter*, X18, SCCO 384/99. As to section
51 hearings under the *CDA* 1998, see *ante*, G–118.

Under the *Funding Order* 2007 fees are payable for preparing and filing a
plea and case management questionnaire where no oral hearing takes
place: Sched. 1, para. 9(3). Fees for oral hearings which fall within the definition of a standard appearance are deemed to be included in the basic
fee: see *post*, G–129. Plea and case management hearings which are not standard appearances are remunerated according to the fees set out in the table
following paragraph 19: *Funding Order* 2007, Sched. 1, para. 9(2). As to standard appearances, see *post*, G–129.

The start of the main hearing

Most trials start when the jury are sworn and evidence is called: *R. v. Rah-　**G–123**
man*, X21, SCCO 119/2000; *R. v. Maynard*, X19, SCCO 461/99; *R. v. Karra*,
X19A, SCCO 375/99. However, the mere swearing of a jury is not conclusive;
there must be a trial in a meaningful sense. There is no meaningful trial
where a jury are sworn and sent away for abuse of process arguments to
proceed, in the knowledge that if the submissions fail, there would be a
discussion as to pleas: *R. v. Brook* [2004] Costs L.R. 178, or where a jury had
been empanelled while counsel continued to take instructions and discuss
pleas with his client who in fact pleaded before the prosecution opened its
case: *R. v. Baker and Fowler* [2004] Costs L.R. 693.

The start of a preparatory hearing is the commencement of the trial for the
purposes of the regulations: *R. v. Jones*, X17, SCCO 527/99: *GFSG*: B8, B8A.

Calculating the length of the main hearing

Length of the main hearing means the number of days of the main hearing　**G–124**
together with the number of days of any *Newton* hearing in relation to the assisted person whose trial is under consideration: *Funding Order* 2001, Sched.
4, paras 1(1) and 2(6); *Funding Order* 2007, Sched. 1, para. 1(1). Thus,
where counsel successfully submits that there is no case to answer, the main
hearing ceases, despite the fact that the trial may continue against the co-

defendants: *Secretary of State for Constitutional Affairs v. Stork, The Times,* October 7, 2005, QBD (Gray J., sitting with assessors). This can lead to harsh anomalies, as where a defendant pleads guilty shortly after a jury have been sworn during an estimated three-week trial; despite preparation for a three-week trial, counsel will be remunerated as for a one day trial: *Meeke and Taylor v. Secretary of State for Constitutional Affairs* [2006] Costs L.R. 1. Non-sitting days cannot be included: *R. v. Nassir,* X13, SCCO 703/98. Where a jury are sworn, but discharged the same day for some reason other than the private or professional convenience of counsel, with a new jury sworn the following day, there may be sufficient continuity to conclude that the trial did in fact proceed, and start of the trial is the date on which the first jury were sworn: *R. v. Gussman,* X14, SCTO 40/99, but part of a day counts as a whole day: *Funding Order* 2001, Sched. 4, para. 5(2)(a); *Funding Order* 2007, Sched. 1, para. 4(2). Applications relating to abuse of process, disclosure and witness summonses are to be treated as part of the main hearing where they are heard during the main hearing: *Funding Order* 2001, Sched. 4, para. 5(2)(a); *Funding Order* 2007, Sched. 1, para. 10(2). The length of a fitness hearing which precedes a trial on indictment must also be included in determining the length of the trial: *Funding Order* 2001, Sched. 4, para. 27(a); *Funding Order* 2007, Sched. 1, para. 26(a). Confiscation proceedings are excluded from the computation: *Funding Order* 2001, Sched. 4, para. 14(2); *Funding Order* 2007, Sched. 1, para. 11(2).

Fees for contested trials

G–125   The calculation of any graduated fee involves arcane formulae: *Funding Order* 2001, Sched. 4, para. 7(1); *Funding Order* 2007, Sched. 1, para. 4. To calculate the correct fee, the appropriate figures should be substituted from the tables of fees and uplifts: *Funding Order* 2001, Sched. 4, para. 8; *Funding Order* 2007, Sched. 1, para. 5. The formula for trials exceeding 10 days differs in that a "length of trial" gradient is added: *Funding Order* 2001, Sched 4, paras 7(1), (2) and 8.

(a) *Representation orders made before October 3, 2005*

G–126   Where a graduated fee case exceeds 25 days, the fee is calculated as though the trial had lasted 25 days, to which is added the appropriate refresher increased by 40 per cent in respect of each additional day after 25 days up to 50 days, and increased by 50 per cent for each day thereafter: *Funding Order* 2001, Sched. 4, para. 26(a), (b); and see *R. v. Maguire* [2006] Costs L.R. 679 In *R. v. Matthews,* unreported January 9, 2007, counsel successfully argued that a length of trial element of the graduated fee formula is payable beyond the 40th day of a trial.

(b) *Representation orders made after October 3, 2005*

G–127   The appropriate refresher is increased by 40 per cent only in respect of each additional day after 40 days up to 50 days, and increased by 50 per cent for each day thereafter.

(c) *Representation orders made on or after April 30, 2007*

G–128   The *Funding Order* 2007 abolished the length of trial uplift. However, it also increased the weight given to page counts and witness uplifts which are the only remaining proxies by which the complexity of a case is calculated.

Standard appearances under Funding Order 2007

G–129   Standard appearances are defined in the *Funding Order* 2007 as appearances which do not form part of the main hearing, and constitute (i) plea and case management hearings (other than the first such hearing); (ii) pretrial reviews; (iii) custody time limit, bail and other applications; (iv) mentions; (v) applications to break or fix trial dates; and (vi) any hearing (except a trial, plea and case management hearing, appeal against conviction or sentence, sentencing hearing following a committal for sentence to the Crown Court, or proceedings arising out of an alleged breach of an order of the Crown Court) which is listed but cannot proceed because of the failure of the assisted person or a witness to attend, the unavailability of a pre-sentence report or other good reason: Sched. 1, para. 1(1). Under the *Funding Order* 2007, an advocate's fees payable for the first plea and case management hearing or pre-trial review and up to four standard appearances are deemed to be included in the basic fee and are not subject to separate remuneration: Sched. 1, para. 9. The fifth and subsequent standard appearances are remunerated as set out in the table following paragraph 19: *ibid.*, para. 9(2).

Trial of Bail Act offences

The trial of any *Bail Act* 1976 offence in the Crown Court entitles counsel who attends to apply for a new "trial" fee for the contested trial or plea: *R. v. Shaw* [2005] Costs L.R. 326; *R. v. Despres* [2005] Costs L.R. 750.   **G-130**

Sendings and transfers to the Crown Court

As to the position before April 30, 2007, see *ante*, G-118.   **G-131**

Where cases are sent or transferred to the Crown Court under the *CDA* 1998, s.51, the *CJA* 1987, s.4 (serious fraud cases) or the *CJA* 1991, s.53 (transfer of certain cases involving children), and are discontinued before the prosecution serve their evidence (cases sent for trial), the advocate is entitled to 50 per cent of the fee calculated on the basis of a guilty plea: *Funding Order* 2007, Sched. 1, para. 18(2), together with an additional 20 per cent of that fee for each additional person represented: para. 18(7)(a). Once the prosecution have served their evidence, discontinuance, the offering of no evidence at a pleas and case management hearing, or the remitting of the case to the magistrates' court at such hearing because the indictment contains no indictable offence, is treated for the purposes of calculating the relevant fee as if each was a guilty plea: *ibid.*, para. 18(3) and (4). An advocate representing more than one person in the latter circumstances is entitled to 20 per cent of the appropriate basic fee for each additional person he represents: para. 18(7)(b).

Dismissal hearings

Where a successful application for dismissal is made under the *CDA* 1998, Sched. 3, para. 2, the *CJA* 1987, s.6, or the *CJA* 1991, Sched. 6, para. 5, with the result that the case is dismissed or remitted back to the magistrates' court, the fee is calculated as if the matter had been disposed of by a guilty plea, together with an attendance fee based upon the total number of days and half days occupied by the hearing: *Funding Order* 2007, Sched. 1, para. 18(5) and (6). A full day's hearing is any court day which begins before and ends after the luncheon adjournment: para. 18(5)(a). An advocate representing more than one person in such circumstances is entitled to 20 per cent of the appropriate basic fee for each additional person he represents: para. 18(7)(b).   **G-132**

Retrials

(a) *Under representations orders made before April 30, 2007*

G–133   Where the same advocate appears at a retrial within one calendar month of the conclusion of the first trial, the retrial fee is calculated at 60 per cent of the normal fee, or 75 per cent if the retrial starts after that date. In either case, the refresher element shall not be reduced: *Funding Order* 2001, Sched. 4, para. 2(5). Where a different advocate conducts the retrial, the graduated fee is calculated in the normal way: *ibid.*, para. 5(5A). However, the mere fact that a jury is discharged does not necessarily make the following trial a retrial. It is submitted that much depends on the circumstances of the discharge and whether the two jury trials can properly be treated as one: see for example, *R. v. Khan* [2005] Costs L.R. 157.

(b) *Under representation orders made on or after April 30, 2007*

G–134   A standard graduated fee is paid for retrials, where the same advocate appears, subject to the following discounts based upon the time elapsed from the conclusion of the first trial to the start of the retrial: *Funding Order* 2007, para. 2(4):

30 per cent   retrial starts within one month

20 per cent   retrial starts after one month

40 per cent   retrial is cracked or becomes a guilty plea within one month

25 per cent   retrial is cracked or becomes a guilty plea after one month.

No discounts are applied where the advocate who conducts the retrial is not the advocate who conducted the original trial: *ibid.*, para. 2(5).

Guilty pleas

G–135   Under the *Funding Order* 2001 a guilty plea included: (a) a trial of a case on indictment discontinued at the pleas and directions hearing for reasons other than a guilty plea: Sched. 4, para. 2(7); and (b) a trial, other than a cracked trial, disposed of by the defendant's guilty plea: *ibid.*, para. 9(5). The *Funding Order* 2007, however, defines a guilty plea as a case on indictment which is disposed of without trial because of the guilty plea, and is not a cracked trial: Sched. 1, para. 1(1)(b). Cases which result in a *Newton* hearing are excluded: *Funding Order* 2001, Sched. 4, para. 2(6)(c); *Funding Order* 2007, Sched. 1, para. 2(6)(c); and see *post*, G–147. Cases where the representation order was made before October 3, 2005, and where there were more than 400 pages of prosecution evidence or 80 prosecution witnesses are also excluded: *Funding Order* 2001, Sched. 4, para. 2(3). Where the representation order was made after October 3, 2005, such guilty pleas fall within the scheme. As to the meaning of prosecution evidence, see *post*, G–137.

The graduated fee for guilty pleas is calculated by reference to the basic fee, together with the appropriate evidence uplift per page as set out in the table of fees and uplifts: *Funding Order* 2001, Sched. 4, paras 7(1) and (2) and 8; *Funding Order* 2007, Sched. 1, paras 6 and 7 (and Table A)

Cracked trials

G–136   A cracked trial is a case on indictment which did not proceed to trial where (a) the defendant pleaded guilty other than at the pleas and directions hearing and there was no *Newton* hearing: *Funding Order* 2001, Sched. 4, para. 2(6)(c) and 9(3); *Funding Order* 2007, Sched. 1, para. 2(5)(c); or (b) the prosecution did not proceed with one or more counts and had not, before the pleas and directions hearing, declared an intention of not proceeding with them: *Funding Order* 2001, Sched. 4, para. 9(3); *Funding Order* 2007, Sched. 1, para. 1(1); or (c) where no pleas and directions hearing took place, the case was listed for trial but was disposed of otherwise: *Funding Order* 2001, Sched. 4, para. 9(4); *Funding Order* 2007, Sched. 1, para. 1(1). The rationale for the cracked trial fee is that it provides some element of compensation for the loss of refreshers and trial length increments which otherwise would have been payable: *R. v. Frampton* [2005] Costs L.R. 527.

The essence of a cracked trial is that after the conclusion of a pleas and directions hearing there are still counts on which the prosecution and defence do not agree so that a trial remains a real possibility: *R. v. Minster*, X23, SCTO 647/99; *R. v. Mohammed*, X27, SCCO 210/2000. A case listed for a plea and directions hearing is ultimately defined by what actually happens at that hearing. If a defendant pleads guilty at what is listed as a plea and directions hearing, the plea obviates the need for such a hearing. Accordingly, an advocate is entitled to a fee for a cracked trial: *R. v. Johnson* [2006] Costs L.R. 852 (*sed quaere*, as this flies in the face of the definition of a "cracked trial": see (a), *ante*). Where an indictment containing two counts was listed for trial following a pleas and directions hearing, but the defendant pleaded guilty to one count, which was acceptable to the prosecution, whereupon the case was put back for sentence, and where, at the adjourned hearing, a formal not guilty verdict was entered on the other count and where the defendant was represented by different counsel on the two occasions, it was counsel who represented him on the first occasion who was entitled to the "cracked trial" fee as what happened on that occasion came within the definition of a "cracked trial" (*viz.* case was one in which pleas and directions hearing took place, case did not proceed to trial, but guilty plea not entered at that hearing): *R. v. Johnson (Craig)* [2007] Costs L.R. 316. Once a meaningful trial has started, a change of plea cannot convert the trial into a cracked trial: *R. v. Maynard*, X19, SCCO 461/99; *R. v. Karra*, X19A, SCCO 375/99; and *Meeke and Taylor v. Secretary of State for Constitutional Affairs* [2006] Costs L.R. 1. Where a jury were discharged on the second day of a trial on a three count indictment, and on the following working day the prosecution added a new lesser count, and, before a new jury were sworn, the defendant offered sufficient pleas to the indictment, counsel was entitled to a fee for the first (abortive) trial, and a cracked trial fee for the later hearing at which pleas were tendered: *Frampton*, *ante*.

Where counsel had been instructed to appear at a plea and case management hearing and at trial (both of which had fixed dates), but over one month later and less than a month before the date fixed for the plea and case management hearing, the prosecution served notice of discontinuance, the matter fell within paragraph 9(4) of Schedule 4 to the 2001 order: *R. v. Wallace* [2008] Costs L.R. 494. *Sed quaere*: see the commentary in *Criminal Law Week* 2008/33/13, and see now paragraphs 2(8) and 18 of Schedule 1 to the 2007 order (*ante*, G–40, G–56).

Cracked trial fees do not apply where a person pleads not guilty at a pleas and directions hearing, but later the same day changes his plea; a guilty plea fee is appropriate: *R. v. Baxter*, X22, SCCO 375/99.

In respect of representation orders made before October 3, 2005 cracked trials fall outside the scheme where the number of pages of prosecution evidence exceeds 250 or prosecution witnesses exceed 80, or where, at the pleas and directions hearing it was accepted that the trial would exceed 10 days (or five days for a Class I offence): *Funding Order* 2001, Sched. 4, para. 2(4) (prior to revocation by S.I. 2005 No 2621, *ante*, G–1). As to the meaning o prosecution evidence, see *post*, G–137. Where the representation order wa made after October 3, 2005, such cracked trials fall within the scheme.

Where the representation order was made before October 3, 2005, the graduated fee for a cracked trial is calculated in the same manner as for a guilty plea, *ante*, G–135. Where the representation order was made after October 3, 2005, cracked trial fees are calculated separately. The fee is calculated by reference to when the case cracked, *i.e.* in the first, second or third part of a period calculated from the date when the court first fixed the date of trial or first ordered that the case should be placed into a warned list to the date of that first fixture or the date of the start of that warned list. The fact that the fixture might later be broken, or the case moved to another warned list is immaterial and does not affect the calculation. Where the number of days in the period cannot be equally divided by three, the remainder is simply added to the last third of the period: *Funding Order* 2001 Sched. 4, Part 3, para. 10(2) and (3); *Funding Order* 2007, Sched. 1, paras (and 7. The fee is payable to the advocate who appeared at the hearing where pleas were entered or the last such hearing if there was more than one: *R. v. Faulkner*, X33, SCCO 201/02.

Calculating the pages of prosecution evidence

G–137   Prosecution evidence includes all witness statements, documentary and pictorial exhibits and notes of interview with any defendant forming part o the committal documents or included in any notice of additional evidence *Funding Order* 2001, Sched. 4, para. 1(2); *Funding Order* 2007, Sched. 1 para. 1(2). The first 50 pages must be excluded for the purposes of the calculation: *Funding Order* 2001, Sched. 4, para. 7(2); *Funding Order* 2007 Sched. 1, para. 4(2). Additional documents cannot be included in the computation unless accompanied by a written notice of additional evidence *R. v. Sturdy*, X9, December 18, 1998, SCTO 714/98. Where one or more no tices of additional evidence have been served, a page count should include the contents of all such notices, unless all sides are agreed that service of a partic ular notice was an administrative error; and it is irrelevant when a notice wa served, or whether it was requested by the defence or prosecution: *R. v Taylor* [2005] Costs L.R. 712 (notice served on day jury retired). Where the Crown have exhibited and served tapes of interview, and defence counsel considers that a transcript of the interview is necessary, the pages of transcrip should be included in the computation: *R. v. Brazier*, X5, SCTO 810/97. Tax ing officers have been directed to include the fullest transcript produced together with the version in the transfer bundle (if shorter), and also t include any video evidence transcripts requested by the judge: *GFSG* A4 A4A. Taxing officers have been directed to exclude title and separator pages *GFSG*: A4A; and any additional edited versions of transcripts placed before a jury: *GFSG*: A5. Fax front sheets which are no more than title pages, duplicat witness statements, whether typed or hand-written, and very short lists of (*e.g* two) exhibits should not be counted: *R. v. El Treki*, X26, SCCO 431/2000. N allowance is made for small or large typefaces or for line spacing. Unused ma terial is also excluded.

Images and photographs

G–138   Pictorial exhibits include images served on CD ROM as well as photographs Where counsel has been served with all the images, those images should g

owards the page count, even if the prosecution shortly before trial decide to
use only a fraction of them. However, where over 33,000 photographs formed
part of the committal documentation, only a sample fraction of which were
copied to the defence and the court for trial purposes, the fact that defence
counsel inspected a further sample of the original photographs did not make
them fall within the definition of "used material". Accordingly, the material
not served on counsel fell outside the page count. As it was reasonable and
proper to view the additional sample, what counsel should have done was to
claim a special preparation fee for that further examination: *R. v. Rigelsford*
[2006] Costs. L.R. 523. *Rigelsford* was considered in *R. v. Austin* [2006] Costs
L.R. 857, where the argument that the page count should include as "pictorial exhibits" nearly 75,000 counterfeit DVDs and inlays on a CD-ROM served
by the prosecution was rejected, albeit not without hesitation.

Fees for leading and junior counsel

(a) *Representation orders made before April 30, 2007*   **G–139**

Leading juniors used to receive 75 per cent of the fee payable to Queen's
Counsel: *Funding Order* 2001, Sched. 4, para. 24(1)(b). As from October 3,
2005, that was increased to 85.71 percent of the fee payable to Queen's
Counsel: para. 24(1)(b), as amended by the *Criminal Defence Service (Funding) (Amendment) Order* 2005 (S.I. 2005 No. 2621). Led juniors, whether led
by Queen's Counsel or junior leading counsel, always receive one-half of the
fee payable to Queen's Counsel: *ibid.*, para. 24(1)(c). As from October 3, 2005,
that was increased to 57.41 percent: para. 24(1)(b), as amended by S.I. 2005
No. 2621. A single advocate may also receive one-half of the fee payable to
Queen's Counsel where a co-defendant on the same indictment is represented
by two advocates provided that the offence on which remuneration for the
single advocate is based is not a Class A offence (murder, manslaughter, etc.):
para. 24(2), (3). However, these percentages do not apply to work falling
within Part 4 of Schedule 4. In such cases payment should be made at the
fixed or hourly fee specified whether or not counsel is led: *Lord Chancellor v.
Singh* [2003] Costs L.R. 62.

(b) *Representation orders made on or after April 30, 2007*   **G–140**

Under the *Funding Order* 2007, fees payable to Queen's Counsel, leading
juniors and led juniors are not directly related, and are calculated from the
relevant tables: see, for example, the tables following paragraphs 5 and 7 of
Schedule 1. Where two or more led juniors are instructed in the same case,
each is paid as if they were the sole junior: Sched. 1, para. 23(1). Where a
junior appears alone, but a co-defendant is represented by two counsel, the
single junior is paid at the same rate as a led junior, unless his claim is for
fees for a Class A offence, when he is paid as a single unled junior: *ibid.*,
para. 23(2) and (3).

Advocates instructed for limited purposes

Advocates retained for a limited purpose are remunerated according to the   **G–141**
specific provisions of the *Funding Orders*. The limited purposes are:

    (a) the cross-examination of witnesses under the *YJCEA* 1999, s.38, which
        is remunerated as if for trial, save that the daily attendance fee is
        calculated by reference to the number of days the advocate actually
        attended court, instead of the number of days of the trial itself:

Funding Order 2001, Sched. 4, para. 28; *Funding Order* 2007, Sched
1, para. 27;

(b) the provision of written or oral advice: see *post*, G–160;

(c) mitigation of sentence on indictment, which is remunerated as for a
sentencing hearing together with a fee based on the fixed hourly specia
preparation rate according to the "reasonable number of hours" taken
Funding Order 2001, Sched. 4, para. 30(1); *Funding Order* 2007, Sched
1, para. 29(1); and an advocate who is discontented with the fee paic
may seek a redetermination: paras 30(2) and 29(2) respectively.

Trial advocates under the Funding Order 2001

G–142   A trial advocate is a person instructed in accordance with a representatior
order to represent the assisted person at the main hearing in the case: para
1(1). The definition must be given its ordinary meaning and does not mear
that counsel must be physically present in court to become entitled to a tria
advocate's fee. Where leading council cracked a case in the absence of junio
counsel, who had been delayed, the junior was nevertheless entitled to receive
the cracked trial fee: *R. v. Johnson* [2005] Costs L.R. 153.

Instructed and substitute advocates under the Funding Order 2007

G–143   An instructed advocate is the first advocate instructed in the case who ha:
primary responsibility for the case, or, where a representation order provide:
for more than one advocate, it means both the first advocate instructed whc
has primary responsibility for those aspects of a case undertaken by a leading
advocate and the first advocate instructed who has primary responsibility fo
those aspects of a case undertaken by a led advocate: art. 1(1).

The new scheme (RAGFS) places great emphasis on continuity o
representation. It seeks to achieve this partly by identifying an "instructec
advocate" who is responsible for advocacy services and partly by paying the
total fee for advocacy to the instructed advocate. An instructed advocatec
remains an instructed advocate at all times, although provision is made fo
the instructed advocate to be changed, where, for example, he is unable tc
conduct the trial because of a clash of commitments, is dismissed by the client
or professionally embarrassed: see Sched. 1, para. 20(9). If the instructec
advocate cannot attend a preliminary hearing, and sends a substitute advocate
he nevertheless remains responsible both for the conduct of the case and the
ultimate payment of the substitute advocate.

The *Funding Order* 2007 places great emphasis on identifying the
instructed advocate. Instructed advocates appointed before the pleas anc
directions hearing must in writing inform the court of their appointment a:
soon as they are appointed, otherwise the advocate who attends the plea
and directions hearing will be deemed to be the instructed advocate. If nc
advocate attends the plea and directions hearing, the advocate who attend
the next hearing will be deemed to be and will be recorded by the court a
the instructed advocate: see Sched. 1, para. 20(1)–(6). Where the represen
tation order is amended after a plea and case management hearing tc
include a second advocate, each advocate must notify the court in writing
whether they are the led or leading advocate. Where no additiona
instructed advocate is notified to the court in writing within seven days o
the plea and case management hearing, the advocate to appear at the nex
hearing is deemed to be the instructed advocate and the court will recorc
in writing whether he is the leading instructed advocate or the lec

instructed advocate, as appropriate to the circumstances of the case: *ibid.*,
para. 20(7).

To give effect to the scheme, emphasise the continuity of representation,
and ensure that all substitute advocates are paid for any RAGFS work they
undertake, the Bar Council has introduced a *Graduated Fee Payment Protocol*.
The protocol is an essential part of the mechanism by which advocates will be
remunerated in future, but it falls outside the immediate scope of this work.
It is available on both the Bar Council's and the Criminal Bar Association's
websites.

Sentencing hearings in cases on indictment

Any person appearing at a sentencing hearing in a case on indictment is **G–144**
entitled to a fixed fee which is enhanced where sentence has been deferred:
Funding Order 2001, Sched. 4, para. 15; *Funding Order* 2007, Sched. 1, para.
12. However, the fee does not apply, (a) where the sentencing hearing follows immediately after and forms part of the main hearing, and (b) where
the court proceeds under its confiscatory powers. In the latter case, separate remuneration is provided: *Funding Order* 2001, Sched. 4, para. 14;
Funding Order 2007, Sched. 1, para. 11, and see *post*, G–149.

A contested application for an anti-social behaviour order at a sentencing
hearing does not attract a separate or additional fee: *R. v. Brinkworth* [2006]
Costs L.R. 512.

Under the *Funding Order* 2001, an advocate instructed solely for the
purpose of mitigation shall be paid the appropriate fee for the sentence
hearing pursuant to paragraph 15, together with a fee calculated by reference to the reasonable number of hours of preparation undertaken for that
appearance multiplied by the hourly rates set out in the table following
paragraph 22 which are appropriate to the category of trial advocate and
length of trial: Sched. 4, para. 30(1). The advocate may apply for redetermination of such fee and shall supply such information and documents as
may be required by the appropriate officer as proof of the number of hours
of preparation: *ibid.*, para. 30(2).

For similar provisions under the *Funding Order* 2007, see *ante*, G–141.

Fitness hearings

A fitness hearing is a hearing to determine whether a defendant is fit to **G–145**
plead or stand trial: *Funding Order* 2001, Sched. 4, para. 27; *Funding Order*
2007, Sched. 1, para. 26. If there is a trial on indictment at any time thereafter, the length of the fitness hearing shall be included in determining the
length of the trial: *Funding Order* 2001, Sched. 4, para. 27(a); *Funding Order*
2007, Sched. 1, para. 26(a). Where a person pleads guilty at any time after
a fitness hearing is held, the advocate may elect to be paid either as if the
fitness hearing was a trial or for the guilty plea: *Funding Order* 2001, Sched.
4, para. 27(c); *Funding Order* 2007, Sched. 1, para. 26(c). Where a person is
found to be unfit, the trial advocate may elect to treat the fitness hearing either as a trial or as a cracked trial: *Funding Order* 2001, Sched. 4, para.
27(b); *Funding Order* 2007, Sched. 1, para. 26(b).

Cross-examination of vulnerable witnesses

Where an advocate is retained solely for the purpose of cross-examining a **G–146**
vulnerable witness under sections 34 and 35 of the *YJCEA* 1999, the gradu-

ated fee shall be assessed as though the matter was a trial, with the length of trial uplift and refresher calculated by reference to the number of days the advocate attended court: *Funding Order* 2001, Sched. 4, para. 28. For similar provision under the *Funding Order* 2007, see *ante*, G–141.

Newton hearings

G–147   Where a *Newton* hearing takes place following a trial on indictment the provisions relating to cracked trials, guilty pleas and sentencing hearings do not apply. The hearing is remunerated as for a contested trial. For the purposes of computation, the length of the *Newton* hearing is added to the main hearing: *Funding Order* 2001, Sched. 4, para. 6(2)(b); *Funding Order* 2007, Sched. 4, para. 2(6). Thus the main hearing starts on the day the plea is entered, even if this occurred during a pleas and directions hearing: *R. v. Gemeskel*, X2, SCTO 180/98. The advocate who attended the main hearing should claim the whole fee and remunerate the other advocate (if any) who attended the *Newton* hearing: *GFSG*: B12, 13.

Where a *Newton* hearing does not take place because the basis of plea was subsequently agreed, the case reverts to a guilty plea or cracked trial as appropriate: *R. v. Riddell*, X3, SCTO 318/98. If the hearing is aborted, the usual rules apply: see *post*, G–162, and *R. v. Ayres* [2002] Costs L.R. 330.

In *R. v. Newton*, 77 Cr.App.R. 13, the Court of Appeal clearly envisaged circumstances in which a sentencing judge could reach a conclusion without hearing evidence. However, the regulations define a *Newton* hearing as one at which evidence is heard for the purpose of determining the sentence of a convicted person in accordance with the *Newton* principles. Accordingly, a *Newton* hearing at which no evidence is called can only be remunerated by a standard appearance fee as it is not a *Newton* hearing for the purposes of the regulations: *R. v. Hunter-Brown*, X29, SCCO, 164/2001.

Adverse judicial comment and reduction of graduated or fixed fees

G–148   Where a trial judge makes adverse observations concerning an advocate's conduct of a graduated or fixed fee case, the appropriate authority may reduce the fee by such proportion as it "sees fit" (2001 order)/ "considers reasonable" (2007 order), having first given the advocate the opportunity to make representations about the extent of the reduction: *Funding Order* 2001, Sched. 1, para. 15(3); *Funding Order* 2007, art. 27. See also *post*, G–220.

(4) Additional fees

Confiscation proceedings

G–149   Hearings under section 2 of the *DTA* 1994 or section 71 of the *CJA* 1988 are excluded from the length computation of the main hearing and are remunerated separately as work for which a daily or half-daily fee is payable: *Funding Order* 2001, Sched. 4, paras 14 and 21; *Funding Order* 2007, Sched. 1, para. 11(2). The same is true of confiscation hearings under the *PCA* 2002: *Funding Order* 2001, Sched. 4, para. 14(1)(c), provided the representation order was made after on or after October 3, 2005 (see S.I. 2005 No. 2621 (*ante*, G–1)); *Funding Order* 2007, Sched. 1, para. 11(2). As there is no statutory provision for payment in respect of confiscation proceedings under the *PCA* 2002 where the representation order was granted before October 3, 2005, applications for payment should be made *ex post facto*

Entitlement to the daily fee arises where the hearing begins before but ends
after the luncheon adjournment; a half-daily fee is paid where the hearing
ends before or begins after the luncheon adjournment: *Funding Order* 2001,
Sched. 4, para. 14; *Funding Order* 2007, Sched. 1, para. 11(2). The appropriate rates are set out in the table following paragraph 19 (*ante*, G–57).

Abuse of process, disclosure and witness summonses' etc.

Applications relating to abuse of process, disclosure or witness summonses   **G–150**
heard before the main hearing are paid by the same fixed daily fee as that for
confiscation hearings: *Funding Order* 2001, Sched. 4, para. 13; *Funding Order*
2007, Sched. 1, para. 10(2), *ante*, G–149. As to remuneration for such applications where they take place as part of the main hearing, see *ante*, G–124.
A hearing merely relating to the failure of the prosecution to comply with an
earlier disclosure order attracts only a standard appearance fee: *GFSG*: 12.

In respect of representation orders granted on or after April 30, 2007,
these provisions were extended to include applications relating to the admissibility of evidence, and an unsuccessful application to withdraw a guilty plea
made by an advocate other than the advocate who appeared at the hearing
where the plea was tendered: *Funding Order* 2007, Sched. 1, para. 10(1)(d)
and (e).

Conferences

(a) *Under the Funding Order 2001*

Conferences are remunerated under the scheme provided that the advocate   **G–151**
satisfies the appropriate officer that the conference was reasonably necessary:
para. 19(1). Counsel can claim fees only up to a pre-determined number of
conferences, each of which cannot exceed two hours. However, where more
than one counsel are instructed, they do not have to claim for the same
conference; thus, a silk and a junior may each claim for different conferences
with the same client: *R. v. Bedford*, X36, SCCO 245/03. The permitted number
of conferences is as follows:

1 conference	trials up to 10 days, guilty pleas;
2 conferences	trials lasting not less than 11 and not more than 15 days;
3 conferences	trials lasting not less than 16 and not more than 20 days;
4 conferences	trials lasting not less than 21 and not more than 25 days;
5 conferences	trials lasting not less than 26 days and not more than 35 days;
6 conferences	trials lasting not less than 36 days and either not more than 40 days, or the case is one where the Commission have elected under article 9A to apply the graduated fee scheme.

The same number of conferences are permitted for cracked trials, *e.g.*
where it was accepted by the court at the pleas and directions hearing that the
trial would not exceed 10 days, one conference of two hours is permitted; if
so accepted that the trial would last not less than 11 and not more than 15
days, two conferences of two hours are permitted, *etc.*

(b) *Under the Funding Order 2007*

G–152   The first three pre-trial conferences or views are not separately remunerated; the fees are deemed to be included in the basic fee: Sched. 1, para 16(2). Thereafter, the permitted number of further conferences or view (each not exceeding two hours) is as follows:

1 conference	trials of more than 20 but less than 25 days
2 conferences	trials of more than 25 days but less than 35 days
3 conferences	trials of more than 35 but less than 40 days

The number of further conferences allowed in respect of cracked trials i similar, save that the anticipated length of trial is that accepted by the court a the plea and case management hearing: Sched. 1, para. 16(3).

(c) *Conferences under both orders*

G–153   Conferences include conferences with expert witnesses: *Funding Orde* 2001, Sched. 4, para. 19 (1); *Funding Order* 2007, Sched. 1, para. 16(1)(a) Travel expenses and the time taken in travelling, including time taken t travel to a conference with a defendant who could not reasonably b expected to attend counsel's chambers, are remunerated at the specifie hourly rate: *Funding Order* 2001, Sched. 4, para. 19(1); *Funding Order* 2007 Sched. 1, para. 16(5). Where such fees are allowed, reasonable travellin expenses may also be claimed: *Funding Order* 2001, Sched. 4, para. 19(1)(c) *Funding Order* 2007, Sched. 1, para. 16(4). The local Bar rule has no ap plication to such fees: *R. v. Carlyle* [2002] Costs L.R. 192.

Views

(a) *Under the Funding Order 2001*

G–154   Where a representation order has been made on or after October 3, 2005 a trial advocate may claim up to one hour (exclusive of travelling time) for view in any one case: Sched. 4, para. 19(1)(aa); and may also claim for tim travelling to and from the view: *ibid.*, para. 19(1)(b). If the client attends, th view also becomes a conference that could not reasonably take place i chambers, and travel expenses can therefore also be claimed: *R. v. Harde Singh* [2002] Costs L.R. 196. Where a view is necessary it is submitted that th local Bar rule does not apply: see *R. v. Carlyle* [2002] Costs L.R. 192.

Paragraph 19(1) as originally drafted related to hourly fees payable fo certain "types" of work which were listed thereafter. The types actually liste were conferences, and the paragraph concluded that where "that fee is a lowed" reasonable travel expenses were payable for "travelling to and from the conference". However, the inclusion of views as a "type" of work as from October 3, 2005 has given rise to an ambiguity. On one interpretation once fee for a "type of work" is "allowed", reasonable travel expenses for that typ of work are also allowed: on the other, travel expenses are payable only fo travelling to and from conferences. It is submitted that the clear intention c the amendment was to treat views in the same way as conferences, and that purposive construction should permit travel expenses for views to be paid.

(b) *Under the Funding Order 2007*

G–155   Under the *Funding Order* 2007, views and conferences are treated alike see *ante*, G–152.

Special preparation

Special preparation is preparation substantially in excess of the amount normally done for cases of the type in question and undertaken because the case involves "a very unusual or novel point of law or factual issue": *Funding Order* 2001, Sched. 4, para. 17(2); *Funding Order* 2007, Sched. 1, para. 14(1)(a). "Very" qualifies both "unusual" and "novel" and the phrase "very unusual or novel" qualifies both the expressions "point of law" and "factual issue": *Meeke and Taylor v. Secretary of State for Constitutional Affairs* [2006] Costs L.R. 1. Remuneration is calculated at an hourly rate for the number of hours "in excess of the amount normally done for cases of the same type": *Funding Order* 2001, Sched. 4, para. 17(3); "the number of hours preparation in excess of the amount the appropriate officer considers reasonable for cases of the same type": *Funding Order* 2007, Sched. 1, para. 14(3)(a).

What falls to be compensated is the extra work caused by the unusual or novel point by comparison with the sort of case involved without the unusual or novel point; as the term is used in relation to the quantification of fees, "type" in this context should be defined as an indication of weight; but the exercise does not include any consideration of the reasonableness of the time claimed; thus, once the determining officer has resolved that the case qualifies for a special preparation fee, he must assess the number of hours worked in excess of the norm and compensate for those hours at the prescribed hourly rate: *R. v. Goodwin* [2008] Costs L.R. 497.

The concept of "normal preparation" done for a case of the same type is wholly artificial. Other than in routine cases of burglary and theft, in virtually all other crimes in the criminal calendar, the circumstances vary infinitely: *R. v. Briers* [2005] Costs L.R. 146. The test is "What is the normal preparation for this offence?" not "What is the normal preparation for a case exhibiting these particular facts": *Briers, ante*; *R. v. Ward-Allen* [2005] Costs L.R. 745.

It is for counsel to differentiate between what he considers to be the normal preparation for a case of that type and the actual preparation that he has carried out: *Briers, ante*; *R. v. Marandola* [2006] Costs L.R. 184.

Very unusual or novel points of law have an obvious meaning, namely a point of law which either has never been raised or decided (novel) or which is outwith the usual professional experience (very unusual): *R. v. Ward-Allen, ante*. Some further assistance can be found in *Perry v. Lord Chancellor, The Times*, May 26, 1994 (*post*, G–225), although it should be noted that that case was not concerned with these regulations.

Very unusual or novel factual issues have a similar meaning, namely a factual issue which either has never been raised or which is outwith the usual professional experience: *R. v. Ward-Allen, ante*. Such issues might cover extremely rare medical conditions, such as Munchausen's Syndrome by Proxy or "pubic symphysitis dysfunction", the exceptional, if not unique, nature of which was held in *R. v. Bishop* [2008] Costs L.R. 808, to justify a special preparation fee where it had contributed to prosecution material of over 600 pages (not served as part of the page count); novel issues might, for example, have included DNA fingerprinting when it was introduced, but it would not qualify now. A case involving "shaken baby syndrome" does not necessarily attract a special preparation fee, unless there are additional medical complications: *R. v. Khair* [2005] Costs L.R. 542. A special preparation fee was allowed in *R. v. Thompson* [2006] Costs L.R. 668 where the defendant was accused of murdering her husband 10 years earlier. Counsel had to consider not only pathology and toxicology reports, but also a psychiatric profile on the husband prepared by a psychiatrist who had never met him, and issues arising in diabetology and physiology. Transcripts of the original coroner's inquest and the defendant's previous trials for theft and attempted murder of another husband were also served.

A special preparation fee would be reasonable where counsel had to check a sample of over 33,000 original photographs of which the prosecution had only copied a representative fraction for use at trial: *R. v. Rigelsford* [2006] Costs. L.R. 523; and see *ante*, G–138. But the mere fact that preparation properly undertaken for a complex three-week rape trial was "wasted" because the defendant decided to plead guilty during the prosecution opening did no justify a special preparation fee: *Meeke and Taylor v. Secretary of State for Constitutional Affairs, ante.*

A large quantity of unused material does not of itself give rise to a novel or unusual factual issue even where it is accepted that detailed examination of the material was necessary: *R. v. Lawrence* [2007] Costs L.R. 138; and even where the trial judge has extended a representation order to allow two juniors to peruse such material: *R. v. Dhaliwal* [2004] Costs L.R. 689. Such work is not remunerated under the graduated fee scheme or indeed at all: *ibid*. No does the mere failure of the scheme to accommodate unused material amoun to as breach of the principle of equality of arms: *R. v. Marandola, ante.*

In respect of respect of representation orders made after August 2, 2004 an advocate can also claim a special preparation fee where the prosecution evidence exceeds 10,000 pages and the appropriate officer considers that it is reasonable to make a payment in excess of the graduated fee which would otherwise be payable: *Funding Order* 2001, Sched. 4, para. 17A(1), and see the *Criminal Defence Service (Funding) (Amendment) Order* 2004 (S.I. 2004 No 2045), art. 3. The fee is calculated by reference to the number of hours which the appropriate officer considers reasonable to read the excess pages, using the current hourly fee rate: *Funding Order* 2001, Sched. 4, para. 17A(2) *Funding Order* 2007, Sched. 1, para. 14(1)(b).

Evidence served electronically

G–157   In respect of representation orders made under the *Funding Order* 2007, a special preparation fee also applies to prosecution evidence served in electronic form only, where the appropriate officer considers it reasonable to make a payment in excess of the usual graduated fee: Sched. 1, para 14(1)(c). The fee is calculated by reference to the number of hours the appropriate officer considers reasonable to view the evidence: *ibid.*, para 14(3)(c). It appears that these provisions are intended to deal with the difficulties encountered in *Rigelsford* and *Austin*: see *ante*, G–138.

Listening to or viewing tapes under the Funding Order 2001

G–158   See paragraph 19(2), and the table following paragraph 22. Each advocate instructed to appear in the main hearing is entitled to be remunerated for listening to tapes: *R. v. Murphy*, X4, SCTO 279/98; *GFSG*: O5, provided that the work was reasonably necessary: Sched. 4, para. 19(1). Listening to tapes when it was always clear that the defendant would plead, would be regarded as premature and therefore unreasonable: *R. v. Olayinka*, X29, SCCO 228/01 Advocates may listen to tapes relating to co-defendants; and they are no restricted to the tapes in the principal case: *R. v. Dalziell* [2003] Costs L.R 651, not following *R. v. Lynch*, unreported, SCCO 66/2000. The fee is calculated in units of 10 minutes listening time. Each tape is rounded up to the nearest 10 minute unit: *R. v. Everitt*, X7, SCTO 672/98.

Listening to or viewing tapes under the Funding Order 2007

There is no provision for any separate payment for listening to or viewing tapes. These are now treated as being rolled up within the whole of the graduated fee.

Provision of written or oral advice

Any advocate instructed solely to provide written or oral advice shall be paid a fee calculated from the reasonable number of hours of preparation for that advice using the appropriate hourly rates in the table following paragraph 22 of Schedule 4 to the *Funding Order* 2001. The advocate may apply for re-determination of such fee under paragraph 20(1)(c) of Schedule 1 and he shall supply such information and documents as may be required by the appropriate officer as proof of the number of hours of preparation: *ibid.*, para. 29.

There are similar provisions in the *Funding Order* 2007: see Sched. 1, para. 28.

(5) Acting for more than one defendant, or in more than one "case"

An uplift of one-fifth for each additional defendant represented may only be claimed where the regulations so provide: *Funding Order* 2001, Sched. 4, para. 23(2); *Funding Order* 2007, Sched. 1, para. 22(2). Where an advocate acts for more than one defendant, the advocate must select the case on which remuneration is to be based (the principal case). Claims may be made for pleas and directions hearings, some aborted hearings, main hearings, appeals against conviction, committals for sentence, proceedings for a breach of a Crown Court order, disclosure, abuse and witness summons hearings, and confiscation proceedings: *Funding Order* 2001, Sched. 4, para. 23(3); *Funding Order* 2007, Sched. 1, para. 22(3). In respect of a trial, the uplift is limited to one-fifth of the basic fee and not the basic fee enhanced by reference to the prosecution evidence, witnesses and length of trial uplift: *Funding Order* 2001, Sched. 4, para. 21(2)(b), *i.e.* where the main hearing in each case was heard concurrently: *R. v. Fletcher*, X6, SCTO 815/97.

The above provisions also apply where the advocate conducts two or more cases concurrently: *Funding Order* 2001, Sched. 4, para. 23(2); *Funding Order* 2007, Sched. 1, para. 22(2). Proceedings arising out of a single notice of appeal against conviction or sentence, or single committal for sentence, constitute a separate "case": para. 1(1) of Schedule 4 to the *Funding Order* 2001, and of Schedule 1 to the 2007 order. However, a committal for sentence together with a committal for breach of a community service order constitute two separate "cases" as the latter is a committal for breach of an earlier order: *R. v. Hines*, X24, SCCO 337/2000. As a case means proceedings on one or more counts of a single indictment, it is submitted that two trials arising from a severed indictment give rise to two separate graduated fees, as the trials are not heard concurrently.

(6) Abortive hearings

a) *Under the Funding Order 2001*

Fixed fees are payable for abortive hearings in certain defined circumstances. These occur where, (a) a bench warrant for non-attendance is issued but not executed within the following three months: Sched. 4, para. 12(1); (b) a listed trial does not proceed for any reason other than an application for postpone-

ment by the prosecution or the defence: *ibid.*, para. 12(1); (c) a listed plea i
adjourned for trial: *ibid.*, para. 12(2); (d) a hearing (other than a trial) canno
proceed because of the non-attendance of the defendant or witnesses or th
unavailability of a pre-sentence report or other good reason: *ibid.*, para. 16(b)
No fee is payable in the last two categories if the hearing forms part of th
main hearing or any other hearing for which remuneration is otherwis
provided: *ibid.*, para. 16(a). In each case, the appropriate fee is specified i
the table set out following paragraph 22.

(b) *Under the Funding Order 2007*

G-163   The payment of such fixed fees is limited to ineffective trials: see Sched. 1
para. 13.

(7) Wasted preparation

G-164   Wasted preparation occurs where an advocate does not represent his clien
because of (a) a clash of listings and the advocate has been unable to secure
change of date for either hearing; or (b) a fixture for a main hearing is altere
by the court despite the advocate's objection; or (c) the advocate withdraw
with leave of the court because of professional embarrassment; or (d) th
advocate is dismissed by the client; or (e) the advocate is obliged to undertak
judicial or other public duties: *Funding Order* 2001, Sched. 4, para. 18(1)
Funding Order 2007, Sched. 1, para. 15(1). A representation order replacing
a single junior with Queen's Counsel acting alone does not entitle junio
counsel to claim a wasted preparation fee in respect of the preparation rea
sonably and properly undertaken; counsel has no redress under th
scheme: *R. v. Schultz*, X10, SCTO 552/98. The hourly fee may be claime
only where eight or more hours of preparation have been undertaken, an
(a) the trial lasted for five days or more, or (b) in the case of a cracked trial
there are more than 150 pages of prosecution evidence: *Funding Order* 2001
Sched. 4, para. 18(3) and (4); *Funding Order* 2007, Sched. 1, para. 15(2)
The wasted preparation fee is calculated by reference to the number o
hours of preparation reasonably carried out by the advocate, who mus
supply such information and documents in support of the claim as may b
required: *Funding Order* 2001, Sched. 4, para. 17(4); *Funding Order* 2007
Sched. 1, para. 15(3) and (5).

(8) Appeals, pleas before venue, committals and other fees

G-165   Graduated fixed fees are also payable in respect of committals for sentenc
(which include plea before venue cases), appeals from magistrates' courts an
breach of Crown Court orders: *Funding Order* 2001, Sched. 4, para. 21(1)
Funding Order 2007, Sched. 4, para. 17; noting briefs: *Funding Order* 2001
Sched. 4, para. 22; *Funding Order* 2007, Sched. 4, para. 19; bail and othe
applications, and mentions when not forming part of a main hearing o
other hearing for which a fixed fee is provided: *Funding Order* 2001, Sched
4, para. 16(c), (d); *Funding Order* 2007, Sched. 4, para. 17(3). The appropri
ate rate is that listed in the table following paragraph 22 in Schedule 4 t
the 2001 order and paragraph 19 in Schedule 1 to the 2007 order. Afte
the Crown Court is seized of a case, any bail applications, or executions o
bench warrants made in a magistrates' court are remunerated as if made i
the Crown Court: *R. v. Bailey*, X16, 378/99. As to trials of *Bail Act* 1976 o
fences, see *ante*, G-130.

(9) Contempt proceedings

Remuneration for proceedings for contempt in the face of the court is fixed **G–166** at discrete daily rates: *Funding Order* 2001, art. 10; and *Funding Order* 2007, art. 13. The fees are fixed and there is no discretion to allow *ex post facto* payment, however regrettable and unfair the result may be: *R. v. Russell* [2006] Costs L.R. 841. Such payments do not fall within the graduated fee scheme and, therefore, such hearings do not form part of the main hearing or the sentencing hearing.

(10) Travel expenses

Travel and hotel expenses may be claimed subject to the usual 40 kilometre **G–167** local Bar rule: *Funding Order* 2001, Sched. 4, para. 25; *Funding Order* 2007, Sched. 1, para. 24 (see generally *post*, G–253). Expenses should not be paid in respect of conferences for which advocates are not entitled to be remuner- ated, unless the conference was abortive due to circumstances beyond the advocate's control: *R. v. Pickett*, X39.

(11) Table of offences

The effect of the table of offences at the end of Schedule 1 to the *Funding* **G–168** *Order* 2007 is set out in the following paragraphs. The principal differences as compared to the table in the *Funding Order* 2001 relate to the insertion of references to new statutory provisions and the creation of two new classes of case, *viz*. Classes J (serious sexual offences) and K (other offences of dishon- esty (high value)). As to value, under the 2001 order, where it mattered, the line was drawn at £30,000. Under the 2007 order, offences are divided into those below £30,000, those where the value is £30,000 or more, but less than £100,000, and those where the value involved is £100,000 or more. As to the method of calculation for the purposes of determining value, see *ante*, G–121. As to conspiracy, incitement and attempt, see *ante*, G–120.

An "armed robbery" (see the *Theft Act* 1968 entries) arises where the of- fender was armed with a firearm or imitation firearm, or was thought by the victim to have been so armed, or was armed with an offensive weapon: *R. v. Stables*, X12, SCTO 102/99.

Where a judge proposes to try an offence under the *Bail Act* 1976, s.6, in respect of a defendant who is first brought up before him for non-attendance, then there is a trial or guilty plea under the graduated fee scheme: *R. v. Shaw* [2005] Costs L.R. 326.

As several statutes are listed under more than one class, the following is a **G–169** list of the statutes and orders featured in the table, with the classes in which they appear—

Air Navigation Order 2005 (S.I. 2005 No. 1970)	H
Aviation Security Act 1982	B
Bail Act 1976	H
Child Abduction Act 1984	C
Crime and Disorder Act 1998	B, C, H
Children and Young Persons Act 1933	B, J
Cremation Act 1902	I
Criminal Damage Act 1971	B, C

Criminal Justice Act 1961	C
Criminal Justice Act 1967	I
Criminal Justice Act 1988	H
Criminal Justice Act 1991	B
Criminal Justice (International Co-operation) Act 1990	B
Criminal Justice (Terrorism and Conspiracy) Act 1998	I
Criminal Justice and Public Order Act 1994	I
Criminal Law Act 1967	I
Criminal Law Act 1977	D
Customs and Excise Management Act 1979	B, C, F, G, H, K
Dangerous Dogs Act 1991	C
Disorderly Houses Act 1751	H
Domestic Violence, Crime and Victims Act 2004	B
Drug Trafficking Act 1994	B, I
Drug Trafficking Offences Act 1986	C
European Communities Act 1972	I
Explosive Substances Act 1883	A, B
Firearms Act 1968	B, C
Firearms (Amendment) Act 1988	C
Forgery Act 1861	F, I
Forgery and Counterfeiting Act 1981	F, G, K
Fraud Act 2006	F, G, K
Hallmarking Act 1973	F, G, K
Identity Cards Act 2006	F
Immigration Act 1971	C
Indecency with Children Act 1960	J
Indecent Displays (Control) Act 1981	H
Infant Life (Preservation) Act 1929	A
Infanticide Act 1938	A
Insolvency Act 1986	G
Magistrates' Courts Act 1980	I
Malicious Damage Act 1861	H
Mental Health Act 1983	D
Merchant Shipping Act 1970	H
Misuse of Drugs Act 1971	B, C, H
Nuclear Material (Offences) Act 1983	B
Obscene Publications Act 1959	H
Offences against the Person Act 1861	A, B, C, H
Perjury Act 1911	I
Post Office Act 1953	H

Prevention of Corruption Act 1906	I
Prevention of Crime Act 1953	H
Prison Act 1952	C
Prison Security Act 1992	B
Proceeds of Crime Act 2002	B
Prohibition of Female Circumcision Act 1985	C
Protection from Eviction Act 1977	H
Protection from Harassment Act 1997	H
Protection of Children Act 1978	J
Public Bodies Corrupt Practices Act 1889	I
Public Order Act 1986	B, C, H
Public Passenger Vehicles Act 1981	H
Road Traffic Act 1960	H
Road Traffic Act 1988	B, H
Road Traffic Regulation Act 1984	H
Sexual Offences Act 1956	D, H, J
Sexual Offences Act 1967	D, H, J
Sexual Offences Act 2003	D, J
Sexual Offences (Amendment) Act 2000	D
Stamp Duties Management Act 1891	F, G, K
Submarine Telegraph Act 1885	C
Suicide Act 1961	B
Taking of Hostages Act 1982	B
Terrorism Act 2000	B, C
Theatres Act 1968	H
Theft Act 1968	B, C, E, F, G, H, K
Theft Act 1978	F, G, H, K
Trade Descriptions Act 1968	H, I
Treason Act 1842	C
Value Added Tax Act 1994	F, G, K
Vehicle Excise and Registration Act 1994	H

Class A: homicide and related grave offences

(i) *Common law offences*
   Murder and manslaughter   **G–170**

(ii) *Offences created by primary or secondary legislation*
   Those contrary to the following provisions:
      Explosive Substances Act 1883, ss.2 and 3;
      Infant Life (Preservation) Act 1929, s.1(1);
      Infanticide Act 1938, s.1(1);
      Offences against the Person Act 1861, s.4.

Class B: offences involving serious violence or damage, and serious drugs offences

(i) *Common law offences*

G–171   Kidnapping and false imprisonment

(ii) *Offences created by primary or secondary legislation*

> Those contrary to the following provisions:
>> *Aviation Security Act* 1982, s.2(1)(b);
>> *Crime and Disorder Act* 1998, s.30(1);
>> *Children and Young Persons Act* 1933, s.1;
>> *Criminal Damage Act* 1971, s.1(2) and (where the value exceeds £30,000) s.1(3);
>> *Criminal Justice Act* 1991, s.90;
>> *Criminal Justice (International Co-operation) Act* 1990, ss.12 and 18;
>> *Customs and Excise Management Act* 1979, s.50 (Class A or B drugs), s.85, s.170(2)(b) or (c) (in relation to Class A or B drugs);
>> *Domestic Violence, Crime and Victims Act* 2004, s.5;
>> *Drug Trafficking Act* 1994, ss.49, 50, 51, 52 and 53;
>> *Explosive Substances Act* 1883, s.4(1);
>> *Firearms Act* 1968, ss.5, 16, 17 and 18;
>> *Misuse of Drugs Act* 1971, s.4 (Class A or B drug), s.5(3) (Class A or B drug), ss.6, 8, 9, 12 and 13;
>> *Nuclear Material (Offences) Act* 1983, s.2;
>> *Offences against the Person Act* 1861, ss.16, 17, 18, 21, 22, 23, 28, 29, 30, 32, 33, 34 and 58;
>> *Prison Security Act* 1992, s.1;
>> *Proceeds of Crime Act* 2002, ss.327, 328, 329, 330, 331, 332, 333, 339(1A);
>> *Public Order Act* 1986, ss.1, 2 and 38;
>> *Road Traffic Act* 1988, ss.1, 3A and 22A;
>> *Suicide Act* 1961, s.2;
>> *Taking of Hostages Act* 1982, s.1;
>> *Terrorism Act* 2000, s s.11, 12, 13, 15, 16, 17, 18, 39, 54, 56, 57, 58 and 59;
>> *Theft Act* 1968, s.8(1) (if "armed"), s.8(2) (if "with weapon"), s.10, s.12A (if resulting in death) and 21.

Class C: lesser offences involving violence or damage, and less serious drugs offences

(i) *Common law offences*

G–172   Permitting an escape, rescue, breach of prison and escaping from lawful custody without force

(ii) *Offences created by primary or secondary legislation*

> Those contrary to the following provisions:
>> *Child Abduction Act* 1984, ss.1 and 2;
>> *Crime and Disorder Act* 1998, ss.29(1) and 30(1);
>> *Criminal Damage Act* 1971, s.1(1) and, where the offence does not also fall within section 1(2) and where the value of the damage is less than £30,000, s.1(3), s.2 and s.3;

Criminal Justice Act 1961, s.22;

Criminal Law Act 1977, s.51;

Customs and Excise Management Act 1979, s.50 (in relation to Class C drugs), s.68A(1) and (2), s.86, s.170(2)(b), (c) (in relation to Class C drugs);

Dangerous Dogs Act 1991, s.3;

Drug Trafficking Offences Act 1986, ss.26B and 26C;

Firearms Act 1968, ss.1, 2, 3, 4, 19, 20, 21(4), 21(5) and 42;

Firearms (Amendment) Act 1988, s.6(1);

Immigration Act 1971, s.25;

Misuse of Drugs Act 1971, s.4 (Class C drug), s.5(2) (Class A drug), s.5(3) (Class C drug);

Offences against the Person Act 1861, ss.20, 24, 26, 27, 31, 37, 47, 59, 60 and 64;

Prison Act 1952, s.39;

Prohibition of Female Circumcision Act 1985, s.1;

Public Order Act 1986, ss.18 to 23;

Submarine Telegraph Act 1885, s.3;

Terrorism Act 2000, s.19;

Theft Act 1968, s.8(1) (other than when "armed");

Treason Act 1842, s.2.

Class D: sexual offences and offences against children

Offences created by primary or secondary legislation

Those contrary to the following provisions: **G–173**

Criminal Law Act 1977, s.54;

Mental Health Act 1983, s.127;

Sexual Offences Act 1956, s.4, s.9, s.10 (other than by man with girl under 13), s.11, s.13 (between male aged 21 or over and male under 16), ss.14, 15, 19, 21, 23, 27, 29, 30 and 31;

Sexual Offences Act 1967, s.5;

Sexual Offences Act 2003, s.3, s.4 (without penetration), ss.11 to 13, 15 to 19, 32, 33, 36, 37, 40, 41, 52, 53, 61 to 67, 69 and 70;

Sexual Offences (Amendment) Act 2000, s.3.

Class E: burglary, etc.

Offences created by primary or secondary legislation

Those contrary to the following provisions: **G–174**

Theft Act 1968, ss.9 and 25

Classes F, G and K: other offences of dishonesty (offences always in Class F)

Offences created by primary or secondary legislation

Those contrary to the following provisions: **G–175**

Forgery Act 1861, ss.36, 37;

Identity Cards Act 2006, s.25(1), (3) and (5).

Classes F, G and K: other offences of dishonesty (offences always in Class G)

Offences created by primary or secondary legislation

G–176   Those contrary to the following provisions:

> *Customs and Excise Management Act* 1979, s.50 (counterfeit notes or coins), s.170(2)(b) or (c) (counterfeit notes or coins);
> *Forgery and Counterfeiting Act* 1981, ss.14 to 17;
> *Insolvency Act* 1986, s.360.

Classes F, G and K: other offences of dishonesty (offences in Class G if value exceeds £30,000, in Class K if value exceeds £100,000 and otherwise in Class F)

Offences created by primary or secondary legislation

G–177   Those contrary to the following provisions:

> *Customs and Excise Management Act* 1979, s.50 (to the extent not specified elsewhere), s.168, s.170(1)(b), s.170(2)(b), (c) (to the extent not specified elsewhere);
> *Forgery and Counterfeiting Act* 1981, ss.1 to 5;
> *Fraud Act* 2006, ss.2, 3, 4, 6, 7, 9 and 11;
> *Hallmarking Act* 1973, s.6;
> *Stamp Duties Management Act* 1891, s.13;
> *Theft Act* 1968, ss.1, 11, 13, 15, 16 and 22;
> *Theft Act* 1978, ss.1 and 2;
> *Value Added Tax Act* 1994, s.72(1)–(8).

Class H: miscellaneous other offences

(i) *Common law offences*

G–178   Keeping a disorderly house, outraging public decency

(ii) *Offences created by primary or secondary legislation*
Those contrary to the following provisions:

> *Air Navigation Order* 2005 (S.I. 2005 No. 1970), art. 75;
> *Bail Act* 1976, s.9(1);
> *Crime and Disorder Act* 1998, ss.1(10), 2(8), 31(1) and 32(1);
> *Criminal Justice Act* 1988, s.139;
> *Customs and Excise Management Act* 1979, ss.13 and 16;
> *Disorderly Houses Act* 1751, s.8;
> *Indecent Displays (Control) Act* 1981, s.1;
> *Malicious Damage Act* 1861, s.36;
> *Merchant Shipping Act* 1970, s.27;
> *Misuse of Drugs Act* 1971, s.5(2) (Class B or C drug); s.11;
> *Obscene Publications Act* 1959, ss.1 and 2;
> *Offences against the Person Act* 1861, ss.35 and 38;
> *Post Office Act* 1953, s.11;
> *Prevention of Crime Act* 1953, s.1;
> *Protection from Eviction Act* 1977, s.1;
> *Protection from Harassment Act* 1997, ss.3(6), 4(1) and 5(5);
> *Public Order Act* 1986, s.3;

Public Passenger Vehicles Act 1981, s.65;
Road Traffic Act 1960, s.233;
Road Traffic Act 1988, ss.2 and 173;
Road Traffic Regulation Act 1984, s.115;
Sexual Offences Act 1956, ss.2, 3, 12, 13 (other than where one partici-
pant over 21 and the other under 16), 22, 24 and 32;
Sexual Offences Act 1967, s.4;
Theatres Act 1968, s.2;
Theft Act 1968, s.12A (but not where death results);
Theft Act 1978, s.3;
Trade Descriptions Act 1968, ss.1, 8, 9, 12, 13 and 14;
Vehicle Excise and Registration Act 1994, s.44.

Class I: offences against public justice and similar offences

(i) *Common law offences*
Embracery, fabrication of evidence with intent to mislead tribunal, pervert-   **G–179**
ing the course of justice and personation of jurors

(ii) *Offences created by primary or secondary legislation*
Those contrary to the following provisions:
Cremation Act 1902, s.8(2);
Criminal Justice Act 1967, s.89;
Criminal Justice (Terrorism and Conspiracy) Act 1998, s.5;
Criminal Justice and Public Order Act 1994, ss.51(1) and (2), 75(1) and
(2);
Criminal Law Act 1967, ss.4(1) and 5;
Drug Trafficking Act 1994, s.58(1);
European Communities Act 1972, s.11;
Forgery Act 1861, s.34;
Magistrates' Courts Act 1980, s.106;
Perjury Act 1911, ss.1 to 7(2);
Prevention of Corruption Act 1906, s.1;
Public Bodies Corrupt Practices Act 1889, s.1;
Trade Descriptions Act 1968, s.29(2).

Class J: serious sexual offences

Offences created by primary or secondary legislation
Those contrary to the following provisions: **G–180**
Children and Young Persons Act 1933, ss.25, 26;
Indecency with Children Act 1960, s.1(1);
Protection of Children Act 1978, s.1;
Sexual Offences Act 1956, ss.1(1), 5, 6, 7, 10, 12 (of person under 16),
16, 17, 20, 25, 26 and 28;
Sexual Offences Act 2003, ss.1, 2, 4 (activity involving penetration), 5 to
10, 14, 25, 26, 30, 31, 34, 35, 38, 39, 47 to 50 and 57 to 59.

G. VERY HIGH COST CASES

Background

Unlike the *ex post facto* and graduated fee schemes, the Very High Cost   **G–181**

Case ("VHCC") regime is not concerned with fee assessment after the completion of a case. VHCCs operate under a contract based system where counsel's tasks and the time allotted for each task are agreed or determined before the work is undertaken.

The VHCC regime was originally intended to apply to cases likely to last for 25 days or longer at trial or where the defence costs (including counsel's fee, disbursements and VAT) of any one defendant (or group of defendants represented by the same firm of solicitors) were likely to exceed £150,000. For representation orders made after August 2, 2004, the criteria were simplified and altered to cover all cases likely to exceed 40 days: *Funding Order* 2001, art. 2 (as amended by the *Criminal Defence Service (Funding) (Amendment) Order* 2004 (S.I. 2004 No. 2045), art. 3). Whether or not a case fulfilled whichever criteria were applicable was a matter for the Legal Services Commission.

Since 2001, VHCCs have been managed under individual case contracts by the Legal Services Commission. On receipt of notification of an appropriate VHCC, the Commission's Complex Crime Unit would, on a case by case basis, issue an individual case contract to a firm of solicitors. Those solicitors would then instruct counsel in the usual way. The rates of remuneration for counsel within the scheme, and the number of hours' preparation to be undertaken within any one month, or during the trial, were matters for counsel to negotiate with the Complex Crime Unit. Although the cab-rank rule did not apply so as to oblige counsel to accept any particular contract, where counsel refused to undertake the work at the rates or upon the terms offered, the Commission could effectively withdraw the representation from counsel and/ or his instructing solicitor.

The *Criminal Defence Service (Funding) (Amendment) Order* 2007 (S.I. 2007 No. 3552) applies to proceedings that the Legal Services Commission classifies as a VHCC on or after January 14, 2008. The 2007 amendment order takes VHCCs out of the scope of the principal order altogether and an entirely new regime has been implemented.

The following paragraphs describe the new regime. The old regime will continue to apply to cases classified as VHCCs prior to January 14, 2008 and this regime is detailed in the first supplement to the 2008 edition of this work.

Definition of VHCCs

G–182   S.I. 2007 No. 3552 (*ante*) substitutes a revised definition of a VHCC which now covers (a) a case which, if it were to proceed to trial, would in the opinion of the commission be likely to last for more than 40 days, and in relation to which the commission considers that there are no exceptional circumstances making it unsuitable to be dealt with as such and (b) a case which in the opinion of the commission, if it were to go to trial, would be likely to last at least 25 days, but not more than 40 days, and in relation to which the commission considers that there are exceptional circumstances making it suitable to be dealt with as a very high cost case.

Very High Costs Case (Crime) Panel

G–183   A "best value" tendering competition has taken place between supplier law firms for places on a new national VHCC Panel. Law firms are not able to conduct any new VHCC cases unless they have secured a place on the panel. Organisations appointed to the panel (mainly comprising solicitors' firms) are known as panel members.

Barristers were not part of this competitive tendering exercise. As part of their tender bid, each panel member will have put forward a proposed defence team (team of lawyers) that would be available to carry out VHCC work. Advocates (barristers or solicitors with rights of audience in the Crown Court) are described as "key members" of the defence team. An individual advocate may have been named on more than one organisation's proposed defence team. Any self-employed advocates who are part of a defence team for an organisation that has successfully become a panel member must sign the Very High Cost Case (Crime) Panel Contract for Panel Advocates in order to work on VHCCs. By signing this document they then become panel advocates and are also appointed to the panel. Any advocates who are employees of a panel member do not have to sign the contract. Therefore, advocates do not apply as individuals to be panel advocates and can only gain membership of the advocates panel by being part of a panel member's defence team.

The *Criminal Defence Service (General) (No. 2) (Amendment No. 3) Regulations* 2007 (S.I. 2007 No. 3550) amend the *Criminal Defence Service (General) (No. 2) Regulations* 2001 (S.I. 2001 No. 1437) to provide, *inter alia*, that in a case which is, or which is likely to be, classified as a VHCC, the right conferred by section 15(1) of the *Access to Justice Act* 1999 (to select a representative) (§ 6–139 in the main work) is to select only a member of the Very High Costs Case (Crime) Panel.

As a result of an insufficient number of the advocates who had been put forward as members of defence teams agreeing to sign the VHCC contract as panel advocates, the *Criminal Defence Service (Funding) (Amendment) Order* 2008 (S.I. 2008 No. 957) further amended the *Criminal Defence Service (Funding) Order* 2007 (S.I. 2007 No. 1174) and makes provision for litigators to instruct advocates who are not members of the Very High Cost Cases (Crime) Panel. In such a case, the litigator may claim payment from the Legal Services Commission in respect of work undertaken by the advocate and authorised in accordance with the contract. Where such a claim is made, the Legal Services Commission must pay the litigator at rates no higher than the rates specified in the order. For the detail, see *ante*, G–81b.

The VHCC Contracts

All panel members must sign the Very High Cost Cases (Crime) Panel   **G–184**
Contract for Panel Members and all self-employed advocates must sign the Very High Cost Cases (Crime) Panel Contract for Panel Advocates (see *ante*, § G–183) in order to work on VHCCs. Panel members and panel advocates who have successfully gained places on the panel will commence their contracts on January 14, 2008 and these will run for a period of 18 months, expiring on July 13, 2009. There is no limit on the number of VHCCs panel members may accept during the terms of their contract; it will simply depend on their capacity and client choice.

Notification of a Very High Cost Case

Under the terms of the contract, the defence team must notify the Complex   **G–185**
Crime Unit as soon as it appears that a case will be, or is likely to be, a VHCC and, in any event, within five working days of (a) the plea and case management hearing or (b) the defence team having identified that the case is or is likely to be a VHCC, whichever is sooner. Under the contract, a case will be deemed to be a VHCC where either, (i) if the case were to proceed to trial, the trial would in the opinion of the complex crime unit be likely to last for more than 40 days and the Commission considers that there are no

exceptional circumstances which make it unsuitable to be dealt with under a contracting arrangement for VHCCs or, (ii) if the case were to proceed to trial, the trial would in the opinion of the Commission be likely to last no fewer than 25 days and no more than 40 days inclusive. Thus far, the definition coincides with the new legislative definitions in the *Funding Order* and the General Regulations. In relation to cases within (ii), however, the contract specifies that the case must also be one prosecuted by the Serious Fraud Office, be a terrorism case or be one to which at least two of the following criteria apply: (a) there are more than five defendants, (b) there are at least 10,000 pages of served prosecution evidence, (c) there are at least 10,000 pages of unused or third party material or (d) the case is a fraud case or one primarily involving serious drug offences (*Funding Order* 2007, Sched. 1, Class B (*ante*, G–171) and the value of the fraud (as described in the indictment or prosecution case statement/ summary) or drugs (as estimated by the prosecution authority) exceeds £1 million.

Quite apart from the obligation imposed by the contract, the *Criminal Defence Service (General) (No. 2) (Amendment No. 3) Regulations* 2007 (S.I. 2007 No. 3550) substitute a new paragraph (1) in regulation 23 (notification of very high cost cases) of the 2001 regulations (*ante*, § 6–177), the effect of which is to require any litigator who has conduct of a case which is, or is likely to be classified as, a VHCC to notify the commission in writing as soon as practicable.

Remuneration

G–186   All VHCC work carried out by defence team members will be paid at the hourly rate(s) specified in Annex 7 to the contracts. The rates have been proportionately reduced from those previously set out in Schedule 3 to the *Funding Order* 2007 (now revoked) (see § G–79 in the first supplement to this work). Further provisions relating to rates of pay and disbursements are set out in Annex 8 which states, *inter alia*, that the complex crime unit will only pay for VHCC work that is agreed in advance, unless certain exceptions apply. An advocate who has signed a contract and whose bid for advocates' panel membership has been accepted by the Commission will be unable to turn away VHCC work on the grounds that the remuneration is too low.

[The next paragraph is G–190.]

H. Preparation and Submission of Claims

(1) The preparation of claims

Every claim

G–190   Every claim must summarise the items of work in respect of which fees are claimed by reference to basic fees, refreshers, and subsidiary fees for conferences, consultations, views, written work and other court attendances where appropriate. The dates of work done, the time taken where appropriate, the sums claimed, the number of defendants represented and the particulars of work done in relation to more than one indictment or retrial must also be stated: *Funding Order* 2001, Sched. 1, para. 14(3). Advocates should always keep full contemporaneous notes of all preparation and times of work un-

706

dertaken: see *post*, G–196. Counsel is also required to supply such further particulars, information and documents as the appropriate authority may require.

(2) Graduated fees

Unlike *ex post facto* cases, there is no mandatory graduated fee form. The use of computer-generated forms is permitted and this allows only the relevant data to be submitted. As to graduated fees generally, see *ante*, G–115 *et seq.*   **G–191**

(3) Ex post facto cases under Schedule 1, para. 15(6)

Ex post facto claims should be made by Queen's Counsel or junior counsel under the *Funding Order* 2001, Schedule 1, para. 15(6). These fees apply in all cases where graduated fees are inapplicable or inappropriate (*ante*, G–116), and counsel has not claimed that exceptional circumstances exist in respect of all or any part of the work done which justifies the fee being assessed at a higher rate. Where work was reasonably undertaken and a claim is made, fees will not exceed the maximum stipulated. Subject to that limitation, fees will be assessed according to the relevant circumstances of the case: see *post*, G–200.   **G–192**

The regulations do not permit an application for *ex post facto* assessment of graduated fees on the grounds that the graduated fee provides inadequate remuneration for the work undertaken. However, counsel may claim that a fixed fee for a committal for sentence, an appeal from a magistrates' court, or proceedings arising out of an alleged breach of a Crown Court order is "inappropriate" taking into account all the relevant circumstances of the case: reg. 9(3). It is submitted that the proper test is whether the appeal, committal or breach was the usual or ordinary committal or appeal, etc., and not whether it was the usual or ordinary theft or other specific offence charged: see *R. v. Legal Aid Board, ex p. R.M. Broudie & Co (a Firm)*, *post*, G–195.   **G–193**

No claims for *ex post facto* fees are anticipated or catered for under the *Funding Order* 2007.

(4) Exceptional cases under the Funding Order 2001, Schedule 1, para. 15(6)

Where counsel claims that, owing to the exceptional circumstances of the case, the maximum rates prescribed for an *ex post facto* determination under Schedule 1, para. 15(2) would not provide reasonable remuneration for any part of his claim, the claim must be submitted for determination under Schedule 1, para. 15(6). That paragraph must be invoked in clear terms. If it is not, counsel cannot complain if the taxing officer fails to address his mind to the relevant factors when arriving at his decision. However, where it is obvious that the given particulars are particulars in support of a claim under paragraph 15(6), the taxing officer should apply that regulation: *R. v. Bryan and Collins*, November 4, 1985, TC C/4.   **G–194**

Nevertheless, it is submitted that for the avoidance of doubt and the preservation of counsel's position, whenever a fee in excess of prescribed statutory maxima is claimed for any single item of work, counsel must clearly state that the claim is made under paragraph 15(6). Where such a claim is made, counsel must additionally give full particulars in support of the claim for determination: Sched. 1, para. 14(4).

Meaning of "exceptional"

G–195   The meaning of the words "exceptional circumstances" and "all the relevant circumstances of the case" was considered by the Divisional Court in *R. v. Legal Aid Board, ex p. R.M. Broudie & Co. (a Firm), The Times*, April 11, 1994, where the phrases appeared in Schedule 1, paragraph 3 of the Costs Regulations (solicitors' standard fees). The Divisional Court did not cavil at the costs appeals committee's ruling that the word "exceptional" should be given its natural and ordinary meaning of "unnatural and out of the ordinary", but held "exceptional" meant exceptional when compared with an ordinary criminal case, not exceptional when compared with other cases of the same type: the taxing authorities should compare the case under consideration with the "usual or ordinary criminal trial" or the "generality of criminal cases", and not with cases of the same type.

(5) Counsel's obligation to keep proper records

G–196   On October 15, 1998, the Remuneration and Terms of Work Committee of the Bar Council resolved that it should be mandatory for counsel in *ex post facto* cases to keep contemporaneous logs recording the date, and the starting and finishing time of work done, and to identify in simple terms the nature of the task. Such logs should be made available to substantiate the claim for fees. The Bar Council further resolved that it would not support claims or appeals by barristers in matters in which no adequate or proper log was kept. Any claim which appears to be excessive and which cannot be substantiated is likely to be reported to the Professional Conduct Committee by the LCD.

The proper and detailed preparation of the original claim is vital. It is counsel's duty to ensure that proper records of time spent in court are kept (DTMD, II/(18)), that appeals to the taxing authority and costs judges are properly supported, and that representations of fact are substantiated: DTMD, II/(41). If counsel fails to supply the proper information at the proper time to enable the taxing officer to perform his statutory function, then he has no-one but himself to blame if he receives fees which he considers inadequate: DTMD, II/(56). Taxing officers can rarely obtain from the case papers all the circumstances relevant to a claim and it is not for the officer to assume or guess at counsel's legitimate and recoverable expenses or other factors not drawn to his attention. It is for counsel to draw all relevant matters to the attention of the taxing officer. Moreover, apart from matters submitted in re-determination, original claims found the basis of appeals to a costs judge unless the costs judge gives leave to adduce fresh evidence. Such leave is rarely given: *post*, G–274.

G–197   In *R. v. Ghadhim Gerhards* (1984) Costs L.R. 463, the taxing master stated:

> "A determining officer cannot be expected properly to take these factors into account unless, when the claim is made, he is supplied with detailed information showing what additional work or conferences are claimed. A general statement, in support of a claimed brief fee, that the case entailed additional preparation during the course of the trial will not do. He must be told on which days it was done and whether or not it was done on days for which a refresher was payable. If the work was done on such a day then clearly a claim must be made that the provisions of regulation 8(2)(b) should apply. That will require counsel to explain under regulation 7(4) [of the 1982 Regulations, now repealed], in respect of each such day, not only the time involved but the reason why the additional work became necessary, since unless there is some special circumstance, routine thinking work, and the ordinary work which counsel always does during a trial is covered by the brief fee or refresher without augmentation. In short, if proper remuneration is to be given, the

burden on counsel accurately to record and to itemise and explain the work he has done, becomes very much heavier than was formerly the case."

It is submitted that the principle stated above is applicable and relevant when some additional and or exceptional work is occasionally undertaken during a trial. It should not apply to long trials where preparation or conferences over and above the norm are a daily or regular feature. In the latter case, the necessity of daily preparation and or conferences should be reflected in enhanced brief fees and refreshers, and the *Ghadhim Gerhards* principle will only apply where some particularly onerous or exceptional piece of work has to be undertaken.

Apportionment of expenses

Expenses should be attributed to the case in respect of which they were incurred. Where expenses have been incurred jointly for more than one case they should be apportioned equally between the cases: DTMD, II/68. **G–198**

(6) Time limits for the submission of claims

No claim by an advocate for fees for work done shall be entertained unless submitted within three months of the conclusion of the proceedings to which it relates: *Funding Order* 2001, Sched. 1, para. 15(1); *Funding Order* 2007, art. 5(3). However, where a confiscation hearing under section 2 of the *DTA* 1994, section 71 of the *CJA* 1988 or Part 2 of the *PCA* 2002 is held more than 28 days after a person has been found or pleaded guilty, a graduated fee claim can be submitted despite the fact that the proceedings have not yet been completed: *Funding Order* 2001, Sched. 1, para. 14(1A); *Funding Order* 2007, art. 5(6). The time limit may be extended for good reason: *Funding Order* 2001, Sched. 1, para. 23(1); *Funding Order* 2007, art. 32(1); for example, where the claim is particularly complicated and difficult to prepare, where a co-defendant's case is awaiting disposal, or because there is a genuine misunderstanding about the submission of a claim. Extensions should be sought before the time limit expires. **G–199**

Where there are no good reasons, the time may be extended in exceptional circumstances, in which case the appropriate authority shall consider whether it is reasonable to reduce the fee: *Funding Order* 2001, Sched. 1, para. 23(2); *Funding Order* 2007, art. 32(2). That provision is designed to cover cases where the advocate is at fault for the delay but it would be too great a penalty to disallow his costs. An advocate should be given a reasonable opportunity to show cause why his costs should not be reduced (*Funding Order* 2001, Sched. 1, para. 23(2); *Funding Order* 2007, art. 32(2)). Any reduction may be challenged by appeal to the taxing master: *post*, G–269. Any reduction in costs made by way of penalty should not normally exceed 20 per cent: *DDO*, para. 5.2.

Notwithstanding that a representation order may be expressed to cover proceedings in the Crown Court "and in the event of [the defendant] being convicted or sentenced ..., advice and assistance in regard to the making of an appeal", the legislation is clear as to the need for a claim in relation to work done in the Crown Court to be submitted within three months of the conclusion of the proceedings in that court, rather than within three months of the date on which an application for leave to appeal to the Court of Appeal was refused: *R. v. White* [2008] Costs L.R. 479 (decided in relation to a like provision relating to claims by solicitors under the 2001 order).

I. Ex Post Facto Assessments

(1) General

G–200   In determining costs in respect of work done under a representation order the appropriate authority shall, subject to and in accordance with the regulations, take into account all the relevant circumstances of the case including the nature, importance, complexity or difficulty of the work and the time involved and shall allow a reasonable amount in respect of work actually and reasonably done: *Funding Order* 2001, Sched. 1, para. 15(1). The words "all the relevant circumstances of the case" are unrestricted: *R. v. Legal Aid Board, ex p. R.M. Broudie & Co. (a Firm), The Times*, April 11, 1994, DC, *ante*, G–195. A comparison with graduated fees is irrelevant as they represent a totally different system of assessing fees: *R. v. Hempsall*, unreported, February 11, 1998, SCTO 928/97; and *R. v. Cheng and Chen* [2007] Costs L.R. 626, SCCO (such a comparison would be flawed, graduated fees being calculated by reference to a standalone statutory scheme which does not draw at all on the methodology used to assess fees *ex post facto*).

G–201   It is impossible to state all the factors or the weight to be attached to any individual factor which may be taken into account in assessing non-graduated fees. Factors which play a substantial role in one case may carry less weight in another. Each case depends upon its own facts. In general terms, however, the major factors are, (a) the importance and gravity of the case; (b) the size and complexity of the matter, including the number of documents examined or perused with due regard to difficulty or length; (c) counsel's skill and specialised knowledge; (d) the degree of responsibility and other burdens placed on counsel; (e) the time reasonably expended by counsel; (f) all other relevant circumstances, including any assessment of the weight of the case and observations made by the trial judge, and travelling and hotel expenses where appropriate.

Ex post facto remuneration effectively ceases in respect of representation orders made on or after April 30, 2007, the *Funding Order* 2007 making no provision for such payments.

(2) The importance and gravity of the case

G–202   The importance of the case includes the importance to each defendant in terms of its consequences to his livelihood, standing, or reputation even where his liberty may not be at stake: *TONG*, para. 1.11(a). The fact that a substantial concurrent civil action involves matters related to the criminal proceedings and is likely to be resolved against the defendant if he is convicted is clearly relevant. The gravity of a case can usually be determined by the charges faced, the maximum terms of imprisonment which such charges attract, and the likely sentence. The fact that the case is heard by a High Court judge is not of itself an indication of its gravity; listing officers cannot always ensure that such judges hear cases of appropriate gravity or difficulty: DTMD, II/(8).

(3) Size and complexity of the case

G–203   Any assessment of the size and complexity of a case is necessarily subjective and coloured by counsel's own past experience and practice. However, the assessment should be based not upon the experience or lack of experience of

counsel, but upon the circumstances of the case. These include the quantity of
documentary, evidential and unused material which had to be examined, the
complexity of the subject matter or the factual background, any unusual
evidential, forensic or legal issues, expert evidence and the number of expert
witnesses, the existence and the number of child witnesses, the number of
defendants represented, the number and nature of the charges, the nature of
the defence, the existence of any potential or real conflicts with co-defendants,
and the length of time spent in preparation and trial. In any event, regard
must be had to the bulk and complexity of the documentary exhibits, the
number of witnesses, counts, and accused, and other factors which indicate
the size of the case: *TONG*, paras 1.11, 2.2, 2.3. The observations of a trial
judge can also be of great assistance to taxing officers in assessing the size,
complexity and weight of a case: see *post*, G–220.

Documents in the case

Earlier editions of *TONG* suggested that the documents in the case should   **G–204**
be counted. The current edition simply observes that in assessing the weight
of a case the taxing officer should take into account the "relevant documents":
TONG, para. 2.3. These can usually be assessed by simply stating the number
of pages of witness statements, exhibits and other material. Where, however,
the number of documents do not accurately reflect the volume of material
examined (where material has been supplied on computer disk, or statements
are of a highly technical or complex nature), counsel should so state. Although the number of pages is a factor, the weight of a case should not be
judged solely thereby: DTMD, II/(2).

(4) Skill and specialised knowledge of advocate

Experience and standing of advocate

An advocate's fees are not usually assessed by reference to the standing and   **G–205**
experience of the individual who undertakes the case but by reference to the
standing and experience of counsel who might normally be expected to handle
a case of that type. The primary consideration is the weight of the case and
not the seniority of counsel: DTMD, II/(37); *TONG*, para. 1.11. The fact that
counsel is a recorder does not of itself require that the fee be enhanced.
Counsel is perfectly entitled to refuse to accept instructions in a case in which
the allowance made in accordance with those principles would not provide remuneration which he considers sufficient to take into account his own standing and experience at the Bar: *R. v. Coleman*, May 24, 1978 (Chief Taxing
Master), approved and followed in DTMD, II/50. Cases of a difficult and deli-
cate nature, such as a charge of gross indecency in a public place by a teacher
of high standing and which involved medical evidence, may well justify the
instruction of mature and experienced counsel: DTMD, II/(19).

Saving of time by advocate

It is not proper to reduce a brief fee where a saving of time results from   **G–206**
counsel's special skill or effort, such as an ability to speak the defendant's
language, with the result that preparation time was shorter than if an
interpreter had been used: DTMD, II/(13). Where, to save costs or shorten
the trial, counsel has properly undertaken work such as preparing admissions
of fact, agreeing evidence, advising his client or attending a pre-trial review,

this should be taken into account even where a separate fee has been allowed for such work: *TONG*, para. 2.11; and see *post*, G–230 and G–242.

(5) Responsibility and burden on advocate

G–207   The degree of responsibility imposed and the burden placed upon counsel in any case is largely but not exclusively reflected in the size, complexity, importance and duration of the case and the issues involved. The longer the case, the greater the burden and strain which may be placed upon counsel.

Representation of two or more defendants

G–208   Representation of more than one accused should be borne in mind when assessing fees. In cases where the defence advocate's burden is increased by different defences put forward or by conflicts between the accused, these factors must be taken into account: *TONG*, para. 2.21.

Murder

G–209   Murder still carries a heavy burden of responsibility and the fees should reflect this: *TONG*, para. 2.16. However simple, a murder trial is always considered as imposing a special burden on an advocate: DTMD, II/(22).

Public and media interest

G–210   Excessive media interest and frequent reporting of the progress of the case require counsel to scan press reports before and during trial to ensure that the client receives a fair trial. Excessive media attention can be a significant additional burden as well as an indication both of public interest and possibly the importance of the case.

Difficult and demanding defendants

G–211   Some defendants place a heavy additional burden on an advocate. They may be demanding, difficult, neurotic, or suffer from depression or personality disorders. This can result in considerable difficulties in obtaining coherent or consistent instructions in conference or otherwise, and in ensuring that the client understands the issues involved. An advocate cannot properly discharge his duties to the court or the defendant unless he obtains and retains the trust and confidence of the lay client. There is a proper distinction to be drawn between the legitimate discharge of what may be called an advocate's pastoral role and the undertaking of unreasonable work. It is submitted that written advice given and conferences held, which are necessary to ensure that the client understands the issues involved and the way in which his case is to be presented, are work reasonably undertaken.

(6) Time reasonably expended by an advocate

G–212   The time expended by an advocate in the preparation and conduct of the case must be reasonable. It is submitted that "reasonable" means what is necessary for the proper conduct of the case and the proper advancement of the defendant's interests. No allowance can be made for any work done in the court below, unless the order for taxation provides otherwise: *TONG*, para. 1.16. Unnecessary preparation, incompetent or prolix advocacy is clearly unreasonable, but such issues are more properly dealt with by way of a reduction in the fees allowed or a wasted costs order.

Change of advocate and preparation by new advocate

An advocate should not be penalised where for good reasons he cannot **G–213**
hold the brief. If a change of advocate is proper and reasonable, a fresh basic
fee should be allowed to the second advocate to hold the brief: *TONG*, para.
2.37. Thus, separate basic fees were properly paid where an advocate successfully applied to sever an indictment and conducted the first trial but was unable to attend when the second trial was fixed the following year (*R. v. Panice*
(1984) Costs L.R. 462), or where an advocate was unable to conduct the trial
because he was detained in a case which overran its estimated length (*R. v.
Davies* (1985) Costs L.R. 472), or where, having prepared a "floater", for
reasons beyond his or his clerk's control, counsel was prevented from appearing (*TONG*, para. 2.55), or where an advocate was dismissed or withdrew
from the case with leave of the court, or where he had to be released due to
prior commitments: DTMD, II/(16) *TONG*, para. 2.56. The fact that an
advocate is part-heard in another case might or might not be a reasonable
ground for returning the brief, depending on the priority in which the cases
were listed and other factors. In general, an advocate who has been instructed
in a case for which a trial date has been fixed should ensure that he does not
accept another brief which would interfere with his availability on that date:
DTMD, II/(47).

Before deciding that a change of advocate was neither reasonable nor **G–214**
proper, the taxing officer must satisfy himself that he has good grounds for
the decision and if justification for the change is required it should be sought
from the advocate who appeared at the first trial. If the change was unnecessary, the second advocate should receive a proper basic fee, but the basic fee
for the original trial or original advocate should be adjusted so that the total
amount will be the same as if one advocate had acted throughout: *TONG*,
para. 2.37. Thus the consequences of an unreasonable change of advocate fall
on the first counsel to be instructed: DTMD, II/(47).

Representing private and publicly funded clients in the same case

An advocate who represents both privately and publicly funded defendants **G–215**
is entitled to a basic fee calculated in the usual way to reflect all work done by
him solely on behalf of the publicly funded client. However, in respect of any
preparation, conferences, views and written work done jointly for the benefit
of both clients, an advocate is entitled to a proportion of the proper fee for
that work which represents the value thereof to the publicly funded client.
But if the advocate has been paid a separate fee by the privately funded client
which wholly remunerates him for all the work he did, he is not entitled to remuneration under the representation order for that work. The position is
clearly different where the amount of the advocate's work has been increased
by the interests of the publicly funded defendant. The application of these
principles is not affected by the number of briefs delivered to an advocate: *R.
v. Noble*; *R. v. Powell-Smith*, May 1991, TC C/16. The taxing officer is entitled
to request an advocate to disclose the amount of fees privately paid: *R. v.
Noble, ante.*

Separate briefs

If delivery of separate but contemporaneous briefs to the same advocate is **G–216**
justified (*i.e.* separate indictments and committals) the fee for the second brief
should be reduced where there is any duplication in the work involved:
TONG, para. 2.20. A basic fee should not be reduced merely because an

advocate appears in more than one case in the same Crown Court on the same day: DTMD, II/(31); *TONG*, para. 2.9.

Wasted time and wasted costs

G-217   A smaller basic fee (or it is submitted, refresher) may be allowed where the taxing officer, having heard an advocate's representations, determines that the court's time has been wasted: *TONG*, para. 2.12. Where the taxing authority is minded to disallow for this reason any amount of a claim for work done and a wasted costs order is made by a court which relates to the same work the taxing authority shall disallow only the greater of two amounts: Sched. 1 para. 16(2). It is submitted that where a wasted costs order is made, it would be unusual for a taxing officer to seek further to reduce the fee. Where the taxing authority has made no such disallowance and a court makes a wasted costs order, the amount of such order is simply deducted from the advocate's fees: *Funding Order* 2001, Sched. 1, para. 16(1); *Funding Order* 2007, art 28(1). As to wasted costs orders, see, §§ 6–54 *et seq.* in the main work, and *Practice Direction (Costs: Criminal Proceedings)* [2004] 2 All E.R. 1070, paras X.1.1 *et seq.*, § 6–114g in the main work.

(7) Other relevant considerations

Fees paid to prosecutors

G-218   The regulations are not restrictive and do not preclude the taxing authority from looking at the fees paid to prosecuting counsel. Prosecuting counsel's fees are part of the material upon which the exercise of judicial discretion is based in determining reasonable remuneration or a reasonable amount: *Lord High Chancellor v. Wright* [1993] 1 W.L.R. 1561, QBD (Garland J.); *Lord Chancellor v. Rees* [2009] L.S. Gazette, January 22, 16, QBD (Sir Charles Gray); and see *R. v. Cheng and Chen* [2007] Costs L.R. 626, SCCO (the fee allowed to prosecution counsel may be used as a useful cross-check to ensure that defence counsel's fee does not fall wholly out of kilter with market forces). Although the taxing officer is not compelled to look at the prosecution fees, it is now the practice for Circuit Taxing Directors to build up links with the Crown Prosecution Service to enable them, in appropriate cases, to see if the prosecution had a particular reason for their fees. Taxing officers should produce written reasons to emphasise in particular cases what might have accounted for a disproportion in allowances: *TONG*, para. 2.15.

Graduated fees and fees in Very High Costs Cases

G-218a   In *Lord Chancellor v. Rees, ante*, G–218, it was held that comparison with fees payable in cases within the Very High Costs Cases scheme might be inappropriate by reason of the particular circumstances of the *ex post facto* scheme which was separate and distinct; and that, likewise, care should be taken when using the graduated fee scheme as a comparator because of the difference between cases under that scheme and those assessed *ex post facto*.

Private fees

G-218b   In *Lord Chancellor v. Rees, ante*, G–218, it was held to be illegitimate to use privately funded cases as comparators in the assessment of publicly funded work; privately funded work was market driven and was the subject of negotiation, whereas publicly funded work was closely regulated.

ees in civil cases

There is no equity between civil and criminal fees: the quantum of fees **G–219**
)aid to barristers in civil cases is not relevant in determining criminal fees: see
?. *v. Martin* [2007] Costs L.R. 128.

Judicial observations and assessments

Before arriving at a final assessment, the taxing officer should also take into **G–220**
account the assessment of the weight of the case by the judge who tried it or
hose who participated in it. To that end the court log should be referred to
)n every taxation and any observations made by the trial judge which are rel-
:vant to taxation should be considered: *TONG*, para. 1.12. Proper regard
nust be given to such observations, but a taxing officer ought not to give ef-
'ect to them if it would produce a result contrary to the relevant regulations
DTMD, II/(12)). In the end, he must form his own judgment: DTMD, II/(3).
Where a trial judge makes adverse comment to the taxing authorities about
an advocate's conduct, for example by stating that a trial had been prolonged
)y two days because of repetitive cross-examination, the advocate concerned
should be given the opportunity of responding: DTMD, II/(3), II/(27); *Practice
Direction (Costs: Criminal Proceedings)* [2004] 2 All E.R. 1070, para. X.1.5, § 6–
114g in the main work; *Funding Order* 2001, Sched. 1, para. 15(3); and *Fund-
ng Order* 2007, art. 27(1). Where observations are made directly to an
advocate by the trial judge, the taxing officer should approach the judge
'or amplification: DTMD, II/(57).

Where no observations are made by a trial judge, a taxing officer should
normally seek guidance from the judge if he considers that an advocate's fees
should be adversely affected, and should be cautious in taking upon himself,
vithout such consultation, a decision which reflects upon the competence of
he advocate: DTMD, II/(14).

(8) The basic fee

Basic fees and brief fees

It is misleading to suggest that the "basic fee" which appears in the regula- **G–221**
ions is synonymous with a brief fee. The "basic fee" is wide enough to include
a brief fee but also extends to all preparatory work, properly carried out by
:ounsel whether or not followed by a hearing: *R. v. Davies* (1985) Costs L.R.
172. The basic fee entitles an advocate to remuneration for preparation,
ncluding preparation for a pre-trial review and, where appropriate, the first
day's hearing including where they take place on that day, short conferences,
onsultations, applications and appearances (including bail applications),
'iews and any other preparation: *Funding Order* 2001, Sched. 1, para.
.5(5)(a). Listening to and annotating tapes in *ex post facto* cases forms part of
he preparation time, and accordingly allowance should be made for the fact
hat the time spent in such a task is likely to exceed tape running time.

Assessing the basic fee

The basic fee is assessed by reference to similar cases, the number of hours **G–222**
pent in preparation and the limits allowed by the *Funding Order* 2001. Fee
issessment depends upon proper and careful assessment of all the relevant
ircumstances including the weight of the case, and the skill and responsibil-
ty involved in its conduct: *TONG*, para. 2.6. Preparation time is of less sig-

nificance when compared with the seriousness of a case, the skill and experience required of counsel, and the responsibility resting upon him: DTMD, II (32); and, accordingly, the application of a simple multiplier to preparation time is not the appropriate method of assessing a basic fee: DTMD, II/(24) *TONG*, para. 2.6; *R. v. Martin* [2007] Costs L.R. 128; and *R. v. Winskill* [2008 Costs L.R. 651 (where it was said that the fee should be assessed by reference to what a hypothetical counsel, capable of conducting the case effectively, bu unable or unwilling to insist on the higher fees sometimes demanded b counsel of pre-eminent reputation, would be content to take on the brief).

In *Loveday v. Renton (No. 2)* [1992] 3 All E.R. 184 at 190, Hobhouse J dealing with a civil claim stated:

> "The brief fee covers all the work done by way of preparation for representation at the trial and attendance on the first day of the trial. But in heavy litigation particularly where there is a team of barristers and experts, additional work i involved in ensuring that the client is properly represented and his case full developed beyond simply appearing in court. In this litigation counsel had to mee together to consider their strategy and tactics and prepare material. They also had t have meetings with their experts, including meetings with experts from abroad prior to their going into the witness box to give evidence. Some of these meeting were lengthy and took place at weekends. Then there was the work involved in th preparation of final submissions."

He later stated (at p. 191) that "the brief fee should be assessed and allowed having regard to the full history of the trial as now known". It is submitted that this observation overrules the general approach adopted in *R. v. Bella* (1986) Costs L.R. 479, to the effect that unexpected matters arising at tria should be ignored in assessing the brief fee, whether counsel's responsibilitie were increased or decreased thereby.

Basic fees cannot and should not be increased to reflect the time taken b counsel to travel to court. Nor can a claim for enhanced payment arise from delay in the determination of fees; such a claim amounts to a claim for inter est, which is not provided for in the regulations and is not in accordance witl the practice of the Bar: DTMD, II/(74). Nor can the fee be enhanced for los of other remunerative work not undertaken because of the necessity of leav ing sufficient time available for dealing with a case which might have beer contested. Such a claim is not recognised by the practice of the Bar as being valid head of claim: DTMD, II/(59); *Loveday v. Renton (No. 2), ante*, at p. 194e and *Lord Chancellor v. Rees, ante*, G–218.

Advocate's familiarity with the case

G–223   Where an advocate has appeared in other trials relating to the same basi facts, it is proper when assessing the basic fee to take into account counsel's fa miliarity with those basic facts in that he did not need to undertake th detailed preparation which would otherwise have been necessary: DTMD, II (7).

Work more properly done by solicitors

G–224   The fact that an advocate does work both in preparation and during th trial which might more properly have been done by instructing solicitors doe not disentitle him from receiving the appropriate recompense out of the pub lic funds: DTMD, II/(5). An advocate's duty is to undertake work which is i the interests of the defendant. If this necessitates work which is more properl done by instructing solicitors, an advocate is entitled to be remunerated in th usual way for the additional burden placed upon him. An advocate's proper remuneration for such extra work is not consequential upon any reduction in the care and conduct costs of his instructing solicitors: DTMD, II/(17), and see DTMD, II/(5).

Preparation and legal research

An advocate is always entitled to remuneration for considering how the law applies to the particular facts of a case, which must include advice on the topic to lay client and solicitors and the preparation of legal argument for submissions before the trial judge. However, taxing officers are entitled to assume that an advocate is familiar with the current substantive and procedural law in the field in which he holds himself out as practising: *Perry v. The Lord Chancellor, The Times*, May 26, 1994 (Garland J.). An advocate may claim for preparation based upon "getting up the law" where legal issues arise which are so unusual or infrequent that an advocate would clearly require substantial preparation time, such as new or changing fields of law; cases which are so unusual or infrequent that substantial preparation time is clearly required; the impact of European law; the proper construction of new legislation; unexpected points of law which arise at the beginning or during the course of a trial which necessitate adjournment for research and argument. Advocates dealing with the ordinary run of criminal cases may not regard themselves as fully equipped to deal with matters arising under specialist legislation governing, for example, pollution, consumer credit or planning. Each case must fall to be decided upon its own facts and counsel's professed expertise: *Perry v. The Lord Chancellor, ante.*

G–225

Preparation and the viewing of unused material

Time spent on preparation includes attendance at a police station or elsewhere to peruse unused material which has not been copied to solicitors: *R. v. Sullivan* (1989) Costs L.R. 490. The fact that counsel has to carry out work at a location away from his chambers by examining such material at a time not wholly under his control should be taken into account as being an "exceptional circumstance" which places an unusual burden on counsel and should be reflected in the basic fee: *Sullivan, ante.*

G–226

Additional preparation resulting from delays and adjournments

Additional preparation may be reasonably necessary where a case is delayed or adjourned or sentence deferred for such period that the advocate is justifiably involved in extra work in refreshing his memory or considering further evidence or reports: *TONG* (1975 ed.), para. 64.

G–227

Not guilty pleas which run short

The basic fee should take into account the length of the hearing plus the full time taken for preparation, the weight of the case, and the skill and responsibility involved in its conduct. Care must be taken to ensure that a fee appropriate to work reasonably undertaken is allowed in those cases where a plea of guilty has been entered on an advocate's timely advice: *TONG*, para. 2.18. Conversely, where defendants are prepared to plead to lesser charges, an advocate will not receive full remuneration for trial preparation if an approach was made to the prosecution only shortly before the trial date: DTMD, II/(67). Even where discussions initiated between solicitors have been unsuc-

G–228

cessful, an advocate once instructed is still required to make an early approach to the prosecutor if his client is prepared to plead to a lesser charge: DTMD, II/(60).

First day's hearing

G–229 The basic fee covers not only preparation of the case, but the value of the advocate's attendance in court on the first day of trial: *TONG*, para. 2.4. Where a case which is listed for trial on a particular day does not begin promptly, and the actual time of the hearing is substantially less than five hours, the brief fee should be adjusted accordingly. But if on the first day an advocate was unable to do any other work whilst necessarily waiting at court for the case to begin and so notifies, or otherwise satisfies the taxing officer, this fact should be taken into consideration when making any such adjustment: *TONG*, para. 2.39, 2.40.

Duration of the trial

G–230 The duration of a trial may reflect the weight of a case. The additional burdens on an advocate usually associated with longer trials may be absent where there is separate representation but no conflict of interest in multi-defendant cases, or an abnormal amount of interpreting, or very lengthy jury deliberations. In such cases, the extra length is compensated for by refreshers: *TONG*, para. 2.8. The basic fee should not be reduced where a trial has been shortened by an advocate's efforts to speed the case or render the issues more intelligible: see *ante*, G–206.

Preparation undertaken during the trial

G–231 Schedule 1, para. 15(5)(b), to the *Funding Order* 2001 provides for a refresher fee for "any day or part of a day during which a hearing continued, including where they took place on that day ... any other preparation." Regulation 8(1)(b) of the *Legal Aid in Criminal Proceedings (Costs) Regulations* 1982 (S.I. 1982 No. 1197) was similarly worded and considered in *R. v. Ghadhim Gerhards* (1984) Costs L.R. 463, *ante*, G–197, where the taxing master ruled that if any work of preparation is reasonably done after the commencement of the trial on a day when a refresher fee is payable, then it can only be remunerated by the payment of an enhanced refresher fee for the day in question, even if the work was done outside normal court hours: but see now *Loveday v. Renton (No. 2)*, *ante*, G–222. If any properly chargeable work of preparation is done during the course of a trial on a day for which no refresher fee is payable, then it must and can only be claimed as part of the brief fee: *ante*, G–197; *TONG*, para. 2.4. As to the position where an advocate is forced to prepare a case during trial because of late instructions, see DTMD, II/28, *post*, G–249.

Retrials

G–232 Time reasonably spent by an advocate in preparation for a retrial should be remunerated at the same rate as for preparation at the first trial and the fee paid as a supplement to the refresher for the first day of the retrial: DTMD, II/(32). In determining what is reasonable, relevant factors include, (a) the lapse of time between the two trials and the extent to which re-preparation was required; (b) the extent to which the issues at the first trial had to be refined or changed for the retrial; (c) whether the same witnesses were called

in the retrial; (d) whether further enquiries had to be made and additional
witnesses called; (e) whether cross-examination of important witnesses was
based on the same assumptions and pursued in the same way as at the first
trial; (f) any additional difficulties caused by changes in the number of
defendants on the indictment: *TONG*, para. 2.36. The extent and degree to
which the evidence of witnesses in the first trial requires to be analysed and
compared with their original witness statements is also a factor: DTMD, II/
(25).

Ex post facto refreshers

For each day on which the hearing continues after the first day, an advocate   **G–233**
is entitled to a refresher unless there is good reason to the contrary: *TONG*,
para. 2.38. There is no justification for paying a smaller refresher while an
advocate is waiting for a jury's verdict than for a day when the advocate is
strenuously cross-examining throughout: *R. v. Mills and Morris* (1993) Costs
L.R. 498. The amount of the refresher will vary according to whether the
advocate has been occupied in court for less or more than a full day. A court
day is normally of five hours' duration, although urgent applications or other
matters may shorten the period available. In such circumstances, a taxing officer should exercise his discretion broadly. He should not count the exact
minutes when considering whether a full refresher has been earned, but
should decide whether, in substance, the time during which counsel has been
prevented from being engaged on other business amounts to one day: *TONG*,
para. 2.42.

Serious fraud cases

In serious fraud cases the trial commences on arraignment and preparatory   **G–234**
hearings therefore form part of the trial: *CJA* 1987, s.8 (§ 4–84n in the main
work). An advocate is thus entitled to a refresher for each day he attends
the preparatory hearing.

Refreshers for days other than full days

Refreshers for less than a full day shall be paid at a rate which is reasonable   **G–235**
having regard to the fee allowable for a full day: Sched. 3, para. 3. For a hearing lasting approximately a half-day the refresher should be rather more than
one-half of a full refresher: *TONG*, para. 2.44. Where a case is interrupted
and an advocate is engaged exclusively in the case (for example in the preparation of schedules) and unable to do other work, such time may, at the taxing officer's discretion, be included for the purpose of calculating the
refresher. Alternatively a separate fee may be allowed for a consultation or
conference: *TONG*, para. 2.45. An advocate should always satisfy the taxing
officer by marking his brief or otherwise recording that the time spent at
court relates exclusively to the case in question and (if appropriate) that he
was unable to do any other work: *TONG*, para. 2.40.

For a hearing of substantially more than five hours on the first or any
subsequent day an additional allowance should be made: *TONG*, para. 2.43.
Logically this should amount to an uplift of that part of the refresher fee
which represents the court hearing.

Weekend sittings

Barristers are not wage earners but professionals who are expected to work   **G–236** unsocial hours from time to time without being remunerated at a higher rate as if they were salaried. An advocate's refreshers in respect of a weekend spent waiting for a jury's verdict should be remunerated in the normal way: *R. v. Mills and Morris* (1993) Costs L.R. 498.

Substitute advocate during trial

G–237   Where the advocate holding the brief does not attend part of the hearing, the amount of the refresher or attendance fee attributed to that part should be assessed having regard to the standing of the advocate who takes his place or holds the brief, whichever is lower: *TONG*, para. 2.47.

As a general rule, payment is only made to the advocate who conducts the case. It is his responsibility to settle with an advocate of equal standing who covered for him. If the other advocate is not called upon to take an active part in the proceedings or if he is very junior, a much lower rate should be allowed—as little as one-quarter in some instances or in the case of a pupil even less: *TONG*, para. 2.52. Nevertheless, where two or more advocates are engaged in the same work for the same client, then provided the multiplicity of advocates is not due to ad hoc devilling, an advocate in different chambers should be paid separately, provided that the aggregate of the fees does not exceed that which would have been paid if only one advocate had been engaged: *TONG*, para. 2.53.

Travel time

G–238   Refreshers should not be increased to reflect the time taken by an advocate to travel to court: *TONG*, para. 2.50; DTMD, II/68.

An advocate's wasted time

G–239   In certain unusual circumstances, an advocate is entitled to claim an attendance fee when his case is not listed for hearing. After a week disrupted by adverse weather conditions, an advocate made every effort to discover whether the court was sitting. Having obtained no useful information he attended court to discover that the day's hearing had been cancelled. As no explanation had been given by the court for wasting his time, he was entitled to a refresher for the wasted day: DTMD, II/38. However, where a case was interrupted by prison officers' strike action so that an advocate had to hold himself in readiness each day to resume the hearing, he was not entitled to refreshers because he had not attended court on the days in question: DTMD, II/(46); and see *ante*, G–222.

In long trials it has been accepted that it is perfectly proper for an advocate to seek, and taxing officers to pay, refreshers for days when the court does not sit (*e.g.* because the judge has another commitment), particularly if the trial judge has directed the advocates not to take on any other work. However, in *Loveday v. Renton (No. 2)* [1992] 3 All E.R. 184 at 190, Hobhouse J. observed that daily refreshers cannot be charged for days the court is not sitting, but that does not mean that advocates should not be remunerated for necessary work which is an incident of the proper representation of their client.

(9) Appearances

G–240   An advocate's attendance at court other than in the course of a substantive hearing may be loosely classified as an appearance. These include bail and other applications and pre-trial reviews, but not, it is submitted, attendances at preparatory hearings: see *ante*, G–234. They also include floaters which are not reached on the day listed for trial. Appearances in non-graduated fees cases cover attendance at applications (including bail applications and adjournments for sentence) and pre-trial reviews together with, where they took place on that day, short conferences where attendance is not covered by the basic or refresher fee: *Funding Order* 2001, Sched. 1, para. 15(5)(c)(iii).

Non-effective cases

Where a case is not reached on the day listed for trial, then if the advocate **G–241** is unable to undertake any other work, he should be allowed a fee for each day or part of a day spent waiting at court. This fee should be about the same as the refresher fee to which he would otherwise have been entitled, but regard will be had to the fact that he has not been actively engaged on the case. Where waiting time is properly spent on preparation, the fee should take that into account. Taxing officers are now directed to allow a fee equal to the maximum amount provided for in Table I in Schedule 3 to the *Funding Order* 2001 for attendance at pre-trial reviews, etc., unless the fee would not provide reasonable remuneration in all the circumstances of the case, in which case the advocate should apply under Schedule 1, para. 15(6). The fee will then be calculated on the same basis as a basic fee save that regard should be had to the fact that counsel was not actively engaged in the case. That fee should therefore be about the same rate as a refresher: *TONG*, para. 2.13.

(10) Conferences and views

The fee for attendance at consultations, conferences and views is **G–242** determined in accordance with the prescribed hourly rate, provided that the fee shall not fall below the minimum amount specified: Sched. 3. Where an advocate holds a conference with prosecuting counsel to discuss pleas, or takes other timely steps to agree pleas and simplify issues, the advocate should be remunerated accordingly: DTMD, II/(49).

A pre-trial conference or consultation of substance with the client, instructing solicitor alone, or the other side should, if justified, be allowed: *TONG*, para. 2.58. It is submitted that this direction must also apply to conferences with expert witnesses.

In assessing the fee, the time justifiably taken travelling to see an accused in prison should be taken into account, normally at the same rate as the conference rate: *TONG*, para. 2.58.

Conferences and consultations during trial

It is assumed that short conferences take place in most trials and the **G–243** refresher takes account of that fact. A conference during trial will not attract a fee unless it is clear that it was of some substance, as for instance where a fresh point of evidence has arisen or is likely to arise: *TONG*, para. 2.59. Refreshers cover "short conferences": *Funding Order* 2001, Sched. 1, para. 15(5)(b), and Sched. 3, para. 1. A short conference is one not exceeding half an hour: *TONG*, para. 2.60. Where no separate fee is allowed for conferences during trial, consideration should be given to reflecting this in the basic fee: *TONG*, para. 2.60.

Views

Preparation does not become a view merely because it is done at a particu- **G–244** lar location. A view means a visit to a location to see a place or some object, or some physical relationship between things at that place, which may have direct evidential value in the case. The visit must occur because proper consideration can be given only to matters seen at the place where they are situated: *R. v. Sullivan* (1989) Costs L.R. 490. The examination of documents other than at an advocate's chambers is not a view. If an examination requires special or other scientific equipment then a visit to the place where such equipment is located in order to conduct the examination can properly be described as a view: *ibid.*

(11) Written work

G–245   Written work covers written advice on evidence, plea, appeal, case stated and other written work: *Funding Order* 2001, Sched. 1, para. 15(5)(b)(ii).

Trial documents and case statements

G–246   It is submitted that a distinction should be drawn between written advices and pleadings which initiate a procedure or process (such as grounds of appeal or a witness summons), and the preparation of documents for use at trial; the former is written work whereas the latter is merely one facet of preparation. Schedules, admissions and agreed statements should form part of an advocate's general preparation. Although defence statements may be said to be a form of pleading, the circumstances in which such documents may go before the jury are limited. It is submitted that such statements form an integral part of the preparation of the case and should be treated as such.

Advice on appeal

G–247   An advocate is entitled to remuneration for written advice on appeal against sentence and/or conviction where it is reasonable to have advised in writing. See also *Practice Direction (Costs: Criminal Proceedings)* [2004] 2 All E.R. 1070, Part XII, § 6–114i in the main work.

Where an advocate forms a final view that there is no prospect of a successful appeal, and so informs the defendant immediately after the conclusion of the case, in the absence of express instructions or special circumstances, the advocate shall not be paid for a subsequent written advice on appeal as it would not be work reasonably done: *Lord Chancellor v. Brennan, The Times*, February 14, 1996 (Hooper J.). Hooper J. observed that *R. v. Neill* (1986) Costs L.R. 475, provided helpful guidance as to what amounted to special circumstances. Relevant factors include the effect on a defendant (a short sentence in a straightforward case can cause as much concern to a defendant as a long sentence), any particular difficulties which occurred in the trial, lack of impact which oral advice given immediately after the conclusion of a trial may have upon a particular defendant, and the fact that negative advice can prevent an unmeritorious appeal which if pursued could cause a defendant to lose part of the time served. It is not reasonable to disallow a negative advice on appeal solely because an advocate after consideration advises that no point of law arises and the only real issue is the length of sentence: *R. v. Neill, ante.*

(12) More than one advocate and noting briefs

Queen's Counsel

G–248   The basic fee for Queen's Counsel appearing with a junior or alone should be assessed in the usual way: *TONG*, para. 2.22. Where leading counsel is briefed on a matter to assist the court in a case more suitable for junior counsel and which comes into the list at very short notice and no suitable junior is available, the fee appropriate to leading counsel should be paid unless he has agreed to accept a lesser amount: DTMD, II/(48).

Junior counsel in cases with Queen's Counsel

The established practice is to allow junior counsel one-half of his leader's   **G–249** brief fee and refreshers unless circumstances justify either more or less: *TONG*, para. 2.30. Where it is clear that the usual practice would result in junior counsel receiving less than fair remuneration for the work done and the responsibility carried by him, then the taxing authority should depart from the usual practice: DTMD, II/(58). In *Glossop v. The Lord Chancellor* [2005] Costs L.R. 359, Hobhouse J. ruled that in assessing junior counsel's fees, taxing authorities are constrained neither by the amount of the fee paid to leading counsel, nor by the fact that leading counsel did not appeal his fees. In the great majority of cases the established practice of paying one-half of the leader's fee applies, but in suitable cases the proportion may well be more (or less). In exceptional cases (*e.g.* where junior counsel has undertaken a great deal of preparatory work and the leader is principally brought in to deal with one important matter which may determine the result of the trial) fair remuneration may require that junior counsel's remuneration exceeds his leader's fee. The *Glossop* principle is still sound and was recently applied in *R. v. Kennedy* [2006] Costs L.R. 662.

Where the leader is also junior counsel, the led junior should normally receive two-thirds of the fee of leading junior counsel: *TONG*, para. 2.31. Where an unled junior appears in a case with Queen's Counsel, the burden on him is greater than that on the led juniors. It will normally be reasonable for him to receive a fee of about two-thirds of the Queen's Counsel's fees: DTMD, II/(24). Where a leader withdraws from a case at a late stage so that his junior has effectively no time to carry out the preparatory work in the normal way but must prepare the case as best he can while the trial is actually in progress, counsel may be compensated by enhanced refresher fees, and in more complex cases the basic fee should be commensurate with that which would have been assessed if counsel had received his instructions in the ordinary way: DTMD, II/(28).

Noting briefs

The fee of a noting junior should not exceed one-half of the refresher ap-   **G–250** plicable to junior counsel: *TONG*, para. 2.33. Where an advocate reasonably sits in on the trial of a co-defendant in order to safeguard his client's interests, he is entitled to a refresher but the amount should reflect the fact that he is not required to take an active part in the trial: *TONG*, para. 2.34.

J. Disbursements and Expenses

(1) Disbursements

A barrister is not entitled to claim for disbursements or expenses other than   **G–251** those permitted under the *Funding Orders*.

(2) **Travelling and accommodation expenses**

Entitlement under the regulations

G–252   Travel and other expenses incidental to appearance at court may be claimed
provided the court is not within 40 kilometres of the advocate's office or
chambers. Unless prior approval for the expenditure has been obtained under
the regulations, or unless the advocate can justify his attendance having
regard to all the relevant circumstances of the case, the amount payable shall
not be greater than that, if any, payable to a trial advocate from the nearest
local Bar or the nearest advocate's office (whichever is the nearer): *Funding
Order* 2001, Sched. 3, para. 5, and Sched. 4, para. 25; *Funding Order* 2007,
Sched. 1, para. 24. As to interim payment of travel and accommodation expenses, see *ante*, G–107, G–108.

Local bars

G–253   An advocate may be able to justify his attendance in a distant court which is
usually serviced by a local bar where:

   (a) the instruction of local counsel might lead to suspicion of prejudice,
       lack of independence or lack of objectivity (*e.g.* cases of local notoriety
       involving public figures or officials);
   (b) there are insufficient local counsel whom instructing solicitors consider
       are sufficiently experienced to undertake the case in question so as to
       give the client a reasonable choice;
   (c) the services of an advocate who has specialised experience and knowl-
       edge of the type of case of an unusual or technical nature are required;
   (d) the advocate has previously been instructed in related matters which
       would assist him in the presentation or preparation of the case in ques-
       tion: DTMD, II/(68), approved in *R. v. Conboy* (1990) Costs L.R. 493;
       and see *R. v. Gussman*, X14, SCTO 40/99 (counsel had represented his
       client seven years earlier on a charge of murder; his knowledge of his
       client's earlier medical condition was relevant to the current charges of
       rape, and this amounted to special circumstances justifying his
       attendance).

It is submitted that a further justification arises where an advocate is forced
to follow a particular judge on circuit who is seized of his case and it was not
reasonable to instruct another local advocate for that particular hearing.
Where an advocate is instructed from outside a local bar for any of the above
reasons it is advisable that he obtains a letter from his instructing solicitor
explaining why he was instructed, and for his clerk to obtain prior approval
for incurring such expenses from the court. This applies also to Queen's
Counsel practising off-circuit: *post*, G–256.

G–254   An allowance will not be paid because counsel, having been instructed as a
member of a local bar, moved chambers to a distant location. Such a move is a
matter of counsel's convenience only: DTMD, II/(11). If counsel chooses to
reside or have his chambers at a distance from the courts in which he usually
practises, he cannot normally expect the extra expense to be taken into account: DTMD, II/(15)1. An advocate is perfectly entitled to refuse to accept
instructions to appear in a case in which he would not receive remuneration
for the unusual expenses which he would be obliged to incur by travelling to
a distant court where it cannot be shown that the circumstances warranted
him personally undertaking that journey: DTMD, II/50. An allowance for expenses will not be justified solely on the grounds that instructing solicitors

normally choose to instruct particular counsel or particular chambers, or that the client specifically asked for the advocate in question, or that counsel had acted for the client in an unrelated matter: DTMD, II/68. A publicly funded person does not have an unrestricted right to choose any advocate in the country for any case, however simple, in which he is involved (DTMD, II/50), nor is he entitled to choose his representative, without regard to the convenience of the court or the cost involved: DTMD, II/73.

[The next paragraph is G–256.]

Queen's Counsel and local bars

Queen's Counsel should not be regarded as being "local" to any particular **G–256** local bar, even though his chambers are in one particular place. Where Queen's Counsel practises on circuit, he should as a general rule receive an amount in respect of travelling and hotel expenses actually and reasonably incurred and necessarily and exclusively attributable to his attendance at a court on the circuit on which he practises: *R. v. Thomas; R. v. Davidson; R. v. Hutton* (1985) Costs L.R. 469. Where Queen's Counsel practises outside his circuit, the "local bar" rules apply: *ante*, G–253.

Expenses reasonably incurred

The reasonableness of an advocate's claim for travel and hotel expenses **G–257** should be judged not by reference to the expenses incurred by other advocates in the same case, but in relation to the demands upon the advocate in putting forward his lay client's case and his own particular circumstances in relation to the conduct of the trial: *R. v. Plews* (1984) Costs L.R. 466; *post*, G–260.

The regulations refer to expenditure "reasonably incurred", whereas earlier regulations referred to expenses "actually and reasonably incurred". In *R. v. Conboy* (1990) Costs L.R. 493, the taxing master observed that the current wording is wider. It is submitted that the alteration acknowledges an advocate's entitlement to recover a reasonable amount in respect of expenses necessarily and exclusively attributable to attendance at court. Thus, where the expense incurred was reasonable, an advocate should recover in full. Where the travel undertaken or accommodation used was reasonable but the cost incurred was excessive, an advocate may only claim for and recover a reasonable amount being a sum no greater than that which he would have incurred had his expenses been reasonable.

Travel to court

In determining what is actually and reasonably incurred the relevant travel **G–258** is that between court and an advocate's chambers: *R. v. Khan*, January 1989, TC C/13. Actual expenses incurred in travelling from an advocate's home to court will only be allowed if his home is nearer to court than his chambers, otherwise his journey is deemed to start from chambers: *R. v. Slessor* (1984) Costs L.R. 438.

(i) *Public transport expenses*

Where expenses are recoverable, travel costs are generally limited to the **G–259** cost of public transport actually incurred, together with the expense incurred in getting from the starting point to the railhead or coach station and the expense incurred from getting from the terminal to the court: *Slessor, ante*.

First class rail travel actually incurred is recoverable: *ibid.*; *TONG*, para. 2.50 as amended; DTMD, II/(75).

(ii) *Car expenses*

G–260   Where an advocate chooses to journey by car, the expenses allowed will not exceed the equivalent cost of public transport: *Slessor, ante*; *Conboy, ante*. The expenses of travel by car will be allowed where public transport is not available or is not reasonably convenient. What is "not reasonably convenient" is a matter for the discretion of the taxing officer. What may be convenient in one case may not be convenient in another. The time spent in getting from the starting point to the railhead, and from the terminus to court is always relevant: if it is considerable, the use of a car may be justified. Taxing officers have been urged to adopt a flexible and broad approach to the problem: *Slessor, ante*. Where the case papers are heavy and bulky, an advocate may be justified in using a car (an example given by the taxing officer in argument in *Conboy, ante*). In *R. v. Plews* (1984) Costs L.R. 466, counsel would have had to catch a 7.15 a.m. train from London to allow him to arrive at court in sufficient time to robe, see his client and solicitor, and to hold any pre-hearing discussions. It was therefore reasonable for counsel, bearing in mind that he had to travel from his home to the station and was faced with a full day in court, to travel by car.

(iii) *Expenses for reasonable travel by car*

G–261   In *Plews, ante*, counsel's claim, based on a mileage rate less than that prescribed for medical practitioners in regulations then current, was considered reasonable, the taxing master observing that a claim based upon the equivalent rate would have been allowed. The usual means of estimating the expenses of travel by car is the standard mileage rate which is calculated by reference to the average cost of running a motor car, including such matters as depreciation, insurance, maintenance, etc., which are referable to the running of a car of the relevant engine capacity. Although the rate is not a precise measure of the actual cost of a particular form of transport, it is intended to provide a mechanism for reimbursing expenses incurred when travelling by car: *Conboy, ante*. Where it is reasonable to incur the expense of travelling by car it must also be reasonable to incur necessary and consequential costs of car parking (if any).

The Legal Services Commission announced an increase in its rates for civil solicitors from 36p per mile to 45p per mile as from April 2, 2001. It is submitted that it is reasonable that similar rates should apply to criminal advocates.

Accommodation expenses

G–262   Hotel or accommodation expenses cannot be divorced from travelling expenses. They should be paid instead of travelling expenses where an advocate reasonably chooses, or by reason of distance is obliged, to stay near a court distant from his chambers rather than travel daily. If travelling expenses are not payable then neither are hotel or accommodation expenses: *R. v. Khan*, January 1989, TC C/13. Where an advocate claims expenses for overnight accommodation and the cost equals or is less than that of the daily travel for which he would be entitled to be reimbursed, such expenses should be allowed. Where the hotel expenses are more than the cost of daily travel, they should be allowed if, having regard to the demands of the case on an advocate, including the need for conferences after court and overnight preparation, the advocate could not have returned home at a reasonable hour: *Plews, ante*. A taxing officer is not obliged to accept an advocate's vouched expenditure on accommodation, but in considering living expenses he should have regard to the average direct cost of suitable accommodation in the vicinity of the court: DTMD, II/75.

Conference travel expenses and travel time

Travel expenses reasonably incurred and necessarily and exclusively attributable to attending a conference should be reimbursed where an advocate attends a conference in prison where the authorities will only produce the client at the place of detention; the same principle applies when the client is a patient in a psychiatric hospital: *R. v. Hindle* (1987) Costs L.R. 486. In assessing the fee for conferences, travel time is not remunerated, but time justifiably taken travelling should be taken into account, normally at the same rate as the conference fee: *TONG*, para. 2.58.   **G–263**

K. Determinations and Appeals

(1) The taxing authorities

The determination of an advocate's costs in the Crown Court rests with the Head of the Court Services, who is the appropriate officer appointed by the Lord Chancellor pursuant to article 2 of the *Funding Order* 2001. Under article 2, the Head of the Court Services may appoint appropriate officers to act on his behalf. On March 1, 1991, four regional teams of experienced taxing officers, designated central taxation units, were established to concentrate on dealing with large claims. These teams determine non-graduated claims where counsel's claim for the basic fee or the solicitor's total costs exceeds £4,000. Each central taxation unit is managed by a taxing director who effectively replaced the circuit taxing co-ordinators and their assistants. Graduated fee claims are determined by Crown Court taxing officers and should usually be paid within 10 working days of receipt of the claim. The time taken to process, determine and pay *ex post facto* claims will vary according to the complexity of the claim, the number of related claims, and the date of receipt of the last related claim.   **G–264**

Under the *Funding Order* 2007, the appropriate officer is the Legal Services Commission: see art. 2.

Applications for re-determination are addressed to the chief clerk of the Crown Court or the regional taxation director as appropriate. The re-determination does not have to be carried out by the original officer, although this is usually the case. Where difficult points of principle arise or large sums are in dispute the matter is referred to the regional taxing director or his assistant. Appeals from re-determinations are heard by costs judges appointed by the Lord Chancellor.   **G–265**

The Lord Chancellor issues target guidelines, usually annually, in respect of taxation, re-determinations and requests for written reasons. These targets are intended to be sufficiently exacting to ensure that the legal professions receive prompt service without adversely affecting performance on initial determinations. They have no statutory effect, being statements of intent. The current targets include: **G–266**

    (a) taxation: 75 per cent of all *ex post facto* claims taxed within three months of being ready to tax; no claim to be untaxed after six months;

(b) re-determination: 75 per cent of all requests to be met within one month; no request to be unmet after two months; and

(c) written reasons: 75 per cent of all requests to be met within two months; no request for written reasons to be unmet after three months.

G–267   Any time which elapses between a taxing officer's request for further information and the provision thereof is discounted for the purpose of meeting these targets.

(2) Guide to the process of determination and appeal

G–268   A brief outline of the various stages of the determination of an advocate's fees is set out below. The paragraphs referred to are those in Schedule 1 to the *Funding Order* 2001. The articles referred to are those of the *Funding Order* 2007 (*ante*, §§ G–6 *et seq.*). The table below is merely intended as a guide to the relevant procedures.

There is no general right of re-determination or appeal in respect of graduated or fixed fees under the *Funding Orders*, although fees can be re-determined after any *ex post facto* assessment of appeals against conviction or sentence, or committals: *ante*, G–193. However, the question of whether a particular cases falls within or without the scheme is susceptible to re-determination: *Funding Order* 2001, Sched. 1, para. 20(1)(b). Under the *Funding Order* 2007, all cases fall within the graduated fee scheme, unless they are contracted as a VHCC. Similarly, there is a right of re-determination, and therefore appeal in respect of decisions to disallow some or all of the hours claimed for special or wasted preparation, conferences, and the classification of an offence not specifically listed within the Table of Offences: *Funding Order* 2001, Sched.1, para. 20(1)(c); *Funding Order* 2007, art. 29(1).

The references in the last column in the tables below are either references to paragraphs in Schedule 1 to the *Funding Order* 2001 or to articles of the *Funding Order* 2007. The former are printed in square brackets for ease of identification.

Stage	Description	[para.]/art.
Submission of Claim		[14] 5
Time limit	Within 3 months of conclusion of proceedings (see *ante* G–199)	[14(1)] 5(3)
Particulars submitted in all cases	In the form and manner directed by the appropriate officer	[14(2)–(6)] 5(3)
Exceptional circumstances cases	Full particulars in support of claim for any item to be considered under para. 15(6).	[14(4)]
Interim payments (40% of total claim less any sum paid)		[5] 18

Stage	Description	[para.]/art.
Definition	Payable where: (a) the basic fee claimed by any counsel in any related proceedings exceeds £4,000, and (b) 3 months have elapsed from the date of the conclusion of related proceedings or the date on which the bill is ready to tax, whichever is earlier.	[4] 17 [4(2)] 17(2) [4(3)] 17(4)
Related proceedings	Proceedings involving the same defendant heard or dealt with together or proceedings involving more than one defendant arising out of the same incident so that defendants are charged, tried or disposed of together.	[4(7)] 17(3)
When the bill is ready to tax	Date of receipt of last bill in related proceedings.	[4(4), (7)] 17(4)
Entitlement	Where counsel is entitled to an interim payment but no interim payment has been made and counsel has submitted his claim.	[4(5), (9)] 17(4), (5)
Time limit	6 months after the conclusion of proceedings against the defendant represented.	[4(5)] 17(5)
Determination and notification of costs; authorisation of payment		
	Costs determined on the basis of work reasonably done.	[15(1)] 23(1)
	Counsel notified of costs payable and payment authorised.	[17(1)] 23(1)
Re-calculation of graduated fee or re-determination of decision to allow special or wasted preparation fee, or classification of offence		
Time limit	Within 21 days of receipt or notification of costs payable.	[20(2)] 29(3)
Particulars to be submitted	(a) Written notice specifying matters in respect of which application is made, grounds of objection and whether counsel wishes to appear or to be represented.	[20(2), (4)] 29(3), (5)
	(b) Documents and information supplied with submission of claim.	[20(3)] 29(4)
	(c) Further information, particulars and documents as required by the appropriate officer.	[20(5)] 29(6)

Stage	Description	[para.]/art.
Re-determination of decision not to allow conference fee (time limit and particulars as above)		29(1)(b)
Re-determination by the appropriate officer		[20(6)] 29(7)
Application for written reasons		[20(7)] 29(8)
Time limit	21 days of notification of the decision	[20(7), (8)] 29(8), (9)
Appeal to costs judge		[21(1)] 30(1)
Time limit	21 days of receipt of written reasons.	[21(2)] 30(2)
Particulars to be submitted to costs judge and appropriate officer	(a) Copy of written representations on application for re-determination. (b) Appropriate officer's written reasons. (c) All documents supplied hereto.	[21(4)] 30(4)
Form of notice of appeal	(a) As directed by the costs judge. (b) Specifying separately each item appealed against, showing amount claimed and determined for each item and the ground of objection. (c) Stating whether appellant wishes to appear or to be represented.	[21(5)] 30(5)
Lord Chancellor's written representations	Where the Lord Chancellor makes written representations, counsel shall have a reasonable opportunity to make representations in reply.	[21(9)] 30(9)
Notification of hearing	The costs judge shall inform counsel of hearing date and give directions as to conduct of appeal.	[21(10)] 30(10)
No further evidence	Unless costs judge otherwise directs no other evidence shall be raised at the hearing nor objection taken which was not raised at redetermination.	[21(11)] 30(11)
Notification of costs judge's decision		[21(13)] 30(13)
Costs	Costs may be awarded where the appeal is allowed.	[21(4)] 30(14)
Appeals to the High Court		[22(1)] 31
Right of appeal	Right of appeal to single QBD judge from costs judge's decision on a point of principle of public importance.	[22(7)] 31(7)

Stage	Description	[para.]/art.
Application for costs judge's certificate	Counsel may apply to the costs judge to certify a point of principle of general importance.	[22(1)] 31(1)
Time limit for application	Within 21 days of notification of costs judge's decision.	[22(2)] 31(2)
Time limit for appeal	Within 21 days from receipt of costs judge's certificate.	
Appeal by Lord Chancellor	Within 21 days of notification of costs judge's decision, the Lord Chancellor may appeal the decision if counsel does not do so.	[22(5), (6)] 31(5)

(3) The enforcement and extension of time limits

Time limits may be extended for good reason by the appropriate authority, **G–269** *i.e.* the appropriate officer, costs judge, or the High Court: *Funding Order 2001*, Sched. 1, para. 23(1)(b); *Funding Order 2007*, art. 32(1). Where for no good reason the time limit is not adhered to, the appropriate authority may in exceptional circumstances extend the time limit and shall consider whether it is reasonable in the circumstances to reduce the costs, subject to granting the advocate a reasonable opportunity to state either orally or in writing why the costs should not be reduced: *Funding Order 2001*, Sched. 1, para. 23(2); *Funding Order 2007*, art. 32 (2). A decision not to extend time, or to reduce costs for claims out of time may be appealed by notice in writing to the senior costs judge specifying the grounds of appeal. The appeal must be instituted within 21 days of the decision being given: *Funding Order 2001*, Sched. 1, para. 23(3); *Funding Order 2007*, art. 32(3); and see *ante*, G–199.

It was held in *R. v. Mahmood* [2008] Costs L.R. 326, that where a 10 per cent penalty was imposed following a delay of over two months in submitting a claim for costs, but where the representative had only received a notice, prior to the case being tried, stating that all late claims would be the subject of a penalty unless there was a good reason, this did not constitute notice to show cause why the claim should not be reduced. The determining officer had clearly not considered the circumstances of the particular case on its own merits.

In *R. v. Roberts* [2008] Costs L.R. 323, the oversight of two fee earners, the holiday of one of those fee-earners (even if well-deserved), and a subsequent systematic firm-wide failure did not constitute "good reason" or "exceptional circumstances" under paragraph 23 so as to justify an extension of time, following a delay of 17 months in submitting a claim for costs. Nor did previous good character constitute "exceptional circumstances", although it was said that it might amount to mitigating circumstances when considering the extent of any reduction in costs (were an extension to be granted under sub-paragraph (2)). This was the case despite a general softening in the attitude to the delay.

A misunderstanding of the legislation cannot amount to "good reason", but could amount to "exceptional circumstances" where the evidence was that other bills that had been submitted late for like reason in the past had been accepted: *R. v. White* [2008] Costs L.R. 479.

In *R. v. Griffin* [2008] Costs L.R. 483, leading counsel had been under the mistaken impression that his junior was going to prepare a taxation note to be agreed between them before submission. However, in the event, his junior submitted his own claim independently and sent a copy of his taxation note to his leader, such note making it plain that he had submitted a claim and asserting, mistakenly, that leading counsel had already submitted his own claim. It was held that as this was already seven months out of time, and leading counsel only submitted his own claim after a further two years, neither the misunderstanding as between leader and junior, nor extreme pressure of work plus some personal pressure over the two years that followed discovery of the fact that his junior had submitted his own claim, could amount to "good reason" for the failure to submit the claim within the three-month time limit; nor could they amount to "exceptional circumstances" so as to justify an extension of time despite the absence of good reason. There had been no obligation on the determining officer to remind counsel that his claim was late and the absence, at the time, of published criteria to be applied to the submission of late claims, did not avail counsel. What was critical to the outcome was the fact that two years before his eventual submission of his claim, he had been alerted by his junior's note to the fact that he would need to submit his own claim and he had failed then to take any steps to address the situation.

(4) Basic principles of taxation and determination

G–270   The paramount duty of all taxing officers was to take account of all the relevant circumstances of a particular case: *R. v. Bellas* (1986) Costs L.R. 479. The relevant circumstances of the case include the nature, importance, complexity or difficulty of the work and the time involved, and the appropriate officer shall allow a reasonable amount in respect of all work actually and reasonably done: *Funding Order* 2001, Sched. 1, para. 1. The general principle to be applied is that work done should be remunerated at the rate appropriate to the date on which it was done and that a reasonable amount should be paid in respect of all work reasonably done. Although the words "fair remuneration" in earlier regulations have been replaced by "reasonable amount" in paragraph 1(2)(b) of Schedule 1, no new principle was created thereby and the test to be applied in the determination and allowance of costs remains unchanged: *DDO*, para. 1D1.

G–271   The phrase "reasonable amount" no longer appears in respect of Crown Court work under the *Funding Order* 2007. All fees, save for those arising under the VHCC scheme, are effectively fixed. Their reasonableness or fairness in any given case or for any given piece of work is no longer relevant to the appropriate remuneration.

In *ex post facto cases*, before arriving at a final assessment the taxing officer should take into account the assessment of the weight of the case by the trial judge: see *ante*, G–220. A taxing officer should also satisfy himself that no allowance is made for any work done in the court below unless the order for taxation provides otherwise: *TONG*, para. 1.16.

(5) Re-determinations and appeals

Graduated fees

G–272   An advocate may only seek re-determination or appeal in respect of graduated fees where, (a) the issue is either whether the graduated fee scheme applied to the relevant proceedings, or (b) complaint is made as to the calcula

tion of the remuneration payable, or (c) where the advocate is dissatisfied with
a refusal to allow a special preparation fee or the number of hours allowed in
the calculation of such fee; or (d) where the advocate is dissatisfied with the
classification of an offence which does not appear in the Table of Offences:
Funding Order 2001, Sched. 1, para. 20(1)(b) and (c); *Funding Order* 2007,
art. 29(3). Under the 2007 order, a re-determination may also be sought in
respect of a decision not to allow an hourly fee in respect of attendance at
conferences or views at the scene of the alleged offence, or of the number
of hours allowed in the calculation of such a fee: see art. 29(1)(b)(i).

Re-determination

On an application for re-determination an advocate shall specify the   **G–273**
grounds of his objection to all or any part of the determination (*Funding Order* 2001, Sched. 1, para. 20(2); *Funding Order* 2007, art. 29(3)(b)) and may
appear in person or through another to make representations: *Funding Order* 2001, Sched. 1, para. 20(4); *Funding Order* 2007, art. 29(5). An advocate
is not obliged to provide fresh information or material to assist the
determining officer in the redetermination. If no additional information is
provided, the determining officer has a duty to redetermine on the basis of
the information already supplied: *R. v. O'Brien* [2003] Costs L.R. 625. Many
appeals which might otherwise have succeeded have failed because the
representations made to the appropriate officer have been perfunctory and
inexplicit: *R. v. Davies* (1985) Costs L.R. 472. Advocates often do not know
the reason for the reduction of their claim until they have obtained the written reasons. Counsel's clerks should, therefore, in suitable cases, ascertain
from appropriate officers the general basis of the original assessment so that
they might make explicit and specific representations, rather than general
representations based upon assumptions which might not be correct: DTMD,
II/(50). In an appropriate case, an advocate may at the review stage submit an
appropriate memorandum to assist the taxing authority in the re-
determination: DTMD, II/(55).

As from January 1, 1994, the General Council of the Bar has agreed that all
requests for fees to be re-determined or for written reasons to be provided
should be signed by counsel personally.

Re-determination should, where possible, be carried out by the officer who
determined costs. Where cases are cited in support of the re-determination,
sufficient references must be given to allow an advocate to identify and look
them up: *R. v. Pelepenko*, X27A, SCCO 186/2001. Where difficult points of
principle arise or a large sum is in dispute, a more senior officer may be
consulted or undertake the re-determination. Re-determination of fees
determined by a central taxing team must always be undertaken by the same
team: *TONG*, para. 1.22.

Further evidence on appeal and supplemental written reasons

On appeal before a costs judge no further evidence shall be received and   **G–274**
no ground of objection shall be valid which was not raised on the application
for re-determination unless the costs judge otherwise directs: *Funding Order*
2001, Sched. 1, para. 21(11); *Funding Order* 2007, art. 30(11). These provisions are strictly applied. A costs judge will rarely accede to a request to adduce further evidence or allow a fresh objection to be raised. Where written
reasons do not address a point raised in the claim, counsel cannot pursue
the matter in the appeal. The proper method of dealing with such an omission is to seek supplemental written reasons from the appropriate officer.

A cogent and detailed memorandum which would have resulted in a successful re-determination and which was submitted to the taxing authorities four weeks after re-determination with no explanation forthcoming for that delay was not received as additional evidence on appeal: DTMD, II/(66).

Appeals

G–275   The right of appeal to a costs judge is effectively limited in that no appeal lies against a determination unless the advocate has applied for a re-determination and, thereafter, for written reasons under the *Funding Order* 2001, Schedule 1, para. 20, or the *Funding Order* 2007, art. 30(1).

An advocate wishing to appeal must have regard to, and be familiar with, the provisions of *Practice Direction (No. 5 of 1994)*, set out in full, at §§ 6–115 *et seq.* of the main work.

Representation, costs and expenses of appeal

G–276   For the purposes of an appeal to a costs judge, an advocate is treated as the appellant and can elect to be represented at the hearing. A successful appellant may be awarded a sum in respect of part or all of any reasonable costs incurred in connection with the appeal: *Funding Order* 2001, Sched. 1, para. 21(14); *Funding Order* 2007, art. 30(14); and see *R. v. Boswell; R. v. Halliwell* [1987] 1 W.L.R. 705 (Leggatt J.).

A barrister without the intervention of a solicitor may accept a brief or instructions, with or without fee, directly from, and represent, another barrister on that other barrister's appeal as to his fees before a costs judge: see *Code of Conduct*, 8th ed., para. 401 (Appendix C–7, *ante*). A professional fee payable by one barrister to another for conducting the former's appeal is capable of constituting part of the costs incurred by the appellant counsel: *R. v. Boswell; R. v. Halliwell, ante.* In assessing such costs the costs judge is entitled to take account of time and skill expended by the appellant or his counsel in the drawing of grounds and preparation of the appeal, and the conduct of the hearing, and travel and subsidence costs: *ibid.* Costs incurred in instructing other counsel are clearly reasonable where there is some technical question on the applicability of some part of the regulations or other issue which legitimately deserves the attention of specialist costs counsel. Costs are not reasonably incurred if trial counsel is available, could easily have represented himself and the only real issue is the weight of the case or the value of a particular item of work undertaken: *Jackson v. Lord Chancellor* [2003] 3 Costs L.R. 395; and *R. v. Martin* [2007] Costs L.R. 128. A successful appellant will ordinarily be entitled to the return of the fee payable in respect of the appeal.

Appeals to the single judge

G–277   As to appeals from a costs judge to the High Court, see the *Funding Order* 2001, Sched. 1, para. 22, and the *Funding Order* 2007, art. 31. The ambit of an appeal is strictly limited to the point of principle certified by the costs judge as being of general importance (such certificate being a pre-condition to an appeal): *Patten v. Lord Chancellor*, 151 N.L.J. 851, QBD (Leveson J.) not following *Harold v. Lord Chancellor* [1999] 1 Costs L.R. 14. Although *Patten* was concerned with the interpretation of regulation 16 of the *Legal Aid in Criminal and Care Proceedings (Costs) Regulations* 1989 (SI 1989 No 343) paragraph 21 of Schedule 1 to the *Funding Order* 2001, is worded in almost

identical terms (as is art. 30 of the *Funding Order* 2007). A refusal of a costs
judge to certify that the matter raises a point of principle of general
importance is not susceptible to judicial review: *R. v. Supreme Court Taxing
Office, ex p. John Singh & Co* [1997] 1 Costs L.R. 49, CA (Civ. Div). As to the
limited scope for a challenge, by way of judicial review, to the substantive decision of a costs judge where a certificate has been refused, see § 6–64 in the
main work.

(6) Recovery of overpayment

Where an advocate receives a sum in excess of his entitlement, the taxing   **G–278**
authority may either require immediate repayment of that excess, or deduct
the excess from any other sum payable to the advocate under the regulations:
Funding Order 2001, Sched. 1, para. 18; *Funding Order* 2007, art. 26. These
provisions apply notwithstanding the fact that a re-determination or appeal
has been or may be requested: *Funding Order* 2001, Sched. 1, para. 18(4);
Funding Order 2007, art. 26(4).

(7) Appeals under VHCCs

Under the arrangements that came into effect on January 14, 2008 (*ante*,   **G–279**
G–181 *et seq.*), both the contracts for panel members and for panel advocates
provide for an appeal to a VHCC Appeals Committee. The details are set out
in Annex 14 to the contract for panel members and Annex 10 to the contract
for panel advocates. The right of appeal is conferred on "the defence team",
rather than on an individual, and paragraph 2.1 of the respective annexes list
the issues in relation to which there is a right of appeal, and paragraph 2.2
lists issues on which there is no right of appeal. An appeal must be lodged
within 10 working days of receipt of the original decision. In an apparent
contradiction, paragraph 7.11 states that in making their decision, the committee may not take into consideration earlier committee decisions, whilst
paragraph 7.15 provides that whilst earlier decisions do not constitute a pre-
cedent, they may be produced by either party at the appeal hearing. The annex does not even hint at any legitimate purpose of producing an earlier decision when there is an embargo on the committee taking it into consideration.
The decision of the appeal committee is final and binding on the parties.
There is no further right of appeal to a costs judge.

APPENDIX J

A Guide to Commencing Proceedings in the Court of Appeal (Criminal Division)

Note: the text of the guide that follows has been subjected to some editorial revision (in relation to such matters as punctuation, use of upper and lower case, abbreviations, manner of citation of legislative references and authorities, and in order to correct a small number of obvious, minor errors). None of these revisions has any effect on the sense of this guide.

Foreword by the Lord Chief Justice of England and Wales

In recent years the Court of Appeal Criminal Division has faced increased   **J–1**
complexity in appeals, not only against conviction but also against sentence,
particularly in the light of the plethora of recent sentencing legislation. Additionally,
the jurisdiction of the court has expanded to encompass a variety of diverse applications and appeals by the defence, the Crown and other interested parties.

This guide provides invaluable advice as to the initial steps for commencing
proceedings in the Court of Appeal Criminal Division generally and in relation to
perhaps unfamiliar provisions.

The first and most important step is, of course, the preparation of the grounds of
appeal. The rules prescribe the form and content of the Notice and Grounds of
Appeal. Practitioners are also required to summarise the facts and outline their arguments concisely. Well drafted grounds of appeal assist the single judge when
considering leave and serve to shorten any hearing before the full court. Ill-prepared
and prolix documents necessarily lead to wasted time spent on preparation and unnecessarily protracted hearings.

It is important that we all take seriously our responsibility to ensure the effective
progression of cases and keep delay to a minimum. Once an application or appeal is
commenced, the responsible officer at the Criminal Appeal Office will be available to
assist with any queries on practice or procedure.

The court could not deal with this volume of work efficiently without the support
of the Registrar and his staff in the Criminal Appeal Office. Their experience and
expertise is invaluable and can always be relied on by those who use the court, not
least those who are unfamiliar with its practice and procedures.

Judge C.J.
October 2008

Introduction

Since the publication of the last Guide to Proceedings in the Court of Appeal   **J–2**
(Criminal Division), the court's jurisdiction has increased. It hears appeals not only
against conviction and sentence, but also against various interlocutory rulings, as well
as other appeals and applications.

This guide provides practical information about how to commence and conduct
proceedings before the court. Once proceedings are commenced, an application will
have its own unique reference number and a case progression officer who can help
with any difficulties or queries about procedure.

The guide is set out as follows:

A. General principles of practice and procedure when applying for leave to appeal
   conviction and sentence.

B. Guidance on appeals against rulings made in preparatory hearings.

C. Guidance on prosecution appeals against 'terminating' rulings.

D. Brief guidance on other appeals in bullet point form showing:

  - the type of appeal,
  - the relevant section of the statute
  - the relevant Criminal Procedure Rules
  - who can apply
  - the forms to be used and time limits
  - respondents' notices,
  - whether representation orders are available
  - whether leave to appeal is required

E. Guidance on applications for a retrial for a serious offence.

A list of all up to date forms referred to in this guide may be accessed from the
HMCS website at *www.hmcourts-service.gov.uk* or the Criminal Procedure Rules Com-

mittee website at *www.justice.gov.uk/criminal/procrules*. Where the *Criminal Procedure Rules* do not provide for a specific form, this guide indicates the appropriate form to be used.

This guide was prepared under my direction by the staff of the Criminal Appeal Office, but principally by Ms Alix Beldam and Ms Susan Holdham. It describes the law and practice of the Court as at 1st October 2008.

Master Venne

Registrar of Criminal Appeals

Terminology

J–3   The *Criminal Appeal Act* 1968 refers to "leave to appeal". This is now referred to as "permission to appeal" in the *Criminal Procedure Rules* 2007. This guide keeps to the terminology used by the Act.

Also consistently with the Act, an "appellant" is referred to without distinction, but it should be borne in mind that it is the accepted practice of the Criminal Appeal Office (CAO) to refer to a person who has served notice of appeal but not been granted leave to appeal as an "applicant" and use the term "appellant" to refer to a person who has been granted leave to appeal.

Any reference to counsel should be read as including a solicitor advocate as appropriate.

A. GENERAL PRINCIPLES OF PRACTICE AND PROCEDURE WHEN APPLYING FOR LEAVE TO APPEAL CONVICTION AND SENTENCE

A1 Advice and assistance

J–4   A1–1 Provision for advice or assistance on appeal is included in the trial representation order issued by the Crown Court. Solicitors should not wait to be asked for advice by the defendant. Immediately following the conclusion of the case, the legal representatives should see the defendant and counsel should express orally his final view as to the prospects of a successful appeal (whether against conviction or sentence or both). If there are no reasonable grounds of appeal, that should be confirmed in writing and a copy provided then, or as soon as practicable thereafter, to the defendant by the solicitor. If there are reasonable grounds, grounds of appeal should be drafted, signed and sent to instructing solicitors as soon as possible. Solicitors should immediately send a copy of the documents received from counsel to the defendant.

A1–2 Prior to the lodging of the notice and grounds of appeal by service of Form NG, the Registrar has no power to grant a representation order. Also, the Crown Court can only amend a representation order in favour of fresh legal representatives if advice on appeal has not been given by trial legal representatives and it is necessary and reasonable for another legal representative to be instructed. Where advice on appeal has been given by trial legal representatives, application for funding may only be made to the Legal Services Commission (LSC).

A1–3 Once the Form NG has been lodged, the Registrar is the authority for decisions about representation orders, in accordance with the principle that the court before which there are proceedings is the court with power to grant a right to representation (*Access to Justice Act* 1999, Sched. 3, affirmed by regulation 10 of the *Criminal Defence Service (General) (No. 2) Regulations* 2001 (S.I. 2001 No. 1437)).

A1–4 Where, in order to settle grounds of appeal, work of an exceptional nature is contemplated or where the expense will be great, legal representatives should submit a Form NG with provisional grounds of appeal and with a note to the Registrar requesting a representation order to cover the specific work considered necessary to enable proper grounds of appeal to be settled.

A2 Form NG and grounds of appeal

J–5   A2–1 Where counsel has advised an appeal, solicitors should forward the signed grounds of appeal to the Crown Court accompanied by Form NG and such other forms as may be appropriate. It should be noted that Form NG and grounds of appeal are required to be served within the relevant time limit in all cases, whether or not leave to appeal is required (*e.g.* where a trial judge's certificate has been granted). However, on a reference by the Criminal Cases Review Commission (CCRC), if no Form NG and grounds are served within the required period, then the reference shall be treated as the appeal notice: rule 68.5(2).

A2–2 Grounds must be settled with sufficient particularity to enable the Registrar, and subsequently the court, to identify clearly the matters relied upon. A mere formula such as "the conviction is unsafe" or "the sentence is in all the circumstances too severe" will be ineffective as grounds and time will continue to run against the defendant.

A2–3 Rule 68.3(1) sets out the information that must be contained in the appeal notice. The notice must … [*see § 7–313q in the main work*].

A2–4 There is now a requirement for the grounds of appeal to set out the relevant facts and nature of the proceedings concisely in one all encompassing document, not separate grounds and advice. The intended readership of this document is the court and not the lay or professional client. Its purpose is to enable the single judge to grasp quickly the facts and issues in the case. In appropriate cases, draft grounds of appeal may be perfected before submission to the single judge (*see further below para. A5*).

A2–5 Any document mentioned in the grounds should be identified clearly, by exhibit number or otherwise. Similarly, if counsel requires an original exhibit or shorthand writer's tape recording, he should say so well in advance of any determination or hearing.

A2–6 Counsel should not settle or sign grounds unless they are reasonable, have some real prospect of success and are such that he is prepared to argue them before the court. Counsel should not settle grounds he cannot support because he is "instructed" to do so by a defendant.

A2–7 Procedure in relation to particular grounds of appeal

A2–7.1 *Applications to call fresh evidence*

A Form W and a statement from the witness in the form prescribed by section 9 of the *CJA* 1967 should be lodged in respect of each witness it is proposed to call. The Form W should indicate whether there is an application for a witness order. The Registrar or the single judge may direct the issue of a witness order, but only the court hearing the appeal may give leave for a witness to be called.

The court will require a cogent explanation for the failure to adduce the evidence at trial. A supporting witness statement or affidavit from the appellant's solicitor should be lodged in this regard (*R. v. Gogana, The Times* July 12, 1999).

If there is to be an application to adduce hearsay and/or evidence of bad character or for special measures, then the appropriate forms should be lodged: rule 68.7(1).

A2–7.2 *Complaints against trial counsel as a ground of appeal*

Where a ground of appeal explicitly criticises trial counsel and/or trial solicitors, the Registrar will institute the "waiver of privilege" procedure. The appellant will be asked to "waive privilege" in respect of instructions to and advice at trial from legal representatives. If he does waive privilege, the grounds of appeal are sent to the appropriate trial representative(s) and they are invited to respond. Any response will be sent to the appellant or his fresh legal representatives for comment. All these documents will be sent to the single judge when considering the application for leave. The single judge may draw inferences from any failure to participate in the process. "Waiver of privilege" is a procedure that should be instigated by the Registrar and not by fresh legal representatives, who should go no further than obtaining a waiver of privilege from the appellant: *R. v. Doherty and McGregor* [1997] 2 Cr.App.R. 218.

A2–7.3 Insufficient weight given to assistance to prosecution authorities

Where a ground of appeal against sentence is that the judge has given insufficient weight to the assistance given to the prosecution authorities, the "text" which had been prepared for the sentencing judge is obtained by the Registrar. Grounds of appeal should be drafted in an anodyne form with a note to the Registrar alerting him to the existence of a "text". The single judge will have seen the "text" when considering leave as will the full court before the appeal hearing and it need not be alluded to in open court.

A3 Time limits

J–6   A3–1 Notice and grounds should reach the Crown Court within 28 days <u>from the date of the conviction</u> in the case of an application for leave to appeal against conviction and within 28 days <u>from the date of sentence</u> in the case of an application for leave to appeal against sentence [*CAA* 1968, s.18 and rule 68.2(1)]. On a reference by the CCRC, Form NG and grounds should be served on the Registrar not more than 56 days after the Registrar has served notice that the CCRC has referred a conviction and not more than 28 days in the case of a sentence referral: rule 68.2(2).

A3–2 A confiscation order (whether made under the *CJA* 1988, the *DTA* 1994 or the *PCA* 2002) is a sentence [*CAA* 1968, s.50]. Where sentences are passed in separate proceedings on different dates there may be two appeals against sentence. Thus, there may be an appeal against the custodial part of a sentence and an appeal against a confiscation order (*R. v. Neal* [1999] 2 Cr.App.R.(S) 352).

A3–3 An application for extension of the 28 day period in which to give notice of application for leave to appeal or notice of appeal must always be supported by reasons why the application for leave was not submitted in time. It is not enough merely to tick the relevant box on Form NG.

A3–4 Such an application should be submitted when the application for leave to appeal against either conviction or sentence is made and not in advance. Notwithstanding the terms of section 18(3) of the *CAA* 1968, it has long been the practice of the Registrar to require the extension of time application to be made at the time of service of the notice and grounds of appeal. This practice is now reflected by *Criminal Procedure Rule* 65.4.

A4 Transcript and notes of evidence

J–7   A4–1 In conviction cases, transcripts of the summing up and proceedings up to and including verdict are obtained as a matter of course. Similarly, the transcript of the prosecution opening of facts on a guilty plea and the judge's observations on passing sentence are usually obtained in sentence cases. There is now an obligation under rule 68.3(2) for counsel to identify any further transcript which counsel considers the court will need and to provide a note of names, dates and times to enable an order to be placed with the shorthand writers. Whether or not any further transcript is required is a matter for the judgment of the Registrar or his staff.

A4–2 Transcript should only be requested if it is essential for the proper conduct of the appeal in the light of the grounds. If the Registrar and counsel are unable to agree the extent of the transcript to be obtained, the Registrar may refer that matter to a judge. In some cases the Registrar may propose that counsel agree a note in place of transcript.

A4–3 In certain circumstances the costs of unnecessary transcript could be ordered to be paid by the appellant. Where transcript is obtained otherwise than through the Registrar, he may disallow the cost on taxation of public funding.

A5 Perfection of grounds of appeal

J–8   A5–1 The purpose of perfection is (a) to save valuable judicial time by enabling the court to identify at once the relevant parts of the transcript and (b) to give counsel the opportunity to reconsider his original grounds in the light of the transcript. Perfected grounds should consist of a fresh document which supersedes the original grounds of appeal and contains *inter alia* references by page number and letter (or paragraph number) to all relevant passages in the transcript.

A5-2 In conviction or confiscation cases, the Registrar will almost certainly invite counsel to perfect grounds in the light of the transcript obtained, to assist the single judge or full court. Where counsel indicates a wish to perfect grounds of appeal against sentence, the Registrar will consider the request and will only invite perfection where he considers it necessary for the assistance of the single judge or full court.

A5-3 If perfection is appropriate, counsel will be sent a copy of the transcript and asked to perfect his grounds within 14 days. In the absence of any response from counsel, the existing notice and grounds of appeal will be placed before the single judge or the court without further notice. If counsel does not wish to perfect his grounds, the transcript should be returned with a note to that effect.

A5-4 If, having considered the transcript, counsel is of opinion that there are no valid grounds, he should set out his reasons in a further advice and send it to his instructing solicitors. He should inform the Registrar that he has done so, but should not send him a copy of that advice. Solicitors should send a copy to the appellant and obtain instructions, at the same time explaining that if the appellant persists with his application the court may consider whether to make a loss of time order *(see further below A-13)*.

A6 Respondent's notice

A6-1 The *Criminal Procedure Rules* 2005 provide for the service of a respondent's notice. Under rule 68.6(1) the Registrar may serve the appeal notice on any party directly affected by the appeal (usually the prosecution) and must do so in a CCRC case. That party may then serve a respondent's notice if it wishes to make representations and must do so if the Registrar so directs: rule 68.6(2). The respondent's notice should be served within 14 days (rule 68.6(4)) on the appellant, the Registrar and any other party on whom the Registrar served the appeal notice (rule 68.6(3)). The respondent's notice must be in the specified form [Form RN], in which a respondent should set out the grounds of opposition (rule 68.6(5)) and which must include the information set out in rule 68.6(6). **J-9**

A6-2 In practice, this procedure primarily applies prior to consideration of leave by the single judge in both conviction and sentence cases. The Attorney General and the Registrar, following consultation with representatives from the Crown Prosecution Service (CPS) and the Revenue and Customs Prosecution Office (RCPO), have agreed guidance on types of cases and/or issues where the Registrar should consider whether to serve an appeal notice and direct or invite a party to serve a respondent's notice before the consideration of leave by the single judge. Examples of when the Registrar might **direct** a respondent's notice include where the grounds concern matters which were the subject of public interest immunity (PII), allegations of jury irregularity, criticism of the conduct of the judge and complex frauds. Cases where it might be appropriate for the Registrar to **invite** a respondent's notice include, for example, homicide offences, serious sexual offences, cases with national profile or high media interest, cases of violence or domestic violence.

A6-3 In conviction cases where leave has been granted or where the application for leave has been referred to the full court, the Crown is briefed to attend the hearing and required to submit a respondent's notice/skeleton argument. In relation to sentence cases where leave has been granted, referred or an appellant is represented on a renewed application, the sentence protocol set out in paragraph II.1 of the consolidated criminal practice direction (§ 7–207a in the main work) will apply. In those cases, a respondent's notice/skeleton argument will have to be served when the Crown indicates a wish to attend or when the Registrar invites or directs the Crown to attend.

A7 Referral by the Registrar

J–10

A7–1 Leave to appeal is required in all cases except where the trial judge or sentencing judge has certified that the case is fit for appeal (*CAA* 1968, ss.1(2) and 11(1A)) or where the case has been referred by the CCRC. The appellant must obtain leave to pursue grounds not related to the Commission's reasons for referral: *CAA* 1995, s.14(4B).

A7–2 Where leave to appeal is required and the Registrar has obtained the necessary documents, he will refer the application(s) either (a) to a single judge for decision under section 31 of the *CAA* 1968 or (b) directly to the full court, in which case a representation order is usually granted for the hearing. However, the Registrar will not grant a representation order when the presence of counsel is not required, *e.g.* where the application refers solely to an amendment of the number of days to be credited as "remand time" and the figure is agreed by the parties. Where an application is referred to the full court by the Registrar because an unlawful sentence has been passed or other procedural error identified, a representation order will ordinarily be granted, but counsel should be aware that the court may make observations for the attention of the determining officer that a full fee should not be allowed on taxation.

A7–3 Where leave to appeal is not required, *e.g.* on appeal by certificate of the trial judge, the Registrar will usually grant a representation order for the hearing. On a reference from the CCRC, it is the Registrar's usual practice to grant a representation order in the first instance, to solicitors for them to nominate and instruct counsel to settle grounds of appeal. Once counsel's details are known, a further representation order will be granted to cover the preparation (including settling grounds) and presentation of the appeal by counsel and further work by solicitors, as necessary in light of the grounds.

A8 Bail pending appeal

J–11

A8–1 Bail may be granted (a) by a single judge or the full court or (b) by a trial or sentencing judge who has certified the case fit for appeal. In the latter case, bail can only be granted within 28 days of the conviction or sentence which is the subject of the appeal and may not be granted if an application for bail has already been made to the Court of Appeal.

A8–2 An application to the Court of Appeal for bail must be supported by a completed Form B, whether or not the application is made at the same time as the notice and grounds are served. The completed Form B must be served on the Registrar and the prosecution at least 24 hours before any application is made to enable the Crown to make representations (either written or oral) about the application and any conditions.

A8–3 An application for bail will not be considered by a single judge or the court until notice of application for leave to appeal or notice of appeal has first been given. In practice, judges will also require the relevant transcripts to be available so they may take a view as to the merits of the substantive application.

A8–4 It is the practice of the court, if bail is granted, to require a condition of residence. An application for variation of conditions of bail may be determined by the Registrar (if unopposed) or a single judge.

A9 Consideration of the applications by single judge

J–12

A9–1 Normally a single judge will consider the application for leave to appeal together with any ancillary applications, *e.g.* for bail or representation order, without hearing oral argument. Counsel may request an oral hearing, but it is only in very rare circumstances that the Registrar would consider it appropriate to grant a representation order for the proceedings before a single judge at an oral hearing, but counsel may appear to argue the applications before the single judge where instructed to do so, usually appearing either *pro bono* or privately funded. Oral applications for leave and bail are usually heard at 9.30 a.m. before the normal court sittings. Counsel appears unrobed. If counsel considers that an application may take longer than 20 minutes, the Registrar must be informed.

A10 Powers of the single judge

A10–1 The single judge may grant the application for leave, refuse it or refer it to the full court. In conviction cases and in sentence cases where appropriate, the single judge may grant limited leave, *i.e.* leave to argue some grounds but not others. If the grounds upon which leave has been refused are to be renewed before the full court, counsel must notify the Registrar within 14 days. In the absence of any notification of renewal, it will be assumed that the grounds upon which leave was refused will not be pursued. **J–13**

The single judge may also grant, refuse or refer any ancillary application.

A11 Grant of leave or reference to full court

A11–1 Where the single judge grants leave or refers an application to the court, it is usual to grant a representation order for the preparation and presentation of the appeal. This is usually limited to the services of counsel only, in which event counsel will be assigned by the Registrar. In such a case the Registrar will provide a brief but does not act as an appellant's solicitor. Counsel who settled grounds of appeal will usually be assigned. However, the Registrar may assign one counsel to represent more than one appellant if appropriate. If it is considered that a representation order for two counsel and/or solicitors is required, counsel should notify the Registrar and provide written justification in accordance with the *Criminal Defence Service (General) (No. 2) Regulations* 2001. **J–14**

A11–2 If solicitors are assigned, it should be noted that by virtue of regulation 13 of the *Criminal Defence Service (General) (No. 2) Regulations* 2001, a representation order can only be issued to a solicitor if he holds a General Criminal Contract (Crime Franchise) with the LSC. A solicitor not holding such a franchise may apply to the LSC for an individual case contract (by virtue of which the solicitor is employed on behalf of the LSC to represent an appellant in a given case). Such a contract is sufficient for the purposes of regulation 13.

A11–3 In some circumstances, the Registrar may refer an application to the full court. This may be because there is a novel point of law or because in a sentence case, the sentence passed is unlawful and regardless of the merits, the sentence should be amended. A representation order for counsel is usually granted. Counsel for the prosecution usually attends a Registrar's referral.

A12 Refusal by the single judge

A12–1 Where the single judge refuses leave to appeal, the Registrar sends a notification of the refusal, including any observations which the judge may have made, to the appellant, who is informed that he may require the application to be considered by the court by serving a renewal notice [Form SJ-Renewal] upon the Registrar within 14 days from the date on which the notice of refusal was served on him. **J–15**

A12–2 A refused application which is not renewed within 14 days lapses. An appellant may apply for an extension of time in which to renew his application for leave: *CAA* 1968, s.31, and rule 65.5(2). The Registrar will normally refer such an application to the court to be considered at the same time as the renewed application for leave to appeal. An application for extension for time in which to renew must be supported by cogent reasons.

A12–3 If it is intended that counsel should represent the appellant at the hearing of the renewed application for leave to appeal, whether privately instructed or on a *pro bono* basis, such intention must be communicated to the CAO in writing as soon as that decision has been made. Whilst a representation order is not granted by the Registrar in respect of a renewed application for leave, counsel may apply at the hearing to the court for a representation order to cover that appearance. In practice, this is only granted where the application for leave is successful.

A13 Directions for loss of time

A13–1 The *CAA* 1968, s. 29, empowers the court to direct that time spent in custody as an appellant shall not count as part of the term of any sentence to which the appellant is for the time being subject. The court will do so where it considers that an application is wholly without merit. Such an order may not be made where leave to appeal or a trial judge's certificate has been granted, on a reference by the CCRC or where an appeal has been abandoned.

A13–2 The mere fact that counsel has advised that there are grounds of appeal will not be a sufficient answer to the question as to whether or not an application has indeed been brought which was wholly without merit: *R. v. Hart*; *R. v. George*; *R. v. Clarke*; *R. v. Brown* [2007] 1 Cr.App.R. 31.

A13–3 The Form SJ, on which the single judge records his decisions, and the reverse of which is used by appellants to indicate their wish to renew, includes:

- a box for the single judge to initial to indicate that that the full court should consider loss of time if the application is renewed and
- a box for the applicant to give reasons why such an order should not be made whether or not an indication has been given by a single judge.

A14 Abandonment

A14–1 An appeal or application may be abandoned at any time before the hearing without leave by completing and lodging Form A. An oral instruction or letter indicating a wish to abandon is insufficient.

A14–2 At the hearing, an application or appeal can only be abandoned with the permission of the court: rule 65.13(2). An appeal or application which is abandoned is treated as having been dismissed or refused by the full court, as the case may be: rule 65.13(4)(c).

A14–3 A notice of abandonment cannot be withdrawn nor can it be conditional. A person who wants to reinstate an application or appeal after abandonment must apply in writing with reasons: rule 65.13(5). The court has power to allow reinstatement only where the purported abandonment can be treated as a nullity (see *R. v Medway*, 62 Cr.App.R. 85; *R. v. Burt, The Independent*, December 3, 2004; *R. v Gran* (2005) 149 S.J. 1186).

A15 Case management duties

A15–1 Rule 65.2 gives the court and parties the same powers and duties of case management as in Part 3 of the rules. In accordance with those duties, for each application received, the Registrar nominates a case progression officer (the "responsible officer"). There is also a duty on the parties actively to assist the court to progress cases. Close contact between counsel and solicitors and the responsible officer is encouraged in order to facilitate the efficient preparation and listing of appeals, especially in complex cases and those involving witnesses.

A15–2 Powers exercisable by the single judge and the Registrar are contained in the *CAA* 1968, s.31. These powers include the power to make procedural directions for the efficient and effective preparation of an application or appeal and the power to make an order under section 23(1)(a) of the 1968 Act for the production of evidence *etc.* necessary for the determination of the case.

A15–3 Procedural directions given by the Registrar may be appealed to a single judge. Those given by a single judge, including a single Lord Justice, are final.

B. Interlocutory Appeals against Rulings in Preparatory Hearings

Appeal against a ruling under section 9 of the Criminal Justice Act 1987 or a decision under section 35 of the Criminal Procedure and Investigations Act 1996 [Part 66 Criminal Procedure Rules 2007]

B1 Where a judge has ordered a preparatory hearing, he may make a ruling as to the admissibility of evidence; any other question of law relating to the case or any question as to the severance or joinder of charges. (s.9(3)(b), (c) and (d) of the 1987 Act/s.31(3)(a), (b) and (c) of the 1996 Act) **J–19**

B2 Under section 9(11) of the 1987 Act/section 35(1) of the 1996 Act the defence or the prosecution may appeal to the CACD (and ultimately to the House of Lords) against such a ruling, but only with the leave of the trial judge, single judge or the full court. As to the scope of a judge's powers in relation to a preparatory hearing and thus the extent of appeal rights, see *R. v. H* (§ 7–286 in the main work).

B3 If the trial date is imminent and the application is urgent, the Registrar should be notified so that he may consider referring the application directly to the full court and make arrangements for listing.

B4 If an application for leave to appeal is made to the trial judge, it should be made orally immediately after the ruling, or within two business days by serving a notice of an application on the appropriate officer of the Crown Court and all parties directly affected: rule 66.4. Notice of appeal or application for leave to appeal [Form NG (Prep)] is to be served on the Registrar, the Crown Court and the parties within five business days of the ruling or the trial judge's decision whether to grant leave: rule 66.2.

B5 The notice and grounds of appeal having been served on the other parties, grounds of opposition should be served in a respondent's notice [Form RN (Prep)] within five business days of service of the appeal notice: rule 66.5.

B6 Defence representatives are usually covered by the Crown Court representation order if one is in force (*Access to Justice Act* 1999, Sched. 3, para. 2(2)).

B7 If the relevant time limits are not complied with, the court has power to grant an extension of time, but cogent grounds in support of the application will be required. Where a single judge refuses leave to appeal or an extension of time within which to serve a notice, the application may be renewed for determination by the full court by serving the notice of refusal, appropriately completed, upon the Registrar within five business days of the refusal being served (rule 66.7).

C. Appeals by a Prosecutor Against a "Terminating" Ruling

Criminal Justice Act 2003, s.58 [Part 67 Criminal Procedure Rules 2007]

C1 Section 58 of the 2003 Act gives the prosecution a right of appeal in relation to a "terminating" ruling: in effect where the prosecution agrees to the defendant's acquittal if the appeal against the ruling is not successful (*R. v. Y.* [2008] 1 Cr.App.R. 34). This is wide enough to encompass a case-management decision (*R. v. Clarke* [2008] 1 Cr.App.R. 33). **J–20**

C2 There is no right of appeal in respect of a ruling that the jury be discharged or a ruling in respect of which there is a right of appeal to the Court of Appeal by virtue of another enactment (s.57(2)). The prosecution should therefore consider whether there is a right of appeal under section 9 of the *CJA* 1987 or section 35 of the *CPIA* 1996.

C3 The prosecution must inform the court that it intends to appeal or request an adjournment to consider whether to appeal (s.58(4)), which will be until the next business day (rule 67.2(2)). The judge has a discretion to adjourn for longer if there is a real reason for doing so (*R. v. H.* [2008] EWCA Crim 483). The prosecution can then ask the trial judge to grant leave to appeal (rule 67.5), although leave to appeal can be granted by the trial judge, the single judge or the full court. The Crown must give the undertaking (as to the defendant's acquittal if the appeal is abandoned or leave to appeal is not obtained) at the time when it informs the court of its intention to appeal. The failure to give it then is fatal to an application to the Court of Appeal for leave: s.58(8); *R. v. Arnold* [2008] R.T.R. 25.

C4 Whether or not leave is granted, the trial judge must then decide if the appeal is to be expedited and if so, adjourn the case. If he decides that the appeal should not be expedited, then he can adjourn the case or discharge the jury (s.59). Leave should be granted only where the trial judge considers there is a real prospect of success and not in an attempt to speed up the hearing of the appeal (*R. v. J.G* [2006] EWCA Crim 3276).

C5 Whether the appeal is expedited or not affects the time limits for service of the notice of appeal [Form NG (Pros)] and respondent's notice [Form RN(Pros)]. If expedited, the appeal notice must be served the next business day after the decision, if not expedited, it must be served within five business days. Similar time limits apply to the service of the respondent's notice. Defence representatives are usually covered by the Crown Court representation order if one is in force (such proceedings being considered incidental within the *Access to Justice Act* 1999, Sched. 3, para. 2(2)). If the relevant time limits are not complied with, the court has power to grant an extension of time.

C6 Expedition does not impose time limits on the Registrar or Court of Appeal. However, if leave has not been granted by the trial judge, the application may be referred to the full court by the Registrar to enable the application and appeal to be heard together to ensure that the matter is dealt with quickly.

C7 The Registrar endeavours to list prosecution appeals where a jury has not been discharged as quickly as possible. He is unlikely to be able to list an appeal in less than a week from the ruling because it is necessary for the prosecution to obtain transcripts, papers to be copied and the judges to read their papers. It is of great assistance if it is anticipated that there is to be an appeal against a ruling where the jury has not been discharged, that a telephone call is made to the Registrar or CAC general office (020 7947 6011) notifying the office even before the appeal notice is sent, so that the list office may be put on notice. The listing of an urgent appeal invariably means that other cases have to be removed from the list.

D. OTHER APPEALS

D1 Prosecution appeal against the making of a confiscation order or where the court declines to make one (save on reconsideration of benefit)

- S.31 of the *PCA* 2002.
- Parts 71 and 72 of the *Criminal Procedure Rules*.
- From April 1, 2008 only the prosecution can appeal.
- Proceedings are commenced by serving a Form PoCA 1 on the defendant and the Crown Court within 28 days of the decision appealed against. [*Proceeds of Crime Act (Appeals under Part 2) Order* 2003, art. 3(2)(a).]
- A respondent's notice PoCA 2 is to be served on the Registrar of Criminal Appeals and the appellant not later than 14 days after receiving PoCA 1.
- An undischarged Crown Court representation order will cover advice and assistance on the merits of opposing the appeal and drafting the respondent's notice, otherwise an application for a representation order can be made to the Registrar [*Access to Justice Act* 1999, ss.12(2)(b), 26]. In any event, where an application for a representation order is made on PoCA 2, the Registrar will consider a representation order for the hearing.

● Leave to appeal can be granted by a single judge or the full court.

D2 Appeal in relation to a restraint order

● S.43 of the *PCA* 2002.
● Parts 71 and 73 of the *Criminal Procedure Rules*.
● The prosecution or an accredited financial investigator can appeal a refusal to make a restraint order. A person who applied for an order or who is affected by the order can apply to the Crown Court to vary or discharge the order and then appeal that decision to the Court of Appeal.
● Proceedings are commenced by serving a form PoCA 3 on the Crown Court within 14 days of the decision being appealed. PoCA 3 must then be served on any respondent, and on any person who holds realisable property to which the appeal relates, or is affected by the appeal, not later than seven days after the form is lodged at the Crown Court. The documents which are to be served with PoCA 3 are set out in rule 73.2(3).
● A respondent's notice PoCA 4 is to be served on the Registrar not later than 14 days after the respondent is notified that the appellant has leave to appeal or notified that the application for leave and any appeal are to be heard together. PoCA 4 is then to be served on the appellant and any other respondent as soon as is practicable and not later than seven days after it was served on the Registrar.
● An application for a restraint order can be made as soon as a criminal investigation has begun. The proposed defendant may not have been charged: *PCA* 2002, s.40. This affects the type of public funding.
● If a defendant has been charged with a criminal offence connected to the restraint order then the restraint proceedings are regarded as incidental to the criminal proceedings and are treated as criminal proceedings for funding purposes [*Criminal Defence Service (General) (No. 2) Regulations* 2001, reg.3(3)(c)] and the Registrar can grant a representation order if a defendant appeals a decision on an application to vary or discharge the restraint order.
● If the prosecution apply for a restraint order in the Crown Court before the subject of the restraint order has been charged with a criminal offence and the subject of that order wishes to appeal a decision on an application to vary or discharge the restraint order then civil legal aid may be available as these proceedings fall within the *Access to Justice Act* 1999, Sched. 2, para. 3. The Legal Services Commission should be contacted for funding within the Community Legal Service scheme.
● Similarly, a person affected by the order who wishes to appeal a decision on an application to vary or discharge the restraint order should apply to the Legal Services Commission for funding within the Community Legal Service scheme.
● Leave to appeal can be granted by a single judge or full court.

D3 Appeal in relation to a receivership order

● S.65 of the *PCA* 2002.
● Parts 71 and 73 of the *Criminal Procedure Rules*.
● An appeal can be brought by:
   (a) the person who applied for the order,
   (b) a person who is affected by the order or,
   (c) the receiver.
The orders against which an appeal will lie are:
   (1) the appointment or non-appointment of a receiver,
   (2) the powers of a receiver,
   (3) an order giving a direction to a receiver, and
   (4) the variation or discharge of a receivership order.
● Proceedings are commenced by serving a Form PoCA 3 on the Crown Court

within 14 days of the decision being appealed. PoCA 3 must then be served on any respondent and on any person who holds realisable property to which the appeal relates, or is affected by the appeal, not later than seven days after the form is lodged at the Crown Court. The documents which are to be served with PoCA 3 are set out in rule 73.2(3).

- A respondent's notice PoCA 4 is to be served on the Registrar not later than 14 days after the respondent is notified that the appellant has leave to appeal or is notified that the application for leave and any appeal are to be heard together. PoCA 4 is then to be served on the appellant and any other respondent as soon as is practicable and not later than seven days after it was served on the Registrar.

- If a defendant has been charged with a criminal offence connected to a receivership order then the receivership proceedings are regarded as incidental to the criminal proceedings and are treated as criminal proceedings for funding purposes [*Criminal Defence Service (General) (No. 2) Regulations* 2001, reg.3(3)(c)] and the Registrar can grant a representation order if a defendant appeals a decision relating to a receivership order.

- If a management receivership order or an application for such an order is made in the Crown Court before a criminal offence has been charged and a person affected by the order (including the proposed defendant) wishes to appeal a decision then civil legal aid may be available as these proceedings fall within *Access to Justice Act* 1999, Sched. 2, para. 3. The Legal Services Commission should be contacted for funding within the Community Legal Service scheme.

- Leave to appeal can be granted by a single judge or the full court.

D4 Appeal against an order of the Crown Court in the exercise of its jurisdiction to punish for contempt – usually a finding of contempt or sentence for contempt

J–24
- S.13 of the *Administration of Justice Act* 1960.
- Part 68 of the *Criminal Procedure Rules*.
- Anyone dealt with by the Crown Court for contempt may appeal.
- Proceedings are commenced by lodging a Form NG at the Crown Court no more than 28 days after the order to be appealed.
- The Registrar may direct a respondent's notice Form RN or the Crown may serve one if they wish to make representations to the court.
- An undischarged Crown Court representation order will cover advice and assistance on appeal. The Registrar will usually grant a representation order for the hearing: *Access to Justice Act* 1999, s.12(2)(b).
- No leave to appeal is required. The appeal is as of right.
- Appeals occur most frequently when an appellant wishes to appeal a sentence for failing to appear at the Crown Court as the failing to appear is dealt with as if it were contempt.

D5 Appeal against a minimum term set or reviewed by a High Court judge

J–25
- Para. 14 of Schedule 22 to the *CJA* 2003
- Part 68 of the *Criminal Procedure Rules*
- A defendant with a mandatory life sentence imposed before December 18, 2003 who has had his minimum term set or reviewed by a High Court judge can appeal.
- Proceedings are commenced by service of Form NG (MT) on the Registrar no more than 28 days after the decision.
- The Registrar may direct a respondent's notice Form RN or the Crown may serve one if they wish to make representations to the court.

- An application for a representation order can be made to the Registrar [*Access to Justice Act* 1999, s.12(2)(b)].
- Leave to appeal is required and can be granted by the full court or a single judge: *Criminal Justice Act 2003 (Mandatory Life Sentences: Appeals in Transitional Cases) Order* 2005 (S.I. 2005 No. 2798), art. 8.

D6 Attorney General's reference of an unduly lenient sentence

- S.36 of the *CJA* 1988.   **J–26**
- Part 70 of the *Criminal Procedure Rules*.
- The Attorney General can refer sentences only in relation to specific offences or sentences [*CJA* 1988, ss.35, 36, and *Criminal Justice Act 1988 (Reviews of Sentencing) Order* 2006] including a minimum term, set or reviewed by a High Court judge [*CJA* 2003, Sched. 22, para 15].
- Although rule 70.3(1) implies there is a specific form to commence proceedings, in practice a standard letter with supporting documents is sent by the Attorney General's office no more than 28 days after sentence.
- If the defendant wishes to make representations to the court he must serve a respondent's notice within 14 days of the Registrar serving the application upon him. Again, there is no specific form designated.
- Representation orders are not issued to respond to an Attorney General's reference but a defendant who appears by counsel is entitled to his reasonable costs from central funds. The cost of instructing leading counsel in addition to or instead of junior counsel is generally not considered reasonable unless there is a compelling reason. It is advisable to consult with the Registrar before leading counsel is instructed.
- The leave of the Court of Appeal is required.

D7 Attorney General's reference of a point of law on an acquittal

- S.36 of the *CJA* 1972.   **J–27**
- Part 70 of the *Criminal Procedure Rules*.
- The Attorney General can refer a point of law to the Court of Appeal for an opinion on the acquittal on indictment of the defendant.
- Although rule 70.3(1) implies there is a specific form to commence proceedings, there is no such form and rule 70.3 sets out what should be included in the reference. The defendant should not be identified.
- There is no time limit.
- If the defendant wishes to make representations to the court he must serve a respondent's notice within 28 days of the Registrar serving the application upon him. Again there is no specific form.
- Representation orders are not issued to respond to an Attorney General's reference but a defendant who appears by counsel is entitled to his reasonable costs from central funds.
- Leave is not required.

D8 Appeal against a finding of unfitness to plead or a finding that the accused did the act or made the omission charged

- S.15 of the *CAA* 1968.   **J–28**
- Part 68 of the *Criminal Procedure Rules*.
- The accused can appeal (by the person appointed to represent the accused) against
  — a finding of unfitness to plead (but not fitness to plead as the defendant can appeal any subsequent conviction in the usual way on the basis he was not fit to plead) or

     — that he did the act or made the omission charged or

     — both findings.

The appeal does not lie until both findings have been made.

- Proceedings are commenced by the service of Form NG on the Crown Court not more than 28 days after the finding made which the accused wishes to appeal.
- The Crown should serve a respondent's notice Form RN if directed by the Registrar or if they wish to make representations to the court.
- There does not appear to be any statutory provision empowering the grant of a representation order. The *Prosecution of Offences Act* 1985, s.19, refers to costs from central funds being available to cover the fees of a person appointed by the Crown Court under section 4A of the *Criminal Procedure (Insanity) Act* 1964. In *R. v. Antoine* ([1999] 2 Cr.App.R 225, CA) this was interpreted to include the costs of an appeal. The *Prosecution of Offences Act* 1985, s.16(4) provides that where the Court of Appeal <u>allows an appeal</u> under Part 1 of the *CAA* 1968 against a finding under the *Criminal Procedure (Insanity) Act* 1964 that the appellant is under a disability, or that he did the act or made the omission charged against him the court may make a defendant's costs order in favour of the accused.
- Leave to appeal may be granted by the Crown Court judge, a single judge or the full court.

D9 Appeal against a verdict of not guilty by reason of insanity

- S.12 of the *CAA* 1968.
- Part 68 of the *Criminal Procedure Rules*.
- The defendant can appeal a verdict of not guilty by reason of insanity.
- Proceedings are commenced by the service of Form NG on the Crown Court not more than 28 days after the verdict.
- The Crown should serve a respondent's notice Form RN if directed by the Registrar or if they wish to make representations to the court.
- There does not appear to be any statutory provision empowering the grant of a representation order. The *Prosecution of Offences Act* 1985, s.16(4), provides that where the Court of Appeal <u>allows an appeal</u> then the court may make a defendant's costs order. If the appeal is not allowed costs from central funds should be available on the same basis as was allowed in *Antoine* (*ante*) in the absence of any statutory provision.
- Leave to appeal may be granted by the Crown Court judge, a single judge or the full court.

D10 Appeal against the order following a verdict of not guilty by reason of insanity or a finding of unfitness to plead

- S.16A of the *CAA* 1968.
- Part 68 of the *Criminal Procedure Rules*.
- An accused who, as a result of a verdict of not guilty by reason of insanity or a finding of fitness to plead has a hospital order, interim hospital order or supervision order made against him may appeal against the order.
- Proceedings are commenced by the service of Form NG on the Crown Court not more than 28 days after the order.
- [As D9, *ante*.]
- [As D9, *ante*.]
- [As D9, *ante*.]

D11 Appeal against review of sentence

- S.74(8) of the *SOCPA* 2005.

- Part 68 of the *Criminal Procedure Rules*.
- A defendant or specified prosecutor may appeal.
- Proceedings are commenced by serving a Form NG (RD) on the Crown Court not more than 28 days after the review.
- A respondent's notice Form RN should be served if directed by the Registrar or if the respondent wishes to make representations to the Court.
- An application for a representation order can be made to the Registrar: *Access to Justice Act* 1999, s.12(2)(b).
- Leave to appeal can be granted by the single judge or full court [*Serious Organised Crime and Police Act 2005 (Appeals under section 74) Order* 2006 (S.I. 2006 No. 2135)].

D12 Appeal against an order for trial by jury of sample counts

- S.18 of the *Domestic Violence, Crime and Victims Act* 2004.   **J–32**
- Part 66 of the *Criminal Procedure Rules*.
- The defendant can appeal.
- An application for the jury to try some counts as sample counts and the judge to try the remainder if the jury convict, must be determined at a preparatory hearing and section 18 confers rights of interlocutory appeal. A Form NG (Prep) must be served on the Crown Court, the Registrar and any party directly affected not more than five business days after the order or the Crown Court judge granting or refusing leave. *(For applications to the Crown Court judge, see Part B above.)*
- A respondent's notice Form RN (Prep) should be served if the court directs or the Crown (or any party affected) wants to make representations to the court.
- Defence representatives are usually covered by the Crown Court representation order if one is in force [*Access to Justice Act* 1999, Sched. 3, para. 2(2)].
- The Crown Court Judge, single judge or full court can grant leave to appeal.

D13 Appeal against an order relating to a trial to be conducted without a jury where there is a danger of jury tampering

- S.9(11) of the *CJA* 1987 and s.35(1) of the *CPIA* 1996.   **J–33**
- Part 66 of the *Criminal Procedure Rules*.
- The prosecution can appeal the refusal to make an order; the defence can appeal the making of an order.
- A Form NG (Prep) must be served on the Crown Court, the Registrar and any party directly affected not more than five business days after the order or the Crown Court judge grants or refuses leave. *(For applications to the Crown Court judge, see Part B above.)*
- A respondent's notice Form RN (Prep) should be served if the court directs or the Crown (or any party affected) wants to make representations to the court.
- Defence representatives are usually covered by the Crown Court representation order if one is in force [*Access to Justice Act* 1999, Sched. 3, para. 2 (2)].
- Leave is required. The Crown Court judge, single judge or full court can grant leave to appeal.

D14 Appeal against an order that a trial should continue without a jury or a new trial take place without a jury after jury tampering

- S.47 of the *CJA* 2003.   **J–34**
- Part 66 of the *Criminal Procedure Rules* (relating to appeals against an order made in a preparatory hearing notwithstanding the ruling will not have been in the context of a preparatory hearing).
- The defendant can appeal.

- As D13, *ante*
- As D13, *ante*
- As D13, *ante*
- As D13, *ante*

D15 Appeal against orders restricting or preventing reports or restricting public access

J–35
- S.159 of the *CJA* 1988
- Part 69 of the *Criminal Procedure Rules*
- A person aggrieved may appeal.
- Applications against orders <u>restricting reporting</u> shall be made within 10 business days after the date on which the order was made by serving Form NG (159) on the Registrar, the Crown Court, the prosecutor and defendant and any other affected person. Applications against orders to <u>restrict public access</u> must be made the next business day after the order was made. If advance notice of an order restricting public access is given, then advance notice of an intention to appeal may be made not more than five business days after the advance notice is displayed.
- A person on whom an appeal notice is served should serve a respondent's notice Form RN (159) within three business days if he wishes to make representations to the court or the court so directs.
- The court may make such order as to costs as it thinks fit (*CJA* 1988, s.159(5)(c)), but not out of central funds – *Holden v. CPS (No. 2)* [1994] 1 A.C. 22, HL.
- A single judge or the full court can grant leave to appeal: *CAA* 1968, s.31(2B).
- Applications for leave to appeal and appeals in relation to reporting restrictions <u>may</u> be heard in private (rule 65.6 (1)). Applications for leave to appeal and appeals relating to restricting public access must be determined <u>without</u> a hearing (rule 65.6(3)).

D16 Appeal against a wasted costs order and appeal against a third party costs order

J–36
- Regulation 3C (costs wasted) and 3E (third party costs) of the *Costs in Criminal Cases (General) Regulations* 1986.
- A legal or other representative against whom a wasted costs order has been made in the Crown Court or a third party against whom a third party costs order has been made may appeal.
- Notice of appeal should be served on the Crown Court within 21 days of the order being made. There is no specific form. The notice should be served on any interested party (including, if appropriate, the Ministry of Justice).
- Any interested party can make representations orally or in writing.
- There is no power to grant a representation order or to order costs out of central funds as these proceedings are civil in nature.
- Leave to appeal is not required.

D17 Appeal relating to serious crime prevention orders

J–37
- S.24 of the *SCA* 2007.
- Part 68 of the *Criminal Procedure Rules.*
- A person subject to the order, an applicant authority or anyone given the opportunity to make representations at the Crown Court about the making, refusal to make, variation or non-variation of an order may appeal.
- Proceedings are commenced by the service of Form NG (SCPO) on the Crown Court not more than 28 days after the order.
- A respondent's notice Form RN (SCPO) should be served if directed by the Registrar or if the respondent wishes to make representations to the court.

- Proceedings before the Crown Court or the Court of Appeal relating to serious crime prevention orders and arising by virtue of section 19, 20, 21 or 24 of the *SCA* 2007 are criminal proceedings for the purposes of section 12(2)(g) of the *Access to Justice Act* 1999 [see the *Criminal Defence Service (General) (No. 2) (Amendment) Regulations* (S.I. 2008 No. 725)]. Accordingly, the Registrar may grant a representation order to a person subject to the order. A person who made representations at the Crown Court can apply to the LSC for funding. The court has discretion to order costs as it thinks fit [*Serious Crime Act 2007 (Appeals under section 24) Order* 2008 (S.I. 2008 No. 1863), Pt 3].
- Leave to appeal can be granted by the Crown Court judge, full court or single judge [S.I. 2008 No. 1863, art. 9].

D18 Appeal against the non-making of a football banning order

- S.14A(5A) of the *Football Spectators Act* 1989. **J–38**
- Part 68 of the *Criminal Procedure Rules*.
- The prosecution can appeal.
- The appeal notice should be served on the Crown Court within 28 days of the decision not to make an order. However, there is no designated form.
- A respondent's notice should be served if directed by the Registrar or if the respondent wishes to make representations to the court. However, again there is no designated form.
- An application for a representation order may be made to the Registrar – *Access to Justice Act* 1999, s.12(2)(b).
- Currently, the Court of Appeal has been given no powers to deal with these appeals.

E. APPLICATION FOR A RETRIAL FOR A SERIOUS OFFENCE

E1 Application by a prosecutor to quash an acquittal and seek a retrial for a qualifying offence

S.76(1) of the Criminal Justice Act 2003 [Part 41 of the Criminal Procedure Rules]

E1–1 There must be new and compelling evidence and it must be in the interests **J–39** of justice for the acquitted person to be retried for a qualifying offence as listed in the *CJA* 2003, Sched. 5, Pt 1 (*CJA* 2003, ss.78, 79: see *R. v. Dunlop* [2007] 1 Cr.App.R. 8, and *R. v. Miell* [2008] 1 Cr.App.R. 23).

E1–2 Proceedings can begin in one of two ways.

(1) By serving notice of the application under section 76 on the Court of Appeal and within two days serving the notice on the acquitted person (s.80). This notice charges him with the offence. It requires the personal written consent of the Director of Public Prosecutions (DPP) (s.76(3)). If the acquitted person is not in custody the prosecution can ask the Crown Court to issue:

    (i) a summons for the acquitted person to appear before the Court of Appeal for the hearing of the application or

    (ii) a warrant for his arrest (s.89(3)).

Once arrested on the warrant the acquitted person must be brought before the Crown Court within 48 hours (s.89(6)).

(2) An acquitted person may be charged with the offence before an application under section 76 has been made. This may be after an arrest in an investigation authorised by the DPP (s.85(2)) or where no authorisation has been given, after arrest under a warrant issued by a justice of the peace (s.87(1)). Having been charged, the acquitted person must be brought before the Crown Court to consider bail within 24 hours (s.88(2)). He can then be remanded in custody or on bail for 42 days whilst an application under s.76 is prepared: s.88(6) unless an extension is granted under subsection (8). Once a notice of application

under section 76 has been served, stating that the acquitted person has previously been charged with the offence, the acquitted person must be brough before the Crown Court to consider bail within 48 hours of the notice being given to the Registrar, if the acquitted person is already in custody under sector 88 (*ante*) (s.89(2)).

E1–3 Thus in either case, bail is dealt with largely by the Crown Court. The Cour of Appeal only considers bail on the adjournment of the hearing of the application under section 76 (s.90(1)).

E1–4 The notice ["Notice of a s.76 application required by s.80(1) *Criminal Justic Act* 2003"] should where practicable be accompanied by the witness statements which are relied on as the new and compelling evidence, the original witness statements unused statements, indictment, paper exhibits from the original trial, any relevan transcripts from the original trial and any other documents relied on: rule 41.2(2).

E1–5 An acquitted person who wants to oppose a section 76 application mus serve a response ["Response of the acquitted person under s.80 *Criminal Justice Ac* 2003"] not more than 28 days after receiving the notice: rule 41.3(2).

E2 Application by a prosecutor for a determination whether a foreign acquittal is a bar to a trial and if so, an order that it not be a bar

S.76(2) of the Criminal Justice Act 2003 [Part 41 of the Criminal Procedur Rules]

E2–1 The prosecution can apply, with the personal written consent of the DP] (s.76(3)) for a determination whether an acquittal outside the UK is a bar to th acquitted person being tried in England and Wales and if it is found to be so, an or der that the acquittal not be a bar. Proceedings can begin in the same way as for a application under section 76(1).

E3 Application for restrictions on publication relating to an application under section 76

S.82 of the Criminal Justice Act 2003 [Part 41 of the Criminal Procedure Rules

E3–1 An application can be made by the DPP for reporting restrictions. This ca be made after a notice of an application for a retrial has been made and may also b made by the court of its own motion (s.82(5)). An application can also be made b the DPP for reporting restrictions <u>before</u> a notice of an application for a retrial if a investigation has been commenced: s.82(6). The application for reporting restriction must be served on the Registrar ["Application for restrictions on publication unde s.82 *Criminal Justice Act* 2003"] and (usually) the acquitted person (rule 41.8(1)).

E3–2 A party who wants to vary or revoke an order for restrictions onpublicatio under section 82(7) may apply to the Court of Appeal in writing at any time after th order was made (rule 41.9(1)).

E4 Representation orders

E4–1 The Registrar will usually grant a representation order to the acquitte person for solicitors and counsel to respond to any of the above applications.

APPENDIX K

Guidelines issued by the Sentencing Guidelines Council

I. GUIDELINES

A. REDUCTION IN SENTENCE FOR A GUILTY PLEA

Guideline

CONTENTS

FOREWORD

K–2   One of the first guidelines to be issued by the Sentencing Guidelines Council related to the statutory obligation to take account of any guilty plea when determining sentence. As set out in the foreword to that guideline[1], the intention was "to promote consistency in sentencing by providing clarity for courts, court users and victims so that everyone knows exactly what to expect". Prior to that guideline there had been different understandings of the purpose of the reduction and the extent of any reduction given.

Since the guideline was issued, there has been much greater clarity but there still remain concerns about some of the content of the guideline and about the extent to which the guideline has been consistently applied. Accordingly the council has undertaken a review of the guideline (in accordance with the statutory obligation placed upon it to do so from time to time[2]); it has also requested that the Judicial Studies Board consider further ways in which judicial training can incorporate the guideline.

The council is extremely grateful to the Sentencing Advisory Panel for the speed and thoroughness with which it has prepared its advice following extensive consultation. The council has accepted almost all the recommendations of the panel; the issues and arguments are set out fully in the panel's advice (see www.sentencing-guidelines.gov.uk). This revised guideline applies to all cases sentenced on or after 23 July 2007.

The council has agreed with the panel that the general approach of the guideline is correct in setting out clearly the purpose of the reduction for a guilty plea, in settling for a reduction no greater than one third (with lower levels of reduction where a plea is entered other than at the first reasonable opportunity) and in continuing to provide for a special approach when fixing the minimum term for a life sentence imposed following conviction for murder.

The council has agreed with the panel that some discretion should be introduced to the approach where the prosecution case is "overwhelming".

The council has not accepted the panel's recommendation in relation to circumstances where a magistrates' court is sentencing an offender for a number of offence where the overall maximum imprisonment is six months. The council continues to consider that there must be some incentive to plead guilty in such circumstances; this is consistent with other aspects of the guideline.

The council has not accepted the panel's recommendation in relation to the "capping" of the effect of reduction on very large fines. The number of such fines is very low and the council was not convinced that the arguments were strong enough to justify a departure from the general approach in the guideline not to "cap" the effect of the reduction. In addition, the revised guideline provides guidance as to when the "first reasonable opportunity" is likely to occur in relation to indictable only offences; emphasises that remorse and material assistance provided to prosecuting authorities are separate issues from those to which the guideline applies and makes clear that the approach to calculation of the reduction where an indeterminate sentence is imposed (other than that following conviction for murder) should be the same as that for determinate sentences.

Since the guideline was issued in 2004, there have been changes in the statutory provisions governing the reduction for guilty plea and in those relating to sentences for public protection. The review has provided an opportunity to bring the guideline up to date and those changes have been incorporated.

The council published a draft guideline in accordance with section 170(8) of the *Criminal Justice Act* 2003 inviting responses by 14 March 2007. A response has been received from the Home Affairs Committee, a response has been received from the Attorney General and seven other responses have been received. A summary of the responses and the decisions of the council has been published separately.

Chairman of the Council
July 2007

A. STATUTORY PROVISIONS

Section 144 *Criminal Justice Act* 2003 provides [the guideline here sets out the text   **K–3** of section 144 of the 2003 Act, set out in the main work at § 5–78].

Section 174(2) *Criminal Justice Act* 2003 provides [the guideline here sets out the text of section 174(2)(d) of the 2003 Act, set out in the main work at § 5–111].

1.1   This guideline applies whether a case is dealt with in a magistrates' court or in the Crown Court and whenever practicable in the youth court (taking into account legislative restrictions such as those relevant to the length of detention and training orders).

1.2   The application of this guideline to sentencers when arriving at the appropriate minimum term for the offence of murder is set out in Section F.

1.3   This guideline can also be found at www.sentencing-guidelines.gov.uk or can be obtained from the Council's Secretariat at 4th Floor, 8–10 Great George Street, London SW1P 3AE.

B. STATEMENT OF PURPOSE

2.1   When imposing a custodial sentence, statute requires that a court must impose   **K–4** the shortest term that is commensurate with the seriousness of the offence(s)[4]. Similarly, when imposing a community order, the restrictions on liberty must be commensurate with the seriousness of the offence(s)[5]. Once that decision is made, a court is required to give consideration to the reduction for any guilty plea. As a result, the final sentence after the reduction for a guilty plea will be less than the seriousness of the offence requires.

2.2   A reduction in sentence is appropriate because a guilty plea avoids the need for a trial (thus enabling other cases to be disposed of more expeditiously), shortens the gap between charge and sentence, saves considerable cost, and, in the case of an early plea, saves victims and witnesses from the concern about having to give evidence. The reduction principle derives from the need for the effective administration of justice and not as an aspect of mitigation.

2.3   Where a sentencer is in doubt as to whether a custodial sentence is appropriate, the reduction attributable to a guilty plea will be a relevant consideration. Where this is amongst the factors leading to the imposition of a non-custodial sentence, there will be no need to apply a further reduction on account of the guilty plea. A similar approach is appropriate where the reduction for a guilty plea is amongst the factors leading to the imposition of a financial penalty or discharge instead of a community order.

2.4   When deciding the most appropriate length of sentence, the sentencer should address separately the issue of remorse, together with any other mitigating features, before calculating the reduction for the guilty plea. Similarly, assistance to the prosecuting or enforcement authorities is a separate issue which may attract a reduction in sentence under other procedures; care will need to be taken to ensure that there is no "double counting".

2.5   The implications of other offences that an offender has asked to be taken into consideration should be reflected in the sentence before the reduction for guilty plea has been applied.

2.6   A reduction in sentence should only be applied to the punitive elements of a penalty[6]. The guilty plea reduction has no impact on sentencing decisions in relation to ancillary orders, including orders of disqualification from driving.

C.   Application of the Reduction Principle

K–5   3.1 Recommended approach

> The court decides sentence for the offence(s) taking into account aggravating and mitigating factors and any other offences that have been formally admitted (TICs)
>
> ⇩
>
> The court selects the amount of the reduction by reference to the sliding scale
>
> ⇩
>
> The court applies the reduction
>
> ⇩
>
> When pronouncing sentence the court should usually state what the sentence would have been if there had been no reduction as a result of the guilty plea.

D.   Determining the Level of Reduction

K–6   4.1   The level of reduction should be *a proportion of the total sentence* imposed, with the proportion calculated by reference to the circumstances in which the guilty plea was indicated, in particular the stage in the proceedings. The greatest reduction will be given where the plea was indicated at the "first reasonable opportunity".

4.2   Save where section 144(2) of the 2003 Act applies[7], the level of the reduction will be gauged on a *sliding scale* ranging from a recommended *one third* (where the guilty plea was entered at the first reasonable opportunity in relation to the offence for which sentence is being imposed), reducing to a recommended *one quarter* (where a trial date has been set) and to a recommended *one tenth* (for a guilty plea entered at the 'door of the court' or after the trial has begun). *See diagram below.*

4.3   The level of reduction should reflect the stage at which the offender indicated a *willingness to admit guilt* to the offence for which he is eventually sentenced:

    (i)   the largest recommended reduction will not normally be given unless the offender indicated willingness to admit guilt at the first reasonable opportunity; when this occurs will vary from case to case (see *Annex 1 for illustrative examples*);

   (ii)   where the admission of guilt comes later than the first reasonable opportunity, the reduction for guilty plea will normally be less than one third;

  (iii)   where the plea of guilty comes very late, it is still appropriate to give some reduction;

(iv) if after pleading guilty there is a *Newton* hearing and the offender's version of the circumstances of the offence is rejected, this should be taken into account in determining the level of reduction;

(v) if the not guilty plea was entered and maintained for tactical reasons (such as to retain privileges whilst on remand), a late guilty plea should attract very little, if any, discount.

In each category, there is a presumption that the recommended reduction will be given unless there are good reasons for a lower amount.

First reasonable opportunity	After a trial date is set	Door of the court/ after trial has begun
======= |	============= |	=========== |
recommended 1/3	**recommended** 1/4	**recommended** 1/10

E. WITHOLDING A REDUCTION

On the basis of dangerousness

5.1 Where a sentence for a "dangerous offender" is imposed under the provisions in the *Criminal Justice Act* 2003, whether the sentence requires the calculation of a minimum term or is an extended sentence, the approach will be the same as for any other determinate sentence (see also section G below)[8].

Where the protection case is overwhelming

5.2 The purpose of giving credit is to encourage those who are guilty to plead at the earliest opportunity. Any defendant is entitled to put the prosecution to proof and so every defendant who is guilty should be encouraged to indicate that guilt at the first reasonable opportunity.

5.3 Where the prosecution case is overwhelming, it may not be appropriate to give the full reduction that would otherwise be given. Whilst there is a presumption in favour of the full reduction being given where a plea has been indicated at the first reasonable opportunity, the fact that the prosecution case is overwhelming without relying on admissions from the defendant may be a reason justifying departure from the guideline.

5.4 Where a court is satisfied that a lower reduction should be given for this reason, a recommended reduction of 20% is likely to be appropriate where the guilty plea was indicated at the first reasonable opportunity.

5.5 A court departing from a guideline must state the reasons for doing so[9].

Where the maximum penalty for the offence is thought to be too low

5.6 The sentencer is bound to sentence for the offence with which the offender has been charged, and to which he has pleaded guilty. The sentencer cannot remedy perceived defects (for example an inadequate charge or maximum penalty) by refusal of the appropriate discount.

Where jurisdictional issues arise

(i) Where sentencing powers are limited to six months' imprisonment despite multiple offences

5.7 When the total sentence for both or all of the offences is six months' imprisonment, a court may determine to impose consecutive sentences which, even allowing for a reduction for a guilty plea where appropriate on each offence, would still result in the imposition of the maximum sentence available. In such circumstances, in order to achieve the purpose for which the reduction principle has been established[10], some modest allowance should normally be given against the total sentence for the entry of a guilty plea.

(ii) Where a maximum sentence might still be imposed

5.8 Despite a guilty plea being entered which would normally attract a reduction in sentence, a magistrates' court may impose a sentence of imprisonment of 6 months for a single either-way offence where, but for the plea, that offence would have been committed to the Crown Court for sentence.

5.9 Similarly, a detention and training order of 24 months may be imposed on an offender aged under 18 if the offence is one which would but for the plea have attracted a sentence of long-term detention in excess of 24 months under the *Powers of Criminal Courts (Sentencing) Act* 2000, s.91.

F. Application to Sentencing for Murder

K–8

6.1 Murder has always been regarded as the most serious criminal offence and the sentence prescribed is different from other sentences. By law, the sentence for murder is imprisonment (detention) for life and an offender will remain subject to the sentence for the rest of his/her life.

6.2 The decision whether to release the offender from custody during this sentence will be taken by the Parole Board which will consider whether it is safe to release the offender on licence. The court that imposes the sentence is required by law to set a minimum term that has to be served before the Parole Board may start to consider whether to authorise release on licence. If an offender is released, the licence continues for the rest of the offender's life and recall to prison is possible at any time.

6.3 Uniquely, Parliament has set starting points[11] (based on the circumstances of the killing) which a court will apply when it fixes the minimum term. Parliament has further prescribed that, having identified the appropriate starting point, the court must then consider whether to increase or reduce it in the light of aggravating or mitigating factors, some of which are listed in statute. Finally, Parliament specifically provides[12] that the obligation to have regard to any guilty plea applies to the fixing of the minimum term, by making the same statutory provisions that apply to other offences apply to murder without limiting the court's discretion (as it did with other sentences under the *Powers of Criminal Courts (Sentencing) Act* 2000).

6.4 There are important differences between the usual fixed term sentence and the minimum term set following the imposition of the mandatory life sentence for murder. The most significant of these, from the sentencer's point of view, is that a reduction for a plea of guilty in the case of murder will have double the effect on time served in custody when compared with a determinate sentence. This is because a determinate sentence will provide (in most circumstances) for the release of the offender[13] on licence half way through the total sentence whereas in the case of murder a minimum term is the period in custody before consideration is given by the Parole Board to whether release is appropriate.

6.5 Given this difference, the special characteristic of the offence of murder and the unique statutory provision of starting points, careful consideration will need to be given to the extent of any reduction and to the need to ensure that the minimum term properly reflects the seriousness of the offence. Whilst the general principles continue to apply (both that a guilty plea should be encouraged and that the extent of any reduction should reduce if the indication of plea is later than the first reasonable opportunity), the process of determining the level of reduction will be different.

6.6 Approach

K–9

1. Where a court determines that there should be a whole life minimum term, there will be no reduction for a guilty plea.

2. In other circumstances,

(a) the court will weigh carefully the overall length of the minimum term taking into account other reductions for which the offender may be eligible so as to avoid a combination leading to an inappropriately short sentence;

(b) where it is appropriate to reduce the minimum term having regard to a plea of guilty, the reduction will not exceed one sixth and will never exceed five years;

(c) the sliding scale will apply so that, where it is appropriate to reduce the minimum term on account of a guilty plea, the maximum reduction (one sixth or five years whichever is the less) is only available where there has been an indication of willingness to plead guilty at the first reasonable opportunity, with a recommended 5% for a late guilty plea;

(d) the court should then review the sentence to ensure that the minimum term accurately reflects the seriousness of the offence taking account of the statutory starting point, all aggravating and mitigating factors and any guilty plea entered.

G. APPLICATION TO OTHER INDETERMINATE SENTENCES

7.1   There are other circumstances in which an indeterminate sentence will be imposed. This may be a discretionary life sentence or imprisonment for public protection. **K–10**

7.2   As with the mandatory life sentence imposed following conviction for murder, the court will be obliged to fix a minimum term to be served before the Parole Board is able to consider whether the offender can be safely released.

7.3   However, the process by which that minimum term is fixed is different from that followed in relation to the mandatory life sentence and requires the court first to determine what the equivalent determinate sentence would have been. Accordingly, the approach to the calculation of the reduction for any guilty plea should follow the process and scale adopted in relation to determinate sentences, as set out in section D above.

Annex 1

First reasonable opportunity

1.   The critical time for determining the maximum reduction for a guilty plea is the first reasonable opportunity for the defendant to have indicated a willingness to plead guilty. This opportunity will vary with a wide range of factors and the court will need to make a judgement on the particular facts of the case before it. **K–11**

2.   The key principle is that the purpose of giving a reduction is to recognise the benefits that come from a guilty plea not only for those directly involved in the case in question but also in enabling courts more quickly to deal with other outstanding cases.

3.   This Annex seeks to help courts to adopt a consistent approach by giving examples of circumstances where a determination will have to be made:

(a) the first reasonable opportunity may be the first time that a defendant appears before the court and has the opportunity to plead guilty;

(b) but the court may consider that it would be reasonable to have expected an indication of willingness even earlier, perhaps whilst under interview;

Note: For (a) and (b) to apply, the court will need to be satisfied that the defendant (and any legal adviser) would have had sufficient information about the allegations

(c) where an offence triable either way is committed to the Crown Court for trial and the defendant pleads guilty at the first hearing in that court, the reduction will be less than if there had been an indication of a guilty plea given to the magistrates' court (recommended reduction of one third) but more than if the plea had been entered after a trial date had been set (recommended reduction of one quarter), and is likely to be in the region of 30%;

(d) where an offence is triable only on indictment, it may well be that the first reasonable opportunity would have been during the police station stage; where that is not the case, the first reasonable opportunity is likely to be at the first hearing in the Crown Court;

(e) where a defendant is convicted after pleading guilty to an alternative (lesser) charge to that to which he/she had originally pleaded not guilty, the extent of any reduction will be determined by the stage at which the defendant first formally indicated to the court willingness to plead guilty to the lesser charge and the reason why that lesser charge was proceeded with in preference to the original charge.

[The next paragraph is K–13.]

B. Overarching Principles: Seriousness

Guideline

Contents

Foreword

K–14   In accordance with the provisions of section 170(9) *Criminal Justice Act* 2003, the Sentencing Guidelines Council issues this guideline as a definitive guideline. By virtue of section 172 of the Act, every court must have regard to a relevant guideline.

The Council was created in 2004 in order to frame Guidelines to assist Courts as they deal with criminal cases across the whole of England and Wales.

The Council has stated that it intends to follow a principled approach to the formulation of guidelines to assist sentencers which will include consideration of overarching and general principles relating to the sentencing of offenders. Following the planned implementation of many of the sentencing provisions in the 2003 Act in April 2005, this guideline deals with the general concept of seriousness in the light of those provisions and considers how sentencers should determine when the respective sentencing thresholds have been crossed when applying the provisions of the Act.

This guideline applies only to sentences passed under the sentencing framework applicable to those aged 18 or over although there are some aspects that will assist courts assessing the seriousness of offences committed by those under 18. The Council has commissioned separate advice from the Sentencing Advisory Panel on the sentencing of young offenders.

This is the first time that it has been possible to produce definitive guidelines not only before new provisions come into force but also before much of the training of judiciary and practitioners.

The Council has appreciated greatly the work of the Sentencing Advisory Panel in preparing the advice on which this guideline has been based and for the many organisations and individuals who have responded so thoughtfully to the consultation of both the Panel and the Council. The advice and this guideline are available on www.sentencing-guidelines.gov.uk or from the Sentencing Guidelines Secretariat. A summary of the responses to the Council's consultation also appears on the website.

Chairman of the Council
December 2004

Seriousness

1.1   In every case where the offender is aged 18 or over at the time of conviction, **K–15**
the court must have regard to the five purposes of sentencing contained in section
142(1) *Criminal Justice Act* 2003:

   (a) the punishment of offenders
   (b) the reduction of crime (including its reduction by deterrence)
   (c) the reform and rehabilitation of offenders
   (d) the protection of the public
   (e) the making of reparation by offenders to persons affected by their offence

1.2   The Act does not indicate that any one purpose should be more important
than any other and in practice they may all be relevant to a greater or lesser degree
in any individual case—the sentencer has the task of determining the manner in
which they apply.

1.3   The sentencer must start by considering the seriousness of the offence, the assessment of which will:

   • determine which of the sentencing thresholds has been crossed;
   • indicate whether a custodial, community or other sentence is the most ap-
     propriate;
   • be the key factor in deciding the length of a custodial sentence, the onerousness
     of requirements to be incorporated in a community sentence and the amount of
     any fine imposed.

1.4   A court is required to pass a sentence that is commensurate with the seriousness of the offence. The seriousness of an offence is determined by two main
parameters; the **culpability** of the offender and the **harm** caused or risked being
caused by the offence

1.5   Section 143(1) *Criminal Justice Act* 2003 provides [see § 5–54 in the main
work].

B. CULPABILITY

1.6   Four levels of criminal culpability can be identified for sentencing purposes: **K–16**
1.7   Where the offender;

   (i) has the **intention** to cause harm, with the highest culpability when an
        offence is planned. The worse the harm intended, the greater the
        seriousness.
   (ii) is **reckless** as to whether harm is caused, that is, where the offender ap-
         preciates at least some harm would be caused but proceeds giving no
         thought to the consequences even though the extent of the risk would
         be obvious to most people.
   (iii) has **knowledge** of the specific risks entailed by his actions even though
          he does not intend to cause the harm that results.
   (iv) is guilty of **negligence**.

Note: *There are offences where liability is strict and no culpability need be proved for the
purposes of obtaining a conviction, but the degree of culpability is still important when
deciding sentence. The extent to which recklessness, knowledge or negligence are involved in
a particular offence will vary.*

C. HARM

1.8   The relevant provision is widely drafted so that it encompasses those offences   **K–17** where harm is caused but also those where neither individuals nor the community suffer harm but a risk of harm is present.

To individual victims

1.9   The types of harm caused or risked by different types of criminal activity are diverse and victims may suffer physical injury, sexual violation, financial loss, damage to health or psychological distress. There are gradations of harm within all of these categories.

1.10   The nature of harm will depend on personal characteristics and circumstances of the victim and the court's assessment of harm will be an effective and important way of taking into consideration the impact of a particular crime on the victim.

1.11   In some cases no actual harm may have resulted and the court will be concerned with assessing the relative dangerousness of the offender's conduct; it will consider the likelihood of harm occurring and the gravity of the harm that could have resulted.

To the community

1.12   Some offences cause harm to the community at large (instead of or as well as to an individual victim) and may include economic loss, harm to public health, or interference with the administration of justice.

Other types of harm

1.13   There are other types of harm that are more difficult to define or categorise. For example, cruelty to animals certainly causes significant harm to the animal but there may also be a human victim who also suffers psychological distress and/or financial loss.

1.14   Some conduct is criminalised purely by reference to public feeling or social mores. In addition, public concern about the damage caused by some behaviour, both to individuals and to society as a whole, can influence public perception of the harm caused, for example, by the supply of prohibited drugs.

D.   The Assessment of Culpability and Harm

K–18   1.15   Section 143(1) makes clear that the assessment of the seriousness of any individual offence must take account not only of any harm actually caused by the offence, but also of any harm that was intended to be caused or might foreseeably be caused by the offence.

1.16   Assessing seriousness is a difficult task, particularly where there is an imbalance between culpability and harm:

- sometimes the harm that actually results is greater than the harm intended by the offender;
- in other circumstances, the offender's culpability may be at a higher level than the harm resulting from the offence

1.17   Harm must always be judged in the light of culpability. The precise level of culpability will be determined by such factors as motivation, whether the offence was planned or spontaneous or whether the offender was in a position of trust.

Culpability will be greater if:

- an offender deliberately causes more harm than is necessary for the commission of the offence, or
- where an offender targets a vulnerable victim (because of their old age or youth, disability or by virtue of the job they do).

1.18   Where unusually serious harm results and was unintended and beyond the control of the offender, culpability will be significantly influenced by the extent to which the harm could have been foreseen.

1.19   If much **more** harm, or much **less** harm has been caused by the offence than the offender intended or foresaw, the culpability of the offender, depending on the circumstances, may be regarded as carrying greater or lesser weight as appropriate.

The culpability of the offender in the particular circumstances of an individual case should be the initial factor in determining the seriousness of an offence.

(i) Aggravating factors

1.20 Sentencing guidelines for a particular offence will normally include a list of aggravating features which, if present in an individual instance of the offence, would indicate *either* a higher than usual level of culpability on the part of the offender, *or* a greater than usual degree of harm caused by the offence (or sometimes both).

1.21 The lists below bring together the most important aggravating features with potential application to more than one offence or class of offences. They include some factors (such as the vulnerability of victims or abuse of trust) which are integral features of certain offences; in such cases, the presence of the aggravating factor is already reflected in the penalty for the offence and **cannot be used as justification for increasing the sentence further**. The lists are not intended to be comprehensive and the aggravating factors are not listed in any particular order of priority. On occasions, two or more of the factors listed will describe the same feature of the offence and care needs to be taken to avoid "double counting". Those factors starred with an asterisk are statutory aggravating factors where the statutory provisions are in force. Those marked with a hash are yet to be brought into force but as factors in an individual case are still relevant and should be taken into account.

1.22 **Factors indicating higher culpability:**
- Offence committed whilst on bail for other offences
- Failure to respond to previous sentences
- Offence was racially or religiously aggravated
- Offence motivated by, or demonstrating, hostility to the victim based on his or her sexual orientation (or presumed sexual orientation)
- Offence motivated by, or demonstrating, hostility based on the victim's disability (or presumed disability)
- Previous conviction(s), particularly where a pattern of repeat offending is disclosed
- Planning of an offence
- An intention to commit more serious harm than actually resulted from the offence
- Offenders operating in groups or gangs
- "Professional" offending
- Commission of the offence for financial gain (where this is not inherent in the offence itself)
- High level of profit from the offence
- An attempt to conceal or dispose of evidence
- Failure to respond to warnings or concerns expressed by others about the offender's behaviour
- Offence committed whilst on licence
- Offence motivated by hostility towards a minority group, or a member or members of it
- Deliberate targeting of vulnerable victim(s)
- Commission of an offence while under the influence of alcohol or drugs
- Use of a weapon to frighten or injure victim
- Deliberate and gratuitous violence or damage to property, over and above what is needed to carry out the offence
- Abuse of power

• Abuse of a position of trust

1.23 **Factors indicating a more than usually serious degree of harm:**

• Multiple victims
• An especially serious physical or psychological effect on the victim, even if unintended
• A sustained assault or repeated assaults on the same victim
• Victim is particularly vulnerable
• Location of the offence (for example, in an isolated place)
• Offence is committed against those working in the public sector or providing a service to the public
• Presence of others *e.g.* relatives, especially children or partner of the victim
• Additional degradation of the victim (*e.g.* taking photographs of a victim as part of a sexual offence)
• In property offences, high value (including sentimental value) of property to the victim, or substantial consequential loss (*e.g.* where the theft of equipment causes serious disruption to a victim's life or business)

(ii) Mitigating factors

K–20   1.24   Some factors may indicate that an offender's culpability is **unusually** low, or that the harm caused by an offence is less than usually serious.

1.25 **Factors indicating significantly lower culpability:**

• A greater degree of provocation than normally expected
• Mental illness or disability
• Youth or age, where it affects the responsibility of the individual defendant
• The fact that the offender played only a minor role in the offence

(iii) Personal mitigation

K–21   1.26   Section 166(1) *Criminal Justice Act* 2003 makes provision for a sentencer to take account of any matters that "in the opinion of the court, are relevant in mitigation of sentence".

1.27   When the court has formed an initial assessment of the seriousness of the offence, then it should consider any offender mitigation. The issue of remorse should be taken into account at this point along with other mitigating features such as admissions to the police in interview.

(iv) Reduction for a guilty plea

K–22   1.28   Sentencers will normally reduce the severity of a sentence to reflect an early guilty plea. This subject is covered by a separate guideline and provides a sliding scale reduction with a normal maximum one-third reduction being given to offenders who enter a guilty plea at the first reasonable opportunity.

1.29   Credit may also be given for ready co-operation with the authorities. This will depend on the particular circumstances of the individual case.

E.   THE SENTENCING THRESHOLDS

K–23   1.30   Assessing the seriousness of an offence is only the first step in the process of determining the appropriate sentence in an individual case. Matching the offence to a type and level of sentence is a separate and complex exercise assisted by the application of the respective threshold tests for custodial and community sentences.

The custody threshold

K–24   1.31   Section 152(2) *Criminal Justice Act* 2003 provides [see § 5–265 in the main work].

1.32   In applying the threshold test, sentencers should note: the clear intention of
the threshold test is to reserve prison as a punishment for the most serious offences;

- it is impossible to determine definitively which features of a particular offence
  make it serious enough to merit a custodial sentence;
- passing the custody threshold does not mean that a custodial sentence should
  be deemed inevitable, and custody can still be avoided in the light of personal
  mitigation or where there is a suitable intervention in the community which
  provides sufficient restriction (by way of punishment) while addressing the rehabilitation of the offender to prevent future crime. For example, a prolific offender who currently could expect a short custodial sentence (which, in advance
  of custody plus, would have no provision for supervision on release) might
  more appropriately receive a suitable community sentence.

1.33   The approach to the imposition of a custodial sentence under the new
framework should be as follows:

(a) has the custody threshold been passed?
(b) if so, is it unavoidable that a custodial sentence be imposed?
(c) if so, can that sentence be suspended? (sentencers should be clear that they
    would have imposed a custodial sentence if the power to suspend had not been
    available)
(d) if not, can the sentence be served intermittently?
(e) if not, impose a sentence which takes immediate effect for the term com-
    mensurate with the seriousness of the offence.

The threshold for community sentences

1.34   Section 148(1) *Criminal Justice Act* 2003 provides [see § 5–126 in the main   **K–25**
work].

1.35   In addition, the threshold for a community sentence can be crossed even
though the seriousness criterion is not met. Section 151 *Criminal Justice Act* 2003
provides that, in relation to an offender aged 16 or over on whom, on three or more
previous occasions, sentences had been passed consisting only of a fine, a community
sentence may be imposed (if it is in the interests of justice) despite the fact that the
seriousness of the current offence (and others associated with it) might not warrant
such a sentence.

1.36   Sentencers should consider all of the disposals available (within or below the
threshold passed) at the time of sentence before reaching the provisional decision to
make a community sentence, so that, even where the threshold for a community
sentence has been passed, a financial penalty or discharge may still be an appropriate
penalty.

Summary

1.37   It would not be feasible to provide a form of words or to devise any formula   **K–26**
that would provide a general solution to the problem of where the custody threshold
lies. Factors vary too widely between offences for this to be done. It is the task of
guidelines for individual offences to provide more detailed guidance on what features
within that offence point to a custodial sentence, and also to deal with issues such as
sentence length, the appropriate requirements for a community sentence or the use
of appropriate ancillary orders.

**Having assessed the seriousness of an individual offence, sentencers must consult
the sentencing guidelines for an offence of that type for guidance on the factors
that are likely to indicate whether a custodial sentence or other disposal is most
likely to be appropriate.**

F.   Prevalence

1.38   The seriousness of an individual case should be judged on its own dimen-   **K–27** sions of harm and culpability rather than as part of a collective social harm. It is legitimate for the overall approach to sentencing levels for particular offences to be guided by their cumulative effect. However, it would be wrong to further penalise individual offenders by increasing sentence length for committing an individual offence of that type.

1.39   There may be exceptional local circumstances that arise which may lead a court to decide that prevalence should influence sentencing levels. The pivotal issue in such cases will be the harm being caused to the community. It is essential that sentencers both have supporting evidence from an external source (for example the local Criminal Justice Board) to justify claims that a particular crime is prevalent in their area and are satisfied that there is a compelling need to treat the offence more seriously than elsewhere.

The key factor in determining whether sentencing levels should be enhanced in response to prevalence will be the level of harm being caused in the locality. Enhanced sentences should be exceptional and in response to exceptional circumstances. Sentencers must sentence within the sentencing guidelines once the prevalence has been addressed. Having assessed the seriousness of an individual offence, sentencers must consult the sentencing guidelines for an offence of that type for guidance on the factors that are likely to indicate whether a custodial sentence or other disposal is most likely to be appropriate.

Published by the Sentencing Guidelines Secretariat, December 2004

C. New Sentences: Criminal Justice Act 2003

Guideline

Foreword

K–28   In accordance with the provisions of section 170(9) *Criminal Justice Act* 2003, the Sentencing Guidelines Council issues this guideline as a definitive guideline. By virtue of section 172 of the Act, every court must have regard to a relevant guideline.

The Council was created in 2004 in order to frame Guidelines to assist Courts as they deal with criminal cases across the whole of England and Wales.

This guideline relates to the new sentencing framework introduced by the *Criminal Justice Act* 2003, which affects the nature of community and custodial sentences. Only those sentences and related provisions which are expected to come into force by April 2005 are dealt with in this guideline. It will be followed by further guidelines in due course. This is an unusual guideline since it covers a range of sentences outside the context of individual offences and does so in readiness for the coming into force of the statutory provisions creating the sentences. It is designed with the object of ensuring a consistent approach when the sentences become available.

This guideline applies only to sentences passed under the sentencing framework applicable to those aged 18 or over.

The guideline is divided into two sections:
- Sections 1 covers the practical aspects of implementing the non-custodial powers namely the new community sentence and the new form of deferred sentence;
- Section 2 deals with the new custodial sentence provisions relating to suspended sentences, prison sentences of 12 months or more, and intermittent custody.[1]

The Act also contains an extensive range of provisions to protect the public from dangerous offenders. These will be dealt with separately.

The Advice of the Sentencing Advisory Panel to the Council (published on 20th September 2004) has been broadly accepted by the Council and forms the basis of this guideline. Further information on the issues covered in this guideline can be found in that Advice or in the discussion document that preceded it. All these documents are available on www.sentencing-guidelines.gov.uk or from the Sentencing Guidelines Secretariat.

Chairman of the Council

December 2004

SECTION 1 PART 1—COMMUNITY SENTENCES

A. STATUTORY PROVISIONS

(i) The thresholds for community sentence

K-30   1.1.1   Seriousness—Section 148 *Criminal Justice Act* 2003 [sets out subsection (1), as to which, see § 5–126 in the main work].

1.1.2   Persistent offenders—Section 151 *Criminal Justice Act* 2003 [sets out subsections (1) and (2), as to which, see § 5–129 in the main work].

(ii) The sentences available

K-31   1.1.3   Meaning of community sentence—Section 147 *Criminal Justice Act* 2003 [sets out subsection (1), as to which, see § 5–126 in the main work].

1.1.4   Offenders aged 16 or over—Section 177 *Criminal Justice Act* 2003 [sets out subsections (1) to (4), as to which, see § 5–130 in the main work].

(iii) Determining which orders to make & requirements to include

K-32   1.1.5   Suitability—Section 148 *Criminal Justice Act* 2003 [sets out subsection (2), as to which see § 5–126 in the main work].

1.1.6   Restrictions on liberty—Section 148 *Criminal Justice Act* 2003 [sets out subsection (1), as to which see § 5–126 in the main work].

1.1.7   Compatibility—Section 177 *Criminal Justice Act* 2003 [sets out subsection (6), as to which see § 5–130 in the main work].

(iv) Electronic monitoring

K-33   1.1.8   Section 177 *Criminal Justice Act* 2003 [sets out subsections (3) and (4), as to which see § 5–130 in the main work].

B. IMPOSING A COMMUNITY SENTENCE—THE APPROACH

K-34   1.1.9   On pages 8 and 9 of the seriousness guideline the two thresholds for the imposition of a community sentence are considered. Sentencers must consider all of the disposals available (within or below the threshold passed) at the time of sentence, and reject them before reaching the provisional decision to make a community sentence, so that even where the threshold for a community sentence has been passed a financial penalty or discharge may still be an appropriate penalty. Where an offender has a low risk of reoffending, particular care needs to be taken in the light of evidence that indicates that there are circumstances where inappropriate intervention can increase the risk of re-offending rather than decrease it. In addition, recent improvements in enforcement of financial penalties make them a more viable sentence in a wider range of cases.

1.1.10   Where an offender is being sentenced for a non-imprisonable offence or offences, great care will be needed in assessing whether a community sentence is appropriate since failure to comply could result in a custodial sentence.

1.1.11   Having decided (in consultation with the Probation Service where appropriate) that a community sentence is justified, the court must decide which requirements should be included in the community order. The requirements or orders imposed will have the effect of restricting the offender's liberty, whilst providing punishment in the community, rehabilitation for the offender, and/or ensuring that the offender engages in reparative activities.

The key issues arising are:
(i) which requirements to impose;
(ii) how to make allowance for time spent on remand; and

774

(iii) how to deal with breaches.

(i) Requirements

1.1.12   When deciding which requirements to include, the court must be satisfied **K–35** on three matters—

(i) that the **restriction on liberty is commensurate with the seriousness** of the offence(s);[2]

(ii) that the **requirements are the most suitable** for the offender;[3] and

(iii) that, where there are two or more requirements included, they are **compatible with each other.**[4]

1.1.13   Sentencers should have the possibility of breach firmly in mind when passing sentence for the original offence. If a court is to reflect the seriousness of an offence, there is little value in setting requirements as part of a community sentence that are not demanding enough for an offender. On the other hand, there is equally little value in imposing requirements that would "set an offender up to fail" and almost inevitably lead to sanctions for a breach.

In community sentences, the guiding principles are proportionality and suitability. Once a court has decided that the offence has crossed the community sentence threshold and that a community sentence is justified, the *initial* factor in defining which requirements to include in a community sentence should be the seriousness of the offence committed.

1.1.14   This means that "seriousness" is an important factor in deciding whether the court chooses the low, medium or high range (see below) but, having taken that decision, selection of the content of the order within the range will be determined by a much wider range of factors.

- **Sentencing ranges must remain flexible enough to take account of the suitability of the offender, his or her ability to comply with particular requirements and their availability in the local area.**

- **The justification for imposing a community sentence in response to persistent petty offending is the persistence of the offending behaviour rather than the seriousness of the offences being committed. The requirements imposed should ensure that the restriction on liberty is proportionate to the seriousness of the offending, to reflect the fact that the offences, of themselves, are not sufficiently serious to merit a community sentence.**

(a) Information for sentencers

1.1.15   In many cases, a pre-sentence report[5] will be pivotal in helping a sentencer decide whether to impose a custodial sentence or whether to impose a community sentence and, if so, whether particular requirements, or combinations of requirements, are suitable for an individual offender. The court must always ensure (especially where there are multiple requirements) that the restriction on liberty placed on the offender is proportionate to the seriousness of the offence committed.[6] The court must also consider the likely effect of one requirement on another, and that they do not place conflicting demands upon the offender.[7]

1.1.16   The council supports the approach proposed by the panel at paragraph 78 of its Aadvice that, having reached the provisional view that a community sentence is the most appropriate disposal, the sentencer should request a pre-sentence report, indicating which of the three sentencing ranges is relevant and the purpose(s) of sentencing that the package of requirements is required to fulfil. Usually the most helpful way for the court to do this would be to produce a written note for the report writer, copied on the court file. If it is known that the same tribunal and defence advocate will be present at the sentencing hearing and a probation officer is present in court when the request for a report is made, it may not be necessary to commit details of the request to writing. However, events may change during the period of an adjournment and it is good practice to ensure that there is a clear record of the request for the court. These two factors will guide the Probation Service in determining the nature and combination of requirements that may be appropriate and the onerousness and intensity of those requirements. A similar procedure should apply when ordering a pre-sentence report when a custodial sentence is being considered.

1.1.17   There will be occasions when any type of report may be unnecessary despite the intention to pass a community sentence though this is likely to be infrequent. A court could consider dispensing with the need to obtain a pre-sentence report for adult offenders—

- where the offence falls within the LOW range of seriousness (see pp.9–10); and
- where the sentencer was minded to impose a single requirement, such as an exclusion requirement (where the circumstances of the case mean that this would be an appropriate disposal without electronic monitoring); and
- where the sentence will not require the involvement of the Probation Service, for example an electronically monitored curfew (subject to the court being satisfied that there is an appropriate address at which the curfew can operate).

(b) Ranges of sentence within the community sentence band

K–37   1.1.18   To enable the court to benefit from the flexibility that community sentences provide and also to meet its statutory obligations, any structure governing the use of community requirements must allow the courts to choose the most appropriate sentence for each individual offender.

1.1.19   Sentencers have a statutory obligation to pass sentences that are commensurate with the seriousness of an offence. However, within the range of sentence justified by the seriousness of the offence(s), courts will quite properly consider those factors that heighten the risk of the offender committing further offences or causing further harm with a view to lessening that risk. The extent to which requirements are imposed must be capable of being varied to ensure that the restriction on liberty is commensurate with the seriousness of the offence.

1.1.20   The council recognises that it would be helpful for sentencers to have a framework to help them decide on the most appropriate use of the new community sentence. While there is no single guiding principle, the seriousness of the offence that has been committed is an important factor. Three sentencing ranges (low, medium and high) within the community sentence band can be identified. It is not possible to position particular types of offence at firm points within the three ranges because the seriousness level of an offence is largely dependent upon the culpability of the offender and this is uniquely variable. The difficulty is particularly acute in relation to the medium range where it is clear that requirements will need to be tailored across a relatively wide range of offending behaviour.

1.1.21   In general terms, the lowest range of community sentence would be for those offenders whose offence was relatively minor within the community sentence band and would include persistent petty offenders whose offences only merit a community sentence by virtue of failing to respond to the previous imposition of fines. Such offenders would merit a 'light touch' approach, for example, normally a single requirement such as a short period of unpaid work, or a curfew, or a prohibited activity requirement or an exclusion requirement (where the circumstances of the case mean that this would be an appropriate disposal without electronic monitoring)

1.1.22   The top range would be for those offenders who have only just fallen short of a custodial sentence and for those who have passed the threshold but for whom a community sentence is deemed appropriate.

1.1.23   In all three ranges there must be sufficient flexibility to allow the sentence to be varied to take account of the suitability of particular requirements for the individual offender and whether a particular requirement or package of requirements might be more effective at reducing any identified risk of re-offending. It will fall to the sentencer to ensure that the sentence strikes the right balance between proportionality and suitability.

**There should be three sentencing ranges (low, medium and high) within the
community sentence band based upon seriousness.**

**It is not intended that an offender necessarily progress from one range to the
next on each sentencing occasion. The decision as to the appropriate range each
time is based upon the seriousness of the new offence(s).**

**The decision on the nature and severity of the requirements to be included in a
community sentence should be guided by:**

    (i)   **the assessment of offence seriousness (low, medium or high);**

    (ii)   **the purpose(s) of sentencing the court wishes to achieve;**

    (iii)   **the risk of re-offending;**

    (iv)   **the ability of the offender to comply, and**

    (v)   **the availability of requirements in the local area.**

**The resulting restriction on liberty must be a proportionate response to the of-
fence that was committed.**

1.1.24   Below we set out a non-exhaustive description of examples of requirements that might be appropriate in the three sentencing ranges. These examples
focus on punishment in the community, although it is recognised that not all pack-
ages will necessarily need to include a punitive requirement. There will clearly be
other requirements of a rehabilitative nature, such as a treatment requirement or an
accredited programme, which may be appropriate depending on the specific needs
of the offender and assessment of suitability. Given the intensity of such interventions, it is expected that these would normally only be appropriate at medium and
high levels of seriousness, and where assessed as having a medium or high risk of re-
offending. In addition, when passing sentence in any one of the three ranges, the
court should consider whether a rehabilitative intervention such as a programme
requirement, or a restorative justice intervention might be suitable as an additional
or alternative part of the sentence.

Low

1.1.25   For offences only just crossing the community sentence threshold (such as
persistent petty offending, some public order offences, some thefts from shops, or
interference with a motor vehicle, where the seriousness of the offence or the nature
of the offender's record means that a discharge or fine is inappropriate).   **K–38**

1.1.26   Suitable requirements might include:

- 40 to 80 hours of unpaid work; or
- a curfew requirement within the lowest range (*e.g.* up to 12 hours per day for a
  few weeks); or
- an exclusion requirement (where the circumstances of the case mean that this
  would be an appropriate disposal without electronic monitoring) lasting a few
  months; or
- a prohibited activity requirement; or
- an attendance centre requirement (where available).

1.1.27   Since the restriction on liberty must be commensurate with the seriousness
of the offence, particular care needs to be taken with this band to ensure that this
obligation is complied with. In most cases, only one requirement will be appropriate
and the length may be curtailed if additional requirements are necessary.

Medium

1.1.28   For offences that obviously fall within the community sentence band such   **K–39**
as handling stolen goods worth less than £1000 acquired for resale or somewhat
more valuable goods acquired for the handler's own use, some cases of burglary in
commercial premises, some cases of taking a motor vehicle without consent, or some
cases of obtaining property by deception.

1.1.29   Suitable requirements might include:

- a greater number (*e.g.* 80 to 150) of hours of unpaid work; or

- an activity requirement in the middle range (20 to 30 days); or
- a curfew requirement within the middle range (*e.g.* up to 12 hours for 2–3 months); or
- an exclusion requirement lasting in the region of six months or
- a prohibited activity requirement.

1.1.30   Since the restriction on liberty must be commensurate with the seriousness of the offence, particular care needs to be taken with this band to ensure that this obligation is complied with.

High

K–40   1.1.31   For offences that only just fall below the custody threshold or where the custody threshold is crossed but a community sentence is more appropriate in all the circumstances, for example some cases displaying the features of a standard domestic burglary committed by a first-time offender.

1.1.32   More intensive sentences which combine two or more requirements may be appropriate at this level. Suitable requirements might include an unpaid work order of between 150 and 300 hours; an activity requirement up to the maximum 60 days; an exclusion order lasting in the region of 12 months; a curfew requirement of up to 12 hours a day for 4–6 months.

(c) Electronic monitoring

K–41   1.1.33   The court must also consider whether an electronic monitoring requirement[8] should be imposed which is mandatory[9] in some circumstances.

Electronic monitoring should be used with the primary purpose of promoting and monitoring compliance with other requirements, in circumstances where the punishment of the offender and/or the need to safeguard the public and prevent re-offending are the most important concerns.

(d) Recording the sentence imposed

K–42   1.1.34   Under the new framework there is only one (generic) community sentence provided by statute. This does not mean that offenders who have completed a community sentence and have then re-offended should be regarded as ineligible for a second community sentence on the basis that this has been tried and failed. Further community sentences, perhaps with different requirements, may well be justified.

1.1.35   Those imposing sentence will wish to be clear about the 'purposes' that the community sentence is designed to achieve when setting the requirements. Sharing those purposes with the offender and Probation Service will enable them to be clear about the goals that are to be achieved.

1.1.36   Any future sentencer must have full information about the requirements that were inserted by the court into the previous community sentence imposed on the offender (including whether it was a low/medium/high level order) and also about the offender's response. This will enable the court to consider the merits of imposing the same or different requirements as part of another community sentence. The requirements should be recorded in such a way as to ensure that they can be made available to another court if another offence is committed.

When an offender is required to serve a community sentence, the court record should be clearly annotated to show which particular requirements have been imposed.

(ii) Time spent on remand

K–43   1.1.37   The court will need to consider whether to give any credit for time spent in custody on remand.[10] (For further detail from the Panel's Advice, see Annex A.)

The court should seek to give credit for time spent on remand (in custody or equivalent status) in all cases. It should make clear, when announcing sentence, whether or not credit for time on remand has been given (bearing in mind that there will be no automatic reduction in sentence once section 67 of the *Criminal Justice Act* 1967 is repealed) and should explain its reasons for not giving credit when it considers either that this is not justified, would not be practical, or would not be in the best interests of the offender.

1.1.38   Where an offender has spent a period of time in custody on remand, there will be occasions where a custodial sentence is warranted but the length of the sentence justified by the seriousness of the offence would mean that the offender would be released immediately. Under the present framework, it may be more appropriate to pass a community sentence since that will ensure supervision on release.

1.1.39   However, given the changes in the content of the second part of a custodial sentence of 12 months or longer, a court in this situation where the custodial sentence would be 12 months or more should, under the new framework, pass a custodial sentence in the knowledge that licence requirements will be imposed on release from custody. This will ensure that the sentence imposed properly reflects the seriousness of the offence.

1.1.40   Recommendations made by the court at the point of sentence will be of particular importance in influencing the content of the licence. This will properly reflect the gravity of the offence(s) committed.

(iii) Breaches

1.1.41   Where an offender fails, without reasonable excuse, to comply with one or more requirements, the 'responsible officer'[11] can either give a warning or initiate breach proceedings. Where the offender fails to comply without reasonable excuse for the second time within a 12-month period, the 'responsible officer' must initiate proceedings.   **K–44**

1.1.42   In such proceedings the court must[12] either **increase the severity of the existing sentence** (i.e. impose more onerous conditions including requirements aimed at enforcement, such as a curfew or supervision requirement) or **revoke the existing sentence and proceed as though sentencing for the original offence**. The court is required to take account of the circumstances of the breach,[13] which will inevitably have an impact on its response.

1.1.43   In certain circumstances (where an offender has wilfully and persistently failed to comply with an order made in respect of an offence that is not itself punishable by imprisonment), the court can **impose a maximum of 51 weeks custody.**[14]

1.1.44   When increasing the onerousness of requirements, the court must consider the impact on the offender's ability to comply and the possibility of precipitating a custodial sentence for further breach. For that reason, and particularly where the breach occurs towards the end of the sentence, the court should take account of compliance to date and may consider that extending the supervision or operational periods will be more sensible; in other cases it might choose to add punitive or rehabilitative requirements instead. In making these changes the court must be mindful of the legislative restrictions on the overall length of community sentences and on the supervision and operational periods allowed for each type of requirement.

1.1.45   The court dealing with breach of a community sentence should have as its primary objective ensuring that the requirements of the sentence are finished, and this is important if the court is to have regard to the statutory purposes of sentencing. A court that imposes a custodial sentence for breach without giving adequate consideration to alternatives is in danger of imposing a sentence that is not commensurate with the seriousness of the original offence and is solely a punishment for breach. This risks undermining the purposes it has identified as being important. Nonetheless, courts will need to be vigilant to ensure that there is a realistic prospect of the purposes of the order being achieved.

Having decided that a community sentence is commensurate with the seriousness of the offence, the primary objective when sentencing for breach of requirements is to ensure that those requirements are completed.

1.1.46 A court sentencing for breach must take account of the extent to which the offender has complied with the requirements of the community order, the reason for breach and the point at which the breach has occurred. Where a breach takes place towards the end of the operational period and the court is satisfied that the offender's appearance before the court is likely to be sufficient in itself to ensure future compliance, then given that it is not open to the court to make no order, an approach that the court might wish to adopt could be to re-sentence in a way that enables the original order to be completed properly—for example, a differently constructed community sentence that aims to secure compliance with the purposes of the original sentence.

1.1.47 If the court decides to increase the onerousness of an order, it must give careful consideration, with advice from the Probation Service, to the offender's ability to comply. A custodial sentence should be the last resort, where all reasonable effort to ensure that an offender completes a community sentence have failed.

- **The Act allows for a custodial sentence to be imposed in response to breach of a community sentence. Custody should be the last resort, reserved for those cases of deliberate and repeated breach where all reasonable efforts to ensure that the offender complies have failed.**
- **Before increasing the onerousness of requirements, sentencers should take account of the offender's ability to comply and should avoid precipitating further breach by overloading the offender with too many or conflicting requirements.**
- **There may be cases where the court will need to consider re-sentencing to a differently constructed community sentence in order to secure compliance with the purposes of the original sentence, perhaps where there has already been partial compliance or where events since the sentence was imposed have shown that a different course of action is likely to be effective.**

SECTION 1 PART 2—DEFERRED SENTENCES

A. STATUTORY PROVISIONS

K–45   1.2.1 Under the existing legislation,[15] a court can defer a sentence for up to six months, provided the offender consents and the court considers that deferring the sentence is in the interests of justice.

1.2.2 The new provisions[16] continue to require the consent of the offender and that the court be satisfied that the making of such a decision is in the interests of justice. However, it is also stated that the power to defer sentence can only be exercised where:

"the offender undertakes to comply with any requirements as to his conduct during the period of the deferment that the court considers it appropriate to impose;".[17]

1.2.3 This enables the court to impose a wide variety of conditions (including residence requirement).[18] The Act allows the court to appoint the probation service or other responsible person to oversee the offender's conduct during this period and prepare a report for the court at the point of sentence i.e. the end of the deferment period.

1.2.4 As under the existing legislation, if the offender commits another offence during the deferment period the court may have the power to sentence for both the original and the new offence at once. Sentence cannot be deferred for more than six months and, in most circumstances, no more than one period of deferment can be granted.[19]

1.2.5   A significant change is the provision enabling a court to deal with an offender before the end of the period of deferment.[20] For example if the court is satisfied that the offender has failed to comply with one or more requirements imposed in connection with the deferment, the offender can be brought back before the court and the court can proceed to sentence.

B. Use of Deferred Sentences

1.2.6   Under the new framework, there is a wider range of sentencing options open to the courts, including the increased availability of suspended sentences, and deferred sentences are likely to be used in very limited circumstances. A deferred sentence enables the court to review the conduct of the defendant before passing sentence, having first prescribed certain requirements. It also provides several opportunities for an offender to have some influence as to the sentence passed—   **K–46**

  (a) it tests the commitment of the offender not to re-offend;

  (b) it gives the offender an opportunity to do something where progress can be shown within a short period;

  (c) it provides the offender with an opportunity to behave or refrain from behaving in a particular way that will be relevant to sentence.

1.2.7   Given the new power to require undertakings and the ability to enforce those undertakings before the end of the period of deferral, the decision to defer sentence should be predominantly for a small group of cases at either the custody threshold or the community sentence threshold where the sentencer feels that there would be particular value in giving the offender the opportunities listed because, if the offender complies with the requirements, a different sentence will be justified at the end of the deferment period. This could be a community sentence instead of a custodial sentence or a fine or discharge instead of a community sentence. It may, rarely, enable a custodial sentence to be suspended rather than imposed immediately.

The use of deferred sentences should be predominantly for a small group of cases close to a significant threshold where, should the defendant be prepared to adapt his behaviour in a way clearly specified by the sentencer, the court may be prepared to impose a lesser sentence.

1.2.8   A court may impose any conditions during the period of deferment that it considers appropriate.[21] These could be specific requirements as set out in the provisions for community sentences,[22] or requirements that are drawn more widely. These should be specific, measurable conditions so that the offender knows exactly what is required and the court can assess compliance; the restriction on liberty should be limited to ensure that the offender has a reasonable expectation of being able to comply whilst maintaining his or her social responsibilities.

1.2.9   Given the need for clarity in the mind of the offender and the possibility of sentence by another court, the court should give a clear indication (and make a written record) of the type of sentence it would be minded to impose if it had not decided to defer and ensure that the offender understands the consequences of failure to comply with the court's wishes during the deferral period.

When deferring sentence, the sentencer must make clear the consequence of not complying with any requirements and should indicate the type of sentence it would be minded to impose. Sentencers should impose specific, measurable conditions that do not involve a serious restriction on liberty.

SECTION 2—CUSTODIAL SENTENCES

PART 1—CUSTODIAL SENTENCES OF 12 MONTHS OR MORE

A. STATUTORY PROVISIONS

K–47 2.1.1 Under existing legislation:

- an adult offender receiving a custodial sentence of at least 12 months and below 4 years will automatically be released at the halfway point and will then be supervised under licence until the three-quarter point of the sentence. [For some, the actual release date may be earlier as a result of release on home detention curfew (HDC).]
- an adult offender receiving a determinate sentence of 4 years or above will be eligible for release from the halfway point and, if not released before, will automatically be released at the two-thirds point. After release, the offender will be supervised under licence until the three-quarter point of the sentence.

2.1.2 Under the new framework, the impact of a custodial sentence will be more severe since the period in custody and under supervision will be for the whole of the sentence term set by the court. Additionally, separate provisions for the protection of the public will be introduced for those offenders designated as "dangerous" under the Act which are designed to ensure that release only occurs when it is considered safe to do so.

2.1.3 Where a prison sentence of 12 months or more is imposed on an offender who is not classified as "dangerous", that offender will be entitled to be released from custody after completing half of the sentence. The whole of the second half of the sentence will be subject to licence requirements. These requirements will be set shortly before release by the Secretary of State (with advice from the Governor responsible for authorising the prisoner's release in consultation with the Probation Service) but a court will be able to make recommendations at the sentencing stage on the content of those requirements.[23] The conditions that the Secretary of State may attach to a licence are to be prescribed by order.[24]

2.1.4 The Act requires that a custodial sentence for a fixed term should be for the shortest term that is commensurate with the seriousness of the offence.[25]

B. IMPOSITION OF CUSTODIAL SENTENCES OF 12 MONTHS OR MORE

(i) Length of sentence

K–48 2.1.5 The requirement that the second half of a prison sentence will be served in the community subject to conditions imposed prior to release is a major new development and will require offenders to be under supervision for the full duration of the sentence prescribed by the court. The Probation Service will be able to impose a number of complementary requirements on the offender during the second half of a custodial sentence and these are expected to be more demanding and involve a greater restriction on liberty than current licence conditions.

2.1.6 As well as restricting liberty to a greater extent, the new requirements will last until the very end of the sentence, rather than to the three-quarter point as at present, potentially making a custodial sentence significantly more demanding than under existing legislation. Breach of these requirements at any stage is likely to result in the offender being returned to custody and this risk continues, therefore, for longer under the new framework than under the existing legislation.

Transitional arrangements

K–49 2.1.7 In general, a fixed term custodial sentence of 12 months or more under the new framework will increase the sentence actually served (whether in custody or in

782

the community) since it continues to the end of the term imposed. Existing guidelines issued since 1991 have been based on a different framework and so, in order to maintain consistency between the lengths of sentence under the current and the new framework, there will need to be some adjustment to the starting points for custodial sentences contained in those guidelines (subject to the special sentences under the 2003 Act where the offender is a "dangerous" offender).

2.1.8   This aspect of the guideline will be temporary to overcome the short-term situation where sentencing guidelines (issued since implementation of the reforms to custodial sentences introduced by the *Criminal Justice Act* 1991) are based on a different framework and the new framework has made those sentences more demanding. As new guidelines are issued they will take into account the new framework in providing starting points and ranges of appropriate sentence lengths for offences and an adjustment will not be necessary.

2.1.9   Since there are so many factors that will vary, it is difficult to calculate precisely how much more demanding a sentence under the new framework will be. The Council's conclusion is that the sentencer should seek to achieve the best match between a sentence under the new framework and its equivalent under the old framework so as to maintain the same level of punishment. As a guide, the Council suggests the sentence length should be reduced by in the region of 15%.

2.1.10   The changes in the nature of a custodial sentence will require changes in the way the sentence is announced. Sentencers will need to continue[26] to spell out the practical implications of the sentence being imposed so that offenders, victims and the public alike all understand that the sentence does not end when the offender is released from custody. The fact that a breach of the requirements imposed in the second half of the sentence is likely to result in a return to custody should also be made very clear at the point of sentence.

- **When imposing a fixed term custodial sentence of 12 months or more under the new provisions, courts should consider reducing the overall length of the sentence that would have been imposed under the current provisions by in the region of 15%.**
- **When announcing sentence, sentencers should explain the way in which the sentence has been calculated, how it will be served and the implications of non-compliance with licence requirements. In particular, it needs to be stated clearly that the sentence is in two parts, one in custody and one under supervision in the community.**
- **This proposal does not apply to sentences for dangerous offenders, for which separate provision has been made in the Act.**

(ii) Licence conditions

2.1.11   Under the Act, a court imposing a prison sentence of 12 months or more   **K–50**
may recommend conditions that should be imposed by the Secretary of State (with advice from the governor responsible for authorising the prisoner's release in consultation with the Probation Service) on release from custody.[27] Recommendations do not form part of the sentence and they are not binding on the Secretary of State.[28]

2.1.12   When passing such a sentence, the court will not know with any certainty to what extent the offender's behaviour may have been addressed in custody or what the offender's health and other personal circumstances might be on release and so it will be extremely difficult, especially in the case of longer custodial sentences, for sentencers to make an informed judgement about the most appropriate licence conditions to be imposed on release. However, in most cases, it would be extremely helpful for sentencers to indicate areas of an offender's behaviour about which they have the most concern and to make suggestions about the types of intervention whether this, in practice, takes place in prison or in the community.

2.1.13   The involvement of the Probation Service at the pre-sentence stage will clearly be pivotal. A recommendation on the likely post-release requirements included in a presentence report will assist the court with the decision on overall sentence length, although any recommendation would still have to be open to review when release is being considered. A curfew, exclusion requirement or prohibited activity requirement might be suitable conditions to recommend for the licence period. A court might also wish to suggest that the offender should complete a rehabilitation programme, for example for drug abuse, anger management, or improving skills such as literacy and could recommend that this should be considered as a licence requirement if the programme has not been undertaken or completed in custody.

2.1.14 The governor responsible for authorising the prisoner's release, in consultation with the Probation Service, is best placed to make recommendations at the point of release; this is the case at present and continues to be provided for in the Act. Specific court recommendations will only generally be appropriate in the context of relatively short sentences, where it would not be unreasonable for the sentencer to anticipate the relevance of particular requirements at the point of release. Making recommendations in relation to longer sentences (other than suggestions about the types of intervention that might be appropriate at some point during the sentence) would be unrealistic. The governor and Probation Service should have due regard to any recommendations made by the sentencing court and the final recommendation to the Secretary of State on licence conditions will need to build upon any interventions during the custodial period and any other changes in the offender's circumstances.

- A court may sensibly suggest interventions that could be useful when passing sentence, but should only make specific recommendations about the requirements to be imposed on licence when announcing short sentences and where it is reasonable to anticipate their relevance at the point of release. The governor and Probation Service should have due regard to any recommendations made by the sentencing court but its decision should be contingent upon any changed circumstances during the custodial period.

- The court should make it clear, at the point of sentence, that the requirements to be imposed on licence will ultimately be the responsibility of the Governor and Probation Service and that they are entitled to review any recommendations made by the court in the light of any changed circumstances.

SECTION 2 PART 2—SUSPENDED SENTENCES OF IMPRISONMENT

A. STATUTORY PROVISIONS

K–51   2.2.1 Section 189 *Criminal Justice Act* 2003 [sets out full text of section 189, as to which, see § 5–321 in the main work].

K–52   2.2.2 Imposition of requirements—Section 190 *Criminal Justice Act* 2003 [sets out full text of section 190, as to which, see § 5–327 in the main work].

K–53   2.2.3 Power to provide for review—Section 191 *Criminal Justice Act* 2003 [sets out full text of section 191, as to which, see § 5–323 in the main work].

K–54   2.2.4 Periodic reviews—Section 192 *Criminal Justice Act* 2003 [sets out full text of section 192, as to which, see § 5–324 in the main work].

K–55   2.2.5 Breach, revocation or amendment of orders, and effect of further conviction—Section 193 *Criminal Justice Act* 2003

Schedule 12 (which relates to the breach, revocation or amendment of the community requirements of suspended sentence orders, and to the effect of any further conviction) shall have effect.

B. IMPOSING A SUSPENDED SENTENCE

K–56   2.2.6 A suspended sentence is a sentence of imprisonment. It is subject to the same criteria as a sentence of imprisonment which is to commence immediately. In particular, this requires a court to be satisfied that the custody threshold has been passed and that the length of the term is the shortest term commensurate with the seriousness of the offence.

2.2.7   A court which passes a prison sentence of less than 12 months may suspend it for between six months and two years (the operational period).[30] During that period, the court can impose one or more requirements for the offender to undertake in the community. The requirements are identical to those available for the new community sentence.

2.2.8   The period during which the offender undertakes community requirements is "the supervision period" when the offender will be under the supervision of a "responsible officer"; this period may be shorter than the operational period. The court may periodically review the progress of the offender in complying with the requirements and the reviews will be informed by a report from the responsible officer.

2.2.9   If the offender fails to comply with a requirement during the supervision period, or commits a further offence during the operational period, the suspended sentence can be activated in full or in part or the terms of the supervision made more onerous. There is a presumption that the suspended sentence will be activated either in full or in part.

(i) The decision to suspend

2.2.10   There are many similarities between the suspended sentence and the community sentence. In both cases, requirements can be imposed during the supervision period and the court can respond to breach by sending the offender to custody. The crucial difference is that the suspended sentence is a prison sentence and is appropriate only for an offence that passes the custody threshold and for which imprisonment is the only option. A community sentence may also be imposed for an offence that passes the custody threshold where the court considers that to be appropriate.   **K–57**

2.2.11   The full decision making process for imposition of custodial sentences under the new framework (including the custody threshold test) is set out in paragraphs 1.31–1.33 of the seriousness guideline. For the purposes of suspended sentences the relevant steps are:

(a) has the custody threshold been passed?

(b) if so, is it unavoidable that a custodial sentence be imposed?

(c) if so, can that sentence be suspended? (sentencers should be clear that they would have imposed a custodial sentence if the power to suspend had not been available)

(d) if not, can the sentence be served intermittently?

(e) if not, impose a sentence which takes immediate effect for the term commensurate with the seriousness of the offence.

(ii) Length of sentence

2.2.12   Before making the decision to suspend sentence, the court must already have decided that a prison sentence is justified and should also have decided the length of sentence that would be the shortest term commensurate with the seriousness of the offence if it were to be imposed immediately. The decision to suspend the sentence should not lead to a longer term being imposed than if the sentence were to take effect immediately.   **K–58**

A prison sentence that is suspended should be for the same term that would have applied if the offender were being sentenced to immediate custody.

2.2.13   When assessing the length of the operational period of a suspended sentence, the court should have in mind the relatively short length of the sentence being suspended and the advantages to be gained by retaining the opportunity to extend the operational period at a later stage (see below).

The operational period of a suspended sentence should reflect the length of the sentence being suspended. As an approximate guide, an operational period of up

to 12 months might normally be appropriate for a suspended sentence of up to 6 months and an operational period of up to 18 months might normally be appropriate for a suspended sentence of up to 12 months.

(iii) Requirements

K–59   2.2.14   The court will set the requirements to be complied with during the supervision period. Whilst the offence for which a suspended sentence is imposed is generally likely to be more serious than one for which a community sentence is imposed, the imposition of the custodial sentence is a clear punishment and deterrent. In order to ensure that the overall terms of the sentence are commensurate with the seriousness of the offence, it is likely that the requirements to be undertaken during the supervision period would be less onerous than if a community sentence had been imposed. These requirements will need to ensure that they properly address those factors that are most likely to reduce the risk of re-offending.

Because of the very clear deterrent threat involved in a suspended sentence, requirements imposed as part of that sentence should generally be less onerous than those imposed as part of a community sentence. A court wishing to impose onerous or intensive requirements on an offender should reconsider its decision to suspend sentence and consider whether a community sentence might be more appropriate.

C. Breaches

K–60   2.2.15   The essence of a suspended sentence is to make it abundantly clear to an offender that failure to comply with the requirements of the order or commission of another offence will almost certainly result in a custodial sentence. Where an offender has breached any of the requirements without reasonable excuse for the first time, the responsible officer must either give a warning or initiate breach proceedings.[31] Where there is a further breach within a twelve-month period, breach proceedings must be initiated.[32]

2.2.16   Where proceedings are brought the court has several options, including extending the operational period. However, the presumption (which also applies where breach is by virtue of the commission of a further offence) is that the suspended prison sentence will be activated (either with its original custodial term or a lesser term) unless the court takes the view that this would, in all the circumstances, be unjust. In reaching that decision, the court may take into account both the extent to which the offender has complied with the requirements and the facts of the new offence.[33]

2.2.17   Where a court considers that the sentence needs to be activated, it may activate it in full or with a reduced term. Again, the extent to which the requirements have been complied with will be very relevant to this decision.

2.2.18   If a court amends the order rather than activating the suspended prison sentence, it must either make the requirements more onerous, or extend the supervision or operational periods (provided that these remain within the limits defined by the Act).[34] In such cases, the court must state its reasons for not activating the prison sentence,[35] which could include the extent to which the offender has complied with requirements or the facts of the subsequent offence.

2.2.19   If an offender near the end of an operational period (having complied with the requirements imposed) commits another offence, it may be more appropriate to amend the order rather than activate it.

2.2.20   If a new offence committed is of a less serious nature than the offence for which the suspended sentence was passed, it may justify activating the sentence with a reduced term or amending the terms of the order.

2.2.21   It is expected that any activated suspended sentence will be consecutive to the sentence imposed for the new offence.

2.2.22   If the new offence is non-imprisonable, the sentencer should consider whether it is appropriate to activate the suspended sentence at all.

Where the court decides to amend a suspended sentence order rather than activate the custodial sentence, it should give serious consideration to extending the supervision or operational periods (within statutory limits) rather than making the requirements more onerous.

SECTION 2 PART 3—INTERMITTENT CUSTODY

A. STATUTORY PROVISIONS

2.3.1   Section 183 *Criminal Justice Act* 2003 [sets out full text of section 183, as to which see § 5–316 in the main work].   **K–61**

2.3.2   Restrictions on power to make orders—Section 184 *Criminal Justice Act* 2003 [sets out full text of section 184, as to which see § 5–317 in the main work].   **K–62**

2.3.3   Licence conditions—Section 185 *Criminal Justice Act* 2003 [sets out full text of section 185, as to which see § 5–318 in the main work].   **K–63**

2.3.4   Further provisions—Section 186 *Criminal Justice Act* 2003:   **K–64**

(1) Section 21 of the 1952 Act (expenses of conveyance to prison) does not apply in relation to the conveyance to prison at the end of any licence period of an offender to whom an intermittent custody order relates.

(2) The Secretary of State may pay to any offender to whom an intermittent custody order relates the whole or part of any expenses incurred by the offender in travelling to and from prison during licence periods.

(3) In section 49 of the 1952 Act (persons unlawfully at large) after subsection (4) there is inserted—

"(4A) For the purposes of this section a person shall also be deemed to be unlawfully at large if, having been temporarily released in pursuance of an intermittent custody order made under section 183 of the *Criminal Justice Act* 2003, he remains at large at a time when, by reason of the expiry of the period for which he was temporarily released, he is liable to be detained in pursuance of his sentence."

(4) In section 23 of the *Criminal Justice Act* 1961 (prison rules), in subsection (3) for "The days" there is substituted "Subject to subsection (3A), the days" and after subsection (3) there is inserted—

"(3A) In relation to a prisoner to whom an intermittent custody order under section 183 of the *Criminal Justice Act* 2003 relates, the only days to which subsection (3) applies are Christmas Day, Good Friday and any day which under the *Banking and Financial Dealings Act* 1971 is a bank holiday in England and Wales."

(5) In section 1 of the *Prisoners (Return to Custody) Act* 1995 (remaining at large after temporary release) after subsection (1) there is inserted—

"(1A) A person who has been temporarily released in pursuance of an intermittent custody order made under section 183 of the *Criminal Justice Act* 2003 is guilty of an offence if, without reasonable excuse, he remains unlawfully at large at any time after becoming so at large by virtue of the expiry of the period for which he was temporarily released."

(6) In this section "the 1952 Act" means the *Prison Act* 1952.

2.3.5   Revocation or amendment—Section 187 *Criminal Justice Act* 2003:   **K–65**

Schedule 10 (which contains provisions relating to the revocation or amendment of custody plus orders and the amendment of intermittent custody orders) shall have effect.

B. Imposing an Intermittent Custody Order

K–66   2.3.6   Intermittent custody must be used only for offences that have crossed the custodial threshold. It is an alternative to immediate full-time custody and so must meet all the criteria that apply to such a sentence, in particular the need to pass the custody threshold and the need to ensure that the sentence is for the shortest term commensurate with the seriousness of the offence.

2.3.7   The prison sentence is not continuous but is interspersed by periods when the offender is released on temporary licence in the community. A court may only impose intermittent custody if the offender consents to serving the custodial part of the sentence intermittently. The court must also make sure that the relevant resources are available in the local area and must consult the Probation Service[36] to confirm that the offender is an appropriate candidate for such a sentence.

2.3.8   This sentence is currently being piloted and this guidance will be reviewed and may need to be developed further in the light of the outcome.

(i) Circumstances when intermittent custody may be appropriate

K–67   2.3.9   Guidance supporting the pilots[37] states that intermittent custody is not intended to be used for sex offenders or those convicted of serious offences of either violence or burglary. There may be other offences which by their nature would make intermittent custody inappropriate and public safety should always be the paramount consideration.

2.3.10   The circumstances of the offender are likely to be the determining factor in deciding whether an intermittent custody order is appropriate. It is only appropriate where the custody threshold has been crossed and where suspending the custodial sentence or imposing a non-custodial sentence have been ruled out. Suitable candidates for weekend custody might include offenders who are: full-time carers; employed; or in education.

2.3.11   The full decision making process for imposition of custodial sentences under the new framework (including the custody threshold test) is set out in paragraphs 1.31–1.33 of the seriousness guideline. For the purposes of intermittent custody the relevant steps are:

(a) has the custody threshold been passed?

(b) if so, is it unavoidable that a custodial sentence be imposed?

(c) if so, can that sentence be suspended? (sentencers should be clear that they would have imposed a custodial sentence if the power to suspend had not been available)

(d) if not, can it be served intermittently?

(e) if not, impose a sentence which takes immediate effect for the term commensurate with the seriousness of the offence.

- **Courts must be satisfied that a custodial sentence of less than 12 months is justified and that neither a community sentence nor a suspended sentence is appropriate before considering whether to make an intermittent custody order.**

- **When imposing a custodial sentence of less than 12 months, the court should always consider whether it would be appropriate to sentence an offender to intermittent custody; primary considerations will be public safety, offender suitability and sentence availability.**

- **Courts should strive to ensure that the intermittent custody provisions are applied in a way that limits discrimination and they should, in principle, be considered for all offenders.**

(ii) Licence requirements

2.3.12   As a primary objective of being able to serve a custodial sentence intermit-   **K–68**
tently is to enable offenders to continue to fulfil existing obligations in the community, and since the time spent in custody is utilised extensively for activities, experience has so far shown that additional, similar, requirements to be completed whilst
on licence are not practical. However, requirements such as curfews, prohibited activity and exclusion requirements might be appropriate in a particular case.

**The practical workings of an intermittent custody sentence will effectively rule
out the use of some of the longer or more intensive community requirements.
Requirements such as curfews, prohibited activity and exclusion requirements
might be appropriate in a particular case.**

(iii) Sentence length

2.3.13   The demands made on the offender by this sentence will generally be con-   **K–69**
siderably greater than for a custodial sentence to be served immediately in full. The
disruptive effect on family life, the psychological impact of going in and out of
custody and the responsibility on the offender to travel to and from the custodial
establishment on many occasions all make the sentence more onerous.

**Once a court has decided that an offender should be sent to prison and has
determined the length of the sentence, it should reduce the overall length of the
sentence because it is to be served intermittently.**

ANNEX A

Time spent on remand—Sentencing Advisory Panel's advice

The Act makes provision for a sentencer to give credit for time spent on remand in   **K–70**
custody where a custodial sentence is passed.[38] It also empowers the court to have
regard to time spent on remand in custody when determining the restrictions on liberty to be imposed by a community order or youth community order.[39] Where an offender has spent several weeks in custody, this may affect the nature of the offence
that is passed. For example, where the court decides that a custodial sentence is justified some sentencers may decide to pass a community sentence instead, on the basis
that the offender has already completed the equivalent of a punitive element in a
sentence. The Panel takes the view that, given the changes in the content of the
second part of a custodial sentence, in such cases it will be more appropriate to pass a
custodial sentence knowing that licence requirements will be imposed on release
from custody (which may be immediate). Recommendations made by the court at the
point of sentence will then be of particular importance in influencing the content of
the licence. This will help to ensure that the record clearly shows the assessment of
seriousness of the offending behaviour.

Whereas the Act clearly states that time spent on remand is to be regarded as part
of a custodial sentence unless the Court considers it unjust,[40] it states that sentencers
passing a community sentence may have regard to time spent on remand, but no further information is given on how this discretion should be exercised. The Panel
recognises that giving credit for time spent on remand is likely to be easier to apply
in relation to punitive requirements rather than the rehabilitative elements of a community sentence. For example, reducing the number of unpaid work hours could be
fairly easy, whereas reducing the length of a rehabilitation programme might not be
appropriate as it could undermine its effectiveness. Where an offender has been kept
on remand, one could take the view that this action was justified by the bail provisions and that the sentencer should not, therefore, feel obliged to adjust the terms of
the community sentence. However, in principle, the Panel recommends that the
court should seek to give credit for time spent on remand in all cases and should
explain its reasons for not doing so when it considers either that this is not justified,
would not be practical, or would not be in the best interests of the offender.

The court should seek to give credit for time spent on remand in all cases. It should make clear, when announcing sentence, whether or not credit for time on remand has been given and should explain its reasons for not giving credit when it considers either that this is not justified, would not be practical, or would not be in the best interests of the offender.

Where, following a period of time spent in custody on remand, the court decides that a custodial sentence is justified then, given the changes in the content of the second part of a custodial sentence, the court should pass a custodial sentence in the knowledge that licence requirements will be imposed on release from custody. Recommendations made by the court at the point of sentence will be of particular importance in influencing the content of the licence.[41]

D. MANSLAUGHTER BY REASON OF PROVOCATION

Guideline

FOREWORD

K–71   In accordance with section 170(9) of the *Criminal Justice Act* 2003, the Sentencing Guidelines Council issues this guideline as a definitive guideline. By virtue of section 172 of the Act, every court must have regard to a relevant guideline. This guideline applies to offenders convicted of manslaughter by reason of provocation who are sentenced after 28 November 2005.

This guideline stems from a reference from the Home Secretary for consideration of the issue of sentencing where provocation is argued in cases of homicide, and, in particular, domestic violence homicides. For the purpose of describing "domestic violence", the Home Secretary adopted the Crown Prosecution Service definition.[1] The guideline applies to sentencing of an adult offender for this offence in whatever circumstances it occurs. It identifies the widely varying features of both the provocation and the act of retaliation and sets out the approach to be adopted in deciding both the sentencing range and the starting point within that range.

This guideline is for use where the conviction for manslaughter is clearly founded on provocation alone. There will be additional, different and more complicated matters to be taken into account where the other main partial defence, diminished responsibility, is a factor.

The Council's Guideline *New Sentences: Criminal Justice Act 2003* recognised the potentially more demanding nature of custodial sentences of 12 months or longer imposed under the new framework introduced by the *Criminal Justice Act* 2003. Consequently the sentencing ranges and starting points in this guideline take that principle into account.

Guidelines are created following extensive consultation. The Sentencing Advisory Panel first consults widely on the basis of a thoroughly researched consultation paper, then provides the Council with advice. Having considered the advice, the Council prepares a draft guideline on which there is further consultation with Parliament, with the Home Secretary and with Ministers of other relevant Government Departments. This guideline is the culmination of that process.

The Council has appreciated greatly the work of the Sentencing Advisory Panel in preparing the advice on which this guideline has been based and for those who have responded so thoughtfully to the consultation of both the Panel and the Council.

The advice and this guideline are available on *www.sentencing-guidelines.gov.uk* or from the Sentencing Guidelines Secretariat at 85 Buckingham Gate, London SW1F 6PD. A summary of the responses to the Council's consultation also appears on the website.

SIGNATURE

Chairman of the Council
November 2005

CONTENTS

MANSLAUGHTER BY REASON OF PROVOCATION

A. STATUTORY PROVISION

1.1 Murder and manslaughter are common law offences and there is no complete **K–73** statutory definition of either. 'Provocation' is one of the partial defences by which an offence that would otherwise be murder may be reduced to manslaughter.

1.2 Before the issue of provocation can be considered, the Crown must have proved beyond reasonable doubt that all the elements of murder were present, including the necessary intent (*i.e.* the offender must have intended either to kill the victim or to cause grievous bodily harm). The court must then consider section 3 of the *Homicide Act* 1957, which provides:

> *Where on a charge of murder there is evidence on which the jury can find that the person charged was provoked (whether by things done or by things said or by both together) to lose his self-control, the question whether the provocation was enough to make a reasonable man do as he did shall be left to be determined by the jury; and in determining that question the jury shall take into account everything both done and said according to the effect which, in their opinion, it would have on a reasonable man.*

Although both murder and manslaughter result in death, the difference in the level of culpability creates offences of a distinctively different character. Therefore the approach to sentencing in each should start from a different basis.

B. ESTABLISHING THE BASIS FOR SENTENCING

2.1 The Court of Appeal in *Attorney General's References (Nos. 74, 95 and 118 of* **K–74** *2002) (Suratan and others)*,[2] set out a number of assumptions that a judge must make in favour of an offender found not guilty of murder but guilty of manslaughter by reason of provocation. The assumptions are required in order to be faithful to the verdict and should be applied equally in all cases whether conviction follows a trial

791

or whether the Crown has accepted a plea of guilty to manslaughter by reason of provocation:

- first, that the offender had, at the time of the killing, lost self-control; mere loss of temper or jealous rage is not sufficient
- second, that the offender was caused to lose self-control by things said or done, normally by the person killed
- third, that the offender's loss of control was reasonable in all the circumstances, even bearing in mind that people are expected to exercise reasonable control over their emotions and that, as society advances, it ought to call for a higher measure of self-control
- fourth, that the circumstances were such as to make the loss of self-control sufficiently excusable to reduce the gravity of the offence from murder to manslaughter.

Bearing in mind the loss of life caused by manslaughter by reason of provocation, the starting point for sentencing should be a custodial sentence. Only in a very small number of cases involving very exceptional mitigating factors should a judge consider that a on-custodial sentence is justified.

The same general sentencing principles should apply in all cases of manslaughter by reason of provocation irrespective of whether or not the killing takes place in a domestic context.

C. Factors Influencing Sentence

K–75   3.1 A number of elements must be considered and balanced by the sentencer. Some of these are common to all types of manslaughter by reason of provocation; others have a particular relevance in cases of manslaughter in a domestic context.

3.2 **The degree of provocation as shown by its nature and duration**—An assessment of the *degree* of the provocation as shown by its nature and duration is the critical factor in the sentencing decision.

(a) In assessing the *degree* of provocation, account should be taken of the following factors:

- if the provocation (which does not have to be a wrongful act) involves gross and extreme conduct on the part of the victim, it is a more significant mitigating factor than conduct which, although significant, is not as extreme
- the fact that the victim presented a threat not only to the offender, but also to children in his or her care
- the offender's previous experiences of abuse and/or domestic violence either by the victim or by other people
- any mental condition which may affect the offender's perception of what amounts to provocation
- the nature of the conduct, the period of time over which it took place and its cumulative effect
- discovery or knowledge of the fact of infidelity on the part of a partner does not necessarily amount to *high* provocation. The gravity of such provocation depends entirely on all attendant circumstances.

(b) Whether the provocation was suffered over a *long or short* period is important to the assessment of gravity. The following factors should be considered:

- the impact of provocative behaviour on an offender can build up over a period of time
- consideration should not be limited to acts of provocation that occurred immediately before the victim was killed. For example, in domestic violence cases, cumulative provocation may eventually become intolerable, the latest incident seeming all the worse because of what went before.

(c) When looking at the *nature* of the provocation the court should consider both the type of provocation and whether, in the particular case, the actions of the victim would have had a particularly marked effect on the offender:

- actual (or anticipated) violence from the victim will <u>generally</u> be regarded as involving a higher degree of provocation than provocation arising from abuse, infidelity or offensive words unless that amounts to psychological bullying

- in cases involving actual or anticipated violence, the culpability of the offender will therefore <u>generally</u> be less than in cases involving verbal provocation

- where the offender's actions were motivated by fear or desperation, rather than by anger, frustration, resentment or a desire for revenge, the offender's culpability will <u>generally</u> be lower.

3.3 **The extent and timing of the retaliation**—It is implicit in the verdict of manslaughter by reason of provocation that the killing was the result of a loss of self-control because of things said and/or done. The intensity, extent and nature of that loss of control must be assessed in the context of the provocation that preceded it.

3.4 The *circumstances of the killing* itself will be relevant to the offender's culpability, and hence to the appropriate sentence:

- in general, the offender's violent response to provocation is likely to be less culpable the shorter the time gap between the provocation (or the last provocation) and the killing—as evidenced, for example, by the use of a weapon that happened to be available rather than by one that was carried for that purpose or prepared for use in advance

- conversely, it is not necessarily the case that greater culpability will be found where there has been a significant lapse of time between the provocation (or the last provocation) and the killing. Where the provocation is cumulative, and particularly in those circumstances where the offender is found to have suffered domestic violence from the victim over a significant period of time, the required loss of self-control may not be sudden as some experience a "slow-burn" reaction and appear calm

- choosing or taking advantage of favourable circumstances for carrying out the killing (so that the victim was unable to resist, such as where the victim was not on guard, or was asleep) may well be an aggravating factor—unless this is mitigated by the circumstances of the offender, resulting in the offender being the weaker or vulnerable party.

3.5 The *context of the relationship* between the offender and the victim must be   **K–76**
borne in mind when assessing the nature and degree of the provocation offered by the victim before the crime and the length of time over which the provocation existed. In cases where the parties were still in a relationship at the time of the killing, it will be necessary to examine the balance of power between one party and the other and to consider other family members who may have been drawn into, or been victims of, the provocative behaviour.

Although there will usually be less culpability when the retaliation to provocation is sudden, it is not always the case that greater culpability will be found where there has been a significant lapse of time between the provocation and the killing.

It is for the sentencer to consider the impact on an offender of provocative behaviour that has built up over a period of time.

An offence should be regarded as aggravated where it is committed in the presence of a child or children or other vulnerable family member, whether or not the offence takes place in a domestic setting.

3.6 **Post-offence behaviour**—The behaviour of the offender after the killing can be relevant to sentence:

- immediate and genuine remorse may be demonstrated by the summoning o
  medical assistance, remaining at the scene, and co-operation with the authori
  ties
- concealment or attempts to dispose of evidence or dismemberment of the bod
  may aggravate the offence.

Post-offence behaviour is relevant to the sentence. It may be an **aggravating**
or mitigating factor. When sentencing, the judge should consider the
motivation behind the offender's actions.

3.7 *Use of a weapon*

(a) In relation to this offence, as in relation to many different types of offence, the
carrying and use of a weapon is an aggravating factor. Courts must consider the
type of weapon used and, importantly, whether it was to hand or carried to the
scene and who introduced it to the incident.

(b) The use or not of a weapon is a factor heavily influenced by the gender of th
offender. Whereas men can and do kill using physical strength alone, wome
often cannot and thus resort to using a weapon. The issue of key importance i
whether the weapon was to hand or carried deliberately to the scene, althoug
the circumstances in which the weapon was brought to the scene will need to b
considered carefully.

The use of a weapon should not necessarily move a case into another
sentencing bracket.

In cases of manslaughter by reason of provocation, use of a weapon may
reflect the imbalance in strength between the offender and the victim and
how that weapon came to hand is likely to be far more important than the use
of the weapon itself.

It will be an aggravating factor where the weapon is brought to the scene in
contemplation of use *before* the loss of self-control (which may occur some
time before the fatal incident).

D. Sentence Ranges and Starting Points

4.1 Manslaughter is a "serious offence" for the purposes of the provisions in th
***Criminal Justice Act* 2003[3] for dealing with dangerous offenders. It is possibl**
that a court will be required to use the sentences for public protectio
prescribed in the Act when sentencing an offender convicted of the offence c
manslaughter by reason of provocation. An alternative is a discretionary lif
sentence. In accordance with normal practice, when setting the minimum ter
to be served within an indeterminate sentence under these provisions, that ter
will usually be half the equivalent determinate sentence.

    4.2 *Identifying sentence ranges*—The key factor that will be relevant in ever
case is the nature and the duration of the provocation.

(a) The process to be followed by the court will be:

identify the sentence range by reference to the degree of provocation

adjust the starting point within the range by reference to the length of time
over which the provocation took place

take into consideration the circumstances of the killing (e.g. the length
of time that had elapsed between the provocation and the retaliation
and the circumstances in which any weapon was used)

(b) This guideline establishes that:

- there are three sentencing ranges defined by the **degree of provocation**—low, substantial and high
- within the three ranges, the starting point is based on provocation taking place over **a short period of time**.
- the court will move from the starting point (based upon the degree of provocation) by considering the length of time over which the provocation has taken place, and by reference to any **aggravating and mitigating factors**

MANSLAUGHTER BY REASON OF PROVOCATION

Factors to take into consideration

1. The sentences for public protection <u>must</u> be considered in all cases of **K–78** manslaughter.

2. The presence of any of the general aggravating factors identified in the Council's Guideline *Overarching Principles: Seriousness* or any of the additional factors identified in this Guideline will indicate a sentence above the normal starting point.

3. This offence will not be an initial charge but will arise following a charge of murder. The Council Guideline *Reduction in Sentence for a Guilty Plea* will need to be applied with this in mind. In particular, consideration will need to be given to the time at which it was indicated that the defendant would plead guilty to manslaughter by reason of provocation.

4. An assessment of the *degree* of the provocation as shown by its nature and duration is the critical factor in the sentencing decision.

5. The intensity, extent and nature of the loss of control must be assessed in the context of the provocation that preceded it.

6. Although there will usually be less culpability when the retaliation to provocation is sudden, it is not always the case that greater culpability will be found where there has been a significant lapse of time between the provocation and the killing.

7. It is for the sentencer to consider the impact on an offender of provocative behaviour that has built up over a period of time.

8. The use of a weapon should not necessarily move a case into another sentencing bracket.

9. Use of a weapon may reflect the imbalance in strength between the offender and the victim and how that weapon came to hand is likely to be far more important than the use of the weapon itself.

10. It will be an aggravating factor where the weapon is brought to the scene in contemplation of use *before* the loss of self-control (which may occur some time before the fatal incident).

11. Post-offence behaviour is relevant to the sentence. It may be an aggravating or

mitigating factor. When sentencing, the judge should consider the motivation behind the offender's actions.

MANSLAUGHTER BY REASON OF PROVOCATION

This is a serious offence for the purposes of section 224 of the Criminal Justice Act 2003

K–79   <u>Maximum penalty:</u> **Life imprisonment**

Type/Nature of Activity	Sentence Ranges & Starting Points
Low degree of provocation: A low degree of provocation occurring over a short period	Sentence Range: 10 years – life Starting Point – 12 years custody
Substantial degree of provocation: A substantial degree of provocation occurring over a short period	Sentence Range: 4 – 9 years Starting Point – 8 years custody
High degree of provocation: A high degree of provocation occurring over a short period	Sentence Range: if custody is necessary, up to 4 years Starting Point – 3 years custody

Additional aggravating factors	Additional mitigating factors
1. Concealment or attempts to dispose of evidence*	1. The offender was acting to protect another
2. Dismemberment or mutilation of the body*	2. Spontaneity and lack of premeditation
3. Offence committed in the presence of a child/children or other vulnerable family member	3. Previous experiences of abuse and/or domestic violence
	4. Evidence that the victim presented an ongoing danger to the offender or another
*subject to para 3.6 above.	5. Actual (or reasonably anticipated) violence from the victim

The Council Guideline New Sentences: Criminal Justice Act *2009 recognised the potential* *more demanding nature of custodial sentences of 12 months or longer imposed under the* *new framework introduced by the* Criminal Justice Act 2003. *The sentencing ranges and* *starting points in the above guideline take account of this.*

E. ROBBERY

K–80   The Sentencing Guidelines Council has issued a definitive guideline on robbery (*Theft Act* 1968, s.8(1) (§ 21–84 in the main work)). It deals with offenders sentenced on or after August 1, 2006. The drafting of the guideline is inconsistent and repetitious. It lacks a coherent structure, and consists, in large part, of a series of lists and bullet points. Accordingly, it is not set out in full here. The following is a summary of its essential contents, but for those wishing to refer to the original, it may be located at <u>www.sentencing</u> <u>guidelines.gov.uk.</u>

796

The foreword states that robbery will usually merit a custodial sentence, but that exceptional circumstances may justify a non-custodial penalty for an adult and, more frequently, for a young offender; that the guideline is not, therefore, intended to mark a significant shift in sentencing practice; and that the sentencing ranges and starting points in the guideline take into account the more demanding nature of custodial sentences of 12 months or more under the *Criminal Justice Act* 2003. The guideline only provides guidance in relation to street robberies, robberies of small businesses, and less sophisticated commercial robberies. No guidance is provided in relation to violent personal robberies in the home and professionally planned commercial robberies.

The sentences suggested by the guideline are determined by the identification of one of three levels of seriousness. These are themselves determined by reference to the type of activity which characterises the offence, and the degree of force or threat present. Level 1 involves a threat and/or minimal use of force. Level 2 involves use of a weapon to threaten and/or use of significant force. Level 3 involves use of a weapon and/or significant force, and the causing of serious injury. Where the offence will fall within a particular level is determined by the presence of one or more aggravating features. However, exceptionally serious aggravating features may have the effect of moving the case to the next level. Aggravating factors which are particularly relevant to the assessment of seriousness are:

(a) the nature and degree of any force or violence used or threatened;

(b) the nature of any weapon carried or used, or the use of which is threatened;

(c) the vulnerability of the victim;

(d) the number of offenders involved and their roles;

(e) the value of the property taken;

(f) the fact that the offence was committed at night or in the hours of darkness; and

(g) the wearing of a disguise.

Mitigating factors which are particularly relevant are:

(a) an unplanned or opportunistic offence;

(b) a peripheral involvement in the offence; and

(c) the voluntary return of the property taken.

Where an offence is committed by a young offender, sentencers should additionally take into account age and immaturity and any group pressure under which the offender may have been acting. Further, in relation to such an offender, the guideline requires that where there is evidence that the offence was committed to fund a drug habit and that treatment might help tackle offending behaviour, the court should consider a drug treatment requirement as part of a supervision order or action plan. In all cases, the court should consider making a restitution or compensation order; in cases where a non-custodial order is made, the court may consider making an anti-social behaviour order.

Starting points and sentencing ranges are prescribed depending on whether the offender is an adult or a young offender. In each case, the starting point is based upon a first time offender who has pleaded not guilty, and who has not been assessed as being dangerous for the purposes of the dangerous offender provisions under the *CJA* 2003, Pt 12, Chap. 5 (ss.224 *et seq.*) (§§ 5–292 *et seq.* in the main work). In the case of young offenders, the starting points are based on a 17-year-old. Sentencers are required to consider whether a lower starting point is justified on account of the offender's age or immaturity. In the case of an adult offender, the starting point for a level 1 offence is 12 months' custody and the sentence range is from a community order (in exceptional circumstances, as stated in the foreword) to three years' custody. The starting point for a level 2 offence is four years' custody and the sentence range is two to seven years. The starting point for a level 3 offence is eight years' custody and the sentence range is seven to 12 years. In the case of the notional young offender, the starting point for a level 1 offence is a community order and the sentence range is from a community order to a 12-month detention and training order. The starting point for a level 2 offence is three years' detention and the sentence range is one to six years' detention. The starting point for a level 3 offence is seven years' detention and the sentence range is six to 10 years' detention.

F. Breach of a Protective Order

K–81   The Sentencing Guidelines Council has issued a definitive guideline relating to the sentencing of offenders who have breached either a restraining order under the *Protection from Harassment Act* 1997, s.5 (§ 19–277f in the main work), or a non-molestation order imposed under section 42 of the *Family Law Act* 1996 (breach being made an offence by section 42A, which is inserted as from a day to be appointed, by the *Domestic Violence, Crime and Victims Act* 2004, s.1). It deals with offenders sentenced on or after December 18, 2006.

Paragraph 2 points out that the facts constituting the breach may amount to a substantive offence in their own right. It advises that in such cases it is desirable that there should be separate counts, and, where necessary, there should be consecutive sentences to reflect the seriousness of the counts and to achieve the appropriate totality. It continues, however, by saying that where there is only the one count, the overall sentence should not generally be affected. If the sole count is the breach, the sentence should reflect the nature of the breach; and if the substantive offence alone has been charged, the fact that it constituted a breach of a court order should be regarded as a matter of aggravation. Where no substantive offence was involved, the sentence should reflect the circumstances of the breach, including whether it was an isolated breach, or part of a course of conduct in breach of the order; whether it was planned or spontaneous; and any consequences of the breach, including psychiatric injury or distress to the person protected by the order.

Paragraph 3 is headed "Factors influencing sentencing". It says that since the order will have been made for the purpose of protecting an individual from harm, the main aim of the sentencer should be to achieve future compliance with the order where that is realistic. The nature of the original conduct or offence is relevant in so far as it allows a judgment to be made on the level of harm caused to the victim by the breach and the extent to which that harm was intended by the offender (para. 3.5). However, sentence following a breach is for the breach alone and must avoid punishing the offender again for the offence or conduct as a result of which the order was made (para. 3.7).

When dealing with a breach, a court will need to consider the extent to which the conduct amounting to the breach put the victim at risk of harm (para. 3.8). Where the order is breached by the use of physical violence, the starting point should normally be a custodial sentence (para. 3.9). Non-violent behaviour and/or indirect contact can also cause (or be intended to cause) a high degree of harm and anxiety. In such circumstances, it is likely that the custody threshold will have been crossed (para. 3.10). Where an order was made in civil proceedings, its purpose may have been to cause the subject of

he order to modify behaviour rather than to imply that the conduct was especially serious. If so, it is likely to be disproportionate to impose a custodial
sentence for a breach of the order if the breach did not involve threats or
violence (para. 3.11). In some cases where a breach might result in a short
custodial sentence but the court is satisfied that the offender genuinely intends
to reform his behaviour and there is a real prospect of rehabilitation, the
court may consider it appropriate to impose a sentence that will allow this.
This may mean imposing a suspended sentence order or a community order
(where appropriate with a requirement to attend an accredited domestic
violence programme) (para. 3.12).

Paragraph 4 deals with matters of aggravation and mitigation. The matters
of aggravation mirror those in the guideline on domestic violence (*post*, Appendix K–82), but there is added the fact that the breach was a further breach
following previous breach proceedings or that it was committed shortly after
the order was made. The matters of mitigation that are listed are that the
breach followed a long period of compliance, or that the victim initiated
contact.

At the end of the guideline there is a table with suggested starting points.
The premise is that the "activity has either been prosecuted separately as an
offence or is not of a character sufficient to justify prosecution of it as an offence in its own right". The first column is headed "Nature of activity" and
the second column is headed "Starting points". There are five entries in the
first column, "Breach (whether one or more) involving significant physical
violence and significant physical or psychological harm to the victim", "More
than one breach involving some violence and/or significant physical or
psychological harm to the victim", "Single breach involving some violence
and/or significant physical or psychological harm to the victim", "More than
one breach involving no/ minimal contact or some direct contact" and "Single
breach involving no/ minimal direct contact". The corresponding entries in
the second column are, "More than 12 months. The length of the ... sentence
will depend on the nature and seriousness of the breaches.", "26–39 weeks'
custody [Medium/High Custody Plus order] (when the relevant provisions of
the *CJA* 2003 are in force)", "13–26 weeks' custody [Low/Medium Custody
Plus order] (when the relevant provisions of the *CJA* 2003 are in force)",
"Medium range community order" and "Low range community order".

G. Domestic Violence

The Sentencing Guidelines Council has issued a definitive guideline for use   **K–82**
in all cases that fall within the Crown Prosecution Service definition of "domestic violence", *viz.* "Any incident of threatening behaviour, violence or
abuse [psychological, physical, sexual, financial or emotional] between adults
who are or have been intimate partners or family members, regardless of
gender or sexuality." It deals with offenders sentenced on or after December
18, 2006. The guideline makes clear that offences committed in a domestic
context should be regarded as being no less serious than offences committed
in a non-domestic context. Indeed, because an offence has been committed in
a domestic context, there are likely to be aggravating factors present that
make it more serious. The foreword, signed by Lord Phillips C.J., as chairman of the council, states that in many situations of domestic violence, the circumstances require the sentence to demonstrate clearly that the conduct is
unacceptable, but that there will be cases where all parties genuinely and
realistically wish the relationship to continue as long as the violence stops. In

such cases, and where the violence is towards the lower end of the scale of seriousness, it is likely to be appropriate for the court to impose a sentence that provides the necessary support.

Paragraph 1 defines "domestic violence" for the purposes of the guideline (*ante*). Paragraph 2 relates to the assessment of seriousness and says nothing new. Paragraph 3 is concerned with matters of aggravation and mitigation. By way of preamble it is stated that the history of the relationship will be relevant to the assessment of seriousness. There follows a non-exhaustive list of aggravating matters, *viz.* abuse of trust or power, that the victim is particularly vulnerable, the exposure of children to an offence (directly or indirectly), using contact arrangements with a child to instigate an offence, a proven history of violence or threats by the offender in a domestic setting, a history of disobedience to court orders and conduct which has forced the victim to leave home. The two matters of mitigation that are listed are positive good character and provocation, but, as to the former, the point is made that the perpetrator of domestic violence may have two personae, and that good character in relation to conduct outside the home should generally be of no relevance where there is a proven pattern of behaviour.

Paragraph 4 deals with the relevance of the wishes of the victim to the sentence. As a matter of general principle, the sentence should be determined by the seriousness of the offence, not by the expressed wishes of the victim. The guideline states that it is particularly important that this principle should be observed in this context, as (a) it is undesirable that a victim should feel a responsibility for the sentence imposed; (b) there is a risk that a plea for mercy made by a victim will be induced by threats made by, or by a fear of the offender; and (c) the risk of such threats will be increased if it is generally believed that the severity of the sentence may be affected by the wishes of the victim. However, there may be cases in which the court can properly mitigate a sentence to give effect to the expressed wish of the victim that the relationship should be permitted to continue. The court must, however, be confident that such a wish is genuine, and that giving effect to it will not expose the victim to a real risk of further violence. Up-to-date information in a presentence report and victim personal statement will be of vital importance. Either the offender or the victim (or both) may ask the court to take into consideration the interests of any children and to impose a less severe sentence. The court will wish to have regard not only to the effect on the children if the relationship is disrupted but also to the likely effect on the children of any further incidents of domestic violence.

The final section of the guideline is headed "Factors to Take into Consideration". It contains nothing new, save that it advises that where "the custody threshold is only just crossed, so that if a custodial sentence is imposed it will be a short sentence, the court will wish to consider whether the better option is a suspended sentence order or a community order, including in either case a requirement to attend an accredited domestic violence programme. Such an option will only be appropriate where the court is satisfied that the offender genuinely intends to reform his ... behaviour and that there is a real prospect of rehabilitation being successful. Such a situation is unlikely to arise where there has been a pattern of abuse."

H. Sexual Offences

K–83   The Sentencing Guidelines Council has issued a definitive guideline on sexual offences, which applies to offenders sentenced on or after May 14

2007. Although its title refers only to the *SOA* 2003, it also deals with offences concerning indecent photographs of children (*Protection of Children Act* 1978, s.1, *CJA* 1988, s.160) and keeping a brothel used for prostitution (*SOA* 1956, s.33A).

The foreword states that guidance from Court of Appeal judgments on offences under the 2003 Act has been incorporated into the guideline; that the guideline uses a starting point of five years for the rape of an adult with no other aggravating or mitigating factors (derived from *R. v. Millberry; R. v. Morgan; R. v. Lackenby* [2003] 1 Cr.App.R. 25) as the baseline from which all other sentences for offences in the guideline have been calculated; and that the more onerous nature of the release on licence regime under the *CJA* 2003 has been taken into account, such that the transitional arrangements in paragraphs 2.1.7 to 2.1.10 of the "New sentences: *CJA* 2003" guideline (*ante*, K–49) do not apply.

The guideline is in seven parts and is set out across more than 140 pages. The following description sets out the key principles and excludes the recitation of ordinary sentencing principles that will be familiar to sentencers and practitioners. To that end, the description is not intended to be a substitute for the guideline, but a quick reference ("pocket sized") guide to it. The description sets the guidelines out in a tabulated form, accompanied by explanatory text. Starting points and sentencing ranges are set out (here, not in the guideline itself) in the form of *x* (*y–z*), with *x* indicating the starting point and *y–z* indicating the sentencing range. Unless otherwise indicated, these figures refer to custodial sentences measured in years.

Part 1: General principles

Part 1 of the guideline sets out various general principles applicable to the imposition of sentences for sexual offences. In particular, save where a distinction is justified by the nature of the offence, the guidelines apply irrespective of the gender of the offender. **K–84**

Starting points and sentencing ranges

Except where otherwise indicated, the starting points and sentencing ranges relate to adult offenders of previous good character convicted following a plea of not guilty. Starting points are based on a "basic offence" (*i.e.* one in which the ingredients of the offence as defined are present, and assuming no aggravating or mitigating factors) in the particular category. References to a "non-custodial sentence" are references to a community order or a fine (although, in most cases, the threshold will have been crossed for a community order). The *sentencing range* is the bracket into which the provisional sentence will fall after consideration of aggravating or mitigating factors (although particular circumstances may require a sentence outside of that range). To that end, the suggested starting points and sentencing ranges are not rigid, and movement within and between ranges will depend upon the circumstances of individual cases and, in particular, the aggravating and mitigating factors present. Previous convictions which aggravate the seriousness of the current offence may take the provisional sentence beyond the range given. Likewise personal mitigation and the reduction for a guilty plea may also take a sentence outside of a range indicated. **K–85**

Aggravating and mitigating factors

Aggravating and mitigating factors which are particularly relevant to each offence are listed in the individual offence guidelines. These lists are non-exhaustive and the factors are not ranked in any particular order. Where a factor is an ingredient of an offence or is used to identify a starting point, it cannot also be an aggravating factor and care will be necessary to avoid double **K–86** counting. Since sexual offences often involve some form of violence as an essential element of the offence, this is included in the starting points. However it will be an aggravating factor if harm was inflicted over and above that necessary to commit the offence. Additionally, regard should be had to the generic list of aggravating and mitigating factors referred to in paragraphs 1.20 to 1.27 of the "Guideline on seriousness" (*ante*, K–19). The foreword states that if an offence is committed in a domestic context, and falls within the definition of "domestic violence", reference should also be made to the additional principles and factors referred to in the "Overarching principles: domestic violence" guideline (*ante*, K–82 *et seq.*). The presence of generic and offence-specific aggravating factors will significantly influence the type and length of sentence imposed.

Young offenders

K–87   As to the culpability of young offenders, Part 7 of the guideline deals with the situation where an offence prescribes a different maximum penalty depending on the age of the offender. Such cases apart, youth and immaturity must always be potential mitigating factors to be taken into account (although not necessarily if an offence is particularly serious). Unless specifically stated, the starting points assume that the offender is an adult.

Victim personal statements

K–88   If a statement has not been produced, the court should enquire whether the victim has had the opportunity to make one. Where there is no statement it should not be assumed that the offence had no impact on the victim.

Pre-sentence reports

K–89   A pre-sentence report should normally be prepared before a sentence is passed since it may address the likelihood of re-offending and it will be in the interests of public protection to provide treatment to sex offenders at the earliest opportunity; a psychiatric report may also be appropriate.

Community orders

K–90   Where a community order is the recommended starting point, the requirements to be imposed are left for the court to decide according to the particular facts of the individual case. Where a community order is the proposed starting point for different levels of seriousness of the same offence or for a second or subsequent offence of the same level of seriousness, this should be reflected by means of the imposition of more onerous requirements.

Ancillary orders

K–91   The guideline states that notification requirements follow automatically upon conviction of an offence; that it is the duty of a sentencer to consider whether to make a sexual offences prevention order under the *SOA* 2003, s.104, and/ or an order disqualifying the offender from working with children under the *CJCSA* 2000, ss.28 and 29; and that sentencers should also consider whether to make confiscation, deprivation or compensation orders.

Treatment programmes

K–92   Treatment programmes are not specifically mentioned in the sentence recommendations, but the summary of general principles concludes by stating that a sentencer should always consider whether, in the circumstances of the individual case, and having regard to the profile of the offending behaviour, it would be sensible to require the offender to take part in a programme designed to address sexually deviant behaviour.

Part 2: Non-consensual offences (*Sexual Offences Act* 2003)

The same starting points apply to all offences dealt with in this part what-   **K–93**
ever the relationship between the offender and the victim (*i.e.* in a relationship, acquaintances, strangers, *etc.*). Extreme youth or old age of a victim is an
aggravating factor; and if the victim is a child, the greater the disparity in the
ages of the offender and victim, the more serious the offence. Youth or immaturity of an offender should also be taken into account. It should be noted
that offenders under the age of 18 convicted of offences contrary sections 11
and 12 should be dealt with under Part 7 of the guideline.

*Parts 2A (rape (ss.1 & 5) and assault by penetration (ss.2 & 6)) and 2B (sexual
assault (ss.3 & 7))*
The planning of an offence indicates a higher level of culpability than an
opportunistic or impulsive offence. Whether an offender's culpability is
reduced because the offender and victim had engaged in consensual sexual
activity on the same occasion immediately before the offence took place will
depend on the nature of the previous activity as compared to the subsequent
activity and timing. There may be cases where the seriousness of the non-
consensual activity overwhelms any other consideration. As to rape, there is
no distinction between starting points for penetration of the vagina, mouth or
anus. As to an assault by penetration, brief penetration with fingers, toes or
tongue may result in a significantly lower sentence where no physical harm is
caused. As to sexual assault, some offences may justify a lesser sentence where
the actions were more offensive than threatening and comprised a single act
rather then more persistent behaviour. Further, where an offence is being
dealt with in a magistrates' court, more detailed guidance will be provided in
the Magistrates' Court Sentencing Guidelines.

Part 2C (causing sexual activity without consent (ss.4, 8 & 31))
The same starting points apply whether the activity was caused or incited
and whether or not the incited activity took place. Some reduction will generally be appropriate where the incited activity did not in fact take place; but
the degree to which the victim may have suffered as a result of knowing or
believing that an offence would take place should be taken into account.

Part 2D (other non-consensual offences (ss.11 & 32 and 12 & 33))
Where an offence can be committed by causing or inciting sexual activity,
the same starting points apply whether the activity was caused or incited and
whether or not the incited activity took place.

Key to table of starting points, *etc.*, for part 2

‡   Denotes that an offence is a "serious offence" for the purposes of the
Criminal Justice Act 2003, s.224

Aggravating factors.
A1:   Offender ejaculated or caused victim to ejaculate
A2:   Background of intimidation or coercion
A3:   Use of drugs, alcohol or other substance to facilitate the offence
A4:   Threats to prevent victim reporting the incident

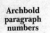

A5:   Abduction or detention

A6:   Offender aware that he or she is suffering from a sexually transmitted infection

A7:   Pregnancy or infection results

A8:   Physical harm caused

A9:   Prolonged activity or contact

A10:   Images of violent activity

Mitigating factors

M1:   Victim is aged 16 or over and previously engaged in consensual sexual activity with the offender on the same occasion and immediately before the offence

M2:   Victim is aged under 16 and the sexual activity was mutually agreed and experimental between two children

M3:   Victim is aged under 16 but offender is a young offender and reasonably believed victim to be aged 16 or over

M4:   Penetration is minimal or for a short duration

M5:   Youth and immaturity of offender

M6:   Minimal or fleeting contact

OFFENCE	TYPE/ NATURE OF ACTIVITY	STARTING POINTS (AND SENTENCING RANGES)			AGG. & MIT. FACTORS	GUIDE-LINE PAGES
		Victim is under 13	Victim 13 or over/ under 16	Victim 16 or over		
Rape 1 (rape) ‡ 5 (rape of a child under 13) ‡	Repeated rape of same victim over a course of time or rape involving multiple victims		15 (13–19)		A1, A2, A3, A4, A5, A6, A7 M1, M2, M3	24–26
	Rape accompanied by any one of the following; abduction or detention; offender aware that he is suffering from a sexually transmitted infection; more than one offender acting together; abuse of trust; offence motivated by prejudice (race, religion, sexual orientation, physical disability); sustained attack	13 (11–17)	10 (8–13)	8 (6–11)		
	Single offence of rape by single offender	10 (8–13)	8 (6–11)	5 (4–8)		
Assault by penetration 2 (assault by penetration) † 6 (assault of a child under 13 by penetration) ‡	Penetration with an object or body part, accompanied by any one of the following; abduction or detention; more than one offender acting together; abuse of trust; offence motivated by prejudice (race, religion, sexual orientation, physical disability); sustained attack	13 (11–17)	10 (8–13)	8 (6–11)	A2, A3, A4, A5, A6, A8, A1 M1, M2, M3, M4	28–30
	Penetration with an object	7 (5–10)	5 (4–8)	3 (2–5)		
	Penetration with a body part where no physical harm sustained by victim	5 (4–8)	4 (3–7)	2 (1–4)		

OFFENCE	TYPE/ NATURE OF ACTIVITY	STARTING POINTS (AND SENTENCING RANGES)			AGG. & MIT. FACTORS	GUIDE-LINE PAGES
		Victim is under 13	Victim 13 or over/ under 16	Victim 16 or over		
Sexual assault 3 (sexual assault) ‡ 7 (sexual assault of a child under 13) ‡	Contact between naked genitalia of offender and naked genitalia, face or mouth of the victim	5 (4–8)	3 (2–5)	3 (2–5)	A1, A2, A3, A4, A5, A6, A8, A9 M1, M2, M3, M5, M6	32–34
	Contact between naked genitalia of offender and another part of victim's body/ Contact with genitalia of victim by offender using part of his or her body other than the genitalia, or an object/ Contact between either the clothed genitalia of offender and naked genitalia of victim or naked genitalia of offender and clothed genitalia of victim	2 (1–4)	12 mths (6–24 mths)			
	Contact between part of offender's body (other than the genitalia) with part of the victim's body (other than the genitalia)	6 mths (4 wks to 18 mths)	Community order (appropriate non-custodial sentence)			

OFFENCE	TYPE/ NATURE OF ACTIVITY	STARTING POINTS (AND SENTENCING RANGES)			AGG. & MIT. FACTORS	GUIDE-LINE PAGES
		Victim is under 13	Victim 13 or over/ under 16	Victim 16 or over		
Causing sexual activity without consent 4 (causing a person to engage in sexual activity without consent) ‡ 8 (causing or inciting a child under 13 to engage in sexual activity) ‡ 31 (causing or inciting a person, with a mental disorder impeding choice, to engage in sexual activity) ‡ **N.B. For the purposes of the offence contrary to s.31, *the starting points applicable are those for victims under the age of 13***	Penetration with any one of the following aggravating factors: abduction or detention; offender aware that he or she is suffering from a sexually transmitted infection; more than one offender acting together; abuse of trust; offence motivated by prejudice (race, religion, sexual orientation, physical disability); sustained attack	13 (11–17)	10 (8–13)	8 (6–11)	A1, A2, A3, A4, A5, A6	38–41
	Single offence of penetration of/ by single offender with no aggravating or mitigating factors	7 (5–10)	5 (4–8)	3 (2–5)		
	Contact between naked genitalia of offender and naked genitalia of victim, or causing two or more victims to engage in such activity with each other, or causing victim to masturbate him.	5 (4–8)	3 (2–5)			
	Contact between naked genitalia of offender and another part of victim's body/ contact with naked genitalia of victim by offender using part of the body other than the genitalia or an object / contact between either the clothed genitalia of offender and naked genitalia of victim, or naked genitalia of offender and clothed genitalia of victim. (*Or causing two or more victims to engage in such activity with each other*).	2 (1–4)	12 mths (6–24 mths)			
	Contact between part of offender's body (other than the genitalia) with part of the victim's body (other than the genitalia)	6 mths (4 wks to 18 mths)	Community order (appropriate non-custodial sentence)			

OFFENCE	TYPE/NATURE OF ACTIVITY	STARTING POINTS (AND SENTENCING RANGES)			AGG. & MIT. FACTORS	GUIDELINE PAGES
		Victim is under 13	Victim 13 or over/under 16	Victim 16 or over		
Sexual activity in the presence of another person 11 (engaging in sexual activity in the presence of a child) (offender 18 or over)‡ 32 (engaging in sexual activity in the presence of a person with a mental disorder impeding choice) ‡	Consensual intercourse or other forms of consensual penetration		2 (1–4)		A2, A3, A4, A5	44, 45
	Masturbation (of oneself or another person)		18 mths (12–30 mths)			
	Consensual sexual touching involving naked genitalia		12 mths (6–18 mths)			
	Consensual sexual touching of naked body parts but not involving naked genitalia		6 mths (4 wks–18 mths)			
Causing or inciting another person to watch a sexual act 12 (causing a child to watch a sexual act) (offender 18 or over) ‡ 33 (causing a person with a mental disorder impeding choice to watch a sexual act) ‡	Live sexual activity		18 mths (12–24 mths)		A2, A3, A4, A5, A10	46, 47
	Moving or still images of people engaged in sexual activity involving penetration		32 wks (26–52 wks)			
	Moving or still images of people engaged in sexual activity other than penetration		Community order (community order to 26 wks' custody)			

Part 3: Offences involving ostensible consent (*Sexual Offences Act* 2003)   **K–95**

It should be noted that an offender under the age of 18 convicted of an offence contrary to section 9, 10, 25 or 26 should be dealt with under Part 7 of the guideline.

Part 3A (offences involving children (ss.9 & 10, 25 & 26, 16 & 17, 18, 19, 14))

Extreme youth of an offender and close proximity in age between the offender and the victim are both factors that will be relevant. As to sexual activity with a child, the same starting points apply whether the activity was caused or incited (causing or inciting offences). As to familial child sex offences, where the victim is over the age of consent, the starting points assume that the offender is a close relative. Further, where the victim was aged 16 or 17 when the sexual activity was commenced and the relationship was unlawful only because it was in a familial setting (*e.g.* offence involves foster siblings, a lodger or *au pair*) the starting points should be in line with generic breach of trust cases. Evidence that the offender has been "groomed" by the offender will aggravate the seriousness of the offence. As to abuse of trust cases, evidence of serious coercion, threats or trauma should move a sentence well above a starting point. The same starting points apply whether the activity was caused or incited (causing or inciting offences).

Part 3B (offences against vulnerable adults (ss.30, 34 & 35, 38 & 39, 36 & 40, 37 & 41))

The period of time during which the sexual activity has taken place will be relevant in determining the seriousness of an offence; although, depending on the particular circumstances, this could amount to aggravation (repeated exploitative behaviour) or mitigation (longer-term relationship where victim has low-level mental disorder). In general, the same starting points should be applied whether (a) the victim has a mental disorder impeding choice, or a mental disorder making him vulnerable to inducement, threat or deception, and (b) the activity was caused or incited (causing or inciting offences).

Key to table of starting points, *etc.*, for part 3

†   Denotes that an offence is a "specified offence" for the purposes of the *Criminal Justice Act* 2003, s.224

‡   Denotes that an offence is a "serious offence" for the purposes of the *Criminal Justice Act* 2003, s.224

Aggravating factors.

A1:   Offender ejaculated or caused victim to ejaculate
A2:   Background of intimidation or coercion
A3:   Use of drugs, alcohol or other substance to facilitate the offence
A4:   Threats to prevent victim reporting the incident
A5:   Abduction or detention
A6:   Offender aware that he or she is suffering from a sexually transmitted infection
A7:   Pregnancy or infection results
A8:   Physical harm caused
A9:   Prolonged activity or contact
A10:   Images of violent activity
A11:   Closeness of familial relationship

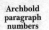
A12:　Number of victims involved

Mitigating factors

M7:　Offender intervenes to prevent incited offence from taking place

M8:　Small disparity in age between victim and offender

M9:　Relationship of genuine affection

M10:　No element of corruption

M11:　Offender had a mental disorder at the time of the offence which significantly affected his or her culpability

OFFENCE	TYPE/ NATURE OF ACTIVITY	STARTING POINTS (AND SENTENCING RANGES)	AGG. & MIT. FACTORS	GUIDE-LINE PAGES
Sexual activity with a child 9 (sexual activity with a child) (offender 18 or over) ‡ 10 (causing or inciting a child to engage in sexual activity) (offender 18 or over) ‡	Penile penetration of the vagina, anus or mouth or penetration of the vagina or anus with another body part or an object	4 (3–7)	A1, A4, A6 M7, M8	52–54
	Contact between naked genitalia of offender and naked genitalia or another part of victim's body, particularly face or mouth	2 (1–4)		
	Contact between naked genitalia of offender or victim and clothed genitalia of victim or offender or contact with naked genitalia of victim by offender using part of his or her body other than the genitalia or an object	12 months (26 weeks to 24 months)		
	Contact between part of offender's body (other than the genitalia) with part of the victim's body (other than the genitalia)	Community order (appropriate non-custodial sentence)		

811

OFFENCE	TYPE/ NATURE OF ACTIVITY	STARTING POINTS (AND SENTENCING RANGES)	AGG. & MIT. FACTORS	GUIDE-LINE PAGES
Familial child sex offences 25 (sexual activity with a child family member) (offender 18 or over) ‡ 26 (inciting a child family member to engage in sexual activity) (offender 18 or over) ‡	**Victim is 13 or over but under 16, regardless of familial relationship with offender/ victim is 16 or 17 but sexual relationship commenced when victim was under 16/ victim is aged 16 or 17 and offender is a blood relative**		A2, A3, A4, A6, A11	56–58
	Penile penetration of the vagina, anus or mouth or penetration of the vagina or anus with another body part or an object	5 (4–8)	M8	
	Contact between naked genitalia of offender and naked genitalia of victim	4 (3–7)		
	Contact between naked genitalia of offender or victim and clothed genitalia of victim or offender	18 months (12 months to 30 months)		
	Contact between naked genitalia of victim by another part of offender's body or an object, or between naked genitalia of offender and another part of victim's body	18 months (12 months to 30 months)		
	Contact between part of offender's body (other than the genitalia) with part of the victim's body (other than the genitalia)	Community order (appropriate non-custodial sentence)		
	Victim was aged 16 or 17 when sexual relationship commenced and relationship was only unlawful because of abuse of trust implicit in relationship			
	Penile penetration of the vagina, anus or mouth or penetration of the vagina or anus with another body part or an object	2 (1–4)		
	Any other form of non-penetrative sexual activity involving naked contact between offender and victim	12 months (6 to 24 months)		
	Contact between clothed part of offender's body (other than genitalia) with clothed part of victim's body (other than the genitalia)	Community order (appropriate non-custodial sentence)		

OFFENCE	TYPE/ NATURE OF ACTIVITY	STARTING POINTS (AND SENTENCING RANGES)	AGG. & MIT. FACTORS	GUIDE-LINE PAGES
Abuse of trust: sexual activity with a person under 18 16 (abuse of position of trust: sexual activity with a child) † 17 (abuse of position of trust: causing or inciting child to engage in sexual activity) †	Penile penetration of the vagina, anus or mouth or penetration of the vagina or anus with another body part or an object	18 months (12 months to 30 months)	A2, A1, A3, A6 M8, M9, M10	60, 61
	Other forms of non-penetrative activity	26 weeks (4 weeks to 18 months)		
	Contact between part of offender's body (other than the genitalia) with part of the victim's body (other than the genitalia)	Community order (appropriate non-custodial sentence)		
Abuse of trust: sexual activity in the presence of a person under 18 18 (abuse of trust: sexual activity in the presence of a child) †	Consensual intercourse or other forms of consensual penetration	2 (1–4)	A2, A3, A4, A5	62, 63
	Masturbation (of oneself or another person)	18 months (12 months to 30 months)		
	Consensual sexual touching involving naked genitalia	12 months (6 months to 24 months)		
	Consensual sexual touching of naked body parts but not involving naked genitalia	26 weeks (4 weeks to 18 months)		
Abuse of trust: causing a person under 18 to watch a sexual act 19 (abuse of position of trust: causing a child to watch a sexual act) †	Live sexual activity	18 months (12 months to 24 months)	A2, A3, A4, A5, A10 M8	64, 65
	Moving or still images of people engaged in sexual activity involving penetration	32 weeks (26–52 weeks)		
	Moving or still images of people engaged in sexual activity other than penetration	Community order (community order–26 weeks custody)		

OFFENCE	TYPE/ NATURE OF ACTIVITY	STARTING POINTS (AND SENTENCING RANGES)	AGG. & MIT. FACTORS	GUIDE-LINE PAGES
Arranging a child sex offence 14 (arranging or facilitating the commission of a child sex offence) ‡	Where the activity is arranged or facilitated as part of a commercial enterprise, even if the offender is under 18	Starting points and sentencing ranges should be increased above those for the relevant substantive offence under sections 9 to 13.	A2, A3, A4, A5, A12	66, 67
	Basic offence assuming no aggravating or mitigating factors	Starting point and sentencing ranges should be commensurate with that for the relevant substantive offence under sections 9 to 13.		
Sexual activity with a person with a mental disorder 30 (sexual activity with a person with a mental disorder impeding choice) ‡ 34 (inducement, threat or deception to procure sexual activity with a person with a mental disorder) ‡ 35 (causing a person with a mental disorder to engage in, or agree to engage in, sexual activity by inducement, threat or deception) †	Penetration with any of the following aggravating factors: abduction or detention; offender aware that he or she is suffering from a sexually transmitted infection; more than one offender acting together; offence motivated by prejudice (race, religion, sexual orientation, physical disability); sustained or repeated activity	13 (11–17)	A2, A1, A3, A4, A5, A6 M9, M11	70–72
	Single offence of penetration of/ by single offender with no aggravating or mitigating factors	10 (8–13)		
	Contact between naked genitalia of offender and naked genitalia of victim	5 (4–8)		
	Contact between naked genitalia of offender and another part of victim's body or naked genitalia of victim by offender using part of his or her body other than the genitalia / Contact between clothed genitalia of offender and naked genitalia of victim or naked genitalia of offender and clothed genitalia of victim	15 months (36 weeks to 3 years)		
	Contact between part of offender's body (other than the genitalia) with parts of victim's body (other than the genitalia)	26 weeks (4 weeks to 18 months)		

OFFENCE	TYPE/ NATURE OF ACTIVITY	STARTING POINTS (AND SENTENCING RANGES)	AGG. & MIT. FACTORS	GUIDE-LINE PAGES
Care workers: sexual activity with a person with a mental disorder 38 (care workers: sexual activity with a person with a mental disorder) ‡ 39 (care workers: causing or inciting sexual activity) ‡	Basic offence of sexual activity involving penetration, assuming no aggravating or mitigating factors	3 (2–5)	A2, A3, A4, A5, A6	74, 75
	Other forms of non-penetrative activity	12 months (6 months to 24 months)	M9	
	Naked contact between part of the offender's body with part of the victim's body	Community order (an appropriate non-custodial sentence)		
Sexual activity in the presence of a person with a mental disorder 36 (engaging in sexual activity in the presence, secured by inducement, threat or deception, of a person with a mental disorder) ‡ 40 (care workers: sexual activity in the presence of a person with a mental disorder) ‡	Consensual intercourse or other forms of consensual penetration	2 (1–4)	A2, A3, A4, A5	76, 77
	Masturbation (of oneself or another person)	18 months (12 months to 30 months)		
	Consensual sexual touching involving naked genitalia	12 months (6 months to 24 months)		
	Consensual sexual touching of naked body parts but not involving naked genitalia	26 weeks (4 weeks–18 months)		
Causing or inciting a person with a mental disorder to watch a sexual act 37 (causing a person with a mental disorder to watch a sexual act by inducement, threat or deception) ‡ 41 (care workers: causing a person with a mental disorder to watch a sexual act) †	Live sexual activity	18 months (12 months to 24 months)	A2, A3, A4, A5, A10	78, 79
	Moving or still images of people engaged in sexual activity involving penetration	32 weeks (26–52 weeks)		
	Moving or still images of people engaged in sexual activity other than penetration	Community order (community order–26 weeks custody)		

Part 4: Preparatory offences (*Sexual Offences Act* 2003, ss.15, 62, 63, 61)

K–97   In addition to the generic aggravating factors, the main factors determining the seriousness of these offences are: the seriousness of the intended offence (which will affect both the offender's culpability and the degree of risk to which the victim has been exposed); the degree to which the offence was planned; the sophistication of the grooming (s.15); the determination of the offender; how close the offender came to success; the reason why the offender did not succeed (*i.e.* whether it was a change of mind or whether someone or something prevented the offender from continuing); and any physical or psychological injury suffered by the victim.

Key to table of starting points, *etc.*, for part 4

†   Denotes that an offence is a "specified offence" for the purposes of the *Criminal Justice Act* 2003, s.224

‡   Denotes that an offence is a "serious offence" for the purposes of the *Criminal Justice Act* 2003, s.224

Aggravating factors.

A2:   Background of intimidation or coercion

A3:   Use of drugs, alcohol or other substance to facilitate the offence

A4:   Threats to prevent victim reporting the incident

A5:   Abduction or detention

A6:   Offender aware that he or she is suffering from a sexually transmitted infection

A13:   Targeting of vulnerable victim

A14:   Significant impact on persons present in the premises

A15:   Targeting of the victim

Mitigating factors

M7:   Offender intervenes to prevent incited offence from taking place

M12:   Offender decides, of his own volition, not to proceed with the intended sexual offence

M13:   Incident of brief duration

OFFENCE	TYPE/ NATURE OF ACTIVITY	STARTING POINTS (AND SENTENCING RANGES)		AGG. & MIT. FACTORS	GUIDE-LINE PAGES
		Victim is under 13	Victim is 13 or over		
Sexual grooming 15 (meeting a child for sexual grooming,*etc.*) (offender over 18) ‡	Where the intent is to commit an assault by penetration or rape	4 (3–7)	2 (1–4)	A2, A3, A6, A5	82, 83
	Where the intent is to the coerce child into sexual activity	2 (1–4)	18 months (12–30 months)		
Committing another offence with intent 62 (committing an offence with intent to commit a sexual offence) ‡	Any offence committed with intent to commit a sexual offence, *e.g.* assault	Commensurate with that for preliminary offence actually committed, but enhanced to reflect intention to commit a sexual offence (2 years where intent to commit rape or assault by penetration)		A3, A6 M12, M13	84, 85
Trespass with intent 63 (trespass with intent to commit a sexual offence) ‡	Intent to commit an assault by penetration or rape	4 (3–7)		A6, A13, A14 M12	86, 87
	Intent is other sexual offence	2 (1–4)			
Administering a substance with intent 61 (administering a substance with intent) ‡	Intent to commit an assault by penetration or rape	8 (6–9)	6 (4–9)	A4, A5, A6, A15, M7	88, 89
	Intent to commit any other sexual offence	6 (4–9)	4 (3–7)		

Part 5: Other offences (*Sexual Offences Act* 2003, ss.64 & 65, 71, 66, 67, 69, 70)

K–99   As to prohibited adult sexual relationships (ss.64 & 65), the most important issue for the sentencer to consider is the circumstances in which the offence was committed and any harm caused or risked. As to exposure (s.66), voyeurism (s.67), intercourse with an animal (s.69) and sexual penetration of a corpse (s.70), a pre-sentence report will be extremely helpful in determining the most appropriate disposal. Where an offence is being dealt with in a magistrates' court more detailed guidance will be provided in the Magistrates' Court Sentencing Guidelines.

Key to table of starting points, *etc.*, for part 5

† Denotes that an offence is a "specified offence" for the purposes of the *Criminal Justice Act* 2003, s.224

‡ Denotes that an offence is a "serious offence" for the purposes of the *Criminal Justice Act* 2003, s.224

Aggravating factors.

A2: Background of intimidation or coercion

A3: Use of drugs, alcohol or other substance to facilitate the offence

A4: Threats to prevent victim reporting the incident

A6: Offender aware that he or she is suffering from a sexually transmitted infection

A16: Evidence of long-term grooming

A17: No effort made to avoid pregnancy or sexual transmission of infection

A18: Intimidating behaviour/ threats of violence to member(s) of the public

A19: Intimidating behaviour/ threats of violence

A20: Victim is a child

A21: Recording activity and circulating pictures/ videos

A22: Circulating pictures or videos for commercial gain (particularly if victim is vulnerable, *e.g.* a child or person with a mental or physical disorder)

A23: Distress to victim (*e.g.* where the pictures/ videos are circulated to persons known to the victim)

A24: Distress caused to relatives or friends of the deceased

A25: Physical damage caused to body of deceased

A26: Corpse was that of a child

A27: Offence committed in funeral home or mortuary

Mitigating factors

M8: Small disparity in age between victim and offender

M9: Relationship of genuine affection

M14: Symptom of isolation rather than depravity

OFFENCE	TYPE/ NATURE OF ACTIVITY	STARTING POINTS (AND SENTENCING RANGES)	AGG. & MIT. FACTORS	GUIDE-LINE PAGES
Prohibited adult sexual relationships: sex with an adult relative	Evidence of long-term grooming when person being groomed was under 18 (offender over 18)	12 months (26 weeks to 24 months)	A2, A3, A4, A16, A6, A17	92, 93
64 (sex with an adult relative: penetration) †	Evidence of grooming of one party by the other when both parties were over 18	Community order (appropriate non-custodial sentence)	M8, M9	
65 (sex with an adult relative: consenting to penetration) †	Sexual penetration with no aggravating factors	Community order (appropriate non-custodial sentence)		
Sexual activity in a public lavatory	Repeat offending and/ or aggravating factors	Community order (appropriate non-custodial sentence)	A18	94, 95
71 (sexual activity in a public lavatory)	Basic offence assuming no aggravating or mitigating factors	Fine (appropriate non-custodial sentence)		
Exposure	Repeat offender	12 weeks (4–26 weeks)	A4, A19, A20	96, 97
66 (exposure) †	Basic offence assuming no aggravating or mitigating factors, or some offences with aggravating factors	Community order (appropriate non-custodial sentence)		
Voyeurism	Offence with serious aggravating factors such as recording sexual activity and placing it on a website or circulating it for commercial gain	12 months (26 weeks to 24 months)	A4, A21, A22, A23	98, 99
67 (voyeurism) †	Offence with aggravating factors such as recording sexual activity and showing it to others	26 weeks (4 weeks to 18 months)		
	Basic offence assuming no aggravating or mitigating factors (*e.g.* offender spies through a hole he or she has made in a changing room wall)	Community order (appropriate non-custodial sentence)		

OFFENCE	TYPE/ NATURE OF ACTIVITY	STARTING POINTS (AND SENTENCING RANGES)	AGG. & MIT. FACTORS	GUIDE-LINE PAGES
Intercourse with an animal 69 (intercourse with an animal) †	Basic offence assuming no aggravating or mitigating factors	Community order (appropriate non-custodial sentence)	A21, M14	100, 101
Sexual penetration of a corpse 70 (sexual penetration of a corpse) †	Repeat offending and/ or aggravating factors	26 weeks (4 weeks to 18 months)	A24, A25, A26, A27	102, 103
	Basic offence assuming no aggravating or mitigating factors	Community order (appropriate non-custodial sentence)		

Part 6A: Indecent photographs of children

This part of the guideline (pp.109—114) deals with offences contrary
to the *Protection of Children Act* 1978, s.1, and the *CJA* 1988, s.160. It is
based on the sentencing levels identified in *R. v. Oliver*; *R. v. Hartrey*; *R. v.
Baldwin* [2003] 1 Cr.App.R. 28, CA, which have been "reviewed". Pseudo-
photographs should generally be treated as less serious than real
photographs, save, for example, where the imagery is particularly gro-
tesque and beyond the scope of normal photography. The presence of any
aggravating factors will substantially increase a sentence. Where it cannot
be established that a victim was under 13, the sentence should be based on
starting points for children aged over 13 but under 16. Inferences should
not be drawn as to the status of unknown material; but using devices to destroy or hide material will amount to the generic aggravating factor of "an
attempt to conceal or dispose of evidence". Where the material is shown or
distributed without the victim's consent, the fact that the victim is over the
age of consent has no bearing on sentence levels even if the material was
made and possessed with the victim's consent. Any profit for the victim,
financial or otherwise, actual or anticipated, should be neutral for sentencing purposes. An offence contrary to the 1978 Act is a serious offence for
the purposes of section 224 of the *CJA* 2003, whereas an offence contrary
to the 1988 Act is a specified offence.

Where the child depicted is aged 16 or 17, the starting points should
reflect the fundamental facts of the case, including that the child is over
the legal age of consent. Sentences should be lower than in cases involving children under 16 where the offender possesses only a few photographs, none of which includes sadism or bestiality, and they are retained
solely for use of the offender.

Aggravating factors.

A2:   Background of intimidation or coercion

A4:   Threats to prevent victim reporting the incident

A28:   Images shown or distributed to others, especially children

A29:   Collection is systematically stored or organised, indicating a sophisticated
       approach to trading or a high level of personal interest

A30:   Images stored, made available or distributed in such a way that they can be
       inadvertently accessed by others

A31:   Use of drugs, alcohol or other substance to facilitate the offence of making
       or taking

A32:   Threats to disclose victim's activity to friends or relatives

A33:   Financial or other gain

Mitigating factors

M15:   Few images held solely for personal use

M16:   Images viewed but not stored

M17:   Few images held solely for personal use and it is established both that the
       subject was aged 16 or 17 and that he or she was consenting

Levels of seriousness

L1:   Images depicting erotic posing with no sexual activity

L2:   Non-penetrative sexual activity between children, or solo masturbation by a child

L3:   Non-penetrative sexual activity between adults and children

L4:   Penetrative sexual activity involving a child or children, or both children and adults

L5:   Sadism or penetration of, or by, an animal

K–102

TYPE/ NATURE OF ACTIVITY	STARTING POINTS (AND SENTENCING RANGES)
Offender commissioned or encouraged the production of level 4 or 5 images	6 (4–9)
Offender involved in the production of level 4 or 5 images	6 (4–9)
Level 4 or 5 images shown or distributed	3 (2–5)
Offender involved in the production of, or has traded in, material at levels 1–3	2 (1–4)
Possession of a large quantity of level 4 or 5 material for personal use only	12 months (6 months to 24 months)
Large number of level 3 images shown or distributed	12 months (6 months to 24 months)
Possession of a large quantity of level 3 material for personal use	26 weeks (4 weeks to 18 months)
Possession of a small number of images at level 4 or 5	26 weeks (4 weeks to 18 months)
Large number of level 2 images shown or distributed	26 weeks (4 weeks to 18 months)
Small number of level 3 images shown or distributed	26 weeks (4 weeks to 18 months)
Offender in possession of a large amount of material at level 2 or a small amount at level 3	12 weeks (4–26 weeks)
Offender has shown or distributed material at level 1 or 2 on a limited scale	12 weeks (4–26 weeks)
Offender has exchanged images at level 1 or 2 with other collectors, but with no element of financial gain	12 weeks (4–26 weeks)
Possession of a large amount of level 1 material and/or no more than a small amount of level 2, and the material is for personal use and has not been distributed or shown to others	Community order (appropriate non-custodial sentence)

Parts 6B to 6D: Abuse of children through prostitution and pornography (*Sexual Offences Act* 2003, ss.47, 48–50)**; exploitation of prostitution** (*Sexual Offences Act* 2003, ss.52, 53, *Sexual Offences Act* 1956, s.33A) **trafficking** (*Sexual Offences Act* 2003, ss.57–59)

K–103

As to offences connected with child prostitution and pornography where a number of children are involved, consecutive sentences may be appropriate leading to cumulative sentences considerably higher than the suggested starting points for individual offences. A more lenient approach may be appropriate where the offender was to a degree also a victim. As to exploitation of prostitution, the degree of coercion (both in terms of recruitment and subsequent control of a prostitute's activities) is

highly relevant; as is the harm suffered as a result, the level of involvement of the offender, the scale of the operation and the timescale over
which it has been run. Mitigation may be available where the offender
had no active involvement in the coercion or control of the victim(s),
where the offender acted through fear or intimidation, or where the offender was trying to escape from prostitution. For causing and inciting
offences, the starting points are the same whether prostitution was caused
or incited, and whether or not the incited activity took place. A fine may
be appropriate for minimal involvement. Where the offence is being
dealt with in a magistrates' court, more detailed guidance will be provided
in the Magistrates' Court Sentencing Guidelines. As to keeping a brothel
used for prostitution, the applicable principles are similar to those for offences of exploitation of prostitution. As to trafficking, the factors to be
taken into consideration broadly correspond to those that relate to
exploitation of prostitution. Additionally, aggravation such as participation in a large-scale commercial operation involving a high degree of
planning, organisation or sophistication, financial or other gain, and the
coercion and vulnerability of victims should move sentences towards the
maximum of 14 years. Where a number of children are involved, consecutive sentences may be appropriate, with total sentences significantly
higher than the suggested starting point for individual offences. The
court should consider making confiscation and deprivation orders.

Key to table of starting points, *etc.*, for parts 6B to 6D

†   Denotes that an offence is a "specified offence" for the purposes of section
      224 of the *Criminal Justice Act* 2003

‡   Denotes that an offence is a "serious offence" for the purposes of section 224
      of the *Criminal Justice Act* 2003

Aggravating factors.

A2:   Background of intimidation or coercion

A3:   Use of drugs, alcohol or other substance to facilitate the offence

A4:   Threats to prevent victim reporting the incident

A5:   Abduction or detention

A6:   Offender aware that he or she is suffering from a sexually transmitted dis-
        ease

A30:   Images stored, made available or distributed in such a way that they can be
        inadvertently accessed by others

A32:   Threats to disclose victim's activity to friends or relatives

A33:   Financial or other gain

A34:   Use of drugs, alcohol or other substance to secure the victim's compliance

A35:   Large-scale commercial operation

A36:   Induced dependency on drugs

A37:   Forcing a victim to violate another person

A38:   Victim has been manipulated into physical and emotional dependence on
        the offender

A39:   Images distributed to other children or persons known to the victim

A40:   Substantial gain (in the region of £5,000 and upwards)

A41:   Personal involvement in the prostitution of others

A42:   High degree of planning or sophistication

A43:   Large number of people trafficked

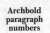

A44:   Fraud

A45:   Financial extortion of the victim

A46:   Deception

A47:   Threats against victim or members of victim's family

A48:   Restriction of victim's liberty

A49:   Inhumane treatment

A50:   Confiscation of victim's passport

A51:   Use of force, threats of force, or other forms of coercion

Mitigating factors

M18:   Offender also being controlled in prostitution or pornography and subject to threats and intimidation

M19:   Using employment as a route out of prostitution and not actively involved in exploitation

M20:   Coercion by a third party

M21:   No evidence of personal gain

M22:   Limited involvement

OFFENCE	TYPE/ NATURE OF ACTIVITY	STARTING POINTS (AND SENTENCING RANGES)			AGG. & MIT. FACTORS	GUIDE-LINE PAGES
		Victim under the age of 13	Victim is 13 or over but under 16	Victim is 16 or over		
Paying for sexual services of a child 47 (paying for sexual services of a child) ‡	History of paying for penetrative sex with children under 18	15 (13–19)	7 (5–10)	3 (2–5)	A34, A5, A4, A32, A6	116–118
	Penile penetration of the vagina, anus or mouth/ penetration of the vagina or anus with any other body part or object	12 (10–16)	5 (4–8)	2 (1–4)		
	Sexual touching falling short of penetration	5 (4–8)	4 (3–7)	12 months (6 to 24 months)		
Child prostitution and pornography 48 (causing or inciting child prostitution or pornography) ‡	Penetrative activity: organised commercial exploitation	10 (8–13)	8 (6–11)	4 (3–7)	A2, A35, A34, A36, A37, A38, A5, A4, A32, A30, A39, A33 M18	120–123
49 (controlling a child prostitute or a child involved in pornography) ‡	Penetrative activity: offender's involvement is minimal and not perpetrated for gain	8 (6–11)	5 (4–8)	2 (1–4)		
	Non-penetrative activity: organised commercial exploitation	8 (6–11)	6 (4–9)	3 (2–5)		
50 (arranging or facilitating child prostitution or pornography) ‡	Non-penetrative activity: offender's involvement is minimal and not perpetrated for gain	6 (4–9)	3 (2–5)	12 months (6 to 24 months)		

OFFENCE	TYPE/ NATURE OF ACTIVITY	STARTING POINTS (AND SENTENCING RANGES)			AGG. & MIT. FACTORS	GUIDELINE PAGES
		Victim under the age of 13	Victim is 13 or over but under 16	Victim is 16 or over		
Exploitation of prostitution 52 (causing or inciting prostitution for gain)† 53 (controlling prostitution for gain)†	Evidence of physical and/or mental coercion		3 (2–5)		A2, A35, A40, A34, A36, A5, A4, A32	126, 127
	No coercion or corruption, but offender is closely involved in victim's prostitution		12 months (6 months –24 months)			
	No evidence that victim was physically coerced or corrupted and involvement of offender was minimal		Community order (appropriate non-custodial sentence)		M18	
Keeping a brothel used for prostitution 33A SOA 1956 (keeping a brothel used for prostitution)	Offender is keeper of a brothel and has made substantial profits in the region of £5,000 and upwards		2 (1–4)		A2, A35, A41, A5, A33	128, 129
	Offender is keeper of a brothel and is personally involved in its management		12 months (6 months 24 months)		M19, M20	
	Involvement of the offender was minimal		Community order (appropriate non-custodial sentence)			
Trafficking 57 (trafficking into the U.K. for sexual exploitation) ‡ 58 (trafficking within the U.K. for sexual exploitation) ‡ 59 (trafficking out of the U.K. for sexual exploitation) ‡	Involvement at any level in any stage of the trafficking operation where the victim was coerced		6 (4–9)		A35, A42, A43, A40, A44, A45, A46, A51 A47, A5, A48, A49, A50	130, 131
	Involvement at any level in any stage of the trafficking operation where there was no coercion of the victim		2 (1–4)		M20, M21. M22	

Part 7: Sentencing young offenders—offences with a lower statutory maximum

The guidelines in this part are intended for cases where the court considers that the facts found by the court justify the involvement of the criminal law, which findings may be different from those on which a decision to prosecute was made. The guidelines relate to sentencing on conviction of a first time offender. Where a young offender pleads guilty to one of the offences dealt with in this part, a youth court may impose an absolute discharge, a mental health disposal, a custodial sentence, or make a referral order. Where a custodial sentence is imposed in the Crown Court, it may be a detention and training order, or detention under section 91 of the *PCC(S)A* 2000 for a period up to the maximum for the offence.

The guideline (as originally drafted) referred to the offences in this part as being contrary to sections 9, 10, 11, 12, 25 and 26 of the 2003 Act. These can be split into two, as slightly different considerations apply to sections 9 to 12 as compared with sections 25 and 26.

As to sections 9 to 12, the guideline was in error in its premise that a person under 18 can commit one of these offences. Each of those offences is defined in such a way that it can only be committed by a person aged 18 or over. If a person under that age does an act proscribed by any of those sections, he does not offend against them. Section 13(1) (not mentioned in the guideline as originally drafted), however, provides that "(1) A person under 18 commits an offence if he does anything which would be an offence under any of sections 9 to 12 if he were aged 18.", and subsection (2) provides for a lesser maximum penalty. A person under 18 who does that which is prohibited by any of those sections would commit an offence under section 13, and should be charged as having committed an offence "contrary to section 13". The guideline has now been corrected in this respect. An offence contrary to section 13 is a specified offence, but not a serious offence for the purposes of Chapter 5 of Part 12 of the *CJA* 2003.

With sections 25 and 26, the position is less clear-cut. It is subsection (1) in each case that creates the offence and age is not an ingredient of the offence; but subsections (4) and (5) contain different penalty provisions according to whether the offender is aged 18 or over or under 18. Where the offender is under 18, the maximum is five years' custody. Taking the section as a whole, it is submitted, on the basis of *R. v. Courtie* [1984] A.C. 463, HL (the effect of the varying penalty provisions in the *SOA* 1956, according to the circumstances of an act of buggery, was to create separate offences), that sections 25 and 26 create distinct offences for those under 18. If this is correct, then these offences are specified offences, but not serious offences, because they carry a maximum of five years' custody and they cannot—by definition—be committed by an 18-year-old. The separate listing of these offences in section 91 of the *PCC(S)A* 2000 (§ 5–358 in the main work) supports this view: an offence under section 25 or 26 committed by an adult carries 14 years' imprisonment and there would have been no need to make special mention of it if there were only one offence.

This view has not been accepted by the Sentencing Guidelines Council as the guideline still shows the offences contrary to sections 25 and 26, when committed by an under 18-year-old, as "serious offences". It is submitted that the better view is that they are "specified", but not "serious" offences.

827

Key to table of starting points, *etc.*, for parts 6B to 6D

†   Denotes that an offence is a "specified offence" for the purposes of section 224 of the *Criminal Justice Act* 2003

‡   Denotes that an offence is a "serious offence" for the purposes of section 224 of the *Criminal Justice Act* 2003

Aggravating factors.

A2:   Background of intimidation or coercion

A3:   Use of drugs, alcohol or other substance to facilitate the offence

A4:   Threats to prevent victim reporting the incident

A5:   Abduction or detention

A6:   Offender aware that he or she is suffering from a sexually transmitted infection

A10:   Images of violent activity

Mitigating factors

M5:   Youth and immaturity of offender

M7:   Offender intervenes to prevent incited offence from taking place

M8:   Small disparity in age between victim and offender

M9:   Relationship of genuine affection

OFFENCE	TYPE/ NATURE OF ACTIVITY	STARTING POINTS (AND SENTENCING RANGES)	AGG. & MIT. FACTORS	GUIDE-LINE PAGES
Sexual activity with a child 13(9) (intentional sexual touching of a person under 16) (offender under 18) †	Offence involving penetration where one or more aggravating factors exist or where there is a substantial age gap between the parties	12-month detention and training order (6- to 24- month detention and training order)	A2, A3, A4, A5, A6 M9, M5	135
	Any form of sexual activity (non-penetrative or penetrative) not involving any aggravating factors	Community order (appropriate non-custodial sentence)		
Causing or inciting a child to engage in sexual activity 13(10) (causing or inciting a child to engage in sexual activity) (offender under 18) †	Offence involving penetration where one or more aggravating factors exist or where there is a substantial age gap between the parties	12-month detention and training order (6- to 24- month detention and training order)	A2, A3, A4, A5, A6 M9, M7, M5	136
	Any form of sexual activity (non-penetrative or penetrative) not involving any aggravating factors	Community order (appropriate non-custodial sentence)		
Engaging in sexual activity in the presence of a child 13(11) (engaging in sexual activity in the presence of a child) (offender under 18) †	Sexual activity involving penetration where one or more aggravating factors exist	12-month detention and training order (6- to 24- month detention and training order)	A2, A3, A4, A5 M5	137
	Any form of sexual activity (non-penetrative or penetrative) not involving any aggravating factors	Community order (appropriate non-custodial sentence)		
Causing a child to watch a sexual act 13(12) (causing a child to watch a sexual act) (offender under 18) †	Live sexual activity	8-month detention and training order (6- to 12- month detention and training order)	A2, A3, A4, A5, A10 M5	138
	Moving or still images of people engaged in sexual acts involving penetration	Community order (appropriate non-custodial sentence)		
	Moving or still images of people engaged in sexual acts other than penetration	Community order (appropriate non-custodial sentence)		

OFFENCE	TYPE/ NATURE OF ACTIVITY	STARTING POINTS (AND SENTENCING RANGES)	AGG. & MIT. FACTORS	GUIDE-LINE PAGES
Sexual activity with a child family member and inciting a child family member to engage in sexual activity 25 (sexual activity with a child family member) (offender under 18) ‡ 26 (inciting a child family member to engage in sexual activity) (offender under 18) ‡‡ **N.B.: As to whether these offences are "serious offences", see *ante*.**	Offence involving penetration where one or more aggravating factors exist or where there is a substantial age gap between the parties	18-month detention and training order (6- to 24- month detention and training order)	A2, A3, A4, A6 M8, M9, M5	139
	Any form of sexual activity that does not involve any aggravating factors	Community order (appropriate non-custodial sentence)		

I. Failing to Surrender to Bail

The Sentencing Guidelines Council has issued a definitive guideline on   **K–107**
failing to surrender to bail (*Bail Act* 1976, s.6(1) and (2) (§ 3–27 in the
main work)). It deals with offenders sentenced on or after December 10,
2007, and only relates to the sentencing of those aged 18 or over.

Assessment of seriousness

The seriousness of an offence is to be determined by: (a) the offender's   **K–108**
culpability (in particular, whether the failure to surrender was intended
to cause harm and, if so, what level of harm), and (b) any harm which the
offence caused, was intended to cause or might foreseeably have caused
(in particular, to what extent the failure to surrender impeded the course
of justice), and "harm" includes not only harm caused to victims and witnesses but also the consequential drain on the police and the courts and
the wider negative impact on public confidence in the criminal justice
system. The same approach to sentencing should be adopted for offences
under both section 6(1) and (2), though the seriousness is likely to be less
for an offence under subsection (2). The assessment of culpability requires
consideration of the immediate reason why the defendant failed to appear, which can range from forgetfulness or fear of the outcome of the
hearing to a deliberate act, and where the failure to surrender was deliberate, it will be relevant whether it was designed to disrupt the system to
the defendant's advantage or whether the defendant simply gave no
thought at all to the consequences. Failure to surrender will always cause
some degree of harm, will inevitably delay justice, and will almost always
waste public money. The circumstances of an offence, and the harm
likely to be caused, will range from failure to appear for a first hearing
but attending shortly afterwards (where the only harm caused is likely to
be financial and procedural), to failure to appear for trial or sentence, especially where the trial does not proceed in the defendant's absence
(where the harm caused may extend to the prevention of justice). Generally, the same approach should be taken whether the failure to surrender
is to a court or to a police station, but the harm caused is likely to be less
in the case of a police station, and there are also circumstances where the
culpability may be less. Where sentence is passed in advance of the offence in respect of which bail was granted, the seriousness of that offence
should not affect the assessment of seriousness, but the nature of that offence may affect the degree or likelihood of harm caused, such as where
it is a violent or sexual offence, and an acquittal for that offence will not
affect the seriousness of the failure to surrender.

Aggravating factors that are particularly relevant to the assessment of
seriousness are: (a) repeated offences under section 6; (b) the absence of
the offender causing a lengthy delay to the administration of justice; and
(c) a determined effort to avoid the jurisdiction of the court or to
undermine the course of justice. Mitigating factors that are particularly
relevant are: (a) prompt voluntary surrender (if initiated by the offender);
(b) misunderstanding (which must be differentiated from a mistake on
the part of the offender); (c) a failure to comprehend the requirements
or significance of bail; and (d) caring responsibilities (where these are the
cause of the failure to surrender). The fact that the offender has a disor-
ganised or chaotic lifestyle (which may be due to dependence on drugs
or alcohol) does not mitigate the seriousness of the offence (though it
may amount to personal mitigation).

Procedural issues

K–109   *As to when to sentence*, the key principle is stated to be that a court should deal with a defendant who fails to surrender as soon as it is practicable, even if the trial or other hearing for the offence in respect of which bail was granted is adjourned. Relevant factors when deciding what is practicable include: (a) when the proceedings in respect of which bail was granted are expected to conclude; (b) the seriousness of that offence; and (c) the type of penalty that might be imposed for that offence and for the failure to surrender. Liability for the section 6 offence should be determined as soon as possible, since it will be central to the issue of whether bail should be renewed; accordingly, a trial should be held on the first appearance after arrest or surrender, unless an adjournment is necessary. Occasions on which it may be more appropriate to sentence both offences together include circumstances where the totality of sentence may affect sentence type and where the harm caused cannot be assessed at an earlier stage.

K–110   *As to sentencing*, the alternatives to immediate custody are a community order, including an electronically monitored curfew requirement and, perhaps, a supervision or activity requirement, and, in more serious cases, a suspended sentence. Where custodial sentences are imposed both for the section 6 offence and for the substantive offence, they should normally be consecutive, but should be concurrent where otherwise the overall sentence would be disproportionate to the combined seriousness of the offences.

K–111   *As to trial in the defendant's absence*, where it has proved possible to proceed to trial or conclude proceedings in the absence of the defendant, this should have no bearing on culpability, but may be relevant to the assessment of harm, if the harm caused by the failure to attend has been reduced or avoided by such a course.

Sentencing ranges and starting points

K–112   The sentencing ranges and starting points relate to persons convicted following a plea of not guilty, and who do not have a conviction which, by virtue of the *CJA* 2003, s.143(2) (§ 5–54 in the main work), must be treated as an aggravating factor. A court should identify the description that most nearly matches the facts of the offence and this will identify a starting point, from which a provisional sentence can be reached. The sentencing range is the bracket into which the provisional sentence will fall after consideration of aggravating or mitigating factors (although particular circumstances, particular matters of aggravation or mitigation or the reduction for a guilty plea may require a sentence outside of that range). A court should give reasons for imposing a sentence of a different kind or outside the range provided in the guideline.

    For a deliberate failure to attend causing delay and/or interference with the administration of justice, the starting point is 14 days' custody, and the range, in a magistrates' court, should be from a community order (low) to 10 weeks' custody, and in the Crown Court, should be from a community order (medium) to 40 weeks' custody, with the type and degree of harm actually caused affecting where in the range the case falls. For a negligent or non-deliberate failure to attend causing delay and/or interference with the administration of justice, the starting point should be a fine, and the range (regardless of court) should be from a fine to a community order (medium). Where the defendant surrenders late, but the case proceeds as planned, the starting point and the range should be a fine.

J. Assault and Other Offences Against the Person

The Sentencing Guidelines Council has issued a definitive guideline on **K–113**
offences of assault that do not result in the death of a victim, but excluding
attempted murder. It deals with offenders sentenced on or after March 3,
2008, and only relates to the sentencing of those aged 18 or over. Additional principles to be considered when the victim is aged 15 or under
and the distinct issues relating to the offence of cruelty to a child (*CYPA*
1933, s.1(1)) are set out in the separate guideline on assaults on children
and cruelty to a child (*post*, § K–131). The foreword states that a separate
guideline on attempted murder will be issued in due course, and that a separate
rate guideline setting out general principles relating to the sentencing of
youths is planned.

Part 1: General principles

Assessing seriousness

The seriousness of an offence is to be determined by (a) the culpability of **K–114**
the offender and (b) the harm caused, intended or reasonably foreseeable,
and guidance on whether sentencing thresholds have been reached is
provided by the guideline on seriousness. Where an offender has previous
convictions, the court must consider whether it should treat any of them as
an aggravating factor, having regard to the nature and relevance of each
offence and the time that has elapsed since the conviction.

Culpability and harm

Where there is an imbalance between culpability and harm, the harm has **K–115**
to be judged in the light of the culpability of the offender and, although the
degree of physical harm actually caused may generally influence the
sentence, the concept of harm also includes the harm that the offence was
intended to cause or might foreseeably have caused. In addition, although
an offender may only be sentenced for the offence of which he has been
convicted, the range of penalties is wide and the degree of harm may be
taken into account when assessing seriousness even when that degree is not
necessary for the offence for which sentence is passed, and the court may
legitimately sentence on the basis of the harm caused within the maximum
available for the offence.

Aggravating and mitigating factors

The guideline refers to the guideline on seriousness for general aggravat- **K–116**
ing and mitigating factors. Care should be taken to avoid "double-counting"
when an essential element of an offence might, in other circumstances, be
an aggravating factor. Aggravating factors particularly relevant to assaults
are: (a) planning an offence; (b) operating in groups or gangs; (c) deliberate
targeting of vulnerable victims; (d) committing an offence against those
working in the public sector or providing a service to the public; (e) using a
weapon to frighten or injure the victim; (f) carrying out a sustained assault
or repeated assaults on the same victim; and (g) the location of the offence
(*e.g.* in an isolated place). Where a number of aggravating factors are present,
the court must consider their combined effect, and particular weight should
be attached to factors involving further degradation of the victim. In accor-

dance with the guideline on seriousness, prevalence may be taken into account but must not take a sentence outside the guidelines.

General considerations: (i) where an offence relates to an attempted honour killing or an effort to force a victim into an arranged marriage, the general aggravating factors of abuse of trust or abuse of power will invariably be present and must be taken into account; (ii) the fact that an offence takes place in the hours of darkness does not itself make an offence more serious, but if it contributed to the isolation of the victim or let the offender take advantage of poor lighting it may be relevant, and in general the timing or location of an offence will be aggravating factors if they were designed to increase the vulnerability of a victim or decrease the chances of discovery; (iii) when considering attacks against public sector workers, the extended harm caused by such assaults should be taken into account, and there will be further aggravation if the worker is also particularly vulnerable; and (iv) save for provocation (see *post*), the guideline does not set out particular mitigating factors, but instead refers to the general factors in the guideline on seriousness.

Use of a weapon and parts of the body: the use of a weapon or part of the body will usually increase the seriousness of an offence. In particular, (a) where an offender carries a weapon to the scene intending to use it or having it available for use should the opportunity or need arise, high culpability is likely to be indicated, and (b) the type of weapon or part of the body and the way it is used will influence the extent of its effect on the assessment of seriousness. In the guideline, in some instances use of a weapon will take the offence into a higher sentencing range, and in other instances it will raise the position of the offence within a particular range by affecting the assessment of seriousness.

Aggravated assaults: when sentencing for a racially or religiously aggravated offence (under the *CDA* 1998, s.29) or for a basic offence that is aggravated by hostility based on race, religion, sexual orientation or disability (under the *CJA* 2003, s.146), the court should determine the appropriate sentence without that aggravation, and then make an addition to the sentence. Factors that would indicate a high level of such aggravation include: (i) the aggravated element was a planned part of the offence; (ii) the offence was part of a pattern of offending by the offender; (iii) the incident was deliberately set up to be offensive or humiliating to the victim or to the group of which the victim is a member; (iv) the nature, timing or location of the offence was calculated to maximise the harm or distress it caused; and (v) the offence is shown to have caused fear and distress throughout a local community. Factors that would make the aggravation less serious include: (i) the aggravated element was limited in scope or duration; and (ii) the motivation for the offence was not hostility based on the victim's race, *etc.*, and the element of hostility or abuse based on prejudice was minor or incidental.

Transmission of infection or disease: an intention to infect another is likely to be treated as a bad example of the offence charged, and culpability is likely to be reduced when an offence is committed recklessly. Matters of personal mitigation may also have particularly high significance.

Provocation: the principles set out in the guideline on manslaughter by reason of provocation and domestic violence should be taken into account, and the court must give careful consideration to the degree to which the offender's personal circumstances (*e.g.* a history of domestic violence or abuse at the hands of the victim, threats made by the victim, or fear generated by the victim's actions) can be said to have provoked the offence. The nature and duration of the provocation and any fear, threat or violence generated by the

actions of the victim must be taken into account, and where the offence
charged was the result of excessive force used in self-defence, the degree of
provocation will often be recognised in mitigation.

Personal mitigation: any matters of personal mitigation, including any
advanced medical condition, should be taken into account, but illness
should not, of itself or by way of general principle, militate against the
imposition of a custodial sentence.

Dangerous offenders
When sentencing for a "specified offence" (within the 2003 Act, s.224), a   **K–117**
court must have regard to the dangerous offender provisions and will need
to consider whether the offender meets the test of dangerousness.

Compensation orders
A court must consider making a compensation order in respect of any   **K–118**
personal injury, loss or damage occasioned. Compensation, however, should
benefit, not inflict further harm on, the victim, and any financial recompense from the offender for an assault or other offence against the person
may cause distress. The views of the victim should be made known to the
court and respected and, if appropriate, acknowledged during sentencing.
It should not, in particular, be assumed that a victim does not want
compensation from the offender.

Ancillary orders
In appropriate circumstances, a court should consider whether to impose   **K–119**
an exclusion order, a drinking banning order, an anti-social behaviour order or a football banning order.

Sentencing ranges and starting points
The sentencing ranges and starting points relate to persons convicted fol-   **K–120**
lowing a plea of not guilty, and who do not have a conviction which, by
virtue of the 2003 Act, s.143(2), must be treated as an aggravating factor. A
court should identify the description that most nearly matches the facts of
the offence and this will identify a starting point, from which a provisional
sentence can be reached. The sentencing range is the bracket into which
the provisional sentence will fall after consideration of aggravating and
mitigating factors (although particular circumstances, particular matters of
aggravation or mitigation, or the reduction for a guilty plea may require a
sentence outside of that range). The provisional sentence may then be
reduced by matters of personal mitigation, which may also take it outside
the appropriate sentencing range. A court should give reasons for imposing
a sentence of a different kind or outside the range provided in the
guideline.

Part 2: Offence guidelines

Offences other than common assault (and its racially, etc., aggravated form)

    See subsequent tables.   **K–121**
    Key to factors to be taken into consideration

A: *Dangerous offenders*: where an offence is a "serious offence" or a "specified offence" within the 2003 Act, s.224, a court must consider the imposition of a sentence for public protection. The guideline only applies to offenders who have not been classed as dangerous.

B: *Personal mitigation*: matters of personal mitigation are often highly relevant to sentencing for this offence, and may justify a non-custodial sentence, particularly in the case of a first-time offender or where there is a guilty plea.

C: *Lack of harm*: the expectation is that this offence will involve little or no physical harm, and so sentencing should largely be guided by the level of culpability. The different maximum penalties of the offences under s.38 of the 1861 Act and s.89 of the 1996 Act are reflected in the guideline.

D: *Intention to cause harm*: this offence requires an intention to cause grievous bodily harm, and so the level of culpability is high and a significant custodial sentence should be expected.

E: *Lack of intention to cause harm*: this offence requires the infliction of a wound or the causing of serious harm, and so the difference between it and an offence under s.18 is the culpability of the offender. This significant difference in culpability and the significantly lower maximum penalty are reflected in the guideline.

F: *Level of harm*: the offences under s.20 and s.47 carry the same maximum penalty but the degree of harm required for s.20 is higher. If an offence under s.20 ought to be sentenced as an offence under s.47, the guideline for the latter should be used.

G: *Self-defence*: if the offender used an unreasonable amount of force in self-defence, this might mitigate sentence but, because of the intention, the offence will still be at the higher end of the seriousness scale, and a lengthy custodial sentence would normally be justified, depending on the degree of harm caused.

I: *Public service*: this offence involves an inherent aggravating factor in that the victim was performing a public service.

J: *Consecutive sentences*: if the offender is also convicted of the offence which gave rise to the arrest, the sentences imposed should normally be consecutive.

K: *Additional factors*: only additional aggravating and mitigating factors specifically relevant to this offence are included in the guideline, and a court must always take into account the full list of factors in the guideline on seriousness.

L: *Racial, etc., aggravation*: for racially, *etc.*, aggravated offences, a court should use the guideline to determine the appropriate sentence and then take account of the relevant aggravation.

Common assault (and its racially, etc., aggravated form)

K–122   As the range of relevant factors is wider for these offences, the guideline approaches them differently. The starting point is normally custody when two or more aggravating factors indicating higher culpability are present, it is normally a community order when one such factor is present, and it is normally a fine when no injury is caused. The level of sentence within each category is determined by whether any of the aggravating factors indicating a more than usually serious degree of harm are present. The aggravating factors indicating higher culpability are: (i) use of a weapon to frighten or harm the victim; (ii) the offence was planned or sustained; (iii) head-butting, kicking, biting or attempted strangulation; (iv) the offence was motivated by, or demonstrated, hostility to the victim on account of his or her sexual orientation or disability; (v) the offence was motivated by hostility towards a minority group, or a member or members of it; (vi) the offence involved an abuse of a position of trust; and (vii) the offence was part of a group action. The aggravating factors indicating a more than usually serious degree of harm are: (i) injury; (ii) the victim was particularly vulnerable or providing a service to the public; (iii) additional degradation of the victim; (iv) the offence was committed in the presence of a child; (v) the offender forced entry to the victim's home; (vi) the offender prevented the victim from seeking or obtaining help; and (vii) previous violence or threats to the same victim. The common mitigating factors are: (i) provocation; and (ii) a single push, shove or blow.

Other factors to take into consideration

Dangerous offenders: racially/ religiously aggravated common assault is a **K–123** "specified offence" under the 2003 Act, s.224, and so a court must consider the imposition of a sentence for public protection. The guideline only applies to offenders who have not been classed as dangerous.

Flexibility: the list of aggravating and mitigating factors is not intended to be exhaustive, and a court must always take into account the full list of factors in the guideline on seriousness. In addition, not all aggravating factors carry the same weight, and so flexibility is required to avoid an over-prescriptive approach to when the custody threshold is passed.

Racial, etc., aggravation: for racially,*etc.*, aggravated offences, a court should use the guideline to determine the appropriate sentence and then take account of the relevant aggravation.

Annexes

Annex A sets out the statutory provisions concerning the offences **K–124** covered by the guideline and the Crown Prosecution Service's guidance on those offences. Annex B sets out extracts from the guideline on seriousness listing various general aggravating factors, divided into those indicating higher culpability and those indicating a more than usually serious degree of harm.

Tables

K–125 **Causing grievous bodily harm with intent/ wounding with intent** (*Offences against the Person Act* **1861, s.18) (indictable only (maximum penalty, life imprisonment), serious offence)**

Type/ nature of activity	Starting point	Sentencing range	Additional aggravating and mitigating factors	Other factors
Life-threatening or particularly grave injury, pre-meditated, involving the use of a weapon acquired prior to the offence and carried to the scene with specific intent of injuring victim	13 years' custody	10 to 16 years' custody		
Life-threatening or particularly grave injury, not pre-meditated **or** Pre-meditated, involving the use of a weapon acquired prior to the offence and carried to the scene with specific intent of injuring victim (but no life-threatening or particularly grave injury)	8 years' custody	7 to 10 years' custody	*Mitigating*: provocation	A, D, G, J
Serious injury or permanent disfigurement **or** Pre-meditated **or** Involving the use of a weapon that came to hand at the scene	5 years' custody	4 to 6 years' custody		
Other	4 years' custody	3 to 5 years' custody		

Inflicting grievous bodily harm/ unlawful wounding (*Offences against the Person Act* **1861, s.20) (either way (maximum penalty, 5 years' imprisonment), specified offence)**

Racially/ religiously aggravated inflicting grievous bodily harm/ unlawful wounding (*Crime and Disorder Act* **1998, s.29) (either way (maximum penalty, 7 years' imprisonment), specified offence)**

Type/ nature of activity	Starting point	Sentencing range	Additional aggravating and mitigating factors	Other factors
Particularly grave injury or disfigurement, pre-meditated, weapon used	3 years' custody	2 to 4 years' custody	*Mitigating*: provocation	A, B, E, F, J, K
Pre-meditated, weapon used **or** Particularly grave injury or weapon used	18 months' custody	12 months to 3 years' custody		
Pre-meditated, no weapon	36 weeks' custody	24 weeks to 18 months' custody		
Other, no weapon	24 weeks' custody	community order (high) to 36 weeks' custody		

K–127   **Assault occasioning actual bodily harm** (*Offences against the Person Act* **1861, s.47**) **(either way (maximum penalty, 5 years' imprisonment), specified offence)**

Racially/religiously aggravated assault occasioning actual bodily harm (*Crime and Disorder Act* **1998, s.29**) **(either way (maximum penalty, 7 years' imprisonment), specified offence)**

Type/ nature of activity	Starting point	Sentenc-ing range	Additional aggravating and mitigating factors	Other factors
Pre-meditated **and either** Injuries just short of grievous bodily harm **or** Weapon used	30 months' custody	2 to 4 years' custody	*Mitigating*: provocation; unintended injury	A, B, J, K
Pre-meditated, relatively serious injury	12 months' custody	36 weeks to 2 years' custody		
Pre-meditated, minor non-permanent injury	24 weeks' custody	12 to 36 weeks' custody		
Other, minor non-permanent injury	community order (high)	community order (medium) to 26 weeks' custody		

Assault with intent to resist arrest (*Offences against the Person Act* 1861, **K–128** s.38) **(either way (maximum penalty, 2 years' imprisonment), specified offence)**

Type/ nature of activity	Starting point	Sentencing range	Additional aggravating and mitigating factors	Other factors
Persistent attempt to resist arrest **or** Use of force or threats of force over and above that inherent in offence	36 weeks' custody	24 weeks to 18 months' custody	*Aggravating*: escape; head butting, kicking or biting; picking up item to use as weapon, even if not used *Mitigating*: genuine belief arrest was unlawful	A, C, H, I, J
Minor non-permanent injury	community order (high)	community order (low) to 26 weeks' custody		
No injury	community order (low)	fine to community order (high)		

K–129   **Assault on a constable in the execution of his duty** (*Police Act* **1996,** **s.89**) **(summary only (maximum penalty, 6 months' imprisonment))**

Type/ nature of activity	Starting point	Sentenc-ing range	Additional aggravating and mitigat-ing factors	Other factors
Sustained assault, minor non-permanent injury	18 weeks' custody	com-munity order (high) to 24 weeks' custody	*Aggravating*: escape; head butting, kick-ing or biting; picking up item to use as weapon, even if not used *Mitigating*: genuine belief arrest was unlawful	C, H, J
Minor non-permanent injury	com-munity order (high)	fine to 18 weeks' custody		
No injury	com-munity order (low)	fine to com-munity order (medium)		

K–130   **Common assault** (*Criminal Justice Act* **1988, s.39**) **(summary only (maximum penalty, 6 months' imprisonment))**

Racially/religiously aggravated common assault (*Crime and Disorder Act* **1998, s.29**) **(either way (maximum penalty, 2 years' imprisonment), specified offence)**

See *ante*, K–122, K–123 for guideline.

K. ASSAULTS ON CHILDREN AND CRUELTY TO A CHILD

K–131   The Sentencing Guidelines Council has issued a definitive guideline (i) supplementing the guideline on assaults and other offences against the person (*ante*, K–113 *et seq.*) by detailing additional principles which apply where the victim of the offence was aged 15 or under and (ii) on the offence of cruelty to a child (*CYPA* 1933, s.1(1)). It deals with offenders sentenced on or after March 3, 2008, and only relates to the sentencing of those aged 18 or over.

Part 1: Assaults on children: general principles

Assessing seriousness

K–132   The seriousness of an offence is to be determined by (a) the culpability of the offender and (b) the harm caused, intended or reasonably foreseeable and guidance on whether sentencing thresholds have been reached is provided by the guideline on seriousness. Where an offender has previous convictions, the court must consider whether it should treat any of them as an aggravating factor, having regard to the nature and relevance of each offence and the time that has elapsed since the conviction. The fact that the victim is a child is likely to aggravate the seriousness of the offence where the offender is an adult.

Aggravation

The fact that the victim of an assault is a child will often mean that the of-   **K–133**
fence involves a particularly vulnerable victim. The most relevant aggravating factors are: (i) the victim is particularly vulnerable; (ii) an abuse of power; (iii) an abuse of a position of trust; (iv) an especially serious physical or psychological effect on the victim, even if unintended; (v) the presence of others, *e.g.* relatives, especially other children; and (vi) additional degradation of the victim. Additional aggravating factors are: (i) sadistic behaviour; (ii) the making of threats to prevent the victim reporting the offence; (iii) the deliberate concealment of the victim from the authorities; and (iv) a failure to seek medical help. The location and particular circumstances of the offence may also be relevant aggravating factors.

Mitigation

The defence of lawful chastisement is only available on a charge of com-   **K–134**
mon assault, and where that defence is not available or is not made out, sentencing for the offence should normally be approached in the same way as for any other assault, even where an offender held a genuine belief that his actions amounted to no more than a legitimate form of physical punishment. However, if an offender has been charged with assault occasioning actual bodily harm and the court has found that he only intended to administer lawful chastisement to the child, and that the injury that was inflicted was neither intended nor foreseen by him, there should be a substantial reduction in sentence and a custodial sentence should not normally be imposed. Where the injury was neither intended nor foreseen, and was not even reasonably foreseeable, then a discharge might be appropriate.

Other factors relevant to sentencing

Adverse effect of the sentence on the victim

Imposition of a custodial sentence will often protect a victim from further   **K–135**
harm and anguish, and some children will be less traumatised once they are no longer living with an abusive carer, but where imprisonment of the offender deprives a child victim of his sole or main carer (and may result in the child being taken into care), it may punish and re-victimise the child. Imposing a custodial sentence on the offender may be the only option, but where other sentencing options remain open, the court should take into account the impact that a custodial sentence for the offender might have on the victim. The court also needs to be aware of the progress of any concurrent family proceedings.

Offenders who have primary care responsibilities

Where the offender is the sole or primary carer of the victim or other de-   **K–136**
pendants, this should potentially be taken into account for sentencing purposes, regardless of whether the offender is male or female. In such cases, an immediate custodial sentence may not be appropriate and, subject to a risk assessment, the offender may be able to resume care of or have contact with the victim.

Part 2: Cruelty to a child

Assessing seriousness

K–137 One category of child cruelty is not automatically more serious than another and, in order properly to assess the seriousness of an offence, its precise nature must be established before consideration is given to a range of contingent factors, including the defendant's intent, the length of time over which the cruelty took place, and the degree of physical and psychological harm suffered by the victim.

Culpability

K–138 Culpability should be the initial factor in determining the seriousness of an offence. An offence may be the consequence of a wide range of factors including: (i) sadism; (ii) violence resulting from any number of causes; (iii) a reduced ability to protect a child in the face of aggression from an overbearing partner; (iv) indifference or apathy resulting from low intelligence or induced by alcohol or drug dependence; (v) immaturity or social deprivation resulting in an inability to cope with the pressures of caring for children; and (vi) psychiatric illness. It might also arise as the result of a momentary lack of control by an otherwise responsible and loving carer. The extent to which any of these factors might have contributed to the commission of an offence will be important in determining the culpability of the offender. A court must strike a balance between the need to reflect the serious view which society takes of the ill-treatment of young children and the need to protect those children, and also the pressures upon immature and inadequate parents attempting to cope with the problems of infancy, and the extent to which remorse should influence sentence will always have to be judged in the light of all the circumstances. The normal starting point should be a custodial sentence, the length of which should be influenced by the circumstances surrounding the offence.

Harm

K–139 It is helpful if the indictment clearly states the nature of the offender's conduct, but even where this is clear, difficulties arise in determining the relative seriousness of the different forms of child cruelty. There is however, a significant distinction between cases of wilful ill-treatment which usually involve positive acts of abuse and physical violence, and cases of neglect which are typified by the absence of actions. There is also a distinction between cases involving physical injury, whether resulting directly from an assault or ill-treatment or resulting from a period of abandonment or neglect, and cases where the harm occasioned is exposure to the risk of harm or lack of proper care, attention or supervision. In addition, whether one form of cruelty is worse than another will depend not only on the degree to which the victim suffers as a result but also on the motivation and culpability of the offender.

Aggravating and mitigating factors

K–140 The guideline refers to the guideline on seriousness for general aggravating and mitigating factors. In particular, care should be taken to avoid "double-counting" when an essential element of an offence might, in other circumstances, be an aggravating factor, and the abuse of trust or abuse of power inherent in the offence have been built into the guideline and should

not be treated as aggravating factors. Relevant aggravating factors are
targeting one particular child from the family and the four additional aggravating factors listed under "Assaults on children: general principles"
(*ante*). The sole relevant mitigating factor is seeking medical help or bringing
the situation to the notice of the authorities.

Other factors relevant to sentencing

Long-term psychological harm
The starting points have been calculated to reflect the likelihood of   **K–141**
psychological harm and this cannot be treated as an aggravating factor.
Where there is an especially serious physical or psychological effect on the
victim, even if unintended, this should result in an increased sentence.

Adverse effect of the sentence on the victim
As in Part 1, *ante*.   **K–142**

Offenders who have primary care responsibilities
As in Part 1, *ante*.   **K–143**

Personal mitigation
The most relevant areas of personal mitigation are likely to be: (i) mental   **K–144**
illness/ depression; (ii) inability to cope with the pressures of parenthood;
(iii) lack of support; (iv) sleep deprivation; (v) domination of the offender
by an abusive or stronger partner; (vi) extreme behavioural difficulties in
the child, often coupled with a lack of support; and (vii) inability to secure
assistance or support services in spite of every effort having been made by
the offender. However, some of these factors could be regarded as an
inherent part of caring for children, especially with young children, and so
before they are accepted in mitigation, there must be evidence that these
factors were present to a high degree and had an identifiable and significant impact on the offender's behaviour.

Factors to take into consideration

Dangerous offenders: the offence is a "specified offence" within the *CJA*   **K–145**
2003, s.224, and so a court must consider the imposition of a sentence for
public protection. The guideline only applies to offenders who have not
been classed as dangerous.

Categories of offence: the same starting point applies regardless of which of
the various ways in which the offence can be committed is in point, and it
already assumes an abuse of trust or power and the likelihood of psychological harm, and is designed to reflect the seriousness with which society as a
whole regards these offences.

Additional factors: only additional aggravating and mitigating factors
specifically relevant to this offence are included in the guideline, and a
court must always take into account the full list of factors in the guideline
on seriousness.

Sentencing ranges and starting points

The sentencing ranges and starting points relate to persons convicted fol-   **K–146** lowing a plea of not guilty, and who do not have a conviction which, by virtue of the 2003 Act, s.143(2) (§ 5–54 in the main work), must be treated as an aggravating factor. A court should identify the description that most nearly matches the facts of the offence and this will identify a starting point, from which a provisional sentence can be reached. The sentencing range is the bracket into which the provisional sentence will fall after consideration of aggravating or mitigating factors (although particular circumstances, particular matters of aggravation or mitigation, or the reduction for a guilty plea may require a sentence outside of that range). The provisional sentence may then be reduced by matters of personal mitigation, which may also take it outside the appropriate sentencing range. A court should give reasons for imposing a sentence of a different kind or outside the range provided in the guideline.

Where there has been (i) serious cruelty over a period of time, (ii) serious long-term neglect, or (iii) a failure to protect a child from either of these, the starting point is six years' custody and the sentencing range is five to nine years' custody.

Where there has been (i) a series of assaults (the more serious the individual assaults and the longer the period over which they are perpetrated, the more serious the offence), (ii) protracted neglect or ill-treatment (the longer the period of ill-treatment or neglect and the longer the period over which it takes place, the more serious the offence), or (iii) a failure to protect a child from either of these, the starting point is three years' custody and the sentencing range is two to five years' custody.

Where there has been (i) an assault resulting in injuries consistent with assault occasioning actual bodily harm, (ii) more than one incident of neglect or ill-treatment (but not amounting to long-term behaviour), (iii) a single incident of long-term abandonment or regular incidents of short-term abandonment (the longer the period of long-term abandonment or the greater the number of incidents of short-term abandonment, the more serious the offence), or (iv) a failure to protect a child from any of these, the starting point is 36 weeks' custody and the sentencing range is 26 weeks' to two years' custody.

Where there has been (i) short-term neglect or ill-treatment, (ii) a single incident of short-term abandonment, or (iii) a failure to protect a child from any of these, the starting point is 12 weeks' custody and the sentencing range is a community order (low) to 26 weeks' custody.

L. SENTENCING IN MAGISTRATES' COURTS

Introduction

K–147   The Sentencing Guidelines Council has issued a guideline on offences for which sentence is frequently imposed in magistrates' courts when dealing with adult offenders, which replaces the guidelines which were effective from January 1, 2004. The foreword and introduction state that they are to apply to all relevant cases appearing for allocation (mode of trial) or for sentence on or after August 4, 2008, not only in magistrates' courts, but also in the Crown Court when dealing with appeals against sentence and when sentencing for summary only offences. The guideline should be consulted when dealing with an either-way offence for which there is no plea or an indication of a not guilty plea, since they will be relevant to the

mode of trial decision, and where an offence is included in this guideline, it
supersedes the equivalent part of the mode of trial guidelines in Part V.51
of the consolidated criminal practice direction (§ 1–75u in the main work).
The guideline will also be relevant to decisions as to committal for sentence.

The Sentencing Guidelines Council has issued an update to these
guidelines to be implemented on January 5, 2009. Changes are made to
Parts 1 (indices), 3 (offence guidelines) and 5 (explanatory material). The
effect of the changes to Part 3 is (i) to include extracts from the guideline
on breach of an anti-social behaviour order (*post*, K–196 *et seq.*) and the
guideline on theft and burglary in a building other than a dwelling (*post*,
K–209 *et seq.*) in these guidelines in the appropriate places, and (ii) to make a
clarificatory amendment to the existing guideline for burglary in a dwelling.
Consequential amendments are made to the section in Part 5 that relates to
ancillary orders, in respect of anti-social behaviour orders, and an amendment is also made to that section in respect of orders disqualifying an offender
from driving, to reflect recent case law.

An update implemented on August 4, 2008, made equivalent changes to
Part 3 in relation to the guideline on causing death by driving (*post*, K–185
et seq.) and modified Part 5 in respect of explanatory material relating to
dangerous offenders (to take account of changes made by the *CJIA* 2008).

Recommendations

The following recommendations are sentence recommendations where   **K–148**
the starting points are based on a first time offender who has pleaded not
guilty. However, the guideline makes plain that they are to be used by
magistrates in making decisions as to whether or not an offender should be
tried or sentenced in the magistrates' court or the Crown Court. What is set
out below is confined to that which is material to the latter decision. It follows, therefore, that the full range of recommendations is not necessarily
set out. For example, in the case of burglary of a dwelling, for a case involving an unforced entry with property of low value being stolen and no aggravating features, the top end of the recommended range is 12 weeks'
custody, which is well within the maximum available to a magistrates' court.
Any description of offence which is of a less serious nature than the descriptions set out below may, therefore, be taken to be suitable for summary
trial.

Whilst the guideline itself lists aggravating and mitigating features for all
the offences, these are only set out below where the presence or absence of
such features is relevant to the decision as to the appropriate court for trial
or sentence.

Burglary in a dwelling

The guideline recommends —   **K–149**
   (i) a starting point of 12 weeks' custody and a range of sentence from a
       high level community order to sentence in the Crown Court for a
       case of forced entry where the goods stolen were not of high value
       and without aggravating features;
  (ii) sentence in the Crown Court where the goods stolen were of high
       value and any aggravating feature was present.

Particular aggravating features mentioned are: (*as indicating higher culpa-*   **K–150**
bility) ransacking, professionalism, a victim deliberately targeted, *e.g.* out of
spite, the carrying of housebreaking implements or weapons; (*as indicating*

greater degree of harm) occupier at home or returning home during burglary, goods stolen being of sentimental value.

As to aggravating features, see *R. v. Saw, post,* § K–441.

Handling stolen goods

K–151   The guideline recommends —

    (i) a starting point of 12 weeks' custody and a range of sentence from six weeks' custody to sentence in the Crown Court for sophisticated offending or the presence of at least two aggravating features;

    (ii) sentence in the Crown Court where the offence was committed in the context of a business, the offender acts as an organiser/ distributor of the proceeds of crime, the offender makes himself available to other criminals as willing to handle the proceeds of thefts or burglaries, the offending was highly organised or professional, or the original offence was particularly serious, *e.g.* armed robbery.

K–152   Particular aggravating features mentioned are: (*as indicating higher culpability*) closeness of offender to primary offence, which may be geographical (arising from presence at or near the primary offence) or temporal (where offender instigated primary offence or, soon after, provided safe haven or route for disposal), high level of profit made or expected; (*as indicating greater degree of harm*) seriousness of the primary offence, including domestic burglary, high (including sentimental) value of goods; threats of violence or abuse of power by offender over others, such as an adult commissioning criminal activity by children or a drug dealer pressurising addicts to steal to fund their habit.

Going equipped for theft

K–153   The guideline recommends a starting point of a high level community order and a range of a medium level community order to sentence in the Crown Court in the case of possession of items for burglary or robbery.

False statements/representations to obtain social security benefits

K–154   The guideline recommends —

    (i) a starting point of 12 weeks' custody and a range of a medium level community order to sentence in the Crown Court for a claim that was fraudulent from the start where the amount obtained exceeded £5,000, but was less than £20,000;

    (ii) sentence in the Crown Court for a claim that was fraudulent from the start and involved large-scale, professional offending.

Vehicle licence/registration fraud (Vehicle Excise and Registration Act 1994, s.44)

K–155   The guideline recommends sentence in the Crown Court in the case of (a) use of number plates from another vehicle, or (b) the forging or altering of licence/ number plates for sale to another.

Assault occasioning actual bodily harm and racially/religiously aggravated versions

K–156   The guideline recommends —

    (i) a starting point of 24 weeks' custody and a range of 12 weeks' custody to sentence in the Crown Court for a pre-meditated assault resulting in minor, non-permanent injury;

    (ii) sentence in the Crown Court for a pre-meditated assault either resulting in relatively serious injury or involving the use of a weapon.

Inflicting grievous bodily harm/wounding and racially/religiously aggravated versions

The guideline recommends —   **K–157**

(i) a starting point of 24 weeks' custody and and a range of a high level community order to sentence in the Crown Court for "other assault" where no weapon has been used;

(ii) a starting point of sentence in the Crown Court and a range of 24 weeks' custody to sentence in the Crown Court for a pre-meditated assault where no weapon has been used;

(iii) sentence in the Crown Court for a pre-meditated assault where a weapon has been used or for any other assault where particularly grave injury results or a weapon has been used.

Assault with intent to resist arrest

The guideline recommends a starting point of sentence in the Crown   **K–158**
Court and a range from 24 weeks' custody to sentence in the Crown Court.

Threats to kill

The guideline recommends sentence in the Crown Court for repeated   **K–159**
threats or a threat accompanied by a visible weapon.

Firearm, carrying in public place (Firearms Act 1968, s.19)

The guideline recommends (but note that certain offences under this sec-   **K–160**
tion are triable only on indictment (not mentioned in the guideline) and certain offences are triable only summarily, as to which, see § 24–57 in the main work)—

(i) a starting point of a high level community order and a range of a medium level community order to sentence in the Crown Court for the carrying of an imitation firearm or an unloaded shot gun without ammunition;

(ii) sentence in the Crown Court for the carrying of a loaded shot gun or for the carrying of a shot gun or any other firearm together with ammunition for it.

Bladed article/offensive weapon (possession of)

The guideline recommends—   **K–161**

(i) a starting point of six weeks' custody and a range of a high level community order to sentence in the Crown Court where the weapon was not used to threaten or cause fear but the offence was committed in dangerous circumstances;

(ii) sentence in the Crown Court where the weapon was used to threaten or cause fear and the offence was committed in dangerous circumstances.

Cruelty to a child

The guideline recommends —   **K–162**

(i) a starting point of sentence in the Crown Court and a range of 26 weeks' custody to sentence in the Crown Court for an assault (assaults) resulting in injuries consistent with actual bodily harm, more than one incident of neglect or ill-treatment (but not amounting to long-term behaviour), a single incident of long-term abandonment or regular incidents of short-term abandonment (the longer the period of abandonment or the greater the number of incidents of short-term abandonment, the more serious the offence) or failure to protect a child from any of the foregoing;

(ii) sentence in the Crown Court for a series of assaults, protracted neglect or ill-treatment, serious cruelty over a period of time or failure to protect a child from any of the foregoing.

Affray

K–163   The guideline recommends 18 weeks' custody as a starting point and a range of 12 weeks' custody to sentence in the Crown Court in the case of a fight involving a weapon or the throwing of objects or conduct causing risk of serious injury.

Harassment (putting people in fear of violence) (Protection from Harassment Act 1997, s.4), and the racially/religiously aggravated version

K–164   The guideline recommends —

(i) a starting point of 18 weeks' custody and a range of 12 weeks' custody to sentence in the Crown Court for a case involving deliberate threats or persistent action over a longer period or an intention to cause a fear of violence;

(ii) sentence in the Crown Court for "sexual threats, vulnerable person targeted".

Breach of a protective order (other than in a domestic context)

K–165   The guideline recommends —

(i) a starting point of sentence in the Crown Court and a range of 26 weeks' custody to sentence in the Crown Court for more than one breach involving some violence and/or significant physical or psychological harm to the victim;

(ii) sentence in the Crown Court for a breach (one or more) involving significant physical violence and significant physical or psychological harm to the victim.

Witness intimidation

K–166   The guideline recommends —

(i) a starting point of 18 weeks' custody and a range of 12 weeks' custody to sentence in the Crown Court for conduct amounting to a threat, staring at, approaching or following witnesses, talking about the case, trying to alter or stop evidence;

(ii) sentence in the Crown Court for threats of violence to witnesses and/or their families or for deliberately seeking out witnesses.

Sexual assault (Sexual Offences Act 2003, ss.3, 7)

K–167   See Part 2 of the sexual offences guideline, *ante*, K–93, and, in particular, the table at K–94.

Child prostitution and pornography

K–168   The guideline recommends that these offences should normally be dealt

with in the Crown Court but that there may be rare cases of non-penetrative
activity involving a victim aged 16 or 17 where the offender's involvement
is minimal and not for gain in which a custodial sentence within the power
of a magistrates' court may be appropriate.

Exploitation of prostitution (Sexual Offences Act 2003, ss.52, 53)
See Parts 6B to 6D of the sexual offences guideline, *ante*, K–103, and, in   **K-169**
particular, the table at K–104.

Exposure (Sexual Offences Act 2003, s.66)
See Part 5 of the sexual offences guideline, *ante*, K–99, and, in particular,   **K-170**
the table at K–100.

Voyeurism (Sexual Offences Act 2003, s.67)
See Part 5 of the sexual offences guideline, *ante*, K–99, and, in particular,   **K-171**
the table at K–100.

Keeping a brothel used for prostitution (Sexual Offences Act 1956, s.33A)
See Parts 6B to 6D of the sexual offences guideline, *ante*, K–103, and, in   **K-172**
particular, the table at K–104.

Indecent photographs of children
See Part 6A of the sexual offences guideline, *ante*, K–101, and, in particu-   **K-173**
lar, the table at K–102.

Failure to comply with the notification requirements applicable to sex offenders
The guideline recommends a starting point of 18 weeks' custody and a   **K-174**
range of six weeks' custody to sentence in the Crown Court for a deliberate
failure to comply or the supply of information known to be false accompanied by long-period of non-compliance or attempts to avoid
detection.

Drugs (possession of Class A)
The guideline recommends —   **K-175**
(i) a starting point of a high level community order and a range of
sentence from a medium level community order to sentence in the
Crown Court for amounts of more than six wraps or tablets;
(ii) sentence in the Crown Court for possession in a prison whether by a
prisoner or another.

Drugs (production, supply, possession with intent to supply, Class A)
The guideline recommends that such cases should normally be dealt with   **K-176**
in the Crown Court, although there may be rare cases involving non-
commercial supply (*e.g.* between equals) of small amounts (*e.g.* one wrap or
tablet) in which a custodial sentence within the powers of a magistrates' court
would be appropriate.

Drugs (supply, possession with intent to supply, Class B and Class C)
The guideline recommends sentence in the Crown Court for any supply   **K-177**

in prison and for any supply other than small scale retail supply or sharing between equals on a non-commercial basis.

Drugs (cultivation of cannabis)

K–178   The guideline recommends sentence in the Crown Court for commercial cultivation.

Dangerous driving

K–179   The guideline recommends sentence in the Crown Court for (a) prolonged bad driving involving deliberate disregard for the safety of others, (b) incidents involving excessive speed or showing off, especially on busy roads or in a built up area, by a disqualified driver, or while driver was being pursued by the police.

Aggravated vehicle-taking (damage to property other than the vehicle taken in accident or to the vehicle)

K–180   The guideline recommends sentence in the Crown Court if the vehicle was taken as part of a burglary or from private premises and the damage caused was valued at in excess of £5,000.

Aggravated vehicle-taking (dangerous driving or accident causing injury)

K–181   The guideline recommends sentence in the Crown Court if there was a course of prolonged bad driving involving deliberate disregard for the safety of others.

Arson

K–182   The guideline recommends sentence in the Crown Court in the case of "significant" damage.

Criminal damage (not arson) and racially/religiously aggravated version of offence

K–183   The guideline recommends sentence in the Crown Court if the value of the damage done was in excess of £10,000.

Identity documents (possession of false or of another's improperly obtained) (Identity Cards Act 2006, s.25(5))

K–184   The guideline recommends —
   (i) a starting point of 12 weeks' custody and a range of a six weeks' custody to sentence in the Crown Court for a small number of documents where there is no evidence of dealing;
   (ii) sentence in the Crown Court for "considerable number of documents possessed, evidence of involvement in larger operation".

M. Causing Death by Driving

The Sentencing Guidelines Council has issued a guideline on the offences   **K–185**
of causing death by dangerous driving (*RTA* 1988, s.1), causing death by
careless driving when under the influence of drink or drugs or having
failed without reasonable excuse either to provide a specimen for analysis
or to permit the analysis of a blood sample (*ibid.*, s.3A), causing death by
careless or inconsiderate driving (*ibid.*, s.2B) and causing death by driving
while unlicensed, disqualified or uninsured (*ibid.*, s.3ZB). The guideline applies to offenders aged 18 or over who are sentenced on or after August 4,
2008, and is based on first-time offenders convicted after trial.

The guideline has an introduction and four parts. Part A sets out factors
relating to the assessment of seriousness, Part B relates to ancillary orders,
Part C contains explanatory material relating to sentencing ranges and
starting points, and a description of the decision making process, and Part
D contains the offence guidelines. The introduction also refers to Annex A
which sets out the statutory definitions of dangerous driving, careless driving and inconsiderate driving, and gives examples.

The introduction makes plain that since the causing of death is common
to all offences covered by the guideline, the factor that is going to have the
greatest weight in determining a starting point for any particular offence
will be the culpability of the offender and, accordingly, the primary task for
the court (apart from s.3ZB cases) will be an evaluation of the quality of the
driving involved and the degree of danger that it foreseeably created. The
degree of intoxication must also be considered where this is an element of
the offence. The introduction further points out that the guideline draws a
distinction between those factors of an offence that are intrinsic to the quality of the driving ("determinants of seriousness") and those which, while
they aggravate the offence (*e.g.* more than one death), are not.

Part A: Assessing seriousness

Determinants of seriousness

There are five determinants of seriousness, for each of which the   **K–186**
guideline sets out examples: (i) the offender's awareness of risk (*e.g.* typified
by a prolonged, persistent and deliberate course of bad driving), (ii) where
the presence of alcohol or drugs is not an element of the offence, the effect of
consumption of any alcohol or drugs (which includes a failure to supply a
specimen for analysis (unless inherent in the offence or charged separately)
and the consumption of legal drugs where this impaired the offender's ability
to drive and the offender knew or should have known about the likelihood of
impairment), (iii) whether the offender was driving at an inappropriate speed,
(iv) whether the offender behaved in a seriously culpable manner, and (v) the
identity of the victim (*e.g.* failing to have regard to, and to take extra care
when driving near, vulnerable road users such as cyclists, motorcyclists, horse
riders, pedestrians and those working in the road).

Examples of (iv), *ante*, are aggressive driving, driving whilst using a hand-
held mobile telephone, driving whilst the driver's attention is avoidably
distracted (*e.g.* reading or adjusting the controls of electronic equipment),
driving when knowingly suffering from a medical or physical condition that
significantly impairs the offender's driving skills (including failure to take
prescribed medication), driving when knowingly deprived of adequate sleep

or rest, particularly where this is caused by commercial concerns, and driving a poorly maintained or dangerously loaded vehicle, again, particularly where this is caused by commercial concerns. A distinction is drawn between ordinary avoidable distractions and gross avoidable distractions (*e.g.* reading or composing a text message over a period of time), but where the degree of impairment is so serious that it is used to determine whether the offence is based on dangerous or careless driving, care must be taken to avoid double counting.

Aggravating and mitigating factors

K–187   Once the court has considered the determinants of seriousness, it must then consider whether any aggravating or mitigating factors affect culpability so as to increase or decrease the starting point, or move the offence into a different sentencing range. When assessing seriousness, the court should have regard to the full list of aggravating and mitigating factors set out in the guideline on seriousness (*ante*, § K–13) and the particular aggravating and mitigating factors applicable to each offence, a key to which is set out, *post*:

Key to aggravating factors:

K–188   1   Previous convictions for motoring offences, particularly offences that involve bad driving or the consumption of excessive alcohol or drugs before driving.

2   Previous convictions for motoring offences, particularly offences that involve bad driving.

3   Previous convictions for motoring offences, whether involving bad driving or an offence of the same kind that forms part of the present conviction.

4   More than one person killed as a result of the offence. Where the number of deaths is high and that was reasonably foreseeable, this is likely to provide sufficient justification for moving an offence into the next highest sentencing range.

5   Serious injury to one or more victims, in addition to the death(s).

6   Disregard of warnings.

7   Other offences committed at the same time, such as driving other than in accordance with the terms of a valid licence, driving while disqualified, *etc.*

8   Irresponsible behaviour such as failing to stop, falsely claiming that one of the victims was responsible, or trying to throw the victim off the car by swerving in order to escape.

9   Irresponsible behaviour such as failing to stop or falsely claiming that one of the victims was responsible for the collision.

10   Driving off in an attempt to avoid detection or apprehension.

Key to mitigating factors:

K–189   11   Alcohol or drugs consumed unwittingly.

12	Offender was seriously injured in the collision, but the greater the driver's fault, the less effect this factor should have on mitigation.
13	The victim was a close friend or relative, but the greater the driver's fault, the less effect this factor should have on mitigation.
14	Actions of the victim or a third party contributed significantly to the likelihood of a collision occurring and/or death resulting.
15	Actions of the victim or a third party contributed to the commission of the offence.
16	The offender's lack of driving experience contributed significantly to the likelihood of a collision occurring and/or death resulting.
17	The offender's lack of driving experience contributed to the commission of the offence.
18	The driving was in response to a proven and genuine emergency falling short of a defence.
19	The offender genuinely believed that he or she was insured or licensed to drive.

Personal mitigation

If the offender can show that he previously had a good driving record, or   **K–190**
can demonstrate remorse or that he provided direct and positive assistance
to a victim at the scene of the accident, this may justify a reduction in
sentence.

Part B: Ancillary orders

An order disqualifying an offender from driving is usually a mandatory   **K–191**
requirement when sentencing for these offences. In principle, the minimum period of disqualification should either equate to the length of the
custodial sentence imposed or the relevant statutory minimum disqualification period, whichever results in the longer period of disqualification.

The court may also consider whether to impose an order depriving the
offender of property, *e.g.*, a vehicle.

Part D: Offence guidelines

Causing death by dangerous driving

There are three levels of seriousness which relate predominantly to the   **K–192**
standard of driving.

Level 1 (starting point 8 years, sentencing range of 7–14 years): driving
that involved a deliberate decision to ignore (or a flagrant disregard for)
the rules of the road and an apparent disregard for the great danger being
caused to others. Determinants of seriousness (as identified *ante*) that will fix
a case at this level include (a) a prolonged, persistent and deliberate course of
bad driving, (b) consumption of substantial amounts of alcohol or drugs leading to gross impairment, and/or (c) a group of determinants of seriousness
which in isolation or smaller number would place the offence in level 2. The
presence of both (a) and (b), particularly if accompanied by aggravating factors will move the offence towards the top of the sentencing range.

Level 2 (starting point 5 years, sentencing range of 4–7 years): driving that created a *substantial* risk of danger. Determinants of seriousness that will fix a case at this level include greatly excessive speed, racing or competitive driving, gross avoidable distraction, driving whilst ability to drive is impaired as a result of consumption of alcohol or drugs, failing to take prescribed medication or a known medical condition, or a group of determinants of seriousness which in isolation or smaller number would place the offence in level 3.

Level 3 (starting point 3 years, sentencing range of 2–5 years): driving that created a *significant* risk of danger. Relevant determinants of seriousness include driving above the speed limit or at a speed that is inappropriate for the prevailing conditions, driving when knowingly deprived of adequate sleep or rest or knowing that the vehicle has a dangerous defect or is poorly maintained or is dangerously loaded, a brief but obvious danger arising from a seriously dangerous manoeuvre, driving whilst avoidably distracted, or failing to have proper regard to vulnerable road users.

Additional aggravating and mitigating factors applicable to sentencing for this offence: 1, 4–8, 10–13, 16, 17 (as to which, see the key, *ante*).

Causing death by careless driving when under the influence of drink or drugs etc.

The legal limit of alcohol is 35µg breath (80mg in blood and 107mg in urine)	Careless/ inconsiderate driving arising from momentary inattention with no aggravating factors	Other cases of careless/ inconsiderate driving	Careless/ inconsiderate driving falling not far short of dangerousness
Level 1 71µg or above of alcohol/ high quantity of drugs OR deliberate non-provision of specimen where evidence of serious impairment	Starting point 6 years Sentencing range 5–10 years	Starting point 7 years Sentencing range 6–12 years	Starting point 8 years Sentencing range 7–14 years
Level 2 51-70µg of alcohol/ moderate quantity of drugs OR deliberate non-provision of specimen	Starting point 4 years Sentencing range 3–7 years	Starting point 5 years Sentencing range 4–8 years	Starting point 6 years Sentencing range 5–9 years
Level 3 35-50µg of alcohol/ minimum quantity of drugs OR test refused because of honestly held but unreasonable belief	Starting point 18 months Sentencing range 26 weeks–4 years	Starting point 3 years Sentencing range 2–5 years	Starting point 4 years Sentencing range 3–6 years

Additional aggravating and mitigating factors applicable to sentencing for this offence: 1, 4, 5, 7, 9, 11–14, 18 (as to which, see the key, *ante*).

Causing death by careless or inconsiderate driving

There are three levels of seriousness defined by the degree of carelessness involved in the standard of driving. A fine is unlikely to be an appropriate sentence for this offence. The most likely requirements to be included in a community order are unpaid work requirements, activity requirements, programme requirements and curfew requirements.

Level 1 (starting point 15 months, sentencing range of 36 weeks–3 years): careless or inconsiderate driving falling not far short of dangerous driving.

Level 2 (starting point 36 weeks, sentencing range of community order (high)–2 years): other cases of careless or inconsiderate driving.

Level 3 (starting point community order (medium), sentencing range (community order (low)–community order (high)): careless or inconsiderat driving arising from momentary inattention with no aggravating feature Examples include misjudging the speed of a vehicle or turning without se ing an oncoming vehicle because of restricted visibility.

Additional aggravating and mitigating factors applicable to sentencing fo this offence: 2, 4, 5, 7, 9, 11, 12, 14, 15, 17 (as to which, see the key, *ante*)

Causing death by driving while unlicensed, disqualified or uninsured

K–195   A fine is unlikely to be an appropriate sentence for this offence.

Level 1 (starting point 12 months, sentencing range of 36 weeks–2 years (i) the offender was disqualified from driving or (ii) the offender wa unlicensed or uninsured and there are two or more aggravating feature from the list, *post*.

Level 2 (starting point 26 weeks, sentencing range of community orde (high)–36 weeks): the offender was unlicensed or uninsured and there wa at least one aggravating factor from the list, *post*.

Level 3 (starting point community order (medium), sentencing range (community order (low)–community order (high)): the offender wa unlicensed or uninsured, with no aggravating factors.

Additional aggravating and mitigating factors applicable to sentencing fo this offence: 3, 4, 5, 9, 11, 12, 17, 19 (as to which, see the key, *ante*).

N. Breach of an Anti-Social Behaviour Order

Summary

K–196   The Sentencing Guidelines Council has issued a guideline on the senten(ing of offenders convicted of breaching an anti-social behaviour order. applies to the sentencing of adult and young offenders, who are sentence on or after January 5, 2009, and is based on first-time offenders (*i.e.* in r(spect of adult offenders, those who do not have a previous conviction fo breach of an anti-social behaviour order and, in respect of young offenders, have its usual meaning) convicted after trial. Since the sentencing framewor for offenders under 18 is significantly different from that for older offender the guidance for young offenders is in the form of principles (see Part E, *post* It is noted that regard should also be had to the approach to sentencing fo breaches of orders set out in the guideline on new sentences (*ante*, K–28 seq.) and the guideline on breach of a protective order (*ante*, K–81).

The guideline is in five parts. Part A sets out section 1(10), and sun marises the effect of section 1(11), of the *CDA* 1998 (§ 5–881 in the mai work), Part B is an introduction, Part C sets out factors relating to the a: sessment of seriousness, Part D contains explanatory material relating sentencing ranges and starting points, a description of the decision makin process, and the sentencing guideline for adult offenders, and Part E se out sentencing principles in relation to young offenders.

Part B: Introduction

K–197   The main aim of sentencing for breach of an order is to achieve t purpose of the order. When sentencing, the primary consideration shou therefore be to reflect the harassment, alarm or distress involved, with t fact that it constituted a breach of a court order (and the consequent har

aused by the undermining of public confidence in the effective administra-
ion of justice) being a secondary consideration.

'art C: Assessing seriousness

This must be assessed by considering the offender's culpability in com-   **K–198**
nitting the offence and the harm which the offence caused, was intended to
ause, or might foreseeably have caused. In order properly to assess the
eriousness of a breach, a court needs to be aware of the purpose of the or-
ler and the context in which it was made. To this end, Annex A sum-
narises the key principles and considerations applicable when making an
›rder. Whereas a breach may be of one or more prohibitions in an order,
he approach to sentencing should be based on an assessment of the serious-
iess of the harm arising from the breach (or intended by the offender)
ather than the number of prohibitions not complied with.

:ulpability and harm

When determining the seriousness of a breach, the court will need to   **K–199**
onsider (a) the degree to which the offender intended to breach the order,
ind (b) the degree to which the offender intended to cause the harm that
·esulted (or could have resulted).

Relevance of the originating conduct

As stated in previous guidelines, the original conduct that led to the mak-   **K–200**
ng of an order is relevant in so far as it indicates the level of harm caused
ind whether this was intended. High culpability and/ or harm may be
ndicated if the breach continues a pattern of behaviour against an identifi-
.ble victim, but the offence may be less serous if there is little connection
)etween the breach and the behaviour that the order was aimed at. The
ourt should examine the prohibitions of the order itself (particularly those
n older orders made without the benefit of the guidance set out in Annex
\), and their necessity and reasonableness in the circumstances.

3reach of an interim order

Breach of such an order is as serious as breach of a final order, and the   **K–201**
ame approach to sentencing should be taken. If the hearing regarding the
inal order can be brought forward, this should be done so that the two is-
ues can be considered together, but sentencing for the interim breach
hould not be delayed for this purpose and should take place as soon as
)ossible. The court should also consider the extent to which an urgent
ieed for specific interim prohibitions was originally demonstrated, or if the
nterim order was sought principally in order to obtain additional time to
›repare a case for the full hearing.

3reach that also constitutes another criminal offence

If the substantive offence only has been charged, the fact that it also con-   **K–202**
titutes breach of an anti-social behaviour order should be treated as an ag-
;ravating factor.

If breach of the order only has been charged, the sentence should reflect
he full circumstances of the breach, which will include the conduct that
ould have been charged as a substantive offence.

Where breach of the order also constitutes another offence with a lower maximum penalty, that penalty is an element to be considered in the interests of proportionality, although the court will not be limited by it.

Aggravating and mitigating factors

K–203 For ease of reference, Annex B sets out the aggravating and mitigating factors in the guideline on seriousness (*ante*, K–13 *et seq.*) that might increase or mitigate the seriousness of an offence. Additional aggravating and mitigating factors are identified in the guideline (*post*).

Personal mitigation

K–204 This is particularly relevant to breach of an anti-social behaviour order since compliance depends on an ability to understand its terms and make rational decisions. Sentence may be mitigated where the offender has a lower level of understanding due to mental health issues or learning difficulties, was acting under the influence of an older or more experienced offender or has complied with an individual support order or intervention order imposed at the same time as the anti-social behaviour order.

Part D: Sentencing guideline—adult offenders

K–205 There are three levels of seriousness:

(i) *serious harm caused or intended*: examples may involve the use of violence, significant threats or intimidation, or the targeting of individuals or groups of people in a manner that leads to a fear of violence;

(ii) *lesser degree of harm intended or likely*: examples may include lesser degrees of threats or intimidation, the use of seriously abusive language or causing more than minor damage to property;

(iii) *no harm caused or intended*: examples may involve being drunk or begging, the prohibited use of public transport, or entry into a prohibited area, provided there is no evidence that harassment, alarm or distress was caused or intended.

K–206 The suggested starting points, *post*, are based on the assumption that the offender had the highest level of culpability (*i.e.* he intended the breach). Care needs to be taken to ensure that there is no double counting when an element of the breach determines the level of seriousness where it might in other circumstances be an aggravating factor. In the most serious cases involving repeat offending and a breach causing serious harassment, together with the presence of several aggravating factors such as the use of violence, a sentence beyond the highest range will be justified.

A conditional discharge is not available as a sentence for this offence.

Nature of failure and harm	Starting point	Sentencing range
Serious harassment, alarm or distress has been caused or where such harm was intended	26 weeks' custody	Custody threshold–2 years' custody

Nature of failure and harm	Starting point	Sentencing range
Lesser degree of harassment, alarm or distress, where such harm was intended, or where it would have been likely if the offender had not been apprehended	6 weeks' custody	Community order (medium)–26 weeks' custody
No harassment, alarm or distress was actually caused by the breach and none was intended by the offender	Community order (low)	Fine (Band B)–community order (medium)

Additional aggravating factors: **K–207**
  (i) offender has a history of disobedience to court orders;
  (ii) breach was committed immediately or shortly after the order was made;
  (iii) breach was committed subsequent to earlier breach proceedings arising from the same order;
  (iv) targeting of a person the order was made to protect or a witness in the original proceedings.
   Additional mitigating factors:
  (i) breach occurred after a long period of compliance;
  (ii) the prohibition(s) breached was/were not fully understood, especially where an interim order was made without notice.

Part E: Sentencing guideline—young offenders
It is noted that the principles covered in Part C apply equally to young   **K–208**
offenders.
Apart from those cases where the court is bound to make a referral order, in less serious cases, such as where the breach has not involved any harassment, alarm or distress, a fine may be appropriate if it will be paid by the offender; otherwise a reparation order. In most cases, however, the appropriate sentence will be a community sentence. The custody threshold should be set at a significantly higher level than for adults, and will usually not be crossed unless the breach involves serious harassment alarm or distress (as to which, see the levels of seriousness, *ante*). Exceptionally, the custody threshold may also be crossed where a youth is being sentenced for more than one offence of breach (committed on separate occasions within a short period) involving a lesser but substantial degree of harassment, alarm or distress. Even where the custody threshold is crossed, the court should normally impose a community sentence in preference to a detention and training order and custody should be used only as a last resort. Where custody is unavoidable, the starting point for sentencing should be four months' detention, with a range of up to 12 months. Where the youth is being sentenced for more than one breach involving serious harassment, alarm or distress, however, the sentence may go beyond that range.
Factors likely to aggravate or mitigate a breach are the same as the ad-

ditional factors listed in the guideline for adult offenders (*ante*) and th
principles relating to personal mitigation (*ante*) also apply. In addition, pee
pressure and lack of parental support may justify mitigation of sentence.

When imposing a community sentence, a court must consider wha
requirements will best prevent further offending and the individual circum
stances of the offender, including his particular stage of intellectual o
emotional maturity. Any requirements imposed must be compatible botl
with each other and with the prohibitions of the anti-social behaviour or
der, if it remains in force, and the combination of both must not be s
onerous as to make further breaches likely.

O. Theft and Burglary in a Building Other Than a Dwelling

Summary

K–209   The Sentencing Guidelines Council has issued a guideline on thes
offences. The guideline applies only to the sentencing of offenders aged 1
and over, who are sentenced on or after January 5, 2009, and is based o
first-time offenders convicted after trial.

The guideline is in five parts. Part A sets out the statutory provisions re
lating to the offences, Part B sets out factors relating to the assessment o
seriousness, Part C relates to ancillary orders, Part D contains explanator
material relating to sentencing ranges and starting points, and a descrip
tion of the decision making process, and Part E contains the offenc
guidelines.

Part A: Statutory provisions

K–210   In addition to setting out the relevant statutory provisions, the mode o
trial and the maximum penalties, Part A states that (i) in relation to bur
glary, the guideline relates solely to cases in which an offender enters
building other than a dwelling as a trespasser with intent to steal or, havin
entered a building as a trespasser, actually goes on to steal, and (ii) th
forms of theft covered by the guideline are theft in breach of trust, theft i
a dwelling, theft from persons, and theft from shops; but that (iii) th
principles in Parts B and C are of general application and likely to be of as
sistance where a court is sentencing for any other form of theft.

Part B: Assessing seriousness

K–211   This must be assessed by considering the offender's culpability in com
mitting the offence and the harm which the offence caused, was intended t
cause, or might foreseeably have caused. When assessing the harm caused
the starting point should be the loss suffered by the victim. However, th
monetary value might not reflect the full extent of the harm and the cour
should take into account the impact of the offence on the particular victin
(*e.g.* where the value of the loss is high in proportion to the victim's financia
circumstances), any harm to a person other than the immediate victim, an
any harm in the form of public concern or erosion of public confidence.

Aggravating and mitigating factors which may affect the seriousness c
the offence must be considered, including those identified in the guidelin
on seriousness (*ante*, K–13 *et seq.*) (and set out in Annex A) and the additiona
factors indentified in each offence guideline. Since the suggested startin
points and sentencing ranges are based on the assumption that the offende
was motivated by greed or a desire to live beyond his means, in order to avoi

ouble counting, such a motivation should not be treated as a factor that
ncreases culpability. The aggravating factors from the seriousness guideline
nost relevant to these offences are planning, offenders operating in groups or
angs and deliberate targeting of vulnerable victims, and the most relevant
ggravating factors indicating a more than usually serious degree of harm are
articularly vulnerable victims, high levels of gain and the high value (includ-
1g sentimental value) of property to the victim or substantial consequential
oss.

The court must also consider the following matters of personal mitiga-
on: return of stolen property (depending on voluntariness and timeliness
f return), whether the offender has been motivated by addiction (in which
ase, while seriousness will not be mitigated, it may be appropriate to
npose a drug rehabilitation requirement, alcohol treatment requirement
r activity or supervision requirement, as part of a community or suspended
entence order), and whether the offender has been motivated by despera-
on or need (which may count as personal mitigation in exceptional
ircumstances).

Part C: Ancillary orders

The ancillary orders which a court must consider are restitution (*PCC(S)A* **K–212**
000, s.148 (§ 5–431 in the main work)), compensation (*ibid.*, s.130 (§ 5–411
1 the main work)), deprivation (*ibid.*, s.143 (§ 5–439 in the main work)) and
onfiscation (*PCA* 2002, s.6 (§ 5–566 in the main work)). Neither restitution
or compensation orders should normally impact or influence the choice of
entence. However, where an offender has acted (as opposed to offered) to
ee assets in order to pay compensation, this is akin to making voluntary
estitution and may be regarded as personal mitigation. In making
ompensation orders, consideration should be given to the wishes of the
ictim and, where it is difficult to ascertain the full amount of the loss suf-
ered, the making of an order for an amount representing the agreed or
kely loss.

Part D: Offence guidelines

Theft in breach of trust

While the seriousness of the offence will generally increase in line with **K–213**
1e level of trust breached, the extent to which the nature and degree of
ust placed in an offender should be regarded as increasing seriousness
ill depend on a careful assessment of the circumstances of each individual
ase, including the type and terms of the relationship between the offender
nd victim. A court should also consider whether a suspended sentence
ould be appropriate, particularly where this may allow reparation to be
ade either to the victim or to the community at large.

Type/ nature of activity	Starting point	Sentencing range
Theft of £125,000 or more **or** theft of £20,000 or more in breach of a high degree of trust	3 years' custody	2–6 years' custody
Theft of £20,000 or more but less than £125,000 **or** theft of £2,000 or more but less than £20,000 in breach of a high degree of trust	2 years' custody	12 months–3 years' custody
Theft of £2,000 or more but less than £20,000 **or** theft of less than £2,000 in breach of a high degree of trust	18 weeks' custody	Community order (high)–12 months' custody
Theft of less than £2,000	Community order (medium)	Fine–26 weeks' custody

K-214   Additional aggravating factors:

    (i) long course of offending;

    (ii) suspicion deliberately thrown on others;

    (iii) offender motivated by intention to cause harm or out of revenge.

    Additional mitigating factors:

    (i) offender has been given inappropriate degree of trust or responsibility;

    (ii) genuine cessation of offending before discovery (particularly wher evidence of remorse);

    (iii) offender reports undiscovered offending;

    (iv) other than in the most exceptional of circumstances, loss of employ ment and any consequential hardship should **not** constitute person mitigation.

Theft in a dwelling and theft from the person

K-215   In respect of theft in a dwelling, it is noted that the guideline does no apply where the offender has been convicted of a burglary, and in respec of theft from the person, it is noted that the guideline does not apply wher the offender has been convicted of robbery. As to the approach, in respec of theft from the person, to issues of local prevalence, see the seriousnes guideline (*ante*, K–13 *et seq.*). Issues of national prevalence should **not** b used by sentencers to justify including a deterrent element as this is alread taken into account in these and other guidelines.

    For the purposes of the table, *post*, property should generally be regarde as having a high monetary value if it is worth more than £2,000 and a victim is vulnerable if he is targeted by the offender because it is anticipated that h will be unlikely or unable to resist the theft (*e.g.* because of youth or age

Type/ nature of activity	Starting point	Sentencing range
Where the effect on the victim is particularly severe, the stolen property is of high value (see *ante*), or substantial consequential loss (e.g. serious disruption to victim's life or business) results, a sentence higher than the range into which the offence otherwise would fall may be appropriate		
Theft from a vulnerable victim (see *ante*) involving intimidation or the use or threat of force (falling short of robbery) or the use of deception	18 months' custody	12 months–3 years' custody
Theft from a vulnerable victim	18 weeks' custody	Community order (high)–12 months' custody
Theft in a dwelling or from the person not involving vulnerable victim	Community order (medium)	Fine–18 weeks' custody

Additional aggravating factors: **K–216**
  (i) offender motivated by intention to cause harm or out of revenge;
 (ii) intimidation or face-to-face confrontation with victim (except where this takes the offence into a higher sentencing range);
(iii) use of force, or threat of force, against victim (not amounting to robbery) (except where this takes the offence into a higher sentencing range);
 (iv) use of deception (except where this takes the offence into a higher sentencing range);
  (v) offender takes steps to prevent the victim from reporting the crime or seeking help (applies only to theft in a dwelling);
 (vi) high level of inconvenience caused to victim, *e.g.* replacing house keys, credit cards, etc., or where the victim is a tourist (applies only to theft from the person).

Theft from a shop
When assessing the level of harm, the circumstances of the retailer (*e.g.*   **K–217**
size) are a proper consideration. However, the seriousness of an individual
case must be judged on its own dimension of harm and culpability and the
sentence on an individual offender should not be increased to reflect the
harm caused to retailers in general by the totality of this type of offending
(*e.g.* higher insurance premiums, cost of preventative security measures).
Whereas the seriousness guideline requires the value of goods to be taken
into account in property offences, where this is associated with other aggravating factors such as the degree of planning and/or operating in a group, care
will need to be taken to avoid double counting.
When taking previous convictions into account, if the offender demonstrates a level of persistent or seriously persistent offending, the community
and custody thresholds may be crossed even though the other characteristics
of the offence would otherwise warrant a lesser sentence.

Type/ nature of activity	Starting point	Sentencing range
Organised gang/ group **and** intimidation or the use or threat of force (short of robbery)	12 months' custody	36 weeks–4 years' custody
Significant intimidation or threats **or** use of force resulting in slight injury **or** very high level of planning **or** significant related damage	6 weeks' custody	Community order (high)–36 weeks' custody
Low level intimidation or threats **or** some planning, *e.g.* a session of stealing on the same day or going equipped **or** some related damage	Community order (low)	Fine—community order (medium)
Little or no planning or sophistication **and** goods stolen of low value	Fine	Conditional discharge–community order (low)

K–218   Additional aggravating factors:
  (i) child accompanying offender where child is involved or aware o
      theft;
  (ii) offender is subject to a banning order that includes the store targeted
       (care to be taken to avoid double counting where offender also being
       sentenced for breach of order);
  (iii) offender motivated by intention to cause harm or out of revenge;
  (iv) professional offending;
  (v) victim particularly vulnerable (*e.g.* small, independent shop);
  (vi) offender targeted high value goods;
  (vii) intimidation, threat or use of force (falling short of robbery) and ad
        ditional damage to property.

Burglary in a building other than a dwelling
K–219   Deliberate and gratuitous violence or damage to property over and above
what is needed to carry out the offence, and abuse of a position of trust are
aggravating factors from the list in Annex A with particular relevance to
this offence.

Type/ nature of activity	Starting point	Sentencing range
Where the effect on the victim is particularly severe, the goods are of particularly high value, the cost of damage or consequential losses is significant, or there is evidence of a professional burglary and/or significant planning, a sentence of more than seven years' custody may be appropriate		
Burglary involving goods valued at £20,000 or more	2 years' custody	12 months'—7 years' custody
Burglary involving goods valued at £2,000 or more but less than £20,000	18 weeks' custody	Community order (high)–12 months' custody
Burglary involving goods valued at less than £2,000	Community order (medium)	Fine–26 weeks' custody

Additional aggravating factors: **K–220**
(i) targeting premises containing property of high value, vulnerable community premises or premises which have been burgled on prior occasion(s);
(ii) possession of a weapon (where this is not charged separately).

II. AUTHORITIES ON OFFICIAL GUIDELINES
A. REDUCTION IN SENTENCE FOR GUILTY PLEA

Introduction
The purpose of this section of this appendix is to give details of authori-   **K–350**
ties considering particular aspects of final guidelines issued by the Sentencing Guidelines Council and which are set out in full or summarised in the previous section of this appendix. There is, however, a fine line that divides cases specifically on some aspect of a guideline from those considering a statutory provision or some more general aspect of sentencing. Accordingly, practitioners looking for authorities on sentencing in relation to one of the guideline subjects should also make reference to the relevant paragraphs of the main work.

Relevant main work references
For sentencing guidelines generally, see section 172 of the *CJA* 2003 (§ 5–   **K–351**
100 in the main work); and for the reduction in sentence for a guilty plea, see section 144 of that Act (*ibid.*, § 5–78), and the authorities set out at §§ 5–79a *et seq.*, and, in particular, §§ 5–82, 5–83a.

B. OVERARCHING PRINCIPLES: SERIOUSNESS

Introduction
As to the purpose of this section of this appendix, see *ante*, K–350.   **K–360**

Relevant main work references
For sentencing guidelines generally, see section 172 of the *CJA* 2003 (§ 5–   **K–361**
100 in the main work); and for the determination of the sereiousness of an offence, see section 143 of that Act (*ibid.*, § 5–54 in the main work).

C. New Sentences: Criminal Justice Act 2003

Introduction

K–370   As to the purpose of this section of this appendix, see *ante*, K–350.

Relevant main work references

K–371   For sentencing guidelines generally, see section 172 of the *CJA* 2003 (§ 5–100 in the main work). As to community sentences generally, see § 5–122 in the main work; as to the restrictions on the imposition of such sentences, see *ibid.*, § 5–125; as to community orders generally, see *ibid.*, §§ 5–130 *et seq.*; as to the requirements that may be included in a community order, see *ibid.*, §§ 5–135 *et seq.*; as to the misleading terminology adopted in this guideline, see *ibid.*, § 5–156a.

Transitional arrangements

K–372   In *R. v. Whittle* (2007) 151 S.J. 398, CA, it was said that whereas paragraph 2.1.9 suggests that any sentence of 12 months or more should be reduced by in the region of 15 per cent to reflect the more onerous nature of the release on licence regime under the *CJA* 2003, where an offender is sentenced to a term of four years or more, the sentencer may be entitled not to reduce the sentence to the full extent or at all; in relation to such sentences, the increased onerousness of the licence conditions would be more or less in balance with the fact that the offender would be entitled to release at the half way point under the new regime instead of at the two-thirds point under the pre-existing regime.

D. Manslaughter by Reason of Provocation

Introduction

K–380   As to the purpose of this section of this appendix, see *ante*, K–350.

Relevant main work references

K–381   For sentencing guidelines generally, see section 172 of the *CJA* 2003 (§ 5–100 in the main work); and for provocation as a defence to a charge of murder generally, see §§ 19–50 *et seq.* in the main work.

Approach to guideline

K–382   Referring to heightened and justifiable public concern about cases involving the stabbing of one teenager by another, the court in *R. v. Daley* [2008] 2 Cr.App.R.(S.) 95, CA, said that the guideline had not been intended to lay down fixed or rigid boundaries.

E. Robbery

Introduction

K–390   As to the purpose of this section of this appendix, see *ante*, K–350.

Relevant main work references

K–391   For sentencing guidelines generally, see section 172 of the *CJA* 2003 (§ 5–

100 in the main work). As to this guideline, see, in particular, § 21–93 in the main work; as to sentencing for armed robbery, for robbery in the course of burglary and for the hijacking of cars, see *ibid.*, §§ 21–91, 21–92 and 21–94 respectively. For examples of the application of the dangerous offender provisions of the 2003 Act to cases of robbery, see *ibid.*, § 5–307.

"less sophisticated commercial robbery"

In *Att.-Gen.'s References (Nos 32, 33 and 34 of 2007) (R. v. Bate)* [2007] **K–392** Crim.L.R. 815, CA, it was held that for the purposes of the guideline on robbery, (i) the boundary between a "less sophisticated commercial robbery" falling within the guideline and a "professionally planned commercial robbery" falling without the guideline is not a hard and fast one and many cases would properly be regarded as falling on either side of the line; and a judge had been entitled to regard as falling within the guideline (and to regard the case as a level 1 case) two robberies during normal working hours (involving prior reconnaissance or information and the use of a stolen car) in which the three unarmed defendants, wearing masks and using a stolen car, had intercepted unaccompanied lorry drivers making deliveries of cigarettes to shops; and (ii) whereas "vulnerability of the victim" as an aggravating factor is expressly stated to be "targeting the elderly, the young, those with disabilities and persons performing a service to the public, especially outside normal working hours", there was nonetheless a low level of vulnerability (and hence aggravation) where the targets of the robberies were delivery drivers working alone, albeit delivering to shops where there were people to receive them.

Whilst the *CJA* 2003, s.172 (§ 5–100 in the main work), requires a court to have regard to a relevant sentencing guideline, a guideline is only a guideline and the guideline on robbery cannot cover each and every category because of the immense variety of circumstances in which offences of robbery are committed, and as such there is a wide spectrum of offences that fall between "less sophisticated commercial robberies" and "professionally-planned commercial robberies", as described in the guideline; where, therefore, four men had "swiftly" robbed the driver of a delivery van in a robbery that was "cynically and callously planned" with one of the men persuading him to drive with them to a secluded place whilst wearing a mask and rubber gloves and being armed with a knife, the case did not fall neatly and cleanly within the category of the "less sophisticated commercial robbery" (which has an indicated starting point of four years' custody) and instead fell within a range of six to 10 years (possibly more for a ring leader); and, in the case of the respondent (40), who acted as the driver of the robbers' vehicle, three years' imprisonment on conviction was unduly lenient given that, although he was not a prime mover and did not wield the knife, it must have been within his contemplation that some degree of threat or force would be used on the victim; taking account, however, of the fact that he suffered from Asperger's syndrome, which made him vulnerable to being manipulated by more sophisticated offenders, the appropriate bracket was six to eight years' imprisonment: *Att.-Gen.'s Reference (No. 147 of 2006) (R. v. Gunner)* [2008] 1 Cr.App.R.(S.) 9(2), CA (substituting six years).

As to there being a category of case that falls between the "less sophisticated commercial robbery" and the "professionally planned commercial robbery", see also *R. v. Eccleston* [2008] 2 Cr.App.R.(S.) 56, CA.

"vulnerability of the victim"

K–393   See *Att.-Gen.'s References (Nos 32, 33 and 34 of 2007) (R. v. Bate)*, *ante*, § K–392.

F. Breach of a Protective Order

Introduction

K–400   As to the purpose of this section of this appendix, see *ante*, K–350.

Relevant main work references

K–401   For sentencing guidelines generally, see section 172 of the *CJA* 2003 (§ 5–100 in the main work); for breach of an anti-social behaviour order, see *post*, K–196 *et seq.*; for breach of a restraining order under the *Protection from Harassment Act* 1997, see *ibid.*, § 19–277i; and for breach of a sexual offences prevention order, see *ibid.*, § 20–334.

G. Domestic Violence

Introduction

K–410   As to the purpose of this section of this appendix, see *ante*, K–350.

Relevant main work references

K–411   For sentencing guidelines generally, see section 172 of the *CJA* 2003 (§ 5–100 in the main work); and for breach of a restraining order under the *Protection from Harassment Act* 1997, see § 19–277i in the main work.

H. Sexual Offences

Introduction

K–420   As to the purpose of this section of this appendix, see *ante*, K–350.

Relevant main work references

K–421   For sentencing guidelines generally, see section 172 of the *CJA* 2003 (§ 5–100 in the main work).

Age of offence/offender

K–422   In *Att.-Gen.'s Reference (No. 70 of 2008) (R. v. W.)*, *The Times*, February 2, 2009, CA, it was said, without making any reference to the guideline, that in cases of serious sexual assault, the age of the offender or the age of the offence could be mitigation although, in many cases, they would not receive much weight, especially if the offender had pressurised his victims into silence; but they did not cease to be factors which could form part of the mitigation, and they were not always of comparatively little weight.

Gender of victim/offender

★K–422a   Sentencing guidelines were put forward on the basis that they should apply irrespective of the gender of the victim or of the offender (see *ante*, K–84), except in specified circumstances where a distinction is justified by the

nature of the offence; Parliament did not seek to distinguish between the
genders in the legislation and neither should the courts: *Att.-Gen.'s Reference
(No. 67 of 2008) (R. v. Edwards (Sharon))*, *The Times*, March 17, 2009, CA.

Ranges

In *R. v. Frew* [2009] 1 Cr.App.R.(S.) 17, CA, the court said that the recom-   **K–423**
mended range for the offence in question was three to seven years' imprisonment and that, in terms of gravity, the particular offence was not at the bot-
tom of the range, yet it substituted a sentence that equated to 27 months after
a trial. Whilst the court said that the guideline emphasised the need for flexibility and variability, the result suggests that the ranges are considerably
wider than those recommended in the guideline. To similar effect, see *R. v. P.
(John James)* [2009] 1 Cr.App.R.(S.) 45, CA (assault by penetration of child
under 13 came within most serious category, with range of 11 to 17 years; appropriate penalty before discount for plea was seven-and-a-half years). For a
case in which the court went above the relevant range without giving reasons,
see *R. v. Olawo, post*, K–434a.

Rape of a child under 13

Actual consent is capable of being a mitigating factor, but careful   **K–424**
consideration has to be given in all cases, and particularly where there is a
significant difference in age, to the extent to which ostensible consent had
been obtained opportunistically, or by means of coercion, which might be
subtle, or exploitation, which could be particularly relevant where there
may have been an element of grooming; in such cases, ostensible consent
might well have little value as mitigation, and in all cases the age difference
would be of great significance; as to a reasonable belief that the victim was
aged 16 or over, this was capable of being mitigation (even where the offender was aged 18 or over (though the guideline only lists such a mistaken
belief as mitigation where the offender is under 18), but the older the offender, the less relevant a mistake as to age would be; in determining the
extent to which mitigation relating to consent or a mistaken belief as to age
can justify departing from the sentencing bracket (of eight to 13 years), it
may be helpful to consider the guideline on penetrative sexual activity with
a person under the age of 16, where the offender does not reasonably
believe that the other person is 16 or over (contrary to section 9 of the
2003 Act), *viz.* a starting point of four years and a sentencing range of three
to seven years; bearing this, and the legislative purpose of creating the
absolute offence under section 5 for victims under the age of 13, in mind,
four years should be the minimum for an offence under section 5, subject to
plea and personal mitigation, in the case of a young adult where there is
ostensible consent and a reasonable belief that the victim was 16 or over: *Att.-
Gen's References (Nos 74 and 83 of 2007) (R. v. Fenn; R. v. Foster)* [2008] 1
Cr.App.R.(S.) 110, CA.

I. FAILING TO SURRENDER TO BAIL

Introduction

As to the purpose of this section of this appendix, see *ante*, K–350.   **K–430**

Relevant main work references

For sentencing guidelines generally, see section 172 of the *CJA* 2003 (§ 5–   **K–431**

100 in the main work); for paragraph I.13 of the consolidated criminal practice direction (which touches on the same issues), see §§ 3–32 *et seq.* in the main work; and for the prior sentencing authorities, see *ibid.*, §§ 3–31, 3–35. To the extent that there are any differences between the provisions of the practice direction and of the guideline, it may be taken that the guideline will prevail so far as concerns sentencing considerations. As to procedure, it is apparent that the guideline has drawn on the practice direction and is generally consistent therewith.

J. ASSAULT AND OTHER OFFENCES AGAINST THE PERSON

Introduction

K–433   As to the purpose of this section of this appendix, see *ante*, K–350.

Relevant main work references

K–434   For sentencing guidelines generally, see section 172 of the *CJA* 2003 (§ 5–100 in the main work).

Use in case of young offenders

★K–434a   In *R. v. Bowley* [2009] 1 Cr.App.R.(S.) 79, CA, where a 17-year-old pleaded guilty to causing grievous bodily harm with intent after stabbing a rival gang member, the court said (i) that the judge had been entitled to look to this guideline for assistance, even though it does not apply to offenders under 18 and (ii) in making use of it, the judge need not have been unduly constrained by the particular sentencing brackets set out therein, because the case was one where an element of deterrence was an essential ingredient of the sentencing decision.

Ranges

K–434b   In *R. v. Olawo* [2008] 2 Cr.App.R.(S.) 113, a sentence of 12 months' imprisonment was imposed by the Court of Appeal for an offence contrary to section 20 of the *Offences against the Person Act* 1861, for which the recommended range was up to 36 weeks' imprisonment. The court said that the fact that the victim was a certified enforcement officer was a seriously aggravating factor, but this is a factor specifically mentioned in the guideline on seriousness (see K–19, *ante*) and is presumably allowed for in the range. No reason was given by the court for going outside the range. For a case in which the court went below the relevant range without giving reasons, see *R. v. Frew, ante*, K–422.

As to whether deterrence is a legitimate reason for going outside the recommended bracket, see *R. v. Bowley, ante*, § 5–434a.

Section 18

Use of a knife

K–434c   In *R. v. Osman* [2008] 2 Cr.App.R.(S.) 89, CA, it was said that the need for the courts to take account of legitimate public concern and to deter the premeditated carrying and use of a knife to inflict an intentional wound by the imposition of condign and/or deterrent sentences was all too obvious; and was reflected in the guideline.

K. Assaults on Children and Cruelty to a Child

ntroduction

As to the purpose of this section of this appendix, see *ante*, K-350.   **K-436**

Relevant main work references

For sentencing guidelines generally, see section 172 of the *CJA* 2003 (§ 5-   **K-437**
00 in the main work).

The four categories of seriousness

In *R. v. S. (Will)* [2009] 1 Cr.App.R.(S.) 40, CA, the offender (30/good   **★K-438**
character/no previous parenting experience) subjected a "challenging" five-
year-old, one of the four children of his (now ex-)partner, to a particularly
harsh regime of discipline. She was shouted at, made to feel unwanted, and
sent to her room for long periods (sometimes day after day). No violence was
used except on one occasion, when the offender put masking tape over her
mouth (for which he later expressed regret). At school, it was noticed that the
child, from being a relatively happy child, became tearful and unsettled. On
pleas of guilty to two counts of "causing cruelty to a child", 30 months'
imprisonment was held to be manifestly and grossly excessive. The court
found that it was clear that the offender's actions were not those of a gratu-
tous bully, but of an inexperienced parent, at the end of his tether, who,
together with the mother, was doing what he mistakenly believed to be the
right thing in respect of what he saw as an ill-behaved child. In particular, it
was said that the judge had wrongly identified the case as falling within the
second of the four categories of seriousness in the guideline, which, the court
noted, should more properly be reserved for cases of actual abuse, either
through physical violence or deprivation of food, clothing, shelter or
attendance. A community order with a supervision requirement (to include a
parenting course) was substituted.

L. Sentencing in Magistrates' Courts

ntroduction

As to the purpose of this section of this appendix, see *ante*, K-350.   **K-439**

Relevant main work references

For sentencing guidelines generally, see section 172 of the *CJA* 2003 (§ 5-   **K-440**
00 in the main work); for paragraph V.51 of the consolidated criminal
practice direction, which is superseded by this guideline so far as it relates
o particular offences dealt with in the guideline, but which also contains
general mode of trial considerations, see § 1-75u in the main work.

Burglary in a dwelling

In *R. v. Saw* [2009] 2 All E.R. 1138, the court observed that when applying   **K-441**
the provisions of the guideline relating to dwelling house burglaries, regard
should always be had to all the matters of aggravation and mitigation listed in
the judgment (as to which, see *ante*, § 21-114).

M. Causing Death by Driving

Introduction

K–442   As to the purpose of this section of this appendix, see *ante*, K–350.

Relevant main work references

K–443   For sentencing guidelines generally, see section 172 of the *CJA* 2003 (§ 5–100 in the main work). For the penalty provisions relating to the offences covered by this guideline, see § 32–6 (causing death by dangerous driving), § 32–47e (causing death by careless or inconsiderate driving); § 32–59 (causing death by careless driving when under the influence of drink or drugs or having failed without reasonable excuse either to provide a specimen for analysis or to permit the analysis of a blood sample) and § 32–63e (causing death by driving while unlicensed, disqualified or uninsured). As to disqualification and endorsement, see §§ 32–167 *et seq.*

N. Breach of an Anti-Social Behaviour Order

Introduction

K–450   As to the purpose of this section of this appendix, see *ante*, K–350.

Relevant main work references

K–451   For sentencing guidelines generally, see section 172 of the *CJA* 2003 (§ 5–100 in the main work). For the power to make an anti-social behaviour order on conviction, see section 1C of the *CDA* 1998 (§ 5–880 in the main work). For authorities considering the imposition of an anti-social behaviour order, see §§ 5–884 in the main work.

O. Theft and Burglary in a Building Other Than a Dwelling

Introduction

K–475   As to the purpose of this section of this appendix, see *ante*, K–350.

Relevant main work references

K–476   For sentencing guidelines generally, see section 172 of the *CJA* 2003 (§ 5–100 in the main work). For previous guidelines in relation to various types of theft, see §§ 21–4c *et seq.*

III. COMPENDIUM OF GUIDELINE CASES

K–1000   The Sentencing Guidelines Council has published a compendium of those cases that it regards as constituting considered guidance and issued over the past 30 years. The list is in two parts, "Generic sentencing principles" and "Offences". It has been updated four times, with some cases having been removed from the original list.

In the first list are: *R. v. Martin (Selina)* [2007] 1 Cr.App.R.(S.) 3 (**approach to sentencing**); *Att.-Gen.'s Reference (No. 4 of 1989) (R. v. Brunt)*, 11

Cr.App.R(S.) 517 (**Attorney-General's references**); *R. v. Montgomery*, 16 Cr.App.R(S.) 274 (**contempt**); *R. v. Bernard* [1997] 1 Cr.App.R(S.) 135 (**health of the offender**); *R. v. Goodyear* [2005] 3 All E.R. 117; *R. v. Kulah* [2008] 1 Cr.App.R.(S.) 85 (**indication of sentence**); *R. v. Buckland* [2000] 1 W.L.R. 1262 (**automatic life sentences**); *R. v. Hodgson*, 52 Cr.App.R. 113; *R. v. Chapman* [2000] 1 Cr.App.R. 77; *R. v. McNee, Gunn and Russell* [2008] 1 Cr.App.R.(S.) 24; *R. v. Kehoe* [2009] 1 Cr.App.R.(S.) 9; *R. v. Davies* [2009] 1 Cr.App.R.(S.) 15 (**discretionary life sentences**); *R. v. M. (Discretionary Life Sentence)*; *R. v. L.* [1999] 1 W.L.R. 485; *R. v. Szczerba* [2002] 2 Cr.App.R.(S.) 86 (**life sentence—specified period**); *R. v. McLean*, 6 Cr.App.R. 26; *R. v. Simons*, 37 Cr.App.R. 120; *R. v. Walsh*, unreported, March 8, 1973 (**taking offences into consideration**); *Att.-Gen.'s Reference (No. 52 of 2003) (R. v. Webb)* [2004] Crim.L.R. 306 (**prosecution duty**); *R. v. Kelly and Donnelly* [2001] 2 Cr.App.R.(S.) 73; *R. v. McGillivray* [2005] 2 Cr.App.R.(S.) 60; *R. v. O'Callaghan* [2005] 2 Cr.App.R.(S.) 83 (**racially aggravated offences**); *R. v. A. and B.* [1999] 1 Cr.App.R.(S.) 52; *R. v. Guy* [1999] 2 Cr.App.R.(S.) 24; *R. v. X. (No. 2)* [1999] 2 Cr.App.R.(S.) 294; *R. v. R. (Informer: Reduction in sentence), The Times*, February 18, 2002; *R. v. P.*; *R. v. Blackburn* [2008] 2 Cr.App.R.(S.) 5 (**discount on account of assistance given to the police**); *R. v. Bird*, 9 Cr.App.R.(S.) 77; *R. v. Tiso*, 12 Cr.App.R.(S.) 122 (**discount on account of lapse of time since offence**); *R. v. Bibi* [1980] 1 W.L.R. 1193; *R. v. Ollerenshaw* [1999] 1 Cr.App.R.(S.) 65; *R. v. Kefford* [2002] 2 Cr.App.R.(S.) 106 (**length of custodial sentences**); *R. v. Nelson* [2002] 1 Cr.App.R.(S.) 134; *R. v. Cornelius* [2002] 2 Cr.App.R.(S.) 69; *R. v. Pepper* [2006] 1 Cr.App.R.(S.) 20 (**length of extended sentences**); *R. v. Lang* [2006] 2 Cr.App.R.(S.) 3; *R. v. S.*; *R. v. Burt* [2006] 2 Cr.App.R.(S.) 35; *CPS v. South East Surrey Youth Court* [2006] 2 Cr.App.R.(S.) 26 (**dangerousness**); *R. v. Reynolds* [2007] 2 Cr.App.R.(S.) 87; *R. v. Johnson* [2007] 1 Cr.App.R.(S.) 112; *R. v. O'Brien* [2007] 1 Cr.App.R.(S.) 75; *R. v. O'Halloran*, unreported, November 14, 2006 ([2006] EWCA Crim. 3148) (**dangerousness: imprisonment for public protection**); *R. v. Brown and Butterworth* [2007] 1 Cr.App.R.(S.) 77; *R. v. Lay* [2007] 2 Cr.App.R.(S.) 4; *R. v. C.*; *R. v. Bartley* [2007] 2 Cr.App.R.(S.) 98 (**dangerousness: extended sentences**); *Att.-Gen.'s Reference (No. 101 of 2006) (R. v. P.)*, unreported, December 8, 2006 ([2006] EWCA Crim. 3335) (**deferment of sentence**); *R. v. Cain* [2007] 2 Cr.App.R.(S.) 25 (**prosecution and defence duty to assist at sentencing**); *R. v. Seed*; *R. v. Stark* [2007] 2 Cr.App.R.(S.) 69 (**sentence length: custodial sentences**); *R. (Stellato) v. Secretary of State for the Home Department* [2007] 2 W.L.R. 531 (**sentence length: licence period**); *Att.-Gen.'s Reference (No. 6 of 2006) (R. v. Farish)* [2007] 1 Cr.App.R.(S.) 12 (**sentence length: minimum sentences**); *R. v. Gordon* [2007] 2 All E.R. 768 (**sentence length: time spent in custody on remand**); *R. v. Tyre*, 6 Cr.App.R.(S.) 247 (**sentence length: joint conviction with a juvenile offender**); *R. v. Davies* [2009] 1 Cr.App.R.(S.) 15 (**sentence length: standard of proof**); *R. v. McGrath* [2005] 2 Cr.App.R.(S). 85; *R. v. Morrison* [2006] 1 Cr. App.R.(S.) 85; *R. v. Lamb* [2006] 2 Cr.App.R.(S.) 11; *R. v. H., Stevens and Lovegrove* [2006] 2 Cr.App.R.(S.) 68 (**anti-social behaviour orders**); *R. v. P. (Shane Tony)* [2004] 2 Cr.App.R.(S.) 63 (**anti-social behaviour order imposed with custody**); *R. v. Sullivan* [2003] EWCA Crim. 1736 (**compensation with custody**); *R. v. Robinson* [2002] 2 Cr.App.R.(S.) 95; *Att.-Gen.'s Reference (No. 64 of 2003)* [2004] 2 Cr.App.R.(S.) 22; *R. v. Woods and Collins* [2006] 1 Cr.App.R.(S.) 83 (**drug treatment and testing orders**); *R. v. Richards* [2007] 1 Cr.App.R.(S.) 120 (**sexual offences prevention orders**); *R. v. Kidd*; *R. v. Canavan*; *R. v. Shaw (Dennis)* [1998] 1 W.L.R. 604; *R. v. Tovey*;

R. v. Smith [2005] 2 Cr.App.R.(S.) 100 (**specimen offences**); *R. v. Perks* [2001] 1 Cr.App.R.(S.) 66; *R. v. Ismail* [2005] 2 Cr.App.R.(S.) 88 (**victim's wishes**); *R. v. Danga*, 13 Cr.App.R.(S.) 408; *R. v. Ghafoor* [2003] 1 Cr.App.R.(S.) 84 (**age for purpose of sentencing**); *R. (W.) v. Southampton Youth Court*; *R. (K.) v. Wirral Borough Magistrates' Court* [2003] 1 Cr.App.R.(S.) 87 (**venue for trial**); *R. v. Sharma* [2006] 2 Cr.App.R.(S.) 63 (**confiscation orders**); *R. v. Oshungbure and Odewale* [2005] 2 Cr.App.R.(S.) 102 (**confiscation proceedings following sentence**); *R. v. Richards (Michael,* [2005] 2 Cr.App.R.(S.) 97 (**confiscation order: obtaining social security benefits by false representations**); *R. v. Debnath* [2006] 2 Cr.App.R.(S.) 25 (**restraining orders**); *R. v. Lees-Wolfenden* [2007] 1 Cr.App.R.(S.) 119 (**suspended sentence orders**); *R. v. Eagles* [2007] 1 Cr.App.R.(S.) 99 (**young offenders: treatment of time spent in custody on remand**).

In the second list are:—

affray—*R. v. Fox and Hicks* [2006] 1 Cr.App.R.(S.) 17;

breach of licence—*R. v. Pick and Dillon* [2006] 1 Cr.App.R.(S.) 61;

burglary (domestic)—*R. v. McInerney*; *R. v. Keating* [2003] 1 All E.R 1089;

counterfeiting and forgery—*R. v. Howard*, 7 Cr.App.R.(S.) 320 (dealing in counterfeit currency); *R. v. Crick*, 3 Cr.App.R.(S.) 275 (counterfeiting coins); *R. v. Kolawole* [2005] 2 Cr.App.R.(S.) 14; *R. v Mutede* [2006] 2 Cr.App.R.(S.) 22; *Att.-Gen.'s Reference (Nos 1 and 6 o, 2008) (R. v. Dziruni and Laby)* [2008] 2 Cr.App.R.(S.) 99 (false passports);

drugs—*R. v. Aramah*, 76 Cr.App.R. 190 (general); *R. v. Aranguren*, 99 Cr.App.R. 347 (importation of Class A); *R. v. Martinez*, (Cr.App.R.(S.) 364 (cocaine); *R. v. Bilinski*, 9 Cr.App.R.(S.) 360 (heroin); *R. v. Mashaollahi* [2001] 1 Cr.App.R. 6 (opium); *R. v. Warrer and Beeley* [1996] 1 Cr.App.R. 120 (Ecstasy); *R. v. Wijs*; *R. v. Rae*; *R v. Donaldson*; *R. v. Church*; *R. v. Haller* [1998] 2 Cr.App.R. 43((importation of amphetamine); *R. v. v. Ronchetti* [1998] 2 Cr.App.R.(S.) 100 (importation of cannabis (prior to reclassification)) *R. v. Maguire* [1997] 1 Cr.App.R.(S.) 130; *R. v. Wagenaar and Pron* [1997] 1 Cr.App.R.(S.) 178 (in transit on high seas); *R. v. Singh (Satvir)*, 10 Cr.App.R.(S.) 402 (possession of Class A with intent to supply); *R. v. Hurley* [1998] 1 Cr.App.R.(S.) 299 (possession of LSD with intent to supply); *R. v. Morris (Harold Linden)* [2001] 1 Cr.App.R. 25 (purity analysis of Class A); *R. v. Djahit* [1999] 2 Cr.App.R.(S.) 142 *R. v. Twisse* [2001] 2 Cr.App.R.(S.) 9; *R. v. Afonso*; *R. v. Sajid*; *R. v Andrews* [2005] 1 Cr.App.R.(S.) 99 (supply and dealing in Class A); *R v. Prince* [1996] 1 Cr.App.R.(S.) 335 (supply to prisoners); *R. v. Her ridge* [2006] 1 Cr.App.R.(S.) 45; *R. v. Xu* [2008] 2 Cr.App.R.(S.) 50 (production/cultivation of cannabis);

explosive offences—*R. v. Martin* [1999] 1 Cr.App.R.(S) 477;

firearms offences—*R. v. Avis*; *R. v. Barton*; *R. v. Thomas*; *R. v. Torrington*; *R. v. Marquez*; *R. v. Goldsmith* [1998] 1 Cr.App.R. 420; *R. v Rehman*; *R. v. Wood* [2006] 1 Cr.App.R.(S.) 77 (exceptional circumstances);

fraud—*R. v. Stewart*, 9 Cr.App.R.(S.) 135; *R. v. Graham*; *R. v. Whatle* [2005] 1 Cr.App.R.(S.) 115 (benefit); *R. v. Feld* [1999] 1 Cr.App.R.(S. 1 (company management); *Att.-Gen.'s Reference (Nos 86 and 87 o 1999) (R. v. Webb and Simpson)* [2001] 1 Cr.App.R.(S.) 141 (tax evasion); *R. v. Czyzewski* [2004] 3 All E.R. 135 (evading excise duty); *F*

v. Palk and Smith [1997] 2 Cr.App.R.(S.) 167 (fraudulent trading); *R.
v. Stevens*, 14 Cr.App.R.(S.) 372 (mortgage fraud); *R. v. Roach* [2002]
1 Cr.App.R.(S.) 12 (obtaining money transfer by deception);

handling stolen goods—*R. v. Webbe* [2002] 1 Cr.App.R.(S) 22;

health and safety offences—*R. v. F. Howe and Son (Engineers) Ltd*
[1999] 2 All E.R. 249; *R. v. Rollco Screw and Rivet Co Ltd* [1999] 2
Cr.App.R.(S.) 436; *R. v. Balfour Beatty Infrastructure Ltd* [2007] 1
Cr.App.R.(S.) 65;

immigration—*R. v. Le and Stark* [1999] 1 Cr.App.R.(S.) 422; *R. v. Ai
(Lu Zhu)* [2006] 1 Cr.App.R.(S.) 5 (failing to produce an immigration
document);

incest—*Att.-Gen.'s Reference (No. 1 of 1989)*, 11 Cr.App.R.(S.) 409;

indecent assault—*Att.-Gen.'s References (Nos 120, 91 and 119 of 2002)*
[2003] 2 All E.R. 955 (general); *R. v. Lennon* [1999] 1 Cr.App.R. 117
(on male);

intimidation of witness—*R. v. Williams* [1997] 2 Cr.App.R.(S.) 221; *R.
v. Chinery* [2002] 2 Cr.App.R.(S.) 244(55);

kidnapping—*R. v. Spence and Thomas*, 5 Cr.App.R.(S.) 413;

manslaughter—*R. v. Chambers*, 5 Cr.App.R.(S.) 190 (diminished
responsibility); *R. v. Furby* [2006] 2 Cr.App.R.(S.) 8 ("single punch");
Att.-Gen.'s Reference (No. 111 of 2006) (R. v. Hussain) [2007] 2
Cr.App.R.(S.) 26 ("motor");

money laundering—*R. v. Basra* [2002] 2 Cr.App.R.(S.) 100; *R. v.
Gonzalez and Sarmineto* [2003] 2 Cr.App.R.(S.) 9 (general); *R. v. El-
Delbi* [2003] 7 *Archbold News* 1 (proceeds of drug trafficking);

murder—*R. v. Jones* [2006] 2 Cr.App.R.(S.) 19; *R. v. Barot* [2008] 1
Cr.App.R.(S.) 31; *R. v. McNee, Gunn and Russell* [2008] 1
Cr.App.R.(S.) 24 (conspiracy); *R. v. Davies* [2009] 1 Cr.App.R.(S.) 15
(minimum term); *R. v. Javed* [2008] 2 Cr.App.R.(S.) 12 (soliciting)

offensive weapons—*R. v. Poulton*; *R. v. Celaire* [2003] 4 All E.R. 869;
R. v. Povey [2009] 1 Cr.App.R.(S.) 42;

perjury—*R. v. Archer* [2003] 1 Cr.App.R.(S.) 86;

perverting the course of justice—*R. v. Walsh and Nightingale*, 14
Cr.App.R.(S.) 671;

pornography—*R. v. Holloway*, 4 Cr.App.R.(S.) 128 (having obscene
articles for publication for gain); *R. v. Nooy and Schyff*, 4 Cr.App.R.(S.)
308 (importation of indecent or obscene publications);

prison breaking (escape)—*R. v. Coughtrey* [1997] 2 Cr.App.R.(S.) 269;

public nuisance—*R. v. Kavanagh* [2008] 2 Cr.App.R.(S.) 86;

riot—*R. v. Najeeb* [2003] 2 Cr.App.R.(S.) 69;

robbery—*R. v. Snowden, The Times*, November 11, 2002 (hijacking of
cars);

sex offenders' register—*Att.-Gen.'s Reference (No. 50 of 1997) (R. v.
V.)* [1998] 2 Cr.App.R.(S.) 155;

theft—*R. v. Dhunay*, 8 Cr.App.R.(S.) 107 (airport luggage); *R. v. Evans*
[1996] 1 Cr.App.R.(S.) 105 ("ringing" stolen cars);

trafficking women for prostitution—*Att.-Gen.'s Reference (No. 6 of
2004) (R. v. Plakici)* [2005] 1 Cr.App.R.(S.) 19;

violent disorder—*R. v. Chapman* (2002) 146 S.J. (LB 242);

K–1001   In addition to the compendium of cases (*ante*), the Sentencing Guidelines Council issued a "guide" for practitioners and sentencers concerning the dangerous offender provisions of the *CJA* 2003 in September, 2007. It has now been updated to take account of the amendments effected by the *CJIA* 2008 which apply to everyone sentenced on or after July 14, 2008. The introduction expressly states that the "guide" is not a "guideline" for the purposes of section 172 of the 2003 Act (§ 5–100 in the main work). Its purpose is to set out clearly the statutory requirements that determine whether one (or more) of the new sentences is available, and to summarise the Court of Appeal (and High Court) guidance regarding the application of those requirements. The guide does not apply to protective sentences under the pre-2003 Act regimes.

Parts 2 and 3 of the guide respectively set out the criteria for imposing sentences under the dangerous offender provisions in respect of offenders aged 18 or over and offenders aged under 18. Part 4 sets out matters in connection with the determination of venue where an offender is under the age of 18. Part 5 deals with the giving of a *Goodyear* indication (*R. v. Goodyear (Practice note)* [2005] 2 Cr.App.R. 20, CA (§ 5–79b in the main work)) in relation to offenders charged with serious or specified offences. Part 6 deals with the assessment of dangerousness. Part 7 sets out matters in connection with the imposition of imprisonment (or custody or detention) for life. Part 8 deals with the choice of whether an extended sentence or a sentence for public protection should be imposed in respect of an offender aged under 18. Part 9 deals with the fixing of "minimum terms", and "custodial terms" and "extension periods". Part 10 deals with questions arising where an offender falls to be sentenced for more than one offence and/or is serving an existing custodial sentence. Part 11 deals with the correction of errors and omissions. Part 12 is a glossary.

There are six annexes. Annex A sets out simple flow charts. Annexes B and C purport to list all serious and specified violent offences; and Annexes D and E purport to do the same in respect of sexual offences. Annex F reproduces sections 225 to 229 of the 2003 Act in amended form, including the new Schedule 15A.

Reduction in Sentences for a Guilty Plea

[1] Published December 2004 (K–2).

[2] *Criminal Justice Act* 2003, s.170(4) (K–2).

[4] *Criminal Justice Act* 2003, s.153(2) (K–4).

[5] *Criminal Justice Act* 2003, s.148(2) (K–4)).

[6] Where a court imposes an indeterminate sentence for public protection, the reduction principle applies in the normal way to the determination of the minimum term (see para. 5.1, footnote and para. 7 below) but release from custody requires the authorisation of the Parole Board once that minimum term has been served (K–4)).

[7] See section A above (K–6).

[8] There will be some cases arising from offences committed before the commencement of the relevant provisions of the *Criminal Justice Act* 2003 in which a court will determine that a longer than commensurate, extended, or indeterminate sentence is required for the protection of the public. In such a case, the minimum custodial term (but not the protection of public element of the sentence) should be reduced to reflect the plea (K–7).

[9] *Criminal Justice Act* 2003, s.174(2)(a) (K–7).

[10] See section B above on page 4 (K–7).

[11] *Criminal Justice Act* 2003, Schedule 21 (K–8).

[12] *Criminal Justice Act* 2003, Schedule 1, para 12(c) (K–8).

[13] In accordance with the provisions of the *Criminal Justice Act* 2003 (K–8).

New Sentences: *Criminal Justice Act* 2003

[1] References to the Probation Service reflect current roles and responsibilities. By the time these provisions come into force, some or all of those roles and responsibilities may be those of the National Offender Management Service (NOMS) (K–28).

[2] *Criminal Justice Act* 2003 section 148(2)(b) (K–35).

[3] *ibid* section 148(2)(a) (K–35).

[4] *ibid* section 177(6) (K–35).

[5] Under the Act, a pre-sentence report includes a full report following adjournment, a specific sentence report, a short format report or an oral report. The type of report supplied will depend on the level of information requested. Wherever it appears, the term "pre-sentence report" includes all these types of report (K–36).

[6] *Criminal Justice Act* 2003 section 148(2) (K–36).

[7] *ibid* section 177(6) (K–36).

[8] *ibid* section 177(3) and (4) (K–41).

[9] unless the necessary facilities are not available or, in the particular circumstances of the case, the court considers it inappropriate (K–41).

[10] *Criminal Justice Act* 2003 section 149 (K–43).

[11] *Criminal Justice Act* 2003 Schedule 8, paragraphs 5–6 (K–44).

[12] *ibid* paragraphs 9–10 (K–44).

[13] *ibid* paragraph 9(2) (K–44).

[14] *ibid* paragraph 9(1)(c) (K–44).

[15] *Powers of Criminal Courts (Sentencing) Act* 2000 sections 1 and 2 (K–45).

[16] *Criminal Justice Act* 2003 schedule 23 repealing and replacing sections 1 and 2 of the 2000 Act (K–45).

[17] *ibid* new section 1(3)(b) as inserted by Schedule 23 to the *Criminal Justice Act* 2003 (K–45).

[18] *ibid* new section 1A(1) (K–45).

[19] *ibid* new section 1(4) (K–45).

[20] *ibid* new section 1B (K–45).

[21] *ibid* new section 1 (3)(b) as inserted by Schedule 23 to the *Criminal Justice Act* 2003 (K–46).

[22] *Criminal Justice Act* 2003 section 177 (K–46).

[23] *Criminal Justice Act* 2003 section 238(1) (K–47).

[24] *ibid* section 250 (K–47).

[25] *ibid* section 153(2) (K–47).

[26] Having reference to the Consolidated Criminal Practice Direction [2002] 2 Cr App R 533, Annex C, as suitably amended (K–49).

[27] *Criminal Justice Act* 2003 section 238(1) (K–50).

[28] *ibid* section 250 (K–50).

[30] The power to suspend a sentence is expected to come into force earlier than the provisions implementing "custody plus" and transitional provisions are expected to enable any sentence of imprisonment of under 12 months to be suspended. This guideline therefore is written in the language of the expected transitional provisions (K–56).

[31] *Criminal Justice Act* 2003 schedule 12, para. 4 (K–60).

[32] *ibid* para. 5 (K–60).

[33] *ibid* para. 8(4) (K–60).

[34] *ibid* section 189(3) and (4) (K–60).

[35] *ibid* schedule 12, para. 8(3) (K–60).

[36] *Criminal Justice Act* 2003 section 184(2) (K–66).

[37] IC Pilot Project "A Brief Guide to Intermittent Custody" 02/03/04 HMPS (K–67).

[38] *Criminal Justice Act* 2003 section 240 (K–70).

[39] *ibid* section 149 (K–70).

[40] *ibid* section 240 (which will, at a future date, replace *Criminal Justice Act* 1967, section 67, by which such period is now deducted automatically) (K–70).

[41] This recommendation only applies to sentences of 12 months and above pending the implementation of 'custody plus' (K–70).

Manslaughter by Reason of Provocation

[1] "Any criminal offence arising out of physical, sexual, psychological, emotional or financial abuse by one person against a current or former partner in a close relationship or against a current or former family member." A new definition of domestic violence was agreed in 2004 (and appears in the CPS Policy on Prosecuting cases of Domestic Violence 2005) "any incident of threatening behaviour, violence or abuse [psychological, physical, sexual, financial or emotional] between adults who are or have been intimate partners or family members, regardless of gender or sexuality" (K–71).

[2] [2003] 2 Cr.App.R.(S.) 42 (K–74).

[3] Sections 224–230 (K–77).

APPENDIX N

Protocols

A. Control and Management of Heavy Fraud and other Complex

Criminal Cases

A protocol issued by the Lord Chief Justice of England and Wales **N–1**

22 March 2005

Introduction

The investigation

  The role of the prosecuting authority and the judge

  Interviews

  The prosecution and defence teams

  Initial consideration of the length of a case

  Notification of cases likely to last more than 8 weeks

  Notification of cases likely to last more than 8 weeks

  Venue

Designation of the trial judge

  The assignment of a judge

Case management

  Objectives

  The assignment of a judge

Case management

  Objectives

  Fixing the trial date

  The first hearing for the giving of initial directions

  The first Case Management Hearing

  Further Case Management Hearings

  Consideration of the length of the trial

  The exercise of the powers

  Fixing the trial date

  The first hearing for the giving of initial directions

  The first Case Management Hearing

  Further Case Management Hearings

  Consideration of the length of the trial

  The exercise of the powers

  Expert Evidence

  Surveillance Evidence

Disclosure

Abuse of process

The trial

Introduction

N–2   There is a broad consensus that the length of fraud and trials of other complex crimes must be controlled within proper bounds in order:

         (i) To enable the jury to retain and assess the evidence which they have heard. If the trial is so long that the jury cannot do this, then the trial is not fair either to the prosecution or the defence.

         (ii) To make proper use of limited public resources: see *Jisl* [2004] EWCA Crim 696 at [113]–[121].

There is also a consensus that no trial should be permitted to exceed a given period, save in exceptional circimstances; some favour 3 months, others an outer limit of 6 months. Whatever view is taken, it is essential that the current length of trials is brought back to an acceptable and proper duration.

This Protocol supplements the *Criminal Procedure Rules* and summarises good practice which experience has shown may assist in bringing about some reduction in the length of trials of fraud and other crimes that result in complex trials. Flexibility of application of this Protocol according to the needs of each case is essential; it is designed to inform but not to proscribe.

This Protocol is primarily directed towards cases which are likely to last eight weeks or longer. It should also be followed, however, in all cases estimated to last more than four weeks. This Protocol applies to trials by jury, but many of the principles will be applicable if trials without a jury are permitted under s.43 of the *Criminal Justice Act* 2003.

The best handling technique for a long case is continuous management by an experienced Judge nominated for the purpose.

It is intended that this Protocol be kept up to date; any further practices or techniques found to be successful in the management of complex cases should be notified to the office of the Lord Chief Justice.

1. The investigation

(i) The role of the prosecuting authority and the judge

N–3   (a) Unlike other European countries, a judge in England and Wales does no

directly control the investigation process; that is the responsibility of the
Investigating Authority, and in turn the Prosecuting Authority and the
prosecution advocate. Experience has shown that a prosecution lawyer
(who must be of sufficient experience and who will be a member of the
team at trial) and the prosecution advocate, if different, should be involved
in the investigation as soon as it appears that a heavy fraud trial or other
complex criminal trial is likely to ensue. The costs that this early preparation will incur will be saved many times over in the long run.

(b) The judge can and should exert a substantial and beneficial influence by
making it clear that, generally speaking, trials should be kept within
manageable limits. In most cases 3 months should be the target outer limit,
but there will be cases where a duration of 6 months, or in exceptional circumstances, even longer may be inevitable.

(ii) Interviews

(a) At present many interviews are too long and too unstructured. This has a   **N–4**
knock-on effect on the length of trials. Interviews should provide an opportunity for suspects to respond to the allegations against them. They
should not be an occasion to discuss every document in the case. It should
become clear from judicial rulings that interviews of this kind are a waste of
resources.

(b) The suspect must be given sufficient information before or at the interview
to enable them to meet the questions fairly and answer them honestly; the
information is not provided to give him the opportunity to manufacture a
false story which fits undisputable facts.

(c) It is often helpful if the principal documents are provided either in advance
of the interview or shown as the interview progresses; asking detailed questions about events a considerable period in the past without reference to
the documents is often not very helpful.

(iii) The prosecution and defence teams

(a) **The Prosecution Team**   **N–5**
While instructed it is for the lead advocate for the prosecution to
take all necessary decisions in the presentation and general conduct of
the prosecution case. The prosecution lead advocate will be treated by
the court as having that responsibility.

However, in relation to policy decisions the lead advocate for the
prosecution must not give an indication or undertaking which binds the
prosecution without first discussing the issue with Director of the Prosecuting authority or other senior officer.

"Policy" decisions should be understood as referring to non-
evidential decisions on: the acceptance of pleas of guilty to lesser counts
or groups of counts or available alternatives: offering no evidence on
particular counts; consideration of a re-trial; whether to lodge an appeal; certification of a point of law; and the withdrawal of the prosecution as a whole (for further information see the "Farquharson Guidelines" on the role and responsibilities of the prosecution advocate).

(b) **The Defence Team**
In each case, the lead advocate for the defence will be treated by the
court as having responsibility to the court for the presentation and general conduct of the defence case.

(c) In each case, a case progression officer must be assigned by the court, prosecution and defence from the time of the first hearing when directions are
given (as referred to in paragraph 3(iii)) until the conclusion of the trial.

(d) In each case where there are multiple defendants, the LSC will need to
consider carefully the extent and level of representation necessary.

(iv) Initial consideration of the length of a case
If the prosecutor in charge of the case from the Prosecuting Authority or the lead   **N–6**

advocate for the prosecution consider that the case as formulated is likely to last more than 8 weeks, the case should be referred in accordance with arrangements made by the Prosecuting Authority to a more senior prosecutor. The senior prosecutor will consider whether it is desirable for the case to be prosecuted in that way or whether some steps might be taken to reduce its likely length, whilst at the same time ensuring that the public interest is served.

Any case likely to last 6 months or more must be referred to the Director of the Prosecuting Authority so that similar considerations can take place.

(v) Notification of cases likely to last more than 8 weeks

N–7 Special arrangements will be put in place for the early notification by the CPS and other Prosecuting Authorities, to the LSC and to a single designated officer of the Court in each Region (Circuit) of any case which the CPS or other Prosecuting Authority consider likely to last over 8 weeks.

(vi) Venue

N–8 The court will allocate such cases and other complex cases likely to last 4 weeks or more to a specific venue suitable for the trial in question, taking into account the convenience to witnesses, the parties, the availability of time at that location, and all other relevant considerations.

2. Designation of the trial judge

The assignment of a judge

N–9 (a) In any complex case which is expected to last more than four weeks, the trial judge will be assigned under the direction of the Presiding Judges at the earliest possible moment.

(b) Thereafter the assigned judge should manage that case "from cradle to grave"; it is essential that the same judge manages the case from the time of his assignment and that arrangements are made for him to be able to do so. It is recognised that in certain court centres with a large turnover of heavy cases (e.g. Southwark) this objective is more difficult to achieve. But in those court centres there are teams of specialist judges, who are more readily able to handle cases which the assigned judge cannot continue with because of unexpected events; even at such courts, there must be no exception to the principle that one judge must handle all the pre-trial hearings until the case is assigned to another judge.

3. Case management

(i) Objectives

N–10 (a) The number, length and organisation of case management hearings will, of course, depend critically on the circumstances and complexity of the individual case. However, thorough, well-prepared and extended case management hearings will save court time and costs overall.

(b) Effective case management of heavy fraud and other complex criminal cases requires the judge to have a much more detailed grasp of the case than may be necessary for many other Plea and Case Management Hearings (PCMHs). Though it is for the judge in each case to decide how much pre-reading time he needs so that the judge is on top of the case, it is not always a sensible use of judicial time to allocate a series of reading days during which the judge sits alone in his room, working through numerous boxes of ring binders.

See paragraph 3(iv)(e) below

(ii) Fixing the trial date

N–11 Although it is important that the trial date should be fixed as early as possible, this may not always be the right course. There are two principal alternatives:

(a) The trial date should be fixed at the first opportunity—i.e. at the first (and usually short) directions hearing referred to in The first hearing for the giving of initial directions. From then on everyone must work to that date. All orders and pre-trial steps should be timetabled to fit in with that date. All advocates and the judge should take note of this date, in the expectation that the trial will proceed on the date determined.

(b) The trial date should not be fixed until the issues have been explored at a full case management hearing (referred to in The first Case Management Hearing), after the advocates on both sides have done some serious work on the case. Only then can the length of the trial be estimated.

Which is apposite must depend on the circumstances of each case, but the earlier it is possible to fix a trial date, by reference to a proper estimate and a timetable set by reference to the trial date, the better.

It is generally to be expected that once a trial is fixed on the basis of the estimate provided, that it will not be **increased** if, and only if, the party seeking to extend the time justifies why the original estimate is no longer appropriate.

(iii) The first hearing for the giving of initial directions

At the first opportunity the assigned judge should hold a short hearing to give **N–12** initial directions. The directions on this occasion might well include:

(a) That there should be a full case management hearing on, or commencing on, a specified future date by which time the parties will be properly prepared for a meaningful hearing and the defence will have full instructions.

(b) That the prosecution should provide an outline written statement of the prosecution case at least one week in advance of that case management hearing, outlining in simple terms:

   (i) the key facts on which it relies;

   (ii) the key evidence by which the prosecution seeks to prove the facts.

The statement must be sufficient to permit the judge to understand the case and for the defence to appreciate the basic elements of its case against each defendant. The prosecution may be invited to highlight the key points of the case orally at the case management hearing by way of a short mini-opening. The outline statement should not be considered binding, but it will serve the essential purpose in telling the judge, and everyone else, what the case is really about and identifying the key issues.

(c) That a core reading list and core bundle for the case management hearing should be delivered at least one week in advance.

(d) Preliminary directions about disclosure: see paragraph 4.

(iv) The first case management hearing

(a) At the first case management hearing: **N–13**

   (1) the prosecution advocate should be given the opportunity to highlight any points from the prosecution outline statement of case (which will have been delivered at least a week in advance;

   (2) each defence advocate should be asked to outline the defence.

If the defence advocate is not in a position to say what is in issue and what is not in issue, then the case management hearing can be adjourned for a short and limited time and to a fixed date to enable the advocate to take instructions; such an adjournment should only be necessary in exceptional circumstances, as the defence advocate should be properly instructed by the time of the first case management hearing and in any event is under an obligation to take sufficient instructions to fulfil the obligations contained in sections 33–39 of *Criminal Justice Act* 2003.

(b) There should then be a real dialogue between the judge and all advocates for the purpose of identifying:

   (i) the focus of the prosecution case;

   (ii) the common ground;

   (iii) the real issues in the case. (Rule 3.2 of the *Criminal Procedure Rules*.)

(c) The judge will try to generate a spirit of co-operation between the court and the advocates on all sides. The expeditious conduct of the trial and a focussing on the real issues must be in the interests of **all** parties. It cannot be in the interests of any defendant for his good points to become lost in a welter of uncontroversial or irrelevant evidence.

(d) In many fraud cases the primary facts are not seriously disputed. The real issue is what each defendant knew and whether that defendant was dishonest. Once the judge has identified what is in dispute and what is not in dispute, the judge can then discuss with the advocate how the trial should be structured, what can be dealt with by admissions or agreed facts, what uncontroversial matters should be proved by concise oral evidence, what timetabling can be required under Rule 3.10 *Criminal Procedure Rules*, and other directions.

(e) In particularly heavy fraud or complex cases the judge may possibly consider it necessary to allocate a whole week for a case management hearing. If that week is used wisely, many further weeks of trial time can be saved. In the gaps which will inevitably arise during that week (for example while the advocates are exploring matters raised by the judge) the judge can do a substantial amount of informed reading. The case has come "alive" at this stage. Indeed, in a really heavy fraud case, if the judge fixes one or more case management hearings on this scale, there will be need for fewer formal reading days. Moreover a huge amount can be achieved in the pre-trial stage, if all trial advocates are gathered in the same place, focussing on the case **at the same time**, for several days consecutively.

(f) Requiring the defence to serve proper case statements may enable the court to identify

(i) what is common ground and

(ii) the real issues.

It is therefore important that proper defence case statements be provided as required by the *Criminal Procedure Rules*; judges will use the powers contained in ss.28–34 of the *Criminal Proceedings and Evidence Act* 1996 [*sic*] (and the corresponding provisions of the *CJA* 1987, ss.33 and following of the *Criminal Justice Act* 2003) and the *Criminal Procedure Rules* to ensure that realistic defence case statements are provided.

(g) Likewise this objective may be achieved by requiring the prosecution to serve draft admissions by a specified date and by requiring the defence to respond within a specified number of weeks.

(v) Further case management hearings

N–14

(a) The date of the next case management hearing should be fixed at the conclusion of the hearing so that there is no delay in having to fix the date through listing offices, clerks and others.

(b) If one is looking at a trial which threatens to run for months, pre-trial case management on an intensive scale is essential.

(vi) Consideration of the length of the trial

N–15

(a) Case management on the above lines, the procedure set out in paragraph 1(iv), may still be insufficient to reduce the trial to a manageable length generally a trial of 3 months should be the target, but there will be cases where a duration of 6 months or, in exceptional circumstances, even longer may be inevitable.

(b) If the trial is not estimated to be within a manageable length, it will be necessary for the judge to consider what steps should be taken to reduce the length of the trial, whilst still ensuring that the prosecution has the opportunity of placing the full criminality before the court.

(c) To assist the judge in this task,

(i) the lead advocate for the prosecution should be asked to explain why the prosecution have rejected a shorter way of proceeding; they may also be asked to divide the case into sections of evidence and explain the scope of each section and the need for each section;

    (ii) the lead advocates for the prosecution and for the defence should be prepared to put forward in writing, if requested, ways in which a case estimated to last more than three months can be shortened, including possible severance of counts or defendants, exclusions of sections of the case or of evidence or areas of the case where admissions can be made.

(d) One course the judge may consider is pruning the indictment by omitting certain charges and/or by omitting certain defendants. The judge must not usurp the function of the prosecution in this regard, and he must bear in mind that he will, at the outset, know less about the case than the advocates. The aim is achieve [*sic*] fairness to all parties

(e) Nevertheless, the judge does have two methods of pruning available for use in appropriate circumstances:

    (i) persuading the prosecution that it is not worthwhile pursuing certain charges and/or certain defendants;

    (ii) severing the indictment. Severance for reasons of case management alone is perfectly proper, although judges should have regard to any representations made by the prosecution that severance would weaken their case. Indeed the judge's hand will be strengthened in this regard by rule 1.1(2)(g) of the *Criminal Procedure Rules*. However, before using what may be seen as a blunt instrument, the judge should insist on seeing full defence statements of all affected defendants. Severance may be unfair to the prosecution if, for example, there is a cut-throat defence in prospect. For example, the defence of the principal defendant may be that the defendant relied on the advice of his accountant or solicitor that what was happening was acceptable. The defence of the professional may be that he gave no such advice. Against that background, it might be unfair to the prosecution to order separate trials of the two defendants.

(vii) The exercise of the powers

(a) The *Criminal Procedure Rules* require the court to take a more active part in case management. These are salutary provisions which should bring to an end interminable criminal trials of the kind which the Court of Appeal criticised in *Jisl* [2004] EWCA 696 at [113]–[121].   **N–16**

(b) Nevertheless these salutary provisions do not have to be used on every occasion. Where the advocates have done their job properly, by narrowing the issues, pruning the evidence and so forth, it may be quite inappropriate for the judge to "weigh in" and start cutting out more evidence or more charges of his own volition. It behoves the judge to make a careful assessment of the degree of judicial intervention which is warranted in each case.

(c) The note of caution in the previous paragraph is supported by certain experience which has been gained of the *Civil Procedure Rules* (on which the *Criminal Procedure Rules* are based). The CPR contain valuable and efficacious provisions for case management by the judge on his own initiative which have led to huge savings of court time and costs. Surveys by the Law Society have shown that the CPR have been generally welcomed by court users and the profession, but there have been reported to have been isolated instances in which the parties to civil litigation have faithfully complied with both the letter and the spirit of the CPR, and have then been aggrieved by what was perceived to be unnecessary intermeddling by the court.

(viii) Expert evidence

(a) Early identification of the subject matter of expert evidence to be adduced by the prosecution and the defence should be made as early as possible, preferably at the directions hearing.   **N–17**

(b) Following the exchange of expert evidence, any areas of disagreement should be identified and a direction should generally be made requiring the experts to meet and prepare, after discussion, a joint statement identifying points of agreement and contention and areas where the prosecution is put to proof on matters of which a positive case to the contrary is not advanced by the defence. After the statement has been prepared it should be served on the court, the prosecution and the defence. In some cases, it might be appropriate to provide that to the jury.

(ix) Surveillance evidence

N–18
    (a) Where a prosecution is based upon many months' observation or surveillance evidence and it appears that it is capable of effective presentation based on a shorter period, the advocate should be required to justify the evidence of such observations before it is permitted to be adduced, either substantially or in its entirety.

    (b) Schedules should be provided to cover as much of the evidence as possible and admissions sought.

4. Disclosure

N–19
In fraud cases the volume of documentation obtained by the prosecution is liable to be immense. The problems of disclosure are intractable and have the potential to disrupt the entire trial process.

    (i) The prosecution lawyer (and the prosecution advocate if different) brought in at the outset, as set out in paragraph 1(i)(a), each have a continuing responsibility to discharge the prosecution's duty of disclosure, either personally or by delegation, in accordance with the Attorney General's Guidelines on Disclosure.

    (ii) The prosecution should only disclose those documents which are relevant (i.e. likely to assist the defence or undermine the prosecution—see s.3(1) of *CPIA* 1996 and the provisions of the *CJA* 2003).

    (iii) It is almost always undesirable to give the "warehouse key" to the defence for two reasons:

        (a) this amounts to an abrogation of the responsibility of the prosecution;

        (b) the defence solicitors may spend a disproportionate amount of time and incur disproportionate costs trawling through a morass of documents.

The judge should therefore try and ensure that disclosure is limited to what is likely to assist the defence or undermine the prosecution.

    (iv) At the outset the judge should set a timetable for dealing with disclosure issues. In particular, the judge should fix a date by which all defence applications for specific disclosure must be made. In this regard, it is relevant that the defendants are likely to be intelligent people, who know their own business affairs and who (for the most part) will know what documents or categories of documents they are looking for.

    (v) At the outset (and before the cut-off date for specific disclosure applications) the judge should ask the defence to indicate what documents they are interested in and from what source. A general list is not an acceptable response to this request. The judge should insist upon a list which is specific, manageable and realistic. The judge may also require justification of any request.

    (vi) In non-fraud cases, the same considerations apply, but some may be different:

        (a) It is not possible to approach many non-fraud cases on the basis that the defendant knows what is there or what they are looking for. But on the other hand this should not be turned into an excuse for a "fishing expedition"; the judge should insist on knowing the issue to which a request for disclosure applies.

        (b) If the *bona fides* of the investigation is called into question, a judge will be concerned to see that there has been independent and effective appraisal of the documents contained in the disclosure schedule and that its contents are adequate. In appropriate cases where this issue has arisen and there are grounds which show there is a real issue, consideration should be given to receiving evidence on oath from the senior investigating officer at an early case management hearing.

5. Abuse of process

(i) Applications to stay or dismiss for abuse of process have become a normal   **N–20**
feature of heavy and complex cases. Such applications may be based upon delay and the health of defendants.

(ii) Applications in relation to absent special circumstances [*sic*] tend to be unsuccessful and not to be pursued on appeal. For this reason there is comparatively little Court of Appeal guidance: but see: *Harris and Howells* [2003] EWCA Crim 486. It should be noted that abuse of process is not there to discipline the prosecution or the police

(iii) The arguments on both sides must be reduced to writing. Oral evidence is seldom relevant.

(iv) The judge should direct full written submissions (rather than "skeleton arguments") on any abuse application in accordance with a timetable set by him; these should identify any element of prejudice the defendant is alleged to have suffered.

(v) The judge should normally aim to conclude the hearing within an absolute maximum limit of one day, if necessary in accordance with a timetable. The parties should therefore prepare their papers on this basis and not expect the judge to allow the oral hearing to be anything more than an occasion to highlight concisely their arguments and answer any questions the court may have of them; applications will not be allowed drag on.

6. The trial

(i) The particular hazard of heavy fraud trials

A heavy fraud or other complex trial has the potential to lose direction and focus.   **N–21**
This is a disaster for three reasons:

(a) the jury will lose track of the evidence, thereby prejudicing both prosecution and defence;

(b) the burden on the defendants, the judge and indeed all involved will become intolerable;

(c) scarce public resources are wasted. Other prosecutions are delayed or—worse—may never happen. Fraud which is detected but not prosecuted (for resource reasons) undermines confidence.

(ii) Judicial mastery of the case

(a) It is necessary for the judge to exercise firm control over the conduct of the   **N–22**
trial at all stages.

(b) In order to do this the judge must read the witness statements and the documents, so that the judge can discuss case management issues with the advocates on—almost—an equal footing.

(c) To this end, the judge should not set aside weeks or even days for pre-reading (see paragraph 3(i)(b)). Hopefully the judge will have gained a good grasp of the evidence during the case management hearings. Nevertheless, realistic reading time must be provided for the judge in advance of trial.

(d) The role of the judge in a heavy fraud or other complex criminal trial is different from his/her role in a "conventional" criminal trial. So far as possible, the judge should be freed from other duties and burdens, so that he/

she can give the high degree of commitment which a heavy fraud trial requires. This will pay dividends in terms of saving weeks or months of court time.

(iii) The order of the evidence

N–23
    (a) By the outset of the trial at the latest (and in most cases very much earlier) the judge must be provided with a schedule, showing the sequence of prosecution (and in an appropriate case defence) witnesses and the dates upon which they are expected to be called. This can only be prepared by discussion between prosecution and defence which the judge should expect, and say he/she expects, to take place: See: *Criminal Procedure Rule* 3.10. The schedule should, in so far as it relates to prosecution witnesses, be developed in consultation with the witnesses, via the witness care units, and with consideration given to their personal needs. Copies of the schedule should be provided for the Witness Service.

    (b) The schedule should be kept under review by the trial judge and by the parties. If a case is running behind or ahead of schedule, each witness affected must be advised by the party who is calling that witness at the earliest opportunity.

    (c) If an excessive amount of time is allowed for any witness, the judge can ask why. The judge may probe with the advocates whether the time envisaged for the evidence-in-chief or cross-examination (as the case may be) of a particular witness is really necessary.

(iv) Case management sessions

N–24
    (a) The order of the evidence may have legitimately to be departed from. It will, however, be a useful for tool for monitoring the progress of the case. There should be periodic case management sessions, during which the judge engages the advocates upon a stock-taking exercise: asking, amongst other questions, "where are we going?" and "what is the relevance of the next three witnesses?". This will be a valuable means of keeping the case on track. Rule 3.10 of the *Criminal Procedure Rules* will again assist the judge.

    (b) The judge may wish to consider issuing the occasional use of "case management notes" to the advocates, in order to set out the judge's tentative views on where the trial may be going off track, which areas of future evidence are relevant and which may have become irrelevant (e.g. because of concessions, admissions in cross-examination and so forth). Such notes from the judge plus written responses from the advocates can, cautiously used, provide a valuable focus for debate during the periodic case management reviews held during the course of the trial.

(v) Controlling prolix cross-examination

N–25
    (a) Setting **rigid** time limits in advance for cross-examination is rarely appropriate—as experience has shown in civil cases; but a timetable is essential so that the judge can exercise control and so that there is a clear target to aim at for the completion of the evidence of each witness. Moreover the judge can and should indicate when cross-examination is irrelevant, unnecessary or time wasting. The judge may limit the time for further cross-examination of a particular witness.

(vi) Electronic presentation of evidence

N–26
    (a) Electronic presentation of evidence (EPE) has the potential to save huge amounts of time in fraud and other complex criminal trials and should be used more widely.

    (b) HMCS is providing facilities for the easier use of EPE with a standard audio visual facility. Effectively managed, the savings in court time achieved by EPE more than justify the cost.

    (c) There should still be a core bundle of those documents to which frequent reference will be made during the trial. The jury may wish to mark that bundle or to refer back to particular pages as the evidence progresses. EPE can be used for presenting all documents not contained in the core bundle.

(d) Greater use of other modern forms of graphical presentations should be made wherever possible.

(vii) Use of interviews

The judge should consider extensive editing of self serving interviews, even when the defence want the jury to hear them in their entirety; such interviews are not evidence of the truth of their contents but merely of the defendant's reaction to the allegation. **N–27**

(viii) Jury management

(a) The jury should be informed as early as possible in the case as to what the issues are in a manner directed by the Judge. **N–28**

(b) The jury must be regularly updated as to the trial timetable and the progress of the trial, subject to warnings as to the predictability of the trial process.

(c) Legal argument should be heard at times that causes the least inconvenience to jurors.

(d) It is useful to consider with the advocates whether written directions should be given to the jury and, if so, in what form.

(ix) Maxwell hours

(a) Maxwell hours should only be permitted after careful consideration and consultation with the Presiding Judge. **N–29**

(b) Considerations in favour include:

(i) legal argument can be accommodated without disturbing the jury;

(ii) there is a better chance of a representative jury;

(iii) time is made available to the judge, advocates and experts to do useful work in the afternoons

(c) Considerations against include:

(i) the lengthening of trials and the consequent waste of court time;

(ii) the desirability of making full use of the jury once they have arrived at court;

(iii) shorter trials tend to diminish the need for special provisions *e.g.* there are fewer difficulties in empanelling more representative juries;

(iv) they are unavailable if any defendant is in custody.

(d) It may often be the case that a maximum of one day of Maxwell hours a week is sufficient; if so, it should be timetabled in advance to enable all submissions by advocates, supported by skeleton arguments served in advance, to be dealt with in the period after 1:30 pm on that day.

(x) Livenote

If Livenote is used, it is important that all users continue to take a note of the evidence, otherwise considerable time is wasted in detailed reading of the entire daily transcript. **N–30**

7. Other issues

(i) Defence representation and defence costs

(a) Applications for change in representation in complex trials need special consideration; the ruling of HH Judge Wakerley QC (as he then was) in *Asghar Ali* has been circulated by the JSB. **N–31**

(b) Problems have arisen when the Legal Services Commission have declined to allow advocates or solicitors to do certain work; on occasions the matter has been raised with the judge managing or trying the case.

(c) The Legal Services Commission has provided guidance to judges on how they can obtain information from the LSC as to the reasons for their decisions; further information in relation to this can be obtained from *Nigel Field, Head of the Complex Crime Unit, Legal Services Commission, 29–37 Red Lion Street, London, WC1R 4PP.*

(ii) Assistance to the judge

N–32   Experience has shown that in some very heavy cases, the judge's burden can be substantially offset with the provision of a judicial assistant or other support and assistance.

B. MANAGEMENT OF TERRORISM CASES

N–33   A protocol issued by Sir Igor Judge P.

January 30, 2007

Terrorism cases

N–34   1. This protocol applies to "terrorism cases". For the purposes of this protocol a case is a "terrorism case" where:

(a) one of the offences charged against any of the defendants is indictable only and it is alleged by the prosecution that there is evidence that it took place during an act of terrorism or for the purposes of terrorism as defined in section 1 of the *Terrorist Act* 2000 [*sic*]; this may include, but is not limited to:

    i. murder;

    ii. manslaughter;

    iii. an offence under section 18 of the *Offences against the Person Act* 1861 (wounding with intent);

    iv. an offence under section 23 or 24 of that Act (administering poison etc);

    v. an offence under section 28 or 29 of that Act (explosives);

    vi. an offence under section 2, 3 or 5 of the *Explosive Substances Act* 1883 (causing explosions);

    vii. an offence under section 1(2) of the *Criminal Damage Act* 1971 (endangering life by damaging property);

    viii. an offence under section 1 of the *Biological Weapons Act* 1974 (biological weapons);

    ix. an offence under section 2 of the *Chemical Weapons Act* 1996 (chemical weapons);

    x. an offence under section 56 of the *Terrorism Act* 2000 (directing a terrorist organisation);

    xi. an offence under section 59 of that Act (inciting terrorism overseas);

    xii. offences under (v), (vii) and (viii) above given jurisdiction by virtue of section 62 of that Act (terrorist bombing overseas);

    xiii. an offence under section 5 of the *Terrorism Act* 2006 (preparation of terrorism acts);

(b) one of the offences so charged includes an allegation by the prosecution of serious fraud that took place during an act of terrorism or for the purposes of terrorism as defined in section 1 of the *Terrorist Act* 2000 [*sic*] and meets the test to be transferred to the Crown Court under section 4 of the *Criminal Justice Act* 1987;

(c) one of the offences charged is indictable only includes [*sic*] an allegation that a defendant conspired, incited or attempted to commit an offence under sub-paragraphs (1)(a) or (b) above;

(d) it is a case (which can be indictable only or triable either way) that a judge of the terrorism cases list (see paragraph 2(a) below) considers should be a terrorism case. In deciding whether a case not covered by sub-paragraphs (1)(a), (b) or (c) above should be a terrorism case, the judge may hear representations from the Crown Prosecution Service.

The terrorism cases list

2. (a) All terrorism cases, wherever they originate in England and **N–35** Wales, will be managed in a list known as the "terrorism cases list" by the Presiding Judges of the South Eastern Circuit and such other judges of the High Court as are nominated by the President of the Queen's Bench Division.

(b) Such cases will be tried, unless otherwise directed by the President of the Queen's Bench Division, by a judge of the High Court as nominated by the President of the Queen's Bench Division.

3. The judges managing the terrorism cases referred to in paragraph 2 will be **N–36** supported by the London and South Eastern Regional Co-ordinator's Office (the "Regional Co-ordinator's Office"). An official of that office or nominated by that office will act as the case progression officer for cases in that list for the purposes of part 3.4 of the *Criminal Procedure Rules*.

Procedure after charge

4. Immediately after a person has been charged in a terrorism case, anywhere **N–37** in England and Wales, a representative of the Crown Prosecution Service will notify the person on the 24 hour rota for special jurisdiction matters at Westminster Magistrates' Court of the following information:

(a) the full name of each defendant and the name of his solicitor of [*sic*] other legal representative, if known;

(b) the charges laid;

(c) the name and contact details of the crown prosecutor with responsibility for the case, if known;

(d) confirmation that the case is a terrorism case.

5. The person on the 24-hour rota will then ensure that all terrorism cases **N–38** wherever they are charged in England and Wales are listed before the Chief Magistrate or other District Judge designated under the *Terrorism Act* 2000. Unless the Chief Magistrate or other District Judge designated under the *Terrorism Act* 2000 directs otherwise the first appearance of all defendants accused of terrorism offences will be listed at Westminster Magistrates' Court.

6. In order to comply with section 46 of the *Police and Criminal Evidence Act* **N–39** 1984, if a defendant in a terrorism case is charged at a police station within the local justice area in which Westminster Magistrates' Court is situated the defendant must be brought before Westminster Magistrates' Court as soon as is practicable and in any event not later than the first sitting after he is charged with the offence. If a defendant in a terrorism case is charged in a police station outside the local justice area in which Westminster Magistrates' Court is situated, unless the Chief Magistrate or other designated judge directs otherwise, the defendant must be removed to that area as soon as is practicable. He must then be brought before Westminster Magistrates' Court as soon as is practicable after his arrival in the area and in any event not later than the first sitting of Westminster Magistrates' Court after his arrival in that area.

7. As soon as is practicable after charge a representative of the Crown Prosecu- **N–40** tion Service will also provide the Regional Listing Co-ordinator's Office with the information listed in paragraph 4 above.

8. The Regional Co-ordinator's Office will then ensure that the Chief Magis- **N–41** trate and the Legal Services Commission have the same information.

Cases to be sent to the Crown Court under section 51 of the Crime and Disorder Act 1998

9. A preliminary hearing should normally be ordered by the magistrates' court **N–42**

in a terrorism case. The court should ordinarily direct that the preliminary hearing should take place about 14 days after charge.

N–43   **10.** The sending magistrates' court should contact the Regional Listing Coordinator's Office who will be responsible for notifying the magistrates' court as to the relevant Crown Court to which to send the case.

N–44   **11.** In all terrorism cases, the magistrates' court case progression form for cases sent to the Crown Court under section 51 of the *Crime and Disorder Act* 1998 should not be used. Instead of the automatic directions set out in that form, the magistrates' court shall make the following directions to facilitate the preliminary hearing at the Crown Court:

> (a) three days prior to the preliminary hearing in the terrorism cases list, the prosecution must serve upon each defendant and the Regional Listing coordinator:
>
>> i. a preliminary summary of the case;
>>
>> ii. the names of those who are to represent the prosecution, if known;
>>
>> iii. an estimate of the length of the trial;
>>
>> iv. a suggested provisional timetable which should generally include:
>>
>>> • the general nature of further enquiries being made by the prosecution;
>>>
>>> • the time needed for the completion of such enquiries;
>>>
>>> • the time required by the prosecution to review the case;
>>>
>>> • a timetable for the phased service of the evidence;
>>>
>>> • the time for the provision by the Attorney General for his consent if necessary;
>>>
>>> • the time for service of the detailed defence case statement;
>>>
>>> • the date for the case management hearing;
>>>
>>> • estimated trial date;
>>
>> v. a preliminary statement of the possible disclosure issues setting out the nature and scale of the problem including the amount of unused material, the manner in which the prosecution seeks to deal with these matters and a suggested timetable for discharging their statutory duty;
>>
>> vi. any information relating to bail and custody time limits;
>
> (b) one day prior to the preliminary hearing in the terrorist cases list, each defendant must serve in writing on the Regional Listing Co-ordinator and the prosecution:
>
>> i. the proposed representation;
>>
>> ii. observations on the timetable;
>>
>> iii. an indication of plea and the general nature of the defence.

Cases to be transferred to the Crown Court under section 4(1) of the Criminal Justice Act 1987

N–45   **13.** If a terrorism case is to be transferred to the Crown Court the magistrates' court should proceed as if it is being sent to the Crown Court, as in paragraphs 10–12 above.

N–46   **14.** When a terrorism case is so sent or transferred the case will go into the terrorism list and be managed by a judge as described in paragraph 2 above.

The preliminary hearing at the Crown Court

N–47   **15.** At the preliminary hearing, the judge will determine whether the case is one to remain in the terrorism list and if so give directions setting the provisional timetable.

N–48   **16.** The Legal Services Commission must attend the hearing by an authorised officer to assist the court.

Use of video link

N–49   **17.** Unless a judge otherwise directs, all Crown Court hearings prior to the trial will be conducted by video link for all defendants in custody.

Security

18. The police service and the prison service will provide the Regional Listing   **N-50**
Co-ordinator's Office with an initial joint assessment of the security risks associated with any court appearance by the defendants within 14 days of charge. Any
subsequent changes in circumstances or the assessment of risk which have the
potential to impact upon the choice of trial venue will be notified to the Regional
Listing Co-ordinator's Office immediately.

[The next paragraph is N-52.]

C. Control and Management of Unused Material in the Crown Court

Introduction

1. Disclosure is one of the most important—as well as one of the most   **N-52**
abused—of the procedures relating to criminal trials. There needs to be a sea-
change in the approach of both judges and the parties to all aspects of the
handling of the material which the prosecution do not intend to use in support of
their case. For too long, a wide range of serious misunderstandings has existed,
both as to the exact ambit of the unused material to which the defence is entitled,
and the role to be played by the judge in ensuring that the law is properly applied.
All too frequently applications by the parties and decisions by the judges in this
area have been made based either on misconceptions as to the true nature of the
law or a general laxity of approach (however well-intentioned). This failure
properly to apply the binding provisions as regards disclosure has proved
extremely and unnecessarily costly and has obstructed justice. It is, therefore, essential that disclosure obligations are properly discharged—by both the prosecution and the defence—in all criminal proceedings, and the court's careful oversight
of this process is an important safeguard against the possibility of miscarriages of
justice.

2. The House of Lords stated in *R. v. H. and C.* [2004] 2 A.C. 134 at 147:

> Fairness ordinarily requires that any material held by the prosecution which
> weakens its case or strengthens that of the defendant, if not relied on as part
> of its formal case against the defendant, should be disclosed to the defence.
> Bitter experience has shown that miscarriages of justice may occur where such
> material is withheld from disclosure. The golden rule is that full disclosure of
> such material should be made.

3. However, it is also essential that the trial process is not overburdened or
diverted by erroneous and inappropriate disclosure of unused prosecution material, or by misconceived applications in relation to such material.

4. The overarching principle is therefore that unused prosecution material will
fall to be disclosed if, and only if, it satisfies the test for disclosure applicable to the
proceedings in question, subject to any overriding public interest considerations.
The relevant test for disclosure will depend on the date the criminal investigation
in question commenced (see the section on Sources below), as this will determine
whether the common law disclosure regime applies, or either of the two disclosure
regimes under the *Criminal Procedure and Investigations Act* 1996 (*CPIA*).

5. There is very clear evidence that, without active judicial oversight and
management, the handling of disclosure issues in general, and the disclosure of
unused prosecution material in particular, can cause delays and adjournments.

6. The failure to comply fully with disclosure obligations, whether by the prosecution or the defence, may disrupt and in some cases even frustrate the course of
justice.

7. Consideration of irrelevant unused material may consume wholly unjustifiable and disproportionate amounts of time and public resources, undermining the overall performance and efficiency of the criminal justice system. The aim of this Protocol is therefore to assist and encourage judges when dealing with all disclosure issues, in the light of the overarching principle set out in paragraph 4 above. This guidance is intended to cover all Crown Court cases (including cases where relevant case management directions are made at the magistrates' court). It is not, therefore, confined to a very few high profile and high cost cases.

8. Unused material which has been gathered during the course of a criminal investigation and disclosed by the prosecution pursuant to their duties (as set out elsewhere in this Protocol) is received by the defence subject to a prohibition not to use or disclose the material for any purpose which is not connected with the proceedings for whose purposes they were given it (s.17 *CPIA*). The common law, which applies to all disclosure not made under the *CPIA*, achieves the same result by the creation of an implied undertaking not to use the material for any purposes other than the proper conduct of the particular case (see *Taylor v. Director of the Serious Fraud Office* [1999] 2 A.C. 177, HL). A breach of that undertaking would constitute a contempt of court. These provisions are designed to ensure that the privacy and confidentiality of those who provided the material to the investigation (as well as those who are mentioned in the material) is protected and is not invaded any more than is absolutely necessary. However, neither statute nor the common law prevents any one from using or disclosing such material if it has been displayed or communicated to the public in open court (unless the evidence is subject to continuing reporting restriction), and moreover, an application can be made to the court for permission to use or disclose the object or information.

Sources

N–53   **9.** It is not the purpose of this Protocol to rehearse the law in detail; however, some of the principal sources are set out here.

10. The correct test for disclosure will depend upon the date the relevant criminal investigation commenced:

    a. In relation to offences in respect of which the criminal investigation began prior to 1 April 1997, the common law will apply, and the test for disclosure is that set out in *R. v. Keane*, 99 Cr.App.R. 1.

    b. If the criminal investigation commenced on or after 1 April 1997, but before 4 April 2005, then the *CPIA* in its original form will apply, with separate tests for disclosure of unused prosecution material at the primary and secondary disclosure stages (the latter following service of a defence statement by the accused). The disclosure provisions of the Act are supported by the 1997 edition of the Code of Practice issued under section 23(1) of the *CPIA* (S.I. 1997 No. 1033)

    c. Where the criminal investigation has commenced on or after 4 April 2005, the law is set out in the *CPIA* as amended by Part V of the *Criminal Justice Act* 2003. There is then a single test for disclosure of unused prosecution material and the April 2005 edition of the Code of Practice under section 23(1) of the *CPIA* will apply (see S.I. 2005 No. 985).

The *CPIA* also identifies the stage(s) at which the prosecution is required to disclose material, and the formalities relating to defence statements. The default time limit for prosecution disclosure is set out in section 13 of the Act (see further at paragraph 13 below). The time limits applicable to defence disclosure are set out in the *Criminal Procedure and Investigations Act 1996 (Defence Disclosure) Regulations* 1997 (S.I. 1997 No. 684).

10. [*sic*] Regard must be had to the Attorney General's Guidelines on Disclosure (April 2005). Although these do not have the force of law (*R. v. Winston Brown* [1995] 1 Cr.App.R. 191) they should be given due weight.

11. Part 25 of the *Criminal Procedure Rules* 2005 (see S.I. 2005 No. 384) sets out the procedures to be followed for applications to the court concerning both sensitive and non-sensitive unused material. Part 3 of the Rules is also relevant in respect of the court's general case management powers, and parties should also have regard to the Consolidated Criminal Practice Direction.

12. Parts 22 and 23 of the *Criminal Procedure Rules* are set aside to make provision for other rules concerning disclosure by the prosecution and the defence, although at the date of this Protocol there are no rules under those Parts.

The duty to gather and record unused material

13. For the statutory scheme to work properly, investigators and disclosure officers responsible for the gathering, inspection, retention and recording of relevant unused prosecution material must perform their tasks thoroughly, scrupulously and fairly. In this, they must adhere to the appropriate provisions of the *CPIA* Code of Practice.   **N–54**

14. It is crucial that the police (and indeed all investigative bodies) implement appropriate training regimes and appoint competent disclosure officers, who have sufficient knowledge of the issues in the case. This will enable them to make a proper assessment of the unused prosecution material in the light of the test for relevance under paragraph 2.1 of the *CPIA* Code of Practice, with a view to preparing full and accurate schedules of the retained material. In any criminal investigation, the disclosure officer must retain material that may be relevant to an investigation. This material must be listed on a schedule. Each item listed on the schedule should contain sufficient detail to enable the prosecutor to decide whether or not the material falls to be disclosed. The schedules must be sent to the prosecutor. Wherever possible this should be at the same time as the file containing the material for the prosecution case but the duty to disclose does not end at this point and must continue while relevant material is received even after conviction.

15. Furthermore, the scheduling of the relevant material must be completed expeditiously, so as to enable the prosecution to comply promptly with the duty to provide primary (or, when the amended *CPIA* regime applies) initial disclosure as soon as practicable after:

- the case has been committed for trial under section 6(1) or 6(2) of the *Magistrates' Courts Act* 1980; or
- the case has been transferred to the Crown Court under section 4 of the *Criminal Justice Act* 1987, or section 53 of the *Criminal Justice Act* 1991; or
- copies of documents containing the evidence are served on the accused in according [*sic*] with the *Crime and Disorder Act* 1998 *(Service of Prosecution Evidence) Regulations* 2005 (S.I. 2005 No. 902), where the matter has been sent to the Crown Court pursuant to section 51 or 51A of the *Crime and Disorder Act* 1998; or
- a matter has been added to an indictment in accordance with section 40 of the *Criminal Justice Act* 1988; or
- a bill of indictment has been preferred under section 2(2)(b) of the *Administration of Justice (Miscellaneous Provisions) Act* 1933 or section 22B(3)(a) of the *Prosecution of Offences Act* 1985.

16. Investigators, disclosure officers and prosecutors must promptly and properly discharge their responsibilities under the Act and statutory Code, in order to ensure that justice is not delayed, denied or frustrated. In this context, under paragraph 3.5 of the Code of Practice, it is provided "an investigator should pursue all reasonable lines of inquiry, whether these point towards or away from the suspect".

17. CPS lawyers advising the police pre-charge at police stations should consider conducting a preliminary review of the unused material generated by the investigation, where this is practicable, so as to give early advice on disclosure issues. Otherwise, prosecutors should conduct a preliminary review of disclosure at the same time as the initial review of the evidence. It is critical that the important distinction between the evidence in the case, on the one hand, and any unused material, on the other, is not blurred. Items such as exhibits should be treated as such and the obligation to serve them is not affected by the disclosure regime.

18. Where the single test for disclosure applies under the amended *CPIA* disclosure regime, the prosecutor is under a duty to consider, at an early stage of proceedings, whether there is any unused prosecution material which is reasonably capable of assisting the case for the accused. What a defendant has said by way of defence or explanation either in interview or by way of a prepared statement can be a useful guide to making an objective assessment of the material which would satisfy this test.

19. There may be some occasions when the prosecution, pursuant to surviving common law rules of disclosure, ought to disclose an item or items of unused prosecution material, even in advance of primary or initial disclosure under section 3 of the *CPIA*. This may apply, for instance, where there is information which might affect a decision as to bail; where an abuse of process is alleged; where there is material which might assist the defence to make submissions as to the particular charge or charges, if any, the defendant should face at the Crown Court; and when it is necessary to enable particular preparation to be undertaken at an early stage by the defence. Guidance as to occasions where such disclosure may be appropriate is provided in *R. v. DPP, ex p. Lee* [1999] 2 Cr.App.R. 304. However, once the *CPIA* is triggered (for instance, by committal, or service of case papers following a section 51 sending) it is the *CPIA* which determines what material should be disclosed.

The judge's duty to enforce the statutory scheme

20. When cases are sent to the Crown Court under section 51 of the *Crime and Disorder Act* 1998, the *Crime and Disorder Act 1998 (Service of Prosecution Evidence) Regulations* 2005 allow the prosecution 70 days from the date the matter was sent (50 days, where the accused is in custody) within which to serve on the defence and the court copies of the documents containing the evidence upon which the charge or charges are based (in effect, sufficient evidence to amount to a prima facie case). These time limits may be extended and varied at the court's direction. Directions for service of these case papers may be given at the magistrates' court.

21. While it is important to note that this time limit applies to the service of evidence, rather than unused prosecution material, the court will need to consider at the magistrates' court or preliminary hearing whether it is practicable for the prosecution to comply with primary or initial disclosure at the same time as service of such papers, or whether disclosure ought to take place after a certain interval, but before the matter is listed for a PCMH.

22. If the nature of the case does not allow service of the evidence and initial or primary disclosure within the 70, or if applicable 50, days (or such other period as directed by the magistrates' court), the investigator should ensure that the prosecution advocate at the magistrates' court, preliminary Crown Court hearing, or further hearing prior to the PCMH, is aware of the problems, knows why and how the position has arisen and can assist the court as to what revised time limits are realistic.

23. It would be helpful if the prosecution advocate could make any foreseeable difficulties clear as soon as possible, whether this is at the magistrates' court or in the Crown Court at the preliminary hearing (where there is one).

24. Failing this, where such difficulties arise or have come to light after directions for service of case papers and disclosure have been made, the prosecution should notify the court and the defence promptly. This should be done in advance of the PCMH date, and prior to the date set by the court for the service of this material.

25. It is important that this is done in order that the listing for the PCMH is an effective one, as the defence must have a proper opportunity to read the case papers and to consider the initial or primary disclosure, with a view to timely drafting of a defence case statement (where the matter is to be contested), prior to the PCMH.

26. In order to ensure that the listing of the PCMH is appropriate, Judges should not impose time limits for service of case papers or initial/primary disclosure unless and until they are confident that the prosecution advocate has taken the requisite instructions from those who are actually going to do the work specified. It is better to impose a realistic timetable from the outset than to set unachievable limits. Reference should be made to Part 3 of the *Criminal Procedure Rules* and the Consolidated Practice Direction in this respect.

27. This is likewise appropriate where directions, or further directions, are made in relation to prosecution or defence disclosure at the PCMH. Failure to consider whether the timetable is practicable may dislocate the court timetable and can even imperil trial dates. At the PCMH, therefore, all the advocates—prosecution and defence—must be fully instructed about any difficulties the parties may have in complying with their respective disclosure obligations, and must be in a position to put forward a reasonable timetable for resolution of them.

28. Where directions are given by the court in the light of such inquiry, extensions of time should not be given lightly or as a matter of course. If extensions are sought, then an appropriately detailed explanation must be given. For the avoidance of doubt, it is not sufficient merely for the CPS (or other prosecutor) to say that the papers have been delivered late by the police (or other investigator): the court will need to know why they have been delivered late. Likewise, where the accused has been dilatory in serving a defence statement (where the prosecution has complied with the duty to make primary or initial disclosure of unused material, or has purported to do so), it is not sufficient for the defence to say that insufficient instructions have been taken for service of this within the 14-day time limit: the court will need to know why sufficient instructions have not been taken, and what arrangements have been made for the taking of such instructions.

29. Delays and failures by the defence are as damaging to the timely, fair and efficient hearing of the case as delays and failures by the prosecution, and judges should identify and deal with all such failures firmly and fairly.

30. Judges should not allow the prosecution to abdicate their statutory responsibility for reviewing the unused material by the expedient of allowing the defence to inspect (or providing the defence with copies of) everything on the schedules of non-sensitive unused prosecution material, irrespective of whether that material, or all of that material, satisfies the relevant test for disclosure. Where that test is satisfied it is for the prosecutor to decide the form in which disclosure is made. Disclosure need not be in the same form as that in which the information was recorded. Guidance on case management issues relating to this point was given by Rose L.J. in *R. v. CPS (Interlocutory application under sections 35/36 CPIA)* [2005] EWCA Crim. 2342.

31. Indeed, the larger and more complex the case, the more important it is for the prosecution to adhere to the overarching principle in paragraph 4 and ensure that sufficient prosecution resources are allocated to the task. Handing the defence the "keys to the warehouse" has been the cause of many gross abuses in the past, resulting in huge sums being run up by the defence without any proportionate benefit to the course of justice. These abuses must end.

The defence case statement

32. Reference has been made above to defence disclosure obligations. After the   **N–56** provision of primary or initial disclosure by the prosecution, the next really critical step in the preparation for trial is the service of the defence statement. It is a mandatory requirement for a defence statement to be served, where section 5(5) of the *CPIA* applies to the proceedings. This is due within 14 days of the date upon which the prosecution has complied with, or purported to comply with, the duty of primary or initial disclosure. Service of the defence statement is a critical stage in the disclosure process, and timely service of the statement will allow for the proper consideration of disclosure issues well in advance of the trial date.

33. There may be some cases where it is simply not possible to serve a proper defence case statement within the 14-day time limit; well founded defence applications for an extension of time under paragraph (2) of regulation 3 of the *Criminal Procedure and Investigations Act 1996 (Defence Disclosure Time Limits) Regulations* 1997 may therefore be granted. In a proper case, it may be appropriate to put the PCMH back by a week or so, to enable a sufficient defence case statement to be filed and considered by the prosecution.

34. In the past, the prosecution and the court have too often been faced with a defence case statement that is little more than an assertion that the defendant is not guilty. As was stated by the Court of Appeal in *R. v. Patrick Bryant* [2005]

EWCA Crim. 2079 (*per* Judge L.J., paragraph 12), such a reiteration of the defendant's plea is not the purpose of a defence statement. Defence statements must comply with the requisite formalities set out in section 5(6) and (7), or section 6A, of the *CPIA*, as applicable.

35. Where the enhanced requirements for defence disclosure apply under section 6A of the *CPIA* (namely, where the case involves a criminal investigation commencing on or after 4 April 2005) the defence statement must spell out, in detail, the nature of the defence, and particular defences relied upon; it must identify the matters of fact upon which the accused takes issue with the prosecution, and the reason why, in relation to each disputed matter of fact. It must further identify any point of law (including points as to the admissibility of evidence, or abuse of process) which the accused proposes to take, and identify authorities relied on in relation to each point of law. Where an alibi defence is relied upon, the particulars given must comply with section 6(2)(a) and (b) of the *CPIA*. Judges will expect to see defence case statements that contain a clear and detailed exposition of the issues of fact and law in the case.

36. Where the pre-4 April 2005 *CPIA* disclosure regime applies, the accused must, in the defence statement, set out the nature of the defence in general terms, indicate the matters upon which the defendant takes issue with the prosecution and set out (in relation to each such matter) why issue is taken. Any alibi defence relied upon should comply with the formalities in section 5(7)(a) and (b) of the Act.

37. There must be a complete change in the culture. The defence must serve the defence case statement by the due date. Judges should then examine the defence case statement with care to ensure that it complies with the formalities required by the *CPIA*. As was stated in paragraph 35 of *R. v. H. and C.*—

> If material does not weaken the prosecution case or strengthen that of the defendant, there is no requirement to disclose it. For this purpose the parties' respective cases should not be restrictively analysed. But they must be carefully analysed, to ascertain the specific facts the prosecution seek to establish and the specific grounds on which the charges are resisted. The trial process is not well served if the defence are permitted to make general and unspecified allegations and then seek far-reaching disclosure in the hope that material may turn up to make them good. Neutral material or material damaging to the defendant need not be disclosed and should not be brought to the attention of the court.

38. If no defence case statement—or no sufficient case statement—has been served by the PCMH, the judge should make a full investigation of the reasons for this failure to comply with the mandatory obligation of the accused, under section 5(5) of the *CPIA*.

39. If there is no—or no sufficient—defence statement by the date of PCMH, or any pre-trial hearing where the matter falls to be considered, the judge must consider whether the defence should be warned, pursuant to section 6E(2) of the *CPIA*, that an adverse inference may be drawn at the trial. In the usual case, where section 6E(2) applies and there is no justification for the deficiency, such a warning should be given.

40. Judges must, of course, be alert to ensure that defendants do not suffer because of the faults and failings of their lawyers, but there must be a clear indication to the professions that if justice is to be done, and if disclosure to be dealt with fairly in accordance with the law, a full and careful defence case statement is essential.

41. Where there are failings by either the defence or the prosecution, judges should, in exercising appropriate oversight of disclosure, pose searching questions to the parties and, having done this and explored the reasons for default, give clear directions to ensure that such failings are addressed and remedied well in advance of the trial date.

42. The ultimate sanction for a failure in disclosure by the accused is the drawing of an inference under section 11 of the *CPIA*. Where the amended *CPIA* regime applies, the strict legal position allows the prosecution to comment upon any failure of defence disclosure, with a view to seeking such an inference (except where the failure relates to identifying a point of law), without leave of the court, but often it will be helpful to canvass the matter with the judge beforehand. In suitable cases, the prosecution should consider commenting upon failures in defence disclosure, with a view to such an inference, more readily than has been the practice under the old *CPIA* regime, subject to any views expressed by the judge.

43. It is vital to a fair trial that the prosecution are mindful of their continuing duty of disclosure, and they must particularly review disclosure in the light of the issues identified in the defence case statement. As part of the timetabling exercise, the judge should set a date by which any application under section 8 (if there is to be one) should be made. While the defence may indicate, in advance of the cut-off date, what items of unused material they are interested in and why, such requests must relate to matters raised in the accused's defence statement. The prosecution should only disclose material in response to such requests if the material meets the appropriate test for disclosure, and the matter must proceed to a formal section 8 hearing in the event that the prosecution declines to make disclosure of the items in question. Paragraphs 4(iv)–(vi)(a) of the Lord Chief Justice's March 2005 Protocol for the Control and Management of Heavy Fraud and Other Complex Criminal Cases should be construed accordingly.

44. If, after the prosecution have complied with, or purported to comply with, primary or initial disclosure, and after the service of the defence case statement and any further prosecution disclosure flowing there from, the defence have a reasonable basis to claim disclosure has been inadequate, they must make an application to the court under section 8 of the *CPIA*. The procedure for the making of such an application is set out in the *Criminal Procedure Rules*, Pt 25, r.25.6. This requires written notice to the prosecution in the form prescribed by r.25.6(2). The prosecution is then entitled (r.25.6(5)) to 14 days within which to agree to provide the specific disclosure requested or to request a hearing in order to make representations in relation to the defence application. As part of the timetabling exercise, the judge should set a date by which any applications under section 8 are to be made and should require the defence to indicate in advance of the cut-off date for specific disclosure applications what documents they are interested in and from what source; in appropriate cases, the judge should require justification of such requests.

45. The consideration of detailed defence requests for specific disclosure (so-called "shopping lists") otherwise than in accordance with r.25.6, is wholly improper. Likewise, defence requests for specific disclosure of unused prosecution material in purported pursuance of section 8 of the *CPIA* and r.25.6, which are not referable to any issue in the case identified by the defence case statement, should be rejected. Judges should require an application to be made under section 8 and in compliance with r.25.6 before considering any order for further disclosure.

46. It follows that the practice of making blanket orders for disclosure in all cases should cease, since such orders are inconsistent with the statutory framework of disclosure laid down by the *CPIA*, and which was endorsed by the House of Lords in *R. v. H. and C.* (*supra*).

Listing

47. It will be clear that the conscientious discharge of a judge' s duty at the PCMH requires a good deal more time than under the old PDH regime; furthermore a good deal more work is required of the advocate. The listing of PCMHs must take this into account. Unless the court can sit at 10am and finish the PCMH by 10.30am, it will not therefore usually be desirable for a judge who is part-heard on a trial to do a PCMH. **N–57**

48. It follows that any case which raises difficult issues of disclosure should be referred to the Resident Judge for directions. Cases of real complexity should, if possible, be allocated to a specific trial judge at a very early stage, and usually before the PCMH.

49. Although this Protocol is addressed to the issues of disclosure, it cannot be seen in isolation; it must be seen in the context of general case management.

Public interest immunity

50. Recent authoritative guidance as to the proper approach to PII is provided **N–58**

by the House of Lords in *R. v. H. and C.* (*supra*). It is clearly appropriate for PII applications to be considered by the trial judge. No judge should embark upon a PII application without considering that case and addressing the questions set out in paragraph 36, which for ease of reference we reproduce here:

"36. When any issue of derogation from the golden rule of full disclosure comes before it, the court must address a series of questions:

(1) What is the material which the prosecution seek to withhold? This must be considered by the court in detail.

(2) Is the material such as may weaken the prosecution case or strengthen that of the defence? If No, disclosure should not be ordered. If Yes, full disclosure should (subject to (3), (4) and (5) below be ordered.

(3) Is there a real risk of serious prejudice to an important public interest (and, if so, what) if full disclosure of the material is ordered? If No, full disclosure should be ordered.

(4) If the answer to (2) and (3) is Yes, can the defendant's interest be protected without disclosure or disclosure be ordered to an extent or in a way which will give adequate protection to the public interest in question and also afford adequate protection to the interests of the defence? This question requires the court to consider, with specific reference to the material which the prosecution seek to withhold and the facts of the case and the defence as disclosed, whether the prosecution should formally admit what the defence seek to establish or whether disclosure short of full disclosure may be ordered. This may be done in appropriate cases by the preparation of summaries or extracts of evidence, or the provision of documents in an edited or anonymised form, provided the documents supplied are in each instance approved by the judge. In appropriate cases the appointment of special counsel may be a necessary step to ensure that the contentions of the prosecution are tested and the interests of the defendant protected (see paragraph 22 above). In cases of exceptional difficulty the court may require the appointment of special counsel to ensure a correct answer to questions (2) and (3) as well as (4).

(5) Do the measures proposed in answer to (4) represent the minimum derogation necessary to protect the public interest in question? If No, the court should order such greater disclosure as will represent the minimum derogation from the golden rule of full disclosure.

(6) If limited disclosure is ordered pursuant to (4) or (5), may the effect be to render the trial process, viewed as a whole, unfair to the defendant? If Yes, then fuller disclosure should be ordered even if this leads or may lead the prosecution to discontinue the proceedings so as to avoid having to make disclosure.

(7) If the answer to (6) when first given is No, does that remain the correct answer as the trial unfolds, evidence is adduced and the defence advanced?

It is important that the answer to (6) should not be treated as a final, once-and-for-all, answer but as a provisional answer which the court must keep under review.".

51. In this context, the following matter [*sic*] are emphasised:

a. The procedure for making applications to the court is as set out in the *Criminal Procedure Rules* 2005, Pt 25 (r.25.1–r.25.5).

b. Where the PII application is a Type 1 or Type 2 application, proper notice to the defence is necessary to allow them to make focused submissions to

the court before hearing an application to withhold material; the notice
should be as specific as the nature of the material allows. It is appreciated
that in some cases only the generic nature of the material can properly be
identified. In some wholly exceptional cases (Type 3 cases) it may even be
justified to give no notice at all. The judge should always ask the prosecution to justify the form of notice given (or the decision to give no notice at
all).

c. The prosecution should be alert to the possibility of disclosing a statement
   in redacted form by, for example simply removing personal details. This
   may obviate the need for a PII application, unless the redacted material in
   itself would also satisfy the test for disclosure.

d. Except where the material is very short (say a few sheets only), or where
   the material is of such sensitivity that do so would be inappropriate, the
   prosecution should have supplied securely sealed copies to the judge
   beforehand, together with a short statement of the reasons why each document is said to be relevant and fulfils the disclosure test and why it is said
   that its disclosure would cause a real risk of serious prejudice to an
   important public interest; in undertaking this task, the use of merely
   formulaic expressions is to be discouraged. In any case of complexity a
   schedule of the material should be provided showing the specific objection
   to disclosure in relation to each item, leaving a space for the decision.

e. The application, even if held in private or in secret, should be recorded.
   The judge should give some short statement of reasons; this is often best
   done document by document as the hearing proceeds.

f. The tape, copies of the judge's orders (and any copies of the material
   retained by the court) should be clearly identified, securely sealed and kept
   in the court building in a safe or stout lockable cabinet consistent with its
   security classification, and there should be a proper register of all such material kept. Some arrangement should be made between the court and the
   prosecution authority for the periodic removal of such material once the
   case is concluded and the time for an appeal has passed.

Third party disclosure

52. The disclosure of unused material that has been gathered or generated by a   **N–59**
third party is an area of the law that has caused some difficulties: indeed, a Home
Office Working Party has been asked to report on it. This is because there is no
specific procedure for the disclosure of material held by third parties in criminal
proceedings, although the procedure under section 2 of the *Criminal Procedure
(Attendance of Witnesses) Act* 1965 or section 97 of the *Magistrates' Courts Act* 1980 is
often used in order to effect such disclosure. It should, however, be noted that the
test applied under both Acts is not the test to be applied under the *CPIA*, whether in
the amended or unamended form. These two provisions require that the material in
question is material evidence, *i.e.*, immediately admissible in evidence in the proceedings (see in this respect *R. v. Reading JJ., ex p. Berkshire County Council* [1996] 1
Cr.App.R. 239, *R. v. Derby Magistrates' Court, ex p. B* [1996] A.C. 487 and *R. v. Alibhai* [2004] EWCA Crim. 681).

53. Material held by other government departments or other Crown agencies
will not be prosecution material for the purposes of section 3(2) or section 8(4) of
the *CPIA*, if it has not been inspected, recorded and retained during the course of
the relevant criminal investigation. The Attorney General's Guidelines on Disclosure,
however, impose a duty upon the investigators and the prosecution to consider
whether such departments or bodies have material which may satisfy the test for
disclosure under the Act. Where this is the case, they must seek appropriate
disclosure from such bodies, who should themselves have an identified point for such
enquiries (see paragraphs 47 to 51, Attorney General's Guidelines on Disclosure).

54. Where material is held by a third party such as a local authority, a social
services department, hospital or business, the investigators and the prosecution
may seek to make arrangements to inspect the material with a view to applying
the relevant test for disclosure to it and determining whether any or all of the ma-

terial should be retained, recorded and, in due course, disclosed to the accused. In considering the latter, the investigators and the prosecution will establish whether the holder of the material wishes to raise PII issues, as a result of which the material may have to be placed before the court. Section 16 of the *CPIA* gives such a party a right to make representations to the court.

55. Where the third party in question declines to allow inspection of the material, or requires the prosecution to obtain an order before handing over copies of the material, the prosecutor will need to consider whether it is appropriate to obtain a witness summons under either section 2 of the *Criminal Procedure (Attendance of Witnesses) Act* 1965 or section 97 of the *Magistrates' Court Act* 1980. However, as stated above, this is only appropriate where the statutory requirements are satisfied, and where the prosecutor considers that the material may satisfy the test for disclosure. *R. v. Alibhai (supra)* makes it clear that the prosecutor has a "margin of consideration" in this regard.

56. It should be understood that the third party may have a duty to assert confidentiality, or the right to privacy under article 8 of the ECHR, where requests for disclosure are made by the prosecution, or anyone else. Where issues are raised in relation to allegedly relevant third party material, the judge must ascertain whether inquiries with the third party are likely to be appropriate, and, if so, identify who is going to make the request, what material is to be sought, from whom is the material to be sought and within what time scale must the matter be resolved.

57. The judge should consider what action would be appropriate in the light of the third party failing or refusing to comply with a request, including inviting the defence to make the request on its own behalf and, if necessary, to make an application for a witness summons. Any directions made (for instance, the date by which an application for a witness summons with supporting affidavit under section 2 of the 1965 should be served) should be put into writing at the time. Any failure to comply with the timetable must immediately be referred back to the court for further directions, although a hearing will not always be necessary.

58. Where the prosecution do not consider it appropriate to seek such a summons, the defence should consider doing so, where they are of the view (notwithstanding the prosecution assessment) that the third party may hold material which might undermine the prosecution case or assist that for the defendant, and the material would be likely to be 'material evidence' for the purposes of the 1965 Act. The defence must not sit back and expect the prosecution to make the running. The judge at the PCMH should specifically enquire whether any such application is to be made by the defence and set out a clear timetable. The objectionable practice of defence applications being made in the few days before trial must end.

59. It should be made clear, though, that 'fishing' expeditions in relation to third party material—whether by the prosecution or the defence—must be discouraged, and that, in appropriate cases, the court will consider making an order for wasted costs where the application is clearly unmeritorious and ill-conceived.

60. Judges should recognise that a summons can only be issued where the document(s) sought would be admissible in evidence. While it may be that the material in question may be admissible in evidence as a result of the hearsay provisions of the *CJA* (sections 114 to 120), it is this that determines whether an order for production of the material is appropriate, rather than the wider considerations applicable to disclosure in criminal proceedings: see *R. v. Reading Justices (supra)*, upheld by the House of Lords in *R. v. Derby Magistrates' Court (supra)*.

61. A number of Crown Court centres have developed local protocols, usually in respect of sexual offences and material held by social services and health and education authorities. Where these protocols exist they often provide an excellent and sensible way to identify relevant material that might assist the defence or undermine the prosecution.

62. Any application for third party disclosure must identify what documents are sought and why they are said to be material evidence. This is particularly relevant

where attempts are made to access the medical reports of those who allege that
they are victims of crime. Victims do not waive the confidentiality of their medical
records, or their right to privacy under article 8 of the ECHR, by the mere fact of
making a complaint against the accused. Judges should be alert to balance the
rights of victims against the real and proven needs of the defence. The court, as a
public authority, must ensure that any interference with the article 8 rights of
those entitled to privacy is in accordance with the law and necessary in pursuit of
a legitimate public interest. General and unspecified requests to trawl through
such records should be refused. If material is held by any person in relation to
family proceedings (*e.g.*, where there have been care proceedings in relation to a
child, who has also complained to the police of sexual or other abuse) then an application has to be made by that person to the family court for leave to disclose that
material to a third party, unless the third party, and the purpose for which disclosure
is made, is approved by rule 10.20A(3) of the *Family Proceedings Rules* 1991 (S.I.
1991 No. 1247). This would permit, for instance, a local authority, in receipt of such
material, to disclose it to the police for the purpose of a criminal investigation, or to
the CPS, in order for the latter to discharge any obligations under the *CPIA*.

Conclusion

63. The public rightly expects that the delays and failures which have been **N–60**
present in some cases in the past where there has been scant adherence to sound
disclosure principles will be eradicated by observation of this Protocol. The new
regime under the *Criminal Justice Act* and the *Criminal Procedure Rules* gives judges
the power to change the culture in which such cases are tried. It is now the duty of
every judge actively to manage disclosure issues in every case. The judge must seize
the initiative and drive the case along towards an efficient, effective and timely resolution, having regard to the overriding objective of the *Criminal Procedure Rules* (Pt
1). In this way the interests of justice will be better served and public confidence in
the criminal justice system will be increased.

TABLE OF CONTENTS

2005

JANUARY

M	T	W	Th	F	Sa	Su
3	4	5	6	7	1	2
10	11	12	13	14	8	9
17	18	19	20	21	15	16
24	25	26	27	28	22	23
31					29	30

FEBRUARY

M	T	W	Th	F	Sa	Su
7	1	2	3	4	5	6
14	8	9	10	11	12	13
21	15	16	17	18	19	20
28	22	23	24	25	26	27

MARCH

M	T	W	Th	F	Sa	Su
7	1	2	3	4	5	6
14	8	9	10	11	12	13
21	15	16	17	18	19	20
28	22	23	24	25	26	27
	29	30	31			

APRIL

M	T	W	Th	F	Sa	Su
4	5	6	7	1	2	3
11	12	13	14	8	9	10
18	19	20	21	15	16	17
25	26	27	28	22	23	24
				29	30	

MAY

M	T	W	Th	F	Sa	Su
2	3	4	5	6	7	1
9	10	11	12	13	14	8
16	17	18	19	20	21	15
23	24	25	26	27	28	22
30	31					29

JUNE

M	T	W	Th	F	Sa	Su
6	7	1	2	3	4	5
13	14	8	9	10	11	12
20	21	15	16	17	18	19
27	28	22	23	24	25	26
		29	30			

JULY

M	T	W	Th	F	Sa	Su
4	5	6	7	1	2	3
11	12	13	14	8	9	10
18	19	20	21	15	16	17
25	26	27	28	22	23	24
				29	30	31

AUGUST

M	T	W	Th	F	Sa	Su
1	2	3	4	5	6	7
8	9	10	11	12	13	14
15	16	17	18	19	20	21
22	23	24	25	26	27	28
29	30	31				

SEPTEMBER

M	T	W	Th	F	Sa	Su
5	6	7	1	2	3	4
12	13	14	8	9	10	11
19	20	21	15	16	17	18
26	27	28	22	23	24	25
			29	30		

OCTOBER

M	T	W	Th	F	Sa	Su
3	4	5	6	7	1	2
10	11	12	13	14	8	9
17	18	19	20	21	15	16
24	25	26	27	28	22	23
31					29	30

NOVEMBER

M	T	W	Th	F	Sa	Su
7	1	2	3	4	5	6
14	8	9	10	11	12	13
21	15	16	17	18	19	20
28	22	23	24	25	26	27
	29	30				

DECEMBER

M	T	W	Th	F	Sa	Su
5	6	7	1	2	3	4
12	13	14	8	9	10	11
19	20	21	15	16	17	18
26	27	28	22	23	24	25
			29	30	31	

2006

JANUARY

M	T	W	Th	F	Sa	Su
2	3	4	5	6	7	1
9	10	11	12	13	14	8
16	17	18	19	20	21	15
23	24	25	26	27	28	22
30	31					29

FEBRUARY

M	T	W	Th	F	Sa	Su
6	7	1	2	3	4	5
13	14	8	9	10	11	12
20	21	15	16	17	18	19
27	28	22	23	24	25	26

MARCH

M	T	W	Th	F	Sa	Su
6	7	1	2	3	4	5
13	14	8	9	10	11	12
20	21	15	16	17	18	19
27	28	22	23	24	25	26
		29	30	31		

APRIL

M	T	W	Th	F	Sa	Su
3	4	5	6	7	1	2
10	11	12	13	14	8	9
17	18	19	20	21	15	16
24	25	26	27	28	22	23
					29	30

MAY

M	T	W	Th	F	Sa	Su
1	2	3	4	5	6	7
8	9	10	11	12	13	14
15	16	17	18	19	20	21
22	23	24	25	26	27	28
29	30	31				

JUNE

M	T	W	Th	F	Sa	Su
5	6	7	1	2	3	4
12	13	14	8	9	10	11
19	20	21	15	16	17	18
26	27	28	22	23	24	25
			29	30		

JULY

M	T	W	Th	F	Sa	Su
3	4	5	6	7	1	2
10	11	12	13	14	8	9
17	18	19	20	21	15	16
24	25	26	27	28	22	23
31					29	30

AUGUST

M	T	W	Th	F	Sa	Su
7	1	2	3	4	5	6
14	8	9	10	11	12	13
21	15	16	17	18	19	20
28	22	23	24	25	26	27
	29	30	31			

SEPTEMBER

M	T	W	Th	F	Sa	Su
4	5	6	7	1	2	3
11	12	13	14	8	9	10
18	19	20	21	15	16	17
25	26	27	28	22	23	24
				29	30	

OCTOBER

M	T	W	Th	F	Sa	Su
2	3	4	5	6	7	1
9	10	11	12	13	14	8
16	17	18	19	20	21	15
23	24	25	26	27	28	22
30	31					29

NOVEMBER

M	T	W	Th	F	Sa	Su
6	7	1	2	3	4	5
13	14	8	9	10	11	12
20	21	15	16	17	18	19
27	28	22	23	24	25	26
		29	30			

DECEMBER

M	T	W	Th	F	Sa	Su
4	5	6	7	1	2	3
11	12	13	14	8	9	10
18	19	20	21	15	16	17
25	26	27	28	22	23	24
				29	30	31

2007

JANUARY

M	T	W	Th	F	Sa	Su
1	2	3	4	5	6	7
8	9	10	11	12	13	14
15	16	17	18	19	20	21
22	23	24	25	26	27	28
29	30	31				

FEBRUARY

M	T	W	Th	F	Sa	Su
			1	2	3	4
5	6	7	8	9	10	11
12	13	14	15	16	17	18
19	20	21	22	23	24	25
26	27	28				

MARCH

M	T	W	Th	F	Sa	Su
			1	2	3	4
5	6	7	8	9	10	11
12	13	14	15	16	17	18
19	20	21	22	23	24	25
26	27	28	29	30	31	

APRIL

M	T	W	Th	F	Sa	Su
						1
2	3	4	5	6	7	8
9	10	11	12	13	14	15
16	17	18	19	20	21	22
23	24	25	26	27	28	29
30						

MAY

M	T	W	Th	F	Sa	Su
	1	2	3	4	5	6
7	8	9	10	11	12	13
14	15	16	17	18	19	20
21	22	23	24	25	26	27
28	29	30	31			

JUNE

M	T	W	Th	F	Sa	Su
				1	2	3
4	5	6	7	8	9	10
11	12	13	14	15	16	17
18	19	20	21	22	23	24
25	26	27	28	29	30	

JULY

M	T	W	Th	F	Sa	Su
						1
2	3	4	5	6	7	8
9	10	11	12	13	14	15
16	17	18	19	20	21	22
23	24	25	26	27	28	29
30	31					

AUGUST

M	T	W	Th	F	Sa	Su
		1	2	3	4	5
6	7	8	9	10	11	12
13	14	15	16	17	18	19
20	21	22	23	24	25	26
27	28	29	30	31		

SEPTEMBER

M	T	W	Th	F	Sa	Su
					1	2
3	4	5	6	7	8	9
10	11	12	13	14	15	16
17	18	19	20	21	22	23
24	25	26	27	28	29	30

OCTOBER

M	T	W	Th	F	Sa	Su
1	2	3	4	5	6	7
8	9	10	11	12	13	14
15	16	17	18	19	20	21
22	23	24	25	26	27	28
29	30	31				

NOVEMBER

M	T	W	Th	F	Sa	Su
			1	2	3	4
5	6	7	8	9	10	11
12	13	14	15	16	17	18
19	20	21	22	23	24	25
26	27	28	29	30		

DECEMBER

M	T	W	Th	F	Sa	Su
					1	2
3	4	5	6	7	8	9
10	11	12	13	14	15	16
17	18	19	20	21	22	23
24	25	26	27	28	29	30
31						

2008

JANUARY

M	T	W	Th	F	Sa	Su
	1	2	3	4	5	6
7	8	9	10	11	12	13
14	15	16	17	18	19	20
21	22	23	24	25	26	27
28	29	30	31			

FEBRUARY

M	T	W	Th	F	Sa	Su
				1	2	3
4	5	6	7	8	9	10
11	12	13	14	15	16	17
18	19	20	21	22	23	24
25	26	27	28	29		

MARCH

M	T	W	Th	F	Sa	Su
					1	2
3	4	5	6	7	8	9
10	11	12	13	14	15	16
17	18	19	20	21	22	23
24	25	26	27	28	29	30
31						

APRIL

M	T	W	Th	F	Sa	Su
	1	2	3	4	5	6
7	8	9	10	11	12	13
14	15	16	17	18	19	20
21	22	23	24	25	26	27
28	29	30				

MAY

M	T	W	Th	F	Sa	Su
			1	2	3	4
5	6	7	8	9	10	11
12	13	14	15	16	17	18
19	20	21	22	23	24	25
26	27	28	29	30	31	

JUNE

M	T	W	Th	F	Sa	Su
						1
2	3	4	5	6	7	8
9	10	11	12	13	14	15
16	17	18	19	20	21	22
23	24	25	26	27	28	29
30						

JULY

M	T	W	Th	F	Sa	Su
	1	2	3	4	5	6
7	8	9	10	11	12	13
14	15	16	17	18	19	20
21	22	23	24	25	26	27
28	29	30	31			

AUGUST

M	T	W	Th	F	Sa	Su
				1	2	3
4	5	6	7	8	9	10
11	12	13	14	15	16	17
18	19	20	21	22	23	24
25	26	27	28	29	30	31

SEPTEMBER

M	T	W	Th	F	Sa	Su
1	2	3	4	5	6	7
8	9	10	11	12	13	14
15	16	17	18	19	20	21
22	23	24	25	26	27	28
29	30					

OCTOBER

M	T	W	Th	F	Sa	Su
		1	2	3	4	5
6	7	8	9	10	11	12
13	14	15	16	17	18	19
20	21	22	23	24	25	26
27	28	29	30	31		

NOVEMBER

M	T	W	Th	F	Sa	Su
					1	2
3	4	5	6	7	8	9
10	11	12	13	14	15	16
17	18	19	20	21	22	23
24	25	26	27	28	29	30

DECEMBER

M	T	W	Th	F	Sa	Su
1	2	3	4	5	6	7
8	9	10	11	12	13	14
15	16	17	18	19	20	21
22	23	24	25	26	27	28
29	30	31				

2009

JANUARY

M	T	W	Th	F	Sa	Su
			1	2	3	4
5	6	7	8	9	10	11
12	13	14	15	16	17	18
19	20	21	22	23	24	25
26	27	28	29	30	31	

FEBRUARY

M	T	W	Th	F	Sa	Su
						1
2	3	4	5	6	7	8
9	10	11	12	13	14	15
16	17	18	19	20	21	22
23	24	25	26	27	28	

MARCH

M	T	W	Th	F	Sa	Su
						1
2	3	4	5	6	7	8
9	10	11	12	13	14	15
16	17	18	19	20	21	22
23	24	25	26	27	28	29
30	31					

APRIL

M	T	W	Th	F	Sa	Su
		1	2	3	4	5
6	7	8	9	10	11	12
13	14	15	16	17	18	19
20	21	22	23	24	25	26
27	28	29	30			

MAY

M	T	W	Th	F	Sa	Su
				1	2	3
4	5	6	7	8	9	10
11	12	13	14	15	16	17
18	19	20	21	22	23	24
25	26	27	28	29	30	31

JUNE

M	T	W	Th	F	Sa	Su
1	2	3	4	5	6	7
8	9	10	11	12	13	14
15	16	17	18	19	20	21
22	23	24	25	26	27	28
29	30					

JULY

M	T	W	Th	F	Sa	Su
		1	2	3	4	5
6	7	8	9	10	11	12
13	14	15	16	17	18	19
20	21	22	23	24	25	26
27	28	29	30	31		

AUGUST

M	T	W	Th	F	Sa	Su
					1	2
3	4	5	6	7	8	9
10	11	12	13	14	15	16
17	18	19	20	21	22	23
24	25	26	27	28	29	30
31						

SEPTEMBER

M	T	W	Th	F	Sa	Su
	1	2	3	4	5	6
7	8	9	10	11	12	13
14	15	16	17	18	19	20
21	22	23	24	25	26	27
28	29	30				

OCTOBER

M	T	W	Th	F	Sa	Su
			1	2	3	4
5	6	7	8	9	10	11
12	13	14	15	16	17	18
19	20	21	22	23	24	25
26	27	28	29	30	31	

NOVEMBER

M	T	W	Th	F	Sa	Su
						1
2	3	4	5	6	7	8
9	10	11	12	13	14	15
16	17	18	19	20	21	22
23	24	25	26	27	28	29
30						

DECEMBER

M	T	W	Th	F	Sa	Su
	1	2	3	4	5	6
7	8	9	10	11	12	13
14	15	16	17	18	19	20
21	22	23	24	25	26	27
28	29	30	31			

2010

JANUARY

M	T	W	Th	F	Sa	Su
4	5	6	7	1	2	3
11	12	13	14	8	9	10
18	19	20	21	15	16	17
25	26	27	28	22	23	24
				29	30	31

FEBRUARY

M	T	W	Th	F	Sa	Su
1	2	3	4	5	6	7
8	9	10	11	12	13	14
15	16	17	18	19	20	21
22	23	24	25	26	27	28

MARCH

M	T	W	Th	F	Sa	Su
1	2	3	4	5	6	7
8	9	10	11	12	13	14
15	16	17	18	19	20	21
22	23	24	25	26	27	28
29	30	31				

APRIL

M	T	W	Th	F	Sa	Su
5	6	7	1	2	3	4
12	13	14	8	9	10	11
19	20	21	15	16	17	18
26	27	28	22	23	24	25
			29	30		

MAY

M	T	W	Th	F	Sa	Su
3	4	5	6	7	1	2
10	11	12	13	14	8	9
17	18	19	20	21	15	16
24	25	26	27	28	22	23
31					29	30

JUNE

M	T	W	Th	F	Sa	Su
7	1	2	3	4	5	6
14	8	9	10	11	12	13
21	15	16	17	18	19	20
28	22	23	24	25	26	27
	29	30				

JULY

M	T	W	Th	F	Sa	Su
5	6	7	1	2	3	4
12	13	14	8	9	10	11
19	20	21	15	16	17	18
26	27	28	22	23	24	25
			29	30	31	

AUGUST

M	T	W	Th	F	Sa	Su
2	3	4	5	6	7	1
9	10	11	12	13	14	8
16	17	18	19	20	21	15
23	24	25	26	27	28	22
30	31					29

SEPTEMBER

M	T	W	Th	F	Sa	Su
6	7	1	2	3	4	5
13	14	8	9	10	11	12
20	21	15	16	17	18	19
27	28	22	23	24	25	26
		29	30			

OCTOBER

M	T	W	Th	F	Sa	Su
4	5	6	7	1	2	3
11	12	13	14	8	9	10
18	19	20	21	15	16	17
25	26	27	28	22	23	24
				29	30	31

NOVEMBER

M	T	W	Th	F	Sa	Su
1	2	3	4	5	6	7
8	9	10	11	12	13	14
15	16	17	18	19	20	21
22	23	24	25	26	27	28
29	30					

DECEMBER

M	T	W	Th	F	Sa	Su
6	7	1	2	3	4	5
13	14	8	9	10	11	12
20	21	15	16	17	18	19
27	28	22	23	24	25	26
		29	30	31		

2011

JANUARY

M	T	W	Th	F	Sa	Su
					1	2
3	4	5	6	7	8	9
10	11	12	13	14	15	16
17	18	19	20	21	22	23
24	25	26	27	28	29	30
31						

FEBRUARY

M	T	W	Th	F	Sa	Su
	1	2	3	4	5	6
7	8	9	10	11	12	13
14	15	16	17	18	19	20
21	22	23	24	25	26	27
28						

MARCH

M	T	W	Th	F	Sa	Su
	1	2	3	4	5	6
7	8	9	10	11	12	13
14	15	16	17	18	19	20
21	22	23	24	25	26	27
28	29	30	31			

APRIL

M	T	W	Th	F	Sa	Su
				1	2	3
4	5	6	7	8	9	10
11	12	13	14	15	16	17
18	19	20	21	22	23	24
25	26	27	28	29	30	

MAY

M	T	W	Th	F	Sa	Su
						1
2	3	4	5	6	7	8
9	10	11	12	13	14	15
16	17	18	19	20	21	22
23	24	25	26	27	28	29
30	31					

JUNE

M	T	W	Th	F	Sa	Su
		1	2	3	4	5
6	7	8	9	10	11	12
13	14	15	16	17	18	19
20	21	22	23	24	25	26
27	28	29	30			

JULY

M	T	W	Th	F	Sa	Su
				1	2	3
4	5	6	7	8	9	10
11	12	13	14	15	16	17
18	19	20	21	22	23	24
25	26	27	28	29	30	31

AUGUST

M	T	W	Th	F	Sa	Su
1	2	3	4	5	6	7
8	9	10	11	12	13	14
15	16	17	18	19	20	21
22	23	24	25	26	27	28
29	30	31				

SEPTEMBER

M	T	W	Th	F	Sa	Su
			1	2	3	4
5	6	7	8	9	10	11
12	13	14	15	16	17	18
19	20	21	22	23	24	25
26	27	28	29	30		

OCTOBER

M	T	W	Th	F	Sa	Su
					1	2
3	4	5	6	7	8	9
10	11	12	13	14	15	16
17	18	19	20	21	22	23
24	25	26	27	28	29	30
31						

NOVEMBER

M	T	W	Th	F	Sa	Su
	1	2	3	4	5	6
7	8	9	10	11	12	13
14	15	16	17	18	19	20
21	22	23	24	25	26	27
28	29	30				

DECEMBER

M	T	W	Th	F	Sa	Su
			1	2	3	4
5	6	7	8	9	10	11
12	13	14	15	16	17	18
19	20	21	22	23	24	25
26	27	28	29	30	31	

2012

JANUARY

M	T	W	Th	F	Sa	Su
						1
2	3	4	5	6	7	8
9	10	11	12	13	14	15
16	17	18	19	20	21	22
23	24	25	26	27	28	29
30	31					

FEBRUARY

M	T	W	Th	F	Sa	Su
		1	2	3	4	5
6	7	8	9	10	11	12
13	14	15	16	17	18	19
20	21	22	23	24	25	26
27	28	29				

MARCH

M	T	W	Th	F	Sa	Su
			1	2	3	4
5	6	7	8	9	10	11
12	13	14	15	16	17	18
19	20	21	22	23	24	25
26	27	28	29	30	31	

APRIL

M	T	W	Th	F	Sa	Su
						1
2	3	4	5	6	7	8
9	10	11	12	13	14	15
16	17	18	19	20	21	22
23	24	25	26	27	28	29
30						

MAY

M	T	W	Th	F	Sa	Su
	1	2	3	4	5	6
7	8	9	10	11	12	13
14	15	16	17	18	19	20
21	22	23	24	25	26	27
28	29	30	31			

JUNE

M	T	W	Th	F	Sa	Su
				1	2	3
4	5	6	7	8	9	10
11	12	13	14	15	16	17
18	19	20	21	22	23	24
25	26	27	28	29	30	

JULY

M	T	W	Th	F	Sa	Su
						1
2	3	4	5	6	7	8
9	10	11	12	13	14	15
16	17	18	19	20	21	22
23	24	25	26	27	28	29
30	31					

AUGUST

M	T	W	Th	F	Sa	Su
		1	2	3	4	5
6	7	8	9	10	11	12
13	14	15	16	17	18	19
20	21	22	23	24	25	26
27	28	29	30	31		

SEPTEMBER

M	T	W	Th	F	Sa	Su
					1	2
3	4	5	6	7	8	9
10	11	12	13	14	15	16
17	18	19	20	21	22	23
24	25	26	27	28	29	30

OCTOBER

M	T	W	Th	F	Sa	Su
1	2	3	4	5	6	7
8	9	10	11	12	13	14
15	16	17	18	19	20	21
22	23	24	25	26	27	28
29	30	31				

NOVEMBER

M	T	W	Th	F	Sa	Su
			1	2	3	4
5	6	7	8	9	10	11
12	13	14	15	16	17	18
19	20	21	22	23	24	25
26	27	28	29	30		

DECEMBER

M	T	W	Th	F	Sa	Su
					1	2
3	4	5	6	7	8	9
10	11	12	13	14	15	16
17	18	19	20	21	22	23
24	25	26	27	28	29	30
31						

Archbold
paragraph
numbers

AL-9

AL-9

Archbold's Criminal Pleading—2009 ed.

Holidays and Notable Dates

Holiday, etc.	2004	2005	2006	2007	2008	2009	2010	2011
New Year's Day	Jan. 1	Jan. 1	Jan. 1	Jan. 1	Jan. 1	Jan. 1	Jan. 1	Jan. 1
New Year Holiday (England)	—	—	—	—	—	—	—	—
New Year Holiday (Scotland)	Jan. 2	Jan. 2	Jan. 2	Jan. 2	Jan. 2	Jan. 2	Jan. 2	Jan. 2
St David's Day (Wales)	Mar. 1	Mar. 1	Mar. 1	Mar. 1	Mar. 1	Mar. 1	Mar. 1	Mar. 1
St Patrick's Day (Ireland)	Mar. 17	Mar. 17	Mar. 17	Mar. 17	Mar. 17	Mar. 17	Mar. 17	Mar. 17
Good Friday	Apr. 9	Mar. 25	Apr. 14	Apr. 6	Mar. 21	Apr. 10	Apr. 2	Apr. 22
Easter Monday	Apr. 12	Mar. 28	Apr. 17	Apr. 9	Mar. 24	Apr. 13	Apr. 5	Apr. 25
St George's Day (England)	Apr. 23	Apr. 23	Apr. 23	Apr. 23	Apr. 23	Apr. 23	Apr. 23	Apr. 23
May Day Holiday	May 3	May 2	May 1	May 7	May 5	May 4	May 3	May 2
Spring Bank Holiday	May 31	May 30	May 29	May 28	May 26	May 25	May 31	May 30
August Bank Holiday	Aug. 30	Aug. 29	Aug. 28	Aug. 28	Aug. 25	Aug. 31	Aug. 30	Aug. 29
St Andrew's Day (Scotland)	Nov. 30	Nov. 30	Nov. 30	Nov. 30	Nov. 30	Nov. 30	Nov. 30	Nov. 30
Christmas Day	Dec. 25	Dec. 25	Dec. 25	Dec. 25	Dec. 25	Dec. 25	Dec. 25	Dec. 25
Boxing Day	Dec. 26	Dec. 26	Dec. 26	Dec. 26	Dec. 26	Dec. 26	Dec. 26	Dec. 26
Christmas Holiday(s)	—	—	—	—	—	—	—	—

Measurement Conversion Tables

The measurements set out below are based upon the following standards set by the *Weights and Measures Act* 1985, Sched. 1, Pts I to V:

YARD = 0.9144 metre; GALLON = 4.54609 cubic decimetres or litres; POUND = 0.45359237 kilograms

Measurements of Length

Imperial Units of Length		Metric Equivalents
Mil	1/1000 inch	0.0254 millimetres
Inch	1000 mils	2.54 centimetres
Link	7.92 inches	20.1168 centimetres
Foot	12 inches	0.3048 metres
Yard	3 feet	0.9144 metres
Fathom	6 feet	1.8288 metres
Cable	60 feet or 10 fathoms	18.288 metres
Chain	22 yards (100 links)	20.1168 metres
Furlong	220 yards	201.168 metres
Mile	1,760 yards (8 furlongs)	1.609344 kilometres
Nautical mile	6080 feet	1.853184 kilometres

Metric Units of Length		Imperial Equivalents
Micron	1/1000 millimetre	0.03937007 mils
Millimetre	1/1000 metre	0.03937007 inches
Centimetre	1/100 metre	0.3937 inches
Decimetre	1/10 metre	3.937 inches
Metre	Metre	1.09361329 yards
Kilometre	1000 metres	0.62137712 miles or 0.53961 nautical miles

919

Measurements of Area

Imperial Units of Area	Metric Equivalents
Square inch	6.4516 square centimetres
Square foot	929.0304 square centimetres
Square yard	0.83613 square metres
Square chain	404.685642 square metres
Rood	1011.714 square metres
Acre	4046.85642 sq. ms or 40.4685642 acres
Square mile	258.998811 hectares

Metric Units of Area	Imperial Equivalents
Square millimetre	0.00155 square inches
Square centimetre	0.155 square inches
Square decimetre	15.5 square inches
Square metre	1.1959 sq. yards or 10.7639 sq. ft.
Are	119.599 sq. yds or 0.09884 roods
Dekare	0.2471 acres
Hectare	2.47105 acres
Square kilometre	247.105 acres or 0.3861 square miles

(Imperial Units of Area column values:)

Square inch — 1/144 square feet
Square foot — 1/9 square yard
Square yard — Square yard
Square chain — 484 square yards
Rood — 1,210 square yards
Acre — 4 roods or 4840 square yards
Square mile — 640 acres

(Metric Units of Area column values:)

Square millimetre — 1/100 square centimetre
Square centimetre — 1/100 square decimetre
Square decimetre — 1/100 metre
Square metre — Square metre
Are — 100 square metres
Dekare — 10 ares
Hectare — 100 ares (1,000 square metres)
Square kilometre — 100 hectares

Measurements of Volume

Imperial Units of Volume		Metric Equivalents
Cubic inch	Cubic inch	16.387064 cubic centimetres
Cubic foot	1,728 cubic inches	28.3168465 cubic decimetres
Cubic yard	27 cubic feet	0.76455485 cubic metres

Metric Units of Volume		Imperial Equivalents
Cubic centimetre	1,000 cubic millimetres	0.06102374 cubic inches
Cubic decimetre	1,000 cubic centimetres	0.03531466 cubic feet
Cubic metre	1,000 cubic decimetres	1.30795061 cubic yards or 35.3147 cu. ft.

Measurements of Capacity

Imperial, Apothecaries and US Units of Capacity

		Metric Equivalents
Minim	Minim	0.0591938 millilitres
Fluid Drachm	60 minims	0.35516328 centilitres
Fluid ounce	8 fluid drachms	2.84130625 centilitres
US fluid ounce	1.0408 UK fluid ounces	29.573522656 millilitres
Gill	5 fluid ounces	1.42065312 decilitres
Pint	4 gills or 20 fluid ounces	0.56826125 litres
US pint	0.8327 UK pints or 16 US fluid ounces	0.47317636 litres
Quart	2 pints or 8 gills	1.1365225 litres
Gallon	4 quarts or 1.20095 US gallons	4.54609 litres
US gallon	0.08327 UK gallons	3.7854109 litres
Peck	2 gallons or 16 pints	9.09218 litres
Bushel	4 pecks or 8 gallons	36.36872 litres
Quarter	8 bushels or 36 pecks	2.9094976 hectolitres
Chaldron	36 bushels or 4½ quarters	13.0927392 hectolitres

Metric Units of Capacity

		Imperial Equivalents
Millilitre	Millilitre	0.28156064 fluid drachms
Centilitre	10 millilitres	0.35195080 fluid ounces
Decilitre	10 centilitres	0.70390160 gills
Litre	10 decilitres	1.75975398 pints or 0.21999924 UK gallons
Dekalitre	10 litres	2.1996924 UK gallons
Hectolitre	10 dekalitres or 100 litres	21.996824 UK gallons

Measurements of Weight

Imperial and Apothecaries Units of Weight		Metric Equivalents
Grain	Grain	64.79891 milligrams
Scruple	20 grains	1.2959782 grams
Pennyweight	24 grains	1.55517384 grams
Drachm	3 scruples or 60 grains	3.8879346 grams
Troy ounce	8 drachms or 480 grains	31.1034768 grams
Dram	1/16 ounce	1.77184519 grams
Ounce	16 drams or 437.5 grains	28.3495231 grams
Troy pound (US)	12 troy ounces or 5,760 grains	373.241721 grams
Pound	16 ounces or 7,000 grains	453.59237 grams or 0.45359237 kilograms
Stone	14 pounds	6.35029318 kilograms
Quarter	28 pounds or 2 stone	12.7005863 kilograms
Cental	100 pounds	45.359237 kilograms
Hundredweight	4 quarters or 112 pounds	50.8023454 kilograms
Short hundredweight (US)	100 pounds	45.359237 kilograms
Ton (UK or long ton)	20 cwt or 2,240 pounds	1.0160469 metric tonnes (tonne)
Ton (US or short ton)	2,000 pounds	0.90718474 metric tonnes

Metric Units of Weight	Imperial Equivalents
Milligram	.001 grams	0.012432 grains
Centigram	.01 grams	0.15432 grains
Decigram	.1 grams	1.5432 grains
Gram	1 gram	0.03527396 ounces or 0.03215 troy ounces
Dekagram	10 grams	0.35273961 ounces
Hectogram	100 grams	3.52739619 ounces
Kilogram	1,000 grams	2.20462262 pounds
Myriagram	10 kilograms	22.0462 pounds
Quintal	100 kilograms	1.9684 hundredweight
Tonne	1,000 kilograms	0.984207 UK tons or 1.10231 US tons

Measurements of Velocity

Per Hour	Per Minute	Per Second
Mile 1.609344 kph	88 feet 26.8224 metres	17.6 inches per second 44.704 centimetres per second
Kilometres 0.62137 mph	16.6667 metres 54.6806 feet	27.7778 centimetres 10.9361 inches

SYSTÈME INTERNATIONALE D'UNITES OR SI UNITS

1. SI units are increasingly being used to report laboratory results. **AL–17**
They have largely replaced earlier systems such as c.g.s. units (centime-
tre, gram, second), m.k.s. or Giorgi units (metre, kilogram, second), and
Imperial units (yard, pound, second).

2. S.I. Units comprise 7 base units and 2 supplementary units. Other
units are derived from these. 18 derived units are currently widely
accepted.

Base SI Units

Physical Quantity	Unit	Symbol
Length	metre	m
Mass	kilogram	kg
Time	second	s
Electric current	ampere	A
Temperature	kelvin	K
Luminosity	candela	cd
Amount of substance	mole	mol
Plane angle*	radian*	rad
Solid angle*	steradian*	sr

*Supplementary Units

Archbold
paragraph
numbers
AL–20

AL–20

Archbold's Criminal Pleading—2009 ed.

Derived SI Units

Physical Quantity	Unit	Symbol
Frequency	hertz	Hz
Energy	joule	J
Force	newton	N
Power	watt	W
Pressure	pascal	Pa
Electric charge	coulomb	C
Electric potential difference	volt	V
Electrical resistance	ohm	Ω
Electric conductance	siemens	S
Electric capacitance	farad	F
Magnetic flux	weber	Wb
Inductance	henry	H
Magnetic flux density	tesla	T
Luminous flux	lumen	lm
Illuminance	lux	lx
Absorbed dose	gray	Gy
Activity	becquerel	Bq
Dose Equivalence	sievert	Sv

Multiples and Subdivisions of SI Units

Prefix	Symbol	Power	Value
exa	E	10^{18}	1,000,000,000,000,000,000
peta	P	10^{15}	1,000,000,000,000,000
tera	T	10^{12}	1,000,000,000,000
giga	G	10^{9}	1,000,000,000
mega	M	10^{6}	1,000,000
kilo	k	10^{3}	1,000
hecto	h	10^{2}	100
deca	da	10	10
–			1
deci	d	10^{-1}	1/10
centi	c	10^{-2}	1/100
milli	m	10^{-3}	1/1,000
micro	μ	10^{-6}	1/1,000,000
nano	n	10^{-9}	1/1,000,000,000
pico	p	10^{-12}	1/1,000,000,000,000
femto	f	10^{-15}	1/1,000,000,000,000,000
atto	a	10^{-18}	1/1,000,000,000,000,000,000

International Time Differences

The following time differences are based upon Greenwich Mean Time (GMT).
British Summer Time (BST) is one hour in advance of GMT.

Country	Hours +/-
Algeria	+ 1 hour
Argentina	- 3 hours
Australia	
South Australia	+ 9½ hours
New South Wales	+ 10 hours
Tasmania	+ 10 hours
Victoria	+ 10 hours
Austria	+ 1 hour
Belgium	+ 1 hour
Bolivia	- 4 hours
Brazil	- 3 hours
Bulgaria	+ 2 hours
Canada	
Newfoundland	- 3½ hours
Atlantic	- 4 hours
Eastern	- 5 hours
Central	- 6 hours
Mountain	- 7 hours
Pacific	- 8 hours
Yukon	- 9 hours
Chile	- 4 hours

Country	Hours +/-
China	+ 8 hours
Columbia	- 5 hours
Czech Lands	+ 1 hour
Denmark	+ 1 hour
Egypt	+ 2 hours
Finland	+ 2 hours
France	+ 1 hour
Germany	+ 1 hour
Ghana	—
Greece	+ 2 hours
Holland	+ 1 hour
Hong Kong	+ 8 hours
Hungary	+ 1 hour
India	+ 5½ hours
Iraq	+ 3 hours
Ireland	—
Israel	+ 2 hours
Italy	+ 1 hour
Jamaica	- 5 hours
Japan	+ 9 hours
Kenya	+ 3 hours

Country	Hours +/-
Luxembourg	+ 1 hour
Malaysia	+ 8 hours
Malta	+ 1 hour
Morocco	—
New Zealand	+ 12 hours
Nigeria	+ 1 hour
Norway	+ 1 hour
Peru	– 5 hours
Philippines	+ 8 hours
Poland	+ 1 hour
Portugal	—
Romania	+ 2 hours
Russia	
Moscow	+ 3 hours
Vladivostock	+ 10 hours
Saudi Arabia	+ 3 hours
Serbia	+ 1 hour
Singapore	+ 8 hours

Country	Hours +/-
South Africa	+ 2 hours
Spain	+ 1 hour
Sri Lanka	+ 5½ hours
Sweden	+ 1 hour
Switzerland	+ 1 hour
Taiwan	+ 8 hours
Thailand	+ 7 hours
Tunisia	+ 1 hour
Turkey	+ 2 hours
Ukraine	+ 3 hours
United Arab Emirates	+ 4 hours
United States	
Eastern	– 5 hours
Central	– 6 hours
Mountain	– 7 hours
Pacific	– 8 hours
Zambia	+ 2 hours
Zimbabwe	+ 2 hours

Stopping Distances

AL-24

Speed (m.p.h.)	Stopping distance (feet)
20	40
30	75
40	120
50	175
60	240
70	315

Useful Contact Details

	Telephone	Email
Courts, etc.		
House of Lords, Judicial Office	(020) 7219 3111	
Royal Courts of Justice	(020) 7947 6000	
Registrar, Criminal Appeals	(020) 7947 6103	
Criminal Appeal Office	(020) 7947 6011	Criminalappealoffice.general@officehmcourts-service.x.gsi.gov.uk
Administrative Court Office	(020) 7947 6205	
Official Bodies		
Home Office	(020) 7035 4848	public.enquiries@homeoffice.gsi.gov.uk
Serious Fraud Office	(020)7239 7272	public.enquiries@sfo.gsi.gov.uk
H.M. Revenue and Customs	0845 010 9000	Enquiries.estn@hmrc.gsi.gov.uk This address handles all enquiries related to VAT, Excise and other duties formerly administered by HM Customs and Excise (with the exception of International Trade)
New Scotland Yard	(020)7230 1212	new.scotland.yard@met.police.uk
City of London Police	(020) 7601 2222	postmaster@cityoflondon.police.uk
British Transport Police	0800 40 50 40	
Others		
Justice	(020) 7329 5100	admin@justice.org.uk
Liberty	(020) 7403 3888	
Bar Council	(020) 7242 0082	

INDEX

LEGAL TAXONOMY
FROM SWEET & MAXWELL

This index has been prepared using Sweet and Maxwell's Legal Taxonomy. Index entries conform to keywords provided by the Legal Taxonomy except where references to specific documents or non-standard terms (denoted by quotation marks) have been included. These keywords provide a means of identifying similar concepts in other Sweet & Maxwell publications and online services to which keywords from the Legal Taxonomy have been applied. Readers may find some minor differences between terms used in the text and those which appear in the index. Suggestions to *sweetandmaxwell.taxonomy@thomson.com*

All references are to paragraph numbers.